# Tax Planning for Troubled Corporations

*Bankruptcy and Nonbankruptcy Restructurings*

**2008 Edition**

**Gordon D. Henderson**
*Of Counsel, Weil, Gotshal & Manges LLP*
*New York*

**Stuart J. Goldring**
*Partner, Weil, Gotshal & Manges LLP*
*New York*

**This volume is current through September 1, 2007**

**Editorial Staff**

Production . . . . . . . . . . . . . . . . . . . . . . . . . . . . . . . . . . . . . . . Diana Roozeboom



ISBN: 978-0-8080-1814-8



CCH

4025 W. Peterson Ave.
Chicago, IL 60646-6085
1 800 248 3248
www.CCHGroup.com

# Highlights of the 2008 Edition

With updated material and expanded coverage, the 2008 Edition is thoroughly updated to account for all new developments that have occurred in this dynamic area of the law since publication of the past edition, including relevant legislation, important IRS rulings and regulations, and new case law.

New and revised discussions and tax planning strategies added to the book include information on the following:

- **IRS Alters Treatment of Corporate Conversions to Disregarded Entity Status for Debt Exchange Purposes.** The IRS has issued two new letter rulings that treat a corporate conversion to disregarded entity status as a technical change in the obligor of the corporation's outstanding debt resulting in a "modification" of the debt for tax purposes but *not* a modification that was so "significant" under the circumstances so as to create a deemed exchange of the debt. This represents a change from the IRS's initial ruling position, which did not consider the conversion to result in even a technical change in the obligor (presumably since the obligor of the debt was not considered to have changed for state law purposes), and thus imposes a more stringent standard for such conversions. *See* the discussion at § 402.5.
- **Regulations Implement Additional Obligations Imposed on Tax Shelter Advisors by the 2004 Act.** The Treasury in late 2006 proposed, and in 2007 finalized, regulations under Code § § 6111 and 6112 implementing the expanded reporting and record-keeping requirements imposed on tax shelter "material advisors" by the amendments to these sections made by the American Jobs Creation Act of 2004. The reporting provisions include a new IRS Form 8918 for this purpose. *See* the discussion at § 403.5.
- **IRS Adheres to Bankruptcy Court Order Retroactively Voiding a Stock Acquisition That Otherwise Might Produce a Code § 382 Ownership Change.** After a Bankruptcy Court issued an order restricting stock transfers that could impair the debtor company's net operating losses, an investor informed the debtor that during the period the court was considering the order, but before the order was issued, the investor had acquired enough stock to have violated the order if the order had been issued before the acquisition. The debtor and the investor then asked the court to declare the acquisition of the excess shares void, and direct that the excess shares be sold in the open market with any profit going to charity. The court so ordered. The IRS ruled that it would adhere to the court's treatment for Code § 382 purposes, so long as the court order remains in effect. *See* the discussions at § § 508.2.4 and 1002.4.1.
- **IRS Rules That, for Purposes of Applying the Code § 382 Five-Percent Shareholder Test, Stock Held by an Investment Advisor for Its Clients Is Not Aggregated, and Instead Should Be Considered Owned Individually by Its**

**Clients.** In this ruling, an investment advisor filed a Schedule 13G with the SEC because it held more than five percent of a loss company's stock. The stock was held for its clients, and though the advisor had the right to vote the stock and keep custody of it, the advisor had no right to keep the dividends or proceeds of sale. The IRS ruled that, for purposes of determining the loss company's five-percent shareholders for Code § 382 ownership change purposes, the stock is not aggregated and treated as held by a single person; instead each client should be treated as the owner of the stock held for its individual account. Moreover, the IRS ruled that the loss company, unless it had actual knowledge to the contrary, could assume that if none of the clients file a Schedule 13G, none of them is a member of any group that is itself a five-percent shareholder. *See* the discussion at § 508.2.8.1.

- **Temporary Regulation Provides That Prepaid Income Whose Recognition the Debtor Has Elected to Defer Will in Most Cases Not Qualify for Built-In Gain Treatment Under Code § 382.** Implementing its prior ruling position, the Treasury issued a temporary regulation denying built-in gain treatment under Code § 382 for most (though not all) prepaid income that a loss company elects to defer. *See* the discussion at § 508.4.3.

- **IRS Continues to Assert That in a Consolidated Return the Code § 108 Attribute Reduction Rules for Cancellation of Debt Should Be Applied on a Consolidated Basis Even for Periods Before the 2003 Consolidated Return Regulations.** The IRS Chief Counsel has reasserted the position that within consolidated groups the Code § 108 attribute reduction rules for excluded cancellation of debt income must be applied on a consolidated basis (except for basis reductions) even for periods before the 2003 effective date of the consolidated return regulations specifically addressing such treatment. *See* the discussion at §§ 804.4.1 and 804.4.5.

- **Proposed Regulations Issued Under Code § 362(e)(2).** The Treasury issued proposed regulations under Code § 362(e)(2), which section seeks to eliminate loss duplications when loss property is transferred to a corporation in a Code § 351 transaction. *See* the discussion at § 804.5.3.

- **Proposed Regulations Would Revise the Consolidated Return Stock Loss Disallowance Rules.** The Treasury has proposed a new regulation—Prop. Reg. § 1.1502-36—that would revise and supplant, beginning on the date it becomes effective, the existing rules for eliminating non-economic and duplicated losses where the stock of a consolidated subsidiary is disposed of at a loss. The new loss duplication rule would apply even to sales of all of the stock of a subsidiary, and generally would require that the tax attributes of the subsidiary be reduced by the amount of the duplicated loss (subject to an election to forgo the stock loss or possibly reattribute certain tax attributes of the subsidiary in lieu of the stock loss). *See* the discussion at § 804.5.4.

- **Treasury Also Seeks in a Proposed Regulation to Apply Code § 362(e)(2) to Consolidated Groups.** The Treasury has also issued a regulation—Prop. Reg. § 1.1502-13(e)(4)—proposing to apply Code § 362(e)(2) within consolidated return groups. Because the consolidated return regulations already contain, and there are already proposed, extensive provisions in Reg. §§ 1.1502-32 and -35 and Prop. Reg. § 1.1502-36 intended to eliminate duplicated losses, practitioners and commentators have questioned whether Code § 362(e)(2) should apply at all to consolidated returns. The proposed regulation is designed to prevent duplicated losses only to the extent such duplicated losses might not somehow already be eliminated by existing consolidated return provisions. *See* the discussion at § 804.5.3.

- **IRS Concludes That It Has the Right to Offset Tax Overpayments Against Unassessed Tax Claims in Bankruptcy Prior to Granting a Tax Refund.** In a series of three rulings and a new temporary regulation, the IRS has stated that unassessed taxes reflected in either a proof of claim filed in a bankruptcy proceeding or in a statutory notice of deficiency may be offset against any tax overpayments for which a refund claim is made. The IRS reasons that the proof of claim and notice of deficiency represent a specific administrative determination of the nature and amount of the tax liability that is entitled to a presumption of correctness, and thus reflects an outstanding liability for purposes of offset under the Tax Code. The IRS did not address the potential implications of the automatic stay in bankruptcy with respect to any such setoff. *See* the discussions at § § 1006.1 and 1012.1.

- **Bankruptcy Court Determines That Bankruptcy Code Section 505(b) Prompt Audit Procedure Discharges Bankruptcy Estate Even in Pre-2005 Act Cases.** In October 2005, Congress specifically included a debtor's bankruptcy estate among the persons to be discharged pursuant to the prompt audit procedure of Bankruptcy Code section 505(b) applicable to a debtor corporation's post-petition tax returns. This change was necessitated by a series of court cases determining that a bankruptcy estate did not benefit from such discharge, and thus any property held by the bankruptcy estate remained subject to a subsequently determined tax deficiency for such tax returns until such time as the assets of the estate could be distributed in accordance with the provisions of the Bankruptcy Code. In a new decision, however, a Bankruptcy Court took exception with such prior cases and held that, at least in a Chapter 11 case, the bankruptcy estate should be considered discharged even in bankruptcy cases commenced before the statutory change. *See* the discussion at § 1011.

- **IRS Deferral of Tax Return Filing Deadline in Disaster Situations Does Not Apply to Bankruptcy Code Time Limitations for Priority Tax Claims.** The IRS has ruled that an IRS postponement of the time to file an income tax return due to a declared disaster or a terroristic or military action does not change the technical due date of the return for purposes of determining the priority of tax claims in bankruptcy. *See* the discussion at § 1015.1.4.

- **Courts Continue to Grapple with the Scope of the States' Waiver of Sovereign Immunity in Bankruptcy Cases.** In the wake of the Supreme Court's 2006 decision in *Central Virginia Community College v. Katz*, lower courts have had to work through the reversal of the sovereign immunity landscape in bankruptcy matters with respect to state governmental authorities. In particular, the courts have had to consider the extent to which Bankruptcy Code section 106, which historically described the breadth of the Congressional abrogation of State sovereign immunity, now serves as a limitation upon what the Supreme Court has declared to have been a general waiver by the States of their sovereign immunity with respect to bankruptcy matters as part of the adoption of the Constitution. *See* the discussion at § 1102.5.2.

- **Eleventh Circuit Holds Chapter 11 Transfer Tax Exemption Applies to Pre-Plan Transfers.** Departing from the decisions of two other Circuit Courts of Appeals, the Eleventh Circuit Court of Appeals upheld the application of the Chapter 11 exemption from transfer taxes to transfers that occur prior to a confirmed Chapter 11 plan where the pre-confirmation transfers are necessary to the consummation of a plan. A petition for writ of *certiorari* has been filed with the Supreme Court to resolve the conflict. *See* the discussion at § 1102.15.

**September 2007**

# About the Authors

**Gordon D. Henderson** has been a partner, and is now of counsel, in the law firm of Weil, Gotshal & Manges LLP in New York City. He received his A.B. degree *magna cum laude* from Harvard College in 1951, where he was elected to Phi Beta Kappa, and his J.D. degree *magna cum laude* from Harvard Law School in 1957, where he was an editor of the *Harvard Law Review*. He has had extensive experience in major bankruptcy cases extending over 25 years. He has Chaired the Tax Section of the New York State Bar Association, the Committee on Corporation Law of the Association of the Bar of the City of New York, and the Policy Advisory Group for the New York Joint Legislative Commission to Study the New York State Tax Laws. He has been a member of the New York City Tax Study Commission. He has been a visiting lecturer on corporation tax law at Yale Law School and has been a frequent speaker at tax institutes and a writer of numerous articles on tax subjects. He served as Special Counsel to the SEC and Associate Director of one of its divisions during the Kennedy Administration. He has also been a member of the Little, Brown Tax Practice Advisory Board.

**Stuart J. Goldring** is a partner in the law firm of Weil, Gotshal & Manges LLP in New York City. He received a bachelor's in Business Administration degree with high distinction from the University of Michigan in 1979 and graduated *magna cum laude* from the University of Michigan Law School in 1982, where he was elected to the Order of the Coif. He also received an LL.M. in Taxation from the New York University School of Law, where he was a Graduate Editor of the *Tax Law Review*. He has extensive experience in advising debtors, creditors, and potential acquirers and investors in troubled companies, spanning over 20 years. He serves on the Executive Committee of the Tax Section of the New York State Bar Association and is Co-Chairman of the Committee on Bankruptcy and Losses. He also served on the former Tax Council of the Association of the Bar of the City of New York, and chaired a special subcommittee of the Tax Council and the Committee on Bankruptcy and Corporate Reorganization with respect to tax-related proposals of the National Bankruptcy Review Commission. He is also a member of the Tax Section of the American Bar Association. He is an adjunct professor of law at New York University Law School on *Bankruptcy Tax*, is a frequent speaker at tax institutes, and has published numerous articles on tax issues relating to financially troubled companies. He is also a member of the Corporate Tax and Business Planning Advisory Board for *Tax Management*.

# Acknowledgments

The authors wish to thank their colleague Martin Bienenstock of Weil, Gotshal & Manges LLP for his helpful suggestions regarding the bankruptcy law portions of this volume; their former partner Jerred G. Blanchard, Jr., now a partner with Ernst & Young LLP, for his assistance and insights in connection with the financially troubled thrift institution and consolidated return portions of this volume; their colleague Kevin M. Richards, also a partner with Ernst & Young LLP, for his assistance in the development of the Eleventh Amendment state immunity discussion; and their secretary Sandra Delacey for her devotion and skill in the transcription of the manuscript.

# Summary of Contents

# Table of Contents

## 4

## Debt Modification

# 6

## Two-Company Reorganizations Involving a Failing Company

## 7

## Utilizing Tax Losses



## 8

## Special Problems of Multi-Company Debtor Groups

## 9

## Liquidating Trusts, Escrows, and the Like

**10**

## Bankruptcy Aspects of Federal Tax Procedure

**11**

**State and Local Tax Aspects of Bankruptcy**

## 12

## Liquidating Bankruptcies

## 13

## Deductibility of Expenses During Bankruptcy

# Introduction: Dealing with the Troubled Corporation

Businesses begin with optimism. Some succeed beyond their dreams. Some meet projections. Some do less well than had been hoped. More than a few—occasionally after many years of success—become failing businesses whose survival is threatened. Some failing businesses can be reorganized and turned into survivors. Others will end up as failed businesses that must be liquidated.

This volume is about failing and failed businesses. A failing business is one whose cash flow becomes insufficient to meet its cash obligations. Indeed, the fundamental problem facing every failing business is the need to reduce its cash obligations. Cash obligations include obligations to pay wages to employees; to pay employment and withholding taxes on such wages; to pay trade creditors for such items as inventory, supplies, utilities, and rent; to purchase capital plant and equipment; and to pay interest and principal on short- and long-term debt.

A failing business will try to solve its cash flow problems initially by cutting operating expenses. If this does not solve the problem, more drastic steps will be taken. The enterprise may consider selling some of its assets to provide funds to pay down debt, thereby shrinking its business. The enterprise may consider asking its various creditors to restructure its debt, perhaps by stretching out due dates for payments of principal and interest or by reducing the amount of principal and interest payable on the debt or by converting debt into equity.

Failing businesses will usually have generated significant net operating losses (NOLs) and, perhaps, various tax credit carryovers. These are valuable assets. Maximizing their use will be an important element of the business plan for the company. Sometimes, perhaps after shrinking its failing business by selling off assets, a failing company may decide to buy an existing successful business whose income can be sheltered for a time by the NOLs and credit carryovers generated by the failing business. Or, instead of being the buyer, the failing company may become a target for a successful company, whose owners see possibilities in combining the two businesses.

A basic question faced by every failing business is whether restructuring the company in one or more of the above ways will be practicable from a business and tax point of view without resorting to proceedings under the Bankruptcy Code, or whether, instead, the business will have to resort to the Chapter 11 reorganization provisions of the Bankruptcy Code.

If restructuring the company—whether within or without a Bankruptcy Code proceeding—does not prove feasible, the company will have to be liquidated. A liquidation, like a restructuring, can occur by consent, without resort to the Bankruptcy Code, or by a liquidating bankruptcy proceeding under Chapter 7, or possibly Chapter 11, of the Bankruptcy Code.

At the same time as company management is deciding on a strategy, the company's creditors and stockholders should be doing their own strategic thinking, keeping in mind the consequences to themselves. Because the various classes of creditors and shareholders will usually have conflicting tax and nontax interests, resolving these conflicts becomes the main problem to be solved in the restructuring process, once a business plan for the survival of the business operation has been developed.

This volume will describe the various transactions that may typically take place in the effort to deal with a failing or failed business and will focus on their tax consequences to the company and its various classes of creditors and shareholders. It will be limited to corporate businesses and will not cover proprietorships or partnerships.

Gordon D. Henderson

Stuart J. Goldring

**September 2007**

# 1

# Developing a Strategy for a Failing Company



## §101 DEVELOPING A PLAN

As a company begins to approach a failing condition, management strategy should include a plan to deal with creditors when and if the time comes that the company will be unable to pay its obligations as they fall due. The plan should include a decision as to whether the company should seek concessions from creditors without resorting to proceedings under the Bankruptcy Code, or whether the makeup of its creditor and stockholder groups suggests that resort to the Bankruptcy Code may be necessary. As the troubles of the company become apparent to the creditors, they, too, should reach a decision on this point. The considerations involved in choosing between a bankruptcy or a nonbankruptcy proceeding are discussed beginning at §201.

## §102 AVOIDING TOO MUCH BUSINESS SHRINKAGE

The strategy for the company should include a plan for preserving its NOLs, capital loss carryovers, ITC carryovers, and foreign tax credit carryovers. Although the company may need to pare down operations in order to save expenses, and it may have to sell off assets in order to pay debts, the company should be careful not to wind down its activities so far as to jeopardize its ability to preserve these tax attributes in the event of a restructuring of its capital or the consummation of an acquisitive transaction. A severe shrinkage of the company's activities may make it difficult or impossible for the company later to surmount the hurdles for survivability of these attributes that are raised by Code §§269, 382 and 383. These provisions are discussed later in this volume.

In addition, the company should be careful in its planning to avoid speculating about the possibility of engaging in a two-company reorganization, as opposed to an internal recapitalization, until it becomes clear that this must be done to save the company. As discussed below in the chapter dealing with two-company reorganizations, the IRS has developed the ruling policy that it will begin to measure the "substantially-all-assets" test and certain aspects of the "continuity-of-interest" test for tax-free reorganizations from the time the company first decides to embark on a two-company, rather than an internal, approach to restructuring. Premature planning for a two-company transaction may therefore have the perverse result of eventually making it impossible for the company to satisfy these tests by the time the company is finally ready to launch the transaction.

## §103 AVOIDING LIABILITY FOR EMPLOYMENT TAXES

A company suffering cash flow problems typically becomes slow in paying its liabilities even before it reaches the point where it cannot pay its obligations as they become due. Management will keep current on those liabilities that as a practical matter cannot be delayed, such as wages, but will fall behind on other items that seem less pressing. In these circumstances, there is a temptation for management to fall behind in paying payroll taxes withheld from its employees. If this occurs, the company may eventually reach the point where it does not have enough cash to pay over the withheld amounts to the appropriate levels of government.

This should be avoided. Penalties can be severe. Code §7501 states that all taxes collected or withheld are to be considered held in trust for the benefit of the United States. Code §7202 provides that a person who is required to collect and pay over taxes and who willfully fails to do so is guilty of a felony and can be fined up to $10,000 or imprisoned for up to five years, or both. Under Code §7215, a person who fails to make withholding tax deposits may be guilty of a misdemeanor and fined not more than $5,000 or imprisoned for not more than one year or both. Code §6672 provides a civil penalty—equal to 100 percent of the taxes withheld—on any person responsible for collecting the tax who willfully fails to collect it or truthfully account for and pay it over.[1] A penalty of up to 15 percent is imposed by Code §6656 for the

---

[1] **§103** The liability for employment taxes arises at the time of withholding, not at the time the withheld amount is due for payment. Consequently, a responsible person cannot avoid the penalty by resigning prior to the date the taxes are due. *See, e.g., Brown v. United States*, 591 F.2d 1136, 79-1 U.S.T.C. ¶9285 (5th Cir. 1979); *Long v. Bacon*, 239 F. Supp. 911, 65-1 U.S.T.C. ¶9289 (S.D. Iowa). A three-year statute of limitations on assessments generally applies for purposes of the Code §6672 penalty—Action on Decision CC-1996-006, July 15, 1996; *see also* Code §6672(b)(3), as added by the Taxpayer Bill of Rights 2 (referencing statute of limitations under Code §6501)—and, effective July 1, 1996, no Code §6672 penalty generally may be assessed unless the IRS first provides a notice of proposed assessment. Code §6672(b). Where, however, the company is subject to an unlimited assessment period for its employment tax liability—as in the case of fraud—the IRS takes the position that an unlimited assessment period similarly applies for purposes of the related Code §6672 penalty. IRS Chief Counsel Advice 200532046, June 30, 2005, *reprinted at* 2005 TNT 156-12.

For a further discussion of the Code §6672 100 percent penalty, particularly where the debtor has filed for bankruptcy under Chapter 11, *see* §§1006.3, 1006.3.2 and 1014 in Chapter 10. *See also* Hertz, Personal Liabilities of the Unsuspecting Executive for Penalties Under Section 6672 and Other Nightmares, 32 Inst. on Fed. Tax'n 1171 (1974).

failure to deposit taxes when due in an appropriate government depository. In addition to these penalties, interest can be imposed on the underpayment.

For possible actions that the debtor company might take—either before filing a bankruptcy petition or in a bankruptcy plan—that might help relieve responsible persons of the 100 percent civil penalty, *see* § § 1006.3.2 and 1016.2 below.

## § 104 POTENTIAL CREDITOR LIABILITY FOR DEBTOR'S WITHHOLDING TAXES

As a failing business moves from bad to worse, creditors may find themselves taking on major responsibilities relating to the control and management of the business. If this is done in the wrong way, the creditor will run the risk of having its claims subordinated to those of other creditors and of becoming subject to liability for unpaid withholding taxes of the debtor.

Where a lender, surety, or other person who is not the employer with respect to an employee or group of employees pays wages directly to the employee or group of employees, or to an agent on their behalf, it will have personal liability to the United States under Code § 3505 for the taxes (with interest) required to be withheld from such wages.[1] Moreover, if the lender, surety, or other person supplies funds to or for the account of the employer for the specific purpose of paying wages and has actual notice or knowledge that the employer will not make timely payment or deposit of the required withholding amounts, it will be personally liable for the withheld taxes (together with interest), although in this instance its liability is limited to 25 percent of the amount it supplied to the employer for this purpose.[2] A creditor's liability under

---

[1] **§ 104** Code § 3505(a). Code § 6303(a) generally requires the Commissioner to give notice of an assessment, within 60 days after making it, to each person liable for the unpaid tax. However, in *Jersey Shore State Bank v. United States*, 87-1 U.S.T.C. ¶ 9131, 107 S. Ct. 782 (1987), the Supreme Court held that the IRS is not required by Code § 6303(a) to give notice of an assessment for unpaid withholding taxes against an employer to a creditor potentially liable under Code § 3505 for "a sum equal to" the unpaid tax. *See* Note, Jersey Shore State Bank v. United States: Lender Liability and Notice—When a Summons Is Enough, 7 Va. Tax Rev. 179 (1987); Note, Taxation: Lender Liability Under I.R.C. § 3505(a), 39 Okla. L. Rev. 348 (1986) (pre-Supreme Court decision).

For a more detailed discussion of Code § 3505, *see, e.g.*, Saltzman, IRS Practice and Procedure, 17.11 (Rev. Second Edition); Goldring & Mayo, Lenders Beware: Potential Liability for Unpaid Employment Taxes, 4 J. Bank Tax'n #1 (Fall 1990); Makel & Chadwick, Lender Liability for a Borrower's Unpaid Payroll Taxes, 43 Bus. Law. 507 (1988); Winston, Lender's Liability for Borrower's Unpaid Employment Taxes, 46 Tex. B.J. 1253 (1983); explanation at Stand. Fed. Tax Rep. (CCH) ¶ 35,006. *See also* Douglas-Hamilton, When Are Creditors in Control of Debtor Companies, 26 Practical Law No. 7, pp. 61, 70-72 (1980) (hereafter Douglas-Hamilton, Creditors in Control); Douglas-Hamilton, Creditor Liabilities Resulting from Improper Interference with the Management of a Financially Troubled Debtor, 31 Bus. Law. 343 (1975).

[2] Code § 3505(b); *see, e.g.*, *United States v. Park Cities Bank & Trust Co.*, 481 F.2d 738, 73-2 U.S.T.C. ¶ 9503 (5th Cir. 1973) (Code § 3505 penalty imposed on bank where bank approved overdrafts, the proceeds of which were deposited in a payroll account from which the employer failed to withhold); *In re Brandt-Airflex Corp.*, 87-1 U.S.T.C. ¶ 9194, 69 B.R. 701 (Bankr. E.D.N.Y. 1987), *rev'd on other grounds*, 78 B.R. 10 (E.D.N.Y. 1987), *aff'd* 843 F.2d 90 (2d Cir. 1988) (held that lender was liable under Code § 3505(b) where the lender approved overdrafts for the payment of net wages but "bounced" employer's checks for the payment of withholding taxes); *United States v. Swiftships, Inc.*, 1995 U.S.

these provisions does not relieve the debtor of its responsibility for any unpaid withholding taxes, except to the extent of amounts actually paid by the creditor.[3]

The IRS may institute collection proceedings against a creditor under these provisions any time within ten years after assessment of the *employer's* tax.[4] Because the employer's tax must generally be assessed within three years after the filing date of its employment tax return (which is treated as occurring no earlier than April 15 of the succeeding calendar year to which the return relates), this means that the collection proceeding against the lender may be brought more than 13 years after the original liability for the tax arose.[5] There is a conflict in the courts as to whether the lender's collection period is further extended automatically by any period for which the employer's statute of limitation on collection is tolled or extended, such as by the automatic stay in bankruptcy or by the employer's agreement to extend the statute of limitations.[6]

Creditors should make special note of these provisions and be certain that, in the circumstances described therein, the withheld taxes are paid to the appropriate taxing authority.[7] Even beyond these particular circumstances, however, creditors (and even prospective purchasers) who take over practical control of the failing company may find that they have become subject to the civil and criminal provisions, discussed

(Footnote Continued)

Dist. LEXIS 17643, 76 A.F.T.R.2d (P-H) 8006 (E.D. La. 1995) (Code § 3505(b) imposes no duty on a lender to investigate outside of its own organization).

[3] Code § 3505(c); *In re Brandt-Airflex Corp., supra* note 2.

[4] Reg. § 31.3505-1(d)(1) (effective August 1, 1995, the collection period was increased from six to ten years to be consistent with the general statute of limitations for collections); Code § 6502(a) and Reg. § 301.6502-1 (statute of limitations for collection extended from six to ten years, effective for all taxes for which the limitations period had not expired by November 5, 1990). *See also United States v. R.C. Ziegler Co., Inc.*, 76 A.F.T.R.2d ¶ 95-5339 (W.D. Wash. 1995) (rejected IRS position that the collection period under Code § 3505 should be interpreted as coterminous with general statute of limitations for collections prior to the effective date of the change in the regulations).

[5] *See* Code § 6501 (a) and (b)(2); *O'Hare v. United States*, 878 F.2d 953, 89-2 U.S.T.C. ¶ 9436 (6th Cir. 1989).

[6] *Compare United States v. Harvis Construction Co.*, 857 F.2d 1360, 88-2 U.S.T.C. ¶ 9524 (9th Cir. 1988) (lender's collection period not extended), *with United States v. Associates Commercial Corp.*, 721 F.2d 1094, 83-2 U.S.T.C. ¶ 9689 (7th Cir. 1983) (extended; viewed absence of any statement in the regulations to parallel suspensions as an oversight). *See also United States v. Olympic Savings and Loan Ass'n*, 677 F. Supp. 1079 (W.D. Wash. 1988) (employer's agreement to extend the statute of limitations on collection of employment withholding taxes also bound lender liable for such taxes under Code § 3505, even though the lender received no notice of the agreement). A similar debate exists with respect to the assessment period for the 100 percent penalty imposed on responsible persons under Code § 6672. *See* IRS Chief Counsel Advice 200532046 (June 30, 2005), *reprinted at* 2005 TNT 156-12.

[7] In this regard, it should be noted that even a late payment of withholding taxes by a company on the eve of bankruptcy is not regarded as a voidable preference in bankruptcy. *See Begier, Jr. v. IRS*, 110 S. Ct. 2258 (1990), discussed in Chapter 10 at § 1005.2. Moreover, even if the company is in bankruptcy, the company may be able to obtain the court's permission to pay such withholding taxes or, as part of a plan of reorganization, direct that such withholding taxes be paid before other prepetition tax claims. *See United States v. Energy Resources Co.*, 110 S. Ct. 2139 (1990), discussed in Chapter 10 at § 1016.2.

above at § 103, that are applicable to responsible corporate officers and other responsible persons, including the 100 percent civil penalty under Code § 6672.[8]

It should be noted that Code § 6672, which imposes a civil penalty on "responsible persons" of 100 percent of the taxes that should have been withheld, does not mention interest. Thus, it has been held that under this provision the "responsible person" has no liability for interest on the unpaid withholding taxes to the extent that it accrues between the date that the employer's tax should have been paid and the date on which the IRS assesses the penalty against the "responsible person."[9] In contrast, Code § 3505, which applies to lenders, mentions interest for such period and makes the lenders to which it applies liable for such interest as well. Moreover, it has

---

[8] *See, e.g., Commonwealth Nat'l Bank of Dallas v. United States*, 665 F.2d 743, 82-1 U.S.T.C. ¶ 9149 (5th Cir. 1982) (Code § 6672 100 percent penalty imposed on creditor, even though creditor's employees did not manage debtor corporation); *Merchants Natl. Bank of Mobile v. United States*, 878 F.2d 1382, 89-2 U.S.T.C. ¶ 9511 (11th Cir. 1989) (same); *Pacific Natl. Ins. Co. v. United States*, 422 F.2d 26, 70-1 U.S.T.C. ¶ 9238 (9th Cir. 1970), *cert. denied* (Code § 6672 100 percent penalty imposed on surety where surety approved wage payments to employees and declined to advance funds for the payment of withheld taxes, even though surety approved and funded payments to nonemployee creditors); *United States v. Vaccarella*, 735 F. Supp. 1421, 90-1 U.S.T.C. ¶ 50,305 (S.D. Ind. 1990), *aff'd sub nom. United States v. Security Pacific Business Credit, Inc.*, 956 F.2d 703, 92-1 U.S.T.C. ¶ 50,125 (7th Cir. 1992) (lender, rather than corporate officers, was liable under Code § 6672 and under Code § 3505(b) where the lender had complete control of the debtor's finances through a lock-box system, exercised veto power over funding requests, directed that other creditors be paid before the IRS, funded net wages through wire transfers directly into the debtor's payroll account, and knew that the debtor had no other source of funds to pay the withholding tax); *Mercantile Bank of Kansas City v. United States*, 856 F. Supp. 1355, 94-2 U.S.T.C. ¶ 50,379 (W.D. Mo. 1974) (Code § 6672 liability *not* imposed, even though bank had the ability to exercise discretionary control over payments and had knowledge that tax payments were not made, because the bank never in fact exercised such control); *United States v. North Side Deposit Bank*, 83-2 U.S.T.C. 9503 (W.D. Pa.) (Code § 6672 100 percent penalty and, alternatively, Code § 3505(b) penalty imposed on bank where funds continued to be lent even after bank directed debtor to have its receivables paid directly to the bank, a bank officer was appointed to manage the receivables, and bank's officers knew of the debtor's inability to continue paying payroll taxes and did not intend to clear any further checks for such taxes); *Caterino v. United States*, 794 F.2d 1, 86-1 U.S.T.C. ¶ 9452 (1st Cir.), *cert. denied*, 107 S. Ct. 1347 (1987) (upheld imposition of Code § 6672 100 percent penalty against the president/principal stockholder of the purchaser of a troubled company, where evidence supported the finding that the president had the "ability to significantly determine the flow and disbursements of funds" of the troubled company and it was undisputed that, having knowledge of the unpaid withholding taxes, the president consciously disregarded his obligation to pay them; the president had arranged or guaranteed substantial loans to the troubled company, was instrumental in installing a new general manager of the troubled company and, as evidenced by an employee's mailing of the withholding tax returns of the troubled company to him for his review, was deferred to regarding management decisions); *United Siding Supply Inc. v. United States*, 95-1 U.S.T.C. ¶ 50,269 (N.D. Okla. 1995) (100 percent penalty imposed on creditor who, pursuant to collateral protection order, had authority to determine which of debtor's creditors would be paid); *Clouse v. United States*, 87-2 U.S.T.C. ¶ 9595 (D. Mich.) (granted IRS motion for judgment notwithstanding the verdict and imposed Code § 6672 100 percent penalty on an employee/principal creditor/minority shareholder who had a "significant voice" in management, co-signed checks on several occasions, received substantial sums in payment of obligations due him, and, given his knowledge of the company's financial position and his experiences as a former 80 percent shareholder of the company's predecessor, should have inquired if any withholding taxes were owing). *See also* Saltzman, *supra* note 1, at ¶ 17.08(2)(a); Makel & Chadwick, *supra* note 1; Hertz, *supra* § 103 note 1, at 1178; Winston, *supra* note 1; Douglas-Hamilton, Creditors in Control, *supra* note 1; Lundgren, Liability of a Creditor in a Control Relationship with Its Debtor, 67 Marq. L. Rev. 523 (1984).

[9] *See United States v. Security Pacific Business Credit, Inc., supra* note 8.

been held that the government can maximize its recovery by recovering the unpaid tax from a "responsible person" and recovering the interest on the unpaid tax from a lender under Code § 3505.[10]

An interesting variation from the approach taken in the foregoing authorities can be found in an IRS Chief Counsel Advice[11] dealing with a situation where a factor had purchased wage claims from employees of a bankrupt company. Pointing to Code § 3401(d)—which provides that if the person for whom the individual performs services does not have control of the payment of wages for such services, the term "employer" means a person having control of the payment of wages—the Chief Counsel held that the factor had become the "employer" and was liable for the withholding of income and employment tax and the payment of the employer's FICA and FUTA taxes on the payments (which presumably were less than the face amount of the wage claims themselves) that it actually made to the employees, and that the debtor would not be obligated to withhold or pay taxes on any payments that it might make of these wages to the factor (even if these payments equaled the face amount of the wage claims).

The issuer of a performance bond to protect a contractor against default by a subcontractor has been held not to be liable for the defaulting subcontractor's federal and state employment taxes.[12] The contractor was the only beneficiary of the performance bond; the federal and state tax authorities were neither stated nor implied beneficiaries.

## § 105 CREDITOR BAD DEBT DEDUCTIONS

Creditors of a failing business will generally want to take appropriate bad debt deductions at as early a date as possible.[1] The amount and timing of the deductions will depend on whether the creditor takes a partial or a complete worthlessness deduction. The creditor who fails to take adequate bad debt deductions may find itself faced with a capital, rather than an ordinary, loss when the debt of the failing business is eventually restructured. As mentioned below at § 502.4, however, bad debt deductions may cause any stock received in exchange for the debt to be treated as Code § 1245 property to the extent of such deductions.

An exception to the foregoing advice may apply where the creditor is, or expects to become, a stockholder while still being a creditor. If the creditor in such a situation were to write down the debt and then later contribute the debt to the capital of the debtor, the debtor could have cancellation of debt consequences under Code § 108

---

[10] Id. In this case, the bank was found to be both a "responsible person" under Code § 6672 and a lender liable under Code § 3505(b). The IRS was allowed to recover the full amount of the unpaid tax from the bank under Code § 6672, and the interest on the unpaid tax from the date the tax was due under Code § 3505(b). The 25 percent limit contained in Code § 3505(b) applied in this case only to the recovery of the unpaid interest.

[11] IRS Chief Counsel Advice 200019009, February 7, 2000, *reprinted at* 2000 TNT 94-99.

[12] *Island Ins. Co. v. Hawaiian Foliage & Landscape Inc.*, 2000 U.S. Dist. LEXIS 16749 (D. Hawaii 2000).

[1] **§ 105** *See generally* Blanchard, Jr., Bennett and Speer, The Deductibility of Investments in Financially Troubled Subsidiaries and Related Federal Income Tax Considerations, 80 Taxes 91 (2002).

that the parties might wish to avoid. In addition, special considerations may apply where the debtor and creditor are members of the same consolidated group (*see* §§ 508.2.4, 804.2, and 804.4).

# 2

# Bankruptcy Versus Nonbankruptcy Restructuring



## §201 CHOOSING BETWEEN BANKRUPTCY AND NONBANKRUPTCY RESTRUCTURING

A fundamental strategic question that most failing companies must face is whether to attempt restructuring outside the provisions of the Bankruptcy Code, or whether instead to seek the protections of the Bankruptcy Code by filing a voluntary petition for reorganization under Chapter 11.

Creditors, for their part, will face the question of whether and when to file an involuntary petition in bankruptcy against the failing company under Chapter 11 (reorganizations) or Chapter 7 (liquidations) of the Bankruptcy Code.

A voluntary petition can be filed by a debtor even if the debtor is neither insolvent in a balance sheet sense nor unable to pay its debts as they become due.[1] However, the petition is likely to be dismissed at the request of any creditor or of the

[1] **§201** 11 U.S.C. §301.

United States Trustee or on the court's own motion if the bankruptcy court does not believe that the protections of the Bankruptcy Code are necessary to allow the debtor to continue as a viable business.[2]

An involuntary petition can be filed by creditors holding noncontingent claims aggregating at least $5,000 in excess of the value of any security for such claims.[3] If the involuntary petition is contested, the petition will be granted only if the debtor is generally not paying its debts (except those that are the subject of a bona fide dispute) as they become due.[4]

The advantages and disadvantages that should be weighed by the failing company and its creditors in deciding whether to utilize the Bankruptcy Code include issues that are discussed immediately below at § § 202-213.

## § 202 EFFECTS ON CUSTOMERS AND SUPPLIERS

Filing for protection under the Bankruptcy Code may in some cases cause the failing company to lose its customers or its suppliers. In such circumstances, there is little chance of saving the company if a bankruptcy petition is filed. Conversely, sophisticated suppliers frequently feel more comfortable dealing with a Chapter 11 debtor-in-possession because their claims for postpetition goods and services are provided administrative (*i.e.*, first) priority status and postpetition payments for postpetition goods and services are not recoverable from those creditors as voidable preferences.

## § 203 COMPARING SPEED AND EXPENSE

If it seems feasible to obtain a restructuring by the consent of the failing company's creditors and shareholders, such a consensual arrangement may in some cases be achieved faster and cheaper than in a bankruptcy restructuring. On the other hand, where there are only a few creditor holdouts to a consensual arrangement, a bankruptcy restructuring may be relatively fast and inexpensive. Indeed, in appropriate cases it may be possible to combine the speed and economy of a largely consensual arrangement with the various advantages that bankruptcy affords (including the ability to bind nonconsenting creditors), by devising a so-called prepackaged bankruptcy plan (*see* § 213 below).

---

[2] 11 U.S.C. § § 105(a), 307, 1112(b); *see, e.g., Zolg v. Kelly* (*In re Kelly*), 841 F.2d 908 (9th Cir. 1988); *In re Phoenix-Piccadilly, Ltd.*, 84 B.R. 843 (Bankr. M.D. Fla. 1988).

[3] 11 U.S.C. § 303.

[4] 11 U.S.C. § 303(h). This subsection also provides that the involuntary petition must be granted if within 120 days before the filing of the petition a trustee or other agent was appointed to take charge of less than substantially all the property of the debtor for the purpose of enforcing a lien against the property.

## §204 BANKRUPTCY PLAN CAN BIND NONCONSENTING CREDITORS OR SHAREHOLDERS

Creditors whose claims would not be impaired by a Chapter 11 plan of reorganization are deemed to have consented to it.[1] As to any class of creditors whose interests would be impaired by the plan, the entire class is deemed to have consented to the plan if those voting in favor represent at least two-thirds in amount, and more than one-half in number, of the claims voted.[2] A class of shareholders whose interests would be adversely affected by the plan is deemed to have consented if at least two-thirds of the shareholders in that class voting on the plan approve it.[3] Even if a class of creditors or shareholders does not consent, the plan may be "crammed down" on that class by the court if the court finds that the nonconsenting class is receiving as much as it would have received in a liquidation and no junior class obtains any distribution.[4]

## §205 CHANGE IN STATUS OF NONRECOURSE DEBT IN BANKRUPTCY

Section 1111(b) of the Bankruptcy Code provides that nonrecourse debt will have general recourse against the debtor in a Chapter 11 bankruptcy proceeding, notwithstanding its contrary terms, unless (1) the property securing the debt is to be sold during the pendency of the Chapter 11 proceeding or pursuant to the Chapter 11 plan or (2) the class of nonrecourse creditors elects to forfeit its unsecured deficiency claims against the debtor, in which case such class of creditors will be entitled to obtain deferred cash payments equal to the full amount of its claims, but the present value of the payment stream need only equal the value of the creditor's interest in the underlying collateral.[1] Absent one of the above exceptions, a nonrecourse creditor may be entitled to obtain distributions of cash or other assets in respect of any deficiency claim, as well as deferred cash payments having an aggregate present value equal to the value of the creditor's interest in the underlying collateral.[2] It is possible, however, that the aggregate of these distributions will not equal the full amount of the creditor's claim.

---

[1] **§204** 11 U.S.C. §1126(f).

[2] 11 U.S.C. §1126(c).

[3] 11 U.S.C. §1126(d).

[4] *See* 11 U.S.C. §1129(b).

[1] **§205** 11 U.S.C. §§506(a), 1111(b)(2), 1129(b)(2)(A)(i)(II). This election may be useful for purposes of avoiding a book writeoff for financial accounting purposes. *See* FASB Statement No. 15, Accounting by Debtors and Creditors for Troubled Debt Restructurings, paragraphs 30-33 (June 1977) (in the case of certain debt restructurings, a creditor may not be required to record a loss in respect of his claim where the aggregate amount of cash payments to be received over time, whether denominated as principal or interest, equals at least the excess of the principal amount of the claim plus accrued interest over the fair value of any other assets received in satisfaction of such claim).

[2] *See* 11 U.S.C. §1129(b)2)(B).

The granting of the unsecured claim under section 1111(b)(1) makes it more difficult or sometimes impossible for a plan proponent to obtain confirmation of a Chapter 11 plan over the lender's dissent pursuant to Bankruptcy Code section 1129(b) (*i.e.*, makes cramdown more difficult). For the plan proponent to obtain confirmation of its plan, at least one class of impaired claims must accept the plan pursuant to Bankruptcy Code section 1129(a)(10). In a single asset real estate case, if the undersecured lender votes its secured claim against the plan, then the class of the single secured claim would reject the plan. If the lender also votes its unsecured deficiency claim against the plan, and the deficiency claim is more than one-third the amount of all unsecured claims in the class of unsecured claims, then the entire class of unsecured claims will have rejected the plan because, pursuant to Bankruptcy Code section 1126(c), two-thirds of the total amount of voted claims must accept for the class to accept. If both classes reject the plan and there is no other class of impaired claims (such as a class of a claim secured by a different asset) that accepts the plan, confirmation must be denied.

Bankruptcy Code section 1111(b)(2) enables an undersecured, nonrecourse lender to minimize writeoffs on its financial statements pursuant to Financial Accounting Standards Board Opinion 15. For example, pursuant to section 1111(b)(2), the lender may elect to have its entire claim (say $3 million) treated as a secured claim even if the collateral's value is only $2 million. Without the election, the lender would hold a secured claim of $2 million and an unsecured deficiency claim of $1 million. There are several consequences of the section 1111(b)(2) election. First, the lender forfeits its unsecured claim. Therefore, if there is any distribution to unsecured claimholders, the lender will not receive its ratable share of such distribution. Second, the lender will be entitled under Bankruptcy Code section 1129(b)(2)(A)(i)(II) to a note in the face amount of the entire claim ($3 million), which note, however, need only have a present value of $2 million. Accordingly, the interest rate can be pegged at a below market rate in order to lower the present value of the note from $3 million to $2 million.

In sum and substance, under the section 1111(b)(2) election the lender forfeits its unsecured deficiency claim and obtains the same present value for its secured claim as if the lender had not made the election. Thus, there is no economic benefit to making the election. In fact, there is an economic loss equal to the loss of the distribution on the unsecured claim that is forfeited. But, by receiving a new note for the full amount of its claim, albeit at a below market interest rate, the lender can sometimes avoid writeoffs under FASB 15.

## §206 BANKRUPTCY MAY BAR USE OF NONVOTING STOCK

Section 1123(a)(6) of the Bankruptcy Code requires a Chapter 11 plan to include in the charter of the corporate debtor a provision

> prohibiting the issuance of nonvoting equity securities, and providing, as to the several classes of securities possessing voting power, an appropriate distribution of such power among such classes, including, in the case of any class of equity securities having a preference over another class of equity securities with respect to dividends, adequate provisions for the

> election of directors representing such preferred class in the event of default in the payment of such dividends . . .

This provision may limit the flexibility to adapt the restructuring plan to the requirements of various provisions of the tax law. For example, for purposes of Code § 382, "stock" generally does not include nonvoting and nonconvertible stock that is limited and preferred as to dividends. The issuance of such limited and preferred nonvoting stock is sometimes helpful in preserving NOLs and other carryovers. It may be, however, that Section 1123(a)(6) of the Bankruptcy Code will be construed to allow the issuance of preferred stock that votes only when dividends fall in arrears.[1] If so, this provision would not limit tax flexibility, since such stock is generally not considered voting stock for tax purposes until the condition precedent to its voting power occurs.[2]

## § 207 CHANGE OF INTEREST LIABILITY IN BANKRUPTCY

The Bankruptcy Code affects the liability of the debtor for interest for the period commencing with the filing of the bankruptcy petition. The debtor remains liable for interest on secured debt to the extent that the security is adequate to provide for the interest as well as the principal.[1] However, interest on unsecured debt is generally not allowed for the period commencing with the bankruptcy case unless the assets of the debtor are sufficient to pay both the interest and the principal on all of the company's debt.[2] These provisions may, however, be varied by contract or by consent of the creditors as part of the Chapter 11 plan of bankruptcy reorganization.

## § 208 BANKRUPTCY STAY OF ASSESSMENT AND COLLECTION OF TAXES

The commencement of a bankruptcy case operates as an automatic stay preventing the collection (and, until recently, the assessment) against the failing company of tax or other claims until relief from the stay is granted, the case is dismissed or closed, or a discharge is denied or granted.[1] This protects the failing company from being harassed by a multitude of lawsuits from different creditors. Moreover, where claims for prepetition taxes are allowed as part of a Chapter 11 plan, the Bankruptcy Code permits the debtor to pay many of these taxes (with interest) over time, not to extend beyond five years after the commencement of the bankruptcy case for bankruptcy cases on or after October 17, 2005. For bankruptcy cases commenced prior to such

---

[1] **§ 206** *See* 5 Collier on Bankruptcy ¶ 1123.01 (15th ed.).

[2] *See, e.g.*, Vermont Hydro-Electric Corp., 29 B.T.A. 1006 (1934), *acq.*, Dec. 8403; Reg. § 1.302-3(a)(3); J. Crestol, K. Hennessey & A. Rua, The Consolidated Tax Return ¶ 2.01[e](supplemented).

[1] **§ 207** 11 U.S.C. § 506(b).

[2] *See* 11 U.S.C. § 502(b)(2) and discussion at § 301.

[1] **§ 208** 11 U.S.C. § 362(a), (c).

date, payment can be made over as long as six years after the assessment of such taxes.[2]

## §209 CANCELLATION OF DEBT RULES IN BANKRUPTCY

As we shall see, Code §108 provides less liberal cancellation of debt (COD) rules for solvent companies outside of bankruptcy than for either companies not made solvent by the cancellation or companies in Chapter 11 proceedings. In particular, the debt-for-stock rules are less liberal for solvent debtors outside bankruptcy. Thus, the reduction of NOLs and other favorable tax attributes caused by a capital restructuring may be smaller if they occur in a Chapter 11 proceeding than if they occur in a consensual proceeding outside bankruptcy. Even though the Code §108 rules are the same for companies that are not made solvent by the cancellation as for companies in Chapter 11 proceedings, the company in a bankruptcy case has the considerable advantage that it need not prove insolvency.

In addition, section 346(j) of the Bankruptcy Code provides special cancellation of debt rules for state and local tax purposes.

## §210 SPECIAL CODE §382 RULES AVAILABLE IN BANKRUPTCY

The substantial changes made by the Tax Reform Act of 1986 give certain companies in Chapter 11 (or similar) proceedings an election to be governed by a special version of Code §382 that is not available outside such proceedings. This special version (discussed at §508.5) is more liberal in many important respects, although, as a price for its application, a limitation is imposed on past interest deductions and on the availability of the Code §108 stock-for-debt exception to COD income. Even if a company elects not to apply this special rule or it is otherwise inapplicable, the regular Code §382 annual limitation is more favorably computed for companies in Chapter 11 proceedings (by valuing their stock after, rather than before, any debt cancellation that is part of the Chapter 11 plan) than for companies outside such or similar proceedings (*see* §508.4).

## §211 BANKRUPTCY LIMITATIONS ON STATE AND LOCAL TAXATION

A ruling as to the state and local tax consequences of a Chapter 11 plan may be requested from the respective state and local tax authorities and, if not granted, from the bankruptcy court.[1] Moreover, Section 346 of the Bankruptcy Code, particularly as applicable to bankruptcy cases commenced prior to October 17, 2005, imposes certain limitations on the way in which state and local governments may tax a restructuring occurring under the Bankruptcy Code.

---

[2] 11 U.S.C. §1129(a)(9)(C).

[1] **§211** 11 U.S.C. §1146(b), formerly §1146(d).

## §212 THE *LTV* CASE: TREATMENT OF CREDITORS IN NONBANKRUPTCY DEBT EXCHANGES

For a time, lower court opinions in the *LTV* bankruptcy case made creditors reluctant to engage in debt restructurings outside bankruptcy, at least where the debt restructuring did not so fundamentally solve the debtor's problems as to make a subsequent bankruptcy proceeding unlikely.

LTV had issued publicly traded bonds for cash. The bonds were issued at a modest discount and so carried some OID. As the prospects for the company dimmed and the old bonds fell in value, the company made an offer to exchange for each $1,000 face amount of old bonds a new $1,000 face amount bond (with modified interest rate, maturity date, and sinking fund provisions) plus 15 shares of common stock. Many of the old bondholders accepted the offer. Less than two months later LTV filed for bankruptcy. In the bankruptcy case, LTV argued that the amount of the allowable claim for those who had accepted the exchange offer was less than for those who had not (even though both held claims with a face amount $1,000). The ground for its argument was that section 502(b)(2) of the Bankruptcy Code disallows claims for interest that has not matured at the date of bankruptcy, including OID. LTV argued that the amount of the OID on the new bonds should be measured by the difference between their face amount and the value, on the date of the exchange, of the old bonds. The Bankruptcy and District Courts agreed.[1] Because the old bonds had fallen in value by the date of the exchange, the amount of OID on the new bonds, as so measured, was greater than the amount of remaining OID on the old bonds. Thus, under these holdings the bondholders who had accepted the exchange were worse off than those who had not, who did not suffer such a reduction in their claims.

The Second Circuit reversed these holdings.[2] Noting that Congress designed the Bankruptcy Code to encourage nonbankruptcy workouts in the first instance, with bankruptcy only as a last resort, the court concluded that the lower court holdings produced the opposite result. If the workout provided only an interim solution and a subsequent bankruptcy proceeding became necessary, these holdings penalized the creditors who participated in the nonbankruptcy workout and gave the debtor and

---

[1] **§212** *In re Chateaugay Corp.*, 109 B.R. 51, 111 B.R. 67 (Bankr. S.D.N.Y. 1990), *aff'd*, 130 B.R. 403 (Bankr. S.D.N.Y. 1991).

[2] *In re Chateaugay Corp.*, 1961 F.2d 378 (2d Cir. 1992); to the same effect, *see Pengo Industries, Inc. v. Licht*, 962 F.2d 543 (5th Cir.), *cert. denied*, 61 U.S.L.W. 3400 (1992). Both the *Chateaugay* and *Pengo* decisions distinguished *In re Allegheny Intl. Inc.*, 100 B.R. 247 (Bankr. W.D. Pa. 1989), which involved an exchange of old equity for new debt. Not only may an exchange of old equity for new debt of the same issuer in a prebankruptcy consensual workout be treated differently from an exchange, in such a consensual workout, of old debt for new debt of the same issuer, but exchanges of interests in one corporation for interests in a different corporation are also likely to be distinguishable. For example, an exchange of equity in one corporation for new debt issued by a different corporation, which was in effect purchasing that equity, was held to create OID for bankruptcy law purposes. *In re ICH Corp.*, 230 B.R. 88 (Bankr. N.D. Tex. 1999), *rev'g*, 219 B.R. 176 (Bankr. N.D. Tex. 1998). The lower court had been influenced by the reasoning in the *Chateaugay and Pengo cases.* But the upper court considered these cases inapposite because the creation of OID on the facts there involved would not discourage consensual workouts in attempts to avoid bankruptcy.

its other creditors a windfall. Accordingly, the Second Circuit held that a nonbankruptcy exchange of old debt obligations for new debt obligations of equal face amount does not create new OID for purposes of section 502(b)(2) of the Bankruptcy Code. However, any OID that remained on the old debt obligations would carry over to the new debt obligations and would be amortized (using the constant interest method rather than the straight line method) over the life of the new debt.

Given the holding by the Second Circuit in the *LTV* case, it is not surprising that the effort to treat market discount—that is, the difference between what an investor paid for the debt in the trading market and the face amount of the debt—as OID disallowed by section 502(b)(2) of the Bankruptcy Code has not been successful.[3]

## § 213 HAVING THE BEST OF BOTH WORLDS: PREPACKAGED BANKRUPTCY PLANS

The advantages offered by a bankruptcy proceeding for restructuring the debt of a failing company are, as indicated in the previous paragraphs, substantial. These include, among other things, an ability to prevent dissident members of a creditor class from blocking a restructuring that is desired by the bulk of the class and, for the tax planner, more favorable tax rules. The chief drawbacks of a bankruptcy proceeding are the potential delay and expense entailed in bankruptcy and possible adverse effects on customer loyalty to the business and its products.

In certain situations, bankruptcy counsel can obtain the advantages of a bankruptcy proceeding while at the same time achieving much of the speed and economy of an out-of-court restructuring. The device employed is a so-called prepackaged bankruptcy plan. A debt restructuring plan is worked out in advance between the debtor and the bulk of the creditors in the affected class or classes. This is incorporated in a bankruptcy plan whose success upon filing is essentially insured, because of those creditors already agreeing to it.[1] Such a plan can be speedily confirmed and consummated with minimum disruption to the business.[2]

A prepackaged plan is not generally feasible, however, where there are large contingent or disputed liabilities that need to be resolved in order to accomplish a successful restructuring, or where a class of debt that needs to be affected is so widely held as to preclude obtaining a prefiling consent from the appropriate percentage of the class. Additionally, even when the requisite portion of each class accepts the plan, there is always a risk that a dissident creditor will object to confirmation on any of numerous grounds, such as that his class is receiving less than it would receive in a Chapter 7 liquidation or the plan is not feasible.

---

[3] *Mt. Rushmore Hotel Corp. v. Commerce Bank*, 146 B.R. 33 (Bankr. D. Kan. 1992).

[1] **§ 213** For the treatment of such agreements under the Code § 382 "option" rules, *see* § 508.2.7.3.

[2] For a discussion of prepackaged bankruptcy plans, *see* Kirschner, Kusnetz, Solarsh & Gatarz, Prepackaged Bankruptcy Plans: The Deleveraging Tool of the '90s in the Wake of OID and Tax Concerns, 21 Seton Hall L. Rev. 643 (1991).

# 3

# Deduction and Accrual of Interest



## §301 INTEREST AND THE FAILING BUSINESS

As a company descends into failing status it may fall behind in interest payments on its debt. As time passes, the company's ability to pay accrued but unpaid interest may become increasingly doubtful. Finally, if the company goes into bankruptcy, the Bankruptcy Code will limit the obligation of the failing company to pay interest for the period commencing with the filing of the bankruptcy petition.[1] Interest on secured debt will be payable if the security is adequate to cover the interest as well as the principal,[2] but interest on unsecured debt for the bankruptcy period will gener-

[1] **§301** 11 U.S.C. §§506(b) (secured claims), 502(b)(2) (unsecured claims for "unmatured interest," including original issue discount, generally disallowed). The computation of OID for bankruptcy law purposes may differ from that for tax purposes. For example, in *In re Chateaugay Corp.*, discussed at §212, the Second Circuit held that the exchange of old debt for new debt of equal face amount did not create OID for bankruptcy law purposes and considered tax authorities that might have produced a different result in certain circumstances to be irrelevant for bankruptcy law purposes. To the same effect, *see* the *Pengo Industries* case, also discussed at §212. Moreover, the *Mt. Rushmore Hotel Corp.* case discussed at §212 held that market discount would not be treated as OID for bankruptcy law purposes. For the tax treatment of market discount, *see* §§403.1.8 and 403.2.8. On the other hand, both the *Chateaugay* and *Pengo* cases distinguished *In re Allegheny Intl., Inc., supra* §212, which dealt with an exchange of old equity for new debt.

[2] Bankruptcy Code section 506(b) provides that, to the extent the security for a secured claim is greater than the claim, there shall be allowed "interest on such claim, and any reasonable fees, costs, or charges provided under the agreement or *State statute* under which such claim arose" (emphasis added). The italicized language was added effective for bankruptcy cases commenced on or after October 17, 2005. P.L. 109-8, §712(d) (2005). In *United States v. Ron Pair Enters., Inc.*, 109 S. Ct. 1026 (1989), decided prior to this legislative change, the Supreme Court held that Bankruptcy Code section 506(b) entitles holders of nonconsensual oversecured claims—such as a tax lien or judicial lien—to

ally not be payable at all unless the assets of the company are sufficient to pay the principal and also the interest on all of its debt in full.[3] A subordination agreement

---

(Footnote Continued)

receive postpetition interest, but *not* fees, costs, or other charges (absent an actual agreement). This is still the case for *federal* tax liens, whereas in newly filed bankruptcy cases a holder of an oversecured *state* tax lien may collect reasonable fees, costs and other charges, to the extent permitted by state statute. Of course, the debtor may raise traditional defenses to payment (*e.g.*, the statute of limitations and estoppel). *See In re Lapiana*, 909 F.2d 221, 90-2 U.S.T.C. ¶50,436 (7th Cir. 1990) (also leaves open possibility for additional equitable relief depending on the circumstances). Conversely, the Supreme Court has held that an *undersecured* creditor is not entitled to postpetition interest on the secured portion of its claim. *United States Assoc. of Texas v. Timbers of Inwood Forest Assocs., Ltd.*, 484 U.S. 365 (1988). The Fifth Circuit has held that where both the value of the collateral and the amount of the creditor's claim fluctuate during the bankruptcy proceeding, the creditor is entitled to interest only for the periods during which his claim is oversecured. *In re T-H New Orleans Ltd. Partnership*, 116 F.3d 790 (5th Cir. 1997).

The allowable rate of interest on oversecured tax claims has been a matter of some uncertainty, but is now specifically addressed in the Bankruptcy Code for bankruptcy cases commenced on or after October 17, 2005. In such cases, new Bankruptcy Code section 511(a) permits interest to accrue on oversecured tax claims at the applicable rate under nonbankruptcy law.

For bankruptcy cases commenced prior to October 17, 2005, the applicable rate of interest on oversecured claims (tax or otherwise) depends, in part, on whether there is a contractual agreement specifying the rate of interest. In the case of *consensual oversecured claims* (that is, claims bearing contractual interest), the courts generally give deference to the parties' agreed interest rate, but may modify the rate in appropriate circumstances. In cases of equity insolvency, imposition of higher default rates of interest are often disallowed. *See, e.g., Fischer Enters., Inc. v. Geremia (In re Kalian)*, 178 B.R. 308 (Bankr. R.I. 1995) (collecting cases; disallowed higher default rate). In the case of *nonconsensual oversecured claims* (such as most oversecured tax claims), the cases are in conflict as to whether the applicable rate is some federal statutory rate (such as the Code §6621 rate), the federal judgment rate, or possibly a general market rate. Nevertheless, the courts generally appear to prefer the applicable non-bankruptcy statutory rate. *Compare In re Greensboro Lumber Co.*, 95-1 U.S.T.C. ¶50,259 (Bankr. M.D. Ga. 1995) (Chapter 7 case; applied Code §6621 rate); *United States v. Rhodey (In re R&W Enterprises)*, 1994 Bankr. LEXIS 2248 (Bankr. N.D. Fla. 1994) (Chapter 7 case; discusses rationale for §6621 rate or, in the case of state tax claims, the applicable state underpayment rate); *Galveston Indep. Sch. Dist. v. Heartland Fed. Sav. & Loan Assn.*, 159 B.R. 198 (S.D. Tex. 1993) (applied state statutory rate under which lien arose, provided the charge could be reasonably characterized as true interest rather than a penalty); *United States Trust Co. v. LTV Steel Company, Inc. (In re Chateaugay Corp.)*, 150 B.R. 529, 539-540 (Bankr. S.D. N.Y. 1993) (in *dicta*, stated that the rate should be determined by reference to applicable state law), *appealed and aff'd on other issues*, 170 B.R. 551 (S.D. N.Y. 1994); *with In re Wasserman*, 151 B.R. 4 (D. Mass. 1993) (Chapter 11; applied federal judgment rate); *In re Kelton*, 137 B.R. 18 (Bankr. W.D. Tex. 1992) (same); *see Goldberg v. City of New York (In re Navis Realty, Inc.)*, 193 B.R. 998 (Bankr. E.D.N.Y. 1996) (Chapter 7 case, applied state statutory rate; concluded that a court should only deviate from the statutory rate where (i) the rate constitutes a penalty or (ii) equity mandates it, citing as an example *Wasserman, supra*, a Chapter 11 case; court found no Chapter 7 case that applied a reduced rate on equitable grounds). *See also* discussion at §1016.1; Note, Supreme Court Decisions in Taxation: 1988 Term—*United States v. Ron Pair Enters.*, 43 Tax Law. 475, 488-489 (1990).

[3] *See* discussion at §1006.1.2; *see, e.g.*, Bankruptcy Code §726(a)(5); *In re Oahu Cabinets Ltd.*, 12 B.R. 160, 163 (Bankr. D. Haw. 1981) (exception to nonpayment of postpetition interest on unsecured claims where existence of surplus after all creditors are otherwise paid in full); *Thompson v. Kentucky Lumber Co. (In re Kentucky Lumber Co.)*, 860 F.2d 674 (6th Cir. 1988) (unsecured creditors not entitled to postpetition interest where debtor was considered insolvent at confirmation but subsequently obtained a large unexpected settlement of a pending lawsuit); *In re Adcom, Inc.*, 74 B.R. 673 (Bankr. D. Mass. 1987) (clearly solvent debtor required to pay postpetition interest on unsecured prepetition tax claim at the Code §6621 rate plus 2.5 percent). Cf. *United States v. Robinson (In re D.C. Sullivan & Co.)*, 929 F.2d 1, 91-1 U.S.T.C. ¶50,156 (1st Cir. 1991), *rev'g in part* a District Court decision, *aff'g* an unpublished bankruptcy court decision (Bankruptcy Act case; where, during pendency of a bank-

will be enforced, however, even as to postpetition interest, provided the agreement unambiguously states that postpetition interest is covered.[4] In addition, a Chapter 11 plan approved by the creditors and stockholders may vary these results.

Two basic questions arise: (1) Will a failing company that uses the accrual method of accounting be able to continue to claim a deduction for the accruing interest? and (2) Will an accrual basis creditor be required to continue to accrue the interest into income?

## §302 DEDUCTION OF UNPAID INTEREST AS EXPENSE

There is authority for the proposition that the failing company may be allowed an interest deduction, even with respect to unsecured debt, for interest accruing during the bankruptcy period on debt that has contractual provisions for interest. For example, in *Zimmerman Steel Co.*,[1] the Eighth Circuit Court of Appeals allowed a deduction for accruing interest on debt providing for stated interest even though there was no reasonable expectation that the accrued interest would actually be paid. Moreover, in Rev. Rul. 70-367,[2] the IRS held that a taxpayer undergoing a Section 77 railroad reorganization under the terms of the prior Bankruptcy Act could continue

---

(Footnote Continued)

ruptcy filed more than 20 years earlier, the debtor became solvent because of trustee's recovery in a lawsuit for misappropriation of the debtor's assets, so that all creditors, both secured and unsecured, could be paid in full, postpetition interest was recoverable by IRS pursuant to Code §6621 on both lien and nonlien tax claims).

*But see In re New Valley Corp.*, 168 B.R. 73 (Bankr. D. N.J. 1994), which, in the context of a Chapter 11 bankruptcy case, held that unsecured claims that, under former Bankruptcy Code section 1124(3) were considered unimpaired due to the payment of their prepetition claim in full in cash, were not entitled to postpetition interest (despite the debtor's solvency), subject only to the requirement that the Chapter 11 plan be proposed in "good faith." Highly critical of this result, Congress repealed Bankruptcy Code section 1124(3) as part of the Bankruptcy Reform Act of 1994. *See* H.R. 5116, 103d Cong., 2d Sess. §213(d) (1994); H. Rep. No. 975, 108th Cong., 1st Sess. §704 (2003).

[4] *See, e.g., Continental Ill. Nat'l Bank and Trust Co. v. First Nat'l City Bank of New York (In re King Resources Co.)*, 528 F.2d 789 (10th Cir. 1976) (generic subordination to principal and interest not sufficient); *Bankers Life Co. v. Manufacturers Hanover Trust (In re Kingsboro Mortgage Corp.)*, 379 F. Supp. 227 (S.D.N.Y. 1974), *aff'd*, 514 F.2d 400 (2d Cir. 1975) (similar provision); *In re Time Sales Corp.*, 491 F.2d 841 (3d Cir. 1974) (same); *In re Envirodyne Indus., Inc.*, 1993 WL 566565, *36 (Bankr. N.D. Ill.) (enforced subordination that expressly included "interest accruing after the commencement of any [bankruptcy] proceeding . . . whether or not allowed"). *Cf. American Iron & Steel Mfg. Co. v. Seaboard Air Line Railway*, 233 US 261 (1914) (discussing exception for solvent debtors).

[1] **§302** *Zimmerman Steel Co. v. Commissioner*, 130 F.2d 1011, 42-2 U.S.T.C. ¶9697 (8th Cir. 1942); *see also Panhandle Refining Co.*, 45 B.T.A. 651, Dec. 12,159 (1941) (nonbankruptcy case; accrual of interest on debt of wholly owned subsidiary to parent); *Butler Consolidated Coal Co.*, 6 T.C. 183 (1946) (receivership case), *acq.*, 1946-1 C.B. 1. *But see Kellogg v. United States (In re Southwestern States Marketing Corp.)*, 95-1 U.S.T.C. ¶50,057, *aff'd without op.*, 82 F.3d 413, 96-1 U.S.T.C. ¶50,165 (5th Cir. 1996) (court holds that no deductions for accrued expense can be taken in the extreme circumstance where taxpayer is so hopelessly insolvent that the expense will never be paid, on the ground that allowance of such a deduction would constitute a distortion of income under Code §461; the expense involved in this case was not interest).

[2] 1970-2 C.B. 37.

to accrue a deduction for interest even though there was no reasonable expectation that the debtor would pay the full amount.

It is interesting to note that the factual summary in Rev. Rul. 70-367 indicated that the debtor's old bonds, together with interest to January 1, 1969, were to be exchanged in the bankruptcy plan of reorganization for new securities aggregating the same face value but comprised of first mortgage bonds, general mortgage bonds, and stock.[3] The interest rate on the new bonds would be different from the interest rate on the old bonds. The plan of reorganization had not been accepted by creditors and had not become operative, however, by the end of 1969. The issue presented in the ruling was whether interest accruing on the old bonds would be deductible for the year 1969, even though it was highly unlikely that the interest for 1969 would ever be paid. (Indeed, it seemed clear that even some of the interest for the period before 1969 would never be paid.) The ruling holds that doubt as to the payment of interest is not a contingency of a kind that postpones an accrual of a deduction for interest; and since the plan of reorganization had not been adopted by the end of 1969, interest on the old bonds at the old rate could continue to accrue as a deduction for the year 1969.[4]

---

[3] The ruling gives no details about the stock; presumably the reference to "face value" refers to the par value or, perhaps, the asset preference (if any) of the stock.

[4] The failing company will also find support for this proposition in IRS Technical Advice Memorandum 8642005, June 30, 1986. Here, an accrual method failing company had fallen behind on principal and interest payments. A debt workout agreement was reached in 1981 that provided, among other things, for a stretch out of payments on its past-due installments of principal and interest. Despite the workout, the company continued to fall behind in interest payments, causing its accrual deductions to exceed its payments and creating increasing doubt that the payments would ever be made. The IRS, citing Rev. Rul. 70-367, *supra* note 2, but not *Zimmerman or Continental Vending*, allowed the accrual deductions, concluding that accrual deductions for interest are proper where it cannot be categorically said at the time of the deductions that the interest would not be paid, even though payment is extremely doubtful.

The technical advice memorandum went on, however, to reach the rather startling conclusion that the previously accrued but unpaid interest, whose payment was stretched out by the 1981 workout agreement, should be brought back into income in 1981 under the tax benefit theory of *Hillsboro National Bank*, 457 U.S. 1103, 83-1 U.S.T.C. ¶9229 (1983). Also, the memorandum referred, in a rather confusing way, to the doctrine of *Mooney Aircraft v. United States*, 420 F.2d 400, 69-2 U.S.T.C. ¶9714 (5th Cir. 1969), as support for its tax benefit position. The result, under the memorandum, is to bring the postponed interest back into income in 1981 but allow it to be deducted again over the revised schedule of due dates. The application of the tax benefit theory in this situation seems wrong because the debtor continued to be liable for the interest, which had already been earned, and only the payment date was postponed. (*Cf.* the earlier R & D tax benefit ruling, Rev. Rul. 72-528, 1972-2 C.B. 481, that was later determined to be wrong and was revoked in Rev. Rul. 85-186, 1985-2 C.B. 84.) However, for many taxpayers, application of this tax benefit concept may prove to be helpful; if they have sufficient NOLs to absorb the tax benefit income and the amount owed is not cancelled or reduced, the result may be simply to freshen up their deductions.

Subsequently, in IRS Litigation Guideline Memorandum TL-103, May 6, 1996, *reprinted at* 2000 TNT 121-83, the IRS took the position that Rev. Rul. 70-367 does not apply under present law and that where the debtor has filed a petition for bankruptcy, the debtor may not deduct accrued interest or OID on unsecured debt from the petition date forward (nor need the creditor report such items as income). The Guideline does not apply to secured debt, to debt that is nondischargeable in bankruptcy, or to debt that is incurred after the bankruptcy petition has been filed. In addition, any previously nondeductible accrued interest or OID will become deductible to the extent payment of such accrued interest or OID is provided for in a confirmed bankruptcy plan. To the same effect, *see*

On the other hand, the IRS subsequently took a contrary position in *In re Continental Vending Machine Corp.*[5] In that case, a company was in Chapter X under the prior Bankruptcy Act. The security for its secured debt was sufficient to cover both the interest and principal on the secured debt, but the remaining assets of the company were not sufficient to provide for interest as well as principal on its unsecured debt. Although the court allowed the company to accrue an interest deduction for the interest on the secured debt, it denied a deduction for interest accruing on the unsecured debt. The court said that a deduction should be denied unless all events have occurred to create a legally binding obligation to pay the interest, and even then a deduction should be denied if payment of the interest is unlikely ever to occur. With respect to these two points, the court emphasized that the legal posture under Chapter X of the prior Bankruptcy Act of interest accruing during the bankruptcy was that no obligation to pay interest existed unless and until there were sufficient assets to pay the principal as well as the interest on all of the debt. This is the same provision that applies under Chapter 11 of the current Bankruptcy Code.[6] The court interpreted this provision to mean that during the years at issue the taxpayer in *Continental Vending* had no legal obligation to pay the interest, because the legal obligation could only arise upon the satisfaction of a later condition, namely, the existence of sufficient assets in a later year to pay the interest as well as the principal on all the debt.[7] Moreover, the *Continental Vending* court indicated that even if this had not been the case, the factual unlikelihood of payment of the interest would be a sufficient ground for denying the deduction. The *Continental Vending* case was followed by the Fifth Circuit in *Kellogg v. United States* (*In re West Texas Marketing Corp.*).[8]

---

(Footnote Continued)

IRS Field Service Advice 1998-459, March 31, 1998, *reprinted at* 2000 TNT 165-74. The IRS also repeated its position with respect to unsecured debt in IRS Technical Advice Memorandum 200449001 (September 7, 2004).

[5] 77-1 U.S.T.C. ¶9121 (E.D.N.Y. 1976).

[6] *See* §301; 3 Collier on Bankruptcy ¶502.02 (15th ed.).

[7] Although the court did not discuss the point, this analysis may provide at least a theoretical basis for distinguishing Rev. Rul. 70-367, for although the substance of the interest rules in old Chapter X and Section 77 proceedings of the prior Bankruptcy Act are the same, Section 77 did not contain statutory language on the point and in such proceedings judges apparently disallowed postpetition interest when, at the time of adopting the plan, assets were not sufficient to pay the interest. 6 Collier on Bankruptcy ¶9.08 (14th ed. 1978); Plumb, The Tax Recommendations of the Commission on the Bankruptcy Laws—Reorganizations, Carryovers and the Effects of Debt Reduction, 29 Tax L. Rev. 227, 307 (1974); *cf. American Iron & Steel Mfg. Co. v. Seaboard Air Line Railway* (U.S.), *supra* §301 note 4 (applying bankruptcy principles to a receivership proceeding). In a Section 77 proceeding, one could perhaps argue, therefore, that the legal liability for the interest continued until the judge decided otherwise. Id.

[8] 155 B.R. 399, 93-2 U.S.T.C. ¶50,637 (Bankr. N.D. Tex. 1993) (Chapter 7 case), *aff'd*, 94-1 U.S.T.C. ¶50,063 (N.D. Tex.), *aff'd*, 54 F.3d 1194 (5th Cir. 1995). Thereafter, as discussed *supra* at note 4, the IRS distributed an internal memorandum describing its litigating position, and most recently summarized its position in IRS Technical Advice Memorandum 200449001 (September 7, 2004). The latter acknowledges the contrary 2001 bankruptcy court decision in *In re Dow Corning Corp.*, discussed below.

Suppose, if the *Continental Vending* approach is to be taken, that under the plan of reorganization for a failing company, each creditor's claim is to include interest up to the plan consummation date at the contract rate provided in the terms of the debt, and the consideration being issued in the plan is to be distributed among the creditors in proportion to these total amounts. Does this change the result?

### EXAMPLE

Assume that a creditor had a claim for principal of $1,000 and that the accrued but unpaid postpetition interest at the contract rate by the consummation date of the plan was $450. If the creditor was given credit in the plan for a total claim of $1,450 and was to receive $10 in cash plus 40 shares of stock of the debtor (worth $800), could the debtor successfully claim that it had been entitled to a deduction for the $450 of interest?

Where the various creditors had differing contract rates of interest, so that a plan of this kind would affect the actual amount of consideration that each creditor would receive, a reasonable argument could be made for the proposition that such a deduction should be allowed to the debtor company, at least by the consummation date of the plan, if not before. Unless the interest claim is satisfied with stock and the stock-for-debt exception to COD income applies, the issue will be academic for most debtors, since cancellation of the accrued interest obligation will produce COD income if the interest has been deducted.[9] If the interest claim is cancelled in exchange for stock, the stock-for-debt exception to COD may apply, and, if so, the tax benefit rule should have no application.[10]

---

[9] *See* discussions at §§404 and 504A.

[10] *See* Asofsky, Discharge of Indebtedness in Bankruptcy After the Bankruptcy Tax Act of 1980, 27 St. Louis U. L.J. 583, 615-616 (1983); cf. *Motor Mart Trust v. Commissioner*, 4 T.C. 931, Dec. 14,427 (1945), *acq.* 1947-1 C.B. 3, *aff'd*, 156 F.2d 122 (1st Cir. 1946) (applied stock-for-debt exception even as to interest; no discussion of tax benefit rule); *Alcazar Hotel, Inc. v. Commissioner*, 1 T.C. 822, Dec. 13,099 (1943), *acq.* 1943 C.B. 1 (same); GCM 25277, 1947-1 C.B. 44; *Columbia Gas Sys. v. United States*, 473 F.2d 1244, 73-1 U.S.T.C. ¶9176 (2d Cir. 1973) (looked to whether exchange of stock for debt was intended also to be an exchange for the accrued interest on the debt, citing *Alcazar Hotel;* held that where a bond is converted into stock pursuant to its terms, which include a "no-adjustment" clause for accrued interest, the extinguishment of the accrued interest results in COD income); Rev. Rul. 67-200, 1967-1 C.B. 15 (COD rules override tax benefit recovery rules; thus, it is a simple step to say that the stock-for-debt exception to COD income should likewise override the tax benefit recovery rules), clarified by Rev. Rul. 70-406, 1970-2 C.B. 16; Rev. Rul. 58-546, 1958-2 C.B. 143 (same); Eustice, Cancellation of Indebtedness and the Federal Income Tax: A Problem of Creeping Confusion, 14 Tax L. Rev. 225, 253 (1959); *but see* Heng & Parker, Tax-Free Debt Repurchase Using Stock-for-Debt Exchanges, 60 Taxes 527, 533-534 (1982) (indicating that the IRS has in certain cases taken the position that interest obligation relieved via the stock-for-debt exception was subject to tax benefit recapture); Note, Discharge of Indebtedness and the Bankruptcy Tax Act of 1980: An Economic Benefit Approach, 50 Fordham L. Rev. 104, 122-123 (1981) (concluding that the cancellation of accrued interest results in COD income to the debtor; in support for this position, the author contrasts Code §354(a)(2)(B), which provides that the general nonrecognition rule in tax-free reorganizations will not apply to the extent a creditor exchanges accrued interest for stock or other property; Code §354(a)(2)(B) was enacted as part of the Bankruptcy Tax Act of 1980, reversing prior case law);

In the fall of 2001, the Bankruptcy Court for the Eastern District of Michigan in *In re Dow Corning Corp.*[11] applied the *Continental Vending* and the *West Texas Marketing* cases to debt that did not contain contractual provisions for interest. Because Bankruptcy Code sections 502(b)(2) and 726(a)(5) make the obligation to pay interest on such debt (which would be at the legal rate on judgments) entirely contingent on there being sufficient assets at the plan consummation date to pay the full amount of the claims plus the legal rate of interest on such claims, the court said this means that the liability for interest on such debt does not arise at all until the plan consummation date. Thus, no accrual interest deduction can arise for such debt before the consummation date.

However, as to unsecured debt containing contract provisions for interest, the *Dow* court said that the *Continental Vending* and *West Texas Marketing* cases were wrongly decided. It held that the all events test for accrual of the interest on such debt is satisfied during the pendency of the case. The court concluded that, although Bankruptcy Code sections 502(b)(2) and 726(a)(5) do provide that interest is not to be paid even on such debt until consummation of the plan, and then only if there are sufficient assets, these Code provisions do not expunge during the pendency of the bankruptcy case the underlying contractual liability for the interest. If at the consummation date there are not sufficient assets to pay such interest, then these provisions may cause that liability to be cancelled, but that cancellation takes effect only at that time. Thus, the taxpayer is entitled to accrue and deduct the stated interest during the pendency of the bankruptcy case. The bankruptcy court further rejected the argument that, in the case of interest, unlikelihood of payment can by itself be used to disallow the deduction. In short, the court held that Rev. Rul. 70-367 properly states even the current law.

The case concludes, however, with a curious twist. The court said that in its view the Bankruptcy Code, in the case of debt containing contractual provisions for interest, allows the creditor to get the higher of the stated or the legal (*i.e.*, the judgment) rate of interest on the debt, provided there are adequate assets to pay it. In the *Dow Corning* case, the contractual rate was 5 percent and the judgment rate was

---

(Footnote Continued)

consider IRS Letter Ruling 6207059980A, July 5, 1962 (merger whereby creditors received stock in exchange for principal and accrued unpaid interest; IRS allocated all stock received to principal; IRS held cancellation of accrued unpaid interest was COD income subject to exclusion under then Code § 108; no mention was made of stock-for-debt exception).

The IRS, in attempting to assert the tax benefit rule in cases where previously deducted items are contributed to capital, has generally lost. *See, e.g., Putoma Corp. v. Commissioner*, 66 T.C. 652, Dec. 33,911 (1976), *aff'd*, 601 F.2d 734 (5th Cir. 1974) (also held that no COD created upon contribution by cash basis creditor/shareholder of previously deducted accrued interest; COD holding reversed, to the extent interest has not been accrued into income by the contributing creditor, by the Bankruptcy Tax Act of 1980 in Code § 108(e)(6)); *Commissioner v. Fender Sales, Inc.*, 338 F.2d 924, 65-1 U.S.T.C. ¶ 9104 (9th Cir. 1965) (salary obligation), *cert. denied*, 382 U.S. 813 (1965); IRS Field Service Advice 200006003, June 11, 1999 (treated contribution of interest to capital as payment of the interest with stock, following *Fender Sales* and disagreeing with *Putoma*), *reprinted at* 2000 TNT 30-68. This conclusion should be unaffected by the Supreme Court's decision in *Hillsboro National Bank*, 457 U.S. 1103, 83-1 U.S.T.C. ¶ 9229, as the satisfaction of the accrued liability with stock or its contribution to capital is not "fundamentally inconsistent" with having taken an earlier deduction for such liability.

[11] *In re Dow Corning Corp.*, 2002-1 U.S.T.C. ¶ 50,155 (Bankr. E.D. Mich. 2001).

6.8 percent. Although one would think that the judgment rate of 6.8 percent would be no more non-contingent for the debt containing lesser stated rates of interest than it is for the debt containing no stated rate of interest, the court held that Dow could accrue and deduct during the pendency of the bankruptcy case interest at the 6.8 percent rate on the debt that called for 5 percent stated interest.

There have, however, been suggestions that Bankruptcy Code Section 726(a)(5) should be construed as providing that the judgment rate of interest completely supersedes contractual rates of interest on unsecured debt.[12] If this view were to prevail, it would seem difficult to justify reaching a different accrual conclusion for unsecured debt having stated interest than for unsecured debt not having stated interest.

## § 303 ACCRUAL OF UNPAID INTEREST AS INCOME

It appears that the creditor may cease to accrue interest income at the point where it becomes relatively clear that the interest will never be paid.[1] For example, in Rev. Rul. 80-361,[2] the IRS held that where the debtor company became insolvent during the middle of the creditor's taxable year, and so by the middle of the taxable year of the creditor it had become clear that the interest was unlikely to be paid, the creditor should continue to accrue interest up to the point where payment became unlikely but could cease accruing interest income from that point forward.[3]

## § 304 AMORTIZATION OF ORIGINAL ISSUE DISCOUNT

In determining whether to continue to accrue unpaid interest, either where the debtor is in bankruptcy or is insolvent, it should make little difference whether such unpaid interest is stated interest or original issue discount (OID). The considerations should be the same as those discussed above at §§ 302 and 303. For example, assume that a creditor purchased a ten-year $1,000 bond, payable in full at maturity, at an original

---

[12] This is suggested in 6 Collier on Bankruptcy 726.02(5) (15th ed. 1997). The Ninth Circuit Court of Appeals, in *In re Samuel Duke Cardelucci*, 2002 U.S. App. LEXIS 6770 (9th Cir. 2002), suggests the same theory, but this was by way of *dictum* (since the debt involved in the case did not carry stated interest).

[1] **§ 303** *But see* authorities cited at § 401, note 5, especially the *European American Bank and Trust Co.* case cited therein, where the loan documents required payments to be applied first to interest, and the facts indicated the interest could all be paid even though perhaps not all of the principal could be paid.

[2] 1980-2 C.B. 164; Rev. Rul. 81-18, 1981-1 C.B. 295 (same; savings and loan association). To the same effect, *see* IRS T.A.M. 9538007, June 13, 1995. For a discussion of the two Revenue Rulings and the underlying case law, *see* Industry Specialization Program Coordinated Issue Paper, Settlement Guideline for Banks and Savings and Loan Associations, from the Office of the IRS National Director of Appeals (June 21, 1993), reprinted in BNA Daily Tax Report for October 7, 1993. *See also* the authorities cited at ¶ 403.2.1.

[3] If the creditor has included accrued interest in income that is later not paid, an ordinary loss deduction should be available. *See* H.R. Rep. No. 833, 96th Cong., 2d Sess. 33 (1980); S. Rep. No. 96-1035, 96th Cong., 2d Sess. 38 (1980). That this is a correct reading of the law was affirmed in IRS T.A.M. 9538007, June 13, 1995.

issue discount of $200. If, subsequently, it becomes apparent that the debtor probably can only pay $900, the creditor at that point should not have to amortize further the $100 of OID as to which payment is unlikely.[1]

Unfortunately, the IRS has taken the opposite position in a Technical Advice Memorandum.[2] The T.A.M. recognizes that there is a "doubtful collectibility" exception for the accrual of interest by holders on the accrual method of accounting; and that if the debt is later exchanged for stock in a tax-free reorganization, the creditor is even allowed a deduction for the unpaid accrued interest to the extent value is not received for it in the reorganization exchange. However, the T.A.M. then takes the position that on both points OID should be treated differently.[3]

The case covered by the T.A.M. involved OID on pay-in-kind debentures. In the three tax years at issue, the debentures traded at less than 10 percent of their face value, and even in the earliest of these years, the issuer had expressed doubt in its annual report about its ability to continue as a going concern. In the third year, the issuer went into bankruptcy. Under the bankruptcy plan for the taxpayer, the debenture holders received stock for their debentures. The IRS held that the "doubtful collectibility" exception that applies under the general accrual rules does not apply to OID. Thus the IRS said that debenture holders had to continue accruing OID for so long as they held the debentures, regardless of the financial condition of the issuer. In addition, the IRS held that the debenture holders could not deduct the unpaid OID in the year of the exchange of the debentures for stock, even to the extent the value of the stock was less than the accrued OID. In our view, the reasons given by the IRS for these holdings, which treat OID differently than accrued interest, are unpersuasive. They are also inconsistent with the legislative history, which specifically says as to the loss deduction point that OID is to be treated the same as accrued interest.[4] The first holding (dealing with the taxation of the OID as income to the creditor) is also inconsistent with a 1996 IRS litigation guideline concluding that, for periods during which an issuer is in bankruptcy, a creditor is not required to include in income any accrued OID on prepetition unsecured debt.[5]

---

[1] **§304** *Accord,* Garlock, Federal Income Taxation of Debt Instruments, Chapter 3, Part 14 (3d ed.). *See also* Calvin & Farias, When Can Holders of Defaulted Debt Cease Accruing Interest Income? J. Taxn. 378 (Dec. 1990).

[2] IRS T.A.M. 9538007, June 13, 1995. For a critique of this T.A.M., *see* Pollack, Goldring & Gelbfish, Uncollectible Original Issue Discount: To Accrue or Not To Accrue, 84 J. Tax'n 157 (1996). *See also* New York State Bar Association, Tax Section, Report on Proposed Legislation to Amend the Market Discount Rules of Sections 1276-78 (June 22, 1999), at n.24 ("We disagree with the position taken in TAM 9538007 (June 13, 1995) that the common law 'doubtful collectibility' exception for accrual basis taxpayers ... does not apply to accrual of OID").

[3] For the same position as to the non-deductibility of a loss from unpaid OID, *see* IRS Letter Ruling 200345049, August 2, 2002.

[4] The legislative history is cited at §§303 n.3, 403.1.6 n.39. As to the loss deduction, the T.A.M. is also inconsistent with IRS Letter Ruling 8933001, August 22, 1988 (Ruling 7).

[5] IRS Litigation Guideline Memorandum TL-103, May 6, 1996, *reprinted at* 2000 TNT 121-83.

## §305 DEDUCTION OF INTEREST BY GUARANTOR

Where a debtor has defaulted on its obligations or its liability is discharged in bankruptcy, and the guarantor of such obligations becomes primarily liable for any amounts owing and any future interest thereon, no deduction is permitted for the payment by the guarantor of interest that accrued prior to the time he became primarily liable.[1] The guarantor generally would not be considered primarily liable until he had no chance of collecting the debt from the original obligor. However, he should be entitled to a deduction for interest arising thereafter, although the IRS disagrees.[2] A guarantor who pays his guarantee on a corporate debt and cannot collect the debt will be entitled generally to a bad debt deduction, which may be either an ordinary business deduction or a capital loss, depending on whether the dominant motive for making the guarantee is a business motive or an investment motive.[3]

---

[1] **§305** *See, e.g., Hynes v. Commissioner,* 74 T.C. 1266, Dec. 37,232 (1980); *Nelson v. Commissioner,* 281 F.2d 1, 60-2 U.S.T.C. ¶9591 (5th Cir. 1960), *aff'g* 17 T.C.M. 888; *Golder v. Commissioner,* 604 F.2d 34, 79-2 U.S.T.C. ¶9451 (9th Cir. 1979), *aff'g* 35 T.C.M. 680; *Integraph Corp. v. Commissioner,* 121 F.3d 723, 97-2 U.S.T.C. ¶50,597 (11th Cir. 1997), *aff'g* 106 T.C. 312 (1996); *Timothy Provost v. Commissioner,* T.C. Memo 1999-178. For a broad general discussion of the tax treatment of guarantees, *see* Miller, The Federal Income Tax Consequences of Guarantees: A Comprehensive Framework for Analysis, 48 Tax Law. 103 (1994).

[2] *See Stratmore v. Commissioner,* 785 F.2d 419, 86-1 U.S.T.C. ¶9274 (3d Cir. 1986), *rev'g* 48 T.C.M. 1369 (1984); *Gregersen v. Commissioner,* T.C. Memo. 2000-325; *cf. Tolzman v. Commissioner,* 43 T.C.M. 1, Dec. 38,466(M), T.C. Memo. 1981-689. *See also Arrigoni v. Commissioner,* 73 T.C. 792, Dec. 36,758, 805-806 (1980) (corporate officer jointly and severally liable under state law for sales and employment taxes that the corporation was required to withhold and pay over to the state was entitled to deduct his payment of the accrued interest thereon; "Since a debt arose immediately between [the corporate officer] and the State when the taxes due and owing were not paid, all interest paid by [the officer] had accrued while he was primarily liable for the taxes"); *but see Abdalla v. Commissioner,* 647 F.2d 487, 81-2 U.S.T.C. ¶9491 (5th Cir. 1981) (appears contrary to *Stratmore,* but perhaps dealt only with interest incurred before the primary debtor was discharged in bankruptcy, in which case the holding would not be inconsistent with *Stratmore*). The IRS, in a 1988 action on decision, disagreed with the conclusion of the Third Circuit in the *Stratmore* case that the guarantor's status ripened from that of a secondary to that of a primary obligor when it could no longer look (because of the discharge of the original obligor in bankruptcy) to the original obligor for payment of the debt. The view of the IRS is that the guarantor remains merely a secondary obligor, and secondary obligors are not entitled to a deduction for interest. The IRS said it would continue to litigate this issue in Circuits other than the Third Circuit. AOD 1998-016, 1988 AOD LEXIS 13.

[3] *See Elliott v. Commissioner,* T.C. Memo. 1997-294; Reg. §1.166-9; IRS Letter Ruling 200706011, September 7, 2007.

# 4

# Debt Modification



## §401 MODIFYING THE FAILING COMPANY'S DEBT

The failing company will eventually face the necessity of working out a formal arrangement for modifying the terms of its debt. This section deals with the tax consequences of debt modifications other than through the issuance of stock or warrants. Exchanges of stock or warrants for debt are covered beginning in Chapter 5.

Debt modifications not involving the issuance of stock or warrants may consist of agreements between the failing company and its creditors (1) to reduce the interest rate on its debt, (2) to defer the payment of interest, (3) to extend the maturity date, (4) to eliminate sinking fund provisions, (5) to modify conversion privileges, (6) to change security provisions, (7) to reduce the principal amount of the debt, or (8) to make more than one of these changes.

Debt modifications present a number of significant tax issues that must be taken into account by the failing company in shaping the particular capital restructuring that will be best for it.[1] One of these issues is whether the debt modification will be treated as an exchange of the old debt for new debt. If it does constitute an exchange, not only may the creditor have taxable gain or loss (or the debtor have cancellation-

---

[1] **§401** For a comprehensive example raising many of the issues discussed in this section, *see* Bacon, Rescue Planning for the Failing or Bankrupt Company, 61 Taxes 931, 935-937 (1983); *see also, generally*, Mandel, Lender Beware: Tax Planning for Troubled Loans in Troubled Times, 80 Taxes 77 (2002); Peaslee, Modifications of Nondebt Financial Instruments as Deemed Exchanges, 95 Tax Notes 737 (April 29, 2002).

of-debt income), but the time-value-of-money provisions of the Internal Revenue Code may apply to the new debt. The latter can greatly complicate matters.[2]

A major issue presented by debt modification is whether the debtor will have cancellation-of-debt (COD) income. If it will, the result may be a reduction of its valuable tax attributes, such as NOLs, credits, and basis. The failing company will want to design a debt modification plan that minimizes its exposure to COD income.

The advent of the "disregarded entity"[3] has created some potential complications. For example, will the change in status of an entity from a regarded one to a disregarded one be treated as an exchange of its debt? *See* §402.5 below. Will recourse debt of a disregarded entity be treated as if it were nonrecourse debt of the owner of that entity? *See* §§403.1.3, 403.2.4 below.

Still another complication has been created by the addition in 1989 of Code §163(e)(5) dealing with certain high yield obligations containing OID or pay-in-kind (PIK) interest provisions. Where the old debt being modified is grandfathered under that provision, new debt exchanged for it will not be grandfathered unless the new debt satisfies certain fairly narrow requirements for a qualified refinancing instrument. *See* §405 below.

Finally, debt modification may result in the need to file a special reporting form with the IRS within a short time after the modification occurs. Some of these reporting obligations apply to creditors reducing debt in ways that produce COD income to debtors, others apply to taxpayers, and yet others apply to certain advisors. *See* §§403.4, 403.5, 404.8 and 407 below.

## §401.1 *Partial Payments of Debt Distinguished*

Before examining the authorities dealing with the consequences of debt modification, we should observe that payments on debt should be distinguished from debt modifications. There may, however, be a question in some cases as to whether it is interest or principal that is being paid, particularly where a partial payment is involved. Absent other indicia of intent from the parties,[4] the general rule in the past

---

[2] For a report that suggests the present value rules applicable to debt-for-debt restructurings reach inappropriate results for financially troubled companies, and which recommends changes in the regulations to change these criticized results, *see* Los Angeles County Bar Association, Taxation Section, Corporate Tax Committee, Report on Restructuring the Debt of Financially Troubled Companies, 2003 TNT 94-126 (May 15, 2003).

[3] *See* Reg. §§301.7701-2(a), 3(a).

[4] To be upheld, any express allocation between principal and interest must be pursuant to a bona fide, arm's-length agreement. Rev. Rul. 63-57, 1963-1 C.B. 103; *see also Huntington-Redondo Co. v. Commissioner*, 36 B.T.A. 116, *acq.* (upheld a second allocation agreement entered into after payment but before year end; "[s]o long as the correct and final allocation was made by the taxpayer within the year of receipt, there is no reason why the return should not be made in accordance with the correct entry"); *Estate of John C. Hagen, Jr.*, 28 T.C.M. 341, Dec. 29,508(M), T.C. Memo. 1969-59 (upheld allocation first to principal, then to interest, of payments received in full discharge of outstanding indebtedness). Although the fact that parties to an agreement have adverse tax interests in an allocation of payments is often indicative of a bona fide, arm's-length agreement, the rulings and cases cited above did not specifically state that adverse tax interests were required. *But consider* IRS Letter Ruling 8650035, September 12, 1986 (where total payments were insufficient to pay principal of

has been that payments occurring before retirement of the debt were normally construed to be applied first to accrued unpaid interest rather than principal,[5] and payments at maturity were assumed to apply proportionately to unpaid interest and principal.[6] The latter presumption has even been applied to debt in default where less

(Footnote Continued)

certain defaulted tax-exempt bonds, IRS allocated all payments to principal and refused to follow express agreement of the parties allocating payments ratably between interest and principal, on the grounds that (1) the parties to the allocation lacked adverse tax interests, in that the payor was a tax-exempt foundation, and (2), moreover, payment of interest was prohibited from accruing on the bonds during the pending receivership proceeding in the absence of full payment); IRS Letter Ruling 200035008, May 23, 2000 (payments on troubled tax-exempt bonds are to be allocated first to interest, as provided by the terms of the bonds, except that payments upon liquidation are to be allocated first to principal, even though this was not provided for in the terms of the bonds), *reprinted at* 2000 TNT 172-37; IRS Field Service Advice 1998-459, March 31, 1998, *reprinted at* 2000 TNT 165-74.

[5] *E.g., European American Bank and Trust Co. v. United States*, 940 F.2d 677, 92-1 U.S.T.C. ¶50,026 (Fed. Cir. 1991), *aff'g* 20 Cl. Ct. 594, 90-2 U.S.T.C. ¶50,333 (1990); *Motel Corp.*, 54 T.C. 1433, Dec. 30,214 (1970), *Estate of D. Buckley*, 37 T.C. 664, Dec. 25,306 (1962), *acq.; Estate of Paul M. Bowen*, 2 T.C. 1, Dec. 13,230 (1943), *acq.; Theodore R. Plunkett*, 41 B.T.A. 700, Dec. 11,045 (1940), *acq., aff'd on other grounds*, 118 F.2d 664, 41-1 U.S.T.C. ¶9373 (1st Cir. 1941); Rev. Rul. 70-647, 1970-2 C.B. 38; IRS Field Service Advice 1998-459, March 31, 1998, *reprinted at* 2000 TNT 165-74.

[6] *See, e.g., Warner Co.*, 11 T.C. 419, Dec. 16,603 (1943), *aff'd per curiam*, 181 F.2d 599, 50-1 U.S.T.C. ¶9291 (3d Cir. 1950) (where no express allocation of amounts received in redemption of debt, IRS proportionate allocation between principal and accrued interest upheld, even though amounts received did not exceed face amount of debt); IRS Letter Ruling 8819068, February 17, 1988 (same); IRS Letter Ruling 8141100, July 17, 1981 (for purposes of determining bond holders' loss on foreclosure of defaulted bonds, amount realized required to be allocated proportionately between principal and accrued interest); *cf.* Watts, Corporate Acquisitions and Divisions Under the Bankruptcy Tax Act: The New "G" Type Reorganization, 59 Taxes 845, 855-856 (1981) (for purposes of the allocation to interest under Code §354(a)(2)(B) (discussed at §403.1.6), stated that "the most likely allocation would seem to be in proportion to the respective amounts of principal (and preholding period interest) and of holding period interest"); Scranton, Corporate Transactions Under the Bankruptcy Tax Act of 1980, 35 Tax Law. 49, 87 (1981) (same issue; "likely" pro-rata allocation); New York State Bar Association, Tax Section, Committee on Bankruptcy and Insolvency, Report on Certain Provisions of H.R. 5043 ("The Bankruptcy Tax Act of 1979"), 33-35 (October, 1979); *see also United States v. Langston*, 308 F.2d 729, 62-2 U.S.T.C. ¶9757 (5th Cir. 1962) (third-party sale; where no express allocation, amount paid for defaulted bonds sold "flat" at a price above face amount was allocated proportionately between principal and accrued interest); *Jaglom v. Commissioner*, 303 F.2d 847, 62-2 U.S.T.C. ¶9519 (2d Cir. 1962), *aff'g* 36 T.C. 126, Dec. 24,790 (1961); *First Kentucky Co. v. Gray*, 190 F. Supp. 824, 60-2 U.S.T.C. ¶9810 (D. Ky. 1960), *aff'd*, 309 F.2d 845, 62-2 U.S.T.C. ¶9830 (6th Cir. 1962) (same).

However, support exists for the position that, in certain cases, amounts paid or received in full satisfaction of a debt may be allocated first to principal and then to accrued interest. *See Newhouse v. Commissioner*, 59 T.C. 783, Dec. 31,885 (1973) (upheld IRS position that proceeds from a foreclosure involving an insolvent cash basis debtor were entirely allocable to principal and, therefore, not deductible in part as interest expense by the debtor; the creditor had allocated the entire foreclosure proceeds to principal, and the court, concluding that this was proper because the usual allocation to interest does not appear applicable in foreclosure proceedings—at least where the creditor has allocated nothing to interest—added that "[w]e find it difficult to believe that a creditor who has foreclosed on the collateral of an insolvent debtor, and who will never get back the full amount of the principal, is required to report a fictitious amount of income designated as interest"); *Petit et al.*, 8 T.C. 228, Dec. 15,576 (1947), *acq.* (where corporate debtor sought an interest deduction with respect to a payment in full satisfaction of its debt pursuant to a settlement of a creditor's collection suit, which payment was "considerably less than face," court required full allocation of payment to principal even though there was no express allocation); *Lackey v. Commissioner*, 36 T.C.M. 890, Dec. 34,500(M), T.C. Memo. 1977-213 (same as *Newhouse*); *see also Drier v. Helvering*, 72 F.2d 76, 4 U.S.T.C. ¶1300 (D.C.

than the full amount of the principal has been paid, although support exists for the proposition that in the latter circumstance the payments should be allocated first to unpaid principal.[7] It has always been wise in the past for the parties to express their intent on this issue rather than rely on presumptions.

As mentioned at §402.15, however, the OID regulations and Reg. §1.446-2(e) provide that (with an exception for certain pro rata prepayments) partial payments are to be applied first to accrued unpaid interest. These regulations do not suggest that this is merely a presumption that can be superseded by expressions of contrary intent. On the other hand, these regulations do not seem to have been written with the situation of a failing company in mind. We would be inclined to speculate that where the debt is in default but a final resolution of it is not being reached, agreements by the parties to allocate more of a partial payment to principal than this rule would allow may be treated (unless the arrangement falls within the pro rata prepayment provisions of Reg. §§1.446-2(e)(4) and 1.1275-2(f)) by the IRS as an amendment of the debt that will have to be tested to determine whether it is significant enough to be treated as a deemed exchange of the existing debt for a new debt. On the other hand, where a final payment is being made, and the payment is not sufficient to cover all the principal and unpaid interest, we question whether the IRS intends this rule to apply or, if it does, whether the courts would uphold it, especially in a case where the parties express a contrary intent.[8] It should be noted that this allocation can be relevant for a few different purposes. For example, from a

(Footnote Continued)

Cir. 1934) (cited with approval in IRS Letter Ruling 8650035, *supra* note 4; despite an express allocation between principal and interest for payments received by taxpayer from the U.S. Treasury with respect to property seized during World War I by the German government, court held that, as the total payments received just equaled the acquisition cost of taxpayer's seized property, all payments were properly allocable to principal; "it seems to us to follow . . . that, without regard to what the payments are called, the inescapable conclusion is that in the transaction there was . . . no income . . . . To hold otherwise would be to . . . substitute form for substance . . ."); IRS Letter Ruling 200035008, May 23, 2000 (payments on troubled tax-exempt bonds are to be allocated first to interest, as provided by the terms of the bonds, except that payments upon liquidation are to be allocated first to principal, even though this was not provided for in the terms of the bonds), *reprinted at* 2000 TNT 172-37. *Cf.* Rev Rul. 73-328, 1973-2 C.B. 296 (the amount realized by a cash basis taxpayer upon an exchange with a third party of bonds of *X* Co. for bonds of *Y* Co., the fair market value of which was less than the principal amount of the *X* bonds, was all allocable to principal, even though there was no express allocation); *Charles T. Fisher v. Commissioner*, 209 F.2d 513, 54-1 U.S.T.C. ¶9212 (6th Cir. 1954), *cert. denied*, 347 U.S. 1014 (third-party sale; in absence of allocation, amount paid in excess of face amount on a sale of notes with accrued interest in default allocated first to principal then to accrued interest); Scranton, *supra*, at 87.

[7] *See* the authorities described in the preceding footnote. *See also* IRS Field Service Advice 1998-459, March 31, 1998, *reprinted at* 2000 TNT 165-74.

[8] The Tax Section of the New York State Bar Association, observing that application of this rule to payments that cancel a debt instrument in its entirety would be contrary to prior law, has recommended that the IRS not so apply it. NYSBA Tax Section, Report on Final OID Regulations, 64 Tax Notes 1747 (Sept. 26, 1994). IRS Letter Ruling 200035008, *supra* notes 3 and 5, is consistent with this conclusion. Without mentioning the above-cited regulations, the IRS held that payments upon liquidation of troubled tax-exempt bonds were to be allocated first to principal, even though this was not provided for in the terms of the bonds. *But cf.* TR-45-1715-95, October 17, 1995, 1995 FSA LEXIS 177 (which suggests that perhaps even in workout situations payments should be allocated first to interest and COD, citing Reg. §§1.446-2(b) and 1.1275-2(a)).

creditor's perspective, the allocation may be the difference between having interest income (if at some earlier date the holder of the debt took the position that it could cease to accrue the interest or, contrary to the IRS's position discussed at §304 above, the OID) or only a partial ordinary loss deduction for the previously accrued interest (if the holder had included the interest in income) with additional capital loss due to the reduced payment of principal. From the debtor's perspective, this translates into the potential for additional interest deductions if the debtor had ceased accruing the interest (that may help to offset income during the current year), with a corresponding amount of additional COD due to the reduced payment of principal, which may be excludable from current income if the debtor is insolvent or in bankruptcy (*see* §404.2 below). The allocation can also affect the amount of the debtor's surviving NOLs and other tax attributes in the context of a Code §382 ownership change to which the special bankruptcy exception in Code §382(l)(5) applies (*see* §508.5.3 below).

## §402 MODIFYING DEBT MAY CONSTITUTE "EXCHANGE" OF OLD DEBT FOR NEW DEBT

Debt modification may be accomplished by amending the terms of the existing debt or by substituting new notes for the existing notes. Such modifications have always presented the tax question as to whether they constitute an exchange of the old debt for new debt, instead of a continuation of the old debt under modified terms. For this purpose, the IRS has indicated it does not matter whether the modification is accomplished by amendment of the old debt instruments or by substitution of new debt instruments. In either case, it is the nature of the changes rather than their form that will govern,[1] the issue being whether, in the language of Reg. §1.1001-1(a), the taxpayer has in substance received something "differing materially either in kind or in extent" from what he had before.

The IRS has also said that the mere fact that the new debt has a different market value than the old debt is not a material factor in determining whether there has been an exchange; rather, one should focus on the changes in terms alone.[2] Although at first blush this seems a surprising statement, because one normally expects the significance of different terms to be reflected in value changes, the fact of the matter is that in the case of a failing company the value of the old debt will reflect not its original terms but its present expectations, which will similarly be reflected in the terms and value of the modified debt. Thus, changes in market value would not be a reliable guide to the materiality of the modifications.

---

1 **§402** Rev. Rul. 81-169, 1981-1 C.B. 429; *see* Rev. Rul. 73-160, 1973-1 C.B. 365; GCM 37884, March 19, 1979.

2 *See* Rev. Rul. 81-169, 1981-1 C.B. 429; GCM 37884, March 19, 1979; GCM 37002, February 10, 1977. But consider Henry, Reissuance Revisited, 42 Tax Notes 91, 95 (January 2, 1989) (suggesting that a change not perceived as material by the marketplace should not be considered material for Code §1001 purposes; Ms. Henry was the principal author of Notice 88-130, 1988-2 C.B. 543, which provided special "deemed exchange" rules applicable only under Code §§103 and 150 for "tender"—often called "variable rate demand"—bonds).

Over the years, a considerable body of law has developed regarding which modifications in terms will be sufficiently "material," within the meaning of Reg. § 1.1001-1(a), to constitute an exchange. Several events in recent years have, however, created considerable upheaval and uncertainty about the extent to which these precedents will still be respected.

The first event was the issuance of regulations to implement the time-value-of-money provisions of Code §§ 483 and 1271-1275, initially in proposed form—once in 1986 and again in 1992 and subsequently in final form in 1994. The impact of these regulations on the present subject is discussed at § 402.15 below. The second event was the Supreme Court opinion in the *Cottage Savings Association* case.[3] The third event was the issuance, in response to the *Cottage Savings* case, of Prop. Reg. § 1.1001-3 in late 1992, and final Reg. § 1.1003-3 in mid-1996.

Curiously, the *Cottage Savings* opinion did not involve a debt modification at all. It involved an actual exchange of one group of home mortgages by a savings and loan association for another lending institution's group of different home mortgages. Nor did the holding of the case plow any new ground. The IRS had asserted the novel position that when a group of individual mortgages is exchanged for a group of other mortgages, the exchange does not involve "materially different" properties if, despite the differences in the individual mortgages, the characteristics of the two groups are similar. The Court rejected this effort, holding that because the individual loans that were exchanged involved different obligors and were secured by different homes, the properties exchanged (*i.e.*, the mortgages) were materially different even if their other terms (*e.g.*, stated maturity or interest rate) and their aggregate value were nearly identical. The Court said that properties are different in a sense that is "material" as long as their owners "enjoy legal entitlements that are different in kind or extent," and it gave as an illustration stock issued by different corporations. None of this departs from prior precedent, and indeed the Court presumably thought it was just applying existing concepts and rejecting the effort of the government to modify them.

However, rather than limiting itself to an expression of intent to adhere to the status quo while rejecting the government's novel idea that a grouping of individual assets could cause the components to lose their individuality for exchange purposes, the Court indulged in some *dictum*.[4] The opinion said that the differences in legal entitlements, which can be found to be material, can be "minimal": "For, as long as the property entitlements are not identical, their exchange" may satisfy the materiality standard. "Under our interpretation of § 1001(a), an exchange of property gives rise to a realization event so long as the exchanged properties are 'materially different'—that is, so long as they embody legally distinct entitlements."

---

[3] *Cottage Savings Ass'n v. Commissioner,* 111 S. Ct. 1503, 91-1 U.S.T.C. ¶ 50,187 (1991), *rev'g and remanding,* 890 F.2d 848, 89-2 U.S.T.C. ¶ 9662 (6th Cir. 1989). For a good discussion of the case, its background, and its implications, *see* Nicholls, *Cottage Savings*: More S&L Problems?, 45 Tax Lawyer 727 (1992); Bacon and Adrion, Taxable Events: The Aftermath of *Cottage Savings*, 59 Tax Notes 1227, 1385 (May 31, 1993).

[4] The authors of the ABA Task Force Report cited in the next footnote disagree with our characterization of these statements as *dictum.*

This *dictum* fueled speculation—some of it from IRS officials—that the Court had so strongly rejected the government's efforts to change the law that instead of merely preserving the status quo, the Court had actually changed the law in a direction opposite to that asserted by the IRS. This speculation raised the question of whether the Court had adopted a "hair trigger" test of materiality that could apply beyond the actual exchange of property that the Court had before it, in which event many debt modifications that heretofore had been considered immaterial might now be found to be material. This would mean that while the Court had not changed the law applicable to the facts in the case before it, it did change the law applicable to different fact patterns that were not involved in the case before it—a rather bizarre result.

This speculation reflects an unfortunate tendency of modern lawyers to ignore the difference between *dicta* and holdings by treating every statement of justifying reasons in a Supreme Court opinion as though it were operative language in a statute or regulation, even though such lawyers are aware that the Justices often had no idea of the ramifications such statements could have if read in this way.

Because of such speculation, the IRS issued Prop. Reg. § 1.1001-3 in December 1992[5] and final Reg. § 1.001-3 in mid-1996, to prescribe standards for determining which debt modifications will be treated as deemed exchanges. The regulation applies only to debt modification, and not to modifications of nondebt financial instruments such as warrants, options, and notional principal contracts.[6]

The regulation first defines what constitutes a "modification." This is essentially any alteration of a right or duty under an instrument, whether the alteration is evidenced by amendment of the instrument or by conduct of the parties. The regulation then declares that only "significant" modifications constitute deemed exchanges (although, as mentioned at § 402.1 below, even insignificant modifications can require recomputation of OID) and sets forth standards for judging what modifications are "significant."

The regulation applies to alterations of the terms of a debt instrument on or after September 24, 1996, although taxpayers may rely on the regulation for alterations after December 2, 1992.

The regulation takes more the form of a legislative than of an interpretative regulation. It is detailed and technical, and includes specially defined terms, such as "modification," "significant modification," and "significant alteration." It has both general and, in some instances, bright-line rules, in each case often with various special limitations and exceptions. The rules can be arbitrary. For example, if the original terms of a debt instrument include an option to defer interest payments,

---

[5] For an excellent discussion of the proposed regulation, *see* Lipton, IRS Issues Proposed Regulations on Debt Modification, 71 Taxes 67 (February 1993). The *Cottage Savings* case, and the proposed regulation, are examined in depth in American Bar Association Section of Taxation Task Force, Report on Prop. Regs. § 1.1001-3: Modifications of Debt Instruments [Parts I-V], 47 Tax Law. 987 (1994); id. [Parts VI-VII], 48 Tax Law. 177 (1994).

[6] When Reg. § 1.001-3 was issued in final form in 1996, the IRS expressly refused to extend its provisions to such nondebt financial instruments. For a discussion of the consequences of modifying such nondebt financial instruments, *see* Peaslee, Modifications of Nondebt Financial Instruments as Deemed Exchanges, 95 Tax Notes 737 (April 29, 2002); *see also* § 402.1 note 14, below.

exercise of the option will not result in a deemed exchange (assuming interest is required on the deferred amount so that there is no change in yield) if the option was held by the issuer, but a contrary result applies if the option was held by the holder. The preamble to the final regulation admits that the rules in the regulation can produce "anomalies . . . (for example, different results for economically similar transactions)." Since Code § 1001 contains no special authorization for legislative regulations, the extent of the validity of the regulation might be questioned. Such a question could in fact be raised at some point by a taxpayer, since the regulation has in many instances reduced the flexibility available to lenders and borrowers to achieve nontaxable workouts.[7] On the other hand, taxpayers will appreciate the certainty provided by the bright-line rules, and in some instances may even seek to take advantage of these to generate gains or losses through modifications that have little economic significance.[8]

Because of the involuted nature of the regulation, it is difficult to describe it completely with fewer and less technical words than are contained in the regulation itself. We shall not try to be that complete here. Unfortunately, each time one is faced with a debt modification, there is probably no substitute for reading the regulation—all of it.[9] What we shall do in the following portions of this section is to summarize the more important of the provisions in the regulation. In the course of this summary, we will discuss the authorities on debt modification as they existed before the issuance of Reg. § 1.1001-3 and the extent to which the regulation has changed them.

Before proceeding with that discussion, we should first address the question of the consequences of an agreement by the parties to cancel only part of a debt, while leaving the remainder outstanding.

**Effect of partial cancellation.** Before the issuance of Rev. Rul. 89-122,[10] we had said on this subject that a mere reduction of the amount of the debt by cancellation of part or all of the principal or accrued but unpaid interest should not be treated as an exchange of the old debt for new debt.[11] To the creditor, we suggested that such a reduction should be treated as a contribution to capital if the creditor is also a shareholder; otherwise it should give rise to a bad debt deduction. For the debtor company, the reduction should give rise to COD consequences under Code § 108.

---

[7] *See* Lipton, The Section 1001 Debt Modification Regulations: Problems and Opportunities, 85 J. Tax'n, 216, 228-229 (1996).

[8] Id.

[9] *See* Goldring, Modifying Debt and Its Consequences, Vol. 20 Tax Strategies for Corporate Acquisitions, Dispositions, Spin-Offs, Joint Ventures, Financing, Reorganizations and Restructurings (Prac. Law Inst. 2006). We would commend the reader to consult, as well, the excellent article by Richard Lipton about the regulation, op. cit. *supra* note 6, and a useful flow chart prepared by Robert Willens and Andrea J. Phillips. Willens and Phillips, A Road Map Through the *"Cottage Savings"* Regulations, Tax Notes, Aug. 5, 1996, p. 765.

[10] 1989-2 C.B. 200. To the same effect, dealing with years before the effective date of the current regulation, *see* IRS Field Service Advice 199910009, December 2, 1998, *reprinted at* 1999 TNT 49-87. *See also* IRS Field Service Advice 1998-459, March 31, 1998, *reprinted at* 2000 TNT 165-74, which also involves pre-effective date years and takes the position that a reduction in principal amount of a debt "arguably" caused a deemed exchange of the "old" debt for the "new" debt, citing Rev. Rul. 89-122.

[11] *See also* Dooher, Review of the Tax Aspects of Real Estate Foreclosures and Workouts, 91 Tax Mgmt. Mem. 220-221 (1985).

However, Rev. Rul. 89-122 held that a mere reduction in the amount of a debt by cancellation of part of the principal constituted a deemed exchange of the old debt for a new debt. This result is surprising and, we believe, wrong.[12] Suppose the parties to a debt that does not provide for prepayment agree to make a prepayment, without penalty, of a portion of the principal together with any unpaid accrued interest thereon. We doubt anyone would contend that this creates a deemed exchange of the remaining portion of the old note for a new note. Indeed, this conclusion is confirmed by Reg. §§1.446-2(e)(4) and 1.1275-2(f). These hold that where such prepayments are made pro rata on each payment remaining under the instrument, the debt will be treated as though it had originally consisted of two instruments: one that is retired by these payments and one that remains outstanding. This does not create a deemed exchange of the portion of the debt that remains outstanding. We do not see why a cancellation, rather than a prepayment, of part of the principal should produce a different result. Suppose a $10,000 loan had been evidenced by ten identical $1,000 notes, and later one of the ten notes was cancelled. In a practical world would anyone contend that there had been a deemed exchange of the other nine notes? Should it make a difference if a single $10,000 note had been issued, which was later broken into ten identical $1,000 notes followed by cancellation of one of the ten notes? Should it make a difference if the separate notes become held by different owners? Just to ask these questions points out the questionable wisdom of the ruling.

However, Reg. §1.1001-3(g) Example 3 takes the same position as Rev. Rul. 89-122. In this Example, a debt instrument provides for $100,000 payable in ten years with annual interest payments of 10 percent. At the end of the fifth year, and after the fifth annual payment of interest, the parties agree to reduce the principal by $20,000. Interest continues to be payable on the reduced principal of $80,000 at 10 percent. The Example holds that the debt is to be tested under the OID rules immediately after the change as a debt issued for $100,000 providing for four annual payments of $8,000 and a payment at maturity of $88,000. Under such an analysis, the yield has been reduced from 10 percent to 4.332 percent; there has been a significant modification and the old instrument is deemed exchanged for a new instrument. We believe that this gives the OID rules an importance that is not merited and that this approach is wrong.

Moreover, we must also note that Reg. §1.446-2(f) says that "all contracts calling for deferred payments arising from the same transaction (or a series of related transactions) are treated as a single contract." (Reg. §1.1275-2(c)(1) contains similar language applicable to instruments with OID.) It goes on to say, however, that this rule generally only applies to contracts involving a single borrower and a single lender. Thus, this rule, to the extent it applies, might produce different results where some of the separate notes are issued (or perhaps later transferred) to different owners.

---

12 *Accord* Adrion, Reducing the Uncertainty Regarding the Amount Realized in Debt-for-Debt Exchanges, Tax Notes, May 30, 1994, at 1169, 1178 n.24.

## *§402.1 Change in Maturity Date*

Before issuance of the §1.1001-3 Regulation, the IRS had fairly consistently held that merely extending (or shortening)[13] the maturity of debt does not in and of itself create an exchange.[14] Because a call (redemption) provision is merely a method of varying the maturity of debt, changes in, or the addition of, a call provision should not, alone or in combination with a change in maturity date, be material.[15] Similarly, the mere addition of a sinking fund provision or the substitution of a serial obligation for a term bond should not be material.[16]

Reg. §1.1001-3(e)(3) indicates that a prepayment of a portion of a debt is not a significant modification. This, as previously indicated, is consistent with Reg. §§1.446-2(e)(4) and 1.1275-2(f).

---

[13] GCM 22901, September 16, 1941; *see* GCM 37002, February 10, 1977; GCM 23148, February 15, 1942.

[14] Rev. Rul. 73-160, 1973-1 C.B. 365 (also added subordination provision, not material); *see West Missouri Power Co. v. Commissioner*, 18 T.C. 105, Dec. 18,920 (1952) (in exchange for old bonds in default, new bonds were issued that extended the maturity date, added a prepayment privilege, changed revenue source from particular tax revenues to percentage of central fund, and provided that interest could be paid partly by issuing new bonds bearing a lower interest rate; these changes were found not material and thus there was no "exchange"), *acq.* 1952-2 C.B. 3; *Shafer v. United States*, 204 F. Supp. 473, 62-1 U.S.T.C. ¶9252 (S.D. Ohio 1962), *aff'd per curiam*, 312 F.2d 742, 63-1 U.S.T.C. ¶9195 (6th Cir. 1962); *Motor Products Corp. v. Commissioner*, 47 B.T.A. 983, Dec. 12,885 (1942) (new bonds issued in exchange for defaulted bonds extended the maturity date, allowed for prepayment, and provided portion of interest could be paid in new bonds; changes held to be mere extension of time for payment, not material and not an "exchange"), *acq.* 1946-1 C.B. 3, *aff'd per curiam*, 142 F.2d 449, 44-1 U.S.T.C. ¶9308 (6th Cir. 1944); *City Bank Farmers Trust Co. v. Hoey*, 52 F. Supp. 665, 42-2 U.S.T.C. ¶9747 (D.N.Y. 1942) (bonds reserved right to partially pay interest in new bonds), *aff'd per curiam*, 138 F.2d 1023, 43-2 U.S.T.C. ¶9627 (2d Cir. 1943); IRS Letter Ruling 8708017, November 21, 1986, (change in schedule of interim principal payments before maturity date was not an "exchange" and thus not a reissuance of the bond for purposes of Code §103); IRS Letter Ruling 8722064, March 2, 1987 (one-month extension of maturity of five-year tax-exempt bonds held not to constitute a material change resulting in a reissuance of the bond for purposes of Code §103, but no opinion expressed as to consequences if there is a series of subsequent extensions of maturity); but consider GCM 37884, March 19, 1979 (expressing "serious doubts" that a change in maturity date can "never" be material); IRS Letter Ruling 8346104, August 18, 1983 (same).

In the case of warrants, the IRS has held that a unilateral extension of the exercise date is a material change, constituting an issuance of new warrants. Rev. Rul. 80-134, 1980-1 C.B. 187. To the same effect, *see* IRS T.A.M. 9129002, March 26, 1991, where modification as to duration and price of an option to purchase land was held to be a termination of the original option, and where the optionor had to recognize ordinary income in the year of modification. *See also* Peaslee, *supra* note 6.

In Technical Advice Memorandum 8642005, June 30, 1986, the IRS held that where a failing debtor, who had deducted previously accrued but unpaid interest, entered into a workout agreement with its creditors whereby the due date for such interest was extended, the tax benefit doctrine required that the previously deducted interest be brought into income at the time of the making of the agreement. Such interest could then be deducted again in accordance with the revised payment schedule. For the reasons expressed at §302 note 4, this seems to be a misapplication of the tax benefit theory.

[15] *West Missouri Power Co. v. Commissioner*, 18 T.C. 105, Dec. 18,920 (1952).

[16] *See* GCM 37884, March 19, 1979 (suggests, but does not decide the issue, that there is no "real difference" between a serial obligation and a term bond and that, therefore, the mere substitution of a serial obligation for a term bond can never be material).

In contrast, Reg. § 1.1001-3(e)(3) changes prior law by providing that the extension of the due dates of payments, whether they be of the maturity date of the instrument or of any payments of interest or principal due before maturity, is a significant modification if it results in a "material" deferral. What is "material" is not defined. (To come within the scope of this provision, the deferral must of course be a "modification." For the treatment of simple late payments as not being "modifications" at all, *see* § 402.11 below.) But a safe harbor is provided for deferrals equal to the lesser of five years or 50 percent of the original term of the instrument, provided the deferred payments are unconditionally payable no later than at the end of the safe-harbor period. The safe harbor is cumulative, so that if some payments are deferred for less than the full safe-harbor period, only the balance remains available for any subsequent deferrals.

The foregoing rules assume that the deferral of payment does not produce a change in yield. If the yield is changed by the deferral because of the absence of compounding of interest, the special rule applicable to yield changes must be applied separately.

Reg. § 1.1001-3(g), Example 2 presents such a case. In the fifth year of a 10-year zero coupon note the parties agree to extend the maturity for two years but make no other change. The Example holds that although this modification is not a significant extension of maturity, it does reduce the yield, and so it must also be tested for significance under the change in yield rules (*see* § 402.3 below).

Even if a modification producing deferral does not rise to the dignity of a "significant modification," it is important to note that it may nonetheless require recomputation of OID. The 1992 Proposed Regulation § 1.1001-3 allowed the IRS to treat any deferral of payments made with a principal purpose of avoiding the time-value-of-money rules as a significant modification. This was dropped from the 1996 final Reg. § 1.1001-3, the preamble stating that the concerns addressed by it had been resolved by Reg. § 1.1275-2(j), which was also issued in 1996. The latter says that if:

> the terms of a debt instrument are *modified* to defer one or more payments and the *modification* does not cause an exchange under section 1001, then, solely for purposes of sections 1272 and 1273, the debt instrument is treated as retired and then reissued on the date of the modification for an amount equal to the instrument's issue price on that date. (Emphasis added.)

This applies to debt instruments issued on or after August 13, 1996. The word "modified" in this provision presumably refers to the Reg. § 1.1001-3 meaning. This conclusion is supported by the fact that the preamble to Reg. § 1.1275-2(j) says that the regulation does not apply to simple late payments, stating that if timely "payment is not made (*other than because of insolvency, default, or similar circumstances*), the final regulations require a deemed reissuance for OID purposes . . . ." (Emphasis added.)

In situations where a "significant modification" of the debt had not occurred for § 1001 purposes, the recomputation of OID thus required by Reg. § 1.1275-2(j) created a fungibility problem for issuers who wanted to consolidate two or more outstanding issues of debt instruments into a single new issue. Under the regulation, OID on the single issue of new debt attributable to each separate issue of the old debt would have to be determined separately, which means that no single set of OID computations could be made for all of the instruments constituting the new issue of debt. This made such a consolidation transaction impracticable. To eliminate this problem, the IRS has issued Rev. Proc. 99-18[17] and Rev. Proc. 2001-21,[18] which give issuers and holders an election to treat certain debt substitutions in a consolidation transaction as a deemed exchange for § 1001 purposes even though the substitution is not a "significant modification" under the § 1001 regulations. By treating the new substitution as though it were a § 1001 exchange, the issue price of the new debt will be determined under § 1273 and thus can be a single price for the entire issue of the new debt. Before this election can be made, a number of conditions must be satisfied. Among them are the requirement that both the new and the old debt be publicly traded; that the OID or premium on both the new and old debt must be *de minimis;* that neither the new nor the old debt be a contingent payment debt instrument or a convertible debt instrument or a tax exempt instrument; and that the issuer and at least one holder of the old debt must agree to make the election. The Revenue Procedure provides that the holder's election can be made by including a statement in the offering documents stating that those who participate in the exchange shall be deemed to have made the election and to have agreed to comply with the provisions of the Revenue Procedure. Consenting holders are treated as though the exchange was a realization event but one that had non-taxable exchange consequences. If the adjusted issue price of the old debt differs from the issue price of the new debt, both the issuer and the electing holders generally must take the differences into account over the life of the new debt (either as OID or as bond premium). The non-electing holders would have no exchange and would recompute the issue price and OID of their debt under Reg. § 1.1275-2(j). Rev. Proc. 99-18 applies to substitutions occurring on or after March 1, 1999, and before March 13, 2001, and Rev. Proc. 2001-21 applies to substitutions occurring on or after March 13, 2001.[19]

Prop. Reg. § 1.1001-3(e)(iii) provided that the addition or deletion of a put or call right is significant if the right has "significant" value at the time of change. This provision of the proposed regulation seemed to go beyond current law. The final regulation contains no specific provision for determining whether the addition of, or a change in, a call provision would be considered significant. For all cases that are not covered by specific rules, however, Reg. § 1.1001-3(e)(1) provides a general rule that a modification will be considered significant only if, based on all the facts, the alterations in rights are "economically significant." In applying this rule, one takes into account all modifications made to the instrument, other than those for which specific rules are provided. (The latter are tested separately, and individually but not collectively, for significance.) Of course, if the new call provision only permits acceleration of payments, it should be covered by the safe harbor for changes in timing of payments that do not defer payments. Similarly, if a holder pays the issuer to waive or defer a call privilege, the payment would change the yield on the debt, and this change in yield would have to be tested for significance under the specific rules for

---

[17] 1999-11 I.R.B. 7.

[18] 2001-9 I.R.B. 2.

[19] Rev. Proc. 99-18 originally applied only to substitutions occurring between March 1, 1999 and June 30, 2000. However, Rev. Proc. 2000-29, 2000-28 I.R.B. 113, eliminated the sunset date.

changes in yield. If the change is not significant under that specific rule, this modification would still have to be tested for significance under the general rule of economic significance of § 1.1001-3(e)(1) mentioned above. This is illustrated by Example 1 in Reg. § 1.1001-3(g).

## *§402.2 Change in Maturity Date and in Subordination or Security*

Before issuance of Reg. § 1.1001-3, the IRS had ruled that a change in maturity date did not create an exchange even when it was coupled with the addition of a subordination provision[20] or a change in collateral.[21]

Reg. § 1.1001-3 provides, as mentioned above (§ 402.1), a specific rule for changes in the timing of payments, and so under the regulation this change will be tested for significance separately from changes in subordination or collateral.

As for subordination, Reg. § 1.1001-3(e)(4)(v) provides a specific rule (which therefore will also be tested separately from other changes) which says that a change in priority of debt is a significant modification if it results in a change in payment expectations.

Another specific rule (which, again, would be tested for significance independently of other changes) is contained in Reg. § 1.1001-3(e)(4)(iv). This distinguishes between recourse and nonrecourse debt for purposes of determining the significance of changes in collateral. For a recourse debt, such a change is significant only if it results in a change in payment expectations. On the other hand, for nonrecourse debt, a change in collateral will be considered significant, unless the collateral is essentially fungible in nature.

## *§402.3 Change in Interest Rate*

Until Rev. Rul. 87-19[22] was issued in 1987, it had been an open question whether a significant change in the interest rate of an instrument in and of itself constituted a

---

[20] Rev. Rul. 73-160, 1973-1 C.B. 365; IRS Letter Ruling 9043060, August 1, 1990 (stretch-out of remaining principal payments on municipal bond did not constitute exchange and thus did not constitute reissuance, citing Rev. Rul. 73-160).

[21] IRS Letter Ruling 8346104, August 18, 1983. *Cf. West Missouri Power Co. v. Commissioner*, 18 T.C. 105, Dec. 18,920 (1952); IRS Letter Ruling 8753014, October 2, 1987 (deferral of sinking fund installments and reduction in reserve fund held not material). To similar effect, *see* IRS Letter Ruling 8907049, November 23, 1988; IRS Letter Ruling 8920047, February 17, 1989; IRS Letter Ruling 8928049, April 18, 1989; IRS Letter Ruling 9833015, May 18, 1998; IRS Letter Ruling 9819043, February 11, 1998; IRS Letter Ruling 9801047, October 3, 1997; Modification of Notes Does Not Result in Sale or Exchange, 89 J. Tax'n 54 (1998). However, modifications to the collateral provisions for tax-exempt bonds that significantly increased expectations of payment were held material under Reg. § 1.1001-1(a) in IRS Field Service Advice 200035020, June 1, 2000, *reprinted at* 2000 TNT 172-46, dealing with years before the effective date of Reg. § 1.1001-3.

[22] 1987-1 C.B. 249. However, in IRS Letter Ruling 8835050, June 8, 1988, the IRS distinguished Rev. Rul. 87-19 and held that a material change had not occurred, where a similar waiver had been executed but for only one year, and the effect of the one-year waiver on the entire yield to maturity was less than 3 basis points (3/100 of 1 percent). IRS Letter Ruling 8932067, May 17, 1989, held that a one-year partial waiver of a similar interest rate adjustment that changed the yield over the

material change in terms, thereby triggering an exchange.[23] Rev. Rul. 87-19 holds that it does. Indeed, the ruling held that a *waiver* of a scheduled future change in interest rates is an "exchange" and that the date of the "exchange" was the date the waiver was agreed to, rather than the later date of the interest rate change.

As this ruling also confirms, however, one should make a sharp distinction between a change made in an existing interest rate by a new agreement of the parties and a change occurring in accordance with the very terms of the original instrument itself. For example, an instrument that from the outset provides that its interest rate will float in relation to a specified objective standard, such as the short-term Treasury bill rate or the prime rate of a particular bank, has generally been viewed as not creating an exchange of old debt for new debt each time the rate changes.[24]

Reg. § 1.1001-3 confirms these positions. Reg. § 1.1001-3(e)(2) provides that a change in the annual yield of an instrument will be considered significant if the modified rate varies from the original rate by more than the greater of 1/4 of one percent (25 basis points) or 5 percent of the annual yield of the unmodified instrument, but not otherwise.

This is a specific rule; thus a change in yield is to be tested independently of other changes. This applies to both fixed and variable rate instruments. But this

(Footnote Continued)

remaining term of the bonds by less than 12.5 basis points (1/8 of 1 percent) was not material. On the other hand, in IRS Letter Ruling 8834090, June 3, 1988, the IRS declined to rule on the materiality of a 1/5 of 1 percent change in the fixed in interest component of a floating interest rate. Rev. Rul. 89-122, 1989-2 C.B. 200 held that a reduction in interest rate from 10 percent to 6.25 percent produced a deemed exchange. No deemed exchange was held to occur where the change at issue was treated under state law as merely a clarification of the existing instrument. IRS Letter Ruling 8952029, September 29, 1989.

The interest rate provided in a debt instrument on late payments of interest probably should not, however, be considered as important for this purpose as the basic interest rate on the debt. In *West Missouri Power Co.*, the court ignored the fact that the interest rate on bonds that were issued in payment of part of the *interest* on refunding bonds was a lower rate than the interest on the refunding bonds themselves. However, the opinion does not indicate what interest rate had been provided in the original bonds for late payments of interest. The IRS has also held that amendment of a bond to add interest on late payments of interest (in this case, the interest on late payments was at the same rate as the interest on principal) was not a material change. IRS Letter Ruling 8920047, February 17, 1989.

[23] *See* Winterer, "Reissuance" and Deemed Exchanges Generally, 37 Tax Law. 509 (1984) (indicates no clear authority either way); Bacon, Rescue Planning for the Failing or Bankrupt Company, 61 Taxes 931, 936 (1983) (indicates that authority exists supporting no exchange where change is in interest rate alone, but then cites Code § 453 "no disposition" ruling); *but see Mutual Loan and Savings Co. v. Commissioner*, 184 F.2d 161, 50-2 U.S.T.C. ¶ 9420 (5th Cir. 1950) (no exchange where maturity date extended, interest rate lowered, and sinking fund provision added to defaulted note); *Truman H. Newberry*, 4 T.C.M. 576, Dec. 14,602 (1945) (no exchange where maturity extended, interest rate lowered and collateral added to defaulted note). The IRS Chief Counsel had stated that a change in interest rate is the "most critical" factor in determining whether an exchange has taken place. GCM 37002, February 10, 1977. *See also* 1986 Prop. Reg. § 1.1274-7(a)(3), Example (2), discussed below at § 402.9.

[24] *See, e.g.*, Winterer, *supra* note 23, at 527, 530 (Case #1) (observing that a variation in interest rate under a floating interest rate is not a "change in terms"); Joint Committee on Taxation, General Explanation of the Revenue Provisions of the Tax Reform Act of 1984, December 31, 1984, at 121 (OID once fixed does not vary even though stated interest rate floats); Prop. Reg. § 1.7872-3(e)(1)(i) (same rule applied in below market interest cases involving term loans).

specific rule does not apply to contingent payment debt instruments, as to which the general rule of Reg. § 1.1001-3(e)(1) applies, and thus a yield change in such an instrument has to be tested for significance in combination with any other changes not covered by specific rules.

Reg. § 1.1001-3(c)(ii) provides, as a general rule, that any change occurring by operation of the original terms of a debt instrument is not a modification, whether it occurs automatically or by operation of an option held by a holder or issuer. However, a number of exceptions are then made to this general rule, including changes in obligor, changes in recourse status, and options exercisable by a holder (rather than an issuer) that can result in a deferral or reduction in any scheduled payment. In addition, for the exercise of an option to be considered pursuant to the original terms of the instrument, the option must be a "unilateral" option. This means that the exercise of the option cannot (i) be contingent on the other party's consent or the consent of a related party or arbiter, (ii) permit the other party to terminate the debt or, in the case of the holder, sell the debt to a related party of the issuer or (iii) require consideration, unless, at the time the debt was issued, the consideration was a *de minimis* amount, a "specified" amount, or an amount based on a formula that uses objective financial information (and other than incidental costs and expenses). The regulation does not define the terms "specified" amount or *de minimis* amount.

## *§ 402.4 Change in Interest Rate and Maturity Date*

Where a change in maturity date is coupled with a change in interest rate, the IRS has generally considered an exchange to have occurred.[25] The courts, however, have not always reached the same conclusion.[26]

---

[25] *See* Rev. Rul. 81-169, 1981-1 C.B. 429 (extending maturity from 15 years to 25 years, lowering interest rate from 9 percent to 8½ percent, and eliminating sinking fund of defaulted note held material); Rev. Rul. 81-281, 1981-2 C.B. 18 (substitution of a 10 percent, 10-year mortgage note at a reduced principal amount for a 7 percent, 30-year mortgage note constituted issuance of "new" obligation for Code § 103 purposes); IRS Letter Ruling 8602038, October 15, 1985; IRS T.A.M. 8451012, August 23, 1984; IRS T.A.M. 8052023, September 25, 1980; IRS T.A.M. 7929061, April 19, 1979; IRS T.A.M. 7902002, June 29, 1978; IRS T.A.M. 7845001, June 23, 1978; *see also, e.g.*, GCM 37884, March 19, 1979; GCM 37002, February 10, 1977. For the possibility that the rate of interest on late payments of interest may be less significant than the basic interest rate, *see* the comment in note 21, *supra*, about *West Missouri Power Co. v. Commissioner* and IRS Letter Ruling 8920047.

[26] *Compare, e.g.*, *Truman H. Newberry*, *supra* note 23 (extending maturity, lowering interest rate, and providing additional collateral of defaulted note held not material); *Mutual Loan and Savings Co.*, 8 T.C.M. 203, Dec. 16,861 (1949) (material), *rev'd, see supra* note 23 (extending maturity from 10 to 44 years, lowering interest rate from 6 percent to a maximum graduated rate of 5 percent, adding call feature and sinking fund provisions of defaulted municipal bonds held not material change); *and C.M. Hall Lamp Co. v. United States*, 97 F. Supp. 481, 51-1 U.S.T.C. ¶ 66,008 (D. Mich. 1951) (involuntary maturity/interest change; court also referred to Florida law that treated refunding bonds as a continuation of the old debt); *with Thomas Watson*, 8 T.C. 569, Dec. 15,676 (1947) (changes in note from a 6 percent, two-year note to a 6 percent, 10-year note, and subsequently to a 30-year note with graduated interest from 1½ percent to 5 percent were material), *acq.*; *Girard Trust Co. v. United States*, 166 F.2d 773, 48-1 U.S.T.C. ¶ 9209 (3d Cir. 1948) (different interest rate, maturity date, and call dates); *and Emery v. Commissioner*, 166 F.2d 27, 48-1 U.S.T.C. ¶ 9165 (2d Cir. 1948) (same).

As mentioned above, Reg. § 1.1001-3 tests changes in maturity separately from changes in interest rates or yield. If neither type of change, considered separately, would be considered significant, combining them in a single change will not make them significant. As also mentioned above, however, one must bear in mind that a change in maturity that affects yield is tested under the change-in-yield rules as well as under the change-in-maturity rules.

## *§ 402.5 Change in Obligor*

Before issuance of Reg. § 1.1001-3, the IRS took the view that a change in obligor could, in certain circumstances, be sufficiently material to constitute an exchange. For example, the IRS viewed the complete substitution of a parent corporation as obligor in replacement of its subsidiary (*i.e.*, a novation) as a material change in terms.[27] Assumptions without novations were often treated differently. The IRS, on several occasions, ruled that no exchange occured where a newly organized holding company parent assumed joint and several liability for its subsidiary's debt, even where such assumption was coupled with the parent's assumption of the subsidiary's conversion obligation to issue stock.[28]

In IRS Letter Ruling 8047021,[29] the IRS found that an operating parent's assumption of a newly acquired subsidiary's indebtedness as part of its acquisition of the subsidiary did not result in gain or loss to the debt holders. The IRS based its determination on alternative theories: First, that there was no exchange and, second, that the exchange was tax-free under the reorganization provisions. In contrast, the IRS held that where a parent (in a split-up) organized two new subsidiaries and each subsidiary acquired half of the parent's assets and assumed half of the parent's debt, there was a material change in terms of the debt, triggering an exchange.[30] The split-up gave the transaction the element of a novation rather than an assumption. The result in this latter ruling would appear to have been affected, however, by Code § 1274(c)(4) (as discussed below), which provides that in certain cases the debt instrument would not be retested to determine whether it provides for adequate stated interest. It had been suggested that one factor the IRS has considered in the

---

[27] *See* GCM 39225, April 27, 1984 (substitution of parent as obligor for subsidiary, including parent's assumption of subsidiary's conversion obligation, material).

[28] IRS Letter Ruling 8504049, October 30, 1984 (parent assumed joint and several liability, held not material); IRS Letter Ruling 8223044, March 9, 1982 (parent also assumed conversion obligation, not material); IRS Letter Ruling 8117091, January 28, 1981 (same); *compare* GCM 37844, March 19, 1979 (suggests combination not material, absent other changes); GCM 37583, June 22, 1978 (IRS original position; parent's assumption of joint and several liability together with conversion obligation material); *see also* IRS Letter Ruling 8509066, December 3, 1984 (assumption of conversion obligation alone, not material).

[29] August 26, 1980.

[30] IRS Letter Ruling 7925065, March 22, 1979.

change-in-obligor rulings is whether the debt is backed by essentially the same assets or additional assets.[31]

Code § 1274(c)(4) provides that if, in connection with the sale or exchange of property, the transferee assumes (or acquires the property subject to) an existing debt instrument, the assumption (or acquisition) shall not be taken into account in determining whether Code § 483 or 1274 applies to such debt instrument, unless "the terms and conditions of such debt instrument are modified (or the nature of the transaction is changed) in connection with the assumption (or acquisition)."[32] In effect, Code § 1274(c)(4) appears to permit a change of obligors in connection with the transfer of property. We would question, however, whether the property transferred must be the original property to which the debt related, at least in the case of acquisition debt. If not, has the "nature of the transaction" changed? Similarly, does a novation change the "nature of the transaction"? The only example given in the legislative history of a change in the "nature of the transaction" is where the existing debt arose in a transaction that was excepted from Code § 483 and the current transaction does not qualify for the exception.[33] Moreover, the regulations under Code § 1274(c)(4) ignore entirely the parenthetical reference to changes in the nature of the transaction and, in determining whether the assumption rule of Code § 1274(c)(4) applies, only consider whether the terms and conditions of the debt have been modified.[34] According to the legislative history, "minor" modifications may be made to the debt instrument without losing the benefits of the assumption rule.[35] The 1986 proposed regulations employed the definition of modification in 1986 Prop. Reg. § 1.1274-1(c), discussed at § 402.15 below. Final Reg. § 1.1274-5(a), as did the 1992

---

[31] *See* Winterer, *supra* note 23, at 514 n.30, 517-518; GCM 37844, February 2, 1979; *cf.* IRS Letter Ruling 8619021, February 6, 1986 (assumption of mortgage-backed bonds by a newly formed stock savings bank upon the merger of a mutual savings bank not a material change).

[32] This section applies to sales and exchanges occurring after June 30, 1985. In addition, proposed regulations provided transitional rules for debt assumptions in connection with sales or exchanges occurring in the first half of 1985. *See* 1986 Prop. Reg. § 1.1274-7(b).

[33] H.R. Rep. No. 87, 99th Cong., 1st Sess. 16, at n.6 (1985) (citing, as an example, Reg. § 1.483-1(f)(6)(iv), Example 4); S. Rep. No. 83, 99th Cong., 1st Sess. 20-21, at n.24 (1985) (same).

[34] *See* 1986 Prop. Reg. § 1.1274-7(a)(1) and 1992 Prop. Reg. § 1.1274-5 (omitting parenthetical). In the event the debt is modified in connection with the assumption (or acquisition of property subject to the debt), the 1986 proposed regulations provided that the modification shall be treated as occurring in a separate transaction immediately before the sale or exchange, unless the seller neither consents to nor participates in the modification (in which case it is treated as occurring in a separate transaction immediately after the sale or exchange). *See* 1986 Prop. Reg. § 1.1274-7(a)(2), (3) (Examples). *Contra Commissioner v. Stanley Co. of America*, 185 F.2d 979, 51-1 U.S.T.C. ¶9129 (2d Cir. 1951) (immediately following the merger of a wholly owned subsidiary into its parent, the parent exchanged new, lower face amount bonds for the subsidiary's old bonds pursuant to an agreement reached with the bondholders prior to the merger and in which the subsidiary participated; held, the parent had COD income upon the exchange), *rev'g*, 12 T.C. 1122 (1949) (reviewed, with five dissenting). The 1992 Prop. Reg. § 1.1274-5 and the final Reg. § 1.1274-5 somewhat revise the rule contained in the 1986 proposed regulations. They provide that the modification will be treated as a separate transaction occurring immediately before the sale and will be attributed to the seller (unless the seller did not know or have reason to know of the modification), unless the seller and buyer jointly elect to have the modification treated as occurring in the hands of the buyer in a separate transaction immediately after the sale.

[35] H.R. Rep. No. 87, 99th Cong., 1st Sess. 16 (1985); S. Rep. No. 83, 99th Cong., 1st Sess. 20-21 (1985).

proposed version thereof, does not contain this definition and instead simply refers to modifications constituting deemed exchanges under Code § 1001.

Reg. § 1.1001-3 addresses the change-in-obligor issue. Reg. § 1.1001-3(c)(2)(i) says that "the substitution of a new obligor, the addition or deletion of a co-obligor," or a change in the recourse nature of the instrument constitutes a modification, even if the change occurs pursuant to the terms of the original instrument. Even if there has been such a modification, the modification will not be deemed to produce an exchange unless it is "significant."

Usually, the threshold question of whether there has been a change in the obligor or a change in the recourse nature of the debts, and thus a modification (whether or not "significant"), involves only a factual analysis. However, an interesting issue on this point potentially arises where the obligor is an entity that changes from one that is "regarded" for federal income tax purposes to one that is "disregarded"—that is, one which is not treated as separate from its owner for all "federal tax purposes"—under Reg. § 301.7701-3 (or vice-versa). This change may take several forms, including an elective state law conversion of a wholly-owned corporation from corporate form into a limited liability company, a merger of the corporation into a limited liability company, or in the case of a limited liability company that previously elected corporate tax treatment, a reversing tax election. If on the facts there has been no change in the rights and obligations of the debtor and the creditors under state law—that is, the disregarded entity remains the only obligor under state law—does the entity becoming "disregarded" nevertheless effectuate, for deemed exchange purposes, a change in the obligor of the debt from the disregarded entity to its parent, or a change in the recourse nature of the debt? The IRS has faced this question in several private letter rulings. Initially, the IRS concluded that, for the limited purpose of applying Reg. § 1.1001-3, such a conversion will not be considered to have produced a change in obligor or a change in the recourse nature of the debt.[36] This seems to us to be the proper result. However, the IRS subsequently treated the conversion as a "modification" due to a change in obligor, but *not* as a "significant" modification under the exception (discussed below) for acquisitions of substantially all of an obligor's assets.[37] The latter rulings did not explicitly address the prospect of a change in the recourse nature of the debt.

Once it is determined on the facts and law that a "modification" has occurred, this leaves the question whether the modification is "significant."[38]

As for nonrecourse debt, Reg. § 1.1001-3(e)(4)(ii) provides that a substitution of a new obligor is not significant.

---

[36] IRS Letter Ruling 200315001, September 19, 2002. For an analysis of this issue, *see* Cummings, The Disregarded Entity Is and Isn't Disregarded, 99 Tax Notes 743 (May 5, 2003); Cuff, Indebtedness of a Disregarded Entity, 81 Taxes 303 (2003); Hoffer, Give Them My Regards: A Proposal for Applying the COD Rules to Disregarded Entities, 107 Tax Notes 327 (April 18, 2005).

[37] *See, e.g.*, IRS Letter Ruling 200630002, April 24, 2006; IRS Letter Ruling 200709013, November 22, 2006.

[38] Where a parent and its subsidiary were co-obligors on various debt instruments, the IRS held that the elimination of the subsidiary as a co-obligor was not, on the facts, a significant modification, because there would be no substantial change in the asset base available to service the debt. IRS Private Letter Ruling 200047046, August 30, 2000.

With respect to recourse debt, a sharp distinction is drawn between an assumption and a novation. Reg. § 1.001-3(e)(4)(iii) provides that the addition or deletion of a co-obligor (an assumption) is *not* a significant modification unless it results in a "change in payment expectations" (which generally requires that the debtor's capacity to pay the debt go from adequate to primarily speculative, or vice versa), or unless it is part of a series of steps that results in the substitution of a new obligor (a novation).[39]

Reg. § 1.1001-3(e)(4)(i) provides that a novation of a recourse debt generally *is* a significant modification. But it makes important exceptions to this rule for substitutions of obligors occurring: (1) in reorganization acquisitions governed by Code § 381, or in nonreorganization acquisitions of substantially all the assets of the original obligor, if the transaction does not result in a change in payment expectations or in a significant alteration of the debt instrument;[40] (2) in Code § 338 transactions; or (3) from the mere filing of a bankruptcy petition. A "significant alteration" is a change that would be a significant modification but for the fact it occurs pursuant to the terms of the debt instrument.

Note that the novation rule and its exceptions can have curious results. Take the case of real estate that is subject to a recourse mortgage. If a purchaser of the building assumes the mortgage in a novation, the question whether this results in a significant modification of the debt will depend on whether the purchase was part of an acquisition of substantially all the assets of the seller—a fact that seems somewhat extraneous to the particular debt instrument itself.

Reg. § 1.1001-3(e)(5)(ii) provides that change in the nature of a debt instrument from recourse (or substantially all recourse) to nonrecourse (or substantially all nonrecourse), or vice versa, is generally a significant modification. (For the possible effect that bankruptcy might have of converting non-recourse into recourse debt, *see* § 205 above.)

While the distinction drawn for recourse debt in Reg. § 1.1001-3 between assumptions and novations (and the exceptions thereto) would seem initially to answer certain of the questions posed immediately above about the scope of Code § 1274(c)(4), Example 6 of Reg. § 1.1001-3(g) makes clear that Code § 1274(c)(4) is applied independently of the debt modification rules and only applies to prevent a reissuance for OID purposes. In that example, a building that is secured by recourse debt is purchased, and the purchaser is substituted as the obligor (a novation). The building does not constitute substantially all of the assets of the seller. The example concludes that, although for Code § 1001 purposes there has been a significant modification and thus a deemed exchange of the debt by the holder as a result of the

[39] In IRS Letter Ruling 199904017, January 29, 1999, the common parent of an affiliated group of corporations assumed notes of one of its subsidiaries that it had previously guaranteed. The subsidiary was a special finance subsidiary whose primary purpose was to issue debt for the parent and its affiliates. Instead of treating the parent's assumption of the subsidiary's debt as a novation, the IRS treated the parent as having been essentially a co-obligor, and analyzed the transaction from that perspective.

[40] This provision was applied in IRS Letter Ruling 9711024, December 12, 1996. This was a Code § 355 spin-off in which the spun-off corporation received substantially all of the assets of its distributing parent and was substituted as obligor on the parent's debt.

novation, Code § 1274(c)(4) prevents the modified debt from being retested for OID purposes (absent any other changes in the debt). What this means is that only the OID consequence of the deemed exchange is avoided; all other potential consequences (such as the possibility of gain or loss to the holder) may still arise through the separate application of Reg. § 1.1001-3.

## *§ 402.6 Relevance of Voluntary or Involuntary Change*

The voluntary or involuntary nature of a change in terms has been cited by a few courts as a factor in determining whether an exchange occurred.[41] A change is unlikely to be considered involuntary for this purpose where the debt is not in default.[42] Although the IRS apparently seems generally to view the involuntary nature of a change in terms as irrelevant,[43] the Chief Counsel has stated in the past that, "as a matter of policy," the IRS will not litigate where there is an involuntary change in terms, except where "the bonds were acquired after [a]default in contemplation of realizing a gain from the change in terms."[44]

Reg. § 1.1001-3 is silent about the effect of the voluntary or involuntary nature of the change, and presumably the IRS will apply its rules equally to both types of change.

## *§ 402.7 Modification Required by Original Debt Terms*

Modifications in the terms of debt occurring as the result of agreements reached after issuance of the debt should be distinguished from modifications occurring as a result of certain features contained in the original debt itself. We have already mentioned fluctuating interest rates (*see* § 402.3, above). Similarly, conversions occurring pursuant to the terms of the original debt may be treated as not involving an exchange.[45] For example, in Rev. Rul. 57-535,[46] certain nonmarketable treasury bonds were converted into marketable treasury notes pursuant to a right contained in the original treasury bonds. The IRS concluded that there had been no exchange. "[In substance and effect,] the holder continued to own the same property, its form being

---

[41] *See, e.g., Mutual Loan and Savings Co. v. Commissioner, supra* note 23; *West Missouri Power Co. v. Commissioner, supra* note 14; *C.M. Hall Lamp Co. v. United States, supra* note 26, *rev'd on other grounds,* 201 F.2d 465, 53-1 U.S.T.C. ¶ 66,049 (6th Cir. 1953); *Truman H. Newberry, supra* note 26; *see also* Bacon, Rescue Planning for the Failing or Bankrupt Company, 61 Taxes 931, at 937 n.45 (1983) ("Some courts may be less likely to find a constructive exchange where the debtor is bankrupt or financially troubled than where it is healthy").

[42] *See* GCM 37002, February 10, 1977 ("The old [City of Philadelphia refunding] bonds were not in default; thus, the exchanges were voluntary").

[43] *See, e.g.,* IRS T.A.M. 8451012, August 23, 1984; IRS T.A.M. 8052023, September 25, 1980.

[44] GCM 37002, February 10, 1977, at n.10.

[45] *See* Winterer, *supra* note 23, at 525-527; National Association of Bond Lawyers, Committee on General Federal Tax Matters, Tax Analysis of "Reissue" Questions Arising from Changes in Bond Terms 9-11 (undated and unpublished).

[46] 1957-2 C.B. 513.

changed pursuant to a right embodied in it when [the holder] acquired it."[47] Similarly, no gain or loss is "realized" (a concept that suggests that no exchange has occurred) upon a holder's exercise of its right to convert convertible debentures into stock of the same corporation.[48] As already mentioned, Reg. §1.1001-3 generally confirms these concepts. Thus, things like changes in yield, changes in maturity, changes from fixed to variable interest or vice versa, are generally not considered modifications if they occur pursuant to the terms of the original instrument. However, the regulation contains certain exceptions (*see* §402.3), including (1) changes that result in the substitution of a new obligor, the addition or deletion of a co-obligor, or a change in the recourse nature of the instrument, and (2) changes that result from the exercise of options given to the holder that result in the deferral or reduction in any scheduled payment.[49] Such changes must be tested for significance to the same extent as if they were not pursuant to the terms of the original instrument.

## *§402.8 Changes Made in Series*

Suppose a debt instrument is changed several times over the years, but each change, if considered separately, would not be treated as a significant modification for Code §1001 purposes. Reg. §1.1001-3(f)(3) provides that these are to be tested cumulatively, as if they had all been done at once. If this cumulative treatment causes them to be classified as significant modifications, then they are so treated at the time the cumulation produces that result. An exception is made for prior changes in yield. Such changes can be ignored if they occurred more than five years before the date of the modification being tested.

Query: can changes pre-dating the effective date of the regulation be ignored? The regulation generally applies only to changes occurring on or after September 24, 1996, but the regulation is silent as to whether the cumulative effect of pre-effective date changes must be taken into account in applying the regulation to later changes. This may be particularly significant for payment deferrals and maturity extensions, since under prior law there were generally no limitations imposed on these. Thus, even changes believed to be comfortably within the parameters of prior law may have to be tested under the regulation upon the occurrence of a later change (even a very modest change) of the same type.

## *§402.9 Changes in Accounting or Financial Covenants*

Reg. §1.1001-3(e)(6) states flatly that a modification that adds, deletes, or alters customary accounting or financial covenants is not a significant modification. What such customary covenants are is not described, but presumably they cannot be

---

[47] 1957-2 C.B. 516.

[48] *See* Rev. Rul. 72-265, 1972-1 C.B. 222.

[49] Reg. §1.1001-3(c)(ii)(2).

considered to include provisions that are covered by other specific rules in the regulation, such as changes in security, etc.

## *§402.10 Deferred or Contingent Changes*

When a change is made that has a delayed effective date, an important question is whether the change will be treated as occurring when it was made or only when it takes effect. Reg. § 1.1001-3(c)(6) states as a general rule that it shall be considered a modification when it is made, even if it is not immediately effective. This is consistent with the approach taken in Rev. Rul. 87-19, mentioned at § 402.3 above. However, exceptions to this rule are made for (1) changes conditioned on reasonable closing conditions, which are thus deemed to occur on the closing date, and (2) changes pursuant to a plan of reorganization in a title 11 or similar case (within the meaning of Code § 368(a)(3)(A)), which are thus treated as occurring when the plan becomes effective.

If, after applying these rules, the modification remains contingent or deferred in effect beyond the date that it is considered a modification, two special rules apply for determining how to test such a contingent or deferred change for significance.

The first special rule is that if a change described in any of the specific rules of significance in the § 1001 regulations will be effective only upon a substantial contingency, the change will be tested for significance only under the general rule of Reg. § 1.1001-3(e)(1) and not under the specific rules of Reg. § 1.1001-3(e)(2) through (5) otherwise applicable to such changes.[50]

The second special rule is that if a change in obligor or security, or a change in the recourse status of the debt is made on a noncontingent but deferred basis, the change will be tested for significance under the general rule of Reg. § 1.1001-3(e)(1) and not under the more specific rules of Reg. § 1.1001-3(e)(4) and (5) otherwise applicable to such changes.

Contingencies regarding the effective date of a change in a debt obligation should be distinguished from contingencies regarding the amounts of payments that are to be made under the debt obligation. The text of this § 402.10 deals with the former types of contingencies, but one needs to keep in mind that contingencies of the latter kind (contingent interest or contingent principal payments) can produce a number of special tax problems.[51]

## *§402.11 Issuer's Failure to Perform*

Typically, in any troubled debt situation, the debtor may fall behind in payments, and discussions will take place between the debtor and the holder, perhaps for a considerable period of time, before any amendment is made in the instrument. Since Reg. § 1.1001-3(c)(1)(i) says that a modification includes alterations evidenced

---

[50] Reg. § 1.1001-3(f)(ii).

[51] These issues are thoroughly explored in Asofsky, A Guide to the Tax Treatment of Contingent Payment Debt Instruments, 56 NYU Inst. on Fed. Tax'n, Chapter 5 (1998). *See also* § 403.1.3 below.

by the conduct of the parties, even if not contained in an express agreement, this typical fact pattern could raise a serious question as to whether the failure to perform is itself a modification. The same question could arise about any late payment, even an inadvertent one. The IRS addressed this problem in Reg. § 1.1001-3(c)(4). This states that the issuer's failure to perform is not itself a modification. Neither is the holder's nonaction, or even its agreement to stay collection or temporarily waive an acceleration clause or similar default right, unless and until two years following the initial failure to perform plus any additional period during which the parties conduct good faith negotiations or during which the issuer is in a title 11 or similar case (as defined in Code § 368(a)(3)(A)). Presumably, if the late payment is later made up, and there is no change in yield, there has never been a modification and the safe-harbor period for modifications constituting deferrals is not even implicated.

## *§402.12 Debt-Equity Issues*

Reg. § 1.1001-3(e)(5)(i) says that any modification of a debt instrument that results in its not being debt is a significant modification. But it then says that for purposes of this paragraph ((e)(5)(i)), any deterioration of the financial condition of the obligor between the date of issuance of the debt and its modification will not be taken into account unless there is a change in the obligor. The IRS seems to have intended the latter qualification to be a broad general rule,[52] and not one that applies only when the tinkering with the debt is minor. However, the limiting phrase "for purposes of this paragraph (e)(5)(i)" makes the qualification literally applicable only when the modification would not also be treated as significant under any of the other paragraphs of the regulation. It does not literally say that if the debt is modified in ways that are considered significant under the other provisions of the regulation, the new instrument will not be treated as equity by looking to the financial condition of the issuer. Accordingly, pending further guidance from the IRS, practitioners should proceed with care.

## *§402.13 Coordination with Code §166*

Code § 166 provides that a partially worthless debt deduction is allowed only to the extent there is a prior charge-off of this amount for book purposes made in the tax year. Suppose a debt that has been partially charged off undergoes a significant modification that causes the holder to recognize gain, thus reversing the previous charge-off for tax (but not for book) purposes. Because the charge-off had occurred for book purposes in an earlier year and thus could not be repeated for book purposes in the current year, the holder could not offset the tax gain by taking a partially worthless debt deduction because it could not satisfy the technical require-

---

[52] *See, e.g.*, 96 Tax Notes Today 164-2 (August 21, 1996) (reporting statements by Thomas J. Kelley, the principal drafter of the regulation, at the ABA annual meeting); BNA Daily Tax Report No. 156, at G-1 (August 13, 1996) (same). *Cf.* IRS Field Service Advice 19991009, December 2, 1998, *reprinted at* 1999 TNT 49-87, and noted at § 508.2.2.3 below.

ment of a current year book charge-off. At the time the IRS issued the final § 1.1001-3 regulations, it eliminated this problem by issuing Reg. § 1.166-3(a)(3), first as a temporary and later as a final regulation, which deems such debt to have been charged off in the year of the modification in the amount of the gain, but not below the fair market value of the debt.

## *§ 402.14 Irrelevance of Installment Sale Authorities*

Code § 453B provides that where an installment obligation for which the holder has elected the installment method of taxation is "satisfied at other than its face value or distributed, transmitted, sold, or otherwise disposed of," gain or loss shall result to the extent of the difference between the basis of the obligation and the amount realized.[53] The IRS has been liberal in ruling that a disposition by a holder does not occur under this provision when the interest rate is increased and the maturity date deferred;[54] the principal amount is reduced;[55] a single promissory note and deed of trust is split into two secured notes;[56] a new obligor assumes liability for the notes or becomes substituted for the old obligor;[57] a new obligor is substituted for the old obligor and the interest rate is increased;[58] or the security for the note is changed.[59] In fact few amendments to promissory notes have been ruled to be dispositions. One that went too far is described in Rev. Rul. 82-188.[60] There, a note that had been convertible into stock was amended by increasing its face amount in exchange for eliminating the right of conversion. This modification was held to be a disposition of the old note. In a later private ruling,[61] the IRS limited the impact of Rev. Rul. 82-188 to situations where the conversion feature had become valuable by the time of the later modification of the debt, so that the modification "locked-in" the value of the conversion feature. The private letter ruling held that elimination of a conversion feature would not create a disposition of the old debt where the conversion feature had virtually no value at the time of the modification.

Most of the installment sale disposition authorities are obviously inconsistent with those dealing with whether modifications of a debt constitute an exchange for purposes of Code § 1001. The tax policy considerations involved are quite different. It is not surprising, therefore, that the IRS has said that the installment sale disposition

---

53 *See* explanation of the installment sale rules at Stand. Fed. Tax Rep. (CCH) ¶ 21,471.

54 Rev. Rul. 68-419, 1968-2 C.B. 196; IRS Letter Ruling 9505011, November 4, 1994, and IRS Letter Ruling 9505016, November 7, 1994 (both involving extensions of maturity date).

55 Rev. Rul. 55-429, 1955-2 C.B. 252, *amplified by* Rev. Rul. 72-570, 1972-2 C.B. 241.

56 Rev. Rul. 74-157, 1974-1 C.B. 115.

57 Rev. Rul. 75-457, 1975-2 C.B. 196; Rev. Rul. 61-215, 1961-2 C.B. 110.

58 Rev. Rul. 82-122, 1982-1 C.B. 80.

59 Rev. Rul. 55-5, 1955-1 C.B. 331; Rev. Rul. 68-246, 1968-1 C.B. 198.

60 1982-2 C.B. 90. This is consistent with Rev. Rul. 72-264, 1972-1 C.B. 131, in which the IRS held that a conversion of an installment note is a taxable "disposition" of the note with the full value of the stock being the amount realized. However, in Rev. Rul. 82-188, should the IRS have treated the additional face amount simply as a purchase of the conversion privilege; and, if so, should OID or imputed interest be computed separately for this new portion of the debt?

61 IRS Letter Ruling 9412013, December 21, 1993.

authorities should not be considered precedent for purposes of applying Code § 1001.[62] Consistent with this approach, but stating the point from the opposite direction, the preamble to Reg. § 1.1001-3 says that "a modification of a debt instrument that results in an exchange under section 1001 does not determine if there has been an exchange or other disposition of an installment obligation under section 453B."[63]

We should note, further, that the installment sale disposition cases have only dealt with the tax treatment of the holder of the note[64] and have not focused on the tax treatment of the obligor. Where the debt modification is sufficient to constitute an exchange for Code § 1001 purposes, but is not sufficient to be a disposition for Code § 453B purposes, obligors of notes that have been reported under Code § 453 by the holders will wonder which set of authorities should apply to their side of the transaction. The language just quoted from the preamble to Reg. § 1.1001-3 does not specifically address this side of the question. The better answer would seem to be that they should apply the Code § 1001 concepts, but in the absence of persuasive precedent, obligors should be able to take the position on this issue that proves most advantageous to them in each particular case.

## *§ 402.15 Effect of Time-Value-of-Money Regulations*

In April 1986, the IRS issued proposed regulations under Code § § 1271-1275, as well as under Code § § 163(e), 446, 482 and 483. The proposed regulations are designed to implement the Tax Reform Act of 1984's time-value-of-money concepts. Most of the 1986 proposed regulations were withdrawn in December 1992 and new proposed regulations were substituted for them. The 1992 proposed regulations differed from the 1986 proposed regulations in a number of respects.

The 1992 proposed regulations provided that they would be effective prospectively only, for debt issued after 60 days following their effective date. Final regulations, which differed in some respects from the 1992 proposed regulations, were issued in 1994. The final regulations apply to debt instruments issued on or after April 4, 1994, and to lending transactions, sales, and exchanges occurring on or after that date. However, the preamble to the final regulations says that taxpayers may rely on the final regulations for such events occurring after December 21, 1992. In addition, that preamble says that for purposes of applying the Code § 6662 understatement penalty, one can rely (1) on the 1992 proposed regulations for such events occurring after December 21, 1992, and before April 4, 1994, and (2) on the 1986 proposed regulations for such events occurring before December 22, 1992.

---

[62] GCM 39225, April 27, 1984; *see also* GCM 37889; March 20, 1979.

[63] This language is stronger than that in the Preamble to the December 1992 proposed regulations, which states: " . . . the determination of whether there is a sale or disposition under section 1001 does not conclusively determine that there has been a disposition of an installment obligation under section 453 of the Code."

[64] The IRS has described in Rev. Rul 72-570, 1972-2 C.B. 241, the way in which the holder of the note is to report his income from the note after the note has been modified in a way that does not amount to a disposition.

Some of the provisions in the 1986 proposed regulations tried to deal with modification itself. Perhaps the most important of these was 1986 Prop. Reg. § 1.1274-1(c), which provided that:

> For purposes of Section 1274, if the issuer and holder (or a successor to either) modify a debt instrument, the modified debt instrument shall be treated as a new debt instrument given in consideration for the unmodified debt instrument (the old instrument) . . . . A debt instrument has been modified if the terms of the new debt instrument differ "materially in kind or in extent," within the meaning of § 1.1001-1(a), from the terms of the old debt instrument . . . . For this purpose, a payment to or from the lender (or a successor) not provided for in the debt instrument shall be treated as a modification of the debt instrument.

An example in the 1986 proposed regulations illustrated this passage by saying that a change in interest rate from 8 percent to 11 percent, coupled with a deferral of payment until maturity of the next two years of interest, is a modification.[65] Another example went even farther, by holding that a change in interest rate from 10 percent to 11 percent is itself a modification.[66] (These examples were not included in the 1992 proposed or the 1994 final regulations, and their content has been superseded by the regulations issued under Code § 1001.)

What may potentially have been an even more profound change is suggested by the last sentence in the passage just quoted from the 1986 Prop. Reg. § 1.1274-1(c): "For this purpose, a payment to or from the lender (or a successor) not provided for in the debt instrument shall be treated as a modification of the debt instrument." This could be read to suggest that any deviation (however small) from the terms of the original instrument in the timing of payments will be a modification. If so, a prepayment of some principal, where the debt instrument did not provide for prepayment without penalty, could result in an "exchange" of new for old debt. If this were the intent, it seems unlikely that one could have avoided the problem by first amending the instrument to permit the prepayment and then arguing that the amendment was not "material." The sentence could also be read, however, as referring not to changes in the timing of payments but to changes in the aggregate amounts payable under the original debt instrument. Or the sentence could be read to refer to both types of changes. Whatever the intent, the sentence seemed overly broad because of its failure to require that the change be "material."

While the 1986 proposed regulations left a considerable amount of confusion regarding the extent to which they superseded the prior law, it is worth noting that the IRS nonetheless continued to issue several rulings that applied traditional concepts under Code § 1001 as to what constitutes an exchange of old debt for new debt, while seeming to ignore the foregoing provisions of the 1986 proposed regulations.[67]

---

[65] 1986 Prop. Reg. § 1.1274-7(a)(3), Example (3). *See also* IRS Letter Rulings 8708017 and 8722064, *supra* note 14.

[66] 1986 Prop. Reg. § 1.1274-7(a)(3), Example (2).

[67] *See* the post-1986 authorities cited in notes 10, 20, and 22 above.

Fortunately, the language quoted above from 1986 Prop. Reg. § 1.1274-1(c) was omitted from the 1992 proposed regulations and the 1994 final regulations. As mentioned earlier, in 1992 the IRS also issued proposed, and in 1996, final regulations under Code § 1001 regarding the extent to which modifications of debt instruments will be treated as exchanges of new for old debt. The intent of the regulation writers since 1992 has been to leave the subject of debt modification, with certain exceptions, to the Code § 1001 regulations. The exceptions are the provisions in Reg. §§ 1.446-2(e)(4) and 1.1275-2(f), dealing with pro rata allocations of prepayments; Reg. § 1.1274-5, dealing with certain assumptions; and Reg. § 1.1275-2(j) which, as discussed above at § 402.1, can cause an OID modification to occur even where a § 1001 exchange of old for new debt has not been deemed to occur.

More importantly, these regulations seem to change the prior rules for determining the allocation of payments as between principal and interest. This change largely erodes the ability of the parties to affect tax consequences by earmarking payments. 1986 Prop. Reg. § 1.446-2(d) provided that each payment under a loan should be treated first as interest to the extent of the accrued unpaid interest, next as prepayment of interest to the extent so earmarked by the parties, and last as principal. The 1992 Prop. Reg. § 1.446-2(e) provided that payments are to be treated first as interest to the extent of accrued unpaid interest and the remainder as principal. The 1994 final Reg. § 1.446-2(e) limits itself to saying simply that payments are to be allocated first to interest to the extent of accrued unpaid interest. 1986 Prop. Reg. § 1.1272-1(e)(2)(ii) provided that each payment (other than a payment of stated interest) on a note having OID should be treated first as a payment of accrued unpaid OID, then as principal (with none treated as prepaid interest). Final Reg. § 1.1275-2(a) is to the same effect, as was the 1992 Prop. Reg. § 1.1275-2(a).

None of the foregoing regulations explicitly deal with the kind of factual circumstances that arise when the debt of a failing business has to be restructured. One wonders, for example, whether these allocation rules were intended to apply in cases where it is unlikely that principal will be paid in full or to payments made in termination of a loan where less than the full amount of principal and interest is paid.[68]

## § 403 CONSEQUENCES OF AN "EXCHANGE" OF OLD DEBT FOR NEW DEBT

Where an exchange of old debt for new debt occurs, both the creditor and the debtor need to determine (1) whether gain or loss or interest income is to be recognized by

---

[68] The Tax Section of the New York State Bar Association has recommended that the rule not be applied on termination of the loan. NYSBA Tax Section, Report on Final OID Regulations, 64 Tax Notes 1747 (Sept. 26, 1994). *Accord* Garlock, Federal Income Taxation of Debt Instruments, Ch. 10, Part 3(D) (3rd ed.). *See* the discussion of this point in § 401.1 above, including the year 2000 letter ruling (IRS Letter Ruling 200035008, May 23, 2000) holding that all payments in liquidation of defaulted tax-exempt bonds should be allocated to principal. On the other hand, IRS Field Service Advice 1998-459, March 31, 1998, *reprinted at* 2000 TNT 165-74, which deals with bankruptcy case transactions that occurred before the effective date of the above final regulations, suggests that the new regulations would apply even in the case of a restructuring of a failing company.

the creditor on the exchange, (2) whether COD income is to be recognized to the debtor on the exchange, and (3) whether Code § 1273 or § 1274 OID or Code § 483 "imputed interest" is to be recognized for either the debtor or the creditor.[1]

The answers depend on whether the exchange constitutes a tax-free recapitalization or a taxable exchange, and on whether the holder of the old debt has applied the Code § 453 installment method of accounting to the old debt. These issues will be examined next.

A preliminary observation, however, is in order. There is little difference in substance between (1) a refinancing or debt modification accomplished by issuing the new debt for cash and using cash to retire the old debt and (2) one accomplished by exchanging a new note for the old note. Yet the tax consequences of the two methods, if the form is respected, can be different. Although in extreme cases there may be some risk that the form adopted by the taxpayer will not be respected, on this issue it appears—at least where there is not a complete overlap between the owners of the old debt and the new debt—that by and large the form adopted by the taxpayer will prevail.[2]

---

[1] **§ 403** *See* explanation of the imputed interest rules of Code § 483 at Stand. Fed. Tax Rep. (CCH) ¶ 22,299.

[2] *See* IRS T.A.M. 8815003, December 11, 1987 (swap with underwriters of old debt purchased by them at a discount in exchange for new zero coupon debt was held to be a recapitalization exchange and not a purchase of old bonds for cash by the debtor followed by issuance of new debt); *see also, e.g., Helvering v. Union Public Serv.*, 75 F.2d 723, 724, 35-1 U.S.T.C. ¶ 9099 (8th Cir. 1935) (upheld independence of cash issuance of new debt and cash redemption of old debt, even though same bank was trustee for both issues and new debt was issued for the stated purpose of raising funds to redeem old debt; in so holding, the court stated that the described transaction "does not involve the substitution or exchange of one issue of bonds for another. The holders of the 2 bond issues were obviously not the same persons. The fact that the new 5% issue was sold for the purpose of retiring old bonds does not alter the conclusion and the case is not distinguishable in character from one in which the old bond issue is retired before maturity out of surplus or funds made available for that purpose by some other means."); *Helvering v. California Oregon Power Co.*, 75 F.2d 644, 645, 35-1 U.S.T.C. ¶ 9064 (D.C. Cir. 1935) (upheld similar transaction where new debt was issued after old debt had been called for redemption); *Congress Square Hotel Co. v. Commissioner*, 4 T.C. 775, Dec. 14,385 (1945), *acq.* (wherein taxpayer, for the express purpose of raising funds to redeem its old bonds, sold to certain underwriters new bonds under a firm commitment underwriting; to the extent old bondholders desired to acquire new bonds rather than receive cash, the underwriters (independent of taxpayer) adopted a special procedure whereby such exchanges were possible; although, at taxpayer's request, Maine residents were given terms of exchange more favorable than that offered to others, the court upheld the independence of the issuance of new bonds for cash and of the redemption of old bonds, finding that the underwriter acted on their own behalf and not as agents for taxpayer); *see also, e.g., Great Western Power Co. v. Commissioner*, 297 U.S. 543, 36-1 U.S.T.C. ¶ 9185 (1936) (citing with approval *Union Public Service and California Oregon Power Co.*); *Bridgeport Hydraulic Co.*, 22 T.C. 215, 217, Dec. 20,301 (1955) (upheld independence of transaction similar to that in *California Oregon Power;* distinguished debt-for-debt exchanges on ground that decision to call old debt occurred prior to contracts for sale of new debt), *nonacq., aff'd per curiam*, 223 F.2d 925, 55-2 U.S.T.C. ¶ 9548 (2d Cir. 1955); *South Carolina Continental Telephone Co.*, 10 T.C. 164, 169, Dec. 16,228 (1948) (although upholding the form of a debt-for-debt exchange, the court stated that, prior to applying the law, it must "be determined as an ultimate fact that the transactions here involved constituted an exchange of petitioner's old bonds for its new bonds"); *cf.* IRS T.A.M. 8538004, May 24, 1985 (taxpayer sold Ginnie Mae certificates at a loss and, five days later, repurchased identical certificates; held that, despite the passage of cash, the two transactions should be considered together, in which case an "exchange" within the meaning of Reg. § 1.1001-1(a) did not occur). There is also a possibility of characterizing a transaction as a repayment of a loan and the creation of a new loan. *See*

## §403.1 *Tax-Free Recapitalization*

The exchange of new debt for old debt constitutes a tax-free recapitalization exchange under Code §§368(a)(1)(E) and 354 where both the old and the new debt constitute a security for purposes of Code §§368 and 354.[3] As a rule of thumb, the original maturity of a debt is what usually provides the dividing line between debt that is a security and debt that is not. Instruments with original maturities of ten years or more usually will be considered securities.[4] Instruments with original maturities of five years or less usually will not.[5] Thus, most trade debt and bank revolving credit debt will not constitute securities. The status of instruments that have an original maturity of between five and ten years is unclear.

The original maturity test is no more than a rule of thumb, however; the maturity of an instrument alone is not necessarily determinative. "Though time is an important factor, the controlling consideration is an overall evaluation of the nature of the debt, degree of participation and continuing interest compared with similarity of the note to a cash payment, the purpose of the advances, etc."[6] In a perhaps extreme example, the Tax Court in *D'Angelo Associates, Inc.*[7] held that a demand note was a security (though not equity) where the debtor corporation could not have paid off the note without selling its business and thus was unlikely to pay the note within

---

(Footnote Continued)

*Buddy Schoellkopf Products, Inc. v. Commissioner*, 65 T.C. 640, Dec. 33,593 (1975) (taxpayer had a loan with insurance company; before maturity, the loan was repaid from proceeds of a second loan taken out from the same insurance company. The new loan also increased the principal amount borrowed and had a different maturity date and interest rate. The court held that the new loan was separate and independent of the old loan, rather than a mere increase in the old loan, with the consequence that the debtor could immediately deduct the unamortized issuance expenses of the old loan rather than having to amortize them over the life of the new loan); to similar effect, *see* the second issue in *Federal National Mortgage Ass'n v. Commissioner*, 90 T.C. 405, Dec. 44,637 (1988), *aff'd*, 896 F.2d 580, 90-1 U.S.T.C. ¶50,105 (D.C. Cir. 1990).

[3] *See* explanation of tax-free recapitalization rules at Stand. Fed. Tax Rep. (CCH) ¶16,433.

[4] *See* Bittker & Eustice, Federal Income Taxation of Corporations and Shareholders §3.03 (5th ed.), ¶12.41[3] (7th ed.); *Burnham v. Commissioner*, 86 F.2d 776, 36-2 U.S.T.C. ¶9544 (7th Cir. 1936), *cert. denied*, 300 U.S. 683 (1937) (unsecured, confess-judgment, ten-year promissory note); Rev. Rul. 59-98, 1959-1 C.B. 76 (bonds with average life of 6$^1/_2$ years when issued were securities).

[5] Id.; *see* Reg. §1.368-1(b); Rev. Rul. 2004-78, 2004-31 I.R.B. 1.

[6] *Camp Wolters Enters., Inc. v. Commissioner*, 22 T.C. 737, 750-751, Dec. 20,430 (1954), *aff'd*, 230 F.2d 555, 56-1 U.S.T.C. ¶9314 (5th Cir. 1956), *cert. denied*, 352 U.S. 826 (1956).

[7] 70 T.C. 121, Dec. 35,128 (1978), *acq*.

a short term.[8] In contrast, in *Bradshaw v. United States*,[9] the Court of Claims held that installment notes ranging in maturity from two and one-half to six and one-half years did not constitute securities. The court found that repayment was not dependent upon the success of the business, that a fair price had been paid, and that no continuing proprietary interest was intended.[10]

In 2004, the IRS issued an important ruling[11] to address what happens when a target corporation security with little remaining maturity is exchanged in an "A" reorganization for an acquiring corporation debt instrument that is identical in all respects (including the short remaining maturity) except for a change in interest rate. Will the short remaining maturity of the new debt prevent it from being classified as a security, so that the exchange of the old debt for the new debt is not a tax-free exchange under Code § 354?

The facts in the ruling were that the T debt had an original maturity of 16 years, but at the time of the merger there were only two years remaining. In the "A" reorganization, the T debt was exchanged for acquiring corporation debt that was identical in all respects (including only a two-year maturity), except that the interest rate had been changed (perhaps to reflect differences in the credit ratings of the target and the acquiring corporation). The interest rate change constituted a significant modification under Reg. § 1.1001-3. The ruling noted that an instrument with a term of less than five years generally is not a security. But the ruling concluded that, because the new debt of the acquiring corporation had the same terms (except interest rate) as the T securities exchanged for them, the new debt of the acquiring corporation represented a continuation of the security holder's investment in the target in substantially the same form, and should be treated as securities within the meaning of Code § 354. We assume the same conclusion should apply if such a new

---

[8] *See also, e.g.*, Rev. Rul. 59-98, 1959-1 C.B. 76 (first mortgage bonds with average term of 6½ years purchased for investment were securities); *United States v. Hertwig*, 398 F.2d 452, 68-2 U.S.T.C. ¶9495 (5th Cir. 1968) (12½ year promissory notes exchanged for patents were securities); *Aqualane Shores, Inc. v. Commissioner*, 269 F.2d 116, 59-2 U.S.T.C. ¶9632 (5th Cir. 1959) (five annual installment notes exchanged for land were securities in that the corporation only had $600 of operating funds and could only pay off the notes if and when it sold the land); *Prentis v. United States*, 273 F. Supp. 460, 67-2 U.S.T.C. ¶9554 (D.N.Y. 1967) (six-month equipment note held to be a security for Code § 351 purposes as the purpose of the note was ultimately to transform it into preferred stock); *George A. Lagerquist*, 53 T.C.M. 530, Dec. 43,830(M), T.C. Memo. 1987-185 (two promissory notes maturing consecutively—the first over years 1 through 4 and the second over year 5 through 9—held to be securities; as evidence of the holder's continuing exposure to the risks of the enterprise, the court noted that the promissory notes were unsecured, subordinate to almost all present and future debt, unregistered, nontransferable without consent of issuer's counsel, nonprepayable, and, as the company was cash-tight, dependent on the success of the business for repayment).

[9] 683 F.2d 365, 82-2 U.S.T.C. ¶9454 (Ct. Cl. 1982).

[10] *See also Piedmont Corp. v. Commissioner*, 388 F.2d 886, 68-1 U.S.T.C. ¶9189 (4th Cir. 1968) (installment notes varying in maturity from two to six years held to be nonsecurities); *Neville Coke and Chemical Co. v. Commissioner*, 148 F.2d 599, 45-1 U.S.T.C. ¶9233 (3d Cir. 1945), *cert. denied*, 326 U.S. 726 (three-, four- and five-year notes held to be nonsecurities as there was no indication that the holder ever intended a long-term investment in the business); *Commissioner v. Sisto Fin. Corp.*, 139 F.2d 253, 44-1 U.S.T.C. ¶9101 (2d Cir. 1944) (unsecured demand notes and secured notes payable in six months or less held to be nonsecurities).

[11] Rev. Rul. 2004-78, 2004-31 I.R.B. 1. For a discussion of some of the implications of this ruling, *see* Friedman, Debt Exchanges After Rev. Rul. 2004-78, 105 Tax Notes 979 (November 15, 2004).

debt instrument were issued in a single company recapitalization exchange (including a deemed exchange resulting from the change in interest rate) rather than in a two company reorganization.

Where both the new and the old debt involved in an exchange are securities so that the exchange is a recapitalization exchange, the consequences are as follows:

### § 403.1.1 Creditor Gain Limited to Boot; No Loss

No gain or loss will be recognized to the creditor except to the extent that the creditor receives "boot." Boot is cash or any property received by the creditor other than stock or a security of the debtor. Boot also includes any "excess principal amount" of the new security over the principal amount of the old security.

The term "principal amount" is an anachronism dating back to the days before the "issue price" OID concept was inserted in the Code. It had been our view that for purposes of interpreting this phrase, as for other tax purposes, the face or principal amount of a debt instrument should not mean its nominal face amount, but the nominal face amount adjusted for any OID or Code § 483 imputed interest.[12] There is a question, however, whether this requires a statutory amendment. For COD purposes, the OID approach was confirmed by the adoption in 1990 of what is now Code § 108(e)(10). The Tax Simplification Act of 1991, § 444, introduced June 26, 1991, but not enacted, would have resolved the matter for Code § § 354 and 356 purposes as well by substituting "issue price" or "adjusted issue price" for "principal amount" in Code § § 354 and 356. Although most of the provisions of the 1991 Act were reintroduced as part of the 1992 Act, this particular provision was not included. Elimination of this provision was intentional, apparently because the staff did not feel the "issue price" concept would work correctly in Code § § 354 and 356 in all circumstances.[13] In light of this history, the words "principal amount" in Code § § 354 and 356 might be construed to mean nominal face amount in some, but not all, circumstances.[14] As noted in § 403.1.2 below, however, OID may nonetheless be created in the new securities issued in the exchange, even if they have the same face amount or principal as the old securities.

Where there is boot, the creditor will recognize gain, if any, but not in excess of the fair market value of the boot[15] (the Tax Simplification Act of 1991, *supra*, would have eliminated the reference to fair market value where the boot consists of an excess amount of securities).

---

[12] *See* Code § 1271 *et seq.* including § 1273(b) and § 1274 (OID); and § 483(b).

[13] *See* Ginsburg and Levin, Mergers, Acquisitions and Buyouts, ¶ 605 note 5 (Aspen, Dec. 2001 ed.).

[14] *See ibid.*; IRS Field Service Advice 200146013, June 27, 2001, *reprinted at* 2001 TNT 223-14 (reads principal amount to mean issue price). *See also* Carrington and Munro, Debt Recapitalization: Planning Opportunities and Pitfalls, 39 Tax Mgmt. Memo. S-353 (1998).

[15] Code § § 354 and 356. For a general discussion of the treatment of boot received in a reorganization exchange, *see* Bittker & Eustice, *supra* note 4, at ¶ 12.44 (6th ed.). *See also* Lipton, Section 1274 and COD Income Due to Modification of the Interest Rate in a Debt Instrument, 68 Taxes 504 (1990).

As mentioned at § 403.1.6, there is one limited exception to the rule that bars recognition of a loss on such an exchange. This exception applies to the extent interest is not paid in the exchange to a creditor that had accrued the interest into income.

### § 403.1.2 Creation of New OID

Prior to its repeal (effective, with certain exceptions, for exchanges after October 9, 1990, except those pursuant to a title 11 or similar case filed before October 10, 1990) by the Revenue Reconciliation Act of 1990, Code § 1275(a)(4) provided a limitation on the creation of new OID in reorganization exchanges. It stated that if new debt is issued in a tax-free reorganization in exchange for old debt, and if the adjusted principal amount of the new debt (after applying the OID provisions, without regard to this reorganization provision) would be *less than* the adjusted principal amount of the old debt (meaning the face amount of the old debt, reduced by the OID created when it was issued and increased by the portion of this OID previously includible in the income of the holder of the old debt), then the adjusted principal amount of the new debt shall be *equal* to the adjusted principal amount of the old debt.

The general intent of this provision was clear: By and large, in a reorganization exchange of old for new debt, the remaining OID on the old debt was to carry over into the new debt and no new OID was to be created. However, the provision did not operate quite so simply. A few examples will illustrate this. In each instance, assume that the old debt had a face amount of $1,000 and OID at issuance of $100, and that $8 of this OID has been includible to date in the income of the holder. Thus, the adjusted principal amount of the old debt is $908.

**EXAMPLE 1**

The old debt is exchanged for new debt with a face amount of $1,000. The new debt is publicly traded and has a value at issuance of $850. Thus, without regard to Code § 1275(a)(4), it would have OID of $150 and an adjusted principal amount of $850.[16] Since $850 is less than $908, the adjusted principal amount of the new debt after application of Code § 1275(a)(4) will be $908 and the new debt will have only $92 of OID (which has carried over from the old debt). The debtor will have no COD income, having exchanged a $908 adjusted principal amount debt for a $908 adjusted principal amount debt.

[16] Code § 1273(b)(3).

### EXAMPLE 2

The new debt has a $1,000 face amount but its public trading market value at issuance is $920. Without regard to Code § 1275(a)(4), the adjusted principal amount of this new debt would be $920. Since this is not less than $908, Code § 1275(a)(4) does not apply. Because the new debt is publicly traded, its OID will be governed by Code § 1273(b)(3), and its adjusted principal amount will therefore be its fair market value. Thus, the new debt will have a $920 adjusted principal amount and only $80 of OID; the exchanging holder will have boot on the exchange of $12 (the fair market value, on these facts, of the difference between the $908 and $920 adjusted principal amounts), which will be recognized to the extent of the holder's gain;[17] and the debtor will have a $12 premium item that it should be entitled to deduct currently as a retirement premium attributable to the redemption of the old debt.[18]

### EXAMPLE 3

The new debt has a nominal face amount of $800 and a public trading market value of $750. Disregarding for the moment Code § 1275(a)(4), the new debt would have an adjusted principal amount of $750 and OID of $50; a holder who had a $908 basis in the old debt would have a loss of $158 (the difference between $908 and $750), but because the loss in a tax-free recapitalization exchange cannot be deducted, his basis in the new debt would be $908; and the debtor would have $158 (the difference between $908 and $750) of COD income. When one then turns to Code § 1275(a)(4), one finds that it does not work properly on the facts of this example. Here, the adjusted principal amount of the new debt (without regard to Code § 1275(a)(4)), $750, is less than $908, and Code § 1275(a)(4), if literally applied, would treat the adjusted principal amount of the new

---

[17] This does not seem an appropriate fact situation in which to construe "principal amount" in Code §§ 354 and 356 to mean nominal face amount, rather than "adjusted issue price." The recognized gain would not be reportable on the installment method because the new debt is publicly traded. *See* Code § 453(f)(4). However, it would increase the holder's basis in the new debt. If the new debt were not publicly traded, and if the other requirements of Code § 453 were met, the boot could be reported on the installment method. *See* Code § 453(f)(6) (flush language). A security (or, for that matter, a nonsecurity) should constitute "property" for purposes of installment method reporting. *Compare* Code § 453(b) *with* Code § 351(d) (excludes debt which is not a "security" from the definition of "property" for purposes of Code § 351); *cf. Duncan v. Commissioner*, 9 T.C. 468 Dec. 16,027 (1967) (prior to Code § 351(d), "property" for purposes of Code § 351 included all debt); Rev. Rul. 77-81, 1977-1 C.B. 97 (same); Prop. Reg. § 1.1274-1(c) (debt of issuer can constitute "property" for purposes of Code § 1274). The text of Prop. Reg. § 1.453-1(f)(2) does not suggest otherwise, although it should be noted that all of the examples contained therein involve the transfer of old stock and none involves the transfer of old debt.

[18] *See* Bittker & Eustice, *supra* note 4, at ¶ 12.27[4][c] (7th ed.). *But see* Lewis, Recognizing Discharge of Indebtedness Income on Bond-for-Bond Recapitalizations, 45 J. Tax'n 370 (December 1976).

debt as being $908, even though its nominal face amount is only $800. This obviously cannot be permitted. The probable intent of the drafter of Code § 1275(a)(4) is that on these facts the adjusted principal amount of the new debt should be $800 (not $908 and not $750), in which event the new debt would have no OID and the debtor would have $108 of COD income. What Code § 1275(a)(4) should have said to accomplish this result is that, where it applies, the adjusted principal amount of the new debt should be the lesser of the adjusted principal amount of the old debt or the nominal face amount of the new debt. Hopefully this is the way it will be interpreted.[19] (In IRS Letter Ruling 9234030, May 27, 1992, the IRS adopted our suggested result.) The creditor who had a $908 basis in the old debt would have a $908 basis in the new $800 adjusted principal amount of new debt. The creditor can treat the $108 difference as amortizable bond premium under Code § 171. *See* Code § 171(b)(4)(B).

As mentioned above, the 1990 Act repealed Code § 1275(a)(4). The repeal is effective for exchanges after October 9, 1990, except for those (1) pursuant to a prior binding written contract, (2) in a transaction described in certain previously filed or released documents, or (3) in a Title 11 or similar case filed before October 10, 1990.

The repeal of Code § 1275(a)(4) makes recapitalization debt-for-debt exchanges substantially less attractive for the debtor company, which is more likely to have COD income. In some cases, this may only represent a timing difference: What is treated today as COD income may be deducted over the life of the new debt by the debtor company as OID. However, these future deductions may not always become available. Their utility, for example, might be limited by the built-in loss restrictions of Code § 382 if there is an ownership change, and, even more frequently, they may be deferred or even eliminated by the "high yield OID or PIK obligations" rule of Code § 163(e)(5) (*see* § 405 below). This is particularly likely to occur where either the old or the new debt is publicly traded. In that case, the issue price of the new debt (and thus the resulting COD and OID) will be determined under Code § 1273 by these market values (which will almost always, when debt restructuring is needed, be low) and not by the Code § 1274 interest-capitalization method (which may create an issue price substantially above the value of the debt). Thus, very significant tax consequences will hang on the question of whether debt is publicly traded within the meaning of Code § 1273. Unfortunately, this could become a source of uncertainty and controversy, given the frequently illiquid nature of the markets for "public" debt of troubled companies.[20] For these reasons, the repeal of Code § 1275(a)(4) conflicts with the goal of the Bankruptcy Code to encourage and facilitate the restructuring

---

[19] Alternatively, one could try to apportion the adjusted principal amount of the old debt between the part that is being exchanged for the new debt and the part that is being forgiven or satisfied with other property. The result should be the same in either case, provided that $800 of the $908 adjusted principal amount of the old debt is apportioned to the new debt.

[20] This problem is alleviated to some extent by the statement in Reg. § 1.1273-2(f)(4) that inclusion of the security in the "yellow sheets" would not by itself cause the security to be considered publicly traded. The yellow sheets do not include sales transactions or bids and offers, but do name the security and dealers who may have an interest in buying or selling the security.

and survival of troubled businesses. The timing of the repeal, in late 1990 when the American economy was in difficulty and there were an extraordinary number of American companies in need of debt restructuring, strikes us as odd, particularly since the repeal was strongly opposed by the National Bankruptcy Conference and by the Tax Section of the New York State Bar Association.

When Code § 1275(a)(4) was repealed, there was also a substantial risk that it would have almost equally adverse consequences for the exchanging creditors in a recapitalization exchange. Code § 354 will not allow them to recognize (by taking a deduction) the economic loss they realize on the exchange. While the 1990 Act committee reports specifically mentioned this consequence, they were silent on the question of whether this disallowed loss could be used by the creditors to offset the OID income they would have on the new debt. Fortunately, the IRS issued in July 1991, with a retroactive effective date, Prop. Reg. § 1.1272-2, which would apply Code § 1272(a)(7) to allow such an offset. This became final in 1994.

### § 403.1.3 Debtor COD Income: Differences Between Recourse and Nonrecourse Debt

If the principal amount of the new security, after adjustment for OID, imputed interest, or bond premium, is less than the similarly adjusted principal amount of the old security, the difference should be treated as COD income to the debtor.[21] *See* the discussion in § 403.1.2 above. The consequences of COD income are discussed beginning at § 404.

A special comment should be made about nonrecourse debt. The COD rules for nonrecourse debt are quite different from the rules for recourse debt. As a general rule, where property securing *recourse* debt is foreclosed upon, the amount of the cancelled debt up to the value of the property is treated as proceeds from the sale of the property, and any excess amount is treated as COD income.[22] In contrast, where property securing *nonrecourse* debt is foreclosed upon, the full amount of the debt is treated as an amount realized from sale of the property, even if the property is worth less than the face amount of the debt.[23] This treatment of nonrecourse debt can be an

---

[21] *See* Code §§ 61(a)(12), 108(a) and (e)(3); Rev. Rul. 77-437, 1977-2 C.B. 28. Code § 108(e)(10), added by the 1990 Act, specifically states that for COD purposes, the debtor in a debt-for-debt exchange will be treated as having satisfied the debt with an amount of money equal to the issue price of the new debt, as determined under Code § 1273 or 1274. *See also* the discussion of the OID issue in § 403.1.2 above.

[22] Reg. § 1.1001-2(a)(1) and (a)(2); Rev. Rul. 90-16, 1990-1 C.B. 12; *Gehl v. Commissioner*, 102 T.C. 784 (1994), *aff'd*, 50 F.3d 12 (8th Cir. 1995), *cert. denied*, 116 Sup. Ct. 257 (1995); *Frazier v. Commissioner*, 111 T.C. 243 (1998).

[23] Code § 7701(g); Reg. § 1.1001-2(a), (b); *2925 Briarpark Ltd. v. Commissioner*, 163 F.3d 313, 99-1 U.S.T.C. ¶ 50,209 (5th Cir. 1999). This difference in treatment between nonrecourse and recourse debt was not noted in *Cozzi v. Commissioner*, 88 T.C. 435 (1987), a case sometimes cited on the question of *when* COD income should be deemed to arise. The case involved nonrecourse debt, yet the court dealt with the discharged amount as being COD income, rather than as proceeds from the effective abandonment of the collateral to the creditor. This error apparently arose because the parties stipulated that the discharge created COD income. This error was noted, and the distinction was crucial to one of the holdings, in *Coburn v. Commissioner*, T.C. Memo 2005-283. *See* § 404.7 below.

unfortunate result for a debtor, since the insolvency and bankruptcy rules of Code § 108 will not apply to such an amount realized.[24] However, in Rev. Rul. 91-31[25] the IRS held that where the amount of nonrecourse debt is reduced without there being a disposition of the property, the amount of the reduction will be treated as COD income. The IRS said it would not follow *Fulton Gold Corp. v. Commissioner*,[26] which suggests there might be a basis reduction instead. (*See also* § 205 above, for the possible effect that bankruptcy might have of converting nonrecourse into recourse debt.)

The existence of entities that are "disregarded entities" for federal tax purposes[27] adds another facet to the question of the recourse versus nonrecourse classification of debt for COD purposes. Where debt of a disregarded entity is fully recourse under state law to the disregarded entity, will it nonetheless be treated as nonrecourse debt of the owner of that entity for COD purposes? The law in this area is far from fully developed, but it would seem appropriate to apply the COD rules by looking to how the debt would be classified if the entity was a *regarded* entity (*i.e.*, consistent with state law).[28]

A further special comment should be made about debt where payment of some or all of the interest or principal payments is contingent. In the case where debt is governed by Code § 1274, the regulations provide that the issue price of the debt for OID purposes is the lesser of the noncontingent principal payments and the sum of the present values of the noncontingent payments.[29] For example, suppose a note of a troubled company with a $5 million face amount and fixed interest is exchanged for a note with contingent interest, a fixed $4 million principal amount, plus an earn-out formula that could provide an additional contingent face amount of up to $1 million. Neither the contingent interest nor the contingent principal can be taken into account in determining the new note's issue price. The result would be that the new note would have a very low adjusted issue price, which can produce quite harsh results,[30] such as greatly increasing the debtor's present COD income and its future OID deductions (which latter may be severely limited by the "high yield OID or PIK obligations" rule of Code § 163(e)(5)-*see* § 403.1.2 above).

---

[24] IRS Letter Ruling 9302001, August 31, 1992.

[25] 1991-1 C.B. 19; IRS Legal Memorandum, dated February 8, 1991, *reprinted at* 98 TNT 53-97. In this ruling, the debt was not held by the seller of the property to the taxpayer. For the relation of this factor to the purchase-price exception to COD income, *see* § 404.1.3. *Accord*, *Parker Properties Joint Venture v. Commissioner*, T.C. Memo. 1996-283.

[26] 31 B.T.A. 519, Dec. 8766 (1934).

[27] *See* Reg. § 301.7701-2(a), 3(a).

[28] For a detailed discussion of this issue, *see* Hoffer, Give Them My Regards: A Proposal for Applying the COD Rules to Disregarded Entities, 107 Tax Notes 327 (April 18, 2005).

[29] Reg. § 1.1274-2(g).

[30] These results are discussed at length, and criticized, in Asofsky, A Guide to the Tax Treatment of Contingent Payment Debt Instruments, 56th NYU Inst. on Fed. Tax'n § 5.08 (1998).

### § 403.1.4 Creditor Holding Period and Basis

To the extent the exchange is tax-free, the basis of the old security to the holder will become the basis of the new security, and the holding period of the old security will be added to the holding period of the new security.[31] If boot is received, the amount of the basis carried over to the new security will be reduced by the fair market value of the boot and increased by any gain recognized on the exchange.[32] The boot will obtain a basis equal to its fair market value and will have a new holding period.[33] If the boot takes the form of an "excess face amount" of new debt, the new debt will have a split holding period, with the boot portion having a new holding period and the other portion a tacked-on holding period.[34]

### § 403.1.5 Installment Method for Debt as Boot

To the extent the boot on the exchange consists of the excess principal amount of the new security, the creditor should be able to apply the installment method of accounting under Code § 453 to any gain that he recognizes on the exchange, assuming that the general requirements of Code § 453 are met.[35]

### § 403.1.6 Amount of New Security Representing Accrued Unpaid Interest on Old Security

Under Code § 354(a)(2)(B), the nonrecognition of gain provisions of Code § 354 do not apply to the creditor to the extent that stock, securities, or other property in a reorganization exchange are attributable to interest accrued on the old securities during the creditor's holding period.[36] The legislative history of the Bankruptcy Tax Act of 1980 indicates that this provision applies to accrued OID as well as to accrued stated interest.[37] It also indicates that it applies whether the creditor is a cash basis or

---

[31] Code § 358(a)(1).

[32] Id.

[33] Code § 358(a)(2).

[34] *Cf.* Rev. Rul. 62-140, 1962-2 C.B. 181 (stock acquired upon exercise of conversion privilege of debentures plus additional cash payment has a split holding period; amount realized upon subsequent sale of stock is first allocated to the stock basis attributable to the cash, in the proportion that the amount of cash paid bears to the fair market value of stock at conversion, with remainder allocated to stock basis attributable to debenture).

[35] *See* Code § 453(f)(6) (flush language). *See* discussions at §§ 403.2.1 and 403.2.6; *see also supra* note 17. Application of the installment method is automatic unless the creditor elects out. Code § 453(d). Code § 453 does not apply, however, if the debt is readily marketable in a public trading market, is issued for publicly traded property, or is issued in certain other circumstances. *See* Code § 453(b)(1), (f)(4), and (j)(2). Special rules apply to dealers. *See* Code §§ 453(b)(2)(A), 453A. For an excellent discussion of the application of Code § 453, *see* Schler, The Sale of Property for a Fixed Payment Note: Remaining Uncertainties, 41 Tax L. Rev. 209 (1986); Ginsburg, Future Payment Sales After the 1980 Revision Act, 39 Inst. on Fed. Tax'n § 43 (1981); Ginsburg, Rethinking the Tax Law in the New Installment Sales World, 59 Taxes 886 (1981).

[36] *See* explanation of these nonrecognition rules at Stand. Fed. Tax Rep. (CCH) ¶ 16,433.

[37] H.R. Rep. No. 833, 96th Cong., 2d Sess. 33 (1980); S. Rep. No. 1035, 96th Cong., 2d Sess. 38 (1980).

an accrual basis taxpayer. To the extent the interest is not paid in the exchange, the creditor that had accrued the interest (including OID) into income recognizes a loss.[38] As mentioned at § 304, the IRS takes a contrary position with respect to OID. The purpose of this provision is to treat this portion of the property as a payment of interest to the creditor. The provision leaves a couple of questions unanswered, however.

For example, suppose the adjusted principal amount of the old security was $100 and the accrued but unpaid interest at the date of the exchange was $20. Suppose further that a new security with a nominal face amount of $80 was issued in exchange for this old security. From the point of view of the creditor, how much of the $80 face amount of the new security should be deemed attributable to the $20 of accrued but unpaid interest? Is the answer $20, or $13.33 (20/120 of $80), or zero?

Before the issuance in early 1986 of the proposed time-value-of-money regulations (discussed above at § 402.9), one could say that, absent an expression of intent by the parties, the answer might be supplied by the general presumption that payments will be applied first to interest when made during the term of the debt and proportionately to interest and principal when made at retirement of the debt.[39] In such case, an allocation could be made to interest, even though the creditor has an overall loss on the exchange. Therefore, the parties should always express their intent. The House Report to the Bankruptcy Tax Act stated that if a plan of reorganization allocated the value received by a creditor between principal and interest, both the creditor and the debtor would be bound by the allocation.[40] The agreement may not, however, allocate more value to principal than the principal amount until an amount equal to the full amount of interest has been allocated to interest.[41] It is unclear whether, or the extent to which, the time-value-of-money regulations are intended to affect the ability of the parties in this situation to determine the allocation, although a literal application of the allocation rules of Reg. § 1.1275-2(a) would suggest that the amount received would have to be allocated first to unpaid interest.

Suppose the new security issued in exchange for the old security is publicly traded and has a value less than its face amount. Before its repeal in 1990, would the Code § 1275(a)(4) reorganization limitation on the creation of new OID apply to the portion of the new security that is deemed attributable to the unpaid interest on the old security? Code § 1275(a)(4) did not expressly provide for an increase in the adjusted principal amount of the old security for accrued but unpaid stated interest,

---

[38] Id. Such loss properly should be an ordinary loss. *Cf. Arrowsmith v. Commissioner*, 344 U.S. 6, 52-2 U.S.T.C. ¶ 9527 (1952). This is further supported by the example in footnote 9 of the House Report to the Bankruptcy Tax Act of 1980, which states that the security holder "may *deduct* $10 [unpaid interest] if that amount previously had been accrued by the [holder] as interest income," suggesting that the loss would be an ordinary loss rather than a capital loss. H.R. Rep. No. 833, 96th Cong., 2d Sess. 33, n.9 (1980) (emphasis added); S. Rep. No. 96-1035, 96th Cong., 2d Sess. 38 (1980). That this is a correct reading of the law was confirmed in IRS T.A.M. 9538007, June 13, 1995.

[39] *Supra* note 38 and § 401.1, notes 6 and 7.

[40] Id.

[41] Id. If the debtor had accrued the interest as a deduction, payment of less than the full amount of the interest would produce COD income to the debtor, unless the prior deduction had not produced a tax benefit. *See* discussion at § 404.

as it does for the portion of OID that has been includible in the income of the holder. It would seem appropriate to apportion the face amount of the new debt between the principal and interest elements of the old debt before, rather than after, applying the OID rules. Code § 1275(a)(4) would then be applied looking solely to the principal portion of the new security.[42] The following three examples, assuming the same facts except as noted, illustrate the allocation possibilities.

### EXAMPLE 1

An old security has an adjusted principal amount of $1,000 and accrued unpaid stated interest of $200. The old security plus interest is exchanged for a new security with a nominal face amount of $1,200 and a trading market value of $1,000. If the allocation of the new security between principal and interest on the old security were made after the application of Code § 1275(a)(4) and the determination of OID, rather than before, the new security would have an adjusted principal amount of $1,000 and OID of $200. The adjusted principal amount would then be allocated between the principal and interest portions of the old security. There would presumably be $200 of OID no matter how that allocation is made. However, if instead, as suggested above, the face amount of the new debt is allocated to the principal and interest portions of the old debt before OID is determined, the results are illustrated in Examples 2 and 3 below.

### EXAMPLE 2

Assume there is an express agreement allocating the entire new security as repayment of the principal of the old security and allowing nothing to interest. Although the nominal face amount of the new security ($1,200) exceeds the adjusted principal amount of the old security ($1,000), the House Report to the Bankruptcy Tax Act of 1980 indicates that the allocation should be respected since the value of the new security ($1,000) does not exceed the adjusted principal amount of the old security.[43] No interest would, therefore, have been paid, and an accrual basis creditor would be entitled to a bad debt deduction for any interest accrued. An accrual basis debtor will have COD income (or attribute reduction) for the

---

[42] *See* Henderson, Developing a Tax Strategy for the Failing Company, 63 Taxes 952, 956 (1985); *cf.* Tatlock, 466 T.M., Bankruptcy and Insolvency: Tax Aspects and Procedure, A-56 (1985) ("Although the literal language of the statute does not appear to permit [accrued but unpaid interest to be added to the adjusted principal amount] (because it does not represent original issue discount), as a theoretical matter it would seem that it should be included").

[43] *See* H.R. Rep. No. 833, 96th Cong., 2d Sess. 33 (1980) (allocation to principal amount of old debt respected as long as no excess value allocated to principal amount of old debt until interest paid in full); *but see* the time-value-of-money regulations, discussed at § 402.9.

accrued interest.[44] The adjusted principal amount of the new security would be $1,000 under Code § 1273(b)(3). The special reorganization rule of Code § 1275(a)(4) would not apply, since the adjusted principal amount of the new security absent Code § 1275(a)(4) was not less than that of the old security (also $1,000). OID on the new security would, therefore, be $200 (its nominal face amount less its adjusted principal amount).

### EXAMPLE 3

Assume there is no express allocation of the new security between principal and interest of the old security. In such case, a ratable allocation may be required.[45] Hence, $1,000 of nominal face amount of the new security, with a market value of $833.33, would be allocated to principal of the old security, and $200 of nominal face amount, with a market value of $166.67, to interest. Because the adjusted principal amount of the portion of the new security allocated to the principal amount of the old security absent Code § 1275(a)(4) would under Code § 1273(b)(3) be in effect its market value of $833.33, which is less than the $1,000 adjusted principal amount of the old security, Code § 1275(a)(4) would apply and the adjusted principal amount of such portion of the new security would be $1,000 and no OID would be created. The adjusted principal amount of the portion of the new security allocated to interest on the old security would under Code § 1273(b)(3) be $166.67, resulting in $33.33 of OID ($200 of face amount of the new security allocable to interest on the old security less $166.67). A cash basis creditor would have immediate interest income of $166.67. Such interest would probably, however, already have been included in income by an accrual basis creditor. If the entire $200 of interest had already been included, the accrual basis creditor would be entitled to an immediate bad debt deduction of $33.33. An accrual basis debtor would, to the extent it deducted interest in excess of $166.67, probably have COD income (or attribute reduction).[46] Going forward, the adjusted principal amount of the new security would be the sum of the respective amounts allocated to principal and interest on the old security, *i.e.*, $1,166.67 ($1,000+$166.67). The OID would be $33.33. In the creditor's hands, the new security, however, would have a split holding period; the $1,000 face-amount portion attributable to the principal amount of the old security would include the old security's holding period since the exchange would be a tax-free recapitalization; and the

---

[44] *See, e.g.*, Rev. Rul. 67-200, 1967 1 C.B. 15, clarified by Rev. Rul. 70-406, 1970-2 C.B. 16 (COD rules apply prior to tax benefit recapture, but after Code § 111 exclusion).

[45] *See* text accompanying note 39 *supra*.

[46] *See* § 404.1.2.

$200 face-amount portion attributable to interest would presumably have a new holding period.[47]

Even though the portion of the new debt allocable to interest on the old debt will produce interest income to a cash basis creditor, it may not produce a deduction for a cash basis debtor. There is no indication in the legislative history of this provision that the cash basis debtor would be able to escape from the general rule that a cash basis debtor cannot get a deduction by paying interest with its own note.[48] Where the debtor was an accrual basis taxpayer, the deduction will already have been accrued. If less than the full accrued amount of interest is paid in the exchange, an accrual basis debtor will have COD income, unless one of the exceptions to COD income applies.[49]

### § 403.1.7 Imputed Interest Rules

The imputed interest rules of Code § 483 apply to debt issued for property if the OID rules of Code §§ 1273 and 1274 do not apply.[50] For present purposes, the main difference between the imputed interest and OID rules is that imputed interest under Code § 483 is not taxed (or deducted) until payments are due (for accrual basis taxpayers) or paid (for cash basis taxpayers), whereas OID is taxed (and deducted) each year even before payment is due or made.[51]

Code § 1274(c)(3)(C) provides that it does not apply (and thus Code § 483 does apply) to sales or exchanges of property if the total payments do not exceed $250,000;[52] for this purpose it says that "all sales and exchanges which are part of the same transaction (or a series of related transactions) shall be treated as 1 sale or exchange."

Suppose creditor *A* only holds one $1,000 nominal face amount of old security, which he exchanges for a new $1,200 nominal face amount security, but this is part of a debt restructuring workout in which the debtor is issuing $100 million of new debt. Creditor *B* has $500,000 of old securities and receives $600,000 nominal face amount of new securities. Does the aggregation rule apply to each creditor separately, so that Code § 483 applies to creditor *A* and Code § 1274 applies to creditor *B*? If so, the

---

47 *Supra* note 34.

48 *See, e.g.*, Rev. Rul. 70-647, 1970-2 C.B. 38.

49 *See* discussion at § 404.1.

50 Code § 483(d)(1). Where debt originally governed by Code § 483 as it existed prior to the Tax Reform Act of 1984 ("old" Code § 483) is modified, it may be unclear whether the provisions of old Code § 483, rather than the current imputed interest or OID rules, are to apply. For a discussion of this potential conflict, *see* Banoff, Tax Aspects of Real Estate Refinancing and Debt Restructuring: The Best and Worst of Times, 64 Taxes 926, 947-953 (1986) (more generally, the article discusses debt restructurings in the context of a real estate partnership).

51 *See* Code § 1272 (OID); Reg. § 1.483-2(a)(1)(i) and (ii).

52 Reg. § 1.1274-1(b)(2)(ii)(B) provides that the determination of the total payments is made at the earlier of (1) the date of the sale or exchange or (2) the contract date. If all or part of the payments are contingent, the maximum of the aggregate amount of payments is used; if such amount is unknown, the $250,000 exception is unavailable.

timing of the debtor's deductions on the security issued to A will differ from that on the identical security issued to *B*. The former will have imputed interest deductible and includible only as payments are due or made and the latter will have OID, deductible and includible over the life of the new security.

Perhaps the drafter of the Code § 1274(c)(3)(C) exception was thinking of the aggregation of transfers by only a single seller/creditor. But he undoubtedly did not think of the present example. The statutory language is ambiguous enough to allow aggregation at either the creditor or the debtor level. It is to be hoped that in cases like this the aggregation concept will be applied at the debtor level, so that both creditor *A* and *B* will be covered by Code § 1274 and neither by Code § 483.[53] Otherwise, large debtors will face compliance problems. The regulations appear to take this approach.[54]

If Code § 483 applies, it should be noted that this provision contained no reorganization exception like the pre-1990 Code § 1275(a)(4). Under Code § 483 as it existed before the Tax Reform Act of 1984, the IRS seemed disposed to interpret Code § 483 as not applying at all to debt exchanges.[55] Such a blanket exception would have a broader potential reach than the more limited Code § 1275(a)(4), with the result that the amount (and not just the timing) of interest imputed under Code § 483 could differ from the amount of Code § 1274 OID.[56] However, the regulations now take the position that Code § 483 does apply to debt exchanges.[57]

### § 403.1.8 Market Discount

The 1984 Act added to Code § 1276 the new concept of market discount for debt issued after July 18, 1984. Market discount is the amount by which the creditor's basis in the debt when he acquires it is less than the adjusted principal amount at that time. Generally, market discount is only created on a purchase in a secondary market. Gain recognized by a creditor will be interest income to the extent of his market discount. However, where a creditor exchanges market discount debt in a tax-free recapitalization exchange, the market discount in the old debt simply transfers over into the new debt.[58] The market discount concept has no impact on the debtor. The debtor receives no deduction for the market discount taxed as interest income to the creditor.

---

[53] The IRS appears to have taken this approach in Reg. § 1.1274A-1(b)(3), Example (2). It does so simply by cross referencing to the aggregation rule in Code § 1274A(d)(1), which is written rather differently.

[54] Reg. § 1.1274-1(b)(2)(ii)(B) and (C); Reg. § 1.1274A-1(b)(2) and (3).

[55] *See* IRS Letter Ruling 7846009, August 15, 1978.

[56] The size of the transaction may affect not only the question of whether Code § 483 instead of Code § 1274 will apply to the transaction, it may also affect the interest rate applied under both sections. Code § 1274A provides that the imputed or OID interest rate under these sections will be nine percent if the face amount of the new debt (without regard to other consideration paid) does not exceed $2.8 million (adjusted for inflation). Code § 1274A contains an aggregation rule that is somewhat different from the Code § 1274(c)(3)(C) aggregation rule, although as mentioned in note 53, *supra*, the IRS appears to give them identical meaning.

[57] Reg. § 1.483-1(a)(1).

[58] Code § 1276(c).

Where new debt is issued after July 18, 1984, for old debt issued before July 18, 1984, the new debt will be considered to have been issued after July 18, 1984, even if the exchange is a recapitalization exchange (unless the new debt has the same maturity and interest rate as the old debt).[59]

The 1993 Act eliminated entirely the grandfathered status of bonds issued on or before July 18, 1984, effective for such bonds purchased after April 30, 1993.

## §403.2 *Nonrecapitalization Exchanges*

Where either the old or the new debt is not a security, the tax-free recapitalization exchange provisions will not apply. The consequences of an exchange of old for new debt in these circumstances will be as follows.

### §403.2.1 Creditor Recognition of Gain or Loss

A creditor will recognize gain or loss on the exchange equal to the difference between its "amount realized" and its adjusted basis in the old debt.[60] To determine the amount realized by the creditors on the exchange, the IRS position is that the OID provisions of Code §§1273 and 1274 generally must be applied to the new debt (and perhaps also Code §1275(a)(4), before its repeal in 1990, *see* §403.2.2 below) in order to determine its adjusted principal amount. Unless the creditor elects out of Code §453 installment treatment, or the transaction does not qualify for installment treatment (because, for example, either the old or the new debt is publicly traded), the installment method of reporting income from the transaction would apply to the taxation of any gain realized by the creditor on the exchange.[61] The installment method does not apply to (1) obligations issued for services or publicly traded property or (2) demand obligations or obligations issued by corporations that are readily tradeable in an established securities market.[62] Nor is it available in certain circumstances for dealer property.[63]

---

[59] Code §1278(a)(1)(C)(iii), as added by the technical corrections portion of the Tax Reform Act of 1986. *See* H.R. Rep. No. 426, 99th Cong., 1st Sess. 885 (1985).

[60] If the old debt is a security but the new debt is not—such that the exchange does not constitute a tax-free recapitalization—the wash sale provisions of Code §1091 are unlikely to apply to disallow any loss. Code §1091 applies only where a loss is sustained on the disposition of "stock or securities" *and* within 30 days the creditor acquires (or has entered into an option or contract to acquire) "substantially identical stock or securities." Thus, it would seem that to fall within the wash sale rule the new debt would have to be a "security," yet in the case of a debt-for-debt exchange such a transaction would presumably qualify as a recapitalization and thus the loss would be disallowed for that reason. On the other hand, if the new debt were sufficiently different from the old debt as not to constitute a "security" for recapitalization purposes, it is possible that such debt would not be considered "substantially identical" to the old debt. *See* Rev. Rul. 76-346, 1976-2 C.B. 247 (substantial differences between the new and the old security, even if the issuer is the same, avoid wash sale treatment).

[61] *See* discussion at §403.2.6; *see also supra* note 17.

[62] Code §453(f)(3), (4), and (j)(2).

[63] *See* Code §§453(b)(2)(A), 453A.

Where the installment method does not apply, the IRS position is that the amount realized by an accrual method creditor will be the adjusted principal amount of the new debt.[64] However, where real doubt exists at the time of the exchange as to the ultimate collectibility of the new debt, an accrual basis creditor may, rather than computing gain or loss (or basis) using the principal amount of the new debt, compute gain or loss (or basis) by reducing the new debt's principal amount for the portion likely to be uncollectible.[65] Collectibility is only sufficiently in doubt for this purpose where the debtor is insolvent in the bankruptcy sense, *i.e.*, its liabilities exceed the fair market value of its assets.[66] Mere financial difficulty is insufficient.[67] This rule is sometimes referred to as the "doubtful collectibility doctrine."

As a practical matter, uncollectibility at the time of the exchange may be difficult to establish if the exchange was voluntary.[68] If the debtor becomes insolvent after the exchange, but prior to the end of the taxable year in which the exchange took place, the IRS position would be that an accrual basis creditor should probably compute

---

[64] Reg. § 15A.453-1(d); Reg. § 1.1001-1(g). Rev. Rul. 89-122, 1989-2 C.B. 200; Rev. Rul. 79-292, 1979-2 C.B. 287; *First Savings and Loan Assn. v. Commissioner*, 40 T.C. 474, Dec. 26,158 (1963); *see also* Schler, *supra* note 35, at 212-216 (discusses the weaknesses inherent in using the principal amount); GCM 37218, August 4, 1977; IRS T.A.M. 8052023, September 25, 1980.

A persuasive argument can be made that the rule in the regulations is wrong, that even for an accrual basis taxpayer, the amount realized from any noninventory sales of property (including exchanges of debt) is limited to the fair market value of the new debt received. *See* Adrion, Reducing the Uncertainty Regarding the Amount Realized in Debt-for-Debt Exchanges, Tax Notes, May 30, 1994 at 1169. Adrion analyzes the authorities under Code § 1001 that support this conclusion. In considering this point, it should also be noted that Code § 1001 applies only to the holder of the debt and does not necessarily govern the tax consequences to the issuer. This point is analyzed in American Bar Association Section of Taxation Task Force, Report on Prop. Regs. § 1.1001-3: Modifications of Debt Instruments [Parts I-V], 47 Tax Law. 987 (1994). Thus, use of the fair market value rule for Code § 1001 purposes could lead to different results for the holder of the debt than for the issuer. One situation where this can occur is where old fixed-payment debt is exchanged for new debt having some payments of interest or principal that are contingent rather than fixed. The holder's amount realized from the exchange includes the fair market value of the contingent payments. Reg. § 1.1001-1(g)(2)(ii). But where the debt is subject to Code § 1274, the issuer cannot take these contingent amounts into account in determining the new debt's adjusted issue price for COD and OID purposes. *See* § 403.1.3 above; Asofsky, A Guide to the Tax Treatment of Contingent Payment Debt Instruments, 56 NYU Inst. on Fed. Tax'n, Chapter 5 (1998).

[65] *See Spring City Foundry Co. v. Commissioner*, 292 U.S. 182, 4 U.S.T.C. ¶ 1276 (1934) ("It is the right to receive and not the actual receipt that determines inclusion"); *cf. Clifton Mfg. Co.*, 137 F.2d 290, 43-2 U.S.T.C. ¶ 9539 (4th Cir. 1943) (income not includible until "collectibility is assured"; "not accruable as long as reasonable doubt exists as to amount collectible by reason of the financial condition or insolvency of the debtor"); *Electric Controls and Service Co. v. Commissioner*, T.C. Memo. 1996-486 (income not accruable when, in the same year that the right to income arises, collection and receipt of the income becomes sufficiently doubtful, or it becomes reasonably certain that the income will not be collected; nor is it accruable if the right to receive it is contingent upon the happening of a future event such as the realization of future profits); GCM 38426, June 26, 1980.

[66] *Moore v. Commissioner*, 45 T.C.M. 557, Dec. 39,845(M), T.C. Memo. 1983-39 (insufficient); *Harmont Plaza, Inc. v. Commissioner*, 64 T.C. 632, Dec. 33,348 (1975), *aff'd*, 549 F.2d 414, 77-1 U.S.T.C. ¶ 9276 (6th Cir. 1977), *cert. denied*, 434 U.S. 955 (delay in payment due to negative cash flow insufficient). *See Greer-Robbins Co. v. Commissioner*, 119 F.2d 92, 41-1 U.S.T.C. ¶ 9406 (9th Cir. 1941) (generally taxpayer's burden to establish bad debt character of accrual).

[67] *Koehring Co. v. United States*, 421 F.2d 715, 70-1 U.S.T.C. ¶ 9242 (Ct. Cl. 1970).

[68] *Cf. Moore*, *supra* note 66 (court reasoned that if taxpayer had any real doubt as to collectibility he would not have extended credit to the debtor).

gain or loss using the principal amount of the new debt adjusted for OID or imputed interest.[69] In such event, however, the creditor may be entitled to a bad debt deduction.[70] However, case law suggests that in such an event, the creditor need not accrue the income at all.[71]

As to a cash basis creditor not using the installment method, there is a direct conflict in authority. The final regulations dealing with sales not reported on the installment method flatly hold that the amount realized would be the fair market value of the new debt.[72] On the other hand, the Code § 1001 regulations equally flatly hold that the amount realized is the adjusted principal amount of the new debt determined under Code § 1273 or § 1274.[73] Reg. § 1.1001-1(g)(3) provides generally that this conflict is to be resolved by applying the Code § 1001 regulations.

Where the old debt had been written down by the holder through a partial bad debt deduction, the exchange could produce a gain that in effect reverses that deduction. This could create a problem for the holder, since a partial worthlessness deduction can be taken only when the reduction is charged off on the holder's books, and that would have occurred in the earlier year but not in the year of the exchange. However, as mentioned at § 402.13 above, this problem has been solved by a regulation provision that deems such a write-off to have occurred.

### § 403.2.2 Creation of New OID on New Debt

The taxable exchange of the old debt for the new debt will come within the scope of Code § 1274 (or, if either the old or the new debt is publicly traded, it will come within the scope of Code § 1273). The analysis here is the same as was discussed above in the case of exchanges qualifying as tax-free recapitalizations, except that a question exists (discussed immediately below) whether Code § 1275(a)(4)—before its repeal in 1990—applied to a taxable exchange.

**Questions under repealed Code § 1275(a)(4).** Code § 1275(a)(4) applied to any debt instrument issued for another debt instrument pursuant to a plan of reorganization "within the meaning of section 368(a)(1)." Code § 368(a)(1)(E) simply says that a reorganization includes a "recapitalization." An argument can be made that an exchange of new for old debt is a recapitalization within the meaning of Code § 368(a)(1)(E) even if, because either the old or the new debt is not a "security," the

---

69 *See, e.g.*, Rev. Rul. 80-361, 1980-2 C.B. 164; Rev. Rul. 81-18, 1981-1 C.B. 295; *Spring City Foundry Co. v. Commissioner*, *supra* note 65.

70 Code § 166.

71 *Electric Controls and Service Co. v. Commissioner*, T.C. Memo. 1996-486, *supra* note 65; *Cuba Railroad Co. v. Commissioner*, 9 T.C. 211, Dec. 15,970 (1947) (no accrual required where "real doubt and uncertainty at the end of the taxable year as to whether the amount due and unpaid would ever be paid"; facts substantiated specific refusal and inability of debtor to pay); *Corn Exchange Bank v. United States*, 37 F.2d 34, 2 U.S.T.C. ¶ 455 (2d Cir. 1930) (interest not accruable where debtor was in actual receivership at the close of the taxable year).

72 *See* Reg. § 15A.453-1(d).

73 Reg. § 1.1001-1(g). As noted in note 64, *supra*, Adrion criticizes this result.

exchange is fully taxable under Code § 354. If this interpretation were to prevail,[74] Code § 1275(a)(4) would apply to a taxable debt-for-debt exchange just as it did to a tax-free one, and in general no new OID would be created. Moreover, application of this interpretation would affect the determination of the "amount realized" by an accrual basis taxpayer. It might even affect the determination of the "amount realized" by a cash basis taxpayer: As mentioned above at § 403.2.1, the Code § 1001 regulations (in flat opposition to the final Code § 453 regulations) hold that the amount realized by a cash basis taxpayer is the adjusted principal amount of the new debt as determined under the OID or imputed interest rules.

If this interpretation did not prevail, then, at least where the entire debt exchange is taxable under Code § 354, Code § 1275(a)(4) would not apply. This would affect the determination of the adjusted principal amount of the new debt and also the amount realized by the exchanging creditors.

A possible middle situation existed where some of the old creditors have a tax-free exchange under Code § 354 and some do not. Before its repeal in 1990, Code § 1275(a)(4) clearly applied to limit the creation of OID on the new debt issued to those having a tax-free exchange. What of the same debt issued to those whose old debt was not a security and who therefore have a taxable exchange? An argument can be made that the language of Code § 1275(a)(4) applied: It applied to "any debt instrument . . . issued pursuant to a plan of reorganization . . . for another debt instrument. . . ." The argument would be that all the new securities were issued "pursuant to" a single plan of reorganization, even if some of the creditors had taxable rather than tax-free reorganization exchanges.

One's decision whether Code § 1275(a)(4) did or did not apply to taxable debt-for-debt exchanges (in either of the circumstances mentioned above) might well have been influenced by whether, for a cash basis taxpayer, the amount realized on the exchange was measured by the fair market value of the new debt (as provided in the Code § 453 regulations) or by the adjusted principal amount of the new debt (as provided in the Code § 1001 regulations). If the amount realized is the fair market value, application of Code § 1275(a)(4) would produce anomalous results for a cash basis taxpayer.[75] This would not be so if the amount realized is the adjusted principal amount of the new debt.

For the effect of the 1990 repeal of Code § 1275(a)(4), *see* § 403.1.2 above.

---

[74] This interpretation was proposed by the Tax Section of the New York State Bar Association, Report of Ad Hoc Committee on Proposed Original Issue Discount Regulations, 34 Tax Notes 363, 376 (January 26, 1987), and by Benjamin Cohen and Richard Reinhold in their memorandum reprinted in 47 Tax Notes 1247, 1248 (June 4, 1990).

[75] In such event, if a cash basis creditor holding a $100 note that is not a security exchanged it for a new security having a $100 face amount but a value of $80, the creditor would be entitled to claim an immediate $20 loss. However, if no OID were created on the exchange, this would come back as capital gain at the time the security was paid off (assuming the market discount rules did not apply in this circumstance).

### § 403.2.3 Imputed Interest Possibilities

For a creditor whose total payments from the exchange will not exceed $250,000, Code § 483 rather than Code § 1274 may apply. The analysis here, and the question of whether the aggregation rule applicable in determining the $250,000 amount should be applied at the debtor rather than the creditor level, is the same as in the case of recapitalization exchanges, which have already been discussed above at § 403.1.

### § 403.2.4 Debtor COD Income

To the extent the adjusted principal amount of the new debt, after adjustment for OID, imputed interest, or bond premium, is less than the adjusted principal amount of the old debt, the debtor will have COD income.[76] For the treatment of nonrecourse debt (including the question whether recourse debt of a "disregarded entity" should be treated as nonrecourse debt of its owner) and debt having contingent payments, *see* § 403.1.3 above. The consequences of COD income are discussed beginning at § 404.

### § 403.2.5 Creditor Holding Period and Basis

Except where the Code § 453 installment method applies, the creditor's basis in the new debt will be its amount realized (as determined above at § 403.2.1), and the creditor will have a new holding period in the new debt.[77]

### § 403.2.6 Availability of Installment Method

The creditor in a taxable exchange should be able to apply the installment method of accounting under Code § 453 to any gain recognized by him on the exchange, assuming the general requirements of Code § 453 are met.[78] As mentioned earlier, Code § 453 does not apply to demand notes or notes issued by a corporation that are readily tradeable in a public market, or to notes issued for publicly traded property, as well as in certain other circumstances.[79]

Moreover, Code § 453 only applies to payments made for property and thus does not apply to payments for services.[80] Many of the holders of nonsecurity claims against a failing company may have been providers of services rather than property. The installment method should not be available to them with respect to debt received in exchange for these claims. This conclusion assumes, of course, that the claims for

---

[76] *See* Code §§ 61(a)(12), 108(a), (e)(3), and (e)(10); Rev. Rul. 77-437, 1977-2 C.B. 28.

[77] *See* Code § 1012 (cost basis); *cf.* Code § 1223 (tacking of holding periods).

[78] *Supra* note 35.

[79] Code § 453(b), (f)(4), and (j)(2).

[80] Code § 453(b) (only applies to dispositions of "property").

services have not somehow been transmuted into debt having the status of property.[81]

### §403.2.7 Payment for Services: Possible Applicability of Code §467

As just mentioned, many of the holders of nonsecurity claims against a debtor will be providers of services rather than property.[82] Where the new debt issued to such creditors is publicly traded, the OID rules of Code §1273 will apply and the new debt may carry OID.[83] However, where the new debt is not publicly traded, the OID provisions will not apply. Code §1274, like Code §453, only applies to debt issued for property, not to debt issued for services.[84] For the same reason, the Code §483 imputed interest provisions would not apply.[85]

On the other hand, Code §467, which was added by the Tax Reform Act of 1984, gives the IRS authority to issue regulations whereby interest consequences similar to OID, though computed at a different rate,[86] would be imposed on deferred payments for services under certain circumstances.

When regulations are issued under this provision, one hopes they will deal with the potential conflict between section 502(b)(2) of the Bankruptcy Code, which disallows postpetition interest in certain circumstances during the period of bankruptcy,[87] and Code §467.

### §403.2.8 Market Discount

The market discount portion, if any, of the creditor's gain in a taxable exchange of old debt for new debt will be taxed as interest income. (This provision does not apply to old debt issued on or before July 18, 1984, unless such old bonds were purchased by the creditor after April 30, 1993.)[88]

---

[81] Even if they have, the "property" probably will not have attained the status of a capital asset. *See* Code §1221(a)(4). For a similar result where stock is issued to a cash basis taxpayer for debt not yet reflected in income, *see* Code §108(e)(7)(B), discussed at §502.4.

[82] *See* explanation of these deferred payment rules at Stand. Fed. Tax Rep. (CCH) ¶21,911.

[83] *See* Code §§1273(b) and 1274(c)(4)(D).

[84] Code §1274(c)(1); *see* discussion at §403.2.6.

[85] Code §483(a)(1).

[86] The Code §467 rate is 110 percent, whereas the Code §§1274 and 483 rates are only 100 percent, of the "applicable Federal rate" (and where Code §1274A applies, the Code §§1274 and 483 rates are 9 percent). Of course, one conceivably could take the position that the new debt is not being issued for services but instead is being issued for property, namely the existing claim for payment.

[87] *See* §103.

[88] *See* Code §1276. *See also* the discussion of market discount at §403.1.8 above.

### §403.2.9 Treatment of Amount of New Security Representing Accrued Unpaid Interest on Old Security

The determination of the portion, if any, of the new debt that is deemed attributable to accrued but unpaid interest on the old debt and the tax treatment of that portion should be the same as was analyzed above in connection with recapitalization exchanges.[89]

## *§403.3 OID Complications with Different Classes of Creditors*

The foregoing portions of this chapter indicated that the tax treatment of an exchange depends on whether (1) the creditor had applied the installment method of reporting for his old debt (in which case the exchange may not result in any disposition by him of his old debt); (2) the exchange is a tax-free recapitalization as to the creditor and, if so, whether any portion of it nonetheless represents a receipt of boot or payment for accrued interest; (3) the exchange is a fully taxable exchange to the creditor; (4) if neither the new nor the old debt is publicly traded, the "$250,000 or less" exception to Code §1274 applies to the particular creditor (with the result that Code §483 applies);[90] (5) the new debt is being issued for services rather than property; and (6) the installment sale provisions apply to any gain recognized on the exchange. One of the important issues that flows from these distinctions, as we have seen, is whether new OID (or imputed interest) will be created on the exchange and, if so, how it will be computed.

Creditors in all of these categories may be included in a general grouping of unsecured creditors to which the parties desire to issue a single class of new securities. If the issuer must compute OID or imputed interest differently for one or more of these categories, considerable complexities could result. Not only may the timing and amount of the debtor's deductions and the creditor's income be affected, but the debtor must comply with the requirements for stamping the debt instrument and providing the IRS at issuance of the new debt with information about its OID[91] and with the annual OID information return requirements.[92]

The issuer should therefore seek ways to minimize these problems as it designs its debt restructuring plan. If the debt is not publicly traded, the simplest way is to provide sufficient stated and currently payable interest to satisfy the test rates under all of Code §§467, 483, and 1274. In other cases the situation may become complex,

---

[89] *See* discussion at §§402, 402.15, and 403.1.6 (discussing allocation to accrued interest). Although Code §354(a)(2)(B) only applies by its terms to reorganization exchanges, the obvious intent of the provision was to establish a general rule applicable to both tax-free and taxable exchanges.

[90] In addition, as discussed *supra* at note 56, the size of the transaction may also affect the interest rate applied under Code §§1274 and 483.

[91] *See* Code §§1275(c) and 6706 (penalties); Reg. §1.1275-3 (Form 8281 must be filed within 30 days of issuance).

[92] *See* Code §6049; Reg. §§1.6049-1 and 1.6049-4 (post-1982); *see* Form 1099-OID, U.S. Information Return for Original Issue Discount.

and the issuer will have to make a series of practical judgment calls on such matters as applicability of Code § 1274 rather than Code § 483.

## *§403.4 Information Reporting by Creditors Creating COD Income*

The 1993 Act added Code § 6050P, which was amended in 1996 and again in 1999. This requires creditors that are certain government agencies and "applicable financial entities" to file information returns with the IRS and with debtors to report discharge of such indebtedness of $600 or more. "Applicable financial entities" include

(1) the FDIC, RTC,[93] and National Credit Union Administration;
(2) any financial institution described in Code § 581 (certain banks, trust companies, and building and loan associations) or Code § 591(a) (mutual savings banks and certain other savings institutions);
(3) credit union;
(4) any subsidiary of an entity described in (2) or (3) that is subject to federal or state supervision by virtue of such affiliation; and
(5) in a provision added in 1999 (but, under regulations, made effective only for COD occurring after 2004), any organization in a significant trade or business of which is the lending of money (such as finance companies and credit card companies, whether or not affiliated with financial institutions).

The reporting obligation applies to any COD income, including cancellations resulting from modifications of debt instruments that produce COD income. The information return is required whether or not the debtor is subject to tax on the debt discharge. Thus, the information return is to be filed even if, under Code § 108 or some other rule of law (as discussed below in § 404), the COD income is not taxable to the debtor. The information is to be filed by the creditor with the Internal Revenue Service on Form 1099-C, with copy to the debtor.

The reporting requirement is effective for discharges after 1993, other than with respect to (i) an organization described in (5) above, which was added by the Tax Relief Extension Act of 1999 but whose application was suspended by the IRS pending issuance of interpretative guidance and did not become effective until 2005,[94] and (ii) governmental entities, which have an earlier effective date of August 6, 1993.

---

[93] Before adoption of this 1993 provision, a 1984 Office of Management and Budget memorandum and Treasury guideline had required similar reporting by Federal agencies on a Form 1099-G except where prohibited by law. The FDIC and RTC believed that such information reporting by them would violate the Right to Financial Privacy Act of 1978. Since the latter permits such reporting if the Internal Revenue Code requires it, the 1993 provision eliminates this problem.

[94] Although the statute made this provision effective for discharges after 1999, the IRS first postponed that date so as to make it effective only for discharges after 2000 (IRS Notice 2000-22, 2000-16 I.R.B. 902), and subsequently extended that postponement to include discharges occurring prior to the first calendar year beginning at least two months after the date that regulatory or other appropriate guidance is given regarding the interpretation of the 1999 provision. IRS Notice 2001-8, 2001-4 I.R.B. 1. This delay was incorporated as the effective date of Prop. Reg. § 1.6050P-2, which could apply only to discharges occurring in any calendar year beginning at least two months after the

Interpretative guidance regarding the scope of item (5) above was issued as proposed regulation § 1.6050P-2 in June 2002, to be effective for discharges of debt occurring in any calendar year beginning at least two months after the date the regulation is made final. This regulation was issued in final form in October 2004, and is effective for COD occurring after 2004. It is described at the end of this § 403.4.

The IRS issued temporary and proposed regulations under the original provisions of Code § 6050P in late 1993, effective for discharges of debt occurring after December 31, 1993.[95] Final regulations (Reg. § 1.6050P-1) were issued in January 1996, to apply to discharges of debt occurring after December 21, 1996.

The 1993 temporary regulations were strongly criticized as being impracticable in many cases. In response to these criticisms, the IRS issued Notice 94-73,[96] which said that before the later of January 1, 1995, or the effective date of final regulations, no penalties would be imposed for failure to report a discharge of indebtedness:

(1) under title 11 of the United States Code;

(2) resulting from the expiration of the statute of limitations for collection;

(3) for an amount other than principal in the case of debt arising from a lending transaction; or

(4) for a person other than the primary (or first-named) debtor in the case of indebtedness incurred before January 1, 1995, that involves multiple debtors.

The preamble to the 1996 final regulations extended the foregoing no-penalty date through December 21, 1996 (and, in some cases, through December 31, 1996).

The 1996 final regulations provide that reporting is required only if the debt discharge occurs as the result of eight identifiable events specified in the regulations.[97] Special rules are included for determining when, and if, reporting is required where the statute of limitations on collectibility of the debt has expired. The final regulations do not require the reporting of discharged interest, although in non-lending cases discharged penalties and fees must be reported. Where multiple debtors are jointly and severally liable for a debt, the return filed for each debtor must reflect the entire amount of the debt discharged. Guarantors, however, are not treated as debtors for purposes of the reporting requirements, even if there has been a default and payment has been demanded from them.

---

(Footnote Continued)

regulation becomes final. This regulation became final in October 2004, and applies to COD occurring after 2004.

[95] Prop. and Temp. Reg. § 1.6050P-1T.

[96] Notice 94-73, IRB 1994-29, July 18, 1994.

[97] The IRS has ruled that COD need not be reported under Code § 6050P if it is reportable under Code § 6041 as compensation for services, and thus is reportable on Form W-2. *See* IRS Legal Memorandum 200130038, May 31, 2001, *reprinted at* 2001 TNT 146-72. It also ruled that no reporting under Code § 6050P was required for an agreement by a credit card company to forgive credit card debt in exchange for the cardholder paying a fee to the bank if certain conditions are met. IRS Letter Ruling 200131027, May 9, 2001.

Neither the proposed and temporary nor the 1996 final regulations (Reg. § 1.6050P-1) address the discharge of disputed debts. The preamble to the final regulations contains the following statement about disputed liabilities:

> The temporary and proposed regulations do not address the reporting requirements under section 6050P in the case of the settlement of a disputed liability. The preamble to the temporary regulations solicited public comment relating to this issue. Several commentators urged that the final regulations include an exception from reporting for settlements of bona fide disputed liabilities.
>
> The determination regarding whether the settlement of a disputed liability results in discharge of indebtedness income under section 61(a)(12) is inherently factual. Thus, it continues to be the position of the IRS and Treasury that this issue should be addressed on a case-by-case basis, rather than by these final regulations. Therefore, the final regulations do not provide an exception from reporting for disputed liabilities. Instead, resolution of the question of whether there may have been a discharge of indebtedness reportable under this section remains the obligation of the applicable financial entity. The IRS and Treasury recognize that a creditor and debtor may take inconsistent positions on this issue. The IRS does not intend to impose penalties for good faith failures to report settlements that constitute discharges of indebtedness.

Final Reg. § 1.6050P-1 contains a provision for coordinating reporting under Code § 6050P with reporting under Code § 6050J for foreclosures or other acquisitions of property in satisfaction of secured debt.

The IRS, on April 1, 1998, issued a Service Center Advice Memorandum describing how the information form should be completed in the following circumstances:[98]

(1) Where several persons are jointly and severally liable on a debt which is forgiven, the full amount of COD income should not be attributed to each such taxpayer. Instead, the amount should be appropriately allocated among them.

(2) The reporting of cancellation of debt is not required with respect to guarantors or sureties on the indebtedness.

(3) When applying the insolvency test of Code § 108(d), a taxpayer's interest in a pension plan or other assets exempt from the creditor's claims should be included as assets of the taxpayer.

(4) The IRS will not issue Forms 1099-C when canceling tax debts of individuals discharged either in a bankruptcy case or as a result of an offer in compromise.

---

[98] Service Center Advice Memorandum 1998-039, April 1, 1998, *reprinted at* 98 TNT 250-34.

The IRS has also held that a creditor should not file an information form merely because it has taken a write-off of the debt as "uncollectible," if the debt has not been forgiven.[99]

The preamble to the 1996 final regulation stated that, pending the issuance of further guidance, no penalties would be imposed for nonreporting by certain foreign entities. This was amplified and expanded in IRS Notice 96-61, 1996-49 I.R.B. 8.

In June 2002, the IRS issued Prop. Reg. §1.6050P-2, and in October 2004 final Reg. §1.6050P-2, to provide guidance regarding the meaning of Code §6050P(c)(2)(D), which was added in 1999 to include as an "applicable financial entity" any organization "a significant trade or business of which is the lending of money," *i.e.*, the type of organization mentioned in item (5) in the first paragraph of this §403.4. Although this language is very broad and might be thought to include any manufacturing or retail or service business that sells goods or services on credit, the legislative history indicated that what Congress really had in mind was credit card and finance companies. Thus, the primary approach of the regulation is to narrow the application of the statutory provision to the types of entity the Congress had in mind. Consistent with this purpose, the regulation contains a general provision stating that "if the principal trade or business of an organization is selling nonfinancial goods or providing nonfinancial services and if the organization extends credit to the purchasers of those goods or services in order to finance the purchases, then, for purposes of section 6050P(c)(2)(D), these extensions of credit are not a significant trade or business of lending money." This exception is not available, however, to a finance subsidiary of such a taxpayer. Three safe harbor provisions are also provided to cover small amounts of lending activity or the initial months of a new taxpayer. The regulation adds a provision to the effect that lending money includes acquiring a loan not only from the debtor at origination but also from a prior holder of the debt, and a provision that treats an entity that is formed or availed by an entity to which Code §6050P applies for the principal purpose of holding indebtedness acquired by that entity as itself having a significant trade or business of lending money. The proposed regulation provided that it would only be effective for debt discharges occurring in any calendar year beginning at least two months after the regulation becomes final. Consistent with this provision, the final regulation applies only to COD occurring after 2004. The notice issuing the proposed regulation added that it may be relied on for prior periods.

---

[99] IRS Field Service Advice 1998-78, August 25, 1992, *reprinted at* 98 TNT 106-33. In fact, if a creditor does file an information return indicating that the debt has been cancelled, this may interfere with any subsequent effort by the creditor to collect the debt. *See In re Crosby*, 261 B.R. 470, 2001-1 U.S.T.C. ¶50,404 (Bankr. D. Kan. 2001). However, Reg. §1.6050P-1(a)(1) suggests that, if a discharge of indebtedness has been deemed to occur under the terms of Reg. §1.6050P, this does not necessarily mean that an actual discharge of debt has occurred for purposes of other Code sections. Indeed, Service Center Advice 200235030, June 3, 2002, *reprinted at* 2002 SCA LEXIS 13, dealt with a case where an individual reported COD income because of an information return filed under Reg. §1.6050P even though the debt was not in fact discharged and was later paid. Nonetheless, if a creditor feels a filing is needed under Reg. §1.6050P for a debt that it does not intend to forgive, the creditor should consider adding language protective of its position.

### *§403.5 Special Information Reporting Required by "Tax Shelter" Regulations and Schedule M-3*

In 2003, the IRS adopted regulations (popularly described as "tax shelter" regulations) intended to help it combat tax shelters and overly aggressive tax planning: *see, e.g.,* Reg. §§1.6011-4, 301.6111-2, and 301.6112-1. These regulations greatly expanded required information reporting in certain areas. Some of their provisions are broad enough to be potentially applicable to debt modifications, even those of a kind not ordinarily thought of as tax shelters.

For example, Reg. §1.6011-4, as originally adopted, requires a taxpayer to file a special disclosure Form 8886 with its tax return if it participates in a transaction that falls within any one of six categories described in the regulation. One category is transactions resulting in a gross loss under Code §165 (including capital losses) exceeding certain dollar limits specified in the regulation. Another category is transactions producing a book-tax difference of more than $10 million (computed on a gross basis, without netting). These two categories, as well as some of the others, can easily apply to various debt restructurings. However, the IRS also issued two revenue procedures to exempt from the scope of the regulations certain transactions that are not likely to involve tax abuse. For example, Revenue Procedure 2004-66[100] provides that the Code §165 loss category in the regulation will not extend to certain losses from the sale or exchange of an asset having a "qualifying basis," which, with certain exceptions, generally means a basis produced entirely by cash payments. Revenue Procedure 2004-67[101] provides that the book-tax category in the regulation will not include, among other things, differences resulting from bad debts, from COD income, or from debt-for-debt exchanges. In 2004, the IRS adopted a new Schedule M-3 to the corporate tax return which also requires disclosure of differences between book income and tax return income.[102] Because the reporting of book-tax differences required on Schedule M-3 could be duplicative of the reporting required by the book-tax category in the regulation, the IRS decided to eliminate this overlap by removing the book-tax category from the regulation for reports required to be filed on or after January 6, 2006.[103]

In addition to the foregoing provisions, Reg. §301.6112-1 requires organizers, promoters, and certain advisors involved in the transactions described in Reg. §1.6011-4 to keep various records, including lists of participants, and to furnish such information to the IRS on request; and Reg. §301.6111-2 requires certain promoters of confidential corporate tax shelters, as therein defined, to register the shelter with the IRS and provide certain information to investors. The American Jobs Creation Act of 2004 considerably expanded and strengthened the impact of these requirements by adding new reporting requirements (amendments to Code §§6111 and 6112), new penalties (amendments to Code §§6662, 6664, 6688, 6700, 6707, 6708, and the addi-

---

[100] 2004-50 I.R.B. 966, *superseding* Rev. Proc. 2003-24, 2003-11 I.R.B. 599.

[101] 2004-67 I.R.B. 967, *superseding* Rev. Proc. 2003-25, 2003-11 I.R.B. 601.

[102] Rev. Proc. 2004-45, 2004-2 C.B. 140.

[103] IRS Notice 2006-6, 2006-5 I.R.B. 385. This elimination was reflected in Reg. §1.6011-4, when it was revised in 2007.

tion of new Code §§6662A and 6707A), and extensions of the statute of limitations where information required to be included in a return or statement by Code §6011 has not been so included (amendment to Code §6501). The decision, mentioned above, to eliminate the book-tax difference category from Reg. §1.6011-4, also applies for purposes of the reporting required by Code §§6111 and 6112 for periods on or after January 6, 2006.[104]

One particular change made by the American Jobs Creation Act of 2004 was an amendment to Code §6111 that granted the IRS authority to require any person who is a "material advisor" with respect to a transaction reportable under Code §6011 to file a return containing certain information about the transaction. A "material advisor" means any person providing any material help or advice with respect to organizing, managing, promoting, selling, implementing, insuring, or carrying out any transaction that, in effect, is reportable under Reg. §1.6011-4(b)(1), if such person receives compensation above certain threshold amounts. This authority has been implemented in Notice 2004-80,[105] effective October 22, 2004 (which uses Form 8264, with modifications, on an interim basis), and in Reg. §301.6111-3, adopted August 3, 2007 (which prescribes new Form 8918 for such reporting). Related amendments regarding the record-keeping requirements imposed on "material advisors" have been reflected in Reg. §301.6112-1, as revised on August 3, 2007.

Persons involved in a debt restructuring should examine the foregoing authorities to determine if any of their special reporting obligations apply to the restructuring.

## §404 COD INCOME OF DEBTOR

We mentioned above that when some or all of a debt is cancelled, the debtor company may have COD income (*see* §§403.1.3 and 403.2.4).[1] For a discussion of

---

[104] For a discussion of the problems created for law and accounting firms by the requirements of Code §§6111 and 6112, see New York State Bar Association, Tax Section, Report on Application of the IRC Sections 6111 and 6112 Material Advisor Rules to Law and Accounting Firms (May 5, 2006), *reprinted at* 2006 TNT 88-79 (May 8, 2006).

[105] 2004-50 I.R.B. 963; *see also* Information Release 2004-138 (Nov. 16, 2004), *reprinted at* 2004 IRB LEXIS 475.

[1] **§404** For an excellent and thorough discussion of the history and application of the COD rules discussed herein, *see* Asofsky, Discharge of Indebtedness Income in Bankruptcy After the Bankruptcy Tax Act of 1980, 27 St. Louis U. L.J. 583 (1983) (hereafter Asofsky, Discharge of Indebtedness). *See also* Asofsky, Reorganizing Insolvent Corporations, 41 Inst. on Fed. Tax'n §§5, 5.04[1] (provides comprehensive example of COD rules); Phelan and Sharp, Kick 'Em While They're Down—A Taxation and Bankruptcy Critique of the Technical and Policy Aspects of the Bankruptcy Tax Act of 1980, 35 Sw. L.J. 833 (1981). For an excellent discussion of the history of Code §108 and the COD rules in and outside of bankruptcy, *see* Plumb, The Tax Recommendations of the Commission on the Bankruptcy Laws—Reorganizations, Carryovers and the Effects of Debt Reduction, 29 Tax L. Rev. 227, 254-281 (1974); Eustice, Cancellation of Indebtedness and the Federal Income Tax: A Problem of Creeping Confusion, 14 Tax L. Rev. 223 (1959). For a flowchart analysis of the COD rules and the OID rules discussed above, *see* Sniderman, Gallagher & Joshowitz, A Tax Overview of Troubled Company Debt Restructuring, 21 Tax Advisor 199 (No. 4 April 1990). *See also* Willens, Formal Bankruptcy Proceedings Can Improve Tax Consequences Where Debtors See Potential Cancellation of Indebtedness Income, BNA Daily Tax Report (Feb. 21, 2007), at J-1.

COD income in respect of disputed or contingent claims, *see* §404.6. For a discussion of the question as to the time when COD income is deemed to arise, *see* §404.8. For a discussion of the principle that a cancellation of a debt does not produce COD income where the cancellation does not enrich the taxpayer, because the issuance of the debt did not increase the gross assets of the taxpayer and thus the cancellation simply prevents the taxpayer from suffering a net loss, *see* discussion at §404.1.5 below. Examples of such items include the release of liability of an accommodation endorser, surety, or guarantor. *See also* §404.1.1, which deals with cancellation of a debt to the extent payment would have given rise to a deduction that has not yet become deductible; and §404.1.2, dealing with the application of the tax benefit theory to the forgiveness of interest that was never paid but was deducted in a prior year, to the extent the deduction never produced a tax benefit.

For a discussion of the different treatment of nonrecourse debt from the treatment of recourse debt where the debt is cancelled by foreclosure upon the collateral securing the debt, *see* §403.1.3. As pointed out there, in the case of nonrecourse debt, the general rule is that the entire amount of the cancelled debt is treated as proceeds from the disposition of the collateral, even where the collateral is worth less than the amount of the debt cancelled. Thus, the cancellation does not produce COD income (and is not subject to Code §108). On the other hand, in the case of recourse debt, the excess, if any, of the amount of the debt cancelled above the value of the collateral foreclosed upon is treated as COD income (to which Code §108 thus applies), rather than as proceeds from the sale of the collateral.

The consequences of COD income are set forth in Code §108, which provides one set of results for taxpayers who are in bankruptcy or who are insolvent (to the extent they are not made solvent by the cancellation) and a quite different set of results for solvent taxpayers (including insolvent taxpayers not in bankruptcy to the extent they are made solvent by the cancellation, that is, to the extent the cancellation causes the fair market value of their assets to exceed their remaining liabilities).[2]

For this purpose, to be "in bankruptcy" means that the taxpayer is under the jurisdiction of the court in a title 11 (Bankruptcy Code) case, but only if the debt cancellation is granted by the court or is pursuant to a bankruptcy plan approved by the court.[3] A taxpayer is "insolvent" if its liabilities exceed the fair market value of its

---

[2] *See* Code §108(a); Department of the Treasury, IRS Publication 908, Bankruptcy 21 (Sept. 1994). Code §108 was enacted as part of the Bankruptcy Tax Act of 1980 and is effective for debt cancellations after 1980, unless occurring in bankruptcy or similar proceedings commenced prior to such date for which an election to apply the Bankruptcy Tax Act was not (or could not be) made. *See* Bankruptcy Tax Act of 1980, §§7(a)(1) and (f); Temp. Reg. §7a.3(b) and (d); *see also* IRS Letter Ruling 8531021, May 2, 1985 (IRS extended time in which COD rules could be elected for pre-1981, post-September 1979 period). For the developmental history of this Code section, *see* Asofsky, Towards a Bankruptcy Tax Act of 1993, 51 NYU Inst. on Fed. Tax'n §§13.02, 13.03 (1993).

[3] Code §108(d)(2). Note that this is narrower than the concept of a "title 11 *or similar* case" (emphasis added) that is defined in Code §368(a)(3) for "G" reorganization and Code §382 purposes. *See* §605.1.1.

Four Tax Court memorandum decisions dealt with this jurisdictional requirement and the meaning of the "only if" phrase in a situation involving the COD treatment of the general partners of a partnership in bankruptcy. Note that, in the partnership context, the COD exception for taxpayers in bankruptcy is applied at the partner level—*see* Code §108(d)(6)—and that the general partners in question did not themselves file for bankruptcy. Rather, the general partners and the partnership

assets; and with respect to any debt discharge, whether the taxpayer is insolvent, and the extent of the insolvency, are to be determined as of the moment immediately before the discharge.[4] In applying the insolvency test, one should take into account assets not reflected on balance sheets, including intangible assets such as goodwill. We also believe that one should be able to include in appropriate cases a reasonable reserve for contingent liabilities.[5] However, the Tax Court in *Merkel* has recently taken a narrow approach to the recognition of contingent liabilities, saying that "any obligation claimed to be a liability" can be taken into account for insolvency valuation purposes only to the extent the taxpayer proves "it is more probable than not that he will be called upon to pay that obligation in the amount claimed. . . ."[6] The Tax Court opinion was affirmed by the Ninth Circuit, with two judges agreeing with the Tax Court but a third filing a vigorous dissent.[7]

The contingencies involved in *Merkel* were potential liabilities as guarantor of a debt, and as secondary obligor on a state sales tax claim. The IRS had argued in *Merkel* that only fixed liabilities, or liabilities whose discharge would produce COD

---

(Footnote Continued)

entered into settlement agreements with the creditors of the partnership, pursuant to which, among other things, the general partners were to be discharged of further liability as general partners and as guarantors of the partnership debt. To effectuate the agreement, the bankruptcy court issued an order subjecting these general partners to the jurisdiction of the court and discharged them from further personal liability as general partners and as guarantors of the partnership debt. The court held that the resulting COD to the general partners from the discharge of their liability (as opposed to the partnership's liability) was the result of a discharge "in a title 11 case" and governed by the rules for taxpayers in bankruptcy. *Gracia v. Commissioner*, T.C. Memo 2004-147; *Mirarchi v. Commissioner*, T.C. Memo 2004-148; *Price v. Commissioner*, T.C. Memo 2004-149; *Estate of Martinez v. Commissioner*, T.C. Memo 2004-150.

[4] Code § 108(d)(3). In the case of individual debtors, it has been held that assets, for purposes of determining solvency, do not include assets that are exempt from claims of creditors. *See, e.g.*, IRS Letter Ruling 9130005, March 29, 1991; IRS Letter Ruling 9125010, March 19, 1991. However, in 1999, the IRS began to take a contrary position, and it persuaded the Tax Court to adopt that contrary position in *Carlson v. Commissioner*, 116 T.C. 87 (2001). This represented quite a change in law, and has been criticized. Ross, Exempt Assets and the Calculation of Insolvency Under § 108: Carlson v. Commissioner, Tax Mgmt. Mem. (June 21, 2001); Note, An Examination of the Section 108 Statutory Insolvency Exclusion and Its Definition of "Assets" as Applied in *Carlson v. Commissioner*, 55 Tax Law 329 (2001).

[5] *See, e.g.*, *Conestoga Transp. Co. v. Commissioner*, 17 T.C. 506, Dec. 18,547 (1951) (decided under prior judicially developed law; going concern value, and reserve for contingencies, taken into account); *J.A. Maurer, Inc.*, 30 T.C. 1273, Dec. 23,182 (1949) (goodwill value taken into account); C. McQueen and J. Williams, Federal Tax Aspects of Bankruptcy § 22:25 (1997 ed.); Phelan and Sharp, *supra* note 1, at 851 nn. 89-90; *but see* Asofsky *et al.*, Conference on the Bankruptcy Tax Act of 1980, 39 Inst. on Fed. Tax'n §§ 57, 57.04[3] at 57-43 (1981) (hereafter Bankruptcy Tax Conference). In determining the extent to which a debt discharge makes the taxpayer solvent, can one take into account the tax liability resulting from the COD income?

[6] *Merkel v. Commissioner*, 109 T.C. 463, 476, 484 (1997), *aff'd*, 192 F.3d 844, 99-2 U.S.T.C. ¶ 50,848 (9th Cir. 1999). The court did not mention the *Conestoga Transp.* case, cited *supra* note 5.

[7] For a further discussion of the *Merkel* case, *see*, Raby and Raby, Measuring Assets and Liabilities for DOI Purposes, 85 Tax Notes 77 (October 4, 1999). The article also discusses three IRS rulings (IRS Letter Ruling 199932013, IRS Technical Advice 199935002, and IRS Technical Advice 199932019), in which the IRS, reversing a long standing position, held that, in the case of individual taxpayers, assets which are exempt from the claims of creditors must nonetheless be taken into account in determining the solvency of those taxpayers for COD purposes.

income (which these would not) could be counted. The court properly rejected these IRS legal arguments.

The court then addressed the issue of the factual burden of proof that the taxpayer must satisfy in order to take contingent liabilities into account. The taxpayer had asserted that if payment of the contingent obligation is neither certain nor remote, the liability should be taken into account by multiplying its face amount by the probability that it will have to be paid. For example, if there is a 20 percent probability of payment of a contingent liability, 20 percent of the face amount should be taken into account. This is the approach that is used for determining the issue of insolvency for purposes of Bankruptcy Code section 548(a)(1)(B).[8] The court rejected this standard saying it was inappropriate for purposes of Code § 108. The court found more congenial the approach taken in Financial Accounting Standards No. 5 (Accounting for Contingencies) which allows accrual only for those loss contingencies that are "likely to occur." But the court did not exactly adopt the FASB No. 5 standard, either. Instead, the court announced the standard mentioned above.

On the facts, the contingent liabilities in *Merkel* seemed quite remote (in fact they never did require any payment). So it is easy to agree with the court's holding that the taxpayers had not proven insolvency for Code § 108 purposes. But it is less easy to agree with the legal standard applied by the court to reach this result. That standard seems to mean that if there is a 49 percent probability that a contingent liability will have to be paid, no amount can be taken into account; it also seems to mean that if the probability is 51 percent, 100 percent of the contingent liability (not just 51 percent) can be taken into account.[9] To us, there seems no more justification for allowing 100 percent recognition when the probability is only 51 percent than for denying all recognition when the probability is 49 percent.

Although the court did not address contingent liabilities that differ from the two that were before it, the court's standard certainly creates considerable doubt whether one can take into account reasonable reserves for product warranties, product liabilities, pending tax disputes, pending tort or contract disputes, and the like. Certainly a prospective buyer of a business would take a reasonable estimation of such contingent liabilities into account in valuing the business. We believe that just as the Code § 108 insolvency test requires that a reasonable estimate be made as to the fair market value of the taxpayer's assets—including its contingent assets—it should also allow a reasonable estimate of the value of the taxpayer's contingent liabilities to be taken into account. However, so long as the contrary view in *Merkel* stands, it provides troubled companies having significant contingent liabilities a strong reason to do their debt workouts in a bankruptcy proceeding (where insolvency need not be proved for Code § 108 purposes, *see* § 404.2 below) rather than outside bankruptcy.

---

[8] *See Covey v. Commercial Nat'l Bank*, 960 F.2d 657 (7th Cir. 1992). A similar approach must be taken for estate tax purposes. *See Estate of Smith v. Commissioner*, 2000-1 U.S.T.C. ¶ 60,366 (5th Cir. 1999).

[9] *See* Raby and Raby, Do Contingent Liabilities Count for Section 108 Insolvency?, Tax Notes (January 12, 1998), p. 205; Lipton, The Tax Court's New Standard for Testing Contingent Liabilities—Will it Work?, 88 J. Tax'n 150 (1998); Dooher, Contingent Liabilities and the Insolvency Exception to Cancellation of Debt Income: Merkel v. Comr., 39 Tax Mgmt. Memo. 195 (1998).

## EXAMPLE

Failing company's balance sheet shows the following assets and liabilities using GAAP accounting:

| **ASSETS** | | |
|---|---|---|
| Cash | | $ 1,000 |
| Inventory | | 10,000 |
| Buildings | $500,000 | |
| Less depreciation | (100,000) | 400,000 |
| Equipment | 200,000 | |
| Less depreciation | (50,000) | 150,000 |
| **Total Assets** | | $561,000 |
| **LIABILITIES** | | |
| Accounts Payable | | $20,000 |
| Bank Debt | | 600,000 |
| Capital Stock | | 100,000 |
| Accumulated Deficit | | (159,000) |
| **Total Liabilities** | | $561,000 |

In fact, an appraisal of the company shows that the buildings and equipment are only worth $250,000; the company has goodwill and going concern value of $50,000; and pending disputed product liability and tax claims against the company are expected to cost it $200,000. Assuming the appraisal is correct, for purposes of the insolvency test the company's assets and liabilities (all of which are fully recourse) are:

| **ASSETS** | |
|---|---|
| Cash | $1,000 |
| Inventory | 10,000 |
| Plant and Equipment | 250,000 |
| Goodwill and Going Concern Value | 50,000 |
| **Total Assets** | 311,000 |
| **LIABILITIES** | |
| Accounts Payable | 20,000 |
| Bank Debt | 600,000 |
| Reserve for Contingencies | 200,000 |
| **Total Liabilities** | $820,000 |

> The company is insolvent to the extent of $509,000 (assuming that the *Merkel* case is construed to allow this reserve for contingencies to be taken into account, or is overruled). If the entire $600,000 of bank debt were cancelled, the company would be treated as an insolvent taxpayer for $509,000 of the cancellation and a solvent taxpayer for $91,000 of the cancellation.[10] If the company was not in bankruptcy when the debt was cancelled, the consequences to the company of the first $509,000 of cancellation would differ from the consequences of the next $91,000 of cancellation. On the other hand, if the debt were cancelled pursuant to a plan of bankruptcy approved by a bankruptcy court, it would not matter whether the company was insolvent before or after the cancellation. In that case the need for, and validity of, an appraisal would not be a concern.

It has been held that the excess of the face amount of nonrecourse debt over the value of the collateral is not counted in determining insolvency.[11] The IRS agrees, except that where it is a portion of the nonrecourse debt itself that is being cancelled, the excess being cancelled is taken into account in determining insolvency.[12]

## *§404.1 Exceptions to Creation of COD Income*

No matter which category the debtor corporation is in, the first question to be examined is whether one of the exceptions to the creation of COD income from debt cancellation applies. Certain of the exceptions are not available to taxpayers in all categories. (Moreover, certain of the exceptions may not be effective for purposes of computing the alternative minimum tax (AMT) for tax years beginning before 1990. *See* §§404.5, 504A.6, 505, 511, and 710.) These exceptions are discussed below.

### §404.1.1 "Lost" Deductions

Code §108(e)(2) provides that no COD income is created from the cancellation of debt to the extent that payment of the liability would have given rise to a deduction that has not yet become deductible. (*See* §404.1.5 for a suggestion that this same result should apply to the forgiveness of interest which had been made non-deductible, such as personal interest or interest whose deductibility is denied by Code §163(l).)

---

[10] *See* Bankruptcy Tax Conference, *supra* note 5, §57.05 at 57-53 (remarks of Paul H. Asofsky and Milton B. Hyman); Eustice, Cancellation of Indebtedness Redux: The Bankruptcy Tax Act of 1980 Proposals—Corporate Aspects, 36 Tax L. Rev. 1, 15 (1980).

[11] *Babin v. Commissioner*, 64 T.C.M. 1357, Dec. 48,651(M), T.C. Memo. 1992-673, *aff'd*, 23 F.3d 1032 (6th Cir. 1994).

[12] Rev. Rul. 92-53, 1992-2 C.B. 48. For a critique of this ruling, *see* Asofsky, Towards a Bankruptcy Tax Act of 1993, 51 NYU Inst. on Fed. Tax'n, ch. 13.

**EXAMPLE**

> Certain of the liabilities of the debtor for current expenses such as wages, interest, and rent are cancelled. If the debtor were a cash method taxpayer, these expenses would not yet have become deductible because they have not been paid. The Code § 108(e)(2) exception to COD income applies. On the other hand, if the taxpayer were an accrual method taxpayer, to the extent these expenses had already accrued as deductions, the Code § 108(e)(2) exception would not apply. Nor would it apply to liabilities of either cash or accrual taxpayers that had to be capitalized.

A potential interpretative question exists as to whether this provision applies where deductibility would be deferred, even if the debt were currently paid. This could happen, for example, where deductibility would be deferred at that time under Code § 461 (the economic performance rules) or 465 (the at-risk rules). There are three possibilities:

(1) the provision applies when the debt is cancelled, notwithstanding that a deduction would have been deferred had the debt been paid at that time;
(2) the provision does not apply in such circumstances; or
(3) COD is created upon the cancellation, subject to reversal if the deferral ends while the return for the year of cancellation is still open.

The latter seems impractical. The second would convert a mere deferral of a deduction event into a total destruction of this exception to COD income, which does not seem consistent with the purpose of this provision. Thus, the first alternative provides the better answer.

Where accrued but unpaid interest is cancelled, and the debt cancellation does not also include in substantial part principal, the cancelled interest may be subject to the below market interest rules of Code § 7872.[13] Under proposed regulations, if the debt would initially have been subject to Code § 7872 had it been made without the cancelled interest, and the principal purpose for the cancellation is to confer a benefit on the debtor (such as to pay compensation or to make a gift, a capital contribution, a dividend-type distribution, or a similar payment to the debtor), the cancellation will be treated as if the interest had in fact been paid to the creditor and then retransferred by the creditor to the debtor.[14] Presumably, this provision would not apply where the cancellation occurs in an out-of-court workout involving a significant portion of the

---

[13] *See* explanation of the rules relating to loans bearing below market interest rates at Stand. Fed. Tax Rep. (CCH) ¶ 44,860.

[14] Prop. Reg. § 1.7872-11(a). The requisite purpose will be presumed in the case of loans between (1) family members, (2) corporations and shareholders, (3) employers and employees, or (4) an independent contractor and a person for whom such independent contractor provides services, *unless* the taxpayer can show by *clear and convincing evidence* that the interest obligation was cancelled for a legitimate business purpose of the creditor who is seeking to maximize satisfaction of a claim (such as in the case of a debtor's insolvency). Id.

debtor's creditors or a bankruptcy or similar insolvency proceeding, as the requisite purpose would be absent.

### § 404.1.2 Tax Benefit Recovery Exclusion

Code § 111 provides that gross income does not include income attributable to the recovery during the taxable year of any amount deducted in a prior year to the extent the deduction did not produce a tax benefit. This exclusion is applied before the Code § 108 rules are applied.[15] Thus, if in a prior year the failing company deducted accrued interest that was never paid, and if in the current year the obligation to pay the interest is forgiven, Code § 111 excludes the cancellation from income to the extent the deduction never produced a tax benefit.[16] Code § 111(c) provides that a deduction that has increased a carryover that has not expired shall be treated as producing a tax benefit. Because of this, and because NOLs now generally survive for 15 years, the Code § 111 exclusion is not likely to be of much practical use in debt forgiveness situations except in unusual circumstances. Only to the extent that Code § 111 does not provide an exclusion is Code § 108 applied to the debt cancellation.[17]

### § 404.1.3 Purchase Price Reduction

This statutory exception, which is found in Code § 108(e)(5), applies only to solvent debtors. It does not apply to insolvent debtors or to debtors in bankruptcy proceedings. The statutory exception provides that where the seller of specific property reduces the debt of the purchaser that arose out of the purchase of the property, the reduction shall be treated by the purchaser and the seller as a purchase price adjustment on that property.[18] The purpose of the exception is to eliminate factual controversy over the question of whether the reduction represented a purchase price adjustment instead of a cancellation of debt. The legislative history indicates that the statutory exception does not apply where the debt has been transferred by the seller to a third party (including a related party); or where the property has been transferred by the buyer to a third party (including a related party); or where the debt is

---

[15] Rev. Rul. 67-200, 1967-1 C.B. 15, *clarified* by Rev. Rul. 70-406, 1970-2 C.B. 16.

[16] Code § 111 provides no benefit where the deduction could have been, but was not, claimed in the prior year and the prior year is barred by the statute of limitations. *See, e.g., First Nat'l Bank*, 22 T.C. 209, Dec. 20,299 (1954), *aff'd*, 221 F.2d 959, 55-1 U.S.T.C. ¶ 9448 (2d Cir. 1955), *cert. denied*, 350 U.S. 887 (1955).

[17] Rev. Rul. 67-200, 1967-1 C.B. 15, *clarified* by Rev. Rul. 70-406, 1970-2 C.B. 16. *See also* Rev. Rul. 58-546, 1958-2 C.B. 546. However, in IRS Letter Ruling 9037033, June 18, 1990, the IRS treated the cancellation of previously deducted accrued interest as COD only to the extent of the debtor's insolvency, and as tax benefit income thereafter. This is clearly wrong. TR-45-1715-95, October 17, 1995, 1995 FSA LEXIS 177, suggests that IRS Letter Ruling 9037033 may no longer represent the view of the national office.

[18] That this treatment applies to the purchaser is not apparent from the statute, but the legislative intent is clear. *See* S. Rep. No. 1035, 96th Cong., 2d Sess. 16 (1980); H.R. Rep. No. 833, 96th Cong., 2d Sess. 13 (1980). In addition, the IRS has held that the cancellation of the accrued interest portion of the debt will not qualify as a purchase price adjustment. IRS Letter Ruling 9037033, June 18, 1990.

reduced other than by agreement between the buyer and seller, such as by the running of the statute of limitations on the debt.[19]

The same legislative history suggests that the statutory exception applies only if the amount of the reduction would otherwise be treated as income from the cancellation of debt.[20] This would suggest that, where the exception does not apply, then the taxpayer—whether or not the taxpayer is solvent or insolvent or in bankruptcy—might look to prior law to determine whether the debt reduction should be treated as a purchase price adjustment.[21] In addition, it seems significant that, although both the statute and the legislative history state that Code § 108 supersedes the prior judicially

---

[19] Id. In IRS Ruling Letter 9037033, June 18, 1990, the IRS applied the statutory purchase price exception for the portion of COD income to which the insolvency exception did not apply, even though the original purchaser of the property had transferred the property to a corporation that also assumed the purchase money indebtedness. Thus, the purchase price adjustment was not made with the original purchaser. However, under the facts of the ruling, the IRS considered the original purchaser to have been essentially an agent for the transferee in making the purchase. In a 1993 Field Service Advice, FSA 1998-421 (dated July 15, 1993), *reprinted at* 98 TNT 234-66, the IRS held that where the original purchaser of the property was merged into a different corporation in a tax-free reorganization to which Code § 381 applied, the different corporation should be treated as the original purchaser for purposes of qualifying for the Code § 108(e)(5) statutory exception. The IRS said that even though Code § 108(e)(5) is not mentioned in § 381 or its regulations as a carryover attribute, it should be so treated. The IRS gave no indication as to whether it would have reached a different result had Code § 381 not applied to the transaction.

[20] Code § 108(e)(5)(C). If, for debt discharges occurring before 1987, a solvent debtor desires to elect to treat certain debt as "qualified business indebtedness" under Code § 108(c) and have the general basis reduction rules apply to the cancellation of such debt (discussed at § 404.3), will such rules govern where the cancellation otherwise would be subject to the purchase price reduction rules? The general basis reduction rules often may be desirable where the purchase price reduction is in respect of fully depreciated property, ITC recapture would be triggered, and/or the debtor has a significant amount of other property with a longer depreciable life. The resolution of this issue depends on whether it can be said that the cancellation would, but for the purchase price reduction rules, be "treated as income to the purchaser from the discharge of indebtedness." Code § 108(e)(5)(C). This language could be read as referring either to (1) the actual inclusion in gross income of any COD income (in which case the general basis reduction rules would apply) or (2) the creation of COD income, whether or not includable in gross income (in which event the purchase price reduction rules would apply). Both readings can be supported. The better reading appears to be the second, that is, that the purchase price reduction rules should govern. *Cf.* Rev. Proc. 85-44, 1985-2 C.B. 504, § 3.03 (advance ruling procedure for basis reduction of selective assets of a solvent debtor inapplicable where purchase price reduction rules apply); S. Rep. No. 1035, 96th Cong., 2d Sess. 16 (1980); H.R. Rep. No. 833, 96th Cong., 2d Sess. 13 (1980).

A solvent debtor in bankruptcy continues to face a similar conflict (even after 1986) where the debtor desires to have the elective basis reduction rules (discussed at § 404.2) apply in respect to certain debt (the cancellation of which otherwise would be subject to the purchase price adjustment rules). The prior analysis applies equally here.

[21] *See also* Asofsky, Discharge of Indebtedness, *supra* note 1, at 623-624; Scranton, Corporate Transactions Under the Bankruptcy Tax Act of 1980, 35 Tax Law. 49, 74 (1981); Bankruptcy Tax Conference, *supra* note 5, at § 57.05[1] (remarks of Paul H. Asofsky), § 57.08 at pp. 57-76 to 57-77 (remarks of Paul H. Asofsky and Richard B. Ruge). Prior case law allowed purchase-price adjustment treatment on appropriate facts, including: A reduction resulting from negotiations between buyer and seller over price rather than a general debt reduction; property having a value not in excess of the reduced debt; and no prior deduction of the cancelled debt. *See Estate of Broadhead v. Commissioner*, 391 F.2d 841, 68-1 U.S.T.C. ¶ 9249 (5th Cir. 1968); *Hirsch v. Commissioner*, 115 F.2d 656, 40-2 U.S.T.C. ¶ 9791 (7th Cir. 1940); *Fifth Avenue-14th Street Corp. v. Commissioner*, 147 F.2d 453. 45-1 U.S.T.C. ¶ 9115 (2d Cir. 1945); *Commissioner v. Coastwise Transportation Co.*, 71 F.2d 104, 4 U.S.T.C. ¶ 1288 (1st Cir.

developed law regarding the insolvency exception from cancellation of debt income,[22] they do not say this regarding the purchase price exception.[23] The IRS, in Rev. Rul. 92-99,[24] has acknowledged the continued existence of the prior judicially developed purchase price exception. At the same time, this ruling stated that the IRS will not follow one aspect of this prior judicial law. In the ruling, individual *A* had purchased an office building from *B* for $1 million. To pay for the building, *A* had borrowed $1 million from *C*, a third-party lender, and had given *C* an interest-bearing nonrecourse note for that amount. A year later, when the value of the building had fallen to $800,000, *C* agreed with *A* to reduce the principal of the note from $1 million to $800,000. *A* was solvent and not in bankruptcy. The ruling noted that the statutory purchase-price-adjustment exception to COD income did not apply to this adjustment, because that exception applies only to adjustments of debt issued to the seller of the property. Here, *B* was the seller and *C* was just a third-party lender. The ruling then addressed the question of whether the judicial purchase-price-adjustment exception would apply. Some of the prior judicial purchase-price exception cases had applied a purchase-price exception to COD income even where the adjustment was made to third-party debt, rather than to debt issued to the seller. These cases included the *Hirsch* case.[25] While the ruling indicates that a judicial exception still exists, it holds that the IRS will not follow these particular cases to the extent the adjustment in the third-party debt is not based on an infirmity that relates back to the original sale (such as the seller's inducement of an inflated purchase price by misrepresentation or fraud).[26] On the facts addressed in the ruling, the debt reduction by the third party was attributable to a later decline in the value of the property, rather than to an infirmity in the original sale. Thus, the ruling holds that it produced COD income. (One should note that where the statutory exception rather than the judicial exception applies, it is not necessary that the debt reduction relate to an infirmity that existed at the time of sale.)

Where the purchase price exception (rather than the general basis reduction rules examined below) applies, the purchase price adjustment results in the recapture of

(Footnote Continued)

1934), *cert. denied*, 293 U.S. 595 (1934); *L.D. Coddon & Bros., Inc.*, 37 B.T.A. 393, Dec. 9959 (1938); *John E. Montgomery*, 65 T.C. 511, Dec. 33,536 (1975).

[22] Code § 108(e)(1); S. Rep. No. 1035, 96th Cong., 2d Sess. 15 n.16 (1980); H.R. Rep. No. 833, 96th Cong., 2d Sess. 12 n.15 (1980).

[23] S. Rep. No. 1035, 96th Cong., 2d Sess. 20 n.24 (1980), also seems to assume that the common law purchase price exception continues to exist.

[24] 1992-2 C.B. 35. *See also* IRS Letter Ruling 9412013, December 21, 1993; TR-45-1715-95, October 17, 1995, 1995 FSA LEXIS 177.

[25] *Supra* note 21.

[26] To similar effect on this point, *see* Rev. Rul. 91-31, discussed *supra* at § 403.1.3. The IRS position in Rev. Rul. 92-99 was in effect adopted by the Tenth Circuit in *Preslar v. Commissioner*, 167 F.3d 1323 (10th Cir. 1999). The loan was a third-party loan and its adjustment was found not to relate to an infirmity at its inception. However, the opinion suggests that the IRS had argued that the common law purchase-price exception did not survive the adoption of Code § 108(e)(5) at all—a position contrary to Rev. Rul. 92-99.

any investment tax credit taken with respect to the portion of the purchase price that is reduced.[27]

In the case of partnerships, application of the statutory exception is complicated by the fact that whereas Code § 108(e)(5) makes the exception unavailable to insolvent or bankrupt debtors, Code § 108(d)(6) provides that in the partnership context, the bankruptcy and insolvency exclusions are applied at the partner rather than at the partnership level. Rev. Proc. 92-92[28] deals with this problem by allowing a partnership to apply the statutory exception without regard to the bankruptcy or insolvency of the partnership. However, Rev. Proc. 92-92 does not apply if any partner adopts a tax reporting position with respect to the debt discharge that is inconsistent with the partnership's treatment of the discharge. The government's concern here is that an insolvent or bankrupt partner might find application of the general attribute reduction rules of Code § 108(b) more advantageous than reduction of the basis of the partnership's property. However, insolvent or bankrupt partnerships should be able to apply the judicial exception without regard to this consistency requirement.

No guidance has been given as to application of the statutory exception to an insolvent debtor who is rendered solvent by cancellation of a mixture of purchase money and other debt.

**EXAMPLE**

> Insolvent debtor owes a seller $1 million on the purchase price of property and owes $2 million to other creditors. The entire $3 million is cancelled and the fair market value of all the debtor's property exceeds its liabilities by $500,000 after the cancellation. Does the statutory purchase price exception apply to $500,000 of the debt cancellation; or to only $150,000 (1/3); or to none? The well-advised debtor will try to avoid this problem by cancelling the debt in the sequence that will produce the desired result.[29]

For application of the purchase price exception to contested purchase price claims, *see* § 404.6.

The availability of either the statutory or the prior case law purchase-price adjustment may not be critical for a taxpayer to the extent the general election (which is discussed below at § 404.2) to adjust basis rather than suffer COD consequences is available to the taxpayer. Where there would be no difference in results, it may be safer to make a protective election to reduce basis. However, the consequences of the

---

[27] Id.; H.R. Rep. No. 833, 96th Cong., 2d Sess. 16 n.23 (1980).

[28] 1992-2 C.B. 505. For a ruling applying Rev. Proc. 92-92 to allow an insolvent partnership to treat a debt cancellation as a purchase price adjustment, *see* IRS Letter Ruling 200336032, June 10, 2003.

[29] *See* IRS Letter Ruling 9037033, June 18, 1990, wherein the IRS respected the sequence set forth in the parties' agreement. The parties had agreed that the amount by which each obligation was reduced would be applied first to unpaid interest and then to principal. Accordingly, the IRS applied the insolvency amount first against the cancellation of the interest.

two rules will often differ. The purchase price adjustment applies to, and only to, the specific property purchased with the reduced debt; it applies to the property as of the time of reduction, even if the property is disposed of before the beginning of the next tax year; it applies without regard to whether the property is depreciable; and it results in investment credit recapture. In each of these respects, the rules applicable to the general basis reduction election will produce different results.

### § 404.1.4 Stock-for-Debt and Contribution-to-Capital Exceptions

The stock-for-debt exception to COD income is discussed at § 504A, and the contribution-to-capital exception is discussed at § 505.

The stock for-debt-exception was repealed by the 1993 Act. The repeal is effective for stock transferred after 1994, except that the repeal does not apply to stock transferred in a title 11 or similar case filed before the end of 1993.

Before the 1993 Act, the contribution-to-capital exception was equally available to nonbankrupt solvent taxpayers and to insolvent and bankrupt taxpayers, whereas the stock-for-debt exception was severely restricted for solvent taxpayers not in bankruptcy. The contribution-to-capital exception also was computed differently than the stock-for-debt exception. The 1993 Act does not directly change the contribution-to-capital exception, but it gives the Treasury authority to issue regulations to coordinate the treatment of contributions of debt to capital with the repeal of the stock-for-debt exception.

Even in those cases where the stock-for-debt exception has been applicable, its availability has not always been enough to protect the failing company's NOLs and other tax attributes from erosion or loss. As we shall see in Chapter 5 (at § § 506-509), whenever stock is issued by the failing company, Code § 382 must be consulted and, when it applies, these attributes may be adversely affected or even lost.

### § 404.1.5 Creation of Debt Did Not Increase Debtor's Gross Assets

It has been held that release of the liability of an accommodation endorser, surety, or guarantor will not produce COD income. This is true even after the guarantee has been triggered and the guarantor has become primarily liable—the theory being that the guarantor has no income because its assets were not initially increased by the making of the guarantee and so there has been no untaxed accretion in wealth. Indeed, this is part of a broader principle that a cancellation which does not enrich the taxpayer, in the sense of allowing the taxpayer to keep an asset received earlier on which it was not taxed, is not COD income.[30] We would suggest

---

[30] *Landreth v. Commissioner*, 50 T.C. 803 (1968); *Payne v. Commissioner*, T.C. Memo. 1998-227; *Bradford v. Commissioner*, 233 F. 2d 935, 56-1 U.S.T.C. ¶9552 (6th Cir. 1956); *Whitmer v. Commissioner*, T.C. Memo. 1996-83; Asofsky, Discharge of Indebtedness, *supra* note 1, at 622-623; Heinlen, The ABC's of Cancellation of Indebtedness Income and Attribute Reduction, 40 Inst. on Fed. Tax'n § § 42, 42.04[6] (1982); Beck, Is Compromise of a Tax Liability Itself Taxable? A Problem of Circularity in the Logic of Taxation, 14 Va. Tax Rev. 153 (1994). The Tax Court has applied this same principle to hold that a taxpayer did not have an amount realized when he transferred appreciated stock in settlement of a liability owed by a third party and not by himself, where he was essentially acting as a guarantor.

that the same result should apply to the forgiveness of nondeductible interest, such as personal interest or interest whose deductibility is denied by Code § 163(l). For the same reason, settlement of a disputed claim for less than the amount claimed generally does not create COD income.[31] The IRS has applied this concept to the acceptance by the IRS of the taxpayer's offer in compromise on a tax liability.[32]

An interesting application of this theory can be found in an opinion of the Court of Appeals for the Fifth Circuit in *Estate of Smith v. Commissioner*.[33] Here, a decedent had received royalties from an oil company on which he had paid full tax, but the oil company subsequently asserted that the royalties had been overpaid and demanded the decedent return $2.4 million of these royalties. After the decedent died, the estate settled the claim for about $682,000. The court held that, for estate tax purposes, the amount of the claim should be valued as of the date of death, but even if this proved to be greater than the amount for which the claim was settled, the court further held that settlement of the claim did not produce COD income. Since the decedent had paid full income tax on the royalties when they were received, the cancellation of the claim for return of part of these royalties did not leave the decedent or the estate with funds that had not previously been brought into income.[34]

Another interesting application of this approach can be found in *U.S. Steel Corporation v. U.S.*,[35] where U.S. Steel issued preferred stock for $100 per share; later exchanged it, when it was worth $165, in a tax-free reorganization for U.S. Steel debentures having a face amount of $175; and later repurchased some of these latter debentures for $118 each. The court observed that if the transactions are viewed as a whole, the corporation had not really increased its capital through the repurchase of the debentures for less than their face amount, because the $100 of cash it received in

---

(Footnote Continued)

*Friedland v. Commissioner*, T.C. Memo 2001-236 (a portion of the holding in this case is criticized in Note, Discharge of Nonrecourse Liability Versus Discharge of Third Party Indebtedness: *Friedland v. Commissioner*, 55 Tax Law. 917 (2002), but in making its criticism, the Note fails to take into account the reasoning described above in the text). The IRS, however, may not always agree that the retention of previously untaxed income is a necessary prerequisite to COD income. *See* IRS Service Center Advice 200038044, August 14, 2000 (forgiveness of asserted penalty for violation of a scholarship contract created COD income), *reprinted at* 2000 TNT 186-62; IRS Information Letter 20020024, January 11, 2002 (stating the IRS disagrees with the view that no COD income is recognized when guarantees for which no value was received are cancelled). On the other hand, in IRS Legal Memorandum 200402004, November 26, 2003, *reprinted at* 2004 TNT 7-28, a corporation had made overcharges for its sales of crude oil that violated price controls. The corporation and its sole owner had joint and several liability to make restitution of the overcharges. The owner was released from liability. The IRS held that the owner was essentially in the position of a guarantor, and release of the owner's liability did not create COD income for the owner. *See also* the discussions at § § 404.1.1 and 404.1.2 above.

[31] *See* the discussion at § 404.6 below; *see also* Asofsky, Discharge of Indebtedness, *supra* note 1, at 621-22; McQueen and Williams, *supra* note 5, at § § 22:18 and 22:19.

[32] IRS Field Service Advice 1998-297, dated May 28, 1992, *reprinted at* 98 TNT 197-93. *See also* the discussion in relation to Example 9, § 404.6.

[33] 198 F.3d 515 (5th Cir. 1999), *non-acq.* 2000-19 I.R.B.

[34] The Fifth Circuit also held that the cancellation satisfied the requirements of both the *Preslar* and *Zarin* cases for application of the contested liability exception from COD income, which is discussed below at § 404.6.

[35] 848 F.2d 1232 (Fed. Cir. 1988).

step 1 was less than the $118 that it had to pay out to cancel the debentures. Since the cancellation of the $57 face amount of the debentures did not leave U.S. Steel with more cash or property than it had before the cancellation, the court held that there was no COD income.

## *§404.2 Insolvent and Bankrupt Taxpayers*

To the extent that the exceptions to COD income mentioned above do not apply, Code § 108 provides identical COD consequences for insolvent taxpayers (but only to the extent of their insolvency immediately before the debt cancellation) and for taxpayers in bankruptcy (whether or not they are insolvent). The great practical advantage to the taxpayer in bankruptcy is that there is no need to prove insolvency, and that these rules (which are more favorable than those applicable to solvent taxpayers not in bankruptcy) apply even to the extent the bankrupt taxpayer's debt is cancelled by more than is necessary to make it solvent.

We should note that the special rule under Code § 108 for bankrupt taxpayers is limited to taxpayers in a case under title 11 of the United States Code.[36] (Moreover, if the cancelled debt was issued by a disregardable LLC owned by the bankrupt corporation, the IRS has informally asserted that the special bankruptcy rule applies only if *both* the corporation and the LLC are under the jurisdiction of the bankruptcy court.[37]) This contrasts with the special rules for bankrupt companies for purposes of the Code § 382 and "G" reorganization provisions, which apply not only in title 11, but also in a *"similar"* case, which includes a receivership, foreclosure, or similar proceeding in a Federal or State court.[38]

The basic rule applicable to insolvent and bankrupt taxpayers under Code § 108 is that COD income is entirely excluded from gross income, so that no income tax (other than perhaps alternative minimum tax for pre-1990 years, *see* § § 404.5, 504A.6, 505, and 708) needs to be paid currently as a result of the debt cancellation; but the debt cancellation does reduce various tax attributes of the taxpayer (such as NOLs), with the result that the debt cancellation may have the consequence of increasing the future income taxes of the debtor.

---

[36] *See* Code § § 108(a)(1)(A) and 108(d)(2). This has been held by the Tax Court to include general partners of a bankrupt partnership, who, for purposes of settlement, were made subject to the jurisdiction of the bankruptcy and discharged from their personal liability as general partners and guarantors of the partnership debt. *Gracia v. Commissioner*, T.C. Memo 2004-147; *Mirarchi v. Commissioner*, T.C. Memo 2004-148; *Price v. Commissioner*, T.C. Memo 2004-149; *Estate of Martinez v. Commissioner*, T.C. Memo 2004-150.

[37] *See* "Officials Highlight Upcoming Consolidated, Corporate Guidance," 2004 TNT 184-3 (September 22, 2004) (reporting comments of Derek Cain, then IRS Deputy Assoc. Chief Counsel (Corporate), that were made at an ALI-ABA conference). This position, however, appears inconsistent with the Tax Court memorandum decisions discussed in the preceding footnote and *supra* note 3, involving the applicability of the exception for bankrupt taxpayers to general partners of a bankrupt partnership.

[38] *See* Code § § 382(l)(5)(G), 382(l)(6), 368(a)(3)(A).

As discussed below, the reduction of the tax attributes occurs only after the determination of tax for the year of the debt cancellation.[39] In addition, as discussed more fully in item (6) below, the regulations clarify that, in the case of an acquisitive tax-free reorganization occurring during the year of the debt cancellation, the tax attributes to which the acquiring corporation succeeds still get reduced.[40]

The tax attributes that are reduced, and the order of their reduction, are as follows:

(1) *Elective Basis Reduction.* To the extent the debtor elects to reduce basis in depreciable property, this reduction is applied before the other attribute reductions listed below.[41] This election should be made by filing Form 982 with the tax return for the tax year in which the debt cancellation occurred. The consequences of this election are the same as the consequences that existed for solvent taxpayers for debt cancellation occurring before 1987, which are discussed at § 404.3 below, except that the order of the property for which the basis is to be reduced was determined, prior to the issuance of new regulations, under rules applicable to prior law under Reg. § § 1.1016-7 and 1.1016-8.[42] New regulations were issued on October 22, 1998, as Reg. § 1.108-4 and § 1.1017-1. These new regulations are effective only for COD occurring on or after October 22, 1998.

The election applies to the basis of property held by the taxpayer at the beginning of the taxable year following the year of debt cancellation. For purposes of the election, "depreciable property" means any property subject to the allowance for depreciation, but only if the basis reduction would reduce the amount of depreciation or amortization otherwise allowable for the period immediately following the reduction. Depreciable property, in addition to property normally subject to the allowance for depreciation, also includes:

(a) any real property treated as inventory, if the debtor so elects;

(b) the stock of a subsidiary with which the debtor files a consolidated return, but only to the extent the subsidiary consents to a corresponding reduction in the basis of its depreciable property; and

(c) an interest of a partner in a partnership, to the extent of the partner's proportionate interest in depreciable property of the partnership, but only if there is a corresponding reduction in the partnership's basis in depreciable property with respect to such partner.

---

[39] Code § 108(b)(4)(A). For a discussion of the attribute reduction rules within the consolidated return context, *see* § § 804.4.1 and 804.4.5 below.

[40] *See* Reg. § 1.108-7(c).

[41] Code § 108(b)(5). For the considerations involved in deciding whether to make such an election, *see, e.g.*, Pollack, How Section 108 Election Permits Debt Cancellation Income to Be Minimized, 62 J. Tax'n 276 (1985) (discusses considerations for solvent debtors, which have equal applicability for corporate insolvent debtors); Scranton, *supra* note 21, at 81; Phelan and Sharp, *supra* note 1, at 853. The IRS has permitted recissions of elective basis reductions where they were made under a mistake of fact or law. IRS Letter Ruling 200208016, November 21, 2001 (S corporation); IRS Letter Ruling 200210044, December 6, 2001 (same); IRS Letter Ruling 200436002, May 6, 2004 (C corporation).

[42] *See* S. Rep. No. 1035, 96th Cong., 2d Sess. 14 (1980); H.R. Rep. No. 833, 96th Cong., 2d Sess. 11(1980); *see* Asofsky, Discharge of Indebtedness, *supra* note 1, at 598; *cf.* Pollack, *supra* note 41.

For authorities amplifying these provisions, *see* § 404.3 below (cancellations occurring before 1987).

(2) *NOLs.* The net operating loss for the year of cancellation (first) and the NOLs to the year of cancellation (second) are reduced next.[43] The latter are reduced in the order of the years in which they arose.[44] Consider the following situation, which often arises. A corporation has current year losses which could be carried back to a prior year, if these losses did not first have to be reduced by the corporation's current year COD. Can the current year losses be carried back before the COD is applied, or must they be reduced by the COD so that only the remaining balance, if any, is available for carryback? Code § 108(b)(4)(A) provides that the attribute reductions compelled by Code § 108 "shall be made after the determination of the tax . . . for the taxable year of the discharge." One must therefore decide whether the carryback should be thought to occur as *part of the determination* of the tax for the COD year, or only *after the determination* of that tax. In other words, should the "determination of the tax . . . for the taxable year of the discharge" be construed to include the determination of tax for prior years, or should the determination of tax for prior years (even though attributable to a current year NOL) be considered beyond the scope of that phrase? If the former, the carryback will be allowed without reduction for the COD. But if it is considered to occur *after* that determination, then the carryback and the attribute reduction arguably would coincide, leaving the answer to depend on an evaluation of the purposes of the two provisions. The IRS finally resolved this issue in favor of the carryback, as explained below, in Temporary Regulations in July 2003, which were made final in 2004.

Prior to these regulations, this issue could be avoided by making an elective basis reduction under Code § 108(b)(5), as described in the preceding paragraph. However, if this was not done, the question remained, and there was disagreement on the answer in the secondary authorities.[45] In a previous edition of this book, we had said we believed the correct answer is that the carryback should be allowed before being reduced by the COD, at least from a policy perspective and, possibly, based on a plain reading of the statute. The basic policy of the Code § 108 exclusion of COD from income would seem to be that the COD should not adversely affect the

---

[43] Code § 108(b)(2)(A) and (4)(B).

[44] Code § 108(b)(4)(B).

[45] Collier on Bankruptcy Taxation, at ¶ TX6.03[4][b][i], while noting that the answer was unclear, stated that the NOL carryback should come before the COD reduction. But another commentator argued to the contrary, except where the carryback would *actually* affect the determination of tax for the current year. Germain, Avoiding Phantom Income in Bankruptcy: A Proposal for Reform, 5 Fla. Tax Rev. 249 (2001). Under the latter view, since a carryback will seldom affect the tax determination for the current year, the carryback would come before the COD adjustment only in very limited situations, one example of which can be found in Reg. § 1.1212-1(a)(3) Ex. 5. *But consider United Dominion Industries, Inc. v. United States,* 121 S. Ct. 1934, 2001-1 U.S.T.C. ¶ 50,430 (2001) (wherein the Supreme Court, in considering the issue of consolidated versus separate company application of the Code § 172(f) 10-year carryback, rejected an argument by the IRS that it should discount the significance of certain adjustments made by the consolidated return regulations to a member's separate company NOL since, according to the IRS, such adjustments had never once made a difference; the Court stated that "whether or not the excluded items have made a difference in the past, or make a difference here, they certainly could make a difference . . . ").

current year cash position of the insolvent or bankrupt company. Thus, a loss carryover from a year before the COD year may be used to reduce the tax liability for the year of the COD, and to the extent it can be so used, it is not reduced by the COD. That much is clearly compelled by the Code § 108(b)(4)(A) language quoted above. This same policy would seem to require that where the NOL for the year of the COD could be carried back to a prior year (if not first reduced by the COD) thereby improving the cash position of the debtor for the year of the COD, the carryback should be allowed, because otherwise the COD would be adversely affecting the current year cash position of the debtor. The same policy is reflected in the Code § 1017 requirement that COD allocated to the reduction of asset basis can affect basis only at the beginning of the *next* tax year, thus not impairing the cash position of the debtor for the COD year. In short, we believe Code §§ 108(b)(4)(A) and 1017 both reflect a policy that COD attribute reduction should affect only the future, not the present or the past.[46] As indicated above, the position we espoused was adopted in mid-July 2003 in Temp. Reg. §§ 1.108-7T(b) and (d), Example 2 and in identical proposed regulations. The preamble to these temporary and proposed regulations said they were clarifying in nature. They applied effective for COD occurring after July 17, 2003. These regulations were made final as Reg. §§ 1.108-7(b) and (d), Example 2 in 2004, effective for COD occurring on or after May 10, 2004.

(3) *R&D and ITC Credit Carryovers.* Carryovers of these credits (and any other credits making up the Code § 38 "general business" credit) to or from the year of cancellation are reduced (at the rate of 33 1/3 cents for each dollar of debt cancellation) in the order in which they would be taken into account in the year of cancellation.[47] No reduction is made, however, in the portion of the credits attributable to the employee stock ownership credit determined under Code § 41.[48]

(4) *Alternative Minimum Tax Credits.* Payments of alternative minimum tax that are available as carryovers from the year of the debt discharge as credits against future regular tax are reduced (at the rate of 33 1/3 cents for each dollar of debt cancellation). This provision was added by the 1993 Act and is applicable to debt discharges occurring in taxable years beginning after December 31, 1993.

---

[46] Support for reading Code §§ 108(b)(4)(A) and 1017 to be consistent in reaching the same result as to the timing of attribute reduction, namely that it should occur only at the beginning of the year following the COD, can be found in *Gitlitz v. Commissioner*, 121 S. Ct. 701, 2001-U.S.T.C. ¶ 50,147 (2001) and one of its predecessor cases, *Farley v. Commissioner*, 202 F. 3d. 198, 2000-1 U.S.T.C. ¶ 50,179 (3d Cir. 2000). For example, the *Farley* court held that Code § 108(b)(4)(A) "clearly provides for the reduction of NOLs to occur at the beginning of the year following the year of the COD" 202 F.3d at 205-206. And the Supreme Court said that Code §§ 1017(a) and 108(b)(4)(A) contain the "same sequencing" language. 121 S. Ct. at 709. Germain, in the article cited in the preceding footnote, argues that because these cases involve S corporation issues at the shareholder level, they are not in point on the present question. However, we believe the approach taken on this issue in these cases provides very helpful support for the position allowing the loss carryback in advance of attribute reduction. As stated in the text, this position is now confirmed in the regulations.

[47] Code § 108(b)(2)(B), (3)(B), and (4)(C).

[48] Code § 108(b)(2)(B).

(5) *Capital Loss Carryovers.* The net capital loss of the year of cancellation (first) and the capital loss carryovers to the year of cancellation (second) are reduced.[49] The latter are reduced in the order of the years in which they arose.[50]

(6) *Basis of Property.* The basis of any property of the taxpayer as of the beginning of the tax year following the year of cancellation is reduced.[51] Unlike the elective basis reduction mentioned above and discussed further below, this automatic basis reduction applies to nondepreciable property in addition to depreciable property, but the aggregate basis of such property will not be reduced by more than the amount by which the tax basis of property held immediately after the cancellation exceeds the aggregate liabilities remaining at that time.[52] Thus, a sale of all the assets to pay the liabilities remaining after the debt discharge will not result in an income tax liability unless the proceeds after the sale exceed the remaining liabilities. Effective for debt cancellations on or after September 11, 1995, Reg. § 1.108-3 also treats as additional basis subject to reduction any intercompany loss or deduction deferred under Code § 267(f) or Reg. § 1.1502-13. The order in which the basis of property is to be reduced was determined under the rules applicable to prior law under Reg. § § 1.1016-7 and 1.1016-8 until new regulations were issued.[53] These new regulations were issued on October 22, 1998 as Reg. § 1.1017-1. These do not have retroactive effect, and determine the order in which the basis of property is reduced only for COD occurring on or after October 22, 1998. Basis reduction under this provision does not result in ITC recapture.[54] Any gain on subsequent disposition of the property will result in Code § 1245 or 1250 ordinary income recapture, in the same manner as for elective basis reductions.[55] One way that at least one taxpayer had found to avoid the automatic basis reduction from COD was to utilize a "G" reorganization of the debtor's assets. During the year that the COD arose, the debtor transferred all of its assets to another corporation in a "G" reorganization. The IRS in a 2001 Field Service Advice memorandum agreed that the basis of these transferred assets was not reduced by the COD, because the automatic basis reduction from the COD is made only as of the beginning of the tax year following the year of cancellation, and in that year the debtor has no property at all. To avail oneself of this device it was necessary that the reorganization be a "G" reorganization, and not just an "F" reorganization.[56] However, there were in 2001 at least two authorities that suggested a different conclusion on the question

---

49 Code § 108(b)(2)(A) and (4)(B).

50 Code § 108(b)(4)(B).

51 Code § § 108(b)(2)(D) and 1017(a).

52 Code § 1017(b)(2).

53 S. Rep. No. 1035, 96th Cong., 2d Sess. 14 (1980); H.R. Rep. No. 833, 96th Cong., 2d Sess. 11 (1980); *see* Pollack, *supra* note 41.

54 Code § 1017(c)(2); Rev. Rul. 81-206, 1981-2 C.B. 9.

55 Code § 1017(d) (33$^{1}/_{3}$ rate reduction effective for taxable years beginning after 1986; prior rate reduction was 50 cents for each dollar of debt reduction); *see* discussion *infra* § 404.3.

56 IRS Field Service Advice 200145009, July 31, 2001 (the IRS in this Advice reasons that a basis reduction would be required in an "F" but not in a "G," but when a reorganization is both an "F" and a "G," "G" primes "F"). *See also* Code § 368(a)(3)(C) ("G" primes all other reorganization types).

whether the basis reduction is avoided in a "G."[57] In 2003, the IRS decided that its 2001 Field Service Advice had been wrong, and corrected its position by issuing Temp. Reg. §§1.108-7T(c) and 1.1017-1T(b)(4) and identical proposed regulations. These regulations provide that in the case of any transaction described in Code §381(a)—such as a "G" reorganization—that ends a taxable year in which the distributor or transferor corporation excludes COD income under Code §108(a), any tax attributes to which the acquiring corporation succeeds—including the basis of property acquired by the acquiring corporation in the transaction—shall reflect the reductions required by Code §108(b). The preamble to these regulations describe them as clarifying in nature; the regulations themselves say they apply to COD occurring after July 17, 2003. These regulations were made final in 2004 as Reg. §§1.108-7(c) and 1.1017-1(b)(4), effective for COD occurring on or after May 10, 2004. These final regulations expand the scope of the temporary regulations by providing that they apply if the taxpayer realizes COD excluded under Code §108(a) *"either during or after* a taxable year in which the taxpayer is the distributor or transferor of assets in a transaction described in section 381(a) . . . " (emphasis added).

(7) *Passive Activity Losses and Credits.* Deductions and credits from passive activities, whose use in earlier years has been suspended under the passive activity loss rules, and which are otherwise available as carryovers from the year of the debt discharge, are reduced. (For the credits, the reduction is at the rate of 33 1/3 cents for each dollar of debt cancellation.) This provision was added by the 1993 Act and is applicable to debt discharges occurring in taxable years beginning after December 31, 1993.

(8) *Foreign Tax Credit Carryovers.* Foreign tax credit carryovers to or from the year of cancellation are reduced (at the rate of 33 1/3 cents for each dollar of debt cancellation) in the order in which they would be taken into account in the year of cancellation.[58]

To the extent the amount of debt cancellation exceeds the amount of tax attributes available to be reduced, the cancellation is simply excluded from income.[59]

Until the late 1990s, the IRS had held that the attribute reduction rules of Code §108 are to be applied on a separate company basis, even for members of a consolidated return group, without affecting the attributes of any other member of the group.[60] However, in the late 1990s the IRS asserted that COD income of one member of the group will reduce the consolidated NOL, even though the member

[57] First, there is an example on p. 34 of H.R. Rep. No. 96-833, 96th Cong., 2d Sess. (March 19, 1980) that states an elective basis reduction made by the debtors just before its "G" reorganization would reduce the basis of the property in the hands of its successor in the "G"; second, IRS Letter Ruling 9226064, March 31, 1992, which is discussed at §508.4.3 below, seems to be to the same effect.

[58] Code §108(b)(1)(E), (3)(B) and (4)(C).

[59] S. Rep. No. 1035, 96th Cong., 2d Sess. 13 (1980); H.R. Rep. No. 833, 96th Cong., 2d Sess. 11 (1980).

[60] *See, e.g.*, IRS Letter Ruling 9650019, September 11, 1996; IRS Letter Ruling 9121017, February 21, 1991. However, in one such ruling, the IRS declined to express an opinion as to the treatment of any excluded COD income in excess of the discharged member's separate tax attributes. *See* IRS Letter Ruling 9122067, March 6, 1991 (holding #24).

did not contribute any of the losses making up the consolidated NOL.[61] The 2001 Supreme Court opinion in *United Dominion Industries, Inc. v. United States*[62] seemed likely to cause the IRS to adhere to that position regarding the reduction of consolidated group NOLs, and perhaps even to lead to efforts to apply certain other aspects of Code § 108 to members of consolidated return groups on a combined group basis, rather than separately to the debtor member having the COD item. Indeed, in 2003, the IRS issued temporary and proposed regulations to do just that. *See* the discussion at § § 804.4.1 and 804.4.5 below.

Code § 108(b)(4)(A) provides that the attribute reductions are made only after the determination of tax for the year of discharge. The intent of this provision appears to be that the reductions can only affect tax liability for years after the year of debt cancellation.

**EXAMPLE**

> Bankrupt debtor corporation in the year of a $2 million debt cancellation has $1 million of taxable income before taking into account a $1.5 million NOL carryover from a prior year. Even though the NOL attribute reduction language of Code § 108(b)(2)(A) refers to reducing NOL carryovers to the year of cancellation, $1 million of the carryover will be used to reduce the taxable income for the year of discharge to zero and only the remaining $500,000 of the carryover, which would otherwise be available as a carryover to the next year, is subject to reduction as a result of the debt cancellation.

If the debtor is a corporation which has made a subchapter S election, Code § 108(d)(7)(A) provides that Code § 108 shall be applied at the corporate level. One consequence of this is that the insolvency test for the cancellation of S corporation debt is to be applied at the corporate level rather than at the shareholder level. Thus, the exception can apply even if the shareholder is solvent. (This differs from the rule applicable to partnerships, where Code § 108(d)(6) provides that the insolvency test for the cancellation of partnership debt is to be applied at the partner, not the partnership level.) Although an S corporation does not generate NOLs in S years, Code § 108(d)(7)(B) provides that any S-period losses for a taxable year whose deductibility has been suspended for that taxable year at the shareholder level because of lack of shareholder basis shall be treated as NOLs subject to the attribute reduction rules.

If these rules could be applied literally and without exception, the following could occur. Suppose an insolvent S corporation has $1 million of debt cancellation

---

[61] IRS Legal Memorandum 200149008, August 10, 2001; IRS Field Service Advice 199912007, December 14, 1998 (mentioning IRS Letter Ruling 9121017, cited in preceding footnote, and saying that the IRS would not adhere to the position taken in that ruling with respect to consolidated attributes), *reprinted at* 1999 TNT 59-56.

[62] 121 S. Ct. 1934, 2001-1 U.S.T.C. ¶ 50,430 (2001).

and no other income or expense. Its shareholder has $1.2 million of suspended losses from the S corporation from prior years, and $700,000 of current income from other sources. The $1 million of debt cancellation would be excluded from taxable income. It would be treated as "tax-exempt income" that, by virtue of Code § 1366(a)(1), increases his zero basis in the S corporation stock to $1 million. Because attribute reduction occurs only after the taxable income for the current year has been computed, the shareholder can deduct $700,000 of his suspended S corporation losses against his $700,000 of other income for the current year, and only the remaining $500,000 of suspended losses are eliminated under the attribute reduction rules.

Since such a literal application of the rules would give the shareholder the benefit of the corporate-level insolvency exemption without having to suffer the full elimination of the suspended corporate losses, the IRS considered that it conflicted with the policy of the attribute reduction rules, and must not have been intended by Congress. Accordingly, it disallowed such use of the suspended losses. Much litigation ensued, producing conflicts among the Courts of Appeal, which were finally resolved by the Supreme Court, which held that the statutory language was so clear and unambiguous that, in fact, it had to be applied literally.[63] The final chapter in this story was written by Congress, which in 2002 amended Code § 108(d)(7) to eliminate the basis increase for the S corporation shareholder. The statutory amendment applies to COD occurring after October 11, 2001, in taxable years ending after that date, with an exception for COD arising before March 1, 2002, pursuant to a plan of reorganization filed with a bankruptcy court on or before October 11, 2001.

The IRS has ruled that no NOL arising from a C corporation year is affected by debt discharges occurring during an S corporation year.[64]

## § 404.3 *Solvent Taxpayers Not in Bankruptcy*

To the extent that the exceptions to COD income discussed above do not apply, debt cancellation for solvent taxpayers not in bankruptcy generally produces immediate taxable income,[65] except to the extent the taxpayer elects (for debt cancellations

---

[63] *Gitlitz v. Commissioner*, 121 S. Ct. 701, 2001-1 U.S.T.C. ¶ 50,147 (2001). The cases preceding this resolution of the issue are described in Lipton and Bots, Gitlitz and Winn, Petitioners v. Commissioner of Internal Revenue, Respondent, 28 J. Corp. Tax'n 3 (Jan./Feb. 2001). The IRS has permitted S corporations to rescind basis elections made when they did not anticipate the Supreme Court opinion in *Gitlitz*. IRS Letter Ruling 200208016, November 21, 2001; IRS Letter Ruling 200210044, December 6, 2001.

The IRS had incorporated its position in Reg. § 1.1366-1(a)(2)(viii), effective for tax years beginning on or after August 18, 1998. This regulation was not mentioned by the Supreme Court in its opinion; but given the reasoning of the opinion, one has to assume that the regulation is invalid.

[64] IRS Letter Ruling 9541001, November 30, 1994.

[65] In addition, Code § 108(g) contains an exception for discharge of "qualified farm indebtedness." The IRS has held that, in the case of a consolidated return, the gross receipts test for determining whether the debtor is a qualified farmer should be applied on a separate corporation basis rather than on a consolidated basis. IRS Field Service Advice 1999-513 (undated), *reprinted at* 1999 TNT 15-82. Two other exceptions—the exception in Code § 108(f) for student loans and an elective basis reduction provision added by the 1993 Act as Code § 108(c) for certain real property indebtedness—are not available for C corporations. The latter provision has been given a rather expansive interpreta-

occurring before 1987) to reduce the basis in depreciable assets (and has such basis to reduce).[66] While COD income is ordinary income, its character for certain provisions of the Code may be determined by the character of the debt that was cancelled. For example, it has been held that COD income will be treated as income from a passive activity for purposes of Code § 469 to the extent the cancelled debt was allocable to passive activity expenditures.[67]

**Election available for debt cancellations occurring before 1987.** The depreciable basis election that was available for debt cancellations before 1987 applied to debtors not in bankruptcy who were solvent both before and after the debt cancellation, and to those who were insolvent before, to the extent the debt cancellation caused the value of their assets afterward to exceed their remaining liabilities.[68]

The election had the same consequences for solvent taxpayers outside bankruptcy as the election to reduce depreciable basis still has for insolvent taxpayers and taxpayers in bankruptcy, except that for the former the order of the property in which basis was reduced was governed under then existing Reg. §§ 1.1017-1 and 1.1017-2.[69]

For purposes of the election, "depreciable property" means any property subject to the allowance for depreciation, but only if the basis reduction will reduce the

---

(Footnote Continued)

tion making it applicable to debt that refinances earlier real estate debt. IRS Technical Advice Memorandum 200014007, December 13, 1999.

[66] Code § 61(a)(12); Tax Reform Act of 1986, Pub. L. No. 99-514, § 822(b)(2) (repeal of basis reduction election of "old" Code § 108(c)). For solvent taxpayers, only "qualified business indebtedness" qualifies for the election. Old Code § 108(a)(1)(C). However, in the case of a corporation, the qualified business indebtedness limitation is irrelevant, because any indebtedness of a corporation is treated as qualified business indebtedness. *See* old Code § 108(d)(4). For a discussion of the considerations involved in deciding whether to make such an election, *see* articles cited *supra* note 41; *see also* Lassila and Putnam, The Discharge of "Qualified Business Indebtedness": Should the Section 108(d)(4) Election Be Made? 36 Tax Executive 365 (1984) (presents an economic decision model).

[67] Rev. Rul. 92-92, 1992-2 C.B. 103.

[68] *See* Code § 108(a)(2)(B); *see also supra* note 5 (liabilities taken into account in insolvency determination).

[69] S. Rep. No. 1035, 96th Cong., 2d Sess. 15 (1980); H.R. Rep. No. 833, 96th Cong., 2d Sess. 13 (1980); *see supra* § 404.2. Rev. Proc. 85-44, 1985-2 C.B. 504, sets forth conditions under which a solvent debtor can obtain advance IRS approval to reduce the basis of selective, rather than all, depreciable property, including:

(1) cancellation not subject to purchase price reduction rules of Code § 108(e)(5);
(2) no plan or intention to dispose of selected properties;
(3) weighted average remaining "useful life" of selected properties (for purposes of Code § 168 ACRS rules) no longer than weighted average remaining useful life of all debtor's depreciable/amortizable property (excluding property fully depreciated at beginning of the taxable year following the taxable year of discharge); and
(4) basis of selected assets will fully absorb the COD income (disregarding salvage value of assets subject to Code § 167 depreciation).

A copy of the ruling and closing agreement must be attached, along with the debtor's election to treat the cancelled debt as "qualified business indebtedness," to the debtor's tax return for the taxable year in which the discharge occurred. *See, e.g.*, IRS Letter Ruling 8602013, August 26, 1985; IRS Letter Ruling 8552020, August 8, 1985; IRS Letter Ruling 8552014, August 8, 1985; IRS Letter Ruling 8552013, August 8, 1985; IRS Letter Ruling 8547029, April 24, 1985; IRS Letter Ruling 8545009, April 24, 1985.

amount of depreciation or amortization otherwise allowable for the period immediately following the reduction.[70]

Depreciable property, in addition to property normally subject to the allowance for depreciation, also includes:

(1) any real property treated as inventory, if the debtor so elects;[71]
(2) the stock of a subsidiary with which the debtor files a consolidated return, but only to the extent the subsidiary consents to a corresponding reduction in the basis of its depreciable property;[72] and
(3) an interest of a partner in a partnership, to the extent of the partner's proportionate interest in depreciable property of the partnership, but only if there is a corresponding reduction in the partnership's basis in depreciable property with respect to such partner.[73]

The election applies to the basis of property held by the taxpayer at the beginning of the taxable year following the year of debt cancellation.[74] This is done in order to avoid interaction between the basis reduction and the reduction of other attributes for bankrupt and insolvent taxpayers,[75] but it applies as well to solvent taxpayers not in bankruptcy. It means that the basis reduction will not apply to assets disposed of during the year of debt cancellation, and that it can apply to assets acquired after the debt cancellation took place. This gives a taxpayer some latitude for tax planning in picking the assets to which the election applies.

---

[70] Code § 1017(b)(3)(B). The legislative history of Code § 1017 gives, as an example of property that would not be depreciable, property subject to a lease where the debtor is the lessor of the property and the lessee is obligated to restore to the lessor the loss in value due to depreciation during the lease. S. Rep. No. 1035, 96th Cong., 2d Sess. 13 n.14 (1980); H.R. Rep. No. 833, 96th Cong., 2d Sess. 11 n.14 (1980). This example is repeated in the regulations. Reg. § 1.1017-1(e). This example appears to be premised on pre-1981 Economic Recovery Tax Act (ERTA) decisions such as *Kem v. Commissioner*, 432 F.2d 961, 963 (9th Cir. 1970), which held that where any possible loss was restored to lessors, salvage value equals original cost; therefore, lessors were not entitled to depreciation deductions. However, Code § 168 has eliminated the concept of salvage value. Code § 168(b)(4) ("salvage value shall be treated as zero"). *See also Simon v. Commissioner*, 68 F.3d 41, 45 (2d Cir. 1995) ("Congress' intent to do away with salvage value is indisputable"); *Liddle v. Commissioner*, 65 F.3d 329, 333 (3d Cir. 1995) ("entire cost or other basis of eligible property is recovered under ACRS eliminating the salvage value limitation of prior depreciation law"). In view of this change in law regarding depreciation, the leased property in the example described above may well be depreciable property today.

[71] Code § 1017(b)(3)(E).

[72] Code § 1017(b)(3)(D). This rule can be applied successively through a chain of corporations as long as the lowest tier subsidiary reduces its basis in actual depreciable property (or realty held as inventory). Id.; S. Rep. No. 1035, 96th Cong 2d Sess. 13 n.15 (1980). For an example in which a parent corporation successfully utilized this technique by contributing the stock of a subsidiary to the capital of another subsidiary, thereby increasing the amount of depreciable assets down through the chain that became available for this election, *see* IRS Letter Ruling 9650019, September 11, 1996.

[73] Code § 1017(b)(3)(C); S. Rep. No. 1035, 96th Cong., 2d Sess. 21-22 n.28; *see* Asofsky, Discharge of Indebtedness, *supra* note 1, at 595-596 (indicates that partnership's adjustment of its basis, in a Code § 754-like manner, would probably be deemed a consent to partner's treatment of partnership interest as depreciable property).

[74] Code § 1017(a). For the application of this rule to cases where the taxpayer is a transferor in a Code § 381(a) transaction and has no subsequent tax year, *see* the discussion at § 404.2(6) above.

[75] S. Rep. No. 1035, 96th Cong., 2d Sess. 14 (1980).

The election is made by attaching a statement with a completed Form 982 to the debtor's tax return for the year of cancellation. A late election will be accepted only if the Commissioner is satisfied that there was reasonable cause for the lateness.[76] An election cannot be revoked without the consent of the Commissioner.[77]

The election can reduce the basis of assets below the amount of remaining liabilities, but not below zero.[78] The reduction in basis does not result in investment tax credit recapture.[79] However, regardless of the character of the property involved, the basis reduction is treated as a depreciation deduction for applying the recapture rules of Code §§1245 and 1250 and any property that is neither Code §1245 nor §1250 property is treated for this purpose as Code §1245 property.[80] This means that any gain subsequently recognized on the sale of property that is not Code §1250 property will be treated as Code §1245 ordinary income recapture to the extent of the basis reduction. For purposes of Code §1250 recapture, the amount of straight-line depreciation that would have been taken on the property is computed without regard to the basis reduction for purposes of determining whether the depreciation taken has exceeded straight-line depreciation.[81] Thus, if the property is held long enough, the basis reduction may not result in Code §1250 recapture.[82]

Where an election has been made to treat subsidiary stock or a partnership interest as depreciable property, both the stock or the partnership interest and the underlying depreciable property of the subsidiary or partnership are tainted by the Code §1245 or §1250 recapture rules.[83] Unless regulations to be issued provide otherwise, recognition of recapture in the underlying assets of the subsidiary or partnership does not appear to remove the recapture taint in the stock or partnership interest, or vice versa.[84] This should be taken into account before electing to reduce basis in subsidiary stock or a partnership interest.

## *§404.4 Effect of COD Income on Earnings and Profits*

Except to the extent that COD income results in a basis reduction, the earnings and profits of a corporate debtor are increased by any COD income.[85] This is true regardless of whether the COD income only produces attribute reduction (other than

---

76 Temp. Reg. §7a.1(d)(1).

77 Code §108(d)(9); Temp. Reg. §7a.1(e).

78 *Cf.* Code §1017(b)(2).

79 Code §1017(c)(2); Rev. Rul. 81-206, 1981-2 C.B. 9.

80 Code §1017(d)(1).

81 Code §1017(d)(2).

82 *See generally* Pollack, *supra* note 41.

83 *See* explanation of these recapture rules at Stand. Fed. Tax Rep. (CCH) ¶¶32,509 and 32,606.

84 Id.; *see also* Scranton, *supra* note 21, at 80.

85 Code §312(l)(1) as amended by the Bankruptcy Tax Act of 1980. The IRS has rejected a taxpayer's assertion that only accumulated earnings and profits, and not current earnings and profits, should be increased under this provision. The taxpayer had a deficit in accumulated earnings and profits that exceeded in amount the taxpayer's current COD income and, but for its COD income, had no current earnings and profits. The taxpayer had made a distribution to its shareholders during the year, and claimed that the distribution was a return of capital. The IRS rejected the taxpayer's position and held

basis reduction) instead of immediate recognition of income and even if it exceeds the amount of attribute reduction and is excluded from income.[86] If a debt cancellation satisfies one of the exceptions to COD income (such as the stock-for-debt exception) other than the Code § 111 exception, however, the cancellation should not increase earnings and profits.[87]

## § 404.5 *Effect of Excluded COD Income on Alternative Minimum Tax*

For tax years beginning before 1990, a special concern for the failing or failed company was that debt cancellation usually (although not always) produced book income under generally accepted accounting principles, even where one of the exceptions to the creation of taxable income, such as the stock-for-debt exception, applies. Thus, where the company reduces its debt and the debt reduction is excluded from regular taxable income because one of the exceptions to COD income applies, the fact that the debt reduction is included in book income could subject the company to the AMT when the AMT included a book income factor, making the AMT particularly inescapable for the failing company. (*See* § § 404.1, 504A.6, 505, 511, and 708.)

The Technical and Miscellaneous Revenue Act of 1988, through an amendment to Code § 56(f)(2), eliminated this problem where the exclusion that applied to COD income was the stock-for-debt exception.[88] Like the stock-for-debt exception (*see* § 504A.1), it applies only to (1) debtors in title 11 cases and (2) insolvent debtors (to the extent the debtor is not rendered solvent). The amendment applies to taxable

---

(Footnote Continued)

that the COD created earnings and profits, causing the distribution to be treated as a dividend. IRS Field Service Advice 1999-540 (undated), *reprinted at* 1999 TNT 15-83.

[86] *See* Strobel & Strobel, The Effect on Earnings and Profits of the Forgiveness of Indebtedness Pursuant to Discharge in Bankruptcy, 12 J. Corp. Tax'n 359 (1985); but consider Scranton, *supra* note 24, at 79-80 (indicating that a different reading of Code § 312(l)(1) may be possible as it relates to attribute reductions other than basis).

[87] *See* S. Rep. No. 445, 100th Cong., 2d Sess. 96 (1988); Joint Committee on Taxation, Staff Description of Amendment Proposing Additional Tax Law Changes and Tax Increases to H.R. 4333, released July 13, 1988, at 72. For pre-1980 authorities, *see* Rev. Rul. 66-353, 1966-2 C.B. 11 (earnings and profits not increased by contributions to capital); *Western Maryland Railway Co. v. United States*, 131 F. Supp. 873, 893-894, 55-1 U.S.T.C. ¶ 49,136 (D. Md. 1955) (excess profits case; in conjunction with a determination of "equity invested capital," the court, in an alternative holding, held that debtor's accumulated earnings and profits was not increased where stock-for-debt exception applied to preclude COD); *cf. Annis Van Nuys Schweppe*, 8 T.C. 1224, Dec. 15,838 (1947), *aff'd per curiam*, 168 F.2d 284, 48-1 U.S.T.C. ¶ 9280 (9th Cir. 1948) (earnings and profits increased since court found that cancellation did not constitute a capital contribution). The "substitution of liability" theory upon which the stock-for-debt exception is grounded (*see* § 504A.3) also supports no increase to earnings and profits. *Cf.* Eustice, Cancellation of Indebtedness and the Federal Income Tax: A Problem of Creeping Confusion, 14 Tax L. Rev. 225, 238-240 (1959) ("There is no present realization of income but rather a transmutation or downgrading of the debt interest into an equity interest, which is purely a capital transaction").

[88] Technical and Miscellaneous Revenue Act of 1988, Pub. L. No. 100-647, 100th Cong., 2d Sess., § 6303.

years beginning after 1986 and applies even where the *de minimis* and proportionality requirements of the stock-for-debt exception have not been met.

The amendment did not eliminate the book-income problem where the debt reduction was excluded from COD income (but not book income) by reason of other provisions, such as the capital-contribution exception, the basis-adjustment exception, etc.

For tax years beginning after 1989, the AMT is computed by using adjusted earnings and profits (ACE) rather than book income as its base. Under the ACE method of computing the AMT, this problem has been eliminated by Code § 56(g)(4)(B), as amended by the Revenue Reconciliation Act of 1989, which provides that earnings and profits for this purpose shall not include any amount excluded from gross income by Code § 108 (or corresponding provisions of prior law).

## *§ 404.6 Contested Liabilities*

The prior discussion assumes that the amount of the debt that is being modified, exchanged, or forgiven is a known, liquidated number. In such cases, one's inquiry relates not so much to determining the amount of the debt discharge, but to the potential consequences of the cancellation.

There are many cases, however, where the amount of the debt is itself in dispute. In the event the disputed claim is settled or adjudicated for less than the claimed amount, the question then becomes whether the difference is COD. As the following examples indicate, disputed claims arise in a wide variety of factual contexts, and the answers are not necessarily the same for each dispute.

**EXAMPLE 1**

Painter agrees to paint a building for a price equal to time and materials. After completing the job, he submits a bill for $100,000. The building owner considers this too much and refuses to pay. Painter sues for $100,000. The court decides the job was worth $90,000, that this is all the painter was entitled to receive, and enters judgment for that amount, which the owner pays. Does the owner have $10,000 of COD income? The answer should be no. Although the painter claimed that $100,000 was due, the owner disputed the validity of that claim, and the court's decision means there never was an obligation for $100,000, only an obligation for $90,000.[89]

---

[89] *See generally*, Culp & Marsh, Avoiding Cancellation of Debt Income Where the Liability Is Disputed, 74 J. Taxation 288 (1991). Because in this example services are involved rather than the sale of property, the purchase price adjustment provisions of Code § 108(e)(5) would not apply.

### EXAMPLE 2

The facts are the same as in Example 1, except that instead of going all the way to court judgment, the parties settle the dispute by agreeing that owner only owes painter $90,000, which owner thereupon pays. The answer is the same as in Example 1.[90]

### EXAMPLE 3

Plaintiff sues defendant for $1 million, alleging damages from environmental pollution and negligence. Defendant disputes liability and finally settles the claim for $200,000. The answer is the same as in Example 2. There never was a debt for more than $200,000, and since defendant has paid that amount, there is no COD.[91]

### EXAMPLE 4

The facts are the same as in Example 3, except that instead of agreeing to pay plaintiff $200,000, defendant settles the case by agreeing to deliver Greenacre to plaintiff on May 10. When the settlement agreement is reached, the parties believe that Greenacre is worth $250,000. However, on May 10 an appraisal shows it to be worth only $210,000. Does defendant have $40,000 of COD? The answer should be no. The disputed claim

---

[90] The fact that settlement rather than judgment is involved should not change the result. *See N. Sobel, Inc. v. Commissioner*, 40 B.T.A. 1263, Dec. 10, 393 (1939); *Zarin v. Commissioner*, 916 F.2d 110, 90-2 U.S.T.C. ¶50,530 (3d Cir. 1990). In each of these cases, the taxpayer contested the validity of the entire amount of the debt but then settled the contest by paying a fraction of the amount claimed. The courts held there was no COD. To the same effect, *see* IRS Letter Ruling 200243034, July 26, 2002 (Ruling 10). For a case involving settlement of a credit card liability where a portion of the liability was liquidated and the remainder (interest and penalties) was not, *see Earnshaw v. Commissioner*, T.C. Memo. 2002-191 (COD was not produced by canceling the unliquidated portion, but was produced to the extent the cancellation extended to the liquidated amount), *aff'd in an unpublished decision*, 2005-2 U.S.T.C. ¶50,666 (10th Cir. 2005).

[91] *See* the authorities cited in the two preceding footnotes. *See also United States v. Hall*, 307 F.2d 238, 1962-2 U.S.T.C. ¶9744 (10th Cir. 1962) (unenforceable gambling debt of $245,000, which parties agreed to settle for $150,000, was satisfied by delivering property worth $148,110; held, neither the $245,000 nor the $150,000 figure was relevant, there was no COD, but taxpayer had gain for the difference between his basis and the $148,110 value of the property transferred).

The Tenth Circuit in the *Hall* case based its decision largely on the fact that the gambling debt was unenforceable. In *Preslar v. Commissioner*, 167 F.3d 1323 (10th Cir. 1999), the Tenth Circuit indicated that this reasoning would no longer be accepted by it because it had ceased to believe that unenforceability of a debt eliminated COD income. But the Tenth Circuit added that the holding reached in the *Hall* case was nonetheless proper, since on the unique facts in that case the original amount of the debt was unliquidated, and the contested liability doctrine can apply where the amount of the debt is unliquidated.

> was settled by an agreement that defendant would transfer Greenacre to plaintiff. Defendant did so. There never was a debt for a liquidated dollar amount, only an agreement to transfer Greenacre. Any fluctuation in the value of Greenacre is irrelevant.[92]

Where the dispute arises over what should be paid for the purchase of property, an overlap can occur between the contested claim doctrine and the purchase price adjustment exception to COD (discussed at § 404.1.3 above).

**EXAMPLE 5**

Purchaser acquires property by giving seller a purchase money note for $500,000. Six months later purchaser discovers that seller had made material misrepresentations to induce the sale and succeeds in rescinding the sale. The $500,000 note is therefore cancelled. Purchaser does not have COD. The rescission means that there never was a valid indebtedness.[93]

**EXAMPLE 6**

The facts are the same as in Example 5, except that the parties settle by allowing purchaser to keep the property and by reducing the $500,000 note to $100,000. Does purchaser have $400,000 of COD? The answer is no. Just as in Example 5, the settlement in this example means there never was a valid indebtedness for more than $100,000.[94] Since there is no COD,

---

[92] *United States v. Hall, supra* note 91.

[93] *See Sobel, supra* note 90. The Court of Appeals for the Tenth Circuit would apparently reach this same result by applying the purchase-price exception to COD income, rather than the contested liability concept. The Tenth Circuit takes the position that the contested liability exception can only apply where the original amount of the debt is an unliquidated amount. *Preslar v. Commissioner, infra* note 94.

[94] This, in fact, is essentially the *Sobel* case, *supra* note 90. *Sobel* treated the issue as a contested liability matter, but on the same facts it could just as easily have been treated as a purchase price adjustment issue, as it was in *Commissioner v. Sherman*, 135 F.2d 68, 43-1 U.S.T.C. ¶9367 (6th Cir. 1943). *See also Preslar v. Commissioner*, T.C. Memo. 1996-543, *rev'd*, 167 F.3d 1323 (10th Cir. 1999), where the taxpayer had agreed to purchase property for $1 million but could assign lot sale contracts to the lending bank and be credited on the loan with 95 percent of their stated contract price, even if the lot purchaser later defaulted. When the FDIC took over the lending bank and refused to accept assignment of lot sales contracts, the taxpayer sued for breach of contract. The case was finally settled by bringing the taxpayer's total payments on the $1 million loan to $550,540. The IRS claimed the remaining $449,460 was COD income. The Tax Court held that the contested claim doctrine applied so that there was no COD income. The court did not address the taxpayer's alternative argument that the purchase price adjustment exception to COD applied. The Court of Appeals for the Tenth Circuit reversed the Tax Court. The Tenth Circuit held that the contested liability doctrine should only apply where the original amount of the loan was unliquidated, and two of the three Tenth Circuit judges in the case believed that the facts did not support the claim that the originally intended amount of the loan was to be something other than its face amount. Thus, the loan was originally in a fixed

one need not reach the question of whether the purchase price reduction exception applies. This situation is to be distinguished from the facts dealt with in Rev. Rul. 84-176.[95] There, a taxpayer ordered six lots of goods. After shipping $1,000x worth of these goods, the seller failed to ship the remainder. Taxpayer refused to pay $1,000x. Seller sued taxpayer, and taxpayer counterclaimed for lost profits resulting from the breach of contract. The parties settled, with the taxpayer paying seller $500x and with the claims and counterclaims being dropped. The ruling holds that the $500x of debt reduction was ordinary income to the taxpayer in payment of damages and was not cancellation of debt income. The critical fact here was that the taxpayer did not dispute that $1,000x was owed for the purchase of the goods delivered. Thus, Code § 108 did not apply.

### EXAMPLE 7

Purchaser acquires property by giving seller a purchase money note for $500,000. A year later, because of an unexpected event the property becomes much less able to produce income and purchaser's ability to pay the note becomes much less certain. The parties agree to reduce the note to $300,000. Does purchaser have $200,000 of COD? Here, the validity of the debt is not disputed. Thus, the contested liability doctrine should not apply. However, if purchaser is still solvent and not in bankruptcy, the statutory purchase price reduction exception of Code § 108(e)(5) should apply to eliminate the COD.

### EXAMPLE 8

The facts are the same as in Example 7, except that when the later unexpected event occurs, purchaser contests its liability to pay more than $300,000. This should not change the conclusions reached in Example 7. Unless the grounds for disputing all or a portion of a liability go to the fundamental question whether the liability was created at all, the contested liability doctrine should not apply.

---

(Footnote Continued)

liquidated amount, and the liability for this full amount was not therefore an unliquidated amount when the loan was made. The third judge disagreed on the facts, and would have affirmed the Tax Court. The majority also held that the purchase price exception did not apply, since the debt was third-party debt, and the debt reduction was not related to fraud or misrepresentation connected to the original sale. *See*, on this latter point, the discussion in § 404.1.3 above.

[95] 1984-2 C.B. 34.

**EXAMPLE 9**

The IRS asserts that a taxpayer has underpaid its taxes, and issues a deficiency notice stating that the taxpayer owes an additional $300,000 in income taxes, plus interest of $20,000 and penalties of $5,000. The taxpayer disputes the claim, and the case is eventually settled by a compromise agreement whereby the taxpayer pays only $40,000 to the IRS. Does the remainder of the amount claimed by the IRS constitute COD income? The answer is no.[96]

The *Zarin* case[97] provides a vivid example of the application of the contested liability doctrine. Zarin incurred $3.4 million of gambling debts. The casino sued, and Zarin defended on the ground that under local law gambling debts were unenforceable. Zarin finally settled the claim by paying $500,000. The IRS argued that the debt cancellation produced COD. The court held it did not, for two reasons. First, because the debt was unenforceable, there never was an indebtedness to be cancelled. To come within the COD rules, there must first be, as required by Code § 108(d)(1), an indebtedness "for which the taxpayer is liable, or . . . subject to which the taxpayer holds property." Neither condition existed here. Second, the claim was a contested claim, and the settlement of the claim determined that no more than $500,000 was owing. The court's conclusion seems eminently correct. Unfortunately, an example used in the opinion to illustrate the contested liability doctrine is over broad, and for this reason the IRS may be unwilling to accept the opinion. After stating that "Under the contested liability doctrine, if a taxpayer, in good faith, disputed the amount of a debt, a subsequent settlement of the dispute would be treated as the amount of debt cognizable for tax purposes," a perfectly correct statement, the court illustrated it with this example. A taxpayer took out a loan for $10,000, refused in good faith to pay the full $10,000 back, and then reached an agreement with the lender to pay back

---

[96] *Eagle Asbestos & Packing Co. v. United States*, 348 F.2d 528 (Ct. Cl. 1965); OM 19866, I-201-84 (Nov. 26, 1984); IRS Field Service Advice 1998-297, dated May 28, 1992, *reprinted at* 98 TNT 197-93; IRS Service Center Advice Memorandum 1998-039, April 1, 1998, *reprinted at* 98 TNT 250-34. These authorities dealing with the compromise of federal tax matters go beyond the general concept regarding contested liabilities because they add as an additional reason for eliminating COD consequences the concept that the compromise is intended to extinguish all tax liabilities arising from the items compromised, including the consequences of the compromise itself. As a result, even if the taxpayer had deducted the interest claimed by the IRS, the extinguishment of the interest liability would not have created COD income. These authorities also indicate that the tax benefit rule would not apply to create income from such a compromise agreement. This represents a change from earlier IRS positions. *See Yale Avenue Corp. v. Commissioner*, 58 T.C. 1062 (1972) (where prior stipulated federal tax liability was later compromised for a lower amount, the difference was held to be COD income, though the parties did not cite the *Bradford* case and so the court expressly (*see* its footnote 5) did not deal with the concept that the avoidance of a loss of assets, rather than the ability to keep assets earlier received without tax, does not produce COD income); Beck, Is Compromise of a Tax Liability Itself Taxable? A Problem of Circularity in the Logic of Taxation, 14 Va. Tax Rev. 153 (1994).

[97] *Zarin, supra* note 90. The IRS, in IRS Legal Memorandum 200039037, July 27, 2000, *reprinted at* 2000 TNT 191-45, has indicated that it disagrees with the holding in the *Zarin* case. However, in this memorandum, the IRS held that, where the gambling casino had told the gambler in advance that it would discount any net losses by 30 percent, the discount did not produce COD income because it was essentially a purchase price reduction.

only $7,000 in full satisfaction of the debt. The court suggested that on these facts there would be no COD. This seems to go too far. If the loan was valid when taken out, and the dispute arose for later reasons, the reduction in the liability should produce COD income, unless additional facts would suggest application of the purchase price exception. *See* Example 7 above.[98] Moreover, if the loan was a cash and not a purchase price loan and the debtor was allowed to keep the $3,000 of cash that was not originally his, even if the ground for the contest related back to the inception of the loan, income of some sort should result from allowing him to keep the cash.

The Tenth Circuit in *Preslar* has disagreed with the *Zarin* opinion.[99] In *Preslar*, the taxpayer had borrowed money to purchase property, and argued that the loan was to be repaid not at original face value but at a formula based on the sales price of the property. A subsequent holder of the debt believed that the full face amount was owed, but because of this dispute the loan was settled for less than the face amount. The taxpayer argued that the contested liability exception applied to eliminate any COD income.[100] The Tenth Circuit, disagreeing with the Tax Court, held that the loan had originally been intended to be repaid at its face amount, and held that the contested liability exception could not apply unless the original amount of the debt was for an unliquidated amount. As indicated above in Example 7, we agree that debt reduction caused by a later-arising dispute or by later uncollectability does not make the contested liability doctrine applicable. This would not require any disagreement with *Zarin*, where the debt was settled for a lesser amount because of a defect in the debt that existed *ab initio, i.e.*, its original unenforceability. The concept of "unenforceability," however, gave the Tenth Circuit difficulty. The court pointed to

---

98 This conclusion is supported by the holding in another gambling debt case, *Rood v. Commissioner*, T.C. Memo. 1996-248. Here a gambling debt that was enforceable under local law was settled for a lesser amount. Although the taxpayer asserted that the aggregate amount of the debt was in dispute, the court found the evidence did not support this, and held the forgiven portion of the debt to constitute COD income.

99 *Preslar v. Commissioner* (10th Cir.), *supra* note 91. The *Preslar* case has been criticized in Note, Challenges to Enforceability of a Debt Do Not Trigger the Contested Liability Exception to the Discharge-of-Indebtedness Income Rule: *Preslar v. Commissioner*, 53 Tax Lawyer 535 (2000). The Fifth Circuit, in *Estate of Smith v. Commissioner*, 198 F.3d 515, 2000-1 U.S.T.C. ¶50,147 (5th Cir. 1999), noted the disagreement of the *Preslar* court with the *Zarin* court, but said it did not have to choose between them because in the case before it both the amount and the enforceability of the debt were being contested by the taxpayer. The taxpayer was an estate. When decedent died, a claim had been made against him which was contested by the estate in its entirety. The estate deducted the entire asserted amount of the claim in computing its estate tax, but succeeded in settling the claim fifteen months later for a much smaller amount. The IRS had argued that only the actual settlement amount could be used as a deduction against the estate tax, and had argued, in the alternative, that if a larger amount could be used for that purpose, the difference between that amount and the settlement amount would represent COD income. The Fifth Circuit disagreed with both conclusions, saying that the estate tax required an estimated amount of the liability as of the date of death based on the facts known as of that date, whereas the estimated value of the contingent liability at the date of death would be irrelevent for purposes of the income tax. For purposes of the latter, the contested liability doctrine would treat the settlement amount as the amount of the debt and thus avoid creating any COD income.

100 The taxpayer had argued in the alternative that the purchase price exception to COD income should apply, but the court held that the loan was a third-party loan that did not qualify for either the statutory or the common law purchase price exception.

the undisputed fact that failure to collect the face amount of a nonrecourse debt because of a decline in value of its security produced COD income, and extrapolated this into a broad conclusion that unenforceability cannot be a defense to COD income. The difficulty with the Tenth Circuit's reasoning is that it fails to recognize the difference between unenforceability caused by later-arising disputes or collection problems (the nonrecourse debt example) and unenforceability attributable to original invalidity of the debt. It is this failure that allows it to make a blanket condemnation of unenforceability as a basis for invoking the contested liability exception to COD income, and that leads to its disagreement with *Zarin*. The Tenth Circuit's entire discussion of *Zarin* might be viewed as *dictum*.

As mentioned at §403.4 above, the preamble to final Reg. §1.6050P contains a recognition by the IRS that the settlement of disputed liabilities does not always create COD income.

## *§404.7 Acquisition of Debt by Related Party*

Code §108(e)(4) provides that "For purposes of determining income of the debtor from discharge of indebtedness, to the extent provided in regulations," the acquisition of outstanding indebtedness by a person related to the debtor from a person who is not so related shall be treated as an acquisition by the debtor. The section adds that such regulations "shall provide for such adjustments in the treatment of any subsequent transactions involving the indebtedness as may be appropriate . . ."

Code §108(e)(4) provides that persons are related to the debtor for this purpose if they bear a relationship to the debtor specified in Code §§267(b) or 707(b)(1). Special family attribution rules are prescribed. In addition, entities treated as a single employer under Code §414(b) or (c) are treated as related. Although this provision was adopted in 1980, no regulations were issued until Prop. Reg. §1.108-2 was released on March 21, 1991.[101]

Not content with waiting for the proposed regulation to become effective, and concerned about earlier transactions, the IRS issued Rev. Rul. 91-47[102] on September

---

[101] The proposed regulation had a March 21, 1991, effective date. For a discussion of the proposed regulation, *see* §803 n.4 below. The regulation was published in final form on December 29, 1992, with modifications. Although the final regulation, like the proposed regulation, was also made effective for transactions on or after March 21, 1991, the IRS subsequently announced that taxpayers could apply the terms of the original proposed regulation, where these differ from the final regulation, for transactions occurring after March 20, 1991, and before December 28, 1992, provided that all related parties are consistent in applying the proposed regulation to the transaction. IRS Notice 93-40, 1993-2 C.B. 331. For comments on the proposed regulation, *see* New York State Bar Association, Tax Section, Committee on Bankruptcy, Report on Acquisitions of Discount Debt by Related Parties Under the New Section 108(e)(4) Regulation, 52 Tax Notes 211 (July 8, 1991); *see also* Lipton, The Tax Consequences to a Debtor from the Transfer of Its Indebtedness, 69 Taxes 939 (Dec. 1991). For prior writings on Code §108(e)(4), *see* Peaslee, Discharge of Debt Through Its Acquisition by a Person Related to the Debtor—An Analysis of Section 108(e)(4), 37 Tax L. Rev. 193 (1982); New York State Bar Association, Tax Section, Report on Related Party Debt Acquisitions Under Section 108(e)(4) of the Code (April 12, 1984).

[102] 1991-2 C.B. 16.

3, 1991. This deals with a situation where an unrelated person (probably an investment banker) formed a corporation that bought debt with the expectation that the debtor would shortly thereafter buy 100 percent of the stock of the corporation, which it did. The ruling says that because the corporation had no purpose except to avoid COD, the unrelated person's ownership of the corporation will be disregarded and the transaction will be treated as though the debtor had acquired its indebtedness "directly or through a related party" and will have COD equal to the difference between the price it paid for the stock and the issue price of the debt.

Final regulations were issued under Code § 108(e)(4) in December 1992. These regulations (Reg. § 1.108-2) provide that the acquisition of debt by a related person (including a person who becomes related on the same day the debt is acquired) from an unrelated person will produce debt cancellation for the debtor.[103] The amount of the debt cancellation is the difference between the adjusted issue price of the debt and the purchase price paid by the holder, if the debt was acquired in a purchase transaction.

The regulations also provide that debt cancellation can occur from indirect related party acquisitions. Indirect transactions are those in which the holder of the debt becomes related to the debtor, if the debt was acquired by the holder in anticipation of this relationship. Debt acquired by the holder less than six months before becoming related is conclusively deemed to have been acquired in anticipation of the relationship. Otherwise, whether such anticipation existed depends on the facts. The debtor is required to make special disclosure on its return, however, if (1) the holder had acquired the debt from 6 months to 24 months before becoming related; or (2) the debt at the time of becoming related represented more than 25 percent of the value of the holder's (and its affiliates') assets (not counting cash and similar items or interests in members of the holder's group). Failure to make such disclosure adds a rebuttable presumption that the debt was acquired in anticipation of the relationship. In the case of such an indirect related party acquisition, the cancellation event occurs when the relationship is established and is measured by the cost of the debt to the related party, provided the debt was acquired by the related party in a purchase transaction within six months before becoming related. Otherwise the fair market value of the debt is generally used for this measurement.

A special rule provides that the fair market value of the debt (rather than cost) is also used to measure the debt cancellation where the principal purpose of the transaction is avoidance of income tax. An example of such a purpose given in the preamble to the regulations is a transaction that shifts the cancellation income from a domestic corporation to a foreign affiliate.

The regulation does not deal with how to measure the cancellation amount where the debt is acquired in a nonrecognition transaction. An example given in the preamble is a merger of the holder into a subsidiary of the debtor in a tax-free

---

103 The IRS has held, however, that where a debt passes from a related creditor to his estate whose beneficiary is also a related person, the acquisition of the debt will not be treated as an acquisition from an unrelated person even though, technically, the estate is not a related person within the meaning of these provisions. Rev. Proc. 2000-33, 2000-36 I.R.B. 257.

reorganization, or the merger of the debtor with the creditor, or vice versa. Future regulations are expected to be issued to cover this subject.

The regulations provide that if the debtor realizes debt cancellation under these provisions, then the debt is deemed to be new debt issued for the amount (cost or fair market value, as the case may be) used in measuring the amount of the debt cancellation. This can produce OID for both the debtor and the holder, and can also invoke the interest disallowance or deferral rules of Code § 163(e)(5) and (7). The holder, however, is not treated as having gain or loss from the transaction: The holder continues to have the same basis in the "new" debt that it had in the "old" debt. To the extent this basis differs from the amount used in measuring the debt cancellation (and thus the issue price for the new debt), the holder may have issue premium or market discount. If the "new" debt is sold by the holder to an unrelated party, the debt continues in the hands of the unrelated party to have its "new" (rather than its original) adjusted issue price.

The IRS has issued a very helpful ruling articulating what happens under the regulations when a subsidiary, S, purchases from an unrelated third party debt of its parent, P (with which it does not file a consolidated return), for an amount that differs from P's adjusted issue price of the debt, and in the next year (in which S has earnings and profits in excess of the value of the debt) distributes the debt (the market value of which has changed once again) to P. Among other things, the ruling holds that P is treated as receiving a dividend in the amount of the fair market value of the debt on the date of the distribution, and may realize COD income or be entitled to an interest deduction depending on the fair market value of the debt on the date of the distribution relative to the debt's adjusted issue price.[104] The ruling also articulates the other adjustments that P and S need to make in the year of S's purchase and the year of the distribution.

If the related party holder disposes of the debt at a loss, the regulations provide that in certain circumstances the allowance of the loss to the related party holder is deferred. The regulation does not apply to direct or indirect acquisitions of debt having a maturity date not more than a year after the acquisition, provided the debt is in fact retired on or before its maturity date. The regulation also contains an exception for certain transactions by securities dealers.

The regulation is effective for transactions after March 20, 1991.[105] The regulation adds that although it does not apply to previous transactions, "section 108(e)(4) is effective for any transaction after December 31, 1980 . . . " The IRS position is that Code § 108(e)(4) did not require implementing regulations to become effective. The final regulations add that "Taxpayers may use any reasonable method of determining the amount of discharge of indebtedness income realized and the treatment of correlative adjustments under section 108(e)(4) for acquisitions of indebtedness before March 21, 1991, if such method is applied consistently by both the debtor and

---

[104] Rev. Rul. 2004-79, 2004-31 I.R.B. 1.

[105] As noted at note 101, *supra*, the IRS has announced that taxpayers may instead apply the terms of the proposed regulation, where these differ from the final regulation, for transactions after March 20, 1991 and before December 28, 1992, if all parties apply this approach consistently.

the related holder." It remains to be seen whether the courts will accept the IRS view that Code § 108(e)(4) is self-executing.[106]

The IRS has been aware that many debtors have taken the position that Code § 108(e)(4) was not self-executing. When the IRS issued the proposed implementing regulations in 1991, the preamble expressed concern that such debtors might later engage in a nonrecognition transaction (under Code § § 332, 351, 368, 721, 731 or the like) that would combine the debtor and the holder in such a way as to eliminate the inherent COD income. As a result, the preamble, as clarified by Notice 91-15,[107] expressed an intention to issue regulations requiring the COD income to be recognized upon such a subsequent nonrecognition transaction.

Although the final regulations also leave the treatment of nonrecognition transactions to future regulations, the IRS had already applied a recognition approach in such circumstances in a private letter ruling.[108] Here, a member of an affiliated group had purchased debt of a subsidiary from a third party at a discount, but the subsidiary had not reported COD income. (As indicated above, the IRS position presumably is that the subsidiary should have reported COD income at that time.) In early 1992 the subsidiary was liquidated into the parent, but just before the liquidation, the parent transferred the debt to another affiliate. The ruling stated it is the position of the IRS that "if a related party acquired indebtedness at a discount in a transaction that would have been . . . [covered by] proposed regulation section 1.108-2 if it had occurred on or after March 21, 1991, and the debtor, for whatever reason, did not realize cancellation of indebtedness income through the application of section 108(e)(4) at the time of the acquisition, such cancellation of indebtedness income must be realized upon the [tax-free]liquidation of the debtor into the holder." The ruling also stated that the transfer of the debt to an affiliate immediately before the liquidation would not change this result. Note that while the IRS takes the view that Code § 108(e)(4) was self-executing back to 1980, the statement in this private ruling suggests that the IRS will apply the second-step effort to catch the COD income upon a later nonrecognition transaction only if the latter occurred on or after March 21, 1991.

For corporations that file consolidated returns, special rules regarding transactions in debt that become intercompany debt can be found in Reg. § 1.1502-13(g)(4). These supercede § 108(e)(4). *See* § 804.4 below.

---

[106] The Tax Court, in *Traylor v. Commissioner*, 59 T.C.M. 93, Dec. 46.456(M), T.C. Memo. 1990-132, accepted the IRS's view, although it is doubtful that the court really considered the issue. The contrary view is supported by the Tax Court's opinion in *Alexander v. Commissioner*, 95 T.C. No. 33 (1990), *aff'd, sub. nom, Stell v. Commissioner*, 999 F.2d 544 (9th Cir. 1993), in which the IRS argued and the court agreed that Code § 465(b)(3) was not effective in the absence of regulations. Code § 465(c)(3)(D) says that Code § 465(b)(3) "shall apply only to the extent provided in regulations." This is similar to Code § 108(e)(4), although the word "only" does not appear in the latter. Perhaps regulations under Code § 108(e)(4) could have been adopted with retroactive effect, but the final regulation does not do this. *See also* § 803 *infra* note 4.

[107] 1991-1 C.B. 139.

[108] IRS Letter Ruling 9253027, October 2, 1992.

## *§404.8 Timing: When Does the COD Item Occur?*

The time at which a debt is deemed to be cancelled is inherently a factual question. In most situations, it will not be difficult to determine when the cancellation occurs, because it will have arisen from an exchange or other agreement between the debtor and the creditor. But in other situations, the timing will be less clear.

A case often cited on the timing of debt cancellation is *Cozzi v. Commissioner*.[109] Here, a nonrecourse loan had been secured by a movie production agreement. The loan agreement provided for payments to be made in each of the years 1977-80. No payments were ever made, and as it quickly became clear the movie was not going to turn profitable, the lender made no effort to foreclose on the production agreement. The obligor had not reported any debt discharge income. When the IRS asserted that the debtor might have had debt cancellation income in 1980, the debtor worked out an agreement with the creditor in 1984 to exchange the collateral for cancellation of the debt. The debtor then claimed that the debt cancellation income did not occur until 1984. The court, clearly influenced by its view that the movie project had been a tax shelter and the parties might never have reported the debt discharge income had the IRS not begun an audit, held—based on an examination of various identifiable events (particularly the payment history under the production agreement)—that the collateral was worthless and effectively abandoned well before 1984, and upheld the assessment of the income for 1980. In the course of its opinion, the court said that when it becomes clear, on a practical assessment of the facts, that a debt will never have to be paid, such debt must be viewed as having been discharged. It agreed with the government's argument that this occurred when the production agreement, which was the sole source for payment of the debt, became worthless and was abandoned by the creditor. (It is interesting to note that, because the parties had stipulated that this was a case involving ordinary income arising from the discharge of debt, and the only issue was when that occurred, the case reads as though it is a COD income case, even though, as we have noted at §403.1.3 above, the cancellation of the nonrecourse debt should not have produced COD income but instead should have been treated as proceeds from the effective abandonment of the production agreement to the creditor.)[110]

In contrast, in *Coburn v. Commissioner*,[111] although the creditor abandoned in 2000 the collateral for a recourse loan that had gone into default in that year, and the creditor made no other effort to collect on the loan, the court held that because the creditor had not said it was canceling the loan, and the statute of limitations to enforce repayment did not run until 2006, the debtor did not have COD income in 2000.

---

[109] 88 T.C. 435 (1987).

[110] The confusion about this distinction in *Cozzi* was pointed out in *Coburn v. Commissioner*, T.C. Memo 2005-283, where the distinction made a determinative difference in the first of the court's alternative holdings.

[111] Id (alternative holding).

In the *Friedman* and *Alpert* cases,[112] S corporations having recourse debts well in excess of the value of their assets were thrown into bankruptcy. The taxpayer shareholders had contended that they had COD income in the year of the bankruptcy filing, asserting that it was quite clear by the end of the year that a portion of the debts involved would not be paid. However, in both cases the court held that the COD income was not realized until the year that the bankruptcy cases were finally closed. The courts stated that, until then, the trustees were still actively administering the estates, collecting and distributing monies, such that it could not be said that an identifiable event had occurred that fixed a discharge of the indebtedness.

### §404.9 *Information Reporting Requirements*

For a discussion of the special reporting requirements that can arise when a transaction involves COD income, even if that income is not taxable to the debtor, *see* §§403.4 and 403.5 above.

## §405 HIGH YIELD OID OR PIK OBLIGATIONS

The Revenue Reconciliation Act of 1989[1] added Code §163(e)(5). This provision applies to "high yield discount" obligations issued by corporations, meaning generally instruments having a maturity of more than five years and a yield more than five percentage points above the applicable federal rate and containing significant OID. For debt to which it applies, this provision disallows a deduction for the portion of the interest that exceeds six percentage points above the applicable federal rate and defers deductions for OID and PIK interest (including PIK interest paid either in new debt or in stock) until cash is paid. The new provision generally applies to instruments issued after July 10, 1989. There is a limited refinancing exception for instruments issued after that grandfathering date to refinance a grandfathered instrument. The refinancing exception is rather narrow: The maturity of the new instrument cannot be later than the maturity of the old instrument; the issue price of the new instrument may not exceed that of the old instrument; the stated redemption price at maturity of the new instrument may not be greater than that of the old instrument; and the interest payments required under the new instrument before maturity must not be less than (or paid later than) the interest payments required under the old instrument. Where debt is modified, this new provision, and the limited refinancing exception, must be taken into account.

---

112 *Friedman v. Commissioner*, 216 F.3d 537, 2000-1 U.S.T.C. ¶50,515 (6th Cir. 2000), *aff'g* T.C. Memo. 1998-196; *Alpert v. United States*, 430 F. Supp. 2d 682, 2006-1 U.S.T.C. ¶50,262 (N.D. Ohio 2006), *aff'd*, 481 F.3d 404 (6th Cir. 2007). The taxpayers in these cases had contended for the earlier date for the COD income because this would increase their basis in their S corporation stock under the law as then in effect (*see* §404.2 above), giving them a chance for a carryback tax refund from losses previously suspended.

1 **§405** Pub. L. No. 101-239, 101st Cong., 1st Sess., §7202(a).

## §406 DEBT PAYABLE IN, OR BY REFERENCE TO, EQUITY

The Taxpayer Relief Act of 1997 added Code §163(l), which disallows deduction of any interest payable on a "disqualified debt instrument." An instrument is a "disqualified debt instrument" if—

(1) a substantial amount of the principal or interest is required to be paid in or converted into, or at the option of the issuer or a related party is payable in, or convertible into, equity of the issuer or a related party (or, for debt issued after October 3, 2004, equity held by the issuer or any related party in any other person),[1]
(2) a substantial amount of the principal or interest is required to be determined, or at the option of the issuer or a related party is determined, by reference to the value of such equity, or
(3) the indebtedness is part of an arrangement which is reasonably expected to result in the foregoing.

For this purpose, principal or interest will be treated as required to be so paid, converted, or determined if it may be so required at the option of the holder or a related party, and there is a substantial certainty the option will be exercised.

The legislative history states that nonrecourse debt secured principally by such equity will be treated as "disqualified." But debt with a conversion feature will not be treated as "disqualified" where the conversion price is significantly higher than the market price of the stock on the issue date of the debt.[2] The legislative history adds that Section 163(l) applies not only to debt issued by a corporation but also to debt "issued by a partnership to the extent of its corporate partners." However, under Section 163(l)(5), the application of Section 163(l) to debt of a partnership with corporate partners (other than through the anti-abuse rule of Treas. Reg. §1.701-2) requires regulations to be promulgated, and is intended to address the use of partnerships by corporations to circumvent the statute.

Code §163(l) does not change the tax treatment of the holder, nor does it affect the characterization of the instrument as debt or equity. All it does is disallow the issuer's deductions for all interest on the debt.

Lenders to troubled companies often like to receive an equity kicker in the form of contingent interest that is either payable in equity or that is measured by the market price of the issuer's equity. If such kicker interest constitutes a "substantial amount of the interest," then the debt will be considered "disqualified" and *none* of the interest on the debt will be deductible.

---

[1] **§406** The parenthetical language was added by the American Jobs Creation Act of 2004.

[2] *See* Joint Committee on Taxation, General Explanation of Tax Legislation Enacted in 1997, 192-3 (1997). In IRS Letter Ruling 200052027, September 29, 2000, a corporation had issued debt and had also issued put options allowing it to sell its stock to the put option holder in certain events. Although the debt and the put options might be issued at the same time, they were not connected, and if an investor who purchased the debt also sold one of the put options, the documents provided that the investor could not satisfy its obligation under the put option by delivering the debt. The IRS ruled that Code §163(1) would not apply to disallow deductions for interest on the debt.

Code § 163(l) applies to debt issued after June 8, 1997 (and its expansion by the American Jobs Creation Act of 2004 applies, as mentioned above, to debt issued after October 3, 2004). But issuers should note that debt which was issued before that date may become subject to the new rule if the debt is significantly modified after that date.

## § 407 SPECIAL REPORTING OBLIGATION

On July 5, 1990, the IRS issued proposed regulations to implement Code § 6043(c).[1] The proposed regulations would have required new Form 8820 (when it was prepared) to be filed to report (1) any acquisition by one or more persons acting together of control (as defined in Code § 304(c)) of a corporation (if the stock acquired is worth $10 million or more), (2) any substantial change (involving $10 million or more) in capital structure of a corporation, including stock-for-stock, stock-for-debt, and other recapitalization exchanges, and (3) any significant net increase (as specially defined) in the corporation's debt. The reporting requirement would have been applied to all such transactions occurring after March 31, 1990. Form 8820 was to be filed by the fifteenth day of the fourth month following the month of the transaction (or, if later, within 120 days after Form 8820 became available). The penalty for noncompliance was $500 per day up to a maximum of $100,000. There could also be criminal penalties.

On October 16, 1992, this proposed regulation was withdrawn, the IRS having concluded that the value of the information that would have been collected did not justify the burden of compliance.

The 1993 Act added Code § 6050P, which requires creditors that are "applicable financial entities" to file information reports regarding discharge of any indebtedness they hold. This provision is discussed at § 403.4 above.

In 2003, the IRS implemented new Reg. §§ 1.6011-4, 301.6111-2, and 301.6112-1, which, although aimed primarily at tax shelters and overly aggressive tax planning, can nonetheless in some instances impose special reporting obligations on taxpayers, promoters, or advisors involved in debt restructurings. These, and the expansion of their impact by the American Jobs Creation Act of 2004, are discussed at § 403.5 above.

## § 408 FOREIGN TAX CREDIT IMPLICATIONS

Where the debtor company has foreign operations, care should be taken that modification of its debt does not result in an adverse change in its foreign tax credit position. This can happen, for example, where the debt is nonrecourse debt secured solely by U.S. property.

Temp. Reg. § 1.861-10T provides that interest expense on "qualified nonrecourse indebtedness" is considered directly allocable to the gross income from the property that secures it. However, this direct allocation rule applies only to debt incurred to

---

[1] **§ 407** Prop. Reg. § 1.6043-4.

purchase, construct, or improve property. Thus, the benefit of this rule can be lost when the debt is refinanced, unless a special refinancing exception contained in the regulation is satisfied.

The refinancing exception permits the refinanced indebtedness to continue to qualify for direct allocation so long as (1) the principal amount of the new debt is not more than 105 percent of the remaining principal amount of the old debt and (2) the term of the new debt is not more than six months longer than the term of the old debt. Certain other requirements must also be satisfied.

## §409 CONSOLIDATED RETURN CONSIDERATIONS

Various of the rules discussed above in this chapter are modified by the consolidated return regulations. *See* the discussion in Chapter 8 below.

# 5

# One-Company Equity-for-Debt Recapitalizations



## §501 EXCHANGING EQUITY FOR DEBT IN ONE-COMPANY RECAPITALIZATIONS

Another method by which a corporation can modify its debt is to issue its stock or warrants in exchange for part or all of the principal or unpaid interest of its debt. The consequences of such an exchange to the debtor corporation and creditor are discussed below.[1]

As we shall see in this chapter, Congress in the years 1980-1986, and again in 1990, adopted several changes to the stock-for-debt exception to COD income and to Code §382. Finally, in 1993, Congress repealed the stock-for-debt exception entirely (with a prospective effective date).[2] All of these changes have greatly increased the

[1] **§501** For examples of many of the issues discussed here, *see* Bacon, Rescue Planning for the Failing or Bankrupt Company, 61 Taxes 931, 938-941 (1983).

[2] The history of these changes is ably described in Asofsky, Towards a Bankruptcy Tax Act of 1993, 51 NYU Inst. on Fed. Tax'n §§13.02, 13.03 (1993). As he points out, the series of laws passed

risk to a troubled company that an exchange of its stock for its debt will impair or destroy its NOLs and other tax attributes. This is unfortunate. Not only will the restructuring and survival of troubled companies be made more difficult, but the changes also seem to have the unfortunate tax policy consequence of exalting form over substance. Had the debt money originally been contributed for stock instead, no problem would exist. Why should NOLs and other valuable tax attributes—which may indeed have been created by the money contributed for the debt—be differently affected if the money becomes equity in two steps, rather than one?

Many of these legislative provisions have also drawn a distinction between stock-for-debt exchanges occurring inside a bankruptcy or similar insolvency proceeding and those occurring outside such proceedings. They have provided more liberal rules for those occurring *in* bankruptcy and similar insolvency proceedings. This too is unfortunate. The distinction gives failing companies a tax incentive to utilize Chapter 11 bankruptcy proceedings for restructuring their debt, thereby perhaps placing burdens on the bankruptcy courts that might otherwise have been avoided. The distinction also has troubling tax policy connotations: Why should the same transaction create different consequences just because it occurs inside, rather than outside, bankruptcy?

Even more astoundingly, the stock-for-debt exception to COD income was repealed without Congress ever having held hearings on the subject. The repeal provision first appeared in the Revenue Bill of 1992, H.R. 11, which passed Congress in the fall of 1992 but was vetoed by President Bush. The repeal provision came as the "revenue raiser" portion for a House member's bill that would have granted tax benefits to certain insurance companies and barge owners.[3] Despite strong objections voiced by those who were aware of the harm such repeal would cause, the repeal provision surfaced once more—and again without any hearings on the subject—when the Senate needed an additional revenue raiser for its version of the 1993 Act. The Joint Committee's estimate of revenue to be raised over five years from this repeal proved to be curiously flexible. In the fall of 1992 it was $286 million, whereas just a few months later—in mid-1993—it had become $622 million. The Conference Committee included the repeal in the final version of the 1993 Act, albeit with a slightly delayed effective date. All of this can only be described as a remarkably casual and troubling way to make major changes in public policy.[4]

---

(Footnote Continued)

subsequent to the Bankruptcy Tax Act of 1980 have "destroyed the foundations" of that thoughtfully prepared Act, with the result that today troubled corporations must "reorganize themselves in what is at best an ambiguous, and at worst a hostile, tax atmosphere." Id. at pp. 13-3, 13-33.

[3] This has been described as a "political pork" bill that should "occupy a special place in the hall of shame." Asofsky, *supra* note 2, at § 13.03[5], pp. 13-32, 13-33.

[4] The repeal is strongly criticized in Newton and Wertheim, Examining the Impact From the Repeal of the Stock-For-Debt Exception, 3 Am. Bankr. Inst. 355 (1995). The authors conclude that the repeal will raise substantially less revenue than was estimated by the Joint Committee, and that even this will be offset by revenue losses from the reduction of jobs and the increase in company liquidations that will be produced by the repeal. The repeal is also criticized in Asofsky, Towards a Bankruptcy Tax Act of 1993, 51 NYU Inst. on Fed. Tax'n § 13.05 (1993).

In addition to impairment of NOLs and other tax attributes, an exchange of stock for debt that produces a Code § 382 ownership change can increase the debtor corporation's exposure to the alternative minimum tax (AMT) for years to which the adjusted current earning (ACE) method of computing the AMT applies (*i.e.*, tax years beginning after 1989). This is because Code § 56(g)(4)(G) provides that, if a Code § 382 ownership change occurs in a taxable year beginning after 1989 at a time when the debtor corporation has a net unrealized built-in loss within the meaning of Code § 382(h), then the basis of the debtor's assets for purposes of computing ACE shall be reduced to fair market value. This adjustment, of course, increases the amount of the AMT. The Revenue Bill of 1992, H.R. 11, which passed Congress in the fall of 1992 but was vetoed by President Bush, contained a provision that would have eliminated this adjustment. However, this provision was not included in the 1993 Act. *See* § 511 below.

Finally, the issuance of stock for debt may result in the need to file a special reporting form with the IRS within a short time after the exchange. *See* § § 403.4, 403.5 and 512.

## § 502 CREDITOR TAX CONSEQUENCES

As discussed more fully below, the tax consequences to a creditor of an exchange of new stock or warrants of the debtor corporation for its old debt depends on the nature and terms of the debt.

### *§ 502.1 Nonsecurity, Nonconvertible Old Debt*

Where the old debt (1) is not a "security" and (2) is not being converted in accordance with its terms into stock or warrants, the exchange of old debt for new stock or warrants of the debtor corporation will be a taxable exchange to the creditor. The stock or warrants will be valued at their fair market value.[1] The portion of the stock and warrants attributable to accrued unpaid interest on the debt will be treated as a payment of interest, and the remainder will be treated as received in exchange for the principal of the debt.[2] If the creditor had Code § 1276 "market discount" in the old debt and has realized gain on the exchange, that gain will be treated as interest income to the extent of the market discount.[3] The basis of the stock and warrants to the creditor will be their fair market value.[4]

---

[1] **§ 502** Even where the stock is subject to transfer restrictions and has no easily ascertainable value, the IRS will normally refuse to treat the transaction as an open transaction and will require a valuation of the stock. *See* T.A.M. 9633001, April 10, 1996.

[2] The manner for determining the portion attributable to unpaid interest was discussed at § § 402 and 403.1.6.

[3] *See* discussion of market discount at § 403.1.8.

[4] Code § 1012.

## §502.2 *Conversion of Convertible Debt to Debtor Stock*

A conversion of convertible debt into debtor corporation stock pursuant to the terms of the debt ordinarily will be tax free to the creditor.[5] Neither gain nor loss can be recognized by the creditor. Accordingly, the creditor's basis, as well as his holding period, in the convertible debt will carry over to the stock received.[6]

However, if the convertible debt was originally received in exchange for property and was reported by the creditor under the Code §453 installment method, the conversion will be treated as a taxable "disposition" of the installment obligation. The IRS will treat the value of the stock (including any excess of that value over the principal amount of the debt) as the amount realized on the disposition, with the result that no part of the conversion will be tax free.[7]

## §502.3 *Old Debt a Security*

If the old debt constitutes a security, the exchange of the old debt for stock of the debtor corporation will qualify as a tax-free recapitalization (an "E" reorganization).[8] Accordingly, the exchanging creditor will not recognize gain or loss, except that gain will be recognized to the extent of the "boot" received, and except that any stock received that is attributable to accrued but unpaid interest on the old debt will be treated as payment of the interest.[9] If the creditor had market discount in the old debt (assuming such debt was issued after July 18, 1984) and had realized gain on the exchange, the market discount will be recognized and treated as interest income to the creditor to the extent of the taxable "boot"; any market discount not recognized on the exchange would carry over to the stock received and will produce ordinary interest income upon profitable disposition of the stock.[10]

Recently, two significant changes have been made regarding the definitions of what constitutes "boot" in such transactions. The first relates to the treatment of warrants.

For many years, the IRS took the position in its regulations that warrants did not constitute either stock or securities of the issuing corporation for purposes of the tax-

---

[5] Rev. Rul. 72-265, 1972-1 C.B. 222.

[6] Id.; Rev. Rul. 62-140, 1962-2 C.B. 181 (if cash payment also required upon conversion, stock acquired will have a split holding period; the holding period of the portion of stock attributable to the cash payment would commence the day following the date of acquisition of the stock; amount realized upon subsequent sale of stock is first allocated to the stock basis attributable to the cash, in the proportion that the amount of cash paid bears to the fair market value of stock at conversion, with the remainder allocated to stock basis attributable to debenture); *see* Albert Ades, 38 T.C. 501, Dec. 25,588 (1962), *aff'd per curiam*, 316 F.2d 734, 63-1 U.S.T.C. ¶9476 (2d Cir. 1963) (issue premium on old debt not deductible upon conversion).

[7] *See* Rev. Rul. 72-264, 1972-1 C.B. 131.

[8] *See* Code §368(a)(1)(E); Reg. §1.368-2(e); Rev. Rul. 77-238, 1977-2 C.B. 115.

[9] Code §§354(a)(2)(B) and 356. For a discussion of the portion attributable to accrued but unpaid interest, *see* §403.1.6.

[10] *See* Code §1276; *see also* discussion of market discount at §403.1.8.

free reorganization provisions of the Code.[11] However, in late 1996, the IRS proposed to amend these provisions to provide that rights issued by a party to the reorganization to acquire its stock will be treated as securities of that corporation for purposes of Code §§354 and 355, and that for purposes of Code §356 such securities will be treated as having no principal amount. The traditional treatment of convertible instruments would not be affected: the preamble to the proposed regulation makes clear that the conversion privilege in a convertible stock or debt will not be treated as being a separate property right for purposes of the reorganization provisions. The amendments, which apply only for purposes of Code §§354, 355, and 356, do not apply for purposes of any other Code section (such as Code §§351 and 382). They became effective in January 1998 and apply to exchanges occurring on or after March 9, 1998.[12] These amendments will open the door for broader use of warrants in debt-for-equity exchanges where the debt constitutes a security.

The second change was the treatment of certain types of preferred stock—"nonqualified preferred stock" as defined in Code §351(g)(2)—as constituting "boot" for purposes of Code §§354, 355, and 356 (except when exchanged for such nonqualified stock or for securities).[13] This new rule is effective for exchanges occurring on or after March 9, 1998.[14] Such stock, though treated as "boot," will still be treated as stock and not as debt for other purposes.

The creditor's basis in his old debt would carry over to any qualifying stock or securities (including warrants) received.[15] Such basis, however, would be (1) increased by any gain (but not interest income, except as noted below) recognized on the exchange and (2) decreased by any money, the fair market value of any boot received and any loss recognized on the exchange.[16] Such basis would be allocated between the stock and securities received in accordance with their relative fair market values.[17] In addition, the stock's basis would include an amount equal to the fair market value of the stock, if any, attributable to accrued stated interest.[18] In the latter

---

[11] *See* Reg. §1.354-1(e) and Reg. §1.355-1(b), as issued in 1955. *See also* the authorities cited in §605.1.4 at note 41.

[12] Reg. §1.354-1(e), Reg. §1.355-1(c), Reg. §1.356-3(b), and Reg. §1.356-6T as issued in January 1998. These changes also allow warrants to be exchanged for warrants tax-free. See the parenthetical language in Reg. §1.356-3(b). However, the regulations continue to make clear that Code §354 does not apply to an exchange of solely securities (including warrants) for stock. Reg. §1.354-1(d) Example 4. Simultaneously with these changes, the IRS also held (reversing its prior position) that security-for-security or security-for-stock exchanges accompanying a "B" reorganization can be tax-free under Code §354, subject to Code §356. Rev. Rul. 98-10, 1998-1 C.B. 643.

[13] Code §354(a)(2)(C).

[14] Reg. §1.356-6. This new rule also applies to warrants to acquire such stock. *See also* Bloom, Certain Preferred Stock Gets The "Boot"—But Does It Fit?, 88 J. Tax'n 69 (1998). Treasury officials have stated that the purpose of the provision was to force taxpayers to issue debt rather than instruments that look like debt.

[15] Code §358(a)(1).

[16] Id.

[17] Reg. §1.358-2.

[18] *See* Code §1012.

event, the stock would have a split holding period;[19] the portion attributable to accrued but unpaid interest would have a new holding period beginning the day after the exchange, and the remaining portion would have a holding period that included the holding period of the old securities.[20] Any "boot" received in the exchange (other than money) would receive a basis equal to its fair market value, and have a new holding period.[21]

Where the stock issued in exchange for the debt is preferred stock, the holder may have Code § 305 deemed-distribution problems (analogous to OID on new debt) with the stock. *See* the discussion of Code § 305(c) at § 504A.3 below.

## *§502.4 Recapture on Subsequent Disposition of Stock*

A creditor that receives stock of a debtor corporation (its parent or a successor corporation)[22] in exchange for old debt is required, to the extent that gain is recognized upon a subsequent disposition of such stock, to "recapture" as ordinary income under Code § 1245 any bad debt deductions taken by the creditor with respect to such debt and any loss claimed by the creditor upon the receipt of the stock in satisfaction of such debt, reduced by any gain recognized upon receipt of the stock.[23] This "recapture" component in the stock is in addition to the market discount component mentioned at § 403.1.8. If the stock is subsequently disposed of in a tax-free transaction (*e.g.*, in a tax-free recapitalization or another type of reorganization), the potential recapture will carry over to the stock received.[24]

**EXAMPLE**

A, a corporate creditor, made a $1,000 short-term loan to B Corporation on July 1, 1980. In 1982, A took an $800 bad debt deduction due to the partial worthlessness of the loan. If on March 1, 1983, B Corporation satisfies the principal amount of the debt with B Corporation stock worth $500, A will have a resulting gain of $300 (the $500 of stock less the $200 of debt that was not deducted). The gain would be ordinary income. If A

---

[19] *Cf.* Rev. Rul. 62-140, 1962-2 C.B. 181.

[20] *See* Code § 1223(1); H.M. Hooper, 26 B.T.A. 758, Dec. 7689 (1932) (holding period of stock or securities excludes day of acquisition, except if acquired pursuant to the exercise of rights, *see* Code § 1223(6)); Rev. Rul. 70-598, 1970-2 C.B. 168 (holding period unaffected by holidays).

[21] Code § 358(a)(2).

[22] The House Report to the Bankruptcy Tax Act defines a "successor corporation" as a corporation that succeeds to the debtor corporation's tax attributes (under Code § 381) in a tax-free transaction. H.R. Rep. No. 833, 96th Cong., 2d Sess. 15 n.22 (1980). A "parent corporation," for purposes of Code § 108(e)(7), is a corporation that owns stock of the debtor corporation possessing (1) at least 80 percent of the total combined voting power of all of classes stock entitled to vote *and* (2) at least 80 percent of the total number of shares of each of the other classes of stock of the corporation. Code §§ 108(e)(7)(D) and 368(c)(1).

[23] Code § 108(e)(7)(A) and (B).

[24] *See* Code § 1245(b).

> later disposes of the B Corporation stock for $1,500, $500 of A's gain is subject to recapture and would be treated as ordinary income. In other words, the entire $800 bad debt deduction is recaptured, less the $300 of gain recognized on the exchange of the stock for the debt.[25]

In the case of a cash basis creditor, any amount that the creditor would have included in income if the old debt had been paid in full, but was not included solely by reason of the cash method of accounting, is treated, for purposes of applying Code § 108(e)(7), as a bad debt deduction allowed with respect to the debt.[26]

## § 503 DEBTOR TAX CONSEQUENCES

No gain or loss is recognized by the debtor corporation upon the issuance of its own stock, including treasury stock.[1]

### *§ 503.1 Stock Issuance Expenses*

Any stock issuance expenses are generally considered to be capital expenditures and are, therefore, not deductible (even upon liquidation).[2] The rule applies whether the stock is common stock or stock that has a limited life.[3] "Stock issuance expenses" include accounting and legal costs (whether incurred before or after the issuance of the stock) in registering stock with the Securities and Exchange Commission and listing stock on an exchange.[4] Fees paid to the registrar and transfer agent[5] and annual fees paid to maintain listing on an exchange are deductible.[6]

---

[25] *See* S. Rep. No. 1035, 96th Cong., 2d Sess. 18 (1980).

[26] Code § 108(e)(7)(B).

[1] **§ 503** Code § 1032.

[2] *See generally* Bittker & Eustice, Federal Income Taxation of Corporations and Shareholders ¶ 5.04[9] (6th ed.); *see also General Bancshares Corp. v. Commissioner*, 326 F.2d 712, 64-1 U.S.T.C. ¶ 9220 (8th Cir. 1964), *cert. denied*, 379 U.S. 832 (1964) (stock dividend expenses); *Simmons Co. v. Commissioner*, 8 B.T.A. 631, Dec. 2909 (1927), *aff'd*, 33 F.2d 75, 5 U.S.T.C. ¶ 1569 (1st Cir.), *cert. denied*, 280 U.S. 588 (1929); *Emerson Elec. Mfg. Co. v. Commissioner*, 3 B.T.A. 932, Dec. 1298 (1926); *cf.* Rev. Rul. 73-463, 1973-2 C.B. 4 (stock issuance expenses paid or incurred by an open-end investment company, other than those incurred during the initial stock offering period, are deductible).

[3] *E.g., Surety Finance Co. of Tacoma v. Commissioner*, 77 F.2d 221, 35-1 U.S.T.C. ¶ 9354 (9th Cir. 1935) (only common stock issued, but corporate existence limited by corporate charter); *Commercial Investment Trust Corp.*, 28 B.T.A. 143, Dec. 8069 (1933), *aff'd*, 74 F.2d 1015 (2d Cir. 1935) (by its terms, preferred stock was to be retired at the rate of 3 percent per year).

[4] *E.g.*, Rev. Rul. 69-330, 1969-1 C.B. 51; *Consumers Water Co. v. United States*, 369 F. Supp. 939, 74-1 U.S.T.C. ¶ 9189 (S.D. Me. 1974).

[5] Rev. Rul. 69-615, 1969-2 C.B. 26.

[6] *Chesapeake Corp. of Va.*, 17 T.C. 668, Dec. 18,578 (1951), *acq.* 1952-1 C.B. 1.

## *§503.2 Unamortized OID or Original Issuance Expense*

Any unamortized original issue discount (OID) or original issuance expenses with respect to the old debt exchanged (or converted) for debtor corporation stock is viewed as a capital expenditure of issuing the new stock. Accordingly, this cannot be deducted by the debtor corporation.[7]

## *§503.3 Deduction on Issuance of Equity*

**For accrued interest.** Interest, in general, may be paid by stock of a debtor corporation, as well as by cash or other assets, and a deduction received therefor.[8] Any portion of stock issued in exchange for old debt that is attributable to accrued but unpaid interest (including OID) will constitute a payment of interest by the debtor corporation to the extent of the fair market value of the stock.[9] In the case of convertible debt, however, if on conversion the debtor is relieved of its obligation to pay interest, the interest attributable to the period during which the debt is converted may not be accrued or deducted and no part of the stock will be deemed attributable to such interest.[10]

Code § 163(l), which was adopted in 1997, creates a significant caveat to the foregoing statement of the general rules. This provision, which is discussed above at § 406, disallows deductions for any interest payable on a "disqualified debt instrument," and an instrument will be so treated if a substantial amount of its principal or interest is payable in equity of the issuer or a related party.

---

[7] *See Chicago, Milwaukee, St. Paul and Pacific Ry. Co. v. United States*, 404 F.2d 960, 967, 69-1 U.S.T.C. ¶9125 (Ct. Cl. 1969); Rev. Rul. 72-238, 1972-1 C.B. 65; Rev. Rul. 72-348, 1972-2 C.B. 97 (conversion); Bittker & Eustice, *supra* note 2, at § 4.61 n.244; consider *Husky Oil Co. v. Commissioner*, 83 T.C. 717, Dec. 41,630 (1984) (same result where debt converted into stock of parent; arguably erroneous result). Debt issuance expenses so treated may include the unamortized portion of the value of warrants issued as debt issuance expenses. IRS Field Service Advice 200011006, November 23, 1999, *reprinted at* 2000 TNT 54-82.

[8] *See Commissioner v. Fender Sales, Inc.*, 338 F.2d 924, 65-1 U.S.T.C. ¶9104 (9th Cir. 1965), *cert. denied*, 382 U.S. 813 (1964) (salary obligation paid with stock); *Central Elec. & Tel. Co. v. Commissioner*, 47 B.T.A. 434, Dec. 12,597 (1942) (exchanged bonds and accrued interest in § 77B Bankruptcy Act case for common and preferred stock, new bonds and voting trust certificates); *Shamrock Oil and Gas Co. v. Commissioner*, 42 B.T.A. 1016, Dec. 11,346 (1940) (bonds and interest coupons for common stock and bonds in a tax-free reorganization), *acq.* 1940-2 C.B. 6; *Hummell-Ross Fibre Corp. v. Commissioner*, 40 B.T.A. 821, Dec. 10,853 (1939) (bonds and accrued interest for preferred stock), *acq.* 1940-1 C.B. 3; *see also* IRS Techical Advice Memorandum 8248010, August 25, 1985. No deduction is allowed, however, when a cash basis debtor issues its own note in payment of interest. Rev. Rul. 70-647, 1970-2 C.B. 38.

[9] *See, e.g.*, Code § 354(a)(2)(B). As mentioned at § 403.1.6, to the extent the payment is less than the amount of post-1969 OID or stated interest that has already been includible in the creditor's income, the creditor would be entitled to a deduction, arguably ordinary in character.

[10] Rev. Rul. 74-127, 1974-1 C.B. 47 (no interest accrued since last payment date prior to conversion was to be paid in any form); *Bethlehem Steel Corp. v. United States*, Ct Cls, 71-1 U.S.T.C. ¶9110, 434 F.2d 1357 (same); *Columbia Gas Sys., Inc. v. United States*, 473 F.2d 1244, 73-1 U.S.T.C. ¶9176 (2d Cir. 1973) (same); *Tandy Corp. v. United States*, 626 F.2d 1186, 80-2 U.S.T.C. ¶9700 (5th Cir. 1980) (same, even though accrued interest and bond premium would have been payable upon the immediate redemption of the debentures had they not been converted).

**For debt repurchase premium.** Where nonconvertible debt is repurchased by voluntary agreement from the holder by the debtor in exchange for debtor stock, and the debtor, as an inducement to the holder to make the exchange, issues stock with a value that exceeds the adjusted issue price of the debt, the IRS has held that the debtor can deduct this premium as interest under Code § 163.[11] Similarly, where the value of the stock issued in exchange for allowed claims exceeded the amount of the claims in a Chapter 11 case, the IRS held that the excess could be deducted as interest.[12] However, if the debt is by its terms convertible, the result is not the same. In such a case, Code § 249 applies to limit the deduction for such a premium to the portion that qualifies as a "normal call premium."[13]

## § 504 NO STOCK-FOR-DEBT EXCEPTION TO COD INCOME

Under current law, the issuance by the debtor of its stock in exchange for its debt will produce COD income if the stock has a fair market value that is less than the adjusted issue price of the debt.[1] This result applies whether or not the debt is a security (in which case the exchange would be an "E" reorganization), and whether or not the exchange is pursuant to a conversion occurring pursuant to the terms of the debt.[2] Under prior law (as described in § 504A immediately below), the stock-for-debt exception to COD income would have changed that result. But the stock-for-debt exception to COD income no longer applies.

## § 504A PRIOR LAW: STOCK-FOR-DEBT EXCEPTION TO COD INCOME

As discussed at § 404, a debtor corporation that cancels part or all of its debt will have cancellation of debt (COD) income, unless one of the exceptions to the COD income rule applies. The consequences of having COD income—which, depending on the status of the taxpayer at the time of the cancellation, may consist of recognition of the income, or the reduction of valuable tax attributes such as NOLs or asset basis—were also discussed in Chapter 4.

---

[11] IRS Letter Ruling 200449001, September 7, 2004. The general rule is that when nonconvertible debt is repurchased for a price above its adjusted issue price, this premium can be deducted as interest. Reg. § 1.163-4(c) and 7(c), and the foregoing letter ruling held this rule applies whether the repurchase is for cash or equivalent, including stock.

[12] IRS Technical Advice Memorandum 200143001, October 26, 2001. Interestingly, the claims for which stock was received included convertible debentures. It appears, however, that the only issue raised by the agent was the general proposition of whether a deduction could be allowed despite the general non-recognition rule of Code § 1032. The IRS concluded that Code § 1032 does not preclude "deductions for payments of premium to creditors *that are otherwise deductible under the Code*" (emphasis added).

[13] Rev. Rul. 2002-31, 2002-1 C.B. 1023. For other arguments, *see* Willens, Determining Deductibility of a 'Premium' in Equity-for-Debt Exchanges, BNA Daily Tax Report (Nov. 8, 2006), at J-1.

[1] **§ 504** Code § 108(e)(8).

[2] Reg. § 1.61-12(c)(2); IRS Technical Advice Memorandum 200606037, October 27, 2005.

Before its repeal in 1993, the most important single exception to the creation of COD income was the stock-for-debt exception. This exception applied, subject to certain limitations, where stock of the debtor was used to satisfy its debt.[1] However, even where this exception was applicable, debt cancellation using stock could raise the possibility of AMT consequences for years beginning before 1990, as discussed at §§404.5 and 504A.6.

As mentioned at §501 above, the Omnibus Budget Reconciliation Act of 1993 repealed the stock-for-debt exception, with a slightly delayed effective date. This was accomplished by an amendment to Code §108(e)(8) and the repeal of then Code §108(e)(10). Congressional hearings were never held on this repeal. The repeal was made generally effective for stock transferred in satisfaction of debt after 1994, except for transfers in a title 11 or similar case filed on or before the end of 1993.

Because of the delayed effective date provisions, particularly the one for transfers made in bankruptcy cases for which petitions are filed by the end of 1993, the stock-for-debt exception to COD income will continue to be applicable to numerous exchanges occurring after 1993. It will also be of continuing interest to those handling audits of returns for prior years. The remaining portions of this §504A will therefore discuss the provisions of the stock-for-debt exception, as it existed before its repeal by the 1993 Act.

## *§504A.1 Unavailability for Solvent Companies Not in Bankruptcy*

The stock-for-debt exception developed as a judicially created common law rule of taxation.[2] Before its repeal in 1993, Congress had narrowed its scope by amendments made to Code §108 in 1980, 1984, 1986, and 1990. As narrowed by the 1984 and 1986 changes, the exception only applied to (1) debtors in title 11 cases[3] and (2)

---

[1] **§504A** For a discussion of the history and application of the stock-for-debt exception, and other consequences of equity-debt exchanges, *see* Bryan, Cancellation of Indebtedness by Issuing Stock in Exchange: Challenging the Congressional Solution to Debt-Equity Swaps, 63 Tex. L. Rev. 89 (1984); Asofsky, Discharge of Indebtedness Income in Bankruptcy After the Bankruptcy Tax Act of 1980, 27 St. Louis U. L.J. 583, 600-621 (1983) (hereafter Asofsky, Discharge of Indebtedness); *see also* Eustice, Cancellation of Indebtedness Redux: The Bankruptcy Tax Act of 1980 Proposal—Corporate Aspects, 36 Tax L. Rev. 1 (1980); Eustice, Cancellation of Indebtedness and the Federal Income Tax: A Problem of Creeping Confusion, 14 Tax L. Rev. 225, 238-240 (1959).

[2] *Commissioner v. Motor Mart Trust*, 156 F.2d 122, 46-1 U.S.T.C. ¶9301 (1st Cir. 1946), *aff'g* 4 T.C. 931, Dec. 14,427 (1945), *acq.* 1947-1 C.B. 3; *Alcazar Hotel, Inc. v. Commissioner*, 1 T.C. 872, Dec. 13,099 (1943) (permitted use of successor corporation stock), *acq.* 1943 C.B. 1; *Capento Sec. Corp. v. Commissioner*, 140 F.2d 38, 44-1 U.S.T.C. ¶9170 (1st Cir. 1944), *aff'g* 47 B.T.A. 691, Dec. 12,843 (1942), *nonacq.* 1943 C.B. 28; *Tower Building Corp. v. Commissioner*, 6 T.C. 125, Dec. 14,947 (1946), *acq.* 1974-1 C.B. 4; GCM 25277, 1947-1 C.B. 44; *but see Claridge Apartments Co. v. Commissioner*, 1 T.C. 143, Dec. 12,896 (1942), *rev'd in part*, 138 F.2d 962, 43-2 U.S.T.C. ¶9663 (7th Cir. 1943), *rev'd on other grounds*, 323 U.S. 141 (1944) (the IRS eventually acquiesced in the Tax Court decision at 1947-1 C.B. 2). *See also Los Angeles Shipbuilding & Drydock v. United States*, 289 F.2d 222, 229, 61-1 U.S.T.C. ¶9329 (9th Cir. 1961); *Woodmont Corp. v. Commissioner*, 5 T.C.M. 291, Dec. 15,110(M) (1946); *Potter & Rayfield, Inc. v. Commissioner*, 5 T.C.M. 119, Dec. 15,027(M) (1946).

[3] A "title 11 case" is defined in Code §108(d)(2) as a case under the Bankruptcy Code, but only if the debt cancellation is approved by the court. This limitation under Code §108 to title 11 cases contrasts with the broader bankruptcy concept that applies for "G" reorganization and Code §382

insolvent[4] debtors (though only to the extent the debtor is not rendered solvent). The 1990 change eliminated certain preferred stock from qualifying for the exception.

With respect to solvent debtors outside bankruptcy—including insolvent debtors, to the extent the debt cancellation makes them solvent—the legislative amendments made the stock-for-debt exception entirely inapplicable. As a result, companies desiring to rely on the stock-for-debt exception often felt compelled to enter Chapter 11 bankruptcy proceedings. This way, the exception applied even if the company was or was made solvent in a balance sheet (marked to market) sense, and the problem of proving insolvency disappeared.

In Rev. Rul. 92-52,[5] the IRS specifically ruled on how one should apply the stock-for-debt exception outside a title 11 case where the debt restructuring leaves the debtor solvent. The ruling gives two examples. In the first, the debt being cancelled was held by only one creditor. In the second, the debt being cancelled was held by two different creditors, but only one of the two creditors received stock.

The ruling holds that, in the first example, the fair market value of the stock plus the value of the other consideration issued is first applied to the amount of the debt being restructured in order to determine the amount of the debt discharge, and then the stock is treated as satisfying the entire remainder of the debt. In short, the stock is considered issued for all of the debt not satisfied with other consideration. What this comes down to is that the stock-for-debt exception applies to the entire amount of the discharge of indebtedness that is attributable to the insolvency, and the attribute-reduction rules do not apply. This holding is illustrated by an example in which a $90,000 debt is exchanged for a $10,000 issue price of new debt plus $20,000 FMV of common stock. The debtor was insolvent by $50,000 before the exchange, but was $30,000 solvent after the exchange. The ruling holds that the debtor has $60,000 of discharge of indebtedness (note that the $20,000 FMV of the stock is taken into account in making this calculation). The ruling further holds that the stock is also treated as satisfying the entire remainder of the debt. Thus, the stock-for-debt exception applies to the $50,000 of the discharge representing the insolvency, and the attribute reduction rules do not apply. The debtor also has $10,000 of COD income (the difference between the $60,000 of debt discharge and the $50,000 of predischarge insolvency).

In the second example, the facts are the same except the $90,000 of debt is split between two holders: A holds $30,000 of it and receives the new $10,000 debt in exchange for it; B holds $60,000 of the old debt and receives $20,000 FMV of common stock in exchange for it. The ruling holds that in such a situation the discharge of indebtedness attributable to insolvency is first allocated to the stock-for-debt ex-

(Footnote Continued)

purposes. The latter extend the concept to include title 11 and *similar* cases, including receivership, foreclosure, or similar proceedings in a federal or state court. Code §§382(l)(5)(G), 382(l)(6), 368(a)(3)(A).

[4] "Insolvent" is defined in Code §108(d)(3) as meaning the excess of liabilities over the fair market value of assets. The application of this test, which is to be applied immediately before the debt cancellation, was discussed in the last chapter. *See* discussion at §404.

[5] 1992-2 C.B. 34.

change, and only the remaining amount is allocated to the other exchange. This was illustrated in the ruling by the observation that the debtor, as in the first example, has $50,000 of insolvency before the exchange; $60,000 of debt discharge (total debt of $90,000 less the $10,000 of new debt and $20,000 FMV of stock exchanged for it); and $10,000 of debt discharge income. In the stock-for-debt exchange, the debtor has $40,000 of debt discharge ($60,000 of debt less the $20,000 FMV of stock). The first $40,000 of the insolvency is allocated to this exchange, and the stock-for-debt exception applies. The balance of the $10,000 of the $50,000 insolvency discharge produces attribute reduction, and the remaining $10,000 of the $60,000 total debt discharge produces income.

## *§504A.2 Consequences of Not Having the Exception*

If the stock-for-debt exception to COD income does not apply, stock issued by a company to its creditors will be treated as having satisfied an amount of debt equal to the fair market value of the stock.[6] Note that this rule applies even to conversions of convertible debt.

## *§504A.3 Scope of the Exception*

Congress did not redefine the stock-for-debt exception in Code § 108. Before the 1993 repeal, Congress had simply preserved it, as it had been developed by the courts, and then added certain limitations.[7] Hence, to find the basic scope of the exception, one must look to prior case law. These cases make it clear that the exception applies even where the stock issued has a value substantially less than the amount of debt being cancelled.[8]

**EXAMPLE**

Bankrupt company has $1 million principal amount of debt, which it satisfies by issuing common stock. Even if the stock is worth only $250,000, the stock-for-debt exception applies to eliminate all COD income.

Aside from the various statutory limitations that were placed on the stock-for-debt exception beginning in 1980, one must not lose sight of the doctrine that substance, rather than form, generally governs tax consequences. This is just as true of the stock-for-debt exception as for other matters. For example, where creditors

---

[6] Pre-1994 Code § 108(e)(10)(A); current Code § 108(e)(8).

[7] *See* pre-1994 Code § 108(e)(8) and (10); S. Rep. No. 1035, 96th Cong., 2d Sess. 17 (1980).

[8] *See* cases cited *supra* note 2. The stock-for-debt exception (rather than the tax benefit rule) should apply to the cancellation of accrued interest as well as principal. *See* Chapter 3 at § 302 note 11, and accompanying text.

were issued stock in exchange for their debt, but the stock was subject to the right of a third party (who had purchased most of the debtor's assets) to buy it for a nominal price in the future, the IRS considered the creditors to have no interest in the stock for purposes of the stock-for-debt exception.[9] The IRS has also stated that the stock-for-debt exception does not apply when stock is issued for cash and the debtor uses the cash to satisfy debt for less than the amount owed on the debt.[10]

### § 504A.3.1 Preferred Stock

The rationale expressed by the courts for the stock-for-debt exception has usually been that the corporation was simply substituting one liability for another. Where limited preferred stock (*i.e.*, nonconvertible and nonparticipating preferred) is issued instead of common stock, this rationale applies if the liquidation value of the preferred equals the amount of debt being cancelled (even if the stock has a lesser value). In the *Capento* case,[11] the debtor successfully avoided COD income by issuing limited preferred stock in cancellation of debt. The stock had a value that was much less than the principal amount of the debt, but it had a liquidation price equal to the cancelled principal. However, where the asset preference of the preferred on liquidation is less than the amount of debt being cancelled, it has long been questioned whether the issuance of such stock would avoid COD income for the excess of the cancelled debt over the liquidation preference.[12] Some support can be found in the *Capento* opinion, nonetheless, for the proposition that such excess does qualify for the stock-for-debt exception. After articulating the substitution of liability theory as a reason for its conclusion, the court added as another reason for its opinion: "Gain is not realized by a corporation in the receipt of the subscription price of its shares . . . and this would seem to be no less true when the subscription price, instead of being newly paid, is the amount which has already been paid in as the principal of a bond loan . . . ."[13] Similar support can be found in the *dictum* with which the First Circuit concluded its opinion in the *Motor Mart* case: "The offer of stock, with its accompanying equity rights in the company, was good consideration for the surrender of the bonds; and this is so *whether the par value of the stock or its then market value was greater or less than the face value of the bonds*. The transaction may be considered a form of

---

[9] IRS Letter Ruling 9015053, January 16, 1990. A different result may apply, however, for purposes of Code § 382(l)(6). *See* § 508.4.1.

[10] IRS Letter Ruling 9231036, April 30, 1992; preamble to Prop. Reg. § 1.382-3(i), (j), (k), (l), (m)(2), (n), and (p) issued under Code § 382(1)(6) (Prop. Reg. § 1.382-3 has since been renumbered as Reg. § 1.382-9). The IRS takes the opposite position, however, for purposes of Code § 382(l)(6). Id. *See* § 508.4.

[11] *Capento Sec. Corp. v. Commissioner, supra* note 2.

[12] *See* Rabinowitz & Jacobson, Reorganization of the Bankrupt Corporation Under IRC Section 368(a)(1)(G): Panacea or Placebo, 42 Inst. on Fed. Tax'n § 10.05[2](1984); Asofsky, Discharge of Indebtedness, *supra* note 1, at 607-608; New York State Bar Association, Tax Section, Report of the Committee on Bankruptcy, The Stock-for-Debt Exception to the Tax Treatment of Income from Discharge of Indebtedness (December 20, 1983) (additionally, the excess of liquidation preference over value may result in constructive dividend consequences under Code § 305).

[13] *Capento Sec. Corp. v. Commissioner, supra* note 2, at 695.

payment to the bonds, not cancellation." (Emphasis added.)[14] The IRS seemed to waffle during the 1980s about the way the stock-for-debt exception applies to limited preferred stock. However, in early 1990 it refused to rule on the issue pending further study;[15] and later that year it issued Rev. Rul. 90-87[16] holding that while limited preferred stock qualified for the stock-for-debt exception, the excess of the debt being cancelled over the liquidation preference of the preferred would constitute COD income (and it is irrelevant for this purpose that the value, and thus the issue price, of the preferred might be less than the liquidation preference). This view was subsequently embodied in the 1990 version of Prop. Reg. § 1.108-1, and in the revised version issued in 1992 and made final in 1994 (which are discussed at § 504A.4.1, below). The regulations limit the amount that qualifies for the stock-for-debt exception to the lesser of the lowest redemption price or lowest liquidation preference (determined at issuance).

The Revenue Reconciliation Act of 1990, by amending pre-1994 Code § 108(e)(10)(B),[17] narrowed the availability of the stock-for-debt exception for preferred stock still further (and differently). This provision[18] says that the exception is not available for "disqualified stock." This is defined as any stock having a stated redemption price if (1) it has a fixed redemption date, (2) the issuer has the right to redeem the stock at one or more times, or (3) the holder has the right to compel redemption of the stock at one or more times. A related amendment to Code § 108(e)(8)[19] provides that "disqualified stock" will not be treated as stock at all for purposes of the *de minimis* and disproportionality requirements of the stock-for-debt exception. Nothing is said in the statute or committee reports about the effect of

---

[14] *Commissioner v. Motor Mart Trust, supra* note 2, at 127. This comment was cited favorably by the IRS in a footnote (though again, apparently as a *dictum*) in several 1987 technical advice memoranda involving stock-for-debt swaps with underwriters. The memoranda, referring to the cases that came after *Capento,* said: "Unlike the Board of Tax Appeals' decision in *Capento Securities Corp.* which identified the par value of the stock as relevant, these cases rejected this factor. Instead, they regarded the face amount of the loan, representing the amount of otherwise taxable income, as the sole measure of exclusion." *E.g.,* Technical Advice Memorandum 8738003, n.6, May 22, 1987; Technical Advice Memorandum 8735006, n.4, May 18, 1987; Technical Advice Memorandum 8735007, n.4, May 18, 1987. However, in another technical advice memorandum issued in 1988 regarding the stock-for-debt exception, the IRS said that: "The cases which follow *Capento* do so on the basis of the substitution of liability theory. [Citing, among others, the *Motor Mart* case] . . . The sole reliance of these cases on the substitution of liability theory [sic]casts some doubt as to the continued viability of the subscription price theory of *Capento.*" Technical Advice Memorandum 8837001, May 10, 1988.

[15] IRS Letter Ruling 9019036, February 9, 1990; *but see* IRS Letter Ruling 8735007, May 18, 1987 (background documents reveal use of straight preferred stock without discussion of the issue). Also consider IRS Letter Ruling 8914080, January 11, 1989 (subsidiary debt exchanged for acquiring company's preferred stock; transaction recast as a first-step deemed recapitalization of the debt for the subsidiary's stock—to which the stock-for-debt exception applied—followed by an exchange of that stock for the preferred stock).

[16] 1990-2 C.B. 32.

[17] This provision was repealed prospectively by the 1993 Act as part of its prospective repeal of the stock-for-debt exception.

[18] For a discussion of this provision, *see* Pollack & Goldring, The Stock for Debt Exception—New Restrictions on the Use of Preferred Stock, 2 Faulkner & Gray's Bankr. L. Rev. #4, p.41 (Winter 1991).

[19] This provision was repealed prospectively by the 1993 Act as part of its prospective repeal of the stock-for-debt exception.

adding a convertible or participating feature to what would otherwise be "disqualified" stock. Such stock as an economic matter has common stock characteristics, and we can discern no policy reason for not treating it as common stock for COD purposes. Aside from this economic point, if the convertibility or participating feature operates, by the terms of the instrument, to affect the redemption price that must be paid by the issuer, the stock would not seem to have a "stated" redemption price.[20] Thus, it should not come within the scope of Rev. Rul. 90-87 or pre-1994 Code § 108(e)(10)(B). However, if these features do not affect the redemption price, one is left with only the economic argument. Except to the extent these exceptions are accepted, the only preferred that one can count on as continuing to qualify for the stock-for-debt exception is "evergreen preferred," that is, preferred that has no fixed redemption date and is neither callable by the issuer nor puttable by the holder. Of course, in the IRS's current view, as reflected in Rev. Rul. 90-87 and Reg. § 1.108-1, such evergreen preferred would qualify for the exception only in the amount of its lowest liquidation preference (determined at issuance).

Note that the consequences of coverage by the Rev. Rul. 90-87 and Reg. § 1.108-1 approach differ sharply from the consequences of being "disqualified stock." Rev. Rul. 90-87 and Prop. Reg. § 1.108-1 allow the stock to qualify for the stock-for-debt exception in the amount of its liquidation preference (even if its value is lower) and to count toward the *de minimis* and disproportionality tests, whereas "disqualified stock" does not qualify at all and is simply treated as paying an amount of debt equal to its fair market value.

Note, further, that this statutory treatment of "disqualified" preferred means that from the tax point of view new "disqualified" preferred is now less attractive than new debt as an instrument for debt restructurings in cases where neither the old nor the new instruments are publicly traded. In such cases Code § 1274 allows the new debt to be taken into account at its Code § 1274 issue price (which may be substantially above its value). But new "disqualified stock" must always be taken into account at value. Thus the use of "disqualified" preferred will often produce more COD income for the issuer and OID-like Code § 305 income to the holder than the use of an equivalent amount of new debt.

The 1990 Code § 108 statutory amendment that creates this new "disqualified" stock status is effective for exchanges after October 9, 1990, except for those (1) pursuant to a prior binding written contract, (2) in a transaction described in certain previously filed or released documents, or (3) in a title 11 or similar case filed before October 10, 1990.

The 1990 Act simultaneously amended Code § 305(c), to subject preferred stock issued at a premium to the economic accrual rules of the OID provisions. This amendment provides that the *entire* premium (subject only to the 1/4 of 1 percent annual exception incorporated from the OID rules) will be subject to such treatment where the stock is required to be redeemed by the issuer or is puttable by the holder.

---

[20] The IRS has ruled that common stock that the issuer had an option to purchase for a price equal to the fair market value of the stock at the time of exercise was not "disqualified" stock for purposes of pre-1994 Code § 108(e)(10)(B). IRS Letter Ruling 9408020, November 29, 1993.

Where the stock is not puttable and the issuer has only the right (but not the obligation) to redeem it, regulations provide that the redemption premium (other than a premium solely in the nature of a penalty for premature redemption) will be brought into income only if, based on all facts and circumstances as of the issue date, the stock will more likely than not be redeemed (subject to a safe harbor test).[21] When such an unreasonable premium is brought into income, the economic accrual method of the OID provisions rather than the former Code § 305 ratable inclusion method will apply. (Note that this new Code § 305(c) distinction, between stock that is mandatorily redeemable and stock that is redeemable only at the option of the issuer, was not made in the Code § 108 definition of "disqualified stock.") The committee reports add that stock that in form is only optionally callable by the issuer may nonetheless be treated as puttable or mandatorily callable if other arrangements effectively require the issuer to redeem the stock. They also say the IRS may treat cumulative dividends as a disguised redemption premium when there is no intention at the time of issuance of the stock to pay them currently. The effective date of the Code § 305(c) amendment is essentially the same as that of the 1990 Code § 108 amendment, except the bankruptcy-case grandfathering provision is narrower and only applies to stock issued pursuant to a *plan* filed before October 10, 1990.

Suppose, for example, that new preferred stock with a liquidation and redemption preference of $100 but a value of $20 is issued in a recapitalization exchange for $100 face amount (and basis) of old debt. Because Code § 354 will not allow the holder to deduct his loss, the holder's basis in the new preferred stock will be $100. Will the Code § 305 redemption premium be zero or $80? If $80, can the holder amortize his $80 excess basis against the deemed Code § 305 distribution? Would the answer differ if the preferred is "disqualified" stock (which has different COD consequences for the issuer than other preferred stock) or if the exchange is a taxable exchange (in which case the holder's basis will be $20) rather than a recapitalization exchange? Obviously, these questions pose issues identical to those presented by Code § 1275(a)(4) and its 1990 repeal (*see* § 403.1.2 above). These questions were not discussed in the 1990 Act committee reports. Example (6) in Reg. § 1.305-5(d) seems to leave the door open for treating the premium as zero, at least if a tax-free recapitalization exchange is involved. However, in view of the repeal of Code § 1275(a)(4), the IRS will no doubt want to treat the redemption premium in the example given as $80. Moreover, it is doubtful that the holder will be able to offset his deemed dividend income by his equivalent basis "premium," unless the IRS adds this privilege in the final regulations it issues to implement the Code § 305(c) amendment.

The cumulative effect of these 1990 amendments to Code §§ 108 and 305(c) is to make preferred stock far less attractive as a mechanism for restructuring old debt than it used to be.

---

[21] Reg. § 1.305-5(b)(1)(3).

### § 504A.3.2 Parent Stock; Successor Stock

The cases make it clear that not only stock of the debtor, but stock of a successor to the debtor, will qualify for the stock-for-debt exception.[22] However, the courts never had occasion to decide whether stock of a parent corporation would qualify, and so, until the IRS ruled on this issue in early 1995, one had to hesitate to use parent stock. This is the primary reason why triangular "G" reorganizations, although authorized by the 1980 Bankruptcy Tax Act amendments to the Internal Revenue Code, had not proved practicable.[23] One can make a strong argument that parent stock should satisfy the test and that this is implicit in Code § 108 and the "G" reorganization provisions adopted in 1980. But it was not until 1995—after the stock-for-debt exception had been prospectively repealed by the 1993 Act—that the issue was addressed. Congress had had an opportunity to clarify this issue when it adopted the Tax Reform Act of 1986, but it failed to do so. The 1986 Act amended Code § 361(b) to provide that the disappearing transferor company in a two-company or triangular reorganization would not recognize gain or loss on the distribution to its creditors of stock or securities in another party to the reorganization. The occasion of this statutory amendment would have been an excellent time for Congress to say whether parent stock could qualify for the stock-for-debt exception. However, a footnote in the Conference Report to the 1986 Act only said that "this provision is not intended, however, to affect the recognition of discharge of indebtedness income by the acquired corporation on a transfer to a creditor."[24] Code § 361 was amended by TAMRA in 1988. Again, however, the parent stock issue was sidestepped. The 1988 committee report contained the same footnote as had the 1986 committee report.[25]

Fortunately, in early 1995, the IRS finally ruled that stock of a parent corporation issued for debt of a subsidiary could qualify for the stock-for-debt exception to COD income at the subsidiary level.[26] In this ruling, the parent of a consolidated return group that was in bankruptcy issued its stock in satisfaction of debt issued by the bankrupt subsidiaries and of debt issued by the bankrupt parent. The IRS ruled that the stock-for-debt exception would apply to the subsidiaries as well as to the parent upon issuance of the parent's stock; that each subsidiary should separately determine whether the conditions of pre-1994 Code § 108(e)(8) had been satisfied as to it, by treating the parent stock as if it had been subsidiary stock of equal value; that each creditor of a subsidiary, for purposes of determining future recapture, is likewise to treat the parent stock received in satisfaction of the subsidiary debt as being stock of the subsidiary whose indebtedness was so satisfied; and that the issuance of parent

---

[22] *Alcazar Hotel, Inc. v. Commissioner, supra* note 2; *Claridge Apartments Co. v. Commissioner, supra* note 2.

[23] On the use of parent stock, *see* Pollack & Goldring, Can Cancellation of Indebtedness Income Be Avoided with Parent Stock? 2 Corp. Tax'n 18 (Jan./Feb. 1990), 3 Corp. Tax'n 12 (July/August 1990). *See also* the explanation of the "G" reorganization provisions in Chapter 6. The IRS refrains from ruling on whether parent stock will qualify. *See, e.g.,* IRS Letter Ruling 9231036, April 30, 1992.

[24] H.R. Rep. No. 841, 99th Cong., 2d Sess. II-844 (1986) (the 1986 Act Conference Report).

[25] H.R. Rep. No. 445, 100th Cong., 2d Sess. 393 n.104.

[26] IRS Letter Ruling 9516025, January 18, 1995.

stock for subsidiary debt would not result in any such debtor subsidiary ceasing to be a member of the consolidated return group. In addition, the total amount of stock that could be issued for unresolved claims was fixed and thus would not be affected by the amount of claims that were eventually allowed; and in this regard the IRS ruled that for purposes of pre-1994 Code §108(e)(8)(B), both for determining the "individual common stock ratio" and for determining the "group common stock ratio," the recoveries of creditors would be determined by treating the amount payable to the unresolved claims as the amount estimated in the plan's Disclosure Statement, without being affected by the ultimate recoveries.

Before the issuance of this favorable IRS letter ruling, taxpayers had to consider whether they could solve the parent-stock problem in some way other than by a direct issuance of parent stock for subsidiary debt. One possible way was by engaging in a first-step recapitalization, wherein the subsidiary's debt is exchanged for subsidiary stock (which qualifies for the stock-for-debt exception), followed by a second-step exchange of such stock for parent stock. In fact, the IRS has favorably ruled on just such a transaction.[27] Moreover, in Rev. Rul. 59-222 (discussed at §§510.2 and 602 below), the IRS recharacterized an exchange of debt of a bankrupt company for stock of an acquiring company as involving a "deemed" first-step recapitalization even though no actual first-step recapitalization physically occurred. The first-step deemed recapitalization was held to qualify for the stock-for-debt exception, and the second-step actual acquisition qualified as a "B" reorganization. The IRS applied this "deemed" recapitalization approach in two letter rulings.[28] The facts of these rulings are similar to those in Rev. Rul. 59-222: In both rulings (1) the debtor was in bankruptcy or a similar insolvency proceeding and (2) the second-step deemed exchange qualified as either a "B" reorganization or an equivalent reorganization solely for stock. However, the IRS confined the application of these rulings to quite narrow facts. In the first of these rulings, the acquiring entity in the second-step reorganization was the corporation that was the parent of the debtor at the time of the first-step deemed recapitalization (rather than an outside acquirer as in Rev. Rul. 59-222). In the ruling, the IRS stated that it would not have issued the ruling had the parent not also been in bankruptcy.[29] It also said that it would not have issued the ruling had the second-step deemed exchange not constituted a "B" reorganization; indeed, it indicated that to the extent the second step did not constitute a "B" reorganization, the transaction would not be treated as though it involved a first-step

---

[27] *See* IRS Letter Ruling 8852039, October 4, 1988. *See also* IRS Letter Ruling 200144001, April 27, 2001 (conversion of a mutual insurance company into a stock company is a good "E" recapitalization, and does not prevent immediate downstream merger into a subsidiary from qualifying under Code §§368(a)(1)(A) and 368(a)(2)(D); the ruling does not involve a failing company or the stock-for-debt exception, and does not mention Rev. Rul. 59-222).

[28] *See* IRS Letter Ruling 8933001, August 22, 1988; IRS Letter Ruling 8914080, January 11, 1989. *See also* IRS Letter Ruling 200144001, April 27, 2001 (conversion of a mutual insurance company into a stock company is a good "E" recapitalization, and does not prevent immediate downstream merger into a subsidiary from qualifying under Code §§368(a)(1)(A) and 368(a)(2)(D); the ruling does not involve a failing company or the stock-for-debt exception, and does not mention Rev. Rul. 59-222). *See also* Pollack & Goldring, *supra* note 23 (analyzing rulings).

[29] *See* IRS Letter Ruling 8933001, August 22, 1988.

deemed recapitalization, and COD would result. This amounts, in essence, to a rejection of the inclusion of parent stock within the stock-for-debt exception. This first ruling was subsequently modified and broadened, however, to delete the requirement for "B" reorganization treatment of the second step.[30] In the second ruling (in which the second-step reorganization involved an independent acquiring entity, as in Rev. Rul. 59-222), it is unclear whether the acquiring corporation was itself in bankruptcy. Thus, it is unclear whether this will be required for similar rulings in the future. In addition, in the first ruling, the IRS ruled that the deemed issuance of the debtor's stock would not result in the debtor ceasing to be a member of its parent's consolidated group (although at one time the IRS was reported to have been reconsidering that position).[31] For a number of years before 1995, the IRS had suspended issuing rulings applying Rev. Rul. 59-222, pending its resolution of the parent stock issue itself.[32] Although the IRS has now favorably resolved the parent-stock issue by issuing IRS Letter Ruling 9516025, discussed above, it remains unclear as to whether the IRS will continue to be reluctant to issue rulings applying Rev. Rul. 59-222. However, the IRS, without mentioning Rev. Rul. 59-222,[33] has ruled that an actual "E" recapitalization may precede an "A" reorganization.

The use of parent stock to satisfy the stock-for-debt exception should not be confused with the use of stock of a successor to satisfy the exception. If the subsidiary remains alive as a separate corporation after the issuance of parent stock for its debt, the successor rule cannot apply. In such a case, unless parent stock is determined to qualify (or the concepts of Rev. Rul. 59-222 apply), the stock-for-debt exception will not apply. However, if the subsidiary merges into the parent and parent stock is issued to the creditors of the subsidiary, the parent has become the successor to the subsidiary. And, as mentioned earlier, stock of a successor has always been considered to qualify for the stock-for-debt exception. Indeed, the IRS has issued a letter ruling holding the stock-for-debt exception to apply where an insolvent subsidiary was merged into its parent in what was held to be a "G" reorganization, and parent stock was issued to the creditors of the subsidiary.[34] The ruling noted that the parent expressly assumed the debt of the subsidiary. The ruling did not mention the successor-stock precedent. However, what is particularly interesting about the ruling is that it went out of its way to hold that because of the merger of the subsidiary into the parent, the parent was deemed to be the issuer of the debt issued by the subsidiary, and so the stock-for-debt exception applied when the parent (simultaneously) issued its stock in satisfaction of that debt.

The 1990 Act added yet another potential twist, and one that is quite unintended, to the parent stock (and even possibly the successor stock) saga. As mentioned at

---

[30] IRS Letter Ruling 9333048, May 28, 1993.

[31] *See* 89 Tax Notes 103-19 (May 15, 1989).

[32] *See* remarks of Tom Wessel, 50 Tax Notes 1049, (March 11, 1991).

[33] IRS Letter Ruling 200144001, April 27, 2001 (conversion of mutual insurance company into a stock company was a good "E," and would not prevent an immediate downstream merger into a subsidiary from qualifying under Code §§368(a)(1)(A) and 368(a)(2)(D); the ruling does not involve a failing company, and does not mention Rev. Rul. 59-222).

[34] IRS Letter Ruling 9122067, March 6, 1991.

§ 504A.3.1, the 1990 Act amended pre-1994 Code § 108(e)(10)(B) (subsequently repealed, prospectively, by the 1993 Act) to provide that "disqualified stock" will not qualify for the stock-for-debt exception. Although this was the only stated purpose of the amendment, the amendment added the phrase "stock of the debtor" to pre-1994 Code § 108(e)(10)(B)(i). If this phrase is construed as defining all that now remains of the stock-for-debt exception, it would seem, quite inadvertently, to have eliminated the possibility that parent stock could qualify for the stock-for-debt exception. It is also possible, although less likely, that this language could be construed as repealing (equally inadvertently) the long-standing successor-stock rule. Fortunately, it seems clear that the IRS has not taken either of these adverse positions. Had the IRS done so, the favorable holding in IRS Letter Ruling 9516025, discussed above, could not have been reached. (The transaction in that ruling was one to which pre-1994 Code § 108(e)(10)(B) applied.)

#### § 504A.3.3 Warrants

The courts have never had occasion to decide whether warrants could qualify for the stock-for-debt exception.[35] However, in a 1999 Field Service Advice, the IRS recognized that, "[b]ecause the warrants constitute an equity interest with respect to common stock, the stock-for-debt exception would arguably apply to the issuance of the warrants."[36]

#### § 504A.3.4 Miscellaneous

The 1984 Act included, in Code § 108(e)(10)(C), a limited stock-for-debt exception for solvent taxpayers outside bankruptcy. This "qualified workout" provision, as it was called, had a delayed effective date. It was not to become effective until 1986 (when the 1976 amendments to Code § 382 were also to become effective). It is interesting to note that the legislative history to the 1984 Act indicated that one of the reasons for delaying the effective date of this "qualified workout" provision was to allow Congress time to study the stock-for-debt exception in relation to the Code § 382 rules regarding NOL carryovers, and that such study would include "consideration of the rules relating to the use of preferred or limited stock, stock of a parent corporation, and stock of a party to a reorganization . . . ."[37] The 1986 Act repealed Code § 108(e)(10)(C) (along with the 1976 amendments to Code § 382) before it became effective. Just as nothing was said about the availability of the stock-for-debt

---

[35] *But cf.* 11 U.S.C. § 346(j)(7) (warrants permitted for state and local tax purposes).

[36] IRS Field Service Advice 200011006, November 23, 1999, *reprinted at* 2000 TNT 54-82, involving a transaction pre-dating the statutory repeal of the stock-for-debt exception. It is interesting to note, nonetheless, that neither the statutory reference in Code § 108 allowing the stock-for-debt exception, nor the later repeal by an amendment to this section of the stock-for-debt exception, refer to warrants: they refer only to "stock." For the treatment of warrants as "securities" for purposes of Code § § 354, 355 and 356 beginning in 1998, *see* § 502.3 above.

[37] Joint Committee on Taxation, General Explanation of the Revenue Provisions of the Deficit Reduction Act of 1984, December 31, 1984, at 168.

exception for parent stock in connection with the 1986 amendment to Code § 361(b), so also nothing was said about it in connection with the 1986 repeal of Code § 108(e)(10)(C), although the 1986 Act did direct the Treasury to study the treatment of informal bankruptcy workouts for purposes of Code § § 108 and 382.[38]

## *§504A.4 Limitations on the Exception*

The Bankruptcy Tax Act of 1980 amended pre-1994 Code § 108(e)(8) to provide two new statutory limitations on the stock-for-debt exception. These two limitations, the *"de minimis"* limitation and a limitation dealing with disproportionate distributions to unsecured creditors, are discussed below.

The Tax Reform Act of 1986 amended Code § 382 to add a third limitation. The third limitation applies when a company in a bankruptcy or similar proceeding qualifies for (and does not elect out of) a special Code § 382 provision that was added by the 1986 Act. This third limitation is discussed at § 508.5. Finally, as mentioned at § 504A, the stock-for-debt exception was repealed entirely by the 1993 Act, with a prospective effective date.

### § 504A.4.1 *"De minimis"* Limitation

The first limitation says that the stock-for-debt exception will not apply "to the issuance of nominal or token shares . . . ." The legislative history of the 1980 Bankruptcy Tax Act gives no guidance as to the meaning of this test. However, it is interesting to note that the heading to pre-1994 Code § 108(e)(8) is "stock for debt exception not to apply in *de minimis* cases." The legislative history uses the words "nominal," "token," and "*de minimis*" interchangeably. Webster's Third New International Dictionary (1981) defines nominal as "being so small, slight, or negligible as scarcely to be entitled to the name: trifling, insignificant." It defines "token" as "having semblance or serving as a sign or sample of the real thing: simulated, minimal, perfunctory." The phrase *de minimis* has long been known to lawyers in the phrase *"de minimis non curat lex,"* which Black's law dictionary defines as: "The law does not care for, or take notice of, very small or trifling matters. The law does not concern itself about trifles." Congress's use of all three of these synonymous words, rather than just one of them, seems to emphasize its desire to prevent the exception from interfering with the basic purpose of Congress to preserve the stock-for-debt exception, so as to "encourage reorganization, rather than liquidation, of financially distressed companies that have a potential for surviving as operating businesses."[39]

One commentator suggests looking by analogy to the definition of "transferor" for purposes of receiving nonrecognition treatment on Code § 351 (incorporation-type) transfers.[40] Reg. § 1.351-1(a)(1)(ii) provides that a person will not be treated as a

---

[38] Tax Reform Act of 1986, Pub. L. No. 99-514, 99th Cong., 2d Sess. (the 1986 Act), § 621(d)(2).

[39] S. Rep. No. 1035, 96th Cong., 2d Sess. 11 (1980).

[40] *See* Mirsky & Willens, The Bankruptcy Tax Act of 1980, 59 Taxes 145, 149 (1981).

"transferor" for Code § 351 purposes where he receives stock or securities for property of "relatively small value" in comparison with the value of the stock or securities he already owns or is to receive for services. For purposes of this test, Rev. Proc. 77-37[41] provides that property will not be considered of "relatively small value" for advance ruling purposes if it equals at least 10 percent of the value of the stock or securities already owned by the person or to be received for services by him.

There is some question as to whether 10 percent, or some other percentage, is the appropriate test. Some practitioners have been known to advise, perhaps out of an excess of caution, that a 15 percent or even a 20 percent number should be used for planning purposes. We believe that 10 percent, and perhaps a substantially smaller number, should satisfy the legal test.[42]

Another question is the amount against which the percentage should be applied: Should it be the total value of the old debt (*i.e.*, the value of all the consideration going to the creditor); should it be the principal amount of the debt being satisfied with stock; or should it be the total principal amount of the debt? Where the debtor is very insolvent, the value-of-the-old-debt test has the greatest appeal to us.[43] Otherwise, the more insolvent a company is, the less opportunity it will have to rely on the stock-for-debt exception to eliminate COD income. This does not seem to be the right result. For example, if the value of a company's debt had shrunk to four cents on the dollar, and if one were to decide that the minimum percentage allowable for the exception was 5 percent, issuance of all stock for this debt would not satisfy the exception unless a value-of-the-old-debt test were applied. Hence, it seems to us that if the debt is worth, for example, 40 cents on the dollar, the issuance of stock worth 10 percent of this value (four cents on the dollar of debt) should satisfy the *de minimis* test, even though the stock is only worth 4/100 of the total face of the debt, and only 4/64 of the amount of the debt being satisfied with stock.

In addition, regardless of the value of the stock received, if the creditors of the failing company received in satisfaction of the debt a significant continuing stock ownership in the company, for example 10 or 15 percent of the company's thereafter

---

[41] 1977-2 C.B. 568.

[42] *See also* Asofsky, Uncertain Limits: The Stock-for-Debt Exception to Discharge of Indebtedness Income, Vol. 1, No. 2 Corp. Tax'n 59, 61 (1988); Gelfeld & Lobl, Tax Planning Opportunities for Debtor Corporations in Chapter 11 Proceedings, 91 Comm. Law. J. 417, 423 (1986). Rev. Proc. 77-37 is presumably a "safe harbor" line. The only authorities holding that the substantive test in the regulation, to which it refers, has been violated involve a much smaller percentage. Rev. Rul. 79-194, 1979-1 C.B. 145 (Situation 2) (1 percent); *Kamborian v. Commissioner*, 56 T.C. 847, Dec. 30,895 (1971), *aff'd*, 469 F.2d 219, 72-2 U.S.T.C. ¶9747 (1st Cir. 1972) (stock worth $5,000 representing 0.8 percent). Other *de minimis* tests used in the tax law usually draw a line that is less than 10 percent. *See, e.g.*, Reg. § 1.305-3(c)(1) (5 percent); Temp. Reg. § 1.338-4T(h)(7) (lesser of 5 percent or $50,000); Code § 4943(c)(2)(C) (2 percent).

[43] *See also* Asofsky, Uncertain Limits, *supra* note 42, at 61. But *see* Tatlock, Bankruptcy and Insolvency: Tax Aspects and Procedure, 466 T.M. A-50, A-51 (1985) (although recognizing the absence of any guidance, the author states that "presumably the determination of whether shares are token or nominal would be based on a comparison of the value of the shares and the amount of the debt [satisfied with stock]"); Bacon *et al.*, Tax Planning for the Financially Troubled Company, 36 Major Tax Plan 14-1, at 14-45 (1984) (remarks of Milton B. Hyman; states belief that percentage should be applied to the amount of the debt satisfied with stock; also states that the test ought to be applied on an aggregate basis to all debts being satisfied with stock, rather than on a creditor-by-creditor basis).

outstanding stock (excluding straight preferred stock), we believe that such stock ownership should also satisfy the *de minimis* test.[44] One needs a test that looks only to the proportion of the stock going to the creditors and not to its value, in order to give meaning to the statutory availability of the stock-for-debt exception for insolvent debtors who are not in bankruptcy. For them, the stock-for-debt exception is limited to the amount of their insolvency. Stock that cancels only enough debt to eliminate insolvency (and not enough to create positive net worth) would not, by definition, have any liquidating value. At best such stock could have only minimal speculative value. Applying a value requirement to the stock could virtually eliminate the stock-for-debt exception for insolvent debtors not in bankruptcy.

The IRS issued its first interpretation of the *de minimis* test in a technical advice memorandum issued in May 1988.[45] Here, pursuant to a bankruptcy plan, creditors received cash plus new preferred stock in exchange for their debt. The stock carried the right to cash preferential dividends, plus a 5 percent participation feature with the common stock. After three years, the holder could convert the preferred stock into common stock of the debtor's parent; after five years, the debtor could redeem the preferred stock.

The memorandum took the position that the stock-for-debt provision in pre-1994 Code § 108(e)(8) "was intended to continue the general notions of the substitution of liability theory underlying the stock for debt rule and to limit the application of the rule in the case of a stock for debt exchange which was essentially a sham transaction." The memorandum concluded that the foregoing stock-for-debt exchange was not a sham.

The IRS said that whether stock was "nominal or token" depended on the facts and circumstances of the individual case, especially those relevant to the economic substance of the transaction and the equity interest created. "Accordingly, consideration must be given to those factors which indicate arm's-length bargaining, including such elements as the existence of sufficiently adverse economic interests on each side of the exchange, the value of the stock exchanged in comparison to the face amount of the debt cancelled, and the value of the stock received in comparison to the total consideration received in discharge of the debt." In the case before it, arm's-length bargaining existed. In addition, the stock represented about 15 percent of the total consideration received for the debt and about 10 percent of the amount of debt (after payment of the cash) that was cancelled in the exchange for stock; these comparisons, the IRS said, "indicate that the . . . preferred stock was a significant part of the consideration used to discharge the debt." Further, the creditors received more value as a result of the exchange than they would have received had the company been

---

[44] In Rev. Proc. 94-26, 1994-13 I.R.B. 21, the IRS did issue a safe harbor for the *de minimis* test for common stock issued to unsecured creditors if its value is at least 15 percent of the value of all stock (including preferred stock and disqualified stock) outstanding immediately after the workout. This revenue procedure is effective only for issuances of stock on or after May 17, 1994. It states that no inference is intended for earlier transactions.

[45] IRS Technical Advice Memorandum, 8837001, May 10, 1988. The interpretation suggested above by the authors, and the holding in Technical Advice Memorandum 8837001, are criticized in Shakow, The Stock-for-Debt *De Minimis* Exception, 41 Tax Notes 1325 (December 19, 1988).

liquidated. "Each of these factors," the IRS concluded, "demonstrates that the . . . preferred stock . . . was not 'nominal or token.'"

The IRS issued another interesting *de minimis* ruling in IRS Letter Ruling 9019036. Here, in a bankruptcy plan governed by Code § 382(l)(5), old-and-cold creditors (within the meaning of that section) of a parent corporation were to receive at least 50 percent of the common stock of the debtor (the only class constituting "stock" for Code § 382 purposes). Creditors who were not old-and-cold were to receive straight preferred and some common, the plan having been designed so that old-and-cold creditors would end up with at least 50 percent of the "stock" so as to satisfy Code § 382(l)(5). No consideration other than stock was given to any creditor. The ruling does not indicate the relation of the value of this consideration to the face amount of debt, but it is understood to have been small, perhaps as little as 1 percent or less. The ruling held that the stock issued to the old-and-cold creditors (who received only common stock) would not be considered nominal or token, but expressed no opinion whether the stock issued to creditors receiving both common and preferred would be considered nominal or token. The IRS obviously believed that the preferred should be ignored (essentially treated as if it were cash) and the common examined separately in determining whether the stock issued was nominal or token.[46]

In the same ruling, a subsidiary corporation, which was also in bankruptcy, had a similar plan, except that subsidiary stock rather than parent stock was to be issued to the subsidiary creditors and each creditor was to receive both common and preferred, allowing the parent to continue to own more than 80 percent of the common stock of the subsidiary. Even though the subsidiary common stock represented at least 10 percent of the total consideration (both common and preferred) to be received by the creditors, the IRS refused to rule whether the *common* stock was nominal or token, thereby ignoring the preferred stock in applying the test. Again, the ruling does not state the relation of the value of this total consideration to the face amount of the debt, but we understand it to have been one percent or less.

Apparently, the IRS was troubled because the preferred stock in this ruling was not "stock" for Code § 382 purposes, and the IRS felt that such stock should not qualify for the Code § 108 stock-for-debt exception. Although this policy judgment was debatable, the matter soon shifted from the realm of debatable judgment to that of debatable (but never debated) Congressional action. As mentioned above at § 504A.3.1, the 1990 Act amended pre-1994 Code § 108(e)(11) and (e)(8) to provide that "disqualified" preferred stock is not to be treated as stock for purposes of the stock-for-debt exception, including the *de minimis* test. The drafter of this legislation apparently shifted his focus from the IRS's concern, however, because "disqualified" stock as defined in the amendment can include stock (such as voting, and, as mentioned above, perhaps even convertible or participating preferred) that is treated as stock for Code § 382 purposes. One can surmise that the drafter's focus shifted to whether the preferred was more "debt-like" than "stock-like" (another debatable concept). But if so, even that concept was not carried through in fully logical fashion,

---

46 The IRS subsequently addressed the treatment of preferred stock in Reg. § 1.108, discussed below in this § 504A.4.1.

because, as discussed above at § 504A.3.1, the result of the amendment is that in some ways "disqualified" preferred is treated even more harshly than debt as an instrument for debt restructuring.[47]

The IRS has since issued Reg. § 1.108-1, dealing with the *de minimis* test. The first proposed version, issued on December 7, 1990, was severely criticized. The IRS took the criticisms to heart, and on November 3, 1992, it withdrew the 1990 proposed regulation and issued a new proposed Reg. § 1.108-1. This was made final in 1994. This regulation covers both the *de minimis* and the proportionality tests and is a very substantial improvement in both substance and style.

So that the reader can better understand the development of the rules in this area, we will first include below the description and analysis we had made of the 1990 proposed regulation. We will then cover the final regulation.

**The 1990 proposed regulation.** On December 7, 1990 (which we feared at the time might be remembered as Pearl Harbor Day for the stock-for-debt exception), the IRS issued Prop. Reg. § 1.108-1 and an accompanying release, both dealing with the stock-for-debt exception's *de minimis* test. The regulation was proposed to be effective for exchanges on or after December 6, 1990. For practical planning purposes one therefore had to consider it currently effective. The release said no inference was intended concerning the meaning of the *de minimis* test for prior periods, but then inconsistently went on to say the IRS would apply the principles underlying the proposed rules to exchanges occurring before December 6, 1990.

The proposed regulation said that in determining whether stock is nominal or token the following three stock ratios were to be considered:

(1) *Stock to debt ratio.* This is the ratio of the value of the stock to the face amount of the portion of the indebtedness it satisfies.
(2) *Stock to consideration ratio.* This is the ratio of the value of the stock to the value of the total consideration exchanged for the debt (*i.e.*, to the value of the debt).
(3) *Stock to total stock ratio.* This is the ratio of the value of the stock issued to the creditors to the value of all the outstanding stock.

"Disqualified" stock was not to be treated as stock for purposes of these ratios, unless it was grandfathered under the effective date rules.

The first of these ratios was stated to be the most important. This is contrary to the approach we had suggested above. By focusing on the amount of debt being cancelled rather than on the value of the debt, it meant that the more insolvent a company was, the harder it would be for the company to qualify for the stock-for-debt exception to eliminate COD income. And by focusing on the value of the stock rather than on its percentage of the outstanding stock, it meant a company not in bankruptcy would find it very difficult to qualify for the stock-for-debt exception.

Moreover, the proposed regulation tightened the screws still further by adding a special rule for the treatment of preferred stock in applying the first ratio. This was

---

[47] Id.

that the first ratio was to be applied separately (1) to each class of preferred stock and (2) to the aggregate of all other stock. (If a class of preferred stock was found to be nominal or token, it would be treated, just as "disqualified" stock is treated, as nonstock for purposes of applying the first ratio to other classes of stock.) For this purpose, preferred stock was defined as stock that has a limited or fixed redemption or liquidation amount and does not have a "meaningful" right to participate in corporate growth; moreover, for this purpose neither a conversion right nor a liquidation preference that exceeds the value of the preferred was to be treated as conferring a "meaningful" right to participate in corporate growth. The release added that generally a higher degree of participation in corporate growth would be required under this proposed regulation than where the concept of "significant" participation in corporate growth is used in other parts of the Code. However, it gave no specific guidance as to what this means. Moreover, nothing was said about a participating stock feature.

The proposed regulation ended with an example, designed to illustrate the workings of the first ratio when both preferred and common stock are issued.[48] On the facts given, the first ratio for the preferred was 95 percent and for the common was 50 percent, and the second ratio (which combined the two classes, if the preferred is not nominal) was 96 percent. No facts were given from which one could calculate the third ratio. Despite these high ratios, the ruling surprisingly refrained from indicating whether the nominal or token test was satisfied by either class.

The release accompanying the proposed regulation set forth "proposed standards" for applying the factors set forth in the regulation, and asked for comments on these proposed standards. The proposed standards were that the stock would not be treated as nominal or token if:

(1) the first ratio for each class of preferred and for the aggregate of the other stock is at least 10 percent and the second ratio is at least 25 percent;

(2) the second ratio is at least 25 percent and the third ratio is also at least 25 percent; or

(3) the unsecured creditors receive only stock (thus the second ratio for them is 100 percent), and the third ratio, when applied to the stock issued to the unsecured creditors, is 90 percent.

These standards sharply differed from the 10 percent safe-harbor standards that we consider appropriate and from our view that satisfaction of any one of the three ratios should suffice. The release did not describe these proposed standards as safe harbors. We understand they were being thought of as ruling guidelines.

In our view, the proposed regulation and accompanying proposed standards turned the *de minimis* test on its head. They seemed to convert a negative test that the

---

[48] The example states that the preferred stock was redeemable but was not "disqualified" stock. Although the example states that the exchange was made by a corporation in a title 11 case, it does not say when the title 11 petition was filed. The redemption feature would, of course, cause the stock to be "disqualified" stock unless the petition had been filed before October 10, 1990.

stock issued not be nominal, token, or *de minimis* into a positive requirement that it be large, substantial, and significant.

At that point in our analysis, we observed that one of the issues not adequately addressed by the legislative history is whether the *de minimis* test should be applied by looking to the stock issued to each creditor on a creditor-by-creditor basis, or instead only to the aggregate of the stock issued to all of the creditors as a group. A good argument can be made, we said, that Congress intended the latter; that Congress intended the proportionality requirement (discussed in the next section) to be the exclusive means of dealing with creditor-by-creditor issues. Indeed, the argument would continue, if that is not the case, then the proportionality requirement is surplusage and serves no purpose at all.

In the 1990 proposed regulation, however, the IRS had not accepted that approach. The language of the proposed regulation was clear in requiring that the first two ratios be applied on a separate creditor-by-creditor basis, while requiring the third ratio to be applied to the creditors as a group.

The issue is hardly an academic one. In almost all cases, debtors will have issued subordinated debt. The subordinated debt will always be worth less than debt that is not subordinated, and thus, when stock is issued in satisfaction of both classes of debt, the amount of debt being cancelled with stock (the first ratio in the proposed regulation) will be greater for the subordinated debt.

**EXAMPLE 1**

Bankrupt debtor has outstanding $100,000 of nonsubordinated debt and $100,000 of subordinated debt. The creditors decide that the nonsubordinated debt is worth 20 cents on the dollar, or $20,000, and the subordinated debt is worth 10 cents on the dollar, or $10,000. The debtor satisfies each class with half stock and half cash. Thus, $10,000 worth of stock and $10,000 in cash is applied to discharge the nonsubordinated debt, and $5,000 worth of stock and $5,000 in cash is applied to discharge the subordinated debt. Under the proposed regulation, the second ratio for each class of debt is 50 percent. However, while the first ratio for the nonsubordinated debt is 11.1 percent, for the subordinated debt it is only 5.26 percent.

The stock consideration issued to the subordinated debt in the foregoing example satisfies the proportionality test with a margin of comfort. It would be anomalous to disqualify it for the stock-for-debt exception by applying as stiff a *de minimis* test as that suggested in the 1990 proposed regulation and its accompanying release. This seemed to us to emphasize the wisdom of dropping the first ratio in the proposed regulation entirely.

**The 1994 final regulation.** On November 3, 1992, the IRS, taking note of the criticisms that had been made, withdrew the 1990 proposed regulation and issued an entirely different proposed Reg. § 1.108-1. This proposed regulation, which was made final in 1994, is a vast improvement in both style and substance.

This regulation takes the salutary approach of combining both the *de minimis* (which it refers to as the nominal or token) test and the proportionality test into a single integrated approach. It can be summarized as follows:

(1) The "nominal or token" portion of the rule is applied on an aggregate basis. That is, it is tested not by looking to the stock issued to each creditor on a creditor-by-creditor basis (as the 1990 proposed regulation had done for its first two proposed ratios), but instead by looking only to the aggregate of all of the stock issued for the aggregate of the unsecured indebtedness involved in the title 11 or insolvency workout. The regulation does not provide a list of relevant ratios or factors to be used in making the nominal or token determination (such as the three ratios contained in the 1990 proposed regulation). It merely says instead that "all relevant facts and circumstances must be considered in making this determination." However, the preamble to the proposed 1992 regulation stated the IRS was considering announcing a guideline that the nominal or token test would be met if the stock-to-total-stock ratio for common stock issued for unsecured debt in the workout is at least 15 percent. The ratio would be computed by comparing the value of the common stock issued for unsecured debt to the value of the total stock of all classes (including disqualified stock) outstanding after the workout. The IRS did issue this guideline as Rev. Proc. 94-26, 1994-13 I.R.B. 21. This Rev. Proc. is only applicable to issuances of stock for indebtedness on or after May 17, 1994, with no inference intended for prior transactions.

(2) The "proportionality" portion of the rules is applied on neither a creditor-by-creditor nor an aggregate basis, but rather on a debt-by-debt basis. This essentially amounts to a class-by-class approach, but only as long as all persons within a class receive identical consideration. This is done by determining for the particular unsecured debt the ratio that the value of stock issued in satisfaction of the debt bears to the portion of the debt that is being satisfied with the stock; and by then comparing that ratio with the ratio that the value of all stock issued for all unsecured debt in the workout bears to the aggregate portion of all unsecured debt that is being satisfied with stock *or that is otherwise being cancelled* in the workout. Thus, the regulation makes clear that the denominator of the latter ratio includes debt that is cancelled in the workout but for which no stock is issued. The regulation illustrates its proportionality rule with the following:

**EXAMPLE 2**

Debtor corporation has three $100,000 unsecured debts. The first is satisfied with $50,000 cash and $20,000 FMV of common stock. Thus, its individual stock ratio is 40 percent (the $20,000 FMV of stock compared to the $50,000 of the debt being satisfied with stock). The second debt is satisfied with $10,000 in cash. Thus, its individual stock ratio is zero. The third debt is satisfied with $5,000 FMV of common stock. Thus, its individual stock ratio is 5 percent. The group ratio is 10.4 percent (the ratio of all the $25,000 FMV stock issued for unsecured debt in the workout to the total $240,000 amount of unsecured debt being satisfied with common stock or *otherwise cancelled* in the workout). Thus, the first debt satisfies the proportionality test, but the second two do not (because their individual stock ratios are less than 50 percent of the group ratio) and the stock-for-debt exception does not apply to them.[49]

(3) For purposes of both the "nominal or token" and the "proportionality" tests, the amount of debt being satisfied with stock is the adjusted issue price of the debt (adjusted for accrued unpaid stated interest) less the amount of other consideration issued for the debt.

(4) Where both common stock and preferred stock (other than disqualified stock) are issued, the tests are applied separately (and first) for the preferred and then for the common stock. Preferred stock is defined for this purpose as any stock (other than disqualified stock) that has a limited or fixed redemption price or liquidation preference and does not upon issuance have a right to participate in corporate growth to a meaningful extent. Preferred stock that is convertible into common stock is not treated as preferred stock if the conversion right represents, in substance, a meaningful right to participate in corporate growth. Common stock is defined for this purpose as any stock other than preferred stock and disqualified stock. As in the 1990 proposed regulation, a right to participate in corporate growth does not include for this purpose any excess of the redemption price or liquidation preference over the FMV of the stock.

(5) The amount of debt being considered satisfied by preferred stock is considered to be the lesser of the lowest redemption price (if any) or lowest liquidation preference (if any) of the preferred stock, determined at issuance, but in no event less than the FMV of the preferred stock or more than the adjusted issue price of the debt. Note that any preferred stock having a redemption price would be disqualified stock, and thus thrown out of both the preferred and the common stock categories, unless it was grandfathered disqualified stock.

(6) The amount of debt being satisfied by common stock is considered to be the adjusted issue price of the debt less the following amounts applied to the debt:

(a) the amount of money;
(b) the issue price (determined under Code § 1273 or § 1274) of any new debt;
(c) the amount of the debt allocated to preferred stock; and
(d) the value of any other property, including disqualified stock.

(7) Secured debt that is undersecured is to be bifurcated into two classes of debt: a secured class to the extent of the value of the property securing the debt and an unsecured class for the balance. The regulation provides that, absent strong evidence to the contrary, the value of the property securing the debt is presumed to equal the value of the consideration issued for the *debt other than* new unsecured debt or common or preferred stock. Presumably, a bankruptcy court determination of a

---

[49] *See also* IRS Letter Ruling 9409037, December 7, 1993 (unsecured creditors received only stock for their claims, but the subordinated unsecured creditors had to give up a portion of their stock to the nonsubordinated unsecured creditors, with the result that the nonsubordinated unsecured creditors satisfied the proportionality test but the subordinated unsecured creditors did not).

debt's secured and unsecured status under Bankruptcy Code section 506(b) would override this presumption.[50] The regulation gives the following example:

**EXAMPLE 3**

> A secured $100,000 debt is exchanged for $10,000 FMV of stock and new secured debt of $70,000. The old debt is thus bifurcated into a secured $70,000 debt and an unsecured $30,000 debt before applying the "nominal or token" and "proportionality" rules.

The "proportionality" test applies only to unsecured debt. By allocating all stock to the unsecured portion of the debt, the proposed regulation sidesteps the awkwardness that would exist in applying the tests if one had to decide how much of the stock should be allocated to the secured portion of the debt.

(8) The preamble to the proposed regulation requested comments on two open issues: (i) the treatment under the "proportionality" test of disputed or contingent claims not satisfied on the effective date of the title 11 or insolvency workout, and (ii) the treatment under the "proportionality" test of claims cancelled that are exempted from discharge of indebtedness treatment by Code § 108(e)(2) because payment of the claim would have given rise to a deduction. Although these two open issues are not addressed in the final regulation, they were addressed in IRS Letter Ruling 9105042,[51] which is discussed at § 504A.4.2. The preamble to the final regulation did say that "contingent liabilities may not be used to increase the denominator inappropriately for purposes of meeting the proportionality test. For example, the mere assertion by a claimant that it is owed a specific amount does not by itself warrant inclusion of the asserted liability in the denominator for purposes of determining the group ratios."

(9) The regulation is purely prospective in nature. It is effective only for issuances of stock for indebtedness pursuant to a plan confirmed by a court in a title 11 case after May 17, 1994 or, if there is no title 11 case, pursuant to an insolvency workout in which *all* issuances of stock for indebtedness occur after May 17, 1994. The preamble says no inference is intended concerning the meaning of the "nominal or token" and the "proportionality" rules for prior periods.

### § 504A.4.2 "Disproportionality" Limitation

The second statutory limitation on the stock-for-debt exception applies only to stock issued to creditors holding unsecured claims. For this purpose, the amount of a secured debt in excess of the fair market value of the security is considered an unsecured claim.[52] The limitation provides that the stock-for-debt exception will not

---

[50] *Cf.* S. Rep. No. 1035, 96th Cong., 2d Sess. 17 n.19 (1980).

[51] February 27, 1990. The first point is also dealt with in IRS Letter Ruling 9516025, January 18, 1995.

[52] S. Rep. No. 1035, 96th Cong., 2d Sess. 17 n.19 (1980). The 1992 Prop. Reg. § 1.108-1 confirms this.

apply with respect to a given creditor's unsecured claim *unless* such creditor receives an amount of stock for his claim constituting at least 50 percent of the stock that he would have received if all the stock received for unsecured claims in the workout had been distributed proportionately on all unsecured claims cancelled or exchanged for stock.[53] Reg. § 1.108-1 makes clear that the phrase"cancelled or exchanged for stock" in the statutory language includes debt that was cancelled but for which no stock was issued.[54]

The 1990 Act amended Code § 108(e) to provide that "disqualified" preferred stock is not to be treated as stock for purposes of the proportionality test.

As discussed at § 504A.4.1 above, Reg. § 1.108-1 covers the proportionality test and commendably integrates it with the nominal or token test. That discussion will not be repeated here.

An interesting application of the proportionality test (that includes a number of points not addressed in the proposed regulations) can be found in IRS Letter Ruling 9105042.[55] This ruling involved the same consolidated group of debtors that had obtained IRS Letter Ruling 8933001,[56] which was discussed at § 504A.3.2 above. It will be recalled that in the earlier ruling, the IRS held that parent stock issued to creditors of the subsidiaries would satisfy the stock-for-debt exception by application of Rev. Rul. 59-222. Under the latter, each subsidiary was deemed to issue its own stock (not parent stock) to its creditors in satisfaction of its debt, and the creditor was then deemed to have exchanged the subsidiary stock for parent stock. Since, in that analysis, it was not really parent stock, but instead was the deemed subsidiary stock, that satisfied the stock-for-debt exception, one would assume that the proportionality test would be applied separately for each subsidiary.

However, one can surmise that this later became impossible, because the subsequent ruling stated that the bankruptcy plan had been amended to lump the corporations into six substantively consolidated groups for bankruptcy purposes. Each substantively consolidated group would become a separate debtor for bankruptcy

---

[53] Pre-1994 Code § 108(e)(8)(B). The term "workout," as used for this purpose, includes a title 11 bankruptcy case, or a receivership, foreclosure, or similar proceeding in a federal or state court, or any other transaction or series of transactions in which a corporation in financial difficulty is substantially restructured. S. Rep. 1035, 96th Cong., 2d Sess. 17 n.20 (1980).

For a further discussion of the application of this proportionality test and its imperfections, *see* Bacon *et al., supra* note 43, at 14-45 to 14-46, 14-54 n.69 (remarks of Milton B. Hyman; points out that limitation does not take into account the existence of different classes or levels of unsecured claims, "mistakenly assuming" that the 50 percent deviation provides sufficient flexibility; questions appropriate application of limitation in a joint workout of affiliated corporations).

In a response dated February 2, 2001, to a request for an advisory opinion on the application of the stock-for-debt exception, the IRS held, among other things, that even if the bankruptcy plan does not provide for a distribution to the prepetition interest portion of a creditor's claim or otherwise treats such portion of the claim separately as a disallowed claim, the prepetition interest is nonetheless an inherent part of the underlying claim and must be taken into account in applying the stock-for-debt exception and its tests.

[54] *Cf.* IRS Letter Ruling 8933001, August 22, 1988 (holding #6).

[55] February 27, 1990.

[56] August 22, 1988. IRS Letter Ruling 9105042 was supplemented by IRS Letter Ruling 9333048, May 28, 1993.

purposes. The creditors of each group, therefore, would be lumped together and would be entitled to receive consideration from the entire group, rather than the original separate debtor corporation. The bankruptcy plan provided for distributions to the creditors of packages consisting of parent stock and other consideration. The 1990 ruling did not revoke the 1988 ruling as to the availability of the stock-for-debt exception (which presumably continued to apply on a separate subsidiary-by-subsidiary basis). But it held that the proportionality test would be applied to each of the six substantively consolidated groups as a unit, and not to each subsidiary separately.

The ruling also contained the following additional interesting elements:

(1) Certain of the creditors held claims against the entire affiliated group under principles of joint and several liability. The ruling held that for purposes of the proportionality test, each such claim would be allocated among the six substantively consolidated groups in proportion to the value of the total consideration paid on the claim by each group.

(2) Intercorporate guarantees existed with respect to certain claims. The ruling held that for purposes of the proportionality test, a guarantor would not be treated as owing a creditor any amount, and any amount paid to the creditor by the guarantor would be treated as a contribution to capital or a dividend by the guarantor to the primary debtor and added to the amount paid the creditor by the primary debtor.

(3) There were a number of disputed claims, and the plan provided for a distribution reserve for payment of such claims. The reserve would be sufficient to pay the same consideration to the disputed claims (as if all were allowed, except that for inflated claims the bankruptcy court could substitute a different amount) as was paid on the allowed claims of the same class. If the disputed claim was later disallowed, the reserve consideration could be distributed among the allowed claims (including disputed claims that had become allowed) in specified ratios. The ruling held that the disputed claims reserved for against a substantively consolidated group would be included, along with the allowed claims against the group, within the phrase "all unsecured creditors participating in the workout" for purposes of applying the proportionality test to the group. The imputed collective allowed amount of the disputed claims would be determined by grossing up the consideration reserved for them to provide the same ratios for allowed claims of the same class. Moreover, payment or disallowance of a disputed claim after consummation of the plan would not change the proportionality determination made at consummation or produce COD for the debtors (thus, postconsummation fluctuations in value would not be taken into account).[57]

(4) The claims included in the proportionality test included all claims receiving stock, without regard to whether they qualified for a different exemption from COD (such as the deductible expense exception).

It should be noted that where there are subordinated as well as nonsubordinated classes of creditors, the proportionality test can produce odd results. The descriptive word "proportionality" (which does not appear in the statute) would seem to suggest

---

[57] The issue presented in paragraph (3) of the text was also presented, and similarly dealt with, in IRS Letter Ruling 9516025, January 18, 1995.

that if each class of creditor received the same percentage of stock in proportion to his total consideration received, the test would be satisfied. But that is not the way it works. The test does not look to the proportion of the consideration received that is stock, but to the amount of debt that is satisfied by stock rather than by other consideration. Thus, even if all the creditors of all classes receive the same package of stock and other consideration, the junior classes whose debt is worth less than the senior classes will receive a smaller proportion of stock for purposes of the proportionality test.[58] In such cases, in order to satisfy the proportionality test, it may be necessary to give the senior classes a smaller proportion of stock than the junior classes in relation to the value of their claims. It would, we think, have been more sensible to include, as an alternative base for the proportionality test, one based on the proportion of total consideration applied to the debt that is represented by stock. This conundrum can easily be illustrated by the example of the proportionality test given in Reg. § 1.108-1, which is described at § 504A.4.1 above. In that example, the stock issued to the first (senior) creditor represented only 29 percent of the total consideration that creditor received, whereas the stock issued to the third creditor represented 100 percent of the total consideration he received. The stock received by the first creditor satisfied the proportionality test in its present form, Whereas the stock received by the third creditor did not. Under the proposed alternative test, the conclusion would be reversed; the stock issued to the third creditor would qualify, whereas the stock issued to the first creditor would not. One might be forgiven for concluding from this example that the proportionality test simply does not make a lot of sense. The regulation seems the best one can do with an imperfectly conceived statute.

## § 504A.5 *Issuance of Stock with Other Consideration*

The Internal Revenue Code is silent on the consequences of the issuance of a package of stock and other property in satisfaction of debt. The issue was, however, discussed in the committee reports to the Bankruptcy Tax Act of 1980. The House Report initially proposed that the stock should be treated as satisfying "a proportion of the debt equal to its proportion of the value of the total consideration."[59] The Senate Report disagreed, providing instead that "cash and other property are to be treated as satisfying an amount of debt equal to the amount of cash and the value of other property, and the stock is to be treated as satisfying the remainder of the debt."[60]

---

[58] For a ruling illustrating this problem, and in which the junior class was held not to satisfy the proportionality test, even though the only consideration received by both classes of unsecured creditors was common stock, *see* IRS Letter Ruling 9409037, December 7, 1993.

[59] H.R. Rep. No. 833, 96th Cong., 2d Sess. 14 (1980).

[60] S. Rep. No. 1035, 96th Cong., 2d Sess. 17 (1980); IRS Letter Ruling 8933001, August 22, 1989. The Senate Report's approach is consistent with the apparent approach prior to the Bankruptcy Tax Act of 1980. *See* IRS Letter Ruling 8014091, January 11, 1980; IRS Letter Ruling 8004063, October 31, 1979, as supplemented by IRS Letter Ruling 8021144, February 29, 1980; IRS Letter Ruling 7926120, March 30, 1979, as supplemented by IRS Letter Ruling 8110139, December 12, 1980; IRS Letter Ruling 7821047,

The Senate Report's change in this regard was apparently accepted by the House. Representative Ullman, then Chairman of the House Ways and Means Committee, stated that, in adopting the Senate's version of the Bankruptcy Tax Act, the House was fully cognizant of the Senate's "changes . . . with respect to issuance of a package of stock and other property in cancellation of debt."[61]

Rev. Rul. 92-52, discussed at § 504A.1, and Reg. § 1.108-1, discussed at § 504A.4.1, confirm that the Senate approach is the one that applies.

### *§ 504A.6 Alternative Minimum Tax Consequences*

Even where the stock-for-debt exception to COD income applies, the debt cancellation may (in some but not all cases) produce book income. This can subject the company to an alternative minimum tax (AMT) for taxable years beginning before 1990.

An amendment to Code § 56(f)(2) eliminated this problem where the stock-for-debt exception applies, effective for taxable years beginning after 1986.[62] *See* § 404.5 above.

The problem does not exist for taxable years beginning after 1989. *See* § 404.5 above. *See also* § 511 below.

## § 505 CONTRIBUTION-TO-CAPITAL EXCEPTION TO COD INCOME

Another significant exception to the creation of COD income, and one closely related to the stock-for-debt exception, is the exception for contributions of debt to capital.[1] This exception only applies where the contributing creditor is already a shareholder. Unlike the stock-for-debt exception, it applies not only to bankrupt or insolvent companies but also to solvent companies outside bankruptcy. However, the contribution of debt to capital does not erase all possibility of COD income. Rather, the corporation will be treated as satisfying the debt with an amount of money equal to the shareholder's adjusted basis in the debt.[2] Thus, if the shareholder's basis in the debt is less than the amount due, the corporation can have COD income.

---

(Footnote Continued)

February 23, 1978; GCM 25277, 1947-1 C.B. 44 (declared obsolete by Rev. Rul. 69-44, 1969-1 C.B. 312), revoking GCM 22528,1941-1 C.B. 193.

[61] Comments of Representative Ullman, Chairman of House Ways and Means Committee, Cong. Rec. H 12,462 (December 13, 1980).

[62] Technical and Miscellaneous Revenue Act of 1988, Pub. L. No. 100-647, 100th Cong., 2d Sess. (TAMRA), § 6303.

[1] **§ 505** Code § 108(e)(6).

[2] Id.

### EXAMPLE

A corporation accrues and deducts (but does not actually pay) a $1,000 liability to a shareholder-employee as salary, and the cash basis employee does not include the $1,000 in income. If the shareholder-employee forgives the debt, the corporation would have COD of $1,000. If the shareholder-employee was on the accrual basis and had included the $1,000 in income, the corporation would have no COD income.[3]

Although it is stated above that the contribution-to-capital exception applies to insolvent and bankrupt companies, the IRS has espoused a significant impediment to the application of the contribution-to-capital exception in such cases. In a 1998 field service advice,[4] the IRS took the position that, when a parent cancels the debt of an insolvent subsidiary, the cancellation is *not* a contribution to capital *except to the extent it makes the subsidiary solvent*. Thus, if the debt is in the amount of $100, and the cancellation leaves the subsidiary solvent only to the extent of $20, there has been only a $20 cancellation that is treated as a contribution to capital and that benefits from the contribution-to-capital exception to COD income. As for the rematining $80 portion of the debt that is not treated as a contribution to capital, the subsidiary has COD income that is excluded under the insolvency or bankruptcy exception and results in a reduction of the subsidiary's tax attributes under Code § 108(b).

The field service advice cites as comparative support for this partial capital contribution theory, but without any discussion, a Tax Court memorandum decision: *Mayo v. Commissioner*.[5] A brief recital of the facts and holding of the case is therefore in order. In that case, the taxpayer shareholder cancelled a $100,000 debt owed him by the debtor corporation in an effort to bring about the sale of the business. After the cancellation, the corporation was still insolvent. The following year, the company preferred and common stock were sold for the aggregate price of approximately $120, with other shareholders also required to cancel or assign their debts at substantial discounts. The taxpayer claimed a bad debt loss for the cancelled $100,000 debt, whereas the IRS argued that the cancellation was a capital contribution. The Tax Court sided with the taxpayer. The court observed that the corporation was hopelessly insolvent even after the cancellation, and viewed the cancellation as reflecting the practical judgment that the debt was uncollectible. Accordingly, contrary to what one might be led to believe from the field service advice, the *Mayo* case at most stands

---

[3] *See* S. Rep. No. 1035, 96th Cong., 2d Sess. 18 n.21 (1980); H.R. Rep. No. 833, 96th Cong., 2d Sess. 15 n.20 (1980). For further examples, *see* Asofsky, Discharge of Indebtedness, Income in Bankruptcy After the Bankruptcy Tax Act of 1980, 27 St. Louis U. L.J. 583, 612-613 (1983).

[4] IRS Field Service Advice 199915005, December 17, 1998, *reprinted at* 1999 TNT 74-79; *but see* IRS Letter Ruling 200537026 (June 17, 2005) (applying exception to the full contributed loan, where (i) the only representation was that the loan had a positive fair market value and (ii) immediately following the contribution, all of the stock of the subsidiary was cancelled and new stock issued in exchange for a second intercompany loan). The cancellation described in the field service advice occurred at the same time as, but was respected by the IRS as independent from, a "D" reorganization of the subsidiary.

[5] T.C. Memo. 1957-9, *acq.*

for the proposition that the cancellation of a *wholly worthless* debt that does not enhance the value of the holder's stock lacks the indicia of a capital contribution.[6] Moreover, not all courts accede to even this general proposition, nor does it necessarily represent the general view of the Tax Court—as the case of *Lidgerwood Mfg. Co. v. Commissioner* illustrates.[7]

In that case, a parent corporation attempted to claim (on an amended return) a bad debt deduction for the cancellation of debts owed to it by two wholly-owned subsidiaries where the cancellation was made to enable the subsidiaries to obtain needed bank loans. The parent received additional shares of the subsidiaries, and the subsidiaries reflected the cancellations as a capital contribution. The parent corporation claimed that it was entitled to the deduction because the debts were totally worthless (and, in the alternative, argued for a partial worthless deduction). The Tax Court disagreed. Concluding that the parent's only purpose in voluntarily canceling the debts was to assist the subsidiary, the Tax Court held that the cancellation was properly treated as a capital contribution. The Tax Court emphasized that "it is the voluntary act of the creditor-stockholder which determines the character of the transaction."[8] The Second Circuit affirmed, stating that:

> even on the assumption that the debtors were insolvent after as well as before the cancellations, wiping out the debts was a valuable contribution to the financial structure of the subsidiaries. It enabled them to obtain bank loans, to continue in business and subsequently to prosper. This was the avowed purpose of the cancellations. Where a parent corporation voluntarily cancels a debt owed by its subsidiary in order to improve the

---

[6] *See also Giblin v. Commissioner*, 227 F.2d 692, 56-1 U.S.T.C. ¶9,103 (5th Cir. 1955) (similarly so holding in the case of a wholly worthless bad debt; moreover, the court asserted that the corporation under the same circumstances would have income; in any other circumstance, the court acknowledged that the "income" authorities cited therein by the IRS supported capital contribution treatment, but did not view such authorities as necessarily determinative of the bad debt loss).

[7] 229 F.2d 241, 56-1 U.S.T.C. ¶9214 (2d Cir. 1956) (suggesting without explanation that the Fifth Circuit's decision in *Giblin*, cited in the preceding footnote, may be distinguishable on its facts, but respectfully disagreeing with it to the extent it expressed opposing views), *aff'g*, 22 T.C. 1152 (1954), *cert. denied*, 76 S. Ct. 848 (1956). *See also* Reg. §1.61-12(a) ("In general, if a shareholder in a corporation which is indebted to him gratuitously forgives the debt, the transaction amounts to a contribution to the capital of the corporation to the extent of the principal of the debt").

The Claims Court in *Celanese Corp. v. United States*, 8 Cl. Ct. 456, 85-2 U.S.T.C. ¶9517 (Cl. Ct. 1985), applied the *Mayo* and *Giblin* cases in a bad debt context. The court distinguished the Second Circuit's decision in *Lidgerwood Mfg. Co.*, dicussed below in text, on the basis that (i) the debt was cancelled by a continuing shareholder and (ii) the shareholder's actions clearly indicated the intent by the shareholder to treat the cancellation as a capital contribution. The court also distinguished the Sixth Circuit's decision in *Bratton v. Commissioner*, 217 F.2d 486 (6th Cir. 1954), which held a shareholder's cancellation of debt to be a capital contribution in a rehabilitation context, because (i) the contributing shareholder remained a shareholder and (ii) there were no findings that the debt had no value, but rather were findings that the corporation was expected to return to profitability, in part as a result of the relinquishment of the debt. *See also Plante v. Commissioner*, 168 F.3d 1279, 99-1 U.S.T.C. ¶50,321 (11th Cir. 1999) (suggesting that a distinguishing fact in the *Giblin* case might be that the debt cancellation in that case was not specifially characterized by the parties as a capital contribution).

[8] 22 T.C. at 1157.

> latter's financial position so that it may continue in business, we entertain no doubt that the cancellation should be held a capital contribution and preclude the parent from claiming it as a bad debt deduction.[9]

Conversely, in Technical Advice Memorandum 200101001, August 7, 2000, the IRS distinguished the *Lidgerwood* case and held that a parent corporation was entitled to a bad debt deduction for an unsecured debt of a subsidiary that was not paid in a Chapter 11 bankruptcy proceeding of the subsidiary, where the parent had consistently claimed a bad debt deduction for the debt, and its motive and effort were to collect as much as it could, just as the other creditors did, on its debt from the subsidiary.

At least two additional (but related) interpretative questions exist with respect to the contribution-to-capital exception. The first is the fact that in some cases the ownership of stock by a creditor may be so unrelated to the cancellation of debt that the cancellation should not be considered a contribution to capital. Although the legislative history contained a rather amorphous reference to this possibility, no definitive guidelines on this issue exist (as is evident from the above discussion).[10] An example of what Congress had in mind would be the extreme case where a holder of $20 million of debt in a public company also happened to own a fraction of 1 percent of the stock (much less than its fraction of the company's debt).[11]

The second question relates to the dividing line between the contribution-to-capital exception and the stock-for-debt exception. To illustrate the issue with the most extreme example, suppose that all the stock of the debtor corporation is also held by its only creditor. Will the contribution-to-capital rule apply if the debt is cancelled without having the corporation issue additional shares of stock, and will the stock-for-debt exception be invoked if additional shares are issued to the creditor? Since, as we have seen, the rules and consequences of the two exceptions are quite different, the question is not an academic one.[12] In several letter rulings, the IRS has followed the form adopted by the taxpayer.[13]

---

[9] 229 F.2d at 243 (internal citations omitted).

[10] *See* S. Rep. No. 1035, 96th Cong., 2d Sess. 19 n.22 (1980).

[11] Id.

[12] *See* Asofsky, Discharge of Indebtedness, *supra* note 3, at 614-615; Pollack & Goldring, Can Cancellation of Indebtedness Income Be Avoided with Parent Stock?, 3 Corp. Tax'n 12, 13-14 (July/August 1990). *See also* Bittker & Eustice, Federal Income Taxation of Corporations and Shareholders §3.13[4][a]at n.278. *Cf. Lessinger v. Commissioner*, 85 T.C. 824, Dec. 42,489 (1985) (Code §351 requirement that property be transferred in "exchange for stock or securities" was satisfied upon a transfer of assets to a wholly owned corporation even though no additional stock or securities were issued). This holding in the case was approved by the Second Circuit in *Lessinger v. Commissioner*, 872 F.2d 519 (2d Cir. 1989).

[13] In IRS Letter Ruling 9018005, November 15, 1989, a parent company's cancellation of debt in its wholly owned subsidiary for additional shares of subsidiary stock was treated as a stock-for-debt exchange for COD purposes, rather than a *de facto* capital contribution. This is inconsistent with *Lidgerwood Mfg. Co.* (discussed in the text above), and appears contrary to the IRS's general position. *See* 89 Tax Notes Today 249-H (December 13, 1989) (comments of David P. Madden, at the time an attorney with the office of the Assistant Chief Counsel). However, adherence to the form adopted is supported by some, except where the creditor has taken a bad debt deduction for the debt (where, it

Where the shareholder-creditor is a corporation that files consolidated returns with the debtor, the consolidated return regulations provide special rules. These can be found in Reg. § 1.1502-13(g) and are described at § 804.4 below.

Additionally, even if the contribution-to-capital exception is applicable, the debt cancellation may have alternative minimum tax (AMT) consequences for years beginning before 1990, as discussed in Chapter 4 (*see* § 404.1). This problem does not exist for tax years beginning after 1989. *See* § 404.5 above.

The capital contribution exception is modified where the contribution is to an S corporation. In the case of S corporation debt, the tax basis of the debt may have been reduced by the pass-through of S corporation losses under Code § 1367. Because the shareholder would similarly have been entitled to such losses had the shareholder originally made a capital contribution rather than a loan, a subsequent capital contribution of the debt will not result in COD income to the extent the shareholder's tax basis in the debt was reduced by the pass-through of any S corporation losses.[14]

### § 505.1 *Modification by 1993 Act*

As the foregoing discussion indicates, the contribution-to-capital exception to COD income differs in important respects from the stock-for-debt exception, yet the two are also related. Although the 1993 Act, which repealed the stock-for-debt exception, did not change the contribution-to-capital exception *per se*, it did authorize the Treasury to issue regulations to coordinate the contribution-to-capital exception with the repeal of the stock-for-debt exception.

## § 506 IMPACT OF STOCK ISSUANCE ON NOLs AND OTHER CARRYOVERS

Whether or not issuance of stock to creditors allows the failing company to avoid COD income through application of the stock-for-debt exception (now no longer

---

(Footnote Continued)

has been suggested, the contribution to capital rule should be applied). *See* Witt & Lyons, An Examination of the Tax Consequences of Discharge of Indebtedness, 10 Va. Tax Rev. 1, 111 (1990). In Technical Advice Memorandum 9830002, March 20, 1998, the IRS also followed the form where the debtor was a fourth tier subsidiary, and all of its stock was owned by the third tier subsidiary, but its debt was held in all three upper tiers. The debt was exchanged for stock of the fourth tier subsidiary. The IRS held this was not a contribution to capital, but was a debt-for-stock exchange. The result on the facts was to produce more COD income than contribution to capital treatment would have produced. In other rulings, the IRS accepted the contribution to capital form and applied Code § 108(e)(6): *See* IRS Letter Ruling 9024056, March 20, 1990; IRS Letter Ruling 9215043, January 14, 1992; IRS Letter Ruling 9623028, March 7, 1996; IRS Letter Ruling 9335024, June 3, 1993; IRS Letter Ruling 200537026 (June 17, 2005) (capital contribution by a foreign parent to an indirect wholly-owned U.S. subsidiary respected). In IRS Technical Advice Memorandum 9822005, January 16, 1998, the IRS ducked the issue where a parent canceled subsidiary debt without receiving additional stock, but where neither of the alternative characterizations would have produced, on the facts, COD income. *See* generally Dubroff, Blanchard, Broadbent & Duvall, Federal Income Taxation of Corporations Filing Consolidated Returns § 33.03[2](2d ed.).

[14] Code § 108(d)(7)(C).

available except for grandfathered cases), it may, quite aside from any such creation of COD income, pose a risk to survival of the company's NOLs, capital loss carryovers, and its ITC, foreign tax, and other credit carryovers.[1] The pertinent provisions are Code §§382 (*see* §§507 and 508) and 269 (*see* §509.1), the remnants of the *Libson Shops* doctrine found in TIR 773[2] (*see* §509.2), and the separate return limitation year (SRLY)[3] and consolidated return change of ownership (CRCO)[4] limitations in the consolidated return regulations (*see* §509). The common thread that runs through these is a policy to the effect that while a corporation and its existing shareholders own its NOLs and other attributes and can freely use them against the corporation's income even if the existing shareholders add more capital to the corporation to generate that income, the existing shareholders should be severely limited in their ability to transfer this right to new owners.

These rules potentially come into play when a failing company issues stock to its creditors in satisfaction of part or all of its debt. In form, if perhaps not in substance, the creditors receiving stock become new stockholders of the corporation.

## §507 OLD CODE §382

§382 One of the major changes made by the Tax Reform Act of 1986 (Pub. L. No. 99-514) was the adoption of an entirely new Code §382. The 1986 Act version of Code §382—which we will refer to as "new" Code §382—is generally effective for changes in ownership occurring after December 31, 1986. However, new Code §382 does not apply—and old Code §382 does apply—to an ownership change resulting from a "G" reorganization or an exchange of stock for debt in a title 11 or similar case, if the petition the case was filed with the court before August 14, 1986.[1]

---

[1] **§506** *See generally* Bittker & Eustice, Federal Income Taxation of Corporations and Shareholders ch. 14 (7th ed.); Nicholls, Net Operating Loss and Section 382, 22 Tax Notes 609 (February 13, 1984); Bacon, Rescue Planning for the Failing or Bankrupt Company, 61 Taxes 931 (1983); Asofsky, Reorganizing Insolvent Corporations, 41 Inst. on Fed. Tax'n §5 (1983); Barr, The Availability of Net Operating Loss Carryovers Following Taxable Changes of Ownership: Section 382(a) of the Internal Revenue Code, 38 Inst. on Fed. Tax'n §5 (1980); Thompson, Planning for the Loss Corporation: The Interaction Among Code Sections 269, 381, Old and New Sections 382 and the Consolidated Return Regulations, 31 Major Tax Plan. 223 (1979); Faber, Net Operating Losses in Corporate Reorganizations Revisited in 1979, 38 Inst. on Fed. Tax'n §4 (1979).

[2] Technical Information Release 773, October 13, 1965. In *Libson Shops, Inc. v. Koehler*, 353 U.S. 382, 57-1 U.S.T.C. ¶9691 (1957), the Supreme Court held that, under the 1939 Internal Revenue Code, a surviving corporation in a merger could not carry over and deduct premerger net operating losses of one business against postmerger income of another business that was operated and taxed separately before the merger.

[3] *See* Reg. §1.1502-1(f).

[4] *See* Reg. §1.1502-1(g).

[1] **§507** 1986 Act §621(f)(5). For this purpose, a "title 11 or similar case" means a case defined in Code §368(a)(3). If a stock-for-debt exchange in a title 11 or similar case is coupled with a stock purchase that occurs either (1) as part of the bankruptcy proceeding, or (2) after the bankruptcy proceeding, it is less than clear from the statutory language how this grandfather rule is intended to apply. Temp. Reg. §1.382-2T(m)(5) resolved this ambiguity favorably to the loss company, by holding that an ownership change "results" from an increase in ownership occurring in such proceeding if such ownership increase must be counted to reach an ownership change.

TAMRA amended the transitional rule applicable to bankruptcy cases filed before August 14, 1986, by (1) allowing loss companies to elect to apply new rather than old Code § 382 and (2) providing that an ownership change which occurs under new Code § 382 during the bankruptcy case, but prior to the completion of the case, will be retested after the bankruptcy case with the dilution in the shareholders' ownership being taken into account.[2]

### EXAMPLE

> If 60 percent of a loss company's stock is acquired during a bankruptcy case, but pursuant to the bankruptcy, shareholders were diluted to 20 percent of the company, the 60 percent purchase would be treated as a 12 percent purchase and the ownership change originally resulting from such purchase would be reversed.

The Conference Report to TAMRA indicates that an amended return can generally be filed to reverse the effect of the earlier ownership change without regard to any otherwise applicable statute of limitations.

Because bankruptcy cases filed before August 14, 1986, may not be resolved until many months or even years thereafter, old Code § 382 continues to be relevant for practitioners even after 1986. Moreover, as we shall see in § 508.2.1 (note 13), old Code § 382 may continue to apply through 1988 with respect to changes in ownership that would trigger the limitations of old Code § 382, but not new Code § 382. We will therefore discuss old Code § 382 here and new Code § 382 in the next section (§ 508).

Old Code § 382(a) will totally destroy a corporation's NOLs and other carryovers[3] if the corporation has a prohibited change in ownership coupled with a prohibited change in business.[4] The change in ownership must occur through purchase or redemption of stock, and a change in business essentially means failure to continue an existing business rather than the addition of a new business.[5]

Where stock is issued to creditors in transactions that are taxable exchanges, the stock will be considered "purchased" for this purpose. If, in addition, the business of

---

[2] *See* Pub. L. No. 100-747, § 6277; Conference Report to TAMRA, H. Rep. No. 1104, 100th Cong., 2d Sess. 238-239 (1988).

[3] Old Code § 383 extends the limitations of old Code § 382 to the availability of the investment credit, the foreign tax credit, the work incentive credit, and capital loss carryovers. *See also S.F.H., Inc. v. Commissioner*, 53 T.C. 28, Dec. 29,775 (1969), *aff'd*, 444 F.2d 189, 71-1 U.S.T.C. ¶ 9454 (3d Cir. 1971) (NOLs disallowed even as to income economically accrued prior to prohibited change in ownership); *Commissioner v. Barclay Jewelry, Inc.*, 367 F.2d 193, 66-2 U.S.T.C. ¶ 9704 (1st Cir. 1966) (same).

[4] For other discussions of old Code § 382(a), *see* Nicholls, Net Operating Loss and Section 382, 22 Tax Notes 609 (February 13, 1984); Asofsky, Reorganizing Insolvent Corporations, 41 Inst. on Fed. Tax'n at § 5.04[2](1983) (provides helpful practical suggestions); Bacon, Rescue Planning for the Failing or Bankrupt Company, 61 Taxes 931, 937-941 (1983) (provides comprehensive examples of old Code § 382(a) as applied to new investments as well as debt-equity exchanges); Barr, The Availability of Net Operating Loss Carryovers Following Taxable Changes of Ownership: Section 382(a) of the Internal Revenue Code, 38 Inst. on Fed. Tax'n § 5 (1980) (change in business discussion).

[5] *See* Code § 382(a)(1)(B) prior to amendment by Pub. L. No. 99-514; Reg. § 1.382-1A(h)(1).

the failing company will be significantly wound down at about the same time or within two years after the purchase, care must be taken to avoid the impact of Code § 382(a). The planner should keep in mind that infusions of capital by new investors or subsequent transfers of stock may add to the amount of the change in ownership that occurs by purchase.

## *§ 507.1 Change-in-Ownership Test*

A change in stock ownership prohibited by old Code § 382(a) occurs where the ten largest shareholders of a corporation have an increase, as of the end of the corporation's taxable year, in their ownership of at least 50 percentage points in the value of the corporation's stock, either through their "purchase" or through the corporation's redemptions of the stock of other shareholders,[6] from that at the beginning of the current or preceding taxable year.[7] For this purpose, "stock" does not include nonvoting stock that is limited and preferred as to dividends.[8] One should bear in mind that 50 percentage points and 50 percent are not the same: a shareholder who has increased his ownership from 10 percent to 20 percent of the stock has a 100 percent increase, but only a 10 percentage point increase.

Old Code § 382(a)(4) defines "purchase" for this purpose as the acquisition of stock whose basis is determined solely by reference to its cost to the holder, except from a person whose stock would be attributed to the holder under Code § 318 (as modified by old Code § 382(a)(3)).[9]

A creditor ("security" holder) who receives stock of a failing company in a wholly tax-free recapitalization exchange will have an increase in ownership, but it will not be by "purchase." A creditor receiving stock in a taxable transaction (including a creditor who receives stock for accrued interest, even in an otherwise tax-free recapitalization) will have an increase in stock ownership by "purchase."

Sometimes a debt restructuring will be part of, or be accompanied by, a transfer of property to the failing company by new investors in a tax-free Code § 351 transaction in which the new investors transfer property to the failing company in exchange for stock.[10] To qualify for tax-free status under Code § 351, the "transferors"

---

[6] Redemptions to pay death taxes to which Code § 303 applies are excluded. Code § 382(a)(1)(B)(ii) prior to amendment by Pub. L. No. 99-514.

[7] Code § 382(a)(1)(A) and (B) prior to amendment by Pub. L. No. 99-514.

[8] Code § 382(c) prior to amendment by Pub. L. No. 99-514. For this purpose, the fact that the limited and preferred stock is convertible into voting common stock is ignored, at least until it is converted. IRS Letter Ruling 8204131, October 29, 1981; *see* IRS Letter Ruling 8350047, September 8, 1983 (old Code § 382(c) of old law applied, rather than 1976 amendments wherein convertible stock is treated as "stock"). In addition, the fact that dividends are noncumulative should be irrelevant. *See Maxwell Hardware Co. v. Commissioner*, 343 F.2d 713, 65-1 U.S.T.C. ¶9332 (9th Cir. 1965) (in *dicta*); *cf. Pioneer Parachute Co. Inc. v. Commissioner*, 162 F.2d 249, 47-2 U.S.T.C. ¶5911 (2d Cir. 1947) (assumes noncumulative preferred stock is "limited and preferred" as to dividends for purposes of the predecessor to Code § 1504); Rev. Rul. 79-21, 1979-1 C.B. 290 (same).

[9] Code § 351(a), and Code § 382(c)(1) prior to amendment by Pub. L. No. 99-514.

[10] For successful use of Code § 351 in this context, *see* IRS Field Service Advice, January 15, 1993, *reprinted at* 98 TNT 201-99. In this case, a business related to the business of the loss corporation was

of property must own, immediately after the transfer, at least 80 percent of the voting power and 80 percent of each class of nonvoting stock of the corporation. For Code § 351 purposes, stock issued for property includes stock issued for securities of the issuer but does not include stock issued for nonsecurity debt of the issuer or for unpaid interest on either type of the issuer's debt that has accrued during the transferor's holding period for the debt.[11] Thus, stock issued in exchange for securities (other than for such interest) in the restructuring can be aggregated with stock issued to the new investors for property to determine whether the 80 percent test is met. If it is, neither the stock issued for securities (excluding interest) nor the stock issued for property will be considered "purchased" for purposes of old Code § 382(a).[12] There is one important caveat: the Regulations provide that even Code § 351 transfers of property will nonetheless constitute "purchase" transactions to the extent the transfer consists of "cash or cash equivalents."[13]

Sometimes the failing company will have a subsidiary that also has an NOL or other carryover. These will be affected by an old Code § 382(a) change in ownership at the parent level. Old Code § 382(a)(1)(B) provides that a change in ownership includes a purchase of stock in a corporation or an interest in a trust or partnership owning stock of the target corporation.

Code § 318 generally applies for purposes of old Code § 382(a). However, Reg. § 1.382-1A(a)(2) makes an important modification in the application of the option portion of Code § 318 for purposes of the "purchase" rule. It states that stock acquired by the exercise of an option (and presumably this includes warrants and convertibles) shall be considered as having been acquired on the date the option was acquired. Applied literally, this means that if the failing company sells a warrant or convertible debt (or convertible nonvoting and limited preferred) that cannot be converted into stock (other than nonvoting limited preferred) until long after the statute of limitations has run on the tax years in which the NOLs and other carryovers are expected to be utilized, these instruments, as a practical matter, will not adversely affect the company's NOLs or other carryovers. Not surprisingly, such instruments with delayed exercisability have sometimes been used by failing companies.

The prohibited increase in ownership by "purchase" (or redemption) must occur over a two-taxable year period. The statute phrases it in terms of a look-back and asks if, as of the end of the tax year, there has been a 50 percentage point increase by purchase (or redemption) by the ten largest holders since (1) the beginning of the current tax year or (2) the beginning of the prior tax year.[14] For planning purposes, however, it is often more useful to examine the question as a look-forward question.

---

(Footnote Continued)

added in a Code § 351 transaction. Because the IRS found there had been no change in business of the loss corporation, it decided it did not need to address the question whether there had been a change in ownership.

[11] Code § 351(d).

[12] IRS Letter Ruling 8213059, December 30, 1981; IRS Letter Ruling 7926120, March 30, 1979, supplemented by IRS Letter Ruling 8110139, December 12, 1980; IRS Letter Ruling 7826020, March 28, 1978.

[13] Reg. § 1.382-1A(e)(1); *see also* Rev. Rul. 75-248, 1975-1 C.B. 125.

[14] *See* Code § 382(a)(1)(A) prior to amendment by Pub. L. No. 99-514.

Assuming that there have been no major stock changes in the recent past, usually it is only changes in stock ownership occurring as a result of the debt restructuring, together with possible infusions of capital from new investors, that will become relevant. In this event, one asks whether, in the current or next tax year, there is likely to be the prohibited change in ownership coupled with a prohibited change in business. The look-forward period may actually be less than a full 24 months. This will be true whenever the change in ownership does not begin until after the start of the current year. It may also occur if the corporation's tax year changes for some reason.

**EXAMPLE**

> A is a shareholder of X corporation, which has a calendar taxable year. On December 31, 1982, A increased, by purchase, its ownership of X corporation by 45 percentage points. If, during 1981 or 1982, A, or another of X corporation's ten largest shareholders, experienced a net increase of 5 percentage points, there would have been a prohibited change in stock ownership. If not, the 45 percentage point purchase will continue to taint any purchase during the next taxable year, 1983. A purchase during 1984 would be unaffected, however, by such earlier 45 percentage point purchase. The look-forward period was, in this case, one year and one day. Had X corporation's 1983 taxable year been prematurely closed, the look-forward period would have been less than 12 months.

During the look-back (or look-forward) period, the changes in each of the ten largest shareholders' percentage ownership of the corporation by "purchase" (or redemption) are computed separately and the net increases of all such shareholders having net increases are totalled (undiminished by net decreases, if any, of any such shareholder).[15]

An interesting question, on which there is surprisingly little authority, is how value changes should affect the 50 percent test. Suppose, for example, that a loss company has two classes of stock, one a straight voting preferred and the other common. P purchases all the common at a time when it is worth only 49 percent of the aggregate value of both classes of stock. However, at the end of the two-year look-forward period, the common has grown in value to become worth more than 50 percent of the aggregate value. The U.S. Claims Court has held that in the absence of a subsequent transaction in the stock, such changes in value should be ignored for Code § 382(a) purposes.[16]

---

[15] Reg. § 1.382-1A(d)(3).

[16] *Hermes Consol., Inc. v. United States*, 88-1 U.S.T.C. ¶ 9220 (Cl. Ct.).

### §507.2 Change-in-Business Test

Even if a prohibited change in stock ownership has occurred, old Code §382(a) will not disallow the debtor corporation's NOLs unless the debtor corporation "has not continued to carry on a trade or business substantially the same as that conducted before" the first increase in ownership that leads to the prohibited change in stock ownership.[17]

Generally, the change in business must occur during the two taxable year "look-forward" (or "look-back") period for purposes of determining a prohibited change in stock ownership. In addition, a substantial change in the trade or business of the corporation in contemplation of a prohibited change in ownership will be treated as a prohibited change in business for purposes of old Code §382(a).[18]

**EXAMPLE**

On January 15, 1985, A, the sole shareholder of X Corporation, sold 20 percent of his X stock to B. On March 1, 1985, X Corporation sold its prior business and bought a different one. On December 15, 1985, A sold 40 percent of his X stock to C. X Corporation is a calendar year taxpayer. Because A's sale to B and C together equals at least 50 percent of X's outstanding stock, there is a prohibited change in stock ownership (as of December 31, 1985 and 1986) under old Code §382(a). In addition, the change in X Corporation's business, because it occurred after January 15, 1985 (the date of the first sale which is taken into account in determining the prohibited change in stock ownership), constitutes a prohibited change in business. Old Code §382(a), therefore, would apply and disallow the carryover of X's Corporation's NOLs to 1985 and 1986 and subsequent years.

It is important to note that the addition of a new business is not a "change in business" for purposes of old Code §382(a).[19] The statutory language phrases the test in terms of a failure of the company to continue "a" trade or business substantially the same as that previously conducted by it.[20] Under the regulations, the discontinuance of more than a minor portion of the business carried on before a prohibited change in ownership commenced constitutes a prohibited change in business.[21] The

---

[17] Code §382(a)(1)(C) prior to amendment by Pub. L. No. 99-514; Reg. §1.382-1A(d)(2)(i).

[18] Reg. §1.382-1A(h)(3); *Coast Quality Constr. Corp. v. United States*, 463 F.2d 503, 72-2 U.S.T.C. ¶9548 (5th Cir. 1972) (pursuant to prearranged agreement of buyer and seller, change in business occurred one day prior to prohibited change in stock ownership).

[19] Reg. §1.382-1A(h)(8); *see Commissioner v. Goodwyn Crockery Co.*, 315 F.2d 110, 63-1 U.S.T.C. ¶9369 (6th Cir. 1963).

[20] *See* Code §382(a)(1)(C) prior to amendment by Pub. L. No. 99-514; *supra* note 17; Barr, *supra* note 4, at §5.04[3].

[21] Reg. §1.382-1A(h)(7).

factors to be taken into account in determining a prohibited change in business include changes in the corporation's employees, plant and equipment, product, location, and customers, as well as other items that are significant in determining continuity of business enterprise.[22] For purposes of determining what is "minor," the regulations further provide that consideration should be given to whether the discontinued activities generated the NOLs.[23] Two examples are given. Both involve three businesses (A, B, and C) comprising 50 percent, 30 percent, and 20 percent, respectively, of the corporation's total business activities (measured in terms of capital invested, gross income, size of payroll and similar factors). In the first example, the corporation's NOLs are substantially attributable to C, and, in the second example, to A. In both cases, the business of C is discontinued. The regulation concludes that in the first case, a prohibited change in business took place, but not in the second.[24]

The courts have been more lenient than the regulations and have allowed a significant diminution in the corporation's loss business.[25] The IRS also took a reasonable approach in a 1993 Field Service Advice, in which it held that the disposition of a major division of a business was not fatal where the losses generated by this division were used against the income of a related business.[26] Moreover, some courts have specifically questioned the validity of the approach taken in the regulations, which place importance on the business that generated the NOLs, whereas the

---

[22] Reg. § 1.382-1A(h)(5); *see S.F.H., Inc. v. Commissioner, supra* note 3; *cert. denied*, 404 U.S. 913 (1972) (business discontinued; irrelevant that business continued by a related entity); *see also* Barr, *supra* note 4, at § 5.06[1][b].

[23] Reg. § 1.382-1A(h)(7).

[24] Reg. § 1.382-1A(h)(7), Examples (1) and (2).

[25] *See Glen Raven Mills, Inc.*, 59 T.C. 1 (1972) (allowed some changes in product line and type of customer); *Clarksdale Rubber Co.*, 45 T.C. 234, Dec. 27,650 (1965) (following the acquisition, permitted corporation to lease its assets to a newly formed sister corporation); *Coast Quality Constr. Corp. v. United States*, 463 F.2d 503, 72-2 U.S.T.C. ¶ 9548 (Fed. Cir. 1972) (permitted disposition of 44 percent of assets, where corporation's management, employees and product remained unchanged); *Commissioner v. Goodwyn Crockery Co.*, 315 F.2d 110, 63-1 U.S.T.C. ¶ 9369 (6th Cir. 1963) (held no prohibited change in business where continued principal product line in same geographic area, although shifted location of corporate offices, reduced number of employees and substantially changed customers); *Wallace Corp. v. Commissioner*, 23 T.C.M. 39, Dec. 26,619(M), T.C. Memo. 1964-10 (1964) (same); *Power-Line Sales, Inc. v. Commissioner*, 36 T.C.M. 190, Dec. 34,264(M), T.C. Memo. 1974-43 (1977) (held no prohibited change in business where preacquisition business continued at reduced level and key employees were retained, even though it changed its name and corporate office); *United States v. Federated Dep't Stores. Inc.*, 170 B.R. 331, 94-2 U.S.T.C. ¶ 50,418 (S.D. Ohio 1994) (operation of only seven out of thirty-one former stores, change of name, discontinuation of a product line producing 40 percent of each store's sales, and management of the stores after the acquisition by an affiliate of the purchaser, held not to constitute a prohibited change in business); *Samson Investment Company v. Commissioner*, T.C. Memo. 1998-271 (substantial contraction of contract oil drilling business including reduction in number of rigs and in number of employees from 500 to 4 caused by market conditions was held not to amount to a change in business before the ownership change, or a failure to continue the business after the ownership change).

[26] IRS Field Service Advice, January 15, 1993, 98 TNT 201-99 (October 19, 1998).

literal statutory language requires only the continuation of "a" trade or business substantially the same as that conducted previously.[27]

In contrast to the regulations under old Code § 382(a), an example in the "continuity of business enterprise" regulations (applicable with respect to tax-free reorganizations and new Code § 382) provides that the sale of two, and the continuation of one, of the taxpayer's three lines of businesses, which businesses were of equal value, satisfies the continuity of business enterprise requirement.[28] An argument could be made that there should be consistency between the continuity-of-business-enterprise regulations and the prohibited change in business requirement in this respect. Because the continuity-of-business-enterprise requirement is applicable with respect to tax-free reorganizations and the prohibited change in business requirement is generally applicable only in taxable transactions, consistency between the two, though desirable, is not essential. Also, the two tests are not consistent in other respects. Nevertheless, because old Code § 382(a) literally requires only the continuation of "a" trade or business, it provides no obvious support for giving a different weight to the business that produced the loss than to other businesses.

Where a corporation's business is permanently terminated, there will automatically be a prohibited change in business.[29] In the regulations under old Code § 382(a), a temporary suspension of a corporation's business (*e.g.*, a suspension due to changing market conditions) is treated similarly to a permanent termination of the corporation's business, unless such temporary suspension is clearly involuntary (*e.g.*, destruction of corporation's plant by fire).[30] Some courts have been more lenient.[31]

Investments in stock, securities, and similar property will not constitute a trade or business unless such activities have historically been the corporation's business.[32]

---

[27] *Euclid-Tennessee, Inc. v. Commissioner*, 352 F.2d 991, 65-2 U.S.T.C. ¶ 9763 (6th Cir. 1965), *cert. denied*, 384 U.S. 940 (1966); *Power-Line Sales, Inc. v. Commissioner, supra* note 25; *see* Asofsky, Reorganizing Insolvent Corporations, *supra* note 4, § 5.04[2].

[28] Reg. § 1.368-1(d)(5), Example (1).

[29] Reg. § 1.382-1A(h)(6); *see Commissioner v. Barclay Jewel, Inc.*, 367 F.2d 193, 66-2 U.S.T.C. ¶ 9704 (1st Cir. 1966) (immediately following prohibited change in stock ownership, business abandoned with no plans to continue it; two years later business reactivated; held prohibited change in business); *Glover Packing Co. v. United States*, 328 F.2d 842, 64-1 U.S.T.C. ¶ 9249 (Ct. Cl.) (corporation suspended its business activities and merely rented out its property; former business reactivated after prohibited change in stock ownership; held prohibited change in business); *Euclid-Tennessee Inc. v. Commissioner*, 41 T.C. 752, Dec. 26,682 (1964), *aff'd*, 352 F.2d 991, 65-2 U.S.T.C. ¶ 9763 (6th Cir. 1965), *cert. denied*, 384 U.S. 940 (1966) (same); *Fawn Fashions, Inc.*, 41 T.C. 205, Dec. 26,395 (1963) (involuntary bankruptcy and sale of assets followed by prohibited change in ownership; held prohibited change in business); *Utah Bit & Steel, Inc.*, 29 T.C.M. 224, Dec. 29,983(M), T.C. Memo. 1970-50 (1970) (following prohibited change in ownership, corporation ceased business and sold its assets; held prohibited change in business); *see also* Barr, *supra* note 4, at § 5.06[2][a].

[30] Reg. § 1.382-1A(h)(6), Examples (1) and (2); cf. Barr, *supra* note 4, at § 5.06[1][a], [2][a].

[31] *Ramsey Co., Inc.*, 43 T.C. 500, Dec. 27,220 (1965) (one-year suspension of business permitted), *nonacq.*; *Clarksdale Rubber Co., supra* note 25; *but cf. Six Seam Co., Inc. v. United States*, 524 F.2d 347, 75-2 U.S.T.C. ¶ 9765 (6th Cir. 1975) (suspension coupled with intention to wind up business operations held prohibited change in business); *Glover Packing Co. v. United States, supra* note 29; *Samson Investment Co. v. Commissioner, supra* note 25.

[32] Reg. § 1.382-1A(h)(4); *Exel Corp. v. United States*, 451 F.2d 80, 71-2 U.S.T.C. ¶ 9731 (8th Cir. 1971) (not trade or business); Rev. Rul. 67-186, 1967-1 C.B. 81; *see* Barr, *supra* note 4, at § 5.06[1] (suggests "similar property" includes land).

Holding companies should therefore be treated as engaged in a trade or business if that has been their historic function.[33]

A parent corporation may in certain instances be considered to be still engaged in a business that it transfers to a subsidiary. In IRS Letter Ruling 8303079,[34] a corporation was engaged in several distinct businesses operating through divisions. As part of a bankruptcy plan of reorganization, the corporation proposed to transfer each of its divisions into newly created subsidiaries. After the reorganization, the corporation would be purely a holding company. The IRS ruled that the mere transfer of the divisions would not cause a change in the trade or business of the parent corporation for purposes of old Code § 382(a).

## § 508 NEW CODE § 382

The new Code § 382 adopted in the Tax Reform Act of 1986 applies to all changes in ownership occurring after December 31, 1986, except for (1) changes pursuant to a plan of tax-free reorganization adopted on or before December 31, 1986 (*see* § 604.2.3) and (2) changes taking place in bankruptcy cases that were filed before August 14, 1986 (*see* § 507 above), as well as in certain specifically grandfathered transactions.[1] What follows is a description of new Code § 382. As we shall see, the statute and legislative history leave unanswered numerous important interpretative questions regarding the application of this new provision. This creates considerable difficulty in planning transactions.

For those who are familiar with the old (pre-1986 Act) Code § 382, new Code § 382 can best be understood if one first notes its similarities and dissimilarities to old Code § 382. These can be summarized as follows:

---

[33] Asofsky, Reorganizing, *supra* note 4, at § 5.04[2].

[34] IRS Letter Ruling 8303079, October 20, 1982; GCM 38951, January 17, 1983 (supporting ruling). Similarly, for purposes of the "continuity of business enterprise" test generally imposed as a precondition to a tax-free reorganization, the IRS in 1985 issued two published rulings permitting in certain cases the attribution of a wholly owned subsidiary's business to its parent. *See* Rev. Rul. 85-197, 1985-2 C.B. 120 (merger of holding company into wholly owned subsidiary; business of subsidiary was attributed to holding company); Rev. Rul. 85-198, 1985-2 C.B. 120 (where a bank holding company merged into a similar unrelated holding company and sold one of its two subsidiaries, both of which had significant business, the continuity of business enterprise test was still satisfied). The rulings do not require that the parent and subsidiary have filed a consolidated return.

[1] **§ 508** *See* 1986 Act § 621(f). For a general discussion of Code § 382 in the acquisition context, *see* Ginsburg & Levin, Mergers, Acquisitions, Buyouts ch. 12 (May 2000). For a flowchart analysis of new Code § 382, *see* Sniderman, Gallagher & Joshowitz, A Tax Overview of Troubled Company Debt Restructuring, Vol. 21, No. 4 Tax Advisor 199 (April 1990). For a history of the development of new Code § 382, *see* Asofsky, Towards a Bankruptcy Tax Act of 1993, 51 NYU Inst. on Fed. Tax'n §§ 13.02, 13.03 (1993). The special rules in Code § 382 for bankrupt corporations were the result of a 1986 compromise of which, Asofsky says, it can be said that "the aphorism that a camel is a horse made by a committee was never more true." One of these special rules, Code § 382(l)(5), he notes "is not the product of any philosophy, but an attempt to reconcile two conflicting statutory proposals by indiscriminately adopting a little of each." Id. at p. 13-21.

For a criticism of new Code § 382, *see* Henderson, Controlling Hyperlexis—The Most Important "Law and . . . ," 43 Tax Law. 177, 186-191 (1989).

(1) New Code § 382, like old Code § 382(a), potentially becomes applicable when there ceases to be a 50-percent continuity of ownership. The change that invoked old Code § 382(a), however, was a 50 percentage point change; the change that invokes new Code § 382 is a *more than* 50 percentage point change.

(2) Whereas new Code § 382 requires the same 50 percent continuity of ownership for reorganizations of all kinds as it does for other types of transactions, old Code § 382(b) imposed only a 20 percent continuity for most reorganization transactions (and did not apply at all to "B" reorganizations). For purposes of satisfying the 20 percent continuity test, however, old Code § 382(b) counted only stock received in exchange for the loss company's stock. It did not generally count stock already owned by the loss company's shareholders in the other corporation. New Code § 382 counts both types of stock ownership for purposes of meeting the 50 percent continuity test. In these, and in almost all other respects, new Code § 382 applies very much the same rules to reorganizations as to stock purchases. Many more reorganizations will be affected by new than by old Code § 382.

(3) New Code § 382 invokes different standards than old Code § 382 for determining which shareholders, and which transactions, are taken into account in measuring the change in ownership. Many more stock shifts are likely to be brought into the net of new Code § 382.

(4) In new Code § 382, as in old Code § 382(a), a change in ownership, coupled with a change in business, will destroy a company's NOLs and other carryovers. (An exception is made for certain ownership changes occurring in a bankruptcy or similar proceeding.) However, for this purpose, new Code § 382 substitutes the reorganization "continuity-of-business-enterprise" concept for the old Code § 382(a) "change-in-business" test. (Under old Code § 382(b), the "continuity-of-business-enterprise" test applied simply because it was a prerequisite to a reorganization.) Under new Code § 382, there must be a continuity of business enterprise for two full years after the change in ownership. In contrast, under old Code § 382(a), the period during which a change in business was prohibited could range from less than one year (in rare cases) to almost three years.

(5) Even when the continuity-of-business-enterprise test is met, new Code § 382 imposes a limitation on the use of NOLs and other carryovers if there has been a change in ownership. This was not true under old Code § 382(a). It was true under old Code § 382(b), although the limitation under old Code § 382(b) was quite different from the limitation under new Code § 382.

(6) The limitation imposed by new Code § 382 is not a reduction of the carryovers themselves; rather, it is an annual limitation on the amount of postchange income that can be sheltered by such carryovers. In general, except for certain ownership changes occurring in bankruptcy or similar proceedings, such income is annually limited to the long-term tax-exempt bond rate times the value of the loss company's stock, as determined immediately *before* the change. Where some or all of the stock is not publicly traded, application of this rule may present valuation difficulties. In valuing the stock of a foreign loss corporation, only items connected with a trade or business conducted in the United States are taken into account.

(7) Under new Code § 382, net built-in losses recognized during the first five years following the change in ownership may be subjected to the same limitation as NOLs. On the other hand, net built-in gains recognized during the first five years following the change may be sheltered by prechange NOLs without regard to the annual limitation (even when there has been a failure to satisfy the continuity-of-business-enterprise test). These rules will apply only if the net built-in loss or the net built-in gain, as the case may be, exceeds the applicable *de minimis* threshold. Before amendment by the Revenue Reconciliation Act of 1989, the threshold was 25 percent of the value of the loss company's assets at the date of the change in ownership. After such amendment, the threshold became the lesser of 15 percent of the fair market value of the assets or $10 million. In contrast, old Code § 382 imposed no limitation on built-in losses and was unaffected by built-in gains.

(8) Under new Code § 382, the taxable year in which the ownership change occurs is divided into two segments, a prechange segment and a postchange segment. The new Code § 382 consequences do not apply to the prechange segment. No such division was made under old Code § 382.

(9) In applying the change in ownership rules, new Code § 382 (unlike old Code § 382) cumulates changes resulting from acquisitive reorganizations with those resulting from purchases and other events.

(10) New Code § 382 contains two special rules that are available only to companies in bankruptcy or similar proceedings. The first (the Code § 382(l)(6) rule) provides that, in determining the annual limitation on the amount of postchange income that can be sheltered by prechange NOLs and other carryovers, the value of the loss company's stock is to be measured by including the increase (if any) resulting from debt cancellation occurring at the time of the ownership change. This allows, for example, the increase in equity value resulting from an exchange of debt for stock to be taken into account in determining the annual limitation, if the exchange occurs in bankruptcy as part of a change in ownership. The second special rule for companies in bankruptcy or similar proceedings (the Code § 382(l)(5) rule) allows such companies to avoid the regular Code § 382 rules altogether. In general, such rule is more liberal than the regular Code § 382 rules. No annual limitation on the use of NOLs applies, and the continuity-of-business-enterprise rule need not be met. Moreover, under this provision, qualified prior creditors count for continuity of interest purposes as much as prior equity holders. Thus, even if the prior equity is totally cancelled by the plan, if prior qualified creditors own at least 50 percent of the equity after consummation of the bankruptcy plan, the use of any prechange NOLs and other carryovers can potentially be preserved. This is not true under the other provisions of Code § 382. However, as part of the price for its availability, it limits past interest deductions and the application of the stock-for-debt exception to COD income. Should this second rule (the Code § 382(l)(5) rule) prove less advantageous than the regular Code § 382 rules, the loss company can elect to have the Code § 382(l)(6) rule apply.

It may be remembered that under old Code § 382(a), although no special rules applied to companies in bankruptcy, an exchange of debt for stock in a tax-free recapitalization was not a "purchase" of stock that counted toward a change in ownership. This is no longer the case under new Code § 382. Moreover, under old Code § 382(b)(7), any creditor who received stock in a tax-free two-company reorganization where the company was in a bankruptcy or similar proceeding was treated as an historic shareholder for purposes of meeting the 20 percent continuity-of-ownership requirement. The special bankruptcy rules in new Code § 382 are not so liberal.

## *§508.1 Overview of New Code §382*

As more fully discussed in the following sections, new Code § 382 imposes an annual limitation on the use of NOLs and other carryovers[2] if there has been a more than 50 point increase in the percentage of the value of the loss corporation's stock owned by its 5 percent shareholders over a three-year testing period. The stock ownership is measured after any "owner shift" or "equity structure shift." The testing period may be shorter than three years in certain cases.

After a more than 50 percentage point change in ownership during the testing period has occurred, the taxable income of a loss corporation available for offset by prechange NOLs and other carryovers is annually limited to an amount equal, in general, to the long-term tax-exempt bond rate times the value of the loss company's stock at the time of the ownership change. The value of the stock is generally measured immediately *before* the change; however, in the case of an ownership change in a bankruptcy or similar proceeding, the value is measured by including the increase (if any) resulting from debt cancellation incident to the transaction. This is the Code § 382(l)(6) rule discussed at § 508.4.2 below. Thus, in certain instances, debt reductions in bankruptcy proceedings may increase the value of the stock for purposes of computing the annual limitation. The value of the stock is reduced, however, by (1) the amount of capital contributions made during the two-year (and perhaps longer) period ending on the change date, (2) redemptions or other corporate contractions in connection with the ownership change, and (3) if nonbusiness assets exceed one-third of total assets at the ownership change date, the net value of the nonbusiness assets at the change date. Moreover, the annual limitation becomes zero if the loss company does not satisfy the continuity-of-business-enterprise test for two years after the change (*see* § 508.3).

Regardless of whether the continuity-of-business-enterprise test is satisfied, the annual limitation is, in general, increased by (1) the amount of built-in gains recognized within five years after the change date, provided the net built-in gains at the change date exceeded the applicable *de minimis* threshold at that date, and (2) any Code § 338 gain recognized by the loss company. On the other hand, if net built-in

---

[2] New Code § 383 extends the limitations of new Code § 382 to ITC, foreign tax credit, work incentive credit, and capital loss carryovers, as well as to alternative minimum tax credit carryovers. Although there is no reference in the statute, the 1986 Act Conference Report, H.R. Rep. No. 841, 99th Cong., 2d Sess. at II-194 (1986), also indicates that passive activity losses and credits were to be covered.

losses at the change date exceeded the applicable *de minimis* threshold at the change date, the built-in losses recognized within five years after the change date may be subject to the annual limitation just as if they were NOLs. These provisions are more fully discussed at § 508.4.

Companies in bankruptcy and similar proceedings may have an alternative, special Code § 382 rule apply to them (the Code § 382(l)(5) rule described in § 508.5), in lieu of the above new Code § 382 limitations. We will refer to this rule in this volume as the "Elective Bankruptcy Rule," although, technically, it applies (assuming the requisite 50-percent control test is satisfied) unless the loss company elects to have the regular Code § 382 limitations apply. The Elective Bankruptcy Rule generally will apply if the loss company's shareholders and creditors (determined immediately before the ownership change) own at least 50 percent of the value and voting power of the stock after the change. Creditors receiving stock are not counted for this purpose unless they have held their debt since at least 18 months before the bankruptcy case was filed—a test whose harshness on publicly traded debt the IRS has sought to ameliorate in Reg. § 1.382-9(d)—or the debt arose in the ordinary course of the loss company's business and is held by the original creditor. This is the only Code § 382 rule that allows qualified debt holders to be treated as though they were equity holders, so that even if all the equity is cancelled under the bankruptcy plan, the qualified debt holders will be treated as if they had been equity holders for purposes of satisfying the continuity of ownership test under this special rule. If the Elective Bankruptcy Rule applies, the prechange NOLs and credit carryovers are recomputed to exclude the amount of any interest deducted during the three preceding taxable years and the current taxable year on any debt that is exchanged for stock during the bankruptcy proceeding; and, in the case of debt to which the (former) stock-for-debt exception to COD income applies, the prechange NOLs and credit carryovers also are reduced by 50 percent of the COD income avoided. Further, a subsequent ownership change within two years will render the NOLs and other carryovers of the loss company essentially useless. If the Elective Bankruptcy Rule applies, the company need not satisfy the continuity-of-business-enterprise requirement.

## *§ 508.2 The "Ownership Change" Test*

For purposes of new Code § 382, an "ownership change" occurs if the percentage of the value of the loss company's stock, owned by one or more 5 percent shareholders, has increased by more than 50 percentage points over the lowest percentage of stock owned by them at any time during the "testing period."[3] Changes are measured only when a "testing date" has occurred at a time when the corporation is a "loss corporation." A company is a "loss corporation" if it has an NOL, capital loss, foreign tax credit, general business credit, or minimum tax credit carryover (or any such loss or credits in the current year) or a net unrealized built-in loss.[4] Note that even a

---

[3] Code § 382(g)(1).

[4] Reg. § 1.382-2(a)(1); Temp. Reg. § 1.382-2T(f)(1). Note that this definition is broader than that found in Code § 382(k)(1).

nominal amount of losses or credits apparently makes a company a "loss corporation." A "testing date" occurs only when certain physical events (generally an "owner shift" or certain issuances or transfers of options) take place; fluctuations in value in the meantime are ignored.[5]

On each "testing date," one must first determine what constitutes the loss company's "stock" and then: (1) determine who is deemed to own it, (2) identify the 5 percent shareholders, (3) measure the increase separately for each such 5 percent shareholder, and (4) aggregate the increases to see if the increases during the "testing period" exceeded 50 percentage points. If they did exceed 50 percentage points, an "ownership change" has occurred, and the date on which this happens is called the "change date."[6]

Where the assets of one corporation are absorbed by another in a Code § 381(a) transaction (*i.e.*, a Code § 332 liquidation or a tax-free reorganization), the survivor must make these determinations in two capacities: one in its capacity as successor to the absorbed corporation and one in its own capacity. The testing periods, testing dates, changes in ownership, and annual limitation may be different for each such capacity.

The statutory and regulatory provisions that define these elements of the change in ownership test are an exercise in intricate complexity that has been geometrically escalated. The statute, itself complicated and difficult to apply, left numerous places where the rules were to be created by regulations. Temporary and proposed regulations were issued in August 1987. These, covering some 170 pages in typewritten form, much of it single spaced, managed to pile definition upon involuted definition, exception upon exception, and special rule upon special rule, to a point where they cannot be applied without an inordinate expenditure of time and mental effort. Even after such effort, in numerous instances one will not be able to tell, with certainty, how the rules apply to the facts before oneself. Seldom has a society required so much time and intellectual effort to be expended, by the government and by taxpayers, for such a relatively trivial (even debatable) social purpose. Particularly perverse is the fact that it is the most fragile of enterprises having the most limited resources, *i.e.*, new ventures suffering start-up losses and failing companies, that must grapple with these provisions. Fortunately, even the IRS began to be troubled by the inordinate complexity involved, and beginning in 1992 it proposed, and in 1994 made final, some important simplifying regulations. Still, the statutory scheme and the regulatory overlay remain absurdly complex.

What follows is a summary of these complicated provisions.[7]

---

[5] *See* Code § 382(l)(3)(D).

[6] *See* Code § 382(j).

[7] For greater detail, *see* the following multi-part articles: Goldring & Feiner, Section 382 Ownership Change, 66 Taxes 427, 619 and 803 (June, September, and November 1988); Silverman and Keyes, An Analysis of the New Ownership Regs. Under Section 382, 68 J. Tax'n 68, 142, and 300 (February, March, and May 1988), 69 J. Tax'n 42 (July 1988).

### § 508.2.1 "Testing Date" and "Testing Period"

The "testing date" is the date on which the loss corporation must determine whether an "ownership change" has taken place. For dates on or after November 5, 1992, the 1994 final regulations define the "testing date" as any date on which there occurs:

(1) an "owner shift" (which term is defined in § 508.2.3 below);
(2) the issuance or transfer (except a transfer between persons who are not 5 percent shareholders, between members of separate public groups, or by reason of death, gift, divorce or separation) of an option, if the issuance or transfer is made for an "abusive principal purpose."[8]

For dates occurring before November 5, 1992, the temporary regulations defined the "testing date" as any date on which there occurred:

(1) an "owner shift";
(2) an "equity structure shift" (but only if it also constitutes an "owner shift");
(3) a transfer of an option to (or by) a 5 percent shareholder (or a person who would be a 5 percent shareholder if the option were exercised); or
(4) an issuance of an option by the loss corporation (or by entities directly or indirectly owning 5 percent or more of the stock of the loss corporation).[9]

One cannot ignore a testing date, even if the facts are such that one is confident that no "ownership change" has occurred. The temporary regulations require a corporation to file a statement with its tax return for each year that it is loss corporation, stating whether any testing dates had occurred during the year, identifying some or all of the testing dates, identifying each testing date on which an ownership change (if any) had occurred, and stating certain other information.[10] *See* § 508.6 below. The fact that, under the temporary regulations, a testing date was created each time a loss company (or certain higher tier entities) issued a compensatory stock option to an employee (no matter how small the option or how little stock the employee owned) meant that, just by reason of the issuance of compensatory options by the loss company, or by certain of its corporate owners, numerous "testing dates" might occur during the year. The 1994 final regulations change, and considerably relax, the substantive option rules for testing dates on or after November 5, 1992. They also create a question whether the reporting obligation in the temporary regulations applies to such testing dates, although this seems to have been inadvertent and the IRS considers the reporting obligation as still effective. *See* § 508.6.

On any testing date, both the final and the temporary regulations provide that all computations of increases in percentage ownership are to be made as of the close of the testing date, and any transactions that took place on that date are treated as

---

[8] Reg. § 1.382-2(a)(4).
[9] Temp. Reg. § 1.382-2T(a)(2).
[10] Id.

occurring simultaneously at the close of the testing date. The latter rule means that where a holder has both an increase and a decrease in the percentage of ownership on the testing date, the two are netted before being taken into account.[11] For example, the IRS has privately ruled that the purchase and sale of stock by underwriters on the same day will be ignored for all purposes of Code § 382.[12] Where, however, the purchase by the underwriters in a firm commitment underwriting and the sale to their customers occur on separate days, there was for a time a risk that both the purchase and the sale would be separately counted, perhaps producing two consecutive ownership changes. Although the IRS has in limited circumstances allowed stock issued on different dates pursuant to a plan related to the formation of a new company to be treated, in essence, as though issued on a single day (*see* § 508.2.5), it has not provided a similar relaxation for stock issued in firm commitment underwritings (though, as mentioned in note 12, the statute contained a special grandfather rule for such underwritings). However, Reg. § 1.382-3(j)(7), issued in 1993, prevents this risk by generally providing that the transitory ownership of stock by an underwriter will be disregarded (*see* § 508.2.8).

Other situations can similarly present the question whether an event having several steps will be treated as producing more than one testing date. A bankruptcy plan, for example, may provide that on the consummation date a block of stock will be issued into an escrow account to satisfy disputed claims. As claims are resolved from time to time, stock will be released from the escrow to those whose claims have been allowed. The IRS has ruled that the successful claimants who receive the released shares will be treated as if they had owned them retroactively back to the consummation date, so that the periodic releases of the shares from escrow will not create a subsequent shift in ownership or separate and additional testing dates. *See* §§ 508.2.7.3 and 508.2.8.1 below. If in such a case the shares for the disputed claims are not placed in an escrow (or a qualified settlement fund) pending resolution of the claims, but under otherwise equivalent circumstances are only issued as and when each disputed claim is resolved, the answer, we submit, should be the same: namely, that the later issuance should not be taken into account as a subsequent shift in ownership. Whether or not an escrow is used, there can be a question—depending on the facts—about how one makes ownership calculations during the interim period between the consummation date and the later date when all contested claims are resolved.

---

[11] Id. The temporary regulations do not indicate whether this netting rule also applies to transactions occurring on other days (including prior testing dates), or is used to determine whether one has become a 5 percent shareholder. It seems that it should, and the letter ruling mentioned in the next footnote confirms the latter point.

[12] IRS Letter Ruling 8809081, December 9, 1987, supplemented by IRS Letter Ruling 8823002, February 10, 1988.

With respect to underwritings, it should be noted that H.R. 4333, 100th Cong., 2d Sess. § 106(d)(15) (hereafter cited as the Technical Corrections Bill of 1988), provides that unless the loss company otherwise elects, an underwriter of any firm commitment offering of stock before September 19, 1986 (January 1, 1989, in the case of certain thrift institutions), will not be treated as acquiring any stock to the extent it is disposed of within 60 days after the initial offering.

The "testing period" is the three-year period (measured in terms of actual days, not taxable years) ending on the "testing date."[13] However, to determine the testing period one does not need to look back before the later of:

(1) May 6, 1986;[14]

(2) the day following the last "ownership change" occurring after May 5, 1986;[15] or

(3) the first day of the earliest of (a) the current taxable year (b) the first taxable year from which there is an NOL or other carryforward and (c) if the loss corporation has a net built-in loss that exceeds the applicable built-in loss threshold (*see* § 508.4), the taxable year in which such loss first accrued.[16] (If the corporation has such a net built-in loss but cannot prove when it first accrued (presumably this means when it first went over the threshold), then the limitation described in this clause (3) does not apply.)[17]

Although one can ignore a testing date that occurs before the beginning of the testing period,[18] in order to be able to calculate the changes in ownership that occur during a testing period, one must make the same determinations regarding ownership interests for the first day of the testing period that one would have to make on a testing date.

---

[13] Code § 382(i)(1); Temp. Reg. § 1.382-2T(d)(1). As mentioned above, a testing date can be created by an equity structure shift that also creates an owner shift. In the case of an equity structure shift resulting from a plan of reorganization adopted before January 1, 1987, a special transition rule exists. The shift will be deemed to occur when the plan was adopted. Temp. Reg. § 1.382-2T(m)(1). *See also* Joint Committee on Taxation, General Explanation of the Tax Reform Act of 1986, May 14, 1986 (JCS-10-87) (the 1986 Blue Book), at 326 n.38a (and accompanying text). A technical correction would codify this treatment. Technical Corrections Bill of 1988, § 106(d)(11).

New Code § 382 applies to ownership changes occurring after 1986. Old Code § 382(b) does not apply to any reorganization occurring pursuant to a plan of reorganization adopted after December 31, 1986. Between the end of 1986 and the end of 1988, however, old Code § 382(a) may continue to have overlapping application with new Code § 382, *i.e.*, old Code § 382(a) applies to any increase in percentage ownership that does not produce an ownership change through that date under new Code § 382 by reason of any transitional rule applicable to the latter. *See* Temp. Reg. § 1.382-2T(m)(7); 1986 Blue Book at 327; Technical Corrections Bill of 1988, § 106(d)(11).

In the case of "G" reorganizations or stock-for-debt exchanges occurring in a title 11 or similar case, new Code § 382 does not apply to any ownership change "resulting" from such reorganization or proceeding if the petition was filed before August 14, 1986. 1986 Act § 621(f)(5). The temporary regulations make clear that (1) an ownership change "results" from an increase in ownership occurring in such proceeding if such ownership must be counted to reach an ownership change (whether at the time of the proceeding or later) and (2) it does not apply for determining if an ownership change (whether at the time of the proceeding or later) occurred *before* 1987 for purposes of selecting the beginning of a new testing period. Temp. Reg. § 1.382-2T(m)(5) (Example).

[14] 1986 Act, § 621(f)(3).

[15] Code § 382(i)(2). Under the special transition rule noted in footnote 13, an equity structure shift produced by a plan of reorganization, adopted before the end of 1986, is deemed to occur when the plan was adopted.

[16] Id. Temp. Reg. § 1.382-2T(d); *see also* 1986 Act Conference Report, *supra* note 2, at II-185.

[17] Code § 382(i)(2); Temp. Reg. § 1.382-2T(d).

[18] Temp. Reg. § 1.382-2T(d)(4).

### § 508.2.2 What Is "Stock"?

One cannot apply the ownership change test without knowing what constitutes the "stock" whose change in ownership is to be measured. The definition of "stock" for this purpose begins with the consolidated return definition, that is, it includes all stock other than preferred stock described in Code § 1504(a)(4) and excludes stock that: (1) is nonvoting, (2) is nonconvertible, (3) is limited and preferred as to dividends, (4) does not participate in corporate growth to any significant extent, and (5) has redemption and liquidation rights that do not exceed its issue price (except for a reasonable redemption or liquidation premium).[19] The temporary regulations, following the legislative history,[20] provide that if such excluded stock later acquires a vote because of dividend arrearages, it will not then be treated as "stock" for purposes of the Code § 382 ownership change test, even if it is so treated for Code § 1504 purposes.[21] Even if Code § 1504(a)(4) stock is not treated as "stock" for ownership change purposes, Code § 382(e)(1) provides that such stock will be taken into account for purposes of valuing the loss company immediately before any ownership change in calculating the annual Code § 382 limitation (*see* § 508.4).

However, this is just the beginning. The statute gives the Treasury power to issue regulations treating "stock" as "not stock" and treating warrants, options, contracts to acquire stock, convertible debt interests, and other similar interests as "stock."[22] The temporary regulations have exercised this power[23] effective for interests:

(1) issued on or after September 4, 1987, or

(2) transferred on or after September 4, 1987, to (or by) a 5 percent shareholder (or a person who would be a 5 percent shareholder if these rules applied).[24]

As we shall see when we discuss the attribution rules and the rules for determining who is a 5 percent shareholder, when the stock of the loss corporation is held through one or more tiers of higher entities, one must determine what is "stock," not only for the loss corporation, but also for these higher tier entities. (Alice had to pass through only one looking glass; the Code § 382 adviser is not so lucky.)

---

[19] Code § 382(k)(6)(A). The meaning of Code § 1504(a)(4) is explored in Winston, What Is Section 1504(a)(4) Preferred Stock?, 76 Tax Notes 111 (July 7, 1997).

[20] 1986 Act Conference Report, *supra* note 2, at II-173, 174.

[21] Temp. Reg. § 1.382-2T(f)(18)(i). Nothing is said about the acquisition of voting rights for other, similar reasons, such as the failure to make sinking fund payments or other redemptions. The regulation refers to stock that is not excluded by Code § 1504(a)(4) "solely because it is entitled to vote as a result of dividend arrearages." This suggests that stock that becomes voting for any other reason (whether alone or in combination with dividend arrearages) will not be covered by this provision. Although such stock, once it becomes voting, might be treated as "not stock" under the special rule discussed next, the result is not the same. The present rule for dividend arrearages applies in all instances; the rule treating stock as "not stock" applies only if three conditions are met.

[22] Code § 382(k)(6)(B).

[23] Temp. Reg. § 1.382-2T(f)(18)(ii) and (iii).

[24] Temp. Reg. § 1.382-2T(m)(4)(iv).

In a private ruling, the IRS has held that restricted stock issued to employees will be treated as "stock" for Section 382 purposes, apparently without regard to whether the employee has made a Code § 83(b) election.[25]

*§ 508.2.2.1 Special Rule for Convertible Stock*

Over the years, the IRS has had various changes of heart about how to treat convertible preferred stock for ownership change purposes.

**Present rule.** Reg. § 1.382-2(a)(3)(ii) provides that "stock" for ownership change purposes includes any convertible stock. In addition, Reg. § 1.382-4(d)(9)(ii) provides that such stock will also be treated as an option if the terms of the conversion feature permit or require the payment of consideration in addition to the stock being converted. This rule does not apply to (i) stock issued on or after July 20, 1988 and before November 5, 1992 or (ii) stock issued before July 20, 1988 and the loss corporation made the election described in Notice 88-67 on or before the earlier of the date prescribed in the Notice or December 7, 1992.

**Prior rules.** The temporary regulations, as originally issued, gave convertible stock a dual status: It was both "stock" and an "option." This had the potential for creating considerable confusion. On June 20, 1988, the Treasury announced in Notice 88-67[26] that it would treat "pure" convertible preferred stock as an option and not as stock. For this purpose, "pure" convertible preferred is stock whose only feature at the time of its issuance, taking it out of the Code § 1504(a)(4) exclusion, is its convertibility feature (*i.e.*, stock issued as *nonvoting* and *nonparticipating* convertible preferred).

The announcement indicated that this status is to be determined at the time the stock is issued; apparently a later addition of voting rights may not change its status. The purpose of the rule was to treat "pure" (*i.e.*, nonvoting and nonparticipating) convertible preferred stock the same as convertible debt, namely, as an option under the option rules (discussed below) and not as stock. The announcement further stated that all other convertible stock would be treated solely as stock (though still subject to being treated, like all stock, as "not stock" if the three tests discussed below under the "stock-treated-as-not-stock" rule are met) and not as an option "as long as the terms of the conversion feature do not permit or require the tender of any consideration other than the stock being converted."

The announcement applied only to convertible stock issued on or after July 20, 1988. Unless the loss company made an election to apply the new rule to stock issued earlier, *all* convertible stock issued before July 20, 1988, is treated as stock (though still subject to being treated, like all stock, as "not stock" if the three tests under the "not stock" rule discussed below are met) and *not* as an option.

---

[25] IRS Letter Ruling 9422048, March 8, 1994. We question whether the final option regulations would treat it also as an option. *See* § 508.2.7.6 below. *Cf.* IRS Letter Ruling 9804033, October 24, 1997 (stock does not count for Section 1504 purposes while subject to a Code § 83 substantial risk of forfeiture; Code § 382 not involved); discussed in Raby and Raby, What Stock Counts—And When?, 79 Tax Notes (May 11, 1998), p. 741.

[26] 1988-1 C.B. 555.

Since the pre-1992 option rules were generally far more dangerous under Code §382 than the stock rules, in those years it was advisable for companies to give serious thought to avoiding issuance of nonvoting convertible preferred stock. On the other hand, the ability to treat convertible preferred as stock if it has voting or participation features, but as an option if it does not, could be a useful planning device. Where convertible preferred is treated as an option, its value for Code §382 purposes is the value of the stock into which it is convertible, whereas the value of convertible preferred treated as stock is the value of the convertible preferred itself. During the early life of the instrument the former will usually be less than the latter. Thus, an ownership change that might be created by issuance of voting convertible preferred might be avoided (at least for a time) by issuing nonvoting, nonparticipating convertible preferred. However, the evergreen nature of an option made the latter instrument a perpetual danger, whereas issuance of the former instrument need not be counted after the three-year testing period has expired.

#### *§508.2.2.2 Stock Treated as "Not Stock"*

The temporary regulations state that "stock" will not be treated as stock if three tests are met:

(1) as of the time of its issuance or transfer to (or by) a 5 percent shareholder, the "likely participation of such interest in future corporate growth is disproportionately small" when compared to the value of such stock as a proportion of the total value of the outstanding stock (a "growth participation" test);

(2) treating the interest as not "stock" would result in an ownership change (an "ownership change" test); and

(3) as of the testing date, the loss corporation's NOLs and net built-in losses are not *de minimis* (a *de minimis* test).[27]

The corporation's NOLs and net built-in losses are considered *de minimis* if they do not exceed twice the annual limitation that would apply if an ownership change occurred on the testing date.[28]

Unfortunately, the temporary regulations give no examples or other guidance as to the meaning of the "growth participation" test. The legislative history, however, suggests that in some cases preferred stock that constitutes stock under Code §1504 solely because it is voting stock probably will fail the "growth participation" test, as

---

[27] Temp. Reg. §1.382-2T(f)(18)(ii).

[28] For purposes of computing the annual limitation, one includes as stock all stock in the ordinary sense (including stock excluded under Code §1504(a)(4) and stock that may be treated as "not stock" under this rule), as well as nonstock interests that are treated as "stock" under the companion rule discussed immediately below. *See* Temp. Reg. §1.382-2T(f)(18)(ii)(C) and (iii)(C).

would the common stock issued to the old shareholders in *Maxwell Hardware*.[29] Numerous other questions remain unclear, however, such as:

(1) whether the three-part test applies only to the ownership interest that was issued or transferred, or whether it applies to the entire class (only part of which may have been issued or transferred at the testing time);
(2) whether the ownership change and *de minimis* tests are only to be applied on the date of issuance or transfer of the interest (the date on which the growth participation test applies), or whether they can also apply on any other testing date; and
(3) whether stock that is treated as not stock is to be so regarded retroactively throughout the testing period, or whether it is to be treated as shifting from stock to nonstock status on the date it satisfies the three tests (which could produce dramatically different results).

For the expression of some important IRS positions on the stock as nonstock issue in particular bankruptcy cases, *see* §§ 508.2.2.4 and 1202.1 below.

*§ 508.2.2.3 Nonstock Treated as "Stock"*

The temporary regulations also provide that an ownership interest (other than options) that would not be treated as stock, under Code § 1504(a)(4), will be treated as stock for purposes of the ownership change rule if three tests are met:

(1) as of the time of its issuance or transfer to (or by) a 5 percent shareholder, such interest offers a "potential significant participation" in the growth of the corporation (a "growth participation" test);

---

[29] 1986 Act Conference Report, *supra* note 2, at II-173. In *Maxwell Hardware Co. v. Commissioner*, 343 F.2d 716 (9th Cir. 1969), new investors purchased a specially tailored preferred stock from a loss company. The stock represented about 30 percent of the company's value, but about 90 percent of its future growth. This result occurred because the company discontinued its former hardware business and started a real estate business, and its preferred stock could be redeemed at any time, at the option of either the company or the holder, by distributing in kind 90 percent of the real estate assets. Under old Code § 382(c), this stock was treated as excludable "nonvoting stock which is limited and preferred as to dividends," even though a voting trust was established that restricted the control of the common shareholders for five years (without shifting control to the preferred shareholders). The reference to *Maxwell Hardware* in the legislative history to new Code § 382 indicates an intention to treat the old common stock in that case as "not stock," and the new preferred stock as "stock," thus causing an ownership change to occur when the preferred stock was issued. Ironically, the definition of "not stock" in the temporary regulations would not produce this result on the actual facts of *Maxwell Hardware;* when the common stock of that company was issued (long before issuance of the preferred), the common stock presumably would not have failed the growth participation test, and because the common stock was not transferred when the preferred stock was issued, the growth participation test would not be applicable to it at that time. Thus, since both classes of stock would be treated as "stock," and the preferred was worth only 30 percent of the total, an ownership change would not have occurred. *Accord*, New York State Bar Association Tax Section Report on "Tracking Stock" Arrangements, 43 Tax L. Rev. 51, 68 (1987).

(2) treating the interest as "stock" would result in an ownership change (an "ownership change" test); and

(3) as of the testing date, the loss corporation's losses are not *de minimis* (a *de minimis* test).[30]

This *de minimis* test is the same as that described under the preceding rule.

As in the case of the preceding rule, the "growth participation" test is the key element in this definition. Again, however, the temporary regulations give no guidance as to its meaning. The statutory provision it implements provides, as mentioned above, that the regulations may treat warrants, options, contracts to acquire stock, convertible debt interests, and other similar interests as stock. As we shall see, most of these are treated as options under the temporary regulations and are subjected to the option rules. Since options are excluded from the scope of the "nonstock is stock" definition, there does not seem to be much that is covered by this definition. However, the preamble to the temporary regulations says that instruments characterized as debt for tax purposes may be treated as "stock" under this rule. Does this refer to situations where the value of the company's assets has fallen below the face amount of the debt by a significant degree, and the debt is then transferred to new owners? The answer is unclear. The same concept could apply to preferred stock. If this is the intention, the rule opens up a frightening degree of uncertainty. Perhaps the Treasury only had in mind debt that carries enough kicker interest to constitute, even at the time of its issuance, a "potential significant participation in the growth" of the company. Perhaps one day we will know the answer to these questions. Moreover, this rule is subject to the same three ambiguities in interpretation that were listed in the discussion of the preceding rule.

The IRS did provide some helpful guidance in a private letter ruling in mid-1994.[31] Here the taxpayer had issued new subordinated notes and debentures. The taxpayer could not represent that it was solvent on the date of their issuance, but it could represent that it expected to have sufficient assets (not taking into account future growth of assets) from cash flow from its projected future earnings and proceeds of anticipated additional debt financing to meet all required payments of principal and interest on the new debt. The IRS ruled that the new debt would not be treated as "stock" for Section 382 purposes, at least until it is reissued or transferred to or by a 5 percent shareholder (or person who would be a 5 percent shareholder if the new debt were treated as stock). For the expression of some important IRS positions on the nonstock as stock issue in particular bankruptcy cases, *see* §§ 508.2.2.4 and 1202.1 below.

---

[30] Temp. Reg. § 1.382-2T(f)(18)(iii).

[31] IRS Letter Ruling 9441036, July 14, 1994. In IRS Field Service Advice 199910009, December 2, 1998, *reprinted at* 1999 TNT 49-87, the IRS held that when debt was modified to make it more likely it could be collected, the mere fact that the debtor did not have enough assets to pay the debt in full at that time did not mean that the debt should be treated as "stock." The same field service advice dealt with the question whether, on the facts presented, warrants should be treated as "stock" (some of which were treated as stock by the IRS and some of which were not).

*§ 508.2.2.4 The* Integrated Resources *Case*

In late 1993, the IRS filed an objection to a bankruptcy plan in the *Integrated Resources* case that was proposed by a group of creditors. The proponents then withdrew the plan. The plan was a liquidating Chapter 11 plan and would have left the stock untouched. But because it was unlikely that the stockholders would ever receive anything, and even the debt was unlikely to be paid in full, the IRS asserted that consummation of the plan would cause the debt to become recharacterized as stock for tax purposes under the nonstock-treated-as-stock regulation discussed at § 508.2.2.3 above, and the stock to be treated as nonstock under the regulation discussed at § 508.2.2.2 above, thereby resulting in an ownership change. Subsequently, the IRS has ruled, in a liquidating bankruptcy where the stock was likely to receive nothing, and even the debt was unlikely to be paid in full, that (i) the debt would not be treated as stock for Code § 382 purposes, and (ii) the cancellation of the stock and its replacement by identical stock issued to trusts having limited transferability would not constitute an owner shift for purposes of Code § 382(g). The *Integrated Resources* case, and this ruling are discussed at § 1202.1 below.

**§ 508.2.3 "Owner Shifts" and "Equity Structure Shifts"**

An "owner shift" occurs whenever any change affects the percentage ownership of a 5 percent shareholder.[32] Thus, it includes any acquisition or disposition (whether taxable or tax-free) by a 5 percent shareholder, any acquisition by a person who becomes a 5 percent shareholder, and any increase or decrease in the outstanding stock of the corporation that affects the percentage ownership of a 5 percent shareholder. Thus, the exchange of nonconvertible debt or straight preferred that is not "stock" for "stock" creates an owner shift if it affects the percentage ownership of a 5 percent shareholder. On the other hand, the IRS has ruled that the conversion of convertible preferred stock into common stock is not an owner shift, apparently on the theory that the values should be considered for this purpose to be equal.[33] The IRS has ruled that the issuance of cash in lieu of fractional shares in connection with a reverse stock split will not be treated as an owner shift.[34]

An "equity structure shift" is any tax-free reorganization exchange in which the loss corporation is a party to the reorganization, other than an "F" reorganization or a divisive reorganization.[35] As the temporary regulations expressly recognize, an equity structure shift that affects the percentage ownership of a 5 percent shareholder is also

---

[32] *See* Code § 382(g)(2); Temp. Reg. § 1.382-2T(e)(1)(i).

[33] IRS Letter Ruling 8811030, December 22, 1987; IRS Letter Ruling 8809081, December 9, 1987, supplemented by IRS Letter Ruling 8823002, February 10, 1988. As discussed at § 508.2.2.1 above, certain "pure" convertible stock might be treated as an option rather than as stock. As to such stock, the foregoing holding would not apply, and the conversion of such stock, which would be treated as only an option, could give rise to an owner shift.

[34] IRS Letter Ruling 9104043, October 31, 1990. *See also* IRS Letter Ruling 9405011, November 3, 1993 (cash in lieu of fractional shares on conversion of preferred into common).

[35] Code § 382(g)(3); Temp. Reg. § 1.382-2T(e)(2)(i).

an owner shift. Because the temporary regulations provide that an equity structure shift that is not also an owner shift will not create a testing date,[36] the equity structure shift concept has significance only under the transition rules applicable to plans of reorganization adopted before 1987, and for purposes of the segregation rules discussed below.[37]

### *§ 508.2.3.1 Restricting Transfers: Available Alternatives*

Because transfers of stock can have such serious consequences under Code § 382, loss companies frequently desire to impose restrictions on the transferability of some or all of their shares. The devices used include contractual restrictions, escrows, charter restrictions, and bankruptcy court orders.

An interesting example is found in IRS Letter Ruling 8949040.[38] A loss company that had undergone an ownership change upon confirmation of its bankruptcy plan qualified for the Code § 382(l)(5) rule. To protect against the possibility of a second ownership change (which, it was thought at the time,[39] might have particularly dire consequences under a Code § 382(l)(5) plan) the loss company had placed all of its stock in an escrow arrangement. Subsequently, the company issued more than 5 percent of its stock to a new investor.

The company wished to restrict the new investor's stock and the stock of all other 5 percent shareholders held in the escrow, but also wished to allow the remainder of its stock, which was widely held, to trade on a stock exchange. The company therefore adopted a charter amendment that prohibited, and declared ineffective, any transfer that would increase the transferee's ownership above 4.5 percent (including certain indirect ownership). The amendment contained a mechanism for undoing purported transfers that violated this restriction. The IRS held that (1) provided the restrictions are enforceable, a purported transferee acquiring shares in violation of the provision would not be treated as acquiring ownership from the transferor, (2) any transfer of an option to acquire shares will be disregarded if its exercise would violate the restriction, and (3) if the charter amendment was declared unenforceable *ab initio*, then ownership of stock in violation of the restriction will be treated as having been acquired on the date actually acquired.

Note that the charter restriction involved in this ruling applied to transactions occurring after confirmation of a bankruptcy plan. For the possibility that transactions adversely affecting the debtor under Code § 382 that occur during pendency of

---

[36] Temp. Reg. § 1.382-2T(a)(2)(i).

[37] Temp. Reg. § § 1.382-2T(m)(1),(4).

[38] September 11, 1989. To similar effect, *see* IRS Letter Ruling 9351011, September 23, 1993; IRS Letter Ruling 9405011, November 3, 1993; IRS Letter Ruling 200024047, March 21, 2000; IRS Letter Ruling 200622013, January 27, 2006. Because transfers of stock of S corporations to nonqualifying holders may destroy the corporation's S election, similar charter restrictions have been included in the charters of S corporations that declare such transfers to nonqualified shareholders to be void *ab initio*, and these have been upheld for tax purposes if they are effective under state law. *See*, for example, IRS Letter Ruling 199935035, June 4, 1999.

[39] *See* § 508.5 note 275.

the bankruptcy case (or relating to such periods) might violate the automatic stay or might be restricted by the bankruptcy court, see the discussion of the *Prudential Lines, Phar-Mor,* and other cases and rulings at §§508.2.4 and 1002.4.1, and the *McLean Industries* and the *Pan Am* cases at §§508.5.1 and 1002.4.1.

In addition, it should be noted that the implementation of such a charter restriction for currently outstanding stock may, in certain cases, constitute a constructive recapitalization of such stock.[40]

### §508.2.4 Worthless Stock Rule, Exempt Transfers, and Restricting Transfers in Bankruptcy

The Revenue Act of 1987 added Code §382(g)(4)(D), which provides that if a person who was a 50 percent shareholder (directly or indirectly) of the loss corporation at any time during the preceding three years treats any of his stock as becoming worthless during any taxable year of such shareholder, and the stock is still held by that person at the close of his taxable year, for purposes of determining whether an ownership change has occurred after the close of his year, he shall be treated as acquiring the stock on the first day of his next taxable year and as not owning it previously. The three-year period means the three 12-month periods ending with the last day of the shareholder's taxable year in which the shareholder treated the stock as worthless.

Note that in applying this rule, the loss corporation needs to know facts that may only be known by the shareholder. Note also that a worthless stock deduction by a person who owns very little stock at that time, but who owned 50 percent at some time during his last three taxable years, invokes this rule. To identify such persons, the loss corporation may have to look back before the beginning of the testing period (where the testing period is less than three years).

In the *Prudential Lines* case,[41] a bankruptcy court, holding that NOLs were property of the bankruptcy estate protected by the automatic stay under the Bankruptcy Code, had permanently enjoined a parent corporation from claiming a worthless stock deduction for stock of its bankrupt subsidiary for any year ending before the effective date of the plan. The action of the bankruptcy court was affirmed by the District Court and by the Second Circuit.[42] The courts took the position that the NOLs

---

40 *See* IRS Letter Ruling 8134205, June 1, 1981 (charter amendment prohibiting the transfer of any stock held by a shareholder unless the shareholder sold an equal percentage of each class of stock owned by him constituted a constructive recapitalization of all the company's stock).

41 *In re Prudential Lines, Inc.,* 107 B.R. 832 (Bankr. D.N.Y. 1989) (preliminary injunction), 3 Bankr. L. Rep. §73,203 (January 4, 1990) (permanent injunction). The bankruptcy court opinion is criticized in Pisem & Glicklich, Was the Bankruptcy Court Lost at Sea? *Prudential Lines* Collides with the Internal Revenue Code, 48 Tax Notes 1553 (September 17, 1990). One wonders whether the authors' criticism should not have been directed instead at Code §382 itself, which causes the debtor corporation's tax consequences to be determined by actions occurring at the shareholder, rather than at the corporate, level. *See* Henderson, Controlling Hyperlexis—The Most Important "Law and . . . ," 43 Tax Law. 177, 186-191 (1989).

42 *In re Prudential Lines, Inc.,* 119 B.R. 430 (S.D.N.Y. 1990), *aff'd,* 928 F.2d 565, 92-2 U.S.T.C. ¶50,491 (2d Cir. 1991), *cert. denied,* 112 S. Ct. 82 (1991). On the other hand, a parent's claim of a worthless stock

of the debtor (whether they might be carried back to produce a refund of previously paid tax or carried forward against income that might or might not be earned in the future) were property of the debtor protected by the automatic stay imposed by Section 362(a)(3) of the Bankruptcy Code, which applies to any act seeking to "obtain possession of property of the estate or of property from the estate or to exercise control over property of the estate." It should be noted that Code § 382(g)(4)(D) only applies if the stock is still held at the close of the tax year for which the worthlessness deduction is claimed. The bankruptcy plan involved required cancellation of all the parent's stock in the subsidiary on the effective date of the plan. As a result, the court did not enjoin the parent from claiming a worthless stock deduction for a year ending after the effective date of the plan. Does this precedent suggest that a bankruptcy court could enjoin (or that the automatic stay prevents) other actions by shareholders—such as transfers of their stock—that could impair the bankrupt's NOLs or other tax attributes? Does it matter that the shareholder involved in the *Prudential Lines* case owned a controlling stock interest?

These questions were first answered by the U.S. Bankruptcy Court for the Northern District of Ohio in the *Phar-Mor* case.[43] Here, the court enjoined transfers of stock by two minority 5 percent stockholders, who actually owned in the aggregate less than 10 percent of the outstanding stock. The debtor had already had changes in ownership aggregating between 38 percent and 44 percent, and transfers by both of these two 5 percent stockholders (but not by either alone) might have possibly triggered an ownership change. In reaching its decision, the court rejected the argument of the two minority stockholders that actions of such a small minority stockholder could not amount to the exercise of "control" over the property of the estate within the meaning of Section 362(a)(3) of the Bankruptcy Code.

Since the *Phar Mor* case, it has become a relatively common practice for debtors to seek bankruptcy court orders restricting stock transfers that could increase the extent of the debtor's change in ownership for Code § 382 purposes (often as part of a debtor's "first day" bankruptcy motions, see § 1002.4.1 below). IRS Letter Ruling 200713015, December 20, 2006, provides an example of such an order and an interesting application of the *Prudential Lines* and *Phar Mor* line of cases.[44] Here, a debtor in bankruptcy asked the bankruptcy court on date 4 to enter an order imposing restrictions on transfers that could impair the company's NOLs, including acquisitions of stock that would bring the purchaser's ownership above a percentage that

(Footnote Continued)

deduction was not actionable where the bankrupt subsidiary could not have made use of the NOLs that were destroyed, particularly given the subsidiary's pending liquidation. *In re White Metal Rolling & Stamping Corp.*, 1998 Bankr. LEXIS 901 (Bankr. D.N.Y. 1998).

[43] *In re Phar-Mor, Inc.*, 152 B.R. 924 (Bankr. N.D. Ohio 1993) 29, 1993.

[44] For examples of other bankruptcy court orders restricting stock transfers, *see* § 1002.4.1 below, and IRS Letter Ruling 200605003, October 28, 2005 (indicating that the IRS would respect the remedial provisions of the order, provided the order is enforceable and, where applicable, is enforced). *See also In re Southeast Banking Corp.*, Bankr. S.D. Fla., Case No. 91-14561-BKC-PGH, order dated July 21, 1994 (in which in a Chapter 7 liquidating bankruptcy case the Bankruptcy Court enjoined pursuant to the automatic stay any transfer that would produce an ownership change); *In re First Merchants Acceptance Corp.*, Case No. 97-1500 (JJF) (Bankr. Del.) (final order, dated March 12, 1998).

was safely below 5 percent. On date 5, the bankruptcy court entered such an order. Shortly thereafter, an investor informed the debtor that between date 4 and date 5 it had acquired enough additional shares in the open market to bring its ownership over 5 percent, an acquisition that would have violated the court's order had it taken place after the order was issued. The debtor determined that the amount acquired would be sufficient to cause an ownership change. The debtor and the investor jointly petitioned the bankruptcy court to rule that the purchase of the portion of the additional shares that would have violated the order should be treated as void *ab initio*, which the bankruptcy court did on date 7. The court ordered that these excess shares should be sold in the open market, with the proceeds not in excess of the investor's cost going to the investor, and any profit going to a qualified charity. This was done, and a request for a ruling was filed with the IRS. The IRS ruled that, for purposes of Code §382, the investor would not be treated as having acquired ownership of the excess shares, so long as the court's order remains in effect and is not set aside by any final order of a court of competent jurisdiction.

This practice of restricting stock transfers received something of a jolt from two dicta issued by the Court of Appeals for the Seventh Circuit in *In the Matter of UAL Corporation*,[45] which involved an appeal from a bankruptcy court injunction preventing the sale of bankrupt United Airlines (UAL) stock by the Trustee of United Airlines' ESOP. The two dicta are (1) that the bankruptcy court should have required a bond to protect the ESOP and its beneficiaries from any loss resulting from the injunction, and (2) that the law probably does not even authorize the granting of such an injunction. These dicta are likely to create considerable controversy.

The facts in the *UAL* case are that when United Airlines filed for bankruptcy in December 2002, more than 50% of its stock (then selling for $1.06 per share) was held by workers through an ESOP. Fearing that a transfer of this stock by the ESOP could jeopardize United Airlines' estimated $1 billion of NOLs, United Airlines sought and obtained (over the objection of the ESOP trustee) an injunction against the sale of the shares. The trustee did not ask for a bond, and none was granted. The injunction soon became moot: on June 26, 2003, the IRS issued Temp. Reg. §1.382-10T (adopted in final form in 2006 without substantive change as Reg. §1.382-10) providing that a transfer by an ESOP to its beneficiaries would not itself be a change in ownership for Code §382 purposes; and on June 27, 2003 (when the stock was trading at 76 cents per share), the ESOP was terminated and its shares were distributed to its beneficiaries. The trustee of the ESOP nonetheless pressed its appeal from the order granting the injunction, arguing that the issuance of the injunction was not authorized by the Bankruptcy Code, and that, although the stock had later recovered in value and was trading at $2.02 per share the day before the appeal was argued, the ESOP beneficiaries should be paid the 30 cent loss in the share price that had occurred between the day the injunction was granted and the day the shares were

---

[45] 412 F.3d 775 (7th Cir. 2005), *vacating*, 2004 U.S. Dist. LEXIS 21918 (N.D. Ill. 2004). *See also* Kusnetz, Loss of Control—The Clash of Codes in the Battle Over a Debtor's Net Operating Losses, Tax Review Paper #243 (Nov. 13, 2006).

distributed to the beneficiaries, that is, during the period that the injunction prevented any sale of the shares.

The Seventh Circuit held that because no bond had been issued, the case was moot and the trustee could not recover, since "a person injured by the issuance of an injunction later determined to be erroneous has no action for damages in the absence of a bond." Had the Seventh Circuit limited itself to this holding, the case would be of little interest. However, before reaching that holding, the court expressed at some length its views about whether the ESOP trustee should have requested a bond, whether the bankruptcy court should have granted that request, and whether the injunction issued by the bankruptcy court was authorized by the law. The court said the lack of financial security for the ESOP investors was "unfortunate," and added that requiring the investors to bear the costs of illiquidity "was both imprudent and unnecessary." Although the court recognized that United Airlines wanted to preserve its $1 billion of NOLs, the court said "there is no reason why [the ESOP] investors who need liquidity should be sacrificed so that other investors (principally today's debt holders) that will own United after it emerges from bankruptcy can reap a benefit; bankruptcy is not supposed to appropriate some investors' wealth for distribution to others." Instead of "cramming one side's position down the throat of the other in bankruptcy," the bankruptcy judge should have crafted a "mutual protection" agreement to protect the parties.

The Seventh Circuit then added that the lack of a security agreement was doubly regrettable because the granting of the injunction was "problematic on the merits." The lower court had relied for its authority on section 362(a)(3) of the Bankruptcy Code, which authorizes blocking "any act to obtain possession of property of the estate or of property from the estate or to exercise control over property of the estate." The Seventh Circuit said that whether or not a debtor's tax benefits are "property" within the meaning of this provision, an ESOP's "sale of stock does not 'obtain *possession* . . . or exercise *control*' (emphasis added) over that interest." The court distinguished the *Prudential Lines* case (it did not mention *Phar-Mor* or any case similar to *Phar-Mor*) on the ground that although the taking of the consolidated-return worthless-stock deduction in the *Prudential* case "would have exercised control" over the debtor's operating losses, "there is no equivalent example of control (or consumption) of a loss carry-forward in an investor's simple sale of stock." (This distinction between the cases seems to us, we confess, quite opaque.) The court then added that the authority for granting the injunction against the United Airlines ESOP was so weak as "to make a bond or adequate protection undertaking *obligatory* before a bankruptcy judge may forbid investors to sell their stock in the market" (emphasis added).

After making these statements, the Seventh Circuit said, nonetheless, that it did not need to reach a conclusion on the merits of these issues, since the absence of a bond had made the case moot. Thus, the statements made by the Seventh Circuit on these issues are merely dicta, but have already led to considerable controversy and will likely lead to further litigation.[46]

The Eighth Circuit, in the *Russell* case,[47] has taken the *Prudential Lines* argument a step further but in a different direction. There, an individual filed a voluntary petition under Chapter 11 and for a time acted as a debtor-in-possession. The individual had substantial NOLs for the two years before he filed in bankruptcy. The individual elected on his returns—the first of which was filed before bankruptcy and the second during bankruptcy—not to carry the NOLs back, but instead only to carry them forward, the practical result of which would have been that the bankruptcy estate would have been denied a substantial refund for prior years' taxes, and the individual would have had the potential benefit of these unused NOLs for years after he was discharged from bankruptcy. The Eighth Circuit held, following *Prudential Lines*, that the NOLs were property of the estate, that the elections made by the individual constituted transfers of that property, and that these elections (even though the Internal Revenue Code makes them irrevocable) could be avoided by the bankruptcy court if, in the case of the election made before the petition was filed, the election was made with the kind of intent necessary to make it a fraudulent conveyance, or, in the case of the election made after the petition was filed, the election was not made in the ordinary course of business. With respect to the irrevocable nature of the elections, the court found that the purpose for the irrevocability requirement was to prevent a taxpayer from manipulating the tax law if he later discovered he should not have made the election. Here, no taxpayer was seeking to escape the consequences of his past decision after discovering it was imprudent; rather, a bankruptcy trustee was seeking to preserve an asset of the bankruptcy estate. Applying this same logic, two courts have held that a corporation may avoid as a fraudulent transfer a pre-bankruptcy revocation of its S election, where the revocation would have left the corporation with a tax liability from the sale of its assets during the subsequent bankruptcy that instead would have fallen on the stockholder if the S election had not been revoked.[48]

---

[46] Even before the Seventh Circuit's decision, some commentators remained critical of the common practice by bankruptcy courts of granting stock trading injunctions to protect a debtor's NOLs. *See, e.g.*, Morris, Imposition of Transfer Limitations on Claims and Equity Interests During Corporate Debtor's Chapter 11 Case to Preserve the Debtor's Net Operating Loss Carryforward: Examining the Emerging Trend, 77 Am. Bankr. L.J. 285 (2003).

[47] *Gibson v. United States (In re Russell)*, 927 F.2d 413, 91-1 U.S.T.C. ¶50,128 (8th Cir. 1991). *Accord In re Feiler*, 210 F.3d 948 (9th Cir. 2000) (also involved prepetition waiver of carryback by an individual debtor). On remand, the bankruptcy court found that the elections could not be avoided; there was no evidence of intent to defraud creditors as to the first election, and the second election was made in the ordinary course of business. *Streetman v. United States (In re Russell)*, 154 B.R. 723 (Bankr. W.D. Ark. 1993). After an appeal to the District Court, remand to the bankruptcy court, and another appeal to the District Court, it was determined that the first election was intended to defraud creditors, and the second election was not made in the ordinary course of business. *Streetman v. United States (In re Russell)*, 187 B.R. 287, ¶95-5280, 95-2 U.S.T.C. ¶50,453 (W.D. Ark. 1995). *See* discussions at §§1006.1.2 and 1006.2.2.

[48] *Guinn v. Lines, et al. (In re Trans-Lines West, Inc.)*, 203 B.R. 653 (Bankr. E.D. Tenn. 1996); *Parker v. Saunders (In re Bakersfield Westar, Inc.)*, 226 B.R. 227 (Bankr. 9th Cir. 1998). *See* discussion at §1006.1.3 below.

Could a court similarly void a Code § 165 worthless stock deduction that is found to violate the *Prudential Lines* concept?[49]

Where, as in the *Prudential Lines* case, the stock is that of a bankrupt subsidiary and the member contemplating the worthless stock deduction is a member of its consolidated return group, Reg. § 1.1502-20 (for the period from January 31, 1991, to March 7, 2002, that it was in effect) greatly changed the consequences for the parent claiming the worthless stock deduction and also for the subsidiary.[50] This regulation, with certain narrow exceptions, generally disallowed any loss from the disposition or deconsolidation of the stock of a subsidiary in a consolidated return group. Under this rule, the parent generally did not get the benefit of a worthless stock deduction.

On the other hand, Reg. § 1.1502-20(g) gave the common parent (which may not be the group member that held the allegedly worthless stock) the right to elect to reattribute to itself any portion of the consolidated NOL or capital loss carryovers that had been generated by the departing member (or any lower tier subsidiary), up to the amount of the loss disallowed to the group on the disposition of that stock. *See* § § 804.5 and 804.7 below. This election was not available, however, to the extent the losses did not exceed the separate insolvencies of the subsidiary whose losses were to be reattributed and any higher tier insolvent subsidiaries (counting only such insolvent companies in the chain). In computing insolvency for this purpose, liabilities owed to higher tier members were *not* taken into account, and preferred stock not held by higher tier members *was* taken into account. The preamble to the regulation says the reason for this insolvency limitation is that "circumvention of *General Utilities* repeal would be possible if losses borne by creditors of the subsidiary [or of higher tier subsidiaries] (rather than by the group) could be reattributed to the common parent . . . ."

To the extent the reattribution election was available, if the common parent exercised the election, the subsidiary, if it issued new stock to creditors and left the group, would not be able to take with it the portion of the group's NOLs and capital

---

[49] For an unusual case where the court held that the *Prudential Lines* concept extended to prevent the transfer of stock in a Subchapter S corporation, *see In re Cumberland Farms, Inc.*, 162 B.R. 62 (Bankr. D. Mass. 1993). The court held that the debtor corporation's indirect interest (attributable to the fact that the corporation was obligated by contract to distribute tax money to the shareholder) in the use of its suspended losses by the shareholder was property of the estate and protected by the automatic stay. However, the court then found sufficient grounds to grant relief from the stay.

[50] Reg. § 1.1502-20 was generally effective for dispositions and deconsolidations of subsidiary stock occurring after January 31, 1991. Worthlessness of stock constitutes a disposition for this purpose. Transition rules are found in Reg. § 1.337(d)-1 for dispositions occurring after January 6, 1987, and in Reg. § 1.337(d)-2 for dispositions and deconsolidations occurring from November 19, 1990, through January 31, 1991. For an excellent discussion as to whether a court would uphold the validity of Reg. § 1.1502-20, *see* Salem, Judicial Deference, Consolidated Returns and Loss Disallowance—Could LDR Survive a Court Challenge?, 43 Tax Executive 167 (1991). *See also* McBurney, The Consolidated Return Regs.' Loss Disallowance Rule—When Is It Vulnerable?, 90 J. of Tax'n 20 (January 1999). Indeed, in *Rite Aid Corp. v. United States*, 255 F.3d 1357, 2001-2 U.S.T.C. ¶ 50,516 (Fed. Cir. 2001), the court held that the duplicated loss portion of Reg. § 1.1502-20 was invalid. As a result, the IRS terminated the application of Reg. § 1.1502-20 for periods after March 7, 2002, and (subject to detailed transition rules) substituted Reg. § § 1.337(d)-2, 1.1502-20(i), 1.1502-32(b)(4)(v), and 1.1502-35; and in turn the IRS in early 2007 has proposed to substitute Prop. Reg. § 1.1502-36 for these prior provisions. *See* § 804.5 below for a discussion of these changes.

loss carryovers that it had created. Given the *Prudential Lines* precedent, could a bankruptcy court enjoin such an election by the common parent, on the ground that the NOLs belong to the subsidiary? Indeed, one wonders what effect this rule might have on the *Prudential Lines* precedent. The Second Circuit, in *Prudential Lines*, focused in part on the fact that under the then current regulations the subsidiary would take its own NOLs with it when it left the group. Does the regulation mean that the subsidiary should no longer be viewed as owning the NOLs it has created?

It is obvious that these rules did not work well. Code § 382(g)(4)(D), which treats the claiming of a worthless stock deduction as an event for Code § 382 purposes, was based on the premise that the parent would get a good deduction, and it was aimed at preventing both the parent and the subsidiary from being able to deduct the same economic loss. With the adoption of Reg. § 1.1502-20, this rule became unnecessary for consolidated return groups and was indeed destructive. The preamble to Reg. § 1.1502-20 acknowledged the problem, but failed to deal with it. However, in 1994 and 2007, the IRS amended the consolidated return regulations in a way designed to reduce at least some of this disharmony.[51] The amendment does so by deferring the time when a worthless stock deduction can be taken into account in a consolidated return context. Under the revised regulation, a worthless stock deduction with respect to a subsidiary member's stock cannot be taken until either (i) substantially all of the subsidiary's assets are disposed of for no consideration, (ii) the subsidiary incurs COD income that is excluded due to the insolvency or bankruptcy of the subsidiary and exceeds the amount of tax attributes subject to attribute reduction under Code § 108, or (iii) another member claims a loss for uncollectibility of the subsidiary's debt without the subsidiary recognizing a corresponding amount of current COD income or gain. The preamble to these regulations, when they were proposed in 1992, indicated that this change was intended to reduce the tension created by the *Prudential Lines* concept among affiliated members. Much of the disharmony created by Reg. § 1.1502-20 was removed when that regulation was replaced, effective March 7, 2002, by Temp. Reg. §§ 1.337(d)-2T, 1.1502-20T(i), 1.1502-32T(b)(4)(v), and 1.1502-35T. These regulations have since been finalized. These new regulations eliminate, for periods after their effective date, the right of a parent to reattribute to itself the losses of a subsidiary; and they reduce the circumstances in which there will be disallowance of the parent's deduction for losses in the

---

[51] *See* Reg. §§ 1.1502-80(c) and 1.1502-19(c)(1)(iii); and former Temp. Reg. § 1.1502-80T. The deferral rule is subject to the anti-avoidance rule of Reg. § 1.1502-19(e). For example, if under the deferral rule discussed in the text below, a member ceases operations but retains more than an insignificant amount of assets for a principal purpose of deferring the time of the worthless stock deduction (or the triggering of an excess loss account), the retained assets will not be taken into account and the member will be considered worthless. *See* Reg. § 1.1502-19(g) Example 6. In the context of a bankruptcy of a subsidiary member, however, it is clear from the preamble to these regulations (when originally issued in proposed form) that the deferral rule was intended to delay a worthlessness event as long as possible. In IRS Technical Advice Memorandum 200549007, August 5, 2005, involving a Chapter 11 liquidating bankruptcy, this was until the effective date of the plan, at which time the member's remaining assets were transferred to a "post-confirmation estate" and its stock was cancelled. For an interesting discussion of this and other aspects of this Technical Advice, see Willens, Conseco's Worthless Stock Loss Appears to Withstand Scrutiny, BNA Daily Tax Report #5 (January 9, 2006), at p. J-1. *See also* § 804 below.

stock of a subsidiary. In early 2007, the IRS proposed to replace these provisions, prospectively, by Prop. Reg. § 1.1502-36 (which would reinstate, in part, the right of the parent to reattribute to itself losses of a subsidiary). *See* the discussion at §§ 804.2 and 804.5 below.

**Exempt transfers.** Code § 382(l)(3)(B) provides that certain transfers at death, by gift, or among spouses will be treated as if the transferee had owned the stock during the time it was owned by the transferor. Thus, such transfers will not create a testing date or produce an owner shift.[52]

Code § 382(l)(3)(C) originally provided that acquisitions of employer stock by an ESOP or TRASOP "shall not be taken into account" in determining whether an ownership change had occurred, provided the plan owned at least 50 percent of the value of the corporation's stock after such acquisition and certain other requirements were met. Distributions by such a plan to plan participants (presumably even if they brought the plan below 50 percent) were similarly not taken into account. (Where a plan never owned the 50 percent necessary to exempt its acquisitions, are distributions by it nonetheless covered by the exemption? The temporary regulations do not discuss this rule and thus provide no answer.) The existence of this ESOP and TRASOP rule meant that one way to exempt a loss corporation from the consequences of Code § 382 could have been to place 50 percent or more of the value of its stock in an ESOP or TRASOP. These ESOP and TRASOP provisions were repealed by the Revenue Reconciliation Act of 1989.[53]

### § 508.2.5 Measuring Increases in Ownership; Valuation Issues

On each testing date, one must determine which 5 percent shareholders have had increases in their percentage ownership, as measured on that testing date, from the lowest percentage of stock owned by them at any time during the testing period.[54] Note that this rule means that a shareholder who owns at least as much stock on the testing date as she owned at the beginning of the testing period may nonetheless be treated as having an increase in ownership. This can occur if the shareholder's ownership dipped between those dates, since the rule looks to the lowest percentage owned by the shareholder at any time during the testing period.[55]

#### EXAMPLE 1

Shareholder A owns 100 percent of the stock at the beginning of the testing period, sells 40 percent to B six months later, and a year thereafter buys the 40 percent back from B. On the testing date created by the latter

[52] Temp. Reg. § 1.382-2T(a)(2)(i)(B); Prop. Reg. § 1.382-2(a)(4).

[53] Revenue Reconciliation Act of 1989, Pub. L. No. 101-239, 101st Cong., 1st Sess. (the 1989 Act), § 7304(d)(1), effective for acquisitions of employer securities after July 12, 1989, other than pursuant to prior binding contracts.

[54] Temp. Reg. § 1.382-2T(a)(1).

[55] Temp. Reg. § 1.382-2T(c)(1).

transaction, A has had a 40 percentage point increase in ownership. If eight months later B again purchases 20 percent from A, on the resulting testing date A would have a 20 percentage point increase and B would also have a 20 percentage point increase.

The increases, so measured, of each 5 percent shareholder having increases are then aggregated to determine if an ownership change has occurred. Decreases by 5 percent shareholders are ignored. As mentioned above in the discussion of the "testing date," a shareholder's increases and decreases that occur on the testing date are netted, and such netting presumably applies also for determining the lowest percentage owned by the shareholder during the testing period.

All of a 5 percent shareholder's increases in ownership occurring during the testing period are cumulated, whether they result from purchases, redemptions of stock by others, or reorganizations. His increases are in turn cumulated with increases by other 5 percent shareholders, even though their transactions might be quite independent. This cumulative rule means that quite unrelated transactions may be combined to produce an ownership change, and that a shareholder may lose the benefit of NOLs and any other carryovers and built-in losses created after he became a shareholder, simply because someone else acquired stock in an unrelated transaction.[56]

**EXAMPLE 2**

On January 10, 1987, individual A purchased 46 percent of the stock of a calendar-year company that was otherwise widely held. The company suffered net losses in 1987 and 1988. On December 31, 1988, individual B purchased 5 percent of the stock from the public. The cumulation of B's purchase with A's purchase results in an ownership change. The NOLs into 1989 and later years from 1987 and 1988 will be limited by new Code § 382, even though only B has "bought in" to the losses and in effect there has only been a 5 percentage point shift in the beneficial ownership of the losses.

The IRS has, however, in a letter ruling adopted a gloss on the general rule, which allows stock issued on different dates, but as part of the same plan, in connection with the formation of a company, to be treated as a single stock issuance. In the ruling[57] the IRS dealt with a case where, incident to forming a company, initial shares were issued to directors on December 27 and, before business operations had commenced, a further 99 percent of the stock was issued to investors on the subsequent February 29. The IRS held that no ownership change resulted from the February 29 issuance "because the issuances to Directors and investors were parts of

---

[56] Temp. Reg. § 1.382-2T(c)(3).

[57] IRS Letter Ruling 9142018, July 18, 1991.

an integrated plan to form Company and the issuances were done with an expedition consistent with the orderly formation of Company." Those who wonder whether the IRS will extend this concept to other integrated plan situations should not let their hopes rise too far, however, because we understand the theory on which this ruling was based was that the company had not really come into existence, for practical purposes, until the February 29 date. This caution against allowing one's hopes to rise too far is reinforced by a subsequent ruling, where the IRS did not apply this concept.[58]

### *§ 508.2.5.1 Valuation Issues*

The ownership change rule refers to changes in the percentage of the value of the corporation's stock. A number of valuation questions are presented. For example, where the corporation has only one class of "stock," should each share be considered for this purpose to be of equal value, or must one take into account control premiums, blockage, and restrictions on transfer? In the latter case, a purchase of 45 percent of the shares of a company whose remaining stock is widely held might create an increase in ownership of more than 50 percentage points, rather than only 45 percentage points, and thus an "ownership change." The IRS has resolved this valuation question under regulations by treating each share of a single class of stock as having identical value for this purpose. Thus, control premiums and blockage discounts would not be taken into account.[59]

Where the company has more than one class of stock, additional problems are created. Code § 382(l)(3)(C) states that "except as provided in regulations, any change in proportionate ownership which is attributable solely to fluctuations in the relative fair market values of different classes of stock shall not be taken into account." It is thus clear that such changes will not by themselves create a testing date. But when a testing date occurs, is it intended that fluctuations from the last testing date are to be counted?

**EXAMPLE**

On January 1, 1988 (the beginning of the testing period), L Corp. has a class of voting preferred that represents 75 percent of its value, and common that represents 25 percent. A owns the preferred, and B owns the common. L does well, and on March 1, 1990, when the common is worth 90 percent of the value, L issues a single share of common stock to an employee. Even if the single share of stock represents an insignificant percentage of the total value of the company's stock and the employee owns no other stock, its issuance by the company will create a testing date (as would even the issuance of an option to acquire such share). Is A's

[58] IRS Letter Ruling 9205020, November 4, 1991.

[59] *See* Reg. § 1.382-2(a)(3)(i) (last three sentences).

> lowest percentage during the testing period 75 percent or 10 percent? Has B had an increase in ownership of 65 percent (even though he engaged in no transactions during the testing period), thus triggering an "ownership change," or zero percent?[60]

Neither the statute nor the legislative history gives any guidance. The preamble to the temporary regulations says that such issues have been reserved for later consideration.[61]

Interestingly, the IRS in late 2003 did issue a ruling that deals with the question illustrated by the above example. IRS Letter Ruling 200411012[62] enunciated a principle for its holding that, were it to be applied to the facts in the example, would conclude that B's percentage increase in ownership was zero. The principle used in the ruling was that (1) "on any testing date, in determining the ownership percentage of any 5% shareholder, the value of such shareholder's stock, relative to the value of all other stock of the corporation, shall be considered to remain constant since the date that shareholder acquired the stock;" and (2) "the value of such shareholder's stock relative to the value of all other stock of the corporation issued subsequent to such acquisition date shall also be considered to remain constant since that subsequent date." The IRS has also ruled, in IRS Letter Ruling 200622011, February 2, 2006, that in applying the first rule just quoted to a situation where there had been two stock-for-stock recapitalizations, "a value-for-value recapitalization of stock of the corporation for other stock of the corporation . . . shall be disregarded, and the exchanging shareholder shall be considered to have acquired such newly issued stock as of the date it acquired the stock exchanged therefor." Despite these favorable rulings, one should be cautious about applying this concept to facts that differ from those involved in the rulings.

---

[60] Note that the voting preferred cannot be treated as "not stock" under the rules discussed above, because the rule allowing Code § 1504 stock to be treated as "not stock" only applies where this would produce an ownership change.

[61] For a case dealing with this same kind of issue under old Code § 382, *see Hermes Consolidated* at § 507.1 above. For a discussion of the similar valuation issue that can arise in deciding whether fluctuations in value of different classes of stock may cause a failure to continue to satisfy the Code § 1504(a)(3) 80 percent ownership requirement for remaining in a consolidated return group, *see* the discussion at § 804.1 below.

[62] December 5, 2003. To the same effect, and using the same language, *see* IRS Letter Ruling 200511008, December 6, 2004, and IRS Letter Ruling 200520011, February 18, 2005. For an interesting discussion of the first ruling, *see* Hoffenberg, Owner Shifts and Fluctuations in Value: A Theory of Relativity, 106 Tax Notes 1446 (March 21, 2005). An IRS Branch Chief was reported to have commented that Code § 382(l)(3)(C) is self executing and mandatory; that nothing in the regulations should be construed as limiting it; and that the IRS letter rulings applying it should not be seen as *the IRS* granting permission to back out fluctuations (the statute "says what it says") but only as approving the particular methods used by those taxpayers on their facts. IRS Official Sheds Light on NOL Carryover Rules, 2006 TNT 35-3 (February 21, 2006).

### § 508.2.6 Determining Who Owns the "Stock": Entity and Family Attribution

For purposes of determining the owners of the "stock" of the loss corporation (or higher tier entities) who may have had an increase or decrease in such ownership, modified Code § 318 attribution rules are applied.[63] These are discussed below.

First, all stock owned by corporations, trusts, partnerships, and other entities is attributed out proportionately to its owners until one reaches an owner who is an individual.[64]

Second, such entities are treated as *not* owning the stock that is attributed out of them.[65]

Third, stock owned by shareholders, partners, and beneficiaries is not attributed to their corporations, partnerships, trusts or estates for any purpose.[66]

Fourth, special family and option attribution rules apply. These are discussed separately below.

In applying these rules, the following conventions apply:

(1) The stockholders of corporations to whom attribution may be made are only those holding instruments that constitute "stock" (as specially defined above) for purposes of the ownership change rules.[67] The temporary regulations make clear that this does not include stock treated as "not stock," but does include nonstock that is treated as "stock" under those rules.[68]

(2) The owners of trusts, partnerships, and other noncorporate entities to whom attribution may be made are only those holding instruments having characteristics similar to such "stock," except that, oddly enough, in the case of such noncorporate entities, one does not take into account nonstock that is treated as "stock."[69]

(3) The following entities are treated as if they were individuals who are unrelated to any other owner (direct or indirect) of the loss corporation (the effect of this rule is that these entities are treated as owning the stock owned or attributed to them, and such stock is not attributed out to their owners);[70]

---

[63] Code § 382(l)(3)(A); Temp. Reg. § 1.382-2T(h).

[64] Stock owned by corporations is attributed to its owners without regard to the 50 percent limitation contained in Code § 318(a)(2)(C). *See also* Code § 382(l)(3)(A)(ii)(I) and Temp. Reg. § 1.382-2T(h)(2)(i). The treatment of stock held by investment companies, ESOPs, and qualified settlement funds for purposes of both the attribution, and the aggregation and segregation rules, is discussed at § 508.2.8.1 below. *See also* §§ 508.2.7.3 and 508.5.1 below.

[65] Code § 382(l)(3)(A)(ii)(II); Temp. Reg. § 1.382-2T(h)(2)(A). As we shall see, this second rule does not apply for purposes of applying certain aspects—the aggregation and segregation rules—of the definition of who is a "5 percent shareholder."

[66] Code § 382(l)(3)(A)(iii); Temp. Reg. § 1.382-2T(h)(3).

[67] Temp. Reg. § 1.382-2T(h)(2)(ii).

[68] *See* id. in conjunction with Temp. Reg. § 1.382-2T(f)(24).

[69] *See* Temp. Reg. § 1.382-2T(h)(2)(ii)(C) in conjunction with Temp. Reg. § 1.382-2T(f)(24).

[70] Temp. Reg. § 1.382-2T(h)(2)(iii). Because this lack of look-through treatment seemed inappropriate in the case of distributions of loss corporation stock by a qualified Code § 401(a) trust to its beneficiaries, the IRS issued Reg. § 1.382-10 (in temporary form in 2003 and adopted as final without substantive change in 2006) to provide a modified look-through treatment in such circumstances.

(a) any entity that owns less than 5 percent of the loss corporation's stock;
(b) any Code § 401(a) trust;
(c) governmental entities;[71] or
(d) any other entities that might be designated by the IRS in the Internal Revenue Bulletin.

**Stock owned by charities.** Neither the Code nor the regulations tell how to treat stock owned by charities. In 1996, the IRS issued a private letter ruling involving this issue.[72] Two unrelated Code § 501(c)(3) organizations decided to combine, by consolidating into a new charitable corporation. Each of the former charities had separately owned a chain of business corporations, some of which were to be consolidated as well. One of the latter was the merger of a profitable subsidiary of former charity B into a loss subsidiary of former charity A. Pursuant to the merger, the target stock formerly owned by charity B was simply canceled, and no new stock was issued. For a period of five years following the consolidation of the two charities, the new charity's board of directors was to be comprised, in equal numbers, of former board members of former charity A and charity B. The IRS ruled that the merger of the two subsidiaries was a good "A" reorganization, and that none of the foregoing transactions resulted in a Code § 382 ownership change of the loss subsidiary. No reasons were given by the IRS for its holdings. But if the five-year makeup of the board of directors of the surviving charity can be considered relevant to only the "A" reorganization holding, the ruling would seem to constitute implicit holdings that the "shareholders" of Code § 501(c)(3) organizations are the entire general public, and that the "shareholders" of charity A need not be segregated into a public group separate from the public "shareholders" of charity B. This would seem to be confirmed by a ruling issued in 1998, where one charity took over another charity that owned a taxable subsidiary. In this case, the target charity did not share in future control of the acquiring charity. However, the ruling held, and again without analysis or explanation, that the transaction would not result in a Code § 382 ownership change for the taxable subsidiary of the acquired charity.[73]

**Family attribution.** An individual and the members of his family (defined as his spouse, parents, children, and grandchildren) are treated as a single individual.[74] This

---

[71] The 1986 Blue Book, *supra* note 13, at 311, says that "governmental units, agencies, and instrumentalities that derive their powers, rights, and duties from the same sovereign authority will be treated as a single shareholder." However, the temporary regulations are silent on this point.

[72] IRS Letter Ruling 9643012, July 19, 1996.

[73] IRS Letter Ruling 9839038, July 1, 1998. Two rulings issued in 2000 take a similar approach. IRS Letter Ruling 200027013, March 31, 2000; IRS Letter Ruling 200028005, April 14, 2000. We understand the latter two rulings involved health maintenance organizations. As for the theory upon which such favorable rulings might be based, in addition to the theory that charities might be deemed ultimately owned by the public, it has been suggested by some that these transactions might be considered gifts—which are exempt from application of Code § 382 (*see* § 508.2.4 above)—because they are, usually, transfers made without consideration. Similarly, in IRS Letter Ruling 200207014, November 15, 2001, the IRS held, without giving any reasons, that the distribution of the stock of a taxable subsidiary of one charity to a related charity did not constitute a Code § 382 ownership change for the taxable subsidiary.

[74] Code § 382(1)(3)(A)(i); Temp. Reg. § 1.382-2T(h)(6).

means that sales among such family members will usually not produce an "owner shift" or "ownership change" (one should also remember that other typical family transfers—those by gift or inheritance—are exempt transfers).

An individual may also be a member of many families. For example, he will be a member of (1) the family consisting of his spouse, parents, children, and grandchildren, (2) his spouse's family, consisting of his spouse and her parents, children, and grandchildren, (3) each of his grandparent's families, consisting of each of his grandparents, and such grandparent's spouse, children, and grandchildren; and so on. Each such "family" is treated as a single individual. To avoid treating the same shares of stock as being owned by multiple owners, however, the temporary regulations provide that an individual will be treated only as a member of the "family" that results in the smallest overall increase in total percentage ownership on the testing date and not as a member of any other "family."[75] Because of this rule, an individual might be treated as a member of one "family" on one testing date and another "family" (with retroactive effect throughout the testing period for purposes of this testing date) on a different testing date.

An interesting question has arisen as to how these family attribution rules should be applied to sibling attribution. It should be noted that the statutory language of Code § 318 does not directly provide that siblings are to be treated as a single individual. However, it does provide that parents and children are to be treated as a single individual. Thus, if a father and his two sons are alive, they can be a family that is treated as a single individual. A question can exist, however, whether for this to happen the father must be alive and own stock, and whether, in any event, this family concept extends to treating siblings as members of each other's family. In 2002, the IRS ruled on a situation where an individual sold his entire stock interest in a company to his brother.[76] The transfer would produce an ownership change for the company unless the two brothers could be considered part of the same "family." Neither of the parents of the brothers was living. The IRS held that because of this the two brothers could not be treated as a "family," and so an ownership change occurred. The language used in the ruling suggests that the result would have been different if a parent had been alive. This exact issue was ultimately decided in the case of *Garber Industries Holding Co. v. Commissioner*.[77] In this case, the taxpayer argued that the brothers should be considered part of the same family by reference to

---

[75] Temp. Reg. § 1.382-2T(h)(6)(iv); *see, e.g.*, IRS Letter Ruling 9030012, April 25, 1990 (held no shift occurred where father sold 100 percent interest in loss company to son-in-law, since both were in the daughter's "family" group); IRS Letter Ruling 199918051, February 9, 1999 (found no shift occurred where there were overlapping family members in two corporations, after applying the smallest increase rule).

[76] IRS Letter Ruling 200245006, July 25, 2002. *See* Willens, Good News in Gauging Existence of an "Ownership Change," BNA Daily Tax Report (January 27, 2003), at J-1.

[77] 124 T.C. 1 (2005), *aff'd*, 435 F.3d 555, 2006-1 U.S.T.C. ¶ 50,109 (5th Cir. 2006). This case is discussed in Raby and Raby, Stock Ownership Tax Attribution and Siblings, 106 Tax Notes 675 (February 7, 2005), and in Willens, When Siblings Are Regarded as Strangers, 110 Tax Notes 1099 (March 6, 2006). Willens argues that the reasoning in the Tax Court and Fifth Circuit opinions is too broad (though the holdings are correct). He argues that stock owned by brothers should not be aggregated for purposes of Code § 382 even if a parent is alive who also owns stock. His position is that the reference in Code § 382(l)(3)(A) to Code § 318(a)(1) makes the latter provision (which does not include brothers in the

their parents and grandparents, even though none of these ancestors was alive. The IRS argued that such attribution could not occur unless such an ancestor was alive. The Tax Court, after carefully analyzing the consequences of each of these arguments, accepted neither one of them, holding instead that such attribution could not occur unless such an ancestor was not only alive but also an actual shareholder. The Fifth Circuit affirmed the Tax Court holding, but its reasoning was somewhat different. The Fifth Circuit pointed out that the Code § 382(l)(3)(A)(i) gloss on the Code § 318 attribution rules says that "an individual and all members of his family" as defined in Code § 318(a)(1) shall be treated as one individual for purposes of Code § 382. Code § 318(a)(1) defines a family as a spouse, children, grandchildren and parents. It does not mention siblings. Thus, if one looks only to this language, and asks whether an individual's family includes his brother, the answer would be no. However, the Fifth Circuit did not stop there. As an alternative ground for decision, the Fifth Circuit concluded that if one considers it appropriate to apply a somewhat broader application of this language—such as by attributing stock up to and down from parents—as the Tax Court did, the better view would be that that the ancestor would not only have to be alive but also would have to own stock. It can be seen that any one of these possible interpretations of the sibling issue can produce quite arbitrary results in particular cases, and a clarification of both the policy and the language of the statute in this area would seem to be in order.

Because a loss corporation may not know about people who own less than 5 percent of its stock, the temporary regulations provide that in applying the family attribution rules one includes only the stock owned by individuals who would be 5 percent shareholders without regard to the family attribution rules, except to the extent the loss corporation has actual knowledge of such smaller holdings on the testing date (or acquires such knowledge before its tax return for the year is filed).[78] For example, suppose a father owns 6 percent of the stock and his son owns 2 percent. The son's stock will not be included in the family aggregation (and thus will be treated as owned by the single 5 percent shareholder consisting of all other less than 5 percent shareholders, rather than the separate 5 percent shareholder consisting of his father and members of his family) unless the loss corporation has, or so acquires, actual knowledge of such ownership.

### § 508.2.7 Option Attribution

In early November 1992, the IRS issued proposed regulations that would radically change, and greatly simplify, the option rules contained in the temporary regulations. These were made final in 1994 and generally apply to testing dates occurring on or after November 5, 1992. The old rules in the temporary regulations

(Footnote Continued)

definition of an individual's "family") the exclusive test for Code § 382(1)(3)(A) purposes, and does not permit reference to the other attribution provisions of Code § 318.

[78] Temp. Reg. § 1.382-2T(h)(6)(iii); Temp. Reg. § 1.382-2T(k)(2). If the loss corporation acquires such knowledge only after its return is filed, it is permitted, but not required, to take it into account. Id.

continue to apply to earlier testing dates. In addition, a loss corporation may elect to apply the old rules (i) to testing dates on or before May 17, 1994, or (ii) if a title 11 or similar case was filed on or before May 17, 1994, to any testing date at or before the time the plan of reorganization becomes effective.[79] Accordingly, we will first discuss the rules contained in the temporary regulations. The new rules will then be described at § 508.2.7.6.

Implementing the authority given in Code § 382(l)(3), the temporary regulations contain their own unique option attribution rules. These are very complicated and take an exceedingly antitaxpayer approach. They have very adverse consequences for loss companies. When the option attribution rules apply on any testing date, they treat the option as having been exercised on that date.[80] The option attribution rule does not apply:

(1) unless its application would produce an "ownership change" on such testing date;[81] and

(2) if, as of the testing date, the loss corporation's NOLs and net built-in losses are not *de minimis* (using the same *de minimis* test that is used for determining when stock is to be treated as "not stock," and vice versa, as described above).[82]

Unlike the other attribution rules, the option attribution rule only applies for purposes of determining whether there has been an ownership change; it does not apply

---

[79] Reg. § 1.382-4(h)(2)(vi) (also specifies time and manner for making election). This election does not alter the effective date rules with respect to the treatment of nonvoting convertible preferred stock as "stock."

[80] Temp. Reg. § 1.382-2T(h)(4)(i). Where the option calls for issuance of additional stock by the corporation, such stock will be treated as outstanding if the option is treated as exercised. Temp. Reg. § 1.382-2T(h)(4)(vii)(A). Thus, if there are 100 shares outstanding, and the company has issued a warrant for 20 shares that is treated as having been exercised, the company will be treated as having 120 shares outstanding. However, Temp. Reg. § 1.382-2T(h)(4)(vii)(C) says that such deemed exercise shall have no effect on the determination of the value of the loss company for purposes of computing the annual limitation, referring to the antistuffing rule that disregards capital contributions made during the two years preceding the change date. This seems correct, so far as it goes. The new money paid (in this case "deemed" paid) on exercise of the option should come within the scope of the antistuffing rule. However, what is left unsaid is whether the value of the option itself should be taken into account as part of the value of the loss company for annual limitation purposes. To ignore it would be contrary to the direction in the Conference Report to "prescribe such regulations as are necessary to treat warrants, options, contracts to acquire stock, convertible debt, and similar interests as stock for purposes of determining the value of the loss corporation." The 1986 Act Conference Report, *supra* note 2, at II-187. Presumably, this provision in the temporary regulations would not apply to convertible stock that is treated as an option. Perhaps, when the Treasury issues its promised amendment to the temporary regulations, regarding the treatment of convertible preferred stock, this point will be clarified.

Where the option calls for the redemption of stock by the corporation, Temp. Reg. § 1.382-2T(h)(4)(vii)(B) provides that such stock will be treated as decreasing the outstanding stock, if it is treated as having been exercised, but in this instance nothing is said about the effect on value for purposes of the annual limitation.

[81] Temp. Reg. § 1.382-2T(h)(4)(i).

[82] Temp. Reg. § 1.382-2T(h)(4)(ix); *see* text accompanying note 28, *supra*.

for determining who is a 5 percent shareholder, except on that fatal testing date when its application would produce an ownership change.[83]

The option attribution rule is applied selectively on a worst-case basis. That is, it is applied separately to each 5 percent shareholder (and each person who would be a 5 percent shareholder if the option were treated as exercised), and as to each such person, it is also applied separately as to each class of options (options with identical terms, issued by the same issuer on the same date) owned by him.[84] The selective nature of this rule means that even where the exercise of all outstanding options would not produce an ownership change, an ownership change may nonetheless be deemed to occur.

**EXAMPLE**

A owns 65 and B owns 35 of the 100 outstanding shares of L Corp. stock. B purchased his shares six months ago. L issues rights allowing each of its shareholders to buy one additional share of stock for each share owned. An ownership change has occurred. B's rights are treated as having been exercised, giving him 70 out of 135 shares considered outstanding, or 52 percent. This produces an ownership change because B has thereby had an increase in ownership of 52 percentage points during the testing period. A's rights are not treated as being exercised, because such exercise would not create, indeed it would defeat, an ownership change. This result is not changed even if both A and B actually exercise their rights, and A thus continues to own 65 percent of the stock. (As we shall see, however, if B's rights lapse unexercised, the ownership change will retroactively be considered not to have occurred).

To make the problem presented by the example above even more vivid, suppose that instead of the corporation issuing rights, the two shareholders contracted to purchase the 100 shares of new stock from the corporation and closed the purchase two months later. As we shall see, contracts to buy or sell stock are treated as "options" under this rule, and so the selective exercise rule would seem literally to apply and an ownership change to result, just as in the case of the rights offering in the Example. This, of course, is an absurd result.

Reaching a more sensible result, the IRS, in IRS Letter Ruling 8903043,[85] held that where an exchange offer of stock for debt, a private placement of stock and a rights offering were all interrelated steps of a single plan, either all three steps had to be treated as consummated or none of them. Similarly, where a merger and a stock sale

[83] Temp. Reg. § 1.382-2T(h)(4)(i).

[84] Temp. Reg. § 1.382-2T(h)(4)(i)(A) and (B).

[85] October 14, 1988.

had to be consummated simultaneously, the IRS held, in IRS Letter Ruling 8930045,[86] that both transactions should be treated as exercised jointly (and neither separately).

A related question of timing can arise where an agreement provides that just before stock of a parent is to be issued to creditors (causing an ownership change), stock of a subsidiary is to be distributed to the parent's old stockholders. Assume that the making of the agreement is to be treated as an option. If respect is given to the timing provided in the agreement, an ownership change of the subsidiary will not occur. If respect is not given to such timing (and the "options" are deemed exercised selectively in the fashion that produces an ownership change), the subsidiary, as well as the parent, will be treated as having an ownership change. The IRS has taken both positions. In IRS Letter Ruling 9216020,[87] the IRS held on such facts that the subsidiary did not have an ownership change. But in IRS Letter Ruling 9317044,[88] on similar facts the IRS held the opposite. However, in the second ruling, the IRS decided the taxpayer was saved by making the 120-day election (described at § 508.2.7.4 below): the IRS held that where the actual exercise date (because of the 120-day election) governed, respect would be given to the timing of the exercise of the two "options" (one to issue subsidiary stock to the old shareholders, and the other to issue parent stock to the creditors), with the result that the subsidiary would not be treated as having suffered an ownership change.

### *§ 508.2.7.1 Evergreen Element*

In addition, the option attribution rule continues to apply throughout the life of the option, even if the option was issued long before the beginning of the testing period. This is known as the "evergreen" element of the option attribution rule, and it makes the option a ticking time bomb ready to explode whenever, in combination with other events, its (selective) deemed exercise would produce an ownership change. This ignores the fact that the owner of an option has owned the equity it represents during the entire period of his ownership. For example, take the case of an option to acquire common stock that has been held for seven years before the testing date. The owner has, in substance, owned the equity represented by the option during that entire time. Had he owned the underlying common stock during that period, it could not create an ownership change if he continued to own it on the testing date. However, if the option is treated as exercised on the testing date, he is treated as acquiring the stock on that date (and not as having had any interest in it previously).

As a result of these provisions, the ownership of an option is treated much more harshly than ownership of the underlying stock. Consequently, corporations should be cautious about issuing options, including, as mentioned above, straight nonvoting convertible preferred stock that is treated as an option.

---

[86] May 2, 1989.

[87] January 17, 1992.

[88] April 30, 1993.

### *§ 508.2.7.2 Lapse of Option*

If an option that has been treated as exercised under this rule later lapses unexercised or the owner irrevocably forfeits his right to acquire the stock, the option will be treated (retroactively) as if it had never been issued. The corporation may file amended returns (subject to the statute of limitations) for the prior years affected by the ownership change that was created by the deemed exercise.[89]

The IRS has held, however, that the redemption of an option is not treated as a lapse or forfeiture. As a result, any ownership change created by an earlier deemed exercise of the option would not be reversed if the option was redeemed, even though it would have been reversed if the option had lapsed.[90] If, however, no ownership change previously occurred, the redemption of the option would be a neutral event.[91]

### *§ 508.2.7.3 "Option" Defined*

An "option" for purposes of the attribution rule is very broadly defined. It includes options to acquire stock from a company or a shareholder, options to sell the stock to the company or others, and options by the company to sell or redeem its own stock. Thus, it includes options, warrants, puts, a convertible debt, an instrument other than debt that is convertible into stock, a stock interest subject to forfeiture, a contract to acquire or sell stock (including underwriting agreements), buy-sell agreements, stock that is callable or redeemable, loan pledge agreements, contingent stock that might be issued in reorganizations, tender offers, and the like.[92] It makes no difference that the option may be contingent or not currently exercisable; such restrictions are ignored.[93] No indication is given in the legislative history or regulations as to whether typical rights of first refusal are included.[94] We had expressed the

---

[89] Temp. Reg. § 1.382-2T(h)(4)(viii).

[90] IRS Letter Ruling 8930034, May 1, 1989; *see also* Sheppard, Why Bankrupts May Still Owe Taxes, and Other Anomalies, 43 Tax Notes 941, 943 (May 22, 1989). In IRS Letter Ruling 8930045, May 2, 1989, certain straight preferred stock was to be exchanged for a new convertible preferred stock under a plan of merger. Before the merger, however, the old preferred stock was redeemed at its stated redemption price. The IRS treated the resulting termination of the preferred stockholders' rights to receive the new convertible preferred as a "forfeiture" because "there was no consideration paid other than the release of mutual obligations."

We wonder whether a *de minimis* payment might be ignored. On this latter point, *see* Rev. Rul. 88-31, 1988-1 C.B. 302 (when an instrument ["Right"] entitles the holder to receive a cash payment equal to $11 less the FMV of the issuer's common stock on the settlement date, subject to a specified ceiling and a $0.10 floor, and the actual settlement price is $0.10, "the return of this *de minimis* amount in all events does not detract from the fact that, in substance, the right has lapsed").

[91] IRS Letter Ruling 8940006, April 20, 1989.

[92] *See* Temp. Reg. § 1.382-2T(h)(4)(v) and (x).

[93] Temp. Reg. § 1.382-2T(h)(4)(iii).

[94] Rights of first refusal have been held not to be options for purposes of Code § 1234; *see Anderson v. United States*, 468 F. Supp. 1085, 79-1 U.S.T.C. ¶ 9329 (D. Minn. 1979), *aff'd without opinion*, 624 F.2d 1109 (8th Cir. 1980), and for purposes of Code § 318(a)(4), IRS Letter Ruling 8038048, June 24, 1980. Because the Code § 382 definition of "option" is broader—for example, by including contract rights to

hope in earlier editions of this volume that the IRS would exclude rights of first refusal from the "option" attribution concept. However, the IRS has since held in a private letter ruling[95] that rights of first refusal constitute "options" for this purpose. Would the IRS extend this view to "rights of first offer" or "come-along," "take-along" rights?

The IRS has held that a letter of intent, which was not intended to be a contract and contemplated that a contract would arise only by a later definitive agreement approved by the boards of both parties, was not an "option." An "option" did arise, however, when the later definitive agreement was approved by the second of the two boards to act (even though the agreement was not signed by the two parties until five days later) because, according to the ruling, the merger agreement became nonwithdrawable "as a legal or practical matter" at such time.[96] Conversely, the IRS has held that a "tentative agreement . . . evidenced by a term sheet representing an agreement in principle" did constitute an option. The IRS and the parties treated the "tentative agreement" as a binding contract.[97] The IRS has in a number of letter rulings applied the concept that a right to acquire stock becomes an option when the right is nonwithdrawable "as a legal and practical matter," although this concept does not appear in the regulations.[98]

In another ruling, the IRS has held that stock appreciation rights were not "options."[99] The rights entitled the employee to the spread between the price of the stock on the grant date and the price on the earlier of termination of employment or the date the employee terminates the stock appreciation right. The rights did not entitle the employees to receive or vote any stock and were nontransferable. The IRS held that while some stock appreciation rights might be treated as stock, or as nonstock treated as stock, or as options, that would not be so as to these stock appreciation rights under the facts and circumstances involved. The ruling letter did not indicate what proportion of the equity these stock appreciation rights were equivalent to, nor whether such proportion was considered a relevant fact.

As mentioned at § 508.2.2.1, in Notice 88-67 the IRS stated that convertible stock will in most instances be treated *either* as an option or as stock, rather than being

---

(Footnote Continued)

buy or sell stock—these authorities do not necessarily apply. *See* 1986 Blue Book, *supra* note 13, at 311 n.33.

[95] IRS Letter Ruling 9321081, March 4, 1993.

[96] IRS Letter Ruling 8847067, August 29, 1988. In yet another ruling, the IRS held that an option arose, after the boards of both companies had approved a merger, when "each board was notified of the other board's approval . . . , and the plan of merger was executed by representatives of the two boards." IRS Letter Ruling 9314024, January 7, 1993.

[97] IRS Letter Ruling 9111064, December 20, 1990.

[98] *See, e.g.*, IRS Letter Ruling 8847067, *supra* note 96; IRS Letter Ruling 8903043, October 14, 1988 (restructuring agreement became an option on date of Board approval, even though executed on a prior date); IRS Letter Ruling 8929018, April 19, 1989 (exchange offer became option when made public); IRS Letter Ruling 9330027, May 3, 1993 (private placement memorandum that represented an offer of stock that could not be withdrawn); IRS Letter Ruling 9345045, August 17, 1993 (confidential restructuring memorandum constituted an offer that could not be withdrawn); *cf.* IRS Letter Ruling 8917007, January 6, 1989 (public offering did not become an option prior to being made public).

[99] IRS Letter Ruling 9147031, August 23, 1991.

treated simultaneously as both, with "pure" convertible preferred (*i.e.*, nonvoting, nonparticipating, convertible preferred) being treated only as an option,[100] and most other convertible stock (unless it requires the payment of additional consideration upon conversion) being treated as only stock. (As mentioned at § 508.2.2.1 above, the 1994 final regulations changed the rules for "pure" convertible preferred once again.) Notice 88-67 also said that the IRS intended to amend the regulations to allow the IRS to provide additional exceptions from the option rules through the issuance of revenue rulings. This intention was carried out on December 22, 1989, by the adoption of Temp. Reg. § 1.382-2T(h)(4)(x)(Z).

Will a shareholder rights plan (or "poison pill") be treated as an option under Code § 382? The Tax Section of the New York State Bar Association recommended that it not be, unless and until a "flip-in" event occurs (*i.e.*, the point at which a hostile bidder has acquired enough stock to give the other shareholders the right to make a bargain purchase of the target's stock).[101] The IRS has so held in Rev. Rul. 90-11.[102] This ruling exercised the power reserved in Temp. Reg. § 1.382-2T(h)(4)(x)(Z) to exempt by revenue ruling certain categories of interests from the option attribution rules. The ruling states that poison pill rights like those described in the ruling are exempt from these rules until the rights can no longer be redeemed for a nominal amount without shareholder approval.

What about an option that has been issued but has a delayed effective date? The IRS has issued a letter ruling in a case where a company stapled a warrant to each share of its outstanding stock. The warrant provided that the company could issue up to three "calls." Each call would set the terms and conditions upon which a shareholder could exercise the warrant to purchase additional company stock. The IRS ruled that the warrant would not be considered an option until a call is issued, and each separate call would be a separate option.[103]

Where a bankruptcy plan involving a change in stock interests is confirmed on one date but is to become effective at a later date, does the confirmation produce an option? The IRS initially held that it does.[104] Under this approach, the selective exercise rule could create an ownership change on the confirmation date that might not have occurred if all the new stock had been actually issued (and the selective exercise rule did not apply) on that date. The IRS reconsidered that position (*see, e.g.*,

---

[100] Note, however, the effective date provisions of Notice 88-67, mentioned at § 508.2.2.1.

[101] Report of the Tax Section of the New York State Bar Association on the Taxation of Shareholder Rights Plans at 56 (July 25, 1988).

[102] 1990-1 C.B. 10.

[103] IRS Letter Ruling 200024047, March 21, 2000.

[104] *E.g.*, IRS Letter Ruling 8902047, October 28, 1988. Interestingly enough, the IRS did not consider an "option" to arise at some date before the confirmation, such as the date the creditor proponents agreed to propose the plan. This was true even in the case of a "prepackaged" bankruptcy plan where the creditors agreeing to the plan before the petition was filed had enough votes to confirm the plan. *See* IRS Letter Ruling 8903043, October 14, 1988 ("prepackaged" bankruptcy plan). *See also* IRS Letter Ruling 9247017, August 24, 1992 ("prenegotiated" bankruptcy plan); IRS Field Service Advice 1999-1200, April 2, 1993 (stock purchase agreement that required bankruptcy court approval to become effective was "too executory to rise to the level of an option" before that approval), *reprinted at* 1999 TNT 122-83.

IRS Letter Rulings 8903043 and 8930045, at § 508.2.7), and in Reg. § 1.382-9(o) provided, effective for testing dates occurring on or after September 5, 1990, that Temp. Reg. § 1.382-2T(h)(4)(i), which contains the option attribution rule (including its selective exercise aspect), and its successor in the final regulations, Reg. § 1.382-4(d), shall not apply to an option created by the solicitation or receipt of acceptances to the plan, or by confirmation of the plan, or under the plan, until the plan becomes effective.[105] *See also* the discussion at § 510 below. The preamble to the final regulation makes clear that this is intended to include prepetition solicitations for prepackaged or prenegotiated plans, if the plan is later confirmed in a title 11 or similar case. It adds that if the plan is not confirmed, the option created by the solicitation or receipt of acceptances to the plan will ordinarily be treated as having lapsed. The regulation also contains an anti-abuse rule: It will not apply if, in connection with the plan of reorganization, the loss company issues stock (including limited preferred stock) or otherwise receives a capital contribution before the effective date of the plan for a principal purpose of using losses or credits that otherwise would be limited or eliminated by the reorganization. The final regulations allow elections to be made (1) to apply the regulation to testing dates before October 5, 1990, or (2) not to apply the rule of the regulation to testing dates before April 8, 1992. The anti-abuse rule applies only to testing dates on or after April 8, 1992.

Suppose a bankruptcy plan contemplates that a certain amount of stock will be issued in escrow to satisfy disputed claims. As claims are resolved, portions of the stock will be released from escrow for distribution to those whose claims have been allowed. The IRS has ruled, in a case where the disputed claims covered by an escrow arrangement that could last for up to 40 years included product liability claims, that "For the purposes of section 382 of the Code, the ultimate recipients of new common stock whose ownership is directly attributable to the terms of the Plan will be deemed to have received any stock actually received by them as of the date of confirmation. Thus, those recipients will be treated as owning the new common stock that they will ultimately receive (or an option to acquire the same amount of new common stock) on the 'testing date' triggered by the transactions proposed in the plan . . . . Actual distributions from the Plan will not trigger a 'testing date'."[106] It

---

[105] On a related issue, where a creditor entitled to receive stock on the effective date of the plan transferred that contingent right *prior* to the effective date, the IRS ruled that the issuance of the stock to the transferee on the effective date would *not* be considered to have occurred *after* the effective date for purposes of determining whether a subsequent ownership change occurs. IRS Letter Ruling 200731020, May 2, 2007.

Before issuance of the 1994 testing date regulations, the IRS had ruled that the confirmation date nonetheless technically remained a testing date. IRS Letter Ruling 9348053, December 3, 1993. Under the 1994 regulations this is not the case, since under these regulations the mere grant of an option does not generally create a testing date. Although in 2007 the IRS issued a ruling holding that the confirmation date did constitute a testing date under the 1994 regulations, the ruling was quickly repudiated by the IRS and, we understand, will be revised. IRS Letter Ruling 200720012, January 25, 2007.

[106] IRS Letter Ruling 9247017, August 24, 1992; *See also* IRS Letter Ruling 9105042, February 27, 1990 (this ruling was subsequently modified by IRS Letter Ruling 9333048, May 28, 1993, to eliminate the escrow feature without changing the result); IRS Letter Ruling 9321081, March 4, 1993; IRS Letter Ruling 9351011, September 23, 1993.

should be noted, however, that such rulings were issued before the 1994 change in the option attribution rules. In 1994, these rules were changed from an approach that generally treated all contingent rights to stock as though they were immediately exercised (if doing so would result in an ownership change), to an approach that takes into account such contingent rights only if they have as a principal purpose the avoidance of an ownership change (*see* § 508.2.7). Nevertheless, with the inception of "disputed ownership funds" (*see* § 904.3 below), the indications are that the IRS will continue to take a pragmatic view of the treatment of such escrow arrangements.[107] For example, a similar problem can arise with respect to stock placed in a qualified settlement fund. In such instance, the IRS has, for Code § 382(l)(5) purposes, treated the stock placed in such a fund on the effective date of the plan as being held by the beneficiaries of the fund, even though the ultimate determination of who they will be has not been made by that date.[108]

In IRS Letter Ruling 8835057,[109] a ruling dealing with a "G" reorganization of a bank by the FDIC, the IRS held that an ownership change occurred on the date the FDIC made an agreement with an acquiring bank holding company giving the FDIC the right (but not the obligation) to go forward with a "G" reorganization restructuring of the bank pursuant to which the bank holding company and the FDIC would end up owning all of the stock of the reorganized bank (and the holding company would also have an option to buy the stock to be issued and owned by the FDIC).

### *§ 508.2.7.4 Exercise of Options; 120-Day Rule*

Generally speaking, when an option is exercised, the exercise is treated as an acquisition of stock by the owner and the prior ownership of the option is in effect ignored.[110] However, the exercise of an option is disregarded if the option was in existence both before and after an ownership change (whether or not it was treated as having been exercised in order to create that change), but only if the person who exercises it is the 5 percent shareholder (or person who would have been a 5 percent shareholder if the option owned by such person had been exercised immediately before the change date) who owned the option immediately before and after the ownership change.[111] An example in the temporary regulations indicates that an

---

[107] *Cf.* IRS Letter Ruling 9516025, January 18, 1995 (treatment of similar escrow arrangement for purposes of the stock-for-debt exception), discussed at § 504A.4.2. *See also* the discussion at § 508.2.1 above and § 508.2.8.1 below.

[108] In several rulings, the IRS has treated stock issued to and held by qualified settlement funds as having been issued to and held by the creditors for certain Code § 382 purposes, that is, it has applied a look through approach, even where the ultimate successful-claimant beneficiary has yet to be determined. *See* IRS Letter Ruling 200442011, October 23, 2003; IRS Letter Ruling 200243034, July 26, 2002; IRS Letter Ruling 9619051, February 8, 1996; IRS Letter Ruling 9012039, December 22, 1989; *but cf.* IRS Letter Ruling 200242035, July 22, 2002; IRS Letter Ruling 9733019, May 22, 1997. *See also* §§ 508.2.8.1 and 508.5.1 below.

[109] June 10, 1988.

[110] Temp. Reg. § 1.382-2T(h)(4)(xii).

[111] Temp. Reg. § 1.382-2T(h)(4)(vi)(A). Such options are also not subject to the attribution rules. Temp. Reg. § 1.382-2T(h)(4)(x)(F).

option issued on the same date as the ownership change will be treated for purposes of this rule as having been outstanding before the change.[112] However, in IRS Letter Ruling 9019036,[113] the IRS indicated that where both options and stock were issued to a new investor pursuant to a bankruptcy plan that produced an ownership change governed by the Elective Bankruptcy Rule (*see* § 508.5), for purposes of determining whether a subsequent ownership change occurred, the stock (but *not* the options) distributed pursuant to the plan would be disregarded and the investor would be treated as owning the stock at the distribution date. The intention behind the holding as to the options is not entirely clear, but it is understood that the IRS was unwilling to apply the "before and after" rule to the options in this circumstance, pending a resolution of the extent to which (if any) option attribution rules apply for purposes of satisfying the 50 percent continuity requirement of the Elective Bankruptcy Rule. The IRS resolved this issue by proposing, on September 5, 1990, Prop. Reg. § 1.382-3(c) and (d), which provide, for ownership changes occurring on or after September 5, 1990, but not for earlier ownership changes, that options on stock of the debtor (or of a controlling corporation *if* the controlling corporation is also in bankruptcy), other than an option owned as a result of being an old stockholder or "old and cold" creditor, will be treated as selectively exercised if that would cause the 50 percent continuity requirement of the Elective Bankruptcy Rule not to be met.

A special rule applies where an option is treated as having been exercised (thus creating an ownership change) and is then actually exercised within 120 days thereafter. The loss corporation may elect, in the statement it is to include with its return, to disregard the option and take into account only the actual purchase of the stock. This election affects only the determination of the change date, not whether an ownership change has occurred.[114] One of the consequences of this rule is to allow the loss company to choose the one of these two dates that results in the higher valuation for purposes of computing its annual limitation. Another consequence is that the amount of the NOLs and net built-in losses that would be affected by the ownership change may differ substantially on the two dates. For example, if the second date is chosen, the NOLs can be used without limit against income arising between the two dates.[115] Another consequence may be to prevent multiple ownership changes. For example, suppose a buyer (perhaps an underwriter) enters into a contract to purchase what will become 51 percent of the stock from the issuer, and on the closing date (which occurs within 120 days), resells the stock to others. Exercise of the 120-day election would move the first change date to the second change date, thereby preventing the resale from triggering a second ownership change and two change dates.

---

[112] Temp. Reg. § 1.382-2T(h)(4)(F)(x)(2) Example.

[113] February 9, 1990.

[114] Temp. Reg. § 1.382-2T(h)(4)(vi)(B). For an illustration of how this rule applies in various different situations, *see* Goldring & Feiner, *supra* note 7, at 819.

[115] For an example involving a tender offer where the election was made to use the closing date rather than the offer date as the change date, *see* IRS Letter Ruling 8822074, March 8, 1988. *See also* IRS Letter Ruling 8834086, June 2, 1988 (debt restructuring exchange offer of stock and new debentures for old debentures).

*§ 508.2.7.5 Exceptions*

The temporary regulations provide that the following options are not subject to the attribution rule:

(1) Options relating to publicly traded stock after they have been continuously held by the same holder for three years, but not after (a) the option becomes "in the money" (the value of the stock exceeds the exercise price) or (b) the option is transferred by or to a 5 percent owner (or a person who would become a 5 percent owner if the option were exercised).[116] Thus, long-outstanding options for publicly traded stock can fall in and out of consideration for purposes of the option attribution rule.
(2) Options to convert debt into a fixed dollar amount of stock at the fair market value prevailing when the right is exercised.[117] Such an option gives the holder no interest in appreciation of the stock while it is outstanding. One wonders why all such options have not been excluded from the option rule.
(3) Rights or obligations of a corporation to redeem its stock created when the stock is issued, but only if it is issued to new shareholders (or those who are treated as new shareholders under the segregation rules discussed below).[118]
(4) Options to issue stock of a corporation in payment of dividends or interest by it.[119]
(5) Rights to foreclose on a pledge under a loan made in the ordinary course of its business by a bank (as defined in Code § 581), certain insurance companies, and Code § 401 trusts.[120] However, finance companies and investment bankers also make loans, as do a host of other people. One wonders why this exemption is so narrow.[121]
(6) Certain buy-sell agreements are exempted, but the exemptions are tricky and unnecessarily narrow.[122] First, there is an exemption for options "en-

---

[116] Temp. Reg. § 1.382-2T(h)(4)(x)(A). For this purpose, options will not be considered to have been transferred if they are exchanged in a reorganization for options of another party to the reorganization, and they are not changed except for the substitution of corporations. Id.

[117] Temp. Reg. § 1.382-2T(h)(4)(x)(B).

[118] Temp. Reg. § 1.382-2T(h)(4)(x)(C).

[119] Temp. Reg. § 1.382-2T(h)(4)(x)(E).

[120] Temp. Reg. § 1.382-2T(h)(4)(x)(G).

[121] Taxpayers had hoped that this explicit but narrow exemption for pledges was simply a safe harbor, which nonetheless left room to argue that pledges simply were not options in any case. The IRS took the opposite position in IRS Letter Ruling 9148015, August 23, 1991, which held that pledges that did not qualify for the explicit exemption constituted options. The NYSBA Tax Section filed a report with the Commissioner on January 30, 1992 expressing the view that this result was contrary to the statute and should be modified. *See* Tax Notes Today, February 6, 1992, p.5. The IRS responded to this—prospectively—in the final regulations issued in 1994. *See* § 508.2.7.6 below.

[122] A buy-sell agreement between the issuing company and several shareholders was held to be an option in IRS Letter Ruling 8929018, April 19, 1989.

tered into between owners of the same entity (or an owner and the entity in which the owner has a direct ownership interest)," with respect to stock in such entity exercisable *only* upon death, *complete* disability, or mental incompetency.[123] Then, there is also an exemption for options exercisable *solely* upon the retirement of the owner if the option is between noncorporate owners of the same entity (or a noncorporate owner and the entity in which the owner has a direct interest) with respect to the owner's stock in such entity, but *only* if *each* of such owners actively participates in the management of the business, and the option is issued at a time when the company is not a loss company.[124] Options described in both of these provisions are also exempt.[125] Note the narrowness of the latter rule and that neither rule applies if the agreement is with a parent of the issuing company. (Also note that if a right of first refusal is considered to be an "option," the inclusion of such a provision in a buy-sell agreement would destroy these exemptions.)

(7) Options whose *exercise* would be disregarded, because they were in existence both before and after an ownership change (whether or not they were treated as exercised at such time), but only so long as they are held by the 5 percent shareholder (or person who would be treated as a 5 percent shareholder if the option were exercised) who owned the option immediately before and after the ownership change.[126] For example, in a supplemental ruling to IRS Letter Ruling 883057 (discussed above), the IRS held that, where an ownership change resulted from an agreement between the FDIC and a bank holding company to acquire a loss bank, with the FDIC receiving a purported 80 percent interest and the bank holding company receiving a purported 20 percent interest and a five-year option to buy out the FDIC's interest, a subsequent exercise of the option by the bank holding company would not result in a second ownership change.[127]

The temporary regulations also provide that two types of transfers of options are to be disregarded. First, transfers made at death, by gift, or among spouses are to be disregarded.[128] The transferee will be treated as having owned the option during the period it was owned by the transferor. Second, transfers of options between persons who are not 5 percent shareholders (including transfers between persons who are members of different segregated public groups) also are disregarded.

---

[123] Temp. Reg. § 1.382-2T(h)(4)(x)(D).

[124] Temp. Reg. § 1.382-2T(h)(4)(x)(H). Does retirement mean only retirement at retirement age, or does it include earlier voluntary or involuntary termination of employment? The answer is unclear, but one hopes the latter is correct.

[125] Id.

[126] Temp. Reg. § 1.382-2T(h)(4)(x)(F).

[127] *See* IRS Letter Ruling 8842059, July 22, 1988; Wilkins & Hyde, NCNB Texas Ruling Breaks New Ground, 40 Tax Notes 1417 (September 26, 1988) (discloses relative percentage interests).

[128] Temp. Reg. § 1.382-2T(h)(4)(xi).

**Transitional rules.** In applying the temporary regulations, the following transitional rules apply:[129]

(1) Options issued before May 6, 1986, are exempt unless they are transferred on or after such date by (or to) a 5 percent shareholder (or person who would be a 5 percent shareholder if the option were exercised).[130] The exercise of such an option is not, however, disregarded.
(2) Options issued or so transferred on or after September 18, 1986, and before January 1, 1987, shall be treated as if they had never been issued if: (a) they lapse unexercised or are irrevocably forfeited by the holder or (b) on the date they were issued there was no significant likelihood they would be exercised within five years and a purpose for the issuance of the option was to cause an ownership change before January 1, 1987.

### *§ 508.2.7.6 1994 Regulations*

In early November 1992, effective for testing dates on or after November 5, 1992, the IRS proposed radically to change and greatly to simplify the option rules. These were made final in 1994 as Reg. § 1.382-4(d), with the same general effective date (*see* § 508.2.7). These regulations abandon (prospectively from their effective date) the selective exercise and deemed exercise rules. They provide as their basic rule that options are generally not treated as exercised on their issuance or transfer or on any subsequent testing date, unless the option is issued or transferred for an abusive principal purpose. For a loss company in a title 11 or similar case, a special exemption for the period before the effective date of the plan of reorganization is provided from this abusive purpose exception for the following options: (1) the solicitation or receipt of acceptances to the plan, (2) the confirmation of the plan, and (3) any option created by the plan.[131]

In essence, an abusive principal purpose is a purpose to postpone the timing of an ownership change (by not having the option taken into account for ownership purposes) while giving the holder (or a related person) the benefit of ownership in the meantime, or by allowing the loss company to derive income to absorb its losses before the ownership change occurs. Since an abusive purpose is one designed not to have the option treated as exercised, the regulation provides that an option designed to be treated as exercised in order to *prevent* an ownership change will not be treated as exercised. Specifically, the regulation provides that an option is treated as exercised on the date of its issuance or transfer if, on that date, the option satisfies either (1) an ownership test, (2) a control test, or (3) an income test. Once an option is

---

[129] Temp. Reg. § 1.382-2T(m)(8).

[130] For the treatment of options exchanged in acquisitive reorganizations and similar transactions, *see* Temp. Reg. § 1.382-2T(h)(4)(x)(A); IRS Letter Ruling 8809081, December 9, 1987, supplemented by IRS Letter Ruling 8823022, February 10, 1988.

[131] Reg. § 1.382-9(o). This regulation contains its own rather different anti-abuse rule, however, which is described at § 508.2.7.3 above.

treated as exercised under this provision, it is treated as exercised on any subsequent testing date.

**The ownership test.** An option satisfies the ownership test if a principal purpose of the issuance, transfer, or structuring of the option (alone or in combination with other arrangements) is to avoid or ameliorate the impact of an ownership change of the loss corporation by providing the holder of the option, prior to its exercise or transfer, with a substantial portion of the attributes of ownership of the underlying stock. Factors taken into account under this test include the relationship, at the time of issuance or transfer of the option, between the exercise price of the option and the value of the underlying stock (an exercise price substantially less than the value of the underlying stock would presumably be suspect, although the proposed version of the regulation had indicated that an exercise price of at least 90 percent of the value of the stock would be acceptable); whether the option provides its holder or a related person with the right to participate in management or other rights ordinarily afforded owners of the underlying stock; and the existence of reciprocal puts and calls.

**The control test.** An option satisfies the control test if a principal purpose of the issuance, transfer, or structuring of the option (alone or in combination with other arrangements) is to avoid or ameliorate the impact of an ownership change of the loss corporation, and the holder of the option and any related persons have, in the aggregate, a direct or indirect ownership interest in the loss corporation of more than 50 percent (determined as if all their options had been exercised and any other *intended* increases in their percentage ownership actually occurred). Persons are related for this purpose if they bear a relationship specified in Code § 267(b) or § 707(b) or if they have a formal or informal understanding among themselves to make a coordinated acquisition of stock. Indirect ownership is determined by application of the constructive ownership rules of Temp. Reg. § 1.382-2T(h), with certain modifications. (Unlike the rest of the final regulations, the control test generally applies only to issuances or transfers of options after March 17, 1994.)

**The income test.** An option satisfies the income test if a principal purpose of the issuance, transfer, or structuring of the option (alone or in combination with other arrangements) is to avoid or ameliorate the impact of an ownership change of the loss corporation by facilitating the creation of income (including accelerating income or deferring deductions) or value (including unrealized built-in gains) prior to the exercise or transfer of the option. Factors taken into account in applying this test include whether the option holder or a related person has made a capital contribution or loan to the loss corporation, unless it is made to enable the loss corporation to continue basic business operations.

The preamble to the final regulation states that an abusive purpose can be treated as a principal purpose even when it is outweighed by the nontax reasons (taken together or separately) for the transaction.

The final regulation also contains important safe harbor provisions. This provides that certain options are not treated as exercised pursuant to the ownership, control, or income tests. The safe harbors are for the following:

(1) *Contracts to Acquire Stock:* A commercially reasonable stock purchase agreement, in which the parties' obligations to complete the transaction are subject only to reasonable closing conditions and that is closed on a change

date within one year after it is made. (This safe harbor only applies to the ownership and the control tests and does not apply for purposes of the income test.)

(2) *Escrow, Pledge, or Other Security Agreements:* This safe harbor applies to options that are part of a security arrangement in a typical lending transaction (including a purchase money loan), if the arrangement is subject to customary commercial conditions. A security arrangement, for this purpose, includes an escrow or pledge or other security agreement, or an option to acquire stock contingent upon default of a loan.

(3) *Compensatory Options:* Compensatory options containing customary terms and conditions provided to employees, directors, or independent contractors or a related person (and not excessive for the services performed) if they are nontransferable and do not have a readily ascertainable fair market value on the date issued, within the meaning of the Code Section 83 regulations.

(4) *Options Exercisable Only Upon Death, Disability, Mental Incompetency, or Retirement:* This safe harbor applies to options between stockholders of a corporation (or a stockholder and the corporation) with respect to stock of the stockholder that is exercisable only upon death, disability, or mental incompetency of the stockholder or, in the case of stock acquired in connection with services, the stockholder's retirement.

(5) *Rights of First Refusal:* This applies to rights of first refusal having customary terms, entered into between stockholders of a corporation (or between the corporation and a stockholder) regarding the corporation's stock.

The regulation defines an option as being any contingent purchase, warrant, convertible debt, put, stock subject to a risk of forfeiture,[132] contract to acquire stock, or similar interest, regardless of whether it is contingent or otherwise not currently exercisable. On the other hand, the IRS has ruled that where a warrant is issued that does not become active until a later "call" is made, no option will be deemed to have been created until the "call" is issued. In this case, however, the terms of the warrant were not stated from the date of the issuance of the warrant but only upon the issuance of the "call," which would specify the terms and conditions upon which the warrant could be exercised.[133] This feature would distinguish this instrument from a case where the warrant is issued with its terms fixed at date of issuance, with the only contingency being the delay in its effective date.

An option that is considered to have been issued or transferred with a principally abusive purpose is treated as having been exercised on such date and on each subsequent testing date until an ownership change occurs. However, once such an ownership change has occurred, then (1) the option is not treated as exercised again

---

[132] Is stock that has been issued but is subject to a substantial risk of forfeiture within the meaning of Code Section 83 treated also as "stock"? IRS Letter Ruling 9422048, cited at § 508.2.2 above, suggests that it is.

[133] IRS Letter Ruling 200024047, March 21, 2000, affirmed and extended in IRS Letter Ruling 200207002, July 17, 2001.

unless the option is later transferred for an abusive principal purpose, and (2) the exercise of the option by the person who held it on the change date (and certain transferees) will not cause another ownership change. However, the stock is not treated as outstanding between the change date and the exercise date. Because of this latter point, the loss corporation may, as an alternative to this treatment, apply a look-back rule pursuant to which, if the loss corporation properly reported the option as abusive on the change date and the option is exercised within three years of the change date, the option can be treated as though it had been actually exercised on the change date (and thus is thereafter treated as the underlying stock).

Unlike the temporary regulations, the regulation contains no "lapse or forfeiture" rule. Thus, the lapse or forfeiture of an abusive option that previously resulted in an ownership change of the loss corporation under the deemed exercise rule does *not* erase the prior change.

The regulation provides that a transfer of an option will not cause it to be treated as being exercised if it is a transfer between persons who are not 5 percent shareholders, between members of separate public groups, or is made by reason of death, gift, divorce, or separation.

The regulation also provides that an option is excluded from the "nonstock is stock" definition that is described in § 508.2.2.3 above. However, the option rules do not affect the determination under general tax principles of whether an instrument is an option or stock.

### § 508.2.8 Definition of 5 Percent Shareholder

Since an "ownership change" is measured by increases in ownership by 5 percent shareholders, the definition of 5 percent shareholder is a key concept. The approach taken in old Code § 382(a) was to apply its limitations only to concentrations of ownership, that is, to increases in ownership by those who ended up as the 10 *largest* shareholders. New Code § 382 takes a different approach: it applies to *both* concentrations and dispersions in ownership. How it does this can best be seen in the simple case of a loss corporation owned only by individuals.

Each individual who owns (after family attribution) 5 percent or more of the stock is a "five-percent shareholder." However, all those individuals who individually own less than 5 percent of the stock are treated under new Code § 382 as a separate "five-percent shareholder," even if they actually own in the aggregate less than 5 percent of the stock. Thus, if individual A acquires from the public 51 percent of the stock (a concentration transaction), she becomes a 5 percent shareholder and an ownership change results because a 5 percent shareholder has increased her ownership by more than 50 percentage points during the testing period ending on that testing date. Conversely, if individual *B*, who owns all the stock of a loss corporation, sells 51 percent of his stock to the public, that is, to individuals, none of whom owns 5 percent or more of the stock (a dispersion transaction), the public becomes a separate 5 percent shareholder and an ownership change results here as well. Because new Code § 382 applies to dispersion as well as concentration transactions, it applies to many more cases than did old Code § 382.

Although transactions between holders who actually or constructively own 5 percent or more of the stock, or between such owners and the public that is treated as a fictional 5 percent shareholder, are counted in applying the ownership change test, transactions within the fictional 5 percent shareholder that is comprised of the public are not. Thus, if a company has no actual 5 percent shareholders, stock can be traded back and forth among the members of the public group (which in the aggregate represents a fictional single 5 percent shareholder) without producing an owner shift or an ownership change.

However, the statute and temporary regulations contain special "aggregation" and "segregation" rules that have the effect of fragmenting, into two or more public 5 percent shareholders, the single public 5 percent shareholder that would be created if only the attribution rules were considered. This has the effect of multiplying the opportunities for creating an ownership change.

The aggregation rules apply when the stock of the loss company is owned by one or more tiers of entities that themselves own (directly or after attribution) 5 percent or more of the loss company's stock; their individual stockholders who separately own (indirectly) less than 5 percent of the loss company will be treated as a separate 5 percent shareholder of the loss company if they own in the aggregate (indirectly) 5 percent or more of the loss company's stock.

**EXAMPLE 1**

Suppose publicly owned P acquires 80 percent of the stock of publicly owned L. If only the attribution rules applied, one would look through P, and because L would be owned both before and after the transaction entirely by individuals owning separately less than 5 percent of the L stock, only one 5 percent shareholder would exist, and no ownership change would have been created. Because of the aggregation rule, however, the public owners of P are treated as a 5 percent shareholder of L that is separate from the other public owners of L, and so an ownership change has occurred because this separate 5 percent shareholder has had a more than 50 percentage point increase in ownership.

Note that the aggregation rule can produce (artificially) a change in stock ownership for Code § 382 purposes even if the aggregation event itself produces no change in beneficial ownership. There must, however, have been an acquisition of the stock during the testing period; otherwise the aggregation event itself will not result in a change in ownership. For example, suppose individuals A and B each own 4 percent of publicly owned L, and L has only one 5 percent shareholder (the public group consisting of all its stockholders). If A and B drop their stock into a new partnership or corporation formed by them, their stock will be aggregated into a new public-group 5 percent shareholder (owning 8 percent of the stock) of L. If A and B had acquired their stock during the current testing period, the aggregation event would produce an 8 percent increase in stock ownership in L (without any change in beneficial ownership) for Code § 382 purposes. If A and B had acquired their stock before the beginning of the testing period, it would not have this consequence.

The aggregation rule is applied before the segregation rule. The latter applies not because tiers of ownership exist, but because certain transactions have taken place.

**EXAMPLE 2**

L, which is owned by a single public group, issues stock in a public offering. Under the segregation rule, the offering will (assuming no actual 5 percent shareholder is created thereby) be treated as creating a new public group that is a 5 percent shareholder separate from the old public-group 5 percent shareholder. The new 5 percent shareholder will be treated as acquiring the stock issued in the public offering, except to the extent the issuer can show that old stockholders actually acquired it, and no cross ownership between the two public groups will be deemed to exist. Thus, if the stock issued in the public offering represented more than 50 percent of the stock outstanding after the offering, the new 5 percent shareholder would have had an increase in ownership of more than 50 percentage points and an ownership change would have occurred.

Reg. § 1.382-3(j)(7) provides that, for purposes of determining who is a 5 percent shareholder, and for purposes of the aggregation and segregation rules, the transitory ownership of stock by an underwriter will be disregarded. This rule is generally effective for stock issuances in taxable years beginning on or after November 4, 1992, with an election available to apply it to earlier periods.

*§ 508.2.8.1 Aggregation Rules*

To apply the aggregation test, one goes to the highest tier entity that owns, directly or indirectly, 5 percent or more of the loss company's stock, and then one applies the following tests:[134]

(1) Each individual who *directly* owns 5 percent or more of the loss company's stock is a 5 percent shareholder.
(2) Each individual who is a 5 percent shareholder of a higher tier entity who *indirectly* owns 5 percent or more of the loss company's stock, counting *only* the stock attributed to him through that entity (and not any loss company stock he might own in another capacity) is also a 5 percent shareholder of the loss company.
(3) If the owners of the highest tier entity, who indirectly own less than 5 percent of the stock of the loss company, indirectly own, in the aggregate, 5 percent or more of the loss company, they constitute what the temporary regulations call the "public group" of that highest tier entity (even if some of them own 5 percent or more of that entity) and are treated as a separate public group of the loss company that is a separate 5 percent shareholder.
(4) If such "public group" of the highest tier entity indirectly owns in the aggregate less than 5 percent of the loss company, that public group is not a

---

134 *See generally* Temp. Reg. § 1.382-2T(g)(1)-(3) and (j)(1).

separate 5 percent shareholder of the loss company; instead, its stock is treated as part of the stock of the public group of the next lower tier entity.

(5) This same procedure is followed down through the tiers, but only at the level of each entity that owns directly or indirectly 5 percent or more of the loss company, until one reaches the loss company.

(6) The loss company's public group, even if it owns less than 5 percent of the loss company's stock, is treated as a separate 5 percent shareholder of the loss company.

The aggregation rules are subject to certain presumptions. These are discussed below following the discussion of the segregation rules.

An "entity" is defined in Reg. § 1.382-3(a), as originally issued, as any corporation, estate, trust, association, company, partnership, or similar organization. On November 20, 1990, the IRS issued a proposed amendment to expand this definition of an "entity" to include groups of persons acting together. The proposed regulation, with modifications, was made final in March 1992. The amendment says that an "entity" includes

> a group of persons who have a formal or informal understanding among themselves to make a coordinated acquisition of stock. A principal element in determining if such an understanding exists is whether the investment decision of each member of a group is based upon the investment decision of one or more other members.

The amended regulation contains three examples to illustrate this group concept. In the first, individuals acted together to purchase 60 percent of the stock (though each of them individually owned less than 5 percent). This produced an ownership change, because their group was treated as an entity. In the second, management of a company facing a hostile takeover convinced a number of potentially friendly investors to purchase stock in the market. Apparently, the investors met separately with management, didn't talk to each other, and didn't know the identity of the others. But those who acted did so on the understanding that the company would assemble a group that in the aggregate would acquire more than 50 percent of the stock. Fifteen of these investors each bought 4 percent of the outstanding stock on a single day. This produced an ownership change because the 15 investors were considered to have acted pursuant to a formal or informal understanding among themselves to make a coordinated acquisition of stock.

In the third example, an investment advisor recommends purchase of a stock to its clients. Acting on this advice, 20 unrelated individuals purchase an aggregate of 6 percent of stock (none of them more than 5 percent). The example holds that because there was no understanding among the clients to make a coordinated acquisition, this purchase did not make them an entity. The example goes on to say that the result would be the same if the advisor was also an underwriter for the offering of the stock. The example further states that the result would be the same if, instead of an investment advisor recommending that clients purchase stock, the trustee of several pension trusts sponsored by unrelated employers causes each trust to purchase the stock, so long as the investment decision made for each trust was not based on the investment decision made for the other. Although the regulation does not say so, presumably the same conclusion would apply to mutual funds or trusts sharing the same advisor.[135] The amended regulation adds that

> the participation by creditors in formulating a plan for an insolvency workout or a reorganization in a title 11 or similar case (whether as members of a creditors' committee or otherwise) and the receipt of stock by creditors in satisfaction of indebtedness pursuant to the workout or reorganization do not cause the creditors to be considered an entity.

The IRS has amplified these concepts in several private letter rulings. For example, the IRS has held that:

— regulated investment companies or institutional investors having the same investment advisor are not members of a group that constitute an "entity" (and thus need not be aggregated) for Code § 382 purposes, merely because the investment advisor had authority to vote the stock, acquire or dispose of stock, use a common custodian, file Schedules 13D or 13G with the SEC with respect to the stock, and communicate with the corporation's management regarding operations, management or capital structure;[136]

— an investment advisor that is considered to beneficially own stock of its clients for Schedule 13D or 13G purposes is not the owner of such stock for Code § 382 purposes, since the investment advisor has no right to keep the dividends or the proceeds of sale from the stock;[137] and

— where an investment advisor files a Schedule 13D or 13G with respect to stock owned by its clients and the clients do not themselves file a Schedule 13D or 13G that confirms the existence of a "group" for securities law purposes, the loss company can rely on the absence of a filing by the clients to determine that the clients are not members of a group that constitute an "entity" for Code § 382 purposes, unless the loss company has actual knowledge to the contrary.[138]

---

[135] It is interesting to note that just eight days after issuing the earlier proposed amendment, the IRS ruled that separate mutual funds that combined into one corporation but kept their separate tax identity as separate series funds should continue to be treated as separate holders. IRS Letter Ruling 9109013, November 28, 1990.

[136] *See, e.g.,* IRS Letter Ruling 200713015 (December 20, 2006); IRS Letter Ruling 9725039 (March 26, 1997) (similarly so ruling, even though one or more directors or employees of the advisor could also be directors or employees of the owners); IRS Letter Ruling 9533024 (May 19, 1995) (same); IRS Letter Ruling 9610012 (December 5, 1995) (two or more investment funds with common investment advisor/manager not considered an "entity," even though the funds also had the same board of directors). *See also* IRS Letter Ruling 200618022, January 18, 2006 (the several defined benefit plan trusts of a bankrupt corporate group, which had deposited their assets into a group trust as permitted by Rev. Rul. 81-100, 1981-1 C.B. 326, should be treated as separate persons and not aggregated).

[137] *See, e.g.,* IRS Letter Ruling 200713015 (December 20, 2006); IRS Letter Ruling 9725039 (March 26, 1997); Private Letter Ruling 9533024 (May 19, 1995).

[138] *See, e.g.,* IRS Letter Ruling 200713015 (December 20, 2006); IRS Letter Ruling 9533024 (May 19, 1995).

In addition, in IRS Letter Ruling 200605003,[139] the IRS held that three sister investment funds (a small investor fund, a large investor fund, and a foreign investor fund) having substantially different owners, but a common investment manager and the same investment objective, and thus almost always investing together in the same proportion based on their respective assets, did not constitute a single entity. The funds provided two sets of representations to the effect that no acquisitions by the funds were with a purpose of acquiring any particular minimum percentage, or for the purpose of changing or influencing the control of the Company.

In IRS Letter Ruling 9619051,[140] the IRS held that stock owned by a qualified settlement fund should be deemed held by the beneficiaries in applying the special bankruptcy rule of Code § 382(l)(5), even though the ultimate determination of who the beneficiaries would be had not yet been made. In IRS Letter Ruling 9510007,[141] the IRS held that stock owned by certain ESOPs should be considered for Code § 382 purposes to be held by the participants in the ESOPs.

**Effective date.** For purposes of determining whether an ownership change took place on any testing date before September 4, 1987, the aggregation rules apply only to stock of the loss company acquired after May 5, 1986, by any first tier entity or higher tier entity, unless the loss company elects to apply all of the aggregation and segregation rules without regard to when the stock was acquired.[142]

The amendment treating a group as an "entity" is to be effective for testing dates on or after November 20, 1990, but for groups formed before that date, it becomes effective (but then arguably retroactively) only if the group increases or decreases pursuant to the plan its ownership relative to the amount it owned on November 19, 1990, by 5 percentage points or more after that date. (If the group consists only of Code § 851 regulated investment companies, Code § 401 qualified plans, Code § 584 common trust funds, or trusts or estates that are clients of a bank trust department, the new rule becomes effective only if the group increases—and not if it decreases—its ownership by such 5 percentage points.) Although the "relative to the amount" language is confusing, we understand the 5 percentage points is meant to relate to the total outstanding stock and not just to the stock owned by the group.

---

[139] October 28, 2005.

[140] February 8, 1996, *replacing* IRS Letter Ruling 9603006, October 10, 1995. To the same effect, *see* IRS Letter Ruling 200442011, October 23, 2003; IRS Letter Ruling 200243034, July 26, 2002; IRS Letter Ruling 9012039, December 22, 1989; *but cf.* IRS Letter Ruling 200242035, July 22, 2002 (although also applying Code § 382(l)(5) as a result of the stock received by a qualified settlement fund, it utilized different reasoning); IRS Letter Ruling 9733019, May 22, 1997 (same). *See also* the discussions at §§ 508.2.1 and 508.2.7.3 above, and § 508.5.1 below.

[141] December 6, 1994. *See also* IRS Letter Ruling 9652019, September 30, 1996. *See also* Reg. § 1.382-10 made final in 2006, holding that a transfer by an ESOP to its beneficiaries will not itself be a change in ownership for Code § 382 purposes.

[142] Temp. Reg. § 1.382-2T(m)(4)(i).

*§ 508.2.8.2 Segregation Rules*

The segregation rules take the public groups that are treated as separate 5 percent shareholders of the loss company and, where they apply, fragment them into additional separate public group 5 percent shareholders of the loss company.

If a particular transaction triggers the segregation rules, the resulting segregation applies only in determining whether an ownership change occurs within a testing period that includes the transaction.[143] Thus, once an ownership change occurs, or the beginning of the testing period has otherwise passed the transaction by, any prior application of the segregation rules resulting from the transaction is ignored.

The transactions giving rise to application of the segregation rules are the following:

(1) *Reorganizations and Stock Issuances by the Loss Company.* In the case of equity structure shifts described in Code § 381(a)(2) (*i.e.*, "A," "C," and nondivisive "D" and "G" reorganizations) to which the loss company is a party, or any other issuance of stock by the loss company to which Code § 1032 applies, the public-group shareholders who receive stock in the transaction are treated as a public-group 5 percent shareholder separate from the public-group 5 percent shareholder that existed before the transaction.[144] Under the presumption against cross-ownership (discussed below), the public group that receives stock in the transaction is deemed to consist of entirely new persons and not to include any members of any preexisting public group.[145]

(2) *Redemptions.* If the loss company redeems any of its stock, each public group before the transaction is segregated into two groups, one from which the redemption is considered to have been made, and one consisting of those who did not redeem any of their stock.[146] Under the presumption against cross-ownership (discussed below), the group from which the stock is redeemed is treated as not owning any stock after the redemption. For this purpose, a redemption includes an acquisition by a loss company of its "stock" in exchange for stock that is not "stock" (*e.g.*, straight "pure" preferred) in an "E" recapitalization.

(3) *Deemed Exercise of Options.* When an "option" *issued* by a loss company to acquire its stock is deemed to be exercised under the option attribution

---

[143] Temp. Reg. § 1.382-2T(j)(2)(i).

[144] Temp. Reg. § 1.382-2T(j)(2)(iii)(B).

[145] This provision does not apply to any public offering before 1989 by building and loan association described in Code § 591 (or its 80 percent parent). Moreover, unless the corporation otherwise elects, an underwriter of any firm commitment offering of stock of such an institution before 1989 will not be treated as acquiring any stock to the extent it is disposed of within 60 days after the initial offering. Temp. Reg. § 1.382-2T(m)(6). The Technical Corrections Bill contains a provision that is similar but broader: it covers *all* thrift institutions described in Code § 591, not just building and loan associations. In addition, it extends the 60-day underwriter rule to *any* loss company (not just thrift institutions) for offerings before September 19, 1986 (January 1, 1989 for thrift institutions). Technical Corrections Bill of 1988, § 106(d)(15).

[146] Temp. Reg. § 1.382-2T(j)(2)(iii)(C).

rules discussed above, and if any of the loss company stock deemed acquired is considered owned by a public group, that public group will be segregated and treated as a separate public-group 5 percent shareholder of the loss company, with no cross-ownership with prior groups, just as in the case of an actual stock issuance discussed above.[147]

However, the IRS has privately ruled that, where a loss company issues transferable rights to acquire its stock to multiple public groups, the rights will be deemed exercised "in the same proportion" as if such rights had been exercised pro rata by each public group.[148] This is similar to the express presumption in the regulations that any rights *actually* exercised by a public group are presumed to be exercised pro rata by each public group. For widely held loss companies, this creates a potential "loophole" in that a loss company that cannot issue stock to the general public because the entire stock issuance would be segregated and thus result in an ownership change might be able to issue tradeable rights to its shareholders because a portion of the stock issued would be treated as acquired by preexisting shareholders. Of course, the loss company has to be careful that, under the deemed exercise rule, the selective exercise of such rights (taking into account the pro rata exercise treatment of the ruling) by one or more public groups or 5 percent shareholders does not result in an ownership change.

Recognizing this artificial difference between stock offerings and distributions of tradeable rights under the segregation rules, the IRS in 1993 amended the regulations to treat the two equally. Reg. § 1.382-3(j)(10) accomplishes this by requiring that a loss company, in choosing to take into account its actual knowledge to override the "no cross-ownership" presumption upon the actual or deemed issuance of stock pursuant to the rights, also take into account all trading in the rights. This is intended to put the burden on the loss company to know who actually owns the rights on any given testing date. And only to the extent that the loss company knows that the current holders are members of the original public groups that received the rights would the pro rata exercise presumptions apply. This change is effective for options issued on or after November 4, 1992, unless the option was issued before May 4, 1993, and the issuer, on or before November 4, 1992, had filed a securities law registration statement for the purpose of such issuance;[149] the change could have retroactive effect, however, if the loss corporation filed an election under Reg. § 1.382-3(j)(14)(iii).

(4) *Transfers by Certain 5 Percent Shareholders*. If an entity or individual that directly owns 5 percent or more of the stock of the loss company transfers any loss company stock to a public group, the public group receiving such stock is segregated from the public groups that existed before the transaction and is treated as a separate 5 percent shareholder.[150]

---

[147] Temp. Reg. § 1.382-2T(j)(2)(iii)(D).

[148] *See* IRS Letter Ruling 9222014, February 26, 1992, referencing Temp. Reg. § 1.382-2T(j)(2)(iii)(F), which employs a pro rata exercise presumption for actual exercises.

[149] *See* Reg. § 1.382-3(j)(14)(ii).

[150] Temp. Reg. § 1.382-2T(j)(3)(i).

(5) *Application at Upper Tier Levels.* The temporary regulations provide that the principles of paragraphs (1) through (4) above will also apply to transactions involving stock of higher tier entities that own 5 percent or more of the stock of the loss company, as they affect the various public-group 5 percent shareholders of the loss company; and to acquisitions of the stock of a higher tier entity by a lower tier entity (including the loss company) that have the effect of a redemption.[151] Anyone seeking to apply this mandate upward through the tiers will find the complexities, and resulting uncertainties and ambiguities, quite mindboggling.

The loss company may elect to combine any public groups first identified in the same taxable year resulting from the application of paragraphs (1) and (3) above (and the comparable portions of paragraph (5) above), if they separately own less than 5 percent of the loss company's stock.[152]

Where a transaction qualifies as more than one type of segregation transaction, the segregation rules are to be applied in the way that creates the *largest* percentage increase by 5 percent shareholders.[153]

**Small issuance and cash issuance exceptions.** In late 1993, the IRS issued Reg. § 1.382-3(j) to provide an exception to the segregation rules for (1) small issuances, and (2) cash issuances.

In general, a "small issuance" is an issuance of stock that (together with all prior issuances during the year) represents 10 percent or less of the loss corporation's outstanding stock as of the beginning of the year, determined either on a class-by-class basis or based on the value of all the company's stock (other than Code § 1504(a)(4) stock), generally at the loss corporation's option.

The cash issuance exception applies (if the small issuance exception does not) to that percentage of stock issued for cash that equals 50 percent of the aggregate percentage of the loss company's stock owned by direct public groups. Thus, if 100 percent of the company's stock is owned by one or more direct public groups, half of the stock issued for cash could qualify for the cash issuance exception (if the small issuance exception did not apply). The cash issuance exception applies only to stock issued solely for cash. A share of stock is not considered issued solely for cash if, as a condition of acquiring that share for cash, the acquirer is required to purchase other stock for noncash consideration, or if the share is acquired upon excercise of an option that was not issued solely for cash or was not distributed with respect to stock.[154]

Stock covered by either exception is treated as having been acquired proportionately by each direct public group that exists before the issuance. The exceptions do

---

[151] Temp. Reg. § 1.382-2T(j)(3)(i) and (iii).

[152] Temp. Reg. § 1.382-2T(j)(2)(iv)(A) and (j)(3)(iii).

[153] Temp. Reg. § 1.382-2T(j)(2)(v)(A).

[154] IRS Letter Ruling 9437043, June 22, 1994, held that where a series of options were exercisable only for cash, but a later series could not be exercised unless the earlier series had been exercised, all of the options would be treated as providing for stock to be issued "solely for cash."

not apply to issuances in equity structure shifts except that the small issuance exception applies to recapitalizations.

In addition, for purposes of the cash issuance exception, any stock issued to 5 percent shareholders is initially included in computing the overall size of the offering from which one calculates the amount of the offering qualifying for the exception. This has the beneficial effect of increasing the amount of stock issued to less-than-5 percent shareholders that may qualify for the cash issuance exception, as illustrated by the following example in the proposed regulation:

**EXAMPLE**

L has 1000 shares outstanding which are owned entirely by less-than-5 percent shareholders comprising two equal public groups. L now issues 200 additional shares of common stock for cash. A acquires 120 of these shares and the public acquires the remaining 80 shares. The issuance does not qualify for the small issuance exception, since it exceeds 10 percent of the company. Applying the cash issuance exception, 50 percent of the cash offering (representing one-half of the 100 percent preissuance ownership interest held by direct public groups) can qualify for the cash issuance exception. The offering for this purpose is the entire 200 shares, inclusive of the shares acquired by A. Thus, the maximum amount of stock that can qualify for the cash issuance exception is 100 shares (50 percent times 200). Because this exceeds the 80 shares actually acquired by the public in the offering, the entire 80 shares qualifies for the exception and is deemed acquired proportionately by the two preexisting direct public groups.

For purposes of both the small issuance and cash issuance exceptions (but not for purposes of determining whether stock is issued solely for cash), multiple issuances are treated as a single issuance if (1) the issuances occur at approximately the same time pursuant to the same plan or arrangement, or (2) a principal purpose of issuing the stock in separate issuances rather than a single issuance is to take further advantage of these exceptions.

The proposed regulation provides its principles will be applied to issuances by entities that directly or indirectly own 5 percent or more of the loss corporation.

In general, the 1993 regulation is effective for stock issuances in taxable years beginning on or after November 4, 1992. However, the loss corporation may elect to apply the new rules retroactively.[155]

**Effective date.** Unless the loss company elects to have all of the aggregation and segregation rules apply without regard to when the stock was acquired, the following effective date provisions apply to the segregation rules. In determining whether an ownership change occurred on any testing date before September 4, 1987, the

---

155 *See* Reg. § 1.382-3(j)(14).

segregation rules described in paragraphs (1) through (3) above shall apply only to equity structure shifts in which more than one corporation is a party to a reorganization. The rules described in paragraphs (4) and (5) above shall apply only to stock of the loss company acquired after May 5, 1986, and to equity structure shifts in which more than one company is a party to the reorganization.[156] For purposes of determining whether an ownership change occurs on any testing date after September 3, 1987, the same restrictions apply unless the transaction involves stock acquired after May 5, 1986.[157] The IRS has held that this transition rule also operates to exempt from the segregation rules any option issued before September 4, 1987, and any stock issued pursuant to exercise of such an option.[158]

**Special mutual fund rule.** Reg. § 1.382-3(k) provides, effective for testing dates after December 31, 1986, that the segregation rules relating to issuances and redemptions do not apply to a mutual fund's issuances and redemptions of its stock in the ordinary course of business, where such stock is redeemable on demand of the shareholder. A loss corporation may, however, choose to apply this rule only to testing dates on or after October 29, 1991.[159] The preamble to the proposed regulation says that issuance or redemption of stock pursuant to a merger of the fund would not be covered by the rule because it would not be considered an ordinary-course-of-business transaction.

### *§ 508.2.8.3 Presumptions*

In applying the aggregation and segregation rules, the following presumptions apply:

(1) If in any segregation transaction described in paragraphs (1) or (3) above (*i.e.*, reorganizations, stock issuances, and deemed exercise of options) the loss company issues rights to acquire its stock to members of more than one public group, any *actual* exercise of those rights will be presumed to be exercised pro rata by each public group.[160] The same principle applies when such concepts are applied to upper tier entities under the segregation rules of paragraph (5) above.[161] As discussed at § 508.2.8.2 paragraph (3) above, before amendment of the regulations in 1993, this presumption potentially allowed widely held loss companies to use distributions of tradeable stock rights to mitigate the segregation effect of a public offering. Reg. § 1.382-3(j)(10) changed this result.

(2) Any new public group created by a segregation transaction described in paragraph (1), (3), or (4) above (and so much of paragraph (5) as involves

---

156 Temp. Reg. § 1.382-2T(m)(4)(i)(B) and (C).

157 Temp. Reg. § 1.382-2T(m)(4)(iii).

158 Rev. Rul. 90-15, 1990-1 C.B. 93.

159 Reg. § 1.382-3(k)(2)(ii).

160 Temp. Reg. § 1.382-2T(j)(2)(iii)(F).

161 Temp. Reg. § 1.382-2T(j)(3)(iii).

the same type transactions) is presumed not to include any members of any public group that existed before the transaction.[162]

(3) Any new public group created by a segregation transaction described in paragraph (2) above (a redemption) or so much of paragraph (5) as involves a redemption type transaction, that owned the stock redeemed before the transaction, is presumed not to own any such stock immediately after the transaction.[163]

(4) In applying the aggregation rules, members of a public group are presumed not to be members of any other public group and not to be related to any other direct or indirect shareholder.[164]

(5) The acquisition by either a 5 percent shareholder or the loss company on any date when a public group created by the segregation rules exists shall be treated as being made proportionately from each public group existing before the acquisition (unless a different proportion is established by either the taxpayer or the IRS).[165]

(6) With respect to any stock of the loss company or higher tier entity subject to the requirements of SEC Schedules 13D or 13G (generally, publicly traded classes of equity securities), the loss company may rely on the existence or absence of such filings as of any date to identify the direct 5 percent shareholders of such entity.[166] This reference to Schedules 13D and 13G has interesting connotations. The drafters of new Code § 382 established its threshold testing level at 5 percent, rather than at some higher or lower percentage of ownership, because they felt that the 5 percent information would be available from these SEC filings and they wanted to drop the threshold as low as possible. However, the Schedule 13D and G concepts do not exactly mesh with the Code § 382 concepts as follows: (a) a person need file one of these Schedules only after his ownership has become more than 5 percent, whereas a person becomes a 5 percent shareholder under Code § 382 when his ownership *reaches* 5 percent; and (b) the SEC concepts of ownership (*e.g.*, voting power alone may count, and various grouping concepts apply) differ from the tax concepts. Moreover, while Schedule 13D must be filed relatively promptly after a transaction occurs, Schedule 13G need only be filed annually. The information contained on these Schedules may not always allow one to determine who is the tax owner of the stock,

---

[162] Temp. Reg. § 1.382-2T(j)(2)(iii)(B), (D), and (j)(3)(i) and (iii).

[163] Temp. Reg. § 1.382-2T(j)(2)(iii)(C).

[164] Temp. Reg. § 1.382-2T(j)(1)(iii).

[165] Temp. Reg. § 1.382-2T(j)(2)(vi).

[166] Temp. Reg. § 1.382-2T(k)(1)(i). *See, e.g.*, IRS Letter Ruling 200713015, December 20, 2006, and IRS Letter Ruling 9533024 (May 19, 1995) (holding that (i) an investment advisor that is considered to beneficially own stock of its clients for Schedule 13D or 13G purposes representing more than 5 percent of the issuer's stock would not be treated as the owner of the stock for Code § 382 purposes, even though it could hold and vote the stock and dispose of it for its clients, where it had no right to keep the dividends or proceeds of sale, and (ii) the debtor could rely on the absence of any filing of a Schedule 13D or 13G by any of these clients to conclude that the clients are not members of a group that constitute an "entity" for Code § 382 purposes, unless it had actual knowledge to the contrary).

or when various transactions by such owner occurred. In such situations, it will not always be clear how one is to apply the instant presumption. The IRS has acknowledged these problems and has ruled that the reference to these Schedules in the regulations should be viewed only as a rule of convenience, and that if the loss corporation has actual knowledge that the person filing the Schedule is not the owner of the stock for tax purposes, the loss corporation can disregard the Schedule's characterization of ownership.[167]

(7) A loss company may rely on a statement, expressly signed under penalties of perjury, by an officer or director of a higher tier entity, to establish the extent to which the interests of the 5 percent owners of such entity have changed during the testing period; provided, however, that the statement is not known to be false by the loss company or is not made by an entity that owns, directly or indirectly, 50 percent or more of the loss company.[168]

(8) If a 5 percent shareholder (whether or not an individual) owns less than 5 percent of the stock of a loss company during the testing period and acquired enough stock to become a 5 percent shareholder on the testing date, the loss company may treat any stock owned by such shareholder prior to that date as being owned by a public group rather than such shareholder.[169]

(9) If a 5 percent shareholder (whether or not an individual) reduces its percentage interest in the loss company below 5 percent during the testing period, the loss company may presume that the percentage owned by such shareholder, immediately after such reduction, continues to be held by that shareholder during the remainder of the testing period (unless the percentage again climbs to 5 percent or more).[170]

The presumptions described in paragraphs (1) through (4) above are subject to the following limitations:

(1) To the extent the loss company has actual knowledge of stock ownership by an individual (or entity) who actually owns directly or indirectly 5 percent of its stock, and such knowledge is obtained on the testing date (or before the tax return for the year is filed), the loss company must take such actual

---

[167] *See, e.g.,* IRS letter rulings cited in prior footnote, and IRS Letter Ruling 9104043, October 31, 1990 (Schedule 13G had been filed by an investment adviser who had power to vote and sell the stock, but no right to dividends or proceeds of sale; filing also aggregated shares owned by entities that would not be aggregated for tax purposes). Where the presumption of paragraph (6) above no longer applies, because the stock is no longer publicly traded, the continued ownership of stock of multiple owners in street name can produce great difficulty for debtors in determining who are 5 percent shareholders. For an interesting example of a procedure used by a debtor to solve this problem that met IRS approval, see IRS Letter Ruling 200622013, January 27, 2006.

[168] Temp. Reg. § 1.382-2T(k)(1)(ii).

[169] Temp. Reg. § 1.382-2T(g)(5)(A) and (j)(1)(v)(A).

[170] Temp. Reg. § 1.382-2T(g)(5)(B) and (j)(1)(v)(B). While this presumption is in effect, the shares owned by such shareholder shall be treated as owned by a public group for purposes of applying the tracing presumption described in paragraph (5) above. Id.

knowledge into account. If such knowledge is not obtained until later, the loss company *may*, but need not, take such knowledge into account for purposes of that testing date.[171]

(2) To the extent the loss company has actual knowledge of cross-ownership between members of public groups, the loss company *may*, but need not, take such actual knowledge into account.[172]

(3) The provision mandating use of actual knowledge does not apply to the presumptions permitted by (8) and (9) above.[173]

(4) If the ownership interests are structured by a shareholder for the purpose of avoiding treating a person as a 5 percent shareholder, then most of the presumptions (and some of the attribution limitations) will not apply if that would produce an ownership change.[174] The preamble to the Temporary Regulations says this will occur even if the loss company has no knowledge regarding the ownership interests involved, which is a startling statement.

The loss company has a duty to inquire as to the stock ownership of any individual who has a 5 percent or greater interest in the loss company, and of any entity above the loss company that has a 5 percent or greater interest in the next lower tier entity, and of any 5 percent shareholder who owns 5 percent or more of the loss company indirectly through any *one* higher tier entity. However, there is no duty to inquire whether the facts are consistent with the presumptions listed in paragraphs (1) through (9) above.[175]

### § 508.2.9 Treatment of Successor Corporation in Tax-Free Liquidations, Reorganizations, and Other Carryover Basis Transactions

The regulations provide that a corporation succeeding to the NOLs and built-in losses of a loss corporation is treated, as to the assets and losses inherited, as a continuation of the loss corporation.[176] Following the transaction, the stock of the successor corporation is treated as stock of the loss corporation for purposes of the ownership change rules. Thus, the NOLs and net built-in losses (and gains) of the successor corporation will be bifurcated; one representing those inherited from the loss company, and the other representing the successor's independent history. The successor must separately account for each, and each will have its own (and different) testing period, testing dates, and, possibly, ownership changes. Effective for testing dates on or after January 1, 1997, a corporation is treated as a successor not only if it succeeds to such NOLs and built-in losses in a Code § 381(a) transaction, but also ("as

---

[171] Temp. Reg. § 1.382-2T(k)(2).

[172] Id.

[173] Id.

[174] Temp. Reg. § 1.382-2T(k)(4).

[175] Temp. Reg. § 1.382-2T(k)(3). For an interesting example of procedures used by a debtor to satisfy its duty of inquiry that met with IRS approval, see IRS Letter Ruling 200622013, January 27, 2006.

[176] Temp. Reg. § 1.382-2T(f)(1)(ii), (iii), (f)(4) and (f)(5).

the context may require") if it acquires assets of another corporation in a carryover basis transaction where there is, in aggregate, a material difference between the basis and value of the acquired assets.[177]

Successors should be careful to preserve the separate identity of the inherited assets, so that they will be able to prove whether future losses (or gains) represent built-in losses or gains inherited from the loss company. If the assets are commingled and cannot be separately identified, the successor may find itself whipsawed on audit.

## *§508.3 The Continuity-of-Business-Enterprise Test*

New Code §382 abandons the change in business test of old Code §382, and substitutes the reorganization concept of continuity-of-business-enterprise (discussed at §604.3.2). Unless the loss company satisfies the continuity-of-business-enterprise test for two years after any ownership change, its annual limitation (starting back at the ownership change date) becomes zero (except for certain built-in gains and Code §338 gains, *see* §508.4 below).[178] The continuity-of-business-enterprise test will usually be easier for loss companies to satisfy than the old change-in-business test. The Conference Report specifically mentions that changes in the location of the loss company's business or the loss company's employees will no longer constitute the problem they did under old Code §382.[179] Presumably, where the loss company discontinues one of three businesses, it should now be irrelevant whether the discontinued business was the one that produced the losses.

This statutory continuity-of-business rule does not apply to ownership changes governed by Code §382(l)(5). However, the IRS has sought to engraft an attenuated form of continuity-of-business requirement on such changes, by adopting Reg. §1.269-3(d). *See* §508.5 below.

## *§508.4 The Annual Limitation on the Use of Carryovers and Built-in Losses*

For any taxable year ending after an ownership change, the amount of a loss corporation's taxable income that can be offset by a prechange loss cannot exceed the Code §382 limitation for the year.[180] In general, the "annual limitation" is the long-term tax-exempt bond rate (as prescribed by the Treasury) for the change date[181]

---

[177] Temp. Reg. §1.382-2T(f)(4) and (5).

[178] Code §382(c). This provision was addressed by the court in the *Berry Petroleum Company* case, which is discussed at §508.4.1.1 below.

[179] 1986 Act Conference Report, *supra* note 2, at II-189.

[180] *See* Code §382(a). For adjustments to Code §172(b) ("Amounts of Carryovers and Carrybacks") to reflect the application of new Code §382, *see* new Code §382(1)(2).

[181] *See* Code §382(f). The long-term tax exempt rate for the change date is the highest rate in effect for any month in the three-calendar-month period ending with the calendar month in which the change date occurs. Code §382(f)(1).

times the value of the stock of the loss corporation immediately *before* the change (and in valuing the stock of a foreign loss corporation, only items connected with a trade or business conducted in the United States are taken into account).[182] For this purpose, stock includes limited preferred stock.[183] Moreover, the Treasury may prescribe regulations treating options and the like as being stock.[184] Even though such regulations have not yet been issued, the IRS has held in a technical advice memorandum that the value of warrants for unissued stock should be treated as stock for annual limitation valuation purposes, notwithstanding the lack of regulations. The memorandum observed that the legislative history suggests that the "stock" value used for the limitation should be a surrogate for the value of the company's assets

---

[182] Code §382(b)(1). *See* Wootton, Section 382 After the Tax Reform Act of 1986, 64 Taxes 874, 882-883 (1986) (which discusses a possible mathmatical approach for approximating the purchase price of a loss company taking into account the annual limitation).

In the case of a foreign loss corporation, Code §382(e)(3) as added by TAMRA §1006(d)(17)(A), effective for any ownership change after June 10, 1987, provides that, in determining the value of the foreign company's stock, there shall be taken into account only items treated as connected with the conduct of a trade or business in the United States, unless otherwise provided in regulations. For this purpose, any equity structure shift pursuant to a plan of reorganization adopted on or before June 10, 1987, would be treated as occurring when the plan was adopted. Id. at §1006(d)(17)(B). If a foreign loss corporation (such as a foreign corporation which has a net built-in loss in its assets) had no items connected with a trade or business conducted in the United States at the time of an ownership change, this provision results in the foreign corporation having a Code §382 annual limitation of zero. *See* 1994 FSA LEXIS 159; IRS Chief Counsel Advice 200238025, September 20, 2002. This may be significant where, for example, the foreign corporation subsequently uses such assets in a U.S. trade or business or such assets are subsequently acquired by a U.S. corporation in a carryover basis transaction, such as through a tax-free liquidation into a U.S. parent corporation. Where the loss corporation is a foreign corporation, there are numerous other areas where questions arise on which there is little guidance to be found in the regulations and other authorities. For a discussion of the numerous issues involved, *see* Barry, The Foreign Aspects of Code Sec. 382: Searching for Answers in a Troubled Global Economy, 80 Taxes 153 (2002).

[183] Code §382(e)(1). It also includes stock that is treated as "not stock" for purposes of the ownership change test, as well as nonstock that is treated as "stock" for that purpose. Temp. Reg. §1.382-2T(f)(18)(ii)(C) and (iii)(C).

[184] *See* Code §382(k)(6)(B); 1986 Act Conference Report, *supra* note 2, at II-187 (express directive to Treasury "to prescribe such regulations as necessary"). The Treasury has not yet issued such regulations. In the temporary regulations it issued dealing with the option attribution rules, however, the Treasury did provide that where an option with respect to unissued or treasury stock is deemed to have been exercised under those rules, the deemed exercise "shall have no effect" on the value of the loss company for annual limitation purposes. The temporary regulations then refer to Code §382(l)(1)(B), the "anti-stuffing" rule, that applies to capital contributions made during the two years preceding the ownership change. Temp. Reg. §1.382-2T(h)(4)(vii)(C). This seems correct so far as it goes: the new money paid (in this case "deemed" paid) on exercise of the option should come within the scope of the anti-stuffing rule. However, what is left unsaid is whether the value of the option itself should be taken into account as part of the value of the loss company for annual limitation purposes. To ignore it would be contrary to the direction of the Conference Report to "prescribe such regulations as are necessary to treat warrants, options, contracts to acquire stock, convertible debt, and similar interests as stock for purposes of determining the value of the loss corporation." 1986 Act Conference Report, *supra* note 2, at II-187. This problem regarding the correct treatment of options has now apparently been resolved. *See* the technical advice memorandum cited in note 180, below. Presumably, the anti-stuffing rationale for the statement in the temporary regulations would not apply to convertible stock that is treated as an "option" under the attribution rules, once the preferred stock has been outstanding for more than the anti-stuffing look-back period. *See* §508.2.7 above.

less the value of its debt. It noted that if the warrants were cancelled, the value of the outstanding stock should increase by the value of the warrants. The memorandum concluded that "the fact that regulations have yet to be issued under section 382(k)(6)(B)(i) of the Code will not preclude the Internal Revenue Service from taking the appropriate position in this case."[185]

Where some or all of the stock or other equity instruments are not publicly traded, appraisals may be necessary to determine their value. Moreover, although prices in the public trading market may be strong evidence of value, they are not always determinative. In a technical advice memorandum,[186] the IRS has held that where the NYSE trading price per share did not include the value of control of the corporation, the Code § 382 value of the corporation's stock may be determined by other evidence and methods, since the value of the stock for this purpose is the value of *all* of the stock of the corporation, and this carries with it control of the corporation. Reiterating this view in a subsequent technical advice memorandum,[187] the IRS nevertheless stated that the use of the public trading price (the "market capitalization approach") is the appropriate starting point even where "exceptional circumstances" justify adjustments to that value for blockage discounts, control premiums and the like. The IRS rejected the taxpayer's argument that market inefficiencies would justify disregarding the public trading price of the taxpayer's stock, and expressed skepticism that it could ever be a sufficient justification. Given the statutory focus on the value of the stock "immediately before" the ownership change, the IRS also rejected the taxpayer's attempt for a year-long averaging of the market price.

If a loss company has various types of losses or tax credit carryovers, the annual limitation is absorbed by the company's tax attributes in the following order: (1) built-in capital losses; (2) prechange capital losses; (3) ordinary built-in losses; (4) other prechange losses (including NOL carryovers); (5) prechange foreign tax credits; (6) business credits; and (7) prechange minimum tax credits.[188] For this purpose, tax credits are "grossed-up" and converted to their deduction equivalent based on the effective marginal tax rate of the taxes offset by the credits.[189]

### § 508.4.1 Adjustments to Value of Loss Company

Certain adjustments must be made to the value of the loss company's stock for purposes of computing the Code § 382 limitation. These adjustments, which are described below, include modifications for stock redemptions and similar corporate contractions (sometimes even if they occur several months later), capital infusions,

---

[185] IRS Technical Advice Memorandum 9332004, April 30, 1993.

[186] Id. Conversely, quoting from the legislative history, the memorandum indicates it would be equally inappropriate to gross up the price of a small control block of shares to determine the value of all the stock, since the value of the whole includes both the high value of the control block plus the lower value of the noncontrol shares.

[187] IRS Technical Advice Memorandum 200513027, December 22, 2004.

[188] Reg. § 1.383-1(d)(2).

[189] Reg. § 1.383-1(e).

and the existence of substantial nonbusiness assets. Special rules also apply to controlled groups and foreign corporations.

**Stock redemptions and similar corporate contractions.** For purposes of the annual limitation, the value of the loss company's stock is reduced by the amount of any stock redemption (or similar corporate contraction) that occurs in connection with an ownership change,[190] even if the redemption (or similar corporate contraction, including a dividend) occurs several months later.[191] For this purpose, the concept of a "similar corporate contraction" refers to transactions that accomplish economic results similar to a redemption by the loss company. One example mentioned in the legislative history is a "bootstrap" acquisition (we might call it today a leveraged buy-out), in which aggregate corporate value is directly or indirectly reduced or burdened by debt to provide funds to the old shareholders, but where the debt, instead of being incurred by the loss company to redeem its own stock, is incurred by a parent or other affiliate to purchase loss company stock, and the loss company is directly or indirectly the source of funds for repayment of the debt.[192]

Not all leveraged acquisitions will be found to constitute a "corporate contraction." The key question is whether the loss company is expected to become directly or indirectly the source of funds for repayment of the debt. For example, in IRS Letter Ruling 200406027,[193] an acquiring company borrowed to purchase the stock of the target, and the target was made a guarantor of some of the debt. Based on the acquiring company's representation that it believed it had sufficient funds to pay the acquisition-related debt without using funds from the target, and that it had no intention to cause the target to make any dividend or loan that would reduce its net asset value below the change date value, the IRS ruled that the acquisition did not involve a corporate contraction. The IRS holding is particularly interesting in light of the plan to include the target in a consolidated group cash sweep program (though the target would receive a receivable for any cash taken from it, and the acquirer represented there was no intention to forgive any of this debt), and to consolidate the target operations with its existing operations.

---

[190] Code § 382(e)(2) and (h)(3)(A).

[191] 1986 Act Conference Report, *supra* note 2, at II-187 (Example 23; value reduced on account of redemption that took place 5½ months after ownership change since redemption was "contemplated in connection with" such ownership change); *see also* discussion of *Berry Petroleum Company* case at § 508.4.1.1. below (loans from loss company to acquiring company, subsequently recharacterized as distributions, occurred seven to 10 months after ownership change and considered to be in connection with the change).

[192] *See* 1986 Act Conference Report, *supra* note 2, at II-187; 1986 Blue Book, *supra* note 13, at 316 n.35; S. Rep. No. 445, 100th Cong., 2d Sess. 45 (1988); *see also* discussion of *Berry Petroleum Company* case at § 508.4.1.1. below. In the statute as originally enacted in 1986, coverage of contractions other than redemptions was accomplished in Code § 382(m)(4) and required regulations to implement it. A technical correction instead made it part of the basic statutory language of Code § 382(e)(2) and (h)(3)(A), effective for ownership changes occurring after June 10, 1987, without the need for regulatory implementation. TAMRA § 1006(d)(1). *See generally* Peischel, Adjustments to the Value of a Loss Corporation for Purposes of Section 382, 30 Corp. Tax'n 3 (2003).

[193] October 10, 2003.

**Capital infusions.** The value of the loss company's stock is to be reduced by the amount of capital contributions made as part of a plan to avoid the limitation.[194] The concept of "capital contribution" is to be broadly construed for this purpose, and includes assets received in Code § 351 transactions and other direct issuances of stock, and property received in tax-free reorganizations (at least if the acquired company was commonly controlled with the loss company).[195] Contributions made during the two years ending on the change date will be treated as being part of such a plan, except as provided in regulations.[196] The IRS has suggested in a Field Service Advice that if debt should be treated as becoming "stock," or if it is actually exchanged for stock, on the change date, it would be treated as a capital contribution for purposes of this rule.[197] The Conference Report states that the regulations are expected to exclude from this "anti-stuffing" rule capital contributions made when the company was formed or before the losses arose, or made to meet basic operating expenses.[198] The latter is of particular import for failing companies. Although regulations to exclude such items from the "anti-stuffing" rule have not yet been issued, the IRS, in a technical advice memorandum issued in a case involving stock issued for cash during the two-year period, has held that "the fact that regulations have yet to be issued under Section 382(l)(1)(B) of the Code will not preclude the Internal Revenue Service from applying an exception to the two-year rule in this case if it is appropriate to do so." The IRS required a specific tracing of the uses to which the cash had been put, and excepted from the two-year rule those proceeds which it considered to have been used "to continue basic operations." It held that these included working capital and payments to fund a lawsuit settlement and to collateralize letters of credit. On the other hand, it held that these did not include the current payments due on two-year-old term debt. The IRS memorandum noted that the items to which it gave favorable treatment were made "for purposes of meeting operating expenses of the corporation arising proximate in time to the time the [capital] contribution was made." But, as to those which it did not give favorable treatment, the IRS said that "in the absence of regulations, under the facts of this case, we consider a capital contribution for the repayment of debt incurred more than 21 months earlier lacks a sufficient proximity in time . . . ," notwithstanding that the money when borrowed may have been used to pay operating expenses.[199]

---

[194] Code § 382(l)(1)(A).

[195] *See* 1986 Blue Book, *supra* note 13, at 318; H. Rep. No. 426, 99th Cong., 1st Sess. 269 (1985).

[196] Code § 382(l)(1)(B).

[197] IRS Field Service Advice 199910009, December 2, 1998, *reprinted at* 1999 TNT 49-87.

[198] 1986 Act Conference Report, *supra* note 2, at II-189. In addition, regulations "may" take into account distributions made to shareholders subsequent to a capital contribution. Id. It would also seem appropriate to net distributions made before a capital contribution if made pursuant to the same plan.

[199] IRS Technical Advice Memorandum 9332004, April 30, 1993. In IRS Letter Ruling 9508035, September 30, 1994, the IRS held—on the particular facts there involved—that proceeds from public stock offerings made some ten months before an ownership change were not subject to the anti-stuffing adjustment, because (1) they were made to meet operating expenses arising proximate in time to the date of the stock offerings, and (2) the proceeds from the offerings were traceable to the payment of expenses necessary to continue basic operations. To similar effect, *see* IRS Letter Ruling

**Special Code § 382(l)(6) rule.** The regulations issued to implement the special Code § 382(l)(6) rule for determining the stock value of bankrupt companies (*see* discussion below at § 508.4.2) provide[200] that where a second ownership change occurs within two years after an ownership change to which the loss company elected to have Code § 382(l)(6) apply, the "anti-stuffing" rule will not include the increase in value from debt conversions taken into account in computing the Code § 382(l)(6) value.

**Substantial nonbusiness assets.** If the nonbusiness assets (*i.e.*, assets held for investment) of the loss company represent one-third or more of the value of its total assets immediately *after* the ownership change, the stock value is reduced by the value of the nonbusiness assets (net of a proportionate share of the company's debt).[201] While it is not completely clear, the change in the language of this rule between the original version proposed by the House of Representatives (H.R. 3838) and the adopted version suggests that cash and marketable securities held as working capital, rather than for investment, would *not* constitute "nonbusiness assets." It is hoped that this will be the interpretation ultimately adopted. Although at least one IRS letter ruling seems to take a contrary approach,[202] the Tax Court has taken a broader view, stating that "when cash and marketable securities are held as an integral part of the taxpayer's business, they will not be characterized as nonbusiness assets."[203] But the Tax Court added it believes Congress intended this test to be a fairly stringent one, more stringent, for example, than the "reasonable needs of the business" test under Code § 537. Because of this "nonbusiness asset" rule, a loss company that has received proceeds from a significant asset sale which it plans to reinvest in active business assets would be well advised to complete the reinvestment before the ownership change (or to postpone the asset sale until after the change). It is interesting to note the lack of symmetry between the nonbusiness asset rule and the continuity-of-business-enterprise rule (discussed at § 508.3). The nonbusiness asset rule punishes a company that sells as little as one-third of its assets (net of related debt) before an ownership change, whereas the continuity-of-business-enterprise rule permits a company to sell as much as two-thirds (and perhaps more) of its assets after an ownership change. The nonbusiness asset rule does not, however, apply to regulated investment companies, real estate investment trusts (REITs), or real estate

---

(Footnote Continued)

9630038, May 1, 1996; IRS Letter Ruling 9706014, November 13, 1996; IRS Letter Ruling 9835027, May 29, 1998; IRS Letter Ruling 200730003, April 27, 2007.

200 Reg. § 1.382-9(n)(2); *accord*, IRS Letter Ruling 9253026, October 2, 1992.

201 *See* Code § 382(l)(4); *see also* discussion of the *Berry Petroleum Company* case at § 508.4.1.1 below. For this purpose, the assets of a 50 percent owned (in vote or value) subsidiary are considered ratably owned by the loss corporation, and the stock and securities of such subsidiary owned by the loss corporation are disregarded. Code § 382(l)(4)(E). There is no express provision for attributing the liabilities of a 50 percent owned subsidiary, although this presumably may be implied. *See also* Peaslee & Cohen, Section 382 as Amended by the Tax Reform Act of 1986, 33 Tax Notes 849, 859 (December 1, 1986).

202 IRS Letter Ruling 9630038, May 1, 1996.

203 *Berry Petroleum Company v. Commissioner*, 104 T.C. 584, 649. This case is discussed at § 508.4.1.1 below.

mortgage investment conduits (REMICs). The legislative history adds that assets funding the reserves of an insurance company or a bank will not be considered nonbusiness assets.[204]

**Foreign corporations.** If the loss corporation is a foreign corporation, its value shall be computed by taking into account only assets and liabilities connected with the conduct of a trade or business in the United States, except as otherwise provided in regulations.[205]

**Controlled (nonconsolidated) groups.** For the special valuation rule applicable to controlled groups of corporations that do not file consolidated tax returns for the entirety of the group, *see* § 508.8 below. (Within consolidated groups, the application of Code § 382 and the determination of the annual limitation are governed by the consolidated return regulations, *see* § 508.7 below.)

### *§ 508.4.1.1 The* Berry Petroleum Company *Case*

During 1995, the Tax Court decided *Berry Petroleum Company,*[206] an important case regarding the application of Code § 382 to companies that are not in bankruptcy, with implications as well for bankrupt companies relying on Code § 382(l)(6). The court held that: (1) the target company satisfied the Code § 382 continuity-of-business test (discussed above at § 508.3) for the two years following its acquisition; (2) the computation of the downward adjustment to stock value for substantial nonbusiness assets is to be made by (a) determining the ratio of nonbusiness assets (discussed at § 508.4.1 above) immediately *after* the ownership change to determine substantiality (causing an asset that became a nonbusiness asset only because of the purchaser's plans for it to be taken into account), but then (b) by reducing stock value only for assets that were also nonbusiness assets immediately *before* the ownership change (which would not include those covered by the foregoing change in plans); and (3) the reduction in stock value for corporate contractions (discussed above at § 508.4.1) includes the amount of dividends paid by the target to the purchasing company after the acquisition, even if there is no contraction in business activities and, perhaps (though this point is only implicit in its holding and was not explicitly discussed by the court), even if the dividends are paid from nonbusiness assets for which a downward adjustment has already been made under the nonbusiness asset rule. The Tax Court's opinion was affirmed by the Ninth Circuit in a short opinion that contained little analysis but which said, "we find the well written Tax Court opinion persuasive in every respect."

---

[204] 1986 Act Conference Report, *supra* note 2, at II-190. The Tax Court opinion in *Berry Petroleum* considers this reference to be limited to "reserves required by law," 104 T.C. at 649, although the Conference Report itself does not express this limitation.

[205] Code § 382(e)(3) as added by TAMRA § 1006(d)(17)(A), effective for ownership changes after June 10, 1987. For the purpose of this effective date rule, equity structure shifts pursuant to a plan of reorganization adopted on or before June 10, 1987, are treated as occurring when the plan was adopted.

[206] 104 T.C. 584 (1995), *aff'd,* 98-1 U.S.T.C. ¶ 50,398 (9th Cir. 1998). In IRS Field Service Advice 200140049, July 6, 2001, the IRS followed *Berry Petroleum* in holding that a dividend can constitute a corporate contraction for purposes of Code § 382.

**Facts.** The facts involved in the case were as follows: Target company, T, which was in the heavy oil business, had gross assets worth about $12.6 million. About $10.6 million of this was made up of four heavy oil operating properties: property A, worth about $7.75 million; property B, worth $2 million; property C, worth $.635 million; and property D, worth $.2 million. The remaining $2 million or so of assets included a $1.588 million note receivable, payable in 15 quarterly installments.

T's owner had decided to get out of the heavy oil business. Although T's owner had received an offer from Company X to buy property A for $7.5 million, the owner believed that the other T properties really constituted net liabilities, because of the contingent environmental liabilities potentially associated with them. The owner did not want to be left with these, and so, instead of selling property A to Company X, the owner sought buyers for the stock of T.

One of these potential buyers was P. P, which had independently known about X's interest in property A, worked out an agreement with X which provided that, if P bid for and succeeded in purchasing the stock of T, X would immediately thereafter buy property A from T for cash. The cash price was to be $1.25 million above the price that P paid for the entire T stock, but not more than $7.75 million. T's owner was unaware of this agreement made between P and X.

P, having made this agreement with X, then offered to buy 100 percent of the stock of T for $6.5 million in cash. The offer was accepted by the owner. And on the same day that P purchased all of the stock of T for $6.5 million, causing T to become part of the P consolidated return group, T sold property A to X for $7.75 million in cash.

T had NOLs of $8.109 million. P and T claimed the benefit of these carryovers in the P consolidated return, valuing the stock of T at $6.5 million for purposes of computing the Code § 382 annual limitation.

Seven months after the stock purchase, T lent $1 million to P. Ten months after the stock purchase, T lent P another $2.6 million. A year after the stock purchase, P's obligation to repay these $3.6 million of loans was cancelled, as a dividend by T to P.

Shortly following the stock purchase, T made additional investments in property D, which it sold for $.2 million some two years and four months after the stock purchase. At the same time, T sold property C for $.25 million. Some three and a third years after the stock purchase, T increased its interest in property B (having earlier offered to sell it) and thereafter spent some $4 million on drilling wells and working the property.

The IRS sought to disallow all use of the T NOLs, taking the position that P had acquired T "for the purpose of dismantling it, selling off its assets, and then utilizing its tax attributes." The IRS conceded that neither Code § 269 nor the consolidated return SRLY limitation applied. Thus the only issue was how to apply Code § 382.

**Continuity-of-business-enterprise.** The IRS argued that T had failed to satisfy Code § 382's continuity-of-business-enterprise requirement. Code § 382(c) provides that, unless the loss company satisfies the Code § 382 continuity-of-business-enterprise test for two years following the ownership change, the Code § 382 annual limitation becomes zero (except for certain built-in gains and Code § 338 gains), retroactively back to the ownership change date. The continuity-of-business-enterprise test that applies for Code § 382 purposes is the same one that applies for Code § 368 reorganization purposes.

The IRS contended that T had failed to satisfy this requirement for the two years following the ownership change, since T had sold its largest operating asset immediately following the ownership change, and during the two years following the ownership change had presumably formed an intention to sell its other operating properties.

The Tax Court held that these facts did not cause T to fail the continuity-of-business test. As for whether T had formed an intention during the two years following the ownership change to sell properties B, C and D, the court said this was irrelevant. What actually happened during those two years, and not what might have happened, is what matters for purposes of the continuity-of-business test. T had continued to hold and operate properties B, C and D throughout the two-year period, and the court held this was sufficient to cause T to satisfy the continuity-of-business test. The reader will note that at the time of the ownership change, properties B, C and D represented only about 22.4 percent of T's gross assets (and perhaps none of its net value, after taking into account the potential contingent liabilities). This is considerably below the one-third level used in Example 1 in Reg. § 1.368-1(d)(5). The opinion does not discuss this point. Instead, it simply emphasizes that P and S were in the same line of business, which Reg. § 1.368-1(d)(3) says has special (although not determinative) significance. Moreover, although the opinion said in a footnote that, following the two-year period, T invested more money in property B, the opinion nowhere suggests that any of the cash held by T during the two-year period constituted an asset that could be counted toward satisfaction of the continuity-of-business-enterprise test.

**Nonbusiness asset adjustment.** The second issue raised by the IRS was the adjustment contained in Code § 382(l)(4), which provides that if a loss corporation has substantial nonbusiness assets, the value of its stock, for purposes of computing the Code § 382 annual limitation, shall be reduced by the amount of these assets. The statutory language refers, in a potentially confusing way, to both the old and the new loss corporation. It reads as follows:

> Sec. 382(l). Certain Additional Operating Rules.—For purposes of this section—
>
> * * *
>
> (4) Reduction in Value Where Substantial Nonbusiness Assets.—
>
> (A) In General.—If, immediately after an ownership change, the *new* loss corporation has *substantial* nonbusiness assets, the value of the *old* loss corporation shall be reduced by the excess (if any) of
>
> (i) the fair market value of the nonbusiness assets of the *old* loss corporation, over
>
> (ii) the nonbusiness asset share of indebtedness for which such corporation is liable.
>
> (B) Corporation Having Substantial Nonbusiness Assets.—For purposes of subparagraph (A)—

> (i) In General.—The *old* loss corporation shall be treated as having substantial nonbusiness assets if at least 1/3 of the value of the total assets of such corporation consists of nonbusiness assets.
>
> * * *
>
> (C) Nonbusiness Assets.—For the purposes of this paragraph, the term "nonbusiness assets" means assets held for investment. [Emphasis added.]

The Tax Court described the purpose of this adjustment for nonbusiness assets as follows:

> To discourage "stuffing" a loss corporation with liquid assets or liquidating its active business assets before an ownership change, the value of the *old* loss corporation is reduced by the value of its nonbusiness assets (adjusted for their share of indebtedness), but only if the *new* loss corporation has substantial nonbusiness assets immediately after the ownership change.

The Tax Court found that the only nonbusiness asset held by T immediately before the ownership change (*i.e.*, T as the *old* loss company) was the $1.588 million note receivable. The court concluded that this note continued to be a nonbusiness asset immediately after the ownership change (*i.e.*, in the hands of T as the "new" loss corporation.) In addition, the court found that because of the agreement between T and X, property A, although a business asset in the hands of the "old" loss corporation, became a nonbusiness asset in the hands of the "new" loss corporation. This means that although the nonbusiness assets of the "old" loss corporation were only some 12 percent of its total gross assets, the nonbusiness assets of the "new" loss corporation were some 74 percent of its total assets.

The Tax Court struggled with three legal questions presented by these facts. First, does one determine the "substantiality" of the nonbusiness assets by looking only to the ratio of those assets in the hands of the "old" loss corporation? Or does one instead look only to the ratio of nonbusiness assets in the hands of the "new" loss corporation? Or do both tests have to be satisfied? Further, when one looks to the assets of the "new" loss corporation, does the one-third test govern what constitutes the "substantiality" of its nonbusiness assets, or does that test have a less precise and more general meaning? On the facts of *Berry*, these questions arise because, as the reader will recall from the statutory language quoted above, the statute defines the "substantiality" of assets (*i.e.*, the one-third rule) only by reference to the "old" loss corporation; yet it also says that the adjustment shall be made only if the "new" loss corporation has "substantial nonbusiness assets."

Second, if one determines that the "substantiality" standard has been met (under whatever of the above interpretations applies), is the downward adjustment to be limited to the amount of the assets that were nonbusiness assets in the hands of the "old" loss corporation, or may it include other assets, like property A, that became nonbusiness assets only in the hands of the "new" loss corporation? The reader will recall that the statute expresses this reduction as being made to the value of the "old" loss corporation by the amount of the nonbusiness assets of the "old" loss corporation, and no reference is made in the statute in this regard to the "new" loss corporation.

Third, there is a question of the extent to which working capital and the like should be treated as a "business" rather than a "nonbusiness" asset. The reader will recall that the statute simply defines "nonbusiness assets" as meaning "assets held for investment."

On the first question, the court decided that the substantiality ratio should be computed by looking only to the proportion of the "new" corporation's nonbusiness assets. Thus, T as the "new" loss corporation had substantial nonbusiness assets (because property A was included in this computation for T as the "new" loss corporation), even though T as the "old" loss corporation did not have substantial nonbusiness assets (because property A could *not* be included in this computation for T as the "old" loss corporation). In determining the "substantiality" of the nonbusiness assets of the "new" loss corporation, the Tax Court's opinion seems to suggest that the one-third test (which is explicitly contained in the statute only for the "old" loss corporation) should be applied.[207] The Ninth Circuit opinion takes the opposite approach, saying that "the test is 'substantial' for the new loss corporation, *not* 1/3." [Emphasis added]. The Ninth Circuit's approach reads Code § 382(1)(4)(B)(i) entirely out of the statute, which violates the most fundamental canon of statutory construction. Moreover, the legislative history makes clear that satisfaction of the one-third test is a condition precedent to application of the reduction for nonbusiness assets. For example, the Conference Committee Report describes the provision by saying "*If* at least one-third of the fair market value of a corporation's assets consists of nonbusiness assets, the value of the loss corporation, for purposes of determining the section 382 limitation, is reduced by the excess of the value of the nonbusiness assets over the portion of the corporation's indebtedness attributable to such assets." [Emphasis added.][208]

As to the second question, on the other hand, the court concluded that the downward adjustment in the value of the T stock for nonbusiness assets had to be limited to the amount of the assets that were nonbusiness assets in the hands of the "old" loss corporation (*i.e.*, in the case of T, they had to be limited to $1.520 million, which represented the $1.588 million note receivable less the indebtedness of T allocable to it).

Finally, as to the third question, although the court noted that (as the legislative history stated) cash and marketable securities held as an integral part of the taxpayer's business will not be characterized as nonbusiness assets, it added that because the examples in the legislative history referred only to reserves of banks and insurance companies, which the court (though not the legislative history) described

---

[207] The Tax Court opinion is less than clear on this point, simply stating that "In addition, 'substantial nonbusiness assets' of the *new* loss corporation is defined by reference to the nonbusiness assets of the *old* loss corporation. Sec. 382(1)(4)(B)(i)." This reference to the one-third Code provision seems to suggest that the one-third test is being applied to determine substantiality for the "new" loss corporation as well.

[208] 1986 Act Conference Report, *supra* note 2, at II-190.

as reserves required by law, a fairly stringent test of what constitutes such need should be applied. The court refused to treat any of T's cash from the sale of property A or of the $1.588 million note receivable as a business asset.

The court, in reaching its conclusion as to the first question, was strongly influenced by a feeling that the result in the case should not depend on whether the decision to make property A an investment asset had been made by the buyer of T rather than by the seller of T. The court said, "We see no practical difference between a corporation's acquiring a corporation that has converted its business assets to investment assets before being sold, and an acquiring corporation's obligating itself, before it contracts to purchase the acquired corporation, to convert those business assets to investment assets immediately after it acquires control of them."

Yet, because the court decided, in answering the second question, that the downward adjustment had to be limited to the amount of assets that were "nonbusiness" assets in the hands of the "old" loss corporation, the court did *not* treat the two situations identically. Had property A been a nonbusiness asset in the hands of the "old" loss corporation, the downward adjustment would have been over $9 million, not the $1.520 million required by the court.

The court's holdings on these two points raise some troubling questions. For example, if "old" T had *no* nonbusiness assets, but "new" T had very substantial nonbusiness assets, no downward adjustment for nonbusiness assets could be made under the court's holding. To us, this suggests that Congress could not have meant that the ratio of nonbusiness assets held by the "old" loss corporation should be ignored and the ratio for the "new" loss corporation should be given the primary significance that the court gave it. As another example, suppose P's acquisition of T had taken the form of a tax-free merger of T into P; that property A remained a business asset in the hands of the combined corporations; but that P held other investment assets (ones that had never been owned by T) that caused the ratio of "nonbusiness" assets held by P immediately after the merger to exceed the one-third substantiality level. Should these unrelated assets held by P result in a downward adjustment, even though the assets that came from T did not themselves meet the substantiality ratio in the hands of either the "old" loss corporation or the "new" loss corporation? We think not.[209]

We disagree with the court's holding as to the first question. We submit that what Congress had in mind was that one should determine the "substantiality" of the nonbusiness assets by looking primarily to the ratio of such assets in the hands of the "old" loss corporation, just as the statute says; and that then one would reduce the stock value only to the extent that those same assets were still held by T an instant later in its capacity as the "new" loss corporation. As applied to the facts in the *Berry* case, this would mean that no adjustment would be made, because the substantiality test would not have been satisfied in the hands of the "old" loss corporation.

Even this interpretation leaves a further question to be addressed. Suppose the facts in the *Berry* case had been that it was the *seller* of T that had intended to convert

---

[209] In fact, we believe that Reg. §§1.382-9(k)(5) and (l)(5), mentioned later in the text, confirm this result.

property A to a nonbusiness asset, but that P's intention was to the contrary. Thus, property A would perhaps have been a nonbusiness asset in the hands of T as the "old" loss corporation, but not in the hands of T as the "new" loss corporation. Here, the "substantiality" ratio would have been met by the "old" loss corporation but not by the "new" loss corporation. We think it would be entirely inappropriate to include the value of property A in the downward adjustment, since it was not a nonbusiness asset in hands of the "new" loss corporation. On this point, we would agree with the Tax Court that P's intention should be taken into account.

Accordingly, we submit that the statutory language should be interpreted to mean that either (i) the substantiality ratio must be met by *both* the "old" and the "new" loss corporation, or (ii) the substantiality ratio is to be computed only by looking to the nonbusiness assets of the "old" loss corporation, and if the required threshold is met, one reduces the stock value only for the nonbusiness assets of the "old" corporation that remain nonbusiness assets in the hands of the "new" loss corporation.

One other point should be mentioned. The Tax Court said that there were no existing or proposed regulations that gave guidance on these questions. The court apparently, however, overlooked the regulations that govern this adjustment in Code § 382(l)(6) cases. These are Reg. § § 1.382-9(k)(5) and (l)(5). Both say that:

> If immediately *after* the ownership change, the loss corporation has *substantial nonbusiness assets (as determined under section 382(l)(4)(B) taking into account only those assets the loss corporation held immediately before the ownership change)*, the value of the loss corporation's prechange assets is reduced by the value of the nonbusiness assets . . . . (Emphasis added.)

For purposes of computing the substantiality test, this language seems to refer only to assets held by the "old" loss corporation, and, by the way it refers to Code § 382(l)(4), seems for purposes of this test to look to their character only in the hands of that corporation. The reference to "immediately after the ownership change" can be read to suggest that these assets must remain nonbusiness assets in the hands of the "new" loss corporation. We submit that this regulation language supports our interpretation of the statutory language.[210]

Some might argue that our proposed interpretation of the statute fails to adequately address the situation where the shift from business to nonbusiness intent is made by the buyer rather than the seller (*i.e.*, the situation in the *Berry* case). We believe the nonbusiness asset test was not designed to deal with that situation. That does not mean that this situation is left unaddressed by the statute. The continuity-of-

---

[210] These two sections from the regulations show how to draw the distinction between pre-change and post-change determinations. The first of these two sections goes on to say that the adjustment for the nonbusiness assets' share of the loss corporation's indebtedness is to be "determined under section 382(l)(4)(D) taking into account the loss corporation's assets and liabilities immediately *after* the ownership change." (Emphasis added.) The second of these sections goes on to say that "the value of the loss corporation's *pre-change* assets is reduced by the value of the nonbusiness assets." (Emphasis added.)

business test and the corporate-contraction test are the provisions designed to deal with that situation.

So long as the *Berry* opinion stands, the practitioner must deal with it. In this respect, we should note that the court, in deciding what is a nonbusiness asset "immediately after" the ownership change, applied a Code § 351 meaning to the phrase "immediately after." This suggests that had P delayed, until even a short time after the ownership change, to make its decision to turn property A into a nonbusiness asset, property A would not have been treated by the court as a nonbusiness asset in the hands of either "new" or "old" T, and thus no downward adjustment to the value of T's stock for nonbusiness assets would have been required. That the court's interpretation would cause such a sharp change in result to occur, simply because of such a modest difference in the time at which P's intention is formed, seems to us to add another reason for preferring our interpretation to that of the court.

As to the Tax Court's suggestion that a rather "stringent" test should be applied in determining whether working capital constitutes a business asset, the court added that its "more stringent test is tempered by a relatively high ceiling of allowable nonbusiness assets (one-third of gross assets) before sec. 382(l)(4) will be triggered. This ceiling effectively exempts reasonable amounts of working capital." The court's reasoning on this point seems flawed. If a company's nonbusiness assets, other than working capital, are sufficiently large by themselves to require an adjustment in stock value, then, if working capital is generally to be treated as a nonbusiness asset, none of the working capital would be sheltered by this one-third test, and such working capital would increase the downward adjustment. Moreover, the court's statement that the legislative history refers only to reserves required by law goes too far: the legislative history does not say that the reserves it mentions are limited to those required by law.

Happily, the court's statements on the working capital point seem to be *dictum*. The only consequence of them was to reject P's argument that some part of the property A sale proceeds should be treated as working capital devoted to the business. But the court noted that P did not supply any factual evidence to support its position, and except for the loans made by T to P, most of these sale proceeds were simply kept invested in short-term securities.

**Corporate contraction.** As the Tax Court observed, the downward adjustment to stock value for corporate contractions connected with the ownership change applies whether the contraction occurs before or after the ownership change, and it does not seem relevant whether the contraction takes the form of a redemption or a dividend. Moreover, as the court noted, there is no requirement that there also be a contraction in the business activity of T.

The key question is whether the contraction is "connected" with the ownership change. Here, the court found that the only reason P needed to obtain cash from T was the drain on P's cash position caused by its purchase of the T stock.

We are puzzled, however, by the court's failure to examine the potential overlap between its downward adjustment for nonbusiness assets and its downward adjustment for the corporate contraction. It will be remembered that the $1.588 million note held by T was payable in quarterly installments. On the theory that money is fungible (a concept the court itself espoused), some of the cash advances that were made by T to P should be considered to have come from the proceeds from that loan. This raises the question whether an item, like the $1.588 million note, that causes a downward adjustment under the nonbusiness asset rule, can also result in a second downward adjustment under the corporate contraction rule if that item is used to make the contraction. We submit that the answer to this question should be no. Such double counting for the same asset should not be permitted.[211]

Of course, the court may have been thinking that if the seller had taken the $1.588 million note out of the company before selling the stock to P, there nonetheless could have been a downward adjustment for the full $3.625 million contraction. The court did not discuss this point. However, had the $1.588 million note not been held by T, P's purchase price would presumably have been reduced, and P may not have had so great a need to obtain cash from T. Thus, the corporate contraction might have been smaller. In short, the money-is-fungible concept should have been applied.

### § 508.4.2 Special Valuation Rule for Companies in Bankruptcy

For companies in a title 11 or similar case, the foregoing rules for valuing the stock of the company (discussed in § 508.4.1) are subject to an important, liberalizing modification. This is contained in Code § 382(l)(6), which applies if the company has elected not to apply a second special liberalizing rule available only to companies in a title 11 or similar case, namely the rule found in Code § 382(l)(5) (discussed below at § 508.5). Code § 382(l)(6), which is available only to companies in a title 11 or similar case,[212] provides that in the case of an ownership change resulting from a "G" reorganization or a stock-for-debt exchange in a title 11 or similar case, the value of the company for the purpose of computing the annual limitation shall reflect the increase in value (if any) resulting from any debt reduction occurring in the transaction.[213] Subsequently issued regulations (discussed below) apply this value enhancement within certain limits whenever an ownership change occurs pursuant to a court

---

[211] Of course, in a sense, the court's opinion even double counts property A, because it takes property A into account for purposes of satisfying the nonbusiness asset substantiality test, and then again because it was the source of the cash for the corporate contraction. The legislative history contains a passage, we believe, that supports our view that none of the adjustments to stock value should be applied in a way that produces double counting. This is a sentence contained in the House Conference Report 99-841, at page II-189 (1986), which says, in connection with the reduction for capital contributions, that "the regulations may take into account, under appropriate circumstances, the existence of substantial nonbusiness assets on the change date . . . and distributions made to shareholders subsequent to capital contributions, as offsets to such contributions."

[212] A "title 11 or similar case" means a case under the Bankruptcy Code or "a receivership, foreclosure, or similar proceeding in Federal or State Court." Code § 368(a)(3)(A). This reference to State proceedings would include, for example, proceedings authorized by Del. Gen. Corp. Law §§ 102(b)(2), 302. Such provisions, where they apply, may prove more efficient than the use of title 11. Note that the "similar case" concept, which applies for "G" reorganization and Code §§ 382(l)(5) and 382(l)(6) purposes, is broader than the bankruptcy rule available for § 108 COD treatment, which applies only to companies in a title 11 case. *See* Code §§ 108(a)(1)(A), 108(d)(2).

[213] Code § 382(l)(6), clarified by TAMRA § 1006(d)(9). In IRS Letter Ruling 8849061, September 15, 1988, the IRS did not give credit for the increased value where the debt was exchanged for stock of the bankrupt's parent and the parent was not in bankruptcy.

approved plan or transaction in a title 11 or similar case, *regardless* of whether there is "G" reorganization or stock-for-debt exchange.

The IRS had early on ruled that the benefit of Code § 382(l)(6) applies even where the creditors receiving the stock will be obligated to sell it for cash to a third party; and that stock will be treated for this purpose as though it had been issued to creditors, where it was sold for cash to third parties and the cash was distributed to the creditors.[214]

In August 1992, the IRS issued proposed regulations regarding the determination of value for purposes of Code § 382(l)(6). These were made final in 1994.[215] These confirm that stock issued for cash that is then used to pay creditors is included in this value (the preamble to the proposed regulation states that such stock issued for cash does not, however, qualify for the then applicable, but since repealed, stock-for-debt exception to COD income), and, as discussed in the example below, the regulations go even further. They also hold that stock for this purpose includes limited preferred stock and stock that is treated as "not stock," but excludes nonstock that is treated as "stock" for ownership change purposes.

The regulation also modifies the definition of the value of the stock of the company (described in § 508.4.1 above) in other ways. It defines the value of the stock immediately after the ownership change (for § 382(l)(6) purposes) as being the lesser of (1) the value of the stock of the company immediately *after* the change (the stock test), or (2) the value of the company's assets (determined without regard to liabilities) immediately *before* the ownership change (the asset test).

The reason for the asset test is to filter out increases in stock that did not result from conversions of debt to stock. In valuing the company's pre-change assets for purposes of the asset test, the preamble to the final regulations makes clear that one is not limited to using the so-called "liquidation value" of the assets. Nor is one limited to tangible assets: if the loss corporation is able to establish the existence and value of any intangible asset, including goodwill or going concern value, that value may be taken into account.

For purposes of the stock portion of this two-part test, the regulation states that the value of stock issued in connection with the ownership change may not exceed the value of any property (including debt of the loss company) received by the loss company for the stock. This eliminates any additional intrinsic value that the stock might have because of the completion of the debt restructuring. There is also a special anti-abuse rule which provides that the value of stock does not include stock issued with a principal purpose of increasing the section 382 limitation "without subjecting the investment to the entrepreneurial risks of corporate business operations." The meaning of this rule is not explained, and it is unclear whether the IRS might seek to apply it to limited preferred stock issued in the restructuring. Consequently, if

---

[214] IRS Letter Ruling 9137041, June 18, 1991, restating IRS Letter Ruling 9130044, August 19, 1990; IRS Letter Ruling 9231036, April 30, 1992. A sale of stock for cash that is then used to pay creditors will not, however, qualify for the stock-for-debt exception to COD income. *See* § 504A.3 above.

[215] Reg. § 1.382-9(i), (j), (k), (l), (m)(2), (n), and (p).

limited preferred stock is issued in the restructuring it would be important for the loss company to document the business purpose for its use.

Significantly, the regulations provide that the general "anti-stuffing" rules discussed in the preceding section do *not* apply in computing the *stock* test, but do apply in computing the asset test (and for this purpose they even include certain contributions made in exchange for debt). Conversely, the adjustments to value in the case of certain corporate contractions (also discussed in the preceding section) do *not* apply in computing the *asset* test, but do apply for purposes of the stock test (but only if the contractions occurred after and in connection with the ownership change). Finally, the adjustment to value for substantial nonbusiness assets applies for purposes of *both* the stock and asset value tests. For this purpose, whether nonbusiness assets are substantial is determined by taking into account only assets held immediately before the ownership change, and in computing the stock (but not the asset) test, one adjusts this downward for the portion of the corporation's debt that is allocable to the nonbusiness assets (taking into account only assets and liabilities immediately after the ownership change).[216]

**EXAMPLE**

Bankrupt company has $700,000 of gross assets and $1 million of debt. Pursuant to a confirmed Chapter 11 plan, a new investor contributes $650,000 of cash to the company in exchange for 100 percent of the common stock (all existing common stock is cancelled), and the old debt is exchanged for $400,000 of new debt and $300,000 in cash. Thus, the value of the company immediately after the ownership change is $650,000. Because the "anti-stuffing" rule does not apply for purposes of the stock test, the full $650,000 is taken into account for this purpose. In addition, such value is less than the company's prechange asset value of $700,000, as computed under the asset test. Accordingly, the value of the company for purposes of computing the Code § 382(l)(6) annual limitation is $650,000—*i.e.*, the lesser of $650,000 (the stock value under the stock test) and $700,000 (the prechange asset value under the asset test).[217]

---

[216] In addition, if a loss corporation is a foreign corporation, only those items treated as connected with the conduct of a trade or business in the United States are taken into account for purposes of applying the stock and assets rules.

[217] The interpretation that the Tax Court gave in the *Berry Petroleum Company* case to the adjustment for nonbusiness assets (which is discussed above at § 508.4.1.1) would require one to determine whether some or all of the $650,000 in cash was a nonbusiness asset, even though it is an asset only of the "new" loss corporation and not of the "old" loss corporation. A downward nonbusiness asset adjustment might then be required if the "old" loss corporation had also held nonbusiness assets of any amount. However, as discussed at § 508.4.1.1, we believe that such an interpretation would be contrary to Reg. § 1.382-9(l)(5) and (k)(5), and also contrary to the meaning of the statute. As suggested at § 508.4.1.1, we believe that for purposes of the nonbusiness asset test, one should ignore a nonbusiness asset held by the "new" loss corporation if it was not also a nonbusiness asset held by the "old" loss corporation.

Thus, even though only $300,000 of the $650,000 of cash contributed by the new investor effectively was distributed to creditors, the entire amount was permitted to be taken into account. This appears to reflect a policy determination that the above transaction should be treated no differently than if the creditors had been paid out 100 percent in cash, and the company obtained new third party financing. In essence, the creditors have agreed to finance the reorganized company.

The regulation provides that the election to apply Code § 382(l)(6) rather than Code § 382(l)(5) must be made by the loss company on a timely filed (including extensions) tax return for the year that includes the change date and that the election is irrevocable.

The final regulation applies to ownership changes occurring on or after March 17, 1994. However, the loss company can elect, on its first tax return filed after May 16, 1994, to apply the provisions of the final regulations to prior ownership changes. This retroactive application can be used even to change an earlier decision to apply Code § 382(l)(5) rather than Code § 382(l)(6) to the pre-March 17, 1994 ownership change.

### § 508.4.3 Adjustments to Annual Limitation; Built-in Gains and Losses and Depreciation

The annual limitation is zero, rather than the number produced by the tax-exempt bond rate formula, if the loss corporation fails to satisfy the continuity-of-business-enterprise test for two years after the ownership change (*see* § 508.3). Whether the formula rate or the zero rate is applicable, however, the annual limitation is increased by

(1) built-in gains recognized during the five years beginning on the ownership change date (the five-year period is extended for certain installment sales[218]), but only for the year in which recognized and only if the net built-in gains at the change date are more than the applicable *de minimis* threshold;[219] and

---

[218] Notice 90-27, 1990-1 C.B. 336, says that where a built-in gain asset is sold before or during the five-year recognition period and, by use of the Code § 453 installment method, the gain is not recognized until after expiration of the period, regulations will be issued to extend the recognition period with respect to that until it is recognized. The regulations will apply the same treatment where the first step in the transaction is a transfer of the assets to an affiliate, causing the gain to become a deferred intercompany gain under the consolidated return regulations, and the second step is an installment sale by the affiliate *before* the end of the 5-year recognition period. The regulations will be effective for installment sales occurring on or after March 26, 1990.

[219] For a discussion of issues relating to the determination of built-in gains and losses, *see* Brock, The Forthcoming Built-In Regulations: Issues for the Government to Address, 95 Tax Notes 97 (April 1, 2002); Los Angeles County Bar Association, Taxation Section, Corporate Tax Committee, Recommendations for Regulations to be Promulgated Under Section 382(h)(6), 2003 TNT 94-130 (May 15, 2003).

(2) the amount of any Code § 338 gain (to the extent such gain is not taken into account in computing recognized built-in gains for such year), but only for the year in which recognized.[220]

This latter provision, as originally adopted in the 1986 Act, would have had the curious result of limiting the adjustment for Code § 338 gain to the portion of that gain that arose between the date of the ownership change and the date of the Code § 338 asset "sale." Such a difference in dates could only occur, of course, in the case of a creeping qualified stock purchase in which the acquisition of more than 50 percent of the stock occurred before the acquisition of the remainder of the 80 percent required to complete a qualified stock purchase. The built-in gain that existed at the date of the ownership change would have increased the Code § 382 limitation only if it satisfied the *de minimis* threshold that generally applies under the built-in gain rule. This result when applied to a Code § 338 event seemed inappropriate, since NOLs do not survive such an event and the event is, in essence, an asset purchase. Fortunately, this result was changed by a technical correction which, in the case of a Code § 338 election, increased the Code § 382 limitation by the lesser of the amount of the Code § 338 gain or the net built-in gain (computed without regard to the *de minimis* threshold).[221]

Built-in losses recognized during the five-year period beginning on the change date are subject to the annual limitation in the same way as are NOLs,[222] provided net built-in losses at the change date exceeded the same *de minimis* threshold as for built-in gains.[223] The legislative history also indicates that built-in losses that exceed the *de*

---

220 Code § 382(h)(1)(C).

221 TAMRA § 1006(d)(3)(A).

222 The inclusion of the change date in the statutory definition of the "recognition period" can create a problem where a deduction on the change date creates an NOL that will be carried forward. If this NOL is subject to the Code § 382 limitation, treating this same deduction as a built-in loss item could produce a double disallowance of deductions. Fortunately, the IRS has ruled that such a deduction will not be treated as a built-in loss, and will not be taken into account in computing net built-in gain or loss. IRS Letter Ruling 200442011, October 23, 2003.

223 *See* Code § 382(h). For purposes of determining the *de minimis* threshold for net built-in losses, however, if 80 percent or more of the value of a loss company's stock is acquired in a single transaction (or in a series of related transactions during any 12-month period), the value of the assets of the loss company shall not exceed the grossed-up amount paid for such stock properly adjusted for debt of the company and other relevant items (*i.e.*, essentially a Code § 338 type computation). Code § 382(h)(8). The IRS has held that for purposes of this section: (i) stock is not acquired for this purpose to the extent it is exchanged for loss corporation stock of the same value; (ii) stock received in exchange for debt of the loss corporation is to be deemed acquired; (iii) stock acquired in a Code § 1032 transaction is to be treated as acquired for this purpose; (iv) stock acquired pursuant to the exercise of rights is to be deemed acquired only to the extent of the cash paid upon exercise of the rights (stock acquired equal to the value of the rights themselves is not treated as acquired); and (v) warrants are not to be treated as stock for purposes of this section. IRS Field Service Advice 199914002, December 4, 1998, *reprinted at* 1999 TNT 69-77. In IRS Field Service Advice 1997-42, November 21, 1997, *reprinted at* 2000 TNT 170-27, X purchased all of the stock of target, which had no NOLs, and shortly thereafter wrote down a number of its assets. For purposes of determining whether target had a net built-in loss on the date of the purchase, the IRS held that the write-downs should be taken into account in valuing the target's assets at the date of the change. However, since the price paid for the stock plus the amount of target's debt at the date of change exceeded the book value of its assets, target obviously had goodwill that was not reflected on its books. This goodwill

*minimis* threshold cannot be carried back to prior years (presumably, this means prior, postchange years).[224]

It should be noted that the net built-in loss rule applies only to the amount of the net (not necessarily the gross) loss. To illustrate, assume that the loss company has built-in gains of 100x and built-in losses of 150x, giving it a net built-in loss of 50x. If the 50x exceeds the threshold and is thus subject to the net built-in loss limitation, it is only the first 50x of the 150x built-in loss recognized that is subject to this limitation. The limitation does not apply to the remaining 100x of built-in loss.

As originally adopted in the 1986 Act, the *de minimis* threshold for net unrealized built-in gains or losses was 25 percent of the value of the company's assets. Section 7205 of the 1989 Act changed the threshold to the *lesser* of (1) 15 percent of the value of the company's assets or (2) $10 million.[225]

For purposes of both the old and new *de minimis* tests, assets are generally computed without taking into account cash, cash items, or marketable securities having a value close to basis.[226] The legislative history to TAMRA indicates that accounts receivable are to be treated as cash items, but that regulations (which are to be prospective only) may exclude from cash and cash items accounts receivable acquired in the ordinary course of business.[227] Regulations are also expected to permit marketable securities to be taken into account in determining whether the threshold has been met in appropriate cases, such as for investment companies, REITs, and REMICs.[228] Presumably, such treatment should also apply to broker-dealers, insurance companies, and banks.[229]

---

(Footnote Continued)

needed to be taken into account in determining whether target had a net built-in loss at the date of the change, and after taking it into account, the IRS found that there was no net built-in loss on the change date.

For a discussion of issues involved in determining built-in gains and losses for purposes of Code § 382(h), *see* Brock, *supra* note 219.

224 1986 Act Conference Report, *supra* note 2, at II-191.

225 The change made by the 1989 Act applies to ownership changes and acquisitions of stock after July 10, 1989. However, it does not apply (1) to any ownership changes *or* acquisitions pursuant to a written binding contract in effect on October 2, 1989 and at all times thereafter before such change or acquisition, (2) in the case of a "G" reorganization, or an exchange of debt for stock in a title 11 or similar case, to any ownership change resulting from such reorganization or proceeding if a petition was filed before October 3, 1989, or (3) to any built-in loss of a subsidiary in an affiliated group on October 2, 1989, where the common parent on that date was subject to a title 11 or similar case, but only if the ownership change or acquisition is pursuant to the plan approved in such proceeding and occurs before two years after the date the petition commencing the proceeding was filed.

226 *See* Code § 382(h)(3)(B)(ii).

227 S. Rep. No. 445, 100th Cong., 2d Sess. 49 (1988); H.R. Conf. Rep. No. 1104, 100th Cong., 2d Sess. 8 (1988).

228 S. Rep. No. 445, 100th Cong., 2d Sess. 49 (1988).

229 *Cf.* Rev. Rul. 88-65, 1988-2 C.B. 32 (rents from the active leasing of automobiles not treated as passive income for purposes of Code § 165(g)(3)(B)); IRS Letter Ruling 9218038, January 29, 1992 (similar holding with respect to interest income of thrift institutions). *See also* Technical Advice Memorandum 9538005, Sept. 22, 1995, holding that dividends, interest, and gains from securities realized by an insurance company would not be treated as interest, dividends, and gains from securities for purposes of applying Code § 165(g), which was revoked by Technical Advice Memorandum 9817002, January 5, 1998.

Assets, for purposes of applying the *de minimis* test, mean gross assets, rather than assets net of liabilities. However, redemptions or other corporate contractions occurring in connection with an ownership change may be treated as reducing the value of the company's assets for this purpose.[230] As originally adopted in 1986, Code § 382 said that redemptions were to be taken into account for this purpose. For example, if in connection with an ownership change a portion of the stock of the loss company is subsequently redeemed for a $100 note bearing adequate interest, the value of the loss company's assets at the change date would be reduced by $100 for purposes of determining the *de minimis* threshold. (If cash were used for the redemption, it is unclear whether the result should be the same, since cash is not generally taken into account for purposes of the threshold.) TAMRA made two changes in the provision. First, it extended the concept to include not only redemptions, but also other corporate contractions, although only for ownership changes occurring after June 10, 1987.[231] Second, for ownership changes on or after June 21, 1988, it provided that redemptions or other corporate transactions would be taken into account for *de minimis* threshold purposes only to the extent provided in regulations.[232] The latter change was made because Congress feared that such transactions might be used to manipulate the threshold.[233]

As originally enacted in 1986, new Code § 382 provided that built-in losses do *not* include depreciation, but may, if regulations so provide, include certain accrued expenses.[234] The Revenue Act of 1987 added depreciation, amortization and depletion deductions (to the extent they are built-in deductions, that is, deductions attributable to the asset's built-in loss on the change date) to the built-in loss concept, effective for ownership changes occurring after December 15, 1987.[235]

TAMRA retroactively eliminated the requirement for regulations to be issued before accrued expenses are to be treated as built-in losses.[236] Such accrued expenses include deductions deferred under Code § 267 or Code § 465.[237] TAMRA also retroactively provided that built-in gains include income items taken into account during the recognition period but attributable to periods before the change date.[238] Examples include accounts receivable of a cash basis taxpayer, gain on completion of a long-term contract reported on the completed contract method but attributable to periods before the change date, and Code § 481 adjustments, as where the loss corporation is required to change to the accrual method.[239]

---

230 Code § 382(h)(3)(A)(ii).

231 TAMRA § 1006(d)(1)(B)(i)-(ii).

232 TAMRA § 1006(d)(28)(A).

233 S. Rep. No. 445, 100th Cong., 2d Sess. 48 (1988).

234 *See* Code § 382(h)(6); 1986 Act Conference Report, *supra* note 2, at II-191.

235 Revenue Act of 1987, Pub. L. No. 100-203, § 10225(b).

236 TAMRA § 1006(d)(22).

237 1986 Act Conference Report, *supra* note 2, at II-191.

238 TAMRA § 1006(d)(22).

239 S. Rep. No. 445, 100th Cong., 2d Sess. 48-49 (1988). FDIC assistance payments received after the ownership change of a bank were considered "built-in gains" to the extent they were taxable to the

As mentioned above, built-in gains can be taken into account for this purpose only when they are "recognized." An interesting question regarding the treatment of prepaid items for built-in gain purposes can be found in a ruling[240] that involved an accrual basis taxpayer whose customers, in accordance with industry practice, paid for the taxpayer's services in advance. Pursuant to Rev. Proc. 71-21, 1971-2 C.B. 549, the taxpayer had elected to defer reporting such payments until such services were performed. (Although Rev. Proc. 71-21 was later modified and superseded by Rev. Proc. 2004-34, 2004 C.B. 991, the modifications would not alter this situation.) When the taxpayer underwent a Code § 382 ownership change, the taxpayer had a balance of such prepaid amounts that had not yet been reflected in income. The IRS held that these did not constitute built-in gain for purposes of Code § 382. It can be argued that this result is wrong, since if the taxpayer had not elected to defer recognition of these income items (or if the items had not qualified for such deferral), these items would have been recognized before the change date and in that way sheltered by the pre-change NOLs. On the other hand, it can be argued that the deferral more accurately reflects the economics of the transaction and that, if the taxpayer elects to defer the recognition of these items, one cost of this deferral is the absence of built-in gain treatment under Code § 382(h) for these items. In 2007, the IRS issued proposed and temporary regulations, Reg. § 1.382-7T, applicable to ownership changes occurring on or after June 14, 2007 (and before June 15, 2010). These provide that recognized built-in gain does not include prepaid income—defined to mean "any amount received prior to the change date that is attributable to performance occurring on or after the change date"—whose recognition the taxpayer had elected to defer until after the change date. The explanation accompanying this proposed and temporary regulation notes that the deferral election provisions (which apply to such things, for example, as prepaid subscription income for newspapers and periodicals) are intended, if they are elected, to match the taxpayer's income better with the expenses of earning that income and, as a result, to reflect more clearly the taxpayer's income both in the year of receipt and in the year of performance. The explanation says that this policy should result in denying built-in-gain treatment for such items. The regulation does not eliminate built-in gain treatment for accounts receivable of a cash basis taxpayer, the gain on completion of a long-term contract, and Code § 481 adjustments. Not only were these items described as built-in gain items in the legislative history to TAMRA, but the explanation accompanying the proposed and temporary regulations argues that these examples are distinguishable in substance from prepaid income as defined in the regulations, because in these examples the income can properly be deemed attributable to the pre-change period because that is the period in which the performance occurred and the expenses were incurred to earn the income.

A potentially different question arises where the income produced reflects income from a wasting asset. During the course of a field examination, the IRS faced

(Footnote Continued)

bank. IRS Letter Ruling 8842059, July 28, 1988, supplementing IRS Letter Ruling 8835057, June 10, 1988; IRS Letter Ruling 8912043, December 27, 1988.

[240] IRS Letter Ruling 199942003, July 9, 1999.

the question whether licensing income from software should be treated as "recognized" gain from the appreciated software for this purpose. In a 1993 field service advice, the IRS declined to take a definite position, but it advised the field in that particular case not to oppose the taxpayer's position that it did so qualify.[241] However, the IRS took what seems to be a contrary position in a 2001 Technical Advice, holding that operating income attributed by the taxpayer to an appreciated patient base (a wasting asset) acquired from a health company did not constitute built-in gain.[242] This position has been modified by IRS Notice 2003-65, which is discussed at the end of this § 508.4.3.

Cancellation-of-debt transactions can themselves affect the computation of built-in gains and losses. For example, one IRS private letter ruling involves a case where a bankrupt company cancelled a debt pursuant to a settlement agreement. The agreement became effective before the date of the company's ownership change, which was produced by a "G" reorganization of the bankrupt company into its subsidiary. Rather than have the normal NOL and other attribute reduction rules of Code § 108 apply, the subsidiary (as the survivor in the "G" reorganization) elected under Code § § 108(b)(5) and 1017 to apply the COD item to a reduction of the basis of the assets received from the debtor. Code § 1017 provides that such a basis reduction is to be made to property held by the taxpayer at the beginning of its first tax year after the date of the debt cancellation. Although the ruling does not indicate whether the tax year of the debtor changed between the date of the debt cancellation and the date of the "G" reorganization, it seems likely that the first tax year following the debt cancellation did not begin before the "G" reorganization. If so, the Code § 1017 basis reduction would not take effect until after the change date. Nonetheless, the IRS held (a holding which has subsequently been confirmed in regulations)[243] that for purposes of determining the debtor's net unrealized built-in gain or loss at the date of the ownership change, as well as for purposes of determining the recognized built-in gain or loss for any recognition period following the ownership change, the basis of the debtor's assets should reflect the basis reductions made under Code § 1017.

In a second ruling,[244] a company that was not in bankruptcy made an agreement to exchange stock for its debt. The making of the agreement produced an ownership change for the company. The later consummation of the agreement produced COD income that was not sheltered by the insolvency exception. Even though the change date preceded the COD income, the two were related and the IRS held that the COD income should be treated as an "item of income" that is attributable to the prechange period within the meaning of Code § 382(h)(6)(A), and thus should enter into the

---

[241] IRS Field Service Advice 1998-415, July 8, 1993, *reprinted at* 98 TNT 229-58.

[242] IRS Technical Advice Memorandum 200217009, December 4, 2001, discussed *infra* note 255. *See also* the discussion of the Code § 1374 authorities and IRS Notice 2003-65 below in this § 508.4.3.

[243] IRS Letter Ruling 9226064, March 31, 1992. *See also* IRS Letter Ruling 9409037, December 7, 1993. Although the IRS subsequently issued a conflicting Field Service Advice 200145009, July 31, 2001, the IRS confirmed its earlier position in Temp. Reg. § § 1.108-7 and 1.1017-1(b)(4). *See* the discussion at § 404.2 above.

[244] IRS Letter Ruling 9312006, March 26, 1993.

computation of the company's net unrealized built-in gain at the change date and its recognized built-in gain during the recognition period.[245]

The second ruling does not say whether the stock-for-debt exception applied in its case to the extent of the company's insolvency. It seems likely that this may have been so, however, in which case the ruling implicitly holds that COD income sheltered by the stock-for-debt exception does not constitute an "item of income." Moreover, neither of these two private letter rulings deals with how one should treat, for built-in gain or built-in loss purposes, COD income that produces attribute reduction other than basis reduction. For example, suppose in the second ruling some of the COD income had not been sheltered by the stock-for-debt exception but had been sheltered by the insolvency exception, with the result that under the Code § 108 attribute reduction rules the debtor's NOLs had been reduced. We would suggest that this COD item should be treated as an "item of income" attributable to the prechange period. In such case, it would be considered an item of unrealized built-in gain at the change date. On the date during the recognition period when it is applied to reduce NOLs (an event similar to being brought into income), it would be removed from the remaining balance of such unrealized built-in gain (just as it would be removed had it been included in income).

One other interesting question is how COD income that is treated as an "item of income" adjustment to net built-in gain is to be treated in computing the *de minimis* threshold of 15 percent (formerly 25 percent) of the value of the company's assets. One letter ruling specifically addressed this point.[246] It held that whereas the COD income increased the "net unrealized built-in gain" and thus the numerator of the threshold fraction, it did not increase the value of the assets in the denominator of the fraction. This result seems correct, since COD income hardly represents an asset (indeed, its tax consequences make it more akin to a liability).

The TAMRA amendments leave the scope of the built-in loss concept unfortunately vague. One question is whether the concept may now apply to liabilities that were only contingent on the ownership change date, but which give rise to deductions during the recognition period. An example would be a product liability claim that relates to an event that occurred before the ownership change but which is resolved during the recognition period. Such a contingent obligation could not have been treated as a built-in loss under the original 1986 Act language: the original 1986 Act language of Code § 382(h)(6) permitted the Secretary by regulation to treat as built-in losses amounts "which *accrue* on or before the change date but which are allowable as a deduction after such date . . ." (emphasis added). A contingent liability does not satisfy the "all events" requirement for accrual until it ceases to be contingent. The TAMRA amendments changed the built-in deduction language to conform to the language used for built-in income. In doing so, they dropped the reference to amounts that "accrue" on or before the change date and instead referred

---

[245] *See also* IRS Notice 87-79, 1987-2 C.B. 387; the discussion at § 508.4.4(2) below; and the discussion of IRS Notice 2003-65 at the end of this § 508.4.3.

[246] IRS Letter Ruling 8923021, March 10, 1989. *See also* Needham, The "Item of Income" Exclusion of Section 382(h)(6)(A)—An Expansion of the Built-in Gain Rule, 51 Tax Notes 373, (April 22, 1991).

to amounts which are "attributable to periods before the change date." Although this language is quite different and could (but need not) be read to produce a different result, there is no indication in the legislative history that Congress intended a different result or, more specifically, that it thought the built-in loss concept should apply to contingent liabilities. More often than not the existence of a contingent liability is not even known at the change date, and even where it is known, its amount cannot be accurately measured. The examples of built-in loss given in the legislative history all relate to items that not only are known but which can be accurately measured at the change date. It is to be hoped that the built-in loss provision will be limited to such items. Indeed, as stated later in this § 508.4.3, the IRS in the final regulations under Code § 1374 included the accrual requirement, and specifically stated that the built-in loss concept does not include contingent liabilities. (For the treatment of contingent liabilities for Code § 382(h) purposes, *see* the discussion of IRS Notice 2003-65 at the end of this § 508.4.3.)

The IRS has ruled[247] that where compensatory stock options were issued by a company before a Code § 382 ownership change had occurred, and exercised after the date of the ownership change, any deduction taken by the company attributable to the exercise of the option will be treated as a recognized built-in loss for the taxable year for which it is allowable as a deduction. The ruling did not indicate whether there had been any change in the value of the stock between the date of the ownership change and the date of exercise.

Losses recognized during the five-year period will be presumed to be built-in losses and thus subject to the annual limitation unless the taxpayer can demonstrate otherwise;[248] conversely, gains recognized during the five-year period will not be considered built-in gains except to the extent the taxpayer can prove otherwise.[249] This makes it important for the loss company to be able to trace assets and to determine their value at the change date. Because of the emphasis these various rules place on stock value and asset values, when there is an ownership change, it will often be advisable for the loss company to obtain appraisals.

If a troubled company has net built-in gains that are not large enough to satisfy the *de minimis* threshold, the company should be careful to realize these gains before, rather than after, an ownership change occurs.

Two additional significant developments relevant to the determination of built-in gains and losses for Code § 382 purposes are (i) the regulations under Code § 1374 addressing the recognition of built-in gains for purposes of the S corporation built-in gains tax, and (ii) IRS Notice 2003-65 describing two alternative approaches to the treatment of built-in gains and losses for Code § 382 purposes which may be applied as safe harbors. These are discussed below.

**Code § 1374 Regulations.** On December 23, 1994, the Treasury issued final regulations under Code § 1374 which imposes a tax on the net built-in gains of S corporations in certain circumstances. The language used in that section to define net

---

[247] IRS Letter Ruling 9444035, August 5, 1994.

[248] *See* Code § 382(h)(2)(B).

[249] *See* Code § 382(h)(3)(A).

built-in gains and losses, including income and deduction items, is essentially identical to that of Code § 382(h), except that the Code § 1374 provision does not include the sentence that makes depreciation, amortization and depletion deductions a built-in loss item.[250]

The Code § 1374 regulation takes the position that in determining whether an item of income or deduction is to be deemed attributable to the period before the change in status and thus is to be treated as a built-in gain or loss item, one should as a general rule apply the accrual method of accounting. If the item would have accrued by the change date, it is to be treated as a built-in gain or loss item for the recognition period.[251] For this purpose, the accrual method is to be applied by taking into account all of the economic performance rules (except for Code § 461(h)(2)(C), which delays accrual for certain workers compensation and tort liabilities until the liability is paid).

To illustrate the application of this test, the regulation contains an example involving a contingent liability of a cash-basis taxpayer. A lawsuit asserting liability had been filed against the taxpayer before the change date, but a judgment had not been rendered against the taxpayer until after the change date. The example holds that the deduction properly claimed by the taxpayer upon payment of the judgment during the recognition period did *not* constitute a built-in loss item, because this amount could not have been accrued and deducted by an accrual-basis taxpayer before the change date.[252] Conversely, a second example presents a case where the judgment was rendered against a cash-basis taxpayer before the change date, although it was not paid until after the change date,[253] and the regulation holds that the deduction for paying this judgment during the recognition period *did* constitute a built-in loss item.

The regulation further provides that COD income, and bad debt deductions, taken into account during the first year of the recognition period constitute built-in gain or loss items if they arise from a debt owed by or to the corporation at the beginning of the recognition period.

The regulation contains an example that distinguishes mineral property from the mineral that might be extracted from it.[254] In the example, a corporation owned appreciated oil and gas property when it made its S election. After becoming an S

---

[250] For purposes of Code § 1374, the Tax Court has held that inventories should be valued at an arm's length price, which presumably must fall between cost and retail value. *Reliable Steel Fabricators, Inc.*, T.C. Memo. 1995-293. The Tax Court has also held that Code § 481 adjustments constitute built-in gains for purposes of Code § 1374, which is the position also taken in Reg. § 1.1374(d)(1), issued in December, 1994. *Argo Sales Co. Inc.*, 105 T.C. No. 7 (1995); *Rondy Inc.*, T.C. Memo 1995-372, *aff'd*, 97-2 U.S.T.C. ¶ 50,546 (6th Cir. 1997).

[251] Reg. § 1.1374-4(b).

[252] Reg. § 1.1374-4(b)(3), Example 2. For a ruling that involves contingent assets and liabilities, *see* IRS Letter Ruling 200329011, March 26, 2003. IRS Letter Ruling 200329011, March 26, 2003, held that a cash basis law firm's contingent fees that were still contingent when it converted to S corporation status did not constitute built-in gain, whereas similar fees that had become non-contingent before that date, but were not paid until after that date, did constitute built-in gain.

[253] Id., Example 3.

[254] Reg. § 1.1374-4(a)(3) Ex. 1.

corporation, the corporation began the production of oil from the property. The example holds that the revenue from that production is not built-in gain for purposes of Code § 1374. Had the S corporation sold the mineral property itself, however, its gain from that sale would have been built-in gain. The IRS has since amplified this concept, making clear that this separation of the property interest from the mineral (including petroleum, timber, or coal) produced from it applies even if the sale of the mineral is treated as a capital gain item under Code § 631.[255]

An interesting application of the Code § 1374 regulation is reflected in IRS Letter Ruling 200644013, June 21, 2006. Here, a company held real estate that would produce Code § 1374 gain. The company transferred the realty to a charitable remainder unitrust under Code § 664, which then sold the realty and invested the proceeds in investment assets. The unitrust was required to distribute to the S corporation the lesser of the trust's income or a fixed percentage of the value of its assets. The ruling held that the annual distributions from the trust to the S corporation will be treated as ordinary income to the extent of the trust's ordinary income, and any balance will be treated as capital gains to the extent, if any, as so characterized under the untitrust rules. The ruling holds that neither the transfer of the real estate to the trust nor the trust's sale of the real estate is a built-in gain recognition event to the S corporation under Code § 1374, but that any annual distribution treated as a distribution of capital gain attributable to the real estate will be treated as a Code § 1374 recognized built-in gain.

When the Treasury proposed the Code § 1374 regulations on December 8, 1992, it left open the question whether it would apply the Reg. § 1.1374-4 interpretations under Code § 382(h): the preamble to the proposed Code § 1374 regulation said "the Treasury Department and the Internal Revenue Service intend no inference regarding rules they may adopt in other regulations, such as under sections 382(h)(6) and 384(c)(1)(B), which contain language similar to section 1374(d)(5)." The preamble to the final regulation is silent on the point. In earlier editions of this book we had expressed the hope that the Treasury would not seek to interpret the two provisions very differently: construing identical language differently when it is placed simulta-

---

[255] Rev. Rul. 2001-50, 2001-43 I.R.B. 343. *See also* Smith and Sobol, New Rev. Rul. Says 'Timmm-Berrr' to Built-In Gains Tax for Natural Resource Companies, 96 J. Taxation 46 (2002). *See also* IRS Letter Ruling 200240002, June 25, 2002 (taxpayer grants customers by agreement to a one-time use of a copyrighted item: income from such agreements made after the S election was made is not built-in gain); IRS Letter Ruling 9712027, December 23, 1996; IRS Technical Advice Memorandum 9727001, September 30, 1996; IRS Letter Ruling 9826017, March 25, 1998; IRS Letter Ruling 9825008, March 16, 1998; IRS Letter Ruling 200205028, October 31, 2001; IRS Letter Ruling 200411015, December 4, 2003. This same concept is reflected in IRS Technical Advice Memorandum 200217009, December 4, 2001, which construes Code § 382(h) rather than Code § 1374. In this Technical Advice Memorandum, a taxpayer purchased a health products business and took the position that its existing patient base was a wasting asset, and that to the extent the value of this base exceeded its basis on the date of acquisition, it had a built-in gain. The taxpayer then treated the operating income attributable to this patient base as a recognized built-in gain for purposes of Code § 382. The taxpayer argued that income from an appreciated wasting asset should be treated as recognized built-in gain, just as the Code now provides that depreciation to the extent of a built-in loss in a wasting asset constitutes a recognition of built-in loss. The IRS rejected the taxpayer's argument, holding that the Code does not treat income from wasting assets symmetrically with depreciation from wasting assets—a position that the IRS has since modified in Notice 2003-65 (discussed below).

neously in different parts of the Code would seem—aside from possible questions as to validity—to escalate hyperlexis to new and more undesirable heights.[256] This issue is now addressed in IRS Notice 2003-65.

**IRS Notice 2003-65.** In late 2003, the IRS issued Notice 2003-65 to deal with certain built-in gain and built-in loss issues presented by Code § 382(h).[257] The Notice presented two different approaches that might be used. The Notice solicited comments on these, and said that after receiving such comments, the IRS expected to publish proposed regulations providing only a single set of rules for identifying built-in items for purposes of Code § 382(h). However, in the meantime, the Notice said that taxpayers could apply either of the two approaches set forth in the Notice as safe harbor methods. The Notice adds that these safe harbors are not meant to be exclusive, and other methods used by taxpayers will be examined on a case-by-case basis.

The two safe-harbor methods articulated in the Notice are the "1374 approach" and the "338 approach."

The "1374 approach" applies the rules of Code § 1374 and its regulations (which have been discussed immediately above) for determining Code § 382(h) built-in gain and loss items, with the modification that depreciation, amortization and depletion deductions are to be treated as built-in loss items (as is required by the last sentence of Code § 382(h)(2)(B), but is not done for Code § 1374 purposes). Under this approach, net built-in gain and net built-in loss are determined as the net amount of gain or loss that would be recognized in a hypothetical sale of all the corporation's assets (including goodwill) immediately before the ownership change. For this purpose, assets are to be valued at fair market value, and then reduced by basis and other items that would be deductible in such a sale at the change date. Under this word formula, one would normally presume that any liabilities that are still contingent at the change date would not be taken into account in determining net built-in gain or loss, but the Notice's discussion of the computation of net built-in gain or loss under the "338 approach" leaves this conclusion in doubt. For purposes of the "338 approach," the Notice provides that net built-in gain or loss is calculated "in the same manner" as under the "1374 approach," and goes on to say that, "[a]ccordingly, . . . contingent consideration (including a contingent liability) is taken into account in the initial calculation" of net built-in gain or loss (without any need for subsequent adjustments). As a practical matter, the inclusion of contingent liabilities would only affect the amount of net built-in gain or loss where the payment of the liability would

---

256 *See generally* Henderson, Controlling Hyperlexis—The Most Important "Law and . . . ," 43 Tax Law. 177 (1989).

257 2003-40 I.R.B. 747. The Tax Section of the American Bar Association, although unable to reach a consensus favoring either the "1374" or the "338" approach set forth in the Notice or one similar to either of them, has issued a report making detailed comments about both of these approaches. *See* American Bar Association, Tax Section, Comments Concerning Notice 2003-65 Under Section 382 of the Internal Revenue Code Regarding the Treatment of Recognized Built-In Gains and Losses, April 29, 2005, *reprinted in* BNA Daily Tax Report (May 3, 2005), BNA Tax Core. *See also* Simon, Compound Complexity: Accounting for Built-In Gains and Losses Under the AMT After an Ownership Change, 107 Tax Notes 477 (April 25, 2005).

not have resulted in a deduction or, presumably, in increased basis (such as where the liability was incurred in connection with the acquisition of an asset).

As under the Code § 1374 regulations, the "1374 approach" generally employs the accrual method of accounting to determine what constitutes *recognized* built-in gain or loss. Thus, liabilities that are still contingent at the change date will not be treated as recognized built-in loss even if they become fixed and are paid during the recognition period. Income earned on assets during the recognition period (such as royalties on a patent) are not treated as built-in gain items because they would not have accrued before the change date. COD income and bad debt deductions arising after the change date are treated as under the Code § 1374 regulations: that is, COD and bad debt deductions taken into account during the first 12 months of the recognition period are treated as recognized built-in gain or loss. This modifies, for users of this safe-harbor provision, the approach allowed by IRS Notice 87-79 (described at § 508.4.4(2) below), though such users may apply the latter for ownership changes occurring before September 12, 2003. If such COD produces a basis reduction under Code § 108(b)(5)—or, we assume, Code § 108(b)(2)(E)—during the 12-month period, the reduction is treated as occurring immediately before the ownership change (thereby, if the asset is sold during the recognition period, producing potential built-in gain or reduced built-in loss), but is not taken into account in computing net built-in gain or loss at the change date.

In contrast, the "338 approach" identifies built-in gain and loss items by comparing the corporation's actual items of income and loss during the recognition period with what they would have been if a Code § 338 election had been made for a hypothetical purchase of all the stock on the change date—presumably utilizing as the hypothetical purchase price of the assets, however, the hypothetical amount realized for purposes of computing net built-in gain or loss, as discussed above. Thus, consideration and liabilities that are still contingent at the change date are valued and taken into account in such computation (without any subsequent adjustments). Contingent liabilities that become deductible during the recovery period are treated as built-in losses to the extent of their estimated value at the change date. On sales or exchanges of assets during the recognition period, the actual gain or loss is compared with the hypothetical Code § 338 basis of the assets to determine built-in gain or loss. Actual depreciation, amortization or depletion that exceeds the hypothetical Code § 338 amount is treated as built-in loss. (Thus, even an asset that has a $40 value and a $40 basis and, thus, no apparent built-in loss, may yield a built-in loss if the actual depreciation in any year is greater than the hypothetical Code § 338 depreciation.) Conversely, and most interestingly, wasting assets that had a built-in gain on the change date can, under this approach, produce an increase in the Code § 382 limitation even if they are not sold or exchanged during the recognition period: this is because amortization or similar deductions on such assets, to the extent of this built-in gain (and thus to the extent they exceed actual amortization or similar deductions on such assets), are treated as though they were built-in gain items—not for producing additional taxable income, but for purposes of increasing the Code § 382 limitation. COD income occurring at any time during the recognition period (not just during the first 12 months, as under the "1374 approach") that is attributable to pre-change debt is treated as built-in gain to the extent of the excess of the basis of the debt over its fair market value at the change date. This modifies, for users of this safe-harbor provision, the approach allowed by IRS Notice 87-79 (described at § 508.4.4(2) below), though such users may apply the latter for ownership changes occurring before September 12, 2003. As under the "1374 approach," if such COD produces a basis reduction under Code § 108(b)(5)—or, we assume, Code § 108(b)(2)(E)—during the recognition period, this is treated as occurring before the ownership change (thereby, if the asset is sold during the recognition period, producing increased built-in gain or reduced built-in loss), although it is not taken into account in computing net built-in gain or loss on the change date.

Both the "1374 approach" and the "338 approach" apply Notice 90-27 (described at § 508.4.3(1) above) for dealing with built-in gain from installment sales, and transfers of built-in gain assets to a consolidated return affiliate of the loss corporation.

The main differences between the two approaches would seem to be the following. First, liabilities that are still contingent at the change date arguably should not be taken into account under the "1374 approach" for net built-in gain or loss purposes, just as they're not for recognized built-in loss purposes. On the other hand, they are taken into account, for both purposes, under the "338 approach." For companies having significant contingent liabilities at the change date, this would seem to make the "1374 approach" more favorable than the "338 approach." Second, built-in gain on wasting assets cannot be taken into account in computing recognized built-in gain under the "1374 approach" unless the assets are sold during the recognition period, but, under the "338 approach," even if the wasting assets are not sold during the recognition period, amortization of that gain can be treated as a built-in gain (not to produce taxable income, but to increase the Code § 382 limitation). For companies having such gain assets that they don't wish to sell, this makes the "338 approach" more attractive. Third, COD attributable to pre-change debt can produce built-in gain under the "1374 approach" only if it is recognized during the first 12 months after the change date, but under the "338 approach" it can produce built-in gain if it is recognized any time during the recognition period. For companies expecting delayed recognition of COD, this can make the "338 approach" more favorable than the "1374 approach." The Notice does not address any special adjustments that may be necessary within a consolidated return context.

The explanation that accompanied the issuance of Reg. § 1.382-7T, which is discussed earlier in this § 508.4.3, expresses concern that the "338 approach," by allowing income items and deduction items to be separated for purposes of computing built-in gains and built-in-losses, may distort the computation of realized built-in gains and realized built-in losses, and requests comments on how this might be addressed.

### § 508.4.4 Additional Rules

The following additional rules are relevant in computing the annual limitation:

(1) **Carryover.** The annual limitation for any given year is increased by the amount of the limitation, if any, for prior taxable years that went unused.[258]

---

[258] Code § 382(b)(2).

(2) **Bifurcation of Year of Change.** The taxable year of an ownership change is bifurcated into a prechange portion and a postchange portion.[259] NOLs and other carryovers from prior taxable years into the change year can be applied to income attributable to the prechange portion of the year without limitation.[260] Income and deductions (other than built-in gains or losses that satisfy the *de minimis* threshold test, as to which a tracing concept must be applied) are allocated between the two portions of the year on a daily proration basis, except to the extent regulations may allow tracing.[261] Tracing could be important to failing companies: For example, COD income arising from the debt restructuring will be in the prechange portion of the year, because the prechange portion of the year includes the change date.[262]

In Notice 87-79,[263] the IRS said that regulations would be issued to allow loss companies to apply tracing. Moreover, it added that "in appropriate circumstances, the regulations will permit income that is realized after the change date, but is properly attributable to the period ending with the change date to be allocated to the pre-change period. For example, it is anticipated that the regulations would permit income from a discharge of indebtedness, which is determined to be integrally related to a transaction resulting in an ownership change, to be allocated to the pre-change period." The notice added that until such regulations are issued, loss companies must use ratable allocation unless a private letter ruling allowing a different method is obtained.

In IRS Letter Ruling 8812065,[264] the IRS, implementing the foregoing, allowed tracing to be applied by a consolidated group and held that discharge of indebtedness income occurring after an ownership change but as part of the ownership change plan could be allocated to the prechange period. It further held that any loss or deduction that had economically accrued on or prior to the change date should be treated as a prechange loss. Letter rulings issued subsequent to TAMRA, however, have generally denied this relation back approach for COD income. Rather, it is the current IRS position that such income is "built-in gain" income and subject to the built-in gain rules (if the built-in gain threshold is met).[265]

The "annual" limitation that applies to the postchange portion of the year is the fraction of the full annual limitation equal to the fraction of a year that the postch-

---

[259] *See* Code § 382(b)(3).

[260] Code § 382(b)(3)(A).

[261] Id.; Code § 382(d). Tracing is mandated, however, for built-in gains and losses and for Code § 338 gain. TAMRA § 1006(d)(3)(B) made clear that this applies only to built-in gains or losses that satisfy the *de minimis* threshold test. *Cf.* 1986 Blue Book, *supra* note 13, at 315-316.

[262] Id. *See also* Lockhart, Section 382 Book-Closing Rules Present Significant Planning Opportunities, 82 J. Tax'n 146 (1995).

[263] 1987-2 C.B. 387. *See* IRS Letter Ruling 9015053, January 16, 1990 (discussing closing-of-the-books allocation for AMT purposes). For the modification of Notice 87-79 by Notice 2003-65, *see* the discussion of the latter notice at the end of § 508.4.3 above.

[264] December 29, 1987.

[265] *E.g.*, IRS Letter Ruling 8923021, March 10, 1989. However, if the COD arises on or prior to the change date, it is properly attributable to the prechange period. IRS Letter Ruling 8917007, January 6, 1989.

ange portion represents.[266] Any NOL generated in the change year is similarly allocated between the prechange and postchange portions.[267] Any carryover of the prechange portion would be subject to the Code § 382 limitations resulting from the ownership change, whereas the postchange portion would not be subject to these limitations.

Beginning in 1990, the IRS instituted a "ceiling rule" in connection with rulings permitting an allocation of income or loss based on an interim closing of the books (rather than a ratable allocation).[268] Under this rule, a loss company may not allocate to either the prechange or postchange period an amount of income or loss in excess of the taxable income or loss for the entire year. Thus, for example, a loss company with a $100 net loss for the taxable year of the ownership change—comprised of $200 of prechange net income and $300 of postchange net loss—would, if it elected tracing, allocate a $100 loss to the postchange period, and would have no income or loss in the prechange period. This result seems unjustified. The statute mandates that the tax year be bifurcated into prechange and postchange segments. The theory for allowing this to be done by tracing rather than proration would seem to be to allow it to be done on an exact basis. Thus, tracing should connote a true separation of the year into independent segments, in which event in this example there would be $200 of prechange income (to be offset first against prechange losses) and $300 of postchange loss unlimited by Code § 382.

Recognizing this, some later letter rulings (although retaining the "ceiling rule") have provided that the "annual" limitation for the postchange period (see below) "will be increased to the extent that net prechange income is offset by net postchange loss."[269] This has been called the "limitation increase" rule. Thus, in the above example, the limitation for the postchange period would be increased by $200 since the postchange loss should have been $300 but, because of the ceiling rule, was only $100. This is still not a perfect solution, however. Although the loss company would end up with at least $300 of unlimited NOL—$100 of postchange NOL and $200 of prechange NOL (due to the increased limitation)—the prechange NOL is saddled with its old carryover period. In contrast, a "pure" tracing approach would allow the entire $300 as a postchange loss with a new 15-year carryover period.

In November 1992, the IRS finally issued Prop. Reg. § 1.382-6 to deal with this subject. This regulation was made final in 1994 and applies to ownership changes occurring on or after June 22, 1994. The regulation retains the "ceiling" rule, but rejects the "limitation increase" rule. The preamble to the regulation says the IRS has decided that the "limitation increase" rule is inconsistent with the approach taken in the regulations (referring essentially to one of the consequences of the ceiling rule) which "generally allows change year losses to offset change year income and gains

---

266 Code § 382(b)(3)(B).

267 Code § 382(d).

268 *See, e.g.*, IRS Letter Ruling 9017020, January 25, 1990 (explains mechanics of rule); IRS Letter Ruling 9021057, February 27, 1990; IRS Letter Ruling 9030023, April 27, 1990.

269 *See, e.g.*, IRS Letter Ruling 9049035, September 11, 1990; IRS Letter Ruling 9049055, September 14, 1990; IRS Letter Ruling 9101008, October 3, 1990.

without regard to the section 382 limitation." It adds that the "limitation increase" rule would have required applying the Code § 382 limitation within the change year, thereby adding undesirable complexity.

The regulation provides consistency rules for corporations in consolidated return or other control groups. It also coordinates with Reg. § 1.1502-76, which applies when a company leaves or joins a consolidated return group, by providing that the allocation rules of Reg. § 1.1502-76 will be applied first before the allocation rules of Prop. Reg. § 1.382-6 are applied.

The regulation requires the ordinary net income or NOL for the change year to be determined and allocated separately from the capital gain or loss for the year. If the loss company has a net overall capital gain for the change year, the portion allocable to each part of the year is first offset by any capital loss carryovers that may be available (subject to the Code § 382 annual limitation for the postchange part of the year); any excess can then be used against the NOL for the change year (without regard to the Code § 382 annual limitation), by applying the NOL first against the net amount of capital gain remaining in the same period, and second against the net amount of capital gain remaining in the other period.

The regulation specifically states that the taxable income or NOL and the net amount of capital gain or loss for the change year are to be determined "without regard to the section 382 limitation . . . " Excluded from the computation are net built-in gains or losses, and, as an anti-abuse rule, "any income or gain recognized on the disposition of assets transferred to the loss corporation during the postchange period for a principal purpose of ameliorating the section 382 limitation."

The regulation provides that the election to apply tracing rather than ratable allocation is irrevocable and must be made on a timely return (including extensions) filed for the change year.[270]

The IRS has applied the "ceiling rule" for purposes of allocating alternative minimum tax (AMT) taxable income (including the ACE, *i.e.*, the adjusted current earnings, adjustment), and for purposes of allocating NOLs and net capital losses for purposes of Code § 384, between the prechange and postchange portions of the year, but has required the 90 percent limitation on the use of NOLs against AMT taxable income to be computed under a different method.[271] *See* § 710 below.

(3) **Determining Limitation After Successive Ownership Changes.** The IRS has ruled that where a company has two successive ownership changes, if the annual limitation for the second change is less than or equals the limitation for the first change, the second limitation supersedes the first. However, if the annual limitation for the first change is less than that for the second change, the first limitation will

---

[270] In IRS Letter Ruling 9819030, February 5, 1998, the IRS applied Reg. § 301.9100-0 *et seq.* to allow a late election to be made, where the tax return had been prepared consistently with the making of the election, but the required treatment regarding the election had not been included. The IRS has been generous in allowing taxpayers an extension of time in which to make the election, when the due date was inadvertently missed. *See* IRS Letter Ruling 200329020, April 7, 2003; IRS Letter Ruling 200306023, October 31, 2002; IRS Letter Ruling 200301026, September 27, 2002; IRS Letter Ruling 200112054, December 21, 2000; IRS Letter Ruling 200125056, March 14, 2001.

[271] IRS Letter Ruling 9734028, May 22, 1997; IRS Letter Ruling 9644004, August 6, 1996; IRS letter Ruling 9341026, July 20, 1993; IRS Letter Ruling 9345045, August 17, 1993.

continue to apply (and the second will not) to the items covered by the first limitation, and the items covered by the first limitation will not be included in the computations for the second limitation and the second limitation will be reduced (but not below zero) by the amount of taxable income which is offset by prechange items subject to the first limitation.[272] The preamble to Temp. Reg. § 1.382-5T(d) made clear that this rule also applies to consolidated return groups covered by Reg. § § 1.1502-90 through 1.1502-99 (discussed at § 508.7 below). For special rules that apply where the second ownership change occurs within two years of the first change, and either Code § 382(l)(5) or Code § 382(l)(6) applied to the first change, *see* § § 508.4.2 above and § 508.5 below.

### § 508.4.5 Multi-Corporate Groups

Before the issuance in early 1991 of proposed regulations, which became temporary regulations in 1996, applying consolidated return concepts to Code § 382 (which are discussed at § 508.7 below), there was considerable doubt about how Code § 382 should be applied to multi-corporate groups, particularly if they filed consolidated returns. The statute was written with a stand-alone company in mind. It did not carve out and eliminate a parent's investment in the stock or debt of its subsidiaries. Nor, in determining the income of a parent corporation to which the annual limitation is to apply, did it carve out and eliminate the parent's income that is attributable to its subsidiaries. Presumably, the statute would be applied separately to the parent, without such carve-outs, and separately to each subsidiary. The proposed and temporary regulations address these problems.

For periods not covered by the temporary and proposed regulations, the following authorities are of interest:

In IRS Letter Ruling 8849061,[273] the IRS did not give a bankrupt loss company credit for the increased value of its stock resulting from the exchange of debt for stock (as discussed at § 508.4.2 above) where parent stock was used and the parent was not in bankruptcy. In addition, in IRS Letter Ruling 9019036,[274] the IRS refused to rule that a subsidiary, which had suffered an ownership change because of an ownership change of its parent, could apply the special bankruptcy rule in Code § 382(l)(5) (*see* § 508.5 below) even though the parent was going to apply that rule.

On at least two occasions, however, the IRS granted taxpayers permission to apply the built-in gain and loss rules on a consolidated basis. As a price of the ruling,

---

[272] Reg. § 1.382-5(d), issued as a temporary regulation in 1996 and made final in 1999. This rule was previously set forth in the following IRS letter rulings: IRS Letter Ruling 9122067, March 6, 1991; IRS Letter Ruling 9125039, March 27, 1991; IRS Letter Ruling 9221023, February 20, 1992; IRS Letter Ruling 9341026, July 20, 1993. For a discussion of a number of issues left unresolved by these rulings, *see* Effect of Successive Ownership Changes on Use of NOLs, 75 J. Tax'n 188 (1991).

[273] September 15, 1988.

[274] February 9, 1990.

the taxpayers agreed to certain basis adjustments to the stock of their subsidiaries upon a disposition of the stock.[275]

## *§508.5 Special Rule for Title 11 and Similar Cases*

Companies in title 11 or similar cases[276] may be eligible to have a special Code §382 rule apply to them. This rule is found in Code §382(l)(5).[277] It applies only to companies which meet its special eligibility requirements.

Companies in title 11 or similar cases which do not meet those eligibility requirements—or which affirmatively elect not to have this special rule apply—can apply a different special rule available to companies in title 11 or similar cases. This is the rule of Code §382(l)(6), which, for annual limitation purposes, allows the value of the stock of such companies to reflect the debt reduction resulting from any stock-for-debt exchange or debt cancellation occurring in the ownership change transaction itself. The Code §382(l)(6) rule was discussed at §§508.4.1 and 508.4.2 above. Here, we will discuss the Code §382(l)(5) rule.

Although the statutory language of Code §382(l)(5) is broad enough to suggest that its special rule could apply to an ownership change occurring at any time during the bankruptcy case, Reg. §1.382-9(a) and the legislative history[278] both state that it applies only to a transaction that is "ordered by the court or is pursuant to a plan approved by the court."

Unless the loss company elects in a timely manner (*see* §508.4.2 above) not to have Code §382(l)(5) apply, this special rule automatically applies *if* the creditors and shareholders immediately before the ownership change own at least 50 percent of the value *and* voting power of the stock of the loss company (or of the controlling corporation if also in bankruptcy) immediately after the ownership change.[279] If applicable, Code §382(l)(5) generally provides for a one-time reduction in the loss company's NOLs and other tax attributes (*see* §508.5.3 below). For purposes of the 50 percent test, stock is taken into account only if (1) it was owned immediately before the ownership change or (2) it was received in exchange for stock or a qualified creditor's interest that was owned immediately before the ownership change. Stock

---

[275] IRS Letter Ruling 8923021, March 10, 1989; IRS Letter Ruling 8849061, September 15, 1988. *See*, more generally, Olson & Bailine, How Do the Ownership Rules Affect Consolidated Returns? 3 Corp. Tax'n No. 2, 4 (July/August 1990).

[276] *Supra* note 212.

[277] As Asofsky points out, this provision "is not the product of any philosophy, but an attempt to reconcile two conflicting statutory proposals by indiscriminately adopting a little of each." Asofsky, Towards a Bankruptcy Tax Act of 1993, 51 NYU Inst. on Fed. Tax'n, p. 13-21 (1993).

[278] *See* 1986 Blue Book, *supra* note 13, at 321; 1986 Act Conference Report, *supra* note 2, at II-192.

[279] *See* Code §382(l)(5)(A). "Stock" for purposes of this provision is defined by reference to the consolidated return definition, and so stock that is excluded from that definition by Code §1504(a)(4)—*i.e.*, straight nonvoting preferred stock—is not counted for purposes of satisfying the postownership-change 50 percent test. The IRS had earlier announced, however, that regulations will provide that such preferred stock held *before* the ownership change will be treated as a creditor's claim. Notice 88-57, 1988-1 C.B. 545. Presumably this means it will be subjected to the special holding period requirements that apply to debt but not to stock.

received for new consideration, or purchased from other stockholders, is not counted.[280] In addition, debt exchanged for stock is not counted unless it was (1) held by the creditor continuously since at least 18 months before the petition in bankruptcy was filed (or the commencement of a similar proceeding) or (2) arose in the ordinary course of the business of the loss corporation and is held by the same creditor since it arose.[281]

Reg. § 1.382-9(d)(2)(iv) provides that indebtedness (other than debt incurred for a principal purpose of being exchanged for stock) arises in the ordinary course of the loss corporation's business if it is incurred in the normal, usual or customary conduct of business, without regard to whether the debt funds ordinary or capital expenditures, and includes trade debt; a tax liability; a liability arising from a past or present employment relationship, a past or present business relationship with a supplier, customer or competitor, or from tort, breach of warranty, or breach of statutory duty; indebtedness incurred to pay an expense deductible under Code § 162 or included in the cost of goods sold; or a claim that arises upon the rejection of a burdensome contract or lease pursuant to the title 11 or similar case, if the contract or lease arose in the ordinary course of the business.

### § 508.5.1 Continuous Ownership Rule

The requirement that the debt be continuously owned by the same creditor since it was either incurred or at least 18 months prior to the bankruptcy can have troublesome, and rather odd, consequences for a public company. For example, turnover of its stock in the trading market will not affect its eligibility for the Code § 382(l)(5) rule, but turnover of its public debt in the trading markets can affect such eligibility. In this regard, it is interesting to note that in the *McLean Industries* case a bankruptcy court, presented with a bankruptcy plan premised on the Code § 382(l)(5) rule where a majority of the common stock was to be distributed to "old and cold" creditors, issued an order before confirmation of the plan directing that transfers of claims subject to Bankruptcy Rule 3001 (that is, claims other than those based on

---

280 *See* 1986 Blue Book, *supra* note 13, at 321-322. This point was confirmed by a technical correction to Code § 382(1)(5)(A)(ii) made by § 1006(d)(7) of TAMRA.

281 Code § 382(l)(5)(E). The Conference Report to the 1986 Act states that debt will be considered as having arisen in the ordinary course of the loss company's business "only if the indebtedness was incurred by the loss corporation in connection with the normal, usual, or customary conduct of its business." 1986 Act Conference Report, *supra* note 2, at II-192. It is irrelevant whether the debt was related to ordinary or capital expenditures of the loss company, Id. In IRS Letter Ruling 9019036, February 9, 1990, the IRS held that debt will satisfy the test even if there are changes in the control of the entity holding the debt, provided that avoidance of the Code § 382(l)(5) rule is not a principal purpose of the change in control. The same ruling similarly held that a claim acquired pursuant to payment of a guarantee, letter of credit, or similar security arrangement of a debt that otherwise satisfied the Code § 382(l)(5) test would assume the status of such debt, even if such payment was made during the 18-month period, provided the security arrangement does not have as its principal purpose the avoidance of the Code § 382(l)(5) rule.

The first of these holdings of IRS Letter Ruling 9019036 is not affected by Prop. Reg. § 1.382-9 (discussed below) and would seem to continue to represent the law, except in the narrow case of the special purpose debt-holding entity affected by the anti-abuse rule contained in Reg. § 1.382-9(d)(4).

bonds or debentures) could not be made without notice, hearing, and court approval.[282] In similar circumstances, the bankruptcy court in the *Pan Am Corporation* case issued a preliminary injunction restricting the trading in claims. The order was based, in part, on the automatic stay provisions of the Bankruptcy Code and the court's broad equitable powers. In that case, the restriction extended to accumulations of 5 percent or more of any class of bonds or debentures.[283] Orders of this type have since become quite common (often being obtained within the first days of a bankruptcy case), and are discussed further at § 1002.4.1 below.

The IRS acted in 1994 to ameliorate the problem of public debt by issuing Reg. § 1.382-9(d). The first version of this regulation was proposed on September 23, 1991. This first version was to be effective for ownership changes after September 19, 1991, and the preamble to it added that for earlier ownership changes the loss company could apply for permission by letter ruling to apply similar principles. The 1991 proposed regulation was withdrawn and a modified proposed regulation was issued on May 10, 1993. The 1993 proposed regulation was made final, with minor changes, in early 1994. This takes a different approach to the effective date issue: it applies to ownership changes occurring on or after March 17, 1994. However, the loss company can elect to apply the terms of the final regulation to prior ownership changes, if it makes the selection on its first tax return filed after March 17, 1994. This latter election can even extend to revoking a prior election made to have Code § 382(l)(6) rather than Code § 382(l)(5) apply to the ownership change.

The 1991 proposed regulation allowed a debtor to treat a portion of a class of "widely-held indebtedness" held on the ownership change date by "less-than-5-percent beneficial owners" as always having been held by them. Thus, trading among these smaller owners would be ignored. The amount that would be so considered was, in general, the least amount owned by them on the "plan date" or the "change date." The loss company would have had to ascertain this ownership on those two dates. The 1991 proposed regulation contained conventions for computing this. A class of debt was "widely-held indebtedness" if it was in registered form and was owned by more than 50 beneficial owners on any day.

The final regulation seeks to obtain a similar objective, but takes a different approach to determining whether "qualified indebtedness" has been owned for the requisite time. "Qualified indebtedness" is the term the regulation uses to refer to both types of debt referred to in Code § 382(l)(5), namely (1) debt that has been held by the same beneficial owner since at least 18 months before the title 11 or similar proceeding commenced, and (2) debt that arose in the ordinary course of the business

---

[282] *In re McLean Indus., Inc.*, Ch. 11 Case Nos. 86 B 12238 through 12241 (Bankr. S.D.N.Y., order dated February 16, 1989); *cf. In re Allegheny Intl., Inc.*, 100 B.R. 241 (Bankr. W.D. Pa. 1988) (established additional procedures as a condition to the court's approval of any transfers of claims, including prior notice to the debtor). *See also* Pisem & Glicklich, *supra* note 41; IRS Chief Counsel Advice 200444002, July 22, 2004.

[283] *See In re Pan Am Corp.*, Case Nos. 91-B-10080 (CB) through 91-B-10087 (CB), Adv. Proc. No. 91-6175A (CB) (Bankr. S.D.N.Y. preliminary injunction order dated October 3, 1991). *See also In re First Merchants Acceptance Corp.*, Case No. 97-1500 (JJF) (Bankr. Del.) (final order, dated March 12, 1998); discussion at § 1002.4.

of the loss corporation and has been owned at all times since by the same beneficial owner.

The basic definition of qualified debt requires the debt to have been continuously held by the same beneficial owner for the requisite period and, as the regulation confirms, imposes a duty of inquiry on the loss company to establish that this requirement has been satisfied.[284] However, the regulation provides three exceptions to this continuous ownership rule. Two of them relax that rule. The first allows debt to be deemed to have satisfied the continuous ownership requirement, even if it has not. This first exception applies only if the holder of the debt does not end up immediately after the ownership change being a 5 percent shareholder of the company. The second exception allows certain transferees of debt to step into the shoes of their transferors, by tacking the latter's holding period to their own, and also allows the tacking of holding periods by the same owner in certain debt-for-debt exchanges. This second exception applies even if the holder does end up being a 5 percent shareholder. The third exception tightens rather than relaxes the continuous ownership rule. It seeks to curb the ability of people to avoid the continuous ownership requirement through the mechanism of housing the debt in a special purpose entity the stock of which, instead of the debt itself, can later be transferred to a new owner. These exceptions are discussed immediately below.

**Certain transfers disregarded.** The first exception is set forth in Reg. § 1.382-9(d)(3). It provides that the loss company may treat debt as always having been owned by the person who owned it immediately before the ownership change if that person is not, immediately after the ownership change, either (a) a 5 percent shareholder, or (b) an entity (called by the proposed regulation a "five-percent entity") through which a 5 percent shareholder owns an indirect interest in the loss company. This rule is obviously designed to eliminate the duty of inquiry for publicly traded debt held in street name—but it goes beyond that. It allows the loss company even to ignore debt transfers of which it has actual knowledge (with a limited exception mentioned below), such as transfers of publicly held debt registered in the beneficial owner's name on the company's books, or transfers of trade claims (which the company could ascertain by comparing the original trade payable with the proof of claim filed in the bankruptcy case). But this relaxation of the continuous ownership rule does not apply to debt held by persons who immediately after the ownership change become 5 percent shareholders or entities.

This exception to the continuous ownership rule is subject to the following limitations:

(1) It does not apply to debt beneficially owned by a person "whose participation in formulating a bankruptcy plan makes evident to the loss corporation (whether or not the loss corporation had previous knowledge)" that the person has not owned the debt for the requisite period. It would appear that the regulation intends this to be the only case in which the company

---

[284] The regulation says that in making this inquiry the loss company may rely on a statement, signed under penalties of perjury, by the beneficial owner.

needs to take into account its actual knowledge of transfers of debt held by persons who do not become 5 percent owners. Thus, unless a debt holder is active in plan formulation, the debt still may be treated as qualified debt even if the company possesses knowledge in its files that the holder has not satisfied the continuous ownership requirement.

(2) Where the loss company has actual knowledge of a coordinated acquisition of debt by a group, through a formal or informal understanding among themselves, for a principal purpose of exchanging the debt for stock, the debt (and any stock received for it) is treated for purposes of this regulation as owned by an entity. The regulation says that a principal element in determining if such an understanding exists is whether the investment decision of each member is based on the decision of one or more other members.

(3) In determining which of its debt owners are, immediately after the ownership change, 5 percent shareholders or 5 percent entities, the loss company must take into account any actual knowledge that it has regarding stock ownership described in Temp. Reg. § 1.382-2T(k)(2) (which includes knowledge acquired up through the date the income tax return for the ownership change year is filed) and any actual knowledge it has of ownership interests described in Temp. Reg. § 1.382-2T(k)(4) (which refers to interests structured to avoid treating a person as a 5 percent shareholder).

(4) Although in determining who is a 5 percent shareholder for purposes of the regulation one applies the definition in Temp. Reg. § 1.382-2T(g) without application of the general option attribution rules, a special option rule does apply: a creditor will not be treated as a qualified creditor if the loss company has actual knowledge immediately after the ownership change that the exercise of an option to acquire or dispose of stock of the loss company would cause the beneficial owner of the indebtedness immediately before the ownership change to be, after the ownership change, either a 5 percent shareholder or a 5 percent entity.

Although the foregoing rules will make it easier for a loss company to come within the scope of Code § 382(l)(5), one should note that certainty in advance planning will still be limited by the fact that status as a 5 percent shareholder or 5 percent entity may not be determinable, and thus may not be known, until after the change date.

**Tacking rules.** The second set of holding-period exceptions provided by the regulation allows the tacking of holding periods in certain circumstances. These tacking rules, which are found in Reg. § 1.382-9(d)(5), apply even if the holder ends up being a 5 percent shareholder or 5 percent entity. The tacking rules fall into two categories. The first allows tacking of holding periods between certain transferors and transferees of debt. The second allows tacking of holding periods of new debt exchanged for old debt held by the same owner.

When the transferor-transferee tacking rules apply, the transferee is treated as having owned the debt while it was owned by the transferor. The tacking rules apply where the transfer

(1) is between parties bearing a relationship to each other described in Code § 267(b) or 707(b) (substituting at least 80 percent for more than 50 percent);[285]
(2) is a transfer of a loan within 90 days after its origination, pursuant to a customary syndication transaction;
(3) is a transfer of newly incurred debt by an underwriter that owned it for a transitory period pursuant to an underwriting;
(4) is a transfer in which the transferee's basis is determined under Code § 1014 or 1015 or with reference to the transferor's basis in the debt;
(5) is in satisfaction of a right to receive a pecuniary bequest;
(6) is pursuant to a divorce or separation agreement within the meaning of Code § 71(b)(2);
(7) is pursuant to a subrogation in which the transferee acquires a claim against the loss company by reason of a payment to the claimant pursuant to an insurance policy or a guarantee, letter of credit or similar security arrangement; or
(8) is a transfer of an account receivable in a customary commercial factoring transaction made within 30 days after the account arose to a transferee that regularly engages in such transactions.

The regulation states that the foregoing transferor-transferee tacking rules do not apply if the transferee acquired the debt for a principal purpose of benefitting from the losses of the loss company by exchanging the debt for stock in the title 11 or similar case, or by selling the debt at a profit that reflects the expectation that Code § 382(l)(5) will apply to the ownership change of the loss company.

The second set of tacking rules provided by Reg. § 1.382-9(d)(5) applies to debt-for-debt exchanges by the same owner. These tacking rules provide that where the loss company satisfies its debt with new debt, either through an exchange of new for old debt or by a modification of the old debt that is treated as an exchange, the owner of the new debt is considered as having owned it for the period he owned the old debt, and the new debt is treated as having arisen in the ordinary course of the business of the loss company if the old debt so arose.

**Anti-abuse rule.** The regulation contains in Reg. § 1.382-9(d)(4) an anti-abuse rule designed to limit efforts to avoid the restriction on debt transfers through the device of placing the debt in an entity, thereby allowing future transfers to take the form of transfers of interests in that entity rather than transfers of the debt itself. This anti-abuse rule provides that debt will not be treated as qualified indebtedness at all if: (a) the beneficial owner of the debt is an entity that is a 5 percent entity

---

[285] The IRS applied this concept to a qualified settlement fund, that it permitted as a qualified transferee of the persons holding claims against the corporation that were satisfied by the qualified settlement fund, in IRS Letter Ruling 200242035, July 22, 2002; IRS Letter Ruling 9733019, May 22, 1997. In other rulings, the IRS has treated claims placed in a qualified settlement fund as still being held by the claimant-beneficiary. IRS Letter Ruling 200518050, January 14, 2005; IRS Letter Rulings 200513016 and 200513017, December 14, 2004; IRS Letter Ruling 200442011, October 23, 2003; IRS Letter Ruling 200243034, July 26, 2002; IRS Letter Ruling 9619051, February 8, 1996; IRS Letter Ruling 9012039, December 22, 1989.

immediately after the change date of the loss company; (b) the entity had an ownership change during the period beginning on the later of either the date 18 months before the filing of the title 11 or similar case or the date the entity acquired the debt and ending on the change date of the loss company;[286] and (c) the debt represents more than 25 percent of the value of the gross assets of the entity (excluding cash and cash equivalents) on the change date of the entity.

The existence of this anti-abuse rule means that as a practical matter the loss company should obtain a statement, signed under penalties of perjury, from its 5 percent entities to the effect that they do not come within the scope of this anti-abuse rule, if the available information does not already make clear that this is the case.

### § 508.5.2 Special Option Attribution Rule

Code § 382(l)(5) does not itself apply any option attribution rule to the determination of whether its 50-percent continuity requirement has been met. However, such a rule has in effect been imposed by Reg. § 1.382-9(e), which provides that for ownership changes occurring on or after (but not before) September 5, 1990, options on the stock of the loss corporation (or of a controlling corporation *if* it is also in bankruptcy), other than options owned as a result of being a prechange shareholder or qualified creditor, will be treated as selectively exercised if that would cause the 50-percent continuity requirement not to be met. Options held as a result of being a prechange stockholder or qualified creditor are not treated as being exercised in applying this rule, if such exercise would result in the ownership of stock by such a person. The regulations provide two relief rules: (1) an option that lapses may be treated as if it had never been issued (except to the extent any person owning the option at any time on or after the change date acquires additional stock or an option between the change date and such lapse), and (2) the loss company can take into account stock acquired by a prechange shareholder or qualified creditor upon the exercise of an option issued pursuant to the plan (but only if the exercise is within three years of the ownership change and is by the person who got the option under the plan).

### § 508.5.3 Consequences of Code § 382(l)(5) Rule

If the Code § 382(l)(5) rule applies (and no election out is made), the annual limitation on the amount of income that can be sheltered by the carryovers or built-in losses, and the continuity-of-business-enterprise requirement,[287] do not apply to the loss company—although certain alternative minimum tax adjustments for built-in losses may still apply (*see* § 511 below) and the IRS has sought indirectly to engraft an

---

[286] Within such period, the ownership change of the entity is determined without regard to whether the entity is a loss corporation and by beginning the testing period no earlier than the latest of the day three years before the entity's change date, the day 18 months before the filing of the title 11 or similar case, or the day the entity acquired the debt.

[287] The inapplicability of the continuity-of-business-enterprise requirement is confirmed in Reg. § 1.382-9(m).

attenuated form of a continuity-of-business requirement by adopting Reg. § 1.269-3(d), which says that absent strong evidence to the contrary, acquisition of control or of property in connection with a Code § 382(l)(5) transaction will be considered made for the principal purpose of avoidance of income tax unless the corporation carries on (except for temporary interruptions) more than an insignificant amount of an active trade or business during and subsequent to the bankruptcy case. *See* § 509.1 below. Instead, the following consequences occur:

(1) The loss company's NOLs and tax credits will be determined as if no deduction was allowed for interest paid or accrued, during the three years preceding the change year and during the prechange portion of the change year, on debt exchanged for stock in the proceeding.[288]
(2) In the case of debt to which the stock-for-debt exception to COD income (*see* § 504A) applies, the loss company's prechange losses and credits will be reduced by 50 percent of the excess of the amount of debt exchanged during the bankruptcy or similar proceeding over the value of stock exchanged for it. For this purpose, the amount of debt exchanged excludes any accrued unpaid interest which reduced the loss company's NOLs in (1) above.[289]
(3) If a second ownership change occurs within two years after the ownership change to which this special bankruptcy rule applied, then (1) Code § 382(l)(5) will not apply to the second ownership change, and (2) the annual limitation with respect to the second ownership change will be zero.[290]

The Code § 382(l)(5) rule will, in many situations, create a significant incentive for companies to use a bankruptcy proceeding for accomplishing their debt restructurings. Even though the rule imposes, among other things, a 50-percent reduction on the availability of the stock-for-debt exception to COD income, the fact that a 50-percent availability remains for companies grandfathered from repeal by that exception, and that the stock-for-debt exception is completely unavailable to solvent

---

[288] Code § 382(l)(5)(B), as amended by TAMRA, § 1006(d)(27). In IRS Field Service Advice 200006004, February 11, 2000, *reprinted at* 2000 TNT 30-64, the taxpayer argued that interest for the year of change should not be disallowed because taxpayer did not have an NOL for this year (although it did have NOLs from prior years). The IRS disagreed, pointing out that disallowance of the interest deduction for the year of change would absorb some of the prior NOLs, thereby reducing the total amount of NOLs to be carried over into periods following the change, which is the purpose of the adjustment.

[289] Code § 382(l)(5)(C), as amended by TAMRA, § 1006(d)(18); *see also* 1986 Act Conference Report, *supra* note 2, at II-192.

[290] Code § 382(l)(5)(D); Reg. § 1.382-9(n)(1). It had originally been feared that the second ownership change might also make Code § 382(l)(5) unavailable retroactively to the first ownership change, but the regulation does not take that position. The IRS has announced that where a defaulted savings and loan association transfers its assets and liabilities to a new interim association, pending a sale of the assets, with the old depositors of the stock institution or members of the mutual institution continuing to own the entire equity interest, in what is known in the savings and loan industry as a "passthrough receivership," the transfer will not constitute an ownership change, and thus will not invoke this second-ownership-change rule. The announcement said that regulations will be issued to this effect. Notice 88-7, 1988-1 C.B. 476.

companies outside bankruptcy, will often make a bankruptcy proceeding more attractive than a nonbankruptcy proceeding for debt restructurings involving the exchange of stock for debt. This is true not only for transactions grandfathered from repeal of the stock-for-debt exception, but also, as explained at the end of this section, for transactions covered by such repeal. Moreover, even if the Code § 382(l)(5) rule is unavailable, the special Code § 382(l)(6) rule (*see* § 508.4.2 above) applicable to companies in bankruptcy (and similar insolvency) proceedings for purposes of the annual limitation—namely, that the value of the stock of the loss company is allowed to reflect the debt reduction occurring in the ownership change transaction itself—will also often make a bankruptcy proceeding more attractive.

It should be noted that there is uncertainty whether a subsidiary, which suffers an ownership change as a result of an ownership change of its parent, can utilize the Code § 382(l)(5) rule. In IRS Letter Ruling 9019036, the IRS refused to rule that it could, even though the parent was going to apply the Code § 382(l)(5) rule. When the IRS issued proposed and temporary consolidated return regulations under Code § 382 (discussed at § 508.7 below), in 1991 and in 1996, it expressly reserved on the question of how Code § 382(l)(5) should apply to consolidated groups.[291]

In certain cases, a company otherwise eligible for the Code § 382(l)(5) rule may find it more advantageous to elect to have the Code § 382(l)(6) rule apply (*i.e.*, the annual limitation and the continuity-of-business-enterprise test). This would be the case, for example, if (1) the 50 percent stock-for-debt exception disallowance proves economically less advantageous than the increased annual limitation resulting from the additional stock value associated with the cancellation of debt in the stock for debt exchange (assuming the continuity-of-business-enterprise test is satisfied) or (2) for business reasons, the creditors and other shareholders are unable or unwilling to retain controlling ownership of the loss company for two years, in which event the annual limitation would allow at least some NOL utilization (whatever the amount) in contrast to the zero annual limitation that would be imposed following a subsequent ownership change within two years following a Code Sec. 382(l)(5) ownership change.

Two other points should be mentioned about situations where the Code § 382(l)(5) rule does *not* apply. First, the fact that the annual limitation on carryovers is a percentage (namely, the long-term tax exempt bond rate) of the value of the loss company's stock emphasizes the importance (even for companies in bankruptcy for which the value of the stock may be determined after the debt restructuring) of the advice given earlier to avoid winding the assets of the company down too far before doing the debt restructuring. Second, the emphasis placed by new Code § 382 on the value of the stock (for purposes of applying the annual limitation) and on the value of the assets (for purposes of applying the built-in gain or loss rules) will make appraisals (and perhaps court determinations of value) advisable in many cases where they were not previously needed for tax purposes.

---

[291] For a series of suggested rulings involving the consolidated application of Code § 382(l)(5), *see* New York State Bar Association, Tax Section, Committee on Bankruptcy, Report on Suggested Bankruptcy Tax Revenue Rulings, Tax Notes, February 11, 1991.

**Effect of 1993 Act repeal of stock-for-debt exception.** The 1993 Act's repeal of the stock-for-debt exception will make use of the Code § 382(l)(5) rule even more advantageous than before repeal. After such repeal, the Code § 382(l)(5) provision will produce little or no reduction of NOLs and other attributes beyond what repeal of the stock-for-debt exception itself produces. Oddly enough, the only reduction required would be in respect of interest actually paid within the current or three preceding taxable years on any debt exchanged for stock in the bankruptcy proceeding. On the other hand, the Code § 382(l)(6) rule will produce substantial limitations on the tax attributes, if any, that are left after repeal of the stock-for-debt exception.

## *§ 508.6 Annual Information Statement Required*

As mentioned above at § 508.2.1, the temporary regulations require a loss corporation to file a statement with its tax return for each year that it is a loss corporation. The contents of the statement has been changed (and, in general, simplified) for tax returns due on or after May 30, 2006, other than returns already filed.[292]

For prior returns, the statement must:[293]

(1) indicate whether any "testing dates" occurred during the taxable year;
(2) identify each "testing date" on which an "ownership change," if any, occurred;
(3) identify the "testing date" that occurred during and closest to the end of each calendar quarter;
(4) identify each "5 percent shareholder" on each such "testing date";
(5) state each such "5 percent shareholder's" percentage ownership on each such "testing date" and the increase in ownership during the "testing period";
(6) disclose the extent to which the loss company relied on the presumptions (discussed in § 508.2.8.3 above) arising from the presence or absence of SEC Schedules 13D and 13G, and from statements signed under penalties of perjury by higher tier entities; and
(7) make any election desired by the loss company to apply the 120-day rule under the option attribution provisions[294] (discussed at § 508.2.7.4 above).

For returns due on or after May 30, 2006 (other than returns already filed), the statement must:[295]

(1) identify each "testing date" that occurred during the taxable year (not just the one closest to the end of each quarter);

---

[292] Temp. Reg. § 1.382-11T (including any amended return filed on or after May 30, 2006, but still before the due date of the original return, including extensions). This regulation expires on May 26, 2009, subject to final regulations.

[293] Temp. Reg. § 1.382-2T(a)(2)(ii), as in effect prior to T.D. 9264 (May 30, 2006).

[294] Temp. Reg. § 1.382-2T(h)(4)(vi)(B).

[295] Temp. Reg. § 1.382-11T. For additional effective date information, see *supra* note 292.

(2) identify each date on which an "ownership change," if any, occurred;

(3) disclose the amount of any tax attributes that caused the company to be a loss corporation (including any net built-in loss, determined for this purpose by treating the testing date as a date on which an ownership change occurred);[296] and

(4) include any applicable elections under the Code § 382 regulations (such as an interim-closing-of-the-books election in the case a mid-year ownership change, *see* § 508.4.4 above).

Where a consolidated return group is involved, Reg. §§ 1.1502-92(e) and -94(d) impose on the common parent the duty to file the statement, and amplifies on the way it applies to consolidated groups.

The temporary regulations do not say what happens if the statement is not filed or is incomplete.

Since a "loss company" includes not only a company with NOLs, but also a company without NOLs but with a net unrealized built-in loss that meets the *de minimis* threshold,[297] and since, as discussed at § 508.2.1, numerous testing dates—at least for dates before November 5, 1992—may occur during the year, many companies will have to file such statements, even when they may be quite confident that no ownership change has occurred. Obtaining the information to complete the statement may be no small task (to begin with, one must understand the temporary regulations). As Professor James Eustice has wryly observed, "perhaps the creation of a 'stock tracing' department will be necessary . . . ."[298] This is not the kind of thing that will gladden the hearts of the struggling management of a failing company.

Happily, the 1994 regulations, by simplifying the option rules, reduced the number of testing dates that may occur. They also created a technical question as to whether they eliminated the requirement for this information statement,[299] although the preamble to the regulations contained language suggesting that the IRS thought the reporting requirement continued to apply. However, in 1996, any doubt was put to rest when the IRS referred to the requirement in Reg. § 1.1502-92A(e), finalized in 1999 as Reg. § 1.1502-92(e).

---

[296] Presumably, specifying such attributes with respect to one testing date during the taxable year (particularly if the date is the date on which an ownership change occurred) will suffice.

[297] Temp. Reg. § 1.382-2T(a)(2)(ii) and (f)(1).

[298] Eustice, Federal Income Taxation of Corporations and Shareholders at S16-10 (5th ed. 1988 Supp. No. 1).

[299] The reporting requirement is in Temp. Reg. § 1.382-2T(a)(2)(ii) (for returns filed before May 30, 2006) and in Reg. § 1.382-11 (for returns filed on or after May 30, 2006), both of which refer only to testing dates described in Temp. Reg. § 1.382-2T(a)(2)(i) which regulation defines only testing dates occurring prior to November 5, 1992. Testing dates occurring on or after November 5, 1992, are defined in Reg. § 1.382-2(a)(4), and there is no cross-reference between this regulation and either Temp. Reg. § 1.382-2T(a)(2)(ii) or Reg. § 1.382-11.

## *§508.7 Consolidated Code §382 Regulations*

On January 29, 1991, the IRS issued proposed regulations to govern the application of Code § 382 to corporations filing consolidated returns.[300] These regulations were adopted, with little change, on June 27, 1996, as temporary regulations.[301] Just two days short of the three year sunset on the 1996 temporary regulations, the IRS finalized these regulations with certain amendments.[302] The regulations do not address the special rules for companies in bankruptcy that are contained in Code § § 382(1)(5) and 382(1)(6). Reg. § 1.1502-97 was reserved for this purpose. So the regulations are of somewhat limited use for companies in bankruptcy. The regulations cover the following points.

### § 508.7.1 Determination of Ownership Change

If Code § 382 were applied on a separate company basis, it would be quite possible for a company to join a consolidated group without having an ownership change, or for a parent to have an ownership change when one or more of its subsidiaries does not.

Rather than using a separate company as their model, the regulations use the concept of a "loss group" or loss subgroup as their model and treat it as though it were a separate company. The definition of a loss group is complicated and differs for NOL versus built-in loss purposes versus SRLY purposes. However, with certain exceptions, for NOL purposes a loss group generally consists of all the members of a consolidated return group except those subsidiaries having SRLY losses that entered the group without an ownership change, and for built-in loss purposes it generally includes all members except those who joined the group within the last five years and either (i) had a net built-in gain at the time and still has one, or (ii) had a SRLY built-in loss at the time as to which no ownership change occurred, and still has a net built-in loss (*see* § 508.7.2 below).[303]

---

300 *See* Prop. Reg. § § 1.1502-90 through -99. *See also* IRS Notice 91-27, 1991-2 C.B. 629, in which the IRS announced certain contemplated changes in the transition and effective date rules for these regulations. These proposed regulations are analyzed in depth in Silberberg, Consolidated Section 382: The Proposed Regulations, 69 Taxes 395 (1991), and in Blanchard, The Single Entity Theory of the Consolidated Section 382 Regulations: A Study in Complexity, 69 Taxes 915 (1991).

301 The 1996 proposed and temporary regulations are now Reg. § § 1.1502-90A through 1.1502-99A. The Tax Section of the New York State Bar Association filed a lengthy report making suggestions for improvements in these regulations. New York State Bar Association, Tax Section, Committee on Net Operating Losses, Report on Regulations concerning the Application of Section 382 to Consolidated Groups (October 7, 1998).

302 These regulations and amendments are analyzed in depth in Goldring and Sontag, Life After the Final Regulations: Consolidated Section 382 and SRLY, Vol. 27 Tax Strategies for Corporate Acquisitions, Dispositions, Spin-Offs, Joint Ventures, Financing, Reorganizations and Restructurings (Prac. Law Inst. 2006).

303 This reflects one of the significant changes from the temporary regulations. Under the temporary regulations, all members were included in the loss group for built-in loss purposes *other than* any member that joined the group within the last five years *with* a SRLY built-in loss. Under the final

A "loss subgroup" refers to a group of affiliated companies that joined the present group. For Code § 382 but not for SRLY purposes, a loss subgroup generally must have a common parent, and when a group of brother-sister companies leaves one consolidated group and joins another, it may be necessary to rearrange their structure in order to take advantage of these rules. Alternatively, under the final regulations, an election can be made to treat such companies as nevertheless comprising a single loss subgroup despite the absence of a common subgroup parent. This election permits greater conformity with the SRLY subgroup rules, thereby increasing the likelihood that the two sets of rules will overlap, in which event the SRLY limitation will not apply (*see* § 509.4 below). The regulations permit this election to be made even with respect to certain ownership changes otherwise governed by the temporary regulations. However, the election may have certain disadvantages in the case of a loss subgroup that does not undergo an ownership change at the time it joined the consolidated group but remains separately tracked. In particular, an ownership change of the *entire* loss subgroup will occur if there is a subsequent ownership change of *any* member of the subgroup (other than upon the member's departure from the consolidated group). As with a loss group, the members comprising a loss subgroup can be different for NOL versus built-in loss purposes. For NOL purposes, all that is required is that each member of the subgroup have been affiliated at some time in the past, whereas for built-in loss purposes, a five-year continuous affiliation requirement applies (*see* § 508.7.2 below).

The ownership change rules are as follows:

(1) *Parent change method.* An ownership change of the parent constitutes an ownership change for the group. This is true even if, on a separate company basis, the subsidiaries would not have had an ownership change. This rule ignores changes in stock ownership of the subsidiaries.

(2) *Supplemental method.* If a 5 percent shareholder of the parent (including any person acting pursuant to a plan with such person) increases his percentage ownership (by any amount) in both the parent and any subsidiary during a three year period (or, if shorter, the period since the last ownership change), the parent generally is treated as if it had issued to that person an amount of parent stock having the same fair market value as the subsidiary stock acquired.[304] This rule applies if it would produce an ownership change when the first rule would not; that is, it operates in addition to, and not in place of, the first rule. The concept of a "plan" is vague, and where there have been any increases in the last three years in the percentage ownership of the parent by any of its 5 percent shareholders, it is difficult

(Footnote Continued)

regulations, only certain SRLY built-in loss members are excluded. Moreover, the loss group cannot, in computing its net built-in loss, obtain advantage of any acquired net built-in gains for five years.

[304] In certain cases, the final regulations condition the application of this rule on the common parent having actual knowledge of the 5 percent shareholder's increase in the subsidiary, or of the plan or arrangement between the 5 percent shareholder and the third party to increase their ownership in the parent and subsidiary, before the due date of the group's tax return for the taxable year of the increase. Although this may provide some comfort in the long term, the group remains potentially exposed to changes that the common parent may not learn about until months later but still prior to the due date of its tax return.

to predict which sales of subsidiary stock to third parties would not be considered part of such a plan. For example, would issuance of 10 percent of a subsidiary's stock to its creditors and issuance of 6 percent of the parent's stock to the parent's creditors be considered part of a "plan" orchestrated by the parent or its new 5 percent shareholders, and thus caught by this rule? Compare the not dissimilar acting-in-concert concept involved in the definition of an "entity" for aggregation rule purposes under Code §382 (§508.2.8.1 above). This is an unfortunate rule. It seems animated by the thought that there is generally no good commercial reason for having stock changes at both the parent and subsidiary level, which simply is not true. Indeed, where the parent is highly leveraged but the subsidiary is not, the subsidiary may be the only viable place for raising new equity money for the group. And it is in just such cases that this rule, if it applied, would have the most disastrous effect, since the subsidiary stock will be so much more valuable than the parent stock. In just such a situation, however, the IRS has ruled favorably on a proposed transaction where a subsidiary issued new stock options to management. There had been recent increases of ownership in the parent by 5 percent shareholders of the parent. The employees granted options in the subsidiary were required to give up any options they had for parent stock, and were required to certify that they were "not acting under any formal or informal understanding with another person who has acquired stock (or options) of subsidiary or parent to make a coordinated acquisition of subsidiary stock (or options)." The IRS ruled the employees would not be treated as acting pursuant to a plan with a holder who has increased ownership in the parent, and thus the granting of the options would not be taken into account for purposes of determining whether the parent had an ownership change.[305]

(3) *Exceptions.* These rules are subject to certain exceptions. They amount to additions, not limitations, to the first two rules. That is, the exceptions can create ownership changes for subsidiaries (or subgroups) on a separate tracking basis even where an ownership change for the group under one of the first two rules has not occurred. The first exception provides that where a subsidiary (or subgroup) joined the group without having an ownership change (either at the time or within six months prior), the subsidiary (or subgroup) will be separately tracked for ownership changes until the earlier of (a) its having an ownership change (under either the separate tracking method or one of the first two rules) or (b) the fifth anniversary of its joining the group. A second exception applies where options (other than certain bilateral contracts which are consummated within a year) are issued to buy more than 20 percent of the stock of a subsidiary, if exercise of the options would produce an ownership change for the subsidiary. A third exception applies where one or more 5 percent shareholders, acting pursuant to a plan, acquire interests in both a subsidiary and higher tier members, with the intention of avoiding (under the first two rules) an ownership change of the subsidiary, if separate tracking would produce an ownership change for the subsidiary.

---

[305] IRS Letter Ruling 9245012, August 3, 1992.

### § 508.7.2 Determination of Built-in Gains and Losses

Except where separate tracking applies, the regulations generally treat loss groups or subgroups as single corporations for purposes of determining the amount of Code § 382 built-in gains or losses—including the determination of whether the $10 million or 15 percent threshold has been met. Accordingly, any built-in gain or loss with respect to intercompany debt or stock held in other members is disregarded for purposes of computing the group's net built-in gain or loss (but, when subsequently recognized, will be taken into account in determining the group's recognized built-in gain or loss).[306] The regulations also make clear that built-in gain or loss includes intercompany deferred items under Reg. § 1.1502-13 (other than amounts deferred with respect to the stock or debt of other members).

For companies or subgroups excluded from the definition of the loss group or subgroup for purposes of the built-in gain or loss computation, built-in gains or losses are determined separately for that company or subgroup.

Significantly, the final regulations classify the members of a loss group or subgroup differently for built-in gain purposes than for built-in loss purposes, and, in the case of built-in losses, employ slightly different definitions for loss groups than for loss subgroups. For built-in gain purposes, all members of the group are taken into account without exception. However, for built-in loss purposes, certain members are excluded. In the case of a loss group, any member acquired within the five-year period preceding the group change is excluded *unless* the member was acquired (i) with a net built-in gain, but has a net built-in loss at the time of the group change, or (ii) with a SRLY built-in loss and either has a net built-in gain at the time of the group change, or underwent an ownership change in connection with, or since becoming, a member of the group. In the case of a loss subgroup, there is a similar five-year continuous affiliation requirement; however, the five years is measured at the time the loss subgroup joins the consolidated group (even if no ownership change occurs at that time), and there is no similar exception to that in the loss group context for a less than five-year-old member that had a net built-in gain that has since become a net built-in loss. Thus, in the subgroup context, the net built-in loss of any less than five-year-old member generally would be subject to Section 382 on a separate

---

[306] The theory for ignoring built-in gain or loss in the stock of a subsidiary is, of course, that one looks through the stock of that subsidiary to its underlying assets, so it is the built-in gain or loss in those assets, rather than in the stock of their owner, that is taken into account for this purpose. This rule can have the interesting consequence of allowing, on the right facts, a built-in loss in the stock to escape the Code § 382 deduction limitations, as is illustrated by IRS Technical Advice Memorandum 200549007, August 5, 2005. Here, a bankrupt corporate subsidiary sold essentially all its assets for cash before its ownership change date. Thus, on its ownership change date there was no built-in gain or loss in its assets. Although the stock of that subsidiary did continue nonetheless to have a large built-in loss, under the rule just mentioned this did not have to be included in the group's Code § 382 net built-in-loss calculation. Although the stock of the subsidiary became worthless during the same taxable year in which it had an ownership change, because the ownership change occurred before the end of that year and the worthless stock deduction is treated by Code § 165(g)(1) as not occurring until the last day of that year, the group's ability to deduct the worthless stock deduction was not limited at all by Code § 382. This Technical Advice is discussed in Willens, Conseco's Worthless Stock Loss Appears to Withstand Scrutiny, BNA Daily Tax Report #5 (January 9, 2006), at p. J-1.

company basis. Notice that, in both contexts, acquired net built-in gains generally cannot be taken into account for built-in loss purposes for a full five years. Because a group's net built-in gain and net built-in loss are determined independently, a loss group or subgroup can have a recognized built-in gain that increases the group's Code § 382 limitation for NOL purposes, and at the same time have a recognized built-in loss that is subject to limitation (computed without regard to any increase for recognized built-in gains).

### § 508.7.3 Continuity of Business Enterprise

A loss group is treated as a single entity in determining whether it satisfies the Code § 382 continuity of business enterprise requirement. The regulations give an example of a group consisting of a parent and two subsidiaries. Each conducts a separate line of business, and each is about equal in value. A year after an ownership change of the loss group, the parent and one of the subsidiaries terminate their businesses, but the other subsidiary continues its business. The group satisfies the continuity of business enterprise requirement.

### § 508.7.4 Annual Code § 382 Limitation

Except where separate tracking of a subsidiary or subgroup applies, the annual limitation for the loss group is based on the value of the stock of the parent, plus the value of any stock of the subsidiaries that is not owned by other members of the group. Thus, the value of intercompany stock is eliminated.

This rule can have particularly unfortunate results for consolidated groups that have very highly leveraged parents, as is the case with many companies that have made leveraged buyouts.

**EXAMPLE**

Parent is formed to buy Target. Target's stock is worth $1 billion. Parent finances the purchase by issuing $950 million of debt and $50 million of stock. Target generates NOLs and two years later Parent has an ownership change. Assume that the stock values of Parent and Target have not changed. The annual limitation applicable to Target's (and Parent's) NOLs will be based on the tax exempt bond rate times the $50 million value of Parent's stock, not the $1 billion value of Target's stock.

### § 508.7.5 Apportioning Code § 382 Limitations to Departing Members

The regulations do not change the general rules that determine the amount of a consolidated loss which is apportioned to a member that leaves the group, and which the departing member takes with it when it leaves the group. It will be recalled that a departing member takes with it the portion of the unused consolidated NOL that it has created, but it should also be recalled that this may be cut down by several things, including: (i) income of the consolidated group earned in the entire taxable year of the member's departure (even the portion of the year after the subsidiary leaves); (ii) excluded COD income of the departing member or, under certain circumstances, of another member incurred during the year (even after the subsidiary leaves); and (iii) for periods before March 7, 2002, the election by a parent deprived of a loss under Reg. § 1.1502-20 on the subsidiary's stock to reattribute to itself an amount of the subsidiary's NOLs equal to that disallowed loss.[307]

The regulations add a further problem. They say that if a Code § 382 limitation applied to the group or subgroup before the member left, any predeparture consolidated attribute that was subject to the consolidated limitation will continue to be subject to a Code § 382 limitation in the hands of the departing member; and, what is more, the departing member's limitation shall be *zero*, except to the extent the common parent (not the subgroup parent) elects to attribute some or all of the consolidated limitation to the departing member. Although the regulations state that only the common parent may make such election, as a practical matter the departing member's consent is also required since the regulations require the departing member to sign the election statement. Obviously, unless such an election is made, the attribute that leaves with the subsidiary will become worthless in the subsidiary's hands. Query: In the light of *Prudential Lines* (discussed at § 508.2.4), can such an election be mandated by a bankruptcy court for a bankrupt subsidiary? *See also* § 804.5 and § 804.7 below.

The final regulations also address the apportionment of any unrealized net built-in gain or loss relating to a prior Code § 382 limitation of the group.[308] Similar to the basic Code § 382 limitation, the common parent may elect to apportion any unrealized net built-in gain, absent which no amount will be apportioned to the departing member. Any unrealized net built-in loss is subject to a mandatory apportionment, based on the relative amount of the *gross* (not the *net*) unrealized built-in loss that leaves the group with the departing member. Thus, even a very valuable member that itself had a net built-in gain (as computed on an individual member basis) at the time of the prior group ownership change may be apportioned part of the group's unrealized net built-in loss at the time of the prior change. Thus, unless an election is made to allocate a portion of the group's Code § 382 limitation to that subsidiary as well, all or part of any subsequently recognized loss (or deduction) with respect to

---

[307] *See* §§ 508.2.4 above and 804.5 below (regarding Reg. § 1.1502-20) and § 804.4.5 (regarding excluded COD income within a consolidated group). Code § 382-related rules regarding losses reattributed under Reg. § 1.1502-20 are contained in Reg. § 1.1502-96(d). As a result of the IRS decision to follow *Rite Aid Corp. v. United States*, 255 F.3d 1357, 2001-2 U.S.T.C. ¶ 50,516 (Fed. Cir. 2001), *supra* note 50, the IRS superseded the Reg. § 1.1502-20 rules for periods beginning March 7, 2002, with Reg. §§ 1.337(d)-2T, 1.1502-20T(i), 1.1502-32T(b)(4)(v), and 1.1502-35T. In early 2007, the IRS proposed to replace these provisions, prospectively, with Prop. Reg. § 1.1502-36, which also provides a limited election to reattribute the subsidiary's losses. *See* the discussion at § 804.5 below.

[308] The temporary regulations had been silent, but in the preamble the IRS solicited comments. Although the final regulations build in some elective retroactivity with respect to these provisions, there remains uncertainty as to the proper apportionment of any unrealized net built-in gain and loss for departing members governed by the temporary regulations.

such built-in loss assets during the remainder of the five-year recognition period may be worthless to the subsidiary.

### § 508.7.6 Effective Date

In general, final regulations § § 1.1502-90 through 99 apply to any testing date on or after June 25, 1999 (even if the testing period began before that date). Certain special effective date and transitional rules apply, however, particularly in the case of liberalizing changes. The temporary regulations generally apply to any testing date on or after January 1, 1997, and before June 25, 1999.

The temporary regulations also have an element of retroactivity. They give taxpayers various alternatives for determining whether ownership changes took place before that date, and if they did, the amount of the limitation. If the computations were not consistent with the new rules, then they require certain adjustments to be made to returns filed after January 1, 1997, to bring them into line with the new rules.

## *§ 508.8 Treatment of Controlled Groups: Not Filing Consolidated Returns*

Code § 382(m)(5) gives the IRS authority to issue regulations covering corporations that do not file consolidated returns but which are under 50 percent or greater common control, for the purpose of making appropriate Code § 382 adjustments to value, built-in gain or loss, and other items so that they will neither be omitted nor taken into account twice.

Reg. § 1.382-8 was issued to achieve these objectives.[309] It does this by generally eliminating from the value of any member of a component group the value of the stock it owns in any other member of the group. This means that the value of the stock of a 50 percent or more owned subsidiary generally will be excluded from the value of the parent's stock for purposes of the parent's Code § 382 limitation computations. (This achieves for unconsolidated companies essentially the same result that applies for consolidated companies, substituting 50 percent for 80 percent ownership.) The value of the subsidiary's stock would be taken into account only for purposes of determining the subsidiary's own limitations. However, the subsidiary may elect to allow the parent instead to include in the parent's value for Code § 382 purposes the value of the parent's stock in the subsidiary, provided that the subsidiary reduces its own value for purposes of its own Code § 382 limitation by the same amount. The election must be made with the tax return for the year of the ownership change.[310]

---

309 The effective date of this regulation, which was issued as a proposed and temporary regulation in 1997, is generally the same as the effective date of the consolidated return regulations discussed above. *See* § 508.7.6.

310 Reg. § 1.382-8(h), as in effect prior to T.D. 9264 (May 30, 2006), and Temp. Reg. § 1.382-8T(h) (effective for thereafter).

This election has served as a trap for the unwary, although the IRS has been liberal in granting extensions of time to make the election.[311] Recognizing this, and that most companies cause their foreign subsidiaries to make a restoration election (there generally being no disadvantage to the election), the IRS in 2006 issued a temporary regulation that reverses the manner in which the election operates in the case of a foreign controlled subsidiary that has items treated as connected with the conduct by it of a U.S. trade or business "that it takes into account" in determining its own value for purposes of a Code §382 limitation.[312] Although not entirely clear, it seems to us that the quoted phrasing means that only foreign *loss* corporations have to make an affirmative restoration election. This reversal is effective for tax returns due on or after May 30, 2006, other than returns already filed.[313]

## §509 CODE §269, TIR 773, CRCOs, AND SRLYs

As mentioned at §506, other issues posed by the issuance of stock to creditors include (1) the potential for disallowance of NOLs and other carryovers under Code §269, (2) the remnants of the *Libson Shops* doctrine found in TIR 773, (3) the consolidated return change of ownership (CRCO) rules, and (4) the separate return limitation year (SRLY) rules in the consolidated return regulations. Each issue is discussed below.[1]

### *§509.1 Tax Avoidance Purpose (Code §269)*

Code §269 allows the IRS to disallow a corporation's deductions (including "built-in" losses) or credits where (1) any person or group of persons have acquired "control" of the corporation, or (2) the corporation acquires carryover basis assets from a corporation not controlled by it or its stockholders and, in either case, the principal purpose of the acquisition is the avoidance of tax by obtaining the benefit of the deductions or credits.[2] "Control" for this purpose means 50 percent in voting

---

[311] *See* IRS Letter Ruling 200445011, July 8, 2004; IRS Letter Ruling 200445012, July 8, 2004; IRS Letter Ruling 200513016, December 14, 2004; IRS Letter Ruling 200513017, December 14, 2004; IRS Letter Ruling 200333014, April 30, 2003; IRS Letter Ruling 200130011, April 24, 2001; IRS Letter Ruling 200202043, October 9, 2001; IRS Letter Ruling 200202044, October 9, 2001; IRS Letter Rulings 200603012 through 200603015, October 11, 2005; IRS Letter Ruling 200604018, October 24, 2005; IRS Letter Ruling 200613024, December 16, 2005; IRS Letter Ruling 200622031, February 14, 2006.

[312] Temp. Reg. §1.382-8T(h).

[313] Temp. Reg. §1.382-8T(h)(4) (including any amended return filed on or after May 30, 2006, but still before the due date of the original return, including extensions). This regulation expires on May 26, 2009, subject to final regulations.

[1] **§509** For a discussion of these provisions and their interrelationship, *see* Stewart & Call, Overlap of NOL Limitation Provisions Causes Unwarranted Complexity, 21 J. Corp. Tax'n 353 (1995).

[2] Code §269(a). For a detailed discussion of Code §269, *see* Bittker & Eustice, Federal Income Taxation of Corporations and Shareholders ¶14.41 (7th ed.); Solinga, A Survey of Legal Factors Helpful in Establishing the Principal Motivation Requirements of Section 269, 64 Taxes 302 (1986); Bowen & Sheffield, Section 269 Revisited, 61 Taxes 881 (1983); Faber, Net Operating Losses in Corporate Reorganizations Revisited in 1979, 38 Inst. on Fed. Tax'n at §4.02[1] (1979).

power or value of the stock of the corporation, and it does not matter whether it was acquired in a taxable or in a tax-free manner.[3] "Principal purpose" means the most important purpose.[4]

---

[3] Code § 269(a). In *Hermes Consolidated, Inc. v. United States*, 88-1 U.S.T.C. ¶9220 (Cl. Ct.), a carefully designed acquisition of a loss company by a profitable company was found to involve acquisition of less than 50 percent of either the vote or value of the target's stock. The loss company had been recapitalized, giving the prior owners voting preferred in exchange for all their common. The profitable company acquired new-issue common. It also assigned to the loss company a contract to purchase an oil refinery. The preferred and common each had equal voting rights on such corporate matters as mergers or liquidations, but on the election of directors each class could elect one of the three directors, with the third being elected by all the shares in the aggregate. The purchasing company had only 49 percent of the aggregate number of shares. The common stockholder also had the right to redeem the preferred stock, and to "put" the preacquisition business of the target to the preferred shareholders. The court found only the voting rights for directors to be relevant in determining what constituted voting power, and it decided that the acquisition involved less than 50 percent of both the voting power and value of the stock of the loss company. In effect, the court held that, whereas the purchasing company did have 50 percent of the voting power for approving or disapproving certain fundamental corporate changes, the fact that it had less than 50 percent control with respect to the election of directors was sufficient to throw its voting power below 50 percent for purposes of Code § 269. The IRS addressed a similar issue in T.A.M. 9452002, August 26, 1994. Here, the IRS concluded that the 80 percent voting power requirement for filing consolidated returns can not be determined mechanically based solely on the election of directors. Where the holder of stock possessing 80 percent of the vote for the election of directors is materially restricted in its management control through various class voting requirements, the IRS held that the mere power to elect directors is not an accurate measure of voting power. The T.A.M. indicated that the same type of analysis should be applied for purposes of Code § 269. The IRS position on the 80 percent issue involved in IRS Technical Advice Memorandum 9452002 was upheld by the Tax Court in a case involving the taxpayer to whom the T.A.M. was issued. *Alumax, Inc. v. Commissioner*, 109 T.C. 133 (1997), *aff'd* (11th Cir. January 21, 1999).

[4] *See* Reg. § 1.269-3(a); *Canaveral Intl. Corp. v. Commissioner*, 61 T.C. 520, 536 Dec. 32,432 (1974). In *U.S. Shelter Corp. v. United States*, 87-2 U.S.T.C. ¶9588 (Cl. Ct.), the court held that where several nontax motivations existed, no single one of which was more important than the tax motivation, but the aggregate of which did exceed the tax motivation, the proper application of the "principal purpose" test is to compare the aggregate of the tax motivations with the aggregate of the nontax motivations. For an interesting case, which follows *U.S. Shelter Corp.* and which further holds that the ratio of tax benefits to the value of the company is not determinative as to the principal purpose of the acquisition, *see United States v. Federated Dep't Stores, Inc.*, 170 B.R. 331, 94-2 U.S.T.C. ¶50,418 (S.D. Ohio 1994) (affirming Bankruptcy Court). For a thorough examination of the authorities under Code § 269, and a holding that Code § 269's principal purpose of tax avoidance was not met where there were important business reasons, both offensive and defensive, for making the acquisition, and for the form of the acquisition, *see* IRS Field Service Advice, January 15, 1993, *reprinted at* 98 TNT 201-99. In this Advice, profitable assets were contributed to the bankrupt loss company in a Code § 351 exchange, accompanied by a stock-for-debt recapitalization of the loss company. For an IRS analysis of the Code § 269 principal purpose test where a profitable company was merged into the loss company, following which most of the assets of the profitable company were sold, *see* IRS Field Service Advice 1998-416, July 9, 1993, *reprinted at* 98 TNT 234-65 (acquisition was structured to preserve tax benefits, but there were also sound business reasons; the IRS discouraged the field against raising the Code § 269 issue). The IRS has also recognized, in a field service advice, that Code § 269 is difficult to apply where the loss company buys a profitable company for cash or debt and where it is unlikely that any interest in the NOLs was given to the shareholders of the target corporation. In this case, the IRS also noted that the companies were likely to go back into bankruptcy, in which case the Code § 269 principal purpose issue would be decided by the bankruptcy court, which the IRS viewed as an unfavorable forum for tax issues. IRS Field Service Advice 1999-1103, July 20, 1992, *reprinted at* 1999 TNT 122-78. In IRS Field Service Advice 1999-754, March 19, 1992, *reprinted at* 1999 TNT 40-53, the IRS suggested that where the two corporations involved in the

Where the creditors in a debt restructuring receive stock that will represent 50 percent or more of the vote or value of all the stock thereafter, they will, at least in form, have satisfied the acquisition of "control" requirement. However, in such a circumstance, the debtor's NOLs and other carryovers will usually have been largely financed by the creditors' money. It would be anomalous to invoke Code § 269 when the company's lack of success finally requires the creditors to convert their debt into equity. In reality, they are simply preserving their existing investment in the NOLs and other tax attributes, rather than acquiring anything.[5] Prior to the 1990 authorities mentioned at the end of this § 509.1, there had been no case or ruling that dealt with this question, and we had expressed the hope that the IRS would not seek to apply Code § 269 in such circumstances.[6]

Nonetheless, we had said that until a favorable case or ruling appears, the parties to a debt restructuring should be careful to focus on the business reasons for the transaction and not to exaggerate tax considerations. Obviously, the more substantial the remaining business operations and prospects of the corporation are, the stronger the case will be. As stressed earlier, a failing company should always try to restructure itself long before it has wound down its business operations to a point where its tax benefits may be more valuable than its remaining business operations.

In addition, the case will be stronger where the creditors at the time of the workout are those who originally lent the money that financed the loss, rather than persons who subsequently purchased the debt from the original lenders, perhaps with a view to participating in the workout. A policy, such as that of Code § 269, that discourages sales of stock in the company cannot be expected to look more favorably on sales of debt.

Frequently in a debt workout, a restructuring of debt, including a satisfaction of debt with equity, will be accompanied by the acquisition of stock by outsiders for infusions of new money into the corporation. For the reasons expressed above, we had expressed the hope that old creditors receiving stock would not be treated by the

---

(Footnote Continued)

transaction were ultimately owned by the same interests, and no outside party acquired any interest in the tax benefits, perhaps Code § 269 should not apply; but *cf.* IRS Field Service Advice 199926011, March 26, 1999 (concluding that Code § 269 applies where a foreign parent rearranged the ownership of its U.S. subsidiaries under a U.S. holding company in order to satisfy the 80/20 test of Code § 861(c)(1)(A) and lower the withholding tax on distributions to the foreign parent), *reprinted at* 1999 TNT 128-28. In *Plain Petroleum Co. v. Commissioner*, T.C. Memo. 1999-241, the Tax Court found, in a case where the tax benefits of the target company dwarfed the value of its business assets, the Code § 269 principal purpose test was not met because the business reasons for the acquisition predominated. To similar effect, *see* IRS Field Service Advice 1998-425, August 11, 1993, *reprinted at* 98 TNT 239-67.

[5] *Cf.* GCM 34185, August 22, 1969 (recognizing the interrelationship between losses and borrowed funds and the continued availability of losses when creditors acquire stock of the loss company). *See also In re Prudential Lines, Inc.*, 119 B.R. 430 (S.D.N.Y. 1990), *aff'd*, 928 F.2d 565, 92-2 U.S.T.C. ¶ 50,491 (2d Cir. 1992), *cert. denied*, 112 S. Ct. 82 (1991) (stating that "[w]hen creditors go unpaid due to the very losses giving rise to the NOL, they ought to be able to realize the value of a NOL carryover as property of the bankruptcy estate upon reorganization").

[6] *See also* Krupsky, Take Over of a Bankrupt Company by a Single Major Creditor, 36 Major Tax Plan. § 1502.5 (1984); Asofsky, Reorganizing Insolvent Corporations, 41 Inst. on Fed. Tax'n at § 5.04[2] (1983); Plumb, The Bankruptcy Tax Act, 33 Major Tax Plan. 8-1, 8-56 (1981).

IRS as part of a group with the new investors and have their acquisitions lumped with those by the new investors to determine if "control" has been acquired.

Because of the lack before 1990 of authority on the foregoing points and the uncertainties inevitably created by subjective standards like the tax-avoidance-motive test, we had said that tax practitioners should try, where possible, to limit the aggregate of the stock going to creditors and new investors in a workout to less than 50 percent in vote or value of the stock that will be outstanding thereafter.

Unfortunately, the IRS took steps in 1990 that would dash the hopes expressed above. First, in IRS Letter Ruling 9019036 (February 9, 1990), the IRS faced a situation where a bankruptcy plan governed by the rule in Code §382(l)(5) provided for issuance of more than 50 percent of the stock to old-and-cold creditors (within the meaning of Code §382(l)(5)) with the balance to go to other creditors and a new investor. The IRS held that an acquisition of "control" within the meaning of Code §269 had occurred, and left the question whether the principal purpose was avoiding tax to the determination of the District Director.

Second, on August 13, 1990, the IRS issued proposed amendments to the regulations under Code §269. These were adopted in final form in December 1991 and do the following things:

(1) Reg. §§1.269-3(d) and 1.269-5(b) provide that where creditors (by themselves or with others) acquire control of a corporation, Code §269 may apply if the acquisition was made with the principal purpose of avoiding federal income tax.

    We think—for the reasons expressed above—that this is a wrong approach; that it is both bad tax policy and bad bankruptcy policy to count creditors in the control group. However, this approach was expressly rejected by the IRS in the preamble to the final regulations.

(2) Reg. §1.269-3(e) provides that in determining for purposes of Code §269 whether an acquisition pursuant to a bankruptcy plan was made for the principal purpose of avoiding federal income tax, the fact that (a) the federal government did not object to confirmation of the plan on this ground (as it is permitted to do under section 1129(d) of the Bankruptcy Code (*see* §1002.8 below)) shall not be taken into account and (b) an actual adjudication against the government under this provision by the bankruptcy court shall not be controlling.[7]

(3) Reg. §1.269-5(a) and (b) provide that an acquisition of control occurs for purposes of Code §269 when one or more persons acquire "beneficial ownership" of the requisite percentage of stock; and that creditors of an insolvent or bankrupt corporation shall not be deemed, for purposes of Code §269, to acquire such a beneficial interest earlier than the confirmation date of the bankruptcy plan.

---

[7] In this regard, consider *In re Rath Packing Co.*, 55 B.R. 528 (Bankr. N.D. Iowa 1985), wherein the bankruptcy court itself raised Bankruptcy Code section 1129(d), stating that it was "not going to allow the IRS to . . . bring an action in tax court several years from now."

For the reasons discussed at § 510 below, we believe this is a sound position.

(4) Finally, as mentioned above at § 508.5, Reg. § 1.269-3(d) seeks to engraft an attenuated form of a continuity-of-business requirement onto Code § 382(l)(5). It provides a rebuttable presumption that an ownership change governed by Code § 382(l)(5) is considered to be made for the principal purpose of avoiding tax unless the corporation carries on more than an insignificant amount of an active trade or business during and subsequent to the title 11 case. Responding to the objection that this amounted to overruling Congress's intention that the continuity of business enterprise requirement would not apply to Code § 382(l)(5) transactions, the final regulations expressly state that this requirement is not the same as the continuity of business enterprise requirement. They add that the determination is based on all the facts, including the amount of business assets that continue to be used, or the number of employees who continue to work in an active trade or business (although not necessarily the historic trade or business). They go on to say that this requirement "may be met even though all trade or business activities temporarily cease for a period of time in order to address business exigencies." This presumption applies only to acquisitions made pursuant to a plan confirmed after August 14, 1990, although the IRS will presumably apply similar concepts (without the presumption) to earlier transactions. The preamble to the final regulation observes that commentators objected that this rule refers only to an acquisition of control, whereas a further step—namely action to combine income from other assets with the losses—should be necessary to invoke Code § 269. The IRS expressly rejected this position, saying that an acquisition of control with a bad motive is enough, by itself, to invoke Code § 269. The IRS reserved the question whether the continuation of a significant amount of business requirement could be satisfied on a consolidated group, rather than an individual company, basis.

Reg. §§ 1.269-3(d), (e) and 1.269-5(b) received their first court test in the *Allis-Chalmers* case.[8] Here, the debtor had received a favorable ruling from the IRS regarding applicability of Code § 382(l)(5), and the bankruptcy court had specifically found, pursuant to Bankruptcy Code section 1129(d), that the principal purpose of the plan was not tax avoidance. The IRS was a party to the bankruptcy proceeding and did not raise any question of tax avoidance in that proceeding. The plan was confirmed. Subsequently the IRS notified the debtor that its future use of NOLs might be challenged under Code § 269.

The debtor sought to enjoin the IRS on grounds of *res judicata* or collateral estoppel. Although the bankruptcy court held that neither doctrine was available, the court was highly critical of the regulations and the IRS action. Interestingly, the court held that even if Bankruptcy Code section 1129(d) did not exist or was not specifi-

---

[8] *Allis-Chalmers Corp. v. Goldberg (In re Hartman Material Handling Systems, Inc.)*, 92-2 U.S.T.C. ¶ 50,325 at n.10 (Bankr. S.D.N.Y.), also discussed at §§ 1002.8 and 1013.3.1.

cally invoked by the court or the parties, a finding that the principal purpose of the plan is not tax avoidance is implied in every confirmation order, since otherwise the plan could not be considered proposed in good faith. The court observed that the regulations added an unfortunate uncertainty that jeopardizes the viability of many reorganizations. "It is essential that a reorganizing company know how to structure its reorganization to preserve its tax benefits. In many cases, this certainty will be necessary to determine the feasibility of a plan . . . . The IRS now seeks to use § 269 to disrupt this process." The court went on to say that:

> This Court believes that the IRS's proposed use of the general provisions of § 269 to attack the tax avoidance purpose of transactions that a court has reviewed and that § 382 was specifically enacted to address is an unfair and improper construction of the statutes.

The court then observed that while, for technical reasons, it could not grant the relief requested (and with which it was clearly sympathetic), the taxpayer had a right to assert the court's confirmation finding of nontax avoidance, in response to any future IRS action under Code § 269, and to defend such action on the basis of "judicial estoppel" (which the court described as a rule against playing "fast and loose with the courts").

## § 509.2 *Technical Information Release 773*

For transactions subject to old Code § 382, the IRS has taken the position that it will seek to apply the 1939 Code *Libson Shops*[9] doctrine to 1954 Code cases where there has been both (1) a 50 percentage point or more shift in the benefits of the NOLs and (2) an old Code § 382(a) change in business.[10] The purpose of this is to seek to cover cases like *Maxwell Hardware Co.*,[11] where a stock structure was cleverly designed to avoid creating an old Code § 382(a) change in ownership as a technical matter, even though it had essentially the same substantive result.

Whether the IRS will be able to succeed in this endeavor is questionable. The circuit courts of appeal are split as to the continuing vitality of *Libson Shops* under the 1954 Code. The Eight and Ninth (and apparently the Sixth) Circuit Courts of Appeals

---

[9] *Libson Shops v. Koehler*, 353 U.S. 382, 57-1 U.S.T.C. ¶ 9691 (holding that NOLs can be used only against income from substantially the same enterprise that created them).

[10] TIR 773 (October 13, 1965). TIR 733 was followed, and the change of business requirement was found not to have been met, in IRS Field Service Advice, January 15, 1993, 98 TNT 201-99.

[11] 343 F.2d 716 (9th Cir. 1969).

have held that *Libson Shops* does not survive under the 1954 Code.[12] The Fourth and Fifth Circuit Courts of Appeals have held to the contrary.[13]

For transactions subject to new Code §382, the *Libson Shops* doctrine is to have no application.[14] Thus, TIR 773 will not be applicable to such transactions.

## §509.3 *Consolidated Return (CRCO)*

For transactions subject to old Code §382, the consolidated return CRCO rule provides, in substance, that if there has been an old Code §382(a) change in ownership of the parent of a consolidated return group, the NOLs and other carryovers of the corporations that were members of the group on the last day of the taxable year prior to the change in ownership can be used only against the income of those old members and not against the income of any corporations that join the group thereafter.[15] This rule applies even if the parent had no subsidiaries at the time of the change in ownership[16] and even though no corporation has had an old Code §382(a) change in business.[17] Where, however, a business of a loss company is dropped down into a newly created subsidiary (in a Code §351 transaction) with which it then files a consolidated return, the subsidiary will be regarded as an "old member" of the loss company's consolidated group. As a result, the NOLs and other carryovers of the loss company may be used against the subsidiary's income.[18]

---

[12] *See Exel Corp. v. United States*, 451 F.2d 80, 71-2 U.S.T.C. ¶9731 (8th Cir. 1971); *United States v. Adkins-Phelps, Inc.*, 400 F.2d 737, 742-743, 68-2 U.S.T.C. ¶9609 (8th Cir. 1968); *Maxwell Hardware Co. v. Commissioner*, *supra* note 11; *compare Frederick Steel Co. v. Commissioner*, 375 F.2d 351, 67-1 U.S.T.C. ¶9279 (6th Cir.), *cert. denied*, 389 U.S. 901 (1976) (1954 Code exclusive), *with Euclid-Tennessee, Inc. v. Commissioner*, 41 T.C. 752, Dec. 26,682, (1964), *aff'd*, 352 F.2d 991, 65-2 U.S.T.C. ¶9763 (6th Cir. 1965), *cert. denied*, 384 U.S. 940 (1966) ("We cannot and do not read *Libson* into the 1954 Code, but its broad principles may be relevant except as the 1954 Code, under limited conditions, permits what the 1939 Code, construed by *Libson*, forbade").

[13] *United States v. Jackson Oldsmobile, Inc.*, 371 F.2d 808, 67-1 U.S.T.C. ¶9231 (5th Cir. 1967); *J.G. Dudley Co. v. Commissioner*, 298 F.2d 750, 62-1 U.S.T.C. ¶9224 (4th Cir. 1962); *see also National Tea Co. v. Commissioner*, 83 T.C. 8, Dec. 41,326; *aff'd*, 793 F.2d 864, 86-1 U.S.T.C. ¶9483 (7th Cir. 1986) (*Libson Shops* still applicable to carryback if not to carryovers); *Clarksdale Rubber Co.*, 45 T.C. 234, Dec. 27,650 (1965) (but *Libson Shops* not applicable where old Code §382 may apply).

[14] H.R. Rep. No. 841, 99th Cong., 2d Sess. at II-194 (1986) (the 1986 Act Conference Report).

[15] Reg. §§1.1502-1(g), -3(e) (ITC carryover), -4(g) (foreign tax credit carryover), -21(d) (NOLs), -22(d) (capital loss carryover). It should be noted that the CRCO regulation, Reg. §1.1502-1(g), states its own change in ownership rule instead of simply cross-referencing to old Code §382(a). In doing so, it says nothing about the special option rule contained in the old Code §382 regulations (discussed at §507.1). It is not known whether this was intentional or inadvertent.

[16] *See* Reg. §1.1502-1(g)(3)(ii).

[17] For more detailed discussions of the CRCO rules, *see* J. Crestol, K. Hennessey & A. Rua, The Consolidated Tax Return §§5.02-.04, 7.05-.06; F. Peel, Consolidated Tax Returns §§8-12 (1985 ed.); Dubroff, Blanchard, Broadbent & Duvall, Federal Income Taxation of Corporations Filing Consolidated Tax Returns §42.04 (2d ed.); Salem, How to Use Net Operating Losses Effectively Under the New Consolidated Return Regulations, 26 J. Tax'n 270 (1967).

[18] Rev. Rul. 84-33, 1984-1 C.B. 186.

For transactions governed by new Code § 382, the legislative history indicated that the CRCO concept was to continue to apply.[19] However, in proposed regulations issued on January 29, 1991, the IRS proposed to eliminate the CRCO rules for consolidated return changes in ownership (CRCOs) occurring after January 28, 1991, and this was confirmed in the temporary regulations issued in 1996.[20] The latter apply to tax years beginning after 1996, but can be made to apply to earlier years ending after January 28, 1991 (provided the consolidated return Code § 382 regulations are similarly applied). However, the CRCO rules continued to apply to Code § 38 credits, including the investment credit, and the foreign tax credit until adoption of new SRLY tax credit regulations in 1998, when the CRCO rules were eliminated for foreign tax credits, with the same effective date as the 1998 SRLY tax credit changes. (*See* § 509.4 below.)[21]

## *§509.4 Consolidated Return (SRLY)*

**Pre-January 29, 1991 transactions.** The NOLs and other carryovers of a corporation that were incurred in a year when it was not a member of its present consolidated return group (a separate return limitation year, or SRLY) cannot be used against the income of other members of the group.[22] The SRLY limitation does not apply to the NOLs and other carryovers of the common parent of the group (though it does apply to those of a predecessor of the common parent).[23] Where the failing company is a subsidiary in a consolidated return group and it has subsidiaries of its own, an issuance of stock in a debt restructuring that causes the failing company to leave its present consolidated return group will bring the SRLY limitation into play for the failing company's subsidiaries (and any tax attributes inherited by the failing company from a predecessor).

**Post-January 28, 1991 transactions.** As in the case of the CRCO limitation, the legislative history of new Code § 382 indicated that the SRLY limitation was to continue to apply under new Code § 382. Some commentators thought that this directive had not been carefully thought through, and that both the SRLY limitation and the CRCO limitation were inconsistent with new Code § 382. Others urged

---

19 1986 Conference Report, *supra* note 14, at II-194.

20 *See* Temp. Reg. § 1.1502-21T(d) and (g); Reg. § 1.1502-21A(d).

21 Reg. §§ 1.1502-3(e)(3), 1.1502-4(g)(3).

22 Reg. §§ 1.1502-1(f), -3(c) (ITC carryover), -4(f) (foreign tax credit carryover), -21(c) (NOLs), -22(d) (capital loss carryover). The SRLY limitation also applies to certain "built-in" deductions. Reg. § 1.1502-15(a). For more detailed discussions of the SRLY limitation, *see* Crestol, *supra* note 17, at §§ 5.02-.04, 7.05-.06; Peel, *supra* note 17, at §§ 8-12; Dubroff, Blanchard, Broadbent & Duvall, *supra* note 17, at §§ 42.02-.03; Goldring and Sontag, Life After the Final Regulations: Consolidated 382 and SRLY, Vol. 27 Tax Strategies for Corporate Acquisitions, Dispositions, Spin-Offs, Joint Ventures, Financing, Reorganizations and Restructurings (Prac. Law Inst. 2006); Salem, *supra* note 17. For an interesting analysis, where income from a business contributed in a Code § 351 exchange to the loss company successfully eliminated the SRLY limitation, *see* IRS Field Service Advice, January 15, 1993, 98 TNT 201-99, (October 19, 1998).

23 Reg. § 1.1502-1(f)(2) and (3) (reverse acquisition rules apply).

retention of the SRLY limitation.[24] In 1991, when the IRS eliminated the CRCO limitation, it did not propose eliminating the SRLY limitation. Instead, on January 29, 1991, the IRS proposed to amend the SRLY rules for acquisitions occurring after January 28, 1991. These proposals were reissued as temporary and proposed regulations in 1996.

The temporary regulations generally apply (and continue to apply) to tax years beginning after 1996 and for which the due date of the tax return (without regard to extensions) is on or before June 25, 1999 (the latter being the effective date of the final regulations), but can be made to apply to earlier years ending after January 28, 1991 (provided the consolidated return Code §382 regulations are similarly applied).[25] This means that for these periods of time both the SRLY limitations and the Code §382 limitations can apply simultaneously to the same NOLs, capital losses, and built-in losses. The 1996 temporary regulations only applied to NOLs, capital losses, and certain built-in losses and deductions. They did not apply to tax credits, to which the prior rules continued to apply until new regulations were issued in 1998 (*see* separate discussion below). The 1996 temporary rules made the following changes to the old SRLY rules (these changes were retained in the final 1999 regulations):

(1) *Unfragmented approach.* Under the old rules, when a parent with subsidiaries, or brother-sister companies, joined a new consolidated return group, the SRLY rules always applied to them on a fragmented basis. That is, they applied to each company separately rather than to the acquired group as a whole. Thus, if one of the acquired companies had a SRLY upon acquisition, its NOLs could be used against only its own future income and not against the income of the other members of the acquired group. The new rules change this by generally applying the SRLY rules to the acquired companies as a group, as if together they were a single company. Whether a group of companies acquired together qualify as a group for this purpose depends on whether it satisfies a special definition. The definition is applied for purposes of applying the NOL rules differently from the way it applies for purposes of the built-in loss rules.

(2) *Cumulative approach.* Under the old rules, a SRLY loss of a member could only be used in a future year in which both the consolidated group and the SRLY member had net income. Thus, if the SRLY loss of S was $100, and in year one of the new group S had $100 of income but other members of the

---

[24] *See* American Bar Association, Tax Section, Comments Regarding Retention of the Consolidated Return SRLY Rules (April 30, 1998). This report notes that critics of the SRLY limitation have pointed to the ease with which its impact can often be minimized or avoided by merging the new member into another member (even by use of a single member LLC as the merger partner, thereby preserving limited liability) or by stuffing income or gain assets into the new member (*see* IRS Field Service Advice, *supra* note 22). The report responds that there is a price to be paid for these techniques, for example the loss of a separate basis in the stock of the new member. The adoption of Reg. §1.1502-20 and its successors (*see* §508.2.4 above and §§804.5 and 804.7 below), which disallow certain losses from disposition of subsidiary stock, do not operate to diminish the benefit of retaining such acquisition basis.

[25] *See* Temp. Reg. §1.1502-21T(c) and (g); Temp. Reg. §1.1502-15T; Reg. §1.1502-15A.

consolidated group had losses of $100, and in year 2 S had no income but other members of the consolidated group had $200 of income, the SRLY loss could not be used in either year 1 or year 2. Under the new rules, one looks to the cumulative income of the SRLY member (or SRLY subgroup) to determine if the SRLY NOL can be used. In the example, S's $100 SRLY NOL could be used by the consolidated return group in year 2.

(3) *Special built-in loss rules.* The new rules apply separately to built-in losses (among other things, as mentioned above, groups and subgroups are defined differently for built-in loss than for NOL purposes), and the new SRLY built-in loss rules are designed to be more consistent with the Code § 382(h) built-in loss rules. Thus, the SRLY built-in loss rules will apply only if the member (or subgroup) has a net unrealized built-in loss as defined in Code § 382(h)(3) when it joins the affiliated group. However, if the net built-in loss threshold of the latter section is satisfied when the member (or subgroup) joins the affiliated group, then all of the built-in losses recognized within a five-year recognition period are subject to the SRLY limitation, without limitation to the amount of the net unrealized built-in loss (as applied for Code § 382 purposes). In addition, the SRLY rules treat all assets and liabilities acquired from a non-corporate transferor in a carryover basis transaction (such as a Code § 351 transfer) as assets and liabilities of a corporation that becomes a member of the group on the date of the acquisition, and thus subject to a SRLY limitation any net unrealized built-in loss in the acquired assets. No similar rule exists for Code § 382 purposes.

On August 3, 1998, the IRS announced[26] the possibility of still further changes to the SRLY limitation rules. The announcement mentioned that while some commentators had urged that the SRLY rules be eliminated in whole or in part, other commentators had argued that the SRLY rules should be retained. These comments left the Treasury and the IRS believing that some form of the SRLY limitation should continue to exist in order to protect the integrity of both the separate return system and the consolidated return system. However, the IRS announcement mentioned that the IRS remained concerned about the complexity that existed in applying the current SRLY rules, particularly in situations where both the SRLY rules and Code § 382 apply. In hopes of reducing this complexity, the IRS said it was considering, among other things, an approach that would replace the current SRLY limitation with an approach modeled on Code § 382. The notice said that, while the existing SRLY temporary regulations base the SRLY limitation on the income *actually* generated by the SRLY member or SRLY subgroup, the approach under consideration would base the limitation on an *expectation* of the amount of income to be generated: in other words, applying the methodology of Code § 382, the limitation would be based on the value of the member's or subgroup's stock at the time it joins the consolidated group (with appropriate adjustments, such as adjustments for recognized built-in

---

[26] IRS Notice 98-38, 1998-2 C.B. 222.

gains, to reflect adjustments that would be made under Code § 382). The IRS asked for comments on the desirability of adopting this approach.

The comments received by the IRS on this concept were not favorable. On June 25, 1999, the IRS adopted final SRLY regulations.[27] In these final regulations, the IRS neither maintained the SRLY rules unchanged nor abandoned them altogether. Instead, it adopted a middle ground of eliminating the SRLY rules for NOL and built-in loss purposes in those situations where a Code § 382 ownership change occurs that results in a Code § 382 annual limitation, thereby producing an overlap between the two sets of rules. Because this overlap rule only applies where a Code § 382 annual limitation applies, the overlap rule does not apply where the corporation applies the Code § 382(l)(5) alternative rather than the annual limitation.

In most cases where a corporation joins a consolidated group, there is both a Code § 382 change in ownership and a SRLY change in ownership. In these circumstances, the new rules provide that the SRLY rules will not apply at all (unless, as just mentioned, the taxpayer applies Code § 382(l)(5) rather than the Code § 382 annual limitation). To take into account the situation where the two events do not in fact occur on the same day, the new regulations provide a six-month window: If the two events occur within six months of each other, the SRLY limitation generally does not apply. There is one principal exception to the six-month rule, namely that when the SRLY event occurs before the Code § 382 event, the SRLY limitation does apply until the tax year following the Code § 382 event.

The overlap concept applies not only where a single corporation is acquired, but also where groups of corporations are acquired. A complicated series of special rules is needed to deal with these situations, since the group of corporations subject to the Code § 382 limitation may differ from the composition of the group subject to the SRLY limitation. A difference in the size of the two groups can arise easily, since the definition of a group for each purpose is different. The SRLY subgroup concept embraces entire subgroups from another group, including even brother-sister combinations that do not have a subgroup parent. On the other hand, the Code § 382 subgroup generally must include a subgroup parent. Under the regulations, the relief provided by the overlap rule does not apply unless the composition of the two groups (the SRLY and the Code § 382 groups) is the same. However, the Code § 382 regulations provide an election to permit the acquisition of brother-sister combinations without a single subgroup, common parent to be considered one Code § 382 subgroup, by treating the subgroup parent requirement as satisfied (*see* § 508.7.1 above). Such election must be made by the common parent with its tax return for the taxable years in which the subgroup members join the consolidated group.

The overlap rules for built-in losses operate the same as the rules for net operating losses where a single corporation is acquired. The symmetry ends when subgroups are involved. As in the temporary regulations, SRLY subgroups for built-in loss purposes are defined differently from those for net operating loss purposes.

---

[27] Reg. §§ 1.1502-15, 1.1502-21, 1.1502-22, and 1.1502-23.

The final regulations also maintain the unfragmented approach and the cumulative approach for dealing with SRLY losses that were contained in the temporary regulations and discussed above.

If the overlap situation does not exist, the SRLY rules remain in place. Also, the overlap exception only applies for NOL and built-in loss purposes; it does not apply to credits.

The final regulations are generally effective for taxable years for which the due date (without extension) of the consolidated return is after June 25, 1999. However, an example contained in the preamble to the final regulations illustrates the fact that a certain amount of retroactivity is possible. In the example, S joins the P group in an overlap transaction in 1996, and the first year for which the final regulation is effective is 1999. In this case, the preamble says that any losses carried by S into the P group are subject to a SRLY limitation in 1996, 1997, and 1998, but are no longer subject to SRLY limitation within the P group starting in 1999.

Although, as just mentioned, these regulations became effective June 25, 1999, they were not published in the Federal Register until July 2, 1999. On September 1, 2000, the IRS announced that it would issue regulations allowing a member, that departed from a consolidated return group during this interim period because of a "qualified stock purchase" and while in its former group had SRLY losses, to elect out of the overlap rules of the final regulations with respect to its former group, if the departing member ceased to be a member of the group before June 26, 1999 or pursuant to a binding contract that was in effect before June 26, 1999.[28] This election would be desirable where the departing member had an NOL that was protected against use by the group by the SRLY limitation under the earlier regulations, but which (without the foregoing election) would have been absorbed by the group under the final regulations. The IRS has, within this limited context, allowed taxpayers the best of both worlds by providing that the election will apply to the departing member, but *not* the former group. Thus, the former group will (by reason of the overlap rule) still absorb the departing member's SRLY losses without restriction; yet, the departing member will report the losses as still existing. Although the former group generally will be tax neutral, since any SRLY losses absorbed would increase any gain, or reduce any loss, recognized by the group upon the member's departure, the group can be better off under certain circumstances (such as where the former group has substantial ordinary income, which can be sheltered by the SRLY losses and has expiring capital loss carryforwards that can be used to shelter the additional stock gain).

**1998 rules for tax credits.** In 1998, the IRS issued temporary and proposed regulations dealing with the application of the SRLY limitation to tax credits. These changed the SRLY treatment of the Code § 38 general business credit, including the investment credit, and the alternative minimum tax (AMT) credit by applying principles similar to those contained in the 1996 temporary regulations for losses. At the same time, they eliminated the SRLY limitation entirely for the foreign tax credit

---

[28] IRS Notice 2000-53, 2000-28 I.R.B. 293.

and for losses associated with the foreign tax credit regime, namely overall foreign losses (OFLs) and separate limitation losses (SLLs).

These new 1998 rules were originally proposed to apply commencing with taxable years beginning on or after January 1, 1997 for which the consolidated income tax return was due (without extensions) on or *before* March 13, 1998.[29] This gave the 1998 temporary regulations some retroactive impact, which proved controversial, so the IRS subsequently changed the effective date to apply commencing with consolidated return years for which the due date (without extensions) of the return was *after* March 13, 1998, with the taxpayer having the right to elect to apply the original effective date.[30] Even this change did not eliminate some of the hardship that could arise from retroactive application of the OFL rules, so the IRS subsequently announced (and amended the temporary regulations to reflect) that a taxpayer could elect to apply the 1998 rules to OFLs only commencing with taxable return years beginning after January 1, 1998.[31]

Elimination of the SRLY limitation on OFLs was made final in the final OFL regulation issued in 1999. In 2000, final regulations were issued that also eliminated the SRLY limitations on the use of foreign tax credits and that adopted the 1998 proposals regarding general business credits and the alternative minimum tax credit, with one modification—the extension of the overlap rule contained in the 1999 SRLY regulations to these credits.[32]

**Waiving SRLY losses for post-1994 acquisitions.** In 1994, the IRS amended the investment adjustment provisions of the consolidated return regulations. Under these amendments, the parent's basis in its stock of a subsidiary is reduced when the subsidiary's NOLs or other carryovers expire unused.[33] This could produce particularly painful results for the parent if the reason that the loss expires unused is that its use was limited by Code § 382 or the SRLY limitation. To help alleviate the impact of this new rule, the new regulation allows the consolidated group, when a subsidiary joins the group having losses from a separate return limitation year, to make an irrevocable election (with the group return for the first year) to treat all or any portion of the loss carryover as expiring for all federal income tax purposes immediately before the subsidiary becomes a member of the consolidated group.[34] This election is discussed below at § 804.7. These new rules apply if the subsidiary becomes a member of the consolidated return group in a consolidated return year beginning on or after January 1, 1995. If, however, the subsidiary became a member of the group in

---

[29] *See* Temp. Reg. amendments to Reg. §§ 1.1502-3T, 1.1502-4T, 1.1502-9T, 1.1502-21T, 1.1502-55T issued January 12, 1998.

[30] *See* the amendments to the regulations cited in the preceding footnote issued March 16, 1998. *See also* Huber, Lubozynski and Pallerro, Consolidated Return Temp. Regs. Modernize SRLY Treatment for Credits and Create OFL Problems, 89 J. Tax'n 12 (1998).

[31] IRS Notice 98-40, Aug. 17, 1998, and the amendments to Temp. Reg. §§ 1.1502-3T and -9T, issued on December 29, 1998.

[32] T.D. 8884, May 25, 2000, eliminating Reg. §§ 1.1502-3T and -4T, and amending Reg. §§ 1.1502-3, 1.1502-4, 1.1502-21, and adding Reg. § 1.1502-55 (and eliminating Reg. § 1.1502-55T).

[33] Reg. § 1.1502-32(b)(2), (3)(iii).

[34] Reg. § 1.1502-32(b)(4) (also provides for certain adjustments to the stock basis of the subsidiary and any higher-tier corporations acquired).

a consolidated return year beginning before January 1, 1995, and the subsidiary had a loss carryover from a separate return limitation year at that time, the expiration of this loss unused (even if it occurs in a year beginning on or after January 1, 1995) does not produce a negative basis adjustment.[35]

## § 510 DETERMINING THE DATE OF THE STOCK-FOR-DEBT EXCHANGE

No difficulty usually arises in determining when the exchange of new stock for old debt occurs in the case of a solvent company that is not in bankruptcy and whose creditors have not taken steps in other ways that give them effective command over the corporation's property. The date of the exchange normally will be the effective date provided in the agreement of the parties.

However, where the company has been placed in bankruptcy or where the creditors otherwise have obtained effective command over all its properties through the commencement of a foreclosure or receivership proceeding, a question arises as to whether there has been in effect a *de facto* recapitalization of the troubled company at that earlier time rather than later, when the actual exchange of stock for debt takes place. Because the institution of such a bankruptcy, foreclosure, or similar proceeding may sometimes occur several years before the debt restructuring plan is finally implemented, the tax stakes riding on the answer to this question are high and include the following:

(1) In which year did the creditors not owning "securities" have gain or loss on the "exchange" of their debt for stock?
(2) In which year did this create a "purchase" of the troubled company's stock for purposes of old Code § 382(a) or an "ownership change" for purposes of new Code § 382? *See* § § 507 and 508 (including the option attribution rule in § 508.2.7) above.
(3) If the recapitalization created some COD income for the troubled company (either because some of the creditors actually received only reduced debt and no stock, or because the conditions for application of the former stock-for-debt exception to COD income (*see* § 504A) were not satisfied), in which year did this arise?
(4) In which year did interest on the old debt cease to accrue?
(5) If the troubled company was a subsidiary in a group filing consolidated returns and the debt restructuring plan reduced the group's stock ownership below the necessary 80 percent level, in which year did the troubled company leave the group? *See* § 804.1 below.

The potential questions noted above arise out of language used in (but not the holdings of) *Alabama Asphaltic*[1] (*see* § 510.1) and its progeny. Before these are ex-

---

[35] Reg. § 1.1502-32(h)(4).

[1] **§ 510** *Helvering v. Alabama Asphaltic Limestone Co.*, 315 U.S. 179, 42-1 U.S.T.C. ¶ 9245 (1942).

amined, however, a special word must be said about a provision in the Bankruptcy Code that may, if the parties are not careful, cause debt to be cancelled well before the actual recapitalization exchange occurs. This is Section 1141(d) of the Bankruptcy Code, which says that, except as the bankruptcy plan or order confirming the plan otherwise provides, the confirmation of the plan by the bankruptcy court discharges the claims against the debtor. The consummation or effective date of a bankruptcy plan occurs generally only some time after the confirmation date, however, when the appeals period for the confirmation order has expired or appeals have been completed. Unless the plan provides that the debt reductions do not occur until the plan becomes effective, the creditors may substantively lose their claims if the plan is disallowed on appeal. Even if the plan is not disallowed, the time of the debt discharge becomes separated from the consummation of the plan. No authority exists to tell us what tax significance, if any, the separation in time would have (except that if the plan is consummated, Reg. § 1.382-9(o)—discussed at § 508.2.7.3 above—treats the consummation date as the controlling date for any stock for debt exchange for Code § 382 ownership change purposes), but cautious taxpayers will see that the plan is drafted in a way that eliminates both the substantive and the tax question.[2]

## *§510.1 The* Alabama Asphaltic *Approach*

In *Alabama Asphaltic*, a troubled company was placed in receivership in 1929 and in bankruptcy in 1930. Its assets were transferred to a new company in 1931 in exchange for all of the new company's stock, which was issued to the creditors of the old company (none of whom, incidentally, were holders of "securities"). The old stockholders received nothing. The transfer constituted a tax-free reorganization of the corporations under the tax statute then in effect, provided it met the continuity-of-interest test. In holding that it did, the Supreme Court said that, in substance, the creditors had become the equity owners of the old company:

> We conclude, however, that it is immaterial that the transfer shifted the ownership of the equity in the property from the stockholders to the creditors of the old corporation. Plainly the old continuity of interest was broken. Technically that did not occur in this proceeding until the [transfer to the new corporation] took place. For practical purposes, however, it took place not later than the time that the creditors took steps to enforce their demands against their insolvent debtor. In this case, that was the date of the institution of bankruptcy proceedings. From that time on they had effective command over the disposition of the property. The full priority rule ... applies to proceedings in bankruptcy as well as to equity receiverships .... It gives creditors, whether secured or unsecured, the right to exclude stockholders entirely from the reorganization plan when the debtor is insolvent .... When the equity owners are excluded and the

---

[2] *See* Witt & Albergotti, G Reorganization Offers Simple, Effective Way to Acquire Bankrupt Corporations, 61 J. Taxation 90, 93 n.28 (1985).

> old creditors become the stockholders of the new corporation, it conforms to realities to date their equity ownership from the time when they invoked the processes of the law to enforce their rights of full priority. At that time they stepped into the shoes of the old stockholders. The [transfer to the new corporation] "did nothing but recognize officially what had before been true in fact."[3]

The Court did not explain why the commencement of the bankruptcy proceedings, rather than the commencement of the receivership proceedings, was the time when the "creditors took steps to enforce their demands against their insolvent debtor." However, in the companion case of *Palm Springs Corp. v. Commissioner*,[4] decided the same day, the Court found that creditors had taken effective control without a bankruptcy proceeding when they resorted to a foreclosure proceeding under a bond indenture. In a number of other cases, where the creditors had not taken steps to exert command over the troubled company, but where there was a substantial overlap between the creditor and stockholder groups, the continuity-of-interest test has been held to be met by issuance of all the new company's stock to the creditors on the ground that it was not necessary to determine whether they received the stock as former creditors or as former stockholders.[5]

In none of these cases did the Court have to face the question of whether the creditors had become equity holders of the old company at the time of "taking command," except for purposes of applying the continuity-of-interest test. A number of authorities can be marshalled in support of the view that the doctrine will be limited to that narrow purpose and that an "exchange" will not generally be deemed to have taken place before it physically occurs. For example, *Helvering v. Southwest Consolidated Corp.*[6] was decided by the Supreme Court in the same year that it decided *Alabama Asphaltic*. In *Southwest*, a troubled company was placed in equity receivership by the creditors, and the assets were transferred to a new company. The old stockholders acquired warrants, some creditors received cash, and the others acquired all of the new corporation's stock. The Court said that the continuity test of *Alabama Asphaltic* was met, but that the transfer did not qualify under the predecessor of the present "C" reorganization provisions because the consideration issued by the new company was not solely voting stock. The Court also concluded that the transaction was not a "D" reorganization, because although the creditors may have become the equity owners of the old company in the *Alabama Asphaltic* sense, they were not "stockholders" for purposes of statutory provisions (like the "D" reorganization provision) requiring "stockholders" to receive the new stock. For purposes of the question presently before us, the holding that creditors had not become "stock-

---

[3] 315 U.S. at 183-184 (citations omitted).

[4] 315 U.S. 185, 42-1 U.S.T.C. ¶9246 (1942).

[5] *See, e.g., United States v. Adkins-Phelps, Inc.*, 400 F.2d 737, 742-743, 68-2 U.S.T.C. ¶9609 (8th Cir. 1968); *Seiberling Rubber Co. v. Commissioner*, 169 F.2d 595, 48-2 U.S.T.C. ¶9343 (6th Cir. 1948); *Norman Scott, Inc.*, 48 T.C. 598, Dec. 28,551 (1967); Rev. Rul. 54-610, 1954-2 C.B. 152.

[6] 315 U.S. 194, 42-1 U.S.T.C. ¶9248 (1942).

holders" is inconsistent with a view that upon taking command of the company, there had been a *de facto* exchange or recapitalization.

The Court in the *Southwest Consolidated* case also concluded that the transfer to the new company was not an "E" recapitalization either, since a recapitalization refers to a reshuffling of the capital structure of an existing corporation. Finally, the Court held that the transfer was not an "F" reorganization, saying that "a transaction which *shifts* the ownership of the proprietary interest in a corporation is hardly" an "F" reorganization.[7] Once again, this holding seems inconsistent with the view that there had been an earlier *de facto* recapitalization. If there had been an earlier recapitalization, the later transfer of assets to the new company would not have involved a shift in proprietary interest. Although it is true that in the *Southwest Consolidated* case the commencement of the receivership proceeding and the transfer to the new company occurred in the same year, so that arguably an earlier *de facto* recapitalization did not occur long enough before the asset transfer to have significance for "D" or "F" reorganization purposes, had the Court thought that the creditors had become equity owners for anything other than continuity of interest purposes, the "D" and "F" reorganization issues presumably would have merited more extended discussion than the short treatment the Court gave them.

An interesting variation on the above authorities is found in a 1998 Technical Advice.[8] Here C, a subsidiary of B, transferred its major asset, the stock of H, to G in exchange for G stock, and liquidated. Both B and C were in bankruptcy. The G stock was distributed, pursuant to an order of the bankruptcy court, directly to the creditors of B (C's parent) to whom C was secondarily liable. The parties treated the acquisition of H by G as a Code § 338 asset purchase. The IRS, on the other hand, held that the transaction constituted both a "G" and a "C" reorganization. The IRS said that the G stock should be considered to have been constructively received by B (C's shareholder) when it was transferred to B's creditors, thereby satisfying Code § 354. The IRS also said that the creditors of B satisfied the continuity-of-interest test, citing *Alabama Asphaltic* for the proposition that creditors of a bankrupt corporation can be treated as having stepped into the shoes of the shareholders for continuity-of-interest purposes. Thus, the constructive distribution of the stock from B to its creditors was treated, for continuity purposes, as if B in turn, distributed the stock to its shareholders (which double distribution, the IRS noted, has been permitted for continuity purposes). The IRS considered it irrelevant that B was also to be promptly liquidated.

## *§510.2 Relevant Rulings and Regulations*

There are also a number of relevant rulings. One is Rev. Rul. 63-104,[9] which held that a subsidiary placed in bankruptcy must continue to file consolidated returns with its nonbankrupt parent. Implicit in this ruling is the assumption that the

---

7 315 U.S. at 203-204 (emphasis added).

8 IRS Technical Advice 9841006, June 25, 1998.

9 1963-1 C.B. 172; *see also* Chapter 8 at § 804.1.

bankruptcy filing does not shift stock ownership. Another is Rev. Rul. 70-367,[10] which held, as discussed in Chapter 3 at § 302, that where a proposed Section 77 Bankruptcy Act plan contemplated that old bonds would be exchanged for a package of new debt (with lower interest) and stock, but the plan had not become effective during the year, the interest at the old rate on the old bonds continued to accrue as a deduction during the year because the old debt had not yet been extinguished by an exchange for the new debt and stock.

Still another relevant ruling is Rev. Rul. 59-222.[11] Under the facts of this ruling, in the same year that a failing company (M) was placed in bankruptcy, a plan was adopted and executed pursuant to which the company was acquired by an existing unrelated corporation (N). The plan provided that the old senior creditors would remain unchanged; that the bank debt would be paid with M's cash;[12] that the unsecured creditors were to receive solely N voting stock (worth 30 to 35 cents on the dollar of their claims); that the old stockholders were to receive nothing; and that M would become a wholly owned subsidiary of N. The ruling held the transaction to be a "B" reorganization, saying:

> The facts in the instant case disclose that, due to the insolvency of M corporation[,] the holders of the subordinated debentures and unsecured claims are, in reality, the owners of the equity remaining in M after giving effect to the lien of the first mortgage bonds. The effect of the transaction is the same as though the debenture holders and unsecured creditors surrendered their claims, received the new issue of M common stock and then exchanged such stock for the stock of N.[13]

The ruling further holds that no gain or loss is recognized to the unsecured creditors of M who held securities of M "as a result of the exchange of such debentures for shares of common stock of N corporation, since it is considered that such debenture holders first exchanged such debentures for common stock of M and then exchanged the stock of M for stock of N corporation."[14] Further, for those unsecured creditors who did not hold "securities," the ruling holds that gain or loss is recognized to them "upon the receipt of stock of N corporation in satisfaction of

---

[10] 1970-2 C.B. 37.

[11] 1959-1 C.B. 80.

[12] The ruling does not say whether the bank loan was unsecured. If it was, it would seem to have been equity in the same way as the unsecured debt. If so, redemption with *M'* s assets would not destroy the "B" reorganization (the bank debt comprised much less than half of the unsecured debt and so would not independently raise a continuity-of-interest problem), although the ruling did not discuss the point. For more on this ruling, *see infra* § 602 note 4.

[13] Id. at 84. The IRS has applied the reasoning of Rev. Rul. 59-222 in private letter rulings upon analogous facts. *See* IRS Letter Ruling 8933001, August 22, 1988; IRS Letter Ruling 8914080, January 11, 1989; *see also* IRS Letter Ruling 8852039, October 4, 1988. For a discussion of these rulings, *see* Pollack & Goldring, Can Cancellation of Indebtedness Income Be Avoided with Parent Stock? 2 Corp. Tax'n 18 (Jan./Feb. 1990), 3 Corp. Tax'n 12 (July/August 1990). *See also* § 504A.3.2 above.

[14] Id.

their claims."[15] Although the facts of Rev. Rul. 59-222 show that the commencement of the bankruptcy proceeding and the completion of the plan occurred in the same year, the language used in the ruling suggests that the IRS considered the deemed recapitalization of M to occur only upon execution of the plan and not at the earlier point of insolvency or filing for bankruptcy. The IRS applied a step transaction analysis, treating the single physical transaction on execution of the plan as if it consisted of a first step recapitalization of M, followed by a second step exchange of all of the new M stock for voting stock of N.

The IRS has also issued private letter rulings under Chapter XI of the prior Bankruptcy Act, which gave recognition to actual "E" recapitalizations that took place immediately before "F" reincorporations at the conclusion of the bankruptcy proceedings.[16] There was no suggestion in these rulings that the recapitalization should be deemed to have occurred at some earlier time.

Also consistent with the foregoing authorities is Reg. § 1.382-9(o), which generally provides that the exchanges contemplated by a bankruptcy plan will not be taken into account for Code § 382 ownership change purposes before the effective date of the plan. *See* the discussion at § 508.2.7.3 above.

Another important precedent is provided in Reg. § 1.269-5, which provides that for purposes of Code § 269, creditors of an insolvent or bankrupt corporation will not be deemed to have acquired beneficial ownership of stock any earlier than the confirmation date of the bankruptcy plan.

## *§ 510.3 Practical Effects*

Among the many practical problems that would arise if a deemed recapitalization of a failing company were considered to have occurred when the creditors took "command" of the company is the fact that it simply is not possible to tell, in most cases, who will end up owning the equity of the company until a plan is physically consummated. Between the time of filing in bankruptcy or the institution of foreclosure or receivership proceedings and the consummation of the restructuring, the values of the company's assets, in many cases, will change significantly. The company may become more, or perhaps less, insolvent: In some cases, it may even move from insolvency to solvency. Only at the end of the proceeding will one know which of the various classes of creditors and stockholders will receive the stock of the restructured company. Literal application of the *Alabama Asphaltic* test for "deemed exchange" purposes would mean that there could be one "exchange" at the time of commencement of bankruptcy and perhaps another "exchange" when the plan is

---

[15] Id.

[16] *See, e.g.*, IRS Letter Ruling 7821047, February 23, 1978; IRS Letter Ruling 8110139, December 12, 1980. To similar effect as to the two-step type of transaction, *see* IRS Letter Ruling 200244001, April 27, 2001 (conversion of a mutual insurance company into stock company was a good "E" recapitalization and would not prevent an immediate downstream merger into a subsidiary from qualifying under Code § § 368(a)(1)(A) and 368(a)(2)(D); since this ruling does not involve a failing company, there was no reason for the IRS to consider whether the recapitalization might be deemed to have occurred at an earlier time).

consummated. Conceivably, there could even be a series of "exchanges" during the intervening period. This would create enormous uncertainty and potential whipsawing of both the IRS and taxpayers. It seems unlikely that a court would tolerate it.

The wisdom—even for determining who are the equity owners for continuity of interest purposes—of looking to the end of the road of a debt restructuring rather than to the commencement of bankruptcy or other insolvency proceedings is reflected in *Atlas Oil & Refining Corporation*.[17] In this case, the court interpreted the *Alabama Asphaltic* test to mean that those creditors who actually received stock under the restructuring plan (and presumably those on the same, or on a junior, priority level who received something of value in the plan) are to be considered "by relation back" those who had become the equity owners of the troubled company. The court said,

> While "effective command" over the properties in an insolvency proceeding is necessary to change the creditors into equity owners to satisfy continuity of interest, the fact that a protected class may have had "effective command" over the assets in such proceedings will not make them equity owners for participation purposes if they do not in fact exercise their right to participate in the equity distribution of the new corporation . . . .
>
> Inasmuch as there is no requirement that any surviving creditor retain his status in the new corporation, and they are all permitted, although fully protected, to share in the new stock distribution, all creditors *receiving stock* may be deemed "former owners" at the time they receive it in determining whether the continuity-of-interest rule is satisfied.[18]

In summary, the *Alabama Asphaltic* principle should not be applied to create a *de facto* recapitalization exchange at some point in time before implementation of the actual restructuring plan. That principle should be confined entirely to continuity-of-interest purposes. However, Rev. Rul. 59-222 does show that, in proper circumstances, the IRS will accept the creation of a first-step recapitalization exchange as part of a two-company restructuring (*see* § 510.2 above and § 602 below).

## § 511 IMPACT OF CHANGE IN OWNERSHIP ON ALTERNATIVE MINIMUM TAX

As mentioned at § 501, an issuance of stock that produces a Code § 382 ownership change in a tax year beginning after 1989 not only can reduce NOLs and other

---

[17] Dec. 24,943, 36 T.C. 675 (1961).

[18] Id. at 688 (emphasis in original; citations omitted). Tillinghast & Gardner, in their article Acquisitive Reorganizations and Chapters X and XI of the Bankruptcy Act, 26 Tax L. Rev. 663 (1971), take the position that the *Atlas* case points the way to the proper application of the continuity-of-interest test in bankruptcy and other insolvency cases under pre-1980 law. As discussed at § 605.1.4, the *Atlas* approach appears to be the one that Congress intended to apply for purposes of the "G" reorganization provisions.

tax attributes, but also can increase the impact of the alternative minimum tax (AMT). In particular, this can happen because an ownership change results in eliminating net built-in losses for purposes of computing the adjusted current earnings (ACE) portion of the AMT.

This is mandated by Code § 56(g)(4)(G), which provides that if a Code § 382 ownership change occurs in a taxable year beginning after 1989 at a time when the debtor corporation has a net unrealized built-in loss within the meaning of Code § 382(h), then the basis of each of the debtor's assets for purposes of computing ACE shall be changed to its proportionate share of the fair market value of the assets (as determined under Code § 382(h)) immediately before the ownership change.

Relief from this ACE adjustment was, for a brief time, in sight. The Revenue Bill of 1992, H.R. 11, which passed Congress in the fall of 1992 but was vetoed by former President Bush, would have eliminated this adjustment.

A corporation frequently will have a different basis for earnings and profits purposes than for regular income tax purposes, caused by different depreciation rates or other adjustments. Thus, a corporation can have net unrealized built-in loss as determined for earnings and profits purposes but not for regular income tax purposes. This difference could have led to some confusion in applying Code § 56(g)(4)(G), because whether an ownership change has occurred may depend on whether there is a net built-in loss on a testing date: Code § 382(g) provides that an ownership change can only occur to a "loss corporation"; and the temporary regulations define the latter to mean a corporation with *either* a loss or tax credit carryover or a net built-in loss.[1] In applying Code § 56(g)(4)(G), should one look to built-in losses as determined for earnings and profits purposes or as determined for regular income tax purposes? The regulations eliminate the confusion by saying that a corporation will not be considered to have an ownership change for purposes of Code § 56(g)(4)(G) unless there has been an ownership change for regular tax purposes.[2] This means that, if the corporation has neither a loss or tax credit carry-over nor a net built-in loss for regular tax purposes, an ownership change will not be deemed to have occurred for ACE purposes even if there is a net built-in loss as computed for earnings and profits purposes. Once such an ownership change has been found to occur, then the regulations further provide that an ACE basis adjusted will be needed only if a net unrealized built-in loss exists in basis as computed for earnings and profits purposes.[3]

As discussed above (at § 508.5.3), Code § 382(l)(5) provides relief from the normal net built-in loss rules of Code § 382 for corporations in bankruptcy that qualify for such provision (and do not elect out), by rendering inapplicable the annual limitation that would ordinarily apply following a Code § 382 ownership change. Code § 382(l)(5) does not, however, undo the fact that an ownership change occurred.

---

[1] **§ 511** Temp. Reg. § 1.382-2T(f)(1). *See generally* Simon, Compound Complexity: Accounting for Built-In Gains and Losses Under the AMT After an Ownership Change, 107 Tax Notes 477 (April 25, 2005).

[2] Reg. § 1.56(g)-1(k).

[3] Id. The built-in loss must exceed the lesser of 15 percent of the fair market value of the assets or $10 million in order for the adjustment to become applicable.

Accordingly, nothing in Code § 382(l)(5) excludes an ownership change that is otherwise governed by Code § 382(l)(5) from the special ACE adjustment for corporations with a net unrealized built-in loss, nor is there any statutory exclusion in Code § 56(g)(4)(G) itself. However, some helpful language can be found in the ACE regulations. The ACE regulations define an "ownership change" for its purposes as "an ownership change under section 382(g) *for purposes of computing the corporation's amount of taxable income that may be offset by pre-change losses or the regular tax liability that may be offset by pre-change credits*" (emphasis added). Thus, based on the italicized language, it may be argued that the regulations limit the applicability of the special ACE adjustment to an ownership change *that gives rise to an annual Code § 382 limitation.*[4] Nevertheless, the IRS takes the position that the special ACE adjustment applies even to ownership changes governed by Code § 382(l)(5).[5]

## § 512 SPECIAL REPORTING OBLIGATION

On July 5, 1990, the IRS issued proposed regulations to implement Code § 6043(c).[1] The proposed regulations would have required new Form 8820 (when it was prepared) to be filed to report (1) any acquisition by one or more persons acting together of control (as defined in Code § 304(c)) of a corporation (if the stock acquired is worth $10 million or more), (2) any substantial change (involving $10 million or more) in capital structure of a corporation, including stock-for-stock, stock-for-debt, and other recapitalization exchanges and (3) any significant net increase (as specially defined) in the corporation's debt. The reporting requirement would have applied to all such transactions occurring after March 31, 1990. Form 8820 was to be filed by the fifteenth day of the fourth month following the month of the transaction (or, if later, within 120 days after Form 8820 became available). The penalty for noncompliance was $500 per day up to a maximum of $100,000. There could also be criminal penalties.

On October 16, 1992, this proposed regulation was withdrawn, because the IRS concluded that the value of the information that would have been collected did not justify the burden of compliance.

However, the IRS subsequently changed its mind in part, and in November 2002 issued Temp. Reg. § 1.6043-4T. Although similar to the 1990 proposal, the scope of the provision has been reduced. The major reduction is that it applies only to transactions covered by Code § 367(a), basically inversions of U.S. corporations into foreign corporations. In addition, under the new provision, the dollar floors have been raised from $10 million to $100 million; the "acquisition of control" provision is limited to a distribution by a corporation to its shareholders of controlling stock of a subsidiary, or an acquisition of control by a corporation of stock of a second corporation. In addition, the "substantial change in capital structure" provision has been changed to

---

4 *See* comment letter to the IRS from Deloitte & Touche, "Comments on Notice 2003-65—Application of Section 56(g)(4)(G)," *reprinted at* 2004 TNT 97-28, May 19, 2004.

5 IRS Chief Counsel Advice 200444002, July 22, 2004.

1 **§ 512** Prop. Reg. § 1.6043-4.

apply to (1) a recapitalization with respect to stock, (2) a redemption (including a deemed redemption) of stock, (3) a merger, consolidation or other combination of one corporation with another corporation or a transfer of substantially all assets of a corporation to one or more corporations, (4) a transfer of all or part of its assets to another corporation in a title 11 or similar case if the transferor distributes stock or securities of the other corporation, and (5) a change in identity, form or place of incorporation. The provision has been deleted that would have required reporting if there has been a significant net increase in the corporation's debt. The reporting corporation must file Form 8806 with its tax return. In addition, it must file with the IRS Forms 1096 and 1099-CAP with respect to each shareholder of record who receives cash, stock, or other property pursuant to the reported transaction, and it must send a copy of Form 1099-CAP to each stockholder. The provision applies beginning in 2002 (with modifications announced in IRS Announcement 2003-7, 2003-6 I.R.B. 450), but sunsets on November 14, 2005. The IRS modified Temp. Reg. § 1.6043-4T once again in December 2003, effective beginning in 2003. The modifications relate only to the reporting requirements, and are designed to help ensure that brokers and shareholders receive information on the corporate transactions. Reporting corporations are required to file their Form 8806 within 45 days after the corporate transaction, and in no event later than January 5th of the year following the transaction. The corporation is permitted to elect on this form to consent to publication by the IRS of information necessary for brokers to file information returns with respect to their customers, and if this election is made, the corporation is not required to file Forms 1099-CAP with respect to shareholders that are clearing organizations, or to furnish Forms 1099-CAP to such clearing organizations.

With some revisions, the 2003 temporary regulation was adopted in final form in 2005 as Reg. § 1.6043-4, effective for transactions occurring after December 5, 2005. The final regulation was revised in general to limit the information reporting to transactions in which the reporting corporation or any shareholder is required to recognize gain (if any) under Code § 367(a). The "acquisition of control" provision was revised to eliminate the distribution by a corporation to its shareholders of controlling stock of a subsidiary. The "change in capital structure" provision was revised to eliminate recapitalizations and redemptions.

Reg. § 1.6045-3 requires brokers to file Forms 1096 and 1099-B for customers who have engaged in a transaction described in Reg. § 1.6043-4.

The 1993 Act added Code § 6050P, which requires creditors that are "applicable financial institutions" to file information reports regarding discharge of any indebtedness they hold. This provision is discussed at § 403.4 above.

The American Jobs Creation Act of 2004 added a new Code § 6043A, which requires information reporting, to the extent required by Treasury forms or regulations, by an acquiring corporation in any taxable acquisition of the assets or stock of another corporation, if any shareholder of the target corporation is required to report gain. *See* § 609 below.

# 6

# Two-Company Reorganizations Involving a Failing Company



## §601 SUBSTITUTE FOR A RECAPITALIZATION

One can accomplish the same reshuffling of capital structure by a two-company reorganization as by a one-company recapitalization.

**EXAMPLE**

> A failing company has $10 million of debt, half of which it wants to convert to stock. It can do this through a one-company recapitalization by exchanging half the debt for new stock. Alternatively, the failing company can transfer all of its assets to Newco, with the old creditors of the failing company receiving $5 million of debt of Newco plus some of the stock of Newco, and with the old stockholders of the failing company receiving stock of Newco.

In some cases, there may be nontax reasons for finding a two-company transaction more attractive than a one-company transaction. For example, the corporate law of the state of the old failing company may contain restrictions that the parties wish to eliminate by reincorporating in a new jurisdiction.

Under the prior Bankruptcy Act and old Code §382, considerable differences existed, for both the corporation and its creditors and shareholders, between a two-company and a one-company reorganization. These differences were analyzed in earlier editions of this book. Under present law the differences between one-company and two-company reorganizations have essentially been eliminated.[1]

On the other hand, as discussed below, significant differences do exist between reorganizations that are carried out in bankruptcy, and reorganizations that are not carried out in bankruptcy. This is because the bankruptcy "G" reorganization provisions are more liberal than the non-bankruptcy reorganization provisions (*see* § 605 below), and because Code § 382 provides more liberal rules for bankruptcy cases than for other cases (*see* § 508 above).

## § 602 DEEMED RECAPITALIZATION PRECEDING THE REORGANIZATION

The two conclusions set forth at § 601 assume that a two-company transaction used as a substitute for a recapitalization will be governed exclusively by the rules applicable to two-company reorganizations and that it will not be treated instead as involving a first-step "E" recapitalization of the failing company followed immediately by a two-company "F" reorganization. Before we discuss the rules applicable to two-company reorganizations, we must examine the possibility that this assumption may well not hold.

The existence of this concern may seem surprising, since the Supreme Court in *Helvering v. Southwest Consolidated Corp.*,[1] a case in which the creditors took over the assets of a failing company in a two-company transaction, held that the transaction did not qualify as an "E" recapitalization because "there was not that reshuffling of a capital structure within the framework of an existing corporation contemplated by the term 'recapitalization'" and did not qualify as an "F" reincorporation because "a transaction which shifts the ownership of the proprietary interest in a corporation is hardly 'a mere change in identity, form, or place of organization.'"[2]

---

[1] **§ 601** Until 2005, one difference that remained was that, although the continuity-of-business and continuity-of-interest requirements under Code § 368 did not apply to "E" recapitalizations, they did apply to all other forms of reorganization, including "F" reorganizations. However, effective for transactions on or after February 25, 2005, Reg. § 1.368-1(b) was amended to delete these continuity requirements for "F" reorganizations, and to confirm that they do not apply to "E" recapitalizations.

Notwithstanding this change for "F" reorganizations, the rule of *Southwest Consolidated* continues to apply to "F" reorganizations—namely, the rule that a *transaction* that *shifts* the proprietary interests in the corporation cannot be an "F" reorganization. *See* Prop. Reg. § 1.368-2. (The release accompanying this 2005 proposed regulation says that this rule continues to be under study by the Treasury.) For comments regarding certain problems in the 2005 proposed regulation and recommendations for changes in them, *see* comment letter to the IRS from KPMG LLP, *reprinted at* 2005 TNT 42-53, March 4, 2005.

[1] **§ 602** 315 U.S. 194, 42-1 U.S.T.C. ¶ 9248 (1942).

[2] Id. at 203-204. The "F" reorganization portion of this quotation continues to be the rule, even after the elimination of the continuity-of-interest rule for "F" reorganizations by the amendment to Reg. § 1.368-1(b). *See* Prop. Reg. § 1.368-2, described at § 601 n.1 above. *Cf.* IRS Letter Ruling 9317011, April 30, 1993, in which a purchasing corporation acquired for cash all of the stock of a target corporation and then as part of the same plan caused target to merge into a second-tier subsidiary of purchaser. The IRS held the second transaction to satisfy the continuity-of-interest requirement for purposes of treating the merger as a tax-free "A" reorganization. In this ruling, which reaches a sensible result, the IRS was obviously willing to consider the transaction that caused the shift in proprietary interest,

We saw at § 510.2, however, that in Rev. Rul. 59-222,[3] a situation that involved the acquisition of the failing company by an outside party (and that, thus, was not a two-company transaction used merely as a substitute for a recapitalization), the IRS held that a recapitalization of the failing company was deemed to occur immediately before the two-company reorganization (which, in that case, was a "B" reorganization).[4]

Shortly thereafter, in its leading liquidation-reincorporation ruling, Rev. Rul. 61-156,[5] the IRS declared a two-company transaction to be an "E" recapitalization and an "F" reorganization. There, Oldco "sold" its assets to Newco for cash, securities and 45 percent of the stock of Newco, the other 55 percent being sold simultaneously to the public. Oldco liquidated, distributing the Newco stock and securities and cash to the Oldco shareholders. The IRS held that the issuance of stock to the public should be treated as a separate transaction, and that if the issuance of stock to the public is thus disregarded, "there is clearly a mere recapitalization and reincorporation coupled with a withdrawal of funds." It held the transaction to be "a reorganization within the meaning of Code sections 368(a)(1)(E) and (F)."

Although the courts have rejected the IRS's invitation in similar cases to treat a reincorporation as involving an "E" recapitalization in addition to an "F" or "D" reorganization,[6] the IRS has issued a number of private rulings in which it found an "E" recapitalization to be coupled with an "F" reorganization.[7] These rulings in-

(Footnote Continued)

namely the stock sale, to be separate from the reorganization transaction, even though the two transactions were part of a single plan.

[3] 1959-1 C.B. 80.

[4] Rev. Rul. 59-222 may well be considered to be just a step-transaction ruling in which the separate steps would have been recognized had they actually occurred (but where they were allowed to be collapsed into one transaction). On the recognition of the separate steps in similar circumstances, *see, e.g.*, Rev. Rul. 76-223, 1976-1 C.B. 103 (threshold amendment of charter to give nonvoting preferred a vote to allow acquisition of only common to qualify as a "B" reorganization recognized because change had continuing significance); Rev. Rul. 77-227, 1977-2 C.B. 120 (recapitalization of purchasing corporation before "A" reorganization to avoid Code § 382(b) recognized because change had continuing significance); Rev. Rul. 78-330, 1978-2 C.B. 147 (forgiveness of debt to avoid Code § 357(c) in a "D" reorganization; Rev. Rul. 78-330 was subsequently modified by Rev. Rul. 2007-08, 2007-7 I.R.B. 469, to the extent it had held that Code § 357(c)(1) applies to an "A" reorganization if it is also a "D" reorganization). The more interesting thing about Rev. Rul. 59-222 is not that it recognized a first-step recapitalization, but that it considered the creditors who received stock in the deemed recapitalization to have sufficient continuity of ownership to participate in a second-step "B" reorganization.

[5] 1961-1 C.B. 62. *See also* IRS Letter Ruling 200505010, October 14, 2004.

[6] *See, e.g., Joseph C. Gallagher v. Commissioner*, 39 T.C. 144, Dec. 25,711 (1962); *Pridemark, Inc. v. Commissioner*, 345 F.2d 35, 65-1 U.S.T.C. ¶ 9388 (4th Cir. 1965).

[7] *See, e.g.*, IRS Letter Ruling 7819071, February 13, 1978 (reincorporation coupled with change in par value of common stock); IRS Letter Ruling 7721014, February 24, 1977 (reincorporation in which old preferred and common became common). These rulings did not involve an actual two-step transaction. All that occurred physically was a reincorporation. The rulings do not specify which company had the "E" recapitalization. The IRS has also ruled that a physical reincorporation followed by a physical recapitalization is an "F" reincorporation followed by an "E" recapitalization of the new company. *See, e.g.*, IRS Letter Ruling 7938044, June 20, 1979; IRS Letter Ruling 8104101, October 30, 1980. *See also* IRS Letter Ruling 200644008, June 23, 2006 (exchanges by some shareholders of their stock for new stock with different terms, followed by merger of the corporation into another

cluded at least two cases under Chapter XI of the prior Bankruptcy Act, in which failing former REITs organized as business trusts structured a bankruptcy workout as involving an actual recapitalization (in which creditors received shares of beneficial interest) followed by an actual reincorporation into corporate form. The IRS, following Rev. Rul. 59-222, held the transactions to be "E" recapitalizations of the old company followed by "F" reincorporations.[8]

On the other hand, the second of the first two private rulings issued in a "G" reorganization of a company that was not a banking institution essentially involved a two-company reorganization used as a substitute for a recapitalization. No acquisition of or by outside interests was involved. The parties did not structure the transaction as involving a first-step recapitalization preceding a second-step two-company transaction. The IRS analyzed the case strictly as a two-company reorganization matter and did not seek to apply Rev. Rul. 59-222 or otherwise suggest that a recapitalization was involved.[9]

Interestingly, in a letter ruling issued in early 2001,[10] the IRS, without referring to Rev. Rul. 59-222, held that the conversion of a mutual insurance company into a stock company immediately precedent to a downstream merger of the insurance company into a subsidiary constituted a good "E" recapitalization, and would not prevent the merger from qualifying under Code § § 368(a)(1)(A) and 368(a)(2)(D).

What difference does it make whether the transaction is treated as a two-step "E" coupled with an "F" or a "B" rather than as a single-step two-company transaction? The first potential difference—and the one of most current significance—relates to the question of whether the transaction would qualify as a reorganization at all if it were treated simply as a two-company reorganization. For instance, although neither the continuity-of-interest nor the continuity-of-business test applies to "E" or, since early 2005, to "F" reorganizations for Code § 368 purposes,[11] at the time of the "F" rulings mentioned above the continuity-of-interest rule did apply to "F" reorganizations. Even today, the *Southwest Consolidated* requirement (that a transaction which itself involves a shift in proprietary interest cannot be an "F" reorganization) continues to

---

(Footnote Continued)

corporation and a simultaneous transfer by some of the Oldco shareholders of property to the surviving company was an "E" recapitalization followed by an acquisitive transaction that qualified as both an "A" reorganization and a Code § 351 transaction); IRS Letter Ruling 200648011, September 6, 2006 (merger of a not-for-profit corporation into another not-for-profit corporation organized under the laws of a different state was both an "E" and an "F" reorganization).

[8] IRS Letter Ruling 7821047, February 23, 1978; IRS Letter Ruling 8110139, December 12, 1980.

[9] IRS Letter Ruling 8521083, February 27, 1985. To the same effect is IRS Letter Ruling 9629016, April 22, 1996, in which a merger of Oldco into Newco, pursuant to which the old security holders and shareholders received all of the Newco stock, was held to be a "G" reorganization. In IRS Field Service Advice 1999-1029, September 22, 1993, *reprinted at* 1999 TNT 81-57, the IRS distinguished Rev. Rul. 59-222 and held that a transaction, which it also found to fail the "G" reorganization requirements, should not be considered to be a good "E" followed by an "F" reorganization.

[10] IRS Letter Ruling 200144001, April 27, 2001 (the ruling did not involve a failing company).

[11] *See* Rev. Rul. 82-34, 1982-1 C.B. 59 ("E" reorganizations); Rev. Rul. 77-415, 1977-2 C.B. 311 ("E" reorganizations); Reg. § 1.368-1(b), as amended effective for transactions occurring on or after February 25, 2005 ("E" and "F" reorganizations).

apply.[12] Thus, even today, the above "F" transactions could not qualify as "F" reorganizations without there being an "E" recapitalization as well. Further, at the time Rev. Rul. 59-222 (a "B" transaction) was issued, the transaction would not have been thought to satisfy the "B" reorganization requirement that the "stock" of the target corporation be acquired for acquirer stock, without there being a first-step recapitalization.

Rev. Rul. 59-222 is a perfect example of a two-company transaction that would not qualify as a reorganization if a first-step recapitalization is not inserted in front of it. Similarly, where stock is issued to creditors and the old stockholders are wiped out, a two-company transaction would not qualify as a "D" reorganization, because *Southwest* holds that the word "stockholders" in the statute does not include creditors, even if they have assumed "command" of the company in the *Alabama Asphaltic* (*see* § 510.1) sense. This means that the "stockholders" of the old company would not be in control of the new company, as is required to satisfy the "D" reorganization requirements. However, a first-step recapitalization would eliminate that problem. Indeed, one of the two reasons given by the Supreme Court for the failure of the transaction involved in *Southwest* to qualify as a reorganization would have been eliminated if the transaction had been treated as involving a first-step "E" recapitalization of the old company.[13] Beginning with Rev. Rul. 59-222, it appears to have been the policy of the IRS to allow (or even to deem) a first-step recapitalization where the result is to ensure that the two-company transaction will qualify as a reorganization. More recently, in the 2005 proposed "net value" regulations (discussed at § 604.3.4 below), the IRS presented an example—Prop. Reg. § 1.368-1(f)(5), Example 9—that arguably suggests that a transaction like that in Rev. Rul. 59-222 can qualify as a "B" reorganization *without* the need for deeming a first-step recapitalization. More likely, however, the example is based on an assumed but unstated application of a deemed first-step recapitalization.

In the past, the second difference that application of an "E" and "F" analysis made was in application of the stock-for-debt exception to COD income. In Rev. Rul. 59-222 and the failing company private rulings that have applied the first-step "E" analysis, the IRS has held the stock-for-debt exception to apply to the issuance of stock to the creditors in the first-step "E" recapitalization. This eliminated the potential problem in a two-company reorganization occurring prior to the Tax Reform Act of 1986 that was posed by Rev. Rul. 70-271, which is discussed below.

The third potential difference related to the application of old Code § 382(a) and (b). A first-step "E" guarantees that the 20 percent continuity of equity ownership requirement of old Code § 382(b) will be satisfied where the new company is simply being used as a substitute for a one-company recapitalization. In addition, there is no risk (another point that is discussed below) that the stock of the *new* company that is

---

[12] *See* Prop. Reg. § 1.368-2, described at § 601 n.1 above.

[13] The statute involved in *Southwest* was the equivalent of the present "C" reorganization. The Supreme Court held that the acquisition failed the "solely voting stock" requirement because the acquiring corporation (1) issued warrants and (2) assumed a liability of the acquired company that was created in the reorganization. The first reason would have disappeared if there were deemed to have been a first-step recapitalization.

issued to nonsecurity creditors of the *old* company will be treated as "purchased" for old Code § 382(a) purposes. While the stock of the old company issued to such creditors in the "E" will be treated as so purchased, the old Code § 382(a) "change in business" test (*see* § 507.2) will not create a problem because—assuming the old company has an active business at the time of the transaction—the old company will immediately disappear in the two-company transaction and there will be no time in which the business can "change" (assuming that the transfer to the new company is not itself a change for this purpose and that one would not consider the new company to be a continuation of the old company for this purpose).[14] In short, application of the two-step "E" and "F" characterization could potentially produce a better result under old Code § 382(a) and (b) than either a one-company "E" or a two-company reorganization that was not deemed to involve a first-step "E." Neither the facts in Rev. Rul. 59-222 nor the facts in the failing company private rulings examined by us have presented this issue, however.

In summary, the IRS appears willing to apply the first-step "E" result preceding two-company transaction where the parties choose to structure an actual initial "E" recapitalization of the old company. This willingness to relax the usual application of the step-transaction doctrine undoubtedly reflects, as much as anything, the unique status of "F" reorganizations. This conclusion is supported by Rev. Rul. 96-29,[15] which indicated that the relaxation of the step-transaction doctrine in certain "F" reorganization cases is not intended to reflect the application of that doctrine in other contexts.[16] But where such a physical recapitalization does not take place, the IRS has not been consistent about deeming one to have occurred. Especially where the two-company transaction is an acquisitive transaction in which the failing company is acquired by a profitable business, one should not assume that a first-step recapitalization of the failing company will be deemed to occur, as it was in Rev. Rul. 59-222.[17] Indeed, many, if not most, two-company acquisitive reorganizations, whether of failing or profitable companies, involve at least some change in the interests issued to

---

[14] The first assumption underlies Code § 269(b). *See* Joint Committee on Taxation, General Explanation of the Revenue Provisions of the Deficit Reduction Act of 1984, December 31, 1984, at 998-99. *But cf.* Bacon, Rescue Planning for Failing or Bankrupt Company, 631 Taxes 931, 945 (1983) (wherein the author in text and footnotes expresses doubt as to whether the effects of old Code § 382(a) could be avoided in a first-step recapitalization).

[15] 1996-1 C.B. 50.

[16] Indeed, the IRS in appropriate cases continues to apply Rev. Rul. 96-29 to allow an "F" reorganization to occur as a separate step in a series of related transactions. For example, *see* IRS Letter Ruling 200544006, July 28, 2005 (in a three-step transaction, the IRS ruled that a conversion of a mutual insurance company into a stock company was both an "E" and an "F" reorganization, followed by its acquisition by a holding company which was ruled a "B" reorganization, followed by a drop down of its stock ruled to be a Code § 351 and a "B" reorganization transaction); IRS Letter Ruling 200546015, August 8, 2005 (reincorporation into Newco was a good "F" reorganization even though it was just the first step in a transaction in which Newco acquired a second corporation in an "A" reorganization); IRS Letter Ruling 200608018, February 24, 2006 (complicated restructuring of corporations ruled to be an "F" reorganization, even though as part of the plan Newco was to receive borrowing proceeds which it would then distribute as a dividend to the transferor).

[17] Krane makes the argument that every two-company transaction of a troubled company should be deemed to have been preceded by an internal recapitalization. Krane, Preserving the Tax Attributes of Financially Corporations, 53 Taxes 802 (1975).

the stockholders of the target company. Yet these are routinely characterized in private and published rulings as one-step transactions without a first-step recapitalization of the target company. As mentioned above, however, the 2005 proposed "net value" regulations may make the deeming of a first-step recapitalization less necessary than in prior years.

## §603 ACQUISITIVE TWO-COMPANY REORGANIZATIONS

The most common use of a two-company reorganization is not as a mere substitute for a recapitalization, but as a mechanism for the combination of the business (as well as NOLs and other tax attributes) of the failing company with the business of an unrelated profitable company.

This can be accomplished either by having the failing company be the target that is acquired by the profitable business (a form that we will call a "Reorg. Out") or, instead, by having the profitable company become the target that is acquired by the failing business (which we will call a "Reorg. In").

In either case, the debt and stock interests in the failing company will be changed as part of the two-company transaction. Where this occurs in a Reorg. In, the failing company will have an "E" recapitalization simultaneously with its acquisitive reorganization. Where it occurs in a Reorg. Out, we have suggested above that the failing company may not always (though it was in Rev. Rul. 59-222) be deemed to have had an "E" recapitalization separate from the two-company transaction.

In recent years, the concept of a "disregarded" entity has become an accepted part of the tax law, and in 2003 the IRS issued temporary and proposed regulations to govern how the "A" reorganization provisions can apply to merger or consolidation transactions where some of the entities involved are disregarded entities.[1] These, with some modifications, were made final in 2006.[2] These regulations are quite flexible and may make triangular transactions easier to accomplish where disregarded entities are involved than where such entities are not involved.

The IRS has also increased the flexibility of "acquisitive" reorganizations by allowing drop-downs of assets following such reorganizations.[3]

In late 2002, the IRS announced that it would try to issue more guidance than it has in the past regarding mergers or other combinations of insolvent companies.[4]

---

[1] **§603** *See* Temp. Reg. §1.368-2T; New York State Bar Association, Tax Section, Committee on Reorganizations, Report on Temporary Regulations §1.368-2T Relating to "A" Reorganizations Involving Disregarded Entities (May 26, 2004), 2004 TNT 103-12 (May 27, 2004).

[2] Reg. §1.368-2.

[3] In 2002, the IRS made clear that this applied to "D" reorganizations as well. Rev. Rul. 2002-85, 2002-52 I.R.B. 986; IRS Notice 2002-77, 2002-52 I.R.B. 997, announcing it will propose amendments to the regulations to reflect this result. Such amendments to Reg. §1.368-2(k) and related provisions were proposed in March and August 2004. *See also* New York State Bar Association, Tax Section, Report on Distributions Following Tax-Free Reorganizations (May 19, 2004), 2004 TNT 99-28 (May 21, 2004), proposing liberalization for upstream distributions following reorganizations; American Bar Association, Tax Section, Comments Regarding Transfers of Assets and Stock Following a Reorganization (February 7, 2005), *reprinted at* 2005 TNT 26-7 (February 9, 2005).

[4] *See* BNA Daily Tax Report (December 20, 2002), at G-7.

This subsequently resulted in the issuance in early 2005 of proposed regulations imposing a "net value" requirement for certain reorganizations and addressing the treatment of creditors as proprietors in insolvency and bankruptcy situations for purposes of the continuity-of-interest requirement.

## § 604 TWO-COMPANY ACQUISITIVE REORGANIZATIONS OUTSIDE BANKRUPTCY

A two-company reorganization of a failing company occurring outside bankruptcy proceedings[1] differs from one accomplished during a bankruptcy proceeding in the following respects: First, the "G" reorganization provisions do not apply; second, there will be less certainty whether the creditors will be considered to constitute proprietary interest holders for purposes of the continuity-of-interest test; third, the creditors do not constitute "stockholders" for purposes of statutory provisions such as old Code § 382(b) and the Code § 368(a)(1)(D) (or "D") reorganization provision; fourth, the stock-for-debt exception (to the extent it still remains under the grandfather provisions in its repeal) to the COD income rules will not apply; and fifth, the special, potentially more liberal rules for survival of losses under new Code § 382 that are applicable only in bankruptcy and similar proceedings will not apply.

### *§ 604.1 Creditor and Shareholder Consequences*

The consequences of a two-company Reorg. Out to the creditors and shareholders of the old company will be the same as the consequences of a one-company recapitalization (*see* § § 403, 502). The same Code provisions govern both transactions, assuming of course that the two-company transaction qualifies as a Code § 368 reorganization.[2] Creditors who did not hold securities will recognize gain or loss on the exchange of their debt for new debt or stock. Creditors whose old debt constituted securities will have a tax-free exchange to the extent they receive new securities (of no greater principal amount) or new stock in exchange for the principal amount of their old debt.[3] The old stockholders will have a tax-free exchange to the extent they

---

[1] **§ 604** We use the phrase "bankruptcy proceedings" here in a somewhat loose sense. The reader should note, however, that for purposes of Code § 108 the bankruptcy rules are limited to title 11 proceedings, whereas for purposes of Code § § 368 and 382 they include both title 11 proceedings and receivership, foreclosure, or similar proceedings in a federal or state court.

[2] *See, e.g.*, explanation of the reorganization provisions at Ginsburg and Levin, Mergers, Acquisitions, and Buyouts, Chapters 6-8 (Aspen Law & Business).

[3] Where the old securities have only a short remaining life, the IRS has issued a ruling making it possible to classify new debt issued in exchange for it as a security, even if the new debt has the same short remaining time to maturity. Rev. Rul. 2004-78, 2004-31 I.R.B. 1. This ruling, which is discussed above at § 403.1, holds that where the new debt has terms that are essentially identical to those of the old security (except perhaps the interest rate), including its short remaining life, the new debt can qualify as a security, since it represents a continuation of the security holder's investment in the target corporation in substantially the same form. For a discussion of some of the implications of this ruling, *see* Friedman, Debt Exchanges After Rev. Rul. 2004-78, 105 Tax Notes 979 (November 15, 2004).

receive new stock in exchange for their old stock.[4] These consequences, including the treatment of boot, issuance of stock or securities for accrued unpaid interest, and the treatment of OID and market discount have previously been discussed in Chapters 4 and 5.

Further, as mentioned at § 502.3 above, for exchanges occurring on or after March 9, 1998, warrants will be treated for purposes of Code §§ 354 and 356 as "securities" having a zero principal amount. This means they can be exchanged tax-free for debt that is a security, for stock (although an exchange of solely warrants for stock will not be tax-free), or for other warrants. Also, as mentioned at § 502.3 above, for transactions occurring on or after March 9, 1998, certain preferred stock will no longer qualify as stock for purposes of Code §§ 354 and 356 (except when exchanged for such nonqualifying preferred stock or for securities).

## *§ 604.2 Target Corporation Consequences*

A two-company Reorg. Out will be tax free to the target corporation, unless Code § 357, the conversion of debt to stock, or the "boot" rules of Code § 361 produce income for the target corporation. The Code § 357 and cancellation-of-debt issues are discussed in the next sections.

Code § 361 treats the consequences of "boot" differently depending on whether it is retained by the target corporation or instead is distributed by the target corporation to its shareholders or creditors. If the "boot" is retained by the target corporation rather than being distributed to its shareholders or creditors, then Code § 361(b) provides that the target corporation will recognize its gain (though not loss) on the reorganization exchange itself to the extent of the fair market value of the "boot" so retained. For purposes of Code § 361(b), "boot" means money or property other than the stock and securities permitted to be received by the target corporation tax free.

On the other hand, if the "boot" is distributed by the target corporation to either its shareholders or its creditors, the target corporation will not recognize gain on the basic reorganization exchange itself, but Code § 361(c) provides that the target will recognize gain (though not loss, except on distributions to creditors) on the "boot" itself when it is distributed by the target corporation to the target corporation's shareholders or creditors. Such gain equals the difference between the fair market value of the "boot" when it is so distributed and its basis in the hands of the target corporation. Since its basis to the target corporation will equal its fair market value at the time of the reorganization exchange,[5] as a practical matter this rule means that the target corporation will be taxable only on the increases (if any) in the value of the "boot" between the time the "boot" is received by the target corporation and the time

---

[4] As mentioned at § 502.3, Code § 354 does not apply to the exchange of solely new securities or warrants for old stock. *See* Reg. § 1.354-1(d), Example 4. Thus, in such an exchange the old stockholder could recognize gain. Presumably the wash sale provisions of Code § 1091, however, would prevent the recognition of loss where, for example, warrants are received by the holder to acquire a like amount of stock. But where very great changes are made in the capital structure of the company, it may be difficult to determine what constitutes a "like amount" of stock.

[5] *See* Code § 358(a)(2), (f).

the "boot" is distributed by it to its shareholders or creditors. Moreover, for purposes of Code § 361(c), "boot" has a narrower definition than for purposes of Code § 361(b). Not only does the Code § 361(c) definition of "boot" exclude stock and securities permitted to be received tax free, it also excludes any other debt of a party to the reorganization and any rights to acquire stock of any party to the reorganization.

In some instances, the target corporation will distribute to its shareholders or creditors property that it did not transfer to the acquiring corporation or receive from the acquiring corporation (that is, retained property). If such retained property is distributed to shareholders of the target, the target corporation will recognize gain but not loss.[6] This is the same as the Code § 311 rule for regular distributions to shareholders. However, if such retained property (as well as any Code § 361(c) "boot" received) is distributed to creditors of the target corporation (or sold), the target corporation will recognize either gain or loss, as the case may be.[7]

The corporation will have a basis in the transferred assets equal to the basis of the target corporation, adjusted for any gain recognized to the target corporation.[8] The NOLs and other carryovers of the target corporation will transfer to the acquiring corporation under Code § 381, except to the extent that Code § § 382 and 383 (or Code § 269, or the SRLY limitation in the consolidated return regulations) operate to reduce or eliminate them.[9] These rules are discussed at § § 508, 509, and 804.

### § 604.2.1 Income from Conversion of Debt to Stock

Assume that the failing company transfers all of its assets to Newco in a statutory merger and that Newco issues only stock in the transaction. All of the liabilities of the old company are thus converted to stock. Assume further that some of these liabilities consisted of trade debts that were not securities; and some of it consisted of long-term debts that qualified as securities.

A statutory merger is treated for tax purposes as a transfer of assets by the target company to the acquiring company in exchange for the consideration issued by the acquiring company (even though in corporate form that consideration goes directly to the stockholders and/or creditors of the target company) followed by a liquidation of the target company. The Newco stock received by the target company will have a basis equal to the basis that the target company had in its assets.[10]

Will the target company recognize gain or loss on the distribution of the Newco stock to its creditors and shareholders? The Tax Reform Act of 1986 (and a technical correction adopted in 1988) amended Code § 361 to say no. For transactions after the enactment of the 1986 Act, Code § 361(c) provides that no gain or loss is to be

---

[6] Code § 361(c)(1), (2).

[7] *See* Code § 361(c)(1), (3). Code § 361(c)(3) disallows recognition of loss on a transfer of property to creditors only to the extent the property is "qualified property," as defined in Code § 361(c).

[8] Code § 362(b).

[9] For an excellent transactional outline of when these limitations apply under the law prior to the 1986 Act, as well as other considerations, *see* Eustice, Carryover of Corporate Tax Attributes, 22 San Diego L. Rev. 117, Appendix A (1985).

[10] Code § 358(a)(1).

recognized to the target corporation on any transfer of the Newco stock to its creditors. However, the committee reports contain a footnote that says "this provision is not intended, however, to affect the recognition of discharge of indebtedness income by the acquired corporation on a transfer to a creditor."[11] Where Newco issues its stock or debt to creditors of the failing company, there can be a question, however, as to whether Code §§108(e)(8) and 108(e)(10) by their terms apply to create COD income, and if they do, there can be a question whether the COD is income to Newco or to the failing company.[12]

**Pre-1986 Act Law.** Under the pre-1986 Act version of Code §361(b), however, the answer was not the same, and for those having cases arising under the prior law (and for an insight into the application of the stock-for-debt exception in two-company reorganizations) it may be useful to explain the problem that existed under old Code §361(b).

It had long been clear under the 1954 Code that the target company would not recognize gain or loss on the Newco stock distributed to its old stockholders.[13] However, with respect to the distribution of Newco stock to the old creditors, the IRS had held in Rev. Rul. 70-271[14] that a distribution of Newco stock to old creditors in a "C" reorganization was to be treated as if the old company had sold the stock for cash and then paid the creditors with the cash, with the result that the old company recognized gain or loss on the stock distributed to the creditors.[15]

This ruling was at least technically distinguishable from the stock-for-debt exception to the COD income rules (*see* §504A). The ruling dealt with the difference between the basis of the stock to the target company and its fair market value, whereas the stock-for-debt exception applies to the difference between the face amount of the debt and the fair market value of the stock. For example, assume that the failing company receives stock of the new company having a value of $80,000 and a basis to the failing company under Code §358 of $50,000, which it distributes to a creditor in satisfaction of a $100,000 obligation issued by the failing company.

---

[11] H.R. Rep. No. 841, 99th Cong., 2d Sess. II-844 (1986); H.R. Rep. No. 100-445, 100th Cong., 2d Sess. 393.

[12] *See* Ginsburg and Levin, Mergers, Acquisitions and Buyouts, §605 (Aspen, May 2000 ed.).

[13] Code §361(c)(4).

[14] 1970-1 C.B. 166; *see also* Rev. Rul. 75-450, 1975-2 C.B. 328 (finder's fee paid with stock of acquirer in a "C" reorganization held to generate gain or loss to target company, on theory of Rev. Rul. 70-271).

[15] Of course, if Code §337 (prior to repeal by Pub. L. No. 99-514) applied to a complete liquidation that was also part of a reorganization, neither gain nor loss would be recognized. *See General Housewares Corp. v. United States*, 615 F.2d 1056 (5th Cir. 1980) (Code §337 applied where portion of stock received in a tax-free reorganization was sold for cash and cash was used to pay creditors); *contra, e.g., FEC Liquidating Corp. v. United States*, 548 F.2d 924, 77-1 U.S.T.C. ¶9160 (Ct. Cl. 1977). The 1986 Act amended Code §361(b) to provide that Code §337 does not apply to liquidations that are part of a reorganization. Although this amendment, by the time the final legislation was passed, refers primarily to new Code §337 (and old Code §337 has been repealed pursuant to the repeal of the *General Utilities* doctrine) and does not have retroactive effect, the original intention, when the legislation was in the House, was clearly to refer to old Code §337 as well and to give the amendment retroactive effect back to the date of the adoption of the 1984 Act. *See* H.R. Rep. No. 426. 99th Cong., 1st Sess. 877, 898, 1090-91, 1321 (1985).

The stock-for-debt exception (assuming it otherwise applies and is not limited by Code § 108) relates to the $20,000 difference between the $100,000 face amount of the debt and the $80,000 value of the stock issued in exchange for the debt. Rev. Rul. 70-271, on the other hand, took the position that the $30,000 difference between the basis of the new company stock and its value resulted in the recognition of gain to the old company. (Had the basis of the stock been $100,000, the old company under Rev. Rul. 70-271 would presumably have recognized a $20,000 loss, while the stock-for-debt exception could have eliminated the $20,000 COD income.)

That the judicially created stock-for-debt exception applies to new company stock issued to the old company's creditors in a two-company reorganization was established in *Alcazar Hotel, Inc.*[16] and *Claridge Apartments Co.*[17] These cases are bankruptcy cases in which assets were transferred to a new company in a bankruptcy reorganization exchange, and stock of the new company was issued to creditors of the old company. Under the rules applicable to reorganizations under the old Bankruptcy Act (which were discussed at the beginning of this chapter), the IRS argued that the old company debt that was satisfied with Newco stock would be considered to have been cancelled, with the result that the basis of the assets of the old company was reduced by the amount of the cancellation, but not below the fair market value of the assets. The taxpayer argued that there was no COD income to the old company and that the new company therefore acquired the unreduced basis of the old company in its assets. The court held that the stock-for-debt exception applied and that COD income had not been created. This holding does not seem dependent in any way on the existence of a bankruptcy proceeding.

Even if Rev. Rul. 70-271 is technically distinguishable from the stock-for-debt exception, it seems entirely contrary to its spirit.[18] It also seems contrary to the spirit of the two-company reorganization provisions. Had the failing company in the prior example issued its own stock in satisfaction of its debt, the stock-for-debt exception (except as limited by Code § 108) would apply to the entire $100,000 debt and no gain or loss would be recognized by the failing company. Conversely, had the new company first assumed the debt and then issued its stock in satisfaction of the debt, the stock-for-debt exception (except as limited by Code § 108) would apply to the entire debt and no gain or loss would be recognized by either company. Since the theory behind tax-free treatment of a two-company reorganization is that the old company is simply continuing in modified form, it was inconsistent with this theory to create gain or loss at the corporate level on the distribution of the new company stock to the creditors of the old company. Indeed, it is particularly anomalous to think that while the new company could issue new debt to the creditors of the old company without creating a tax to the old company, it could not issue stock to those creditors without creating gain or loss to the old company.

---

[16] *Alcazar Hotel, Inc. v. Commissioner*, 1 T.C. 872, Dec. 13,099 (1943).

[17] *Claridge Apartments Co. v. Commissioner*, 1 T.C. 163, Dec. 12,896 (1942), *rev'd*, 138 F.2d 962, 43-2 U.S.T.C. ¶ 9663 (7th Cir. 1943), *rev'd on other grounds*, 323 U.S. 141, 44-2 U.S.T.C. ¶ 9532 (1944) (the IRS eventually acquiesced in the Tax Court decision, at 1974-1 CB2).

[18] It appears that the IRS never considered the stock-for-debt exception to COD income when it wrote Rev. Rul. 70-271 and 75-450. *See* GCM 34272 March 12, 1970; GCM 36147, January 27, 1975.

In short, Rev. Rul. 70-271 appears to be wrong. But its existence meant that the IRS could assert that the conversion of debt to stock in a two-company reorganization produced gain to the old company that did not exist in a one-company recapitalization, where the old company had unrealized gain in its assets. Of course, such gain was more likely to exist in a profitable company than in a failing company. Failing companies are more likely to have unrealized losses than unrealized gains in their assets. In such a case, Rev. Rul. 70-271 would produce a loss for the old company, which taxpayers could seek to use for their own advantage.

As discussed earlier at §602, the Rev. Rul. 70-271 problem would not have existed if (1) the transaction was structured as a Reorg. In with an accompanying "E" recapitalization of the failing company or (2) an "E" recapitalization of the failing company were to occur before the Reorg. out.

Even if Rev. Rul. 70-271 is found to be wrong or if it was avoided in one of the ways just mentioned, the failing company still had to take into account the fact that pre-1994 Code §108(e)(10) severely limited the availability of the stock-for-debt exception to COD income in the case of solvent companies that are not in bankruptcy. These rules were discussed at §504A. Moreover, as we have discussed at §504A.3, stock of the parent of an acquiring company could not be presumed to qualify for the stock-for-debt exception, although the private letter ruling issued by the IRS in 1995 is helpful.

### §604.2.2 Liabilities

If the two-company reorganization takes the form of a "D" reorganization, and if that reorganization is a divisive reorganization governed by Code §355, Code §357(c)(1) causes the old company to recognize gain to the extent that the liabilities assumed by, or taken subject to, the new corporation exceed the aggregate basis of the assets transferred to the new corporation.[19] Code §357(c)(1) also applies to Code §351 exchanges. Where liabilities of the old company are satisfied with Newco stock, the new company should not be considered as having first assumed these liabilities (giving rise to a Code §357(c) problem) and then to have satisfied them with its own stock.[20] Hence, it is only the liabilities that continue to exist after the transaction that should be taken into account for purposes of Code §357(c).

For transfers or assumptions in connection with reorganizations occurring before October 22, 2004, Code §357(c)(1) also applied to acquisitive "D" reorganizations governed by Code §354. It had even been held that if under this prior law a transaction was both an "A" and an acquisitive "D" reorganization, Code §357(c)(1) applied, even though it would not apply to an "A" reorganization that was not also a "D" reorganization.[21] Because the potential for such overlap problems could still exist after the 2004 amendment if the transfer was also covered by Code §351, the IRS

---

[19] Code §357(c)(1).

[20] *Cf. Western Maryland Railroad Co. v. United States*, 131 F. Supp. 873, 892-894 (D. Md. 1955).

[21] Rev. Rul. 75-161, 1975-1 C.B. 114, *declared obsolete by* Rev. Rul. 2007-08, 2007-7 I.R.B. 469.

continued to study the problem. Finally, in Rev. Rul. 2007-08,[22] the Service decided that the purpose of the 2004 amendment had been to treat all acquisitive reorganizations alike, and to exempt them from Code § 357(c)(1), at least if the transferor liquidated. Thus, it held that a transaction that is an "A," a "C," an acquisitive "D," or a "G" reorganization to which Code § 354(b)(1) applies, will not be subject to Code § 357(c)(1) even if the transaction is also covered by Code § 351.

### § 604.2.3 Survival of Tax Attributes

Because a tax-free two-company reorganization will always involve the acquisition of control of a corporation or the tax-free transfer of assets, Code § 269 (discussed in the one-company recapitalization context at § 509.1 above) will usually be potentially applicable to the transaction, and the parties will need to be able to satisfy the requirement that tax avoidance is not the principal purpose of the transaction. The consolidated return SRLY rules (discussed at § 509.4) may also become applicable.

With respect to Code § 382, as we have seen at § 508 above, under new Code § 382 essentially the same Code § 382 rules apply to the survival of NOLs (and, by virtue of Code § 383, the survival of other types of carryovers) in two-company reorganizations as in one-company recapitalizations. These rules (which may apply, in a two-company reorganization, to either company) were discussed at §§ 508 and 511 and will not be repeated here. In addition, Code § 384 must be taken into account (*see generally* Chapter 7, Utilizing Tax Losses, and particularly § 709). The consolidated return rules also must be taken into account. *See* Chapter 8.

**Old Code § 382 considerations.** Even after the 1986 Act, old Code § 382 continued to apply to "G" reorganizations in bankruptcy cases filed before August 14, 1986 (as well as other tax-free reorganizations pursuant to plans adopted on or before December 31, 1986). Under old Code § 382, the survival of NOLs (and, by virtue of old Code § 383, other carryovers) in two-company reorganizations was governed by old Code § 382(b). Unlike old Code § 382(a), old Code § 382(b) did not contain a "change-in-business" test to harm the survival of NOLs and other carryovers (although, as will be discussed below, the continuity-of-business-enterprise test applicable to two-company reorganizations applied and imposed a similar, though somewhat different, requirement). On the other hand, old Code § 382(b) provided that the NOLs would be reduced or eliminated unless the stockholders of the loss corporation owned, as a result of owning stock of the loss corporation, at least 20 percent of the fair market value of the outstanding stock of the surviving corporation,[23] For this purpose, stock did not include nonvoting stock that is limited and

---

[22] 2007-7 I.R.B. 469. For earlier IRS thinking about Code § 357 liability assumption issues, *see* IRS Announcement 2003-37, 2003-24 I.R.B. 1025 (May 6, 2003) (which includes an analytical memorandum explaining the IRS substantive thinking in the area). *See also* IRS Letter Ruling 200414046, May 19, 2003 (suggests disallowing step-up in basis for liabilities in excess of basis on assets acquired in a Code § 351 transaction where the transferors were foreigners not subject to tax in the exchange for this excess).

[23] Code § 382(b)(1), prior to amendment by Pub. L. No. 99-514.

preferred as to dividends.[24] For each percentage that the old stockholders fell below the 20 percent line, the NOLs and other carryovers were reduced by a percentage that is five times as large.[25] Thus, if the old stockholders of the loss company owned only 10 percent of the stock of the surviving corporation, 50 percent of the NOLs and other carryovers would be destroyed.[26]

Even if in some circumstances the creditors of the loss company may be considered to have become equity owners, at least if they have taken "command" of the failing company by the institution of some type of creditor's proceeding, *Southwest*[27] teaches that the word "stockholders," when used in the statute, refers to the holders of the old stock and not to creditors. Thus, where the two-company reorganization occurs outside bankruptcy, the creditors of the loss company cannot be counted as stockholders of the loss company for purposes of satisfying the 20 percent test of old Code § 382(b). (As we shall see, the rule is different in a bankruptcy proceeding.)

Old Code § 382(b)(6) provided that where the acquiring company is a subsidiary of another company, parent stock issued in the reorganization would be treated as subsidiary stock for old Code § 382 purposes in an amount equal to the fair market value of the stock of the subsidiary. This rule permitted a small subsidiary of a large parent to acquire for parent stock a target company with an NOL and to preserve that NOL even if a direct acquisition of the assets of the target company by the parent would result in severe reduction of the NOLs.[28] However, because, as noted at § 504A.3.2, before 1995 there was considerable uncertainty as to whether parent stock would satisfy the stock-for-debt exception, triangular reorganizations were not practicable for failing companies in years to which the stock-for-debt exception had applied (unless there was minimal debt cancellation).

### § 604.2.4 Preemption of Old Code § 382(a) by Old Code § 382(b)

In a two-company Reorg. Out in which stock is issued to short-term creditors, could both old Code § 382(a) and (b), or only the latter, apply to the transaction?

---

24 Code § 382(c), prior to amendment by Pub. L. No. 99-514; *see* § 507.1, note 8.

25 Code § 382(b)(2), prior to amendment by Pub. L. No. 99-514. The 20 percent continuity test is applied company by company. Thus, for example, where eight loss companies merge at once, it is impossible for the stockholders of each of the companies to receive at least 20 percent of the surviving company's stock. As a result, in such circumstance, the loss of some NOLs and other carryovers is inevitable. *See Consolidated Blenders, Inc. v. United States*, 785 F.2d 259, 86-1 U.S.T.C. ¶ 9270 (8th Cir. 1986).

26 For a detailed discussion of old Code § 382(b), *see* B. Bittker & J. Eustice, Federal Income Taxation of Corporations and Shareholders § 16.23 (1979, with Supp.); Faber, Net Operating Losses in Corporate Reorganizations Revisited in 1979, 38 Inst. on Fed. Tax'n § § 4,4.02[2] (1979).

27 315 U.S. 194, 42-1 U.S.T.C. ¶ 9248.

28 Because of the consolidated return SRLY rules, however, the NOLs of the target can be used only against the income of the acquiring company and not against the income of other members of the group. *See* Reg. § 1.1502-1(f), -22(c).

**EXAMPLE**

Failing company merges into Newco. Holders of securities in the failing company receive securities of Newco; short-term creditors of the failing company receive 50 percent of the stock of Newco; and the stockholders of the failing company receive the remaining 50 percent of the Newco stock. Assuming that the transaction qualifies as an "A" reorganization, old Code § 382(b) applies to the transaction, but its 20 percent continuity test is satisfied. Does old Code § 382(a) apply as well? If so, the merger involves a "purchase" of 50 percent of the stock of Newco by the short-term creditors because they have a taxable exchange, with the result being that, if the ten-largest-shareholders and the change-in-business portions of the old Code § 382(a) test are also met, the NOLs of the failing company will be destroyed.

There is reason to believe that old Code § 382(b) was intended to preempt old Code § 382(a) in the case of stock issued for the target in two-company reorganizations. The basic design of old Code § 382 was that old Code § 382(a) was to apply to stock acquisitions and old Code § 382(b) was designed to apply to asset acquisitions of a loss company. There is no indication that Congress intended both limitations to apply to stock issued in the same transaction.[29] However, we know of no authority directly in point on this question.

## *§ 604.3 Two-Company Reorganization Requirements*

A two-company reorganization outside bankruptcy must satisfy the traditional requirements for a tax free reorganization. These include the statutory rules for the applicable reorganization form and the non-statutory business purpose,[30] continuity-of-interest, continuity-of-business-enterprise, and (for transactions after the adoption of 2005 Prop. Reg. § 1.368-1(f) in final form) net-value tests.

---

[29] If old Code § 382(a) could apply to stock issued in a two-company reorganization, could old Code § 382(b) apply to a one-company transaction that the IRS considers to be an "F" reorganization? The IRS has held a number of one-company transactions to be "F" reorganizations. *See, e.g.,* Rev. Rul. 72-206, 1972-1 C.B. 105 (mere change of name); Rev. Rul. 79-150, 1979-1 C.B. 149 (conversion of Brazilian public company S.A. to a private company held to be both a Code § 1036 and an "F" transaction); Rev. Rul. 72-420, 1972-1 C.B. 473 (conversion of Antilles N.V. to a Dutch B.V. held to be both a Code § 1036 and an "F" transaction). If such transactions could be deemed to involve a deemed two-company transaction, old Code § 382(b) could apply. However, in such a transaction, the 20 percent continuity of stock interest required by old Code § 382(b) would presumably always be satisfied.

[30] For factors to consider in establishing business purpose in the context of a transfer to a loss corporation, *see* IRS Letter Ruling 8941004, July 11, 1989.

### § 604.3.1 Form of Reorganization

A two-company Reorg. Out of a nonbankrupt failing company can take the form of an "A" reorganization, *i.e.*, a statutory merger or consolidation.[31] This is the most flexible form of two-company reorganization, since it permits the widest latitude in regard to the forms of stock or boot that can be issued in the reorganization, and it does not impose any requirement that "substantially all the assets" be transferred by the old company to the new company.

A "C" reorganization will not be attractive for a Reorg. Out because it limits the consideration that can be issued to solely voting stock of the new corporation plus the assumption of liabilities[32] and because the new corporation must acquire "substantially all of the properties" of the old corporation.[33] A failing company will inevitably have been shrinking its assets, and there will often be uncertainty as to when one begins to measure the assets of the old company for purposes of applying the "substantially all" test. The measurement date may be the date on which the plan of reorganization was formulated, rather than the date of transfer.[34] This could cause difficulty since in some cases the concept of a two-company reorganization may have been hatched (despite the advice given—*see* §§ 102 and 605.1.3—in this volume) simultaneously with the decision to shrink assets.

As for a "D" reorganization, this provision also applies only if "substantially all" of the assets of the old corporation are transferred to the new corporation,[35] although the courts seem to have been more lenient in applying the "substantially all" test to "D" reorganizations than to "C" reorganizations.[36] In addition, a "D" reorganization will exist only if the shareholders of the old company end up owning at least 50 percent of the voting power and value of all of the stock of the surviving company.[37] For this purpose, the shareholders of the old company do not include creditors of the old company who receive stock of the new company.[38]

A two-company acquisitive reorganization of a failing company by a profitable company generally cannot qualify as an "F" reorganization.[39] An "F" reorganization is limited to a change in form of one corporation with little change in stock owner-

---

[31] *See* Code § 368(a)(1)(A).

[32] Although Code § 368(a)(2)(B) permits "boot" to be issued as well if the aggregate of the "boot" and liabilities assumed do not exceed 20 percent of the fair market value of the property of the old corporation, this provision seldom proves to be of practical use.

[33] *See* Code § 368(a)(1)(C).

[34] *See generally* B. Bittker & J. Eustice, Federal Income Taxation of Corporations and Shareholders ¶ 12.24[2][c] (7th ed.); and the discussion in § 605.1.3 *infra*.

[35] This requirement is imposed by Code § 354(b) in the case of a nondivisive "D" reorganization. In this volume, we are dealing only with nondivisive reorganizations.

[36] In "D" more than in "C" reorganizations, the courts have generally focused on the transfer of business assets rather than total assets. *See James Armour, Inc.*, 43 T.C. 295, Dec. 27,071 (1965); *American Mfg. Co.*, 55 T.C. 204, Dec. 30,399 (1970); *Smothers v. United States*, 642 F.2d 894, 81-1 U.S.T.C. ¶ 9368 (5th Cir. 1981).

[37] *See* Code § 368(c)(2).

[38] *Helvering v. Southwest Consol Corp.*, 315 U.S. 194, 42-1 U.S.T.C. ¶ 9248 (1942).

[39] *See* Code § 368(a)(1)(F).

ship and does not apply to acquisitive transactions. The requirements for meeting the "F" reorganization test have been set forth in Prop. Reg. § 1.368-2(m) issued August 12, 2004.

Because of the limitations on applicability of the "C," "D," and "F" reorganization provisions, a two-company Reorg. Out of a failing company that is not in bankruptcy will usually take the form of an "A" reorganization. Where the transaction is a Reorg. In, however, a "C" reorganization will be feasible, because in that case it is only the profitable company that will need to meet the substantially-all-assets test.[40]

### § 604.3.2 Continuity-of-Interest Test

As discussed at § 510.1, the *Alabama Asphaltic* case[41] and its progeny teach that creditors of the old company who receive stock in the new company can sometimes be treated as equity owners of the old company for purposes of satisfying the continuity-of-interest test. On March 10, 2005, the Treasury issued Prop. Reg. § 1.368-1(e)(6) to clarify this area.

Before issuance of that proposed regulation, it was generally said that this concept applies only where the creditors have taken command of the old company by the institution of an appropriate bankruptcy or other creditor's proceeding. Where no such proceeding was commenced, creditors of a failing company who received stock of the new company have sometimes been counted for purposes of satisfying the continuity-of-interest test where they also owned the stock of the former company.[42] However, where these special circumstances plus the clear insolvency (a factual question) of the old company do not exist, the creditors of the old company who receive stock in the new company will not count toward satisfying the continuity of

---

[40] For a discussion of the difficulties and possibilities of an insolvent corporation undergoing a non-"G" tax-free reorganization, *see* Bacon, Rescue Planning for Failing or Bankrupt Company, 631 Taxes 931, 944-945 (1983); Asofsky, *et al.*, Conference on the Bankruptcy Tax Act of 1980, 39 Inst. on Fed. Tax'n § § 57, 57.09[8] at 57-113 (1981)(hereafter Bankruptcy Tax Conference) (remarks of Richard L. Bacon); Faber, *supra* note 26, at § 4.01[2][a]; Plumb, The Tax Recommendations of the Commission on the Bankruptcy Laws—Reorganizations, Carryovers and the Effects of Debt Reduction, 29 Tax L. Rev. 227, 231-237 (1974) (hereafter Plumb, Bankruptcy Committee Tax Recommendations—Reorganizations); Tillinghast & Gardner, Acquisitive Reorganizations and Chapter X and XI of the Bankruptcy Act, 26 Tax L. Rev. 663, 671-686, 690-697 (1971).

[41] *Helvering v. Alabama Asphaltic Limestone Co.*, 315 U.S. 179, 42-1 U.S.T.C. ¶ 9245 (1942). In IRS Letter Ruling 200350016, August 28, 2003, a company in bankruptcy issued all of its new stock to its short-term creditors (there were no security holders). The old stock was cancelled and the stockholders received nothing. The ruling held that, although the short-term creditors would be treated as former equity holders for purposes of the "G" reorganization continuity-of-interest requirement pursuant to *Alabama Asphaltic*, they would not be treated as shareholders or security holders for purposes of Code § § 354 and 355. This ruling is discussed at § 709 below.

[42] *See, e.g.*, *United States v. Adkins Phelps, Inc.*, 400 F.2d 737, 68-2 U.S.T.C. ¶ 9609 (8th Cir. 1968); *Seiberling Rubber Co. v. Commissioner*, 169 F.2d 595, 48-2 U.S.T.C. ¶ 9343 (6th Cir. 1948); *Norman Scott, Inc. v. Commissioner*, 48 T.C. 598, Dec. 28,551 (1967); Rev. Rul. 54-610, 1954-2 C.B. 152. Where these special circumstances exist, one wonders what might happen if a significant portion of the debt held by such creditors had been redeemed before the reorganization. *See* the discussion of this issue in § 605.1.4, Interim Distributions, below.

interest test. In that case, the consideration issued to the stockholders of the old company must by itself satisfy the applicable continuity-of-interest requirements.[43] In this regard, it should be noted that even if the company might be insolvent in a balance sheet sense, this does not mean that its stock does not have value, in which case it cannot be ignored for continuity-of-interest purposes.[44] (We should note that, although the new proposed continuity-of-interest regulation generally seems to require that the stock of the old company be taken into account if it receives any value in the transaction regardless of the insolvency of the company, the simultaneously issued "net value" regulations—which are discussed at § 604.3.4 below—ignore stock for purposes of the net value rule if the value of the issuer's liabilities exceeds the value of its assets.)

Prop. Reg. § 1.368-1(e)(6) was issued in 2005 to liberalize and clarify the rules regarding the extent to which creditors are to be considered equity holders for continuity-of-interest purposes. The proposed regulation is to be effective for transactions occurring after the date it is published as a final regulation. This proposed regulation says that a creditor's claim against a target corporation may be considered a proprietary interest, for continuity-of-interest purposes, if the target is in a title 11 or similar case *or* if the corporation is insolvent. In such cases, the proposed regulation provides that, if any class of creditor receives an equity interest in the acquiring corporation in exchange for part or all of its claim, a proportion of the most senior class to receive an equity interest and all equal classes (based on the overall proportion of all such classes that receives a proprietary interest), and 100 percent of all junior classes, will be considered proprietary interests in the old corporation. Shares of stock for which any consideration is received would also be considered proprietary interests. The proposed regulation further provides that, if a creditor's claim is bifurcated into a secured and an unsecured claim pursuant to an order in a title 11 or similar case, or pursuant to an agreement between the creditor and the debtor, that bifurcation will be respected for purposes of applying these rules. For further discussion of the proposed regulation, *see* § 605.1.4 below.

Aside from determining who should be treated as the old equity holders, it should be noted that to satisfy the continuity-of-interest requirement, the new equity need not be issued pro rata to the old equity holders. The continuity-of-interest test is applied not to each equity holder individually but to the group of equity holders in

---

[43] For these requirements, *see generally* Bittker & Eustice, *supra* note 34 at § 12-21.

[44] *See* IRS Field Service Advice 200008012, November 8, 1999, *reprinted at* 2000 TNT 39-64, holding that stock issued for such old stock could satisfy the requirements for an "A" reorganization, citing *Norman Scott v. Commissioner, supra* note 42. *But see* Rev. Rul. 73-233, discussed at § 605.1.4 below. Also, it should be noted that the explanation accompanying the 2005 proposed "net value" regulations indicated that the IRS would consider *Norman Scott* to fail the new net-value test, and thus would no longer qualify as a good "A" reorganization, because the value of the corporate assets was apparently less than the value of the corporate liabilities. *See also* New York State Bar Association, Tax Section, Committee on Bankruptcy and Losses, Report on Reorganizations Involving Insolvent Subsidiaries (November 7, 2003), 101 Tax Notes 761 (November 10, 2003), making recommendations regarding tax-free treatment for upstream restructurings (through mergers, liquidations, or conversions into disregarded entities) and sideways restructurings (through mergers or otherwise) of non-bankrupt but insolvent subsidiaries.

the aggregate. There is also the question of what measuring date should be used to determine if the continuity-of-interest test has been satisfied. Before the issuance of Reg. § 1.368-1(e)(2) in 2005, the continuity-of-interest test was applied as of the closing date of the transaction, rather than the contract date. Thus, fluctuations in value between the contract and the closing date could, depending on the terms of the contract, create a problem. This regulation is a liberalizing provision that allows the continuity-of-interest test to be applied, in most cases, as of the last business day before the contract becomes binding, if the contract provides for a fixed consideration. If the contract is modified, the modification date is (with certain exceptions) treated as the controlling date; for public tender offers, the announcement date is generally treated as the controlling date. The regulation contains special provisions regarding escrow clauses, and certain contingent consideration provisions. In March 2007, this provision was modified in certain aspects and changed into Temp. Reg. § 1.368-1T(e)(2).[45]

Finally, there is the question of what percentage of the old equity must be exchanged for new equity to satisfy the continuity-of-interest test. For advance ruling purposes, the IRS has for many years required that 50 percent of the aggregate consideration going to the former equity holders consist of stock, even though some cases had approved smaller percentages.[46] On this point, it is interesting to note that an example in the foregoing 2005 Reg. § 1.368-1(e)(2) and in Temp. Reg. § 1.368-1T(e)(2) concludes that the continuity-of-interest test is met if 40 percent of the aggregate consideration issued for the former equity consists of stock. Thus, the IRS has presumably abandoned its 50 percent requirement for rulings.

The continuity-of-interest test applies to the transferor corporation and its owners, but does not apply to the transferee.[47] Thus, where it is difficult for the failing company to satisfy the continuity-of-interest test in a Reorg. Out, it might be possible to structure the transaction so that the company is the acquiring corporation in a Reorg. In.

---

[45] One commentator has observed that cash option mergers may have special difficulty in qualifying for this new liberalizing provision. *See* Willens, Applying the New 'Continuity of Interest' Regulations, 72 BNA Daily Tax Report (April 16, 2007), at J-1.

[46] Rev. Proc. 74-26, 1974-2 C.B. 478; Rev. Proc. 77-37, 1977-2 C.B. 568; *see also* Rev. Rul. 66-224, 1966-2 C.B. 114 (50 percent continuity in the form of stock, by value, adequate); *John A. Nelson Co. v. Helvering*, 296 U.S. 374, 36-1 U.S.T.C. ¶ 9019 (38 percent stock, 62 percent cash held to satisfy continuity test); *Miller v. Commissioner*, 84 F.2d 415, 36-2 U.S.T.C. ¶ 9324 (6th Cir. 1936) (25 percent continuity sufficient); *May B. Kass v. Commissioner*, 60 T.C. 218, Dec. 31,970 (1973), *aff'd by court order*, 491 F.2d 749 (3d Cir. 1974) (16 percent not enough). *See also* New York State Bar Association, Tax Section, Report on Treatment of Variable Stock Consideration in Tax-Free Corporate Reorganizations (February 4, 2004), 2004 TNT 25-12 (February 6, 2004) (making recommendations regarding the treatment of contingent, including escrowed, stock interests for purposes of the continuity-of-interest test); New York State Bar Association, Tax Section, Report on Continuity of Interest and Pre-Closing Stock Value Fluctuation (January 23, 2004), 2004 TNT 17-21 (January 27, 2004) (recommending that changes in value between contract date and closing date be ignored for continuity-of-interest purposes); and New York State Bar Association, Tax Section, Report on Proposed Regulations Regarding Continuity of Interest and Pre-Closing Stock Value Fluctuation (November 29, 2004), *reprinted at* 2004 TNT 233-12 (December 3, 2004) (making further recommendations on the latter subject). Reg. § 1.368-1(e)(2) issued in 2005 reflects the suggestions made in the foregoing bar reports.

[47] *See* Bittker & Eustice, *supra* note 34 at ¶ 12-21.

The IRS has held that the continuity-of-interest test does not apply to either an "E" or an "F" reorganization.[48]

### § 604.3.3 Continuity-of-Business-Enterprise Test

The regulations under Code § 368 have long required that a reorganization involve "a continuity of the business enterprise under . . . modified corporate form."[49] In 1980, the IRS amended the regulations by expanding on the requirements for meeting the continuity-of-business-enterprise test.[50] As amended, the regulations require that the transferee corporation either (1) continue the old corporation's historic business or (2) use a significant portion of the old corporation's historic business assets in its business. Where the old company had more than one line of business, the regulations state that the new company need continue only a "significant line of business" of the old company. This is illustrated by an example involving a target company that had three equal lines of business.[51] It sold two of these and then transferred the sales proceeds plus the third line of business to the acquiring company. The example states that the continuity-of-business-enterprise requirement was met because of the transfer of the third line of business. Another example makes clear that the transfer of the proceeds from the sale of a business does not satisfy the continuity-of-business-enterprise test, *i.e.*, that the use of the sales proceeds in the acquiring company's business is not sufficient.[52] A further example indicates that if the asset sale is made by the acquiring company rather than by the old company, the consequences will be as adverse as if the old company had made the sale: Continuity of business enterprise will be lacking.[53]

In some circumstances, the qualifying business is not being conducted by the target company itself but instead by a subsidiary thereof. In appropriate circumstances, the IRS has permitted the attribution of a wholly owned subsidiary's business to its parent.[54] In addition, the IRS has ruled that a transfer by the acquiring corporation in a merger of a business acquired from the target to a wholly owned subsidiary of the acquiring corporation does not violate the continuity-of-business-

---

48 *See* Rev. Rul. 82-34, 1982-1 C.B. 59 ("E" reorganizations); Reg. § 1.368-1(b) ("E" and, for transactions occurring on or after February 25, 2005, "F" reorganizations).

49 Reg. § 1.368-1(b). The continuity-of-business-enterprise test applies only to the transferor corporation, not to the transferee. Rev. Rul. 81-25, 1981-1 C.B. 132.

50 Reg. § 1.368-1(d).

51 Reg. § 1.368-1(d)(5), Example (1). *See also* Rev. Rul. 88-48, 1988-1 C.B. 117, which held that the substantially-all-assets test for a "C" reorganization was satisfied where target sold one of two equal businesses, and then transferred the second business plus the proceeds from the sale of the first business to the acquirer in the "C" reorganization. Note, however, that such a situation could cause a substantial reduction in the Code § 382 NOL limitation under the Code § 382 substantial nonbusiness assets rule, discussed at § 508.4.1 above.

52 Reg. § 1.368-1(d)(5), Example (4).

53 Reg. § 1.368-1(d)(5), Example (5).

54 *See* Rev. Rul. 85-197, 1985-2 C.B. 120, and Rev. Rul. 85-198, 1985-2 C.B. 120, also mentioned *supra* at § 507.2.

enterprise requirement.[55] Until 1998, the issue was an uneasy one, however, because the regulations did not discuss this possibility and the foregoing were essentially the only authorities on the subject. However, in early 1998 the IRS issued Reg. § 1.368-1(d), which not only adopts the approach taken in these authorities but considerably liberalizes them for transactions occurring after January 28, 1998. This new regulatory provision expressly permits a corporation to satisfy the continuity-of-business-enterprise requirement even if the acquired business is transferred to one or more 80 percent controlled subsidiaries that are members of the acquiring corporation's qualified group.[56] A qualified group consists of a group of corporations that satisfy the control requirement of Code § 368(c). At least 80 percent of the control of the transferee corporation must be held by a single corporation in the group: it is not enough that the group owns 100 percent of the lower tier corporation, if no single member of the group owns 80 percent thereof. Where this qualified group definition is satisfied, the assets acquired in the reorganization can be dropped down to remote subsidiaries, can be sprinkled among subsidiaries, and in some circumstances can even be transferred to partnerships.

At the same time that this liberalized continuity-of-business-enterprise regulation was issued, the IRS also issued Reg. § 1.368-2(k), which provides that the requirements for triangular reorganizations will be considered met even if the assets or stock are dropped down one or more tiers within the qualified group. But for this triangular-reorganization purpose, such drop downs must, as to each transfer, be to a corporation that is directly controlled by the transferor within the meaning of Code § 368(c). An amendment to Reg. § 1.368-2(k) was proposed in March 2004 to make clear that this same result extends to forward triangular mergers and to "D" reorganizations.[57] The March proposed regulation was revised in August 2004. This extended its coverage to distributions to certain other corporations or partnerships.

Rather than continue a significant line of business of the old company, the new company can satisfy the continuity-of-business-enterprise test by using a significant portion of the old company's historic business assets (as opposed to proceeds from the sale of assets) in its business. This is illustrated by an example involving a target

---

[55] Rev. Rul. 81-247, 1981-2 C.B. 87.

[56] Even though the 1998 continuity-of-business-enterprise liberalizing regulations apply to "D" reorganizations, the failure of Code § 368(a)(1)(C) to refer to "D" reorganizations can cause some concern as to whether dropdowns can cause problems in "D" reorganizations. *See* Beller, "D" Reorganizations and Dropdowns: An Uneasy Match, 90 Tax Notes 1757 (June 21, 1999). Happily, the IRS in 2002 made clear that dropdowns can take place in "D" reorganizations. Rev. Rul. 2002-85, 2002-52 I.R.B. 986; IRS Notice 2002-77, 2002-52 I.R.B. 997, announcing IRS will amend the regulations to confirm this result. Such an amendment to Reg. § 1.368-2(k) was proposed in March 2004. This amendment was also designed to incorporate the holding in Rev. Rul. 2001-24, 2001-1 C.B. 1290, to the effect that the same principle extends to forward triangular mergers. The March proposed regulation dealt only with transfers to corporations controlled by the transferor. This proposed regulation was withdrawn and a revised proposed regulation issued in its place in August 2004, which extended its scope to distributions to corporations or partnerships. The revised proposed regulation included amendments to Reg. § 1.368-2(f), (j), and (k). The use of "disregarded" entities may also enhance flexibility in this area. *See* § 603 above.

[57] *See also* New York State Bar Association, Tax Section, Report on Distributions Following Tax-Free Reorganizations (May 19, 2004), 2004 TNT 99-28 (May 21, 2004), suggesting liberalization for upstream distributions following reorganizations.

company that manufactured components for computers and an acquiring company that manufactured computers.[58] The target company had sold all of its output to the acquiring company. After the acquiring company decided to begin buying all of its components abroad, the target company merged into the acquiring company. It no longer manufactured components but the acquiring company retained the equipment of the old company as a backup source of supply. This was held to satisfy the continuity-of-business-enterprise test, even though the acquiring company did not continue the old company's business.

Although the continuity-of-business concept does not apply for Code § 368 purposes to "E" or "F" reorganizations,[59] as mentioned at § 508.3 above the reorganization concept of continuity-of-business-enterprise does apply for purposes of new Code § 382. As for Old Code § 382, however, there were significant differences between the reorganization continuity-of-business-enterprise concept and the change-in-business test of old Code § 382(a). The latter required that the corporation continue to conduct a business "substantially the same as that conducted before" the first step in the change in ownership described in that section. Further, the regulations under old Code § 382(a) placed special emphasis on whether the business continued by the corporation was the one that produced its NOLs.[60]

### § 604.3.4 Net -Value Test

In 2005, the IRS issued Prop. Reg. § 1.368-1(b)(1) to provide that a requisite to reorganization treatment is an exchange of net value, as defined in Prop. Reg. § 1.368-1(f). The new provision is to become effective when it is issued as a final regulation.[61] The new provision focuses on the extent to which insolvent corporations can qualify for Code § 368 reorganization treatment. It generally requires that there be an exchange of property for stock. The purpose of the new provision is to distinguish reorganizations from sales, and it adopts the view that transfers of property in exchange for the assumption of liabilities or in satisfaction of liabilities resemble sales, and should not be entitled to the nonrecognition of gain or loss that is available

---

[58] Reg. § 1.368-1(d)(5), Example (2).

[59] *See* Rev. Rul. 82-34, 182-1 C.B. 59; ("E" reorganization); Reg. § 1.368-1(b) ("E" and, for transactions occurring on or after February 25, 2005, "F" reorganizations).

[60] *See* the discussion at § 507.2. To the extent that a troubled company governed by old Code § 382 could find it easier to satisfy the continuity-of-business-enterprise test than the old Code § 382(a) change-in-business test (*see* § 507.2), a two-company reorganization could thus prove preferable to a one-company recapitalization, provided that the other hurdles to a successful two-company reorganization could be surmounted.

[61] For a thorough and detailed analysis of the proposed regulation, *see* Blanchard, Hooker and Vogel, Underwater Assets and Insolvent Corporations: Reflections on Treasury's Recently Proposed Regulations and Related Matters, 59 Tax Law. 107 (2005). *See also* New York State Bar Association, Tax Section, Report on Proposed Regulations Regarding Organizations, Reorganizations and Liquidations Involving Insolvent Corporations (January 20, 2006), *reprinted at* 2006 TNT 15-10 (January 24, 2006) (expressing serious reservations); American Bar Association, Tax Section, Comments Concerning Subchapter C No-Net-Value Regulations Proposals (April 24, 2006), *reprinted at* 2006 TNT 79-16 (April 25, 2006).

for corporate reorganizations. The provision also ignores the issuance of stock that has no liquidating value. Thus, even if a creditor of an insolvent company might be considered to hold a proprietary interest for purposes of the continuity-of-interest test, that liability could cause the company to fail the net-value test unless the liability is extinguished (*e.g.*, cancelled or converted into stock) in the transaction.

Specifically, Prop. Reg. § 1.368-1(f) provides that for an exchange of net value to exist there must be both a surrender of net value and a receipt of net value. Whether there is a surrender of net value is generally determined by looking to the assets and liabilities of the target corporation prior to the exchange. The value of the assets must exceed the value of the liabilities. This rule ensures that a target transfers at least some of its property in exchange for stock, rather than for the assumption or satisfaction of liabilities. Whether there is a receipt of net value from the acquiring corporation is determined by looking to the assets and liabilities of the acquiring corporation after the exchange. Again, the value of the assets must exceed the value of the liabilities. This rule prevents the issuance of worthless stock (worthless as determined in a liquidating sense) from being treated as issued in exchange for assets.

Without more, this statement of the general rule would lead one to conclude that an insolvent corporation—that is, one whose liabilities exceed its assets—could not qualify as a target for a Code § 368 reorganization. However, the proposed rule contains the important concept that a liability (other than a liability to the acquiring corporation) that is extinguished in the reorganization is disregarded. This allows a corporation that is insolvent immediately before the transaction to qualify for a Code § 368 reorganization if it is made solvent in the transaction. For example, assume target corporation T has assets worth $100, and liabilities of $100 to A and $50 to P. P acquires T's assets in exchange for P stock. T distributes to A its share of the P stock, T's stock is cancelled, and T dissolves. If P is solvent after the transaction, the transaction satisfies the net value test. This is so because, although the $50 liability to P cannot be ignored ($50 of T's assets are considered to have been transferred to P in satisfaction of that liability instead of for P stock), the $100 liability to A can be ignored for purposes of the net value test since it is not assumed by P and is extinguished in the transaction.

This portion of the proposed regulation (unlike the clarifications to the continuity-of-interest regulations issued simultaneously, which require liabilities constituting proprietary interests to be valued at fair market value) contains no guidance on how the amount of the liabilities of a corporation should be valued for purposes of the rule. The release accompanying the proposed regulation says the IRS is giving consideration to various approaches, such as providing that liabilities represented by debt instruments would be valued at their issue price determined under Code §§ 1271-1275, or that all liabilities would be valued at fair market value; in addition it is considering whether the amount of non-recourse debt in excess of the value of the property securing it could be ignored.

The proposed regulation provides that the net-value requirement does *not* apply to "E" or "F" reorganizations, or to a very limited class of "D" reorganizations.

## §605 TWO-COMPANY ACQUISITIVE REORGANIZATIONS IN BANKRUPTCY

The Bankruptcy Tax Act of 1980 (Pub. L. No. 96-589) repealed the old insolvency reorganization provisions contained in Code §§371-374 and replaced them with the new "G" reorganization (effective generally for bankruptcy or similar proceedings commenced after 1980).[1] The Senate Report noted that the new provision was intended "to facilitate the rehabilitation of corporate debtors in bankruptcy," and to this end it was "designed to eliminate many requirements which have effectively precluded financially troubled companies from utilizing the generally applicable tax-free reorganization provisions of present law."[2] For example, it does not require a statutory merger as in an "A" reorganization or the issuance of solely voting stock as in a "C" reorganization, and the former shareholders of the old company need not control the new company as in a "D" reorganization.

However, as will be discussed below, Congress retained a substantially-all-assets test in the "G" reorganization provision and, although it indicated that this test should be applied in a more relaxed way in "G" reorganizations than in other reorganizations, taxpayers could not risk utilizing the provision until they knew how the IRS would apply this directive. Congress did not reckon with the sometimes glacial pace at which the Treasury Department and the IRS move to implement new legislation. Four years passed before the IRS issued its first interpretation of the "G" reorganization provision as it applies to nonbanking companies. This occurred through the issuance of two private rulings, one in late 1984 and one in early 1985.[3] A third ruling was issued in late 1988,[4] and others in 1992[5] and 1993.[6] These changed the "G" reorganization from a source of only academic interest to a practical planning tool. Because private rulings do not constitute precedent, however, until regulations or published rulings are issued addressing various "G" reorganization issues, taxpayers may wish to seek a private ruling. The IRS's proposed regulations in early 2005 (addressing certain continuity-of-interest issues) is a start.

---

[1] **§605** Code §368(a)(1)(G); Bankruptcy Tax Act of 1980, §7(c)(1) (effective date). A corporation in a bankruptcy proceeding commenced prior to 1981, but after September 30, 1979, may have elected (or, in limited cases, may still elect) to apply the new "G" reorganization (and COD) rules. *See* Bankruptcy Tax Act of 1980, §7(f); Temp. Reg. §7a.3(b) and (d); *cf.* IRS Letter Ruling 8531021, May 2, 1985 (the IRS extended time to elect COD rules). For reasons favoring the addition of an insolvency reorganization provision to the ranks of Code §368(a)(1), *see* Plumb, Bankruptcy Committee Tax Recommendations—Reorganizations, Carryovers and the Effects of Debt Reduction, 29 Tax L. Rev. at 243-251 (1974).

[2] S. Rep. No. 1035, 96th Cong., 2d Sess. 35 (1980).

[3] IRS Letter Ruling 8503064, October 24, 1984; IRS Letter Ruling 8521083, February 27, 1985.

[4] IRS Letter Ruling 8909007, November 30, 1988.

[5] IRS Letter Ruling 9229039, April 23, 1992; IRS Letter Ruling 9217040, January 28, 1992; IRS Letter Ruling 9313020, December 30, 1992 (life insurance companies), supplemented by IRS Letter Ruling 9428014, April 15, 1994.

[6] IRS Letter Ruling 9335029, September 3, 1993; IRS Letter Ruling 9409037, December 7, 1993. *See also* IRS Letter Ruling 9629016, issued on April 22, 1996.

The "G" reorganization provisions permit triangular "G" reorganizations. However, until 1995 these remained of only academic interest because the IRS had not yet indicated whether parent stock would qualify for the stock-for-debt exception to COD income. The issuance of a favorable private ruling letter in 1995 (discussed at § 504A.3.2 above) changed this for companies to which the stock-for-debt exception was still applicable. Because triangular "G" reorganizations have not proven popular, however, they will not be discussed in this volume.[7] (As indicated at § 602, perhaps a first-step "E" recapitalization of the old company would facilitate a favorable triangular ruling.)

In addition, the "G" reorganization provisions permit divisive "G" reorganizations. However, divisive reorganizations have seldom proved useful in a bankruptcy context, and so they will not be discussed in this volume, except to note that there has been at least one instance we know about in which a Code § 355 transaction was indeed used in a bankruptcy proceeding. In this case, a group of corporations which were not insolvent but were in financial difficulty needed to refinance their debt. They were told that this could not be done unless they restructured by separating some operations, and related debt, from others. This was to be accomplished by doing a divisive reorganization (a Code § 355 transaction that was characterized as a "G" reorganization).[8]

## *§ 605.1 "G" Reorganization Requirements*

A "G" reorganization must satisfy the continuity-of-interest test and the continuity-of-business-enterprise test, as well as the technical statutory requirements for the "G" reorganization form itself. Each of these aspects of a "G" reorganization differs somewhat from its counterpart in the regular reorganization provisions.[9]

---

[7] For a discussion of triangular "G" reorganizations, *see* Asofsky, Reorganizing Insolvent Corporations, 41 Inst. on Fed. Tax'n §§ 5, 5.05 (1982) (hereafter Asofsky, Reorganizing); Tatlock, 540 T.M., Bankruptcy and Insolvency: Tax Aspects and Procedure; Watts, Corporate Acquisitions and Divisions Under the Bankruptcy Tax Act: The New "G" Type Reorganization, 59 Taxes 845, 851-852 (1981). *See also* IRS Letter Ruling 8909007, November 30, 1988 (involved a forward "G" reorganization, followed by a drop-down of the assets; no COD ruling requested). IRS Letter Ruling 199941023, July 14, 1999, involved the transfer of substantially all of the assets of a mutual insurance parent into a second tier subsidiary, with stock of the first tier subsidiary being issued to the policy holders of the parent. This was held to be a good "G" reorganization.

[8] IRS Letter Ruling 200345049, August 2, 2002. *See also* IRS Letter Ruling 200403060, September 30, 2003 (which involved a number of Code § 355 transactions of companies in bankruptcy; the ruling does not say whether they were "G" reorganizations). For earlier comments on divisive reorganizations in bankruptcy, *see, e.g.*, Watts, *supra* note 7, at 852; Scranton, Corporate Transactions Under the Bankruptcy Tax Act of 1980, 35 Tax Law. 49, 84-86 (1981).

[9] For other discussions of the "G" reorganization provisions, *see, e.g.*, Witt & Albergotti, G Reorganization Offers Simple, Effective Way to Acquire Bankrupt Corporation, 61 J. Taxation 90 (1985); New York State Bar Association, Tax Section, Committee on Bankruptcy, Report on Reorganizations Under Section 368(a)(1)(G); Recommendations for Proposed Regulations, 85 TNT 231-85 (October 25, 1985) (hereinafter NYSBA, "G" Reorganization Report); Asofsky, Reorganizing, *supra* note 7; Bacon, Rescue Planning for Failing or Bankrupt Company, 631 Taxes 931 at 941-948 (1993); Rabinowitz & Jacobson, Reorganization of the Bankrupt Corporation Under IRC 368(a)(1)(G): Panacea or Placebo, 42 Inst. on

### § 605.1.1 Form of "G" Reorganization

Under Code § 368(a)(1)(G), a "G" reorganization is:

> . . . a transfer by a corporation of all or part of its assets to another corporation in a title 11 or similar case; but only if, in pursuance of the plan, stock or securities of the corporation to which the assets are transferred are distributed in a transaction which qualifies under section 354, 355, or 356.

The phrase "Title 11 or similar case" is defined in Code § 368(a)(3) as meaning a case under the Bankruptcy Code or "a receivership, foreclosure, or similar proceeding in a Federal or State court."[10] The same provision says that a transfer of assets of a corporation shall be treated as made in a "Title 11 or similar case" if and only if a party to the reorganization is under the jurisdiction of the court in the case and the transfer is pursuant to a plan of reorganization approved by the court.[11]

Code § 368(a)(3)(C) states that if a transaction would qualify as a "G" reorganization and would also qualify under any of the other regular reorganization provisions or under Code § 332 or § 351, then the transaction shall be treated as qualifying only as a "G" reorganization, except for purposes of Code § 357(c)(1).[12]

For a discussion of the Code § 332 aspect of this provision, and also of the possibility that a liquidation that does not qualify under Code § 332 because the subsidiary is insolvent might be made to qualify as a "G" reorganization, *see* § 802 below. For a discussion of the special limitations imposed on qualification under Code § 351 in a title 11 or similar case, *see* § 906.

As can be seen, the formal requirements imposed on a "G" reorganization in Code § 368 are easy to meet. All that is needed is that the transaction involve a transfer of assets from one corporation to another pursuant to a plan of reorganization approved by a bankruptcy court that has jurisdiction over at least one of the parties to the transaction. The more stringent requirements for a "G" reorganization are imposed by Code § 354, as discussed at §§ 605.1.2 and 605.1.3.

---

(Footnote Continued)

Fed. Tax'n § 10 (1984); Watts, *supra* note 7; Plumb, The Bankruptcy Tax Act, 33 Major Tax Plan. 800, 801.2 (1981).

[10] What constitutes a "similar proceeding" is unclear. Asofsky, *et al.*, Conference on the Bankruptcy Tax Act of 1980. 39 Inst. on Fed. Tax'n ¶ 57.09[8] at pp. 57-110 to 57-111 (remarks of Richard L. Bacon).

[11] *See* Plumb, The Bankruptcy Tax Act, *supra* note 9, at § 801.2(C) (discusses what constitutes a "plan of reorganization"). It should be noted that unlike the "G" reorganization provisions that apply to corporations in bankruptcy or a "similar case," the COD rules applicable to corporations in bankruptcy only apply to corporations in "similar cases" to the extent they can prove their insolvency. *See* Code § 108(a)(d)(2).

[12] *See* S. Rep. No. 1035, 96th Cong., 2d Sess. 36 (1980); H.R. Rep. No. 833, 96th Cong., 2d Sess. 31 (1980); Bacon, *supra* note 9, at 945 (a failed "G" reorganization should still be able to be tested as an "A" or "C" reorganization); NYSBA, "G" Reorganization Report, *supra* note 9, at 53-54 (same). Code § 357(c)(1), which deals with the consequence of a transfer of liabilities in excess of basis, is discussed in the "G" reorganization context at § 605.2. *See also* § 604.2.2 above.

### § 605.1.2 Receipt of Acquiring Company's Stock or Securities

According to Code § 354(a),

> No gain or loss shall be recognized if stock or securities in a corporation a party to a reorganization are, in pursuance of the plan of reorganization, exchanged solely for stock or securities in such corporation or in another corporation a party to the reorganization.

As mentioned at § 605.1.1, a "G" reorganization must involve a distribution that qualifies under Code § 354. A literal reading of Code § 354(a) would suggest that a transaction will not qualify as a "G" reorganization unless at least some of the stock or securities issued by the acquiring company are distributed by the old company to someone who held stock or a security of the old company.[13] This is an unfortunate requirement, because it means that if a failing company has no debt other than trade debt or bank short-term loans, a "G" reorganization structured as a Reorg. Out will not be available if the stockholders of the failing company are to be wiped out and all of the stock as well as debt of the new company is to be issued to the creditors of the failing company.

It seems that the impediment created by this language in Code § 354 was completely unintended by Congress. No such impediment existed under prior Code § § 371-374, and the legislative history evidences no intention to alter the prior law on this point.[14] The IRS has so far not been willing to interpret the statute in a way that eliminates this impediment entirely. It has, however, relaxed it as far as possible while still leaving it in existence, by requiring in five of the private letter rulings mentioned at § 605 that at least *one* person or entity that holds a security of the old company will receive stock in the new company.[15] Presumably it would be equally satisfactory if at least one person who held a security in the old company received a

---

[13] *See, e.g.*, Asofsky, Reorganizing Insolvent Corporations, 41 Inst. on Fed. Tax'n § § 5.00, 5.02[1][c][ii] (raises and then discards three possible methods of reading the distribution-to-a-stock-or "security"-holder requirement out of the statute).

[14] The only reason given in the legislative history for requiring that a "G" reorganization involve a distribution that "qualifies" under Code § 354 was to ensure that substantially all of the assets of the financially troubled corporation are transferred to the acquiring corporation. S. Rep. No. 1035, 96th Cong., 2d Sess. 35 (1980). *See also* NYSBA, "G" Reorganization Report, *supra* note 9, at 6-7; Plumb, The Bankruptcy Tax Act, 33 Major Tax Plan, at ¶ 801.2(D)(3) (1981).

[15] IRS Letter Ruling 8503064, October 24, 1984; IRS Letter Ruling 8521083, February 27, 1985; IRS Letter Ruling 8909007, November 30, 1988; IRS Letter Ruling 9335029, September 3, 1993; IRS Letter Ruling 9629016, April 22, 1996. *See also* IRS Technical Advice 9841006, June 25, 1998 (the stock of acquiring company was distributed directly to creditors of the target company's shareholder to whom the target company had secondary liability; distribution was held to be a constructive distribution to the shareholder). In IRS Field Service Advice 1999-1029, September 22, 1993, *reprinted at* 1999 TNT 81-57, the IRS found that a transaction could not be a "G" reorganization because no stock of the acquiring company was issued to a former stockholder or security holder of the failing company, but instead was issued only to short-term creditors. Various tax groups have recommended the "removal" of this requirement altogether, either through regulations or statutory amendment. *See* NYSBA, "G" Reorganization Report, *supra* note 9, at 8-9; American Bar Association, Tax Section, Committee on Corporate Stockholder Relationships, Legislative Recommendation No. 1984-6 (To Modify "G" Reorganization Provisions) (July 23, 1984). *Cf.* Watts, *supra* note 7, at 847, 857 n.41

security of the new company[16] or if at least one stockholder of the old company received stock in the new company.[17] With the adoption in 1998 of regulations that treat warrants as securities having a zero principal amount for purposes of Code §§354 and 356 (as discussed at §502.3 above), it may now be possible to satisfy this requirement by distributing warrants to at least one holder of a security or of stock in the old company. However, because Code §354 does not apply to an exchange of solely securities for stock, it will still not be possible to satisfy this requirement by distributing only warrants to a holder of stock of the old company.

An open question remains, however, as to whether the issuance of stock to a former stockholder of the old company will satisfy this requirement if the old company was clearly insolvent. The answer should depend on the nature of the transaction in which the new stock is issued to the old stockholder. If the old stockholder simply receives nominal shares for the sole purpose of trying to satisfy the Code §354(a) test, it is doubtful that the test will be deemed to have been met. However, consider a situation in which all of a significant class of former shareholders receive stock in the new company in recognition of their ability substantially to delay the transaction by forcing the creditors into a "cram down" proceeding to wipe out the stockholders. Here, a distribution of the new stock to the former stockholders has real significance and we believe it should be accepted as satisfying the requirement.

The receipt of stock or securities of the acquiring company by a stockholder or security holder of the target company should only be of practical concern in a "G" reorganization structured as a Reorg. Out (*i.e.*, where the debtor company is the transferor). If the "G" reorganization is structured as a Reorg. In, this requirement should easily be met because the target company would generally be a solvent and profitable company.

If structuring the transaction as a Reorg. Out is not possible, the failing company may consider undergoing a first-step recapitalization, converting its short-term creditors to stockholders and/or security holders.[18]

With respect to banking institutions, however, the IRS for a time took a more lenient approach than with respect to other corporations. In IRS Letter Ruling 8835057 (June 10, 1988), supplemented in IRS Letter Ruling 8842059 (October 21,

(Footnote Continued)

(suggesting possible regulatory approach, or, in absence thereof, a statutory amendment, proposed language for which he has set out in a footnote).

[16] Indeed, it was so held in IRS Letter Ruling 9313020, December 30, 1992, when, in addition, certain variable life and annuity contracts were held to be securities.

[17] It is interesting to note, however, that in IRS Letter Ruling 9629016, April 22, 1996, where a debtor corporation merged into Newco in a "G" reorganization in which old security holders received 95 percent and the old shareholders received 5 percent of the Newco stock, the ruling contained a representation that at least one holder of a security of the debtor would receive stock in exchange for that security, but it did not contain a similar representation regarding the receipt of Newco stock by the old shareholders.

[18] *See supra* §602; Watts, Corporation Acquisitions and Divisions Under the Tax Act: The New "G" Type Reorganization, 59 Taxes 845, 846-847 (1981); Thompson, Planning for the Loss Corporation: The Interaction Among Code Sections 269, 381, Old and New 382 and the Consolidated Return Regulations, 31 Major Tax Plan. 223, 293 (1979).

1988), the IRS ruled that a transfer of all of the assets and liabilities of a bank to a new bank, in a transaction in which the old shareholders received nothing and all of the stock of the new bank was issued for cash to the FDIC and an acquiring bankholding company, satisfied the "G" reorganization requirements, because "under these unique circumstances and as a result of the [old bank's] insolvency, the depositors own, in substance, the entire equity interest in [the old bank], and the deposits they have in [the old bank] will continue in [the new bank]." As mentioned at §608.3, below, this ruling could not be issued today.

### §605.1.3 Substantially-All-Assets Test

Under Code §354(b), Code §354(a) will not apply to a purported "G" reorganization unless:

(A) the corporation to which the assets are transferred acquires substantially all the assets of the transferor of such assets; and

(B) the stock, securities, and other properties received by such transferor, as well as the other properties of such transferor, are distributed in pursuance of the plan of reorganization.

Similar "substantially all" language appears in the Internal Revenue Code in connection with the "C," the "D," and the reverse merger (*i.e.*, the Code §368(a)(2)(E)) reorganization provisions. The current ruling position of the IRS with respect to these other acquisitive reorganization provisions is that the "substantially all-assets" test is satisfied where there is a transfer of assets representing at least 90 percent of the fair market value of the net assets of the transferor and at least 70 percent of the transferor's gross assets.[19] The courts, however, have been more lenient, especially in the case of "D" reorganizations.[20]

If, for purposes of the IRS guidelines, one could measure the failing company's assets only at the moment of transfer to the new company, application of the guidelines might not create much of an impediment to "G" reorganizations. However, as we have seen in §604.3.1 and as indicated by the rulings discussed later in this section, the measurement of the old company's assets for purposes of this test probably begins at least as far back as the time when a plan to engage in the two-company reorganization comes into existence.[21] So applied, the IRS 70-percent-of-

---

[19] Rev. Proc. 77-37, §3.01, 1977-2 C.B. 568.

[20] *See, e.g., James Armour, Inc.*, 43 T.C. 295, Dec. 27,071 (1965) (transfer of only 51 percent of corporation's assets, consisting of all its operating assets); *American Mfg. Co.*, 55 T.C. 204, Dec. 30,399 (1970) (transfer of all corporation's operating assets, representing 20 percent of total assets); *Smothers v. United States*, 642 F.2d 894, 81-1 U.S.T.C. ¶9368 (5th Cir. 1981) (transfer of 15 percent of net assets, representing all the operating assets); *Atlas Tool Co.*, 78 T.C. 86, Dec. 35,124 (1978), *aff'd*, 614 F.2d 860, 80-1 U.S.T.C. ¶9177 (3d Cir. 1980), *cert. denied*, 449 U.S. 836 (1980) (25 percent of gross assets transferred).

[21] In contrast, the measuring date was the merger date in IRS Letter Ruling 9629016, April 22, 1996. However, this ruling involved a simple recapitalization of the old company by way of a merger into Newco, and did not include an acquisitive transaction. Query: was this the reason why the merger

gross-assets and 90-percent-of-net-assets tests would, if applied to "G" reorganizations, make it impossible for most failing companies to engage in a "G" reorganization. The problem is not the 90-percent-of-net-assets portion of this test. Where the company is insolvent, it will not have any net assets, and thus presumably this portion of the test would be irrelevant. The problem lies in the 70-percent-of-gross-assets portion of the test, because the failing company will inevitably have been disposing of assets, often in considerable quantities, in the effort to slim down its operations, cut costs, and reduce some of its debt.

Congress made clear that the substantially-all-assets test should be applied in a more lenient way in the "G" reorganization context than in the context of the other reorganization provisions. The Senate Report said:

> The "substantially all" test in the "G" reorganization provision is to be interpreted in light of the underlying intent in adding the new "G" category, namely, to facilitate the reorganization of companies in bankruptcy, or similar cases for rehabilitative purposes. Accordingly, it is intended that facts and circumstances relevant to this intent, such as the insolvent corporation's need to pay off creditors or to sell assets or divisions to raise cash, are to be taken into account in determining whether a transaction qualifies as a "G" reorganization. For example, a transaction is not precluded from satisfying the "substantially all" test for purposes of the new "G" category merely because, prior to a transfer to the acquiring corporation, payments to creditors and asset sales were made in order to leave the debtor with more manageable operating assets to continue in business.[22]

The Senate Report adds, in a footnote, that this stated intent is not relevant to interpreting the substantially all test for purposes of the other reorganization categories.[23] We might add that we rather doubt that the relaxed standard will apply to the profitable company in a "G" reorganization that is cast as a Reorg. In.

As to this latter point, IRS Letter Ruling 8710027 (December 8, 1986) confirms the authors' conclusion that the "substantially-all-assets" test will not be relaxed for the non-Chapter 11 company in a "G" reorganization that is cast as a Reorg. In. In the ruling, a company in Chapter 11 acquired a non-Chapter 11 company in a statutory merger. The latter company, which had been a Subchapter S company, distributed immediately before the merger a note equal to its accumulated adjustments account. This distribution had the effect of reducing the value of the acquired company's net worth to zero. Thus, although the acquiring company received more than 70 percent of the acquired company's gross assets, it received none of its net assets. The IRS held that this caused the merger to fail the "substantially-all-assets" requirement for a "G"

---

(Footnote Continued)

date rather than the earlier plan formulation date was permitted to be used as the measuring date in this ruling?

[22] S. Rep. No. 1035, 96th Cong., 2d Sess. 35-36 (1980).

[23] Id. at 36 n.5.

reorganization, although it did not prevent the merger from qualifying as an "A" reorganization.

As for "G" reorganizations cast in the form of a Reorg. Out, the first three "G" reorganization rulings issued for nonbanking institutions required that more than 50 percent of the fair market value of the *gross* assets and more than 70 percent of the fair market value of the *operating* assets held by the old failing company at the measuring date must be transferred to the new company.[24] "Operating assets" for this purpose were defined as assets other than cash, accounts receivable, investment assets, and assets taken out of operation prior to the measuring date with the intention of effecting a sale thereof.[25]

The measuring date chosen in these three rulings was the date on which the old company (or its trustee in bankruptcy) decided that it could no longer be viably operated as an independent going concern. In the first and third of the rulings, this date occurred sometime after the commencement of the bankruptcy proceedings.[26] In the second ruling, this date occurred before the bankruptcy proceedings were instituted.[27] Each of these first three rulings indicated that, prior to the applicable measuring date, the failing company intended to continue its operations as an independent going concern; and that any dispositions or distributions of the failing company's assets before the measuring date were undertaken with the intention of continuing as an independent going concern and were done to finance its continuing operations and to minimize its operating losses. The measuring date in one subsequent "G" reorganization ruling was the date the plan of rehabilitation for the insurance company involved was filed, and nothing was said about the intentions of the insurance company before that date.[28] In another "G" reorganization ruling, the measuring date was the effective date of the bankruptcy plan, and the ruling indicated that any disposition of assets before that date was done with the intention of continuing as an independent going concern.[29] In still a later ruling, the measuring date also appears to have been the effective date of the bankruptcy plan, and the ruling excluded from operating assets any assets that were taken out of operation before that date with the intention of effecting a sale thereof.[30]

---

[24] IRS Letter Ruling 8503064, October 24, 1984; IRS Letter Ruling 8521083, February 27, 1985; IRS Letter Ruling 8909007, November 30, 1988. Later rulings take the same approach: IRS Letter Ruling 9229039, April 23, 1992 and IRS Letter Ruling 9217040, January 28, 1992; IRS Letter Ruling 9313020, December 30, 1992; IRS Letter Ruling 9335029, September 3, 1993; IRS Letter Ruling 9409037, December 7, 1993; IRS Letter Ruling 9629016, April 22, 1996 (representation in this ruling referred to 50 percent of the fair market value of the gross assets and 90 percent of the fair market value of the operating assets).

[25] Id.

[26] IRS Letter Ruling 8503064, October 24, 1984; IRS Letter Ruling 8909007, November 30, 1988.

[27] IRS Letter Ruling 8521083, February 27, 1985.

[28] IRS Letter Ruling 9313020, December 30, 1992. To the same effect, *see* IRS Letter Ruling 199941023, July 14, 1999.

[29] IRS Letter Ruling 9335029, September 3, 1993.

[30] IRS Letter Ruling 9409037, December 7, 1993. To similar effect, *see* IRS Letter Ruling 9629016, April 22, 1996 (the measuring date was the merger date).

Because the measuring date selected by the IRS in these rulings depends upon the subjective intent of the failing company or its trustee in bankruptcy, it becomes extremely important to cut square corners regarding the time at which such an intent is formulated.[31] The failing company and its trustee should avoid "contingency planning" speculations about the possibilities of two-company reorganizations until the last moment at which it becomes necessary to abandon the thought of rescuing the company through a one-company internal recapitalization.

In 1991, the IRS ruled that a merger of an insolvent subsidiary into its parent constituted a "G" reorganization.[32] The security holders of the subsidiary received stock and debt of the surviving parent, plus an interest in certain litigation claims. The only representations made about the assets of the subsidiary were that there had been no dispositions of assets to creditors before the bankruptcy petition date that were not undertaken for the purpose of the subsidiary's operating as a going concern; that immediately after the merger the parent possessed all of the assets owned by the subsidiary before the merger, except assets used to pay expenses of the reorganization; and that the parent would continue the subsidiary's historic business.

The IRS has ruled that assets transferred by the target company, at the direction of the acquiring company in a merger, directly to a subsidiary of the acquiring company would qualify as assets transferred to the acquiring company for purposes of the substantially all test.[33]

### §605.1.4 Continuity-of-Interest Test

The legislative history of the "G" reorganization provision made clear that the continuity-of-interest rules developed by the courts in prior years with respect to failing companies should continue to apply to "G" reorganizations, and that they should be adjusted to accommodate the fact that the present Bankruptcy Code has modified the "absolute priority" rule that used to apply under the old Bankruptcy Act.[34]

The absolute priority rule required that distributions to creditors and shareholders follow the strict priority of their seniority. The Bankruptcy Code modified this so that plans of bankruptcy reorganization may now provide for distributions that are not in strict accordance with the absolute priority of each class of creditor and shareholder. As a result, under the present Bankruptcy Code junior creditors and even stockholders will often receive stock or other consideration under a bankruptcy plan of reorganization even when they would receive nothing if the failing company were liquidated. The Senate Report stated:

---

[31] Proposals for regulations and the development of a safe harbor test in regulations or a revenue procedure have been made to the IRS. *See, e.g.,* NYSBA, "G" Reorganization Report, *supra* note 9, at 9-23.

[32] IRS Letter Ruling 9122067, March 6, 1991.

[33] IRS Letter Ruling 9409037, December 7, 1993.

[34] *See* S. Rep. No. 1035, 96th Cong., 2d Sess. 36 (1980); *see also* Plumb, Bankruptcy Commission Tax Recommendations—Reorganizations, *supra* note 1, at 239-243.

> It is expected that the courts and the Treasury will apply to "G" reorganizations continuity-of-interest rules which take into account the modification by [the Bankruptcy Code] of the "absolute priority" rule. As a result of that modification, shareholders or junior creditors, who might previously have been excluded, may now retain an interest in the reorganized corporation.
>
> For example, if an insolvent corporation's assets are transferred to a second corporation in a bankruptcy case, the most senior class of creditor to receive stock, together with all equal and junior classes (including shareholders who receive any consideration for their stock), should generally be considered the proprietors of the insolvent corporation for "continuity" purposes. However, if the shareholders receive consideration other than stock of the acquiring corporation, the transaction should be examined to determine if it represents a purchase rather than a reorganization.
>
> Thus, short-term creditors who receive stock for their claims may be counted toward satisfying the continuity-of-interest rule, although any gain or loss realized by such creditors will be recognized for income tax purposes.[35]

This passage suggests that Congress intended to adopt a "relation back" rule essentially like that in *Atlas Oil & Refining Corp.*[36] (*see* § 510.3): Namely, one looks to those creditors who actually receive stock and considers that the most senior class of creditors to receive stock, plus all interests equal and junior to them, are the equity owners of the corporation who must receive a substantial portion (50 percent for IRS ruling purposes) of their total consideration in the form of stock if the transaction is to qualify as a reorganization.[37] (*See* § 608 for special rules that apply to banks and thrift institutions.)

On March 10, 2005, the Treasury issued Prop. Reg. § 1.368-1(e)(6) to provide additional guidance on the continuity-of-interest requirement. The explanation accompanying the proposed regulation stated that the regulation is intended to imple-

---

[35] S. Rep. No. 1035, 96th Cong., 2d Sess. 36-37 (1980). In IRS Field Service Advice 1999-1029, September 22, 1993, *reprinted at* 1999 TNT 81-57, the IRS held that, where a new owner had purchased the short-term indebtedness of the target corporation shortly before the purported "G" reorganization, the purchased debt was too recently acquired to satisfy the continuity-of-interest test.

[36] 36 T.C. 675 (1961).

[37] An interesting treatment of creditors as satisfying the continuity-of-interest test can be found in IRS Technical Advice 9841006, June 25, 1998. Here, C, a subsidiary of B, transferred its assets to G in exchange for G stock and liquidated. Both B and C were in bankruptcy. The G stock was issued directly to the creditors of B. C was secondarily liable to these creditors, though the IRS apparently did not consider this significant. The IRS treated the transaction as a constructive distribution of the G stock to B, C's shareholder, and then by B to B's creditors. The transaction was held to be both a "G" and a "C" reorganization, with B being the "stockholder" for Code § 354 purposes, but the creditors satisfying the continuity-of-interest test. Citing *Alabama Asphaltic* (*see* § 510.1 above), the IRS said that where the transferor corporation is in bankruptcy, the creditors of the bankrupt corporation can be treated as having stepped into the shoes of its shareholders for continuity-of-interest test purposes. For another interesting ruling in this area, *see* IRS Letter Ruling 200350016, August 28, 2003, discussed at § 709 below.

ment the *Atlas Oil* approach and, in "G" reorganization cases, to implement the intentions expressed in the Senate Report.

Thus, the 2005 proposed regulation says that a creditor's claim against a target corporation may be considered a proprietary interest, for continuity-of-interest purposes, if the target is in a title 11 or similar case *or* if the corporation is insolvent. In such cases, the proposed regulation provides that, if any class of creditor receives an equity interest in the acquiring corporation in exchange for part or all of its claim, a proportion of the most senior class to receive an equity interest and of all equal classes, and 100 percent of all junior classes, will be considered proprietary interests. (Shares of target stock for which any consideration is received would also be considered proprietary interests.) The proposed regulation further provides that if a creditor's claim is bifurcated into a secured and an unsecured claim pursuant to an order in a title 11 or similar case, or pursuant to an agreement between the creditor and the debtor, that bifurcation will be respected for purposes of applying these rules.

Before the issuance of the proposed regulation, a number of interpretative questions existed.[38] The proposed regulation addresses many of these. These will now be discussed.

**Partially secured creditors; treatment of senior claims.** Partially secured creditors present one interpretative question regarding the continuity-of-interest rules. To begin with, assume that there is a class of secured creditors whose collateral covers part but not all of their claims against the failing company. If they receive cash or debt in satisfaction of the adequately secured portion of their claim, but stock for the inadequately secured portion, will the cash or debt received by them count against satisfaction of the continuity-of-interest test? Or, instead, will such creditors be treated as having two classes of debt—a senior class in respect of the portion of their secured claim that is adequately secured, and a junior class in respect of the inadequately secured portion? The Bankruptcy Code treats such creditors as having two classes of debt.[39] We believe that a similar approach should apply for purposes of the continuity-of-interest test. Prior to the issuance of the 2005 proposed regulation, there was no direct authority in point.[40]

The 2005 proposed regulation addresses this problem in a way that is consistent with the suggested approach. It contains a provision stating that if a creditor's claim is bifurcated into a secured and an unsecured claim pursuant to an order in a title 11 or similar case, or pursuant to an agreement between the creditor and debtor, the bifurcation and the allocation of consideration to each of the claims will be respected.

---

[38] For other discussions of these interpretative questions (discussed below) and suggested resolutions, *see* NYSBA, "G" Reorganization Report, *supra* note 9, at 41-53; Asofsky, Reorganizing, *supra* note 7, at § 5.02[2]; Plumb, The Bankruptcy Tax Act, *supra* note 9, at ¶ 801.2(E) (excellent discussion of history and application).

[39] 11 U.S.C. § 506.

[40] The Senate Report to the Bankruptcy Tax Act of 1980 did indicate that the Bankruptcy Code rule segregating such secured creditors into two classes should apply for purposes of interpreting. Code § 108. S. Rep. No. 1035, 96th Cong., 2d Sess. 17 n.19 (1980). There is no reason to think that Congress would have intended a different rule for purposes of the continuity of interest test. *See also* NYSBA, "G" Reorganization Report, *supra* note 9, at 41-43.

But beyond this, the proposed regulation contains an additional provision that provides an even more liberal bifurcation rule. This sets forth a general rule (which does not depend on the claims being secured in whole or in part) that treats the claims of the most senior class of creditors to receive a proprietary interest in the issuing corporation and the claims of all equal classes of creditors (together, the senior claims) differently from all junior claims. The senior claims are treated as in part being creditor claims, and in part being proprietary interests. The part that is treated as proprietary interests is determined by multiplying the fair market value of all senior claims in the aggregate by a fraction, the numerator of which is the fair market value of the proprietary interests received in the aggregate in exchange for the senior claims, and the denominator of which is the sum of all consideration of all kinds received in the aggregate for such claims. Then, only the consideration issued for the proprietary interest portion of the claims is taken into account for continuity-of-interest purposes. To illustrate the effect of this rule, assume there are two equal senior creditors, A and B. They together hold aggregate senior claims with a face of $150 and a value of $100, for which the acquiring entity issues $50 worth of its stock (of which $30 worth is issued to creditor A and $20 worth is issued to B) plus $50 of other value (of which $20 is issued to creditor A and $30 to creditor B). Under the proposed regulation, 50 percent of each these creditors' claims (or $25 worth each, $50 in the aggregate) is treated as a proprietary interest. Although A received $25 of stock for his proprietary interest, B received only $20 of stock (plus $5 of other consideration) for his $25 proprietary interest. Thus, only $45 of this $50 proprietary class is treated for continuity-of-interest purposes as having been exchanged for the issuer's stock, and $5 of it for other consideration. The additional $5 of stock issued to creditor A, although taken into account for purposes of the proportionality ratio, is treated as having been paid on a true creditor claim and thus ignored for purposes of computing the measure of continuity-of-interest.

Even after application of the foregoing two-class rule to secured creditors, the need to count as equity owners for purposes of the continuity-of-interest test the most senior class of creditors to receive stock means that, absent application of the more liberalizing bifurcation rule announced in the proposed regulation, even a small proportion of stock issued to a senior class of creditors may cause a transaction to fail the continuity-of-interest test. The adoption of the more liberalizing rule in the proposed regulation would change this result.

## EXAMPLE

A failing company has four classes of creditors and one class of stockholders. The company is insolvent. The most senior class of creditors will receive cash in satisfaction of their claims, and the stockholders will be wiped out. The bankruptcy plan contemplates that the fourth class of creditors will receive 50 percent stock and 50 percent debt in satisfaction of their claims, that the third class of creditors will receive debt in satisfaction of their claims, and that the second class of creditors will receive (on a pro-rata basis) 5 percent stock and 95 percent cash in satisfaction of their claims. Prior to the adoption of the more liberalizing bifurcation rule in the proposed regulation, the issuance of some stock to

> the second most senior class of creditors means that all of the class 2, 3, and 4 creditors must be counted as equity holders for purposes of the continuity-of-interest test. Assuming that the amount of cash and debt issued in the aggregate to the class 2, 3, and 4 creditors vastly exceeds the value of the stock issued to them, the transaction will fail the continuity-of-interest test. However, if no stock had been issued to the class 2 creditors, only the class 4 creditors would be counted as equity owners and the continuity-of-interest test would be satisfied. Under the more liberalizing bifurcation rule in the proposed regulation, only 5 percent (not 100 percent) of the class 2 claims would be considered a proprietary interest. Thus, if the stock issued to the class 2 and 4 creditors exceeded in value the debt issued to the class 3 creditors, the continuity-of-interest test would be satisfied.

Where it is desired to issue some kind of equity interest to a senior class of creditors in such a situation, consideration should be given by the failing company to issuing warrants or convertible debt rather than stock to these creditors. Such equity-flavored instruments will presumably not be taken into account as if they were stock for purposes of the continuity-of-interest test.[41] However, it would be desirable to obtain a ruling on the proposed transaction.

**Interim distributions.** Frequently, during the course of a bankruptcy proceeding, there will have been distributions of cash or property to creditors over a period of time before a two-company reorganization takes place. This raises the question of whether all distributions to creditors during the entire bankruptcy proceeding, or perhaps even before the bankruptcy proceeding, must be taken into account if those same creditors are in a class that receives stock in a two-company transaction.

The first three private rulings issued in "G" reorganizations of nonbanking institutions addressed this question and held that one would take into account distributions to creditors beginning with the date used to measure compliance with the "substantially-all-assets" test, namely, the date on which the failing company or its trustee in bankruptcy decided that the company could no longer be viably operated as an independent going concern.[42]

In 1998, the IRS issued temporary Reg. § 1.368-1T, effective for transactions occurring after January 28, 1998. This stated as a general rule that proprietary interests in target corporations could not be taken into account for continuity-of-interest purposes if, prior to and "in connection with" a potential reorganization, they

---

[41] Warrants have never been considered stock for purposes of Code § 354. *See* Pre-1998 Reg. § 1.354-1(e); Rev. Rul. 78-408, 1978-2 C.B. 203; *Wm. H. Bateman*, 40 T.C. 408 (1963); *Helvering v. Southwest Consol. Corp.*, 315 U.S. 194, 200-01 (1942). As discussed at § 502.3 above, the 1998 regulations treat warrants as securities having a zero principal amount for purposes of Code § § 354, 355, and 356. This new leniency toward warrants applies only for purposes of these three sections, however, and not for any other purpose. Moreover, this new treatment of warrants as securities would seem, if anything, to confirm that they are not to be considered stock for reorganization purposes. Thus, there seems little doubt that warrants will still not count for continuity-of-interest purposes.

[42] IRS Letter Ruling 8503064, October 24, 1984; IRS Letter Ruling 8521083, February 27, 1985; IRS Letter Ruling 8909007, November 30, 1988.

are redeemed. The regulations in effect treated pre-reorganization redemptions of proprietary interests for this purpose the same as post-reorganization redemptions. In drafting these regulations, the IRS had rejected suggestions by commentators that redemptions should not adversely affect continuity where the source of the funds was the target corporation itself, and not directly or indirectly the acquiring corporation.[43] These new regulations did not specifically deal with the special problems of troubled corporations, but there is no reason to believe that the IRS intended the new regulations to change the result in the "G" reorganization rulings just mentioned. Presumably the IRS would still draw the line between those distributions to creditors that are treated as being "in connection with" the reorganization, and those that are not, at the place it did in those "G" reorganizations. When this temporary regulation was adopted in final form as Reg. § 1.368-1(e), this language was changed but the substance was retained. The 2005 proposed amendments to the continuity-of-interest rules in Prop. Reg. § 1.368-1(e)(6) add a sentence which says that a proprietary interest in a target corporation is not preserved to the extent it is redeemed prior to the potential reorganization. We similarly assume that this was not intended to change the line between those distributions to creditors that are treated as being "in connection with" the reorganization, and those that are not.

**Consideration issued to shareholders.** Another set of interpretative questions relates to the treatment of consideration issued to stockholders where the company was insolvent and the creditors do not receive consideration equal to the full amount of their claims. For example, suppose the creditors receive value equal to 30 cents on the dollar for their claims, but the shareholders nevertheless receive some consideration. If the shareholders receive only stock, will the continuity-of-interest test be satisfied by looking only at the stock received by the shareholders and ignoring the stock and other consideration going to the creditors? Conversely, if the stockholders receive only nonstock consideration, such as warrants or cash, will the transaction fail the continuity-of-interest test without regard to the amount of stock issued to the creditors? The answer to these questions should depend in part on whether the only reason for issuing consideration to the old shareholders was to try to satisfy the continuity-of-interest test, or instead whether it reflected the bargaining power of the shareholder group that now exists because of the Bankruptcy Code's modification of the "absolute priority" rule.

In *Detroit-Michigan Stove Co. v. United States*,[44] the creditors of a corporation in bankruptcy received 30 cents on the dollar for their claims but the stockholders of the old corporation received 25 percent of the stock in the new corporation. The parties took the position that the stock satisfied the continuity-of-interest requirement. The court, however, concluded that the old corporation's stock was worthless because of the absolute priority rule; that the stock received by the old shareholders was "gratuitous stock"; and that the continuity-of-interest test was not satisfied. This case

---

[43] Silverman and Weinstein, The New Continuity of Interest/Continuity of Business Enterprise Regs, 80 Tax Notes (July 20, 1998), pp. 357, 359.

[44] 121 F. Supp. 892, 54-1 U.S.T.C. ¶9436 (Ct. Cl. 1954).

has been properly criticized.[45] Businessmen do not give away a 25 percent interest in a significant corporation, and one must assume that the stock received by the old shareholders reflected the strength of their bargaining position despite the potential application of the absolute priority rule. Now that the absolute priority rule has been modified, a holding such as the *Detroit-Michigan* holding would seem to be particularly inappropriate, except where the old shareholders receive only token shares designed to try to meet the continuity-of-interest test without regard to what the creditors receive.[46]

Even where the stock issued to the old shareholders reflects their bargaining power under the Bankruptcy Code, one must consider Rev. Rul. 73-233,[47] which held that a disproportionate amount of stock received by minority stockholders as an inducement to get them to vote in favor of a tax-free merger represented taxable compensation paid by the other shareholders in consideration of the vote by the minority shareholders. The ruling treated the transaction as if the majority shareholders had received the extra shares and then retransferred them to the minority shareholders. If this ruling were correct, then stock issued to shareholders in a bankruptcy reorganization where the creditors receive less than 100 cents on the dollar might be treated as being given to the old stockholders only to get them to vote in favor of the bankruptcy plan of reorganization. In this case, the stock would not be treated as being received in exchange for the old stock, but instead would be treated as being received by the creditors who in turn paid it to the old stockholders as compensation for their vote.

This ruling seems to us to be wrong. The voting power of stock is an inherent characteristic of the stock itself. The premium value in minority stock attributable to the fact that it may be able to block a major corporate transaction such as a merger is no different than the premium value normally attributable to majority stock. Both reflect the value of the stock itself.[48]

Given the present state of the law, and until adoption of the 2005 proposed regulation mentioned above, one cannot be sure whether consideration issued to the old shareholders will be taken into account, or indeed will be treated as the only consideration taken into account for purposes of the continuity-of-interest test.[49] So

---

[45] Tillinghast & Gardner, Acquisitive Reorganizations and Chapters X and XI of the Bankruptcy Act, 26 Tax L. Rev. 663, 680 (1971).

[46] *See also* NYSBA, "G" Reorganization Report, *supra* note 9, at 50-52.

[47] 1973-1 C.B. 179.

[48] Support for this view can, indeed, be found in Rev. Rul. 81-282, 1981-2 C.B. 78. This ruling holds that a donor of stock to charity has not parted with his entire interest (or an undivided fraction thereof) in stock, as required for a charitable deduction by Code § 170(f)(3), where he retains the right to vote the contributed stock. The ruling observed that "the right to vote stock is inherent in the ownership of common stock and, as such, is a property right. This right gives the holder a voice in the management of the corporation and is crucial in protecting the stockholder's financial interest. Therefore, the right to vote the stock of *X* is a substantial right in that stock." The ruling did not cite Rev. Rul. 73-233.

[49] *See* S. Rep. No. 1035, 96th Cong., 2d Sess. 37 (1980) ("However, if the shareholders [of a debtor corporation] receive consideration other than stock of the acquiring corporation the transaction should be examined to determine if it represents a purchase rather than a reorganization"); NYSBA,

long as this uncertainty continues, wisdom suggests that, in transactions where an advance ruling is not obtained, the only consideration issued to shareholders should be stock, rather than cash or even equity-flavored securities such as convertible debt or warrants, and that the plan should be designed so that the continuity-of-interest test is satisfied whether one looks only to what the old shareholders received or instead to what all the creditors (starting with the most senior class to receive stock) and shareholders received. However, in IRS Letter Ruling 9409037 (December 7, 1993) stock of the acquiring company was issued to the unsecured creditors and warrants were issued to the stockholders of the target company. The IRS ruled that continuity was satisfied because more than 50 percent of the total consideration received by the former shareholders and unsecured creditors consisted of common stock of the acquiring company. Thus, in this ruling, the IRS did not look only to the former shareholders to see whether continuity had been satisfied, but it did take them into account. In making the 50 percent computation, the ruling ignored target debt that had been acquired by the acquiring company before the merger.[50]

The 2005 Prop. Reg. § 1.368-1(e)(6) would resolve this issue by not limiting the concept of a proprietary interest to a shareholder class that receives stock in the transaction. Instead, it would treat the most senior class of creditors receiving stock in the transaction, plus all equal and junior classes, and the shareholders, as being the holders of the proprietary interests.

### § 605.1.5 Continuity-of-Business-Enterprise Test

The continuity-of-business-enterprise test applies to "G" reorganizations as well as to other reorganizations. The legislative history of the "G" reorganization provision is silent on the question of whether this test, like the other tests discussed above, should be applied more leniently to "G" reorganizations. The first two private rulings issued in "G" reorganizations of nonbanking companies simply contained statements to the effect that the new company would continue the business of the old company "in a substantially unchanged manner after the consummation of the transaction."[51]

### § 605.1.6 Net-Value Test

In 2005, the IRS issued Prop. Reg. § 1.368-1(b)(1) to provide that a requirement for a Code § 368 reorganization, including a "G" reorganization, is an exchange of net value, as defined in Prop. Reg. § 1.368-1(f). This new requirement, which would be

(Footnote Continued)

"G" Reorganization Report, *supra* note 9, at 49-50 (states that Senate Report language apparently envisions a "highly solvent" debtor and that the Senate Report's adoption of the relation back doctrine should generally apply to solvent, as well as insolvent, debtors in bankruptcy); Asofsky, Reorganizing, *supra* note 7, at § 5.02[2] (indicates that where shareholders of debtor receive more than a nominal value for their stock, the IRS would probably contend that continuity should be tested by only looking to the shareholders).

50 *Cf.* IRS Letter Ruling 9629016, April 22, 1996, described at § 605.1.2, note 17, above.

51 IRS Letter Ruling 8503064, October 24, 1984; IRS Letter Ruling 8521083, February 27, 1985.

effective when issued as a final regulation, is discussed at § 604.3.4 above. That discussion is equally applicable here.

### § 605.1.7 Failing Company as Acquirer

Although it is common to think of "G" reorganizations as involving the acquisition of the failing company by a profitable company (something we might call a "G-out"), it is important to note that a "G" reorganization can equally involve the acquisition by the failing company of a profitable company (something we might call a "G-in"). As mentioned above, all that is needed to meet the basic "G" reorganization definition is that there be a transfer of assets by one corporation to another in a title 11 or similar case and that "any party" to the reorganization be under the jurisdiction of the bankruptcy court, if the transaction is pursuant to a plan of reorganization approved by the court.[52] Thus, a transfer of substantially all its assets by a profitable company to a bankrupt company pursuant to a plan of bankruptcy reorganization, followed by a liquidation of the profitable company, will qualify as a "G" reorganization.

Although Congress intended that more lenient rules be applied to "G" than to other reorganizations with respect to such matters as application of the continuity-of-interest and substantially-all-assets tests, what Congress obviously had in mind was the application of these tests to the failing company. Such leniency is necessary to make a "G" reorganization work where the failing company is acquired by a profitable company. However, it is not necessary where the failing company is itself the acquiring entity. Neither the continuity-of-interest nor the continuity-of-business-enterprise tests apply to acquiring entities in tax-free reorganizations.[53] Because leniency in application of these rules to the profitable company in a G-in is not necessary in order to facilitate combinations of these companies with failing companies, one should assume that neither the IRS nor the courts will apply these more lenient standards to G-ins.

Where the failing company finds it difficult to satisfy even the more lenient rules for a G-out, a G-in may prove to be a useful planning device. Any reshuffling of the capital structure of the failing company that precedes or accompanies a G-in will be treated as a separate "E" recapitalization. Under new Code § 382, the same Code § 382 rules will apply to a G-in as to a G-out, even if there is a first-step "E." As noted at § 507.1, however, under old Code § 382, a first-step "E" may involve an old Code § 382(a) "purchase" of stock of the failing company if nonsecurity creditors receive its stock in exchange for their debt. The provisions of old Code § 382(b) will apply to the G-in in the same way that they apply to a G-out: The 20-percent-continuity-of-equity-interest test applies to the loss company whether it is the acquiring or the acquired company.

---

[52] *See* Code § 368(a)(1)(G) and (3)(A).

[53] *See* Rev. Rul. 81-25, 1981-1 C.B. 132 (no business continuity required for transferee); Bittker & Eustice, *supra* § 604.3.1 note 34, at § 14.11, p. 14-30 (continuity-of-interest test does not apply to transferee).

## §605.2 *Consequences to Creditors, Shareholders, and Corporation*

The consequences to the creditors and shareholders of exchanges made pursuant to a "G" reorganization are the same as were discussed above with respect to reorganizations occurring outside bankruptcy.[54]

The consequences to the corporation are also generally the same, except that Code §§382(l)(5) and 382(l)(6), which apply only to companies in a title 11 (bankruptcy) or similar case, apply to "G" reorganizations. The latter provisions are discussed at §§508.4.2 and 508.5 above. In addition, for companies in bankruptcy, any COD incurred in the "G" reorganization should be governed by the bankruptcy exception to COD income, whereas for companies in "similar cases," the inclusion of any COD income generally will depend on the applicability of the insolvency exception. *See* the discussion at §404.2 above.

**Prior Law.** At various times in the past, there have been other differences in the corporation's treatment. First, for those transactions governed by old Code §382, old Code §382(b)(7) provided that any creditor of the bankrupt company who receives stock in a "title 11 or similar case" shall be treated as a stockholder immediately before the reorganization for purposes of applying the 20 percent equity continuity test of old Code §382(b).

Second, prior to the total repeal of the stock-for-debt exception in 1994, the Code §108(e)(10) limitation on applicability of the stock-for-debt exception (other than the limitation applicable to certain preferred stock) did not apply in bankruptcy proceedings (*see* §504A.1).

Before the 1986 amendment to Code §361(b), there was a further exception, which has been made academic by that amendment. This related to the question of whether, under old Code §361(b), a distribution of boot to creditors would satisfy the requirements for avoiding tax at the corporate level on the boot. Although both old Code §361 and former Code §371 contained identical language to the effect that the corporation will not recognize gain from the receipt of boot if it distributes it "in pursuance of the plan of reorganization," it has been commonly assumed that old Code §361 required the distribution to be to shareholders, whereas the regulations under Code §371 made clear that distributions to creditors qualified as well.[55] The legislative history of the Bankruptcy Tax Act of 1980 indicates that Congress intended distributions of boot to creditors to qualify for nonrecognition to the corporation in "G" reorganizations.[56] In effect, this constituted a special rule for "G" reorganizations under old Code §361. The 1986 amendment to Code §361 eliminated this interpretative problem and changed the rules, not only for "G" reorganizations, but also for all other two-company reorganizations. *See* §604.2 above.

---

[54] *See* §604.1 and Chapters 4 and 5.

[55] Reg. §1.371-1(b).

[56] H.R. Rep. No. 833, 96th Cong., 2d Sess. 34 n.10 (1980); S. Rep. No. 1035, 96th Cong., 2d Sess. 38 n.10 (1980); *see* Asofsky, Reorganizing, *supra* note 7, at §5.02[3][a] (indicating a possible need for regulations in this area).

### *§605.3 Payment of Expenses of Creditors and Shareholders*

A representation traditionally required in advance rulings for nonbankruptcy reorganizations is that each party to the reorganization and the shareholders and creditors will each pay their own expenses. In a bankruptcy proceeding, it is typical that various committees of stockholders and creditors are formed and that the representatives of these committees will be paid fees and expenses out of the assets of the bankrupt corporation as part of the plan of bankruptcy reorganization.

In this regard, it is interesting to note that the first nonbank "G" reorganization private letter ruling issued by the IRS contained a representation to the effect that the old company, the new company, and the creditors and shareholders of the old company "will each pay their own expenses in connection with the proposed transaction, except that Target will pay the reorganization expenses of the creditors and shareholders that are solely and directly related to the reorganization."[57]

## §606 EFFECT OF STOCK CANCELLATION ON EARNINGS AND PROFITS

A two-company reorganization, particularly if it occurs in a bankruptcy proceeding, is very likely to result in the elimination of some of the prior stock interest in the failing company. Where the interest of a stockholder is extinguished in a transaction that does not constitute a "title 11 or similar case" within the meaning of Code §368(a)(3)(A), the cancellation of the stock interest has no effect on the earnings and profits account of the corporation. However, the Bankruptcy Tax Act of 1980 added Code §312(l)(2), which provides that where the interest of a shareholder is terminated or extinguished in a title 11 or similar case, the amount of any deficit in the earnings and profits of the corporation will be reduced (but positive earnings and profits will not be created) by the paid-in capital attributable to the interest of the shareholder so terminated or extinguished.[1] This rule appears to apply only to a complete termination or extinction of the interest of a shareholder; where the shareholder receives some new stock in exchange for his old stock, the earnings and profits of the corporation would apparently not be affected.

## §607 RECAPTURE POTENTIAL IN STOCK RECEIVED BY CREDITORS

As stated at §502.4, where a creditor receives stock of a debtor corporation in satisfaction of his indebtedness, such stock shall be treated as Code §1245 property and any gain recognized on a subsequent sale or exchange will be subject to Code

---

[57] IRS Letter Ruling 8503064, October 24, 1984.

[1] **§606** For the rationale behind this adjustment, *see* Plumb, Bankruptcy Commission Tax Recommendations—Reorganizations, Carryovers and the Effects of Debt Reduction, 29 Tax L. Rev. at 323-341 (1974).

§ 1245 ordinary income recapture to the extent of the deductions allowed to the creditor as bad debt deductions or as an ordinary loss on the receipt of the stock.[1] This Code § 1245 recapture amount is reduced by any gain included in the creditor's gross income on receipt of the stock. The Code § 1245 taint carries over into any property received tax-free in an exchange for the stock.

Not only does this provision apply to stock of the debtor but Code § 108(e)(7)(C) and (D) provides that stock of a successor corporation, as well as stock of a parent corporation (of the debtor or a successor to the debtor), will be treated as stock of the debtor corporation for this purpose.

## § 608 SPECIAL PROBLEMS OF FINANCIALLY TROUBLED THRIFT INSTITUTIONS

Savings and loan associations and mutual savings banks borrow their funds on a short-term basis (mostly from depositors) and lend them on a long-term basis (mostly in the form of mortgages). Sharply rising interest rates, a few years ago, brought financial distress to the industry. The regulatory authorities found it necessary to rescue many such institutions, either through capital contributions from the regulatory authorities or by combining failing institutions with more healthy ones. At the same time, in order to allow such institutions to compete more effectively with commercial banks, legislation was adopted in 1982 that expanded the powers of such institutions, and this made them more attractive as vehicles for new investment by investors. Where the thrift institution takes the form of a mutual rather than a stock corporation, the infusion of new capital by investors requires the conversion of the mutual association into a stock association, followed by the sale of stock to the new investors.

A mutual thrift association does not issue equity interests that are separate from its deposit accounts. The entire equity interest in the association resides in the depositors, in the form of a right to share in the surplus, if any, of the association when it is liquidated. In addition, depositors (and sometimes borrowers) will have the right to vote on various corporate matters. Because these institutions have no equity interest that is separate from the deposit accounts, two-company transactions involving them do not easily fit into the reorganization provisions of the Internal Revenue Code.

The primary problem presented is how to determine whether the acquisition of such an institution will satisfy the continuity-of-interest test.[1] The IRS took the position that the interest of a depositor in a mutual thrift association was a dual ownership interest, consisting primarily of a cash equivalent and secondarily (and to a very minor degree) of an equity interest. Thus, where a mutual association com-

---

[1] **§ 607** Code § 108(e)(7).

[1] **§ 608** *See, e.g.*, Soukup, The Continuity-of-Proprietary-Interest Doctrine and Thrift Institution Mergers, 12 J. Corp. Tax'n 141 (1985); *see also* Note, Availability of Tax-Free Reorganization Treatment for Mergers Involving Hybrid Securities: Paulsen v. Commissioner, 39 Tax Law. 349 (1986) (hereafter Note—*Paulsen*); Bacon, Rescue Planning for Failing or Bankrupt Company, 631 Taxes 931, 946-947 (1983).

bined with another mutual association, and where the depositors in the acquired entity obtained precisely the same type of dual interest in the new entity that they had in the old, the IRS ruled that the continuity of interest requirement was satisfied.[2] On the other hand, where a stock association was acquired by a mutual association, with the result that the stockholders of the acquired company received deposit accounts in the acquiring mutual association, the IRS ruled that the continuity-of-interest requirement was not met, because the stockholders of the acquired entity did not receive a substantial enough portion of the consideration for their stock in the form of an equity interest.[3] After losing a number of cases on this issue, the IRS finally prevailed in the Supreme Court in 1985 in the *Paulsen* case,[4] and this decision has eliminated a great deal of the uncertainty in this area. The Court's opinion made clear that the merger of two mutual associations will satisfy the continuity-of-interest test, as will the acquisition of a mutual association by a stock association.[5] In both cases the depositor in the acquired entity receives nothing but an equity interest for the portion of his old deposit interest that represented equity. It is only the acquisition of a stock association by a mutual association that will not satisfy the test.

The failure of an acquisition of a savings institution to qualify as a reorganization will have significant adverse consequences at the corporate level. Where the target company's mortgages are older mortgages with an interest rate that is lower than the present market, their value will be substantially less than their face amount. If the transaction is taxable, the acquiring corporation will not inherit the target company's basis in the mortgages, but instead will have a much lower fair market value basis.

---

[2] Rev. Rul. 69-3, 1969-1 C.B. 103; Rev. Rul. 69-646, 1969-2 C.B. 54; Rev. Rul. 78-286, 1978-2 C.B. 145. The IRS has applied the same result where a mutual thrift association was converted into a mutual holding company. This was done in two steps: first a conversion of the mutual association into a stock association, and second a transfer of that stock to a new mutual holding company. These transactions were treated as an "F" reorganization of the mutual savings institution into the stock institution, followed by a Code §351 drop-down of the stock of the latter in exchange for mutual interests in the mutual holding company. The continuity-of-interest test was deemed satisfied for the "F" reorganization, and the mutual interests issued by the holding company were accepted as stock for purposes of Code §351. *See* IRS Letter Ruling 9741020, July 10, 1997; IRS Letter Ruling 9741011, July 9, 1997; IRS Letter Ruling 9712016, December 19, 1996. *See also* Rev. Rul. 2003-48, 2003-19 I.R.B. 863 (in addition to the Code §351 analysis, the ruling allowed "B" reorganization treatment as an alternative); IRS Letter Ruling 200544006, July 28, 2006 (to the same effect, involving a mutual life insurance company; it should be noted, as well, that this ruling held the conversion to be an "E" as well as an "F" reorganization, the significance of which is discussed at §608.4 below).

[3] Rev. Rul. 69-6, 1969-1 C.B. 145.

[4] *Paulsen v. Commissioner*, 469 U.S. 131, 85-1 U.S.T.C. ¶9116 (1985) (merger of state-chartered stock savings and loan into a federally chartered mutual savings and loan did not qualify as an "A" reorganization); *see also* Note—*Paulsen, supra* note 1.

[5] Although deposit liquidation accounts will be treated as equity for continuity-of-interest purposes, when two mutual associations merge with each other or a stock association acquires a mutual, they will not be treated as stock for Code §1504 purposes, so as to interfere with the ability of the acquiring stock association to file consolidated returns with its parent. *See, e.g.*, IRS Letter Ruling 8750015, September 10, 1987; IRS Letter Ruling 8742016, July 21, 1987. Nor will they be treated as stock for purposes of applying the reorganization rules to a subsequent acquisition of the acquiring stock association in a tax-free reorganization. *See, e.g.*, IRS Letter Ruling 8750048, September 15, 1987; IRS Letter Ruling 8748033, August 17, 1987; IRS Letter Ruling 8830053, May 3, 1988 (reversing a contrary position taken in IRS Letter Ruling 8737044, June 15, 1987).

This will result in income to the acquiring corporation when it collects the principal on the mortgages. The bad debt reserves of the target corporation may also be recaptured into its income, and any NOLs will not pass over to the acquiring entity. Even where the acquisition of a mutual thrift association constituted a reorganization, there was considerable doubt as to how old Code § 382(b) would apply to the transaction.

## *§ 608.1 "G" Reorganizations of Banks and Thrift Institutions: 1981-1988*

In order to facilitate acquisitions of failing financial institutions and to provide a mechanism for bypassing the position taken by the IRS in *Paulsen,* Congress amended the "G" reorganization provisions in 1981 by adding special, more lenient "G" reorganization rules for banks, described in Code § 585, and savings institutions, described in Code § 593.[6] For these, new Code § 368(a)(3)(D) was added, which provided as follows:

(1) In the case of banks, the federal or state agency supervising the bank would be treated as a court for purposes of the "G" reorganization provisions.[7]

(2) In the case of savings institutions (savings and loan associations, cooperative banks, and mutual savings banks):

(a) The "G" reorganization provisions would apply even though no actual insolvency proceeding has commenced, if the Federal Home Loan Bank Board, the Federal Savings and Loan Insurance Corporation (FSLIC), or an equivalent state authority certified that the failing institution "is insolvent or that it is unable to meet its obligations as they become due or will be unable to do so in the immediate future."[8]

(b) No stock or securities of the acquiring institution had to be issued to the target institution or its depositors, but only if the substantially-all-assets test of Code § 354(b)(1) was met and in addition "substantially all of the liabilities of the transferor immediately before the transfer become, as a result of the transfer, liabilities of the transferee."[9] The first portion of this rule meant that the continuity-of-interest test was completely eliminated for thrift institution "G" reorganizations. The legislative history made clear that this rule covered all possible combinations of stock and mutual thrift institutions, including stock acquiring mutual, stock acquiring stock, mutual ac-

---

[6] *See generally* Blanchard, The Taxation of Federally Assisted Acquisitions of Troubled Financial Institutions, 44 Tax Law. 1037 (1991); Kliegman, Troubled Thrift Reorganizations—The Short Happy Life of Section 368(a)(3)(D), 64 Taxes 281 (1986) (discusses "G" reorganizations and conversions and acquisitions of mutual and stock savings and loans; also discusses the consequences of proposed and pending legislation to repeal the "G" reorganization provisions applicable to failing financial institutions, portions of which were subsequently enacted).

[7] Code § 368(a)(3)(D)(i)(I).

[8] Code § 368(a)(3)(D)(i)(II) and (iii).

[9] Code § 368(a)(3)(D)(ii).

> quiring mutual, and mutual acquiring stock.[10] This meant that the *Paulsen* holding would have no application in a "G" reorganization of a thrift institution. With respect to the "substantially all" aspects of the rule, as a practical matter, the FDIC or FSLIC, as an inducement to attracting a stronger institution to acquire a struggling thrift institution, may be required to strip out certain of the assets and liabilities of the failing institution before it is acquired by the stronger institution. The IRS has issued letter rulings holding that these "stripped out" assets and liabilities need not be taken into account for purposes of applying the Code § 368(a)(3)(D) substantially-all-assets and substantially-all-liabilities tests.[11]

At the same time, old Code § 382 was amended in 1981 by the addition of old Code § 382(b)(7)(B), which provided that deposits in the transferor would be treated as stock for purposes of applying the old Code § 382(b) test.[12]

The judicial continuity-of-business-enterprise test continued to apply to a "G" reorganization of a thrift institution. In this regard, the IRS has ruled that the test will be satisfied if the acquiring entity assumes all of the deposits of the target entity and either (1) will continue to hold at least 50 percent of the fair market value of the assets, including mortgages and other loans, that were held by the target institution at the time of adoption of the plan of reorganization (except for dispositions occurring in the ordinary course of business), or (2) will continue the target corporation's historic business.[13]

In 1996, the IRS issued an interesting Technical Advice Memorandum[14] addressing the question whether the formation of an interim entity, in the nature of a bridge bank, for the failing institution constituted a separate "G" reorganization, or whether it should be ignored. Here, the failing savings institution was placed under federal receivership. The federal banking agency organized an interim entity as a federal mutual savings institution and transferred substantially all the business and assets of the failing savings institution to that interim entity. Shortly thereafter, the interim entity was converted into a federal stock savings institution, which in turn was acquired by an unrelated holding company. The question presented was whether the transfer of the business to the interim entity and the subsequent conversion of the interim entity into a stock savings institution constituted two "G" reorganizations or

---

[10] Joint Committee on Taxation, General Explanation of the Economic Recovery Tax Act of 1981, August 1, 1981, at 152.

[11] *See, e.g.*, IRS Letter Ruling 8212027, December 23, 1981; IRS Letter Ruling 8226082, March 30, 1982.

[12] *See also* General Explanation of the Economic Recovery Tax Act of 1981, *supra* note 10, at 153 ("it is intended that section 269 is to apply as under current law to [all tax-free] reorganizations;" for such purpose, depositors in a thrift institution are treated as shareholders and deposits in the institution are treated as stock); IRS Letter Ruling 8307024, November 12, 1981 (applying Code § 382(b), prior to amendment by Pub. L. No. 99-514); Soukup, *supra* note 1, at 165 n.70 (concluding that the SRLY rules apply including restrictions on use of "built in" deductions).

[13] Rev. Proc. 83-81, 1983-2 C.B. 598, clarifying Rev. Proc. 82-83, 1982-1 C.B. 474.

[14] IRS Technical Advice Memorandum 9623004, February 13, 1996. This modified IRS Letter Ruling 8411060, December 14, 1983.

only one "G" reorganization. The important consequence to the taxpayer here was that having two reorganizations rather than one would result in three rather than two taxable years, thereby reducing its carryover period for its losses. The IRS held that the transfer to the interim entity should be ignored, both because this would be more consistent with the legislative purpose of the "G" reorganization provisions for financial institutions, and because the step-transaction doctrine should produce the same result. This holding produced much the same result that was created for later transactions by the regulations under Code § 597, discussed at § 608.3.2 below.

These liberalized "G" reorganization provisions applied, of course, only if the target company transferred its assets to an acquiring corporation, that is, where there was a two-company transaction. Although the statute placed no limitation on the character of the acquiring corporation, prior to July 22, 1985, the IRS would not issue rulings unless the acquiring corporation was a bank or other financial institution described in Code § 585 or § 593.[15]

The Tax Reform Act of 1986 placed a "sunset" limit on these liberalized "G" reorganization rules (except for the rules that treat the regulatory authorities as a court). It provided that they would not apply to acquisitions made after December 31, 1988.[16] The 1986 Act also included a special provision, applicable until the end of 1988, that liberalized the new Code § 382 limitations for thrift institutions.[17] It did this by modifying the special Code § 382 provision (the Code § 382(l)(5) rule) that applies in bankruptcy (*see* § 508.5) to provide:

(1) that the former shareholders and creditors of the loss institution need only own 20 percent, rather the 50 percent, of the stock after the transaction;[18]

(2) that deposits in the loss institution would be treated as stock for all Code § 382 purposes, both before and after the transaction;

(3) that stock issued to others as part of the same transaction (if the stock was issued in an equity structure shift or Code § 351 transaction) would be governed by the same rules; and

(4) that the loss institution's NOLs would not be reduced by interest paid or accrued on debt (such as deposits) converted to stock, or by 50 percent of the amount that would be COD income but for the stock-for-debt exception.

---

[15] Rev. Proc. 85-34, 1985-2 C.B. 430, *revoking* Rev. Proc. 85-22, 1985-1 C.B. 550, § 5.19. In other instances, the IRS was relatively willing to issue rulings. *See, e.g.*, IRS Letter Ruling 8307024, February 23, 1983 (mutual savings bank to national bank); IRS Letter Ruling 8251055. December 29, 1982 (state mutual savings and loan to publicly held mutual saving and loan); IRS Letter Ruling 8223022, June 16, 1982 (merger of two mutual savings banks).

[16] Tax Reform Act of 1986, Pub. L. No. 99-514 § 904. This provision also would have repealed Code § 597 for acquisitions after December 31, 1988.

[17] Code § 382(l)(5)(F).

[18] In Notice 88-57, 1988-1 C.B. 545, the IRS announced that it would issue regulations holding that deposits can satisfy the 20 percent test even if they do not have voting power. A technical correction to Code § 382(l)(5)(F) by the 1988 Act confirmed, similarly, that deposits can satisfy the 20 percent test even if they do not have voting power. *See also* 1986 Blue Book at 323 n. 38.

The 1981 legislation also added former Code § 597 to provide that troubled thrift institutions would not have income from, and need not reduce the basis of their assets for, money or property contributed to their capital by FSLIC, the latter provision thereby reversing the normal rule of Code § 362(c). Code § 597, as adopted in 1981, did not apply to contributions from the FDIC, and although the IRS at first ruled that these should be treated as nonshareholder capital contributions, the IRS changed its mind and in 1988 held FDIC assistance payments taxable to the bank.[19]

Although the 1981 elimination of the continuity-of-interest requirement for "G" reorganizations of savings institutions did not extend to banks, as a matter of ruling policy, the IRS, as illustrated by IRS Letter Ruling 8835057 (June 10, 1988), supplemented in IRS Letter Ruling 8842059 (October 21, 1988), took a liberal view toward allowing banks to satisfy the continuity-of-interest test for "G" reorganization purposes. In that ruling, where the bank was insolvent and all its old stockholders received no interest in the new bank to which its assets and liabilities were transferred (and whose stock was issued for cash to the FDIC and an acquiring bank holding company), the IRS ruled that the depositors owned, in substance, the entire equity interest in the bank and that this satisfied the "G" reorganization requirement. The deposit accounts, however, were neither stock nor securities, and so this ruling in effect read out of the statute the requirement that at least some stock or a security be issued to a former security holder or stockholder. The ruling also considered the deposit accounts in the new bank as constituting sufficient continuity of interest. As we shall see at § 608.3, Congress, in the legislative history of the 1989 Financial Institutions Reform, Recovery and Enforcement Act (FIRREA) legislation, criticized this approach and indicated such deposit continuity will no longer satisfy the "G" reorganization requirement.

### § 608.1.1 Allowance of Losses Compensated by Tax-Exempt Financial Assistance

From the point of view of the U.S. Treasury, an ongoing problem that continues to result in a loss of tax revenues is that, with respect to pre-FIRREA acquisitions of troubled thrift institutions, FSLIC almost always entered into assistance agreements that provided tax-free loss assistance to acquirers of the troubled thrifts by compensating them for the difference between the book value and sales proceeds of "covered assets" (which typically consisted of nonperforming or troubled loans, real estate owned through foreclosure, and often other assets as well) and by providing the acquirers with yield maintenance guarantees, under which the acquirers were guaranteed a minimum return on such covered assets. On March 4, 1991, the Treasury Department issued a report in which it (1) concluded that deductions should not be allowed for losses that are reimbursed with tax-exempt financial assistance and (2)

---

[19] The 1988 ruling held that FDIC contributions were taxable to a bank, even where the bank issued a note, where there was no realistic expectation of repayment, *see* IRS Letter Ruling 8835057, June 10, 1988, and IRS Letter Ruling 8842059, July 28, 1988. These rulings reflected a change from the IRS's prior position, which treated FDIC assistance payments as nonshareholder capital contributions. *See* IRS Letter Ruling 8243025, July 22, 1982.

recommended that, to stave off anticipated litigation of this conclusion, Congress enact clarifying legislation disallowing such deductions.[20]

Effective for pre-FIRREA financial assistance "credited" on or after March 4, 1991, with respect to (i) assets disposed of and charge-offs made in tax years ending on or after that date and (ii) loss carryovers to taxable years ending on or after that date, Section 13224 of the 1993 Act implemented the Treasury Department's recommendation.[21] These changes in effect treat tax-exempt financial assistance credited with respect to losses on dispositions of covered assets on worthless debts as compensation for such losses, such that, for purposes of Code §§165, 166, 585, and 593, the amount of such tax-exempt assistance will reduce the amount of the otherwise allowed loss, bad debt deduction, or addition to a reserve for bad debts. In this connection, the amount of financial assistance deemed received is the gross amount thereof, without reduction for any offsets allowed under the assistance agreement. Assistance generally is deemed "credited" for purposes of the new provisions when the taxpayer makes an approved debit entry to a special reserve account required to be maintained under the assistance agreement to reflect the asset disposition or write-down. Also, an amount will be deemed to have been "credited" before March 4, 1991, if the taxpayer has disposed of the related asset without FSLIC approval prior to that date. The Committee reports indicate that to the extent FSLIC assistance results in the disallowance of a deductible bad debt loss or charge-off, the assistance should not produce an AMT net positive current earnings and profits adjustment.

---

[20] Department of the Treasury, Report on Tax Issues Relating to the 1988/1989 Federal Savings and Loan Insurance Corporation Assisted Transactions (March 4, 1991), at 16-17. Substantial doubt surrounds the government's position as to the deductibility of losses on covered assets, particularly in cases in which the IRS issued a favorable private letter ruling concluding that losses on covered assets would be allowed notwithstanding the acquirer's receipt of tax-exempt financial assistance under Code §597 reimbursing the losses. *See, e.g.*, IRS Letter Ruling 8943033, July 28, 1989, and IRS Letter Ruling 9010077, December 14, 1989, holding, among other things, that Code §265 did not apply to disallow losses recognized on dispositions of covered assets merely because the losses directly increased the amount of the tax-exempt financial assistance FSLIC would be obligated to pay to the acquirer under the assistance agreement. In IRS Field Service Advice 1999-980 (c. 1993), *reprinted at* 1999 TNT 75-40, the IRS advised that, rather than contest in the bankruptcy courts the deduction by the taxpayer for bad debts for which the taxpayer was compensated by FSLIC, the agents should settle, particularly because the bankruptcy court might well view disallowance of the deduction as undercutting the legislative purpose behind treating the FSLIC contributions as being nontaxable income.

[21] Several companies have contested the retroactive disallowance caused by the 1993 legislation. For an opinion in the early stages of one of these cases, *see Centex Corp. v. United States*, 48 Fed. Cl. 625 (2001) and 49 Fed. Cl. 691 (2001) (motions for partial summary judgment). In 2003, the plaintiffs prevailed and obtained a judgment from the Court of Claims for some $28.5 million. *Centex Corp. v. United States*, 55 Fed. Cl. 381 (2003), *aff'd*, 395 F.3d 1283, 2005-1 U.S.T.C. ¶50,157 (Fed. Cir. 2005), *reh'g denied, en banc*, 2005 U.S. App. LEXIS 10224 (Fed Cir. Apr. 26, 2005). *See also, e.g., Local Oklahoma Bank N.A. v. United States*, 59 Fed.Cl. 713 (2004); *First Nationwide Bank v. United States*, 9431 F.3d 1342, 2006-1 U.S.T.C. ¶50,114 (Fed. Cir. 2005) (First Nationwide was awarded $70,108,647 in damages).

## §608.2 Changes Made by TAMRA

Section 4012 of the Technical and Miscellaneous Revenue Act of 1988[22] liberalized the foregoing rule, as follows:

(1) The sunset dates for the liberalized "G" reorganization and Code § 382 rules for thrift institutions were extended to December 31, 1989;

(2) Effective for acquisitions after November 10, 1988, (a) the liberalized provisions for thrift institutions were extended to banks, and (b) a thrift institution would qualify for these benefits even if it failed to meet the requirement in Code § 593 that it satisfy the 60 percent asset test of Code § 7701(a)(19)(C); and

(3) The Code § 597 exclusion from income (without basis reduction) for FSLIC assistance payments was extended to FDIC assistance payments.

TAMRA also cut back on the liberality of the Code § 597 rule as follows: 50 percent of the tax-free assistance payments would reduce (in order) preassistance NOLs, subsequently recognized built-in losses (computed without regard to the *de minimis* test and including losses on loans, marketable securities, and property acquired in foreclosure) and current year interest deductions. If the tax attributes available for reduction in the year of the contribution were insufficient to absorb the entire 50 percent amount, the excess was to be carried forward to reduce the following year's recognized built-in portfolio losses and interest deductions. Preassistance NOLs and built-in losses were to be measured as of the date that the FDIC or FSLIC determined the institution needed financial assistance (not the date of actual payment and not, necessarily, the date of the assistance agreement), and as of the date of any subsequent revision or modification of such determination. An exception to the 50 percent attribute reduction rule applied where the assets of the institution were acquired in a taxable acquisition and the assistance payments were made to the acquirer.

In 1988, the IRS also issued Notice 88-7,[23] which states that a transfer of the assets and liabilities of a savings and loan association to an interim mutual institution created by FSLIC, pending transfer of the assets and liabilities by FSLIC to a qualified purchaser, will not be treated as a Code § 382 ownership transfer where, in substance, the equity owners of the old association continue to own the entire equity interest in the mutual interim association.

---

[22] Pub. L. No. 100-647, 100th Cong., 2d Sess. (TAMRA). *See generally* Blanchard, *supra* note 6.

[23] 1988-1 C.B. 476. *See also* IRS Letter Ruling 9021054, February 27, 1990, applying Notice 88-7 to hold that where a consolidated return parent had a savings subsidiary whose assets (including some parent stock) were transferred to such an interim association, parent's purchase of parent stock from the interim association will not result in a change in ownership of parent.

## § 608.3 *Changes Made by FIRREA*

By 1989, a reaction had set in against the use of special tax benefits to help salvage troubled thrift institutions and banks. Congress substantially curtailed these benefits as part of the Financial Institutions Reform, Recovery and Enforcement Act of 1989,[24] which became law on August 9, 1989, but which was made effective as of May 10, 1989.[25] In essence after FIRREA, financial institutions became subject to the same "G" reorganization and Code § 382 rules as any other corporation (except that the bank regulatory authorities are treated as a bankruptcy court and assistance payments are treated as ordinary income).

Specifically, FIRREA made the following changes:

(1) *Liberalized "G" Reorganization Rules Ended.* The sunset date for the liberalized "G" reorganization provisions of Code § 368(a)(3)(D) for banks and thrift institutions was moved up to May 9, 1989, except for the rule that treats the regulatory authorities as a court. The House Committee Report also went out of its way to criticize IRS Letter Ruling 8835057,[26] which was mentioned above at § 608.1. The report stated that although "no inference should be drawn as to the correctness of this ruling under prior law, the committee intends it to be clear that such a transaction would not qualify for tax-free reorganization treatment following the enactment of this bill."[27]

(2) *Special Code § 382 Rule Eliminated.* Similarly, the Special Code § 382(1)(5) rule for banks and thrift institutions was terminated effective for transactions occurring on or after May 10, 1989.

(3) *Code § 597 Exclusion of Assistance Payments Ended.* Code § 597was amended, effective May 10, 1989, to eliminate the tax-free nature of assistance payments made to troubled financial institutions. The Treasury was given broad authority to issue regulations governing the income, and basis, consequences of such payments. Code § 597 articulates the intention that where assets of a troubled financial institution are acquired in a taxable acquisition, such assistance payments will generally be taken into account by the transferor institution.

### § 608.3.1 IRS Notice 89-102

With the passage of FIRREA, the IRS soon issued Notice 89-102[28] to provide preliminary guidance under Code § 597, pending issuance of regulations. The Notice applies to financial assistance received or accrued on or after May 10, 1989. The principal points made in Notice 89-102 can be summarized as follows.[29]

---

[24] Pub. L. No. 101-73, 101st Cong., 1st Sess. (FIRREA), § 1401. *See generally* Blanchard, *supra* note 6.

[25] Special effective date rules were provided for acquisitions completed or binding contracts made before September 8, 1989.

[26] June 10, 1988.

[27] H.R. Rep. No. 54, 101st Cong., 1st Sess. 26 (1989).

[28] 1989-2 C.B. 436.

[29] *See* McCurley & Simon, FIRREA Changes the Rules Governing Acquisitions of Troubled Financial Institutions, 45 Tax Notes 617-625 (October 30, 1989).

### *§608.3.1.1 Rules Applicable to Taxable Asset Acquisitions*

(1) *Cash Assistance.* In the case of a taxable acquisition by an acquiring corporation ("Acquirer") of the assets of a financially troubled bank or savings institution ("Target"), cash financial assistance payments received from the applicable federal agency ("Agency")[30] will be treated as ordinary income to Target immediately before the acquisition. This will be so even if the payment is made directly to Acquirer rather than to Target, and even if the Agency receives an equity interest in the Target.

(2) *Net Worth Notes.* If the financial assistance takes the form of a net worth note, the amount of the income is the issue price of the note, computed under the OID rules. Acquirer's basis in the note will be that same issue price. The Notice says that the OID rules are to be applied in the following manner: The note will be treated as not issued for property (even if it was issued for property transferred to the Agency); Acquirer will be treated as the first holder; and any discount will be computed beginning on the date Acquirer acquired the note. In the case of a subsequent retroactive adjustment to the amount of the note, the adjustment will be given effect in Target's return for the year of acquisition as if included in the original note, provided the adjustment is made within 180 days of the date of acquisition. Adjustments made more than 180 days after the acquisition will not affect Target and will be treated as a new separate note. The Notice says that the income tax consequences of such a "new" note will be borne by Acquirer, but does not specify what these consequences should be.

(3) *Loss Guarantees.* Where the financial assistance takes the form of a guarantee against loss or a put, the assets covered by the guarantee or put will be treated as having a value not less than the guaranteed value for purposes of computing Target's gain or loss on the sale and Acquirer's basis in the assets. Amounts paid pursuant to the guarantee against loss or put will be treated as an amount realized in exchange for the covered asset; to the extent the amounts exceed basis, they will be treated as federal financial assistance that must be treated as ordinary income by Acquirer.

(4) *Acquirer's Basis Allocation.* In applying Code §1060 and Reg. §1.1060-IT(d) to determine the basis of the acquired assets, Acquirer, after allocating the purchase price to Class I assets (including the amount of any financial assistance paid in cash), must next allocate the purchase price to any net worth note, and then to any assets covered by a guarantee against loss or put (the guarantee or put are not treated as separate assets but instead affect the value of the covered assets), before allocating consideration to Class II through Class IV assets.

(5) *Yield Maintenance Agreements.* If the Agency provides assistance in the form of a Yield Maintenance Agreement (a guarantee of yield on certain assets), the payments will generally be treated as interest income, and the right to receive the payments will not be treated as a separate asset to which basis may be allocated.

(6) *Expense Reimbursements.* If the Agency provides expense reimbursements or indemnity rights to Acquirer, these are not treated as separate assets to which basis is

---

[30] The Agency may be the FDIC, FSLIC, or Resolution Trust Corporation (the successor to FSLIC).

allocated, and Acquirer does not have to bring them into income, but Acquirer may not deduct (or include in basis) the amounts of cost or expense to which they relate.

(7) *Advance Payments.* The foregoing rules assume that the Agency assistance is provided at the time of the acquisition by Acquirer. Where the assistance is provided in a taxable year that precedes the acquisition, the Target—but only if it is not part of a consolidated return group—may elect to defer the tax consequences to it of the assistance until the earlier of (a) 36 months from the date the assistance is provided or (b) the date Target's assets or stock is acquired.

#### *§ 608.3.1.2 Rules Applicable to Stock Purchase Acquisitions*

(1) *Code § 338 Elections.* When Acquirer makes a taxable purchase of 80 percent or more of the stock of Target (within the meaning of Code § 338), a Code § 338 election can be made. The Notice provides two liberalizations of the normal Code § 338 rules. First, Code § 338 can be applied without regard to whether Code § 351 applies. Thus, a "purchase" of stock can include a Code § 351 acquisition of stock. Second, the Code § 338 consistency rules do not apply. Where Target was a member of a consolidated return group, a Code § 338(h)(10) election can be made.

(2) *If Code § 338 Election Not Made.* If a Code § 338 election is not made, the tax treatment to Target of financial assistance payments, net worth notes, guarantees against loss or puts, reimbursements, and the like are essentially the same as in a taxable asset acquisition. They produce the same kind and amount of income and have the same effect on basis and asset values for all purposes (including Code § 382 or Reg. § 1.1502-15 built-in gain or loss computations). Yield Maintenance Agreements will not constitute built-in gain for purposes of Code § 382 or Reg. § 1.1502-15.

#### *§ 608.3.1.3 Treatment of Bridge Banks*

In some cases the federal bank agency will transfer the assets and liabilities of a Target to a new, interim, banking or savings institution created by it for purposes of continuing the operations of Target pending its acquisition. The Notice provides the following rules relating to such Bridge Banks:

(1) *Carryover Basis Transaction.* The transfer of assets and liabilities from Target to Bridge Bank will be treated as a carryover basis transaction described in Code § 381(c). The Bridge Bank will be treated as a continuation of the Target for all purposes.[31]

---

[31] For the creation of a similar result in a pre-1989 transaction by ignoring the Bridge Bank as an entity separate from the target, *see* IRS Technical Advice Memorandum 9623004, February 13, 1996. Prior to issuance of Notice 89-102 it had been unclear whether creation of the Bridge Bank broke the consolidation with its parent. Where separate returns were filed by conservators or receivers for the Bridge Bank, there was the potential for creating a separate taxable year between the time the assets were placed in receivership and the time they were transferred to a new acquirer. The foregoing technical advice held that such a separate tax year should be ignored by the subsequent acquirer for NOL carryback purposes even for pre-FIRREA transactions.

(2) *No Code § 382 Ownership Change.* The transfer *will not* be treated as an ownership change for purposes of Code § 382.

(3) *Consolidated Returns.* Where Target was a subsidiary member of a consolidated return group, the Bridge Bank will be treated as Target's successor, will continue as a member of the group and will use the same taxpayer I.D. number as Target.[32]

(4) *Successor Treatment.* Where Target was a common parent of a consolidated return group (or was not a member of a group), the Bridge Bank will similarly be treated as a successor of Target. The tax year will not change, the group will not terminate, and the taxpayer I.D. number will stay the same.

(5) *Multiple Transfers.* The foregoing rules assume that the assets of only one Target are transferred to the Bridge Bank. Where assets of more than one financially troubled institution are transferred, the Notice says that special rules will be devised.

### § 608.3.2 The Regulations Under Code § 597

Several criticisms were made of the manner in which Notice 89-102 carried out Congress's directive in Code § 597. First, the deferral mechanism did not properly match the income recognized by reason of the receipt of the financial assistance with the losses incurred by the Target. Second, as a consequence of the limitation in Code § 56(d)(1) on alternative minimum tax (AMT) NOLs to 90 percent of pre-NOL alternative minimum taxable income (AMTI), Notice 89-102 did not properly ensure that a Target with NOLs and built-in losses equal to or exceeding the amount of the financial assistance did not incur a federal income tax liability as a result of the assistance. Third, Notice 89-102 created significant doubt as to tax ownership of Target assets subject to Agency puts or loss guarantees by stating that this issue would remain governed by general income tax principles. Finally, by treating the Bridge Bank as a continuing member of the Target's old consolidated return group, Notice 89-102 essentially required the common parent of that group to report the income or loss of a corporation under the control of an Agency that frequently asserted claims against that common parent and, hence, often was not disposed to provide the common parent with the requisite financial information to prepare the consolidated return.[33]

After carefully considering the relevant issues, the IRS and the Treasury Department issued proposed regulations under Code § 597, published on April 23, 1992, that proposed numerous changes in the manner in which Code § 597 is to be implemented, many of which were quite sensible.[34] These regulations were finalized on December 21, 1995. Although the final regulations adopted the bulk of the proposed

---

[32] Id.

[33] *See generally* New York State Bar Association Tax Section, Report on Section 597 Proposed Regulations, 58 Tax Notes 769 (February 8, 1993) (the "NYSBA" Section 597 Report"); Blanchard, *supra* note 6.

[34] Generally, the proposed regulations stated that the new rules (if finalized) will apply to tax years ending on or after April 22, 1992, subject to an elective application of the new rules to prior years governed by Code § 597, as amended by FIRREA, provided certain conditions are met. *See* Prop. Reg.

regulations without significant modification, there were several meaningful changes. The most notable of the provisions of the final regulations, and the more meaningful differences between the proposed and final regulations, can be summarized as follows:

(1) *Repeal of AMT and Other Limitations on NOLs.* In order to assure the Target that no federal income tax liability will be incurred unless the amount of the financial assistance exceeds its NOLs and built-in losses, the regulations under Code § 597 provide that the limitations imposed by Code § 56(d)(1) (limiting AMT NOLs to 90 percent of pre-NOL AMTI), Code § 382, Code § 383, and the consolidated return regulations[35] do not apply to limit Target's use of its tax attributes to shelter income attributable to the financial assistance.[36]

(2) *Deferral of Income.* A significant change made by the regulations under Code § 597 is the implementation of a broad deferral mechanism designed generally to match assistance income with available offsetting deductions. In lieu of the 36-month deferral allowed by Notice 89-102 with respect to advance payments, one of two alternative formulas will apply, depending upon whether there is "continuing equity" in the Target or Acquirer. Under the regulations, "continuing equity" exists only if, as of the close of the taxable year, the Target is not (a) a Bridge Bank, (b) in Agency receivership, or (c) treated as a new entity that has purchased the assets of the Target in a "taxable transaction" (see paragraph "3" below).[37]

(a) *Absence of Continuing Equity.* In the absence of continuing equity in the Target or Acquirer, the amount of income that must be included by the Target during a tax year is limited to the sum of: (i) the excess of the Target's liabilities over the adjusted bases of its assets reduced by any bad debt reserves (referred to as the "excess debt amount") at the *beginning* of the tax year, plus (ii) the so-called "current loss amount." Under the proposed regulations, the current loss amount was defined as the excess for the tax year of the Target's deductions allowed by Chapter 1 of the Code (other than NOL and capital loss carryovers) over its gross income, determined

(Footnote Continued)

§ 1.597-7. As discussed below, the final regulations retain the same general effective date. *See* Reg. § 1.597-7(b).

[35] Principally, the separate return limitation year rules in Reg. §§ 1.1502-15 and 1.1502-21(c).

[36] Reg. § 1.597-2(c)(5). In addition, Reg. § 1.597-4(c) provides that the imposition of Agency control over Target (such as the appointment of the FDIC as receiver for an insolvent bank), the creation of a Bridge Bank to own all of the Target's assets, the cancellation of the Target's stock, and a deconsolidation election by the consolidated group of the Target (discussed in paragraph "4" below), do not cause an ownership change with respect to the Target.

[37] Reg. § 1.597-1(b). Under the proposed regulations, "continuing equity" existed for any tax year if one or more persons who owned, directly or indirectly (including ownership through related persons within the meaning of Code § 267(b)), 5 percent or more (by vote or value) of the Target's stock at any time during the two-year period before the Target was first placed under the Agency control or first received assistance (whichever is earlier) have such 5 percent ownership of the Target's stock (or the Acquirer's stock) on the last day of the tax year. Prop. Reg. § 1.597-1(b). Thus, the revised definition in the final regulations no longer requires tracing the identity of the Target's shareholders after the assistance transaction.

without regard to the financial assistance.[38] This formulation of the current loss amount was criticized because it failed to distinguish between losses of equity capital and losses of creditor money, with the result that assistance income might improperly be accelerated to offset current losses attributable to equity capital.[39] The final regulations eliminate this problem by treating equity capital as the first capital lost and by not requiring an inclusion of assistance income to offset this loss. This is done by defining the current loss amount as the excess of (i) the Target's current loss (still defined as the amount by which its non-carryover deductions exceed its gross income other than financial assistance) over (ii) the amount by which the adjusted bases of the Target's assets at the beginning of the year exceed its liabilities.[40]

The final regulations (like the proposed regulations) conclusively presume that at some point in the Target's life, the basis of its assets equalled or exceeded the total amount of its liabilities that are outstanding at the beginning of the year in question. This may not always be the case in the real world.[41] Thus, the formula will not always achieve an appropriate deferral of income to match deductions.

---

[38] Prop. Reg. § 1.597-2(c)(2). To illustrate the formula under the proposed regulations, suppose T has assets with a basis of $100 and liabilities of $100. The assets have declined in value to $60, as a consequence of which T receives $40 of financial assistance from an Agency in Year 2. If T disposes of assets with a basis of $50 and fair market value of $30 in Year 1, then T will have an NOL carryover of $20 to Year 2, an excess debt amount at the beginning of Year 2 of $20 ($100 of liabilities less the sum of $50 of basis in original assets and $30 of basis in assets received in the Year 1 disposition), and no current loss amount. As such, under the formula, T would have current income of only $20 with respect to the $40 of financial assistance, all of which would be offset by the $20 NOL carryover. If T disposes of the assets in Year 2, then T will have no excess debt amount at the beginning of Year 2 and will have a current loss amount of $20, again resulting in $20 of current income under the proposed formula and taxable income of zero. In both cases, T will have a built-in loss of $20 available to offset the remaining $20 of financial assistance income that would be recognized in subsequent periods.

[39] *See* preamble to final regulations, 60 F.R. 66091, 66092 (December 21, 1995).

[40] Reg. § 1.597-2(c)(2)(ii). To illustrate the formula of the final regulations, suppose T has assets with a basis of $100 and liabilities of $90. The assets have declined in value to $60, as a consequence of which T receives $40 of financial assistance from Agency in Year 1. In Year 2, T sells assets with a basis of $50 for $30, recognizing a loss of $20. T has no other income or deduction in Year 2.

The deferral formula requires T to include financial assistance in income to the extent of the sum of (i) the amount by which T's liabilities exceed the adjusted bases of its assets (T's excess debt amount) plus (ii) T's current loss amount. T has no excess debt amount in either Year 1 or Year 2, because that test is applied as of the beginning of each taxable year. However, in Year 2, T does have a current loss of $20. Under the proposed regulations, this would require T to include $20 of the assistance in income. By contrast, under the final regulations, T's current loss amount is only $10 (the amount by which its $20 current loss exceeds the $10 excess of T's $100 asset basis at the beginning of Year 2 over its $90 in liabilities). Thus, under the final regulations, only $10 of the $40 of financial assistance is required to be included in T's income in Year 2, thereby permitting T to utilize a $10 net operating loss carryover or carryback from Year 2 against other taxable income of T in prior or future periods.

[41] For example, the stock of a financial institution may have been purchased at a premium over the basis of its assets, after which the institution was completely liquidated into Target in a transaction qualifying under Code § 332. *See generally* the NYSBA Section 597 Report, *supra* note 33. The basis of the subsidiary's assets in the hands of the parent financial institution would be a carryover basis

(b) *Existence of Continuing Equity.* If continuing equity is present, then the amount of income that must be included by the Target during a tax year is the sum of: (i) the excess debt amount at the beginning of the year, plus (ii) the greater of (A) the current loss amount for the Target or (B) a similar amount computed for the Target's consolidated return group (if any), plus (iii) the so-called "carryover amount," plus (iv) any additional amount required to insure that the total amount of assistance is taken into income ratably over the six taxable years immediately following the year of deferral.[42]

Under the proposed regulations, the carryover amount was defined as the amount of any NOL carryover of the Target (or, if the carryover is a consolidated return year of the Target's current consolidated return group, the NOL carryover of that group) to the tax year. This resulted in a duplication of the excess debt amount (liabilities in excess of basis) to the extent that the excess debt amount was attributable to losses incurred in prior periods.[43] To avoid this duplication, the final regulations effectively define the carryover amount as the excess of the proposed regulations' definition over the excess debt amount.[44]

(3) *Deemed Sale Treatment.* Notice 89-102 did not impose deemed sale treatment in connection with a stock acquisition, but merely expanded the availability of the elections under Code § 338(g) and 338(h)(10). By contrast, the regulations under Code § 597 deem certain events to be "taxable transfers" resulting in a deemed sale of all of the Target's assets. Under the regulations, a "taxable transfer" of the Target's assets occurs if:[45]

(a) the Target transfers to other than a Bridge Bank (i) any deposit liabilities and, in connection with the same transaction, financial assistance is pro-

---

(Footnote Continued)

under Code § 334(b), such that the stock purchase premium disappears and is not reflected in the assets received from the subsidiary. For example, suppose P, a bank with $100 in asset basis and $80 in liabilities, borrows an additional $60 and then purchases all of the stock of T for $80. T likewise has assets with a basis of $100 and liabilities of $80. Subsequently, T is liquidated under Code § 332. P's basis in the T assets under Code § 334(b) will be $100, and P will inherit T's $80 of liabilities. Thus, the combination of P's purchase of the T stock at a premium over T's $20 net asset basis and P's financing of 75% of the stock purchase price results in P having total liabilities of $220 and a total asset basis of $200 following the liquidation of T.

[42] Reg. § 1.597-2(c)(3). In addition, a Target with continuing equity must include in income the entire remaining balance of its deferred account in the tax year in which it liquidates, ceases to do business, transfers (other than to a Bridge Bank) substantially all its assets, or is deemed to transfer all its assets under Reg. § 1.597-5(b). Reg. § 1.597-2(c)(4)(iii)(B).

[43] As a result, under the proposed regulations, it would be rare that a Target with continuing equity would not have to pay some current federal income tax in connection with the receipt of financial assistance. For analysis and criticism of this result, *see* the NYSBA Section 597 Report, *supra* note 33.

[44] Reg. § 1.597-5(d)(1)(iii).

[45] Reg. §§ 1.597-5(a)(1), (b). This represents a significant expansion of the events contained in the proposed regulations.

vided,[46] or (ii) any asset for which the Agency has any financial obligation; or

(b) (i) the Target leaves its old consolidated return group, joins another group, or issues stock such that the stockholders owning the Target before the imposition of Agency control or the provision of any financial assistance own 50 percent or less in vote or value of the outstanding Target stock, and (ii) in each instance, the event occurs while the Target is under Agency control, while Target is a Bridge Bank, while Target has a positive balance in its deferred financial assistance account, or in connection with a transaction in which financial assistance is provided.

As a result, most "open bank" transactions will be treated as transactions in which the Target has sold its assets to a new entity. A side benefit is that such Targets would have no "continuing equity" and, thus, would be subject to the less harsh of the deferral-of-income formulas discussed at paragraph "2" above.

The purpose of the deemed sale provision is to end the deferral and accelerate the built-in losses to match the final income inclusion when the Target is acquired by the Acquirer, whether that acquisition is a stock or asset acquisition. Thus, in cases in which the Target is under Agency control, is receiving financial assistance (currently or on a deferred basis) or is a Bridge Bank, this provision will prevent a transaction (such as a "G" reorganization) that continues the tax attributes of the Target if a significant shift in the equity ownership of the Target occurs.[47]

(4) *Deconsolidation Election for Bridge Banks and Targets.* Similar to Notice 89-102, the regulations under Code § 597 provide that a Bridge Bank:

(a) generally will be treated as a continuation of the Target that must be treated as a corporation for federal income tax purposes;[48]

(b) will succeed to the tax attributes of the Target without being deemed to have experienced an ownership change under Code § 382;[49] and

(c) generally will be treated as a member of the Target's consolidated return group, if any.[50]

---

[46] According to the preamble, the term "in connection with" is to be broadly construed.

[47] Even if a "G" reorganization could be structured by the Acquirer, normally an ownership change will occur for purposes of Code § 382, which, due to the repeal of the special insolvent financial institution provision in old Code § 382(l)(5), would result in a zero limitation on the Target's NOLs. Thus, there is no tax incentive to structure a tax-free reorganization of a financial institution under Agency control after the enactment of FIRREA.

[48] Reg. § 1.597-4(b), (d). For an interesting ruling that applies this same concept to a pre-1989 transaction, by simply ignoring the separate status of the Bridge Bank entity, *see* IRS Technical Advice Memorandum 9623004, February 13, 1996. The IRS has issued rulings under Reg. § 1.597 holding that mutual savings associations can satisfy the definition of a Bridge Bank. IRS Legal Memorandum 199952004, July 27, 1999, *reprinted at* 2000 TNT 1-85; IRS Chief Counsel Advice 200013003, March 31, 2000, *reprinted at* 2000 TNT 64-49.

[49] Reg. §§ 1.597-4(d)(1) and 1.597-4(c).

[50] Reg. § 1.597-4(f).

To avoid the problems accompanying the inclusion of a Bridge Bank or Target under Agency control in the Target's consolidated return group, the regulations under Code § 597 provide the group with an election to deconsolidate the Target,[51] and, in certain limited cases, deem a deconsolidation election to be made (including the case in which a Bridge Bank is formed to acquire Targets owned by more than one consolidated return group).[52] However, the price payable for such deconsolidation is a "toll charge" that may be fairly onerous. This toll charge may be summarized as follows:[53]

(a) The Target must include in income its excess debt amount immediately before the deconsolidation (with certain adjustments), and all Code § 481 adjustments are accelerated.[54] In effect, the inclusion of the excess debt amount represents the amount of financial assistance that would be includable in income by the Target if the Agency were to restore the Target's solvency at the time of the deconsolidation.

(b) The members of the consolidated return group owning stock in the Target are generally treated as owning stock of a corporation that has become a nonmember, thereby triggering any excess loss accounts and any other items (such as deferred intercompany gains and losses) that trigger upon a company becoming a nonmember.[55]

(c) If the Target is insolvent (*i.e.*, its liabilities exceed the fair market value of its assets), the members of the consolidated return group owning stock in the Target are allowed a worthless stock deduction under Code § 165(g), subject to the loss disallowance rule of Reg. § 1.1502-20 (for which purpose the excess debt amount included by the Target is treated as an extraordinary

---

[51] Reg. § 1.597-4(g).

[52] *See* Reg. § 1.597-4(g)(6).

[53] *See* Reg. § § 1.597-4(g)(2), (3).

[54] In contrast, the proposed regulations had treated excess debt amount as recognized by the members of the group owning stock of the Target (rather than the Target itself). However, this would have had the result of precluding any Target losses that are subject to the SRLY rules from being available to offset such income. For this reason, as well as the discontinuity created by the new investment adjustment rules (as discussed in note 55, *infra*), the NYSBA Section 597 Report, *supra* note 33, sensibly recommended that the toll charge be treated as Target income.

[55] In contrast, the proposed regulations had treated the members as having disposed of their Target stock outside of the group. To mitigate the income attributable to any excess loss account in such stock that would result from such disposition, the excess debt amount that was includable under the proposed regulations by the owning members was treated as earnings and profits of the Target. This admirable goal ran into problems, however, when Treasury issued the new investment basis adjustment rules in Reg. § 1.1502-32(b), which "delinked" investment basis adjustments from earnings and profits. Under the new investment basis rules, stock basis adjustments reflect a consolidated subsidiary's taxable income or loss, increased by any tax-exempt income and decreased by any nondeductible, non-capital expenditures. Thus, the treatment under the proposed regulations would not have eliminated an excess loss account in the Target's stock. The final regulations, by treating the excess debt amount as *Target* income, ensure that a positive adjustment to the basis of the Target stock will occur under Reg. § 1.1502-32(b) prior to the deconsolidation such that any excess loss account in the Target stock will be reduced or eliminated.

gain disposition).[56] Thus, to the extent a loss is recognized in connection with a disposition of the Target stock or worthlessness of such stock under Code § 165(g), a substantial portion (if not all) of that loss will be disallowed.[57] As discussed at § 804.5.2 below, Reg. § 1.1502-20 was superseded for periods after March 6, 2002, by Reg. § § 1.337(d)-2T and 1.1502-35T.

(d) Finally, after the deconsolidation of a Bridge Bank or Target under Agency control, the Bridge Bank or Target will be viewed as a new corporation with no NOL carryovers but with a non-interest-bearing account receivable for assistance equal to the excess debt amount.[58]

Consistency is required with respect to the deconsolidation election; thus, in connection with an Agency's acquisition of control of two or more financial institutions that are members of the same consolidated return group, an election to deconsolidate one Target cannot be made unless the election has been made, or deemed made, with respect to every subsidiary placed in Agency receivership within the preceding five years.[59] Under the proposed regulations, the election (or nonelection) for the first subsidiary placed in receivership governed all future subsidiaries placed in receivership.[60]

(5) *Transfers of Money and Property to Agency.* Under the regulations, if an acquiring bank issues its obligation or stock to the Agency in connection with its acquisition of the Target, the instrument is disregarded and, hence, is not included in the acquiring corporation's basis in the assets of the Target. However, the acquirer may increase its basis in the Target's assets (and thereby offset or recover the basis shortfall) if and when the Agency disposes of the instrument to a person other than the Agency or a controlled entity, with the increase being equal to the amount of cash and fair market value of other property received by the Agency in exchange for the instrument.[61]

(6) *Assets Protected Against Loss.* Unlike Notice 89-102, the regulations under Code § 597 provide that the Target must be treated for federal income tax purposes as the owner of any assets subject to an Agency guarantee or otherwise protected

---

[56] Reg. § § 1.597-4(g)(2)(v) and 1.597-3(e). Because Reg. § 1.597-4(f)(3) provides that the regulations under Code § 597 take precedence over conflicting provisions of the consolidated return regulations, this rule regarding the worthlessness of Target stock held by owning members preempts the consolidated return test for worthlessness in Reg. § 1.1502-80(d). In addition, the preamble states that this rule also preempts the applicable worthlessness tests under Code § 165.

[57] In IRS Letter Ruling 9712018, December 19, 1996, the IRS granted Code § 9100 relief to a taxpayer who wanted to reattribute to itself losses of its insolvent bank subsidiary so as not to lose the deduction for worthless stock allowed by Reg. § 1.597-4(g) upon a deconsolidation election. Although taxpayer had failed to make the required election under Reg. § 1.1502-20(g)(5), Code § 9100 relief was granted to parent to make this election.

[58] Reg. § 1.597-4(g)(4).

[59] Reg. § 1.597-4(g)(5)(i)(B).

[60] Reg. § 1.597-4(g)(2(ii).

[61] *See* Reg. § 1.597-5(d)(1)(iii). This increase was not permitted under the proposed regulations. As a result, under the proposed regulations, the basis shortfall would have resulted in ordinary income to the acquirer required to be included ratably over six years.

against loss by the Agency, even if the Agency would otherwise be treated as the owner of such assets under general income tax principles.[62]

(7) *Forgiveness of Tax Liability.* The regulations under Code § 597 generally provide that, in the case of an institution without continuing equity, the IRS will not collect any federal income tax attributable to financial assistance or an actual or deemed sale of the institution's assets while under Agency control if the tax would be borne by the Agency.[63] The determination of whether the tax would be borne by the Agency is within the sole discretion of the IRS.[64] In addition, the following rules apply:

(a) Any federal income tax payable by a Target with continuing equity must always be collected. However, in most "open bank" transactions in which the Agency has determined that banking policies are better served by keeping the Target's doors open for business, the regulations treat the transaction as a taxable sale of assets (*see* paragraph "3" above), thereby accelerating loss to match the inclusion of financial assistance income and generally dispensing with the need for the deferral of tax collection in such transactions.[65]

(b) The regulations under Code § 597 will not impede the collection of a consolidated return group's several liability for federal income tax;[66] thus, even if the IRS determines not to attempt to collect federal income tax from the Target, it will not be prohibited from collecting the tax from other members of the Target's consolidated return group.[67]

(c) Any federal income tax the IRS has refrained from collecting under these rules nonetheless must continue to be assessed and used to offset potential refunds of federal income tax in future or past periods.[68]

(d) Finally, the IRS must not assert transferee liability for any federal income tax attributable to the financial assistance (or to any deemed or actual asset sale) against the Acquirer, unless, in the case of a deemed taxable asset transfer resulting from a change in the ownership of Target stock, either (i)

---

[62] Reg. § 1.597-3(a).

[63] Reg. § 1.597-6(a).

[64] Id. In this connection, the IRS is directed to disregard any tax sharing, indemnity or other similar obligations imposed on the Agency or any other member of the Target's consolidated return group.

[65] *See generally* the NYSBA Section 597 Report, note 33, *supra,* in which the point was made that, because the deferral rules applicable to Targets with continuing equity frequently do not properly match income and deductions, some delay in collection of the tax imposed upon such institutions may be appropriate; however, the Treasury rejected this criticism. In the Treasury's view, to permit noncollection from a Target *with* continuing equity would contravene an essential policy of FIRREA; namely, to remove any income tax subsidy for assisted transactions in which all other creditors and stockholders retain their rights.

[66] Reg. § 1.1502-6(a) generally provides that each member of a consolidated return group is severally liable for all of the federal income tax due for each consolidated return year during which it is a member.

[67] Reg. § 1.597-6(a).

[68] Reg. § 1.597-6(d).

shares of the old Target remain outstanding or (ii) consideration is paid for those shares.[69]

(8) *Effective Date.* The regulations generally apply to taxable years ending on or after April 22, 1992, and do not apply to financial assistance received or accrued in connection with an Agency-assisted acquisition occurring before April 22, 1992.[70] An irrevocable election is available to apply the final regulations (in lieu of Notice 89-102) to prior taxable years unless either (i) a Code § 338 election was available but not made for the Target, or (ii) the statute of limitations has expired.[71] The final regulations also permit a taxpayer to rely on the proposed regulations to the extent the taxpayer acted in reliance on the proposed regulations prior to December 21, 1995, and provided such reliance is reasonable and consistent with the policies of Code § 597.[72]

## *§ 608.4 Other Conversions of Thrift Institutions*

Prior to FIRREA, a serious practical impediment to the use of the liberalized "G" reorganization provisions for savings institutions was the requirement, mentioned at § 608.1, for a certification from the Federal Home Loan Bank Board or similar authority that the institution is essentially a failing institution.[73] Announcement of any such certification to the public before the institution has consummated the additional financing or merger that solves its problems could create a depositor's run on the institution. As a result, a "G" reorganization generally was not used unless the financing or the merger could have been completed without the need for advance disclosure to and approval from the depositors of the failing institution.

Prior to FIRREA, a popular method for revitalizing a struggling savings institution, without use of the "G" reorganization device, was the conversion of a mutual association into a stock association, followed by sale of the stock to investors that raises new capital for the institution. Indeed, conversion of a mutual into a stock association may be a viable option after the enactment of FIRREA, provided the conversion is completed before the institution is placed under Agency control.

---

[69] Reg. § 1.597-6(e) (this differs slightly from the proposed regulations). This could present problems in those cases in which a holding company has filed suit against the Agency for its assumption of control over a subsidiary financial institution and actually recovers damages from the Agency. The recovery likely will occur long after the date of the taxable transfer and may be treated under the origin of the claim doctrine as consideration for the Target's stock. In that case, the new owner of the Target may find the Target has transferee liability under the final regulations for the old Target's income tax attributable to financial assistance, even though the acquisition may otherwise have been structured to avoid such liability.

[70] Reg. § 1.597-7(b).

[71] Reg. § 1.597-7(c). The proposed regulations required taxpayers making this election to extend the statute of limitations for all items for three years from the date of filing the election. The final regulations require such an extension only for items affected by the regulations.

[72] Reg. § 1.597-7(d)(2).

[73] Effective for acquisitions on or after May 10, 1989, FIRREA amended Code § 368(a)(3)(D) to eliminate the requirement for Agency certification of insolvency in the case of a thrift.

Sometimes the stock sold to investors is stock of the converted stock association itself. Sometimes it is stock of a parent holding company. The IRS established a rulings pattern for transactions of this kind in Rev. Rul. 80-105.[74]

In the case described in Rev. Rul. 80-105, the assets and liabilities of the mutual institution were transferred to a new stock institution. As mentioned in the preceding section, the interest of a depositor in a mutual savings institution is a dual interest representing a deposit claim plus an equity interest in the form of a right to surplus upon liquidation of the institution. In the ruling, the depositors received deposit claims in the new institution identical to those they had in the old institution, plus an interest in a "liquidation account" established by the new institution. The "liquidation account" was designed to represent a continuation of the equity interest the depositors had in the old mutual association and was an amount equal to the net worth of the mutual association at the time of the conversion. The old depositors would have the right to receive this amount upon liquidation of the new institution before any liquidation distribution could be made on its stock. A depositor who ceased being a depositor before the new institution was liquidated would lose his interest in the account.

The stock of the new institution was to be issued pursuant to nontransferable subscription rights. These rights were to be offered first to those who were depositors in the mutual institution. To the extent they did not subscribe, the rights would be offered successively to borrowers from the institution, to employees, and then to the public. The ruling held that the conversion constituted an "F" reorganization. The issuance of stock to new investors was treated as a separate transaction. Private rulings following this pattern have held that old Code § 382(b) would not apply to the conversion, citing Reg. § 1.381(b)-1(a)(2), which says that, in the case of an "F" reorganization, "the tax attributes of the transferor corporation enumerated in section 381(c) shall be taken into account by the acquiring corporation as if there had been no reorganization."[75]

Establishment by the new stock company of a liquidation account for the depositors of the old mutual association was necessary to provide continuity of equity interest.[76] Until 1985, the IRS insisted that the issuance of subscription rights for the stock of the new company to the depositors of the old mutual company was also a necessity for establishing continuity and obtaining a ruling. This was a curious position because it is well established that warrants are not stock and do not provide continuity as a general matter. The IRS had even ruled that if the rights were for stock in the successor stock corporation, the issuance of the rights was governed by Code § 307, but if the rights were for stock in a holding company, they constituted boot.[77] In

---

[74] 1980-1 C.B. 79.

[75] *See, e.g.*, IRS Letter Ruling 8539078, July 3, 1985; IRS Letter Ruling 8448032, August 27, 1984; IRS Letter Ruling 8447042, August 20, 1984; IRS Letter Ruling 8438035, June 19, 1984; IRS Letter Ruling 8407063, November 16, 1983.

[76] As mentioned in note 5, *supra*, such liquidation accounts are not treated as stock of the new company for consolidated return purposes or for purposes of determining whether a subsequent acquisition of the new company is a tax-free reorganization.

[77] *See, e.g.*, IRS Letter Ruling 8509083, December 5, 1984.

1985, however, the IRS finally issued a favorable ruling in a case that did not involve the issuance of subscription rights to the old depositors.[78]

The IRS has subsequently issued several rulings applying the "F" reorganization concept to the conversion of a mutual association into a stock association, which then becomes a subsidiary of a new mutual association holding company whose mutual interests are issued to the old depositors. Although the corporate mechanics in these rulings are somewhat complicated, the transactions have been treated as though the mutual association was converted into a stock association, with the stock being issued to the old mutual association depositors; and then as though this stock was dropped into a new mutual holding company whose mutual ownership interests were issued in exchange for that stock. These steps were treated as an "F" reorganization plus a Code § 351 drop-down. The rulings hold that the receipt of the stock interest for the old mutual interest, and the later exchange of the stock interest for the new holding company mutual interest would satisfy the continuity-of-interest doctrine; and that the holding company mutual interest would be treated as stock for purposes of Code § 351.[79]

In transactions patterned on Rev. Rul. 80-105, the IRS required a representation to the effect that the fair market value of the assets of the mutual savings institution, on a going concern basis, will exceed the amount of its liabilities at the time of the conversion. In most of these cases, the mortgage portfolio of the savings institution will have a sales value substantially less than the amount of the deposit liabilities, although conventional bank accounting will reflect the mortgage portfolio at face value rather than market value for balance sheet purposes. In such cases, it may often be the off-balance sheet going-concern value of the institution which allows it to make the representation. The fact that investors are willing to purchase stock in the converted institution confirms the validity of the representation.

The corporate law mechanics for converting a mutual institution into a stock institution are governed by the applicable federal or state law. Some of these laws will make clear that the stock company is an entirely new corporation, in which case it would seem likely that the conversion involves a two-company transaction. However, other laws may be equally clear in indicating that no new corporate entity is created, and that only an amendment of the corporate charter of the mutual institution takes place. In such a case, it may well be that a two-company transaction is not involved at all.[80] The one-company conversion arguably qualifies as an "E" recapitali-

---

[78] *See, e.g.*, IRS Letter Ruling 8535051, June 4, 1985.

[79] IRS Letter Ruling 9741020, July 10, 1997; IRS Letter Ruling 9741011, July 9, 1997 (the fact that in this ruling the new stock savings institution simultaneously made a public offering for some of its stock did not change these results); IRS Letter Ruling 9712016, December 19, 1996; IRS Letter Ruling 200051006, September 8, 2000.

[80] For other instances where a conversion was found to be a one-company transaction, *see* Rev. Rul. 79-150, 1979-1 C.B. 149 (conversion of a Brazilian public company S.A. to a limited private company involves a Code § 1036 exchange of stock for stock of the same corporation and was a one-company transaction as well as an "F"); Rev. Rul. 72-420, 1972-1 C.B. 473 (conversion of an Antilles N.V. into a Dutch B.V. involves a Code § 1036 exchange and was a one-company transaction as well as an "F"); *see also* Rev. Rul. 54-269, 1954-2 C.B. 114 (Connecticut special act corporation surrendered its charter and received new charter under general corporation law but was held to be the same corporation).

zation, in which case one need not worry about the continuity-of-interest test because it does not apply to "E" reorganizations.[81] However, the IRS before 2004 refused to issue rulings in such instances except on an "F" reorganization basis, which before 2004 did require satisfying the continuity-of-interest test.[82] On August 12, 2004, the IRS issued Prop. Reg. § 1.368-1(b) which holds that neither the continuity-of-business nor the continuity-of-interest requirements apply to either "E" or "F" reorganizations for Code § 368 purposes. These proposed regulations were made final in 2005, effective for transactions occurring on or after February 25, 2005.[83]

Where the conversion of a mutual institution into a stock institution is accomplished as an "F" (but not as an "E") reorganization, it will be governed for new Code § 382 purposes by the owner shift rather than the equity structure change rules. Because the depositors holding liquidation accounts would generally be treated as shareholders, the conversion itself would not produce an ownership change.[84] Before 1989, the subsequent public offering of stock by the stock institution would not produce an ownership change either, if all the stock (including deposits treated as stock) was owned by less than 5-percent holders. (This might not be true, however, if the public offering was done by a firm commitment underwriting; *see* § 508.2.1 above.) The Treasury regulations issued to treat public offerings as equity structure shifts and to treat the less-than-5-percent purchasers in the public offering as a

---

[81] *See, e.g.*, Rev. Rul. 82-34, 1982-1 C.B. 59 (continuity of interest and business enterprise not required in an "E" recapitalization); Rev. Rul. 77-479, 1977-2 C.B. 119; *Commissioner v. Neudstadt's Trust*, 131 F.2d 528, 42-2 U.S.T.C. ¶ 9751, (2d Cir. 1942). These two rulings were declared obsolete as of February 25, 2005, when the Treasury incorporated this rule in its amended Reg. § 1.368-1(b).

[82] The reason for this is to be found in GCM 35292, April 3, 1973, which underlay Rev. Rul. 73-510, 1973-2 C.B. 387 (conversion of mutual insurance company into stock insurance company was a two-company "F"). The GCM stated that the one-company conversion actually involved in the case might have been a sufficient change to be tantamount to the creation of a new company. The General Counsel required the published ruling to state as a fact that a two-company transaction was involved, however, in order to make it more clear why the "F" characterization applied. The IRS now apparently considers most conversions of domestic companies to be tantamount to a two-company transaction.

In IRS Letter Ruling 9207028, November 19, 1991, the IRS ruled that a conversion of a mutual savings bank into a stock savings bank, as an interim step leading to a taxable sale of all of the stock of the stock savings bank to a bank holding company, constituted an "E" recapitalization. The mechanics of the conversion are not clearly described in the body of the private letter ruling. Thus, it cannot be determined whether the conversion was accomplished via a transfer of all of the assets of the mutual savings bank to a new stock bank constituting a separate corporation. Accordingly, it cannot be determined whether this ruling indicates a more lenient IRS view on the question of whether such conversions constitute two-company "F" reorganizations or one-company "E" recapitalizations.

However, the more lenient view can be found in IRS Letter Ruling 200544006, July 28, 2005, which held that a conversion of a mutual life insurance company into a stock company was both an "E" and an "F" reorganization.

[83] A related Prop. Reg. § 1.368-2 continues to be studied by the IRS. For comments regarding certain problems and recommendations for changes in the proposed regulation, *see* comment letter to the IRS from KPMG LLP, *reprinted at* 2005 TNT 42-53, March 4, 2005.

[84] Act Conference Report, H. R. Rep. No. 841, 99th Cong., 2d. Sess. 11-844 at 11-193 (1986).

separate 5-percent shareholder do not apply to thrift institutions before 1989.[85] For 1989 and after, however, public offerings by all stock institutions will be subject to the "segregation" rules of the Code § 382 regulations, which generally treat the less-than-5 percent purchasers as a single 5-percent shareholder for purposes of determining whether an ownership change occurs. Regulations proposed in 1992 would, however, provide certain exceptions to the segregation rules. *See* § 508.2.8.2, above.

Should the conversion of a mutual institution into a stock institution be treated as an "E" reorganization, a problem could result under new Code § 382. The "E" would be an equity structure shift, and if regulations were issued that aggregated those participating in the "E" as a separate 5-percent shareholder (and did not exempt thrifts until 1989), then the less-than-5-percent holders in the old depositor group would become a separate 5-percent holder, and the less-than-5-percent purchasers in the public offering would become another separate 5-percent holder. If this public offering involved more than 50 percent of the value of the stock an ownership change would result. If regulations are issued treating one-company reorganizations as being subject to the new Code § 382 aggregation rules, they should, like the public offering regulations, exempt thrifts until 1989.

## § 609 SPECIAL REPORTING OBLIGATION

For the special reporting obligation that may apply to certain reorganization transactions, *see* § § 407 and 512 above.

The American Jobs Creation Act of 2004 added Code § 6043A which, to the extent provided in Treasury forms or regulations, provides for information reporting by the acquiring corporation in any taxable acquisition of stock in or assets of another corporation, if any shareholder of the target corporation is required to recognize gain.

---

[85] *See* id. at II-194, apparently referring to all thrift institutions. Temp. Reg. § 1.382-2T(m)(6) implemented this for domestic building and loan associations. TAMRA at § 1006(d)(15) contains a similar provision, but applies it to all thrift institutions described in Code § 591.

# 7

# Utilizing Tax Losses



## §701 INTRODUCTION

By the time the failing company has scaled back its unsuccessful operations to the point where they can sustain themselves profitably, the company—at least for debt restructurings to which the stock-for-debt exception to COD income still applied—will typically have generated far more NOLs and ITC carryovers than it can use in its scaled down activities. This is less likely to be the case for debt restructurings to which the 1993 repeal of the stock-for-debt exception to COD income applies, but even in such cases this situation may still arise. These tax benefits are valuable assets of the failing company. As we have discussed in the prior chapters, the workout plan for the company should be designed to preserve and use these tax benefits. Beyond this, the workout plan for the company should include a program for using these benefits. The liberal 15-year carryover rules (extended by the 1997 Act to 20 years for NOLs arising in years beginning after August 5, 1997) give the failing company plenty of time to use these benefits. However, because of the time value of money, the benefits will be more valuable the faster they are used.

If, as is typically the case, the remaining activities of the failing company will not utilize these tax benefits very rapidly or in full, management must consider how best to utilize these benefits.

Traditionally, the primary focus has been on considering acquisitions that will permit other profitable businesses to combine with the failing company's scaled down activities and tax benefits. Various forms can be used for such a combination of profitable businesses with the failing company, all having the goal of using the NOLs and other tax benefits of the failing company against the future income and gains of the profitable business.[1] In accomplishing these transactions, one needs to use care to structure them in the way that offers the best opportunity for preserving as much as possible of the NOLs and other tax benefits of the failing company. One might use a variety of approaches to reach this goal, including purchasing of assets of a profitable business, purchasing stock of a profitable business, combining with a profitable business in a tax-free reorganization, combining with a profitable business in a Code § 351 transaction, or investing in a profitable business through a partnership. These approaches are discussed in § § 702 through 706 below.

However, over the years, the ability in these transactions to preserve the failing company's tax benefits for future use has been progressively diminished. This has come about through changes such as the adoption of new Code § 382; the elimination of the stock-for-debt exception to COD income; the adoption of Code § 384, to eliminate the use of the failing company's NOLs and other tax benefits against the built-in gains of a profitable company that it combines with; and the adoption of Reg. § 1.1502-28, which causes the excluded COD income of a consolidated group member to reduce the NOLs and other tax benefits, not just of that member, but also of other members of the group. These changes can cause the combined enterprise to lose many of the tax benefits of the failing company, including basis in the failing company's assets because of basis reductions (often to less than fair market value) resulting from excluded COD income. As a result, failing companies have more frequently than in the past explored the question of utilizing their tax benefits, not by making combinations with profitable businesses in an effort to preserve these benefits for future use against the future income of the profitable business, but instead by making taxable sales of their assets, thereby currently using their tax benefits to offset the amount realized from such sales and preserving for the purchaser a fair market value basis for the assets acquired (and perhaps even a Code § 197 amortization deduction for goodwill and similar intangibles acquired in the purchase). In accomplishing such transactions, one needs to take care to structure them in a way to avoid their being characterized as tax-free transactions, or as coming under the consolidated return and/or common-control regulations. Such taxable transactions, often now referred to informally as "Bruno's" transactions (because they were successfully employed in the *Bruno's* bankruptcy) are discussed at § 709 below.

A word should be said about the extent to which the failing company can obtain certainty about the amount of its NOLs and other carryovers that will survive into future years. Although the debtor may be able to obtain an IRS ruling on the consequences of certain transactions involved in its restructuring, such a ruling will not extend beyond the effect of these transactions to determine the amount of the

---

[1] **§ 701** For a general discussion of particular acquisition transactions which provide certain tax advantages, *see* Joint Committee on Taxation, Federal Income Tax Aspects of Mergers and Acquisitions 17-24 (JCS-6-85) (March 29, 1985); *see also* Nicholls, Net Operating Loss and Section 382, 22 Tax Notes 609, 614-617 (Feb. 13, 1984); Bowen & Sheffield, Section 269 Revisited, 61 Taxes 881 (1983); Thompson, Planning for the Loss Corporation: The Interaction Among Code Section 269, 381, Old and New Sections 382 and the Consolidated Return Regulations, 31 Major Tax Plan. 223, 280-294 (1979).

company's NOLs and other carryovers. Nor will an audit for a year from which the company claims carryovers do any more than determine the tax liability for that earlier year; it will not bar the IRS (or the taxpayer) from later—even after the statute of limitations for the loss year has run—recomputing the amount of those carryovers (absent a closing agreement to the contrary). The statute of limitations that governs an NOL or other carry forward is the statute for the year to which the benefit is carried forward, rather than the earlier year in which it was incurred.[2] Thus, when a taxpayer seeks to apply in a current year an NOL that was incurred ten years earlier, neither the taxpayer nor the IRS generally are barred from seeking to recompute the amount of that NOL.

## §702 PURCHASING ASSETS OF A PROFITABLE BUSINESS

A direct taxable purchase of the assets of a profitable business by a loss company is the classic way for a loss company to acquire a profitable business since Code §269 cannot apply to the transaction. Nor does Code §384 apply. Moreover, because the assets of the profitable business are combined in the same corporation with the operations of the loss company itself, the separate-return-limitation-year (SRLY), consolidated-return-change-in-ownership (CRCO) and "reverse acquisition" limitations in the consolidated return regulations on the use of NOLs will not apply.

Code §269 applies wherever (1) control of a corporation (meaning 50 percent of the voting power or value of the stock) is acquired or (2) assets of a corporation not controlled by the acquirer are acquired with a carryover basis, but in either case only if the principal purpose of the acquisition is to make use of a tax benefit.[1] Where the loss company purchases the assets of a profitable business for cash or notes, no change in control of any company is involved nor are assets acquired in a tax-free carryover basis transaction. Thus, Code §269 will not apply to the transaction, without the need for the taxpayer to prove that tax avoidance was not the principal motivation for the transaction.

Of course, if stock constituting at least 50 percent of the voting power or value of the loss company (in addition to cash or notes) were issued in the asset purchase transaction, the control portion of the Code §269 test would be met (and Code §382 would also have to be considered). If, however, the seller of the assets already owned stock of the loss company, the control test would be satisfied by an issuance of stock amounting to less than 50 percent of the voting power or value of the loss company. Moreover, if the notes issued in the transaction were payable over a long period of time and the purchase price exceeded the fair market value of the assets or stock acquired, the IRS reserves the right to assert that Code §269 applies.[2]

---

[2] Rev. Rul. 56-285, 1956-1 C.B. 134; Rev. Rul. 81-88, 1981-1 C.B. 85; IRS Letter Ruling 9504032, Oct. 31, 1994. Of course, a different rule applies where an NOL or other benefit is being carried back, rather than being carried forward. In the carryback case, it is the statute of limitations for the later year in which the loss or other benefit arose, not the earlier year to which it is carried, that governs.

[1] **§702** Code §269(a).

[2] *See* Rev. Rul. 63-40, 1963-1 C.B. 46.

## §703 PURCHASING STOCK OF A PROFITABLE BUSINESS

Sellers of companies usually prefer to sell stock rather than assets. The IRS determined in Rev. Rul. 63-40[1] that where the loss company first attempts to buy assets, but is forced to buy stock, the transaction will be treated as a direct taxable purchase of assets (to which Code §269 would not apply) if the profitable company is immediately liquidated into the loss company. This ruling, however, was based on the law as it existed before the adoption of Code §338 (*see* §707). Under the law in effect at the time of the ruling, the immediate liquidation of the profitable company caused the transaction to be governed by old Code §334(b)(2), with the result that the acquiring company obtained a new basis in the assets of the target company just as if it had purchased assets. On the other hand, under Code §338, the liquidation of the target company will be a tax-free transaction, giving the acquiring company a carryover basis in the assets of the target company, unless the acquiring company makes a Code §338 election for the target company.

If a Code §338 election is made, the approach taken in Rev. Rul. 63-40 should apply: the transaction has the same consequences as if there had been a taxable purchase of assets. The result should be the same even if the target is not liquidated.

On the other hand, if a Code §338 election for the target is not made, the liquidation of the target does not produce the same tax consequences as a taxable purchase of assets. Thus, the holding of Rev. Rul. 63-40 (that Code §269 does not apply) would not seem apposite. The transaction should be treated as an acquisition of stock that comes within the scope of Code §269, but Code §269 should not apply if the principal purpose of the stock acquisition was not tax avoidance. Moreover, a private ruling issued by the IRS indicates that if the purpose of the stock acquisition was not tax avoidance: (1) the subsequent liquidation of the profitable company need not satisfy its own separate tax avoidance test; and (2) Code §269(b) will not apply to the liquidation of the profitable company into the loss company, provided there has been "little or no" change in ownership of the loss company.[2] To the extent the

---

[1] **§703** Id.

[2] IRS Letter Ruling 8648038 (August 29, 1986). The ruling focuses primarily on Code §269(b), as added by the Tax Reform Act of 1984, which provides that if a corporation (1) acquires at least 80 percent of the stock of a target corporation, (2) does not make a Code §338 election, and (3) liquidates the target corporation within two years for the primary purpose of utilizing losses or credits "which the acquiring corporation would not otherwise enjoy," the IRS may disallow the use of such losses or credits. The Conference Report to the 1984 Act stated that this provision was not intended to affect the NOLs or credits of a purchasing loss corporation that acquires a profitable target corporation that it liquidates within two years, where the transaction results in "no change in ownership" of the purchasing loss corporation. H.R. Rep. No. 861, 98th Cong., 2d Sess. 1222 (1984). The IRS held that Congress did not mean literally "no change," but instead "little or no change," a concept that comes from Rev. Rul. 63-40. In the case considered in the letter ruling, the purchasing loss company had issued less than 3.2 percent of its stock (plus cash and notes) in the taxable acquisition of the profit company.

There is no indication in the ruling whether the purchasing loss company and the profitable target company filed consolidated returns, or whether, if they did, the NOLs of the purchasing company were subject to the SRLY limitations. If a consolidated return was not being filed, or if the SRLY limitations applied, the liquidation would have been the only way the purchasing company's NOLs could have been used against the income of the target. The failure of the ruling to mention

liquidation would allow the acquiring loss company to utilize built-in gains of the profitable target company (rather than just the profits it earns after the purchase), however, the issue becomes academic for acquisitions made after December 15, 1987, because Code § 384, adopted by the Revenue Act of 1987, would prevent the NOLs and built-in losses of the acquiring company or its affiliates from being used for five years against such built-in gains. *See* § 708 below.

When the profitable company is not liquidated into the loss company and no Code § 338 election is made, the transaction will come within the scope of Code § 269 (and Code § 384, if 80 percent control has been acquired) because the loss company will have acquired control of the profitable company. As a result, the loss company will need to be able to carry the burden of showing that the principal purpose for the acquisition and any subsequent liquidation was not to make use of its tax losses, but rather to obtain the economic profits from the profitable business.[3]

Tax avoidance is the "principal purpose" of the transaction within the meaning of Code § 269 only if it is the single most important among many purposes.[4] Where the loss company pays no more than a fair price for the profitable business, the acquisition in most cases should satisfy the nontax avoidance test. The economic benefits from the purchase of the profitable business would be the dominant reason for the acquisition, and the ability to utilize the losses of the loss company would constitute a secondary benefit. The parties should, of course, avoid making any statements that would suggest that utilization of the losses is the primary benefit to be obtained from the transaction. Because it is far better not to have to rely on satisfying the subjective motivation test, however, the loss company should prefer to make an asset acquisition rather than a stock acquisition.[5]

---

(Footnote Continued)

these matters may suggest that the IRS reads the legislative history of Code § 269(b) as indicating they are irrelevant. This seems appropriate; if one assumes that the acquisition of the stock of the profitable target was not principally tax motivated, the subsequent liquidation of the target would not be covered by Code § 269(a) because of the common control exception, and thus would not be covered by Code § 269 at all if it does not fall within the provisions of Code § 269(b). *See* Reg. § 1.269-3(c)(2); B. Bittker & E. Eustice, Federal Income Taxation of Corporations and Shareholders ¶ 14.41[3][e](7th ed.).

[3] Code § 269(a)(1) and (b).

[4] *See* Reg. § 1.269-3(a); *Canaveral Int'l Corp. v. Commissioner*, 61 T.C. 520, 536, Dec. 32,432 (1974). In *U.S. Shelter Corp. v. United States*, 87-2 U.S.T.C. ¶ 9588 (Cl. Ct. 1987), the court held that where several nontax motivations existed, no single one of which was more important than the tax motivation, but the aggregate of which did exceed the tax motivations, the proper application of the test is to compare the aggregate of the tax motivations with the aggregate of the nontax motivations.

[5] *See Vulcan Materials Co. v. United States*, 446 F.2d 690, 71-1 U.S.T.C. ¶ 9449 (5th Cir. 1971), *cert. denied*, 404 U.S. 942 (1971). In this case, although the loss company acquired the profitable company by way of merger and the case was a carryover basis asset acquisition, the court treated it as an acquisition of control of the profitable company by the loss company. Because the record was devoid of any evidence of motivation other than a statement by the acquiring company to the effect that the acquisition would allow the losses of the loss company to shelter the income of the profitable company, the court found the principal purpose of the transaction to be tax avoidance. The court went out of its way to suggest, however, that the result would have gone the other way had there been evidence of business motivation as the primary purpose.

In *Briarcliff Candy Corp.*, 54 T.C.M. 667, Dec. 44.222(M), T.C. Memo. 1987-487, a loss company purchased all of the common stock of a profitable company. The taxpayer requested summary

Where the loss company purchases the stock of the profitable company and does not liquidate the profitable company, the ability to shelter the income of the profitable company with the NOLs of the loss company will depend on the consolidated return regulations. The SRLY limitations will not prevent the NOLs of the loss company from sheltering income of the newly acquired profitable company if (1) the loss company is the common parent of the consolidated return group, and the NOLs were generated by the common parent and not by a predecessor of the common parent, or (2) the NOLs were generated by the loss company while it was a member of the same consolidated return group that continues after the acquisition of the profitable company.[6] To achieve this result, however, there must not have been a CRCO[7] or a reverse acquisition,[8] or a Code § 382 event[9] that reduces the NOLs.[10]

## § 704 ACQUISITIONS THROUGH TAX-FREE REORGANIZATIONS

The last chapter discussed the possibility of combining a profitable business with the loss business through a tax-free reorganization.[1] We pointed out at § 603 that the reorganization could take the form of either a "Reorg. Out" or a "Reorg. In." In either event, assuming that the reorganization takes the form of an asset acquisition, Code § 269 will apply to the transaction because it will involve the acquisition of assets with a carryover basis. Thus, the parties will bear the burden of showing that tax avoidance was not the principal purpose of the acquisition. In addition, the taxpayers must surmount the hurdles of Code § 382 (*see* § 508) and the consolidated return SRLY, CRCO and reverse acquisition rules (*see* § § 509, 804); and Code § 384 will prevent the NOLs and net built-in losses of the loss company or its affiliates from being used against any net built-in gains of the profitable company (*see* § 708 below).

---

(Footnote Continued)

judgment, arguing, on the basis of Rev. Rul. 63-40, 1963-1 C.B. 46, that Code § 269 does not apply in such circumstances if there is no significant change in the ownership of the acquiring loss company. The court, correctly pointing out that the taxpayer's reliance on Rev. Rul. 63-40 in this context was misplaced, denied the motion.

In *U.S. Shelter Corp. v. United States*, 87-2 U.S.T.C. ¶ 9588 (Cl. Ct. 1987), the court found that the acquisition by a profitable company of a much smaller loss company in a tax-free "D" reorganization was motivated more by nontax than by tax considerations. Factors influencing the court were (1) an acquisition program that included more nonloss than loss companies, (2) the loss company was not a shell, (3) the business of the loss company was continued for at least two years, and (4) efforts were made to make the loss business profitable. The court rejected the government's argument that the magnitude of the NOLs (in this case $3.4 million) relative to the other assets of the loss company (gross assets $17 million, net assets $1.7 million) should compel a finding of primary tax avoidance.

[6] *See* Reg. § § 1.1502-1(f)(1) and (2), and -21(c).

[7] *See* Reg. § § 1.1502-1(g) and -22(d).

[8] *See* Reg. § § 1.1502-1(f)(3) and (g)(4), and -75(d)(3).

[9] *See* Reg. § 1.1502-22(e).

[10] *See* discussions at § § 507 and 508.

[1] **§ 704** *See* Chapter 6.

## §705 BUSINESS COMBINATIONS UNDER CODE §351

Another possible mechanism for combining a profitable business with the loss business on a tax-free basis is the use of Code §351.

### EXAMPLE

Failing company has generated substantial NOLs and ITC carryovers, which it will not be able to utilize for a long time, if ever, against the income of its scaled down business. Profitable company operates a number of successful businesses in division form. Profitable company contributes one of these successful divisions to the failing company in exchange for stock of the failing company representing 80% of the voting power and 80% of each class of nonvoting stock of the failing company.

The transaction described in this example would constitute a tax-free Code §351 contribution of assets by the profitable company to the loss company in exchange for stock of the loss company representing control of the loss company as defined in Code §368(c)(1), provided the taxpayers can show that there is a valid business purpose for the contribution and not just a desire to save taxes.[1]

Because the assets received by the loss company will have a carryover basis and also because control will have been acquired, Code §269 will apply to the transaction just as it applies to combinations accomplished through tax-free reorganization, that is, the parties will have to satisfy the requirement that tax avoidance was not the principal purpose of the transaction.[2] Because the assets of the profitable business will have become part of the loss company itself, however, the SRLY and other limitations in the consolidated return regulations will not limit the ability of the loss company to utilize its losses against the income of the profitable business. Assuming that the transaction does not also qualify as a tax-free reorganization under Code §368,[3] the limitations of old Code §382(b) will not apply to the transaction. Nor will the loss company stock acquired by the profitable company be treated as having been "purchased" for purposes of old Code §382(a), except perhaps to the extent that the

---

[1] **§705** *See* Code §351(a). Beginning in the late 1990's, the IRS has become much more aggressive in seeking to disallow Code §351 treatment based on an alleged lack of business purpose. *See generally*, Leeds, The IRS Expands Business Purpose Requirement for Transfers to Corporations, 29 J. Corp. Tax'n 3 (2002); IRS Field Service Advice 200135001, July 16, 1999, *reprinted at* 2001 TNT 171-13; IRS Field Service Advice 200125007, March 9, 2001, *reprinted at* 2001 TNT 122-26. As the latter two rulings show, where built-in gain property is transferred, the IRS may also seek to apply Code §482 to reallocate the income back to the transferor.

[2] *See* Code §269(a).

[3] *See* Reg. §1.382-1A(e)(1). It should be noted that if the profitable company distributed the stock received from the loss company in a Code §354 transaction, and if the assets transferred to the loss company represented substantially all of the assets of the profitable company and the other requirements of a "G" reorganization were met, the transaction would constitute a "G" reorganization rather than a Code §351 transaction if the loss company was in bankruptcy. *See* Code §368(a)(3)(C).

property contributed by the profitable company consisted of cash or cash equivalents.[4] Under new Code § 382, however, the stock issued in the Code § 351 transaction will constitute an owner shift, with the result that the new Code § 382 loss limitations may come into play. In addition, although Code § 384 does not automatically apply (as it does in certain reorganization transactions) to prevent the NOLs and net built-in losses of the acquiring loss company or its affiliates from being used against any net built-in gains acquired in a Code § 351 transaction (unless it is also a reorganization), Code § 384(f) gives the IRS authority to issue regulations that could make Code § 384 apply to such a transaction. In addition, the concept of a predecessor/successor in Code § 384(c)(7) is undefined (although such concept traditionally would be thought to be limited to Code § 381(a) transactions, in the absence of regulations[5]). Where property with built-in gain is acquired, the IRS may also seek to apply Code § 482.[6]

## § 706 INVESTMENT IN BUSINESS PARTNERSHIP

Another way for the loss company to acquire a portion of a profitable business has been to participate in a partnership that purchases the profitable business.[1]

**EXAMPLE**

Promoters desire to do a leveraged buyout of the assets of a profitable company. They form a limited partnership, which purchases the assets of the profitable company. The general partner is a corporation owned by the promoters. The limited partner is a company having NOLs. The limited partnership is expected to generate taxable income. For an initial period of time, profits are allocated at the rate of 10% to the corporate general partner and 90% to the loss company. Cash is not distributed currently to the loss company. Instead it is used to pay down debt. The profits allocated to the loss company build up its capital account. After a period of time, the profit-sharing ratio flips so that 90% of the profits are allocated to the general partner and 10% to the loss company. Following the flip, the loss company receives interest on its capital account, and has its capital account paid out over an extended period of time, such as 20 years.

---

[4] *See* Reg. § 1.382-1A(e); Rev. Rul. 75-248, 1975-1 C.B. 125.

[5] For example, the regulations under Code § 382 originally defined a predecessor/successor solely in relation to Code § 381(a) transactions; it was only later that the definition was expanded to include certain non-reorganization carryover basis transfers. *Compare* former Temp. Reg. § 1.382-2T(f)(4), (5) (1988) *with* Reg. § 1.382-2(a)(5), (6).

[6] *See, e.g.*, IRS Field Service Advice 200135001, July 16, 1999, *reprinted at* 2001 TNT 171-13; IRS Field Service Advice 200125007, March 9, 2001, *reprinted at* 2001 TNT 122-26.

[1] **§ 706** For a more detailed discussion, *see* Wootton, Section 382 After the Tax Reform Act of 1986, 64 Taxes 874, 886-889 (1986); Ferguson, Profiting from Tax Losses, 60 Taxes 1010, 1017-1019 (1982) (pre-1986 Act; also discusses utilization of losses through leasing).

Transactions of this type are usually referred to as "Leslie Fay" transactions, after the prototype for this type of transaction.[2]

The *Leslie Fay* transaction presented no problems under Code § 269, old Code § 382, or the consolidated return regulations. The tax question presented was whether the allocation of profits and losses of the partnership would be respected as satisfying the substantial economic effect requirement of Code § 704(b). The interest paid on the loss company's capital account in the early *Leslie Fay* transactions typically was set at a rate below general market interest rates, and certainly below the rate paid on the most junior subordinated debt issued by the partnership in the leveraged buyout. The IRS was unhappy with these arrangements, because it believed that the present value of the expected cash flow from these capital accounts (taking into account the interest expected to be paid) was less than the amount of profits credited to them. In the regulations issued under Code § 704(b) in late 1985,[3] the IRS expressed its dissatisfaction in an example.[4] The example focuses on the portion of the profits shifted from the general partner to the loss company partner before the flip (80 percent where the loss company has a 90 percent initial profit allocation and a 10 percent residual profit allocation). The example holds that the allocation of profits to the loss company will not be considered to have "substantial economic effect" under Code § 704(b) if the interest rate prescribed for the loss company's capital account is sufficiently low that (1) the present value of the loss company's cash distributions from these "excess" profits is less than (2) the present value of the general partner's federal tax savings resulting from the allocation of these "excess" profits to the loss company prior to the flip.[5] This determination is to be made on formation of the partnership.[6]

Compliance with these regulations requires a sufficiently high rate of interest to be provided on the loss company's capital account. The drafters of the regulations assumed that this requirement would make *Leslie Fay* transactions uneconomic for the general partner. They apparently assumed that the loss company's capital account would have to carry an interest rate equal to or in excess of the rate payable on the partnership's most junior subordinated debt. The regulations, however, do not specify what interest rate is to be applied for present value purposes. Some advisers decided that these regulations did not make *Leslie Fay* transactions as uneconomic as the Treasury had thought. The Treasury then warned that it would take further steps to discourage them.[7] The Tax Reform Act of 1986 gave the Treasury explicit authority in new Code § 382(m)(3) to accomplish this by regulations, including power to tax the loss company partner by disallowing the use of its NOLs against its partnership

---

[2] *See* proxy statement of *Leslie Fay, Inc.*, April 8, 1982.

[3] Reg. § 1.704-1(b).

[4] Reg. § 1.704-1(b)(5), Example (9).

[5] The regulations do not say how the profits should in fact be allocated where the allocation in the partnership agreement in a *Leslie Fay* transaction lacks substantial economic effect.

[6] *See, e.g.*, explanation of the "substantial economic effect" requirement at Stand. Fed. Tax Rep. (CCH) ¶ 25,424.012.

[7] *See* testimony of Assistant Treasury Secretary Mentz on Pass-Through Entities Before the House Ways and Means Subcommittee on Select Revenue Measures (June 9, 1986).

income, or to reallocate some of that income to the other partner. Such regulations may be retroactive to the date of enactment of the 1986 Act.[8] *Leslie Fay* transactions will therefore become an extinct species, except probably where the loss company partner has a share of partnership profit and loss essentially proportionate to its share of the partnership capital.

When Congress enacted Code § 384 in 1987 (*see* § 709 below), it similarly provided in Code § 384(f) that the Treasury could adopt regulations, intended to have prospective effect only, to prevent avoidance of the purposes of Code § 384 (to prevent use of losses against acquired built-in gains) through the use of the partnership provisions of Subchapter K, including, among other things, the "ceiling" rule of Code § 704(c).[9]

## § 707 ACQUISITION OF LOSS COMPANY AND AVOIDANCE OF DEEMED CODE § 338 ELECTION

Up to this point, we have been focusing on transactions whereby the loss company acquires a profitable business, or is acquired by a profitable business, with the objective of combining its operations and tax benefits with those of the profitable business. We should, however, take note of a different transaction, which also carries with it the need to preserve and make use of the loss company's NOLs and other tax benefits.

This is where one or more investors purchase the stock of a loss company with the objective of continuing its operations and supplementing them through the acquisition of profitable businesses by the loss company. Such a transaction must surmount all of the hurdles of Code §§ 269 and 382, the consolidated return regulations, and Code § 384. The point we wish to add here is that if the stock of the loss company is purchased by a corporate purchaser in a transaction that meets the requirements for a qualified stock purchase within the meaning of Code § 338,[1] all of the NOLs and other tax benefits of the loss company will be destroyed if a Code § 338 election is made for the company.

The corporate purchaser will naturally be careful not to make an affirmative Code § 338 election.[2] (This will be particularly true after 1986, because of the repeal of the *General Utilities* doctrine by the Tax Reform Act of 1986.) However, it must also avoid doing anything that would cause a "deemed" Code § 338 election to have occurred. The best way for the corporate purchaser to do this is to file a "protective carryover basis" election under the Code § 338 regulations.[3]

---

[8] H.R. Rep. No. 841, 99th Cong., 2d Sess. II-195 (1986).

[9] H.R. Rep. No. 495, 100th Cong., 1st Sess. 973-74 (1987).

[1] **§ 707** *See* Code § 338(d)(3).

[2] *See, e.g.*, explanation of the consequences of an election under Code § 338 at Stand. Fed. Tax Rep. (CCH) ¶ 16,288.014.

[3] *See* Temp. Reg. § 1.338-4T(f)(6). A protective carryover basis election is made by filing, within the period for filing a Code § 338 election, a statement to such effect with the District Director for each internal revenue district in which each corporation required to join in making the election files its tax return. Temp. Reg. § 1.338-4T(f)(6)(ii) (Q&A 1). The same regulation further describes the contents of

## §708 CODE §384

Congress adopted Code §384 in the Revenue Act of 1987, effective for acquisitions after December 15, 1987. The provision was heavily amended, with retroactive effect, by the Technical and Miscellaneous Revenue Act of 1988.[1] This provision applies to prevent a loss company (and any members of its affiliated group) from using its pre-acquisition NOLs and net built-in losses (as well as net capital losses and credit carryovers) against any net built-in gains of a company (1) the "control" of which is acquired (directly or through one or more other corporations) by the loss company, or (2) whose assets are acquired by the loss company in a reorganization described in subparagraph (A), (C), or (D) of Code §368(a)(1).[2] The provision also applies if it is the gain corporation that acquires the loss company. "Control" for this purpose means the ownership of stock that meets the 80 percent requirements of Code §1504(a)(2), without regard to whether the corporation is an "includible corporation" under Code §1504(b).

The Code §384 restriction against use of the loss company (or group) losses against the net built-in gains of the gain company (or group) applies not only to its losses from years before the year of the acquisition, but also to its losses for the pre-acquisition portion of the year of acquisition. Code §384(c)(3) provides as a general rule that the losses for the acquisition year shall be allocated ratably to each day in the year, except as provided in regulations.

Interpreting this provision, the IRS has issued a Technical Advice[3] dealing with the following facts. For the year of acquisition, the acquiring loss group had net losses. For the portion of the acquisition year when it was included in the loss group's consolidated return (the post-acquisition portion), the gain group had net profits. The taxpayer argued that for purposes of determining the pre- and post-acquisition allocation of losses, the loss group's income and losses for the year should be computed separately from the gain group's income and losses for the consolidated return year. Thus, the gain group's profits for that year would not reduce the amount of the loss group's losses for that year that could be allocated between the pre-acquisition and post-acquisition portions of the year. The IRS rejected this argument, saying the income or loss for the acquisition year available for allocation is the consolidated income for the year, which includes the gain group's income (other than its recognized net built-in gain) for the portion of the year that it is in the group. To

---

(Footnote Continued)

the statement and specifies which corporations are required to join in the election. *See* Henderson, Tax Planning for Taxable Stock Acquisitions Under the Section 338 Temporary Regulations, 38 Maj. Tax Plan. Ch. 2 (1986).

[1] **§708** TAMRA, §204(m). The effective date language provided, however, that for acquisitions before March 31, 1988, the acquirer could elect not to have the amendments apply. The election had to be made within a certain time and is irrevocable.

[2] In IRS Letter Ruling 8916071 (January 26, 1989), Code §384 applied where the reorganization qualified as both a "D" and a "G" reorganization.

[3] IRS Technical Advice Memorandum 200447037, August 24, 2004. The IRS also denied the taxpayer's request for specific tracing vs. daily ratable allocation, saying that the request had not been timely made.

illustrate, if the loss group had a $100 loss for the acquisition year and the gain group had $200 of income (not counting any of its recognized net built-in gain) included in the consolidated return, in the IRS view there is no consolidated loss to be allocated to either portion of the year. Thus, even though the loss group did have a post-acquisition loss, in the IRS view none of it is available for allocation to reduce the gain group's tainted net built-in gain. The IRS position in this Technical Advice seems to have been heavily influenced by the *United Dominion Industries* case, which is discussed at § 804.4.5 below.

Although regulations have never been issued under Code § 384 allowing use of the specific-tracing method rather than the daily-ratable method for allocating income and loss between the pre-acquisition and post-acquisition portions of the year of acquisition, the IRS has issued letter rulings allowing specific tracing in some cases.[4] In these rulings, it has applied the concepts, including the ceiling rule, reflected in Reg. § 1.382-6 (which is discussed at § 508.4.4 above).

The IRS has also ruled that post-acquisition NOLs can be used against pre-acquisition built-in gains, even when pre-acquisition NOLs also exist but cannot be used because of the Code § 384 barrier.[5]

The concept of net built-in gain utilizes the Code § 382(h) definitions, including the *de minimis* threshold. The Code § 384 restriction applies to built-in gains recognized within the five-year recognition period after the acquisition date. The IRS has announced, however, that where a built-in gain asset is sold before or during the recognition period and, by use of the Code § 453 installment method, the gain is recognized after expiration of the period, regulations will be issued to extend the recognition period with respect to that gain until it is recognized.[6] The regulations will apply the same treatment where the first step in the transaction is a transfer of the asset to an affiliate, causing the gain to become a deferred intercompany gain under the consolidated return regulations, and the second step is an installment sale by the affiliate before the end of the five-year period.[7] The regulations will be effective for installment sales occurring on or after March 26, 1990. Although years have passed since this announcement, no such regulations have been issued or proposed.

The Code § 384 restriction does not apply where the built-in gain company and the loss company were part of the same commonly controlled group of companies (using a more than 50 percent of vote and value test) for the five-year period before

---

[4] IRS Letter Ruling 9734028, May 22, 1997; IRS Letter Ruling 9644004, August 6, 1996. These rulings provide that each member's income and loss is to be allocated by tracing between the pre-and post-acquisition portions of the year. In other words, the allocation was on an individual company, not a combined group basis. The Technical Advice cited in the preceding footnote would obviously disagree with that approach. The taxpayer in the Technical Advice Memorandum did not ask for individual company separation, but only loss-group vs. gain-group separation, either for purposes of the daily-ratable or specific-tracing allocation.

[5] IRS Letter Ruling 9804013, October 22, 1997.

[6] Notice 90-27, 1990-1 C.B. 336.

[7] Id.

the acquisition (or such shorter period that they were in existence). This exception has posed several interpretational problems.[8]

All members of the same affiliated group immediately before the acquisition (determined, to the extent provided in regulations, without regard to Code §1504(b)) are treated as a single corporation for purposes of computing such things as the threshold for net built-in gains and losses (but not for purposes of the commonly controlled exception).

Once Code §384 applies to a corporation, it extends to any predecessor or successor.[9]

Code §384(f) gives the Treasury power, which Congress intends to be exercised with prospective effect only, to adopt regulations to prevent avoidance of the purposes of Code §384 through use of the partnership provisions of Subchapter K, including, without limitation, the "ceiling rule" of Code §704(c).[10]

The burden of proof under Code §384 is the reverse of that under Code §382. That is, for purposes of Code §384 any gain recognized by the gain company will be considered a built-in gain (and thus subject to the Code §384 limitation) except to the extent the taxpayer can prove otherwise.

A loss company making an acquisition of a profitable company will want to keep sufficient records to be able to prove whether the target company had any built-in gains, and their amount, at the time of acquisition. It will also want to be able to trace the assets acquired. Otherwise, the loss company may find the IRS claiming that gains recognized on other property during the five years after the acquisition are subject to the limitation.

## §709 TAXABLE SALES OF ASSETS; "BRUNO'S" TRANSACTIONS

The foregoing sections of this chapter have dealt with techniques designed to preserve the failing company's NOLs and other tax benefits for future use against the income of a profitable business, either through purchasing the assets or stock of such a business or by combining with such a business in a tax-free transaction. However, changes in the law over the years have progressively reduced the value of these benefits for such future use. These changes include the elimination of the stock-for-debt exception to COD income, the adoption of new Code §382, the adoption of Code §384 disallowing use of the failing company's NOLs and other tax benefits against the built-in gains of the profitable business, and the adoption of Temp. Reg. §1.1502-28T (which was thereafter finalized as Reg. §1.1502-28) causing the failing

---

[8] *See* letter from Gilbert D. Bloom of KPMG Peat Marwick to Thomas Wessel, 89 TNT 81-22 (April 22, 1989); and letter from Mark H. Kavey and Biruta P. Kelley of Scribner, Hall & Thompson, 89 TNT 102-26 (May 12, 1989) (responding to Mr. Bloom's letter).

[9] For a general discussion of Code §384, *see* Ginsburg & Levin, Mergers, Acquisitions, and Buyouts §1207.2.5 (May 2000); Silverman and Keyes, How Stock Acquisitions Will Trigger Section 384, J. Taxation 74 (February 1990), and Limiting Built-In Gains and Losses After Asset Acquisitions, 72 J. Taxation 238 (April 1990); Glicklich, Section 384: Less Left for Loss Corporations, 16 J. Corp. Tax'n 23 (Spring, 1989).

[10] H.R. Rep. No. 495, 100th Cong., 1st Sess. 973-74 (1987).

company's excluded COD income to reduce the tax benefits not only of the failing company but also of the other members of its consolidated return group. As a result, increasing attention has been focused by failing companies on making taxable sales of their assets, thereby making present use of their tax basis and NOLs against amounts realized from such sales, and preserving for the buyers a fair market value basis in the assets and, perhaps, giving them the opportunity to claim a Code § 197 amortization deduction for goodwill and other intangibles received in the sale.

These transactions have come to be called "Bruno's" transactions, because they were successfully employed in the *Bruno's* bankruptcy. To make them work, one must be careful to ensure that they are not treated as "G" or other acquisitive or divisive reorganizations, or as Code § 351 transactions.

One way of accomplishing such a transaction is illustrated in a Chief Counsel Advice responding to a field agent's effort to treat such a transaction as a Code § 351 transaction or as a "G" reorganization.[1] Here, Company A and its affiliates were in bankruptcy. Pursuant to a confirmed Chapter 11 plan, Company A engaged in the following transactions: Company A formed new Company B. Company A sold some of its assets to B for cash. It then (1) distributed an undivided interest in certain Division assets to its creditors in exchange for cancellation of an amount of their debt equal to the fair market value of the assets, which assets the creditors then contributed to B for B stock and B notes, and (2) sold the remaining portion of such Division assets directly to B and distributed the B stock and B notes it received to its creditors. Company A, which still retained some assets and continued in business, then cancelled its existing stock and distributed new A stock to its creditors. Thus, when the transactions were all completed, B owned the Division assets, and the creditors owned stock of both A and B and B notes. The Chief Counsel held that the direct and indirect transfer of the assets to B was a taxable sale of assets by A. Although the Chief Counsel analyzed the transaction as a transfer by A of *all* of the Division assets directly to B in exchange for B stock and notes followed by the distribution of all the B stock and notes to the creditors, the transaction did not meet the requirements for a "D" or "G" reorganization or a Code § 355 transaction, because A had only short-term creditors. Thus, the transaction did not meet the requirement for a "tax-free" reorganization that at least some amount of stock or securities of the acquiring company (*i.e.*, B) be issued to a stockholder or security holder of the failing company (*i.e.*, A).[2] Moreover, the failing company did not meet the requirement for an acquisitive "G" reorganization that it liquidate. Nor was the transaction a Code § 351 transaction, because (1) A was not a "transferor" for Code § 351 purposes, since it was

---

[1] **§ 709** IRS Letter Ruling 200350016, August 28, 2003. This Advice is discussed in Willens, "Bruno"-Type Bankruptcy Arrangement Secures IRS Seal of Approval, BNA Daily Tax Report (January 5, 2004), at J-1. *See also* Woll, Post Bruno's Bankruptcy Planning: An Analysis of Taxable Emergence Structures, 4 DePaul Bus. & Comm. L.J. 277 (2006), which discusses in detail the Bruno's transaction, and a variant thereon, the "Grandfather Structure."

[2] The Advice specifically noted that although the short-term creditors would be treated as former shareholders of A for purposes of the "G" reorganization continuity-of-interest requirement under the *Alabama Asphaltic* case, "this treatment has not been extended to determine status as a shareholder or security holder for purposes of sections 354 or 355." *See* the discussions of the continuity-of-interest concept at §§ 510.1, 604.3.2, and 605.1.4 above.

under an obligation to transfer any B stock it received to its creditors,[3] and (2) Code § 351(e)(2) provides that Code § 351 shall not apply to a transfer of property of a debtor pursuant to a plan while the debtor is in bankruptcy (or in a similar case) to the extent the stock received in the exchange is used to satisfy the indebtedness of the debtor.[4]

We might add that in structuring such a transaction, one should avoid (1) the new company from being affiliated with the debtor corporation in a way that causes it to be part of its consolidated return group if the objective is to utilize the debtor's NOLs against gains recognized in the sale, since consolidation may cause any recognition of gain by the debtor company to be deferred; (2) the common control and related party rules of Code § 267 to the extent that losses from the disposition of some of the assets would be needed to offset gain recognized on the disposition of the rest of the assets, since Code § 267 would operate to disallow or defer the loss; and (3) the anti-churning rules of Code § 197(f)(9), if the acquiring company wants to amortize the acquired goodwill or other Code § 197 intangibles.

## § 710 THE INESCAPABLE ALTERNATIVE MINIMUM TAX

The Tax Reform Act of 1986 made it virtually certain, and it is generally still the case, that a corporation will have to pay at least some tax in any year in which it has income, even if the corporation has unused NOLs or credit carryovers.

The Act accomplished this by changing the corporate minimum tax to an alternative minimum tax (AMT), by expanding its scope, and by providing that (1) NOLs cannot offset more than 90 percent of the corporate alternative minimum taxable income,[1] (2) foreign tax credits may not offset more than 90 percent of the AMT liability,[2] (3) ITCs may not offset more than approximately 25 percent of the minimum tax liability, (4) most other credits are not allowed against the AMT

---

[3] In an interesting footnote (*see* note 6 in the Advice), the Advice leaves open the proposition that, had the creditors been security holders, the creditors might themselves have been considered the equitable owners of the property for Code § 351 purposes, citing some early case law. *See, e.g., Helvering v. Cement Investors, Inc.*, 316 U.S. 527 (1942) (bondholders of a bankrupt corporation were treated as the equitable owners of the company's assets and regarded as the transferors under the predecessor to Code § 351; the Court refrained from considering, since the issue was not properly before it, the government's argument that a taxable event occurred in connection with the bondholders' acquisition of their equitable interest in the assets in substitution of their bonds). However, under Code § 351(e)(2) (discussed in the text below), which was enacted as part of the Bankruptcy Tax Act of 1980, the receipt of stock by the creditors in such circumstance would still have resulted in a taxable transfer of the assets to B.

[4] For a more detailed discussion of Code § 351(e)(2), *see* Asofsky, Reorganizing Insolvent Corporations, 41 Inst. on Fed. Tax'n § 5.03 (1983), at pp. 5-34-5-38 (discussing the legislative history and the interpretational issue presented when the debtor retains a portion of the stock).

[1] **§ 710** Code § 56(d)(1) (the 90% limitation for NOLs was suspended for NOLs utilized in 2001 and 2002, and for NOL carrybacks from 2001 and 2002). Moreover, NOLs arising in years beginning after 1986 must be adjusted, for AMT NOL purposes, by eliminating tax preference and similar items. Code § 56(d)(2).

[2] Former Code § 59(a)(2), repealed by P.L. 108-357, § 421(a)(1) (2004) (effective for taxable years after 2004).

liability, and (5) the combination of NOLs, ITC, and foreign tax credits cannot reduce the AMT liability to less than 10 percent of what it would have been without these adjustments.[3] This has been relaxed over the years by the repeal of the 10 percent ITC limitation effective for property placed in service after 1990, by a two-year suspension of the NOL 90 percent limitation for 2001 and 2002, and by the repeal of the foreign tax credit limitations effective for taxable years after 2004. Because the AMT corporate tax rate is 20 percent, the presence of one or more of these limitations with respect to any particular year means that a corporation that has current income generally will have to pay at least a two percent tax (20 percent times 10 percent of its AMT income), even if it has NOLs or credit carryovers far in excess of its current income.

The IRS has ruled that when the loss company elects for purposes of Code §382 to allocate income and loss between the prechange and postchange portions of the year of an ownership change, alternative minimum taxable income and deductions will be allocated in accordance with the rules for allocating regular income and loss (which are discussed at §508.4.4 above), except that the 90 percent limitation on using NOLs against AMTI must be computed independently. Specifically, it has ruled that the 90 percent limitation must be applied "independently of the section 382 limitation. The amount of the alternative minimum tax net operating losses that . . . [may be used] in computing . . . AMTI for the change year may not exceed the lesser of the amount allowable under the 90 percent limitation of section 56(d)(1)(A) and the amount allowable under section 382. The 90 percent limitation is based on the total AMTI for the change year, without regard to any allocation of the change year's AMTI to the pre-change and post-change periods."[4] This is just one example of many areas where the application of Code §382 to the AMT poses an additional level of considerations.[5]

The income base used for AMT purposes is larger than the base for the regular income tax: it disallows deductions for certain tax preferences and, for taxable years starting before 1990, added 50 percent of the amount by which book income exceeded regular taxable income. The book income tax preference meant that failing companies had to be particularly sensitive to the book accounting treatment of their income both before and after any debt or stock restructuring takes place.

One special problem for failing companies is that debt cancellation often (although not always) will produce book income under generally accepted accounting principles, even where no taxable income is created (because, for example, one of the exceptions to the creation of COD income, such as the stock-for-debt exception, applies). Thus, for years beginning before 1990, where the company reduces its debt and the debt reduction is excluded from regular taxable income, the fact that the debt reduction is included in book income can subject the company to the AMT. Code

---

[3] Former Code §38(c)(2), repealed by P.L. 101-508, §11813(b)(2)(B) (1990) (effective for property placed in service after 1990).

[4] IRS Letter Ruling 9734028, May 22, 1997; IRS Letter Ruling 9644004, August 6, 1996; IRS Letter Ruling 9341026 (July 20, 1993); IRS Letter Ruling 9345045 (August 17, 1993).

[5] *See, e.g.*, Simon, Compound Complexity: Accounting for Built-In Gains and Losses Under the AMT After an Ownership Change, 107 Tax Notes 477 (April 25, 2005).

§ 56(f)(2) eliminates this problem for stock-for-debt exchanges, for taxable years beginning after 1986, but does not solve the problem in other cases. *See* § 404.5 above. Now that the basis for the AMT has shifted from book income to earnings and profits (for taxable years beginning after 1989), the problem is eliminated by Code § 56(g)(4)(B). *See* § 404.5 above.

The imposition of an alternative minimum tax on companies having unused NOLs and other carryovers will make it more difficult to revitalize failing companies.

As discussed at § 511 above, the AMT can also be increased if a Code § 382 ownership change occurs in a tax year beginning after 1989 at a time when there is a net built-in loss in the basis of assets as determined for earnings and profits purposes. In such event, the earnings and profits basis of the assets must be marked to market value for purposes of the AMT adjusted current earnings (ACE) adjustment.

# 8

# Special Problems of Multi-Company Debtor Groups



## §801 INTRODUCTION

More frequently than not in today's business world, failing companies will not be free-standing single corporations but instead will be part of a multi-company consolidated return group. In some such cases, certain companies in the group may be solvent and profitable while others may be troubled and may even go into bankruptcy proceedings. In other cases, the entire group may consist of troubled companies and all of them may go into bankruptcy proceedings. Each of the various companies will have debt outstanding in the hands of its affiliates and its outside creditors. Occasionally, outside owners may own a portion of the subsidiaries' stock.

The existence of multiple corporations and multiple creditor or stockholder interests complicates tax planning for the failing company. Bankruptcy practice permits, in certain, although not all, cases, a "substantive consolidation" of related companies for purposes of a bankruptcy workout.[1] The companies are treated essentially as a single corporation, and the bankruptcy plan will generally provide that the creditors and stockholders of the various corporations will end up owning the debt and the stock of a single corporation.[2] The Internal Revenue Code does not provide

[1] **§801** *See* Bankruptcy Rule 1015(b). Substantive consolidation of two or more debtors' estates in effect results in the pooling of the assets and liabilities of the debtors, and the elimination of intercompany claims and of duplicate claims by creditors.

[2] Over the years, it has become a relatively common practice for bankruptcy courts to allow substantive consolidation without the need for eliminating the separate corporate existence of the subsidiaries—recognizing that the liquidation of the subsidiary debtors could have adverse federal and/or state tax consequences for the debtors, by affecting their federal or state NOLs or tax basis.

for such a convenient approach. Each corporation will generally be recognized as a separate taxable entity, and consolidation of the creditor or stockholder interests in them as part of a workout will involve tax consequences each step of the way.[3] In at least one limited instance, however, the IRS has given tax significance to a substantive consolidation.[4] In this instance, the IRS gave effect to substantive consolidation for purposes of applying the proportionality requirement for the stock-for-debt exception (*see* § 504A.4.2 above). But aside from this exception, the IRS view generally is that bankruptcy substantive consolidation does not apply (*i.e.*, does not merge the entities) for federal income tax purposes.[5] Thus, whether or not some or all of the companies in a multi-company group are "substantively consolidated" for bankruptcy law purposes, the tax consequences for the companies generally will be governed independently by the tax Code and Regulations as though this had not occurred.

What follows is a discussion of the problems that typically arise when one or more members of a multi-company group become financially troubled and need to restructure their debt or stock, whether inside or outside of bankruptcy.

## § 802 LIQUIDATIONS OF INSOLVENT COMPANIES

The tax adviser will often find that a failing subsidiary will be capitalized with a relatively nominal amount of stock, all of which will be owned by the parent, and that the parent will have made very large open account advances or other loans to the subsidiary. The subsidiary will have generated substantial NOLs, some of which may not have been used by the other members of the group.

If the subsidiary is solvent, a liquidation of the subsidiary into the parent would normally be tax free under Code § 332 and the parent would succeed to the subsidiary's NOLs under Code § 381. If the subsidiary is insolvent (that is, its liabilities exceed its assets), however, Code § 332 does not apply because Code § 332(b)(2) provides that the liquidating distribution must be "in complete cancellation or

---

(Footnote Continued)

The first bankruptcy court case so holding was *In re Standard Brands Paint Co.*, 154 B.R. 563 (Bankr. C.D. Cal. 1993). In a 2005 decision, however, the Third Circuit Court of Appeals in *In re Owens Corning*, 419 F.3d 195 (2005), *cert. denied*, 126 S. Ct. 1910 (2006), denied the debtors' attempt at substantive consolidation on multiple grounds, but asserted that "perhaps the flaw most fatal to the Plan Proponents' proposal is that the consolidation sought was 'deemed' (*i.e.*, a pretend consolidation for all but the Banks)." In this regard, the court queried: "If Debtors' corporate and financial structure was such a sham before the filing of the motion to consolidate, then how is it that post the Plan's effective date this structure stays largely undisturbed, with the Debtors reaping all the liability-limiting, tax and regulatory benefits achieved by forming subsidiaries in the first place?" *See also* 'Give-ups' Run Against Absolute Priority Rule, 47 Bankr. Ct. Dec. (LRP Publications), February 20, 2007, at 7.

[3] *See* Asofsky, Bacon, Hyman, Klee, Singer, Tatlock and Ruge, Conference on the Bankruptcy Tax Act of 1980, 39 Inst. on Fed. Tax'n §§ 57, 57.09[8] at 57-141 (remarks of Milton B. Hyman); IRS Letter Ruling 7905078, November 1, 1978.

[4] *See* IRS Letter Ruling 9105042, February 27, 1990, discussed at § 504A.4.2 above.

[5] IRS Field Service Advice 199952016, December 30, 1999 (bankruptcy consolidation of several related partnerships does not merge or consolidate the partnerships for tax purposes), *reprinted at* 2000 TNT 1-95.

redemption of all its stock . . . ." In that case, the parent would get a worthless security deduction for its stock under Code § 165(g), and the NOLs and other tax attributes of the subsidiary would disappear.

Suppose, however, the subsidiary is solvent, but it has both preferred and common stock outstanding, and although the assets are sufficient to provide at least a partial distribution to the preferred stock, they are not sufficient to provide any distribution to the common stock. Judicial decisions have held that that this does not qualify as a Code § 332 liquidation.[1] In such case, the parent could claim a worthless security loss for the common stock under Code § 165(g) and a loss on its preferred under Code § 331, and the NOLs and other tax attributes of the subsidiary would disappear.[2] Although the validity of these decisions is widely accepted, in 2005 the IRS decided to eliminate any doubt by issuing Prop. Reg. § 1.332-2(b), which says that "Section 332 applies only when the recipient corporation receives at least partial payment for each class of stock that it owns in the liquidating corporation."

Because application of Code § 332 and the carryover of the subsidiary's NOLs may hinge on a distribution to the common stock, there could be significant factual questions as to whether the indebtedness of the subsidiary to the parent should be characterized as debt or as equity for tax purposes; and further, if equity, whether it should be treated as preferred stock or instead as a contribution to capital (and thus as part of the common stock).[3] There seems little likelihood, however, that the IRS would accept any recharacterization of parent-held intercompany debt as equity that would result in the subsidiary being solvent and the transaction qualifying under Code § 332. Even if the IRS were to view the debt as having in substance become equity, the IRS would most likely insist that the seniority of the such obligation would have to be respected, with the result that the debt would in effect be treated as preferred stock.[4] Indeed, the Chief Counsel's Office has even taken this position where the auditing IRS agent, rather than the taxpayer, argued against respecting the seniority of the instrument.[5]

Where consolidated returns are filed, the tax consequences of a non-Code § 332 liquidation may differ from those where separate returns are filed. This happens because Reg. § 1.1502-13(g) provides that the parent's bad debt deduction is treated at

---

[1] **§ 802** *Commissioner v. Spaulding Bakeries, Inc.*, 252 F.2d 693, 58-1 U.S.T.C. ¶ 9320 (2d Cir. 1958); *H.K. Porter Co., Inc.*, 87 T.C. 689, Dec. 43,405 (1986).

[2] For a thorough discussion of this and related matters, *see* Blanchard, Jr., Bennett and Speer, The Deductibility of Investments in Financially Troubled Subsidiaries and Related Federal Income Tax Considerations, 80 Taxes 91 (2002). *See also* Rev. Rul. 2003-125, 2003-2 C.B. 1243 (conversion of insolvent corporation into a disregarded entity allows shareholder a worthless security loss under Code § 165(g)), *applied in* IRS Letter Ruling 200706011, September 7, 2006, and in IRS Letter Ruling 200710004, December 5, 2006; Willens, Securing an Ordinary Loss Deduction for Worthless Holding Company Stock, BNA Daily Tax Report (March 22, 2007), at J-1; Willens, A 'Solvent' Liquidation Can Be Taxable, 115 Tax Notes 581 (May 7, 2007).

[3] For an excellent and thorough discussion of these issues, *see* Plumb, The Federal Income Tax Significance of Corporate Debt: A Critical Analysis and a Proposal, 26 Tax L. Rev. 369 (1971).

[4] Compare the 2005 proposed continuity-of-interest regulations described at §§ 504A.3.2 and 605.1.4 above, in which the seniority of debt classes is determinative of the way the continuity-of-interest test should be applied.

[5] IRS Letter Ruling 200706011, September 7, 2006.

the debtor level as a deemed satisfaction of the debt, thereby, on these facts, producing COD for the debtor subsidiary. Moreover, these same consolidated return regulations provide that the Code § 108 exclusions from income for COD in insolvency or bankruptcy do not apply to intercompany debt. *See* § 804.4 below. The resulting inclusion of the deemed COD income will, in effect, offset the effect of the parent's bad debt deduction on the consolidated return. However, this same deemed COD income will increase the parent's basis in its stock of the subsidiary. In substance, therefore, the consolidated return regulations convert bad debt deductions on consolidated subsidiary debt into additional basis in the stock of the subsidiary, and thus into a potential worthless stock deduction. For the time between the adoption of the 1995-1996 amendments to Reg. § 1.1502-13 and March 7, 2002, the pre-2002 regulations made the parent's claim of a bad debt deduction for debt obligations of its subsidiary largely fruitless, because for that period of time the parent's deduction for loss from subsidiary stock was severely limited or entirely disallowed by Reg. § 1.1502-20.[6] This latter risk of total disallowance has become less for stock becoming worthless after March 7, 2002, because of the replacement of Reg. § 1.1502-20 by Reg. § 1.337(d)-2 (which also provides elective relief for prior periods) and Reg. § 1.1502-35T. *See* § 508.2.4 above and § 804.5 below.

One should keep in mind that Code § 368(a)(3)(C) provides that if a transaction would qualify under Code § 332 and also would qualify as a "G" reorganization, it is to be treated as a "G" reorganization. Although the liquidation of an insolvent subsidiary would not qualify under Code § 332, this provision is a reminder that in some circumstances a transaction that might fail to so qualify may nonetheless be structured to qualify as a "G" reorganization if either the parent or the subsidiary is in bankruptcy. To accomplish this, presumably stock or securities of the parent would need to be transferred to the subsidiary and, in turn, transferred to at least one holder of a security or stock of the subsidiary (such as, possibly, the subsidiary's parent).[7] For transactions occurring after the 2005 proposed regulation announcing the addition of a net value test for reorganizations (*see* §§ 604.3 and 605.1 above) becomes final, the transaction would also have to satisfy that net value test to qualify as a "G" reorganization. Indeed, the IRS has issued a ruling treating the liquidation of an insolvent subsidiary by merger into the parent as a "G" reorganization.[8] In this ruling, stock and debt of the parent were issued to security holders of the insolvent subsidiary, and the parent continued to own the subsidiary's assets and conduct its business. The ruling also held that the issuance of the parent's stock in satisfaction of

---

[6] In this circumstance, however, the parent might have been able under Reg. § 1.1502-20(g) to elect to allocate to itself a portion of the unused NOLs of the subsidiary, but only to the extent they exceeded the insolvency of the subsidiary and each higher-tier member, determined without regard to certain intercompany debt.

[7] *See* Asofsky, Reorganizing Insolvent Corporations, 41 Inst. on Fed. Tax'n §§ 5, 5.02(l)(e) (1983). As discussed earlier at § 605.1.2, the IRS has taken the position in private letter rulings (supported by a technical reading of the statute) that to qualify as a "G" reorganization, among other prerequisites, at least one securityholder or stockholder of the target corporation must receive some stock or securities of the acquiring corporation (although, possibly, only a nominal amount). *See* IRS Letter Ruling 8521083, February 27, 1985; IRS Letter Ruling 8503064, October 24, 1984.

[8] IRS Letter Ruling 9122067, March 6, 1991, discussed at § 504A.3.2 above.

the subsidiary's debt qualified for the stock-for-debt exception (*see* § 504A.3.2 above), and we can surmise that obtaining this exception may have been the motivation for the liquidation. It has yet to be determined, however, whether a liquidation of a solvent or insolvent subsidiary into its parent can be a "G" reorganization in the absence of the issuance of stock or a security of the parent to outside securityholders or stockholders of the subsidiary.

It is interesting to note that the 2005 proposed regulation expressly notes that a transaction which fails to qualify as a Code § 332 liquidation due to insolvency may nonetheless qualify as a "C" reorganization.[9] As the proposed regulation illustrates, even if the transaction does constitute a reorganization, the parent would still get a worthless security loss for its common stock in the subsidiary under Code § 165(g), due to the lack of equity value.[10] Future such transactions would also have to meet the new net value test, as mentioned in the preceding paragraph.

## § 803 SATISFACTION OF SUBSIDIARY DEBT WITH PARENT STOCK

Prior to adoption of the Bankruptcy Tax Act of 1980, the IRS had ruled that all debt of a company constituted property that could be transferred to the company tax free under Code § 351.[1] This permitted creditors who did not hold securities to exchange their debt for stock of the debtor corporation in a tax-free rather than a taxable exchange, even though the transaction did not qualify as a recapitalization under Code § § 368(a)(1)(E) and 354.

### EXAMPLE 1

> Failing company in 1978 restructured its capital by cancelling its old stock and issuing 75 percent of its new stock to its former security holders and 25 percent to other creditors in cancellation of their debt. The issuance of 75 percent of the stock to the old security holders is tax free under Code § 354 as a recapitalization exchange. However, because all of the creditors of the company were transferors of property for purposes of Code § 351 prior to its amendment in 1980, by virtue of their exchange of their old debt for new stock, the exchanges by both classes of creditors were tax free under Code § 351 because such transferors owned 80 percent or more of all of the stock immediately after the exchange.

Many multi-company bankruptcy proceedings utilized this device for structuring multi-company workouts.

---

[9] *See* Prop. Reg. § 1.332-2(e) Example 1, and the discussion in the preamble to the proposed regulation.

[10] Id.

[1] **§ 803** *See, e.g.*, Rev. Rul. 77-81, 1977-1 C.B. 97.

### EXAMPLE 2

Parent and each of its ten subsidiaries had debt of various classes outstanding in the hands of outside creditors. In a single plan of bankruptcy reorganization involving all of these companies, the debt of the subsidiaries as well as debt of the parent was transferred to the parent in exchange for debt and stock of the parent. Prior to the Bankruptcy Tax Act of 1980, assuming that the creditors of the parent (consisting of both security and nonsecurity holders) and the subsidiaries end up owning 80 percent of the stock of the parent, the transfers of the debt of both the subsidiaries and the parent to the parent in exchange for parent stock were tax-free exchanges under Code §351. A transfer of a security of the parent in exchange for parent stock will also constitute a tax-free recapitalization exchange. In addition, none of the stock issued by the parent in these exchanges was treated as "purchased" for purposes of old Code §382(a).

The Bankruptcy Tax Act of 1980 made two significant changes in the rules applicable to such transactions. First, it amended Code §351(d) to provide that "property," for Code §351 purposes, does not include either (1) nonsecurity debt of the issuer or (2) accrued but unpaid interest on any debt of the issuer. The reason for these changes was to equate the treatment of these interests under Code §351 with their treatment under a Code §368 reorganization.[2] Second, it added Code §108(e)(4), which states that, to the extent provided in regulations, the acquisition of debt by a related person will be treated as an acquisition of the debt by the debtor for COD income purposes.[3] Related persons are broadly defined for this purpose to include, *inter alia*, all members of an affiliated group.[4] Regulations to implement this provision

---

[2] S. Rep. No. 1035, 96th Cong., 2d Sess. 43 (1980).

[3] *See* Code §108(e)(4)(A). For excellent discussions of the workings of, and issues involved in, the related person rule of Code §108(e)(4), *see* Peaslee, Discharge of Debt Through Its Acquisition by a Person Related to the Debtor—An Analysis of Section 108(e)(4), 37 Tax L. Rev. 193 (1982); New York State Bar Association, Tax Section, Committee on Bankruptcy, Report on Related Party Debt Acquisitions Under Section 108(e)(4) of the Code (April 12, 1984). As mentioned in the text, final regulations under Code §108(e)(4) were issued in 1992. Proposed regulations had been issued in 1991.

[4] *See* Code §§108(e)(4)(A) and 267(b)(3) and (f). As mentioned in the text, final regulations under Code §108(e)(4) were issued in 1992. Proposed regulations had been issued in 1991. The 1991 proposed regulations are analyzed and criticized in New York State Bar Association, Tax Section, Committee on Bankruptcy, Report on Acquisitions of Discount Debt by Related Parties Under the New Section 108(e)(4) Regulation (June 21, 1991). In two private letter rulings, the IRS took the position that Code §108(e)(4) is currently operative despite the apparent need for implementing regulations. *See* IRS Letter Ruling 8923021, March 10, 1989 (holding that where the debtor was merged into S and, at least one day prior to the merger, the parent of S acquired outstanding notes of the debtor, Code §108(e)(4) applied for purposes of determining whether S had COD income upon the parent's acquisition of the notes); IRS Letter Ruling 8922080, March 9, 1989. Similarly, the Tax Court, in a memorandum decision applied Code §108(e)(4) without any discussion (or apparent consideration) of whether such section is self-implementing. *Traylor v. Commissioner*, 59 T.C.M 93. Dec. 46,456(M), T.C. Memo. 1990-132; *see also* Sheppard, How To Avoid COD Income, and How Not To Do It, 90 TNT 222-5 (October 31, 1990) (describing procedural background of case, and other Code §108(e)(4) issues). It is highly questionable that Code §108(e)(4) is self-implementing. *Cf. Alexander v. Commissioner*, 95 T.C. No. 33 (1990) (reviewed decision) (holding that the portion of Code §465 that

(Reg. § 1.108-2) were issued in final form in December 1992. These are discussed at § 404.7 above.

As a result of these changes, the transfer of parent nonsecurity debt (or of accrued interest on parent security debt) to the parent in exchange for parent stock will no longer qualify as a transfer of property for Code § 351 purposes, either for permitting the transfer by such creditors to be tax free to them or for purposes of treating these creditors as being part of the "transferor" group in order to bring transfers by others within a group that reaches the 80 percent level necessary to satisfy Code § 351. In contrast, the acquisition of subsidiary debt by a parent in exchange for parent stock presumably will still qualify as a transfer of property for Code § 351 purposes. However, whether such a transfer will create COD income for the subsidiary depends on the application of the regulations implementing Code § 108(e)(4), or, if consolidated returns are filed, on the application of Reg. § 1.1502-13(g), and the treatment of parent stock for purposes of the stock-for-debt exception (*see* § 504A.3).

Because of these problems and because of the difficulties with Code § 332 liquidations (as discussed at § 802) the tax adviser for multi-company debtors may find it more useful to consider downstream rather than upstream workout plans.[5]

## § 804 CERTAIN CONSOLIDATED RETURN CONSIDERATIONS

The existence of a failing company within a consolidated return multi-company group raises a number of important considerations under the consolidated return regulations.

---

(Footnote Continued)

states that it "shall apply only to the extent provided in regulations prescribed by the secretary" was not self-executing, but required implementing regulations), *aff'd, sub. nom, Stell v. Commissioner*, 999 F.2d 544 (9th Cir. 1993). Prop. Reg. § 1.108-2, issued in March 1991, contained the cryptic statement that "[a]lthough this regulation is not proposed to apply to transactions before March 21, 1991, section 108(e)(4) is effective for any transaction after December 31, 1980 . . . ." The final regulations issued in 1992 say the same thing.

[5] For a general discussion of downstream mergers of parents into subsidiaries, *see* B. Bittker & J. Eustice, Federal Income Taxation of Corporations and Shareholders ¶ 12.63[2][b](7th ed.) For a time, the IRS had placed downstream mergers of parent corporations into less-than-80 percent owned subsidiaries on its list of transactions on which rulings would not be issued. Rev. Proc. 96-22, 1996-1 C.B. 662. But this prohibition on rulings was deleted in Rev. Proc. 99-3, and the IRS now will rule favorably on such transactions. *See* IRS Information Letter 2000-0001, March 31, 2000. However, the tax advisor should note that Treasury has proposed legislation that would tax the parent on its gain in its subsidiary's stock if the parent owns less than 20 percent of the stock of the subsidiary. Aside from the "A" reorganization treatment, the IRS has also ruled that a downstream fusion of a parent into its subsidiary can qualify as a "C" reorganization. IRS Letter Rulings 200037001 and 200037002, April 27, 2000.

## §804.1 *Inclusion of Bankrupt Corporations*

To begin with, Rev. Rul. 63-104[1] holds that a subsidiary placed in bankruptcy must continue to file consolidated returns with its nonbankrupt (or, for that matter, bankrupt) parent.[2] *But see* the discussion of IRS Notice 2004-37, below. As we have mentioned previously, it is implicit in this ruling that the bankruptcy filing does not create some kind of "deemed" recapitalization shift in stock ownership.[3] Thus, the subsidiary will remain part of the consolidated return group unless and until its actual stock ownership is changed in a way that removes it from the group. This approach was confirmed in Reg. § 1.1504-4(d)(2)(vii), issued under Code § 1504(a)(5), which authorizes the IRS to issue regulations defining when options and other interests shall be treated as stock for consolidated return affiliation purposes. This provides that an "option" for this purpose does not include:

> options created by the solicitation or receipt of acceptances to a plan of reorganization in a title 11 or similar case . . . , the option created by the confirmation of the plan, and any option created under the plan prior to the time the plan becomes effective.

The *Continental Airlines* case[4] serves as an interesting illustration. Both Continental Airlines and its consolidated subsidiary, Eastern Air Lines, were in bankruptcy. Continental's stock in Eastern was admittedly worthless, yet Eastern continued to file a consolidated return with Continental. Continental expressed concern that a portion of its continuing losses would go to offset income recognized by Eastern in future liquidation sales. Accordingly, in an attempt to deconsolidate Eastern, Continental sought a bankruptcy court order authorizing it "to abandon all legal or equitable interest in any stock of Eastern and extinguishing such interest so that the Debtors will not be deemed to be owners of Eastern stock for any purpose, including without

---

[1] **§ 804** 1963-1 C.B. 172.

[2] *See also* IRS Letter Ruling 8444063, July 31, 1984 (permission to discontinue filing consolidated returns denied where parent and subsidiary were both in bankruptcy, even though subsidiary's records were in disarray, held by a trustee and not immediately accessible to parent); IRS Letter by Ruling 8713005, December 10, 1986 (same but only subsidiary in bankruptcy; also no indication if a trustee in bankruptcy had been appointed); *cf.* IRS Letter Ruling 9048003, August 22, 1990, and IRS Letter Ruling 9048004, August 22, 1990 (subsidiaries in receivership denied permission to deconsolidate from parent company for periods prior to the parent's dissolution under state law); IRS Letter Ruling 8544018 (July 30, 1985) (casualty insurance subsidiary seized by state regulators and dissolved for state law but not federal income tax purposes still required to consolidate); *cf.* IRS Letter Ruling 199952038, September 30, 1999 (life insurance company placed in receivership ceased to be a life insurance company, and became a non-life company, when its insurance liabilities were taken over by governmental guaranty funds, and thereafter the company had to be included in the consolidated return group as a non-life company). Conversely, where an affiliated group has never previously filed consolidated returns and a subsidiary in bankruptcy (or its trustee, if appointed) refuses to consent to its inclusion in a consolidated return, the affiliated group will be precluded from filing a consolidated return. *See George A. Fuller Co. v. Commissioner*, 92 F.2d 72, 37-2 U.S.T.C. ¶ 9407 (2d Cir. 1937).

[3] *See* § 602.

[4] *See In re Continental Airlines, Inc.*, Ch.11, Case Nos. 90-932 through 90-984 (Bankr. S.D.N.Y. motion dated November 12, 1991).

limitation federal income tax purposes . . . ." Subsequently, Continental Airlines entered into a Stipulation and Order with Eastern Air Lines.[5] The order was appealed by the Department of Labor.[6]

When a subsidiary leaves a consolidated return group, the group (and the subsidiary) may suffer adverse tax consequences, including the triggering of deferred intercompany items and excess loss accounts, and changes in the availability of the subsidiary's tax benefits, such as NOLs and built-in losses. Thus, most consolidated return groups will want to protect against the inadvertent breaking of the consolidated group.

The *Federated Department Stores* case[7] provides an interesting illustration of the kind of problems that can arise. Allied Stores was a subsidiary in the Federated consolidated return group. Allied had issued preferred stock to third parties. The preferred stock provided that its holders had the right to elect two directors of Allied in the event that dividends on the preferred stock fell into arrears for six consecutive quarters. The preferred stock had in fact fallen into arrears, and during the pendency of the Federated and Allied bankruptcy case the stock was about to become voting stock. This would have broken Allied out of the consolidated return group, and the parties estimated that this would have cost the group (including Allied) $234 million. The court granted the request of Allied to amend its charter to remove these prospective voting rights of the preferred stock during the bankruptcy case and until a confirmed bankruptcy plan became effective. (Allied indicated that even without this order it was prepared to argue that the automatic stay imposed upon the filing of its bankruptcy petition precluded the attachment of new voting rights to its stock during the pendency of the case, but obviously it preferred to get the order.) The preferred stock was actually worthless (the bankruptcy plan provided that the holders of the Allied preferred stock would receive nothing for their stock), and the bankruptcy court refused to compensate the holders of the stock for this prospective loss of voting rights (which did not, of course, eliminate their right to vote on the bankruptcy plan itself).[8]

---

5 *See In re Continental Airlines, Inc.*, Ch.11, Case Nos. 90-932-90-984, Stipulation and Order, December 26, 1991. Eastern had filed an objection to the motion in the Continental bankruptcy and a complaint against Continental in its bankruptcy, asserting among other things, that, based on the *Prudential Lines* case (*see* §508.2.4), Continental's motion violated the automatic stay in Eastern's bankruptcy case because the abandonment and extinguishment of Continental's stock interest in Eastern would result in an ownership change of Eastern under Code §382, thus limiting the future use of Eastern's NOL carryforwards and increasing Eastern's tax liability on future liquidation sales. *See Shugrue v. Continental Airlines Holdings, Inc.*, Ch. 11, Case No. 89-B-10488, "Original Complaint," (Bankr. S.D.N.Y., dated November 27, 1991); in the *Continental* case *supra* note 4, *see* objection dated November 27, 1991.

6 *See amicus curiae* brief filed by the Pension Benefit Guaranty Corporation in support of Department of Labor's Appeal (April 17, 1992).

7 *In re Federated Department Stores, Inc.*, 1991 Bankr. LEXIS 743 (Bankr. S.D. Ohio), *aff'd*, 133 B.R. 886 (S.D. Ohio 1991).

8 A similar situation arose in the *Eastern Air Lines* bankruptcy case. There, the bankruptcy court approved a Stipulation and Order enjoining the preferred stockholders from asserting any voting rights until the day after the effective date of a Chapter 11 plan. *See In re Ionosphere Clubs, Inc.*, Ch. 11, Case No. 89-B-10448 (BRL) (Bankr. S.D.N.Y.), Stipulation and Order dated May 31, 1991. This was preceded by a temporary restraining order and a motion similar to that in *Federated* (dated May 9,

Code § 1504(a)(3) provides that a subsidiary is includible in a consolidated return only if the group owns stock of the subsidiary that possesses (1) at least 80 percent of the voting power of its stock and (2) at least 80 percent of the total value of its stock (not including certain nonvoting, nonparticipating, limited preferred stock). Code § 1504(a)(5)(C) authorizes the issuance of regulations that would allow the value test to be considered met if the group relies on a "good faith determination" of value; and Code § 1504(a)(5)(D) authorizes the issuance of regulations that would allow the group to disregard an "inadvertent ceasing" to meet the value test because of changes in relative values of different classes of stock. As of this writing, regulations had not been issued under these provisions. However, in Notice 2004-37,[9] the IRS announced an intention to issue proposed regulations under these provisions in the future. The Notice also announces the tests that the IRS will apply in the meantime under these concepts for determining whether the 80 percent value test has been met. The Notice says that if the group has made a good faith determination that the value test has been met, the "good faith determination" test can be considered satisfied, if the group wishes, until certain "designated events" occur, at which time another good faith determination would become necessary. Similarly, the Notice says that if the value test ceases to be met because of a change in the relative values of different classes of stock that was not caused by a "designated event," the value test can be considered met until a "designated event" occurs. The "designated events" include certain transactions in the stock by members of the group, certain distributions on the stock to a member of the group, and the claiming by the group of a worthless stock deduction for any of the stock. The Notice says that the IRS will not challenge the group if the group takes the position that these "good faith" or "inadvertent" standards are met. On the other hand, it says that the Notice does *not require* the taxpayer to take the position that the value test is met, if in fact it is not met. There is no indication that the issuance of this Notice was triggered by IRS concern about what can happen in the bankruptcy context. Nor is any indication given as to whether the IRS intends the rules announced in the Notice to modify the approach taken in Rev. Rul. 63-104, mentioned at the beginning of this § 804.1. This is a significant question, because these rules, if they applied in bankruptcy, could have a considerable impact on bankruptcy practice.

For a discussion of similar multi-class valuation issues that can arise in determining whether an ownership change has taken place for purposes of Code § 382, *see* § 508.2.5.1 above.

Some interesting problems can arise out of the fact that the common parent has the authority to act as the sole agent for the subsidiary members of the group with respect to all matters relating to the tax liability of the consolidated group. Reg. § 1.1502-77(a) provides that the parent "shall be the sole agent for each subsidiary in the group, duly authorized to act in its own name in all matters relating to the tax

(Footnote Continued)

1991). *Cf.* IRS Letter Ruling 200725026, March 20, 2007 (advance waiver of voting rights by requisite percentage of holders in accordance with the terms of the preferred stock).

[9] 2004-21 I.R.B. 947. For recommendations regarding possible content of the proposed regulation, *see* New York State Bar Association, Tax Section, Report on Notice 2004-37 (November 18, 2004), *reprinted at* 2004 TNT 226-13 (November 23, 2004).

liability for the consolidated return year." In IRS Field Service Advice 200051002, September 15, 2000, a group consisted of a parent, *P*, and subsidiaries *S1* and *S2*. *S1* was placed in receivership. *P* had filed consolidated returns for the group for years 1 through 3, but the sole remaining officer of *P* refused to file returns of any kind for years 4 and 5. The receiver believed that *S1* had overpaid its taxes for year 4, and that the filing of consolidated returns for years 4 and 5 would produce a carryback refund for years 1 through 3. *S1* was not a financial institution to which Reg. § 301.6402-7, issued under Code § 6402(j)—and discussed below at § 806.2.5—applies. Thus, the only provision that in any way addressed this situation was the last sentence of Reg. § 1.1502-77(a), which says: "Notwithstanding the provisions of this paragraph [appointing the common parent as sole agent for the group], the District Director may, upon notifying the common parent, deal directly with any member of the group in respect of its liability, in which event such member shall have full authority to act for itself." Note that this does not make the subsidiary an agent for the other members of the group, nor does it authorize the subsidiary to file a separate, rather than a consolidated, return.

The IRS held that, while *S1* was required to continue to file consolidated returns, the District Director should apply this last sentence of Reg. § 1.1502-77(a) to "break the common parent's agency" to act for *S1* for the years 1 through 5; and *S1* should file a consolidated return for the group for years 4 and 5 and amended returns for years 1 through 3. However, such actions by *S1* would be only on its own behalf, and could not bind the other members of the group, because the last sentence of Reg. § 1.1502-77(a) allows *S1* only "to act for itself" and does not make it an agent for the group. Thus, the returns, though required to be in form and content consolidated returns, could be filed only on behalf of *S1*. Since the IRS would not be protected against claims by the other members of the group if it paid any of the refunds to *S1*, the IRS would deny the claims for refund, and *S1* would have to sue for the refunds in an action in which the other members of the group were interpleaded. Obviously, this is a very cumbersome procedure, which suggests the desirability of bringing all members of a consolidated return group before the court in the first instance where this is possible.

## *§ 804.2 Excess Loss Accounts*

Where the parent has an excess loss account with respect to the stock of a subsidiary that has a cancellation of debt item, the cancellation of debt may, in certain cases, cause the excess loss account to be triggered into income and to generate ordinary income rather than capital gain.

The pre-1994 regulations that dealt with these matters did not work very well. In 1994, however, the IRS amended the consolidated return investment adjustment and excess loss account regulations.[10] The new regulations provide a more coherent result. The new regulations are effective for tax years beginning on or after January 1, 1995. For such years, however, they require retroactive application of their concepts to

---

[10] Reg. § § 1.1502-11, 1.1502-19, 1.1502-31, 1.1502-32, 1.1502-33, 1.1502-76, and 1.1502-80.

events occurring in prior years, to the extent these may affect basis and excess loss computations used in post-1994 years. The 1994 regulations were further amended in August 2003, on a retroactive basis, to reflect the 2003 amendments to the consolidated return attribute reduction rules (*see* the discussion at § 804.4.5 below) and to limit the amount of the excess loss account that is triggered into income by the COD. Under this limitation, the amount of the excess loss account in the stock of the debtor corporation that is brought into income is limited to the portion, if any, of the COD that is not absorbed by the consolidated attribute reductions required by Code § 108 and the related consolidated return regulations.[11] We will first describe how the new regulations deal with these issues, and then how the prior regulations did so.

**1994 regulations.** The reason that certain cancellation of debt income of a subsidiary may trigger the parent's excess loss account in the stock of that subsidiary is that the excess loss account is triggered into income when the stock of a member is disposed of.[12] For excess loss account purposes, the stock of a subsidiary is deemed disposed of when (1) substantially all of the subsidiary's assets are treated as disposed of for no consideration (other than relief of indebtedness), abandoned, or destroyed for federal income tax purposes, (2) a debt of the subsidiary is discharged, to the extent it produces neither income nor attribute reduction under Code § 108 or § 1017, or (3) a member claims a loss for uncollectibility of the debt of a subsidiary, and the subsidiary does not have a corresponding amount of current COD income or gain.[13] The COD portion of this rule (item 2 above) backstops the worthlessness rule (item 1 above), since, after the subsidiary's indebtedness is discharged, the subsidiary is unlikely to be treated as worthless under the first rule.

Under the pre-1994 regulations, the stock of a subsidiary was also considered disposed of when its parent claimed a worthless stock deduction for it under Code § 165(g), but under the 1994 regulations a worthless stock deduction cannot become effective until the subsidiary's stock is deemed disposed of, as described above.[14] By so deferring the treatment of a consolidated loss subsidiary's stock as worthless, the present regulations alleviate the tension caused by authorities like *Prudential Lines*,

---

[11] Reg. § 1.1502-19.

[12] Reg. § 1.1502-19(b)(1). The excess loss account is generally triggered whenever the group ceases to own the stock of the subsidiary, even if no gain or loss is taken into account. For example, a Code § 355 distribution outside the group will trigger the excess loss account of the group in the distributed stock. *See* Reg. § 1.1502-19(g) (example 3) and IRS Field Service Advice 200022006, December 9, 1999, *reprinted at* 2000 TNT 108-61.

[13] Reg. § 1.1502-19(c)(1)(iii).

[14] Reg. § 1.1502-80(c). The purpose of these deferral rules is to defer, not disallow, a worthless stock deduction. However, the terms of this regulatory provision could have the unintended effect of preventing a group from ever claiming a worthless stock deduction for worthless stock of a subsidiary if the subsidiary leaves the group before satisfying the "deemed disposition" rules. Consequently, in T.D. 9118, March 18, 2004, this provision was changed by adopting Temp. Reg. § 1.1502-80T(c), to provide that for this purpose the deferral ends immediately before the time the subsidiary ceases to be a member of the group. The temporary regulation applies to taxable years beginning after March 18, 2004 and before March 19, 2007 (but only through July 18, 2007), with taxpayers permitted to apply it back to taxable years beginning on or after January 1, 1995. This provision was reproposed in early 2007 with nonsubstantive changes (*see* preamble to REG-157711-02), and became final on July 18, 2007, effective for tax returns due without extension after such date, and with the same permissive retroactive application. T.D. 9341.

which protect the tax attributes of such subsidiary in bankruptcy. (The *Prudential Lines* decision is discussed at § 508.2.4.)

This deferral of an excess loss account trigger or, alternatively, a worthless stock deduction is subject to the anti-avoidance rule of Reg. § 1.1502-19(e). Thus, for example, if a member ceases operations but retains more than an insignificant amount of assets with a principal purpose to avoid triggering an excess loss account, the retained assets will not be taken into account and the member will be considered worthless.[15] In the context of a bankruptcy of a subsidiary member, it is clear from the preamble to the 1994 regulations (when originally issued in proposed form) that this deferral was intended to delay a worthless stock deduction as long as reasonably possible. In IRS Technical Advice Memorandum 200549007,[16] involving a Chapter 11 liquidating bankruptcy, this was until the effective date of the plan, at which time the member's remaining assets were transferred to a "post-confirmation estate" and its stock was cancelled.

When the excess loss account is triggered into income, the resulting gain is treated as being from a sale or exchange of the subsidiary's stock.[17] As mentioned above, regulations issued in 2003 limit the amount of the excess loss account that is triggered into income to the portion, if any, of the COD that is in excess of the portion that is absorbed by the Code § 108 consolidated return attribute reductions.[18] Such gain, however, is treated as ordinary income to the extent of the amount by which the subsidiary is insolvent immediately before the disposition. For this purpose, the subsidiary's liabilities include any amount to which preferred stock would be entitled if the subsidiary were liquidated immediately before the disposition, and any former liabilities that were discharged to the extent that they produced attribute reduction under Code § 108 or § 1017.[19] The amount treated as ordinary income is reduced by certain distributions made by the subsidiary to the parent.

**Pre-1994 regulations.** The pre-1994 regulations provided that all of the shares of a subsidiary would be deemed to have been disposed of "on the last day of each taxable year of such subsidiary in which any of its stock is wholly worthless (within the meaning of Code § 165(g)), or in which an indebtedness of the subsidiary is discharged if such discharge would have resulted in 'cancellation of indebtedness income' but for the insolvency of the subsidiary."[20] This language, of course, did not mesh very well with the special bankruptcy COD rule contained in the prior Bankruptcy Act or with the present provisions of Code § 108, because it did not take into account that the reason companies in bankruptcy do not have COD income is that

---

15 *See* Reg. § 1.1502-19(g) (example 6).

16 August 5, 2005. For an interesting discussion of this Technical Advice, including an analysis of how the deduction for the worthlessness of the stock of a consolidated return subsidiary can, with appropriate planning, escape the limitations of Code § 382, see Willens, Conseco's Worthless Stock Loss Appears to Withstand Scrutiny, BNA Daily Tax Report #5 (January 9, 2006), at p. J-1; and § 508.7.2 above. *See also* § 508.2.4 above.

17 Reg. § 1.1502-19(b)(1).

18 Reg. § 1.1502-19.

19 Reg. § 1.1502-19(b)(4).

20 Pre-1994 Reg. § 1.1502-19(b)(2)(iii).

they are in bankruptcy and not because (indeed, whether or not) they are insolvent. Moreover, this provision did not take into account the consequences of attribute reduction that apply to bankrupt companies, or to insolvent companies, under Code § 108.

Under these pre-1994 regulations, where the excess loss account was triggered by the worthlessness of the subsidiary's stock or its COD income, the triggering of the excess loss account produced ordinary income rather than capital gain to the extent the subsidiary was insolvent. For this purpose, a subsidiary was insolvent to the extent that (1) the sum of all its existing liabilities, plus all of its liabilities which were discharged during consolidated return years but did not result in COD income because of the insolvency of the subsidiary, plus the amount of limited preferred stock, exceeded (2) the fair market value of its assets.[21] Ordinary income treatment did not apply, however, to the extent that the excess loss account was attributable to losses of the subsidiary which reduced long term capital gains rather than ordinary income of the group.[22] The theory of this provision was that, where it applied, the subsidiary's debt that was discharged presumably produced ordinary losses that were utilized by other members of the group. Thus, when the debt was forgiven, the other members of the group should have an offsetting amount of ordinary income, in effect reversing the previously deducted ordinary losses.[23]

Prior to the adoption of Code § 312(l) in 1980 and of Code § 1503(e) by the Revenue Act of 1987 and its amendment by TAMRA in 1988, there was a defect in the way the consolidated return investment adjustments applied to COD income excluded from income because of insolvency or bankruptcy, including the way they affected the excess loss account. The defect was caused by the coupling of (1) the IRS position that COD income excluded by the insolvency or similar exceptions increases the earnings and profits of the debtor (except to the extent it results in basis reduction),[24] with (2) the fact that the pre-1994 earnings and profits investment adjustment provisions of the consolidated return regulations gave the parent a positive adjustment in its basis for the stock (including its excess loss account) of the subsidiary for the undistributed earnings and profits of the subsidiary for the taxable year.[25] A literal application of this basis adjustment provision would operate to eliminate the excess loss account to the extent of the COD income excluded by the insolvency exception. Because, at least for pre-1988 Act years, this would undercut the presumed purpose of the consolidated return provision that triggers the excess loss account (if any) into income upon such debt cancellation, the IRS ruled that this upward adjustment in basis should not apply where the earnings and profits of the subsidiary were generated by COD income excluded because of the insolvency

---

[21] Pre-1994 Reg. § 1.1502-19(a)(2)(ii).

[22] Id.

[23] *See* GCM 39303, June 28, 1984.

[24] Rev. Rul. 75-515, 1975-2 C.B. 117. This rule was added to the Internal Revenue Code by the Bankruptcy Tax Act of 1980 as Code § 312(1), which is discussed in Chapter 4 at § 404.4.

[25] Pre-1994 Reg. § 1.1502-32(b). The earnings and profits of the parent are increased in the same amount. Pre-1994 Reg. § 1.1503-33(c)(4)(ii).

exception.[26] Since this ruling was contrary to the literal wording of the consolidated return regulations, there was doubt whether it would be upheld in court without an amendment to the regulations.[27] The Treasury did not amend the regulations. But it did litigate the matter. In *Wyman-Gordon*,[28] a case involving pre-1980 Act years, the Tax Court upheld the IRS position, saying that because the consolidated group had enjoyed the benefit of the loss member's NOLs (and the COD had not produced attribute reduction under the pre-1980 Act rules), allowance of a positive basis adjustment for related debt cancellation to eliminate the resulting excess loss account would amount to allowing a double deduction for the same loss.[29] The Tax Court went on to suggest that this disallowance of an upward basis adjustment would not be necessary for years governed by the Bankruptcy Tax Act of 1980, to the extent that the COD income resulted in attribute reduction under the attribute reduction rules that were added by that Act to Code § 108. (The validity of this conclusion is discussed at § 804.3, immediately below.)

The issue was litigated once again for a pre-1988 year in the *CSI Hydrostatic Testers* case.[30] This time, the opposite result was achieved, since the case involved a post-1980 tax year (and thus Code § 312(l) applied). Like *Wyman-Gordon*, it involved events that occurred before the effective date of Code § 1503(e). The subsidiary had COD income, some of which produced attribute reduction, and some of which exceeded the attributes available for reduction, but all of which was excluded from income under Code § 108. The court held that the language of pre-1994 Reg. § 1.1502-32 required the basis of the parent's stock of the subsidiary to be increased (or the excess loss account decreased) by the earnings and profits of the subsidiary and that the legislative history to Code § 312(l) showed that Congress intended it to require earnings and profits of the subsidiary to be increased by COD income to the extent this was not applied to reduce basis under Code § 1017. The court said that the

---

[26] IRS Tech. Adv. Mem. 8447006, July 27, 1984; GCM 39303, June 28, 1984. These rulings only talk about the basis adjustment, and do not suggest that the earnings and profits of the parent would not be increased.

[27] *See Woods Investment Co. v. Commissioner*, 85 T.C. 274, Dec. 42,315 (1985), *acq.* (IRS bound by result in consolidated return regulations, although resulting in unintended benefit to taxpayers; involved effect of Code § 312(k) on subsidiary earnings and profits and parent basis in subsidiary); IRS Announcement 86-32 (IRS decided not to appeal *Woods Investment Co.*, although disagreed with substantive result, and will revise regulations); Action on Decision 1986-039 (although disagreeing with result, recommended acquiescence and stated that the regulation will be revised); Axelrod, The Basis for Using E&P in Consolidated Return Basis Adjustments, 12 J. Corp. Tax'n 228 (1985); *cf. Henry C. Beck Builders, Inc. v. Commissioner*, 41 T.C. 616, Dec. 26,652 (1964) (rejected IRS's attempt to cure *ad hoc* a gap in the pre-1966 consolidated return regulations). Congress, in the Revenue Act of 1987, Pub. L. No. 100-203. § 10222(a), overruled *Woods Investment Co.* prospectively by adding Code § 1503(e).

[28] *Wyman-Gordon Co. and Rome Industries, Inc. v. Commissioner*, 89 T.C. 207, Dec. 44.084 (1987). The court distinguished *Woods Investment Co. v. Commissioner, supra* note 24, saying that whereas *Woods* involved regulation language that mandated the result desired by the taxpayer in that case, the investment adjustment regulations do not mandate the result desired by *Wyman-Gordon* because they do not specifically mention COD income. This reasoning is not entirely convincing.

[29] The IRS took the same position in IRS Field Service Advice 1999-543 (undated), *reprinted at* 1999 TNT 15-84.

[30] *CSI Hydrostatic Testers Inc. v. Commissioner*, 103 T.C. 398 (1994), *aff'd*, 76 A.F.T.R.2d ¶ 95-5291 (5th Cir. 1995).

adoption of Code § 312(l), coupled with the failure of the IRS to amend its regulations, gave the court no choice. This distinguished the case from *Wyman-Gordon*, and the court refused to read an exception into the regulations. For the portion of the COD income that produced attribute reduction of the subsidiary's NOLs, the IRS asserted an alternative argument that the COD item should not create a net increase in the parent's basis in the subsidiary's stock (or reduce its excess loss account), because the NOL attribute reduction should be treated as an "absorption" of the NOLs within the meaning of Reg. § 1.1502-32(b)(2)(ii), thereby creating an offsetting reduction in the parent's basis in the subsidiary's stock (or increase in the excess loss account). The court rejected this argument as well, saying that the phrase "absorption" as used in these regulations had always meant the use of the NOLs, not their elimination.

At almost the same time as the *Wyman-Gordon* decision was rendered, Congress, in the Revenue Act of 1987, adopted new Code § 1503(e), which provides (as amended by TAMRA in 1988) that solely for the purpose of determining gain or loss on disposition of a subsidiary's stock and the amount of any inclusion in income of an excess loss account, the upward investment adjustment to the stock's basis under the consolidated return regulations will not include earnings and profits from debt cancellation excluded from income by Code § 108, to the extent such excluded income does not reduce tax attributes other than basis.[31] This adopted the result in *Wyman-Gordon*, but did not deal with the part of the *CSI Hydrostatic Testers* case that involved COD income which did reduce tax attributes other than basis. Code § 1503(e) applies to dispositions of stock occurring after December 15, 1987. TAMRA, which added the reference to excess loss accounts, contains a special transition rule for dispositions occurring before January 1, 1989. As indicated above and in § 804.3, the 1994 consolidated return investment adjustment and excess loss account regulations eliminate the defects in the prior rules that were dealt with in *Wyman-Gordon* and *CSI Hydrostatic Testers* cases.

**Other pre-1994 excess loss account problems.** The excess loss account of a troubled subsidiary may be triggered into income by events other than COD income of the subsidiary.[32] The pre-1994 regulations provided that the stock of a subsidiary would be deemed to have been disposed of for excess loss accounts purposes, not only in the COD income case mentioned above, but also in the following circumstances:

(1) On the last day of each taxable year of the subsidiary for which the Commissioner is satisfied that 10 percent or less of the face amount of any

---

[31] Because Code § 312(l) (discussed at § 404.4 above) provides that COD income that produces basis reduction does not increase earnings and profits, it would seem unnecessary for Code § 1503(e) to mention earnings and profits arising from such debt cancellation. Congress referred to it, however, because Congress wanted to be sure to eliminate upward basis adjustments that taxpayers may have made in such circumstances before the effective date of Code § 312(I). *See* H.R. Rep. No. 100-495, 100th Cong., 2d Sess. 963 (1987).

[32] *See* pre-1994 Reg. § 1.1502-19(b); Reg. § 1.1502-19(c).

obligation for which the subsidiary is primarily or secondarily personally liable is recoverable at maturity by its creditors;[33] or

(2) On the day on which a member transfers an obligation for which the subsidiary is primarily or secondarily personally liable to any non-member for an amount which is 25 percent or less of the face amount of the obligation.[34]

The 1994 regulations eliminated these two rules.

## *§804.3 Other Investment Adjustment Problems*

The court in the *Wyman-Gordon* case (discussed at §804.2) suggested that the opportunity for a double deduction, resulting from a potential mismatching between the earnings and profits rules[35] and the consolidated return investment adjustment provisions,[36] was eliminated by the adoption of the Code §108 attribute reduction rules in the Bankruptcy Tax Act of 1980, to the extent such attribute reduction applies. The same assumption underlies Code §1503(e) adopted in 1987 (and also discussed immediately above), because that section does not apply where COD income produces attribute reduction (other than basis reduction). As will be explained below, these assumptions were not entirely free of difficulties; but finally the elimination of any mismatching was addressed in a different and better fashion in the 1994 changes to the investment adjustment regulations.

**Pre-TAMRA analysis.** It is not so clear as the *Wyman-Gordon* court assumed, however, that the opportunity for an extra deduction was eliminated by the adoption of the attribute reduction rules in the Bankruptcy Tax Act of 1980. The reason such an opportunity could potentially still exist, even where attribute reduction occurs, is that the earnings and profits rules were not identical to the pre-1994 investment adjustment provisions. For earnings and profits purposes, for example, when a corporation's loss produces an NOL, the loss reduces earnings and profits. For pre-1994 investment adjustment purposes, however, if the NOL is not simultaneously used by the consolidated group against income of a current or prior year, there is no net reduction in the basis of the stock of the loss member. The earnings and profits deficit produced by the loss is a negative adjustment,[37] but the unused NOL becomes a positive adjustment.[38] A reduction in basis to reflect the loss does not take place unless and until the unused NOL is "absorbed" by the group in a future tax year.[39]

Assume, however, that before the NOL is absorbed against income of the group in a later year, the loss member has COD income that eliminates the NOL. The COD

---

[33] Pre-1994 Reg. §1.1502-19(b)(2)(iv).

[34] Pre-1994 Reg. §1.1502-19(b)(2)(v).

[35] Code §312(l) provides, in substance, that COD income produces earnings profits unless it is applied to reduce basis. *See* §404.4 above.

[36] Pre-1994 Reg. §1.1502-32(b)(1) and (2).

[37] Pre-1994 Reg. §1.1502-32(b)(2)(i).

[38] Pre-1994 Reg. §1.1502-32(b)(1)(ii).

[39] Pre-1994 Reg. §1.1502-32(b)(2)(ii).

income increases the earnings and profits of the loss member under Code § 312(1) (*see* § 404.4); and this will produce a positive investment adjustment[40] (a result which was not changed by Code § 1503(e), but which has been changed by 1994 Reg. § 1.1502-32). Thus, unless some other provisions could be found in the consolidated return investment adjustment rules that required an offsetting negative adjustment to be made, the consequence of the creation of the NOL and its elimination by debt cancellation would be a net positive (rather than a "net zero") investment adjustment. This will produce the extra deduction problem that the *Wyman-Gordon* court assumed would no longer exist. This was the very problem that troubled the IRS in the portion of the *CSI Hydrostatic Testers* case that dealt with COD income that produced NOL reduction.

An offsetting negative adjustment would occur, however, if the NOL could be considered to have been "absorbed" by the group, within the meaning of the investment adjustment regulation, when it was eliminated by Code § 108. Although such a reading would require a strained application of the word "absorbed," it would eliminate the extra deduction problem;[41] it would be consistent with the goal Congress sought to achieve with its adoption in 1987 of Code § 1503(e); and it would produce the result that Congress assumed would occur under the investment adjustment regulation (although Congress provided no analysis to back up its assumption).[42] The court in the *CSI Hydrostatic Testers* case, however, rejected this interpretation.

When the attribute that is reduced by COD income is asset basis, rather than an NOL, no similar interpretative hurdles need to be surmounted in order to avoid an extra deduction problem. Code § 312(1) provides that earnings and profits are not increased by COD income that reduces basis. Therefore, no stock basis increase occured at that time under the pre-1994 consolidated return investment adjustment provisions. The result is that a future increase in earnings and profits (and stock basis) is substituted for a present increase. When the asset is disposed of, there will be an increase in earnings and profits because of the earlier asset basis reduction.

Where the attribute that is reduced is an investment or foreign tax credit, the end result is similar but the timing is different. Here, unlike the basis reduction case, earnings and profits are increased under Code § 312(1) by the COD income that is applied to reduce such credits. This in turn will produce an increase in stock basis under the consolidated return investment adjustment provisions. In the later year, however, when the tax credit would otherwise have been used to reduce tax liability,

---

[40] Reg. § 1.1502-32(b)(1)(i).

[41] Indeed, the IRS took this position in IRS Field Service Advice 1999-543 (undated), *reprinted at* 1999 TNT 15-84.

[42] The Conference Report said that Code § 1503(e) would not eliminate the upward basis adjustment for earnings and profits arising from excluded COD income "where the amount excluded was applied to reduce tax attributes, such as net operating losses, *that were immediately reflected in basis* under the consolidated return regulations." H.R. Rep. No. 100-495, 100th Cong., 1st Sess. 963 (1987) (emphasis added). The court in the *CSI Hydrostatic Testers* case refused to give this statement any significance, saying "[i]t is well settled that the view of one Congress as to the construction of a statute or a regulation adopted many years before is not entitled to substantial weight."

there will be an offsetting decrease in earnings and profits (and thus stock basis) because of the additional tax liability resulting from the elimination of the credits.

In summary, asset basis reduction—which should be considered more in the nature of a postponement of income than a loss of a tax attribute—produces an increase in stock basis but this is deferred; and credit reduction produces an immediate basis increase followed by a later offsetting decrease.

**Post-TAMRA analysis.** The Conference Report to TAMRA, without changing any statutory language, contained the following statement:

> In connection with the provisions of section 1503(e) of the Code relating to cancellation of indebtedness income, the conferees clarify that an upward basis adjustment through the inclusion of cancellation of indebtedness income in earnings and profits for purposes of section 1503(e) is permitted only to the extent that a tax attribute that was reduced under section 108 *had resulted* in a downward basis adjustment in the parent's stock of the subsidiary. It is also clarified that the upward adjustment for cancellation of indebtedness income cannot exceed the amount of the tax attribute that was reduced.[43]

This language, if it were given effect, creates a new problem. The problem, which is caused by the use of the past tense in the portion of the above passage that we have italicized, arises where the attribute being reduced is a credit. As we discussed above, an unused credit will not have produced a previous downward basis adjustment. Its destruction, however, will produce a downward basis adjustment in the future year in which its use would have reduced the loss company's tax liability. This happens because the loss of the credit increases the tax liability in the future year, which reduces earnings and profits and thus, under the investment adjustment rules, reduces the parent's basis in the stock of the subsidiary. It would therefore, as we stated above, seem appropriate to increase earnings and profits, and thus basis, for debt cancellation that reduces tax credits. The quoted language, if applied to credit reductions, would seem to prevent this result. It is not clear that this was intended. Under the holding in the *CSI Hydrostatic Testers* case, however, this language would not be given any effect.

**1994 regulations.** The effect of COD income on investment adjustments to subsidiary stock also is addressed in the 1994 consolidated return regulations. These provide a positive basis adjustment for excluded COD income of the subsidiary only if there would be a corresponding negative basis adjustment resulting from the reduction of the subsidiary's tax attributes.

The pre-1994 investment adjustment regime generally adjusts stock basis by reference to the earnings and profits of the subsidiary. In contrast, the 1994 regulations "delink" the determination of stock basis of a subsidiary from the calculation of that subsidiary's earnings and profits. Instead, under the 1994 investment adjustment regime, the stock basis of the subsidiary is increased or decreased, each year, for the

---

[43] Conference Report to TAMRA, H. Rep. No. 1104, 100th Cong., 2d Sess. 18-19 (1988) (emphasis added).

subsidiary's taxable income or loss, as adjusted, for such year.[44] The subsidiary's loss is taken into account to the extent it is absorbed in such year or is carried back in that year to be absorbed in a prior year; otherwise, the loss is carried forward and taken into account in the year in which it is absorbed (or expires).[45] Other adjustments to taxable income or loss include:

(1) an upward adjustment for "tax-exempt" income, which is income that is permanently excluded from the subsidiary's gross income;[46] and
(2) a downward adjustment for noncapital, nondeductible expenditures, which generally are deductions or losses recognized by the subsidiary that are both permanently disallowed as deductions or losses for federal income tax purposes and not allowable as increases to the tax basis of the subsidiary's property.[47]

Under the 1994 rules, COD income that is excluded from gross income under either the bankruptcy or insolvency exception is treated as tax-exempt income to the extent it reduces tax attributes under the attribute reduction rules of the Code (giving rise to an upward adjustment), and such amount is also treated as a noncapital nondeductible expense (giving rise to a downward adjustment).[48] The reduction of the subsidiary's tax attributes (including credits) is treated as a noncapital, nondeductible expense because such reduction is not taken into account in determining stock basis and is permanently taken into account in determining the subsidiary's income.[49] Thus, by treating excluded COD income as tax-exempt income only to the extent of the attribute reduction resulting therefrom, the rules provide for offsetting positive and negative adjustments to the extent that the subsidiary's own attributes are reduced. However, depending on the magnitude of the subsidiary's excluded COD income, attributes of other members of the group may be reduced under Reg. § 1.1502-28 or its predecessor, Temp. Reg. § 1.1502-28T (for debt cancellations after August 29, 2003). In such event, the debtor subsidiary may have the upward adjustment for the excluded COD income while another member of the group has a downward adjustment for the reduction of its tax attributes (*see* discussion at § 804.4.5 below).[50]

When the 1994 regulations were still in proposed form, there was a question whether purchase price adjustments excluded from COD income of a subsidiary under either the common law exception for purchase price adjustments or Code § 108(e)(5) would be treated as noncapital, nondeductible expenses, giving rise to a negative adjustment in the parent's basis in its stock of the subsidiary. This problem

[44] Reg. § 1.1502-32. The approach of the 1994 regulations is consistent with the approach of Code § 1503(e), which precluded taxpayers from using earnings and profits in computing stock basis of a subsidiary for purposes of determining gain or loss on disposition.

[45] Reg. § 1.1502-32(b)(3)(i), (iii)(A).

[46] Reg. § 1.1502-32(b)(3)(ii)(A).

[47] Reg. § 1.1502-32(b)(3)(iii)(A).

[48] Reg. § 1.1502-32(b)(3)(ii)(C) and -32T(b)(3)(ii)(C).

[49] Reg. § 1.1502-32(b)(3)(iii)(B) and -32T(b)(3)(iii)(A).

[50] Reg. § 1.1502-32T(b)(5), Example 4(b).

was eliminated in the final 1994 regulations, which specifically provide that a purchase price adjustment excluded from COD income of the subsidiary does not result in any adjustment to the parent's basis in the subsidiary's stock.[51]

## *§804.4 COD Income and Transactions in Intercompany Debt*

### §804.4.1 Member COD Income from Nonintercompany Debt

Where a debtor that is a member of a consolidated return group realizes COD income on a debt that is not intercompany debt (that is, the debtor and the creditor are not both members of the consolidated return group when the COD income arises), the question has long been whether the attribute reduction rules of Code §108 apply on a separate company or a consolidated basis. Until new regulations were issued in 2003, there was nothing explicit in the consolidated return regulations that required that a consolidated approach be taken to the application of Code §108. Accordingly, Code §108 generally was, at least before the latter 1990s, applied to the nonintercompany debt as if separate returns were filed. Although the IRS had earlier held that the basis and other attribute adjustments required by Code §108(b) are to be applied as if the debtor member were filing a separate return,[52] in the late 1990s it asserted that attribute reduction—at least NOL reduction—can occur to consolidated attributes, even those not supplied by the debtor member.[53] Finally, in August 2003, the IRS issued regulations (which were originally issued in temporary form, and then finalized in 2005) that apply most (but not all) attribute reductions on a hybrid form

---

[51] Reg. §1.1502-32(b)(5), Example 4(d).

[52] *See, e.g.*, IRS Letter Ruling 9121017, February 21, 1991. It is interesting to note, however, that the IRS applied the Code §108 proportionality requirement of the stock-for-debt exception on a substantively consolidated group rather than an individual company basis in IRS Letter Ruling 9105042, February 27, 1990 (which is discussed at §504A.4.2 above). The consolidated return group had been divided, for bankruptcy plan purposes, into six substantively consolidated groups. Except for the application of the proportionality requirement, this substantive consolidation was not given tax effect.

[53] IRS Legal Memorandum 200149008, August 10, 2001; IRS Field Service Advice 199912007, December 14, 1998, stating that to this extent the IRS will not adhere to IRS Letter Ruling 9121017, February 21, 1991. The IRS has taken the same position in litigation, but has not done so consistently. *See Peoplefeeders, Inc. v. Commissioner*, T.C. Memo. 1999-36 (issue presented, but case resolved on other grounds), and IRS reply brief, dated May 1, 1998; and news article at 1999 TNT 84-18 (April 30, 1999) (reporting on a panel discussion at the ABA's Spring 1999 Tax Section meeting). The foregoing authorities assert that NOL reductions should be applied on a consolidated basis. They do not involve other types of attributes. Both the field service advice and *Peoplefeeders, Inc.* involved the cancellation of intercompany debt prior to the 1995 amendments to Reg. §1.1502-13, where the taxpayer claimed that the COD on the intercompany debt reduced the separate debtor member's tax attributes, while at the same time obtaining advantage of the creditor member's corresponding bad debt deduction. As discussed in the text below, the consolidated return regulations now turn-off the application of Code §108(a) in this context and thus force the recognition of the COD income, neutralizing on a group basis the bad debt deduction. For a discussion of the potential complexities involved in applying Code §108(b) to consolidated attributes, *see* Dubroff, Blanchard, Broadbent & Duvall, Federal Income Taxation of Corporations Filing Consolidated Returns §33.06[1] (2d ed.); and Axelrod, What's "Reasonable" Before the Consolidated COD Regulations?, 115 Tax Notes 745 (May 21, 2007).

of a consolidated basis, which first exhausts the attributes of the debtor member. Although the attribute reduction regime of these regulations only applies to excluded COD income after August 29, 2003, the IRS has expanded its position that for prior periods attribute reduction should occur on a single entity, consolidated basis.[54] *See* the discussion at § 804.4.5 below.

Even when these attribute reductions were generally being made as if separate returns were being filed, there were (and still remain) two exceptions to such separate return treatment. These are: (1) if the debtor has deductions or losses that have been suspended or deferred under the consolidated return intercompany transaction rules, the suspended and deferred deductions are treated as attributes that can be reduced under Code § 108(b);[55] and (2) if the debtor is required under Code § 108(b) to reduce the basis of property that it received in an intercompany transaction (to which the 1995 amendments to Reg. § 1.1502-13 apply), all or part of any gain deferred by the transferring members in connection with such intercompany transaction may be accelerated and includable in the transferor's income in the current year.[56] Even under the 2003 regulations, the IRS continues the separate company application of the jurisdictional requirements of Code § 108(a). Thus, whether Code § 108(a) excludes the COD from income depends on whether the debtor member itself is insolvent or in bankruptcy (regardless of whether any of the other members are insolvent or in bankruptcy).

As discussed in the subsequent paragraphs, the treatment differs where the debt is intercompany debt.

### § 804.4.2 COD Income on Intercompany Debt (Including Intercompany Transfers of Intercompany Debt)

Where the COD income occurs on intercompany debt (that is, both the debtor and the holder are members of the consolidated return group when the COD income arises), the consolidated return regulations governing intercompany transactions override the general application of Code § 108, by providing that Code § 108(a) will not apply to exclude COD income on intercompany debt.[57] Consequently, all COD income on intercompany debt will be includable, and thus no basis or other tax attribute reductions will be made under Code § 108(b) for COD items on such intercompany debt. Since the holder of the debt (which is also a member of the consolidated return group) will presumably have a bad debt deduction for its basis in the portion of the debt that gives rise to the COD income, the two items will offset

---

[54] In 2006, an IRS Chief Counsel Advice went farther than the IRS had in prior pronouncements (noted above), and took the position that the consolidated attributes of all members of a consolidated return group (including NOLs and AMT credits) are subject to reduction for a member's excluded COD income and that the only attribute that is not a consolidated attribute is tax basis. IRS Chief Counsel Advice 200714016, December 1, 2006. The Advice did not consider the treatment of any tax attributes that were subject to a SRLY limitation. For a critique of the IRS's analysis, see Axelrod, *supra* note 53.

[55] Reg. § 1.108-3.

[56] *See* Reg. § 1.1502-13(d)(3), Example 4.

[57] Reg. § 1.1502-13(g)(3)(ii)(B)(2). *See also* Reg. § 1.1502-13(g)(5), Example 3.

each other, in whole or in part, in computing the consolidated return net taxable income. Indeed, this is the purpose of this portion of the consolidated return regulations: the goal is to cause simultaneous matching of income and deductions on such items so that they have a neutral effect on consolidated income, and to prevent shifting of one or more of these items to other members of the group.[58]

The consolidated return regulations produce this result by stating that "if a member *realizes* an amount (other than zero) of income, gain, deduction, or loss, directly or indirectly, from the assignment or extinguishment of all or part of its remaining rights or obligations under an intercompany obligation" (emphasis added), then the obligation is treated as if it had been satisfied immediately *before* the realization event for the cash or property received for it, or if none, for its fair market value;[59] and, to the extent the debt remains outstanding, to have been reissued immediately *after* that event for that same consideration.[60] Certain exceptions are provided from this treatment,[61] including amounts "realized" from the conversion of an obligation into stock of the obligor.

To illustrate this general rule, if the holder were to cancel (and not as a contribution to capital) $40 of a $100 intercompany debt which is worth face, the debt would be treated as having been satisfied for $60 in cash. The obligor would have $40 of COD income, which would be offset by the $40 bad debt deduction of the holder (assuming the holder had a $100 basis in the debt). The remaining $60 face of debt would be treated as having been reissued for $60 (its fair market value).[62] Suppose, however, the remaining $60 face amount of debt had a fair market value of only $20. In that case, the holder would have an $80 bad debt deduction, the obligor would have $80 of COD income, and the remaining $60 face amount of debt would be deemed to have been reissued for $20. Although this deemed reissuance would produce substantial original issue discount on the reissued "new" intercompany debt, the AHYDO interest disallowance provisions of Code §163(e)(5) would not

---

[58] *See* Dubroff, Blanchard, Broadbent, & Duvall, Federal Income Taxation of Corporations Filing Consolidated Returns §33.03[1] (2d ed.).

[59] Reg. §1.1502-13(g)(3)(i)(A), and (ii). On December 21, 1998, the IRS proposed to amend Reg. §1.1502-13(g)(3)(i)(A) to make it applicable to any realization event, even if no income, gain, deduction, or loss is realized. The amendment would not become effective until published in final form. For comments suggesting further changes in the regulation, *see* comments of the AICPA, dated August 11, 1999, *reprinted at* 1999 TNT 156-11; comments of Deloitte & Touche, dated August 24, 1999, *reprinted at* 1999 TNT 171-30. The 1998 proposed regulation was withdrawn, and a revised version was proposed, on September 28, 2007 (although the earlier proposed regulation continues to have some interim effect pending final regulations).

[60] Reg. §1.1502-13(g)(3)(iii). The provision also applies, even without a realization event, if the intercompany obligation ceases to be an intercompany obligation, as where the debtor or creditor leaves the group. *See* discussion below, at §804.4.3.

[61] Reg. §1.1502-13(g)(3)(i)(B), and (g)(4).

[62] *See* Reg. §1.1502-13(g)(5), Example 3. The textual example is for illustrative purposes only. If the debt is worth face, the cancellation would normally be a contribution to capital, or a payment for services, or the like.

apply. The consolidated return regulations provide that Code § 163(e)(5) does not apply to obligations issued as intercompany obligations.[63]

The regulations treat a partial bad debt deduction claimed with respect to intercompany debt the same as a partial extinguishment of the debt.[64] To illustrate, suppose that $100 of debt has a fair market value of $60, and the holder claims a partial bad debt deduction of $40. The debt is treated as having been satisfied for $60, thereby creating $40 of COD income (which offsets in the consolidated return the $40 partial bad debt deduction). And the reissued "new" intercompany debt of $60 face amount is treated as having been reissued for $60.

Even more surprisingly, the regulations treat any transfer of intercompany debt among group members as a deemed satisfaction and reissuance of the debt. The deemed satisfaction and reissuance are generally treated as occurring at fair market value or, in the case of a sale, at the price paid.[65] Thus, even a transfer of the debt among members can result in the current recognition of income or loss. Though this strikes one as surprising, the purpose of this rule is to prevent a member from transferring to other members the tax consequences of economic changes that have arisen in the hands of the first member.

An even more startling result is that the portion of the regulations quoted above is intended to supersede the nonrecognition provisions of the Code.[66] The only clue to the existence of this purpose is the use of the word "realizes," which apparently was used in the most technical sense. Thus, whether the member would normally *recognize* the item involved becomes irrelevant. Such "realization" events include transactions given nonrecognition status under such provisions as Code § 332 and § 351. Further, it appears to have been intended that the "realization" of *any* amount with respect to an intercompany debt causes the entire intercompany debt to be treated as having been satisfied immediately before the event; and, to the extent the debt remains outstanding, to have been reissued immediately after the event.[67]

The language used in this portion of the regulations leaves their application unclear for a number of basic transactions. For example, how is a contribution of intercompany debt to the capital of the debtor member by its member parent to be treated? To illustrate this point, suppose that *P* contributes to the capital of *S* a $50 face amount *S* debt which has a fair market value of $10. The contribution to capital would normally not be considered a realization event for *S*. If one accepts the view

---

[63] Reg. § 1.1502-80(e). This nonapplicability of Code § 163(e)(5) only exists, however, for intercompany obligations issued in consolidated return years beginning on or after July 12, 1995.

[64] *See* Reg. § 1.1502-13(g)(3)(i)(A), and (5), Example 3.

[65] Reg. § 1.1502-13(g)(3)(ii)(A), and (iii). The December 21, 1998, proposed amendments to this regulation would provide that when the debt is transferred for property, it is treated as satisfied for an amount equal to the issue price (determined under Code § § 1273 and 1274) of the "new" reissued debt. The 1998 proposed regulation was withdrawn, and a revised version was proposed, on September 28, 2007. The revised version eliminates the application of the original issue discount rules of Code § § 1273 and 1274 in these circumstances, and substitutes the obligation's fair market value or, in some cases, the amount realized on the transfer of the obligation.

[66] *See* Andrew I. Dubroff, Obligations of Members, paper delivered at the September 26-27, 1996, ALI-ABA Course of Study on Consolidated Tax Return Regulations, pp. 18-24. This is confirmed in the December 21, 1998, proposed amendment to Reg. § 1.1502-13(g)(5), Example 2.

[67] Id.

that it is not a realization event for *P* either (there are possible counter-arguments),[68] then this portion of the consolidated return regulations would not apply, and Code § 108(e)(6) would apply. This would treat the contribution as if *S* had discharged the debt for an amount equal to *P*'s basis in the debt, thereby resulting in zero realization of income or loss to *S* if *P* had a $50 basis in the debt.[69] *P* would have an additional $50 contributed basis in the stock of *S*. On the other hand, if one considers that either *P* or *S* had a realization event from the contribution, and if one further considers that this portion of the regulation, when it applies, overrides Code § 108(e)(6), then the consolidated return regulations would treat the debt as having been retired for $10 immediately before the contribution to capital. *S* would have $40 of COD income, and *P* would have a $40 bad debt deduction.[70] *P* would have a $50 increase in its basis in the stock of *S*, but $40 of this would be an "extraordinary gain" item under Reg. § 1.1502-20(c),[71] with the result that *P* would effectively be precluded from ever taking a loss for the additional stock basis resulting from the worthless portion of the intercompany debt.[72] *P* might argue against this result by taking the position that Code § 108(e)(6) is not superseded by Reg. § 1.1502-13(g)(3). Or *P* might argue that the capital contribution should be considered eligible for the exception in Reg. § 1.1502-13(g)(3)(i)(B)(3) for transactions involving the "conversion" of an obligation into stock of the obligor. Or, in appropriate circumstances, the parties might seek to avoid this controversy entirely, through advance planning, by having P contribute $50 to *S*, which *S* applies in a separate transaction to retire the $50 in intercompany debt.[73]

---

[68] The arguments pro and con on this point are set forth in some detail in Dubroff, Blanchard, Broadbent, & Duvall, Federal Income Taxation of Corporations Filing Consolidated Returns § 33.03[2] (2d ed.). *See also* § 505 above; and IRS Letter Ruling 9836004, March 25, 1998 (non-prorata contribution of X corp. stock to X by an X shareholder is not a realization event for the shareholder).

[69] And *P* would have no recognition of income or loss, but would simply add its basis in the *S* debt to its basis in the *S* stock.

[70] The December 21, 1998, proposed amendment to Reg. § 1.1502-13(g)(3) would treat the extinguished debt as satisfied for an amount equal to the issue price (determined under Code § 1273 or 1274) of a "new" debt issued on the date of the transaction, with identical terms, to a third party for property that is not publicly traded. The amount for which the extinguished debt is treated as satisfied would therefore depend primarily on whether such debt was itself publicly traded debt. Assuming that, in the example presented in the text, the *S* debt contributed was *not publicly traded* debt and provided for adequate interest over its remaining term, the proposed amendment would treat the debt as having been satisfied for $50 (based on the issue price of an equivalent new debt determined under Code § 1274) immediately before the contribution to capital, with the $50 thereafter contributed to capital. Thus, there would be no COD income to *S* and no deduction for *P*. The 1998 proposed regulation was withdrawn, and a revised version was proposed, on September 28, 2007. The revised version would *not* treat a Code § 351 contribution of the debt in exchange for stock as creating a deemed exchange of the old debt for a "new" debt before the exchange. Presumably the same result would apply to a contribution of the debt to capital.

[71] Had the consolidated return "realization" concept not applied to the transaction, none of *P*'s $50 increase in its *S* stock basis would be "extraordinary gain."

[72] *See also* the discussion at § 804.5 below.

[73] Id. *See generally* the discussion of this example at Dubroff, Blanchard, Broadbent, & Duvall, Federal Income Taxation of Corporations Filing Consolidated Returns § 33.03[2] (2d ed.). The December 21, 1998, proposed amendment to the regulation would eliminate the "conversion" argument by

### § 804.4.3 When Intercompany Debt Ceases to be Intercompany Debt

When outstanding intercompany debt loses its status as intercompany debt, such as when either the holder or the obligor leaves the group (or when the debt is sold by the holder to an outsider), the consolidated return rules provide that the debt is treated as though it had been redeemed immediately *before* the transaction that terminated its intercompany status, and to have been reissued immediately *after* that transaction.[74] Since the redemption is deemed to occur while the debt is still intercompany debt, Code § 108(a) will not apply to exclude any resulting COD from income. On the other hand, because the reissuance of the "new" debt is deemed to occur immediately after it loses its intercompany status, the "new" debt is not protected from the AHYDO interest disallowance provisions of Code § 163(e)(5).

If the reason the debt loses its intercompany status is that the holder sold the debt to an outsider for cash, the transaction is treated for both the buyer and the debtor as if the "new" debt had been issued immediately after the sale for that amount of cash; if instead the debt loses its intercompany status because either the debtor or the creditor became nonmembers, the "new" debt is treated as being issued for an amount of cash equal to its fair market value immediately after the debtor or creditor became a nonmember.[75]

### § 804.4.4 When Nonintercompany Debt Becomes Intercompany Debt

When nonintercompany debt becomes intercompany debt (such as when a member buys another member's debt from an outsider, or when the outside obligor or holder joins the consolidated return group), the consolidated return regulations make the related-party acquisition rules of Code § 108(e)(4) inapplicable.[76] Instead, the debt generally is treated as though it had been satisfied, and a "new" debt issued to the holder, immediately after the debt became an intercompany debt.[77] In this instance, the regulations provide that "the attributes of all items taken into account from the satisfaction are determined on a separate entity basis, rather than treating S and B as divisions of a single corporation."[78] Among other things, this means that Code § 108(a) is *not* made inapplicable to this transaction.[79] On the other hand, Reg.

(Footnote Continued)

limiting the conversion rule to conversions provided by the terms of the instrument. This limiting language is not included in the 2007 proposed revision of this regulation.

74 Reg. § 1.1502-13(g)(3)(i), (ii), (iii).

75 Reg. § 1.1502-13(g)(3)(iii). Prop. Reg. § 1.1502-13(g)(3)-(7) issued September 28, 2007, would change this result by causing *both* the deemed redemption of the old debt and the deemed issuance of the new debt to occur immediately before the transaction.

76 Reg. § 1.1502-13(g)(4)(i), (ii)(A).

77 Id. However, the regulations do incorporate the exceptions in Reg. § 1.108-2(e). *See* Reg. § 1.1502-4(i)(B), providing limited exceptions.

78 Reg. § 1.1502-13(g)(4)(ii)(C).

79 *Compare* Reg. § 1.1502-13(g)(3)(ii)(B)(2) *with* Reg. § 1.1502-13(g)(4)(ii)(C), and Example 3 *with* Example 4 in Reg. § 1.1502-13(g)(5) (where Example 3 mentions insolvency as a relevant factor, but Example 4 does not).

§ 1.1502-80(e) would still apply, thereby making the AHYDO provisions of Code § 163(e)(5) inapplicable to the "new" debt.

### § 804.4.5 Does Code § 108 Apply on a Separate Company or on a Group Basis in a Consolidated Return Group?

As mentioned above at § 804.4.1, until the late 1990s, Code § 108 was in practice normally applied on an individual company basis to members of a consolidated return group. To begin with, the jurisdictional requirements for Code § 108(a)—namely, the need for "the taxpayer" to be insolvent or in bankruptcy—has been applied only at the separate debtor corporation level. That is, they have applied only if the debtor corporation met their requirements, whether or not the other members of the group or the group as a whole met them. Secondly, attribute reduction under Code § 108(b) was limited to the attributes of the debtor corporation. If these did not absorb the full amount of the debt cancellation, the remainder of the cancellation produced no further attribute reduction. The attributes of the other members were not reduced.[80]

The IRS began to reconsider at least the second of these conclusions in the late 1990s. This IRS change in position toward a consolidated approach to the application of Code § 108(b) attribute reduction was greatly assisted by the Supreme Court's decision in the *United Dominion Industries* case, wherein the taxpayer had applied a group approach (and *the IRS* had taken a separate company approach) to certain consolidated return NOL computations outside the Code § 108 area.[81] That case involved a consolidated return group that sought to obtain the benefit of the special 10-year NOL carryback allowed for the portion of the NOL deduction that consists of product liability losses. Although the United Dominion group had aggregate losses and thus a group NOL, the members of the group having product liability loss deductions had all been profitable. The question thus presented was whether the portion of the group NOL that represented product liability losses should be limited to the portions of the separate company NOLs that were product liability losses (in which case no 10-year carryback would be available, since none of the members having product liability losses had separate company NOLs) or whether instead this portion should be computed on an aggregate basis as if the group were a single entity. The Supreme Court decided that the computation should be on a single entity basis, not a separate company basis, and so the 10-year carryback was available. The opinion was placed on the narrow ground that the consolidated return regulations contain only one definition of an NOL, namely that of a consolidated NOL.

The case did not involve, nor did the opinion mention, the question of how to apply Code § 108 jurisdiction or attribute reduction in a consolidated return. However, it led to some speculation as to whether, and if so how far, the single entity concept should apply to these issues. As mentioned above at § 804.4.1, the IRS in the

---

[80] *See* IRS Letter Ruling 9121017, February 21, 1991.

[81] 121 S. Ct. 1934, 2001-1 U.S.T.C. ¶ 50,430 (2001). The approach taken in this case was followed in a matter involving apportionment of a CERT (corporate equity reduction) deduction for Code § 172 purposes, in IRS Chief Counsel Advice 200305019, December 13, 2002.

late 1990s began to assert that the NOL attribute reduction under Code § 108 should apply to the consolidated group NOL, not just to the separate NOL of the debtor.[82] So far as we know, before 2003 the IRS did not seek to apply the other aspects of Code § 108 on a group basis, and had unofficially indicated that basis reduction only occurred on a separate company basis (in absence of elections under Code §§ 108(b)(5) and 1017(b)(3)(D) to reduce depreciable property first and to treat a consolidated subsidiary's stock basis as depreciable to the extent the subsidiary agrees to reduce its depreciable asset basis). Concerns had been expressed by commentators that any effort to apply the attribute reduction provisions on a group basis would involve great complexity.[83]

However, in 2003 and 2004, the IRS issued a series of temporary and proposed regulations, which were made final in 2005,[84] that, with an important jurisdictional exception, do apply a hybrid consolidated approach to the COD-attribute reduction provisions of Code § 108; and in audits of periods pre-dating the regulations, the IRS has asserted a single entity, consolidated approach to attribute reduction (other than for tax basis) and has taken the position that this applies to all consolidated attributes, including AMT credits.[85]

The jurisdictional exception in the regulations is that where COD is to be excluded from income because of the debtor's bankruptcy or insolvency, the determination of bankruptcy or insolvency is limited to the debtor member itself (*i.e.*, it is to

---

[82] IRS Legal Memorandum 200149008, August 10, 2001, *reprinted at* 2001 TNT 237-27; IRS Field Service Advice 199912007, December 14, 1998, *reprinted at* 1999 TNT 59-56.

[83] *See* Dubroff, Blanchard, Broadbent & Duvall, Federal Income Taxation of Corporations Filing Consolidated Returns § 33.06[1] (2d ed.); Blanchard, Jr., Bennett and Speer, The Deductibility of Investments in Financially Troubled Susidiaries and Related Federal Income Tax Considerations, 80 Taxes 91, 107 n.194 (2002). To the same effect, *see* Axelrod, What's "Reasonable" Before the Consolidated COD Regulations?, 115 Tax Notes 745 (May 21, 2007).

[84] *See* T.D. 9089, Sept. 4, 2003, adopting Temp. Reg. §§ 1.1502-19T, 1.1502-21T, 1.1502-28T, 1.1502-32T. These temporary regulations were generally effective for COD arising after August 29, 2003. However, the changes to the investment basis adjustments were effective for consolidated returns due after August 29, 2003 (without extension), but could be applied retroactively by taxpayers if so desired. *See also* T.D. 9098, December 11, 2003, amending Temp. Reg. § 1.1502-28T, and T.D. 9117, March 12, 2004, amending Temp. Reg. § 1.1502-13T and -28T, and issuing Prop. Reg. § 1.1502-11. These amendments to the Temporary Regulations contained their own effective dates, some of which related back to August 29, 2003. Prop. Reg. § 1.1502-11 was proposed to be effective when it is adopted in final form, though taxpayers will be allowed to apply its provisions to earlier periods. For a detailed discussion of these provisions, *see* Daley and Friedel, Section 108 Attribute Reduction for Consolidated Groups (Parts 1 and 2), 31 J. Corp. Taxation (Jan./Feb. 2004 and March/April 2004), at 3. The foregoing regulations and amendments were adopted in final form effective March 22, 2005. T.D. 9192, March 22, 2005; *see* Reg. §§ 1.1502-11, 1.1502-13, 1.1502-19, 1.1502-21, 1.1502-28, and 1.1502-32. The final regulations may be applied retroactively to discharges otherwise governed by the temporary regulations, if a debtor so desires. Although in most cases the operative differences between the final and temporary regulations will be minor (if any), the final regulations in particular added certain provisions pertaining to subsidiary acquisitions and dispositions and the timing consequences of end-of-year transactions (which provisions are effective for debt cancellations after March 21, 2005).

[85] *See* IRS Chief Counsel Advice 200714016, December 1, 2006 (relying on the *United Dominion Industries* case). For a critique of the IRS's analysis, see Axelrod, *supra* note 83.

be determined on a separate company basis).[86] Thus, in the case of insolvency, only the debtor member's own assets and liabilities are taken into account.

After this jurisdictional test is made on a separate company basis, the attribute reductions resulting from the excluded COD of the debtor member are made on a consolidated basis.[87] Rather than treating the aggregate of the consolidated group's attributes as a single pool to be reduced in the order provided by Code § 108(b), however, the consolidated approach is modified by applying the following three-step approach:

(1) Reduce the attributes of the separate debtor member, including the debtor's basis in the stock of another member (*e.g.*, a subsidiary of the debtor), but not below zero.

If the debtor's basis in the stock of another member is reduced in the first step, then:

(2) Reduce the attributes of such subsidiary member *to the extent of* the reduction in such member's outside stock basis, just as if the subsidiary had incurred an equivalent amount of COD itself (this is referred to as the "look-through" rule). As discussed below, this can cause the reduction in the basis of the stock in the subsidiary of the debtor to cascade downward.[88]

To the extent the first step does not absorb all the COD (and after applying the second step), then:

(3) Reduce the consolidated attributes of all members (other than the basis in their assets) to the extent such attributes would be available to offset income of the debtor (including certain SRLY or other separate return NOLs of other members which nonetheless are available for use against the income of the debtor member, either because (i) the debtor is a member of the SRLY subgroup or (ii) the SRLY limitations do not apply, such as due to the SRLY § 382 overlap rules).

Significantly, where the attribute to be reduced is basis, the reduction required by the regulations is generally limited to the basis of the debtor's assets, the reason being that the basis of the assets of another member is not directly available to offset the income of the debtor.[89] But where the debtor reduces its stock basis in another

---

[86] Reg. § 1.1502-28(a)(1).

[87] *See* Reg. § 1.1502-28(a)(2)-(4).

[88] Where multiple members of the group incur excluded COD in the same tax year, the first two steps must be fully applied with respect to each member (starting with the highest tier member and fully completing both steps before repeating the steps for the next tier member(s) on down) before proceeding to the third step. Reg. § 1.1502-28(b)(1).

[89] Similarly, the basis-in-excess-of-liabilities limitation applicable to basis reductions, *see* § 404.2(6) above, applies on a separate company basis. For purposes of this limitation, however, the final regulations (unlike the temporary regulations) provide that the stock basis of a subsidiary that has an excess loss account shall be zero, rather than being a negative basis. Reg. § 1.1502-28(b)(3)(ii) and (iii). Accordingly, if a debtor member has positive tax basis in one subsidiary and an excess loss account in

member, the regulations adopt a look-through approach whereby corresponding adjustments must be made to the attributes (including NOLs) attributable to the lower-tier member—in effect, viewing such members as a partial extension of the debtor. The mechanic the regulations employ for this purpose is to treat the lower-tier member as a debtor that has COD excluded from income in the amount of the stock basis reduction. Where there is a chain of corporations below the debtor, these adjustments can cascade downward. The regulations provide that the reduction in stock basis will not be treated as a Code § 1245 item (thereby making it subject to ordinary income recapture) to the extent the reduction flows downward and reduces attributes of the lower-tier member, the theory being that the excluded COD should produce ordinary taxable income for the group only once (just as the COD would have done if included in income).[90]

The primary philosophy of the regulations is that any group attribute that might become available to benefit the debtor should be considered eligible for possible reduction. The concept here is that the purpose of the Code § 108 insolvency and bankruptcy exceptions to COD income is to defer, not eliminate, tax on such COD income. For example, since an NOL generated by another member of the consolidated return group might be available for use against future income generated by the debtor, that NOL is eligible for reduction. A second philosophy reflected in the regulations is that the location of tax attributes and the location of future tax liability within the group should be preserved as much as possible. Thus, the regulations provide that the first attribute reductions should be made in the attributes of the debtor member itself (including the push down attribute reductions to attributes of the debtor's subsidiaries, discussed above), and only after these have been exhausted should reductions be made in the attributes of other members.

The application of the regulations, including the resulting investment basis adjustments in stock of the members, can produce considerable complexity. For example, the consolidated NOL must be allocated among the members of the consolidated return group, so as to determine how much is attributable to the debtor and how much to each of the other members. Special rules for making this allocation are contained in Reg. § 1.1502-21.

To the extent a debtor's COD is used to reduce the attributes of other group members (not including the attributes of the debtor's subsidiaries due to the push down of any stock basis reduction), the basis of the debtor's stock held by the group is *increased* and the basis of the stock of the other member is *reduced*.[91]

Where the stock of one or more loss members of the group is sold, or deemed disposed of for the purpose of triggering an excess loss account, in the same year that the COD arose, circular computations as to the use of NOLs and resulting investment adjustments can produce problems, and these are partially addressed and otherwise "reserved" in Reg. § 1.1502-11. The regulations also coordinated the application of the

(Footnote Continued)

another subsidiary, the two do not offset—absent possible self-help, such as by contributing the stock of one subsidiary to the other.

[90] *See* Reg. § 1.1502-28(b)(4).

[91] *See* Reg. § 1.1502-32(b)(3)(C).

excess loss account rules with respect to any trigger of an excess loss account due to there being insufficient attributes to reduce, by providing that the excess loss account will not be triggered into income by more than the amount of the COD that is applied to it.[92] Nevertheless, the resulting income inclusion can produce a trap for the unwary in the event that the NOLs of the group, or at least any NOLs that would otherwise be available to offset such income, would be fully (or substantially) reduced by the debtor's COD. Although Code § 108(b)(4)(A) provides that the reduction of attributes occurs after the determination of tax for the year, and the regulations make clear that any income inclusion from the triggering of an excess loss account due to insufficient attributes is income in that year,[93] Reg. § 1.1502-11 (as amended in 2005) effectively overrides Code § 108(b)(4)(A) and precludes any NOLs that would otherwise be reduced by the COD from first being used against the income from the excess loss account.[94]

Where the consolidated approach to attribute reduction would reduce substantial attributes of members other than the debtor, the taxpayers might wish to consider certain self-help measures, including the possibility of taking steps to deconsolidate either before or after the COD is created. In the preamble to the temporary regulations, the IRS had indicated that it might adopt rules or take other action to thwart transitory transactions, or other transactions designed to avoid application of the consolidated COD rules;[95] however, in the preamble to the final regulations, the IRS stated it had decided not to adopt any additional rules at this time, as it believed that general tax principles (including the step transaction doctrine) could be applied to disregard certain transactions that are designed to undermine the application of the consolidated COD rules.[96] Even so, the final regulations added certain provisions pertaining to subsidiary deconsolidations and other structural changes of the group which in some cases reduce and in other cases increase possible self-help measures.

As finalized in 2005, the consolidated COD regulations change the timing of attribute reduction in respect of a debtor subsidiary that merges or otherwise combines with another member of the group in an acquisitive tax-free reorganization or Code § 332 liquidation after incurring excluded COD income. Such a transaction ordinarily closes the subsidiary's taxable year (even though the group's year continues). Accordingly, one would anticipate that the subsidiary's tax attributes as of such time would be required to be reduced for the excluded COD, in accordance with Reg. § 1.108-7(c). The final regulations, however, delay the attribute reduction until the end of the successor's taxable year and look to the successor's combined attributes.[97]

---

[92] Reg. § 1.1502-19(b)(1)(ii). *See also* § 804.2. The regulations make clear that the income inclusion resulting from the triggering of the excess loss account must be taken into income in the same year, thereby causing or adding to any circular computations (as discussed in the text below). Reg. § 1.1502-28(b)(6)(ii). This provision was added to the prior temporary regulations in March 2004.

[93] Id.

[94] *See* Reg. § 1.1502-11(c)(2)(viii) (last sentence).

[95] *See* the introductory and explanatory language in T.D. 9089.

[96] *See* introductory and explanatory language in T.D. 9192.

[97] Reg. § 1.1502-28(b)(9) (treats the successor as realizing the excluded COD income; provides an equivalent rule where the common parent is the merging or transferor member), -28(c) Example 7.

Depending on the circumstances, this may provide additional planning opportunities, or an unexpected danger.

Also added in the final regulations are specific rules pertaining to departing members where excluded COD income is incurred during the consolidated return year. These rules operate to ensure that the NOL and other consolidated attributes attributable to a departing subsidiary (whether or not the debtor member) remain available for attribute reduction.[98] In addition, these rules require the application of the stock basis "look-through" rule (step 2 above) as to any corporation whose stock basis is reduced if such corporation is a member of the same consolidated group with the debtor member (*i.e.*, the member with excluded COD income) on the last day of the debtor member's year.[99] The latter provision can come into effect in the following situations, among others:

- The debtor member has a subsidiary and the debtor member itself deconsolidates (including as a result of a group termination), thereby terminating the debtor member's taxable year and in turn causing the deconsolidation of the subsidiary, which thereafter remains owned by the debtor member.
- A non-debtor subsidiary deconsolidates from the group on the last day of the group's taxable year through a partial sale or distribution of its stock, such that the debtor member continues to own a portion of the subsidiary's stock.[100]

Note that a non-debtor subsidiary that deconsolidates mid-year (other than by reason of the deconsolidation of the debtor member) generally will not be subject to the look-though rule.

The final regulations also require the application of the look-through rule to a corporation that joins the consolidated group of the debtor member on the first day of the taxable year following the COD, if and to the extent that the debtor member previously owned stock in such corporation and reduced the stock basis by the excluded COD.[101] Thus, this provision captures certain "creeping" consolidations where the subsidiary (by happenstance or otherwise) joins the consolidated group on the first day following the taxable year of the COD.

What we have said so far in this § 804.4.5 relates only to non-intercompany debt. We must not conclude without pointing out, as we did at § 804.4.2, that the consolidated return regulations make Code § 108 inapplicable to intercompany debt that runs from one group member to another, and so the questions discussed here regarding the interpretation of Code § 108 in the consolidated return context do not

---

[98] Reg. §§ 1.1502-21(b)(2)(ii)(A), -28(b)(8), and -28(c) Example 6; *see also* Reg. § 1.1502-28(b)(11) (in the circumstance where the debtor member deconsolidates on the same day that it realizes excluded COD income, this provision makes clear that the "next day" rule of Reg. § 1.1502-76 does *not* apply to move the COD event outside the group and into the next year); Letter Ruling 200442011 (October 23, 2003) (Ruling #16) (similarly holding that the "next day" rule does not apply, even prior to the adoption of the preceding regulation).

[99] Reg. § 1.1502-28(a)(3)(ii).

[100] Reg. § 1.1502-28(c), Example 5.

[101] Reg. § 1.1502-28(a)(3)(ii).

arise as to such debt, but only as to debt running between a member and a nonmember. It should be noted, however, that to the extent this overriding of Code § 108 might make a group, in some particular fact situation, worse off than it would have been had it filed separate returns, the existence of the *Rite Aid* case (discussed at § 804.5 below) might lead the taxpayer involved to raise the question whether the overriding of Code sections in this way is included within the Congressional authority to issue consolidated return regulations.[102] Indeed, in order to forestall the uncertainties that such attacks on this or other provisions in the consolidated return regulations might have, by mid-2002 efforts had already begun in Congress to buttress the legislative authority for the consolidated return regulations. These efforts culminated in the American Jobs Creation Act of 2004, which added new language to Code § 1502 which says that, in writing consolidated return regulations, "the Secretary may prescribe rules that are different from the provisions of chapter 1 that would apply if such corporations filed separate returns." In an unusual provision, the Act says that this provision is "effective for tax years beginning before, on, or after the date of the enactment of this Act."

## *§ 804.5 Gains and Losses on Member Stock;* Rite Aid, *Its Antecedents and Progeny*

Substantial revisions were made during the 1990s and the 2000s to the investment adjustment, excess loss account, and intercompany transaction portions of the consolidated return regulations. The focus of many of these changes has been on implementing in the consolidated return context the repeal of the *General Utilities* doctrine, by ensuring the recognition of corporate gains while preventing deductions for noneconomic losses and deduction duplications. The theory reflected in these revisions is that consolidated income should be computed, as much as possible, as though the members of the consolidated return group were only divisions of a single corporation.

Since divisions of a single corporation do not issue stock, giving tax significance to subsidiary stock is largely inconsistent with this model.[103] Consequently, as with prior consolidated return approaches, it is necessary to make various adjustments in order to deal properly with such stock. One of the purposes of such adjustments must be to prevent the existence of member stock from creating double deduction or double income inclusion problems.

---

[102] This point is made as to this and other Code sections in the article cited in Blanchard, Jr., Bennett and Speer, The Deductibility of Investments in Financially Troubled Subsidiaries and Related Federal Income Tax Considerations, 80 Taxes 91, 113-114 (2002), and, in Silverman and Zarlenga, *Rite Aid*: A Tough Pill for the Government to Swallow, 94 Tax Notes 1343 (March 11, 2002); and as to other Code sections in Schler, Consolidated Return Loss Disallowance: Conceptual Issues, 95 Tax Notes 899, 921-22 (May 6, 2002). The authors point out the potential chaos such attacks might create, unless they are forestalled by appropriate strengthening of the legislative authority for the consolidated return regulations.

[103] The same may be said of intercompany debt. However, as seen in the prior section, neutrality is not always achieved.

To illustrate such problems, suppose a subsidiary (*S*) formed by the parent corporation (*P*) has a $100 operating loss which also reduces by $100 the value of the *S* stock held by *P*. If the consolidated group can deduct both the $100 operating loss and the $100 stock loss, the group will be taking $200 of deductions for what represents only a $100 economic loss for the group. Similarly, suppose *P* has a $100 basis in the stock of *S*, *S* in turn has a $100 basis in its assets, and *P* sells some of its *S* stock at a $2 loss. If *P* could deduct its $2 loss in the *S* stock without *S* having to suffer a $2 diminution in the basis of the *S* assets, a double deduction could become possible. Conversely, suppose *S* has a $100 profit that increases the value of the *S* stock in the hands of *P* by $100. If the group is taxed on both the $100 operating profit and the $100 stock gain, the group will be taxed on $200 of income when it had only $100 of economic gain.

One way to protect against such double deduction or double income inclusion problems is by causing transactions occurring at the subsidiary level to produce an investment adjustment in the *S* stock held by the parent. The consolidated return regulations do this. But, because of timing and other problems, including complexities caused when *S* has not always been a member of the group, even such adjustments do not entirely solve the problem. This is particularly true when the stock transaction precedes the realization event at the subsidiary level, or when *P* and *S* have not been members of the same consolidated return group throughout their entire existence.

As a back stop against potential double deduction problems, and in order to buttress the repeal of *General Utilities* in 1986, the consolidated return regulations take the further step of disallowing all losses by members on stock of the parent corporation,[104] and disallowing certain losses by members on stock of member subsidiaries.

### § 804.5.1 Reg. § 1.1502-20 Limitation on Losses from Dispositions of *S* Stock, and *Rite Aid*

The disallowance of certain losses from the disposition of subsidiary stock has gone through a checkered historical development.[105] The 1986 Act, in connection with its repeal of the *Generall Utilities* doctrine, adopted Code § 337(d), authorizing regulations designed to prevent circumvention of this repeal through such things as the consolidated return regulations. A primary concern at the time was the so-called "son of mirrors" type of transaction, which can be illustrated as follows. *S* has a single capital asset with a basis of $0 and value of $100. *P* purchases the *S* stock for $100. *S* sells the capital asset to *P* for $100, recognizing a capital gain of $100 and increasing *P*'s basis in *S* to $200. *P* sells the *S* stock for $100, recognizing a capital loss of $100. Thus, the *P* group has no net income, yet has achieved a stepped-up basis in *S*'s assets. *P*'s $100 capital loss deduction in this example is a deduction for a "noneconomic" loss, noneconomic in the sense that neither the group nor its members have suffered a $100 loss in real value terms (although *S* realized $100 of

---

[104] Reg. § 1.1502-13(f)(6).

[105] This history for the period before 2003 is recounted in detail in Vogel and Hering, New Loss Disallowance Regulations—Welcome to the Age of Tracing and Appraisals, 96 J. Taxation 327 (2002).

economic gain, this value was already reflected in the *S* stock when *P* bought the stock for $100). Obviously, deductions for noneconomic losses should not be allowed.

To address this problem, the IRS issued in 1990 and 1991 Reg. §§1.337(d)-1 and -2 and 1.1502-20. Reg. §1.337(d)-2, intended as a transitional rule, disallowed a loss on a sale of *S* stock unless (1) *P* disposed of all its *S* stock in a single transaction to an unrelated party (or had a worthless stock loss for the stock of *S*) and (2) *P* established that the loss was not attributable to *S*'s recognition of built-in gain on the disposition of an asset, where that built-in gain was already economically reflected directly or indirectly in *P*'s basis in *S* (a noneconomic loss). Reg. §1.1502-20, which was issued in 1991 as the permanent rule, took a broader approach. It generally disallowed a loss from the disposition of *S* stock except to the extent the loss exceeded (1) extraordinary gains (very broadly defined) reflected in the basis of the *S* stock, (2) cumulative annual net positive basis adjustments, unreduced by annual net negative basis adjustments, included in the basis of the *S* stock and (3) so-called "duplicated losses," which are primarily NOLs, capital losses, and asset basis available to the subsidiary in its first taxable year after leaving the consolidated return group in excess of the sum of the value of the subsidiary's equity and the amount of its liabilities.[106]

The duplicated loss concept can be illustrated by the following example. *P* forms new *S* and contributes $100 in cash. *S* buys an asset for $100, and the asset declines in value to $30. *P* sells the *S* stock for $30, recognizing a loss of $70. If *S*, which no longer is in the *P* group, later sells the asset for $30, another loss of $70 arises (subject to the limitations of Code §382). (These are essentially the facts presented in the *Rite Aid* case, which is discussed below.) The duplicated loss provision of Reg. §1.1502-20 disallowed *P's* $70 loss. The "duplicated loss" concept differs from the "noneconomic loss" concept, because in the duplicated loss case the group has indeed suffered an economic loss (*i.e.*, here the $70 decline in value of the *S* asset while *S* was a member of the group), but the loss is duplicated because to allow both *S* and *P* to deduct this $70 loss is to permit two deductions for this one economic loss. Yet, it should be noted that, on these particular facts, the two deductions would have been allowed had a consolidated return not been filed. The duplication of the instant loss was not created by a distortion in the application of the consolidated return concept. Thus, the purpose behind the regulations went beyond just eliminating duplicated deductions that would not have been allowed had separate returns been filed. This duplication was viewed as inconsistent with the general treatment of a consolidated return group as divisions of a single corporation. The regulations were less diligent in protecting

---

[106] A statement also had to be filed with the parent's return. These provisions are quite technical, and they offered the possibility for some aggressive tax planning. However, the IRS has been quick to apply substance over form concepts to attack transactions that might technically satisfy this loss allowance rule, but which violate its substantive purpose. *See* IRS Technical Advice Memorandum 200006014, October 22, 1999. Because of the asymmetry between the loss disallowance and the gain recognition rules, and because of the very technical nature of the limited loss allowance formula, taxpayers need to plan their transactions so as to take advantage of steps, such as preliminary intercompany transactions, that might improve the tax result (without violating the substance of the loss disallowance rule), and, in addition, so as to avoid transactions that might exacerbate the problems. Examples of such (both good and bad) planning can be found in White, Loss Disallowance Regulations Flanked? 41 Tax Mgmt. Memo. 248 (2000), discussing IRS Field Service Advice 200012046, December 9, 1999, *reprinted at* 2000 TNT 59-88.

the group against double recognition of income. Indeed, in the case of parent stock, the gain limitation until May 16, 2000, was essentially restricted to situations where the issuance of parent stock might otherwise create a zero basis problem.[107]

Where the disallowed loss was a loss by the group on stock of a consolidated subsidiary, Reg. § 1.1502-20(g) attempted to soften the impact of the loss disallowance provision by giving the common parent (which may not be the group member that held the *S* stock) the right to elect to reattribute to itself any portion of the unused consolidated NOL or capital loss carryovers that have been generated by *S* (or any lower-tier subsidiary of *S*), up to the amount of the loss disallowed to the group on the *S* stock.[108] This election was not available, however, to the extent the losses did not exceed the separate insolvencies of the subsidiary whose losses were to be reattributed and any higher-tier insolvent subsidiaries (counting only such insolvent companies in the chain). In computing insolvency for this purpose, liabilities owed to higher-tier members were *not* taken into account, and preferred stock not held by higher-tier members *was* taken into account. The reason for this insolvency adjustment was that the IRS felt the group ought not to benefit by losses that were economically suffered by investors outside the chain in which the loss subsidiary is owned. For a discussion of this reallocation provision as it may be impacted by the *Prudential Lines* precedent, *see* § 508.2.4 above.

The Reg. § 1.1502-20 disallowance of most losses realized on subsidiary stock under Reg. § 1.1502-20 raised the question whether the consolidated return regulations provided an incentive for capitalizing subsidiaries with debt rather than stock. The answer generally was no, because after applying the consolidated return intercompany transaction and investment adjustment rules, the parent would not end up with better deductions for the debt than it would have had for an equivalent amount of stock, and might well end up with a much worse result. Some marginal benefit might be obtained in certain circumstances from the use of debt under Reg. § 1.1502-20, but it is also the loss disallowance rules which created the potentially worse downside. Leveraging a subsidiary with intercompany debt will, through interest deductions, reduce the net income of the subsidiary and thus reduce the amount of stock loss that would be disallowed on account of the "positive investment adjustment" factor of Reg. § 1.1502-20(c)(1)(ii), in connection with a subsequent disposition of the subsidiary's stock. However, as discussed at § 804.4, if the value of the subsidiary declines, the parent will not receive the benefit of any bad debt deduction or loss in respect of the intercompany debt. In contrast, were the monies initially contributed as equity capital, the facts may or may not support a disallowance of the stock loss under Reg. § 1.1502-20; each case will be different. Thus, a worse result could obtain by the leverage than would have occurred if the parent had invested only in stock.

---

[107] *See* Reg. § 1.1502-13(f)(6)(ii). This provision ceased to apply on May 15, 2000. For periods on or after May 16, 2000, Reg. § 1.1032-3 may limit the recognition of gains on parent stock in certain limited circumstances, as noted in 2007 Prop. Reg. § 1.1502-13(f)(6)(ii).

[108] The reattribution election had to be made within a limited period of time. In a case where an audit adjustment changed the expectations of the parties, the IRS has allowed a late election to be made, where all of the tax years of the parties were still open so that the interests of the government were not prejudiced. IRS Letter Ruling 200029014, April 12, 2000.

Because Reg. § 1.1502-20 went beyond eliminating double deductions within the consolidated return group, questions were raised as to the validity of its scope.[109] Attention focused particularly on the effort of the regulation to eliminate "duplicated losses," where the second loss occurs in *S* after it leaves the consolidated return group (see the example of the duplicated loss concept given above). The double loss in this situation (*P*'s loss in its *S* stock and *S*'s later loss in its asset) is not created by the filing of consolidated returns or by the consolidated return regulations. Rather, the two losses in this situation would be available even if only separate returns had been filed by *P* and *S*. Since allowing the two losses in this situation would not violate *General Utilities* repeal, questions were raised as to the validity of this portion of the regulation. The question was ultimately tested in the *Rite Aid* case,[110] and the Court of Appeals for the Federal Circuit held in that case that the duplicated loss aspect of Reg. § 1.1502-20 was invalid.

The court noted that the duplicated loss was not a problem created by the filing of consolidated returns, would have been allowed if separate returns had been filed, and is allowed by Code § 165. The court concluded that "in the absence of a problem created from the filing of consolidated returns, the Secretary is without authority to change the application of other tax code provisions to a group of corporations filing a consolidated return." Because of the absence of a conflict between circuits, the Solicitor General refused to petition for certiorari.

In the American Jobs Creation Act of 2004, when the Congress amended Code § 1502 to provide that the consolidated return regulations could provide different results than might apply under the Code if separate returns were filed (and to this extent disagreeing with the reasoning of the *Rite Aid* opinion), the Congress took the unusual step of providing in § 844(b) of the Act (a provision not included in the Code) that despite this amendment the Code should be construed to treat Reg. § 1.1502-20(c)(1)(iii) (as in effect in 2001) as being inapplicable to the facts in the *Rite Aid* case. Thus, the Congress indicated that it did not disagree with the result reached in that case, only with some of the reasoning.

The *Rite Aid* opinion made it important for the IRS to amend Reg. § 1.1502-20, and the 2004 amendment to Code § 1502 gave it enhanced power to depart from separate return results in preparing such amendments (so long as it does not overrule the result in *Rite Aid*).

### § 804.5.2 Post-*Rite Aid* Regulations §§ 1.337(d)-2 and 1.1502-35

On January 31, 2002, the IRS in Notice 2002-11[111] announced that, although it disagreed with the Federal Circuit opinion, the sound administration of the tax law would not be served by continuing to litigate the validity of the duplicated loss

---

[109] *See, e.g.*, Salem, Judicial Deference, Consolidated Returns and Loss Disallowance—Could LDR Survive a Court Challenge?, 43 Tax Executive 167 (1991).

[110] *Rite Aid Corp. v. United States*, 255 F.3d 1357, 2001-2 U.S.T.C. ¶ 50,516 (Fed. Cir. 2001).

[111] 2002-7 I.R.B. 526. Although some practitioners have raised the question whether the *Rite Aid* decision invalidated more aspects of the regulation than the duplicated loss portion, we believe the better view (also the IRS view) is that it did not.

component of Reg. § 1.1502-20, and, further, that because the duplicated loss factor is interrelated with other aspects of that regulation, new regulations would be issued governing loss disallowance on dispositions of *S* stock by members of consolidated groups. Somewhat unexpectedly, these new regulations ended up being issued in two installments. On March 7, 2002, the IRS issued the first installment of new temporary and proposed regulations.[112] These dealt with aspects of the stock loss disallowance provisions of Reg. § 1.1502-20 other than the duplicated loss aspect. Simultaneously with their issuance, however, the Treasury announced in Notice 2002-18[113] that additional regulations would later be issued to deal with the duplicated loss aspect, and that these would also be effective as of March 7, 2002.

**First installment: Reg. § 1.337(d)-2.** The primary regulation in the March 2002 first installment of regulations was Temp. Reg. § 1.337(d)-2T (which, as discussed below, was finalized in 2005 with only minor change). From March 7, 2002, forward, this regulation, as supplemented by the later issued duplicated loss regulations (primarily Reg. § 1.1502-35 discussed below), governs the allowability of losses on sales of *S* stock. This new regulation is similar to old Reg. § 1.337(d)-2, though it is more liberal in allowing losses. It continues to disallow a loss on *S* stock resulting from a "son of mirrors" type transaction, namely a loss attributable to an increase in the basis of *P*'s *S* stock resulting from a sale while *S* was still in the group of an *S* asset that had a built-in gain when *S* joined the group (*i.e.*, a noneconomic loss). But for economic losses it eliminates the requirement in old Reg. § 1.337(d)-2 that the group must dispose of its entire interest in *S* in a single transaction to an unrelated buyer if it is to recognize its loss in the *S* stock. Consistent with *Rite Aid*, the new regulation does not contain the loss duplication rule that was in Reg. § 1.1502-20, nor on the other hand does it permit the reattribution of losses from *S* to *P*. The basic rule of the new regulation essentially is that *P*'s loss in the *S* stock will not be disallowed to the extent *P* can show that the loss or basis is not attributable to the recognition of built-in gain (clarified in 2004 to mean the built-in gain less the directly related expenses, including federal income taxes, incurred in recognizing the gain) that was in an *S* asset when *S* joined the group. The burden of proof being on the taxpayer, taxpayers will have to be careful to establish values and bases of *S* assets when an *S* joins the group. This involves tracing, and perhaps appraisals, which can prove expensive. This is something the IRS tried to avoid in Reg. § 1.1502-20.

When Temp. Reg. § 1.337(d)-2T was issued, the general assumption was that it required tracing. But because the reliance of this test on valuations can produce great complexity in many (though not all) cases, this test can impose substantial administrative burdens on taxpayers and the IRS. As a result, the IRS has come to the view that other interpretations of the Regulation might be possible. On September 15, 2004,

[112] Temp. Reg. §§ 1.337(d)-2T, 1.1502-20T and 1.1502-32T(b)(4)(v). Various amendments to the first two of these regulations were issued on May 31, 2002, and an amendment to the third was issued on August 18, 2004. A further amendment to Temp. Reg. § 1.337(d)-2T was issued on March 18, 2004, in T.D. 9118, which provides that in computing recognized built-in gain one can reduce the gain by the directly related expenses of the disposition, including federal income taxes. This amendment applies to transactions occurring on or after March 18, 2004, but the taxpayer can choose to apply it to those occurring on or after March 7, 2002.

[113] 2002-12 I.R.B. 644.

the IRS issued Notice 2004-58,[114] which said that "in addition to other methods that may be appropriate" for satisfying the taxpayer's burden of proof under Temp. Reg. § 1.337(d)-2T, the IRS will accept the "basis disconformity method," which the Notice then describes. This method disallows loss on a deconsolidation of subsidiary stock in an amount equal to the least of the gain amount, the disconformity amount, or the positive investment adjustment amount. All of these terms are defined at length in the Notice. This new method is intended to be easier to compute in many cases than the tracing method, and the IRS seems to favor it, even though the new method can produce different results (including results more favorable to taxpayers in some cases) than the tracing test. The Notice further adds that "a consolidated group is not required to adopt the same method for each disposition or deconsolidation of a share of subsidiary stock." The Notice describes variations on the tracing and disconformity approaches which it is studying, and adds that the IRS intends to promulgate regulations that will prescribe a single set of rules.

Temp. Reg. § 1.337(d)-2T contained substantial transition rules, including the ability to elect to apply the new regulation (or, alternatively, Reg. § 1.1502-20 but without its duplicated loss factor) to prior open years to which Reg. § 1.1502-20 would otherwise apply. Simultaneously with the release of Notice 2004-58, the IRS issued amendments to the regulations to allow taxpayers to change these prior elections, so that any election made could be done with knowledge of the new approaches permitted by the Notice.[115] Any group that had made an election was well advised to carefully review Notice 2004-58 and consider whether to change its prior election. The time periods for making such a change were set forth in the aforesaid amendments.

This first installment of new regulations was made final, with no real substantive changes, on March 3, 2005, as Reg. §§ 1.337(d)-2, 1.1502-20(i), and 1.1502-32(b). The Treasury, in the preamble to the final regulation package, also confirmed the continuing applicability of Notice 2005-58 while the IRS continued to study alternative approaches. The effective dates in the temporary regulations were essentially retained.[116]

**Second installment: Reg. § 1.1502-35.** Shortly before the IRS issued Temp. Reg. § 1.337(d)-2T, the IRS learned of a new transaction, reportedly done by Bank of America, that caused it concern. The new transaction did not involve a built-in gain asset of *S*, so it is not the traditional "son of mirrors" transaction. Rather, it is a duplicated loss transaction, but unlike *Rite Aid*, both aspects of the duplicated loss take place within the consolidated group. Here is a description of the transaction. *P*

---

[114] 2004-39 I.R.B. 1, September 15, 2004. A detailed discussion of the background to this Notice, and of the concepts reflected in it (including examples), can be found in Nelson and Peabody, New Interpretations of the LDR Regime: The Basis Disconformity and Presumption Models, 103 Tax Notes 943 (August 30, 2004). The Notice is discussed in Salem, LDR: Light at the End of the Tunnel?, 105 Tax Notes 1273 (November 29, 2004); Schler, LDR: What to Do?, 105 Tax Notes 1585 (December 13, 2004) (a response to a portion of the Salem article); Sheppard, Elect Your Subsidiary Loss, 104 Tax Notes 894 (August 30, 2004); Sheppard, Elect Your Subsidiary Loss, Part 2, 106 Tax Notes 1129 (March 7, 2005).

[115] T.D. 9154, Aug. 26, 2004, amending Temp. Reg. §§ 1.1502-20T and 1.1502-32T.

[116] *See* letter from Lawrence Axelrod to Treasury Department, dated May 6, 2005, *reprinted at* 2005 TNT 91-24, suggesting an alternative approach.

has an asset with a basis of $100 and a value of $20. *P* contributes the asset to preexisting *S* in a Code § 351 exchange for perpetual preferred stock with a par and market value of $20. *P*'s basis in the preferred stock is $100, and *P* sells it to an unrelated purchaser for $20. *P* has a recognized loss of $80. Because the preferred stock is described in Code § 1504(a)(4), *P* continues to consolidate with *S*. *S* later sells the asset for $20, and the group recognizes a second loss of $80.

It would seem that a consolidated return deduction for one of these losses should be denied. Yet the language of the March 2002 regulation did not catch this, because the deduction did not arise from an *S* asset having a built-in gain when *S* joined the group. Consequently, simultaneously with its release of the new regulation, the IRS issued Notice 2002-18. This reiterated the IRS view that a consolidated group should not be able to benefit more than once from one economic loss, and announced that the IRS would issue new regulations to prevent a consolidated group from obtaining the benefit from a loss on stock (or another asset that reflects the basis of stock) and also a loss or deduction from another asset that reflects the same economic loss. The Notice added that in a situation like that in the foregoing example, the regulations would take the approach of deferring or otherwise limiting the loss on the stock. The Notice said the regulation would apply to dispositions of stock (or another asset that reflects the basis of the stock) occurring on or after March 7, 2002.

This second installment of new regulations—this set dealing with duplicated losses—was issued in proposed form in October 2002.[117] Although these were strongly criticized,[118] they were, with some revisions, adopted as temporary and proposed regulations on March 11, 2003.[119] The primary regulation is Temp. Reg. § 1.1502-35T. They are effective retroactively to transactions occurring on or after March 7, 2002, but only if such events take place during a taxable year for which the original return is due (without regard to extensions) after March 14, 2003. (For a discussion of the IRS position regarding disallowance of duplicative losses for prior periods, *see* the discussion of IRS Legal Memorandum 200423027 at the end of this § 804.5.2.) The Explanation that accompanied release of these proposed and temporary regulations said the Treasury would continue to study the comments received in response to the proposed regulations, and that the Treasury would even be considering alternative regimes to prevent duplicated losses within the consolidated return.[120] These regulations were made final, without substantive change, in 2006 as Reg. § 1.1502-35. The release accompanying the final regulation noted that the Treasury had received many comments about Reg. § 1.337(d)-2 and Temp. Reg. § 1.1502-35T; that the Treasury continues to study these provisions; and that the Treasury intends in the near future to issue proposed regulations that will address the subjects covered in both of these regulations in a single integrated regulation. Indeed, in January 2007,

---

117 REG-131478-02 Doc 2002-2392, *reprinted at* 2002 TNT 208-1.

118 *See, e.g.*, New York State Bar Association Section of Taxation, Report on Temporary Regulation § 1.337(d)-2T and Proposed Regulation § 1.1502-35T, 2003 TNT 43-35 (February 28, 2003).

119 Temp. Reg. §§ 1.1502-21T(b)(1), 1.1502-32T(a), (b), (c), (h)(6), and 1.1502-35T. Various amendments to these regulations were issued on March 12, May 8, and June 3, 2003. Temp. Reg. § 1.1502-32T was also amended on August 29, 2003 by T.D. 9089. Temp. Reg. § 1.1502-35T was also amended on March 18, 2004 by T.D. 9118.

120 *See* Preamble to T.D. 9048, 68 Fed. Reg. 12287 (March 14, 2003).

the IRS did issue new proposed regulations that would supersede Reg. § § 1.337(d)-2 and 1.1502-35. *See* the discussion at § 804.5.4 below.

Reg. § 1.1502-35 states in its first sentence that its purpose is to prevent a group from obtaining more than one tax benefit from a single economic loss. The Explanation in the 2003 preamble to the regulation in its proposed and temporary form observes that the regulation is intended to address at least two situations in which a group may obtain more than one tax benefit from a single economic loss. In one situation, the group first absorbs an inside loss that *S* recognizes (*e.g.*, an *S* NOL, deferred deduction, or a loss inherent in an asset) while it is a member of the group, and later another member of the group recognizes a loss on *S*'s stock that is duplicative of that first loss. In the second situation, a group member first recognizes a loss on a non-deconsolidating disposition of some of *S*'s stock, and that stock loss duplicates a loss that *S* later recognizes while it is a group member.

The first situation can be illustrated by the following example that was given in the Explanation to the October 2002 proposed regulations.[121]

**EXAMPLE**

In year 1, *P* forms *S* with a contribution of $80 in exchange for 80 *S* shares (100%) of *S* common stock. In year 2, *P* contributes asset A with a basis of $70 and a value of $20 to *S* in exchange for an additional 20 shares of *S* common stock. In year 3, *S* sells asset A and recognizes a $50 loss, which offsets income of *P* in the consolidated return. Under the basis adjustment rules of Reg. § 1.1502-32, *P*'s basis in each share of *S* common stock is reduced by a pro rata share of the $50 loss. The 80 shares acquired in year 1 now have a basis of $40 and the 20 shares acquired in year 2 have a basis of $60. In year 4, *P* sells the 20 shares acquired in year 2 and recognizes a $40 loss, which offsets income of *P* on the group's return. Thus, the group has obtained a total tax benefit of $90 from the single $50 economic loss.

An example of the second situation is the case described above that was mentioned in Notice 2002-18.

As can be seen, both of these examples involve so-called stuffing transactions, that is, transactions in which an asset with a built-in loss is contributed to a subsidiary in a Code § 351 transaction. Although, as the Explanation to the regulations points out, a later taxable disposition of the remaining *S* stock by *P* would (because of the basis adjustments required by Reg. § 1.1502-32) offset the excess tax benefit, it also noted that a group has various non-taxable alternatives to ensure that this does not happen, including retention of the remaining *S* shares, or a Code § 332 liquidation of *S*.

All of the examples given in the regulation involve such Code § 351 stuffing transactions. These are the duplicated loss transactions that most concerned the IRS. However, the IRS rejected suggestions, made when the regulation was proposed, that

---

[121] *See* Preamble to Prop. Reg. 1.1502-35 at 6 Fed. Reg. 65060 (October 23, 2002).

the regulation be simplified by limiting its scope to such transactions, because, the IRS said, it is concerned about the potential for duplicated losses in other contexts.

Reg. § 1.1502-35 addresses the duplicated loss problems by imposing three rules, namely, (1) a basis redetermination rule, (2) a loss suspension rule, and (3) a loss expiration rule.

***Basis redetermination rule.*** The first rule, the basis redetermination rule, requires in certain circumstances a reallocation of the basis of the *S* stock held by members of the group. It applies if, immediately before certain dispositions and deconsolidations of a share of *S* stock, any share of *S* stock owned by a member has a basis in excess of value. The effect of the rule is to reallocate basis from high basis shares to low basis shares owned by group members, if a subsidiary loss share is transferred or if the subsidiary has a loss share outstanding when it deconsolidates. The purpose of this basis redetermination rule is to reduce or eliminate the kind of loss duplication that can occur (as in the Example described above) where a member of the group holds different blocks of stock of another member with different bases, and then disposes of only the high basis shares, a duplication that would not occur (or at least would be less) if only the average share basis had been used.

The rule applies differently if, immediately after a disposition by the group of a subsidiary loss share, the subsidiary remains a member of the group, than it does if immediately before a deconsolidation of the subsidiary, any share of the subsidiary's stock (whether or not it is disposed of by the group) is a loss share. The specific provisions of the loss redetermination rule, which are complex, can even apply to situations that do not involve loss duplication. Since this goes beyond the stated purpose of the regulation, in these cases the regulation may be subject to challenge, either as to its application, or as to its validity.[122]

The basis redetermination rule can extend beyond loss duplication not only in ways that are harmful to taxpayers, but also, as the Explanation of the regulation points out, it can be used in ways that are helpful to taxpayers. The rule can be used to shift the location of gain and loss within a group, and even to eliminate gain. The Explanation notes that such results are unintended and would be contrary to the purpose of the regulation. Accordingly, since the IRS does not intend that the rule be used for these purposes, the regulation contains an anti-abuse rule. This provides that, if a transaction is structured with a view to, and has the effect of, deferring or avoiding the recognition of gain on a disposition of stock by invoking application of the basis redetermination rule, and the stock loss attributable to the transferred shares or the duplicated loss of the subsidiary member that is reflected in the subsidiary stock owned by members of the group is not significant, the basis redetermination and loss suspension rules will not apply.

***Loss suspension rule.*** The second rule, the loss suspension rule, applies if, after application of the basis redetermination rule, a member of a consolidated return group recognizes a loss on the disposition of *S* stock, and *S* is a member of the group

---

[122] *See* Yates, Vogel, Hering and Hoffenberg, The Final Factor—Temp. Reg. 1.1502-35T Takes a New Approach to Barring Duplicated Losses, 98 J. Taxation 263 (2003). This article contains both an analysis and a critique of the regulation. *See also* Mombrun and Johnson, Loss Disallowance Post-Rite Aid: The IRS and Treasury Revisit the Treatment of Subsidiary Stock Losses, 81 Taxes 21 (2003).

immediately after the disposition. In that event, the selling member's loss in the *S* stock is suspended to the extent of the duplicated loss that exists in *S*. Because a suspended loss reflects *S*'s unrecognized or unabsorbed deductions and losses, the suspended loss is reduced, with the result that it will not later be allowed, as *S*'s deductions and losses are taken into account (*i.e.*, absorbed) in determining the group's consolidated income or loss. This reduction in the suspended loss in the *S* stock occurs through the consolidated return basis adjustment rules of Reg. § 1.1502-32 as the group's basis in the *S* stock is reduced for the group's use of *S*'s deductions and losses.

The purpose of the loss suspension rule is to eliminate the loss duplication that can occur where the group first sells the *S* stock at a loss and then later realizes its loss in the duplicated loss assets (or, for example, later utilizes a previously incurred NOL). It accomplishes this by suspending (and ultimately disallowing) the loss in the stock, while allowing the deduction for the later arising loss in the duplicated loss assets. As will be explained below, in § 804.5.4, the approach of Prop. Reg. § 1.1502-36 is the opposite: where the loss on the *S* stock is realized before the loss on the underlying duplicated loss assets, it would allow the loss on the *S* stock but reduce the basis in the underlying loss assets, thereby disallowing the loss on the duplicated loss assets.

The loss suspension rule could, in certain cases, disallow a deduction for an economic loss. As a result, the rule contains a safe harbor provision that says the loss suspension rule is not to be applied in a manner that permanently disallows an otherwise allowable deduction for an economic loss. This safe harbor treatment applies on the earlier of the date of the deconsolidation of *S* or the date on which the *S* stock is determined to be worthless. Unlike the basis redetermination rule, the loss suspension rule does not seem to go beyond the purpose of the regulation to prevent duplicated losses. But like that rule, it is complex and can impose substantial factual and record keeping burdens on taxpayers.

***Loss expiration rule.*** The third rule, the loss expiration rule, applies if the *S* stock is treated as worthless under Code § 165; or if a member disposes of *S* stock and on the day following the disposition *S* is not a member of the group and does not have a separate return year (for example, *S* is dissolved in a taxable transaction when it is insolvent). The rule provides that all NOLs and capital loss carryovers that are attributable to *S* under Reg. § 1.1502-21 shall be treated as expired, to the extent they are not absorbed in the year that includes the worthless deduction or the stock disposition (or a carryback year). The purpose of this rule is to prevent *P* from claiming a loss for the stock of *S* and then, in a future year, also using the carryovers of *S* which presumably reflect the same economic loss. Because this third rule took a different form in the October 2002 proposed regulation, the regulation allows the group an election to apply a transitional rule if the worthless loss deduction, or the taxable stock disposition occurs on or after March 7, 2002, and before March 14, 2003. In 2004, the IRS amended the loss expiration rule to provide that the *S* losses will not be eliminated when a member takes a worthless stock deduction for its *S* stock if in the following year *S* has a separate return year (which does not include being part of a consolidated group that contains any member of the former group, except a lower-tier subsidiary of *S*).[123]

Reg. § 1.1502-35(g) contains some anti-avoidance rules, the most important of which is Reg. § 1.1502-35(g)(3), described as an anti-loss reimportation rule. This rule provides that, if a group member is allowed a loss on the disposition of a share of stock of a subsidiary member with respect to which there is a duplicated loss (allowed and not suspended, because the stock sale causes the subsidiary to leave the group, with the result that the duplicated loss assets are no longer in the group), and within 10 years after the subsidiary member ceases to be a member, the subsidiary (or a successor) again becomes a member of the group (or any successor group) when the subsidiary (or any successor) still owns the duplicating loss asset, the duplicated loss will be disallowed when the group sells the asset.

Needless to say, the provisions of Reg. § 1.1502-20 and Reg. § 1.337(d)-2 (and the related transition rules in Reg. § 1.1502-20 for progressing from the first to the second of these), and the provisions of Reg. § 1.1502-35, involve great complexity and the need for very careful tax planning and record keeping.[124] The same will be true when taxpayers need to progress from these regulations to Prop. Reg. § 1.1502-36. *See* the discussion at § 804.5.4 below.

Just before the -35 regulations were made final, a very interesting Chief Counsel's Advice was issued dealing with a transaction that was carefully designed to avoid all the duplicated loss provisions of Temp. Reg. § 1.1502-35T.[125] Here, Target (the parent of a consolidated return group) entered into a contract to be acquired by a member of the Acquiring group in a tax free reorganization. The parties took the following steps: First, in anticipation of the reorganization, various members of the Target group transferred loss assets to another member of the Target group (Target Sub) in exchange for new shares of Target Sub stock (the "loss shares"). Second, Target Sub issued new shares to unrelated third persons and to a member of the Acquiring group, which issuances caused Target Sub to cease to be a member of the Target group. Third, the Target Sub "loss shares" were sold to unrelated third persons, and the Target group deducted the loss. Fourth, Acquiring group acquired stock of Target and thus the Target group. The combination of the Target Sub shares acquired by the Acquiring group in step two and the Target Sub shares indirectly acquired by the Acquiring group in step four was sufficient to cause Target Sub to become a member of the Acquiring consolidated return group. Fifth, the loss assets transferred in the first step were sold by the Acquiring group and it deducted the losses. The taxpayer argued that the -35T regulations did not disallow either deduction, for the following reasons: the loss suspension rule did not apply to disallow the loss on the sale of the Target Sub shares because that rule only suspends losses realized on shares of a member of the group, and Target Sub had ceased to be a member of the group before the group sold its shares and realized its loss on the

---

[123] This amendment is effective for worthlessness determinations and liquidations after March 18, 2004, but the group may apply it back to March 7, 2002.

[124] For penetrating discussions of both the planning and the tax policy issues involved, *see* Blanchard, Jr., Bennett, and Speer, *supra* note 83; Schler, *supra* note 102.

[125] IRS Chief Counsel Advice 200724021, March 6, 2007.

shares; and, similarly, the anti-loss reimportation rule did not apply to disallow the loss on the sale of the assets because that rule also applies only if the loss shares are sold when the issuer is still a member of the group, and Target Sub had ceased to be a member before the loss shares were sold. The Chief Counsel Advice concedes that, if the independence of the steps in the transaction can be respected, the taxpayer's analysis is correct. However, the Advice takes the position that the step transaction doctrine applies on these facts to collapse the steps, with the result that the -35T regulation disallows the stock loss, or if that is not accepted, it disallows the later asset loss. The IRS preference for disallowing the stock loss rather than the asset loss in this case reflects the basic approach of the -35T regulation, which, as mentioned above, addresses the duplicated loss problem primarily by suspending (and ultimately disallowing) the stock loss, while allowing the later asset loss.

As we shall see at § 804.5.4 below, the -35T(g)(3) anti-loss reimportation rule was revised in April 2007 to eliminate the technical defect in its application that was relied on by the taxpayer in the foregoing case, by making it apply even if the initial stock loss sale occurs after the issuer ceases to be a member of the group. For other later developments, see the discussions in § 804.5.3 below (relating to Code § 362(e)(2) added in 2004, and the issuance of Prop. Reg. § 1.1502-13(e)(4) in 2007, with respect to the transfer of loss assets in a Code § 351 transaction or as a capital contribution) and in § 804.5.4 below (relating to the issuance in 2007 of Prop. Reg. § 1.1502-36 to replace the -35 regulation).

**Prior periods not addressed by -35 Regulations.** Reg. § 1.1502-35 only applies to losses occurring on or after March 7, 2002. This leaves the question of what should be done where similar types of duplicative losses arise before that date. The IRS addressed this question in a 2004 Legal Memorandum,[126] which posed the question as follows: "If an economic loss is reflected in the asset of a subsidiary and in the subsidiary's stock, can the consolidated group recognize a loss on the disposition of the subsidiary's stock, as well as the disposition of the loss asset?" The answer it gave was "no." As the primary authority in support of that position, it cited *Charles Ilfeld Co. v. Hernandez.*[127] The Memorandum described the doctrine of this case, which applies both within and outside the consolidated return context, as being that "taxpayers are not entitled to a loss or deduction that is economically duplicative of a prior deduction unless a Code or regulatory provision explicitly authorizes the duplicative benefit."[128] Applying this doctrine, the Memorandum enunciated a much more simple way than was set forth in Reg. § 1.1502-35 for dealing with duplicated losses involving stock of a subsidiary and an asset of that subsidiary. The holding of

---

[126] IRS Legal Memorandum 200423027, May 17, 2004, *reprinted at* 2004 TNT 109-29.

[127] 292 U.S. 62 (1934).

[128] Although a number of cases had allowed duplicative losses, the Memorandum distinguished these as involving situations where the duplicative loss was specifically allowed by the Code or a regulation. These cases are: *Gitlitz v. Commissioner*, 531 U.S. 206 (2001); *Woods Investment Co. v. Commissioner*, 85 T.C. 274 (1985), *acq.*, 1986-2 C.B. 1; *Wyman-Gordon v. Commissioner*, 89 T.C. 207 (1987); and *CSI Hydrostatic Testers, Inc. v. Commissioner*, 103 T.C. 398 (1994), *aff'd per curiam*, 62 F.3d 136 (5th Cir. 1995). The *Gitlitz* case is discussed at § 404.2 above, and the other cases at §§ 804.2 and 804.3 above. The Memorandum distinguished the Federal Circuit's decision in *Rite Aid*, on the ground that it was not about disallowing duplicated loss, but rather about disallowing all loss.

the Memorandum is simply that the *second* of the two such losses to occur in the consolidated group is to be disallowed. Moreover, if the group claims a loss on the disposition of subsidiary stock and the subsidiary leaves the group with the underlying economic asset loss unrecognized (as in *Rite Aid*), the doctrine is not to be applied at all because the group has not enjoyed the benefit of the second loss.

The Memorandum does not preclude the possibility that some other provision might also apply to prevent the duplicative losses in the transactions it covers.

**Subsequent statutory change.** As mentioned above, the duplicated loss transactions that were of the most concern to the IRS in its creation of Reg. § 1.1502-35 were those that involved Code § 351 stuffing transactions, that is, transactions in which an asset with a built-in loss is contributed to a subsidiary in a Code § 351 transaction. The primary, although not the exclusive, focus of the -35 regulations is on such transactions. We should note, however, that the Code § 351 duplicated loss aspect of the -35 regulations may be largely superseded, for transactions occurring after October 22, 2004, by the addition, in the American Jobs Creation Act of 2004, of new Code § 362(e)(2), and by Prop. Reg. § 1.1502-13(f)(4). These new provisions are discussed immediately below in § 804.5.3 and in § 804.5.4.

When the -35 regulations were made final in 2006, the accompanying explanation said that the Treasury had not addressed in them the application of Code § 362(e)(2) to transactions between members of a consolidated group. Indeed, the only references to Code § 362(e)(2) in the final -35 regulations are statements that the transactions involved in each of its examples were completed before October 22, 2004, and therefore are not subject to Code § 362(e)(2).[129] Subsequently, in January 2007, the IRS issued Prop. Reg. § 1.1502-13(e)(4) reflecting the proposed application of Code § 362(e)(2) to consolidated return groups. *See* § § 804.5.3 and 804.5.4 below.

### § 804.5.3 Addition in 2004 of Code § 362(e)(2)

As mentioned in the preceding section, the primary, although not the exclusive, focus of Reg. § 1.1502-35 is on so-called stuffing transactions, namely, transactions that involve the transfer of an asset with a built-in loss to a subsidiary in a Code § 351 transaction (or as paid-in surplus or as a contribution to capital). The IRS concern with the potential for duplication of losses through such transactions soon extended beyond the consolidated return area. This culminated in the addition of new Code § 362(e)(2), which was adopted in the American Jobs Creation Act of 2004, effective for transactions occurring after October 22, 2004.[130]

---

[129] For this, and other reasons, the final regulations were strongly criticized in Friedel, Final Consolidated Return Regs. Preventing Loss Duplication: Worse Than Useless (Parts 1 & 2), 33 J. Corp. Tax'n #4 and #5 (July/Aug. and Sept./Oct. 2006).

[130] For a discussion of Code § 362(e)(2), and a related provision, Code § 362(e)(1), which marks to market net built-in loss property imported from a foreign or tax-exempt transferor, *see* Cummings and Hanson, New Limitations on Corporate Built-in Losses, 107 Tax Notes 1553 (June 20, 2005); and Eisenberg, Limitations on Importation and Transfer of Built-in Losses: Untangling the New Basis Adjustment Rules, 107 Tax Notes 869 (May 16, 2005) (the latter article does not address the consolidated return aspects of these new provisions). For a strong criticism of Code § 362(e), *see* Kahn

This new provision states that where a U.S. taxpayer transfers property in a Code §351 transaction (or as paid-in surplus or as a contribution to capital) having an aggregate basis in excess of the fair market value of the property, the transferee's aggregate basis in the property is limited to the aggregate fair market value of the property immediately after the transaction. Any such reduction in aggregate basis is to be allocated among the transferred properties in proportion to their built-in loss immediately before the transaction.

The transferor and transferee are allowed to elect, however, to reduce the basis of the stock received by the transferor rather than the basis of the assets transferred to the transferee. The procedure for making such an election is set forth in IRS Notice 2005-70.[131]

On October 23, 2006, the IRS issued a proposed regulation under Code §362(e)(2): Prop. Reg. §1.362-4. This proposed regulation incorporates and expands on the election procedures contained in IRS Notice 2005-70, and among other things, provides that: (1) where securities as well as stock are issued in a covered transaction, both the asset basis adjustment and the foregoing elective stock-basis alternative must take into account and include both the securities and the stock; (2) where there are several transferors of property, the provision is to be applied on a separate company-by-company (as distinguished from an aggregate) basis; (3) if the transaction is a reorganization but is also described in Code §351, this provision applies; and (4) the section will *not* apply in situations where the duplication of loss is automatically eliminated by the Code, such as in a Code §368(a)(1)(D) acquisitive reorganization or a Code §355 distribution, where the stock is distributed and receives a substituted basis.

Illustrating how any duplicated loss provision can become very complex in practice, the proposed regulation observes that, even if neither the transferor nor the transferee are subject to the U.S. tax system at the time of a transfer of property that is described in Code §362(e)(2), the section will nonetheless apply if later either the property transferred or the stock or securities received in the exchange do enter the U.S. tax system. To ease the compliance burden this could create, the regulation provides that in such a case the parties need not apply the provision to transfers that occurred more than two years before the assets become subject to the U.S. tax system, if neither the original transfer nor the later entry of any portion of the assets into the U.S. tax system was undertaken with a view to reducing the U.S. tax liability of any person, or to duplicating loss by avoiding the application of Code §362(e)(2).

**Code §362(e)(2) and consolidated returns: Prop. Reg. §1.1502-13(e)(4).** Neither the language of Code §362(e)(2) nor its legislative history makes any mention of, or exception for, consolidated returns, nor does Prop. Reg. §1.362-4 propose any exemption. However, the preamble to Prop. Reg. §1.362-4 stated that the IRS planned to give additional guidance regarding the application of Code §362(e)(2) to transfers

(Footnote Continued)

and Kahn, Prevention of Double Deductions of a Single Loss: Solutions in Search of a Problem, 26 Va. Tax Rev. 1 (2006).

[131] 2005-41 I.R.B. 694.

between members of a consolidated return group. The IRS finally proposed such guidance in January 2007 in Prop. Reg. § 1.1502-13(e)(4).

As the preamble to Prop. Reg. § 1.1502-13(e)(4) notes, there is a threshold question as to whether Code § 362(e)(2) should apply at all to a consolidated return group. The question is pertinent because consolidated return investment adjustments in Reg. §§ 1.1502-32 and loss duplication rules in 1.1502-35 (and new Prop. Reg. § 1.1502-36) are themselves intended to eliminate duplication of deductions in the consolidated return context. Thus, arguably, application of Code § 362(e)(2) to a consolidated return group is duplicative, and might even in some circumstances produce elimination of a single deduction for an economic loss. Although continuing to study the question, the IRS currently remains concerned that such other provisions might not fully eliminate all double deduction problems, and therefore has tentatively concluded that Code § 362(e)(2) should apply—essentially on a standby basis—to cover such situations. Consistent with this standby role, the proposed regulation would suspend application of Code § 362(e)(2) until certain specified "section 362(e)(2) application events" occur, at which time it would apply the section only to the extent the consolidated return investment adjustment system and Prop. Reg. § 1.1502-36 have not already eliminated (as they would usually have done) and can no longer eliminate the remaining potential loss duplication.

The proposed regulation preserves the right of the parties to elect to reduce the transferor's stock basis rather than the transferee's asset basis, and gives the parties the choice to make this election either at the time of the original Code § 351 transfer or only later if and when a "section 362(e)(2) application event" occurs. In either case, the election only applies to the amount of potential duplication that still exists at the time of the "section 362(e)(2) application event." Because the election is irrevocable and has the same consequences whether made at the time of the original Code § 351 transfer or only later at the time of the "application event," it would seem taxpayers should generally delay making the election until an "application event" occurs, so that they can make the election in light of all the facts at that time. The suspended application of Code § 362(e)(2) involves great complexity in application and will create a substantial record keeping and compliance burden.

In addition to the provisions of Prop. Reg. § 1.1502-13(e)(4), related provisions dealing with Code § 362(e)(2) were included in Prop. Reg. §§ 1.1502-32(c) and 1.1502-36.

**For periods before Prop. Reg. § 1.1502-13(e)(4) becomes effective.** As mentioned above, the issuance of Prop. Reg. § 1.1502-13(e)(4) is the first time that the IRS has addressed the question of the application of Code § 362(e)(2) to a consolidated return group. But this proposed regulation provides that it will apply only to transfers on or after the date it becomes final. What should taxpayers do about prior periods? A literal application of Code § 362(e)(2) to a consolidated return group will not only usually be unnecessary to eliminate duplication of losses (due to the consolidated return investment adjustments in Reg. § 1.1502-32, and to Reg. § 1.1502-35), but it could in some situations even result in a double disallowance of a loss. For example, if the election to reduce *P*'s stock basis is made under Code § 362(e)(2), a later sale of the asset by *S* at a loss could produce a second reduction in the stock basis, creating an artificial gain in the stock that, if and when recognized, would eliminate the benefit of the single deduction allowed for the group's economic loss. Various approaches have been suggested, including taking the position that other provisions in the consolidated return regulations should be interpreted to prevent such a double disallowance—*see* Reg. § 1.1502-32(a)(2), stating that "P's basis in S's stock must not be adjusted under this [regulation] and other rules of law in a manner that has the effect of duplicating an adjustment"—or that Prop. Reg. § 1.1502-13(e)(4) can be relied upon for applying the suspended application approach of the regulation during this prior period.[132]

As discussed at § 804.5.2 above, the -35 regulations address duplicated loss problems by imposing three rules, namely, (1) a basis redetermination rule, (2) a loss suspension rule, and (3) a loss expiration rule. New Code § 362(e)(2) essentially supersedes the second of these rules in a Code § 351 situation. This is because the second of these rules, by its terms, does not apply unless there is a duplicated loss, and the application of new Code § 362(e)(2) eliminates such duplication in a Code § 351 transaction. However, the first of these rules applies by its terms even if there is no loss duplication. Thus, unless the transferor and the transferee elect under new Code § 362(e)(2) to reduce the basis of the transferor's stock rather than the transferee's assets, the first of these rules could still have an impact. The third of these rules, which deals with loss expiration rather than basis and asset stuffing, would essentially be unaffected by new Code § 362(e)(2).

### § 804.5.4 Prop. Reg. § 1.1502-36 and Temp. Reg. §§ 1.1502-35T(g)(3) and (g)(6)

**Prop. Reg. § 1.1502-36.** Prop. Reg. § 1.1502-36, issued in January 2007 (the "-36 proposed regulation"), would replace, beginning on the date it becomes effective, the provisions of Reg. §§ 1.337(d)-1 and -2 and 1.1502-35. The purpose of the new provision, like the purpose of these earlier regulations, is to prevent the deduction of noneconomic and duplicated losses.

The -36 regulation would apply whenever a consolidated group member transfers a loss share of subsidiary stock. For this purpose, a "transfer" is defined to include any event in which (a) the holder ceases to own the share in a taxable transaction, (b) the holder and the issuer cease to belong to the same group, (c) the share is acquired by a nonmember, or (d) the share is treated as worthless. Like the -35 regulation, the -36 proposed regulation would impose three rules. The three -36 rules are: (1) a basis redetermination rule, (2) a basis reduction rule, and (3) a subsidiary attribute reduction rule. The first two of these rules are similar to the first two of the -35 rules, though they differ in details. However, the third -36 rule takes a quite different approach than did the third -35 rule. Where the stock loss precedes the realization of the duplicating asset loss, the -35 rule seeks to suspend (and ultimately disallow) the stock loss while allowing the asset loss. In contrast, the -36 rule would allow the stock loss but disallow the later duplicating asset loss by reducing the basis or other duplicating loss attributes.

***Basis redetermination rule.*** Where the group has both high basis and low basis shares, this rule requires in effect that the basis of the shares generally be averaged. The purpose is to prevent a transfer of only the high basis shares from creating more

---

[132] *See* Milner and Clary II, As Proposed, Section 362(e)(2) Does Not Apply to Intercompany Transactions, Unless It Does, 34 Corp. Tax'n 3 (2007).

loss than would occur if the basis of all the shares held by the group is averaged. Thus, the basis redetermination rule only applies where there is a transfer of loss shares (but could impact gain shares transferred at the same time). Among other things, under the rule both positive and negative investment adjustments that have previously been made to the shares are reallocated, first, so as to reduce or eliminate loss on preferred shares, and then to reduce basis disparity on all shares. This rule, in effect, seeks to reduce or eliminate both noneconomic and duplicated losses.

***Basis reduction rule.*** If, after application of the basis redetermination rule, any transferred share remains a loss share (even if it only became a loss share by application of the redetermination rule), the basis of the share is subject to reduction under this second rule. The purpose of this rule is to reduce or eliminate any noneconomic losses that remain after application of the redetermination rule. The basis reduction rule operates by reducing the basis of each transferred loss share (but not below value) by the lesser of the share's "disconformity amount" or its "net positive adjustment."

The "disconformity amount" is the excess of the share's basis over its allocable portion at the transfer date of the issuer's net inside tax attributes. The issuer's net inside tax attributes are the sum of the issuer's loss carryovers, deferred deductions, cash, and asset basis, reduced by the issuer's liabilities.

The "net positive adjustment" is computed as the greater of zero and the sum of all investment adjustments (excluding distributions) that have been applied to the basis of the transferred loss share. All items of income, gain, deduction and loss that have been reflected in the share's basis are taken into account.

***Attribute reduction rule.*** If any transferred share remains a loss share after application of the foregoing two rules, the subsidary's duplicating loss attributes (*e.g.*, asset basis, loss carryovers, deferred deductions) are subject to reduction. This rule seeks to reduce or eliminate duplicated losses: the rule is intended to ensure that the group does not recognize more than one loss with respect to a single economic loss, regardless of whether the group chooses to dispose of the subsidary's stock before or after the subsidary recognizes the loss with respect to its assets. The rule requires the subsidary to reduce its tax attributes by the lesser of the net stock loss or the aggregate inside loss (the latter defined generally as the excess of the subsidary's tax attributes, reduced by the amount of the subsidiary's liabilities, over the value of all of the subsidary's shares). By focusing on reducing the subsidiary's tax attributes, rather than on suspending or disallowing the group's loss in the stock of the subsidiary, the -36 rule allows the deduction for the loss on the shares, but disallows the use of the duplicating asset basis or other tax attribute of the subsidiary.

This attribute reduction rule also gives the group an election to reduce—instead of the subsidary's tax attributes—the basis in the subsidary's shares, or to reattribute the subsidary's tax attributes within the group (though this latter election can only be made if the subsidary ceases to be a member of the group and only for certain attributes). This reattribution election is particularly complex, and has the effect, through tiering up of the adjustments, of also reducing the basis of the subsidary's shares.

Where the consolidated group contains several tiers of subsidiaries, the -36 regulation provides detailed rules about how to apply the foregoing adjustments through the various tiers.

As the reader can tell from even this brief summary, the proposed -36 regulation is exceedingly complex. The good news is that it only applies, and only needs to be considered, when a group transfers a share of a subsidiary that is a loss share. But where that occurs, the regulation will impose heavy analytical and record keeping burdens on taxpayers, and require an expenditure of large amounts of administrative time by both the taxpayer and the government.

**Temp. Reg. §§1.1502-35T(g)(3) and (g)(6).** In April 2007, the IRS issued an amended -35T(g)(3) anti-loss reimportation rule. The amendment corrects the defect that the taxpayer had relied on in the case described in Chief Counsel Advice 200724021, discussed above at §804.5.2. This defect is that the original anti-loss reimportation rule applied only if the loss on the subsidiary stock occurred when the subsidiary was a member of the group. The taxpayer in that Advice had sought to avoid that rule by first deconsolidating the subsidiary before selling its loss stock. The amended rule provides that losses reflected in the basis of subsidiary stock at the time of deconsolidation may not be recognized and reimported into the group, regardless of whether the stock losses are recognized when the subsidiary is a member of the group.

At the same time, the IRS issued -35T(g)(6). This is a new anti-avoidance rule which provides that "if a taxpayer acts with a view to avoid the purposes of this section, appropriate adjustments will be made to carry out the purposes of this section." These new -35T(g)(3) and (g)(6) provisions are effective for events occurring on or after April 10, 2007.

## *§804.6 Consolidated §382, SRLY, and CRCO Rules*

As discussed at §508.7 above, the consolidated return regulations provide special consolidated rules for the application of Code §382.

Similarly, the members of a consolidated return group must take into account the consolidated SRLY limitations. These were discussed at §509.4 above. In this regard, it should be noted that if a member has a built-in loss when it joins a consolidated return group, the SRLY limitation applies to that built-in loss.[133] For earlier years, the group also had to take into account the CRCO limitations, which were discussed at §509.3 above.

## *§804.7 Leaving or Joining a Consolidated Group: Tactical Considerations for Buyer and Seller*

Finally, we should point out that special considerations arise where a member leaves a consolidated return group.[134] A member can leave in a number of different ways, including a taxable or tax-free acquisition of its stock by an unrelated company

---

133 Temp. Reg. §1.1502-15T, applicable to losses recognized in years beginning on or after January 1, 1997, with the right for the taxpayer to elect to apply this rule to certain earlier years.

134 For a further discussion, *see* Hyman and Hoffman, Consolidated Returns: Summary of Tax Considerations in Acquisition of Common Parent or Subsidiary Member of Affiliated Group, 33 Tax Law. 383 (1980); Henderson, Side Effects of Leaving a Consolidated Return Group, 27 Inst. on Fed. Tax'n 711 (1969).

or the acquisition of its assets in a taxable or tax-free acquisition. In any such case, the parties should be careful to draft a tax allocation agreement that takes into account the consequences of the transaction under the consolidated return regulations. These consequences include the possible triggering into income of deferred inter-company accounts and excess loss accounts, the deemed redemption and reissuance of debt that ceases to be intercompany debt, and the withdrawal from the group of the portion of the consolidated NOL carryovers that have been generated by the departing member (unless the member "leaves" through a taxable asset transaction, including a Code § 338(h)(10) transaction, in which case the member entity remains in, or is treated as liquidating into, the consolidated return group). A portion of the consolidated ITC carryovers and other carryovers may also depart with the subsidiary. However, the subsidiary remains severally liable for the consolidated tax liability of the group while it was a member of the consolidated return group. This includes the consolidated return tax liability for the group for the entire year in which the subsidiary leaves, including the portion of the year after the subsidiary has left.

Moreover, income or deductions realized by other members of the group for the portion of the year after the subsidiary has left may affect the subsidiary itself. For example, the portion of the consolidated NOL carryover attributable to the subsidiary will be reduced by income of the other members of the group for the entire taxable year, including the portion of the year after the subsidiary has left. Similarly, under the consolidated COD-attribute reduction regulations, discussed at § 804.4.5 above, the subsidiary attributable NOL may be reduced as a result of excluded COD income incurred by other members of the group throughout the entire year. In addition, where a departing subsidiary is a direct or indirect subsidiary of a member of the group that has excluded COD, and a portion of the subsidiary's stock will continue to be held (directly or indirectly) by the debtor member, the timing of the subsidiary's departure may affect whether the stock basis "look-through" rule applies to the subsidiary. Under that rule, any COD-basis reduction of a group member's stock must in turn reduce the attributes of that member. In general, this will only be of concern when the departing subsidiary leaves the group on the last day of the group's taxable year or at the same time as the debtor member.

The consolidated COD-attribute reduction regulations also have implications for a subsidiary just joining the group. Aside from the normal considerations of subjecting another corporation's attributes to potential reduction as a result of any excluded COD income that may be incurred by another member of the group in the current year or in the future, it is also possible for a new subsidiary to have its attributes reduced as a result of excluded COD incurred by a member of the group in the preceding year. This will only occur when a portion of the subsidiary's stock was owned (directly or indirectly) by the debtor member as of the end of the preceding year (*i.e.*, a "creeping" consolidation) *and* the tax basis of such stock was reduced due to the COD (*see* § 804.4.5 above).

The consolidated Code § 382 regulations add yet another wrinkle to be taken into account when a member leaves a consolidated group. As discussed at § 508.7.5 above, these regulations say that if a Code § 382 limitation applied to the losses of the selling consolidated return group, any predeparture consolidated attribute that was subject to that consolidated limitation will not only continue to be subject to that Code § 382 limitation in the hands of the departing member, but the departing member's Code § 382 limitation for this attribute will be *zero*, except to the extent the old common parent (not the subgroup parent) elects to attribute some or all of the consolidated limitation to the departing member. Obviously, unless such an election is made, the attribute taken by the departing member when it leaves the group will be worthless in its hands. This issue, like those above, must be included in the negotiations between the seller and the buyer of the departing member.[135]

In addition to the foregoing matters, when a troubled corporation is sold by a consolidated return group in a taxable transaction that would produce a loss for the selling group, the selling group needs to take into account (1) for sales before March 7, 2002, the loss disallowance rules of former Reg. § 1.1502-20, and its related loss reattribution election in Reg. § 1.1502-20(g) which can help mitigate that disallowance, (2) for transactions after March 6, 2002, the revised and more limited loss disallowance rule of Temp. Reg. §§ 1.337(d)-2T and 1.1502-35T, and (3) for periods after it becomes effective, the loss disallowance rule of Prop. Reg. § 1.1502-36 (*see* the discussion starting at § 804.5.2 above). Similarly, where the troubled corporation is purchased by a consolidated return group and the troubled corporation brings with it capital loss or NOL carryovers or built-in losses, the purchasing group needs to take into account the stock basis reduction problem that can arise if these attributes expire unused, and it needs to consider the loss waiver election that helps mitigate at least part of that result.[136] These latter points are discussed immediately below.

**Disallowed stock loss and loss reattribution election.** Where the consolidated group sold the stock of a troubled member *S*, before March 7, 2002, in a taxable transaction that would normally have generated a stock loss for the selling consolidated group, former Reg. § 1.1502-20 potentially applied to disallow some, and perhaps all, of that loss. A possible opportunity for mitigating this result, however, was provided by former Reg. § 1.1502-20(g). This gave the common parent of the selling group (which may not be the member that held the *S* stock and had the disallowed loss)[137] an election to reattribute to itself some or all of the consolidated NOL or capital loss carryovers that had been generated by *S* (or any lower-tier subsidiary of *S*), but not in excess of the loss otherwise disallowed to the group on the *S* stock. This election was not available, however, to the extent the losses did not exceed the separate insolvencies (as specially computed for this purpose) of the subsidiary whose losses were to be reattributed and any higher-tier insolvent subsidiaries (counting only such insolvent companies in the chain). *See* §§ 508.2.4 and 804.5.1 above. This election could be made by *S* and the common parent of the selling group. Although notice of the election must be given to the purchaser of *S*, the purchaser's consent was not needed. Obviously, where *S* is being sold at a loss in a taxable transaction, this reattribution election should be included in the items to be negoti-

---

135 Since these losses will be subject to the lesser of the Code § 382 limitation inherited from the selling group and the new Code § 382 limitation created by the sale, *see* § 508.4.4 above, one need not allocate more of the old limitation than this lesser amount.

136 *See* Reg. §§ 1.1502-32(b)(3)(iii)(A) (expiring loss carryover is a noncapital, nondeductible expense for which a negative stock basis adjustment is required) and 1.1502-32(b)(4) (waiver of SRLY losses).

137 Where these reattributed losses are subject to a SRLY limitation, a common parent that is only a holding company may have difficulty using them. An alternative choice was to make a Code § 338(h)(10) election, which allows the selling group to recognize the loss on the asset sale and shift *S*'s carryovers to *S*'s immediate parent.

ated between the buyer and the seller of *S*. For a discussion of these former provisions, *see* § 804.5.1 above. For periods after March 6, 2002, Reg. § 1.1502-20 was superseded by Temp. Reg. § 1.337(d)-2T and Temp. Reg. § 1.1502-35T and thereafter by final Reg. § 1.337(d)-2 and Reg. § 1.1502-35. Temp. Reg. § 1.1502-20T was issued to provide transition rules, including rules for making or changing elections for prior years. In early 2007, the IRS issued Prop. Reg. § 1.1502-36 which would supersede, commencing with its effective date, all of these earlier regulations. *See* §§ 804.5.2 and 804.5.4 above.

**Stock basis reduction for expiring losses; loss waiver election.** A different problem can arise where the stock of *S* is purchased in a taxable transaction by a consolidated return group, and *S* has capital loss or NOL carryovers which it retains (either because *S* was a stand-alone company or was part of a consolidated group that did not reattribute these items to the former common parent). The purchase of the *S* stock will subject these losses to the limitations imposed by Code § 382 and to the SRLY rule. The same problem can be created where *S* has built-in losses.[138] Because these limitations impose a risk that some or all of these losses will expire unused, the purchaser must be especially wary about the consolidated return rule requiring a reduction in the basis of the *S* stock when any of *S*'s loss carryovers or recognized built-in losses expire unused.[139] Although this basis reduction rule reaches a correct result where the *S* stock basis has not previously been reduced because of these disallowed losses (as would be the case if *S* stayed in its old group or was acquired in a carryover basis transaction), the rule does not produce the right result where the stock is purchased for a market price that reflects the reduced value caused by these economic losses.

To illustrate, assume that *S* was formed by its prior parent by an investment of $100. If *S* generates a $60 NOL that is not absorbed by the prior group, the prior parent's basis in the *S* stock remains $100 until the loss is either used or expires unused, when it is reduced to $40. If, on the other hand, *X*, a member of a different consolidated group, purchases the *S* stock for $40 while the $60 NOL still exists (and the $60 NOL is not reattributed to the selling group), *X*'s basis in the *S* stock is only $40. Because the purchase subjects *S*'s $60 NOL to the Code § 382 and SRLY limitations, the risk is increased that some or all of the loss may expire unused. If *S*'s $60 of NOLs do expire unused, *X* will have to reduce its $40 basis in the *S* stock by $60, thereby giving *X* a $20 excess loss account in the *S* stock.

Because this latter result is inappropriate, the regulations have added a loss waiver rule to allow at least partial mitigation of its effect.[140] This permits *X* and *S* (without the need for consent from the former group—indeed, the election is available to *X* and *S* even if *S* was not acquired from a consolidated return group) to elect to treat some or all of the *S* losses as expiring immediately before *S* joins the purchasing consolidated return group (and immediately after *S* leaves its former consolidated

---

[138] If the loss is realized after *S* is purchased but the loss expires unused because of the built-in loss limitation, the new group must reduce the basis of the *S* stock by the amount of the expired loss.

[139] Reg. § 1.1502-32(b)(3)(iii). This rule only applies if *S* joins the purchasing group in a year beginning on or after January 1, 1995. *See* § 509.4 above.

[140] Reg. § 1.1502-32(b)(4).

return group, if it was acquired from such a group). If the election is made, *X*'s basis in the *S* stock will not be reduced by these losses; the election does not solve the built-in loss problem, however, because it applies only to loss carryovers that arose before the purchase of the *S* stock. The election can even be made where the *S* stock is acquired in a carryover basis transaction, with certain benefits for the *X* group in that situation as well.[141]

Although it was not designed to do so, where *S* joined the new group before March 7, 2002, the loss waiver election could potentially benefit the seller of *S*, if the seller is a consolidated return group that has a loss disallowed on the sale of the *S* stock under old Reg. § 1.1502-20. It did this by providing an alternative to the old Reg. § 1.1502-20(g) loss reattribution election discussed above. This alternative existed because the waiver eliminated the waived losses from the "duplicated loss" category, thereby reducing the loss disallowance and increasing the loss which the former group could deduct upon the sale of the *S* stock.[142] Whether the capital loss this would preserve for the selling group was as valuable as the loss reattribution election depended on the particular facts and circumstances.

For transactions after March 6, 2002, however, the elimination of the "duplicated loss" category in determining the allowable loss on the disposition of *S* stock (*see* § 804.5 above) meant that a consolidated return seller of *S* could obtain this same benefit without requiring *X* to make the waiver election. As a consequence, in May 2003 the IRS issued temporary and proposed regulations[143] that give *X* an election to rescind such a waiver for transactions before March 7, 2002, to the extent the seller elects to apply Reg. § 1.1502-20 without regard to the loss duplication factor, or elects to apply Temp. Reg. § 1.337(d)-2T. However, the rescission will only apply to the part of the loss carryovers that did not exceed the duplicated loss with respect to the disposition of the *S* stock. This new provision permits increases, but not decreases, in the amount of loss carryovers available to *X*, and the election must be made in a timely filed return (including extensions) for a year that includes May 7, 2003.

## § 805 DOUBLE DEDUCTION PROBLEMS

Suppose a parent corporation (*P*) invests $2 million in a subsidiary (*S*). *S* loses the $2 million, producing a $2 million NOL. *P*'s investment in *S* becomes worthless. If *P* and *S* can deduct both the $2 million NOL and a $2 million bad debt or Code § 165(g) worthless stock deduction, $4 million of deductions will have been realized for only a $2 million investment. Double deductions for the same loss are not permitted. On the other hand, *P* and *S* are separate entities, and the separateness of a corporate entity is

---

[141] These benefits are discussed in Stewart, Boley & Thompson, Utilization of the Loss Reattribution and Loss Waiver Elections by Consolidated Groups, 25 J. Corp. Tax'n 341 (1998).

[142] *See* IRS Letter Ruling 9814028, December 24, 1997. In circumstances where this election makes sense, a Code § 338(h)(10) election may be an alternative that should be considered.

The interplay between the loss reattribution and the loss waiver rules is analyzed in detail in Stewart, Boley & Thompson, *supra* note 141. *See also* Dubroff, Blanchard, Broadbent & Duvall, Federal Income Taxation of Corporations § § 51.06[6], 71.01, 71.02, Chapter 72 (2d ed.).

[143] Temp. Reg. § § 1.1502-20T(i)(3)(viii), -20T(i)(5), and 1.1502-32T(b)(4)(vii).

generally to be respected. On the facts just stated, the question presented is which of these two potentially conflicting policies will prevail.

## *§805.1 Separate Returns*

This question was addressed in the separate-return context in the *Marwais Steel*[1] case. *P* and *S* filed separate returns. *P* loaned money to *S* which *S* then lost, producing an NOL in *S*. *P* took a bad debt deduction for the loan, and then contributed the debt to the capital of *S*. Although Code § 108(e)(6), as amended in 1980, would now cause *S* to have COD income attributable to the difference between the face amount of the debt and *P*'s basis in it,[2] this was not the law during the years involved in the *Marwais* case. Thus, *S*'s NOL was not reduced. Thereafter, *P* liquidated *S* and attempted to use *S*'s NOL against its own income. The court denied the NOL deduction, on the ground that allowance of the deduction would give *P* a double deduction for the same loss.

A variation on this fact pattern was presented in the *Textron* case.[3] Here, the investment by *P* in *S* that became worthless was an equity investment in *S*, and *S* was not liquidated. Instead, *P* contributed more funds to *S* for the acquisition of profitable assets. The income from the assets absorbed *S*'s NOLs, which were not challenged by the IRS. Although the IRS challenged *P*'s worthless stock deduction on the ground that this deduction produced a double deduction for the same loss, the court held for the taxpayer. The court hinted, however, that it might have disallowed use of the NOL deduction to *S* had that issue been before it, and the IRS subsequently indicated that it may seek to disallow use of the NOL deduction in any similar case, at least where *P* and *S* are related companies.[4] This problem was ultimately addressed not by arbitrarily denying *S*'s NOL but by ensuring that Code § 382 applied to the transaction: The *Textron* case was the inspiration for the adoption in 1987 of Code § 382(g)(4)(D),[5] which is discussed at § 508.2.4 above.

Suppose *P* buys the *S* stock for $100 when *S* has an asset having a basis and a value of $100. The *S* asset declines in value to $20. *P* sells the *S* stock for $20. *S* later sells its asset for $20. Where *P* and *S* have filed separate returns, the *Rite Aid* case (discussed at § 804.5 above) seems to confirm that *P* and *S* are both entitled to a $80 deduction. However, *S*'s deduction will be limited by Code § 382.

---

[1] **§ 805** *Marwais Steel Co. v. Commissioner*, 354 F.2d 997, 66-1 U.S.T.C. ¶ 9138 (9th Cir. 1966).

[2] Code § 108 does not similarly affect *S* when *P* claims a worthless stock deduction under Code § 165(g) for its equity investment in *S*.

[3] *Textron, Inc. v. United States*, 561 F.2d 1023, 77-2 U.S.T.C. ¶ 9539 (1st Cir. 1977).

[4] *See* GCM 37961, May 24, 1979; GCM 39158, April 21, 1983. *See also* Natbony, Twice Burned or Twice Blessed—Double Deductions in the Affiliated Corporation Context, 6 J. Corp. Tax'n 3 (1979). In IRS Legal Memorandum 200423027, described at § 804.5.2 above, the IRS cited *Textron* for the proposition that the *Ilfeld* doctrine, also described at § 804.5.2 above, should not be applied to deny the first loss where the later, duplicative loss has not yet been claimed.

[5] *See* H.R. Rep. No. 495, 100th Cong., 1st Sess. 971-972 (1987).

## §805.2 Consolidated Returns

Where *P* and *S* file consolidated rather than separate returns, the investment adjustment provisions of the consolidated return regulations are designed to prevent the allowance of double deductions. *See* §804.5 above. If *S* has a $2 million NOL that is used by the group, *P*'s basis in *S* is reduced (perhaps producing an excess loss account) by $2 million.[6]

The result under the pre-1994 investment adjustment regulations is fairly straightforward where the investment in *S* is held by *P*. Where other members of the group have also invested in *S*, the result under those regulations was not so straightforward. This is illustrated by a 1983 technical advice memorandum, involving pre-1980 taxable years, in which *P* owned *S1* which in turn owned *S2*.[7] *S1* had acquired the *S2* stock for $0.5 million and *P* had loaned $2 million to *S2*. *S2* generated $2 million of NOLs. These were used by the group, providing a $1.5 million excess loss account in the *S2* stock owned by *S1* (and a $2 million reduction in the basis of the *S1* stock owned by *P*). *P* had claimed a $2 million bad debt deduction for its loan to *S2*, which it then cancelled, whereupon *S2*, which had become worthless, was liquidated. The insolvency exception prevented *S2* from having COD income. The debt cancellation, however, increased *S2*'s earnings and profits by $2 million thereby restoring *S1*'s basis in the *S2* stock to $0.5 million, which *S1* then claimed as a worthless stock deduction. The result: the group had claimed a total of $4.5 million of deductions for an economic loss of only $2.5 million. To avoid this result, the IRS required the transaction to be recharacterized as if *P* had cancelled the debt only after *S2* had been liquidated, thereby resulting in a capital contribution to *S1*. Perhaps a more appropriate characterization would have been to treat the debt cancellation as a contribution by *P* to the capital of *S1*, which in turn contributed it to *S2*. Under the 1994 regulations, this problem does not arise and such recharacterization becomes unnecessary.

For post-1980 years, the combination of the attribute reduction rules contained in Code §108, the provisions of Code §1503(e) as added in 1987 and 1988 (discussed at §804.2 above), Reg. §1.1502-13(f) (discussed at §804.5 above), Reg. §1.1502-20 and its successors Temp. Reg. §§1.337(d)-(2)T and 1.1502-35T (discussed at §804.5 and §804.7 above), and the 1994 rules deferring a worthless stock deduction in Reg. §§1.1502-19(c)(1)(iii) and 1.1502-80(c) including subsequent amendments (all discussed at §804.2 above), should eliminate double deduction problems. Indeed, former Reg. §1.1502-20 with Reg. §1.1502-13(f) went even farther, by often eliminating even a single deduction for a realized economic loss.

---

[6] Pre-1994 Reg. §1.1502-32(b)(1) and (2); present Reg. §1.1502-32(b)(2) and (3). Even before the investment adjustment provisions were included in the regulations, the Supreme Court denied a worthless stock deduction to *P* in such circumstances on the ground that this would produce a double deduction. *Charles Ilfeld v. Hernandez*, 292 U.S. 62, 4 U.S.T.C. ¶1261 (1934); *accord*, *McLaughlin v. Pacific Lumber Co.*, 293 U.S. 351, 355, 35-1 U.S.T.C. ¶9015 (1935). These cases were cited with approval in IRS Legal Memorandum 200423027, described at §804.5.2 above.

[7] IRS Tech. Adv. Mem. 8337010, May 25, 1983; GCM 39158, March 1, 1984.

## §806 SPECIAL BANKRUPTCY CONSIDERATIONS

As discussed in Chapter 10, special problems may be encountered where some (but not all) of the members of a consolidated group for tax purposes are in bankruptcy.

### *§806.1 Consolidated Return Liability Issues Where Less Than All Members Are in Bankruptcy*

For example, can the IRS assess and collect any pre-bankruptcy tax deficiency of the group against the nonbankrupt members while other members (particularly, the common parent) are in bankruptcy (*see* §1007); and, if so, can the nonbankrupt members petition the Tax Court, or otherwise judicially challenge, the assessment (*see* §1009)? Moreover, even though one member of the group receives a discharge in bankruptcy, each nonbankrupt member ultimately remains responsible for the entire amount of any group tax deficiency with respect to the taxable years for which the bankrupt member was discharged (*see* §1014.2). Given these issues, consideration should be given, in connection with the bankruptcy of any member, to bringing the other members of the group into bankruptcy as well.

An interesting variation on these questions can be found in the *Imperial Corporation* case.[1] Here, during the pendency of a bankruptcy case involving a parent, the consolidated return group had taxable income attributable to income of a subsidiary. The parent was of course severally liable for the tax. The IRS asserted that the tax should be entitled to a first priority status as an administrative expense in the bankruptcy proceeding of the parent. The court denied this, saying that the IRS had not proved that the tax was an expense that benefitted the bankruptcy estate of the parent. The court also held that the tax liability was not entitled to a seventh priority, because it was not for pre-bankruptcy taxable years. Thus, the tax liability was entitled only to status as a general unsecured claim in the parent's bankruptcy case.

### *§806.2 Determining Ownership of Consolidated Return Refunds Generated by a Loss Member*

Where a consolidated subsidiary has losses that produce a consolidated group refund from a consolidated net operating loss carryback, a question arises as to whether the loss subsidiary is entitled to all or a portion of the refund that the IRS is required to pay to the common parent. The courts have begun to address this question with increasing frequency. Further, while the IRS has not attempted to answer this question generally, the IRS, pursuant to a grant of regulatory authority, has issued regulations providing for the payment of income tax refunds to a fiduciary of an insolvent financial institution that is a member of an affiliated group to the extent the IRS determines that the refund is attributable to losses or credits of the insolvent financial institution.[2]

---

[1] **§806** *In re Imperial Corp. of America*, No. 90-01585-LM11 (Bankr. S.D. Cal., June 17, 1991).

[2] Code §6402(i) and Reg. §301.6402-7.

### § 806.2.1 Where a Subsidiary's NOL Is Applied Against Its Own Income

The common parent of the consolidated group generally has the authority to act as the sole agent for the subsidiary members of the group with respect to all matters relating to the tax liability of the consolidated group. In particular, the common parent is authorized to file claims for refund, and any refund will be paid directly to the common parent and will discharge the IRS of any liability in respect thereof to any subsidiary member of the consolidated group.[3] Similarly, any tentative carryback adjustment of taxes under Code § 6411 is to be made by the common parent and any refund from such adjustment is to be paid directly to and in the name of the common parent.[4] While the IRS ordinarily will pay a tax refund to the common parent, there is neither a statutory provision nor anything in the consolidated return regulations that determines which member of the consolidated group is entitled to the tax refund.

The cases that have addressed the question of whether the common parent or the loss subsidiary is entitled to the tax refund have uniformly concluded it is the loss subsidiary to the extent that both the loss carryback and the prior year's income being offset are attributable to the subsidiary.[5] This result is based primarily on the theory that the consolidated return regulations authorizing the IRS to pay the refund to the common parent are basically procedural regulations that do not entitle the common parent to the tax refund, and that to allow the common parent to keep the refund would unjustly enrich the common parent because such a refund is attributable to tax payments made by, and tax benefits generated by, the loss subsidiary. Most of the

---

[3] Reg. § 1.1502-77(a). The last sentence of the regulation, however, provides that the district director may, upon notifying the parent, deal directly with any subsidiary member of the consolidated group, and in such event that subsidiary will have full authority to act for itself. This provision, including both its application and its limitations, was applied in IRS Field Service Advice 200051002, September 15, 2000, which is described at § 804.1 above.

[4] Reg. § 1.1502-78.

[5] *See, e.g., Western Dealer Management, Inc. v. England* (*In re Bob Richards Chrysler-Plymouth Corp.*), 473 F.2d 262 (9th Cir. 1973), *cert. denied sub. nom.*, 412 U.S. 919 (1973); *Jump v. Manchester Life & Casualty Management Corp.*, 579 F.2d 449, 78-2 U.S.T.C. ¶ 9557 (8th Cir. 1978), *aff'g* 438 F. Supp. 185 (E.D. Mo. 1977); *Capital Bancshares, Inc. v. FDIC*, 957 F.2d 203, 92-1 U.S.T.C. ¶ 50,201 (5th Cir. 1992) (tax refund held to be property of the bank subsidiary and payable by the IRS to the FDIC as receiver where the losses carried back were entirely attributable to the bank and the bank could have used them to generate the refund had it filed separate returns); *FDIC v. Mercer Bancorp*, 1990 U.S. Dist. LEXIS 16589 (W.D. Mo.) (FDIC, as the receiver for subsidiary, was entitled to entire refund where all losses carried back and all prior income were attributable to subsidiary); *In re Revco D.S., Inc.*, 111 B.R. 631 (Bankr. N.D. Ohio 1990) (brought as an interpleader action by the government to determine which member of the consolidated group was entitled to a tax refund; the court determined that the subsidiary was entitled to the refund to the extent that subsidiary's loss offset prior income of the subsidiary); *United States of America v. Bass Fin. Corp.*, No. 83 C. 706 slip op. (N.D. Ill. 1984) (in an interpleader action, held that the FSLIC, as the receiver for a bankrupt subsidiary, was entitled to the entire tax refund where prior income of the subsidiary was offset by losses of the subsidiary as well as losses of other group members; although approximately 2 percent of the refund was attributable to the carryback of losses of other group members, such other members failed to raise an objection); *In re Florida Park Banks, Inc.*, 110 B.R. 986 (Bankr. N.D. Fla. 1990) (tax refund is property of subsidiary where subsidiary's losses alone would have been sufficient to offset the entire prior income of the subsidiary, even though other members' losses were also carried back).

courts have indicated that this result could be changed by an express agreement among the parties allocating the benefit of the refund.

In the leading case on this question, *In re Bob Richards Chrysler-Plymouth Corp.*,[6] a bankrupt subsidiary sued the common parent of the consolidated group of which the subsidiary was a member for a tax refund received by the parent. The refund was attributable to a carryback of net operating losses incurred by the subsidiary to offset income of the consolidated group in prior taxable years, which income likewise was attributable to the bankrupt subsidiary. The Ninth Circuit stated that "[a]bsent any differing agreement we feel that a tax refund resulting solely from offsetting the losses of one member of a consolidated filing group against the income of that same member in a prior or subsequent year should inure to the benefit of that member."[7] The court reasoned that to allow the common parent to keep the tax refund would unjustly enrich the common parent.

Although the *Bob Richards* case did not involve a tax allocation agreement, because the subsidiary was indebted to the parent, the parent argued that it was entitled to keep the refund as a setoff against the debt owed to it by the bankrupt subsidiary. The Ninth Circuit held that the parent could not offset the amount of the refund against the subsidiary's debt to it because the requisite mutuality of debts and credits did not exist.[8] This was because the parent held the refund solely in its capacity as agent of the consolidated group and, therefore, the parent was acting as a trustee with a duty to return the refund to the bankrupt subsidiary.[9]

### §806.2.2 Where a Subsidiary's NOL Is Applied Against Income of Other Corporations

A more difficult question is whether a loss subsidiary is entitled to a refund resulting from the carryback of its net operating loss against other group members' income. *Jump v. Manchester Life & Casualty Management Corp.*[10] indicates that, absent an express agreement to the contrary, the refund does *not* belong to the subsidiary. In that case, the conservator for a bankrupt subsidiary sued the common parent of the consolidated group for a refund paid to the parent that was obtained by offsetting the subsidiary's losses against the income of all the members of the consolidated group. Each member of the group had calculated its tax liability on an individual basis and paid the amount of such liability to the common parent. The Eighth Circuit held that the bankrupt subsidiary was entitled to receive only that portion of the refund that was attributable to taxes the subsidiary effectively had paid during the carryback period and that it was not entitled to recover any portion of the refund attributable to

---

[6] *Supra* note 5.

[7] 473 F.2d at 262.

[8] Id.

[9] *Accord In re Revco D.S., Inc., supra* note 5; *see also Capital Bancshares, Inc. v. FDIC, supra* note 5 (common parent was not entitled to tax refund even though it had borrowed money from third party lenders for the benefit of the bank subsidiary and had pledged the tax refund to the lenders, because the parent had no asset to pledge).

[10] *Supra* note 5.

taxes paid by other members of the consolidated group. In reaching this decision, the court reasoned that, absent an express agreement to the contrary, there is nothing in the regulations or case law that would entitle a loss member to recoup the tax benefit derived by another member of the group using the losses of the loss member.[11] The conservator had argued that the parent breached a fiduciary duty to the subsidiary by converting a "valuable asset" of the subsidiary, *i.e.*, its losses, to its own use without compensation. The Eighth Circuit found, however, that the loss was not a valuable asset of the bankrupt subsidiary because (1) the subsidiary was liquidated and, thus, could not use its losses in future years, and (2) the subsidiary was not in a position to bargain with the other group members to be currently compensated for the use of its losses since, by previously agreeing to file consolidated returns, the subsidiary could not refuse to file consolidated returns.[12]

### §806.2.3 Stacking Order for Applying Losses of Several Members

Another factual variation that may arise is where an insolvent or bankrupt subsidiary and another member of the consolidated group each have losses that contribute to a consolidated net operating loss carryback that results in a refund. In some cases the tax refunded may have been attributable entirely to income of the subsidiary; in others it may have been attributable to income of several group members. Under the consolidated return regulations, the consolidated net operating loss would offset the group's income for prior years on a pro rata basis, rather than first applying the insolvent or bankrupt member's loss to offset the income of the group or of that subsidiary.[13] This pro rata approach could result in only a portion of the subsidiary's losses being used and the unused portion of the losses being apportioned to the subsidiary when it departs from the group. In *In re Florida Parks Bank, Inc.*,[14] the FDIC, as successor in interest to a bankrupt thrift that was a member of a consolidated group, sued the common parent of the group for a tax refund attributable to a net operating loss carryback, which was comprised of losses of the bankrupt thrift and other members of the group. The FDIC argued that it was entitled to the entire refund because the losses of the bankrupt thrift, taken alone, would have been sufficient to generate the refund for taxes, all of which had been previously paid by the thrift. The Bankruptcy Court, without mentioning the normal pro rata approach of the consolidated return regulations, held that the FDIC was entitled to the entire refund.[15]

---

[11] 579 F.2d at 454.

[12] Id. at 453-454.

[13] Reg. §1.1502-21(b)(3).

[14] *Supra* note 5.

[15] This is similarly the approach employed under the subsequently released Code §6402(i) regulation applicable to insolvent financial institutions; *see* §806.2.5. Consider also *United States of America v. Bass Fin. Corp., supra* note 5 (bankrupt subsidiary recovered entire tax refund even though approximately 2 percent of refund was attributable to losses of other group members; the court stated that although *Jump* might suggest a different result, the other group members did not raise the issue).

The trustee for the common parent had argued that certain "policy statements" adopted by the boards of both the parent and the subsidiary should control the allocation of the refund. The court held, however, that such statements did not constitute a binding agreement because too many essential elements were missing, such as the effective date and which subsidiaries were covered; even if such statements were binding, they failed to address the allocation of the refund under the facts of the case.[16]

### § 806.2.4 Effect of Tax Allocation Agreement

As mentioned earlier, the parties in the cases discussed above did not have a tax allocation agreement that determined the ownership of the refunds involved.[17] Nevertheless, the courts in these cases frequently indicated that, had a valid tax-sharing agreement addressed the issue, its terms would have prevailed.

Such a tax-sharing agreement was involved in the 1993 *Franklin Savings Corp.* case,[18] and its terms governing this issue were upheld. In this case, the conservator for a bankrupt subsidiary sued the bankrupt common parent of the consolidated group for a refund obtained by offsetting the subsidiary's losses against the subsidiary's prior year income. The tax-sharing agreement among the parties provided that the subsidiary should calculate and pay to the parent its tax liability on an individual basis, and should obtain the benefit from the parent of any refund attributable to the subsidiary's losses. The parent's reimbursement obligation, however, was to be reduced to the extent the parent forgave any of the subsidiary's liability to the parent under the tax-sharing agreement.

The parent had in fact earlier forgiven approximately $100 million that would otherwise have been due from the subsidiary under the tax-sharing agreement. The refund involved in the case was for only $10 million. Thus, under the terms of the tax-sharing agreement, the parent was entitled to the refund.

The bankruptcy court held that a tax-sharing agreement can validly allocate the benefit of a tax refund, if the agreement is enforceable under state law. The conservator had argued that the agreement violated the fairness and overreaching standards of corporate law and the unconscionability test of constructive trust law. The court, however, found that the agreement was neither unfair nor unconscionable. The parent was therefore entitled to the tax refund.

---

[16] 110 B.R. at 988.

[17] For a discussion of such agreements, with a particular focus on their role in bankruptcy situations, see Ponikvar and Kestenbaum, Aspects of the Consolidated Group in Bankruptcy: Tax Sharing and Tax Sharing Agreements, 58 Tax Law. 803 (2005).

[18] *Franklin Savings Corp. v. Franklin Savings Ass'n (In re Franklin Savings Ass'n)*, 159 B.R. 9 (Bankr. D. Kan. 1993), *aff'd*, 182 B.R. 865 (D. Kan. 1995). Just as the court in this case considered the fairness of the tax allocation agreement in judging its validity, other courts, influenced by *Prudential Lines* (*see* § 508.2.4 above), are likely to do the same, perhaps couching the inquiry as one of determining whether the agreement was supported by adequate consideration. *See* Berenson, Net Operating Losses and the Bankrupt Member of a Consolidated Return Group, 39 Tax Mgmt. Memo. S-145 (1998); *In re White Metal Rolling & Stamping Corp.*, 217 B.R. 981, 1998 U.S. Dist. LEXIS 3890 (S.D.N.Y. 1998).

A more far reaching result along these lines was reached in the 2001 *First Central Financial Corporation*[19] case. Here, both an insurance company subsidiary and its holding company parent were in bankruptcy. Although the subsidiary had paid all of the taxes, the tax allocation agreement limited its obligations and rights to paying the amount of its separate return liability. The court held this limited the portion of a consolidated return refund that the parent had to pay to the subsidiary, even though this was less than the amount of tax the subsidiary had actually paid. As in the *Franklin Savings* case, the court also held that the portion of the refund that the parent was obligated to pay to the subsidiary should not be considered to have been held in constructive trust for the subsidiary, and thus the subsidiary has only the status of a regular unsecured creditor in its efforts to collect this amount from the parent's bankruptcy estate. Had a constructive trust been imposed, the subsidiary would receive the full amount of its contractual claim. In contrast, as an unsecured contract creditor, it would have to stand in line with other creditors, and thus would be less likely to receive full payment of its claim. The reasoning given by the courts in this case for their refusal to impose a constructive trust is important. They noted that the purpose of the constructive trust remedy is the prevention of unjust enrichment. In the absence of a tax allocation agreement, the retention of the refund by the parent on these facts might well result in unjust enrichment of the parent, in which case a constructive trust remedy might be available. But here a tax allocation agreement did exist, and there was no indication of any fraud or misconduct by the parent. Thus, enforcement of the tax allocation agreement would not leave the parent unjustly enriched. The courts noted that there is a special tension between the constructive trust law and bankruptcy law in this type of situation, which should require courts to proceed cautiously. By creating a separate allocation mechanism outside the scope of the bankruptcy system, the constructive trust doctrine could wreak havoc with the priority system ordained by the bankruptcy law. This latter point raises an interesting question. It seems anomalous that a corporation which had obtained a contract right should be worse off in bankruptcy than one which had done nothing in this regard. Perhaps in future cases the courts might consider trying to fashion their constructive trust remedy to be one which confers no higher priority in bankruptcy than a contract right would create.

### §806.2.5 Regulations Under Code §6402(j)

In 1988, the Congress addressed some of these issues by adopting Code §6402(i)—now Code §6402(j)—which authorizes the IRS to issue regulations providing for the payment of income tax refunds to the statutory or court-appointed fiduciary of an insolvent subsidiary in a consolidated group, to the extent the IRS determines that the refund is attributable to losses or credits of that subsidiary. Although the statutory language authorizes regulations that could apply to any consolidated return group, the IRS has so far limited its exercise of this authority to

---

[19] *Superintendent of Ins. v. First Central Financial Corp.* (*In re First Central Financial Corp.*), 269 B.R. 481, 2002-1 U.S.T.C. ¶50,186 (2001), which was affirmed by the District Court and by the Court of Appeals. 377 F.3d 209 (2d Cir. 2004).

refunds and other adjustments payable to certain fiduciaries, such as the FDIC or the Resolution Trust Corporation (RTC), of insolvent financial institutions.[20]

Under this regulation, if the insolvent financial institution incurs a loss during a taxable year in which it is a member of a consolidated group and if certain notice requirements are satisfied, then the fiduciary of the insolvent financial institution generally can act as agent for the consolidated group of which the financial institution is a member for the following purposes: (1) filing the consolidated tax return for the year in which the financial institution incurs a loss; (2) filing a claim for refund or application for tentative carryback adjustment arising from the loss incurred by the financial institution; and (3) additional matters for which permission is granted by the IRS.[21] If a claim for a refund or an application for a tentative carryback adjustment is filed by the fiduciary for the insolvent financial institution, the IRS can, in its sole discretion, but is not obligated to, pay to the fiduciary all or any portion of the refund or tentative carryback adjustment that the IRS finds is attributable to the losses or credits of the financial institution.[22]

While the regulation determines the party to whom a refund or tentative carryback adjustment will be paid, it is not determinative of which member of a consolidated group (including the financial institution) is entitled to the refund.[23] According to the preamble to the final regulation, this determination will be made in accordance with the principles discussed above in this § 806.2.[24]

Other notable aspects of the regulation are:

(1) the general rule that the waiver of loss carrybacks must be made on a consolidated basis does not apply; instead, the fiduciary may elect separately whether or not to waive the loss carryback period for the insolvent financial institution;[25]

---

[20] Reg. § 301.6402-7. The regulation is effective January 30, 1992, and applies to refunds and tentative carryback adjustments paid after December 30, 1991. The preamble to the previously issued temporary regulation indicates that the IRS was willing to benefit the FDIC and the RTC in this way because the IRS had entered into side agreements with these agencies providing for repayment to the IRS of any erroneous payments to these agencies. T.D. 8387, 1992-1 C.B. 306.

In the preamble to the temporary regulation, the IRS solicited comments regarding application of the regulation to other insolvent corporations. The IRS requested that any comments address how, under a broadened rule, the IRS could protect itself against being whipsawed without entering into an agreement with each insolvent corporation. In the preamble to the final regulation, the IRS noted that no comments regarding expansion of the scope of the regulation were received. T.D. 8446, 1992-2 C.B. 306.

In IRS Field Service Advice 1999-515 (undated), *reprinted at* 1999 TNT 15-125, the IRS held that Code § 6402(i)—now Code § 6402(j)—did not apply to the facts before it, since the refund arose from an amended return rather than from a carryback to an earlier year. The IRS advised the field to ask the bankruptcy court to allow the IRS to pay the refund into the court and to have the court decide who should receive it.

[21] Reg. § 301.6401-7(c).

[22] Reg. § 301.6402-7(g) and (h).

[23] Reg. § 301.6402-7(g).

[24] T.D. 8446, *supra* note 20.

[25] Reg. § 301.6402-7(e)(5).

(2) if the insolvent financial institution and another group member both have losses in the same taxable year, the insolvent financial institution's losses are considered used up first against prior year income of the group, rather than on the usual pro rata basis, which is an approach that favors refunds to the insolvent subsidiary (and, as indicated above, departs from the normal pro rata approach of the consolidated return regulations);[26]
(3) the regulation does not resolve the question of which corporation, the common parent or the insolvent financial institution, is entitled to a refund where the common parent and the fiduciary each file a refund claim on a different basis;[27] and
(4) the regulation adopts subgroup principles so that the fiduciary may, as an agent, generally claim refunds with respect to the losses and credits of the financial institution's subsidiaries as well as the losses and credits of the financial institution itself.[28]

---

[26] Reg. § 301.6402-7(g)(2)(iii); *see In re Florida Parks Bank, Inc., supra* note 5, and discussed at § 806.2.3 (which employed this approach as a substantive matter).

[27] Preamble to T.D. 8387, *supra* note 20.

[28] Reg. § 301.6402-7(h)(1).

# 9

# Liquidating Trusts, Escrows, and the Like



## §901 INTRODUCTION

Liquidating trusts and their close relatives, escrows and liquidating partnerships, are useful devices that can serve a number of different functions in bankruptcy restructurings. For example, the failing company may have assets that are no longer essential to its continuing business and that it would like to sell in order to raise funds to pay creditors as part of its bankruptcy workout, but that cannot easily be sold except at distressed prices by the time the bankruptcy plan is expected to be consummated. These assets can be distributed out of the failing company and placed in a liquidating trust for the benefit of its creditors. The trustee will be given power to sell the assets at a reasonable pace, and to preserve them in the meantime, with the proceeds to be distributed to the former creditors, who are now beneficiaries of the liquidating trust.

As another example, the failing company may have equipment that is useful in its business. The creditors, as part of the debt restructuring, may wish to acquire direct ownership of the equipment, in order to have more control over the assets than they might have if the assets remained in the company and the creditors continued only to have a claim against the company. The assets might even be leased to the company pending their sale. If the ultimate objective is to sell these assets as quickly as possible, a liquidating trust may be a useful device for this purpose. If they are not to be sold within a reasonably short period of time, then a limited partnership or limited liability company will prove more appropriate.

As still another example, by the time a plan of reorganization is reaching the point where it can be confirmed, there may still be a number of claims filed against the debtor corporation which are being contested. Rather than delay the bankruptcy reorganization until these disputes can be resolved, it may be desirable to distribute to an escrow holder a fund of money or other assets (including perhaps some of the new debt or stock being issued in the bankruptcy reorganization) to be used to satisfy these claims. The failing company can be discharged of its obligations and allowed to leave the bankruptcy proceeding as a restructured company free of these claims. The disputed claims can then be resolved without affecting the company, and, as they are resolved, the assets placed in escrow can be distributed to the successful claimants. Excess funds may be returned to the failing company, or may be distributed to the other creditors, depending on the terms of the plan of reorganization that established the escrow fund.

The creditors will usually want the liquidating trust, limited partnership, limited liability company, or escrow account to be treated as a pass-through entity for tax purposes rather than as an association taxable as a corporation. As we shall see, pass-through tax treatment is easier to achieve when the entity is not formed to resolve disputed claims and where it holds only passive investment assets. From a nontax perspective, a liquidating trust or an escrow agreement or a limited liability company will almost always have a greater practical appeal than a limited partnership because the administrators of the former entities do not have personal liability for the activities of the entity the way that a general partner of a limited partnership does.

As for liquidating trusts, a trust cannot achieve pass-through tax treatment under the special rules for liquidating trusts unless the trust is intended only to liquidate the assets as promptly as reasonably possible and the management powers of the trustee are severely restricted.[1] If broader management powers are needed, then, for trusts formed before 1997, the trust ran the risk that it would be taxable as a corporation, and so a limited partnership or limited liability company had to be considered. Limited partnerships established for this purpose do not present major tax difficulties. The difficulty with limited partnerships lies instead in finding an appropriate individual or entity willing to take on the personal liability of a general partner. Where the applicable state law permits, use of a limited liability company may offer a way to sidestep personal liability.[2] For trusts formed on or after January 1, 1997, the so-called check-the-box entity classification regulations[3] have changed the consequences for the trust that fails to meet the special requirements for trust status as a liquidating trust. Under these regulations, such a nonqualifying liquidating trust will be classified as a business entity, and thus taxed as a partnership unless it elects to be taxed as a corporation.[4] In effect, the trust can achieve pass-through treatment, rather

---

[1] **§901** *See* Reg. §301.7701-4(d).

[2] For example, Rev. Rul. 2004-41, 2004-18 I.R.B. 845, holds that the classification of an LLC as a partnership for tax purposes will not make the members personally liable for federal employment taxes, if the state law provides that members of an LLC are not liable for the debts of the LLC.

[3] Reg. §§301.7701-1, 2, and 3.

[4] Reg. §301.7701-3. *See* IRS Letter Ruling 200517020, December 20, 2004 (a trust created to liquidate the business of a partnership was still classified as a partnership).

The January 1, 1997 changes to Reg. §§301.7701-2 and 3 created the additional rule that a non-corporate business entity which has only a single member will be entirely disregarded for tax purposes, unless it elects to be treated as a corporation. Liquidating trusts, escrows or similar entities

than corporate treatment, as a business trust under these new regulations. This is a change from prior law, under which business trusts formed before 1997 are generally taxed as corporations. Nonetheless, where the trust fails to qualify as a liquidating trust and instead is classified as a partnership, the parties need to be careful to prevent the entity from being treated as a publicly traded partnership, since under Code §7704 a publicly-traded partnership is taxed as a corporation. The regulations under Code §7704 provide various mechanisms for restricting trading in ways that avoid that risk. Care also must be taken to determine whether the entity fits the requirements for a "qualified settlement fund" (the latter are discussed below at §904.2), since, whether or not a trust fits the requirements for being treated as a liquidating trust or a partnership, it will be taxed as a qualified settlement fund if it meets the requirements for a qualified settlement fund. Where none of a liquidating trust, business trust, escrow, partnership, or limited liability company satisfies the need of a particular case, the parties may find it desirable to use a corporation, even though it is not a pass-through entity for tax purposes.

Liquidating trusts are used where illiquid assets are involved that can only be converted into cash or cash equivalents over a period of time. Limited partnerships or limited liability companies—and, for those formed on or after January 1, 1997, business trusts—are useful where illiquid assets are involved that require more management than would be possible in a liquidating trust. Escrow or custodian accounts are useful where liquid assets can be placed into the account, and the account holder becomes a stake-holder for the assets pending resolution of disputes regarding their ownership. Where disputed claims are involved, escrow accounts can also be used to hold interests in liquidating trusts or limited partnerships.

A liquidating trust with properly narrow management powers to allow it to be classified as a trust will generally be treated as a grantor trust, although the IRS has

---

(Footnote Continued)

set up for creditors of failing companies will seldom, if ever, have only a single beneficiary. Therefore, we do not discuss these "disregarded entity" regulations in any detail in this book.

However, we would note here that for periods after January 1, 1997 and before the effective date of the 2007 regulations that are discussed in the next paragraph, if an LLC or other non-corporate business entity is a single-member entity that is to be treated under Reg. §§301.7701-2 and 3 as disregarded for tax purposes, the owner (and not the entity) is liable for the employment and similar federal taxes arising from the entity's activities as if the entity did not exist. *McNamee v. Dept. of the Treas.*, 2007 U.S.T.C. ¶50,515 (2d Cir. 2007); IRS Field Service Advice 200114006, December 18, 2000; IRS Field Service Advice 200105045, November 1, 2000; IRS Notice 99-6, 1999-1 C.B. 321. Thus, although in such a "disregarded" case the IRS may be able to collect the tax from the single owner, the IRS cannot collect the tax from the assets of the limited-liability LLC itself. *See* IRS Chief Counsel Advice 200235023, June 28, 2002, which discusses the liability treatment, under each of the various taxpayer elections available, for both multi-member and single-member LLCs.

These "disregarded entity" rules created problems in the administration of federal employment taxes and certain excise taxes for both taxpayers and the IRS. Consequently, in August 2007, the IRS issued regulations to eliminate the disregarded status of an entity for purposes of the obligations to report and pay employment taxes and certain excise taxes, to be effective commencing January 1, 2009, with respect to employment taxes, and January 1, 2008, with respect to excise taxes. Reg. §§1.34-1 through 6, 1.136-4 and -8, and 301.7701-2. The release issuing these final regulations provides that, for employment taxes for periods before January 1, 2009, the owner may continue to apply IRS Notice 99-6, as modified in that release, and that IRS Notice 99-6 will become obsolete as of January 1, 2009.

carved out a middle category of trust with slightly more management power (but not enough to cause it to be treated as an association taxable as a corporation) that will be treated as a Code § 641 (taxable) trust.

Before adoption of the Tax Reform Act of 1986, a properly structured escrow account was treated as a suspense account rather than as a separate taxable entity. The income in the escrow account was not taxable until the beneficial owners of the account became known, at which time all of the income accumulated in the account for their benefit was taxable to them.[5] The 1986 Act changed the treatment of escrow accounts in a noncodified provision, which was eventually codified by the 1988 Act by adding Code § 468B(g). This states that nothing shall be construed as providing that an escrow account, settlement fund or similar fund is not subject to current tax, and authorizes the Treasury to issue regulations taxing them as a "grantor trust or otherwise."

The 1986 Act also added Code § 468B, which provides that "designated settlement funds" will be treated as separate taxable entities and will be taxed at the highest rates applicable to estates and trusts. A "designated settlement fund" is a fund established by a taxpayer pursuant to a court order for the purpose of satisfying present or future tort claims against the taxpayer (or a related person) arising out of personal injury, death or property damages. The taxpayer must not have a reversionary interest in the "designated settlement fund," the fund must extinguish the taxpayer's tort liability for the claims, and a majority of its administrators must be independent of the taxpayer.

The IRS did not issue any regulations under Code § 468B(g), or its 1986 Act predecessor, until 1992, when it issued regulations for "qualified settlement funds," discussed at § 904. These expanded the designated settlement fund approach to a broader class of claims (*i.e.*, most tort, breach of contract, "violation of law," and some environmental claims but specifically not debt work-out claims). These regulations also relax some of the designated settlement fund requirements, such as the prohibition of reversions and the requirement for independent trustees, but they make qualified settlement fund status mandatory, not elective, for entities that meet the qualified settlement fund requirements.

In early 1999, the IRS issued an additional proposed regulation[6] under Code § 468B(g), which was made final in 2006. This regulation (Reg. § 1.468B-9) deals with the taxation of "disputed ownership funds." A disputed ownership fund is, in general, defined as an escrow account, trust or other fund, other than a qualified settlement fund, (1) established to hold money or property subject to conflicting claims of ownership, (2) that is subject to the continuing jurisdiction of a court, and (3) which provides that nothing can be distributed without court approval. These

---

[5] *See* Rev. Rul. 70-567, 1970-2 C.B. 133; Rev. Rul. 64-131, 1964-1 C.B. 485; IRS Letter Ruling 7821076, February 24, 1978. *See also* Rev. Rul. 71-119, 1971-1 C.B. 163. Rev. Rul. 71-119, Rev. Rul. 70-567, and Rev. Rul. 64-131 (to the extent of its third situation) were declared obsolete for funds or accounts established after August 16, 1986 by Rev. Rul. 92-51, 1992-2 C.B. 102.

[6] Prop. Reg. § 1.468B-9. At the same time, the IRS issued proposed regulations (which have since been finalized in part) dealing with escrows formed in connection with sales or exchanges of property. These are not uniquely relevant to troubled companies and will not be discussed in this book.

"disputed ownership funds" are taxed (1) as qualified settlement funds if they hold only passive assets, or (2) as C corporations otherwise, or (3) under a more appropriate alternative method of taxation if the claimants obtain a ruling letter approving such alternative method. While this regulation remained in proposed form, the IRS issued rulings in 2003 and 2004 allowing a "disputed ownership fund" entity to be taxed as a grantor trust, with the entity creating the fund being treated as the grantor. *See* § 904.3 below.

In 2006, Code § 468B(g) was amended by adding a new subparagraph[7] to provide a special exemption for settlement funds established to resolve environmental claims under CERCLA (the Comprehensive Environmental Response, Compensation and Liability Act of 1980). These settlement funds or escrows are usually established in consent decrees between the Environmental Protection Agency ("EPA") and the settling parties under the jurisdiction of a federal district court. To qualify, the settlement fund must (1) be established and controlled by a government entity pursuant to a consent decree issued by a federal district court; (2) be created to receive settlement funds for the sole purpose of resolving claims under CERCLA; and (3) on termination, any remaining funds must be disbursed to the government agency. For this purpose, a government agency means the United States or any state or any subdivision of the foregoing. The provision provides that any such qualifying fund shall be treated as beneficially owned by the United States and exempt from federal tax.

This Chapter 9 focuses primarily on the tax treatment of the liquidating trust or other entity to which the failing company might transfer some of its assets, rather than on the timing of any deduction the failing company might have as a result of such transfer. For the timing of such deductions, *see generally* Code § 461 and the regulations thereunder.

## § 902 LIQUIDATING TRUSTS

The typical use of a liquidating trust can be illustrated by the following example:

**EXAMPLE**

> A failing company has worked out a plan of bankruptcy reorganization that is satisfactory to its creditors and shareholders. Part of the plan requires that various tracts of real estate, an abandoned factory, and certain equipment be set aside for the benefit of the unsecured creditors. However, these assets are not in great demand, and it will not be possible to sell them for reasonable prices except over a period of time. Accordingly, these assets are distributed to a bank as trustee of a liquidating trust. The beneficial owners of the liquidating trust are the unsecured creditors. The failing company retains no interest in the trust or its

---

[7] Code § 468B(g)(2).

> property, and its transfer of the property to the trust discharges its liability to the creditors. The trustee's powers are limited to preserving the assets and selling them as rapidly as reasonably possible. All income from the assets and all proceeds from their sale are required to be distributed promptly to the beneficiaries. The trust is to terminate within three years although it can be extended for up to another five years if necessary in order to liquidate the assets. The certificates of beneficial interest are transferable by the beneficiaries.

The key tax question presented by such a trust is whether it will qualify for taxation as a trust rather than as a partnership or a corporation and, if so, whether it will be taxable as a grantor trust, of which the creditor-beneficiaries will be treated as the grantors.[1]

The tax law makes a sharp distinction between donative trust arrangements and business trusts that are created to operate a profitable business. Business trusts formed before 1997 are generally taxable as corporations.[2] Those formed after 1996 are treated as partnerships, unless they elect to be treated as corporations or are publicly-traded entities.[3] However, the regulations also recognize the existence of two types of trusts which, although they are motivated by commercial rather than donative intentions, can be taxed as trusts. These are fixed investment trusts and liquidating trusts.[4] The distinction between a business trust and a fixed investment trust lies in the fact that in a fixed investment trust the trustee has no power under the trust agreement to vary the investment of the certificate holders.[5] A power to "vary the investment" means "some kind of managerial power over the trusteed funds that enables [the trustee] to take advantage of variations in the market to improve the investment of all beneficiaries."[6] The mere existence of such a power is enough to cause a trust to be taxed as a corporation if it was formed before 1997, and

---

[1] **§902** *See also* Del Negro, Liquidating Trusts—Their Nature and Uses, 38 Inst. on Fed. Tax'n §23 (1980); Brod, Exercise Caution in Forming Section 337 Liquidating Trusts, 59 Taxes 44 (1980).

[2] Pre-1997 Reg. §301.7701-4(b). If the entity had more corporate than noncorporate characteristics, it would be taxed as a corporation. *Morrissey v. Commissioner*, 296 U.S. 344, 36-1 U.S.T.C. ¶9020 (1936). A business trust that did not have more corporate than noncorporate characteristics would, however, be classified as a partnership. Rev. Rul. 88-79, 1988-2 C.B. 361.

[3] Post-1996 Reg. §§301.7701-3, and 4(b) and Code §7704. *See, e.g.,* IRS Letter Ruling 200517020, December 20, 2004 (a trust created to liquidate the business of a partnership was still classified as a partnership).

[4] Reg. §301.7701-4(c) and (d). In the case of a liquidating trust established for the benefit of shareholders, the shareholders are treated as the grantors. *E.g.,* Rev. Rul. 75-379, 1975-2 C.B. 505. In the case of such a trust established for the benefit of creditors, the creditors are treated as the grantors. These results assume that the corporation retains no interest in the trust or its property, and does not remain liable (or at least primarily liable) for the debts the trust is established to satisfy. On the other hand, where the debtor retains a reversionary interest in the trust property, then the debtor may be the grantor of the trust. *See,* however, the discussion of the *Holywell* case at §902.1.

[5] *See* Reg. §301.7701-4(c).

[6] Rev. Rul. 75-192, 1975-1 C.B. 384; Rev. Rul. 89-124, 1989-2 C.B. 262 (right to transfer additional securities to an investment trust in exchange for an interest in the trust held, on the particular facts, not a power to vary the investment).

to be taxed as a partnership or a corporation if it was formed thereafter, even if the power is not exercised.[7] A power to sell the assets, even to sell them at the most opportune time, is not a power to "vary the investment," provided the funds cannot be reinvested but instead must be distributed to the beneficiaries.[8]

In 1986, the fixed investment trust regulations were amended to provide that:

> an investment trust with multiple classes of ownership interests will ordinarily be classified as an association or a partnership . . . ; however, an investment trust with multiple classes of ownership interests, in which there is no power under the trust agreement to vary the investment of the certificate holders, will be classified as a trust if the trust is formed to facilitate direct investment in the assets of the trust and the existence of multiple classes of ownership interests is incidental to that purpose.[9]

The examples that illustrate this principle[10] do little to delineate where multiple classes of ownership will be deemed to satisfy the "incidental" exception. One example states that where an originator of a mortgage interest trust retains an interest in the trust that is identical to that of the investors except that it is subordinated to their interests in the pool of mortgages, the two classes of interests "are substantially equivalent to undivided interests in the pool of mortgages, coupled with a limited recourse guarantee running from . . . [the originator] to the holders of the . . . [other]certificates." Thus, the multiple classes will be treated as incidental and the trust will be classified as a trust.[11] One needs to exercise caution in applying these examples. The IRS has provided little guidance in this area, and some that it has given has proved inconsistent. For example, in 1989 the IRS privately ruled that a subsequent transfer by a sponsor of such a subordinated interest would make the incidental exception inapplicable.[12] More recently, however, in Rev. Rul. 92-32,[13] the

---

[7] Id.

[8] *See* Rev. Rul. 78-149, 1978-1 C.B. 448; Rev. Rul. 75-379, 1975-2 C.B. 505; *see also* Rev. Rul. 86-92, 1986-2 C.B. 214 (limited power of sponsor to provide substitute bonds of the same character and quality for those specified in investment contracts that fail during the first 90 days of the investment trust was not a power to vary investment; rather, such power was merely incidental to the organization of the trust); Rev. Rul. 57-112, 1975-1 C.B. 494 (fixed investment trust which held fee interests in oil and gas properties permitted to lease such properties so long as it retained a passive interest, *e.g.*, a royalty interest, rather than an active interest, *e.g.*, a working interest); IRS Letter Ruling 8626030, March 26, 1986 (trust's holding of a royalty interest in certain working interests in oil and gas properties through a general partnership interest did not create a power in the trustee to vary the investment because the partnership agreement was sufficiently limited).

[9] Reg. § 301.7701-4(c)(1). The phrase "an association or a partnership" in the above quotation was changed in late 1996, as part of the check-the-box regulations, to read "a business entity under § 301.7701-2."

[10] *See* Reg. § 301.7701-4(c)(2).

[11] Reg. § 301.7701-4(c)(2), Example (2).

[12] IRS Letter Ruling 8929030, April 21, 1989.

[13] 1992-1 C.B. 434. *See also* IRS Letter Ruling 9620004, February 1, 1996, which involved a bond trust holding U.S. treasury bonds. The trust had three classes of interest—one class representing a right to specified interest payments on the underlying bond, a second class representing the right to principal payments on non-callable bonds, and a third class representing the right to principal payments on

IRS changed its mind and ruled that such subordinated interests could even be sold initially to the public at the same time as the other interests in the trust, without adversely affecting the status of the trust as a fixed investment trust. Oddly enough, when the IRS amended these regulations to incorporate the check-the-box concept, it did nothing to clarify this issue.

A fixed investment trust that meets the foregoing standards does not have to have as its objective the liquidation of assets. A liquidating trust, on the other hand, must have that objective. Proceeds will not be considered to have been reinvested by a fixed investment trust or a liquidating trust if they are placed for a short period of time in bank certificates of deposit or Treasury bills, pending their distribution to the beneficiaries.[14]

The regulations describe the requirements for a "liquidating trust" as follows:

> (d) *Liquidating trusts.* Certain organizations which are commonly known as liquidating trusts are treated as trusts for purposes of the Internal Revenue Code. An organization will be considered a liquidating trust if it is organized for the primary purpose of liquidating and distributing the assets transferred to it, and if its activities are all reasonably necessary to, and consistent with, the accomplishment of that purpose. A liquidating trust is treated as a trust for purposes of the Internal Revenue Code because it is formed with the objective of liquidating particular assets and not as an organization having as its purpose the carrying on of a profit-making business which normally would be conducted through business organizations classified as corporations or partnerships. However, if the liquidation is unreasonably prolonged or if the liquidation purpose becomes so obscured by business activities that the declared purpose of liquidation can be said to be lost or abandoned, the status of the organization will no longer be that of a liquidating trust. Bondholders' protective committees, voting trusts, and other agencies formed to protect the interests of security holders during insolvency, bankruptcy, or corporate reorganization proceedings are analogous to liquidating trusts but if subsequently utilized to further the control or profitable operation of a

(Footnote Continued)

callable bonds and any interest payments due on them after the first call date. The trust instrument had provided that a holder of all of the interest certificates and principal certificates for a bond could tender those certificates in exchange for that bond. An amendment was proposed to this trust to allow a holder to substitute STRIPS for interest certificates in making such a redemption exchange, with the STRIPS being held in the trust to support the remaining outstanding interest certificates that weren't turned in. The STRIPS would be for payments of interest from U.S. government bonds that are identical to the amounts called for by the interest certificates. The trust received a ruling that this modification would not cause the trust to fail to be treated as a fixed investment trust. The parties had not requested a ruling as to whether the trust constituted a fixed investment trust before the proposed amendment, and the IRS did not rule on that fundamental issue. Presumably, however, the IRS would not have issued the ruling if it thought that the existence of the three classes of beneficial interest made the trust ineligible for classification as a fixed investment trust.

[14] Rev. Rul. 75-192, 1975-1 C.B. 384.

going business on a permanent continuing basis, they will lose their classification as trusts for purposes of the Internal Revenue Code.[15]

The IRS has ruled, for example, that where uncompleted residential housing was distributed by a bankrupt entity to a liquidating trust for its creditors, the trustee could complete the residences before selling them because this was reasonably necessary for the orderly liquidation of the assets.[16] Similarly, the IRS ruled that a fixed investment trust which held fee interests in oil and gas properties could lease the properties without being treated as involved in managing the investment, but only if it retained passive interests, such as royalty interests, rather than active interests, such as working interests.[17] Where the property placed in a liquidating trust was nonincome-producing real estate, the liquidating trust could receive cash to carry the expenses of the property during its expected period of liquidation.[18]

Trusts that qualify as either fixed investment trusts or liquidating trusts are generally treated as grantor trusts under Code § § 671-677.[19] Not only are the original beneficiaries treated as grantors of the trust, but each purchaser or donee of a trust unit is also treated as a grantor.[20] In effect, the beneficiaries are treated as if the trust did not exist. Each beneficiary will have his own cost basis in the underlying assets of the property held by the trust and will report the activities of the trust with respect to his portion of the assets as if the trust were not there.[21] The trustee will be required to file a Form 1041 each year, showing as an attachment to the form the information regarding the receipts and expenditures of the trust.[22] The trustee will usually also send similar information to each of the beneficiaries.

The IRS has also issued regulations dealing with the reporting obligations of widely-held fixed investment trusts and widely-held mortgage trusts.[23] Since these

---

[15] Reg. § 301.7701-4(d).

[16] Rev. Rul. 63-228, 1963-2 C.B. 229.

[17] Rev. Rul. 57-112, 1957-1 C.B. 494.

[18] Rev. Rul. 80-150, 1980-1 C.B. 316.

[19] *See, e.g.*, Rev. Rul. 80-150, 1980-1 C.B. 316; Rev. Rul. 78-175, 1978-1 C.B. 144; Rev. Rul. 77-349, 1977-2 C.B. 20; Rev. Rul. 75-379, 1975-2 C.B. 505; Rev. Rul. 75-192, 1975-1 C.B. 384; Rev. Rul. 72-137, 1972-1 C.B. 101; Rev. Rul. 70-545, 1970-2 C.B. 7; Rev. Rul. 63-228, 1963-2 C.B. 229; IRS Letter Ruling 9603013, October 18, 1995; IRS Letter Ruling 9528017, April 14, 1995; IRS Letter Ruling 7904133, October 30, 1978; IRS Letter Ruling 7843025, July 25, 1978.

[20] *See* GCM 38791, August 28, 1981; Reg. § 1.671-2(e), discussed at the end of this § 902. *See,* however, the discussion of the *Holywell* case at § 902.1 below.

[21] Id.

[22] In addition, the trustee also may be required to "backup withhold" on distributions to the creditors or shareholders. *See* Code § 3406; IRS Letter Ruling 8606011, November 5, 1985. *See also* IRS Letter Ruling 9626056, April 11, 1996 (a foreign business entity which had not engaged in business in the United States obtained judgment against two U.S. individuals for damages they caused to the foreign business. The individuals filed for bankruptcy and their assets were placed in U.S. liquidating trusts. The trustees sought to withhold 30 percent from all of the distributions to the foreign entity. The latter obtained a ruling to the effect that the damage payments would constitute foreign source income, even though paid from a U.S. liquidating trust, and thus no withholding was required under Code § 881).

[23] *See* Reg. § 1.671-5.

are not generally employed as liquidating trusts in failing company situations, these regulations are not discussed in this book.

The transaction in which the liquidating trust is formed and its certificates of beneficial interest are distributed to the creditors or shareholders will be a taxable transaction to them. In such case, the basis of the initial beneficiaries in their trust certificates and in the underlying assets will be the fair market value of the assets at the time of the distribution of the certificates of beneficial interest to the initial owners.[24] Where the certificates of beneficial interest are publicly traded, the initial public trading price for the certificates will be deemed to be the basis of the initial holders in the underlying assets. Since each subsequent purchaser of a certificate of beneficial interest will have his own separate cost basis in his certificate and in his share of the underlying assets, the beneficiaries will have to adjust the figures supplied by the trustee for purposes of computing their federal income tax consequences from transactions by the trust. Consistent with this treatment, a certificate holder in a fixed investment trust or liquidating trust who exchanges his interest in the trust for his proportionate share of each of the trust's assets does not recognize gain or loss.[25]

The IRS has issued guidelines indicating when it will generally rule that a trust will be classified as a liquidating trust.[26] These general guidelines, which are not specifically designed for liquidating trusts formed in bankruptcy cases, provide that a trust will be classified as a liquidating trust if it meets the following conditions:

(1) The governing instrument provides that the trust is organized for the primary purpose of liquidating the assets with no objective to conduct a trade or business.

(2) The trust contains a fixed or determinable termination date that is generally not more than three years from its creation and that is reasonable on all the facts and circumstances. However, if the trust holds installment obligations received incident to a Code § 337 liquidation, it may extend beyond three years until the maturity of the obligation.

(3) The investment powers of the trustee are limited to powers to invest in demand and time deposits in banks or savings institutions, or temporary investments such as short-term certificates of deposit or Treasury bills.

(4) The trust does not receive transfers of any listed stocks or securities, any readily marketable assets or any operating assets of a going business.[27] The trust does not receive or retain cash in excess of a reasonable amount to meet claims and contingent liabilities.

---

[24] *See* GCM 38791 (August 28, 1981).

[25] *See* Rev. Rul. 90-7, 1990-1 C.B. 432.

[26] Rev. Proc. 82-58, 1982-2 C.B. 847, *amplified by* Rev. Proc. 91-15, 1991-2 C.B. 484. *See* Brod, Section 337 Liquidating Trusts Revisited—The IRS Revises Rev. Proc. 79-1, 59 Taxes 286 (1981).

[27] However, the IRS earlier allowed a general partnership interest in land and a 50-percent general partnership interest in an unspecified "venture" to be held by a liquidating trust. IRS Letter Ruling 7827055, April 10, 1978.

(5) The trust does not receive transfers of any unlisted stock of a single issuer that represents 80 percent or more of the stock of such issuer and does not receive transfers of any general or limited partnership interests.[28]

(6) The trust is required to distribute at least annually the proceeds from the sale of assets or income from investments. The trust may retain a reasonable amount of proceeds or income to meet claims and contingent liabilities.

Although the foregoing guidelines for advance rulings require that a liquidating trust generally not last for more than three years, the case law is more favorable. The courts will allow the trust to last as long as is necessary to make an orderly liquidation of the property, and favorable holdings have been obtained in cases where the trust lasted for many years.[29]

Some of these ruling guidelines, particularly the requirement that the term of the trust generally not exceed three years, have proved difficult to meet in bankruptcy cases. In 1994, the IRS issued a special revenue procedure which sets forth ruling guidelines for liquidating trusts created pursuant to bankruptcy plans in Chapter 11 cases, which contains somewhat more relaxed requirements.[30] This Revenue Procedure also contains a checklist to be completed by taxpayers when they request a ruling under its provisions. The Revenue Procedure provides that a ruling will generally be issued treating an entity formed in a Chapter 11 case as a liquidating trust if it meets the following conditions:

(1) It is created pursuant to a Chapter 11 plan for the primary purpose of liquidating the assets, with no objective to conduct a trade or business "except to the extent reasonably necessary to, and consistent with, the liquidating purpose of the trust."

(2) The plan and disclosure statement explain that the transfer to the liquidating trust for the benefit of creditors (or shareholders) must be treated for tax purposes as a transfer of the assets to the creditors (or shareholders), and as a deemed transfer by them to the trust. The ruling request must explain

---

[28] The IRS has favorably ruled, however, that a liquidating corporation can transfer 79 percent of the stock of a subsidiary to a liquidating trust and 21 percent to a limited partnership. (It may or may not have been significant that the partnership had operating characteristics.) IRS Letter Ruling 8529097, April 25, 1985. However, the IRS had earlier allowed a liquidating trust to hold 100 percent of the stock of the subsidiaries of a liquidating corporation. IRS Letter Ruling 7835020, May 30, 1978. *See also* IRS Letter Ruling 7827055, *supra* note 27, wherein the IRS earlier allowed a liquidating trust to hold a general partnership interest. The authors are also familiar with a recent case where the IRS authorized a liquidating trust to hold 100 percent of the stock of a corporation.

[29] *See, e.g.*, Broadway-Brompton Buildings Liquidation Trust, 34 B.T.A. 1089, Dec. 9490 (1936), *acq.* 1938-2 C.B. 4 (trust assets were apartment houses, storerooms and a public garage which trustees as directed by trust instrument made persistent efforts to sell, while leasing in the meantime; trust could last for 15 years if property not sold earlier); *Cebrian, Trustee v. United States*, 181 F. Supp. 412, 149 Ct. Cl. 357, 60-1 U.S.T.C. ¶9305 (1960) (liquidating trust formed by bondholders' committee lasted almost 30 years); *Tyrrell Williams, Trustee*, 3 T.C.M. 591, Dec. 13,999(M) (1944) (trust instrument provided trust could last as long as 20 years); *Wilson Syndicate Trust*, 1 T.C.M. 377, Dec. 12,930-F (1943) (trust was liquidating trust even though significant property had not been sold after 20 years).

[30] Rev. Proc. 94-45, 1994-2 C.B. 684.

whether the debtor will incur any tax liability on the transfer, and if so, how the liability will be paid.

(3) The plan, disclosure statement, and trust instrument must provide that the beneficiaries of the trust will be treated as the grantors of the trust and deemed owners of the trust assets. The trust instrument (or plan if there is no separate trust instrument) must require the trustee to file returns for the trust as a grantor trust pursuant to Reg. § 1.671-4(a).

(4) The plan, disclosure statement, and trust instrument must provide for consistent valuations of the transferred property by the trustees and creditors (or equity-interest holders), and those valuations must be used for all federal income tax purposes.

(5) Whether or not there is a reserve established for disputed claims (and, as discussed at § 904.3 below, Reg. § 1.468B-9 specifically provides that such a reserve for disputed claims created by a liquidating trust can be treated as a "disputed ownership fund"), all of the trust's income must be treated as subject to tax on a current basis, and the ruling request must explain how the trust's taxable income will be allocated and who will be responsible for payment of any tax due.

(6) The trust instrument must contain a fixed or determinable termination date that is generally not more than five years from the date of creation of the trust and that is reasonable based on all the facts and circumstances.[31] The trust term may be extended for a finite term, if provision for this is made in the plan and trust instrument, and the extension is made subject to the approval of the bankruptcy court upon a finding that the extension is necessary. The court approval must be obtained within six months of the beginning of the extended term.

(7) If the trust is to hold any operating assets of a going business, or a partnership interest in a partnership that holds operating assets, or 50 percent or more of the stock of a corporation with operating assets, the ruling request must explain why this is necessary.

(8) If the trust is to receive transfers of listed stocks or securities or other readily marketable assets, the ruling request must explain why this is necessary. The trust is not permitted to receive or retain cash or cash equivalents in excess of a reasonable amount to meet claims and contingent liabilities (including disputed claims) or to maintain the value of the assets during liquidation.

(9) The investment powers of the trustee, other than those reasonably necessary to maintain the value of the assets and to further the liquidating purpose of the trust, must be limited to powers to invest in demand and time deposits, such as short-term certificates of deposit, in banks or other savings institutions, or other temporary, liquid investments, such as Treasury bills.

---

[31] IRS Letter Ruling 200407002, November 3, 2003, approved a liquidating trust that could last for 10 years.

(10) The trust must be required to distribute at least annually to the beneficiaries its net income plus all net proceeds from the sale of assets, except that the trust may retain an amount of net proceeds or net income reasonably necessary to maintain the value of its assets or to meet claims and contingent liabilities (including disputed claims).

(11) The ruling request must contain representations that the trustee will make continuing efforts to dispose of the trust assets, make timely distributions, and not unduly prolong the duration of the trust.[32]

Although it is clear that a liquidating trust may defend against claims, the Revenue Procedure does not specifically state that a liquidating trust may pursue affirmative causes of action that might increase the assets in the trust. The IRS, however, has issued several rulings holding that this is permissible.[33]

As mentioned above, the fixed investment trust portion of the regulations contains a general prohibition against multiple classes of beneficial interests, with an exception (whose parameters are vague) for multiple classes that are "incidental." Take the case of a liquidating trust established by a bankrupt company for the benefit of two different classes—one senior to the other—of its creditors. The senior creditors receive Class A interests in the trust and the junior creditors receive Class B interests. The Class B interests are subordinate to the Class A interests. Will the liquidating trust be classified as a trust? The answer is apparently yes. The liquidating trust portion of the regulations[34] does not contain the prohibition against multiple classes of ownership that is found in the fixed investment trust portion.[35] This could be construed to mean that the prohibition against all but "incidental" multiple classes of interest does not apply to liquidating trusts. A liquidating trust of this kind would not seem to violate any particular tax policy. We are aware of a case where the IRS has ruled favorably on a liquidating trust having multiple classes of interest. This ruling was issued before Rev. Proc. 94-45, and the latter does not contain any language which would limit the use of multiple classes of interest. Indeed, the breadth of the fifth paragraph in the ruling guidelines contained therein (*i.e.*, the generality of the reference to the requirement that the ruling request explain "how the trust's taxable income will be allocated and who will be responsible for payment of any tax due") suggests that multiple classes are acceptable. However, whenever a liquidating trust with multiple classes of interest is contemplated, it would be desirable to consult the IRS staff and perhaps request a ruling. The ability to use multiple classes of beneficial interest is very important in bankruptcy cases. In most such cases, there will be different classes of creditors with different priorities, and

---

[32] Examples of rulings issued under this provision include IRS Letter Ruling 200034022, May 26, 2000; IRS Letter Ruling 9801035, October 1, 1997; IRS Letter Ruling 9836024, June 8, 1998; IRS Letter Ruling 9752039, September 25, 1997.

[33] IRS Letter Ruling 9752039, September 25, 1997; IRS Letter Ruling 9836024, June 8, 1998; IRS Letter Ruling 9801035, October 1, 1997; IRS Letter Ruling 200119019, February 6, 2001; IRS Letter Ruling 200213020, December 21, 2001 (this ruling does not involve a Chapter 11 case).

[34] Reg. § 301.7701-4(d).

[35] Reg. § 301.7701-4(c).

perhaps also equity interests with still other priorities, that must be satisfied. Often, instead of requiring that assets be distributed to each class in accordance with strict priority, so that the highest class must be paid in full before the next class can receive anything, the bankruptcy plan will provide that some or all of the classes will share in each recovery in specified percentages. To be useful in a Chapter 11 case, a liquidating trust must be able to reflect such arrangements.

A potential new problem was created for liquidating trusts by the issuance in mid-1997 of proposed regulations under Code § 671, but rectified in new temporary and proposed regulations issued in 1999[36] and made final in 2000. The problem arose if the original owner of an interest in a liquidating trust makes a transfer of that interest by gift or bequest. The proposed regulations created a question whether the portion of the trust represented by that interest might cease to be a grantor trust and might instead become a taxable trust under the rules for non-grantor trusts.

The cause of the problem arises as follows. In 1996, because of concern about application of the grantor trust rules to foreign grantors, Code § 672(f) was amended to provide that the grantor trust rules could in general be applied only to the extent they resulted in amounts being taxed to U.S. citizens or residents or domestic corporations. An exception from this new rule was made for any portion of a trust from which the only amounts distributable during the lifetime of the grantor are to the grantor or the grantor's spouse.[37]

In mid-1997, the IRS issued proposed regulations to implement Code § 672(f).[38] The preamble to the proposed regulations stated that they "are not intended to change the result of existing law with respect to trusts used for business purposes." Consistent with this approach, the proposed regulations provide that the exemption for trusts (or portions thereof) that during the "lifetime" of the grantor limit their amounts distributable to the "grantor or the spouse of the grantor" applies to grantors that are corporations.[39]

This leaves the question as to who is the "grantor" of the trust. The IRS decided to include in the proposed regulations a definition.[40] This would apply broadly to all of the grantor trust provisions, and would not be limited to Code § 672(f). The definition begins by stating that the "grantor" includes any person who either creates a trust or directly or indirectly makes a gratuitous transfer of property to a trust. This creates no problem, because presumably the original beneficiary of a fixed investment or liquidating trust would be deemed to satisfy this definition. The potential problem created by the wording of the proposed regulations arose only where the

---

[36] Prop. Reg. § 1.671-2(e)(1), (2).

[37] Code § 672(f)(2)(A)(ii).

[38] Prop. Reg. §§ 1.643(h)-1; 1.671-2(e); 1.672(f)-1; 1.672(f)-2; and 1.672(f)-(3). These provisions, other than § 1.671-2(e), were made final in 1999.

[39] Reg. § 1.672(f)-3(b)(4), Examples 4 and 5. The Examples involve a foreign corporation. This same concept applies to domestic corporate grantors, as is made clear by the statement in Reg. § 1.671-2(e)(1) that "a grantor includes any person . . ." Domestic corporations need not be specifically mentioned in Reg. § 1.672(f)-3(b), because, for them, the exemption is unnecessary since the normal grantor trust rules are made inapplicable by Code § 672(f) only where the grantor is a foreign person or entity.

[40] Prop. Reg. § 1.671-2(e).

original beneficiary makes a transfer of the trust interest to another person. Where the transfer is for fair value, the proposed regulations eliminated any problem by specifically stating that the term "grantor" includes such a nongratuitous transferee from a "grantor."[41] This is even illustrated by an Example, in which A makes an investment in a fixed investment trust, and B subsequently acquires A's entire interest in the trust for fair market value, the Example stating that B will be treated as a "grantor" of the trust.[42]

But what happens if the transfer by the original grantor is by gift or bequest, *i.e.*, a gratuitous transfer? The proposed regulations addressed this problem by containing a specific provision that treated such a gratuitous transferee as also being a "grantor" if the "transfer is of an interest in a fixed investment trust."[43] No similar provision was included for interests in liquidating trusts, thereby raising the question whether the IRS intended to treat the two differently. If it did, a problem would exist for all liquidating trusts, whether they have foreign beneficiaries or not. Where a gratuitous transfer occurs, that portion of the trust would cease to be a grantor trust and would be taxable under the non-grantor trust rules. This would represent a change in law. There would seem to be no tax policy reason for treating liquidating trusts differently from fixed investment trusts for this purpose. In an earlier edition of this book, we expressed the hope that the failure to mention liquidating trusts in the exemption for gratuitous transfers was an oversight that would be corrected when final regulations were issued, but we advised those who draft liquidating trusts to take care to include adequate administrative provisions to deal with this potential problem in the meantime. Happily, because of comments including ours, the IRS eliminated this problem when it amended the proposed regulation and issued it as a temporary and proposed regulation in 1999, which was made final in 2000, by stating that a grantor includes any person who acquires an interest in a trust from a grantor of the trust if the trust is either a fixed investment trust or a liquidating trust.[44]

## *§902.1 The* Holywell *Case*

In early 1992, the Supreme Court decided *Holywell Corp. v. Smith*.[45] This curious case must be kept in mind when dealing with liquidating trusts. Here, several affiliated corporations and an individual, who as debtors had filed bankruptcy cases,

---

[41] Prop. Reg. § 1.671-2(e)(2)(i).

[42] Prop. Reg. § 1.671-2(e)(5), Example 2.

[43] Prop. Reg. § 1.671-2(e)(2)(ii).

[44] Reg. § 1.671-2(e)(3). The example was also changed by eliminating the statement that the interest was transferred for fair value, thereby indicating that even a gratuitous transfer would achieve the same result. Reg. § 1.671-2(e)(6), Example 2.

[45] 112 S. Ct. 1021, 92-1 U.S.T.C. ¶50,110, *rev'g* 911 F.2d 1539, 90-2 U.S.T.C. ¶50,509. The *Holywell* case was distinguished and held inapplicable in two situations where the property was returned to the debtor, subject to its obligation to make payments to creditors, because the facts were found not to involve the creation of a trust. IRS Field Service Advice 1999-736, May 1, 1992, *reprinted at* 1999 TNT 122-122 (corporate taxpayer); *In re Andrew G. Shank*, 240 B.R. 216 (Bankr. D. Md. 1999) (individual debtor).

transferred all or substantially all of their assets to a single trustee. The trustee was to liquidate the assets, apply the proceeds for the benefit of their creditors, and return any excess to the debtors. The bankruptcy plan made no provision for the payment of taxes on gains from the asset sales or on other income of the trust; the IRS had participated in the bankruptcy proceedings and had not objected to this aspect of the plan.

The trustee took the position that he was not responsible for paying the tax on these liquidating sales or on any other income of the trust. His position, and that of the creditor-beneficiaries, was that the debtors' reversionary interests made the trust a grantor trust of which the debtors were the grantors, so that the debtors were the ones who were responsible for any such tax. From the government's point of view, this created an interesting problem: the debtors did not have enough assets left to pay the tax. The IRS took the position that the trust was taxable on the income and that the trustee should pay the tax. The lower courts sided with the trustee, showing little sympathy for the government's problem since the government could have protected itself in the bankruptcy proceedings. The Supreme Court, however, sided with the government.

As to the corporate debtors, the Supreme Court observed that Code § 6012(b)(3) provides that a trustee in a title 11 case, a receiver, or an assignee who has "possession of or title to all or substantially all of the property or business of a corporation . . . shall make the return of income for such corporation in the same manner and form as corporations are required to make such returns." The Court held that the trustee was such an assignee. In so holding, the Court rejected the argument that Code § 6012(b)(3) was intended to apply only when the assignee was in effect acting as an agent winding up the business for a dissolving corporation or was conducting the day-to-day business of a distressed corporation, and ignored the fact that the corporation itself was under separate management. The Court next observed that Code § 6151(a) provides that when a return of tax is required, the person required to make the return shall pay the tax. Thus, the Court concluded, the trustee was required to file the return for the corporations and pay the tax that the corporations would have had to pay had the plan not assigned their property to the trustee. In the course of this analysis, the Court paid no attention to the reversionary interest retained by the corporate debtors. Presumably the Court considered that its holding regarding the applicability of Code § 6012(b)(3) rendered that issue moot as to the corporate debtors. The Court did not address the other issues that lurk in the background of the case and are affected by the Court's holding, such as when the debtor corporations are treated as paying the creditors and when the creditors are treated as having been paid.

This corporate portion of the *Holywell* case should not often apply to liquidating trusts that are used in the restructurings of distressed corporations where the purpose of the restructuring is to revive the corporation and allow it to continue in business. In such situations, liquidating trusts typically receive much less than "substantially all" of the corporate debtor's assets, in which event Code § 6012(b)(3) does not apply.

The Court next turned to the effect of the transfer by the individual debtor's bankruptcy estate of its assets to the trustee. The Court observed that Code § 6012(b)(3), which governed the corporate portion of the case, does not apply to transfers by individuals; it applies only to transfers by corporations. The Court then noted that Code § 6012(b)(4) requires a fiduciary of a trust to file a return for the trust.

And the Court concluded that because Code § 6151(a) provides that any person required to make a return must also pay the tax, the trustee was required to pay the tax. This syllogism, as phrased by the Court, must startle anyone familiar with the fact that the Code requires returns to be filed for many flow-through entities that are not taxable entities, such as S corporations, partnerships, and grantor and many other trusts. The Court's analysis, in fact, begs the question: Code § 6151(a) only applies "when a return of *tax* is required," and in flow-through cases the very point is that the return does not show a tax due by the flow-through entity.

The Court did not, of course, intend, despite this unfortunate analysis, to read the substantive pass-through provisions out of the law. The Court did go on to address the reversionary-interest grantor-trust issue. In answer to the trustee's (and creditors') argument that the reversionary interest in the debtor made the debtor the grantor of the trust who thus should be taxed on its income under the grantor trust rules, the Court took the position that the debtor was not the grantor because the assets had not been returned by his bankruptcy estate to him and then placed by him in the trust but instead had been transferred directly by his bankruptcy estate to the trust. Thus, held the Court, the debtor had not himself contributed anything to the trust and could not be treated as the grantor. The opinion does not address the question whether the right of reversion might have been viewed as having been distributed by the bankruptcy estate to the debtor, thereby transferring grantor status from the estate to the debtor. The quite narrow way in which the Court addressed the reversionary interest question suggests that a different result might be achieved simply by varying the terms of the relevant documents: had the bankruptcy plan in the *Holywell* case provided that the assets should be treated as having been returned to the debtor and then placed by him in the trust, arguably the individual debtor would have been treated under the Court's analysis as the grantor.[46]

The Court never addressed the question of whether the creditors should have been treated as the grantors of the trust and therefore taxed on its income. As mentioned above, the traditional view has been that the creditor (or shareholder) beneficiaries of a liquidating trust are its grantors and should be taxed on its income under the grantor trust rules, at least in the typical case where the transfer itself satisfies the debtor's obligations and the debtor has no further interest in the trust. One reason for the absence of this analysis in the opinion can perhaps be found in the retention by the debtors in the case of a reversionary interest. Another reason may be that the trustee and the creditors were trying to escape tax liability entirely by shifting it to the debtors. In any event, there has been no indication that the IRS will try to use the *Holywell* holding to overturn the traditional treatment of more typical liquidating trusts. Indeed, the reverse is true. The issuance of Revenue Procedure 94-45, which is discussed above, confirms this. Indeed, it is interesting to note that in the second

---

[46] The case of *In re Sonner*, 53 B.R. 859, 85-2 U.S.T.C. ¶9810 (Bankr. E.D. Va. 1985), had so held. The Supreme Court noted that this case was distinguishable from the facts in *Holywell* and expressed no opinion on its holding. In addition, the Committee Report for Code § 468B(g), quoted in § 904 below, would support the same conclusion. *Sonner* was followed on this point, and *Holywell* distinguished, in *Duval Country Ranch Co. v. Seattle-First Nat'l Bank*, SD Tex., C.A. No. C-91-208, May 1, 1993; *Smith v. Bank of New York*, 161 B.R. 302 (S.D. Tex. 1993).

ruling guideline contained in that Revenue Procedure, which says that a transfer to a liquidating trust for creditors must be treated for all purposes of the Code as a transfer to the creditors, the IRS added a footnote which simply said that "the tax consequences associated with the creation of a bankruptcy liquidating trust were not addressed in *Holywell* . . ." When the Supreme Court's opinion in *Holywell* was issued, we had advised in these pages that it would be desirable for the particularly cautious advisor to have the bankruptcy plan state that the creditors should be deemed to have received the assets and then placed them in the liquidating trust. In this regard, it is interesting to note that the second and third ruling guidelines contained in Revenue Procedure 94-45 require this to be done, if one wants to get a ruling.

Finally, as was true of the corporate-debtor portion of the case, the Court never addressed the other consequences to the parties that might be affected by its holding, such as the question of when the debtor is to be treated as having made a payment to the creditors and when they are to be treated as having received it. For the more typical liquidating trust, Revenue Procedure 94-45, as mentioned above, does address this question.

As might be imagined, the *Holywell* case had a sequel. The trustee had filed suit against the plan proponent, which was a bank that was the primary creditor of the debtors, to recover the taxes imposed on the trust plus the resulting expenses of the trustee. The plan had made no provision for the payment of taxes, and the disclosure statement contained no discussion of tax issues. Even though the judge in the case had earlier invited the parties to consider tax issues, the bank's officers subsequently testified that the bank had never considered the tax consequences of the plan.

On formation of the trust the bank had agreed to indent the trustee for any claims made against him as a result of any provision of the plan. The court held that this language compelled the bank to reimburse the trustee for the taxes imposed on the trust. The court also held that under state law the bank's failure to disclose the tax issues in the disclosure statement and to provide for taxes in the plan constituted negligent misrepresentation as to the consequences and feasibility of the plan; that the bank intended the trustee to rely on the disclosure statement; and that this not only provided a second basis for the bank being liable to reimburse the trustee for the taxes, but in addition made it liable for any other damages the trustee had suffered.[47]

An interesting contrast to the liquidating structure employed in the *Holywell* case can be found in a recent private letter ruling.[48] Here, a consolidated group of companies had filed a Chapter 11 bankruptcy proceeding. Later deciding that its liabilities substantially exceeded its assets, the debtors proposed a "liquidating" Chapter 11 plan, pursuant to which the assets of the debtors would be liquidated and

---

[47] *Smith v. Bank of New York, supra* note 46. In a subsequent proceeding, the court held that the trustee was not personally liable to the debtors. *Holywell Corp. v. Smith*, 85 AFTR 2d ¶2,000-473 (11th Cir. Jan. 26, 2000); and *In re Holywell Corp.*, 177 B.R. 991 (S.D. Fla. 1995), *aff'd without op.*, 95 F.3d 57 (11th Cir. 1996). *See also In re Holywell Corp.*, 1997 U.S. Dist. LEXIS 10606 (S.D. Fla. 1997); *Holywell Corp. v. United States*, 82 AFTR 2d ¶98-5324 (W.D. Va. 1998); *Gould v. United States*, 2000 U.S. App. LEXIS 22311 (4th Cir. 2000).

[48] IRS Letter Ruling 200445020, November 12, 2003, *supplemented by* IRS Letter Ruling 200509001, March 11, 2004.

the debtors would cease to survive. Rather than distributing their assets to a liquidating or similar fund of some kind, the debtors planned to retain them during the liquidation process, and distribute them or their proceeds to the creditors ultimately found to be entitled to them. If anything were to remain after paying all of the debtors' creditors (considered unlikely), such excess would be paid to the shareholders of the parent. The group had considerable NOLs, which it hoped to use against any gains arising during the liquidation process. The plan provided that the parent's shares of stock would be converted into newly issued shares having identical terms to the shares given up, but with the new shares being deposited into a trust that severely limited their transferability. The IRS ruled that neither the confirmation nor the consummation of the bankruptcy plan would result in an ownership change under Code § 382, thereby preserving the NOLs for use against the liquidation of the assets. The ruling did not address the COD implications of the plan.

## § 903 CODE § 641 TRUST

In at least three instances, the IRS has treated a liquidating trust as a Code § 641 (taxable) trust, rather than as a grantor trust, where the powers of the trustee were greater than the normal powers of a liquidating trustee. In the first of these rulings,[1] a court appointed a bank as custodian of shares of a land trust during litigation over ownership of the shares. The bank was to receive the earnings on the shares, and was given discretion to manage the underlying property, to vote at stockholders' meetings, to approve or disapprove reorganization or refinancing transactions, to invest the earnings in government securities, and to retain counsel. The IRS ruled that where the fiduciary is given such broad discretionary powers of administration and management, a trust is established that is taxable under Code § 641. As a result, the bank was required to file a Form 1041 each year and, as trustee, to pay tax on the income of the trust.

In the second ruling,[2] debtor corporations in a Chapter 11 bankruptcy proceeding deposited money into a fund held by a disbursing agent for creditors. The debtors were then discharged and released from bankruptcy proceedings. The disbursing agent was given power (1) to make distributions pursuant to bankruptcy court orders, (2) to invest the assets in a money market account backed by government securities at a specified bank pursuant to an order of the bankruptcy court, (3) to increase the fund by avoiding transfers of the debtors' property that were voidable under the Bankruptcy Code, (4) to increase the fund by pursuing causes of action of the debtors for money claims and for liability of officers and directors, (5) to contest disputed claims made against the debtors, and (6) to retain investigators, attorneys

---

[1] **§ 903** Rev. Rul. 69-300, 1969-1 C.B. 167.

[2] IRS Letter Ruling 8524052, March 19, 1985; GCM 39368 (February 21, 1985). *See also* IRS Letter Ruling 8916030, January 19, 1989. In IRS Field Service Advice 1999-736, May 1, 1992, *reprinted at* 1999 TNT 122-122, the IRS distinguished GCM 39368. Here, the successor corporation in a bankruptcy held distributions of assets "in trust" for holders of disputed claims. The IRS held that this was simply a disputed claims reserve account which did not create a trust or other separate entity.

and accountants. The IRS stated that although powers (3) and (4) above were part of the purpose of liquidating the assets in the fund, the fact that they permitted the fund to be increased and were designed to make the fund productive required a ruling that the fund was a trust taxable under Code § 641, and not an escrow account or a grantor trust.

Neither of these authorities contain any real discussion of the reason why the entities involved were classified as trusts rather than as corporations for tax purposes.

The third ruling[3] also holds that Code § 641 applies, but it takes a quite different approach. In this ruling, a Chapter 11 plan of reorganization was created for three corporations. Pursuant to the plan, a fund was established for the benefit of the unsecured creditors. Certain assets were transferred to the fund, and the fiduciary of the fund was also authorized to prosecute any cause of action arising under Chapters 3 and 5 of the Bankruptcy Code. The fiduciary of the fund had power to invest and reinvest its assets in cash equivalents. The bankruptcy court retained jurisdiction over the fund. Upon the transfer to the fund, the bankrupt companies were relieved of further liability to the unsecured creditors and were thus able to continue their business free of such claims.

The two prior rulings (Rev. Rul. 69-300 and IRS Letter Ruling 8524052) specifically held that the funds there involved were to be taxed as trusts under Code § 641, and the latter ruling also specifically stated that the creditors were to be treated as beneficiaries. Although these rulings did not go into detail about how subchapter J should apply to the trusts, the clear implication is that the regular subchapter J rules—including those for deductions for current distributions to beneficiaries—would apply to them.

The third letter ruling, which was issued in 1988, also holds that Code § 641 is to be applied. But there the similarity to the earlier rulings ends. The 1988 ruling holds that the regular rules of subchapter J are not to apply to the fund. Rather, the fund is to be taxed in the same way as the bankruptcy estates of individuals and partnerships were taxed before the adoption of the Bankruptcy Tax Act of 1980.

The 1988 ruling cites as authority the two revenue rulings that articulated the way in which individual and partnership bankruptcy estates were taxed before 1980, namely Rev. Rul. 68-48[4] and Rev. Rul. 78-134,[5] which held that the assets and liabilities of an individual or partnership in bankruptcy should be treated as an estate (not as a trust) under Code § 641, taxable at the tax rates applicable to individuals. Tax returns were to be filed on Form 1041 for the estate. The estate was to be entitled to a single $600 exemption under Code § 642(b). However, the estate was a special type of estate: The rulings held (on the theory that the creditors were not really "beneficiaries" of the estate) that none of the other provisions of subchapter J (such as the deductions for distributions, the concept of distributable net income, and the

---

[3] IRS Letter Ruling 8848019, August 31, 1988.

[4] Rev. Rul. 68-48, 1968-1 C.B. 301.

[5] Rev. Rul. 78-134, 1978-1 C.B. 197.

pass-through of tax liability to the beneficiaries in certain instances) were to apply to such an estate.

The 1988 ruling does not specify whether the fund involved is to be treated as an estate or as a trust. (An estate gets a $600 exemption under Code § 642(b), whereas a trust gets only a $300 or $100 exemption, depending on its terms.) However, because of its reliance on Rev. Ruls. 68-48 and 78-134, the 1988 ruling implies that the fund should be treated as an estate. What the ruling does specify is that, because the fund involved functions in a way similar to the estates described in Rev. Ruls. 68-48 and 78-134, the fund should be taxed under Code § 641 and allowed an exemption under Code § 642(b), but the remainder of subchapter J is not to apply to the fund. The fiduciary must file a return on Form 1041 and pay any tax due.

This holding means that income of the fund will potentially be subject to a double tax: one tax at the fund level (which would not enjoy the benefit of any NOLs of the bankrupt corporation), plus a potential second tax at the creditor level when the after-tax fund income is distributed to the creditors.[6] This contrasts with the result that could apply if the fund were classified as a Code § 641 trust (to which pass-through tax concepts could apply, thus resulting in only one tax on the trust income), or if the fund were classified as a liquidating trust (which would result in only one level of tax on the trust income).

Can the 1988 ruling be reconciled with the two earlier rulings? Rev. Rul. 69-300 did not involve a bankruptcy case and can be distinguished on that ground. But IRS Letter Ruling 8524052 seems indistinguishable and inconsistent. The theory of the 1988 ruling seems to be that if a fund is established in a bankruptcy case, the fund must, for that reason alone, take on the special characteristics described in Rev. Ruls. 68-48 and 78-134. This logic does not seem compelling. The latter rulings dealt with a special problem peculiar to the bankruptcies of individuals and partnerships: bankruptcy required these taxpayers to divide, amoeba-like, into two entities, one being the bankruptcy estate and the other being their nonbankruptcy existence. Both should be taxed as much the same as possible, and the special bankruptcy "estate" status specially created for them under Code § 641 by these rulings sought to do that. Just as the individual or partnership had no beneficiaries, neither did the "estate." But this problem does not exist for corporate bankruptcies. The corporation does not divide upon a filing in bankruptcy. Bankruptcy does not create a new taxable entity for a corporation. That being so, when assets leave that corporate solution and are placed in a noncorporate fund for the creditors, the consequences of leaving the corporate solution and the classification of the fund should be treated as if the bankruptcy did not exist.

The fund involved in the 1988 ruling apparently was not authorized to engage in any business activity. If it had been, there could be a question whether the entity would have become taxable as a partnership or corporation rather than as an estate

---

[6] The IRS argued, in its preamble to the final regulations issued under Code § 468B, that double taxation does not result in such circumstances. However, the IRS assertion is valid only where the debtor is fully taxable (and does not have NOLs that would have sheltered the trust income had the trust not been formed or had the trust been treated as a debtor-grantor trust) and where the creditor also is fully taxable (and is not a tax-exempt entity, or a taxable entity with available NOLs).

or trust under Code § 641. It should be noted that estates of bankrupt individuals and partnerships under pre-1980 law were allowed to engage in business without losing their "estate" status.[7] Whether the IRS would extend that concept to a fund of the type involved here has yet to be seen.

With the advent of the check-the-box entity-classification regulations effective beginning in 1997, the need, in order to achieve pass-through tax status, to treat an entity as a § 641 trust if it does not qualify as a liquidating trust, has been greatly diminished. Under these regulations, such an entity formed after 1996 can be taxed as a partnership unless it elects to be taxed as a corporation (or unless it has publicly-traded interests).

Moreover, now that the IRS has ruled that a liquidating trust may pursue positive causes of action that may increase the assets in the trust fund,[8] and now that the Revenue Procedure (*see* § 902 above) containing a checklist for bankruptcy plan liquidating trust rulings allows the trust to conduct a trade or business "to the extent reasonably necessary to, and consistent with, the liquidating purpose of the trust" (*see* § 902 above), there is much less likelihood that one will need to resort to a § 641 trust or any entity other than a liquidating trust in most circumstances.

## § 904 ESCROW AND SETTLEMENT FUND ACCOUNTS FOR DISPUTED CLAIMS

### *§ 904.1 Escrow Accounts*

The use of an escrow account can be illustrated by the following example:

**EXAMPLE**

The bankruptcy plan for the failing company provides that the unsecured creditors will receive certificates of beneficial interest in a liquidating trust plus cash and stock of the debtor. The validity of a number of claims filed by the unsecured creditors is being contested, and the contests may take several years to resolve. Rather than holding up the completion of the bankruptcy proceeding, the plan of reorganization provides that a specified proportion of the units of beneficial interest, cash and stock will be set aside in an escrow account held by a bank as escrow agent pending resolution of the disputed claims. In the meantime, the debtor is discharged from bankruptcy. The escrow agent is given power to invest the earnings on the escrow fund in certificates of deposit or Treasury bills. Distributions of the units of beneficial interest, cash and stock and the

[7] *See* S. Rep. No. 1035, 96th Cong., 2d Sess. 28-29 (1980).

[8] IRS Letter Ruling 9752039, September 25, 1997; IRS Letter Ruling 9836024, June 8, 1998; IRS Letter Ruling 9801035, October 1, 1997; IRS Letter Ruling 200119019, February 6, 2001; IRS Letter Ruling 200213020, December 21, 2001 (this ruling does not involve a Chapter 11 case).

earnings thereon will be made to successful claimants as their claims are upheld. Any balance remaining in the escrow account after resolution of all of the claims will be returned to the debtor.

Prior to the Tax Reform Act of 1986, a fund like that in the example was treated as an escrow account and not as a trust or a corporation.[1] The income earned by the escrow account was not taxable currently either to the potential beneficiaries or to the escrow agent; however, in the taxable year when it was determined that a particular person was entitled to a share of the account, the interest or other earnings that had previously been received with respect to that share were all taxable to that person.[2]

The Tax Reform Act of 1986 changed this established pattern of law. It added new Code § 468B, which applies to certain settlement funds created pursuant to court orders in cases involving claims for personal injury, death, or property damage. The types of funds covered by that section are called "designated settlement funds." The section provides that: (1) "economic performance," within the meaning of Code § 461(h), will be deemed to occur when payments are made into such a designated settlement fund; and (2) the designated settlement fund will be taxed on its income as a separate entity at the maximum rates applicable to trusts and estates. A "designated settlement fund" is a fund established by a taxpayer pursuant to a court order for the purpose of satisfying present or future tort claims against the taxpayer (or a related person) arising out of personal injury, death or property damage. The taxpayer must not have a reversionary interest in the designated settlement fund, the fund must extinguish the taxpayer's liability for the claims, and the majority of its administrators must be independent of the taxpayer. "Designated settlement funds" are discussed at § 904.2 below.

The 1986 Act then added two provisions that were not included in the Code. The first was a special transition rule for a fund that had been set up for such tort claims by a company in bankruptcy.[3] The second was the following far-reaching provision:[4]

---

1 **§ 904** *See, e.g.,* Rev. Rul. 71-119, *supra* § 901 note 4 (to settle Securities Act litigation, cash was deposited in court with a special master who was to receive proofs of claim and determine who was entitled to receive the fund and its earnings); Rev. Rul. 70-567, *supra* § 901 note 4 (proceeds of wrongful death action placed in bank escrow account until court could determine proper distribution of proceeds and interest earned on them); IRS Letter Ruling 8443113, July 27, 1984 (funds set aside under control of trustee pending resolution of disputed claims in a Section 77 Bankruptcy Act proceeding); IRS Letter Ruling 8012024, December 26, 1979 (funds placed in escrow pending resolution of disputed claims filed in Chapter 11 proceeding). For a discussion of escrow accounts generally, *see* Jacobs, Escrows and Their Consequences, 39 Inst. on Fed. Tax'n § 5 (1980). As noted at § 901 note 4 *supra,* Rev. Rul. 71-119 and Rev. Rul. 70-567 were declared obsolete by Rev. Rul. 92-51 for funds or accounts established after August 16, 1986.

2 *See* Rev. Rul. 70-567, 1970-2 C.B. 133; Rev. Rul. 64-131, 1964-1 C.B. 485; IRS Letter Ruling 7821076, February 24, 1978; IRS Agent Orange Letter Ruling, issued as IRS News Release IR 90-79 (May 11, 1990). As noted at § 901 note 4 *supra,* Rev. Rul. 70-567 and Rev. Rul. 64-131 (as to its third situation) were declared obsolete by Rev. Rul. 92-51 for funds or accounts established after August 16, 1986.

3 Tax Reform Act of 1986, Pub. L. No. 99-514, § 1807(a)(7)(C); for a ruling dealing with this special fund, *see* IRS Letter Ruling 9822057, March 5, 1998.

4 Tax Reform Act of 1986, § 1807(a)(7)(D).

> (D) CLARIFICATION OF LAW WITH RESPECT TO CERTAIN FUNDS.—
>
> (i) IN GENERAL.—Nothing in any provision of law shall be construed as providing that an escrow account, settlement fund, or similar fund is not subject to current income tax. If contributions to such an account or fund are not deductible, then the account or fund shall be taxed as a grantor trust.
>
> (ii) EFFECTIVE DATE.—The provisions of clause (i) shall apply to accounts or funds established after August 16, 1986.

Although this latter provision was labeled a "clarification" of law, the legislative history[5] stated that it reverses the holding in Rev. Rul. 71-119.[6] It also says that this provision applies "except as provided in regulations." There were, of course, two significant problems with this provision: (1) it was not in the Code, so it was hard for anyone to find; and (2) it did not tell how to determine the "grantor," who will be taxed on the income of such a fund.

The 1988 Act eliminated these problems by codifying this provision, with added broad regulatory authority, as Code § 468B(g), which reads as follows:

> (g) CLARIFICATION OF TAXATION OF CERTAIN FUNDS.—Nothing in any provision of law shall be construed as providing that an escrow account, settlement fund, or similar fund is not subject to current income tax. The Secretary shall prescribe regulations providing for the taxation of any such account or fund whether as a grantor trust or otherwise.

This 1988 amendment was treated as a technical correction retroactive to August 16, 1986. The Committee Report says the regulations are "to identify the person that is subject to current tax on the income from such an account or fund." It adds that:

> It is anticipated that these regulations will provide that if an amount is transferred to an account or fund pursuant to an arrangement that constitutes a trust, then the income earned by the amounts transferred will be currently taxed under Subchapter J of the Code. Thus, for example, if the transferor retains a reversionary interest in any portion of the trust that exceeds 5 percent of the value of that portion, or the income of the trust may be paid to the transferor, or may be used to discharge a legal obligation of the transferor, then the income is currently taxable to the transferor under the grantor trust rules.[7]

---

[5] Joint Committee on Taxation, Explanation of Technical Corrections to the Tax Reform Act of 1984 and Other Recent Legislation 42 (May 13, 1987).

[6] *Supra* note 1.

[7] S. Rep. No. 445, 100th Cong., 2d Sess. 468 (1988); H. Rep. No. 795, 100th Cong., 2d Sess. 377-378 (1988).

By the end of 1991, regulations had not yet been issued under this provision. However, the IRS had issued one ruling under this provision holding that an escrow account established in settlement of litigation for breach of contract was to be treated as a Code §641 trust.[8] Establishment of the fund extinguished the liability of the transferor, and the transferor had no reversionary interest in the fund. The fund was not treated as a grantor trust. On the other hand, in 1991 the IRS issued a ruling (also dealing with a litigation settlement fund that did not elect to be treated as a "designated settlement fund" under Code §468B) holding that the fund should not be treated as a trust. Instead, the IRS applied pre-1986 Act rules to the interest earned by the fund in the years 1985-1990, that is, it held that the fund would not be taxed on the interest income, and that the accumulated interest would be taxed to the beneficiaries of the fund in the year that a determination is made that they are entitled to it.[9] These rulings were followed by several rulings holding that Rev. Rul. 71-119 will be applied to escrow accounts formed before August 16, 1986, the effective date of Code §468B(g).[10]

In 1992, the IRS issued regulations under Code §468B(g) expanding the "designated settlement fund" concept to certain other specified types of claims by creating an entity called a "qualified settlement fund," which is discussed at §904.2 below.

As for other types of escrow accounts, however, the IRS was quite slow in issuing regulations under Code §468B(g). No governing regulations were issued until 2006 (although, as discussed below, proposed regulations were issued in 1999). For escrow accounts established prior to the issuance of final regulations, we had advised, and continue to so advise for any type of escrow for which regulations are not yet finalized, that because taxpayers will not be able to take the position that there is no current taxation of such funds, care should be taken to provide in the documents establishing such funds a reasonable means for taxing their income. Even in the absence of regulations under Code §468B(g), courts will pay attention to the mandate that someone be subjected to current taxation on the income from such funds. This is illustrated by the case of *Rameau A. Johnson*.[11] Here, automobile dealers deposited a portion of their proceeds from the sale of vehicles into a fund to secure payment of service contracts they had issued on the vehicles. The Tax Court held that the funds should be treated as grantor trusts under traditional grantor trust concepts, with the dealers considered the grantors. The court cited Code §468B(g) for the proposition that someone had to be currently taxable on the income from such funds. Because no regulations had yet been issued under that provision, the court found it comforting that it could decide that these particular funds constituted grantor trusts—and very likely the existence of Code §468B(g) helped it reach that conclusion.

---

[8] IRS Letter Ruling 8916030, January 19, 1989.

[9] IRS Letter Ruling 9129018, April 19, 1991.

[10] *See* IRS Letter Ruling 9252021, September 28, 1992; IRS Letter Ruling 9252024, September 28, 1992; IRS Letter Ruling 9741019, July 10, 1997.

[11] 108 T.C. No. 22 (1997).

Finally, in 1999 the IRS issued proposed regulations (none of which became final until 2006) designed to deal with the following types of Code § 468B(g) funds: (1) escrow and trust accounts used in Code § 1031 like-kind exchanges; (2) pre-closing escrows used in sales or exchanges of property; (3) contingent-at-closing escrows to deal with contingencies existing at the closing of certain sales of property; and (4) disputed ownership funds established under the jurisdiction of a court to hold property subject to disputed claims of ownership. The first three of these types of funds are not uniquely relevant to troubled corporations, and will not be discussed in this book. The fourth category, however, is especially relevant to troubled corporations. The regulation dealing with this "disputed ownership fund" category is Reg. § 1.468B-9. It was made final in 2006, and is discussed at § 904.3 below. Although, as the proposed regulation had stated, this regulation generally applies only to entities formed after its effective date of February 3, 2006, the proposed and final regulation both state that for entities formed before that date the IRS will not challenge a "reasonable, consistently applied method of taxation for income earned by the fund, transfers to the fund, and distributions made by the fund."

## *§ 904.2 Designated and Qualified Settlement Funds*

**Designated settlement funds.** As mentioned at § 901, Code § 468B contains special provisions for "designated settlement funds." These are funds established to settle claims against the settlor arising out of personal injury, death or property damage.[12] A primary reason for establishing such funds is to allow an accrual-method defendant to satisfy the "economic performance" requirements of Code § 461(h) by a payment to a fund that extinguishes his liability to a class of plaintiffs, even if all the ultimate members of the class, and the allocation of the recovery among them, have not yet been determined. This is provided by Code § 468B(a), which says that "economic performance" shall be deemed to occur as "qualified payments" are made by an accrual basis taxpayer to a "designated settlement fund."

Code § 468B(b)-(d) provides, in broad outline, that such a fund is a separate taxable entity taxable at the highest rates applicable to estates and trusts. The fund must be established by a court order, must extinguish completely the transferor's tort liability with respect to the claims, must not receive contributions other than "qualified contributions," and must be administered by persons, a majority of whom are independent of the transferor. "Qualified contributions" do not include stock or indebtedness of the contributor or a related person,[13] and the contributor may not have a reversionary interest in the fund. Contributions to the fund are not income to the fund. The fund takes a fair market value basis in such contributions.

---

[12] However, Code § 468B(e) provides that "designated settlement fund" treatment is not available for Workers' Compensation Act claims or contested liabilities within the meaning of Code § 461(f). For a general discussion of "designated settlement funds" and "qualified settlement funds," *see* Germain, Avoiding Phantom Income in Bankruptcy: A Proposal for Reform, 5 Florida Tax Rev. 249 (2001).

[13] This limitation does not apply to a "qualified settlement fund." *See* Reg. § 1.468B; IRS Letter Ruling 9552009, September 25, 1995; IRS Letter Ruling 200006029, November 10, 1999.

The drafters of this provision intended that a designated settlement fund should not be able to engage in a trade or business, and so the deductions available to a designated settlement fund in computing its taxable income are limited essentially to administrative expenses. Distributions by the fund to its beneficiaries are not deductible by the fund, but in the event the fund distributes property to its beneficiaries, the distribution is treated as a taxable sale of the property by the fund. Finally, the transferor must elect to have the fund treated as a designated settlement fund.

In late 1992, when the IRS issued regulations providing for "qualified settlement funds" (discussed immediately below), the IRS also adopted Reg. §1.468B, which provides that designated settlement funds shall generally be subject to the regulations regarding qualified settlement funds, and that a fund that does not qualify as a designated settlement fund but does meet the requirements of a qualified settlement fund will be treated as a qualified settlement fund.

The rather unique status of "designated settlement funds" and "qualified settlement funds" under the Internal Revenue Code can result in some interesting state tax questions. Such funds are not pass-through tax entities, yet they are not treated as corporations or trusts under the Internal Revenue Code. Few state income tax statutes contain special provisions for such funds, and so a question can exist as to how, if at all, they should be taxed under such state laws. The New York State Tax Department addressed this question in a 1994 advisory opinion.[14] On the particular facts there involved, the Department held that the qualified settlement fund should not be classified as a corporation under New York State law because its activities did not amount to the conduct of a business. Nor should it be taxed as a trust under New York State law, since New York mirrors the federal definitions of a trust, and the federal regulations specifically state that a qualified settlement fund is not treated as a trust for federal income tax purposes. Thus, the Department held that the qualified settlement fund involved there would not be subject to New York State income tax. Pennsylvania has also ruled that qualified settlement funds are not subject to the Pennsylvania Corporate Net Income or Capital Stock Franchise Taxes.[15]

As mentioned above at §901, a 2006 amendment to Code §468B(g) creates a special exemption for CERCLA settlement funds and provides that such funds shall be treated as beneficially owned by the United States. Presumably this language should exempt such funds not just from federal but also from state and local tax.

**Qualified settlement funds.** In regulations issued in late 1992 (Reg. §§1.468B-0 through 1.468B-5), the IRS liberalized and expanded the designated settlement fund concept by creating an entity called a "qualified settlement fund." In summary, a fund is a qualified fund if—

---

[14] TSB-A-94(2)I (February 1, 1994). To the same effect, TSB-A-95(14)C, TSB-A-95(5)I (August 3, 1995). In TSB-A-97(12)C and TSB-A-97(4) (May 19, 1997), the New York State Tax Department extended this result to funds established at the behest of the U.S. government which the IRS had agreed in a closing agreement to treat as though they were "qualified settlement funds," although they technically did not qualify as such.

[15] Pennsylvania Department of Revenue, No. CRP-06-002, August 29, 2006. Pennsylvania has also ruled that a designated settlement fund subject to Code §468B is not subject to the Pennsylvania Personal Income Tax. Pennsylvania Department of Revenue, No. PIT-07-006, July 3, 2007.

(1) It is established pursuant to an order of, or merely with the approval of, a government authority and is subject to the continuing jurisdiction of that authority.

(2) It is established to resolve or satisfy one or more contested or uncontested claims stemming from an event that has given rise to at least one claim asserting liability—

(a) Under the federal Comprehensive Environmental Response, Compensation and Liability Act of 1980; or

(b) Arising out of a tort, breach of contract, or violation of law;[16] or

(c) Designated by the IRS in a Revenue Ruling or Revenue Procedure.[17]

(One should note the ability to use a qualified fund for contested claims: a designated settlement fund cannot be used for such claims.)

(3) The fund or account is a trust *or* its assets are segregated from other assets of the transferor (and related persons). This allows something as simple as a separate bank account to be a qualified fund.

Special rules are applied to govern situations when a fund is established before all three of these requirements are met, but thereafter all three are met.[18] The regulations specifically exclude from the liabilities for which a qualified settlement fund may be set up: (1) liabilities under Workers' Compensation Acts or self-insured health plans; (2) liabilities to refund the purchase price of, repair or replace, products sold in the ordinary course of trade; (3) liabilities designated by the IRS in a ruling or revenue procedure; and (4) most important from the perspective of this book—obligations of the transferor "to make payments to its general trade creditors or debtholders that relate to a title 11 or similar case (as defined in section 368(a)(3)(A)), or a workout." The preamble of the regulations makes clear that this last exclusion

---

[16] In IRS Letter Ruling 9503022, Oct. 26, 1994, the IRS held that a fund created by court order to hold tax payments during litigation over constitutionality of the tax was a qualified settlement fund.

[17] As noted above, a "designated settlement fund" must provide for the full satisfaction, and not just the partial satisfaction, of the claims for which it is set up. As for "qualified settlement funds," a conflict of authority has arisen as to whether the same requirement applies. The IRS position is that it does not. *See* IRS Field Service Advice 200113025, December 13, 2000, *reprinted at* 2001 TNT 63-33 (the fact that claimants against the fund might have other avenues for collecting on their claims did not prevent the fund from being a qualified settlement fund). On the other hand, after a full discussion of the issue, a lower court ruled against the IRS on this point. *United States v. Brown*, 2001-2 U.S.T.C. ¶50,5019 (D. Utah 2001). The latter opinion held also that the particular fund involved would not qualify as a qualified settlement fund for another reason, namely that it was set up simply to return the value of assets to clients of a brokerage firm where there was no dispute as to the right to the assets. This lower court decision was reversed in *United States v. Brown*, 348 F.2d 1200 (10th Cir. 2003).

[18] An illustration can be found in IRS Letter Ruling 200623003, November 30, 2005. Here transfers were made to the fund before all three of the requirements had been met. After stating the general rule that transfers to qualified settlement funds are deductible in the year of their transfer to the fund, the IRS stated that with respect to transfers to the fund that were made before all three requirements had been met, the transfers are deemed to be made on the first date when the fund satisfied all three requirements. *See* Reg. §1.468B-1(j)(1). An exception to this timing is where the transferor and the fund administrator jointly make a "relation back" election to treat earlier transfers as occurring on the later of (i) January 1 of the calendar year in which all three requirements were met or (ii) the date as of which only the requisite governmental approval of the fund was lacking. Reg. §1.468B-1(j)(2).

does not apply to other liabilities that are settled in a title 11 case, such as tort liabilities.

The regulations provide that the fund does not fail to qualify as a qualified fund if it is established to satisfy not only qualifying liabilities but also other types of claims, provided that these other claims arise from the same event or related series of events.[19] As for such other types of related claims, economic performance does not occur upon transfer to the fund; it usually will not occur until the claims are paid by the fund. Although the types of claims that a qualified fund may hold are thus restricted, the IRS has observed that otherwise "the regulations contain no restrictions or prohibitions with respect to either the types of transactions to which a qualified settlement fund may be party or the types of assets which a qualified settlement fund may hold." This observation was made in a ruling that dealt with a qualified fund which had a claims settlement facility that it wanted to make available for use by other entities. The fund proposed to sell undivided interests in this facility to other entities, following which the fund and these other entities would contribute the facility to a subchapter T cooperative corporation. The latter would bill each entity only for the work it did for that entity, and would return patronage dividends only to the entity that produced the patronage funds. The IRS held that neither the sale of the interests in the facility nor the ownership of the interests in the coop would hurt the status of the fund as a qualified settlement fund.[20]

Qualified settlement fund treatment for funds that meet its requirements is mandatory, not elective;[21] and a fund that fails to satisfy all of the conditions for a designated settlement fund, including the election condition, but which satisfies the requirements for a qualified settlement fund, will be treated as a qualified settlement fund.

**Taxation of qualified settlement funds.** When the 1992 regulations were issued, the IRS had considered but rejected an elective approach to the taxation of qualified settlement funds because this could result in inconsistent tax treatment for similar funds and situations. However, in an amendment to the regulations proposed in 1999 and made final in 2006 (and discussed at the end of this section), the IRS amended the qualified settlement fund regulations to allow a very limited election to treat a qualified settlement fund as a grantor trust established by the transferor to the fund.

We shall first describe the basic qualified settlement fund set of tax provisions that apply where this 2006 exception would not be available or is not elected. Under

---

[19] Reg. § 1.468B-1(c)(2); IRS Letter Ruling 200442024, October 15, 2004; IRS Letter Ruling 200704004, October 31, 2006 (counsel fees); IRS Letter Ruling 200709035, November 9, 2006 (counsel fees); IRS Letter Ruling 200717013, January 26, 2007 (counsel fees). If the other claims do not arise from the same event or related series of events, the fund will not be treated as a qualified settlement fund. IRS Ruling 9549026, September 8, 1995.

[20] IRS Letter Ruling 9803019, October 17, 1997; *see also* IRS Letter Ruling 9805019, October 30, 1997; IRS Letter Ruling 200444004, November 3, 2004.

[21] This point was affirmed in *O'Cheskey v. United States*, 2002-1 U.S.T.C. ¶ 50,197 (N.D. Tex. 2001) (fact that parties did not intend to create a qualified settlement fund is irrelevant; the provision is not elective). *See also United States v. Brown*, 348 F.2d 1200 (10th Cir. 2003), where it seems clear the parties did not intend to create a qualified settlement fund, and the court emphasized that treatment of an entity as a qualified settlement fund is not elective.

these basic rules, a qualified settlement fund must use a calendar taxable year and the accrual method of accounting. It is taxable at the highest tax rate applicable to trusts and estates on its taxable income.[22] Its deductions are limited essentially to administrative expenses and do not include trade or business type expenses. This latter restriction is liberalized to the extent of providing that should the fund hold a partnership interest, its pass-through deductions from the partnership are available, though this is true only to the extent of income from that same partnership for the same tax year, and it is available only for partnership interests acquired before February 15, 1992 and even then only for years ending before January 1, 2003. The fund takes a fair market value basis in property contributed to it, and such contributions are not taxable as income to it. The fund gets no deduction for distributions to its beneficiaries,[23] and any distributions of property by it to its beneficiaries are treated as a sale of such property by the fund. The fund does not get the special lower rate of tax on capital gains that is available to other taxpayers, nor is the fund subject to the alternative minimum tax. For purposes of the procedural and reporting provisions of subtitle F of the Code, the fund is treated as a corporation. However, since it is only the procedural provisions for corporations that apply to the fund, the preamble to the regulations makes clear that Code § 382 does not apply to the fund.

The regulations also provide that a transferor to the fund must treat the transfer as a sale or exchange for the fair market value of the property contributed. However, a transfer of the transferor's own debt obligation is not treated as a sale of property by the transferor. The transferor may transfer its own debt or stock to the fund, but if this is not publicly traded, the transferor must provide appraisals to support any deductions it claims for the value of such items.[24] Economic performance does not occur for an accrual method transferor to the extent the transferor or a related person has a right of reversion (1) that is certain to occur; or (2) that is exercisable currently and without the agreement of an independent unrelated person (like a court) or a person having an adverse interest (like the claimants).[25] In such case, economic performance occurs when the right of reversion lapses. Similarly, economic perform-

---

[22] To the same effect, *see* IRS Letter Ruling 200533003, May 16, 2005. As discussed at § 901 above, in 2006 a new subsection (2) was added to Code § 468B(g) to create an exemption from tax for certain CERCLA settlement funds, whose beneficiaries would be governmental units.

[23] However, an interesting variation on this general rule was applied in IRS Letter Ruling 200149013, August 27, 2001, where all of the stock of the debtor company was contributed to the qualified settlement fund. The company continued to operate its business, and on termination of the trust anything left in the trust would go to charity. Reg. § 1.468B-2(b)(2) provides that the fund may not deduct payments for legal fees incurred by, or on behalf of, claimants. This concept was applied in, *e.g.*, IRS Letter Ruling 9609041, December 4, 1995; IRS Letter Ruling 200717013, January 26, 2007.

[24] IRS Letter Ruling 9733019, May 22, 1997, dealt with a qualified settlement fund that received notes and all of the stock of the transferor. The transferor was allowed a deduction for the value of the stock, but was not allowed a deduction for the principal amount of the notes until the principal was paid to the fund. *See also* IRS Letter Ruling 200006029, November 10, 1999. To the same effect, *see* IRS Letter Ruling 200442011, October 23, 2003 (Ruling #8; entitled to deduction "in the tax year Taxpayer makes [the] principal payments" on the notes transferred to the trust).

[25] For an example of a reversion that did not prevent economic performance, *see* IRS Letter Ruling 9720006, January 31, 1997; IRS Letter Ruling 200623003, November 30, 2005.

ance does not occur on the contribution of the transferor's debt (or the debt of a related party), but only as principal payments are made.

If the transferor recovers a distribution from the fund, the distribution is taxable to the transferor at fair market value, except to the extent provided by the tax benefit rule of Code § 111(a) if the transferor did not receive a tax benefit for its contribution to the fund.[26]

The formation and funding of a qualified settlement fund has no direct tax effect on the beneficiaries, and distributions are generally taxed to the beneficiaries just as if the distributions were made directly by the transferor.[27]

The regulations impose various information reporting requirements on transferors and on the funds themselves. In this regard, it is interesting to note that the IRS has issued private letter rulings holding that a designated settlement fund did not have to file any information returns reporting payments to beneficiaries, where the fund administrator could not determine how much, if any, of the payments would constitute taxable income to the beneficiaries, and where no portion of the payments constituted interest within the narrow meaning of Code § 6049(a).[28]

The regulations are effective on January 1, 1993. However, for funds established after August 16, 1986 and before February 15, 1992 (when proposed regulations were published) that would satisfy the requirements of a qualified fund, the IRS will not challenge a reasonable and consistently applied method of taxing the fund and

---

[26] *See* IRS Letter Ruling 200623003, November 30, 2005.

[27] Reg. § 1.468B-4. For a discussion of the consequences where the beneficiaries of an ESOP are claimants, and the qualified settlement fund makes payments to the ESOP which in turn distributes these to its beneficiaries, *see* IRS Letter Ruling 200604039, October 31, 2005.

[28] IRS Letter Ruling 9405010, November 3, 1993. For a similar holding that information reporting need not occur where the payments to claimants were presumably return of basis rather than income, *see* IRS Letter Ruling 9645011, August 5, 1996. For a similar holding dealing with distributions from the qualified settlement fund to pay refunds of property tax or to pay attorneys' fees to class counsel, *see* IRS Letter Ruling 200106021, November 7, 2000. To similar effect on lack of need, on the facts of the case, to withhold or do information reporting on distributions to class-action beneficiaries, or to treat the fund's payment of attorney's fees to class counsel as being income to its beneficiaries, *see* IRS Letter Ruling 200609014, December 1, 2005 and IRS Letter Ruling 200610003, December 1, 2005, both of which rulings are discussed in Wood, Rulings Make Qualified Settlement Funds More Attractive, 111 Tax Notes 673 (May 8, 2006). Also to similar effect are a number of rulings in 2006 regarding the treatment of class action settlements in mutual fund litigation, *e.g.*, IRS Letter Ruling 200712004, December 12, 2006. For a different result with respect to withholding and information reporting where the amounts distributable were apparently includable in the claimants' gross income, but not on the counsel fee point, *see* IRS Letter Ruling 200602017, September 28, 2005, and IRS Letter Ruling 200602016, September 28, 2005. *See also* IRS Letter Ruling 200442011, October 23, 2003 (qualified settlement fund not required to file information returns under Code § 6041 for payments made for personal physical injuries or physical sickness pursuant to Code § 104). In IRS Private Letter Ruling 199945023, August 12, 1999, a qualified settlement fund (QSF) had been established to pay damages to equity investors in a certain partnership. The QSF was funded with monies that would be used to pay the plaintiffs if the trading market values of the partnership interests failed to reach certain levels by a certain date. The defendant was also required to contribute funds to the QSF to guarantee a certain rate of return on the monies deposited in the QSF. The IRS held that the QSF need not file Forms 1099-INT, Forms 1099-MISC or Form 1099-B for its distributions of principal. However, the ruling contained a caveat that the IRS did not have enough facts to rule whether the distribution of the QSF's net investment income constituted a distribution of fixed or determinable income requiring reporting under Code § 6041.

transfers to and from it for the period from its inception until January 1, 1996. Reasonable methods include treating the fund as a grantor trust or a complex trust of which the transferors are the grantors,[29] or treating the fund as if it were a designated settlement fund. For funds established in the interim between February 14, 1992 and January 1, 1993, the IRS will not challenge a reasonable and consistently applied method of taxation for that interim period, but starting January 1, 1993 the method prescribed by the regulations will apply to such funds.

Moreover, the IRS will not challenge use of the cash method of accounting for either type of grandfathered fund for periods before January 1, 1996.

Grandfathered funds may also elect to apply the final regulations retroactively.[30]

**Grantor trust treatment of certain qualified settlement funds.** In 2006, the IRS amended the regulations[31] to allow a qualified settlement fund that has only one transferor to elect to be treated as a grantor trust of which the transferor is the grantor. Thus, all of the property and income of the fund would be taxed as if the property had not yet been transferred by the transferor. Under this proposal, an electing transferor would not have a taxable event upon the transfer of its assets to the fund, nor would it be able to treat such transfer or any other payments to the fund as satisfying the "economic performance" requirements for deductibility. The election applies only to qualified settlement funds established after February 3, 2006, with a limited exception for those established previously if all years of all the parties are still open back to the date of establishment of the fund.

### *§904.3 Disputed Ownership Funds*

In 1999, the IRS proposed a regulation (Reg. §1.468B-9) which would create an entity called a "disputed ownership fund." This regulation, with some changes, was made final in 2006. The regulation defines a "disputed ownership fund" as an escrow account, trust, or fund other than a qualified settlement fund that satisfies the following requirements:

(1) The fund must be established to hold money or property subject to conflicting claims of ownership.
(2) The fund must be subject to the continuing jurisdiction of a court.
(3) Money or property cannot be distributed from the fund to a claimant without court approval.
(4) The fund is not a qualified settlement fund.

---

[29] For an example of such treatment, *see* IRS Letter Ruling 9340046, October 8, 1993. However, in IRS Technical Advice Memorandum 9617004, January 5, 1996, a qualified settlement fund was denied such transitional relief where it had filed returns paying tax, but had reserved the right to seek a ruling that the fund should be treated as a grantor trust. Since in fact the transferors had not paid tax on the income of the fund, but had only reserved a right to do so, the IRS said that the trust did not qualify for transitional relief.

[30] For an example of such treatment, *see* IRS Letter Ruling 9340055, October 8, 1993.

[31] Reg. §1.468B-1(k).

(5) The fund is not a title 11 bankruptcy estate itself or a part thereof (as distinguished from a fund that might be created by that estate).[32]
(6) The fund is not a liquidating trust (except that the trustee of a liquidating trust established pursuant to a confirmed title 11 plan may, in the liquidating trust's first taxable year, elect to treat an escrow or other fund that holds assets of the liquidating trust that are subject to disputed claims as a disputed ownership fund).

Accordingly, an escrow or other segregated fund established under a confirmed Chapter 11 plan (classically called a "disputed claims reserve") to hold pending distributions that are subject to disputed claims of unsecured creditors generally should be treated as a disputed ownership fund.

A disputed ownership fund is to be taxed as follows:

(1) as a qualified settlement fund if all of the assets transferred to it are passive investment assets; or
(2) as a C corporation in all other cases; except that
(3) if there is a more appropriate method of taxing the fund, the claimants to the fund may submit a private letter ruling request proposing such an alternative method of taxation.

In any event, for purposes of the procedural and reporting provisions of Subtitle F of the Code, the fund is to be treated as a corporation.

The property transferred to the fund is not treated as income to the fund nor does the fund get a deduction for distributions of the property to a claimant. The fund's basis in property transferred to it is the fair market value on the date of transfer, unless the transferor claims ownership of the transferred property after the transfer, in which case the fund takes the transferor's basis. A transferor to the fund must treat the transfer as a sale of the property for fair market value, unless the transferor claims ownership of the property after the transfer to the fund.

The regulation provides that economic performance will occur for the transferor upon the transfer to the fund (it is not delayed until the fund makes a transfer to the claimant), but this is only so if the transferor and related parties are not claimants and have no right to receive payments or distributions from the fund. Nor does economic performance occur when the transferor transfers its own debt or that of a related person to the fund.

Where the transferor claims ownership in the assets after they are transferred to the fund, neither the transfer of the property to the fund, nor the transfer by the fund back to the transferor, is treated as a sale or exchange of the property, nor is the transferor taxed on any distributions it receives from the fund. In addition, where the transferor is a claimant, distributions made by the fund to claimants other than the

---

32 The preamble to the final regulations states that the reason for this requirement is to avoid a conflict with Code § 1398, which provides rules for taxing bankruptcy estates of certain individual debtors, and Code § 1399, which provides in all other cases that no separate taxable entity results from the commencement of a bankruptcy case.

transferor are deemed to be made first to the transferor, and then from the transferor to the recipient of the distribution. This latter rule is intended to put the transferor-claimant in the same position for determining the deductibility of the transfer as it would have been in if the property had not been transferred first to the disputed ownership fund.

The regulation contains an interesting provision that says that if the fund has an unused NOL or capital loss carryover or tax credit carryover when it is terminated, the claimants to whom the fund's net assets are distributable will succeed to and take into account these tax benefits.

The regulation is to apply only to funds established after February 3, 2006, but the regulation adds (as the IRS had indicated in the proposed regulation) that for funds established after August 16, 1986, but on or before February 3, 2006, the IRS will not challenge a reasonable, consistently applied method of taxation for income earned by the fund, transfers to the fund, and distributions made by the fund. Applying this provision as it appeared in the proposed regulation, the IRS issued three letter rulings allowing a fund, established to hold assets to be distributed pursuant to the results of a court interpleader action, to be treated as a grantor trust with the sole creator of the fund treated as the grantor.[33] A more recent ruling applying this same "reasonable method" provision to a similar fund approved a different approach. Here, the parties were allowed to apply the proposed version of Reg. § 1.468B-9 (in effect as if it were final) to treat the fund as a disputed ownership fund and, since the fund assets were all passive investment assets, to have the fund taxed as if it were a qualified settlement fund.[34]

## § 905 LIMITED PARTNERSHIPS

A limited partnership can be used to serve essentially the same function as a liquidating trust, but it can have much broader management powers than a liquidating trust without running the risk of being taxable as a corporation.[1] A limited partnership, however, would require finding an appropriate individual or entity willing to take on the function of a general partner.[2] The IRS has issued advance ruling guidelines in this area.[3] In order to preserve the pass-through status of the

---

[33] IRS Letter Ruling 200411020, December 9, 2003; IRS Letter Ruling 200414016, November 20, 2003; IRS Letter Ruling 200411017, November 20, 2003.

[34] IRS Letter Ruling 200714007, January 8, 2007.

[1] **§ 905** *See, e.g.*, IRS Letter Ruling 8614027, January 3, 1986 (primary purpose for partnership was to find buyers for properties received in a Code § 337 liquidation, including nonproducing properties and shut-in wells, as well as a reserved one-third interest in certain oil and gas properties previously sold; in the interim, partnership was fully empowered to continue to operate such properties); IRS Letter Ruling 8629038, April 18, 1986. A properly structured business trust or limited liability company may also be characterized, for federal income tax purposes, as a partnership, rather than as an association taxable as a corporation. Rev. Rul. 88-79, 1988-2 C.B. 361; Rev. Rul. 88-76, 1988-2 C.B. 360.

[2] *See* Reg. § 301.7701-2(d)(2).

[3] *See* Rev. Proc. 89-12, 1989-1 C.B. 798, *amplified by* Rev. Proc. 91-13, 1991-1 C.B. 477, *modified by* Rev. Proc. 92-87, 1992-2 C.B. 496, *supplemented by* Rev. Proc. 92-33, 1992-1 C.B. 782.

partnership, it is important to restrict the transferability of the partnership interests sufficiently to avoid having the partnership treated as a corporation under the publicly-traded-partnership provisions of Code § 7704. Where a limited partnership is used, the IRS will treat the distribution of the limited partnership interests to the creditors or shareholders as involving a distribution to them of the assets that were placed in the partnership, followed by their deemed contribution of these assets to the partnership.[4] The basis of the partners in their limited partnership interests and the basis of the partnership in its assets will be determined accordingly.

## § 906 LIMITED LIABILITY COMPANIES

In recent years, a new form of entity, namely the limited liability company, has become available in many states. This entity can be structured so as to qualify as a partnership for tax purposes, yet none of its members need have personal liability for the obligations of the entity. Such an entity can offer the tax advantages of a limited partnership while offering the non-tax advantages generally associated with corporate form. In order to obtain pass-through tax treatment, the limited liability company must of course be structured so as to satisfy the tax rules for classification as a partnership rather than as a corporation.[1] In addition, it is important to restrict the transferability of the interests in the limited liability company sufficiently to avoid having the company treated as a corporation under the publicly-traded-partnership provisions of Code § 7704.

## § 907 BUSINESS TRUSTS

For entities formed after 1996, the new check-the-box entity-classification regulations make it possible to consider a business trust as an alternative form of organization, where the entity cannot qualify as a liquidating trust. Under these regulations, a business trust is classified as a business entity under Reg. § 301.7701-2.[1] This latter regulation generally treats such an entity as a partnership, unless it elects to be treated as a corporation. Thus, pass-through tax treatment can be achieved even for such an entity. However, in order to achieve this result, the entity must not be treated as a publicly traded partnership under Code § 7704. Care should be taken in drafting any such instrument to comply with the regulations under Code § 7704, which provide certain safe havens for avoiding publicly-traded status.

---

[4] *See, e.g.*, IRS Letter Ruling 8529097, April 25, 1985 (in which a corporation, in a Code § 337 liquidation, formed both a liquidating trust and a limited partnership), discussed *supra* § 902 note 28; IRS Letter Ruling 8248080, August 31, 1982.

[1] **§ 906** Rev. Rul. 2004-41, 2004-18 I.R.B. 845, holds that the members of a limited liability company that is treated as a partnership for federal tax purposes do not have personal liability for the federal employment taxes of the entity, if under the applicable state law the members of the limited liability company are not liable for its debts.

[1] **§ 907** Reg. § 301.7701-4(b).

## §908 CORPORATIONS

On occasion, a corporation will be used instead of a liquidating trust or a limited partnership. The corporation can be given broad management powers, unlike the trustee of a liquidating trust, and a corporation avoids the need to have a general partner who is liable for partnership obligations.

### EXAMPLE

A failing company transfers certain of its assets to a newly formed corporation. The plan of bankruptcy reorganization provides that the shares of the corporation will be distributed to the creditors in partial satisfaction of their claims.

Code §351 will not apply to the transfer of assets to the corporation in the example. To begin with, the IRS takes the position that if a corporation is formed only to liquidate assets, Code §351 will not apply to its formation.[1] Moreover, the Bankruptcy Tax Act of 1980 added new Code §351(e)(2), which provides that a transfer of the property of a debtor pursuant to a plan while the debtor is under the jurisdiction of a court in a title 11 or similar case (as defined in Code §368(a)(3)(A)) will not qualify under Code §351, to the extent that the stock (or, before the 1989 amendment removing securities from the purview of Code §351, securities) received in the exchange are used to satisfy the indebtedness of the debtor.[2]

Thus, the transfer of assets by the debtor to the corporation in the above example will be one in which the debtor recognizes gain or loss and the corporation receives a new basis. Code §351(e)(2) applies whether the corporation to which the assets were transferred is a new corporation or an existing corporation having other activities. Where less than all of the stock of the transferee corporation is transferred to the creditors, only a proportionate part of the gain or loss on the transfer of property by the debtor to the corporation will be recognized.[3]

The purpose of Code §351(e)(2) is to treat the transaction described in the above example as if the debtor had distributed the assets to the creditors and they in turn had contributed them to the corporation. This prevents the debtor from placing high basis, low value assets in the corporation and thus giving the creditors the benefit of a basis higher than value.[4]

The foregoing discussion assumes, of course, that the facts of the transaction do not cause it to qualify as a Code §368 reorganization.

---

[1] **§908** Rev. Rul. 55-36, 1955-1 C.B. 340; IRS Letter Ruling 7817101, January 27, 1978.

[2] For a more detailed discussion of this provision and planning opportunities, *see* Asofsky, Reorganizing Insolvent Corporations, 41 Inst. on Fed. Tax'n §§5, 5.03 (1983).

[3] S. Rep. No. 1035, 96th Cong., 2d Sess., 43 (1980).

[4] Id.

# 10

# Bankruptcy Aspects of Federal Tax Procedure



## §1001 INTRODUCTION

The Bankruptcy Code imposes special procedural rules affecting federal tax matters for restructurings of failing companies in bankruptcy proceedings. These procedural rules can have a profound impact on both the procedure and the substance of federal tax results.

At the outset, we should point out that the Bankruptcy Code rules draw some sharp distinctions between "prepetition" and "postpetition" taxes. "Prepetition" taxes are taxes (including employment taxes) incurred but unpaid prior to the filing of the bankruptcy petition.[1] Conversely, "postpetition" taxes generally are taxes incurred after the filing of the bankruptcy petition and during the administration of the bankruptcy case.[2] As discussed at § 1015.1.1, prior to the bankruptcy reforms in 2005, an increasing number of courts (including three Circuit Courts) had held that income taxes relating to the year of the bankruptcy filing should be bifurcated between the prepetition and postpetition portions of the year for purposes of determining priority of payment.[3] Nevertheless, effective for bankruptcy cases commenced on or after October 17, 2005, any income or gross receipts taxes for taxable years ending after the petition date (and during the administration of the bankruptcy case) should be treated in their entirety as a postpetition tax. A tax on or measured by some event, such as a tax on the payment of wages or an excise tax on a sale or other transaction, generally should be considered to have been incurred on the date of the event.[4]

Changes to many of the procedural bankruptcy rules discussed in this chapter were the subject of a report prepared by the National Bankruptcy Review Commission and submitted to Congress on October 20, 1997.[5] The Commission was established pursuant to the Bankruptcy Reform Act of 1994 as an independent commission to investigate and evaluate issues relating to the Bankruptcy Code, including tax-related issues. Following the submission of the Commission's report, Congress failed in five consecutive congressional sessions to adopt any major bankruptcy reform legislation, but ultimately succeeded in the sixth. On April 20, 2005, with the Republicans in control of the Congress and George W. Bush as Chief Executive, the "Bankruptcy Abuse Prevention and Consumer Protection Act of 2005" was enacted.[6] In most respects, the 2005 Act is the same legislation considered in the prior

---

[1] **§ 1001** *See* IRS Manual, Part 4 (Examining Process), Ch. 27 (Bankruptcy), Exhibit 4.27.1-1, Item 67 (5/25/99); IRS Manual, Part 5 (Collecting Process), Ch. 9 (Bankruptcy), Exhibit 5.9.1-1 (3/1/06) (Glossary of Common Insolvency Terms).

[2] *Cf.* 11 U.S.C. § 350 (administration of bankruptcy case continues until closing of case).

[3] *See infra* § 1015 note 27.

[4] *See, e.g.*, 124 Cong. Rec. H 11,112 (daily ed. September 28, 1978) (statement of Rep. Edwards), S 17,428 (daily ed. October 6, 1978) (statement of Sen. DeConcini); IRS Manual, Part 4 (Examining Process), Ch. 27 (Bankruptcy), Exhibit 4.27.1-1, Item 67 (5/25/99); *In re Bleimeister*, 251 B. R. 383, 394 (Bankr. D. Ariz. 2000).

[5] The Commission's recommendations are reprinted in the BNA Daily Tax Report (October 21, 1997), at p. L-38. The entire report is available through the Government Printing Office website at www.access.gpo.gov. But be prepared with plenty of paper. The report totals 1028 pages in length (excluding dissenting views and Appendices).

For a further discussion of many of the tax proposals considered by the Commission, *see* Report of the American Bar Association Task Force Concerning the Tax Recommendations of the National Bankruptcy Review Commission (dated April 15, 1997), *reprinted at* 97 TNT 90-22; Assn. of the Bar of the City of New York, Response to Certain Proposals Made to the National Bankruptcy Review Commission Relating to Tax Issues, 52 The Record 418 (1997). For a slightly earlier look at possible bankruptcy reforms, *see* Report of the National Bankruptcy Conference Bankruptcy Code Review Project, presented at ALI-ABA Conference, June 10-12, 1993 (Bankruptcy Reform Circa 1993); Asofsky, Towards a Bankruptcy Tax Act of 1993, 51 NYU Inst. Fed. Tax'n § 13.02 (1993).

[6] The legislative history to the 2005 Act includes H.R. Rep. 109-31, 109th Cong., 1st Sess. (April 8, 2005). No similar report was released by the Senate Judiciary Committee in respect of the 2005 legislation.

congressional sessions. Although the Act includes significant changes to the tax-related provisions of the Bankruptcy Code, only in limited respects did it follow the recommendations of the National Bankruptcy Review Commission.[7]

Touted as effectuating major reforms in consumer bankruptcy and representing a fundamental shift in bankruptcy policy from one that views individual debtors as basically honest and hard-working to one of distrust, the 2005 Act is also expected to have a significant impact on corporate bankruptcies. For example, given the tightening of various time periods in the Bankruptcy Code (including with respect to a debtor's exclusive right to file a Chapter 11 plan) and the first time adoption of exceptions to the blanket discharge previously accorded reorganizing corporate debtors, it has been speculated that over time there may be a significant rise in the number of corporate "liquidating" bankruptcies—both true liquidating bankruptcies and bankruptcies involving the transfer of the debtor's business as a going concern to a new corporation to be owned by the former creditors.[8]

For those of you interested in the congressional process and the making of legislation, the remainder of this section traces the long and arduous path from Commission report to final legislation. During 1998, following the submission of the Commission's report, several legislative initiatives were considered by Congress to amend the Bankruptcy Code, primarily focusing on consumer bankruptcies. The most significant of these were H.R. 3150, which was passed by the House of Representatives on June 10, 1998, and S. 1301, which was passed by the Senate on September 23, 1998. The House bill included significant changes to the tax-related provisions of the Bankruptcy Code (the same ones ultimately enacted in the 2005 Act), whereas the Senate bill did not. Although the House-Senate conferees ultimately acceded to the tax-related provisions of the House bill with only minor changes,[9] the resulting bill met with significant opposition in the Senate (and from the White House) and was not passed during the 1998 Congressional session. During the 1999 Congressional session, the conference version of H.R. 3150 was reintroduced as H.R. 833, and was passed by the House of Representatives on May 5, 1999 (again with only minor changes).[10] Although the complimentary bill in the Senate, S. 625, was reported out of the Senate Judiciary Committee, it was not voted on by the Senate during 1999. The Senate subsequently approved the bill, with certain amend-

---

[7] In 1998, when first proposed in legislative form, the tax-related changes were criticized by the private bar for their departure from the Commission's recommendations. *See, e.g.*, American Bar Association, Tax Section, Report on the Tax Provisions of H.R. 3150, 51 Tax Law. 635 (1998); Rep. Gekas Slights Commission/Tax Committee, Bankr. Ct. Dec. (March 17, 1998), at p. A1. *See also* BNA Daily Tax Report (February 2, 2000), at G-7.

[8] *See, e.g.*, Levin and Ranney-Marinelli, The Creeping Repeal of Chapter 11: The Significant Business Provisions of the Bankruptcy Abuse Prevention and Consumer Protection Act of 2005, 79 Am. Bankr. L.J. 603 (2005).

[9] *See* Tax Notes Today, 98 TNT 195-63 (October 8, 1998) (reprinting the tax-related provisions of the bill).

[10] *See* Tax Notes Today, 1999 TNT 87-41 (May 6, 1999) (reprinting tax related provisions of H.R. 833).

ments to the tax-related provisions, on February 2, 2000.[11] The bill, although stalled for most of the year in conference, was approved by the House of Representatives on October 12, 2000 and by the Senate on December 7, 2000, as H.R. 2514.[12] Still dissatisfied with the consumer bankruptcy provisions, however, President Clinton "pocket vetoed" the bill following Congress' adjournment. The bill was promptly reintroduced in the House of Representatives (H.R. 333) and the Senate (S. 220, later renumbered S. 420), with the support of President Bush. Although the House and Senate bills were both approved in March 2001, the Senate bill contained a number of controversial last-minute amendments that ultimately precluded its enactment during 2001 and 2002.[13] The bill was again reintroduced (with limited changes) in the House of Representatives (H.R. 975) in 2003, and passed by the House of Representatives on March 19, 2003.[14] In a further effort to get the bill back on legislative track, the House of Representatives, in January 2004, incorporated the text of H.R. 975 into a Senate passed bill (S. 1920) that would permanently extend the bankruptcy relief provisions of Chapter 12 applicable to farmers, and approved the amended Senate bill, sending it back to the Senate with a request for a conference. Nothing more happened with the bill in 2004. However, with an all Republican majority in Congress (as a result of the November 2004 elections), it seemed inevitable that the reform bill would finally become law in 2005. The bill was promptly reintroduced in the Senate (S. 265) in February 2005, and passed by the Senate on March 10, 2005. The bill was then passed with minimal debate by the House of Representatives on April 14, 2005, and signed into law by President Bush on April 20, 2005.

## §1002 STEPS IN A BANKRUPTCY PROCEEDING

The procedures relating to the tax aspects of a bankruptcy case can best be understood if they are viewed against the background of the steps that typically occur in the bankruptcy proceeding. Therefore, we begin by summarizing below the steps that take place in a typical Chapter 11 restructuring of a failing corporation under the Bankruptcy Code.[1]

---

[11] *See* BNA Daily Tax Report (February 9, 2000), at I-22 (reprinting tax related provisions of S. 625); BNA Daily Tax Report (February 2, 2000), BNA TaxCore, for a side-by-side comparison of the tax-related provisions of H.R. 833 and S. 625.

[12] *See* BNA Daily Tax Report (October 13, 2000), at L-6 (reprinting tax related provisions of H.R. 2514); and 2000 TNT 241-58 (Conference Report explanation of tax related provisions).

[13] The tax provisions in both bills are identical. *See* BNA Daily Tax Report (March 16, 2001), BNA TaxCore (reprinting tax related provisions of S. 420).

[14] *See* BNA Daily Tax Report (March 21, 2003), BNA TaxCore (reprinting tax related provisions of H.R. 975).

[1] **§1002** For a discussion of limited liability companies and the bankruptcy process, *see* Assn. of the Bar of the City of New York, Limited Liability Companies and Bankruptcy, 51 The Record 46 (1996).

## *§1002.1 Filing the Petition*

Most Chapter 11 cases are initiated by the filing of a voluntary petition by the debtor. A voluntary petition can be filed even if the failing corporation is not insolvent in either a "bankruptcy" or an "equity" sense, although an implicit prerequisite to a debtor's right to file a bankruptcy petition is that the filing be made in "good faith" and not merely to delay or frustrate legitimate efforts of creditors to enforce their rights.[2] This is a more liberal rule than that which applied under the old Bankruptcy Act and is a far more lenient test than applies under the current Bankruptcy Code to the filing of an involuntary petition by a creditor. However, a debtor may only withdraw a voluntarily filed petition for "cause" (which, under appropriate circumstances, may include avoiding the stigma of bankruptcy and poor advice from counsel).[3] An involuntary petition will generally be dismissed unless the debtor has not been paying its debts as they become due.[4]

On occasion, a voluntary or involuntary petition that has been filed under Chapter 11 of the Bankruptcy Code will be shifted to a liquidating bankruptcy proceeding under Chapter 7, or vice versa. For example, if a petition has been filed for relief under Chapter 7 (liquidation), the debtor, as a matter of right, or the bankruptcy court, on request of a party in interest, may convert the case to a Chapter 11 (reorganization) case.[5] Conversely, if a Chapter 11 petition is filed, the debtor as a matter of right may or the bankruptcy court, on request of a party in interest and the

---

[2] In *In re Devine,* 131 B.R. 952, 955 (Bankr. S.D. Tex. 1991), the bankruptcy court held that the fact the debtors waited 241 days after the IRS assessment to file their bankruptcy petition—which meant that the assessed tax liability would not be a priority claim (*see* §1015)—did *not* amount to bad faith, "especially since the IRS had the opportunity to file tax liens throughout the 241-day period and neglected to do so." On the other hand, a debtor who filed before the 240-day period expired could not obtain a dismissal of his bankruptcy petition for the sole purpose of refiling after the 240-day period. *Leach v. United States* (*In re Leach*), 130 B.R. 855, 92-1 U.S.T.C. ¶50,144 (Bankr. 9th Cir. 1992); *cf. In re William Scott and Maria J. Profit,* No. 687-08918-W13, (Bankr. Or. March 2, 1989) (refiling after the 240-day period constituted bad faith). In *Maggard & Maggard v. Commissioner* (*In re Maggard & Maggard*), 1992 U.S. Dist. LEXIS 10684 (C.D. Cal. 1992), however, the district court disagreed, holding that the bankruptcy court has the discretion to find that the IRS would not have been legally prejudiced by a dismissal where the IRS had not taken any collection action in the 234 days preceding the bankruptcy or, alternatively, could condition the dismissal on no refiling for another six days. *See generally* John J. Rapisardi, Bad Faith Chapter 11 Filings—An Elusive and Undefined Concept, N.Y.L.J., Jan. 20, 2000, at 3.

[3] *See* 11 U.S.C. §§707(a), 1112(b); *In re Stephenson,* 262 B.R. 871 (Bankr. W.D. Okla. 2001) (debtor's motion to dismiss was denied where the creditors would be prejudiced by losing the assurance of receiving at least partial payment out of the recovery of certain tax refunds).

[4] Even if the debtor has been paying its debts as they become due, the involuntary petition will not generally be dismissed if a custodian was appointed within 120 days before the filing of the petition. *See* 11 U.S.C. §303, which provides that an involuntary petition will generally be dismissed *unless* (1) the debtor is generally not paying its debts as they come due or (2) a custodian was appointed within 120 days before the filing of the petition. 11 U.S.C. §303(a) and (h); 11 U.S.C. §101(11) (definition of "custodian"). For this purpose, a "custodian" excludes a trustee, receiver, or agent appointed or authorized to take charge of less than substantially all of the property of the debtor for the purpose of enforcing a lien against such property. 11 U.S.C. §303(h)(2).

[5] 11 U.S.C. §706(a) and (b).

establishment of cause, must generally convert the case to a Chapter 7 case.[6] It would appear that where there is a reasonable likelihood that reorganization is possible, the bankruptcy court would try to retain the case in Chapter 11 or, on request of a party in interest, convert the case to Chapter 11.[7]

In a small business case (one generally where the debtor has fixed liabilities of $2 million or less, and no committee of unsecured creditors),[8] the debtor corporation must append to its voluntary petition or file within a week of the bankruptcy court's acceptance of an involuntary petition, among other things, its most recent federal income tax return.[9]

## *§1002.2 Debtor-in-Possession Versus Trustee*

In a Chapter 11 case, unless a bankruptcy trustee is appointed, the debtor corporation will remain operating as a "debtor-in-possession."[10] Thus, the only change to the debtor corporation upon the initiation of a bankruptcy case will be the atmosphere in which it is operating. Its actions outside the ordinary course of business will require the approval of the bankruptcy court.[11] Accordingly, the debtor corporation generally will be prohibited from paying any prepetition taxes without the prior court approval. Many debtor corporations promptly seek permission to pay certain types of taxes (such as withholding taxes and sales and use taxes, and sometimes even property taxes, license fees, and the like) given the disruptive effect the deferred payment of such taxes could have on the debtor's operations, the debtor's high degree of confidence that such taxes ultimately would be paid under a Chapter 11 plan, and/or the "trust fund" nature of the taxes.[12] Not all courts are

---

[6] *See* 11 U.S.C. §1112 (no conversion permitted as of right by the debtor where a trustee has been appointed, the case was involuntarily commenced in Chapter 11 or the case was previously converted to Chapter 11 on other than the debtor's request; bankruptcy courts had greater discretion prior to the Bankruptcy Abuse Prevention and Consumer Protection Act of 2005).

[7] *See* H.R. Rep. No. 595, 95th Cong., 1st Sess. 318-20 (1977).

[8] 11 U.S.C. §101(51C), (51D) (excludes real estate companies); Interim Bankruptcy Rule 1020.

[9] 11 U.S.C. §1116(1) (if no return has ever been filed, the small business debtor must certify to such fact under penalty of perjury).

[10] 11 U.S.C. §§1101(1), 1107, and 1108.

[11] Unauthorized actions outside the ordinary course of business may be avoided pursuant to Bankruptcy Code section 549(a). In *Gibson v. United States (In re Russell)*, 927 F.2d 413, 91-1 U.S.T.C. ¶50,128 (8th Cir. 1991), discussed at §1006.2.2, a divided Eighth Circuit remanded for further factual development whether the making of an "irrevocable" election to forgo an NOL carryback (as opposed to the filing of the tax return) is outside "the ordinary course of business," such that the election could be avoided under Bankruptcy Code section 549(a). On remand, the bankruptcy court initially found that the tax election was made within the ordinary course of business; however, the district court subsequently reversed (*see* discussion at §1006.2.2). *Streetman v. United States (In re Russell)*, 154 B.R. 723, 728-730, 93-1 U.S.T.C. ¶50,309 (Bankr. W.D. Ark. 1993), *aff'd*, 1994 U.S. Dist. LEXIS 7185 (W.D. Ark. 1994), *reh'g denied*, 1994 U.S. Dist. LEXIS 7160, *appeal after remand, rev'd*, 187 B.R. 287, 95-2 U.S.T.C. ¶50,453 (W.D. Ark. 1995).

[12] For examples of these "first day" motions and orders, *see, e.g., In re UAL Corp.*, Ch. 11 Case No. 02-B-48191 (Bankr. N.D. Ill.), motions and interim orders dated December 9, 2002, and final orders dated December 11, 2002 (included withholding taxes, sales and use taxes, transportation taxes, security fees, business license fees, landing fees, passenger facility charges and other similar govern-

equally receptive to such requests, however.[13] In addition, the debtor corporation will have to deal with the numerous creditor and equity holder committees that typically are formed in bankruptcy cases to protect the respective interests of their members,[14] or alternatively, in a small business case, with greater scrutiny by the United States trustee for its judicial district.[15] The United States trustee is selected by the United States Attorney General and has oversight responsibility for the bankruptcy cases within its jurisdiction. As such, it is generally regarded as a party in interest in such cases.[16]

In contrast to the United States trustee, a bankruptcy trustee will only be appointed for a debtor's estate by the bankruptcy court (1) "for cause," including fraud, dishonesty, incompetence or gross mismanagement of the affairs of the debtor by current management, (2) if the appointment is otherwise in the interests of the creditors, equity security holders and other interested parties, or (3) if grounds otherwise exist to convert the case to a Chapter 7 liquidation or to dismiss the case, but the bankruptcy court determines that the appointment of a trustee is in the best interests of the creditors and the estate.[17]

Short of the appointment of a bankruptcy trustee, the bankruptcy court will, as appropriate, appoint an examiner to investigate allegations of fraud, dishonesty, incompetence, misconduct, mismanagement or management irregularities (current or past) in cases where (i) the debtors fixed unsecured debts (other than for good,

(Footnote Continued)

ment and airport charges); *In re US Airways Group, Inc.*, Ch. 11 Case No. 02-83984 (SSM) (Bankr. E.D. Va.), motion dated August 11, 2002, and order dated August 12, 2002 (included sales and use taxes, franchise taxes, transportation taxes, business license fees and passenger facility charges); *In re Global Crossing Ltd.*, Ch. 11 Case No. 02-40187 (REG) (Bankr. S.D.N.Y.), motions and orders dated January 28, 2002 (included sales and use taxes, gross receipts taxes, federal excise taxes and business license fees); *In re Ames Department Stores, Inc.*, Chapter 11 Case No. 01-44217 (REG) (Bankr. S.D.N.Y.), motions and orders dated August 20, 2001 (included sales and use taxes, prepetition employee obligations and custom duties); *In re Armstrong World Industries, Inc.*, Case No. 00-4471 (JJF) (Bankr. D. Del.), motions and orders dated December 6, 2000 (included sales and use taxes, property taxes, franchise taxes and trust fund taxes generally, as well as prepetition employee obligations and custom duties).

[13] *See generally* Jenks, Ridgway, and Purnell, TM 790, Corporate Bankruptcy, at III.B. For a general discussion of "first day" orders with respect to non-tax payments, *see, e.g.*, Cieri, Fitzgerald and Miller, Forum Shopping, First Day Orders, and Case Management Issues in Bankruptcy, 1 DePaul Bus. & Comm. L.J. 515 (2003).

[14] *See* 11 U.S.C. § 1102 (providing for appointment of creditor and equity holder committees). In certain limited circumstances—which generally would involve the Pension Benefits Guaranty Corp. (PBGC), the Resolution Trust Corp. (RTC), or the Environmental Protection Agency (EPA)—the federal government may serve as a member of a committee. *See* 11 U.S.C. § 101(41) (as amended by the Bankruptcy Reform Act of 1994). The bankruptcy court may dispense with a meeting of creditors and equity holders in bankruptcy cases filed on or after October 17, 2005, if the debtor solicited acceptances to its plan prior to the filing of the bankruptcy case (*i.e.*, in "pre-packaged" bankruptcy cases). 11 U.S.C. § 341(e).

[15] *See, e.g.*, 28 U.S.C. § 586(a)(7).

[16] 28 U.S.C. § § 581 *et seq.*

[17] 11 U.S.C. § § 1104(a) (third criteria effective for bankruptcy cases commenced on or after October 17, 2005) and 1105 (permits bankruptcy court to terminate trustee's appointment).

services, or taxes or insider debts) exceed $5 million or (ii) such appointment is in the interests of the creditors, equity security holders and any interested parties.[18]

## *§1002.3 Reporting by Debtor-in-Possession*

Whether the debtor is operating as a debtor-in-possession or a bankruptcy trustee is appointed, the duties, powers, and limitations of the debtor-in-possession and trustee are, with relatively few and minor exceptions, identical.[19] Therefore, unless otherwise indicated, all references herein to a debtor-in-possession equally apply to a Chapter 11 trustee.

As one of the first orders of business, a debtor-in-possession must prepare and file with the bankruptcy court a list of creditors, a schedule of assets and liabilities, and a statement of affairs.[20] In addition, "as soon as practicable," a Chapter 11 plan should be filed (*see* §1002.6).[21] To expedite the bankruptcy case, a debtor may file a plan at the same time it files a voluntary petition.[22]

## *§1002.4 Stay of Action Against Debtor*

Upon the filing of either a Chapter 7 or 11 petition, whether voluntary or involuntary, there is, with limited exceptions, a suspension (called an "automatic stay") of, *inter alia,* (i) any litigation or proceeding against the debtor with respect to a prepetition claim, (ii) any act to obtain possession of or exercise control over property of the bankruptcy estate, and (iii) any effort to create, perfect, or enforce a lien against the property of the estate.[23] This includes any action by any government to collect or

---

[18] 11 U.S.C. §104(c).

[19] 11 U.S.C. §1107(a) (in contrast to a trustee, a debtor-in-possession has no right to compensation and no obligation to perform investigative duties); *see* 11 U.S.C. §§704 and 1106(a) (duties of a trustee); *see also Local Union No. 38, Sheet Metal Workers' Int'l Assoc., AFL-CIO v. Custom Air Systems, Inc.*, 333 F.3d 345, 347-348 (2d Cir. 2003) (generally treating a debtor-in-possession and a bankruptcy trustee as equivalent in power), *vacated and remanded on other grounds,* 357 F.3d 266 (2d Cir. 2004). Subject to bankruptcy court approval, a debtor-in-possession (as well as a trustee) has the power to assume or reject any executory contract of the debtor. 11 U.S.C. §365(a) and (d) (in a Chapter 11 case, the executory contract may generally be assumed or rejected any time prior to confirmation of the Chapter 11 plan; in a Chapter 7 case, if not expressly assumed or rejected generally within 60 days after the order for relief, the contract is deemed rejected). An executory contract arguably includes an offer in compromise for federal taxes (made pursuant to Reg. §301.7121-1(d)(1); *see also* IRS Form 656) and related collateral agreements—IRS Chief Counsel Advice 200027050, May 16, 2000, *reprinted at* 2000 TNT 132-66; former IRS Manual §57(13)l.23(12) (December 7, 1988)—but does not include an extension of the statute of limitations. *See Bilski v. Commissioner,* 67 T.C.M. 2150 (1994) (involved an extension under Form 872-A), *aff'd,* 69 F.3d 64 (5th Cir. 1995).

[20] 11 U.S.C. §1106(a)(4).

[21] 11 U.S.C. §1106(a)(5).

[22] 11 U.S.C. §1121(a); *see* discussion of "prepackaged" bankruptcy plans at §213.

[23] 11 U.S.C. §362(a) (general rule), (b) (exceptions, including the creation of a lien with respect to certain *ad valorem* property taxes), and (n) (exception in small business cases with respect to certain serial filings). *See Wekell v. United States,* 14 F.3d 32 (9th Cir. 1994) (automatic stay effective upon filing even where the filing of the petition was *ultra vires*); *Fleet National Bank v. Gray (In re BankVest Capital Corp.)*, 2003 U.S. Dist. LEXIS 4876 (D. Mass. 2003) (involuntary bankruptcy).

recover any prepetition tax deficiency, other than the assessment of the tax or the issuance of a notice of deficiency (*see* § 1007).[24] Also, the commencement or continuation of any Tax Court proceeding concerning a corporate debtor's tax liability is expressly suspended (*see* § 1009).[25]

The automatic stay has also been held to apply to, and thus effectively preempts, any receivership proceeding that was previously instituted with respect to the debtor corporation's assets.[26]

### § 1002.4.1 Actions Affecting Debtor's Tax Benefits

In *In re Prudential Lines, Inc.*,[27] the bankruptcy court held (and the district court and Second Circuit affirmed) that a debtor's NOL carryovers were property of the bankruptcy estate protected by the automatic stay. Accordingly, in furtherance of the stay, the court permanently enjoined a nonbankrupt parent corporation from claiming a worthless stock deduction for its stock in the debtor for any year ending before the effective date of the debtor's Chapter 11 plan. (As discussed at § 508.2.4, had the parent claimed the worthless stock deduction, the debtor's use of its NOLs would have been limited under Code § 382.) Going a step further, the bankruptcy court in the *Phar-Mor* bankruptcy case determined that, due to the potential harm to the debtor's NOLs, the sale of the debtor's stock by two minority 5 percent shareholders was prohibited by the automatic stay "as an exercise of control over the NOL."[28]

Similarly, in *In re Southeast Banking Corp.*,[29] involving a Chapter 7 liquidation, the bankruptcy court enjoined pursuant to the automatic stay any transfer that would produce an ownership change. In *In re First Merchants Acceptance Corporation*,[30] the

---

[24] Tax assessments in bankruptcy cases commenced before October 22, 1994 are also stayed. *See* 11 U.S.C. § 362(b)(9) (effective on or after October 22, 1994).

[25] 11 U.S.C. § 362(a)(8), *as amended by* P.L. 109-8, § 709 (2005) (in the case of individual debtors, the referenced amendment limits the stay of Tax Court proceedings to prepetition taxes).

[26] *Gilchrist v. General Electric Capital Corp.*, 262 F.3d 295 (4th Cir. 2001) (holding in the alternative that (1) the bankruptcy court's jurisdiction is exclusive once a bankruptcy petition is filed and (2) even if general equitable considerations could modify the statutory grant of jurisdiction, the equities favored bankruptcy particularly in the case of complex corporate liquidations; interestingly, the court failed to address the fate of the creditors who filed the bankruptcy petition in violation of an order of the receivership court and had been held in contempt).

[27] 107 B.R. 832 (Bankr. D.N.Y. 1989) (preliminary injunction), 3 Bankr. L. Rep. (CCH) ¶ 73,203 (1990) (permanent injunction), *aff'd*, 119 B.R. 430 (S.D.N.Y. 1990), *aff'd*, 928 F.2d 565, 92-2 U.S.T.C. ¶ 50,491 (2d Cir.), *cert. denied*, 112 S. Ct. 82 (1991). *Prudential Lines* was favorably cited in *Gibson v. United States (In re Russell)* (8th Cir.), *supra* note 11. In that case, which is discussed at §§ 508.2.4 and 1006.1.3, the applicability of the automatic stay was not involved. Rather, at issue was whether a debtor's irrevocable election to forgo an NOL carryback constituted a transfer of property that could be avoided under other sections of the Bankruptcy Code. *Cf. In re Luster*, 981 F.2d 277, 93-1 U.S.T.C. ¶ 50,009 (7th Cir. 1992) (Bankruptcy Act case; in a case involving pre-1980 Act law, prepetition NOL carryforwards of an individual debtor assumed to be "property" but were not transferable to the debtor's bankruptcy estate).

[28] *In re Phar-Mor, Inc.*, 152 B.R. 924 (Bankr. N.D. Ohio 1993).

[29] Bankr. S.D. Fla., Case No. 91-14561-BKC-PGH, order dated July 21, 1994.

[30] *In re First Merchants Acceptance Corp.*, Case No. 97-1500 (JJF) (Bankr. D. Del.) (final order, dated March 12, 1998).

bankruptcy court enjoined any party or acquiring group from acquiring or accumulating more than a specified number of shares (representing approximately 5% of the debtor's outstanding shares), subject to 30 days prior notice and, in the event the debtor interposed an objection to the transfer, subject to a final nonappealable order of the court. In *In re Magellan Health Service, Inc.*,[31] any accumulation of shares of 4.75% or more of any class of stock was enjoined, and any sales of stock by a person owning such amount of stock was subject to 20 days prior notice, unless waived by the debtors. Courts in other cases similarly have imposed varying forms of stock restrictions.[32] Some recent court orders have also required special filings by persons already owning in excess of a specified percentage of stock as of the time the order became effective.[33]

In a 2006 private letter ruling, the IRS considered a similar stock trading order which, in addition, specified the remedial consequences of engaging in a restricted transfer (this is in contrast to most orders to date which simply declare the transfer or acquisition void, and leave the remedial consequences for later determination, if necessary).[34] The IRS held that, so long as the order is in effect and not declared unenforceable, and provided that the debtor complies with the prompt enforcement requirements of the order and, to the extent a purported transferor or transferee does not initially comply with the remedial provisions of the order, the debtor continues to seek enforcement of the order at the end of a taxable year, the purported transferee will not be treated as owning the shares that were the subject of the restricted transfer. As discussed below, however, the imposition of trading restrictions may be faced with renewed challenges, in whole or in part, to their enforceability.

In *In re McLean Industries, Inc.* (a 1989 bankruptcy case),[35] the court ordered that transfers of claims subject to Bankruptcy Rule 3001 (that is, claims other than those based on bonds or debentures) could not be made without prior notice, hearing, and court approval, where the debtor's plan, which was premised on Code § 382(l)(5), required that a majority of the stock be distributed to "old and cold" creditors (*see* §§ 508.2.3 and 508.5). Although the bankruptcy court's authority to restrict claims trading under Bankruptcy Rule 3001 (which was narrowed effective August 1, 1991) has been questioned,[36] bankruptcy courts have, in appropriate cases, continued to

---

[31] Bankr. S.D.N.Y., Ch. 11 Case No. 03-40515 (PCB), order dated March 11, 2003.

[32] *See also, e.g., In re The FINOVA Group Inc.*, Ch. 11 Case No. 01-0697 (PJW) (Bankr. D. Del.) (order dated March 12, 1998).

[33] *See, e.g., In re Northwest Airlines Corporation*, Ch. 11 Case No. 05-17930(ALG) (Bankr. S.D. N.Y.) (final order, dated October 28, 2005); *In re Mirant Corporation*, Ch. 11 Case No. 03-46590 (DML) (Bankr. N.D. Tex July 22, 2003); *In re UAL Corporation*, Ch. 11 Case No. 02-B-48191 (Bankr. N.D. Ill.), motions dated December 9, 2002, and resulting interim and final orders (entered from December 10, 2002, through February 6, 2003), and preliminary injunction dated February 24, 2003; *In re US Airways Group, Inc.*, Ch. 11 Case No. 02-83984 (SSM) (Bankr. E.D. Va.), motion dated August 11, 2002, interim order dated August 12, 2002, and an amended and final order dated October 2, 2002.

[34] IRS Letter Ruling 200605003, October 28, 2005. The remedial mechanism was substantially identical to those contained in various charter restrictions previously approved by the IRS. *See* § 508.2.3.1 above.

[35] Bankr. D.N.Y., Ch. 11 Case Nos. 86 B 12238 through 12241, order dated February 16, 1989.

[36] *See* Morris, *infra* note 45; Fortgang & Mayer, Developments in Trading Claims and Taking Control of Corporations in Chapter 11, 13 Cardozo L. Rev. 1 (1991).

restrict claims trading based, in part, on the automatic stay provisions and its equitable powers under section 105(a) of the Bankruptcy Code.[37] These restrictions generally focus on precluding the acquisition or accumulation of claims above a specified dollar amount, set at an amount below the level of unsecured claims that would reasonably be expected to result in the claim holder becoming a 5 percent shareholder in the event of a debt-for-equity recapitalization of the debtor (in an attempt to benefit from the first exception to the continuous ownership requirement for Code §382(l)(5) treatment, discussed at §508.5.1 above).[38] More recently, some trading orders have been crafted to allow the accumulation of claims so long as the holder is required to sell-down sufficiently in advance of the effective date of a plan that seeks to benefit from Code §382(l)(5) to below an amount that under the plan would result in the holder becoming a 5 percent shareholder.[39] The Bond Market Association in conjunction with the Loan Syndications and Trading Association have drafted a form of claims trading order with a bias toward allowing increased trading in claims.[40]

As these trading orders have become more common, bankruptcy courts have been more willing to restrict trading in a debtor corporation's shares and claims in

---

[37] *See, e.g., In re Pan Am Corp.*, Case Nos. 91-B-10080 (CB) through 91-B-10087 (CB), Adv. Proc. No. 91-6175A (CB) (Bankr. S.D.N.Y.) (preliminary injunction order, dated October 3, 1991) (prohibited the sale or transfer of all general unsecured claims and certain transfers of publicly traded bonds and debentures); *In re First Merchants Acceptance Corporation, supra* note 30 and accompanying text (instituted pretransfer notice procedure with respect to certain stock acquisitions and any transfer or acquisition of unsecured claims, other than certain claims for which "old and cold" treatment was clearly unavailable). *See also* Jerome, Blauner & Drain, Bankruptcy Courts Impose New Roadblocks to Claims Trading, 4 Faulkner & Gray's Bankr. L. Rev. #1, 30 (Spring 1992). Not wasting any time, the debtor in *In re Munsingwear, Inc.* (Bankr. Minn.), stated in its initial "Notice and Order" to creditors and other parties in interest (dated July 9, 1991), with respect to the commencement of the bankruptcy case, its "position that the automatic stay bars trading in debentures and other claims because such trading threatens a substantial asset of the estate, the Net Operating Loss Carryforward."

[38] *See, e.g., In re Service Merchandise Co., Inc.*, Ch. 11 Case No. 399-02649 (Bankr. M.D. Tenn.) (order entered April 6, 2000) (required certifications from substantial claim holders, and notice from anyone selling a claim of $1 million or more; and precluded acquisitions by substantial claim holders unless the amount of non-qualifying claims fell below 40% of total claims); *In re UAL Corporation* (Bankr. N.D. Ill.), *supra* note 33 (required notice of ownership by existing substantial claimholders, and subject to certain exceptions, at least 15 days prior notice of any acquisitions by persons who were, or would become, substantial claimholders; included special provisions for certain lease transactions); *In re US Airways Group, Inc.* (Bankr. E.D. Va.), *supra* note 33 (similar, although not identical, provisions).

[39] *See, e.g., In re Mirant Corporation*, Ch. 11 Case No. 03-46590 (DML) (Bankr. N.D. Tex. July 22, 2003) (imposing special notice requirements on substantial claim holders and purchasers, except for purchasers who enter into a so-called "sell down" agreement pursuant to which the purchaser agrees to reduce its claim position below the proscribed level in the order prior to the later of (i) the confirmation of a plan that relies on Code §382(l)(5) or (ii) 60 days after receiving a "sell down" notice); *In re Northwest Airlines Corporation, supra* note 33 (to similar effect, with special leveraged lease related provisions); *In re Delta Air Line, Inc.*, Ch. 11 Case No. 05-17923 (PCB) (Bankr. S.D. N.Y.) (revised final order, dated December 20, 2005) (employing exclusively a sell-down procedure).

[40] The form of order is modeled, in part, on the trading order in *In re Mirant Corporation, supra* note 39, and can be accessed at http://www.lsta.org/story.asp?id=1532. *See* Kusnetz, Loss of Control—The Clash of Codes in the Battle Over a Debtor's Net Operating Losses, Tax Review Club, paper #243 (November 13, 2006); Scinta, Trade Groups Want Rules Eased on Trading of Chapter 11 Securities, Dow Jones Daily Bankruptcy Review (January 19, 2005).

connection with the "first day" motions that a debtor files at the outset of its bankruptcy case.[41]

Even when the bankruptcy court acts promptly, there may be a gap of days or weeks between the debtor's motion and the court's approval. During this period, it is not unusual for a widely-owned debtor company to see significant trading activity in its stock, with the potential for investors in distressed securities to acquire ownership stakes of 5 percent or more at relatively low prices. This appears to be what occurred in IRS Letter Ruling 200713015.[42] The debtor in that ruling had, on date 4, asked the bankruptcy court to enter an order imposing restrictions on transfers that could impair the company's NOLs, including stock acquisitions that would bring the purchaser's ownership above a percentage that was safely below 5 percent. On date 5, the bankruptcy court entered the order. Shortly thereafter, an investor informed the debtor that between date 4 and date 5 it had acquired enough additional shares in the open market to bring its ownership over 5 percent, an acquisition that would have violated the court's order had it taken place after the order was issued. Moreover, the debtor determined that the amount acquired, if required to be taken into account, was sufficient to cause an ownership change for Code § 382 purposes. The debtor and the investor jointly petitioned the bankruptcy court to declare the purchase of the portion of the additional shares that would have violated the order as void *ab initio*. The bankruptcy court so declared, and ordered that the excess shares be sold in the open market with the proceeds first going to the investor to the extent of its cost and any profit going to a qualified charity. The IRS ruled that, for purposes of Code § 382, the investor would not be treated as having acquired ownership of the excess shares, so long as the bankruptcy court's order remains in effect and is not set aside by any final order of a court of competent jurisdiction.

However, the manner in which bankruptcy courts view such restrictions may have received something of a jolt from two dicta issued by the Court of Appeals for the Seventh Circuit in an appeal of an injunction in the *United Airlines (UAL)* bankruptcy case preventing the sale of United Airlines stock by the Trustee of United Airline's ESOP.[43] The two dicta are (1) that the bankruptcy court in the *UAL* case should have required a bond to protect the ESOP and its beneficiaries from any loss resulting from the injunction, and (2) that the law probably does not even authorize the granting of such an injunction. These dicta are likely to create considerable controversy.

The facts in the *UAL* case are that when United Airlines filed for bankruptcy in December 2002, more than 50% of its stock (then selling for $1.06 per share) was held by workers through an ESOP. Fearing that a transfer of this stock by the ESOP could

---

41 *See, e.g., In re Northwest Airlines Corporation, supra* note 33; *In re UAL Corp.* (Bankr. N.D. Ill.), *supra* note 33; *In re US Airways Group, Inc.* (Bankr. E.D. Va.), *supra* note 33; *In re Ames Department Stores, Inc.*, Ch. 11 Case No. 01-42217 (REG) (Bankr. S.D.N.Y.) (order dated August 20, 2001); *In re Casual Male Corp.*, Ch. 11 Case No. 01-41404 (REG) (Bankr. S.D. N.Y.) (order dated May 18, 2001). Motions for these orders are filed with the bankruptcy court on the first day of the bankruptcy case, and any hearings are scheduled as soon thereafter as possible—hence the name "first day" orders.

42 December 20, 2006.

43 *In the Matter of UAL Corporation*, 412 F.3d 775 (7th Cir. 2005), *vacating*, 2004 U.S. Dist. LEXIS 21918 (N.D. Ill. 2004).

jeopardize United Airlines' estimated $1 billion of NOLs, United Airlines sought and obtained (over the objection of the ESOP trustee) an injunction against the sale of the shares. The trustee did not ask for a bond, and none was granted. The injunction soon became moot: on June 26, 2003, the IRS issued Temp. Reg. § 1.382-10T (adopted in final form in 2006 as Reg. § 1.382-10) providing that a transfer by an ESOP to its beneficiaries would not itself be a change in ownership for Code § 382 purposes; and on June 27, 2003 (when the stock was trading at 76 cents per share), the ESOP was terminated and its shares were distributed to its beneficiaries. The trustee of the ESOP nonetheless pressed its appeal from the order granting the injunction, arguing that the issuance of the injunction was not authorized by the Bankruptcy Code, and that, although the stock had later recovered in value and was trading at $2.02 per share the day before the appeal was argued, the ESOP beneficiaries should be paid the 30 cent loss in the share price that had occurred between the day the injunction was granted and the day the shares were distributed to the beneficiaries, that is, during the period that the injunction prevented any sale of the shares.

The Seventh Circuit held that because no bond had been issued, the case was moot and the trustee could not recover, since "a person injured by the issuance of an injunction later determined to be erroneous has no action for damages in the absence of a bond." Had the Seventh Circuit limited itself to this holding, the case would be of little interest. However, before reaching that holding, the court expressed at some length its views about whether the ESOP trustee should have requested a bond, whether the bankruptcy court should have granted that request, and whether the injunction issued by the bankruptcy court was authorized by the law. The court said the lack of financial security for the ESOP investors was "unfortunate," and added that requiring the investors to bear the costs of illiquidity "was both imprudent and unnecessary." Although the court recognized that United Airlines wanted to preserve its $1 billion of NOLs, the court said "there is no reason why [the ESOP] investors who need liquidity should be sacrificed so that other investors (principally today's debt holders) that will own United after it emerges from bankruptcy can reap a benefit; bankruptcy is not supposed to appropriate some investors' wealth for distribution to others." Instead of "cramming one side's position down the throat of the other in bankruptcy," the bankruptcy judge should have crafted a "mutual protection" agreement to protect the parties.

The Seventh Circuit then added that the lack of a security agreement was doubly regrettable because the granting of the injunction was "problematic on the merits." The lower court had relied for its authority on section 362(a)(3) of the Bankruptcy Code, which authorizes blocking "any act to obtain possession of property of the estate or of property from the estate or to exercise control over property of the estate." The Seventh Circuit said that whether or not a debtor's tax benefits are "property" within the meaning of this provision, an ESOP's "sale of stock does not 'obtain *possession* . . . or exercise *control*' (emphasis added) over that interest." The court distinguished the *Prudential Lines* case (it did not mention *Phar-Mor* or any case similar to *Phar-Mor*) on the ground that although the taking of the consolidated-return worthless-stock deduction in the *Prudential* case "would have exercised control" over the debtor's operating losses, "there is no equivalent example of control (or consumption) of a loss carry-forward in an investor's simple sale of stock." (This distinction between the cases seems to us, we confess, quite opaque.) The court then added that the authority for granting the injunction against the United Airlines ESOP was so weak as "to make a bond or adequate protection undertaking *obligatory* before a bankruptcy judge may forbid investors to sell their stock in the market" (emphasis added).[44]

After making these statements, the Seventh Circuit said, nonetheless, that it did not need to reach a conclusion on the merits of these issues, since the absence of a bond had made the case moot. Thus, the statements made by the Seventh Circuit on these issues are merely dicta, but will be fodder for investors and creditors seeking to challenge the imposition of trading restrictions.[45]

The conflict demonstrated by the foregoing cases is this: Once one decides that NOL carryovers and other tax benefits are "property" of the debtor, they become protected by the automatic stay. Code § 382 causes a debtor's tax benefits to be affected by actions at the shareholder or creditor level, rather than the debtor level. Therefore, at least some actions at the shareholder or creditor level may be restrained by the automatic stay. What remains somewhat unclear is how far this restraint on shareholder or creditor action extends.[46] The culprit here, of course, that creates these conflicts is Code § 382, which causes investor level actions to affect corporate level tax attributes, a result fundamentally at odds with a two-tier tax system.

A similar situation can arise where the debtor is a Subchapter S corporation. For example, in *In re Cumberland Farms, Inc.*,[47] a creditor of a 25 percent individual shareholder (H) in a debtor S corporation (S) sought to sell at public auction the individual's shares in S. The losses of S allocable to H had exceeded H's tax basis in its shares, resulting in a "suspended loss" to H under Code § 1366(d)(2). At issue was the continued survival of such losses, which S asserted benefited the bankruptcy estate by alleviating the need for any tax distributions in the event of future income.

---

[44] Although criticizing the Seventh Circuit's reasons for narrowly construing Bankruptcy Code section 362(a)(3), a Pennsylvania bankruptcy court has posited a "balancing of interests" test that takes into account the nexus between the conduct at issue and the property interest of the debtor, the degree of impact on the debtor, and the competing legal interests at issue. *See Allentown Ambassadors, Inc. v. Northeast Am. Baseball, LLC (In re Allentown Ambassadors, Inc.)*, 361 B.R. 422, 440 (Bankr. E.D. Pa. 2007). Although admittedly lacking in certainty, the court observed that a party can always seek clarification of the automatic stay's scope or ask the court to modify the stay, and a debtor can always seek a "non-automatic" stay under Bankruptcy Code section 105(a). Id. at 440 n.40.

[45] This was recently witnessed in the *Dana Corporation* bankruptcy case, *In re Dana Corp.*, Case No. 06-10354 (BRL) (Bankr. S.D. N.Y.) (filed in 2006). *See, e.g.*, Motion of American Real Estate Holdings Limited Partnership for Determination that the Automatic Stay Does Not Apply to Restrict Claims Trading or, in the Alternative, Relief from the Automatic Stay, dated April 17, 2006; and the bankruptcy court's earlier order, dated April 4, 2006, which required that the debtor provide to the creditors' committee prior to the court's next scheduled hearing on the debtor's claims trading motion a written report regarding whether the use of Code § 382(l)(5) was a "reasonable possibility." Pre-dating the *UAL* case, *see also* Morris, Imposition of Transfer Limitations on Claims and Equity Interests During Corporate Debtor's Chapter 11 Case to Preserve the Debtor's Net Operating Loss Carryforward: Examining the Emerging Trend, 77 Am. Bankr. L.J. 285 (2003) (questioning the bankruptcy court's authority to impose such restrictions).

[46] *See also* Pisem & Glicklich, Was Bankruptcy Court Lost at Sea? *Prudential Lines* Collides with the Internal Revenue Code, Tax Notes 1553 (September 17, 1990) (suggesting other ramifications); Sheppard, Preserving NOL Carryovers in Bankruptcy: The Progeny of *Prudential Lines*, 91 TNT 182-9 (August 30, 1991); Larson, The Bankruptcy Court Overlooks Tax Law in *In re Prudential Lines Inc.*: An NOL Should Not Be Property of a Bankruptcy Estate, 29 Willamette L. Rev. 23 (1993).

[47] 162 B.R. 62 (Bankr. D. Mass. 1993).

Although the creditor indicated its willingness to comply with existing transfer restrictions, such that the purchaser would be a qualified Subchapter S shareholder, under the tax law the sale would still result in the elimination of H's suspended losses. In response to the creditor's motion for clarification of the scope of the automatic stay, the bankruptcy court held that, although the suspended loss was personal to H, the benefit of the suspended loss was property of the estate and thus protected by the automatic stay (citing *Prudential Lines*). However, the bankruptcy court found adequate cause to grant relief from the automatic stay. In particular, the court observed that S and its other stockholders had (in the court's view) certain practical ways to protect themselves, and that in this case (unlike *Prudential Lines*) the party "competing" with the estate and its creditors was not the stockholder, but a creditor itself.[48]

Prior to *Cumberland Farms*, we queried whether the automatic stay would preclude individual shareholders of a closely held corporation from making, or terminating, a Subchapter S election (absent prior court approval). In both cases, the answer now appears to be yes.[49]

---

[48] The reverse fact pattern arose in *In re Forman Enterprises, Inc.* In that case, the debtor S corporation had generated income in prior years and made tax distributions to its shareholders and, in the year at issue, had generated a loss which the shareholders carried back to obtain a refund of the prior year taxes. The bankruptcy court considered whether the shareholders were required to turn their refunds over to the S corporation for the ultimate benefit of the creditors under a theory of unjust enrichment or constructive trusts, or as an avoidable postpetition transfer of the debtor's property (namely, the loss). Although initially denying the shareholders' motion to dismiss, the bankruptcy court ultimately held in favor of the shareholders on all grounds, and concluded under the circumstances that "the NOL and the [shareholders'] right to use it were not property of the debtor's bankruptcy estate." *The Official Comm. of Unsecured Creditors v. Forman (In re Forman Enterprises, Inc.)*, 273 B.R. 408, 2002-1 U.S.T.C. ¶50,338 (Bankr. W.D. Pa. 2002) (denying the shareholders' motion to dismiss), and 281 B.R. 600 (Bankr. W.D. Pa 2002), discussed further at §1006.2.2, below.

[49] *See, e.g., Hanrahan v. Walterman (In re Walterman Implement Inc.)*, 2006 Bankr. LEXIS 921 (Bankr. N.D. Iowa 2006) (a debtor's "right to use, benefit from, or revoke its subchapter S election falls within the broad definition of property of the estate;" revocation held to violate automatic stay), discussed at §1006.2.2 below; *cf. Guinn v. Lines, et al. (In re Trans-Lines West, Inc.)*, 203 B.R. 653, 97-1 U.S.T.C. ¶50,252 (Bankr. E.D. Tenn. 1996) (corporate debtor possessed a "property interest" in its Subchapter S status), discussed at §1006.1.3 below; *Parker v. Saunders (In re Bakersfield Westar, Inc.)*, 226 B.R. 227, 98-2 U.S.T.C. ¶50,843 (Bankr. 9th Cir. 1998) (same). Consider, however, *Hauptman v. Director of Internal Revenue*, 309 F.2d 62, 62-2 U.S.T.C. ¶9724 (2d Cir. 1962), *cert. denied*, 372 U.S. 909 (1963) (Bankruptcy Act case; upheld prebankruptcy Subchapter S election even though corporation's bankruptcy was imminent; purpose of statute was to give tax benefits to shareholders). Consistent with the above cases, and as discussed at §1003 below, the filing of an S corporation for bankruptcy does not terminate its status as an S corporation. *See, e.g., Mourad v. Commissioner*, 387 F.3d 27, 2004-2 U.S.T.C. ¶50,419 (1st Cir. 2004) (so holding; court expressly refrained from considering the implications of an attempted shareholder revocation of S status pre- or post-bankruptcy, but "recognize[d] the logic in appellant's contention that it is unfair to assess tax liability on shareholders who do not receive the income on which they are obliged to pay the tax").

Aside from the automatic stay, a shareholder's unilateral action that results in the termination of Subchapter S status may violate such shareholder's fiduciary duty under state law. For example, in *A.W. Chesterton Co., Inc. v. Chesterton*, 128 F.3d 1, 97-2 U.S.T.C. ¶50,809 (1st Cir. 1997), decided under Massachusetts state law, a *minority* shareholder in an S corporation was held to have breached his fiduciary duty to the S corporation *and* the other shareholders when he threatened to transfer (in preparation for a later sale) a portion of his shares to a nonqualifying Subchapter S shareholder. The shareholder was therefore enjoined by the court from engaging in the proposed transfer. It made no

On differing grounds, the courts generally have concluded that the IRS's revocation of the tax-exempt status of a debtor corporation under Code § 501(c)(3) does not violate the automatic stay. In *In re Heritage Village Church and Missionary Fellowship, Inc.*,[50] the Fourth Circuit reached this conclusion on the narrow grounds that the revocation was not in itself an "act to collect, assess, or recover a claim against" the debtor and thus was not within the scope of the automatic stay. Thus, the court held that, as relates to the revocation, there was no express provision in the Bankruptcy Code indicating congressional intent to supersede the Anti-Injunction Act in Code § 7421 (which prohibits suits in any court "for the purpose of restraining the assessment or collection of any tax"). In contrast, the district court in *In re Universal Life Church, Inc.*[51] held that the revocation at issue constituted the commencement or continuation of an administrative proceeding or other action against the debtor with respect to prepetition taxes, and thus would have violated the automatic stay but for an express exception permitting the commencement of an action to enforce a government's "police or regulatory power."[52] The court explained that such exception did not extend to actions that conflict directly with the control of property of the estate or simply further the government's pecuniary interest, but rather was meant to apply to violations of fraud, environmental protection, consumer protection, safety or similar police or regulatory laws. Viewing the IRS's regulation and review of tax-exempt organizations as akin to a type of fraud detection by assuring proper use of charitable monies, the court concluded (and the Ninth Circuit affirmed) that the revocation implements a police power in advancing the government's policies underlying the charitable purposes exemptions of the federal tax code. Notably, both the Fourth Circuit in *Heritage Village* and the district court in *Universal Life* concluded that the corporation's tax-exempt status was not a property right and thus was not in and of itself protected by the automatic stay.

Also under the exception for the enforcement of a government's regulatory and police power, the IRS was permitted to bring an action seeking to enjoin a debtor from promoting allegedly illegal tax schemes (which injunction was subsequently granted).[53]

---

(Footnote Continued)

difference that there were no transfer restrictions imposed by the corporate charter; instead, the relevant factors were the expectations and implicit understandings of the shareholders. In this regard, the court observed that it was the shareholders' expectations, in unanimously electing Subchapter S status, that no shareholder would take any action that would adversely affect the Subchapter S status.

[50] 851 F.2d 104, 88-2 U.S.T.C. ¶ 9476 (4th Cir. 1988).

[51] 191 B.R. 433 (E.D. Cal. 1995), *aff'd*, 128 F.3d 1294, 97-2 U.S.T.C. ¶ 50,764, *amended on reh'g*, 1997 U.S. App. LEXIS 36358 (9th Cir. 1997) (only issue on appeal to Ninth Circuit was the application of the "police power" exception to the automatic stay of collection actions), *cert. denied*, 118 S. Ct. 2367 (1998).

[52] *See* 11 U.S.C. § 362(b)(4).

[53] *United States v. Fisher*, 2004 U.S. Dist. LEXIS 277 (N.D. Tex. 2004) (IRS permitted to bring action), and 2004 U.S. Dist. LEXIS 2222 (N.D. Tex. 2004) (injunction granted).

### §1002.4.2 Expiration/Lifting of Stay

The automatic stay generally remains in effect until the bankruptcy case is either closed or dismissed or, in a case under Chapter 11, a discharge is granted or denied.[54] The stay may, however, on request of a party in interest and after notice and a hearing, be modified, vacated or even retroactively annulled (1) "for cause," including lack of adequate protection of the interest of the party objecting to the continuation of the stay, or (2) with respect to the stay of an act against specific property, if the debtor does not have any equity in the property and "the property is not necessary to an effective reorganization."[55] That the property is the debtor's only asset is insufficient to make it "necessary;" rather, it must be shown as well that an effective reorganization is in prospect.[56]

## *§1002.5 Filing Proofs of Claims*

To establish a claim against the debtor relating to a prepetition period, a creditor must file a "proof of claim" (and a stockholder must file a "proof of interest")[57] with the bankruptcy court.[58] A proof of claim will be deemed filed, however, if the claim

---

[54] 11 U.S.C. §362(c)(2); *see, e.g., Saunders v. United States (In re Saunders)*, 240 B.R. 636, 99-1 U.S.T.C. ¶50,445 (S.D. Fla. 1999), *rev'g*, 1996 Bankr. LEXIS 1928 (Bankr. S.D. Fla. 1996) (discussing when an order of discharge is considered granted—whether when orally granted by the judge or when entered on the docket; the district court favored the former, but not all courts agree). The general rule is potentially different as relates to the stay of any "act against property of the estate." However, in a case under Chapter 11, this difference will seldom, if ever, have any significance. In this regard, *compare* the effect of 11 U.S.C. §362(c)(1), which provides that, in respect of an act against property of the estate, the automatic stay remains in effect until all such property is gone; and 11 U.S.C. §1141(b), which provides that the confirmation of a Chapter 11 plan revests all property of the estate in the debtor, except to the extent the plan or confirmation order provides otherwise; *with* 11 U.S.C. §1141(d), which provides, with certain specified exceptions, that the confirmation of the plan discharges the debtor of its preconfirmation obligations.

[55] 11 U.S.C. §§362(d) (authority of bankruptcy court to lift stay; special provisions apply with respect to secured real property and in single asset real estate cases), 362(g) (party opposing relief has burden of proof on all issues other than debtor's equity in the property); *see also* discussion at §1007.6; *see also* 11 U.S.C. §361 (illustrations of "adequate protection").

[56] *See United Savings Assoc. of Texas v. Timbers of Inwood Forest Assocs., Ltd.*, 108 S. Ct. 626, 632 (1988).

[57] Although only proofs of claim will be discussed hereafter, a similar procedure applies to proofs of interest.

[58] 11 U.S.C. §501(a); *see also* Bankruptcy Rule 3001 (describing the form and other aspects of the proof of claim); *NLRB v. Bildisco & Bildisco*, 104 S. Ct. 1188, 1198 n.10 (1984). In certain cases, a creditor may be able to establish that other filings with the court (*e.g.*, pleadings or the like) constitute an informal proof of claim. *See, e.g.*, Bienenstock, Bankruptcy Reorganizations 632 (1987 with 1989 Supp.); *In re Harper*, 138 B.R. 229 (Bankr. N.D. Ind. 1991) (collecting cases); *see also In re International Horizons, Inc.*, 85-1 U.S.T.C. ¶9212 (11th Cir.), discussed *infra* at §1014.1.

A "claim" for this purpose means a right to payment or a right to an equitable remedy for breach of performance if such breach gives rise to a right to payment, whether or not such right is reduced to judgment, liquidated, unliquidated, fixed, contingent, matured, unmatured, disputed, undisputed, secured, or unsecured. 11 U.S.C. §101(5).

was identified in the schedule of liabilities filed by the debtor-in-possession with the court (except for claims listed as disputed, contingent, or unliquidated).[59]

Moreover, to expedite the filing of claims and aid in the formulation of a plan, the bankruptcy court will establish a "bar date" by which all proofs of claim must be filed.[60] Claims not filed by such date are generally barred.[61] For bankruptcy cases commenced on or after October 22, 1994, a governmental authority is guaranteed at least 180 days in which to file a claim.[62] A timely filed claim may be amended after the bar date as long as the amendment relates to the original claim (*i.e.*, does not constitute a new claim) and depending on the prejudice to the estate or reorganization.[63]

A timely filed claim is generally deemed allowed unless the debtor or a party-in-interest objects.[64] In general, if a party objects, and after notice and a hearing, the court will determine the validity and amount of the claim.[65] Moreover, the court is required to estimate contingent or unliquidated claims where not to do so would unduly delay the administration of the case.[66]

A similar "bar date" procedure may, but need not, be employed for administrative expense claims—that is, claims arising during the administration of the bankruptcy case—that are not otherwise paid in the ordinary course of business.[67] In such instance, any late filed claim will only be permitted for cause.[68]

For a more detailed discussion of the claims process as relates to the IRS, *see* § § 1010 and 1013 below.

---

[59] 11 U.S.C. § 1111(a); Bankruptcy Rule 3003(c)(2). In addition, if a creditor does not timely file a claim, the debtor-in-possession or a codebtor, surety, or guarantor may file a proof of claim on the creditor's behalf up to 30 days after the bar date. 11 U.S.C. § 501(b), (c); Bankruptcy Rules 3004, 3005. *See* discussion at § 1010.

[60] *See* Bankruptcy Rule 3003(c)(3) (may extend bar date "for cause").

[61] Bankruptcy Code section 502(b)(9), which was added by the Bankruptcy Reform Act of 1994, codifies this principle. A late-filed claim may be permitted if the creditor (1) received inadequate notice of the bar date or (2) can establish excusable neglect (which is an equitable determination, taking into account all relevant circumstances surrounding the creditor's omission and any negative impact that the claim would have on the administration of the case or the confirmation of the plan). *See, e.g., Pioneer Inv. Serv. Co. v. Brunswick Assocs. Ltd. Partnership*, 113 S. Ct. 1489 (1989); Miller & Tanenbaum, High Court Clarifies "Excusable Neglect," The Natl. L.J., May 24, 1993, at 18; Koger & True, The Final Word on Excusable Neglect? 98 Comm. L.J. 21 (1993); Bienenstock, *supra* note 58, at 632; 8 Collier on Bankruptcy ¶ 3003.05[5] (15th ed.); *In re Hudson Oil Co.*, 100 B.R. 72 (Bankr. D. Kan. 1989) (granting leave to file a late claim for environmental clean-up costs).

[62] 11 U.S.C. § 502(b)(9).

[63] *See* discussion at § 1010.2; *see also* Bienenstock, *supra* note 58, at 633 (supplement).

[64] *See* 11 U.S.C. § 502.

[65] *See, e.g.*, 11 U.S.C. § 502(b).

[66] 11 U.S.C. § 502(c). *See* discussion at § 1010.1.

[67] *See* 11 U.S.C. § § 503(b), 1108; *see also* 11 U.S.C. § 549 (postpetition payments not authorized by the Bankruptcy Code require court approval).

[68] 11 U.S.C. § 503(a) (effective for cases commenced on or after October 22, 1994).

## *§1002.6 Filing the Chapter 11 Plan*

Where a trustee has not been appointed, the debtor has an "exclusive period" (generally 120 days) for filing a Chapter 11 plan.[69] The exclusive period is frequently extended by the bankruptcy court but also may be reduced.[70] If a debtor has filed a plan within the requisite period, no other party in interest may file a plan thereafter, provided the debtor's plan is accepted within the statutorily prescribed period (generally 60 days after filing, subject to extension by the bankruptcy court).[71]

In the case of a debtor that elects to be considered a "small business,"[72] the debtor's exclusive period for filing a plan generally is limited to 100 days, and all plans must be filed within 160 days (which periods may be shortened by the bankruptcy court for cause).[73]

## *§1002.7 Contents of the Chapter 11 Plan and Disclosure Statement*

The Chapter 11 plan usually will provide the treatment to be received by each class of creditors and stockholders. It will specify the terms of debt or stock cancellation, the debt or stock modification, and the issuance of stock, cash, or other property for the debt or stock of the debtor company.[74] The plan must also provide adequate means to implement any reorganization of the debtor.[75] Because the Bankruptcy Code does not define what the effective date of a Chapter 11 plan is, the plan itself should state the effective date as of which the distributions contemplated by the plan are deemed to commence.[76]

---

[69] 11 U.S.C. §1121(b).

[70] *See* 11 U.S.C. §1121(d) (bankruptcy court authority to extend or reduce 120-day period for cause on request for party in interest following notice and a hearing; exclusivity period cannot be extended beyond 18 months after the petition date or, in involuntary cases, the order for relief, for bankruptcy cases commenced on or after October 17, 2005).

[71] Id.; 11 U.S.C. §1121(c) (for bankruptcy cases filed on or after October 17, 2005, statutory period cannot extend beyond 20 months after the petition date or, in involuntary cases, the order for relief).

[72] *See* 11 U.S.C. §101(51C) (generally covers companies with noncontingent liquidated debts of less than $2 million, excluding real estate companies, and no committee of unsecured creditors is appointed).

[73] 11 U.S.C. §1121(e).

[74] *See* 11 U.S.C. §§1122, 1123. For a description of supplemental provisions that the IRS might seek to have included in the plan, and for a list of provisions that the IRS should ensure are contained in the plan, *see* IRS Manual, Part 5 (Collecting Process), Ch. 9 (Bankruptcy), §8.14.2 (3/1/07), at ¶3.

[75] *See* 11 U.S.C. §1123(a)(5).

[76] *See supra* text accompanying note 2 at §510 (cautioning that the Chapter 11 plan be drafted so that the effective date of the plan and the date at which the claims against the debtor are discharged are the same). Under Bankruptcy Code section 1141(d), the confirmation of the plan by the bankruptcy court generally discharges all claims, unless either (i) the plan or order confirming the plan provides otherwise or (ii) the plan provides for the liquidation of all or substantially all of the debtor's property and the debtor does not engage in business after the consummation of the plan. However, for bankruptcy cases commenced on or after October 17, 2005, such section excludes from discharge, in the case of a corporate debtor, (i) any tax or customs duty with respect to which the debtor either made a fraudulent return or willfully attempted in any manner to evade or defeat the

In addition, the accompanying disclosure statement must contain "adequate information," meaning that it must contain information that would permit a reasonable creditor or equity holder to make an informed judgment on the plan.[77] Accordingly, the disclosure statement should include an analysis of the probable tax consequences of the plan, even if simply to state that there are none.[78] Moreover, effective for bankruptcy cases filed on or after October 17, 2005, the Bankruptcy Code expressly requires "a discussion of the potential material Federal tax consequences of the plan to the debtor, any successor to the debtor, and a hypothetical investor typical of the holders of claims or interests in the case."[79] In an extreme case, the plan proponent in the *Holywell* case,[80] which involved the transfer of assets to a liquidating trust (*see* § 902.1), was held liable for negligent misrepresentation where it failed to investigate the tax consequences of the plan (including who would be liable for the payment of current and postconfirmation taxes on asset sales), the plan did not make provision for the payment of taxes, and the disclosure statement failed to include an analysis of the tax consequences of the plan.

## *§1002.8 Approval and Confirmation of the Chapter 11 Plan*

The Chapter 11 plan, once filed, will be submitted, together with a court-approved disclosure statement,[81] for a vote of the impaired classes of creditors and stockholders.[82] Only a percentage of each such class of creditors and stockholders need generally accept the plan for the plan to be binding on the entire class.[83]

---

(Footnote Continued)

tax or duty, and (ii) certain commercial agreements and obligations obtained in a false or fraudulent manner. *See* 11 U.S.C. § 1146(d)(6), *added by* P.L. 109-8, § 708 (2005).

[77] *See* 11 U.S.C. § 1125(a)(1), (b).

[78] *See, e.g., In re Malek*, 35 B.R. 443 (Bankr. E.D. Mich. 1983); *In re Metrocraft Pub. Services, Inc.*, 39 B.R. 567 (Bankr. N.D. Ga. 1984) (should discuss, at least briefly, the effect of the plan on the future availability of the company's tax attributes, so that the creditors may evaluate the actual after-tax position of the debtor); *cf. In re The Leslie Fay Companies, Inc.*, 207 B.R. 764, 775-781 (Bankr. S.D.N.Y. 1997) (tax disclosure cited as a factor in establishing feasibility; also assisted in establishing reasonableness of tax planning in the presence of a last-minute objection to confirmation).

[79] 11 U.S.C. § 1125(a)(1), *as amended by* P.L. 109-8, § 717 (2005).

[80] *Smith v. The Bank of New York*, 161 B.R. 302 (Bankr. S.D. Fla. 1993).

[81] In a "small business" case, the debtor may solicit votes based on a conditionally approved disclosure statement, so long as it provides adequate information to each creditor and stockholder solicited (and may even dispense with a disclosure statement if the court determines that the plan itself provides adequate information). A final hearing on the disclosure statement may then be combined with the confirmation hearing on the plan. 11 U.S.C. § 1125(f).

[82] 11 U.S.C. §§ 1125, 1126; *see Phoenix Mutual Life Ins. Co. v. Greystone III Joint Venture (In re Greystone III Joint Venture)*, 995 F.2d. 1274 (5th Cir. 1991), *cert. denied*, 113 S. Ct. 72 (1992) (substantially similar interests may not be divided into separate classes in order to manipulate vote); *Boston Post Road Ltd. Partnership v. FDIC (In re Boston Post Road Ltd. Partnership)*, 21 F.3d 477 (2d Cir. 1994), *cert. denied*, 115 S. Ct. 897 (1995) (same).

[83] *See* 11 U.S.C. § 1126(c) (as to creditors, acceptance requires at least two-thirds in amount and more than one-half in number of the allowed claims of the class that are voted); 11 U.S.C. § 1126(d) (as to stockholders, acceptance requires at least two-thirds in amount of the allowed interests of the class that are voted).

If any class rejects (or is deemed to reject) the plan, such class may, nevertheless, be "crammed down." That is, it may be forced to accept the plan, if the bankruptcy court, at the request of the proponent of the plan, determines that such class has been treated fairly and in an equitable manner and that the plan does not discriminate unfairly against such class.[84] In general, this means that such class would at least receive what it would have received in a straight liquidation, that no other class of similar claims receives disproportionate treatment, and that no junior class receives anything unless the dissident class is paid in full.

### § 1002.8.1 Tax Avoidance Purpose May Impede Confirmation

As a condition to confirmation, the Chapter 11 plan must be proposed in good faith.[85] In one case, the "good faith" requirement was invoked as the basis for rejecting a plan that would have preserved the corporate shell of the debtor with no assets but with an NOL.[86]

Moreover, if the principal purpose of the Chapter 11 plan is the avoidance of taxes, the bankruptcy court *sua sponte*, or at the request of any governmental tax entity, may not confirm the plan.[87] Once confirmed, tax avoidance is not grounds for revoking the plan.[88] In fact, one bankruptcy court has stated that implied in every confirmation order is a finding that the principal purpose of the plan is not tax avoidance: Otherwise, the plan would not be proposed in good faith and could not be

---

[84] 11 U.S.C. § 1129(b).

[85] 11 U.S.C. § 1129(a)(3).

[86] *See In re Maxim Indus., Inc.*, 22 B.R. 611 (Bankr. D. Mass. 1982). The bankruptcy court relied on the underlying policy of the Bankruptcy Code (as best exemplified by the "no discharge" rule of Chapter 7) against trafficking in corporate shells and bankrupt partnerships. Id. at 613; H. Rep. No. 595, 95th Cong., 1st Sess. 384-385 (1987); S. Rep. No. 989, 95th Cong., 2d Sess. 98-99 (1978). Also note that the bankruptcy court had insisted that a copy of the plan and disclosure statement be served on the IRS, even though the IRS was not a creditor. *See also* Bacon, *et al.* Tax Planning for the Financially Troubled Company: A Panel Discussion, 36 Major Tax Plan. 14-1, 14-61 (1984) (remarks of Kenneth N. Klee) (hereafter Bacon, Panel Discussion).

[87] 11 U.S.C. §§ 1129(d) (in any hearing, the burden of proof is on the governmental unit), 101(27) ("governmental unit" defined). The ability of the bankruptcy court to raise the issue of tax avoidance *sua sponte*—despite the literal language of the statute, which states that the request must be made by a governmental unit—is grounded in the court's broad equitable powers under Bankruptcy Code section 105(a). *See* § 1013.5; *see also In re The Rath Packing Co.* (Bankr. N.D. Iowa), discussed *infra* this section; *Allis-Chalmers Corp. v. Goldberg (In re Hartman Material Handling Systems, Inc.)*, 141 B.R. 802, at n.10, 92-2 U.S.T.C. ¶ 50,325 (Bankr. S.D.N.Y. 1992).

[88] *See In re McLean Indus., Inc.*, 132 B.R. 267, 91-2 U.S.T.C. ¶ 50,465 (Bankr. S.D.N.Y. 1991). In the *McLean Industries* case, the debtors and the unsecured creditors' committee sought a postconfirmation determination, pursuant to Bankruptcy Code section 105(a), that the principal purpose of the plan was not tax avoidance and that the NOLs vested as property of the reorganized debtor upon confirmation. The court denied the motion, viewing it as a postconfirmation request for a determination under Bankruptcy Code section 1129(d), to which the moving parties were not entitled. The court did not consider the motion as asking for a determination of tax liability, which would have required a determination under Code § 269. Nevertheless, the court commented on whether the debtors would have been entitled to such a determination; *see* discussion at § 1013.3.1.

confirmed.[89] However, this does not necessarily preclude the IRS from subsequently attacking the debtor's use of its NOLs and other tax benefits postconfirmation under Code § 269.[90]

In *In re The Rath Packing Company*, the bankruptcy court considered whether tax avoidance was the principal purpose for the proposed Chapter 11 plan.[91] The plan called for substantially all the assets of the debtor to be distributed to creditors, leaving the reorganized debtor as little more than a corporate shell. The common stock of the reorganized debtor was to be owned 52 percent by existing shareholders, 17 percent by the creditors and 31 percent by an investor group that would purchase its stock for cash. The bankruptcy court found that, although a primary reason for preserving the corporate shell was to exploit the NOLs of the debtor by purchasing profitable corporations and sheltering their income, the publicly held status of the debtor was equally important; accordingly, the court held that the "principal" (*i.e.*, most important) purpose of the plan was not tax avoidance. To illustrate the principal purpose test, the court looked to Code § 269 and the example in Reg. § 1.269-3(b)(1) (involving the transfer to a loss corporation of a profitable business).[92]

It is interesting to note that the court in *Rath Packing* had itself raised the tax avoidance issue (although the IRS had orally suggested the issue at an earlier plan modification hearing), stating that it was "not going to allow the IRS to . . . bring an action in tax court several years from now." Thus, the court apparently believed that its determination for plan confirmation purposes also resolved the issue of tax avoidance under Code § 269.

An example of a bankruptcy court denying confirmation on tax avoidance grounds (at the behest of the IRS) is *In re Scott Cable Communications, Inc.*[93] The debtor in that case proposed a prepackaged liquidating Chapter 11 plan that contemplated the sale of substantially all of its assets pursuant to a sale agreement previously approved by the bankruptcy court but expressly conditioned to occur only after confirmation of the plan. It was the debtor's position that, by the sale occurring after the confirmation date, the tax that would be incurred upon the sale would not be an administrative expense of the bankruptcy case and thus would only be entitled to payment after all distributions under the plan (which distributions were ostensibly to previously secured claims). Although the bankruptcy court disagreed with the debtor's position and held that the tax would, under the circumstances, nevertheless be considered an administrative expense (which in itself made the plan nonconfirmable due to its failure to provide full payment for all administrative claims), the court went on to find that the principal purpose of the Chapter 11 plan was tax avoidance.

---

[89] *Allis-Chalmers Corp. v. Goldberg* (*In re Hartman Material Handling Systems, Inc.*), *supra* note 87.

[90] *See* Reg. § 1.269-3(e), discussed in § 509.1. *See also* the McLean Industries case, *supra* note 88, discussed at § 1013.3.1.

[91] 55 B.R. 528 (Bankr. N.D. Iowa 1985).

[92] *See also* Bacon, Panel Discussion, *supra* note 86, at 14-61.

[93] 227 B.R. 596 (Bankr. D. Conn. 1998) ("Memorandum and Order on Objection to Confirmation"); *see also* court pleadings: "United States of America's Objection to Confirmation of Debtor's Plan of Reorganization," dated November 16, 1998, and Debtor's Response thereto, dated November 18, 1998.

In this regard, the court cited certain declarations by the debtor in its disclosure statement that the principal purpose of the plan was to structure a plan acceptable to the junior noteholders and that payment of the tax would eliminate any recovery to the junior noteholders.

In the *Allis-Chalmers* case,[94] the court considered the *res judicata* and collateral estoppel effect for Code § 269 purposes of a determination by the court, for plan confirmation purposes, that the principal purpose of the Chapter 11 plan was not tax avoidance. The case involved a creditor takeover pursuant to a confirmed Chapter 11 plan. At issue was the future availability of the debtor's tax losses and the validity of the Code § 269 regulation that states that such a determination is not controlling for Code § 269 purposes.[95] Commenting on the regulation, the bankruptcy court stated that it was "at a loss to decipher how the power to promulgate regulations gives the IRS the authority to determine the effect of an order of a court" and concluded that the regulations are nothing more than the IRS's position on how the applicable statutes should be interpreted. On the more substantive issue, the court held that *res judicata* did not apply (since only the future use of the tax losses were at issue) and that a confirmation ruling on tax avoidance cannot collaterally estop the IRS from making a subsequent Code § 269 challenge "to attempts to use the NOLs *after* transactions not specifically contemplated in [the debtor's] plan of reorganization."[96] The court observed that the issue of tax avoidance under Code § 269 necessarily involved the examination of all facts and circumstances leading up to *and following* the acquisition of control, and that the bankruptcy court in making its ruling as to confirmation does not have the opportunity to examine the totality of events with respect to the use of NOLs that have not been claimed as deductions (*i.e.*, used to offset income) at the time of confirmation.

It should be noted that the reorganized debtor in the *Allis-Chalmers* case was to be used as an acquisition vehicle.[97] One wonders what the court would have done if the debtor had had an ongoing business against which its NOLs were projected to be used. This question as well as similar ones are discussed at § 1013.3, below. Moreover, although the bankruptcy court did not affirmatively hold that the IRS was barred from raising a Code § 269 challenge to a debtor's use of its NOLs to offset income from transactions specifically contemplated in the Chapter 11 plan, its holding clearly creates that implication. The legislative history to Bankruptcy Code section 1129(d) similarly indicates that the IRS should be barred in such circumstances, even where the bankruptcy court does not expressly rule on the purpose of the plan.[98] Most telling is the fact that Congress specifically rejected a Senate proposal that would have provided that, if the taxing authority did not request the bankruptcy court to

---

[94] *Allis-Chalmers Corp. v. Goldberg (In re Hartman Material Handling Systems, Inc.), supra* note 87. *See also* discussion at § 509.1.

[95] *See* Reg. § 1.269-3(e), discussed at § 509.1.

[96] 141 B.R. at 812 (emphasis added).

[97] *See* Jacobs, The Bankruptcy Court's Emergence as Tax Dispute Arbiter of Choice, 45 Tax Law. 971, 1008 (1992).

[98] 123 Cong. Rec. H 11,115 (daily ed. September 28, 1978) (statement of Rep. Edwards), S 17,432 (daily ed. October 6, 1978) (1statement of Sen. DeConcini).

rule on the purpose of the plan, the taxing authority would not be barred from later asserting tax avoidance motives with respect to the debtor's postconfirmation use of its tax benefits. Rather, legislative statements made at the time of enactment state that the Bankruptcy Code does "not provide a basis by which a tax authority may collaterally attack confirmation of a plan of reorganization other than under section 1144 [which applies in the case of fraud, *see* § 1002.9]."[99]

## *§1002.9 Finality of Plan; Reopening the Bankruptcy Case*

The order confirming the Chapter 11 plan becomes final ten days after the date the bankruptcy court enters the order, provided no appeal of the order is made within such period.[100] The debtor (or the proponent of a plan) may modify the plan even after confirmation so long as the plan has not been "substantially consummated."[101]

Even after the confirmation order becomes nonappealable, a discharge granted to a debtor can be revoked and the case reopened if a party in interest within 180 days of the confirmation order demonstrates that the order was procured by fraud.[102] In addition, upon the happening of certain events—such as a material default by the debtor under the confirmed plan—the bankruptcy court may, even after confirmation, convert the case to Chapter 7 or dismiss the case (although such a dismissal may not necessarily return the parties to their pre-bankruptcy positions, *see* § 1014.1).[103] Other remedies may also be available in the event the debtor defaults on its plan obligations (such as state court actions, enforcement of liens, commencement of a second bankruptcy, etc.).[104]

---

[99] Id.

[100] *See* Bankruptcy Rules 3020(e) and 8002.

[101] 11 U.S.C. § 1127(b). "Substantial consummation" occurs when any one of the following three events take place: (1) all or substantially all of the property proposed by the plan to be transferred is actually transferred; (2) the debtor or its successor assumes the business or management of all or substantially all of the property dealt with by the plan; or (3) the commencement of distributions under the plan. 11 U.S.C. § 1101(2).

[102] *See* 11 U.S.C. § 1144; *see, e.g., Tenn-Fla Partners v. First Union Nat'l Bank of Fla. (In re Tenn-Fla Partners)*, 226 F.3d 746 (6th Cir. 2000); *In re Hertz*, 38 B.R. 215 (Bankr. S.D.N.Y. 1984).

[103] *See* 11 U.S.C. §§ 1112(b) (lists grounds; changes made in 2005 generally require dismissal or conversion if any of the listed grounds exist, "absent unusual circumstances"), 348 (effect of conversion), and 349 (effect of dismissal), discussed further at § 1014.1 below; *see also In re Compco Corp.*, 1990 Bankr. LEXIS 38 (Bankr. N.D. Ill. 1990) (plan need not provide for retention of bankruptcy court jurisdiction); *State of Ohio v. H.R.P. Auto Center, Inc. (In re H.R.P. Auto Center, Inc.)*, 130 B.R. 247 (Bankr. N.D. Ohio 1991) (considered relative merits of conversion v. dismissal); *Florida Peach Corp. v. Commissioner*, 90 T.C. 678, Dec. 44,689 (1988) (bankruptcy court tax determination binding even though Chapter 11 case subsequently dismissed; judgment was not vacated by Bankruptcy Code section 349(b) as Bankruptcy Code section 505(a) is not one of the enumerated provisions to which such section applies).

[104] *See, e.g.*, Ahart and Meadows, Deferring Discharge in Chapter 11, 70 Am. Bankr. L.J. 127, 131-140 (1996); IRS Chief Counsel Advice 200016017, February 23, 2000 (Issue and Answer #3), *reprinted at* 2000 TNT 79-35.

Although recognizing that the law is unclear, the IRS has taken the position that, once the debtor has "substantially defaulted" on its payments under a Chapter 11 plan, all tax payments under the plan, including any deferred payments with respect to priority tax claims (*see* § 1016.1 below), become immediately collectible and that the IRS can employ its full administrative collection authority.[105] In this regard, the IRS has cautioned that the debtor generally should not be considered to be in substantial default unless (i) the debtor has missed a series of plan payments and has ceased making any payments under the plan,[106] and (ii) the IRS has sent the debtor notice giving the debtor a brief period to cure (such as 15 to 30 days) and the debtor has failed to do so.[107] Where the debtor has only missed some payments and is still actively making some payments under the plan, the IRS Chief Counsel has stated that the IRS should limit any administrative collection to the plan payments then due.[108] To avoid unnecessary litigation, the IRS Manual recommends that the IRS, during negotiations of the Chapter 11 plan, obtain a default provision that is consistent with this position and makes clear that the IRS is able to use its normal administrative collection authority.[109]

The bankruptcy court also may reopen a Chapter 11 case, upon motion by a party in interest, "to administer assets, to accord relief to the debtor, or for other cause."[110] This rule cannot be used to circumvent the 180-day period in which a request must be filed to revoke confirmation on grounds that the order was procured

---

105 *See, e.g.*, IRS Chief Counsel Advice 200146058, November 16, 2001, *reprinted at* 2001 TNT 223-68; IRS Chief Counsel Advice 200022010, February 22, 2000, *reprinted at* 2000 TNT 108-66; IRS Chief Counsel Advice 200016017, February 23, 2000, *reprinted at* 2000 TNT 79-35. *But consider In re Decker's General Contracting, Inc.* (Bankr. D. N.J. August 28, 2000), No. 97-15083 (JHW) (consent order) (court increased rate of repayment to IRS but did not require immediate repayment in full where debtor missed several successive payments to the IRS; court indicated that any subsequent failure would result in the reopening and conversion of the case to Chapter 7). *See also* § 1008 at note 3, below (discussing tolling of statute of limitations on collection).

106 *See* IRS Chief Counsel Advice 200146058, *supra* note 105.

107 *See* IRS Chief Counsel Advice 200022010, *supra* note 105; IRS Chief Counsel Advice 200016017, *supra* note 105.

108 *See* IRS Chief Counsel Advice 200146058, *supra* note 105.

109 IRS Manual, Part 5 (Collecting Process), Ch. 9 (Bankruptcy), § 8.14.2 (3/1/07), at ¶ 3(L) and (M).

110 11 U.S.C. § 350(b). *See* Fed. R. Civ. P. 60; Bankruptcy Rule 9024 (waiving one-year limitation of Rule 60(b)); *Dearing v. United States (In re Catt)*, 96-2 U.S.T.C. ¶ 50,422 (1996) (reformation of plan more than three years after confirmation to correct for a clerical error was not an abuse of discretion); *City of White Plains, N.Y. v. A & S Galleria Real Estate, Inc. (In re A & S Galleria Real Estate, Inc.)*, 1998 Bankr. LEXIS 101 (Bankr. S.D. Ohio 1998) (reopened case to determine existence of tax lien with respect to prepetition taxes and the allowance of other taxes as administrative expenses); *Mass. Dept. of Rev. v. Crocker (In re Crocker)*, 362 B.R. 49 (Bankr. 1st Cir. 2007) (upheld the reopening of a bankruptcy case to determine the dischargeability of taxes owed to the Massachusetts Dept. of Revenue and the IRS, in part based on the fact that it involved multiple taxing authorities and thus was more efficiently handled by the bankruptcy court). A bankruptcy case that was dismissed prior to full administration cannot be reopened under Bankruptcy Code section 350(b), but in "extraordinary circumstances" or situations of "extreme and undue hardship," may be able to be reopened for limited purposes under Bankruptcy Rule 9024, which incorporates Fed. R. Civ. P. 60. *See Phoenix Bond & Indemnity Co. v. MCM Enter., Inc.*, 319 B.R. 157 (S.D. Ind. 2005).

by fraud.[111] In addition, laches may constitute a bar to an action that has been delayed too long.[112]

Regardless of whether the bankruptcy court reopens the Chapter 11 case, the bankruptcy court generally can still determine if a particular debt was discharged in the case.[113]

## §1003 BANKRUPT CORPORATION AS TAXABLE ENTITY

For bankruptcy law purposes, the filing of a bankruptcy petition creates a separate "estate" in bankruptcy.[1] When the debtor is a corporation, however, this separate estate has no tax significance. No new or separate taxable entity is created.[2] The debtor corporation continues unchanged as the taxable entity. This is true even if a trustee in bankruptcy is appointed. The filing of the petition does not, for example, affect the corporation's taxable year,[3] its ability to be included in a consolidated federal income tax return,[4] or its status as a Subchapter S corporation,[5] or, in the case of a limited liability company, the tax status of such company.[6] For examples of where debtors have obtained, or sought to obtain, equitable relief from the bankruptcy court in order to preserve or sever a preexisting consolidated group, *see* discussion at §804.1.

However, a corporation in bankruptcy is excluded from the personal holding company tax, unless a major purpose of instituting or continuing the bankruptcy is to

---

[111] Bankruptcy Rule 9024; *see BFP Investments, Inc. v. BFP Investments Limited,* 2005 U.S. App. LEXIS 22243 (11th Cir. 2005) (unpublished decision). *Cf. IRS v. Kostoglou (In re Kostoglou),* 1993 U.S. Dist. LEXIS 11697 (N.D. Ohio).

[112] H. Rep. No. 595, 95th Cong., 1st Sess. 338 (1977); S. Rep. No. 989, 95th Cong., 2d Sess. 49 (1978); *see also In re Rundle,* 1991 Bankr. LEXIS 1875 (Bankr. N.D. Ill. December 13, 1991); *United States v. Ashe,* 228 B.R. 457, 98-2 U.S.T.C. ¶50,675 (C.D. Cal. 1998).

[113] *See, e.g., Menk v. Lapaglia (In re Menk),* 241 B.R. 896, 910 (Bankr. 9th Cir. 1999); *In re Chester E. Ehrig,* Order Denying Motion to Dismiss, Adv. No. 03-0142-R (Chapter 7), Bankr. N.D. Okla. (Sept. 12, 2003), *reprinted at* 2004 TNT 10-19.

[1] **§1003** *See* 11 U.S.C. §541 (describing property included in the estate).

[2] Code §1399; *Callahan v. UMWA 1992 Plan (In re Callahan),* 304 B.R. 743 (W.D. Va. 2003) (so holding; rejected any distinction between Chapter 7 and Chapter 11, and held that such treatment was also applicable to premiums under the Coal Industry Retiree Health Benefits Act, which had been held under earlier case law to constitute "taxes"). This is also true for state and local income tax purposes. 11 U.S.C. §346(b), *as amended by* P.L. 109-8, §719 (2005); and former 11 U.S.C. §346(c).

[3] *See* Rev. Rul. 69-600, 1969-2 C.B. 241; Reg. §1.6012-2(a)(2); *see also* Mrs. Grant Smith, 26 B.T.A. 1178, Dec. 7768 (1932), *nonacq.* (Chapter VII liquidation).

[4] Rev. Rul. 63-104, 1963-1 C.B. 172, *declared obsolete,* CC-2003-005 January 16, 2003. *See* Reg. §1.1502-75(h)(3). *See also* discussion at §804.1; and GCM 12207, XII-2 C.B. 83 (1933).

[5] *See Mourad v. Commissioner,* 121 T.C. 1 (2003), *aff'd,* 387 F.3d 27, 2004-2 U.S.T.C. ¶50,419 (1st Cir. 2004) (Chapter 11 case; even though bankruptcy trustee appointed); *In re Stadler Assoc., Inc.,* 186 B.R. 762, 95-2 U.S.T.C. ¶50,589 (Bankr. S.D. Fla. 1995) (appointment of Chapter 7 trustee does not terminate debtor corporation's Subchapter S status). *See also Williams v. Commissioner,* 123 T.C. No. 8 (2004) (bankruptcy filing of individual shareholder does not create a short year or interim allocation with respect to S corporation losses).

[6] *Gilliam v. Speier (In re KRSM Properties LLC),* 318 B.R. 712 (Bankr. 9th Cir. 2004).

avoid the tax.[7] Absent such exclusion, a debtor corporation might otherwise find itself incurring a personal holding company tax due to its inability to make distributions to its stockholders while in bankruptcy. Unfortunately, there is no provision exempting a REIT in bankruptcy from the annual distribution requirements of Code § 857(a)(1). Thus, a REIT that is unable to make the requisite distributions in any given taxable year due to the restrictions of bankruptcy may lose the benefits of REIT status for such year.

From a procedural perspective, a corporation filing for bankruptcy will lose its status as the "tax matters partner" with respect to any partnerships for which it held such role.[8] However, one member of a consolidated group filing for bankruptcy will not cause a non-filing member of the group to lose its status as the tax matters partner of any partnership in which the non-filing member owns a direct interest.[9]

## § 1004 NOTICES TO IRS

Upon the commencement of the bankruptcy case or, in an involuntary bankruptcy, upon the bankruptcy court's formal approval of the petition (called an "order for relief"), notice will automatically be transmitted to the IRS by the clerk of the bankruptcy court (or any other person as the court may direct).[1] In addition, whether or not the IRS is scheduled as a creditor, the IRS will automatically receive separate notice of the first meeting of creditors, the bar date for filing proofs of claims, and the hearings on (and the time fixed for filing objections to) the disclosure statement and

---

[7] Code § 542(c)(9). This section similarly applies to any corporation in a receivership, foreclosure or similar proceeding in a federal or state court. Id.; Code § 368(a)(3)(A).

[8] *See* Reg. § 301.6231(a)(7)-1(l)(iv) (designation as tax matters partner terminates upon the "partnership items" of the tax matters partner becoming "nonpartnership items"); Temp. Reg. § 301.6231(c)-7T (upon a partner becoming a debtor in bankruptcy, or the appointment of a receiver for the partner, all partnership items of the partner for which the IRS could make a claim in the bankruptcy or receivership proceeding are treated as "nonpartnership items"); *Computer Programs Lambda, Ltd. v. Commissioner*, 89 T.C. 198 (1987).

[9] *See, e.g.*, IRS Field Service Advice 200203007, September 28, 2001, *reprinted at* 2002 TNT 14-93; IRS Field Service Advice 200122023, February 23, 2001, *reprinted at* 2001 TNT 107-20. The filing of the partner member, however, will convert all "partnership items" of a non-partner member (*i.e.*, the partnership items that are taken into account in determining the group's consolidated taxable income and thus the several tax liability of the non-partner member) into "nonpartnership items" and, thus, preclude such persons from being considered a "partner" under Code § 6231(a)(2)(B) for purposes of the administrative partnership procedures in Code §§ 6221 *et seq. But consider Katz v. Commissioner*, 2003 U.S. App. LEXIS 13584 (10th Cir. 2003) (2:1 decision; held that the resolution of a loss allocation issue required a partnership level proceeding because the *process* of allocating losses among partners is not itself an "item" and thus cannot become a "nonpartnership item" upon the filing of the partner for bankruptcy).

[1] **§ 1004** Bankruptcy Rules 2002(f)(1) and (j)(3) in conjunction with 11 U.S.C. §§ 301 and 303(h); *see also* Reg. § 301.6036-1(a)(1), as amended by T.D. 8172, 1998-1 C.B. 383 (no separate notice required to be filed alerting IRS to appointment or authorization to act of a bankruptcy trustee, debtor-in-possession or other like fiduciary in a bankruptcy case). In a receivership or other nonbankruptcy proceeding where all or substantially all of the debtor's assets are subject to the proceeding, the receiver or similar fiduciary is required to notify the IRS in writing within ten days of his appointment or authorization to act. *See* Reg. § 301.6036-1(a)(2).

confirmation of the plan, and any other notices required to be provided to all creditors pursuant to Bankruptcy Rule 2002.[2] Such notices will be sent to the District Director of the IRS for the district in which the case is pending.[3] Local court rules may provide for additional notices.[4]

In contrast, where the IRS is served in connection with an adversary proceeding, a copy of the summons and complaint must also be served on the civil process clerk at the office of the U.S. Attorney for the district in which the action is brought *and* the Attorney General of the United States at Washington, D.C.[5] An adversary proceeding includes, among other things, a proceeding to recover money or property (such as a preference action); to determine the debtor's tax liability or the validity, priority, or extent of a tax lien; to obtain an injunction or other equitable relief; or to obtain a declaratory judgment relating to any of the foregoing.[6] A proceeding being initiated against the IRS should be careful to name the "United States" as a defendant, since federal agencies generally cannot be sued in their own name.[7]

A matter of general confusion has been whether an objection to an IRS proof of claim may be served only on the IRS (the claimant) or must comply with the service of process rules for an adversary proceeding.[8] Bankruptcy Rule 3007 provides that a

---

[2] Bankruptcy Rules 2002(a), (b), (f), and (j)(3). All notices to creditors are required to contain the name, address, and taxpayer identification number of the debtor; however, the absence of such information does not invalidate the effect of the notice. 11 U.S.C. §342(c) (effective for bankruptcy cases commenced on or after October 22, 1994).

[3] Bankruptcy Rule 2002(j)(3) (for Chapter 11 cases). In a Chapter 7 case, no specific department or office of the IRS is specified. *See, e.g., Roeder v. IRS (In re Benny's Leasing, Inc.)*, 166 B.R. 823 (Bankr. W.D. Pa. 1993) (notice of bar date sent to IRS Service Center held sufficient), *aff'd*, 187 B.R. 484 (W.D. Pa. 1995), *recons. denied*, 189 B.R. 350 (W.D. Pa. 1995). *See* Bankruptcy Rule 9036 (permits electronic transmission of any notice, upon written request and court approval); IRS Legal Memorandum 200212031, January 12, 1999, *reprinted at* 2002 TNT 57-56 (approving an "Electronic Bankruptcy Noticing Trading Partner Agreement" between the Bankruptcy Court for the District of South Carolina and the IRS).

[4] *See, e.g., In re Griffin Oil Co.*, 149 B.R. 419 (Bankr. E.D. Tex. 1992) (involving the Beaumont division of the Eastern District of Texas); *In re Vaughn*, 151 B.R. 87 (Bankr. W.D. Tex. 1993) (involving the Western District of Texas); *In re Gold*, Case No. 892-81381-288 (Bankr. E.D. NY 11/15/2001), *reprinted at* 2002 TNT 4-9 (memorandum and order; involving the Eastern District of New York).

[5] Bankruptcy Rule 7004(b)(4) (governing service by first class mail); *In re Warren* (Bankr. N.D. Tex., July 25, 1991), *reprinted at* 91 TNT 179-27 (debtor's motion to adjudicate his tax liability dismissed for failure to serve the Attorney General of the United States in Washington, D.C.).

[6] Bankruptcy Rule 7001. *See, e.g., In re Tanner* (Bankr. D. Nev., July 7, 1995) (objection to IRS proof of claim seeking an offset should have been brought as an adversary proceeding), *reprinted at* 95 TNT 170-9.

[7] *Core Group, Inc. v. United States Dept. of Treas., IRS (In re Core Group, Inc.)*, 2007 U.S.T.C. ¶50,175 (Bankr. M.D. Pa. 2006) (adversary proceeding against the "United States Department of the Treasury, Internal Revenue Service" for a preferential transfer was dismissed without prejudice for failing to name the proper party).

[8] *See, e.g., United States v. Hernandez (In re Hernandez)*, 173 B.R. 430 (N.D. Ala. 1994); *United States v. Arthur's Industrial Maintenance, Inc. (In re Arthur's Industrial Maintenance, Inc.)*, 93-1 U.S.T.C. ¶50,092 (W.D. Va. 1993) (served U.S. Attorney and did not serve either the IRS or the U.S. Attorney General in Washington, D.C.; unlike the bankruptcy court, the district court believed that the plain language of the bankruptcy rule and Advisory Committee Notes required compliance with service of process rules for adversary proceeding; nevertheless, the IRS was held to have waived its right to object when the U.S. Attorney on behalf of the IRS appeared at the initial hearing and did not object to the service

copy of the objection with notice of the hearing "shall be mailed or otherwise delivered to the claimant," thus suggesting that service on the IRS alone is sufficient. However, the filing of an objection to a proof of claim initiates a "contested matter" governed by Bankruptcy Rule 9014,[9] which provides that, in "a contested matter . . . not otherwise governed by these rules," the service of process rules for adversary proceedings govern. Most courts require compliance with the service of process rules for adversary proceedings.[10]

Even if service is improper, however, the noticing party may still be able to demonstrate (depending on the jurisdiction) that adequate notice was given under the circumstances, *i.e.*, that the notice was reasonably certain to apprise the interested parties of the pendency of the action and afforded them a reasonable time to object.[11] Alternatively, the bankruptcy court in the *Arthur's Industrial Maintenance* case[12] noted that the court could treat the objection to service as a motion to quash service and retain the case while the debtor obtained proper service.

## §1005 RECOVERY OF CERTAIN PREPETITION TAX PAYMENTS, VOIDING TAX LIENS, AND SOVEREIGN IMMUNITY

Faced with an impending bankruptcy, or in recognition of the company's financial situation, actions may be undertaken by the company's officers prior to the corporation's filing for bankruptcy to pay certain outstanding tax obligations (*e.g.*, employment withholding and other "trust fund" taxes). Similarly, the IRS may undertake to obtain payment of any unpaid taxes. This could entail, among other things, setting off

---

(Footnote Continued)

of process); *In re Morrell*, 69 B.R. 147, 87-1 U.S.T.C. ¶9142 (N.D. Cal. 1987) (must comply with service of process rules for adversary proceedings); *In re Brown* (Bankr. W.D. Va. July 2, 1992), *reprinted at* 92 TNT 143-19 (discussing issue).

[9] *See* Advisory Committee Notes to Bankruptcy Rule 3007, *reprinted at* Collier Pamphlet Edition, Bankruptcy Rules 177 (1998 version); *Laughlin v. United States (In re Laughlin)*, 210 B.R. 659, 97-2 U.S.T.C. ¶50,606 (Bankr. 1st Cir. 1997) (discussing the difference between a contested matter and an administrative matter; motion to abate tax penalties initiated a contested matter); *cf. In re Stavriotis*, 977 F.2d 1202 (7th Cir. 1992).

[10] *See, e.g., United States v. Traficante (In re Traficante)*, 99-1 U.S.T.C. ¶50,527 (Bankr. 1st Cir. 1998) (an abbreviated manner of service permitted under locals rules cannot override the express requirements of the national rules). *But consider In re Taylor*, 132 F.3d 256, 262 (5th Cir. 1998) (indicating that a motion requesting a determination of a debtor's tax liability, where no proof of claim has been filed, would be considered a contested matter under Bankruptcy Rule 9014 and *not* an adversary proceeding), *reh'g denied, en banc*, 140 F.3d 1040 (5th Cir. 1998).

[11] *Compare, e.g., In re Griffin Oil Co., supra* note 4 (notice held inadequate in the circumstances); *In re Arthur's Industrial Maintenance, Inc., supra* note 8; *United States v. Lewis (In re Lewis)*, 142 B.R. 952 (D. Col. 1992) (despite inadequate notice, government arrived at hearing prepared to argue legal issues), *with In re Laughlin* (Bankr. 1st Cir.), *supra* note 9 (notice to IRS through Special Procedures Staff did not cure procedural defect); *In re Sousa*, 2001 Bankr. LEXIS 974 (Bankr. 1st Cir. 2001) (IRS attorney's admission of actual notice in time to avoid default did not overcome improper service). For a discussion of what constitutes adequate notice to a governmental agency, *see United States, Small Business Admin. v. Bridges*, 894 F.2d 108 (5th Cir. 1990).

[12] *Supra* note 8.

any tax refunds claimed, filing notices of tax lien, or levying upon and seizing corporate assets.

As discussed below, although occurring before bankruptcy and, thus, before the imposition of the automatic stay, certain prepetition tax payments (whether voluntary or involuntary) may be recoverable by the debtor corporation under the Bankruptcy Code. For example, such payments may constitute a "voidable preference" within the meaning of the Bankruptcy Code. In addition, certain prepetition tax liens (particularly unfiled tax liens) may be avoided in bankruptcy, and any assets seized by the IRS but not yet sold as of the commencement of the bankruptcy case may be required to be returned to the debtor. Prior to the Bankruptcy Reform Act of 1994, a serious impediment to any proceeding to recover tax payments was the government's sovereign immunity.

## *§1005.1 Sovereign Immunity*

As a sovereign entity, the United States is immune from suit absent an express waiver.[1] Such immunity necessarily extends to its agencies, including the IRS.[2]

Examples of express waivers include the refund provisions of the Internal Revenue Code and actions against the IRS for damages under Code §§7430 through 7433 (relating to court costs and attorneys' fees, unauthorized disclosure of returns and return information, the failure to release certain tax liens, and unauthorized collection actions).

In addition, in bankruptcy cases, Bankruptcy Code section 106 provides a waiver of the sovereign immunity of the United States and certain other governmental authorities.[3]

As part of the Bankruptcy Reform Act of 1994, Congress expanded the waiver of sovereign immunity contained in Bankruptcy Code section 106. In so doing, Congress overruled the Supreme Court's decision in the *Nordic Village* case (*see* §1005.1.3) and

---

1 **§1005** *See, e.g., United States v. Nordic Village Inc.*, 112 S. Ct. 1011, 92-1 U.S.T.C. ¶50,109 (1992) (waiver must be "unequivocally expressed"); *United States v. Mitchell*, 100 S. Ct. 1349, 1351-1352, 68-1 U.S.T.C. ¶410 (1980); *United States v. King*, 89 S. Ct. 1501, 1503 (1969). In the case of states, the Eleventh Amendment to the U.S. Constitution offers similar sovereign immunity protection. *See* discussion at §1102.5 below.

2 *See generally* 14 Wright, Miller & Cooper, Federal Practice and Procedure, Civil 2d, §3655 (1985 ed. with Supp.).

3 By its terms, the waiver of sovereign immunity contained in Bankruptcy Code section 106 applies to "any" governmental unit, including states and local governments. *See* 11 U.S.C. §101(27) (defining "governmental unit"). However, the constitutionality of such an abrogation of sovereign immunity as applied to the states has been a prime matter of contention since the Supreme Court's decision in *Seminole Tribe of Florida v. Florida*, 116 S. Ct. 1114 (1996). *See* discussion at §1102.5 below. Notwithstanding, cases cited in this section that involve a state generally remain valid authority in respect of the legal principle for which such cases are cited for purposes of applying Bankruptcy Code section 106 to governmental units other than the states.

The courts have also reached conflicting conclusions as to whether Bankruptcy Code section 106(a) waives a foreign government's immunity under the Foreign Sovereign Immunities Act, 28 U.S.C. §§1602-1611. *See* Shmuel Vasser, Waiver of Foreign Sovereign Immunity Under Bankruptcy Code §106, N.Y.L.J., June 5, 2003.

intended to overrule the Supreme Court's decision in a similar case involving a state's Eleventh Amendment immunity (*see* § 1102.5), which cases effectively constrained a bankruptcy court's ability to order or enforce monetary recoveries against a governmental authority. Although expansive in effect, the 1994 changes generally were intended to conform Bankruptcy Code section 106 to Congress's original intent at the time the Bankruptcy Code was enacted. The net effect of these changes generally was to treat the federal government like any other creditor, particularly in the case of tax claims.

As discussed in the next section, Bankruptcy Code section 106(a) operates to subject the United States and certain other governmental units to most provisions of the Bankruptcy Code, notwithstanding any assertion of sovereign immunity. In addition, Bankruptcy Code sections 106(b) and (c) provide a limited waiver of sovereign immunity where the governmental unit has filed a proof of claim in the bankruptcy case or, in the case of setoff, otherwise has a claim against the estate (*see* § 1005.1.2).[4]

Nothing in Bankruptcy Code section 106 is intended to create any independent substantive claim for relief or cause of action.[5] Rather, the only purpose of Bankruptcy Code section 106 is to do away with the defense of sovereign immunity to the extent provided therein.

### § 1005.1.1 General Application of Bankruptcy Code Provisions: Bankruptcy Code Section 106(a)

Bankruptcy Code section 106(a) expressly abrogates the sovereign immunity of the United States and other governmental units with respect to most operative provisions of the Bankruptcy Code (although such abrogation of immunity may, nevertheless, not apply to the states or to foreign governments, as noted above[6]). As had been suggested by the Supreme Court, section 106(a) specifically enumerates those provisions to which it applies. These include Bankruptcy Code sections:

- 105 (equitable powers)

---

[4] As with Bankruptcy Code section 106(a), the constitutionality of Bankruptcy Code sections 106(b) and (c) as applied to the states' Eleventh Amendment immunity had been seriously questioned as a result of the Supreme Court's decision in *Seminole, supra* note 3, but should no longer be in dispute. *See* discussion at § 1102.5.

[5] 11 U.S.C. § 106(a)(5). *See, e.g., United States v. Braeview Manor Inc. (In re Braeview Manor Inc.)*, 268 B.R. 523, 2001-1 U.S.T.C. ¶ 50,383 (N.D. Ohio 2001) (sovereign immunity barred objection to levy action based on nominee status; only defenses that could be asserted were those under Code § 7426, since Bankruptcy Code section 106 cannot be used to create new cause of action). *But compare Field v. Montgomery County, MD (In re Anton Motors, Inc.)*, 177 B.R. 58 (Bankr. D. Md. 1995) (§ 106 did not apply to a state law fraudulent conveyance action brought under Bankruptcy Code section 544 where such an action could not be brought against the County under state law); *United States v. Field (In re Abatement Environmental Resources, Inc.)*, 2003 U.S. District LEXIS 11989 (D. Md. 2003) (agrees with *Anton Motors*), *rev'g*, 2003-1 U.S.T.C. ¶ 50,151 (Bankr. D. Md. 2002); *with Liebersohn v. IRS (In re C.F. Foods, L.P.)*, 265 B.R. 71, 2001-2 U.S.T.C. ¶ 50,599 (Bankr. E.D. Pa. 2001) (offhandedly distinguished *Anton Motors* on the basis that it involved a state governmental unit).

[6] *See supra* note 3, and § 1102.5, below.

- 346, 1146 (special state tax provisions)
- 362 (automatic stay)
- 502, 503 (allowance of claims, interests and administrative expenses)
- 505 (determination of tax liability)
- 524 (effect of discharge)
- 542 through 553 (covering voidable preferences, fraudulent transfers, avoidable postpetition transactions, impermissible setoffs, and the like)
- 1141 (confirmation of plan; discharge of claims)[7]

The bankruptcy court may hear and determine any issue arising with respect to the application of any such section to a governmental unit.[8] Thus, for example, the bankruptcy court may determine the amount and dischargeability of a corporate debtor's tax liability under Bankruptcy Code section 505 or 1141, whether or not the IRS or any other taxing authority filed a proof of claim affirmatively waiving its sovereign immunity.

In addition, the bankruptcy court may issue against a governmental unit any kind of legal or equitable order, process, or judgment under the above sections or the Bankruptcy Rules, including an order or judgment awarding a money recovery.[9] By expressly permitting money recoveries, Bankruptcy Code section 106(a) makes clear that the Supreme Court's decision in *Nordic Village* is overruled and that the United States, like any other creditor, is subject to the preference and avoidance provisions of the Bankruptcy Code.[10]

However, a bankruptcy court may not award punitive damages against a governmental unit based on the abrogation of sovereign immunity under Bankruptcy Code section 106(a).[11] Also, as discussed further below, any order or judgment for cost or fees under the Bankruptcy Code or the Bankruptcy Rules against a governmental unit must be consistent with the fees and expense limitations of 28 U.S.C. § 2412(d)(2)(A) under the Equal Access to Justice Act (which generally limit attorney fees to $125/hour, except for cost-of-living increases since 1996 and special circumstances).[12]

---

[7] 11 U.S.C. § 106(a)(1). The other enumerated sections are Bankruptcy Code sections 106 (thus, it applies to itself), 107, 108, 303, 363 through 366, 506, 510, 522, 523, 525, 722, 724, 726, 728 (prior to its deletion), 744, 749, 764, 901, 922, 926, 928, 929, 944, 1107, 1142, 1143, 1201, 1203, 1205, 1206, 1227, 1231, 1301, 1303, 1305, and 1327. *Consider supra* note 5 and accompanying text.

[8] 11 U.S.C. § 106(a)(2).

[9] 11 U.S.C. § 106(a)(3). For a discussion of what is meant by a "money recovery," see *United States v. Torres (In re Torres)*, 432 F.3d 20, 2006-1 U.S.T.C. ¶ 50,112 (1st Cir. 2005) (does not permit damage claim for emotional distress as a sanction under a bankruptcy court's equitable powers).

[10] *See* § 1005.1.3; *see also* H. Rep. No. 835, 103d Cong., 2d Sess. 42 (1994); 140 Cong. Rec. H 10,766 (daily ed. October 4, 1994) (statement of Rep. Brooks, containing section-by-section analysis of the final bill).

[11] 11 U.S.C. § 106(a)(3); *see infra* § 1007 note 111, for cases where punitive damages had been imposed against the IRS for violating the automatic stay.

[12] 11 U.S.C. § 106(a)(3). Quoted in its entirety, 28 U.S.C. § 2412(d)(2)(A) reads as follows:

> "fees and other expenses" includes the reasonable expenses of expert witnesses, the reasonable cost of any study, analysis, engineering report, test, or project which is found by the court

The enforcement of any order, process, or judgment against a governmental unit must be consistent with appropriate nonbankruptcy law. In this regard, any money judgment by a bankruptcy court against the United States is treated as if rendered by a district court.[13] Thus, an order against a governmental unit will not be enforceable by attachment or seizure, but will be enforceable in the same manner and subject to the same nonbankruptcy procedures as other judgments against such governmental unit.[14]

We question whether the prohibition against punitive damages and the restriction on cost or fees based on 28 U.S.C. § 2412(d)(2)(A) applies to a waiver of sovereign immunity under Bankruptcy Code sections 106(b) and (c). Although a plain reading of the statute arguably suggests not, most courts thus far have applied such limitations to all waivers.[15]

In addition, it should be observed that 28 U.S.C. § 2412(d)(2)(A)—which is quoted in full in footnote 12—only relates to the quantification of the fees and expenses and not the qualification requirements of the Equal Access to Justice Act. This is significant since, as discussed at § 1007.7 below, there are multiple bases upon which a debtor potentially may seek (and has often recovered) fees and expenses depending on the circumstances, each with its own culpability and/or qualification requirements.[16] For example, in the case of violations of the automatic stay, such sources may include, depending on when the violation occurred, (i) contempt sanc-

(Footnote Continued)

> to be necessary for the preparation of the party's case, and reasonable attorney fees (The amount of fees awarded under this subsection shall be based upon prevailing market rates for the kind and quality of the services furnished, except that (i) no expert witness shall be compensated at a rate in excess of the highest rate of compensation for expert witnesses paid by the United States; and (ii) attorney fees shall not be awarded in excess of $125 per hour [$75/hour for costs relating to civil actions commenced before March 29, 1996] unless the court determines that an increase in the cost of living or a special factor, such as the limited availability of qualified attorneys for the proceedings involved, justifies a higher fee).

This definition is substantially identical to the definition of "reasonable litigation costs" in Code § 7430(c)(1)(A). *See also Cozean v. Commissioner*, 109 T.C. 227 (1997) (same limitations on fees held to apply to accountants authorized to practice before the IRS); *Ragan v. Commissioner*, 135 F.3d 329, 98-1 U.S.T.C. ¶ 50,209 (5th Cir. 1998), *cert. denied*, 119 S. Ct. 176 (1998) (accountant fees were recoverable as reasonable litigation costs, and not subject to the cap on attorney fees, to the extent such fees were for the preparation of an analysis or report that aided in taxpayer's defense).

[13] 11 U.S.C. § 106(a)(4).

[14] 140 Cong. Rec. H 10,766 (daily ed. October 4, 1994) (statement of Rep. Brooks, containing section-by-section analysis of the final bill).

[15] *See, e.g., Florida Dept. of Rev. v. Omine (In re Omine)*, 485 F.3d 1305, 1316-1319 (11th Cir. 2007), *rev'g in relevant part*, 2006 U.S. Dist. LEXIS 8396 (M.D. Fla. 2006). Many cases have applied the limitations without any apparent consideration of the potential distinction. *See, e.g., In re Jove Engineering, Inc.*, 92 F.3d 1539, 96-2 U.S.T.C. ¶ 50,469 (11th Cir. 1996); *Price v. United States*, 42 F.3d 1068 (7th Cir. 1994); *Baird v. United States (In re Baird)*, 2005-1 U.S.T.C. ¶ 50,173 (Bankr. M.D. Ala. 2004); *United States v. Washington (In re Washington)*, 184 B.R. 172 (S.D. Ga. 1995). *See also United States v. Lile (In re Lile)*, 43 F.3d 668, 95-1 U.S.T.C. ¶ 50,031 (5th Cir. 1994) (counsel conceded application of limitations).

[16] *See, e.g., Thibodaux v. United States (In re Thibodaux)*, 201 B.R. 827, 833-835, 96-2 U.S.T.C. ¶ 50,534 (Bankr. N.D. Ala. 1996) (allowed costs under contempt power, even though taxpayer did not meet qualifications of Code § 7430); *cf. Brown v. United States (In re Brown)*, 211 B.R. 1020, 97-2 U.S.T.C. ¶ 50,814 (Bankr. S.D. Ga. 1997).

tions, (ii) Bankruptcy Code section 362(h), (iii) the Equal Access to Justice Act, and (iv) Code § 7430, the complementary statute to the Equal Access to Justice Act in tax cases. The legislative history to Bankruptcy Code section 106(a) does not indicate any express intention to change this result. Nevertheless, some courts have read the provisions of Bankruptcy Code section 106(a) as effectively requiring compliance with the qualification requirements of the Equal Access to Justice Act or Code § 7430, as the case may be.[17]

Significantly, the Eleventh Circuit in *In re Jove Engineering, Inc.*,[18] held that "a district court exercising its discretion to award attorney fees under [its contempt powers] must consider the criteria of § 7430." The court reached this conclusion on the basis that Bankruptcy Code section 106(a) requires that the enforcement of any order or process of judgment must be "consistent with appropriate nonbankruptcy law." It therefore remanded the case to the district court to award attorney fees "consistent with § 7430 and § 2412(d)(2)(A)." Although such language is highly suggestive, whether the Eleventh Circuit intends that the district court actually apply the qualification requirements of Code § 7430 is unclear. In fact, in *In re Brown*,[19] the bankruptcy court characterized as *dicta* the Eleventh Circuit's statement as to the need for consistency with Code § 7430, and rejected any such consistency requirement on the grounds that only the "enforcement" of an award of attorney fees, not the statutory basis for the award or the amount imposed, must be consistent with appropriate nonbankruptcy law.[20]

With respect to any IRS violation of the automatic stay that occurs after July 22, 1998, or of the postdischarge injunction imposed by Bankruptcy Code section 524 with respect to discharged debts that occurs after July 22, 1998, and that is in connection with the collection of any federal tax, the recovery of damages is circum-

---

[17] For example, in *Matthews v. United States*, 184 B.R. 594 (Bankr. S.D. Ark. 1995), the court found that the IRS's action in violating the automatic stay was actionable and awarded compensatory damages as contempt sanctions and under Bankruptcy Code section 362(h). However, with respect to the issue of fees and expenses, the court reasoned, based on the requirement for consistency with 28 U.S.C. § 2412(d)(2)(A) but given that the violation involved the attempted collection of taxes, that its exclusive authority to award fees and expenses derived from Code § 7430. Thus, the debtor was required to establish that it was the "prevailing party" as such term is defined in Code § 7430 (*see* discussion at § 1007.7.4), which it failed to do. The court's (leap of) reasoning in this instance appears somewhat spurious. *But consider In re Jove Engineering, Inc.*, discussed in text. *See also In re Torres*, 2002-1 U.S.T.C. ¶ 50,268 (Bankr. D. P.R. 2002), *aff'd in part and rev'd in part*, 309 B.R. 643, 2004-2 U.S.T.C. ¶ 50,379 (Bankr. 1st Cir. 2004), *rev'd in part*, 432 F.3d 20, 2006-1 U.S.T.C. ¶ 50,112 (1st Cir. 2005).

[18] *Supra* note 15. *See also* its companion case, *Hardy v. United States*, 97 F.3d 1384, 96-2 U.S.T.C. ¶ 50,635 (11th Cir. 1996) (mirrors statements/holdings in *Jove Engineering*).

[19] *Brown v. United States (In re Brown)*, *supra* note 16. *But see In re Torres*, *supra* note 17 (read *Jove Engineering* as requiring compliance with qualification requirements of Code § 7430, without any discussion of possible contrary position; denied costs due to taxpayer's failure to file an administrative claim for damages with the IRS in accordance with the regulations).

[20] The bankruptcy court, which was within the Eleventh Circuit, also factually distinguished its case from *Jove Engineering* on the basis that the Eleventh Circuit had previously held in *In re Brickell Investment Corp.*, 922 F.2d 696, 91-1 U.S.T.C. ¶ 50,056 (11th Cir. 1991), that, unlike a district court, a bankruptcy court is not definitionally a court to which Code § 7430 applies. The statutory authority of the bankruptcy court to award fees under Code § 7430 is discussed at § 1007.7.4 below.

scribed by Code § 7433. As a result, any recovery of fees and expenses incurred by the debtor in seeking relief from such a violation (including any attorney fees incurred in bringing the action for damages) generally will require compliance with Code § 7430, including the qualification requirements (*see* § 1007.7 below). Under Code § 7433(b), certain costs of the action (such as court fees and costs of witnesses) may be recoverable without regard to Code § 7430.

Apart from Bankruptcy Code section 106(a), Bankruptcy Code section 342(g)(2) prohibits the imposition of any monetary penalty for a violation of the automatic stay (or for a creditor's failure to return to the debtor its property following the filing of the bankruptcy case as required by the Bankruptcy Code) in a bankruptcy case filed on or after October 17, 2005, unless the violation occurs after the creditor receives notice of the bankruptcy case (or in an involuntary case, of the order for relief) in accordance with Bankruptcy Code section 342.

Nothing in the statute or legislative history addresses the potential interaction between Bankruptcy Code section 106(a) and the setoff language in Bankruptcy Code section 106(c) as it relates to monetary recoveries. As discussed below, the setoff language of Bankruptcy Code section 106(c) can be read as not only waiving a government's sovereign immunity in respect to a setoff of claims but in fact mandating such a setoff. Several courts have adopted this interpretation as it relates to monetary recoveries otherwise permitted by Bankruptcy Code section 106(b).[21] Whether, or to what extent, this interpretation will also be applied in respect of recoveries otherwise permitted under Bankruptcy Code section 106(a) is unclear. Logically, however, it should not apply in respect of recoveries pursuant to preference and other avoidance actions.[22]

### § 1005.1.2 Further Right to Monetary Recoveries: Bankruptcy Code Sections 106(b) and (c)

In general, when it comes to tax and related claims, it will be unnecessary—given the expansive waiver in Bankruptcy Code section 106(a)—to rely on Bankruptcy Code section 106(b) or (c). Bankruptcy Code sections 106(b) and (c) provide a limited (additional) waiver of sovereign immunity with respect to monetary recoveries. These sections provide that:

> (b) A governmental unit that has filed a proof of claim in the [bankruptcy] case is deemed to have waived sovereign immunity with respect to a claim against such governmental unit that is property of the estate and that arose out of the same transaction or occurrence out of which the claim of such governmental unit arose.
>
> (c) Notwithstanding any assertion of sovereign immunity by a governmental unit, there shall be offset against a claim or interest of a govern-

---

[21] *See infra* note 46 and accompanying text.

[22] *See, e.g., Ellenberg v. DeKalb County, Georgia* (*In re Maytag Sales and Service, Inc.*), 23 B.R. 384, 390 (Bankr. N.D. Ga. 1982).

mental unit any claim against such governmental unit that is property of the estate.

An important distinction between these two sections is that Bankruptcy Code section 106(b) permits an affirmative recovery unlimited by the amount of the government's claim, whereas Bankruptcy Code section 106(c) provides only for an offset *but* applies whether or not the government's claim is related.[23]

A further difference between these sections, which was clarified by the 1994 amendments, is that Bankruptcy Code section 106(b) requires the filing of a proof of claim as a precondition to waiver, whereas Bankruptcy Code section 106(c) does not. Thus, in the case of setoff, the mere existence of a government "claim" within the meaning of the Bankruptcy Code (which is broadly defined to include contingent and unliquidated rights) is apparently sufficient to support a waiver.

**Proof of claim requirement.** With the exception of the proof of claim issue, the current provisions of Bankruptcy Code sections 106(b) and (c) are substantially identical to their pre-1994 Act predecessors—former Bankruptcy Code sections 106(a) and (b), respectively.

Under prior law, both sections were silent as to the need for filing a proof of claim. Although most courts interpreting former Bankruptcy Code section 106(a) required either that a proof of claim be actually filed in the bankruptcy case[24] or that the government otherwise have taken affirmative action of an equivalent nature so as to rise to the level of an "informal" proof of claim,[25] a number of courts continued to

---

[23] *See* H. Rep. No. 595, 95th Cong., 1st Sess. 317 (1977); S. Rep. No. 989, 95th Cong., 2d Sess. 29-30 (1978). Subject to equitable considerations, a third party cannot compel the debtor to assert a setoff claim it has chosen to relinquish. *See, e.g., Merritt Commercial Savings & Loan, Inc. v. Guinee*, 766 F.2d 850 (4th Cir. 1985) (after stating general rule, concluded that surety had equitable right to compel setoff to prevent unjust enrichment of principal at the expense of the surety).

[24] *See, e.g., 995 Fifth Avenue Assocs., L.P. v. New York Dep't of Tax'n (In re 995 Fifth Avenue Assocs., L.P.)*, 963 F.2d 503, at n.1 (2d Cir.), *cert. denied*, 113 S. Ct. 395 (1992) ("the only reasonable construction of [former] § 106(a) is that waiver will arise only if a claim is actually filed"); 2 Colliers on Bankruptcy ¶ 106.02. *See also Prudential Lines, Inc. v. United States Maritime Administration (In re Prudential Lines, Inc.)*, 79 B.R. 167 (Bankr. S.D.N.Y. 1987) (government did not waive its immunity under former Bankruptcy Code section 106(a) by merely considering whether to file a proof of claim; court set bar date to encourage filing of proof of claim).

[25] *See, e.g., Sullivan v. Town & Country Home Nursing Services, Inc. (In re Town & Country Home Nursing Services, Inc.)*, 963 F.2d 1146 (9th Cir. 1992) (state agency waived its sovereign immunity by offsetting postpetition amounts due debtor against prepetition amounts owing to state; state's affirmative actions were sufficient to effect a waiver of the state's sovereign immunity and constituted an "informal" proof of claim). However, the court's opinion also suggests that sovereign immunity may be waived even if the state's actions had fallen short of constituting an "informal" proof of claim. To such extent, the court's decision represents a minority view. *See, e.g., The Official Comm. of Unsec. Creditors of Operation Open City v. The New York State Dep't of State (In re Operation Open City, Inc.)*, S.D.N.Y., 170 B.R. 818 (1994) (follows *Town & Country*); *Taylor v. United States (In re Taylor)*, 148 B.R. 361, 93-1 U.S.T.C. ¶ 50227 (S.D. Ga. 1992) (to same effect); *United States v. Inslaw, Inc.*, 113 B.R. 802 (D. Colo. 1989); *Gower v. Farmers Home Administration (In re Davis)*, 20 B.R. 519 (Bankr. M.D. Ga. 1982); *cf. California State Board of Equalization v. Kupetz (In re Vanguard Manufacturing Co.)*, 145 B.R. 644 (Bankr. 9th Cir. 1992) (state's receipt and acceptance of an unauthorized postpetition payment was not the type of affirmative conduct necessary to trigger a waiver of sovereign immunity).

But *see, e.g., Unicare Homes, Inc. v. Four Seasons Care Center, Inc. (In re Four Seasons Care Center, Inc.)*, 19 B.R. 681 (Bankr. D. Minn. 1990) (disagreeing that conduct of a kind involved in Town &

hold the mere existence of a "claim" sufficient.[26] Intended as a clarifying change, the current provision expressly requires the filing of a proof of claim by the governmental unit.[27] However, certain legislative history raises anew the issue of whether the establishment of an "informal" proof of claim will satisfy this requirement.[28] The Fourth Circuit has held that it will not.[29]

A similar proof of claim issue existed in respect of former Bankruptcy Code section 106(b), with some courts focusing on the reference in that section to an "allowed" claim or interest as the basis for requiring a filed claim. This reference was deleted without comment by the 1994 amendments, and the introductory phrase "notwithstanding any assertion of sovereign immunity" was added. Thus, it now appears relatively clear that no proof of claim is necessary.

Where a proof of claim is necessary to effect a waiver, it is irrelevant whether the proof of claim is filed after the debtor's action against the government is initiated, so long as it is in fact filed during the suit. In effect the waiver created by the filing works retroactively.[30]

**"Same transaction or occurrence" requirement.** The requirement in current Bankruptcy Code section 106(b) that the estate's claim arise "out of the same transaction or occurrence" as the government's claim (for which a proof of claim is filed) is intended to effect a waiver of sovereign immunity with respect to "compulsory counterclaims," as defined in Rule 13(a) of the Federal Rules of Civil Procedure, which uses the same phrase.[31] This generally requires that a "logical relationship"

---

(Footnote Continued)

Country results in a waiver of sovereign immunity); *Cohen v. Illinois Dep't of Public Aid (In re Ramos)*, 12 B.R. 250 (Bankr. N.D. Ill. 1981); *Posey v. United States Dep't of Treas.*, 156 B.R. 910 (W.D.N.Y. 1993).

[26] *See, e.g., Mims v. United States (In re The Craftsman, Inc.)*, 163 B.R. 88 (Bankr. N.D. Tex. 1994); *Profilet v. United States (In re Johnson)*, 163 B.R. 890 (Bankr. S.D. Fla. 1993). *Cf. Flynn v. IRS (In re Flynn)*, 169 B.R. 1007 (Bankr. S.D. Ga. 1994) (so concluding in *dicta*), *aff'd in part and rev'd in part*, 185 B.R. 89 (S.D. Ga. 1995). In support, these courts observed that former sections 106(a) and (b) had omitted language from prior proposals that would have expressly required the filing of a proof of claim.

[27] The filing of a claim by the debtor or another person on behalf of the government under Bankruptcy Code section 501(c) does not constitute a waiver of the government's sovereign immunity. It must be the government's own action. *See* H. Rep. No. 595, 95th Cong., 1st Sess. 317 (1977); S. Rep. No. 989, 95th Cong., 2d Sess. 29-30 (1978).

[28] A section-by-section analysis of the 1994 amendments included in the Congressional Record for the House of Representatives states that the current provision only applies where a proof of claim is "actually filed" and that the amendment has the effect of overruling contrary case law, such as *Sullivan v. Town & Country Nursing Home Services, Inc., supra* note 25; *Mims v. United States (In re The Craftsman, Inc.), supra* note 26; and *In re Gribben* (S.D.N.Y.), *infra* note 55. 140 Cong. Rec. H 10,766 (daily ed. October 4, 1994) (statement of Rep. Brooks). It is unclear whether the reference to the *Town & Country* and *Gribben* cases was intended to refer only to the portion of those decisions suggesting that certain government actions could effect a waiver of sovereign immunity even if they do not rise to the level of an "informal" proof of claim or whether it extends to informal proofs of claim as well.

[29] *Aer-Aerotron, Inc. v. Texas Dep't of Transp.*, 104 F.3d 677 (4th Cir. 1997).

[30] *See, e.g., WJM, Inc. v. Massachusetts Dep't of Public Welfare*, 840 F.2d 996, 1004 (1st Cir. 1988); *Brown v. United States (In re Rebel Coal Co.), infra* note 35, at 321 n.1; *995 Fifth Avenue Assocs., L.P. v. New York Dep't of Tax'n (In re 995 Fifth Avenue Assocs., L.P.), supra* note 24.

[31] *See* H. Rep. No. 595, 95th Cong., 1st Sess. 317 (1977); S. Rep No. 989, 95th Cong., 2d Sess. 29-30 (1978). Some courts have strictly applied the notion of the "compulsory counterclaim" rule such that once the government's proof of claim is either fully paid or discharged, Bankruptcy Code section

exist between the two claims, taking into account "the totality of the claims, including the nature of the claims, the legal basis for recovery, the law involved, and the respective factual backgrounds."[32]

**Preference and other avoidance actions.** Prior to the Bankruptcy Reform Act of 1994, with its general abrogation of sovereign immunity for actions under the Bankruptcy Code (*see* § 1005.1.1), former Bankruptcy Code section 106(a)—now section 106(b)—was the principal provision upon which a waiver of sovereign immunity in preference actions could be based, if at all. By its nature, a preference action only exists where the IRS has obtained payment. Thus, a proof of claim is never filed for the collected tax. The absence of a filed claim, combined with the Supreme Court's decision in *Nordic Village* (discussed at § 1005.1.3 below), left many debtors unable to pursue valid preference actions. Because most courts required a filed claim before a waiver could be demonstrated under former Bankruptcy Code section 106(a), without a claim there could be no monetary recovery and thus generally no preference action (*see* § 1005.1.3).

Very often, however, prepetition payments obtained by the IRS are insufficient to satisfy all outstanding prepetition taxes, with the result that a proof of claim is filed for the remainder. In this instance, whether former Bankruptcy Code section 106(a) applied depended upon whether the preference action and the claim for the unpaid taxes satisfied the "same transaction or occurrence" test. This remains the central issue under current Bankruptcy Code section 106(b)—although resort to this section generally should be unnecessary with respect to federal taxes given new Bankruptcy Code section 106(a), *see* § 1005.1.1.

As one might expect, the courts have taken very disparate positions.[33] For example, some courts would permit a preference action where the unpaid tax is

(Footnote Continued)

106(b) is no longer applicable. *See, e.g., Moulton v. United States (In re Moulton)*, 146 B.R. 495 (Bankr. M.D. Fla. 1992) (involving IRS violation of postconfirmation injunction imposed by Bankruptcy Code section 524(a)(2) against acts to collect discharged debts), discussed, *infra*, at note 47 and accompanying text. However, this appears inconsistent with the fact that, unlike the compulsory counterclaim rule, monetary recoveries pursuant to a waiver under Bankruptcy Code section 106(b) are not limited to the amount of the government's related claim.

[32] *Burlington N.R. Co. v. Strong*, 907 F.2d 707, 711-712 (7th Cir. 1990) (nonbankruptcy case applying "compulsory counterclaim" rule); *see, e.g., United States v. Aronson*, 617 F.2d 119, 80-1 U.S.T.C. ¶ 9440 (5th Cir. 1980) (logical relationship exists when "the same operative facts serves [sic] as the basis of both claims or the aggregate core of facts upon which the claim rests activates additional legal rights, otherwise dormant, in the defendant"; held that IRS assessments were not logically related to taxpayer's prior tax refund suit where, among other things, different taxable years were involved), *quoting Plant v. Blazer Fin. Service, Inc. of Ga.*, 598 F.2d 1357, 1361 (5th Cir. 1979); *Maddox v. Kentucky Finance Co.*, 736 F.2d 380, 382 (6th Cir. 1984) (four-factor test including "logical relationship"); *Federman v. Empire Fire and Marine Ins. Co.*, 597 F.2d 798, 812 (2d Cir. 1979) (three-factor test including "logical relationship").

[33] *See, e.g., United States v. Pullman Constr. Indus., Inc.*, 153 B.R. 539 (N.D. Ill. 1993), *aff'g* 142 B.R. 280 (Bankr. N.D. Ill. 1992) (collecting cases), *appeal dismissed*, 23 F.3d 1166 (7th Cir 1994). *See also* IRS Litigation Guideline Memorandum GL-51, February 26, 1991, at part II.C.1, *reprinted at* 2000 TNT 91-42, as *supplemented by* IRS Litigation Guideline Memorandum GL-51A, June 4, 1992, *reprinted at* 2000 TNT 91-43.

literally the unpaid portion of the precise tax satisfied by the preference[34]—for example, where the preference satisfies $100 of the debtor's $200 income tax liability for 1989, and the claim is for the remainder—whereas others apparently would not.[35] On the other hand, some courts have taken a more liberal view and would permit a preference action so long as the underlying tax is the same type of tax (such as an income tax or employment-related tax).[36]

Moreover, it has been argued—although, in most cases, without success—that the filing of a proof of claim by one governmental agency (such as the Department of Labor) operates as a waiver with respect to preference and other avoidance actions against another governmental agency (such as the IRS) in that both claims emanated from the same "occurrence": namely, the bankruptcy filing.[37] On the positive side,

---

[34] *See, e.g., United States v. Pullman Constr. Indus., Inc., supra* note 33 (involved nontrust fund employment taxes, possibly for different periods); *Ellenberg v. Dekalb County, Georgia (In re Maytag Sales and Service, Inc.), supra* note 22; *Levit v. United States (In re V.N. DePrizio Constr. Co.)*, 1994 Bankr. LEXIS 1252 (Bankr. N.D. Ill.). *See also In re 995 Fifth Avenue Assocs., L.P., supra* note 24 (held that New York State had waived its immunity from suit with respect to the debtor's action for a refund of the "gains tax" paid upon the sale of certain real property allegedly exempt from tax under then Bankruptcy Code section 1146(c), now section 1146(a), when it filed an administrative claim for additional gains tax in connection with the sale).

[35] *Brown v. United States (In re Rebel Coal Co.)*, 944 F.2d 320 (6th Cir. 1991) (involved civil penalties under the Mine Safety Act; court stated that "even if the garnishment [which was the subject of the preference action] and the government's claim were based on the same judgment, the relationship between the claims would be insufficient"); *but see Murray v. Withrow (In re PM-II Assocs., Inc.)*, 100 B.R. 940, 943 (Bankr. S.D. Ohio 1989) (involving similar facts). *Consider also Graham v. United States (In re Graham)*, 981 F.2d 1135, 93-1 U.S.T.C. ¶50,255 (10th Cir. 1992) (claim for attorneys' fees incurred to pursue litigation of tax claims did not arise out of the same transaction or occurrence as the tax payments that were the subject of the litigation).

[36] *See In re Malmart Mortgage Co.*, 109 B.R. 1 (Bankr. D. Mass. 1989) (pre-*Begier*; involved employment withholding taxes, in part for different periods). *Consider also United States v. Pullman Constr. Indus., Inc., supra* note 33, concluding that:

> The United States seeks payment of the amount of taxes that Pullman has failed to pay the IRS. Pullman seeks to recoup payments already made to the IRS on account of its tax arrearage . . . . Thus, both claims arise from Pullman's failure to make timely payments of withheld taxes, withheld FICA taxes and unemployment taxes. Further, since one of the elements of Pullman's preference claim under section 547(b) is that it owed a debt to the United States for unpaid taxes, many of the factual and legal issues overlap. Consequently, by filing its proofs of claims, the United States is deemed to have waived its sovereign immunity with respect to Pullman's preference claim.

[37] *Hoffman v. State of Connecticut (In re Zera)*, 72 B.R. 997 (D. Conn. 1987) (claim for unemployment taxes filed by the State's Department of Labor did not arise out of "same transaction or occurrence" as the debtor's preference action against the State's Department of Revenue with respect to sales and use tax), *appealed and* aff'd *on other issues sub nom. In re Willington Convalescent Home Inc.*, 850 F.2d 50 (2d Cir. 1988), *aff'd, Hoffman v. Connecticut Dept. of Maintenance*, 109 S. Ct. 2818 (1989); *Unicare Homes, Inc. v. Four Seasons Care Centers, Inc. (In re Four Seasons Care Centers, Inc.), supra* note 25; *White v. Shalala (In re Pace Enters. of Columbia, Inc.)*, 171 B.R. 444 (Bankr. D.C. 1994); *but see Storey v. City of Toledo (In re Cook United, Inc.)*, 24 C.B.C. 128 (1990) (preference action against the city's department of revenue upheld under former Bankruptcy Code section 106(a) where proof of claim was filed by the city's department of public utilities). *See also* Gravis & Koger, If at First You Don't Succeed . . . : An Alternative Remedy After *Nordic Village*, 66 Am. Bankr. L.J. 423, 427-429 (1992), concluding that the better result would be to find a waiver.

however, the presence of such a claim should operate as a waiver for purposes of effectuating a setoff under current Bankruptcy Code section 106(c)—for which the "same transaction or occurrence" test does not apply. In this regard, the Seventh, Ninth and Tenth Circuits have held, as a matter of law, that all agencies of the United States are treated as a single governmental unit, except when acting in some distinctive private capacity (such as the FDIC when acting in its receivership capacity).[38]

It has also been suggested that, absent a waiver under Bankruptcy Code section 106, the provisions of the Tucker Act, 28 U.S.C.A. § 1491(a)—which generally permit suits against the United States to be brought in the United States Claims Court in cases not sounding in tort—might permit trustees to sue the IRS in the Claims Court for monetary recoveries based on the avoidance provisions of the Bankruptcy Code.[39] However, the district court in *In re Julien Company*[40] rejected just such an argument, as it would vitiate the effect of Bankruptcy Code section 106 and permit the general waiver of the Tucker Act to supersede the more specific waiver provisions of the Bankruptcy Code. Moreover, the Federal Tort Claims Act expressly excludes damage claims arising from the assessment or collection of taxes.[41]

**Damages for stay violations; overlapping provisions.** Prior to the 1994 changes, the issue of waiver frequently arose in the context of a damage claim against the IRS under Bankruptcy Code section 362(h) or for civil contempt sanctions for violations of the automatic stay (*see generally* § 1007.7 below). Although most courts had held, in the aftermath of *Nordic Village*, that the IRS was immune to such actions where no

---

[38] *United States v. Maxwell*, 157 F.3d 1099 (7th Cir. 1998) (involved the Small Business Administration and the U.S. Navy), *reh'g, en banc, denied*, 1998 U.S. App. LEXIS 30851 (1998); *Turner v. Small Business Admin. (In re Turner)*, 84 F.3d 1294 (10th Cir. 1996) (rejected type of analysis adopted in William Ross, Inc., below); *Doe v. United States*, 58 F.3d 494 (9th Cir. 1995) (upheld jurisdiction over an asserted damage claim against FBI where judgment could be offset against IRS claim for back taxes). *See also Aetna Casualty & Surety Co. v. LTV Steel Co., Inc. (In re Chateaugay Corporation)*, 94 F.3d 772, 96-2 U.S.T.C. ¶ 50,458 (2d Cir. 1996) (involved IRS; implicitly reached the same conclusion); *Gibson v. United States (In re Gibson)*, 176 B.R. 910 (Bankr. D. Ore. 1994) (involved EPA and HUD; discusses conflicting authorities).

Similarly, state agencies have also been viewed as part of a single governmental unit for this purpose, but only to the extent state law supports the setoff of obligations involving different state agencies. *See, e.g., Wallach v. New York State Dep't of Tax'n and Finance (In re Bison Heating & Equip., Inc.)*, 177 B.R. 785 (W.D. N.Y. 1995) (upheld jurisdiction over avoidance action against New York State Department of Taxation and Finance where claims had been filed by the State Department of Labor; recognizing that the Department of Taxation would become entitled to a priority claim with respect to any recovery, the court only upheld jurisdiction to the extent the amount subject to recovery would exceed the amount that would have to be repaid on account of the resulting priority claim); *but see, e.g., William Ross, Inc. v. Biehn Const. Inc. (In re William Ross, Inc.)*, 199 B.R. 551, 556 (Bankr. W.D. Pa. 1996) (court could not "ignore the fact" that Bankruptcy Code section 101(27) defines a "governmental unit" to include "a department, agency, or instrumentality" and, as such, felt "constrained" to respect each as a separate unit for setoff purposes); *Bezner v. East New Jersey State Prison (In re Exact Temp., Inc.)*, 231 B.R. 566 (Bankr. D. N.J. 1999) (same).

[39] *See* Gravis & Koger, *supra* note 37, 429-437; *see also* 28 U.S.C.A. § 1346(a)(2), which effectively extends the Tucker Act to the district court for monetary claims of less than $10,000.

[40] *Marlow v. United States (In re Julien Co.)*, 1993 U.S. Dist. LEXIS 15226 (W.D. Tenn.).

[41] *Sec* 28 U.S.C. § 2680.

proof of claim was filed,[42] a few courts continued to reject IRS claims of sovereign immunity, reasoning that the "power to enjoin" necessarily confers the "power to sanction."[43] Where, however, the IRS had filed a proof of claim, both former Bankruptcy Code sections 106(a) and (b) generally provided a basis for waiver. Under former Bankruptcy Code section 106(a), most courts held that a damage claim against the IRS for attempting to collect a prepetition tax in violation of the automatic stay was "property of the estate"[44] and arose out of the "same transaction or occurrence" as the IRS's proof of claim for such taxes.[45]

One might think that having established a waiver under former Bankruptcy Code section 106(a), which permits an affirmative monetary recovery, the debtor would be entitled to immediate cash damages. However, reading such section together with former Bankruptcy Code section 106(b), which provided that any claim against the government "shall be offset" against "allowed" claims of the government, most courts required that any damage awards first be offset against any allowed claims of the government, thereby precluding the government from being put in the position of having to pay the debtor currently while being forced to attempt to recover its own claim in the bankruptcy.[46] Thus, the debtor generally had to await the

---

[42] *See, e.g., Pearson v. United States (In re Pearson)*, 917 F.2d 1215 (9th Cir. 1990) (no indication whether a proof of claim was filed, *but see* the *Pinkstaff* case, *infra* note 45, limiting holding), *cert. denied sub nom. Moore v. United States*, 111 S. Ct. 1590 (1991); *United States v. McPeck, infra* note 46, referring to *Small Business Admin. v. Rinehart*, 887 F.2d 165 (8th Cir. 1989); *In re Shafer*, 146 B.R. 477 (D. Kan. 1992) (post-*Nordic Village;* stated that monetary sanctions are not the only ways of handling contemptuous behavior), *amended on other grounds*, 148 B.R. 617 (1992); *Taborski v. IRS (In re Taborski)*, 141 B.R. 959, 92-1 U.S.T.C. ¶50,281 (N.D. Ill. 1992) (post-*Nordic Village*). *Consider also In re Graham, supra* note 35, at 1139-1142 (did not involve stay violation; also suggested alternatives to monetary sanctions).

[43] *See, e.g., In re Tyson*, 145 B.R. 91, 92-2 U.S.T.C. ¶50,527 (Bankr. M.D. Fla. 1992) (court analyzed issue from the perspective of former Bankruptcy Code section 106(c), although it appears that former Bankruptcy Code section 106(a) would have also applied on the facts); *see also infra* note 50; *cf. Kolb v. United States (In re Kolb), infra* §1007 note 98 (pre-*Nordic Village*).

[44] "Property of the estate" is defined extremely broadly and, in general, includes all legal or equitable interests of a debtor corporation whether acquired before or after the commencement of the bankruptcy case. *See* 11 U.S.C. §541. Thus, virtually any claim against a governmental unit by a debtor corporation for a monetary recovery should be considered "property of the estate."

[45] *See, e.g., Pinkstaff v. United States (In re Pinkstaff)*, 974 F.2d 113 (9th Cir. 1992); *United States v. Lile (In re Lile)*, 161 B.R. 788 (S.D. Tex. 1993) (collecting cases), *aff'd in part and rev'd in part*, 95-1 U.S.T.C. ¶50,031 (5th Cir. 1994); *In re Lile*, 96 B.R. 81, 89-2 U.S.T.C. ¶9506 (Bankr. S.D. Tex. 1989); *United States v. Bulson (In re Bulson)*, 117 B.R. 537, 91-1 U.S.T.C. ¶50,023 (Bankr. 9th Cir. 1991), *aff'd without opinion*, (9th Cir. August 17, 1992) (per curiam); *Taborski v. IRS (In re Taborski), supra* note 42; *In re Solis, infra* note 46; *In re Long, infra* note 46; *cf. United States v. McPeck, infra* note 46. *But see Davis v. IRS, infra* note 46 (concluding that the stay violations and the failure to pay taxes raise separate, unrelated issues of fact and law); *United States v. Academy Answering Service, Inc. (In re Academy Answering Service, Inc.)*, 100 B.R. 327, 89-2 U.S.T.C. ¶9424 (N.D. Ohio) (no offset or recovery allowed even though proof of claim was filed).

[46] *See, e.g., United States v. McPeck*, 910 F.2d 509, 512-513, 90-2 U.S.T.C. ¶50,593 (8th Cir. 1990); *In re Solis*, 137 B.R. 121, 127-128 (Bankr. S.D.N.Y. 1992); *In re Long*, 142 B.R. 234, 238 (Bankr. S.D. Ohio 1992); *Davis v. IRS*, 136 B.R. 414, 420-421 (E.D. Va. 1992); *In re Hyndman*, 1991 Bankr. LEXIS 1027 (Bankr. M.D. Fla.); *see also Rhodes v. IRS (In re Rhodes)*, 155 B.R. 491 (W.D. Ark. 1993) (as sanctions for violating stay, IRS was ordered to satisfy the balance of any unpaid portion of its claim). The IRS, in a 1991 internal litigation memorandum, observed that "[t]his approach was not advocated by the govern-

ultimate determination of the government's claim (*i.e.*, until the amount of the government's "allowed" claim was determined) before it knew the extent of any monies due it.

In general, the 1994 changes do not alter the interaction of the statutory successors to these sections: namely, current Bankruptcy Code sections 106(b) and (c), respectively. Although current Bankruptcy Code section 106(c) omits the reference to an "allowed" claim in former Bankruptcy Code section 106(b), presumably it would still be necessary to determine the possible extent of the government's claim before an actual cash recovery would be permitted. As such, one suspects that, as a practical matter, most debtors will still have to await the ultimate determination of the government's claim before the extent of any actual cash recovery is known.[47]

As discussed above at § 1005.1.1, the general abrogation of sovereign immunity under new Bankruptcy Code section 106(a) in respect of damage claims excludes punitive damages and restricts awards of cost or fees. Although the applicability of such limitations with respect to a waiver under Bankruptcy Code section 106(b) or (c) is arguably unclear, most courts have thus far applied such limitations irrespective of the basis for the waiver of sovereign immunity. As discussed at § 1007.7 below, any damage claims against the IRS for violations of the automatic stay after July 22, 1998, in connection with the collection of federal tax, are circumscribed by Code § 7433. Bankruptcy Code section 342(g)(2) also prohibits the imposition of any monetary penalty for a violation of the automatic stay in a bankruptcy case filed on or after October 17, 2005, unless the creditor has received prior notice of the bankruptcy case (or in an involuntary case, of the order for relief) in accordance with that section—although the interplay between that section and Code § 7433 is not entirely clear.

**Damages for violating discharge; postconfirmation actions.** In contrast to stay violations, whether, prior to the 1994 changes, a damage claim could be brought under the Bankruptcy Code for an IRS violation of the postconfirmation injunction imposed by Bankruptcy Code section 524(a)(2) against acts to collect discharged debts depended, in part, upon whether, at the time the damage action was brought, any allowed claim for taxes remained unpaid. In this regard, some courts held that, inasmuch as former Bankruptcy Code section 106(a) was intended to effect a waiver with respect to "compulsory counterclaims," once the government's claim was extinguished, former Bankruptcy Code section 106(a) no longer applied.[48] Still others focused on the fact that the assets of the estate have since revested in the debtor, and that the damage claim thus belongs to the debtor, not the estate. If the claims are not property of the estate, neither former Bankruptcy Code section 106(a) nor (b) ap-

(Footnote Continued)

ment in McPeck and appears inconsistent with the plain language of section 106 and its legislative history." Nevertheless, the IRS recognized the benefits of such approach and encouraged it. IRS Litigation Guideline Memorandum GL-51, February 26, 1991, at part II.C.2, *reprinted at* 2000 TNT 91-42. In contrast, preference claims are not subject to offset. *See, e.g., Ellenberg v. Dekalb County, Georgia (In re Maytag Sales and Service, Inc.)*, *supra* note 22, at 390.

[47] *But see Indiana Dept. of Rev. v. Williams*, 301 B.R. 871, 879 (S.D. Ind. 2003).

[48] *See, e.g., Moulton v. United States (In re Moulton)*, *supra* note 31 (discussing authorities, but upholding sanctions, *see infra* note 50).

plied.[49] This is similarly true of current Bankruptcy Code sections 106(b) and (c). However, a few courts, representing a distinct minority, held that the IRS's sovereign immunity was waived under former Bankruptcy Code section 106(c).[50] These courts distinguished *Nordic Village*, reasoning that *Nordic Village* precluded only the recovery of money judgments (in that case, an unauthorized payment), not the issuance of sanctions, and that any other interpretation would make the injunction virtually meaningless insofar as the IRS is concerned. In addition, the Sixth Circuit recently held, in the context of a *liquidating* Chapter 11 plan, that the debtor's claim for certain postconfirmation tax refunds constituted property of the estate for purposes of determining jurisdiction under current Bankruptcy Code section 106(b).[51] The court stated that, "[a]lthough there may be some situations in which distinguishing post-petition property from property of the estate might help maintain the integrity of the plan of reorganization, we agree with [the district court's holding in *In re Price*[52]] that where the debtor does not obtain a discharge and postconfirmation property is committed to the plan of reorganization, it would be arbitrary to exclude post-petition property from the property of the estate."

In contrast, new Bankruptcy Code section 106(a) expressly abrogates the IRS's sovereign immunity in respect of discharge violations, other than as relates to punitive damages and recoverable costs or fees (*see* § 1005.1.1). However, any damage claims against the IRS for violations of the discharge injunction after July 22, 1998, in connection with the collection of federal tax, are circumscribed by Code § 7433 (*see* § 1007.7.1).

### § 1005.1.3 Pre-1994 Act: Declaratory and Injunctive Relief

Prior to the 1994 amendments to Bankruptcy Code section 106—which apply to all bankruptcy cases, regardless of when commenced—Bankruptcy Code section 106(c) provided that:

> notwithstanding any assertion of sovereign immunity—
>
> (1) any provision of [the Bankruptcy Code] that contains "creditor," "entity" or "governmental unit" applies to governmental units; and

---

49 *See, e.g., In re Germaine*, 152 B.R. 619, 624 (Bankr. 9th Cir. 1993); *Brown v. United States (In re Brown)*, 159 B.R. 1014 (Bankr. S.D. Ga. 1993) (sovereign immunity waived as to damage action for violating the automatic stay, but not for violating postconfirmation injunction); *In re Adams*, 1993 Bankr. LEXIS 2105 (Bankr. E.D. Mich. 1993).

50 *See, e.g., Moulton v. United States, supra* note 31 (presents a prime illustration of the potential for abuse in the absence of appropriate sanctions); *Daniels v. United States (In re Daniels)*; 150 B.R. 985 (Bankr. M.D. Ga. 1992); *United States v. Johns (In re Johns)*, 184 B.R. 161 (M.D. Fla. 1995); *see also infra* § 1014 note 14.

51 *Gordon Sel-Way, Inc. v. United States (In re Gordon Sel-Way, Inc.)*, 270 F.3d 280, 2001-2 U.S.T.C. ¶ 50,720 (6th Cir. 2001).

52 *Price v. United States (In re Price)*, 130 B.R. 259, 260-261 (N.D. Ill. 1991) (Chapter 13 case).

(2) a determination by the court of an issue arising under such a provision binds governmental units.

Accordingly, a bankruptcy court could issue declaratory and injunctive relief against a governmental unit in furtherance of any provision of the Bankruptcy Code that, by its terms, used one of the three "trigger" words—"creditor," "entity," or "governmental unit"—whether or not the government had filed a proof of claim.

Thus, for example, former Bankruptcy Code section 106(c) also permitted the bankruptcy court to determine the amount and dischargeability of a corporate debtor's tax liability under Bankruptcy Code section 505 or 1141, whether or not the IRS filed a proof of claim affirmatively waiving its sovereign immunity. The IRS had repeatedly, although generally unsuccessfully, objected to being bound by such determinations under the former Bankruptcy Act.[53]

Initially, the courts were split as to whether former Bankruptcy Code section 106(c) also permitted monetary relief. In the *Nordic Village* case,[54] the Supreme Court held that it did not. Examining the language of Bankruptcy Code section 106(c), the Court held that, although such section could be interpreted to permit monetary relief, a more narrow interpretation was equally (if not more) plausible.[55] As such, the Court held that Bankruptcy Code section 106(c) did not contain an "unequivocal textual waiver" of the government's immunity from a suit for monetary relief. The Court noted that because of the need for an express waiver, it could not look to legislative history for clarification.

In *Nordic Village*, an officer and shareholder of a corporation that had previously filed for bankruptcy withdrew funds from the company's account and used the funds to satisfy his personal tax liability. The corporation had sought to avoid the unauthorized postpetition transfer of funds under Bankruptcy Code section 549(a) and to recover the funds from the IRS under Bankruptcy Code section 550(a). Bankruptcy Code section 550(a) is also the operative provision for the recovery of, *inter alia*, voidable preferences under Bankruptcy Code section 547, fraudulent transfers under Bankruptcy Code section 548, unauthorized postpetition transactions under Bank-

---

[53] *See* The Supreme Court decision in *Nordic Village, supra* note 1, at 1016; *Neavear v. Schweiker (Matter of Neavear)*, 674 F.2d 1201, 1204 (7th Cir. 1982).

[54] *Supra* note 1.

[55] In so holding, the Court adopted the position of the plurality in *Hoffman v. Connecticut Dept. of Income Maintenance*, 492 U.S. 96 (1989), a 1989 Supreme Court decision involving the scope of former Bankruptcy Code section 106(c) as it related to a state's Eleventh Amendment immunity in the context of a voidable preference action and a "turnover" proceeding under Bankruptcy Code section 542(b). Because the deciding vote in *Hoffman* rested on Eleventh Amendment grounds, the holding in *Hoffman* was not determinative of the issue of federal sovereign immunity. *See* IRS Litigation Guideline Memorandum GL-51, February 26, 1991, *reprinted at* 2000 TNT 91-42, *as supplemented by* IRS Litigation Guideline Memorandum GL-51A, June 4, 1992, *reprinted at* 2000 TNT 91-43; Richman, More Equal Than Others: State Sovereign Immunity Under the Bankruptcy Code, 21 Rutgers L.J. 603 (1990). In enacting the Bankruptcy Reform Act of 1994, Congress expressly intended to overrule this case. *See* H. Rep. No. 835, 103d Cong., 2d Sess. 42 (1994); *but see* discussion at §1102.5 (1994 amendments as applied to the states generally held unconstitutional).

ruptcy Code section 549, and recoverable prepetition setoffs under Bankruptcy Code section 553(b).[56]

(In fact, the legislative history ignored by the Court included an express statement that Bankruptcy Code section 106(c) permitted preference actions against governmental units.[57] It was in keeping with this intent that the Bankruptcy Reform Act of 1994 amended Bankruptcy Code section 106 generally to permit monetary recoveries in connection with declaratory and injunctive relief.[58])

The Supreme Court distinguished its earlier decision in *United States v. Whiting Pools, Inc.*,[59] wherein it upheld a bankruptcy court order requiring that, under Bankruptcy Code section 542(a), the IRS turn over tangible property of the debtor that it had seized before the debtor filed for bankruptcy but as to which the debtor retained ownership as of the bankruptcy filing. Thus, such proceedings were not barred by sovereign immunity.[60]

Similarly, in the *USA Rent-a-Car* case, the bankruptcy court permitted the trustee's recovery of cashier's checks received by the IRS but not yet presented to the issuing bank and enjoined by the IRS from presenting (and the bank from honoring) the checks. The debtor's principal had used company funds to obtain the cashier's checks, which he then delivered to the IRS in satisfaction of his personal liability for unpaid withholding taxes of the debtor and related entities. The court distinguished *Nordic Village*, which involved substantially similar facts, in that there the checks had already been presented and the funds applied to the principal's tax liability.[61]

The Supreme Court's decision did not consider whether a bankruptcy court could still undertake to determine whether a given transfer was a voidable transfer, even if unable to grant affirmative monetary relief.[62] For example, what if a corporate

---

[56] In this regard, *see, e.g., Hankerson v. United States Dept. of Education*, 138 B.R. 473 (E.D. Pa. 1992) (sovereign immunity barred recovery of prepetition setoffs). However, an unauthorized setoff of prepetition amounts during the bankruptcy case has been held by some courts sufficient to effect a waiver of sovereign immunity under former Bankruptcy Code section 106(a) and constitute an "informal" proof of claim. *See, e.g., Gribben v. United States (In re Gribben)*, 158 B.R. 920 (S.D.N.Y. 1993) (sovereign immunity waived); and cases discussed *supra* note 25.

[57] *See* 124 Cong. Rec. H 11,091 (daily ed. September 28, 1978) (statement of Rep. Edwards), S 17,407 (daily ed. October 6, 1978) (statement of Sen. DeConcini); *see infra* note 68, regarding the weight generally accorded legislative statements.

[58] H. Rep. No. 835, 103d Cong., 2d Sess. 42 (1994).

[59] 462 U.S. 198, 83-1 U.S.T.C. ¶9394 (1983); *see Nordic Village, supra* note 1, at 1017.

[60] *Cf. Hoffman v. Connecticut Dept. of Income Maintenance, supra* note 55, at 104 (referring to position in government's brief). *See also Quillard v. United States (In re Quillard)*, 150 B.R. 291, 93-1 U.S.T.C. ¶50,110 (Bankr. D.R.I. 1993) (debtor could bring voidable preference action to avoid levy on funds still on deposit).

[61] *Hyman v. Sun Bank of Tampa Bay (Matter of USA Rent-a-Car/Florida, Inc.)*, 149 B.R. 695 (Bankr. M.D. Fla. 1992).

[62] *Consider*, for example, *Graham v. United States (In re Graham)*, *supra* note 35 (suggesting possible forms of nonmonetary or alternative relief); *Staats v. United States (In re Frederick Petroleum Corp.)*, 144 B.R. 758, 92-2 U.S.T.C. ¶50,362 (Bankr. S.D. Ohio 1992), (bankruptcy court would not permit the debtor to amend its complaint to seek a recovery of unauthorized postpetition payments to the IRS absent a waiver of sovereign immunity that permitted monetary recoveries); *Marlow v. United States (In re Julien Co.)*, 1992 Bankr. LEXIS 2482 (Bankr. W.D. Tenn. 1992) (denied declaratory request to void transfers to IRS since ultimate aim of request was to receive a judgment for monetary recovery), *aff'd*

debtor did not seek to recover in actual dollars the amount at issue, but, rather, sought a declaratory order applying the amount in question to postpetition taxes of the corporation? Was this an impermissible form of monetary relief? Did it make a difference if, for example, the debtor also disputed the underlying tax liability of the corporation upon which the voidable transfer was based, such that the debtor might be due a refund?[63] Many of these questions are now being answered in the state tax context, in the wake of the Supreme Court's decisions in *Seminole Tribe of Florida v. Florida* and *Central Virginia Community College v. Katz* (*see* discussion at § 1102.5 below).

## *§1005.2 Voidable Preference*

The payment of certain taxes within 90 days prior to a debtor's bankruptcy filing may constitute a voidable preference under Bankruptcy Code section 547(b) and, subject to a possible defense based on sovereign immunity (which, as discussed above, is unlikely after the Bankruptcy Reform Act of 1994), generally may be reclaimed by the debtor-in-possession.[64] In general, a preferential payment is a payment (1) to a creditor, (2) for or on account of an antecedent debt owed by the debtor before the payment was made, (3) made while the debtor is insolvent (there is a rebuttable presumption of insolvency), and (4) that enables the creditor to receive more than he would have in a Chapter 7 proceeding.[65]

---

(Footnote Continued)

*on other grounds*, 1993 U.S. Dist. LEXIS 15226 (W.D. Tenn. 1993); *Brown v. United States* (*In re Larry's Marineland of Richmond, Inc.*), 166 B.R. 871 (Bankr. E.D. Ky. 1993) (upheld trustee's right to bring action to disallow IRS claim under Bankruptcy Code section 502(d) until IRS remits any amounts avoidable under Bankruptcy Code section 548).

63 *Consider Sheffel v. New York* (*In re Lehal Realty Assocs.*), 133 B.R. 9 (Bankr. S.D.N.Y. 1991) (bankruptcy court had jurisdiction to determine the reach and scope of the exemption from transfer taxes under then Bankruptcy Code section 1146(c), now section 1146(a), but could not order state to refund taxes already paid since state had not waived its sovereign immunity by filing a claim in the bankruptcy); *In re Lopez Dev., Inc.*, 154 B.R. 607 (Bankr. S.D. Fla. 1993) (to same effect; however, the bankruptcy court "ordered and directed [the State] to process the application for refund according to its normal procedures").

64 *See* 11 U.S.C. § 550 (authorizing recovery of avoided transfers, but with certain limitations such as in the case of a subsequent good faith transferee for value, *see infra* note 106). Even those courts that have found a waiver of the government's right to sovereign immunity do not permit the debtor interest on the reclaimed amounts, even though ordinarily allowed in preference cases. *See, e.g., In re Pullman Const. Indus., Inc.*, discussed *infra* this section; *In re Husher*, 131 B.R. 550 (E.D.N.Y. 1991), *rev'd on other grounds*, 1992 U.S. Dist. LEXIS 8376 (E.D.N.Y.) (held no waiver of sovereign immunity); *Ballard v. State of Wisconsin* (*In re Ballard*), 1991 U.S. Dist. LEXIS 13111 (W.D. Wis.).

65 *See* 11 U.S.C. § 547(b) (requirements), (f) (rebuttable presumption of insolvency), (g) (debtor-in-possession generally bears the burden of proof), 546(a) (action generally must be brought during the first two years of the bankruptcy case); *In re Tenna Corp.*, 801 F.2d 819, 86-2 U.S.T.C. ¶ 9696 (6th Cir. 1986) (tax payment was not voidable preference because IRS did not receive a greater share of the debtor's assets than it would have received in a Chapter 7 proceeding; anticipated costs of Chapter 7 proceeding should be taken into account in determining amount recoverable); *Lemelman v. Brown* (*In re S.N. Brown Electrical Corp.*), 136 B.R. 598 (Bankr. E.D. Mass. 1992) ("deferred taxes" listed on the debtor's books were not liabilities for purposes of determining the debtor's "insolvency" where the debtor's continuing operating losses would eliminate necessity of paying the taxes); *In re Greasy Creek*

Ordinary course payments of taxes (*e.g.*, estimated taxes) that are timely made are not voidable preferences, however.[66] In addition, in *Begier, Jr. v. IRS*,[67] the Supreme Court held that any voluntary payment over of withholding taxes to the IRS during the 90-day preference period was not voidable, because such taxes are held "in trust" for the IRS under Code § 7501 and, thus, not property of the debtor. In so holding, the court concluded—based on legislative statements made at the time of enactment of the Bankruptcy Code and the House Report—that "reasonable assumptions" should govern the tracing of trust-fund taxes and that one such assumption is that "any voluntary prepetition payment of trust-fund taxes out of the debtor's assets is not a transfer of the debtor's property."[68] The Supreme Court did not deal with

---

(Footnote Continued)

*Coal Co.*, 84-2 U.S.T.C. ¶9651 (Bankr. S.D. W. Va.); *see also* IRS Litigation Guideline Memorandum GL-39, September 4, 1993, *reprinted at* 2000 TNT 121-38; Bienenstock, Bankruptcy Reorganizations, at 364-398 (1987 with Supp.); Note, Tax Payments: Are They Voidable Preferences in Low-Asset Bankruptcies?, 10 Cardozo L. Rev. 341 (1988).

[66] *See* 11 U.S.C. § 547(b)(2) (only applies to payment of antecedent debts), (c)(2) (exception for payment in ordinary course of business; broadened effective for bankruptcy cases commenced on or after 10/17/05) and (a)(4) (for preference purposes, a tax is considered incurred on the date last payable without penalty, including any extension); H. Rep. No. 595, 95th Cong., 1st Sess. 372-374 (1977); 124 Cong. Rec. H 11,114 (daily ed. September 28, 1978) (statement of Rep. Edwards), S 17,431 (daily ed. October 6, 1978) (statement of Sen. DeConcini); *Barry v. State of Arkansas* (*In re Wieser*), 86 B.R. 157 (Bankr. W.D. Ark. 1988) (estimated taxes); *Orrill v. Orrill* (*In re Orrill*), 226 B.R. 563 (Bankr. E.D. La. 1997) (held that election on tax return to apply tax overpayment to succeeding year's taxes is treated as the payment of estimated taxes, *citing* Code § 6513(d), and is not recoverable as a preference as it is not a payment of an antecedent debt).

However, prepetition transfers from a tax escrow, established in favor of a purchaser of property, including transfers to the county for the timely payment of property taxes, were preferential transfers, where the purchaser would otherwise have had an unsecured claim against the debtor which would have received only partial payment. *Carmel v. Orr* (*In re Lakeside Comm. Hospital, Inc.*), 200 B.R. 853 (Bankr. N.D. Ill. 1996). In contrast, transfers by a bank to *itself* of tax refund monies remitted by the IRS to a designated bank account at the taxpayer's instructions and in accordance with the terms of a refund anticipation loan agreement were held to be protected under the "ordinary course" exception. *See Kleven v. Household Bank F.S.B.*, 2003 U.S. App. LEXIS 13228 (7th Cir. 2003) (noting conflicting case law in the case of a first-time refund transaction). For a discussion of the potential application of the "ordinary course" exception in the context of continual late payments, *see* Lawniczak, Courts Defining Ordinary Course of Business in a Preference Case More Liberally, 31 Bankr. Ct. Dec. (LRP Pub., Aug. 12, 1997), at p. 3. *See also The Official Plan Committee v. United States* (*In re Valley Steel Products Company, Inc.*), 214 B.R. 202 (E.D. Mo. 1997) (holding that tax payments after the accrual of penalties is not in the ordinary course even though pursuant to an agreed payment plan, and that IRS's agreement to forgo filing its tax liens did not constitute a contemporaneous exchange of value for the installment payments).

[67] 110 S. Ct. 2258 (1990). *See also Levit v. Ingersoll Rand Fin. Corp.* (*In re Deprizio*), 874 F.2d 1186 (7th Cir. 1989) (although the preference period for payments to or on behalf of insiders is one year, rather than 90 days, the one-year preference period for insiders did not apply to the payment of withholding taxes for which debtor's officers would have had Code § 6672 liability).

[68] 110 S. Ct. at 2267; *see also* H. Rep. No. 595, 95th Cong., 1st Sess. 372-373 (1977); legislative statements quoted *infra* at § 1006 note 171; *United States v. O'Rourke* (*In re L & S Concrete Services, Inc.*), 129 B.R. 208 (E.D. Wash. 1991) (irrelevant that actual monies paid traceable to accounts receivable, so long as payment is voluntary). Following *Begier*, the bankruptcy court in *In re Russman's*, 125 B.R. 520 (Bankr. E.D. Tenn. 1991), held that the transfer of monies from a commingled account to a segregated fund labeled "tax escrow" (which monies were only later, after the case was converted to Chapter 7, specifically identified as representing unpaid sales taxes) was sufficient identification to entitle the State to the escrowed funds, including the accrued interest. Interestingly, the *Russman* case involved

involuntary payments; but in a lower court decision that preceded the Supreme Court decision, it was held that where the payment is involuntary, in that the IRS obtained payment of outstanding trust fund taxes during the preference period by levying upon the debtor's accounts receivable, the payment was voidable absent some reasonable ability to trace the seized funds to the unpaid taxes.[69] While some subsequent cases have similarly distinguished between voluntary and involuntary payments,[70] others have not.[71] The IRS takes the position that there should be no distinction where the subject of the IRS levy is the debtor's general bank account and

(Footnote Continued)

sales taxes (held by the court to be "trust fund" taxes) that were collected during the debtor's Chapter 11 case, but prior to its conversion to Chapter 7, and where the estate did not have sufficient funds to pay all Chapter 11 administrative expenses in full. Accordingly, absent a finding that the escrowed funds were held "in trust" for the benefit of the State, the State would have been entitled to only partial payment. *See* 11 U.S.C. §726(b) (subordinating preconversion administrative expenses).

It should be noted that the U.S. Supreme Court has generally cautioned against reliance on legislative statements where such statements are merely "passing comments" or "casual statements" of a member of Congress and has stated that the legislative intent is generally to be found in committee reports. *Garcia v. United States*, 469 U.S. 70 (1984), *reh'g denied*, 469 U.S. 1230 (1985). Nevertheless, the legislative statements cited above (and throughout this chapter) comprise but a small part of 27 identical pages in the Congressional Records of both the House and Senate, which add considerable detail to the sparse committee reports. Such statements were apparently carefully prepared in advance and are generally considered authoritative source material. Accordingly, in *Begier*, the Supreme Court stated (in note 5 of its opinion) that such statements are "persuasive evidence of Congressional intent." *See also In re Pacific-Atlantic Trading Co.*, 64 F.3d 1292, 1300 (9th Cir. 1995); *Burns v. United States (In re Burns)*, 887 F.2d 1541, 1548-1550, 89-2 U.S.T.C. ¶9630 (11th Cir. 1989) (quoting from various circuit court opinions regarding the weight accorded the joint statements). However, not all portions of such statements have been received by the Supreme Court with equal deference, where, for example, assertions as to existing law could not be supported upon closer scrutiny. *See United States v. Noland*, 116 S. Ct. 1524, 1528, 96-1 U.S.T.C. ¶50,252 (1996).

[69] *See Christison v. United States (In re Hearing of Illinois, Inc.)*, 110 B.R. 380 (Bankr. C.D. Ill. 1990), *rev'd on other grounds*, 960 F.2d 613, 92-1 U.S.T.C. ¶50,188 (7th Cir. 1992). In an analogous context where the IRS seeks to recover *unpaid* prepetition trust fund taxes *during* the debtor corporation's bankruptcy case, the courts generally have recognized (consistent with the legislative statements referenced above) that the application of the "lowest intermediate balance" rule to trace trust funds held in a commingled account is a reasonable tracing assumption. *See infra* §1006.3 at note 171 and accompanying text. Of course, this provides little assistance if the intermediate balance was zero. *See also* IRS Litigation Guideline Memorandum GL-39, September 4, 1993, *reprinted at* 2000 TNT 121-38.

[70] *See, e.g., United States v. Paul Borock (In re Ruggeri Elec. Contr., Inc.)*, 199 B.R. 903, 96-2 U.S.T.C. ¶50,695 (Bankr. E.D. Mich. 1996) (any reasonable basis to trace seized funds to trust fund taxes ceased upon prior issuance of injunction in favor of union freezing debtor's bank account), *aff'd*, 214 B.R. 481, 97-2 U.S.T.C. ¶50,998 (E.D. Mich. 1997) (discusses cases); *Wasden v. Florida Dept. of Rev. (In re Wellington Foods, Inc.)*, 165 B.R. 719, 94-2 U.S.T.C. ¶50,307 (Bankr. S.D. Ga. 1994) (in *dicta*). *Consider also Hoffman v. United States (In re Jones & Lamson Waterbury Farrel Corp.)*, 208 B.R. 788 (Bankr. D. Conn. 1997) (collateral proceeds relinquished by a secured creditor to the IRS to obtain a release of an IRS tax lien and, per an agreement between the debtor and the IRS, applied to unpaid trust fund taxes, were not a voidable preference; court viewed payment as coming from the secured creditor, not the debtor; alternatively, court held that payment was "voluntary" in that there was no distraint, levy or other legal proceeding involved).

[71] *See, e.g., Taylor v. Commonwealth of Mass. Dept. of Rev. (In re Nash Concrete Form Co.)*, 1994 Bankr. LEXIS 1118 (Bankr. D. Mass. 1994) (seizure of available bank account was sufficient to establish nexus), *remanded by* 159 B.R. 611 (D. Mass. 1993) (similarly espousing such position); *Front Office Assoc., Inc. v. Clark (In re Front Office Assoc., Inc.)*, 142 B.R. 24 (Bankr. D.R.I. 1992) (did not even raise potential distinction).

the IRS applies the seized funds to the debtor's unpaid trust fund taxes upon receipt.[72] In the IRS's view, the simple fact that the bank account was available to be levied upon—and that the debtor thus had the ability to pay the trust fund taxes—should support a "reasonable assumption" that the seized funds were trust fund taxes.[73]

One bankruptcy court has concluded that the Supreme Court did not mean exactly what it said: namely, that "any" voluntary prepetition payment of trust fund taxes is not a voidable preference.[74] Rather, such court concluded that a "fundamental basis" for the Supreme Court's application of the "voluntary payment" was the existence of commingled funds in an amount sufficient to satisfy the tax obligation paid, and, accordingly, that, to the extent that the balance in the commingled account dropped (even temporarily) below the amount of the trust fund taxes, a voluntary payment of such taxes during the 90-day preference period would be a voidable preference. This overlooks the fact, however, that the Supreme Court, although considering the type of tracing employed by the bankruptcy court as reasonable, nevertheless concluded, based on the House Report, that the preferred approach was to treat all voluntary prepetition payments of trust fund taxes as nonvoidable.[75]

Providing an interesting case illustration is the decision in *In re Pullman Construction Industries, Inc.*[76] In this case, the debtor had fallen behind in its required deposits of the trust fund portion of its employment taxes. Within the 90-day period preceding its bankruptcy, but prior to the due date for its quarterly employment tax return for the taxes at issue, the debtor made eight payments to the IRS. The first four contained no designation and were applied by the IRS to the non-trust fund portion of the debtor's quarterly employment tax liability. The fifth, although designated by the debtor to the payment of trust fund taxes, was misapplied by the IRS to the non-trust fund portion. The remaining three were properly applied by the IRS to the payment of trust fund taxes in accordance with the debtor's instructions. The debtor sought to recover as a preferential transfer the first five payments.

---

[72] IRS Chief Counsel Advisory 200029002 (July 21, 2000), *reprinted at* 2000 TNT 142-66. The principal support for this position is the 1993 district court and 1994 bankruptcy court decisions in *In re Nash Concrete Form Co., supra* note 71. This position was recently rejected by the district court in *United States v. Natale (In re TCB Carpet Services Inc.)*, 2000-2 U.S.T.C. ¶50,820 (N.D. Ill. 2000) (even though the debtor paid wages out of the general account).

[73] In cases where the seized amounts were initially applied to non-trust fund taxes, the IRS Chief Counsel has advised against reallocating such funds following the commencement of the bankruptcy case, recognizing that the initial allocation "undercuts any argument that the funds were held in trust prior to remittance by the taxpayer." IRS Chief Counsel Advisory 200029002 (July 21, 2000), *supra* note 71.

[74] *Wendy's Food Systems v. State of Ohio (In re Wendy's Food Systems)*, 133 B.R. 917 (Bankr. S.D. Ohio 1991).

[75] *See Wasden v. Florida Dept. of Rev. (In re Wellington Foods, Inc.), supra* note 70, at 725-726 (so concluding).

[76] 186 B.R. 88 (Bankr. N.D. Ill. 1995), *amended*, 190 B.R. 618 (1996), *aff'd*, 210 B.R. 302, 97-2 U.S.T.C. ¶50,652 (N.D. Ill. 1997). This decision followed the parties' earlier litigation—which pre-dated the Bankruptcy Reform Act of 1994—wherein both the bankruptcy court and the district court found that the IRS had waived its sovereign immunity by filing a proof of claim for the unpaid portion of the debtor's employment tax liability (*see supra* note 33).

Ultimately, the court held that only a portion of the payments were recoverable.[77] The court first considered, per *Begier*, whether the five payments (all of which were made prior to any formal collection action) were voluntary, and easily concluded that all were. For this purpose, the court applied the same standard of "voluntary" as that used by the courts in determining whether a taxpayer's designation of a tax payment must be adhered to by the IRS (*see* § 1016.2 below). The court then determined the extent to which such payments could be fairly said to represent trust fund taxes.

As to the first three payments, the IRS was able to establish "by evidence with a clear inference"—the debtor's handwritten worksheets which were included in the stipulated record—that $341,230.19 of the amount paid represented trust fund taxes. No similar evidence existed for the fourth payment. As to the fifth payment of $119,716, although initially misapplied by the IRS, the debtor's designation was controlling. Accordingly, the court held that $460,946.19 of the amount paid represented funds held in trust for the IRS that could not be recovered.

As to the remaining amounts, the court, although initially denying any recovery on the basis that such payments were not "for or on account of an antecedent debt," subsequently amended its decision and allowed recovery in part. At issue was the proper interpretation of Bankruptcy Code section 547(a)(4), which provides, for preference purposes, that "a debt for a tax is incurred on the day when such tax is last payable without penalty, including any extension." In its amended decision, the court determined that, as the debtor was required to deposit its employment taxes with the Federal Reserve Bank (or other authorized depository) in advance of filing its employment tax return, such taxes became an antecedent debt—and thus recoverable—when the debtor failed to deposit such taxes and became subject to the failure-to-deposit penalty.

The debtor could not, however, recover from the IRS prejudgment interest on the preferential payment. Although Bankruptcy Code section 106 expressly waives the government's sovereign immunity in preference actions generally, the court held that such waiver does not encompass prejudgment interest.[78]

Where the trust fund payment is recovered, the potential liability of any responsible person or creditor for such unpaid trust fund taxes (*see* §§ 103, 104, and 1006.3) generally would be resurrected, subject to a later payment of such taxes under a Chapter 11 plan or otherwise (*see* § 1016.2).[79]

From a slightly different perspective, courts have been reluctant to apply a trust concept and *Begier*-type analysis in favor of a *taxpayer* who uses a payroll tax service or other agent for making tax deposits and whose tax monies are caught up in *the agent's* bankruptcy.[80]

---

[77] Although an issue in many cases, the IRS here stipulated that the five payments enabled it to receive more than if the debtor had been liquidated in a Chapter 7 proceeding.

[78] *See* also note 64, *supra*.

[79] *See, e.g.*, IRS Legal Memorandum 199949034, September 14, 1999, *reprinted at* 1999 TNT 238-50.

[80] *See, e.g., Wyle v. S&S Credit Co. (In re Hamilton Taft & Co.)*, 53 F.3d 285 (9th Cir. 1995), *appeal dismissed as moot and vacated*, 68 F.3d 337 (9th Cir. 1995) (case settled); *In re S & S Lumber Co., Inc.*, 178 B.R. 397 (Bankr. M.D. Pa. 1995); *Morin v. Elmira Water Board (In re AAPEX Systems, Inc.)*, 273 B.R. 35,

Presenting a further perspective on *Begier*, the debtor in *In re U.S. Wireless Corp., Inc.*,[81] had prior to filing bankruptcy remitted to the IRS employment taxes due in respect of an employee's exercised stock options. A liquidating trust established under the debtor's chapter 11 plan thereafter sought to recover (as a fraudulent transfer) the "withholding tax" portion from the employee. The employee argued that, under *Begier*, the debtor's remittance of such taxes established that such amounts were not property of the debtor and therefore unrecoverable. The court disagreed, explaining that the remitted amounts did not reflect amounts actually "collected" or "withheld" from the employee and, thus, no "trust" was created under Code § 7501.

In *In re The Warnaco Group, Inc.*,[82] the debtor successfully recovered from a temporary employment service as a voidable preference amounts paid to the employment service for services rendered during the preceding five months. The court rejected the employment service's attempt to have itself viewed as some sort of intermediary, rather than as the real provider of services (with the temporary workers on its payroll).

In contrast, in *In re Firstpay, Inc.*,[83] the Chapter 7 trustee for a payroll services firm sought to recover under various theories, including voidable preference, client employment tax monies that it had paid to the IRS in respect of its clients' taxes. The court had little problem concluding that no voidable preference had occurred, in that the payments were made on behalf of the firm's clients and not with respect to an antecedent debt owed by the firm to the IRS.

## *§ 1005.3 Recoverable Setoffs*

Under Bankruptcy Code section 553(b), a setoff of a prepetition overpayment against unpaid prepetition taxes within 90 days prior to the bankruptcy filing is not a voidable preference and is effectively permitted (although the statutory language is very convoluted) except to the extent such overpayment was incurred during such 90-day period.[84] Thus, for example, a debtor corporation could not recover "excess" estimated tax payments that the IRS setoff against prior year deficiencies, where the bankruptcy filing occurred more than 90 days after the end of the taxable year of the

(Footnote Continued)

2002-1 U.S.T.C. ¶ 50,234 (Bankr. W.D. N.Y. 2002), *aff'd sub. nom. Morin v. Frontier Business Technologies*, 288 B.R. 663 (W.D. N.Y. 2003) (held that monies paid over to the IRS by the debtor (a payroll tax service) on the taxpayer's behalf were a voidable preference to the taxpayer, even though the debtor had filed the requisite agency form with the IRS under Code § 3504; court exhibited a general reluctance to extend *Begier*, as well as finding an inability to trace in the circumstances).

[81] *The Liquidating Trust of U.S. Wireless Corp., Inc. (In re U.S. Wireless Corp., Inc.)*, 333 B.R. 688 (Bankr. D. Del. 2005).

[82] *Authentic Fitness Corp. v. Dobbs Temp. Help Servs., Inc. (In re Warnaco Group, Inc.)*, 2006 U.S. Dist. LEXIS 4263 (S.D. N.Y. 2006).

[83] 2006-2 U.S.T.C. ¶ 50,530 (Bankr. D. Md. 2006).

[84] *See also* 11 U.S.C. § 542(b). For this purpose, it makes no difference whether the debtor was insolvent at the time of the setoff.

overpayment.[85] However, had the bankruptcy filing occurred within such 90-day period, the full amount of the overpayments could be recovered since the "overpayment" relating to estimated taxes was not considered to arise until the end of the taxable year.[86]

It should be noted that Bankruptcy Code section 553 only preserves (rather than authorizes) a creditor's right of setoff.[87] Thus, in the first instance, any setoff by the IRS must be in compliance with Code § 6402 ("Authority to Make Credits and Refunds") and the regulations thereunder.

## *§ 1005.4 Voiding Tax Liens and Recovering Seized Assets*

A properly filed (perfected) tax lien is not a voidable preference.[88] If, however, the tax lien is not perfected or enforceable as against a third party purchaser (whether or not then existing) as of the commencement of the bankruptcy case, it may be avoided under Bankruptcy Code section 545(2).[89]

---

[85] *Remillong v. United States,* 131 B.R. 727 (Bankr. D. Mont. 1991).

[86] For the latter proposition, *see also Midkiff v. Dunivent* (*In re Midkiff*), 271 B.R. 383 (Bankr. 10th Cir. 2002) (refund arose at end of year, not when tax return is filed); *Harbaugh v. United States* (*In re Harbaugh*), 89-2 U.S.T.C. ¶ 9608 (W.D. Pa. 1989), *aff'd without opinion,* 902 F.2d 1560 (3d Cir. 1990) (refund accrues at end of taxable year); *In re Glenn,* 207 B.R. 418, 97-1 U.S.T.C. ¶ 50,188 (E.D. Pa. 1997) (irrelevant that interest does not start to accrue on refund until a later date); *In re Thorvund-Statland,* 158 B.R. 837 (Bankr. D. Idaho, 1993); *Sticka v. Mellon Bank (DE) Natl. Assn.* (*In re Martin*), 167 B.R. 609 (Bankr. D. Or. 1994); *In re Franklin Sav. Corp.,* 177 B.R. 356, 95-1 U.S.T.C. ¶ 50,163 (Bankr. D. Kan. 1995); *but see Hankerson v. United States* (*In re Hankerson*), 133 B.R. 711 (Bankr. E.D. Pa. 1991), *rev'd on other grounds,* 138 B.R. 473 (E.D. Pa. 1992) (held that overpayment is incurred on the date the IRS authorizes the refund, rather than end of the taxable year; thus, issue was whether IRS authorization was within 90 days of bankruptcy filing); *cf. Dougherty v. United States* (*In re Dougherty*), 187 B.R. 883, 886, 95-2 U.S.T.C. ¶ 50,623 (Bankr. E.D. Pa. 1995) (refund arose no earlier than the filing of the tax return claiming the refund).

[87] *See, e.g.,* H. Rep. No. 595, 95th Cong., 1st Sess. 377 (1977); S. Rep. No. 989, 95th Cong., 2d Sess. 91-92 (1978).

[88] 11 U.S.C. § 547(c)(6). *See, e.g., Reitmeyer v. Internal Revenue Service* (*In re Totten*), 82 B.R. 402 (Bankr. W.D. Pa. 1988) (properly filed tax lien was not a voidable preference due to 11 U.S.C. § 547(c)(6)); *Borque v. United States* (*In re Borque*), 123 F.3d 705, 97-2 U.S.T.C. ¶ 50,630 (2d Cir. 1997) (duplicate lien filing does not render lien avoidable).

[89] *See, e.g., Stanford v. Butler* (*In re Stanford*), 826 F.2d 353 (5th Cir. 1987) (unrecorded tax lien for local property taxes not avoidable under Bankruptcy Code section 545(2) since, under Texas law, an unrecorded tax lien on realty is enforceable against a bona fide purchaser); *United States Leather, Inc. v. City of Milwaukee* (*In re United States Leather, Inc.*), 271 B.R. 306 (Bankr. E.D. Wis. 2001) (tax lien for prepetition Wisconsin water and sewer charges that came into existence postpetition and was not retroactively effective as of the beginning of the year was avoidable); *Robinson v. United States* (*In re Carolina Resort Motels, Inc.*), 85-2 U.S.T.C. ¶ 9628 (Bankr. D.S.C.); *Ducote v. United States* (*In the Matter of de la Vergne, II*), 156 B.R. 773 (1993) (IRS lien could be avoided where notice of tax lien was rendered unenforceable due to misspelling of debtor's last name), *aff'd,* 1994 U.S. Dist. LEXIS 6843 (E.D. La.); *United States v. LMS Holding Co.* (*In re LMS Holding Co.*), 50 F.3d 1526, 95-1 U.S.T.C. ¶ 50,201 (10th Cir. 1995) (where debtor acquired property subject to a tax lien, the tax lien remained perfected and could not be avoided even though not refiled in the debtor's name).

However, the failure of the IRS to timely refile notices of tax lien that expired after the commencement of the bankruptcy case was held not to affect the existence of the liens, but only the priority vis-a-vis other liens. *Global Sales Corp. v. United States,* Case No. Sa 85-00147 JB, Adv. No. SA91-3511 JB (Bankr. C.D. Cal. May 8, 1992). *See also United States v. Lowe* (*In re Hansen*), 1993 U.S.

Ordinarily, some of the properties afforded protection if acquired by a bona fide purchaser are listed in Code § 6323(b) and include, among other things, securities, motor vehicles, and personal property. The issue this presented was whether Code § 6323(b) affords a debtor-in-possession or bankruptcy trustee, standing in the shoes of a hypothetical purchaser, the ability to avoid a filed tax lien. The 2005 bankruptcy reforms clarified that the answer is no, effective for bankruptcy cases commenced on or after October 17, 2005.[90] Accordingly, Bankruptcy Code section 545(2) cannot be used to override the IRS's priority under Code § 6323.[91]

Although some lower courts early on had held that a debtor-in-possession could utilize Code § 6323(b) to avoid an IRS lien,[92] such success was short lived. Highly critical of these decisions, the Sixth Circuit rejected the position that Code § 6323(b) afforded any benefit under Bankruptcy Code section 545(2), on two grounds:[93]

- First, on the ground that, whereas a bona fide purchaser for purposes of Bankruptcy Code section 545(2) means "one who has purchased property for value without notice of any defects in title of the seller," a purchaser for purposes of Code § 6323 requires "adequate and full consideration in money or money's worth"—a significantly higher standard;[94] and
- Second, as relates to motor vehicles, as to which Code § 6323(b) requires that the purchaser have actual possession,[95] on the basis that the Bankruptcy Code does not impute possession to the hypothetical purchaser. Although involving a bankruptcy trustee, the court made clear that its analysis applies equally to a debtor-in-possession in that a debtor-in-possession and a hypothetical purchaser are two separate persons. The attributes of the one cannot be imbued to the other.

---

(Footnote Continued)

Dist. LEXIS 5593 (W.D. Tex.) (refilings did not violate stay and did not transfer any new property interest to creditor; lower court found that Bankruptcy Code section 108(c) protected the IRS liens from expiring).

[90] 11 U.S.C. § 545(2), *as amended by* P.L. 109-8, § 711 (2005).

[91] The 2005 amendment also protects the priority of any state or local taxing authority under a similar provision of state or local law.

[92] *See, e.g., United States v. Sierer*, 139 B.R. 752 (N.D. Fla. 1991) (distinguished cases under Chapter 13); *In re Znider*, 150 B.R. 239 (Bankr. C.D. Cal.), *vacated on other grounds*, 167 B.R. 603 (C.D. Cal. 1993).

[93] *United States v. Hunter (In re Walter)*, 45 F.3d 1023, 95-1 U.S.T.C. ¶ 50,072 (6th Cir. 1995). *Accord Battley v. United States (In re Berg)*, 121 F.3d 535, 97-2 U.S.T.C. ¶ 50,665 (9th Cir. 1997) (involving a security); *Janssen v. United States (In re Janssen)*, 213 B.R. 558, 97-2 U.S.T.C. ¶ 50,860 (Bankr. 8th Cir. 1997), *rev'g in relevant part* 96-2 U.S.T.C. ¶ 50,588 (Bankr. N.D. Iowa 1996) (also involving a security). For a discussion of the conflicting decisions, *see* Bowmar, The Bankruptcy Trustee as "Bona Fide Purchaser" Under Section 545(2) Against Federal Tax Liens on Personal Property, 29 Unif. Comm. Code L.J. 168 (1996).

[94] *See* Code § 6323(h)(6).

[95] *See* Code § 6323(b)(2). Possession is not required in the case of a purchaser of securities or personal property.

As relates to the latter proposition, most courts agreed that a trustee does not have "hypothetical possession."[96] The IRS later adopted the Sixth Circuit's reasoning and conclusions as its litigating position.[97]

Aside from Bankruptcy Code section 545, which specifically governs the avoidance of statutory liens, it is possible that an unfiled tax lien may also be avoided under Bankruptcy Code section 544(a)(1)—which treats a debtor-in-possession (or trustee) as a hypothetical judicial lien creditor—or under another part of section 544(a). Whereas some courts have applied section 544(a) to statutory liens, others have held that section 545 is exclusive.[98] A "statutory lien" is a lien arising solely by force of a statute (on specified circumstances or conditions).[99]

In contrast to the creation of a tax lien, a seizure of the debtor's assets pursuant to a tax lien may constitute a voidable preference.[100] This will frequently depend on whether the IRS is considered to have recovered more by way of the seizure than it would have recovered were the debtor to liquidate under Chapter 7.[101] Alternatively, a debtor-in-possession (or trustee) may be able to obtain the "turn over" of the seized property pursuant to Bankruptcy Code section 542(a) unless the property was sold (or otherwise transferred to a third party) in good faith before the IRS had actual

---

96 *See* the Sixth Circuit's decision (citing cases), and *cf. Sierer, supra* note 92 (citing cases). *But see Fandre v. IRS* (*In re Fandre*), 167 B.R. 837 (Bankr. E.D. Tex. 1994).

97 *See* IRS Litigation Guideline Memorandum GL-39A, July 12, 1996, *reprinted at* 2000 TNT 91-35.

98 *Compare Gonzales v. United States* (*In re Silver*), 303 B.R. 849 (Bankr. 10th Cir. 2004) (supports potential application of both provisions), *supplemented by*, 305 B.R. 381 (2004); *In re HDI Partners*, 202 B.R. 524, 97-1 U.S.T.C. ¶50,102 (Bankr. S.D. Fla. 1996) (applied both provisions), *with In re Sullivan*, 254 B.R. 661 (Bankr. D. N.J. 2000) (concludes that section 545 is exclusive, based on apparent legislative intent, comprehensive regime for avoidance of statutory liens, and the basic maxim that the more specific provision controls over the more general); *Goldstein v. Griffing* (*In re Goldstein*), 297 B.R. 766 (Bankr. D. Ariz. 2003) (section 545 is the exclusive provision for statutory liens).

99 11 U.S.C. §101(53). A statutory lien does *not* include a security interest or judicial lien, whether or not such interest or lien is provided by or is dependent on a statute and whether or not such interest or lien is made fully effective by statute. Id.

100 *See, e.g., United States v. Daniel* (*In re R & T Roofing Struc. & Comm. Framing, Inc.*), 887 F.2d 981, 89-2 U.S.T.C. ¶9607 (9th Cir. 1989) (IRS seizure of debtor's general office bank account pursuant to a tax lien for unpaid employee withholding taxes was a preferential "transfer," even though the tax lien was perfected more than 90 days prior to the filing of the bankruptcy petition; because the withheld taxes were not held in a segregated account and could not be traced to the seized funds, the seized funds were not amounts held "in trust" for the IRS under Code §7501); *In re Cleveland Graphic Reproductions, Inc.*, 78 B.R. 819 (Bankr. N.D. Ohio 1987) (rejected argument that seizure of assets was in ordinary course of business and thus not avoidable). *But see Fandre v. IRS* (*In re Fandre*), *supra* note 96.

101 In this regard, it should be noted that, under Chapter 7, tax liens generally are subordinated in right to non-tax secured claims and all administrative and priority claims (including priority tax claims). *See* 11 U.S.C. §724(b). As such, under Chapter 7, any tax claim that, but for the tax lien, would be a priority tax claim will be so classified and paid accordingly. *See Barstow v. United States* (*In re Markair, Inc.*), 308 F.3d 1038 (9th Cir. 2002), *cert. denied*, 123 S. Ct. 2575 (2003) (subordination under Bankruptcy Code section 724(b) only applies to statutory tax liens, and not to contractual or judicial liens obtained by the IRS); *United States v. Morgan* (*In re Morgan*), 196 B.R. 758 (E.D. Ky. 1996) (distinguishing setoff right from tax lien for purposes of Bankruptcy Code section 724(b); held setoff right preserved). It is therefore entirely possible that a tax claim with a properly filed tax lien could fare less well under Chapter 7.

notice or knowledge of the bankruptcy filing.[102] In such event, the IRS would be entitled to adequate protection of its secured interest.[103] In effect, Bankruptcy Code section 542(a) ensures that any assets of the debtor that might be essential to a successful reorganization are available to the debtor corporation.[104] The failure of the IRS to turn over estate property in a timely manner would be a violation of the automatic stay.[105]

---

[102] *See United States v. Whiting Pools, Inc.* (S. Ct.), *supra* note 59; 11 U.S.C. § 542(c) ("good faith" defense); *see also Schieffler v. United States (In re Howk)*, 1990 Bankr. LEXIS 2772 (Bankr. E.D. Ark.) (IRS had "good faith" defense, even though transfer to third party occurred after IRS received notice of bankruptcy case; court held that, because a "freeze code" was promptly entered into the IRS computer but, due to the limitations of the computer systems, was not operative until after the transfer, the IRS did not have "effective notice" when the transfer occurred); Note, Bankruptcy and Turnover Proceedings Against the IRS: A Path Toward Reorganization and Rehabilitation Fraught with Pitfalls, 4 Whittier L. Rev. 87 (1982).

In accord with the developing case law, the IRS has indicated that it will no longer attempt to distinguish between tangible property (long recognized to be properly the subject of turnover by the Supreme Court in *Whiting Pools*) and intangible property (such as bank accounts), but, rather, will evaluate whether turnover is warranted solely based upon adequate protection considerations. *See* IRS Litigation Guideline Memorandum GL-67, August 29, 1997, *reprinted at* 2000 TNT 102-53; *see also* IRS Chief Counsel Advice 200247025, November 22, 2002, *reprinted at* 2002 TNT 227-63. For earlier discussions and case law regarding whether a debtor retains a property interest in cash or cash equivalents that have been levied upon but not paid over prior to bankruptcy, *see, e.g., Camacho v. United States*, 190 B.R. 895, 96-1 U.S.T.C. ¶ 50,103 (D. Alaska 1995), *recons. denied*, 195 B.R. 114, 96-1 U.S.T.C. ¶ 50,104 (D. Alaska 1996), *appeal dismissed*, 131 F.3d 1289, 97-2 U.S.T.C. ¶ 50,931 (9th Cir. 1997); *Brown v. Evanston Bank (In re Brown)*, 126 B.R. 767 (N.D. Ill. 1991); *In re Anaheim Electric Motor, Inc.*, 137 B.R. 791 (Bankr. C.D. Cal. 1992) (holding that accounts receivable are not cash equivalents, but discussing authorities to the contrary); Falk, Recovering Prepetition Levies and Seizures by the IRS, 4 Faulkner & Gray's Bankr. L. Rev. #1, 21 (Spring 1992). *See also United States v. Challenge Air Intl., Inc. (In re Challenge Air International, Inc.)*, 952 F.2d 384, 92-1 U.S.T.C. ¶ 50,090 (11th Cir. 1992) (upheld turnover of accounts receivable that were levied upon prepetition but still held by the third party as of the bankruptcy filing); *West Aire Refrigeration Co. v. United States (In re West Aire, Inc.)*, 131 B.R. 871 (1991) (same); *contra Silverman v. Johnson Controls, Inc. (In re Sigmund London, Inc.)*, 139 B.R. 765, 92-2 U.S.T.C. ¶ 50,421 (Bankr. E.D.N.Y. 1992); *In re Eisenbarger*, 160 B.R. 542, 93-2 U.S.T.C. ¶ 50,538 (Bankr. E.D. Va. 1993) (case-by-case analysis; not subject to turnover where tax liability exceeds value of receivable at issue).

[103] *See United States v. Whiting Pools, Inc., supra* note 59 at 211-212. *See also* IRS Litigation Guideline Memorandum GL-67, August 29, 1997, *reprinted at* 2000 TNT 102-53.

[104] Id. at 208.

[105] *State of California Empl. Dev. Dept. v. Taxel (In re Del Mission Limited)*, 98 F.3d 1147 (9th Cir. 1996) (no discussion of adequate protection); *A & J Auto Sales, Inc. v. United States (In re A & J Auto Sales, Inc.)*, 223 B.R. 839, 98-1 U.S.T.C. ¶ 50,416 (D. N.H. 1988) (collecting cases), *reh'g denied* (June 24, 1998), *reprinted at* 98 TNT 145-8; *cf. Gouveia v. IRS (In re Quality Health Care)*, 215 B.R. 543, 97-2 U.S.T.C. ¶ 50,695 (Bankr. N.D. Ind. 1997) (IRS failure to comply did not violate automatic stay because trustee did not offer or provide IRS with any adequate protection for its lien interest); *In re Giles*, 271 B.R. 903 (Bankr. M.D. Fla. 2002) (non-tax case to same effect); *In re Martha Fitch*, 217 B.R. 286 (Bankr. S.D. Cal. 1998) (collecting cases involving repossessed cars for which return is sought; based on state law, court viewed debtor's property interest to be a statutory right to redeem the car rather than the car itself).

## §1005.5 *Treatment of IRS Claim in Connection With an Avoidable Transfer*

As discussed above, a debtor-in-possession may recover under the avoidance provisions of the Bankruptcy Code various prepetition transfers of money and other property.[106] These include preferential transfers (*see* §1005.2), recoverable setoffs (*see* §1005.3), and seized property (*see* §1005.4). In addition, a debtor-in-possession may recover under Bankruptcy Code section 548 property that was fraudulently conveyed. In many of these cases, the IRS will have applied the payment or property transferred in satisfaction of the debtor's outstanding tax liability. Where the payment or property is thereafter recovered, the IRS's claim against the debtor will be resurrected.

Although the resulting claim technically arises during the bankruptcy, Bankruptcy Code section 502(h) provides that the claim "shall be determined, and [generally] shall be allowed . . . , the same as if such claim had arisen before the date of the filing of the petition."[107] Thus, the IRS generally should be treated no differently than if the avoidable transfer had not occurred.[108] This does not preclude the debtor from avoiding any tax lien (*see also* §1005.4) and thus rendering the IRS claim unsecured, since the voiding of the tax claim does not give rise to a new claim.[109] Nor, on the other hand, should it prevent the IRS from thereafter seeking court approval to set off its claim against any mutual prepetition obligations it has to the debtor.

An important exception to this same-as-before treatment is contained in Bankruptcy Code section 502(d), which is intended to ensure a creditor's compliance with the recovery provisions of the Bankruptcy Code. Such section *requires* the bankruptcy court to *disallow any prepetition claim* of a creditor from whom any money or other property is recoverable *unless* the creditor has repaid the amount or returned the property. And "any" claim means exactly what it says: All prepetition claims of the creditor, not only the claim that is the subject of the particular recovery provision, are required to be disallowed.

---

[106] *See* 11 U.S.C. §550, authorizing recovery of avoided transfers, with certain exceptions such as in the case of subsequent good faith transferees for value with no knowledge of the voidability of the original transfer. *See, e.g., Liebersohn v. IRS (In re C.F. Foods, L.P.)* (Bankr. E.D. Pa.), *supra* note 5 (court rejected argument that the IRS was a "mere conduit" for monies paid by the debtor to the IRS on behalf of a limited partner of the debtor, where the IRS refunded some but not all of the monies to the limited partner); *Richardson v. United States (In re Anton Noll, Inc.)*, 277 B.R. 875 (Bankr. 1st Cir. 2002), *aff'g*, 2001 Bankr. LEXIS 346 (Bankr. D. R.I. 2001) (Chapter 7 trustee could not recover company funds paid to the IRS by the CEO for his own benefit where the funds were initially represented by a company check made out to "cash" which the CEO then endorsed and presented to the bank for a "treasurer's check" payable to the IRS; the CEO was the initial transferee; the IRS was a subsequent good faith transferee for value).

[107] This provision also applies to any claim arising due to the recovery of an unauthorized postpetition transfer under Bankruptcy Code section 549.

[108] *See, e.g., Fleet National Bank v. Gray (In re Bankvest Capital Corp.)*, 375 F.3d 51 (1st Cir. 2004), and *In re Gibout*, 2000-2 U.S.T.C. ¶50,583 (Bankr. E.D. Mich. 2000), illustrating the application of Bankruptcy Code section 502(h).

[109] Id.

From an IRS/creditor's perspective, the potential reach of section 502(d) is frightening. For example, most courts have held that section 502(d) applies to disallow a creditor's claims even if the statutory period during which the debtor-in-possession can bring an avoidance action has expired.[110] Thus, the IRS and other creditors must be vigilant in examining whether any payments or property received or obtained from the debtor are properly recoverable, or else risk their claims being disallowed. Moreover, the Ninth Circuit Court of Appeals recently took the surprising position that a creditor's defense of an avoidance action (in that case, the City of El Paso's assertion that its statutory lien was valid) constituted a refusal to turn over or release the property such that, upon the court adjudication that the transfer (the imposition of the lien) was avoidable, section 502(d) applied and instantaneously disallowed the City's claims. In effect, the Ninth Circuit requires that the creditor first return the property, leaving control of the property with the debtor-in-possession until the avoidance action is resolved.[111] This is in direct conflict with the view of the Fifth Circuit Court of Appeals, which held that a creditor (there, the IRS) should be afforded a reasonable period of time to comply with the court order before its claims are dismissed, and concluded that five days was not a reasonable period.[112] Aside from these two decisions, very few courts appear to have considered the issue.[113]

Finally, although not surprisingly, even if a creditor's claims are disallowed by section 502(d) due to the creditor's failure to return the improperly transferred

---

[110] *See* Collier on Bankruptcy ¶ 502.05[2][a] (15th rev. ed. 1999); *El Paso City v. America West Airlines Inc.* (*In re America West Airlines Inc.*), 217 F.3d 1161 (9th Cir. 2000); *United States Lines, Inc., et al. v. United States* (*In re McLean Industries., Inc.*), 196 B.R. 670 (S.D.N.Y. 1996), *aff'g*, 184 B.R. 10 (Bankr. S.D. N.Y. 1995). *See also* Steinberg and Fruchter, Bankruptcy Code Section 502(d): Back Door to Avoidance, 28 Unif. Comm. Code L. J. 73 (1995) (discussing majority and minority views). An avoidance action generally must be brought within two years of the commencement of the bankruptcy or, if longer, one year after the appointment of a trustee. *See* 11 U.S.C. § 546(a). An avoidance action with respect to an unauthorized postpetition transfer under Bankruptcy Code section 549 generally must be brought within two years of the unauthorized transfer. *See* 11 U.S.C. § 549(d).

[111] *El Paso City v. America West Airlines Inc.* (*In re America West Airlines Inc.*) (9th Cir.), *supra* note 110.

[112] *Campbell v. United States* (*In re Davis*), 889 F.2d 658 (5th Cir. 1989), *cert. denied*, 495 U.S. 933 (1990) ("The legislative history and policy behind Section 502(d) illustrates that the section is intended to have the coercive effect of insuring compliance with judicial orders"). Factually, the Fifth Circuit decision involved an administrative freeze imposed by the IRS on any refunds while an asserted tax deficiency remained in dispute. The Fifth Circuit upheld the freeze, until a "reasonable period of time" after the tax deficiency was fully adjudicated. The reader should be careful not to rely on the Fifth Circuit for its position of set off in this case in light of the Supreme Court's 1995 decision in *Citizen's Bank of Maryland v. Strumpf*, discussed at § 1006.1.1 below.

[113] *See In re Red Dot Scenic, Inc.*, 313 B.R. 181 (Bankr. S.D. N.Y. 2004) (holding that a creditor's claim was disallowed under section 502(d) unless, prior to the court's decision, the creditor had turned over the monies, plus interest, determined in prior proceedings to have been fraudulently transferred; the court rejected the creditor's contention that the trustee should first have attempted collection of the prior judgment); *Seta Corp. of Boca, Inc. v. Atlantic Computer Systems* (*In re Atlantic Computer Systems*), 173 B.R. 858 (S.D. N.Y. 1994) (adopted Fifth Circuit's view); Collier on Bankruptcy ¶ 502.05[1], [2][a] (15th rev. ed. 1999). *See also Holloway v. IRS* (*In re Odom Antennas, Inc.*), 340 F.3d 705, 2003-2 U.S.T.C. ¶ 50,634 (8th Cir. 2003) (involving a related but different issue, the Eighth Circuit favorably cited the Fifth Circuit's decision).

property in a timely manner, the creditor must still turn over the property assuming an avoidance action was timely brought.

Another area of contention involving section 502(d) is whether the bankruptcy court can invoke that section to disallow a *previously* allowed claim within the context of a subsequently brought avoidance action. More recent decisions have concluded that it can.[114]

An action to disallow a claim under section 502(d) can be raised either as a defense to an asserted claim or as an affirmative cause of action.[115] If the section 502(d) disallowance action is brought prior to a resolution of the substantive avoidance action, any claim in question will be treated as a disputed claim until the avoidance action is resolved.[116]

## §1006 TAX PAYMENT AND REPORTING REQUIREMENTS IN BANKRUPTCY

Whether the debtor corporation is operating as a debtor-in-possession or a trustee has been appointed, the reporting and payment obligations are generally the same. These are described below.

### *§1006.1 Prepetition Taxable Years*

The Bankruptcy Code provides that, if for any prepetition taxable year a tax return has not been filed, the debtor-in-possession in a Chapter 11 case must supply any information with respect to such unfiled tax return that the IRS may require in light of the condition of the debtor's books and records and the availability of the information.[1] Only in a small business case filed on or after October 17, 2005, does the Bankruptcy Code impose on the debtor corporation an affirmative obligation to file timely tax returns and other required government filings.[2] The Internal Revenue Code goes further. It requires all debtors-in-possession or trustees to file any unfiled

---

[114] *Compare TWA Inc. Post Confirmation Estate v. City & County of San Francisco Airports Comm'n* (*In re TWA Inc. Post Confirmation Estate*), 305 B.R. 221 (Bankr. D. Del. 2004) (permitted); *Peltz v. Gulfcoast Workstation Group* (*In re Bridge Info. Sys., Inc.*), 293 B.R. 479 (Bankr. E.D. Mo. 2003); *Rhythms Netconnections, Inc. v. Cisco Systems, Inc.* (*In re Rhythms Netconnections*), 300 B.R. 404 (Bankr. S.D. N.Y. 2003), *with Caliolo v. Azdel, Inc.* (*In re Cambridge Indus. Holdings Inc.*), 2003 Bankr. LEXIS 794 (Bankr. D. Del. 2003) (not permitted); *LaRoche Indus., Inc. v. Gen. Am. Transp. Corp.* (*In re LaRoche Indus., Inc.*), 284 B.R. 406 (Bankr. D. Del. 2002).

[115] *Enron Corp. v. Avenue Special Situations Fund II, LP* (*In re Enron Corp.*), 340 B.R. 180 (Bankr. S.D. N.Y. 2006).

[116] Id (also holding that a claim in the hands of a transferee remains subject to later section 502(d) disallowance action, just as if such claim was still held by the transferor).

[1] **§1006** 11 U.S.C. §1106(a)(6) (also insulates trustee from personal liability for supplying such information).

[2] 111 U.S.C. §1116(6)(A). A small business case generally is one where the debtor has fixed liabilities of $2 million or less, and no committee of unsecured creditors is appointed. 11 U.S.C. §101(51C), (51D) (excludes real estate companies); Interim Bankruptcy Rule 1020.

returns or else suffer the possible imposition of penalties for failure to do so.[3] Similarly, a bankruptcy court may order the debtor to file its tax returns.[4] A debtor (and any responsible officer or controlling person)[5] that fails to comply with such an order may be held in contempt of court and subject to appropriate sanctions, including dismissal of the bankruptcy case or conversion of the case to Chapter 7.[6] Moreover, effective for bankruptcy cases commenced on or after October 17, 2005, the Bankruptcy Code provides for the dismissal or conversion of the case when the debtor (i) fails to timely file any tax return that becomes due (with extensions) after the commencement of the bankruptcy case *and* (ii) does not rectify the situation within 90 days of the IRS's request for dismissal or conversion due to the debtor's failure to so file.[7]

Where a trustee has been appointed, a 1963 ruling indicates that any form or return he files with the IRS should be accompanied by a copy of the order appointing him as trustee.[8] More recent IRS instructions and publications do not mention any such requirement.[9]

The debtor-in-possession, however, generally is precluded from *paying* prepetition taxes (including employment withholding taxes) without first obtaining court

---

[3] *See* Code § 6012(b)(3), requiring that a receiver or bankruptcy trustee, who has possession of or holds title to all or substantially all the property or business of a corporation (whether or not the property or business is being operated), file income tax returns for the corporation; Reg. § 1.6012-3(b)(4); *In re Hudson Oil Co.*, 88-2 U.S.T.C. ¶ 9554 (Bankr. D. Kan.) (applied to prepetition taxable years); *see also In re Hahn*, 200 B.R. 249 (Bankr. M.D. Fla. 1996); Code § 6658(a) (relieved only from penalties for failure to *pay* prepetition taxes); IRS Field Service Advice 1999-1040, June 29, 1992 (discusses purpose of fiduciary's filing obligation; factually involves the appointment of a trustee concurrent with confirmation of the Chapter 11 plan), *reprinted at* 1999 TNT 91-40. Effective for bankruptcy cases commenced on or after October 22, 1994, the IRS may formally demand that any unfiled tax returns be filed without it violating the automatic stay. *See* 11 U.S.C. § 362(b)(9)(C).

[4] *See infra* note 6; *see also United States v. Farrell (In re Farrell)*, 241 B.R. 348, 99-1 U.S.T.C. ¶ 50,499 (Bankr. M.D. Pa. 1999) (Chapter 13 case; court declined to do so where IRS failed to establish, or even allege, that it was unable to file an accurate proof of claim without the debtor's tax returns, that the debtor was uncooperative or that the debtor refused to supply relevant financial information under Bankruptcy Rule 2004).

[5] *See* Bankruptcy Rule 9001(5).

[6] *See, e.g., In re Hahn, supra* note 3 (individual's bankruptcy case dismissed for failure to comply with repetitive bankruptcy court orders to file prepetition tax returns; found that failure demonstrated lack of good faith in filing the bankruptcy case); *Jablonski v. IRS*, 204 B.R. 456 (W.D. Pa. 1996) (to similar effect), *aff'd*, 114 F.3d 1172 (3d Cir. 1997); *In re International Art Galleries, Inc.*, No. 87-00353, (Bankr. D. Haw. July 31, 1990) (debtor failed to file tax returns for the taxable year preceding bankruptcy and all postpetition taxable years, despite multiple court orders; court refused to confirm debtor's plan of reorganization until returns were filed and, following the conversion of the case to Chapter 7, held both the debtor and the "controlling officer" in contempt of court for their continued failure; the officer could "purge himself of contempt," however, were he still to file the tax returns—at his own expense, if necessary); *In re Berryhill*, 127 B.R. 427 (Bankr. N.D. Ind. 1991).

[7] 11 U.S.C. § 521(j) (applies to all bankruptcy cases, including Chapter 7, and applies to *all* tax returns, including state and local tax returns).

[8] Rev. Rul. 63-104, 1963-1 C.B. 172.

[9] *See* Instructions to Form 1120 (U.S. Corp. Income Tax Return), p.2. (no mention of need to include copy of appointment); IRS Publication 908, Bankruptcy (July 1996) (same).

approval.[10] In most cases, this means that payment will be made only pursuant to a confirmed Chapter 11 plan. In some cases (such as a "pre-packaged" Chapter 11 plan), this may be merely a delay of a couple of months; however, in other cases, the delay may be several years. Although this delay provides the debtor the time necessary to get its economic affairs in order and to formulate a plan, many debtors promptly seek permission to pay certain types of taxes—such as withholding taxes and sales and use taxes, and sometimes even property taxes, license fees and the like—given the disruptive effect the deferred payment of such taxes could have on the debtor's operations, the debtor's high degree of confidence that such taxes ultimately would be paid under a Chapter 11 plan, and/or the "trust fund" nature of the taxes.[11] The principal focus of such requests generally is the payment of "trust fund" and other "responsible person" taxes, *i.e.*, those prepetition taxes for which the directors, officers or employees of the debtor may be personally liable in the event of nonpayment or where payment is unduly delayed (*see* §§1006.3 and 1102.4 below). However, such orders have, in some cases, included other prepetition taxes where, for example, the administrative costs of complying with the automatic stay is disproportionately high relative to the amount payable (such as oversecured property taxes where the state or local taxing authority continues to be entitled to interest at an above market rate). Not all courts are equally receptive to such requests, particularly to the extent such payments are seen as a departure from the normal Bankruptcy Code priorities for the payment of prepetition claims and viewed as unfairly favoring certain creditors over others.[12]

As discussed at §1012.1, any portion of a "quickie" refund of prepetition taxes received during the bankruptcy case that is subsequently determined to have been excessive is regarded as an administrative expense of the bankruptcy, and thus treated in the same fashion as a *postpetition* tax (*see* §1006.2 below).

**FUTA payments.** The fact that a payment to a state unemployment compensation fund is made late will not affect the debtor corporation's offset for such payment against any FUTA amounts payable, provided such failure was not the fault of the debtor-in-possession.[13]

### §1006.1.1 Setoff of Prepetition Taxes

Because of the potentially long delay in the payment of prepetition taxes and the associated risks of payment, one can readily understand the IRS's desire to set off any overpayment of taxes against any outstanding tax deficiencies (or other government obligations). Ordinarily, a creditor is precluded, without first obtaining bankruptcy

---

[10] 11 U.S.C. §549; *In re Bulk Transport, Inc.*, 83-1 U.S.T.C. ¶9133 (Bankr. E.D. La. 1983) (any payment without court approval is voidable). *See also* discussion at §1006.3 (a debtor's continuing obligation to pay over any withheld or collected taxes).

[11] For examples of these motions and orders, *see supra* §1002.2 at note 12.

[12] *See generally* Jenks, Ridgway, and Purnell, 790 T.M., Corporate Bankruptcy, at III.B.

[13] Code §3302(a)(5). *See In re Hospital General San Carlos, Inc.*, 88-1 U.S.T.C. ¶9214 (Bankr. D.P.R. 1988) (debtor permitted to set off payments made to a state unemployment fund against FICA liability to the extent otherwise creditable against debtor's FUTA liability).

court approval, from exercising whatever rights it may have in the non-bankruptcy context to set off mutual prepetition obligations.[14] Local rules or general court orders may sometimes permit the setoff of certain prepetition tax obligations, although the validity of such rules and orders is questionable.[15] Significantly, as part of the bankruptcy reform legislation passed in 2005, Congress excluded from this prohibition certain income tax offsets.

Effective for bankruptcy cases commenced on or after October 17, 2005, the IRS can setoff without bankruptcy court approval any *income* tax refund with respect to a taxable period that ended before the filing of the bankruptcy petition (or in the case of an involuntary bankruptcy, before the order for relief) against any *income* tax liability owing for another prepetition taxable period where such setoff would be permitted absent bankruptcy.[16] Moreover, where applicable nonbankruptcy law would not have permitted a setoff of an income tax refund due to "a pending action to determine the amount or legality of a tax liability," the IRS can *hold* the refund pending the resolution of the action unless the bankruptcy court, upon motion and after notice and hearing, grants the IRS adequate protection for its secured claim.[17] Although this change in law may rightfully ease the process of setoff where the tax liability owed by the debtor is fully agreed, it prematurely permits setoff where the debtor can still properly dispute such liability in bankruptcy but has not yet commenced an action. It also shifts the burden to the debtor-in-possession within the income tax context to seek release of a withheld refund, thereby freeing such administrative holds (or freezes) from the scope of the Supreme Court's decision in *Strumpf*, discussed below.

Aside from the foregoing exception—which is limited to income taxes and to bankruptcy cases commenced on or after October 17, 2005—the extent to which the IRS generally is precluded from setting off the over- and underpayments of prepetition taxes of corporate debtors is unclear, particularly in light of cases in the Seventh Circuit, as discussed below at § 1006.1.1.1. In addition, the IRS takes the position, based on the Supreme Court's decision in *Citizen's Bank of Maryland v. Strumpf*,[18] that a temporary freeze on the remittance of a debtor's tax refunds while the IRS seeks setoff approval from the bankruptcy court does not run afoul of the automatic stay

---

[14] *See* 11 U.S.C. §§ 362(a)(7) and 553(a) (automatic stay of setoffs); *consider also* the discussion at § 1006.1.1.4, below (automatic stay does not apply to equitable recoupment). Outside of bankruptcy, the decision to offset over- and underpayments is, under Code § 6402(a), entirely within the IRS's discretion. *See, e.g., Northern States Power Company v. United States*, 73 F.3d 764, 96-1 U.S.T.C. ¶ 50,022 (8th Cir. 1995), *cert. denied*, 117 S. Ct. 168 (1996); *see also infra* note 45. *See also* IRS Chief Counsel Advice 200014033 (April 7, 2000), *reprinted at* 2000 TNT 69-62, concluding that the IRS may recover "nonrebate" erroneous refunds (*i.e.*, amounts inadvertently refunded to a taxpayer that are not due to an asserted correction to the taxpayer's tax liability) pursuant to the IRS's common law right of setoff.

[15] *See* § 1007 at notes 7-8.

[16] 11 U.S.C. § 362(b)(26).

[17] Although the statute does not specifically limit the term "tax liability" in the context of an administrative hold to solely "income" tax liabilities, presumably the latter was intended and should be inferred since the statute presents the administrative hold as an "exception" to the situation where the setoff of a prepetition income tax refund against a prepetition income tax liability is not permitted.

[18] 516 U.S. 16 (1995).

(provided the freeze is for an amount equal or less than the offsetting obligation).[19] In the IRS's view, a "temporary" freeze generally would include the time necessary for the IRS to complete a pending audit of the debtor.[20]

In *Strumpf*, the Supreme Court held that a bank's temporary imposition of an "administrative hold" upon a debtor's checking account while it sought court approval to setoff the balance of the account against an outstanding loan to the debtor was not itself a "setoff" in violation of the automatic stay. The Court recognized that, to conclude otherwise, would be to render the bank's right of setoff effectively meaningless (as illustrated by the very facts in *Strumpf*) by providing the debtor the opportunity to deplete or withdraw its account before the bankruptcy court could approve the setoff.[21] The Court stated that for there to be a prohibited "setoff" within the meaning of the Bankruptcy Code a creditor's actions in refusing to pay must not only constitute a setoff under state law, but (whether or not required under state law) must be with the intent of permanently settling the debtor's obligations without court approval.[22] Courts generally have interpreted this as requiring the creditor to

---

[19] *See* IRS Manual, Part 5 (Collecting Process), Ch. 9 (Bankruptcy), § 4.4 (3/1/07), at ¶¶ 6 and 7 (requiring that IRS determine within up to 60 days of discovering that a refund is being retained whether to (i) issue the refund, (ii) seek permission to set it off, or (iii) continue to retain it). As discussed above, at text accompanying *supra* notes 16 and 17, effective for bankruptcy cases commenced on or after October 17, 2005, Bankruptcy Code section 362(b)(26) generally permits an IRS-imposed freeze with respect to refunds of prepetition income taxes where there is a pending dispute as to the debtor's prepetition income tax liability, and permits the amounts to be setoff where no dispute exists. If there is more than one outstanding income tax liability, the IRS may choose which liability to set off with the tax refund, regardless of the relative bankruptcy priority of the tax liabilities. *See, e.g., In re Lybrand*, 338 B.R. 402 (Bankr. W.D. Ark. 2006), and authorities at § 1013.5 n. 144.

[20] IRS Chief Counsel Advice 200217005, December 21, 2001, *reprinted at* 2002 TNT 82-86 (Issue 2b; cautioning, however, that "in cases where the Service expects some difficulty with concluding its audit process in an expeditious manner, [local area counsel] may want to consider acquiring the debtor's consent to the freeze or to file a motion to lift stay, or otherwise petition the court, to allow [the IRS] to keep the freeze in place").

[21] The Court also observed that it would eviscerate the exception in Bankruptcy Code section 542(b), concerning the turnover of property of the estate. Such section provides that an entity that owes a debt to a debtor that is matured, payable on demand, or payable on order, generally must pay such debt to, or upon order of, the trustee or debtor-in-possession "except to the extent that such debt may be offset . . . against a claim against the debtor."

[22] *Consider In re Schiller*, 98-1 U.S.T.C. ¶ 50,445 (Bankr. D. Nev. 1998) (filing of amended proof of claim by the IRS that reclassified a previously unsecured claim as secured, and indicated that the change in status was due to an "offset" of a recently agreed tax overpayment, violated the automatic stay; court rejected IRS contention that the amended claim did not effectuate the setoff but only asserted the IRS's "right" of setoff). The approach taken by the IRS in *In re Schiller* was consistent with the directive in the IRS Manual at the time. *See* former IRS Manual, Part 34 (General Litigation), Ch. 10 (Bankruptcy Code Cases), § 2.6 (1/16/98), at ¶ 2(B), stating that, when the IRS puts a freeze on a debtor's tax refund or overpayment, it has "the affirmative obligation to promptly seek relief from the stay, or, when a refund is retained prior to confirmation of a Chapter 11 or 13 plan, a proof of claim notifying the parties of the retention of the refund should be filed." Nevertheless, the IRS's practice does not always adhere to the IRS Manual's directive. *See, e.g., United States v. Holden*, 2000-2 U.S.T.C. ¶ 50,666 (D. Vt. 2000) (Chapter 13 case; IRS violated automatic stay where it imposed an open-ended freeze on refunds, did not limit the freeze to the amount of unpaid taxes, did not seek court permission to setoff, and sought to use the freeze as leverage to obtain payment; IRS agent testified that the freeze was implemented consistent with IRS policy).

promptly seek court approval. In *Strumpf*, the bank's motion for setoff was filed five days after imposition of the hold. In another case, a delay of three to five weeks was considered too long; yet, in other cases, longer delays have been permitted.[23] The Supreme Court's criterion for a prohibited setoff would suggest, as the IRS asserts, that the IRS should similarly be able to "temporarily" freeze a debtor's tax refunds while it promptly seeks court approval to setoff, although (as indicated above) the IRS takes a liberal view of what constitutes a temporary freeze and thus at what point it is required to seek court approval to either setoff or extend the freeze. In addition, however, the Supreme Court also considered certain other aspects of the automatic stay, which some courts believe distinguish the IRS's situation from that of a bank.

In *Strumpf*, the debtor, in addition to asserting that the bank's hold constituted an impermissable setoff, argued that the hold also violated the automatic stay in that it constituted an act "to obtain possession of property of the estate or of property from the estate or to exercise control over property of the estate"[24] and "to collect, assess, or recover a [prepetition] claim against the debtor."[25] The Supreme Court dismissed this argument on the grounds that it was premised on the notion that the bank took something ("property of the estate") from the debtor. The Court stated that a bank account is in fact "nothing more or less than a [contractual] promise to pay, from the bank to the depositor." As such, the bank's temporary refusal to pay was simply the refusal to perform, rather than the retention of the debtor's property. In contrast, the courts have long recognized that a debtor's right to a tax refund is itself property of the estate.[26] Based principally on this difference, some courts have held

---

(Footnote Continued)

For cases predating the Supreme Court's opinion, which may still provide helpful guidance or authority, *see, e.g., Duguay v. IRS*, 85-2 U.S.T.C. ¶9616 (Bankr. W.D.N.Y. 1985) (IRS's retention of debtor corporation's prepetition tax refund in a "suspense account" for purposes of setting off the refund against unpaid prepetition taxes is not a violation of the automatic stay; under New York law, mere "refusal to pay" is not setoff, affirmative steps required); *United States v. Reynolds*, 85-2 U.S.T.C. ¶9610 (4th Cir. 1985) (held that, in absence of controlling federal or state law, the mere retention of assets in a "suspense account" is a setoff in violation of the automatic stay); *United States v. Norton*, 717 F.2d 167, 83-2 U.S.T.C. ¶9583 (3d Cir. 1983) (Pennsylvania law leads to same conclusion); *Hudson v. United States (In re Hudson)*, 168 B.R. 449 (Bankr. S.D. Ga. 1994) (retention of refund "without expeditiously" seeking relief from the stay violated the stay).

23 *Compare In re Calore Express Company, Inc.*, 199 B.R. 424, 430 (Bankr. D. Mass. 1996) (in earlier proceeding, a three- to five-week delay was held to be too long), *aff'd sub. nom., United States v. Fleet National Bank (In re Calore Express Company, Inc.)*, 2000 U.S. Dist. LEXIS 19950 (D. Mass. 2000), *rev'd*, 288 F.3d 22 (1st Cir. 2002) (reversed on various issues due to the failure of the bankruptcy court to hold an evidentiary hearing on issues of intent and equity); *with Stewart v. Army & Air Force Exchange Service (In re Stewart)*, 253 B.R. 51, 2000-2 U.S.T.C. ¶50,778 (Bankr. E.D. Ark. 2000) (wherein a delay of 3 1/2 months was apparently not considered too long); and *In re Shortt*, 277 B.R. 683, 2002-2 U.S.T.C. ¶50,530 (Bankr. N.D. Tex. 2002) (bankruptcy court granted the Army & Air Force Exchange Service (AAFES) retroactive relief from the automatic stay for an earlier setoff of the debtor's income tax refund, despite a six month delay in seeking relief). The IRS has adopted a more liberal approach in this regard. *See* IRS Manual authority, *supra* note 19.

24 11 U.S.C. §362(a)(3).

25 11 U.S.C. §362(a)(6).

26 *See, e.g., Segal v. Rochelle*, 382 U.S. 375, 66-1 U.S.T.C. ¶9173 (1966); *Gibson v. United States (In re Russell)*, 927 F.2d 413, 91-1 U.S.T.C. ¶50,128 (8th Cir. 1991).

that a temporary freeze of a debtor's tax refunds by the IRS, even if not constituting a setoff, nevertheless violates the automatic stay.[27]

The Supreme Court also declared, however, from a more fundamental perspective, that it would not interpret the automatic stay in a way that would proscribe what the "exception" under Bankruptcy Code section 542(b) (involving the repayment to the debtor of a matured debt or a debt payable upon demand, *see* note 21 above) and the general rule of Bankruptcy Code section 553(a) (governing setoffs) "were plainly intended to permit: the temporary refusal of a creditor to pay a debt that is subject to setoff against a debt owned by the bankrupt." This has been viewed by some courts as the real holding of the case, to the point of dismissing as *dicta* the Court's treatment of a bank account as a promise to pay and not as estate property.[28] In contrast, debtors challenging such an IRS refusal will no doubt assert the fundamental axiom that any exemptions from the automatic stay must be strictly construed, and debate the applicability of Bankruptcy Code section 542(b) to tax refund claims.

The situation changes, though, where, for example, a claimed income tax refund relates to a taxable year which is already under examination by the IRS or which the IRS selects for examination in response to the refund claim. The IRS Chief Counsel has informally expressed the view that, in such instance, because the examination will determine whether an overpayment in fact exists, the failure to issue the claimed refund pending the outcome of the examination is not a violation of the automatic stay.[29] This, of course, assumes that the examination is not artificially prolonged.

---

[27] *See, e.g., United States v. Harchar*, 2007 U.S. Dist. LEXIS 47028 (N.D. Ohio 2007); *Holden v. United States (In re Holden)*, 236 B.R. 156, 99-2 U.S.T.C. ¶50,747 (Bankr. D. Vt. 1999) (so concluding, but also factually distinguishable as it involved an open-ended administrative freeze with no affirmative attempt by the IRS to obtain court approval prior to the debtor's motion for sanctions), *aff'd*, 2000-2 U.S.T.C. ¶50,666 (D. Vt. 2000) (district court distinguished IRS's actions factually, without addressing the propriety of a temporary IRS freeze). *Cf. In re Calore Express Company, Inc., supra* note 23 (bankruptcy and district courts held that the setoff of mutual postpetition obligations constitutes "an act to obtain possession of property of the estate or of property from the estate or to exercise control over property of the estate" under section 362(a)(3) of the Bankruptcy Code and thus violates the automatic stay; First Circuit reversed on other grounds).

But *see Stewart v. Army & Air Force Exchange Service (In re Stewart)* (Bankr. E.D. Ark), *supra* note 23 (in defense of the IRS's retention of the tax refund and dismissal of the debtor's recovery action, the court asserted that "it is well settled" that a creditor may hold the debtor's funds pending a timely motion for relief; note that, factually, the debtor did not commence its action until approximately 3½ months after the IRS had withheld the refund, at which point the IRS apparently had still not sought bankruptcy court relief; the court also stated that, to obtain relief from the stay under Bankruptcy Code section 362(d) and Bankruptcy Rule 4001, the IRS must affirmatively seek it and that a request for relief in the answer to a complaint for turnover does not suffice); *In re Stienes*, 2002 Bankr. LEXIS 945 (Bankr. D. N.J. 2002) ("The administrative freeze on the [tax] refund was validated by the Supreme Court in *Strumpf*").

[28] *See, e.g., Jimenez v. Wells Fargo Bank, N.A. (In re Jimenez)*, 335 B.R. 450, 457-59 (Bankr. D. N.M. 2005) (discussing the limited nature of the opinion, and citing authorities); *but see, e.g., United States v. Harchar* (N.D. Ohio), *supra* note 27, at n.12 (arguing against such a reading).

[29] IRS Chief Counsel Advice 200217005, December 21, 2001, *supra* note 20 (but indicates "it has long been the position of the Service and the courts that the Service may credit an overpayment only against a tax which has been formally assessed or for which a statutory notice of deficiency has been issued," and that a filed proof of claim is not sufficient); IRS Chief Counsel Advice 200051009, November 2, 2000, *reprinted at* 2000 TNT 248-69. *Cf. Harchar v. United States*, 2006 Bankr. LEXIS 3033

If the IRS timely seeks court approval, courts generally will allow the IRS to set off any overpayment of *prepetition* taxes against any unpaid prepetition taxes.[30] The debtor's liability for the prepetition tax must be sufficiently determined to be considered an "outstanding" liability.[31] In this regard, the IRS Chief Counsel in a 2002 internal advice stated that "it has long been the position of the [IRS] and the courts that the [IRS] may credit an overpayment only against a tax which has been formally assessed or for which a statutory notice of deficiency has been issued," and that the filing of a proof of claim in a bankruptcy case is not sufficient.[32] In 2007, however, the

(Footnote Continued)

(Bankr. N.D. Ohio 2006) (rejected such arguments in the context of a summary judgment motion wherein the debtor had alleged contrary facts which had to be treated as true), *aff'd*, 2007 U.S. Dist. LEXIS 47028 (N.D. Ohio 2007).

30 *See, e.g.*, *Segal v. Rochelle* (S. Ct.), *supra* note 26; *In re G.S. Omni Corp.*, 835 F.2d 1317 (10th Cir. 1987) (per curiam) (right of setoff unaffected by failure to file proof of claim); *In re Pleasant*, 320 B.R. 889 (Bankr. N.D. Ill. 2004) (readily granted retroactive relief from the stay to permit setoff where the IRS did not receive timely notice of the bankruptcy); *Crawford v. Dept. of Treas. IRS (In re Crawford)*, 2001-2 U.S.T.C. ¶50,769 (Bankr. W.D. Wis. 2001); *Weems v. United States (In re Custom Center, Inc.)*, 163 B.R. 309, 316-17, 94-1 U.S.T.C. ¶50,199 (Bankr. E.D. Tenn. 1994) (reviewing conflicting decisions on the effect of failing to assert right of setoff in a proof of claim); *In re Lawson*, 1995 Bankr. LEXIS 1438 (Bankr. D. Idaho 1995) (IRS permitted to setoff tax refund first against its general unsecured claim and then any remainder against its priority claim); *In re W.L. Jackson Mfg. Co.*, 50 B.R. 506, 85-2 U.S.T.C. ¶9543 (Bankr. E.D. Tenn. 1985) (irrelevant that refund claim not filed until after bankruptcy petition); *Harbaugh v. United States (In re Harbaugh)*, 89-2 U.S.T.C. ¶9608 (W.D. Pa. 1989), *aff'd without opinion*, 902 F.2d 1560 (3d Cir. 1990) (allowed setoff without prior court approval where IRS was unaware of bankruptcy; debtor's right to refund was a prepetition asset, because taxable year in which overpayment arose ended before the petition date; court observed that, for subsequent bankruptcy cases, the bankruptcy court has issued a standing order permitting the IRS to set off amounts within the first 60 days of bankruptcy); *In re Alibrandi*, 1990 Bankr. LEXIS 1002 (Bankr. N.D.N.Y.) (current setoff allowed "absent compelling circumstances"). *Cf. In re Shortt*, *supra* note 23 (granted retroactive relief to a previously effectuated setoff of an income tax refund).

Only in limited instances is a setoff not permitted, chief among which is where the claim to be offset is disallowed under Bankruptcy Code section 502(b). *See* 11 U.S.C. §553(a). *See also Southeast Bank, N.A. v. Grant (In re Apex Intl. Mgmt. Services, Inc.)*, 155 B.R. 591 (Bankr. M.D. Fla. 1993) (disallowed IRS setoff against amounts paid by Air Force, where IRS failed to timely assert setoff rights and the debtor reasonably relied on such failure).

The IRS, however, is not required to invoke its right of setoff. For example, in *Robert W. Sawyer v. United States*, 86-2 U.S.T.C. ¶9745 (N.D. Ind.), *rev'd on other grounds*, 831 F.2d 755, 87-2 U.S.T.C. ¶9573 (7th Cir. 1987), the chief operating officer of a Chapter 7 debtor remained subject to penalty under Code §6672 for failing to pay over withheld employment taxes where the IRS complied with a claim for refund of income taxes filed by the trustee of the debtor's estate rather than utilizing the refund as a setoff against the debtor's withholding tax liability.

31 *See* Reg. §301.6402-1 (IRS "may" credit any overpayment of tax against "any outstanding liability for any tax"); *United States v. Helig-Meyers Company* (E.D. Va.), discussed *infra* note 32.

32 IRS Chief Counsel Advice 200217005, December 21, 2001, *supra* note 20 (Issue 2; containing citations). In *United States v. Helig-Meyers Company*, 2003-1 U.S.T.C. ¶50,287 (E.D. Va. 2003) (affirming bankruptcy court decision, but remanding for further proceedings), the IRS, contrary to the position espoused in the text, sought bankruptcy court approval to setoff a pending tax refund against a proof of claim for "unassessed deficiencies in income taxes." The asserted deficiencies were based on an ongoing examination of the debtors' tax returns. While the IRS's motion was pending before the bankruptcy court, the IRS due to a computer error issued a check for the refund, which the debtors subsequently agreed to hold pending the outcome of the motion. The bankruptcy court proceeding on the motion (disregarding the later appeal) spanned approximately a year during which the IRS issued a "30-day letter" to the debtors describing the proposed adjustments, and the debtors objected

IRS issued Rev. Rul. 2007-51 and 2007-52. Although the first ruling formalizes the IRS's position with respect to a tax for which a statutory notice of deficiency was sent, the second ruling *reverses* the IRS's position as relates to a filed proof of claim. Similar in presentation, the rulings reasoned that both the notice and claim represent a specific administrative determination of the nature and amount of a tax debt that is entitled to a presumption of correctness, and thus reflect an outstanding liability. (The IRS similarly extended this position to "quickie" refunds. *See* § 1012.1 below.) The IRS did not address the potential implications of the automatic stay with respect to any such offset. In general, even if bankruptcy court approval to setoff is denied (and no exception to setoff applies), the IRS should still be regarded to the extent of its general right of setoff as holding a secured claim and thus entitled, on request, to "adequate protection" of its secured interest in the event the debtor seeks a refund of the overpayment.[33] As discussed above, the IRS's right to adequate protection in such instance is specifically provided for in the income tax context for bankruptcy cases commenced on or after October 17, 2005. On the other hand, a court generally will not allow an overpayment of *postpetition* taxes to be set off against unpaid prepetition taxes, nor will the IRS be treated as having a security interest in such overpayment.[34] It is generally irrelevant for purposes of setoff whether the tax claim would otherwise

---

(Footnote Continued)

to the proof of claim. The bankruptcy court ultimately denied the IRS's motion, concluding that "setoff is premature and cannot be made until there has been a valid assessment." On appeal, the district court found IRS Chief Counsel Advice 200217005 (discussed in the text above) to be particularly instructive, and similarly concluded that the IRS had failed to establish that it had a right of setoff under Code § 6402 and Bankruptcy Code section 553. Nevertheless, the court directed that the refund be held in escrow in an interest bearing account until the underlying tax liability was determined.

33 *See* 11 U.S.C. § 506(a), which treats a creditor's claim, which is otherwise unsecured, as a secured claim to the extent such claim is subject to setoff under Bankruptcy Code section 553 (involving mutual prepetition debts); 11 U.S.C. § 363(e), which provides for adequate protection of a creditor's interest in collateral; and 11 U.S.C. § 362(d), which provides that the lack of adequate protection is cause for lifting the automatic stay and permitting setoff. *See also* Bienenstock, Bankruptcy Reorganizations, at 416-418 and 159-236 (1987 with Supp.) (discussing setoff rights and adequate protection); *In re Stienes, supra* note 27 (permitted IRS setoff; debtors could not satisfy their burden that IRS was adequately protected).

According to the IRS, the concept of a "right of setoff" for purposes of determining whether a federal tax claim is secured should be determined without regard to whether a setoff would be "permitted" under Code § 6402 (such as due to the absence of an assessment or statutory notice of deficiency), but should only depend on whether a right of setoff otherwise exists under common law. IRS Chief Counsel Advice 200217005, December 21, 2001, *supra* note 20 (Issue 2a). This may prove too fine a distinction, however, given that secured status depends on the claim being "subject to setoff under section 553" of the Bankruptcy Code. It also seems incongruous that the IRS could be viewed as having a secured claim on the one hand, but not the effective means of enforcing it on the other hand (due to the limitations of Code § 6402).

Where the IRS has withheld (or set off) the overpayment in violation of the automatic stay and only seeks adequate protection after the fact, some courts, as a form of sanction, have denied adequate protection. *See, e.g., In re Hawkins*, 224 B.R. 334 (Bankr. E.D. La. 1998).

34 *See, e.g., Cooper-Jarrett, Inc. v. Central Transport, Inc.*, 726 F.2d 93 (3d Cir. 1984); *Prudential Ins. Co. v. Nelson*, 101 F.2d 441 (6th Cir.), *cert. denied*, 308 U.S. 583 (1939); *In Re Rocor International, Inc.*, 2005-2 U.S.T.C. ¶ 70,245 (Bankr. W.D. Okla. 2005) (not permitted to setoff postpetition fuel excise tax refund against prepetition heavy vehicle highway use tax). For a discussion of the ability to effectuate a setoff *postconfirmation, see* § 1006.1.1.3 below.

be subordinated to a claim of a third party.[35] Some courts have held, though, that the bankruptcy court has discretion not only to determine whether a setoff is appropriate, but also to delineate the allocation of the set off where there are claims of different rankings (*e.g.*, a priority claim versus a general unsecured claim) that could be subject to the setoff.[36]

Whether a tax overpayment is a pre- or postpetition obligation for purposes of setoff depends on when the overpayment is considered to "arise" (which is the terminology used in Bankruptcy Code section 553 in discussing permissible setoffs). Most courts consider an overpayment of income tax that occurs due to the payment of estimated taxes or the carryback of current year losses to "arise" as of the end of the debtor's taxable year, regardless of when the tax return or refund claim is filed or allowed.[37] This is also in accord with the 2005 exemption of certain income tax offsets, where both the income tax refund and income tax liability are for taxable periods ended before the filing of the bankruptcy petition (or in the case of an involuntary bankruptcy, before the order for relief). Thus, a tax overpayment due to the overpayment of estimated taxes for, or the carryback of losses from, a taxable year ending *prior to* the bankruptcy should be regarded as a prepetition overpayment, even if the tax return is filed or the refund granted postpetition. Less clear is the proper treatment for setoff purposes of an income tax refund due in respect of the year of the bankruptcy filing. It may be argued that the entire refund should be considered to be postpetition because the refund does not arise until year end. In addition, in a

---

[35] *See, e.g., Rochelle v. United States*, 521 F.2d 844, 75-2 U.S.T.C. ¶9792 (5th Cir. 1975) (Bankruptcy Act case; unpaid employment and excise taxes of a bankrupt partnership were subject to set off against a refund due the bankrupt general partner individually, even though claims of partnership creditors are generally subordinated to claims of partner creditors), *modified on other grounds*, 526 F.2d 405 (1976), *cert. denied*, 426 U.S. 948 (1976); *In re Silver Eagle Company*, 262 B.R. 534 (Bankr. D. Or. 2001) (Chapter 7 case; IRS permitted to setoff tax refund against tax penalty claim, despite subordinated treatment afforded non-pecuniary loss penalties in Chapter 7); *In re Sound Emporium, Inc.*, 70 B.R. 22, 87-1 U.S.T.C. ¶9134 (W.D. Tex. 1987) (IRS permitted to set off debt owed by the U.S. Army to the debtor against unpaid withholding and employment taxes, even though a third party had a security interest in such debt). *But see Superpumper Inc. v. Nerland Oil, Inc. (In re Nerland Oil, Inc.)*, 2002 U.S. App. LEXIS 18725 (8th Cir. 2002) (unfiled IRS lien on third party's promissory note arose prior to third party's offsetting claim and thus precluded setoff). *Consider also United States v. Offord Finance, Inc. (In re Medina)*, 205 B.R. 216 (Bankr. 9th Cir. 1996) (upheld IRS setoff since right to setoff against proceeds from government contracts existed prior to IRS notice of assignment of proceeds); *In re Calore Express Company, Inc., supra* note 23 (involving similar issue, with First Circuit reversing on the proper application of Massachusetts' law and the timing of when a right of setoff arose).

[36] *Compare United States v. Martinez*, 2007 U.S. Dist. LEXIS 6163 (M.D. Pa. 2007) (permitting bankruptcy court allocation), *on remand*, 2007 Bankr. LEXIS 1168 (Bankr. M.D. Pa. 2007) (explaining reason for allocation), *with In re Daniels*, 2007 Bankr. LEXIS 847 (Bankr. S.D. Ala. 2007) (allocation is within IRS's statutory discretion).

[37] *See* authorities at § 1005.3 note 85 (involving overpayment of estimated taxes); *Rozel Indus., Inc. v. IRS (In re Rozel Indus., Inc.)*, 120 B.R. 944 (Bankr. N.D. Ill. 1990) (involving loss carryback). *See also Gordon Sel-Way, Inc. v. United States (In re Gordon Sel-Way, Inc.)*, 98-2 U.S.T.C. ¶50,676 (Bankr. E.D. Mich. 1998) (involved prepetition FUTA taxes that were paid postpetition), *rev'd on other grounds*, 239 B.R. 741 (E.D. Mich. 1999) (held that refund arose postpetition), *aff'd*, 270 F.3d 280, 2001-2 U.S.T.C. ¶50,720 (6th Cir. 2001); *Harris v. IRS (In re American Payroll Network, Inc.)*, 98-2 U.S.T.C. ¶50,680 (Bankr. N.D.N.Y. 1998) (refund of penalties that were paid prepetition, but abated postpetition, arose prepetition).

reversal of prior law, a 2005 change in the priority provisions of the Bankruptcy Code governing income tax liabilities for the year of the bankruptcy filing effectively treats the entire liability as a postpetition administrative expense (*see* § 1015.1.1 below). However, the more appropriate treatment appears to be to allocate the refund between the pre- and postpetition portions of the year on an equitable basis.

For example, the courts have consistently allocated tax refunds received by an individual debtor in respect of the year of the bankruptcy filing, treating the prepetition portion as "property of the estate" (rather than a postpetition asset belonging to the individual debtor).[38] In general, such courts have prorated the tax refund, given that the individual's earnings were presumed to be fairly regular and the overpayment generally resulted from excessive tax withholdings.[39] In *Segal v. Rochelle*,[40] however, which involved the definition of estate "property" under the former Bankruptcy Act, the tax refund was due to a loss carryback generated in the year of the bankruptcy filing, but attributable to losses incurred entirely in the prepetition portion of the year. In such instance, the Supreme Court held that the tax refund was "sufficiently rooted in the prebankruptcy past" that it should be regarded entirely as estate "property." In a footnote to its opinion, the Court made mention of the fact that the Fifth Circuit in its lower court decision had stated that had a portion of the losses been incurred postpetition, a proration of the refund in the ratio of the losses before and after the filing date would be indicated.[41] The only case to apparently address this issue in the setoff area is the 1982 bankruptcy court decision in *In re Wilson*.[42]

---

38 *See, e.g., Barowsky v. Serelson (In re Barowsky)*, 946 F.2d 1516 (10th Cir. 1991); *In re Webb*, 234 B.R. 96 (Bankr. W.D. Mo. 1999); *In re Haedo*, 211 B.R. 149 (Bankr. S.D.N.Y. 1997). Courts have generally employed this approach even when the tax refund is due to an earned income credit (in those cases where the credit was not considered exempt property for bankruptcy purposes). *See, e.g., Williamson v. Jones (In re Montgomery)*, 224 F.3d 1193, 2000-2 U.S.T.C. ¶ 50,865 (10th Cir. 2000), and the cases cited therein; *In re Picard*, 2000 Bankr. LEXIS 21 (Bankr. M.D. Fla. 2000).

39 *See, e.g., In re Barowsky, supra* note 38, at 1518 n.1 (indicating that the debtors had not challenged the bankruptcy court's use of a pro rata formula); *In re Haedo, supra* note 38, at 153 (recognizing that courts generally use a pro rata allocation, but remanding to determine if another allocation was more appropriate; the court observed that the parties had not indicated whether, for example, the refund was due to a loss carryback or possibly an overpayment of the prior year's taxes that the debtors elected to carry over and treat as an estimated tax payment). However, where an individual debtor could show that the only tax payments for the year were made postpetition, the refund of the overpaid amounts was properly allocable to the postpetition portion of the year (and thus belonged to the debtor). *In re Christie*, 233 B.R. 110 (Bankr. 10th Cir. 1999) ("We are convinced the cases indicate that the most important factor in making that determination is not whether the tax liability is based, in whole or in part, on the debtor's prepetition earnings, but whether the refund was generated, in whole or in part, by the debtor's prepetition payments").

40 *Supra* note 26 (Bankruptcy Act case).

41 382 U.S. at 380 n.5, *referring to* 336 F.2d 298, 302 n.5 (5th Cir.). Based on *Segal*, the IRS Chief Counsel's office recommends "that as a general matter the Service assert its right to set off the entire amount of [an income tax refund or] tentative carryback adjustment since it appears that most if not all of the losses were incurred before the petition date. In appropriate cases, a setoff of a portion of the carryback would be proper if the debtor clearly shows that the carryback adjustment is attributable only in part to a loss incurred before the filing of the bankruptcy petition." IRS Legal Memorandum 200235024, July 5, 2002, *reprinted at* 2002 TNT 170-13.

42 29 B.R. 54 (Bankr. W.D. Ark. 1982). This case was cited as an illustration for when a prepetition tax refund arises in *In re Rozel Industries, Inc.*, 120 B.R. 944, 950 (Bankr. N.D. Ill. 1990).

Consistent with the foregoing authorities, the bankruptcy court allocated a portion of the tax refund to the prepetition portion of the year and held that such portion was subject to setoff by the IRS's prepetition claim. The court reasoned that, having concluded that the allocable portion of the tax refund is property of the estate, "it would be anomalous to now hold that it concurrently lacked sufficient specificity and mutuality to permit an offset by the United States under 11 U.S.C. § 553."

A sister concept to the right of setoff is the doctrine of equitable recoupment, discussed at § 1006.1.1.4, below. Although more limited in general application, prior bankruptcy court approval is *not* required to invoke the doctrine of equitable recoupment.

### *§ 1006.1.1.1 The Pettibone Corporation Case and Its Progeny*

Prior to 1994, it appeared well settled that the setoff of over- and underpayments of prepetition taxes, whether of a corporate, individual, or other debtor, during the pendency of the automatic stay was precluded absent bankruptcy court approval.[43] However, as a result of the Seventh Circuit decision in the *Pettibone Corporation* case[44]—which, in the context of a multi-year audit of a corporate debtor, distinguished the type of "setoff" permitted by the Internal Revenue Code from that prohibited by the Bankruptcy Code—there developed considerable uncertainty as to whether, or in what circumstances, the IRS is precluded from offsetting mutual prepetition tax obligations of corporate debtors. For bankruptcy cases commenced on or after October 17, 2005, this uncertainty has been substantially resolved by legislation which, as discussed in the preceding section, permits the setoff of prepetition income tax refunds against prepetition income tax liabilities.

In the *Pettibone Corporation* bankruptcy case, the issue of setoff arose postconfirmation. Although proofs of claims were filed during the bankruptcy case, Pettibone's final tax liability for its prepetition taxable years was not resolved until several years after confirmation. As finally agreed, Pettibone had underpaid its taxes in some years and overpaid its taxes in others. As it generally does outside bankruptcy, the IRS applied the so-called continuous offset method, which offsets the earliest overpayments against the earliest underpayments, and calculated interest at the applicable rate for the net amount outstanding for any given period.[45] Pettibone contended that this constituted an impermissible setoff under Bankruptcy Code section 553(a),

---

43 *See infra* note 50.

44 *Pettibone Corp. v. United States*, 34 F.3d 536 (7th Cir. 1994), *aff'g* 161 B.R. 960 (N.D. Ill. 1993), *aff'g* 151 B.R. 156 (Bankr. N.D. Ill. 1992).

45 For a discussion of the continuous offset method and interest netting, *see* Treasury Dept., Study on Netting of Interest on Tax Overpayments and Underpayments (April 18, 1997), *reprinted at* BNA Daily Tax Report #76 (April 21, 1997). So-called "zero" netting is now required for periods beginning after July 22, 1998 (*i.e.*, for interest accruing after October 1, 1998), and also applies to prior periods if certain conditions are met. *See* Code § 6621(d); IRS Chief Counsel Advice 200407015 (August 5, 2003), *reprinted at* 2004 TNT 31-45 (illustrating netting in certain two company situations); Rev. Proc. 2000-26, 2000-24 I.R.B. 1257; Rev. Proc. 99-43, 1999-2 C.B. 579 (provides guidance for prior periods).

in violation of the confirmed plan and confirmation order, and sought a refund of the overpayments plus interest.

Under the plan, Pettibone and the IRS were to determine by agreement and/or litigation what tax or refund was owing, and any tax determined to be owing was to be paid in installments. The plan did not recognize any right of setoff by the IRS and, pursuant to the confirmation order, any act to offset a discharged debt was enjoined. Pettibone therefore asserted that the overpayments and underpayments had to be kept separate, with separate interest calculations. Moreover, in calculating interest, Pettibone accrued postpetition interest on the overpayments but, in accord with the general prohibition against postpetition interest on unpaid prepetition taxes (*see* § 1006.1.2 below), did not accrue postpetition interest on the underpayments.

The district court disagreed and approved the continuous offsetting of overpayments on the following grounds:

> First, we are inclined to agree with the IRS that the setting off of tax overpayments with tax underpayments is an accounting method prescribed by the Internal Revenue Code [Code § 6402(a)] and not the type of "setoff" or "offset" contemplated by the Bankruptcy Code. Secondly, if the IRS did perform "setoffs" within the meaning of the Bankruptcy Code, the setoff of mutual debts is specifically allowed by the Code, 11 U.S.C. § 553, and we do not agree with Pettibone that the Confirmation Order, [the postdischarge injunction of] section 524, or the Plan prohibit such setoffs.[46]

On appeal, the Seventh Circuit agreed with the district court that this was not the type of setoff contemplated by the Bankruptcy Code. The court reasoned that, by undertaking an examination of 13 years at once, the IRS effectively transformed the 13-year stretch into one accounting period; that the nominal "underpayments" and "overpayments" within the audit period were merely intermediate steps to determine Pettibone's taxes; that the tax liability for each taxable year was interdependent, as exemplified by the ability of a corporation to carry back losses from one year to another; and that this interdependence acquires special significance during an audit when multiple years are open simultaneously. Thus, the Seventh Circuit's holding

---

[46] *Cf. In re Pigott*, 330 B.R. 797 (Bankr. S.D. Ala. 2005) (concluding that Code § 6402(a) precludes a prepetition tax overpayment from being part of the bankruptcy estate until after reduction for any unpaid tax liabilities). Although the *Pettibone* district court affirmed the bankruptcy court's decision, it rejected the bankruptcy court's reasoning. In the bankruptcy court's view, an overpayment and an underpayment involving the same taxpayer lacked "mutuality" (as required by Bankruptcy Code section 553), since a taxpayer's right to a refund is dependent on the IRS's right of offset under Code § 6402. In contrast, the district court stated that the very fact that Pettibone was seeking a refund of overpaid taxes and that the IRS was attempting to offset amounts owed the IRS by Pettibone indicated mutuality, and the court observed that the cases that have found mutuality lacking have done so only on the basis that one of the debts at issue did not arise prepetition or that the parties to the debt were different. 1993 U.S. Dist. LEXIS 16801, at 8.

would initially appear limited to the offset of under- and overpayments within the same audit period.[47]

As a practical matter, however, the interdependence of which the Seventh Circuit spoke is not necessarily restricted to the taxable years within an audit period. Frequently, there are carryover adjustments from one audit period to another, NOL carrybacks to otherwise closed years, and similar problems. Thus, it is possible that courts will take a more expansive view of the Seventh Circuit's holding and apply it across all prepetition tax years.

In a surprising decision, the district court in *In re Midway Industrial Contractors, Inc.*,[48] took the Seventh Circuit's "interdependence" rationale one step further: Not only were the under- and overpayments not within the same audit period, but they involved different taxes. In that case, a corporate debtor had filed a "quickie" refund claim and the IRS sought to set off under Code § 6411(b) outstanding employment tax penalties for late deposits. Applying an expansive interpretation of the Seventh Circuit's "interdependence" rationale, the district court held that a corporation's income tax and employment tax liability were in fact interdependent and that the setoff under Code § 6411(b) was not an impermissible setoff within the meaning of the automatic stay provisions of the Bankruptcy Code. To illustrate this proposition, the court focused on the ability of corporations to deduct their employment tax liabilities for income tax purposes. However, this loses sight of the fact employment taxes are calculable separate and apart from the debtor's own income taxes and are deductible merely as ordinary business expenses.

The court also cited as support a line of cases dealing with the issue of post-bar date amendments which have permitted the addition of a post-bar date claim for income taxes to date back to a timely claim for employment taxes (and vice versa) on the basis that such claims are of the same generic nature. However, the preponderance of cases have held to the contrary (*see* discussion at § 1010.2). Such cases notwithstanding, any reliance on bar date authorities appears strained in light of the differing bankruptcy policy and equitable considerations underlying the allowance of post-bar date amendments.[49]

As indicated above, the Seventh Circuit's decision in *Pettibone* and, more particularly, the district court's decision in *Midway Industrial* represent a departure from prior case law as to what constitutes a setoff within the meaning of Bankruptcy Code section 553.[50] The Seventh Circuit attempted to distinguish the bulk of these cases on the basis that they involved individuals:

---

[47] After discussing the issue of setoff, the court further concluded, in light of the facts of the case, that the provision of Pettibone's plan providing for "payment in full" of all taxes should be read as an agreement to pay taxes as determined by normal IRS operating procedures.

[48] 178 B.R. 734 (N.D. Ill. 1995).

[49] It should be noted that a majority of courts have also held that each taxable year, even for the same tax, gives rise to a distinct claim in bankruptcy. Thus, if the bar date analogy were apt, this would suggest a contrary result even on the facts of *Pettibone*.

[50] *See, e.g., Still v. United States (In re W.L. Jackson Mfg. Co.)*, 50 B.R. 498, 85-2 U.S.T.C. ¶9543 (Bankr. E.D. Tenn. 1985) (approving setoff of income tax under and overpayments); *Rozel Indus. v. IRS (In re Rozel Indus., Inc.)*, *supra* note 37 ("Section 553 does not grant [a right of setoff], but it does not restrict or impair such a right if it exists under other applicable law. The applicable law in this case is

> Unlike corporations, natural persons rarely shift tax consequences across years. When the end of the year closes the books on taxes, applying refunds from one year to debts from another more closely resembles the traditional notion of a setoff.

As part of a broader decision, the Second Circuit, in *In re Chateaugay Corporation*,[51] disagreed with the *Pettibone* line of authorities and rejected the argument that the crediting of under- and overpayments under Code §6402(a) is something other than an ordinary right of setoff. The Second Circuit thus observed that the IRS, like any other creditor, must obtain the permission of the bankruptcy court before setting off (or crediting) any amount against a prepetition claim.

At least one court, though, in an analogous situation (involving an anticipated refund claimed as exempt property by an individual debtor), described as "the emerging view" the IRS's right to credit under- and overpayments under Code §6402(a), with only the resulting refund being considered estate property.[52]

In *In re Coastal Bus and Equipment Sales, Inc.*,[53] the IRS sought relief from the automatic stay "out of an abundance of caution" to setoff a corporate debtor's *prepetition income* tax overpayments against unpaid *postpetition payroll* tax liabilities (incurred prior to the debtor's conversion from Chapter 11 to Chapter 7). Interestingly, the court asked the parties to consider the applicability of the doctrine of equitable recoupment (discussed below at §1006.1.1.4), since recoupment—unlike setoff—is not an act precluded by the automatic stay. The IRS's conclusion, however, was that "[s]ince different taxes and periods are involved here, and no single transaction, item, or taxable event is involved, the doctrine of recoupment has *no*

(Footnote Continued)

§6402(a)"; court observed that the exercise of a setoff under Code §6402(a) would violate the automatic stay); *In re Rush-Hampton Indus., Inc.*, 159 B.R. 343 (Bankr. M.D. Fla. 1993), *aff'd and rev'd in part*, 98 F.3d 614, 96-2 U.S.T.C. ¶50,613 (11th Cir. 1996) (IRS setoff of income tax overpayment against unpaid employment taxes in violation of automatic stay; although bankruptcy court subsequently approved offset for the tax and prepetition interest owing, it refused to "reward the IRS for offsetting prior to receiving relief from the automatic stay by allowing [it] to offset postpetition interest"; the Eleventh Circuit, however, also permitted the IRS to offset postpetition interest); *Matter of Johnson*, 136 B.R. 306, 308 (Bankr. M.D. Ga. 1991) ("the IRS' right to setoff derives from §6402(a)"; held IRS not permitted to setoff an income tax refund owed to Chapter 13 debtor against an income tax liability for a prior year because IRS was adequately protected under the plan); *In re Miel*, 134 B.R. 229 (Bankr. W.D. Mich. 1991) (IRS setoff of a claimed income tax refund against an income tax liability for a prior year violated automatic stay; however, IRS was not held in civil contempt where notice of bankruptcy proceeding was sent to wrong address); *cf. United States v. Norton*, *supra* note 22 (where the issue was the retention of an overpayment in a "suspense account," the IRS argued that no violation of the automatic stay occurs absent a setoff as defined in Code §6402; also involved income taxes, as in *Johnson and Miel*); *In re Harris*, 19 B.R. 624 (Bankr. E.D. Pa. 1982) (government admitted and court effectively concluded that a Code §6402 setoff is a setoff within the meaning of Bankruptcy Code sections 362 and 553; also involved income taxes, as in *Johnson and Miel*). *See also* cases cited at Stand. Fed. Tax. Rep. (CCH) ¶39,470.072 (setoff either held in violation of automatic stay, or court approval obtained).

[51] *Aetna Casualty & Surety Co. v. LTV Steel Co., Inc.* (*In re Chateaugay Corp.*), 94 F.3d 772, 780-781, 96-2 U.S.T.C. ¶50,458 (2d Cir. 1996).

[52] *Jones v. IRS (In re Jones)*, 2007-1 U.S.T.C. ¶50,266 (Bankr. M.D. Ga. 2006).

[53] 330 B.R. 328 (Bankr. D. Mass. 2005).

*application* to the facts of this case" (emphasis added). Surprisingly, the court disagreed. Recognizing that it was adopting an interpretation more favorable to the IRS than the IRS itself espoused, the court held that "the taxes and tax years at issue here form a unified whole where recoupment is singularly appropriate." In support, the court quoted extensively the Seventh Circuit's reasoning in *Pettibone* regarding the interdependence of taxable years.[54] As discussed at § 1006.1.1.4, the IRS was right, recoupment should not have applied.

### *§ 1006.1.1.2 Interagency Setoffs by IRS*

The federal government's ability to effectuate, with bankruptcy court approval, an interagency setoff of other federal obligations of a debtor against tax overpayments generally depends upon (1) the extent to which such a setoff is permitted under applicable nonbankruptcy law and (2) the "mutuality" of the other federal obligation and the tax overpayment.[55] In addition, some courts have held that the failure to assert a setoff right specifically in a proof of claim constitutes a waiver of such claim.[56] A creditor may, however, generally rescind a waiver unless another party to the proceeding has detrimentally relied on the waiver and the court invokes estoppel.[57] Although bankruptcy courts have discretion whether to allow a setoff of prepetition obligations, applying general principles of equity,[58] such discretion must be exercised with due consideration for the Bankruptcy Code's general preservation of a creditor's right of setoff subject to the automatic stay.[59]

---

[54] Adopting the Seventh Circuit's distinction between corporations and individuals, the same court a month later refused to apply recoupment to the offsetting of prepetition overpayments and underpayments of an *individual* debtor. *Beaucage v. United States (In re Beaucage)*, 334 B.R. 353 (Bankr. D. Mass. 2005) (but granted relief from stay to allow setoff), *aff'd*, 342 B.R. 408 (D. Mass. 2006).

[55] *See* 11 U.S.C. §§ 553(a) (only addresses the setoff of prepetition obligations), 362(a) (restricting the setoff of prepetition claims). The general ability to set off mutual postpetition obligations has nevertheless been recognized in case law. *See, e.g., In re Calore Express Company, Inc., supra* note 23 (ability to setoff mutual postpetition obligations is similarly subject to the automatic stay; First Circuit reversed on other grounds).

[56] *Compare In re Calore Express Company, Inc.* (1st Cir.), *supra* note 23, at 39-40 (First Circuit held that "as a general matter, a creditor's silence in the early stages of bankruptcy proceedings, at such as the filing of a proof of claim, does not waive the right of setoff," but found that the inclusion of express statements in the proof of claim can constitute a waiver; discusses differing judicial standards for "waiver"), *with United States v. Continental Airlines (In re Continental Airlines)*, 143 F.3d 536 (3d Cir. 1998), *cert. denied*, 119 S. Ct. 336 (1998) (involved postconfirmation setoff; stated that setoff right must be asserted timely and in accordance with other provisions of the Bankruptcy Code). *See also* authorities cited *supra* note 30.

[57] *In re Calore Express Company, Inc., supra* note 23 (discussed in First Circuit decision).

[58] *See, e.g., United States v. Arkison (In re Cascade Roads, Inc.)*, 34 F.3d 756, 763-766 (9th Cir. 1994) (denied setoff; found government misconduct); *In re Sauer*, 233 B.R. 715, 725-726 (Bankr. D N.D. 1998) (permitted setoff where only justification for denial would be to enhance the debtor's ability to reorganize).

[59] *See, e.g., In re Calore Express Company, Inc.* (1st Cir.), *supra* note 23 (First Circuit decision discusses breadth of bankruptcy court discretion; lower courts had denied setoff where the IRS did not assert its setoff right, despite multiple opportunities, until after the debtor's assets had been sold and the proceeds readied for distribution; First Circuit reversed due to insufficient consideration of the facts);

In *In re Chateaugay Corporation*,[60] the Second Circuit held that, contrary to suggestions in various cases and legislative history,[61] there did in fact exist a common law right of setoff of tax refunds against debts owed to other federal agencies. Due to the years in issue, the Second Circuit specifically did not address whether the enactment of Code § 6402(d) in 1984 (often called the "tax intercept statute"), and the related provision 31 U.S.C. § 3720A, were intended to be the exclusive method for government agencies to offset debts owed them against tax refunds. Such sections authorize (and, in fact, mandate) that the Treasury set off against a tax overpayment certain debts of other federal agencies upon compliance with certain statutory and regulatory requirements, including proper notice to the IRS from the other federal agency.[62] However, in *In re HAL, Inc.*[63] the Bankruptcy Appellate Panel for the Ninth Circuit treated the IRS's statutory and common law rights of setoff as coexisting rights.

For offsetting debts to be considered "mutual," the two debts must be "in the same right and between the same parties, standing in the same capacities."[64] As such, the courts have held that, in order for offsetting debts of two governmental agencies to be considered mutual, (i) the two agencies must be properly considered as a single creditor or, in the parlance of the Bankruptcy Code, a single governmental unit, and (ii) the offsetting debts must be both prepetition (or both postpetition) obligations.[65]

The Seventh, Ninth and Tenth Circuits, representing the majority view, have held that, for all purposes of setoff under the Bankruptcy Code, all agencies of the United

(Footnote Continued)

*N. J. Nat'l Bank v. Gutterman (In re Applied Logic Corp.)*, 576 F.2d 952, 957-58 (2d Cir. 1978) ("The rule allowing setoff, both before and after bankruptcy, is not one that courts are free to ignore when they think application would be 'unjust'").

60 *Supra* note 51.

61 *See, e.g.*, Conference Report to the Deficit Reduction Act of 1984, H. Conf. Rep. No. 861, 98th Cong., 2d Sess. 1413 (1984) ("Present law does not provide authority for the IRS to offset tax refunds against nontax debts owed to Federal agencies").

62 *See, e.g.*, IRS Service Center Advice 200137049, August 1, 2001, *reprinted at* 2001 TNT 180-77. Effective for tax refunds payable after January 1, 1998, the rules governing the tax refund offset program are set forth in 31 C.F.R. § 258.2. *See* Reg. § 301.6402-6(n) (cross-referencing such rules). These rules are issued under 31 U.S.C. § 3720A, and administered by the Financial Management Service, another bureau of the Treasury. For prior rules, *see* Reg. § 301.6402-6 (effective for tax refunds payable after April 15, 1992 through January 1, 1998), and former Temp. Reg. § 301.6402-6T (effective for tax refunds payable from January 1, 1986, through April 15, 1992).

63 *Hawaiian Airlines, Inc. v. United States (In re HAL, Inc.)*, 196 B.R. 159 (Bankr. 9th Cir. 1996), *aff'd*, 122 F.3d 851 (9th Cir. 1997).

64 *In re Calore Express Company, Inc., supra* note 23; *Barnett Bank of Tampa v. Tower Environmental, Inc. (In re Tower Environmental, Inc.)*, 217 B.R. 933, 939-940 (Bankr. M.D. Fla. 1997).

65 Id.; *In re Chateaugay Corp.* (2d Cir.), *supra* note 50; *Boston & Maine Corp. v. Chicago Pac. Corp.*, 785 F.2d 562 (7th Cir. 1986). *See also* 5 Collier on Bankruptcy ¶ 553.03[3](15th ed. rev.). The second requirement—as it relates to offsetting prepetition obligations—is quite often referred to as being an independent requirement rather than a part of the concept of "mutuality." This is due to the separate reference to such requirement in Bankruptcy Code section 553(a), in contrast to its predecessor provision under the former Bankruptcy Act. *See* section 68a of the former Bankruptcy Act. As discussed above, *supra* note 55, generally the ability to offset postpetition obligations is not governed by Bankruptcy Code section 553(a), but is recognized in the case law.

An exception to the general ability to offset postpetition debts occurs where the Chapter 11 case has been converted to Chapter 7 and the offsetting debts are again treated as being from different periods. *See, e.g., In re W.L. Jackson Mfg. Co., supra* note 50, at 505.

States constitute a single governmental unit, except those acting in some distinctive private capacity (such as the FDIC when acting in its receivership capacity).[66] A small minority of courts have, for bankruptcy purposes, felt constrained by the definition of "governmental unit" in Bankruptcy Code section 101(27), which defines a "governmental unit" to include, in addition to the United States itself, "a department, agency, or instrumentality of the United States." From this separate delineation, such courts have concluded that each agency should be treated as its own governmental unit, and not part of a single governmental unit comprised of the United States as a whole.[67]

As discussed earlier,[68] an overpayment generally arises as of the end of the taxable year for purposes of setoff (regardless of when the tax return or refund claim is filed or allowed) and, thus, would be a prepetition obligation if the taxable year ended prior to the bankruptcy filing. However, with respect to an overpayment relating to the taxable year of the bankruptcy filing, it is possible that the overpayment may be allocated in whole or in part to the prepetition portion of such year (depending on the events during the year responsible for such overpayment) and to such extent be considered a prepetition obligation for purposes of setoff. The remainder of the overpayment, if any, would be considered a postpetition obligation.

A procedural point that has arisen from time to time is whether the IRS or Treasury—in contrast to the United States government generally and the agency that requested the offset, more specifically—is a properly named party to an action asserting a violation of the automatic stay as a result of an interagency setoff pursuant to Code § 6402(d) against a pending tax refund.[69] As mentioned above, Code § 6402(d) *requires* the Treasury to offset against a tax refund certain debts of other federal agencies that comply with specific notice and certification requirements. Prior to 1998, the IRS assisted in the maintenance of the "Debtor Master File," which is the database of persons with delinquent government non-tax debts against which any pending tax refunds is checked in order to effectuate an offset pursuant to Code § 6402(d).[70] Effective January 1, 1998, the Financial Management Service (FMS), another branch of the Treasury, administers the database, receives the interagency

---

[66] *United States v. Maxwell*, 157 F.3d 1099 (7th Cir. 1998), *reh'g, en banc, denied*, 1998 U.S. App. LEXIS 30851; *In re HAL, Inc.* (9th Cir.), *supra* note 63; *Turner v. Small Business Administration* (*In re Turner*), 84 F.3d 1294 (10th Cir. 1996) (*en banc*); *see also In re Chateaugay Corporation* (2d Cir.), discussed *supra* at note 51 (which involved a right of setoff in bankruptcy and implicitly reached the same conclusion); *In re Whimsy, Inc.*, 221 B.R. 69 (S.D.N.Y. 1998); *Lopes v. United States*, 211 B.R. 443 (D.R.I. 1997), and the authorities at § 1005.1.2 note 38. Outside of bankruptcy, the treatment of the departments and agencies of the United States as a unitary creditor is well established. *See, e.g., Cherry Cotton Mills v. United States*, 66 S. Ct. 729, 46-1 U.S.T.C. ¶ 9218 (1946).

[67] *See, e.g., Shugrue v. Fischer* (*In re Ionosphere Clubs, Inc.*), 164 B.R. 839, 842-843 (Bankr. S.D.N.Y. 1994) (collecting cases). A similar conflict arises in respect of state agencies, although the ability to set off obligations involving different state agencies will depend on the law of the particular state. *See* authorities at § 1005.1.2 note 38.

[68] *See* text accompanying notes 37-42 *supra*.

[69] This is aside from the fact, as discussed at § 1004 above, that in any event the proper party is probably the United States government, since federal agencies generally cannot be sued in their own name.

[70] *See, e.g.*, IRS Legal Memorandum 200205046, December 19, 2001, *reprinted at* 2002 TNT 23-70; *see also* regulatory history, *supra* note 62.

requests, and effectuates the offset (with notice of the offset thereafter provided to the IRS).[71] In view of the Treasury's administrative function in effectuating an interagency offset, Code § 6402(f) provides that:

> No court of the United States shall have jurisdiction to hear any action, whether legal or equitable, brought to restrain or review a reduction authorized by [Code § 6402(c) (offset of past due support), (d) (interagency setoff) or (e) (past due state income tax obligations)]. No such reduction shall be subject to review by the Secretary [of the Treasury] in an administrative proceeding. No action brought against the United States to recover the amount of any such reduction shall be considered to be a suit for a refund of tax. This subsection does not preclude any legal, equitable, or administrative action against the Federal agency or State to which the amount of such reduction was paid . . . .[72]

Thus, some bankruptcy courts have dismissed the IRS and Treasury as a party from an action asserting a violation of the stay as a result of an interagency setoff,[73] while others have entertained such actions without any discussion of this statutory allocation of responsibility.[74]

### *§ 1006.1.1.3 Setoff of Prepetition Taxes Postconfirmation*

A separate issue as to which the courts are divided is whether a right of setoff under Bankruptcy Code section 553(a) takes precedence over the discharge provisions of the Bankruptcy Code. By its terms, Bankruptcy Code section 553(a) preserves a creditor's right to offset mutual prepetition debts subject only to the automatic stay (which terminates upon discharge), and a debtor-in-possession's right to use, sell, or lease property as provided in Bankruptcy Code section 363. On the other hand, Bankruptcy Code section 1141, which provides for the general discharge of prepetition debts, makes no exception for the setoff of prepetition debts. Similarly, Bankruptcy Code section 524(a)(2) reads as an absolute injunction against any act "to collect, recover or offset" any discharged debt as a personal liability of the debtor (subject to a contrary provision in the Chapter 11 plan or other agreement, as

---

71 *See* 31 C.F.R. § 285.2 (governing regulation).

72 *See also* 31 C.F.R. § 285.2(n) (similarly so providing).

73 *See, e.g., Bourne v. IRS (In re Bourne)*, 2001 U.S. Dist. LEXIS 11449 (E.D. Tenn. 2001) (dismissed IRS as a party, since the IRS had no financial interest, and substituted the Dept. of Housing and Urban Development, which was the agency which received the refund by way of offset); *Blake v. U.S. Dept. of Education (In re Blake)*, 235 B.R. 568 (Bankr. D. Md. 1998) (holding the Department of Education, not the IRS, responsible for the violation).

74 *See, e.g., In re Lafanette*, 208 B.R. 394 (Bankr. W.D. La. 1996) (but nevertheless declined to find the IRS in contempt or award monetary damages for the IRS's technical violation, since it was merely following the "law of the land" without knowledge of the bankruptcy filings); *cf. Stucka v. United States (In re Stucka)*, 77 B.R. 777 (Bankr. C.D. Cal. 1987) (involving an offset under Code § 6402(c) for past-due child support, court held the IRS, the State and the county in willful violation of the stay, with the debtor's fees and cost to be borne equally among them).

prescribed by statute).[75] Thus, the courts have had to decide which of these sections control.

Following the Ninth Circuit's decision in *In re De Laurentiis Entertainment Group, Inc.*,[76] the district court in the *Pettibone Corporation* case[77] (discussed in § 1006.1.1.1 above) held that Bankruptcy Code section 553(a), and thus the IRS's right of setoff, took precedence over the discharge provisions of the Bankruptcy Code. Only a handful of cases appear to have considered this issue in the context of a Chapter 11 plan. In establishing the primacy of Bankruptcy Code section 553(a), the Ninth Circuit in the *De Laurentiis* case concluded that the underlying policies served in preserving a creditor's right of setoff (which are based in equity and fairness) outweighed the limited inroad to the policies of finality and discharge served by Bankruptcy Code section 1141.[78] The court rejected the decisions in the Chapter 13 area, which, up to that point, generally had interpreted the virtually identical language in Bankruptcy Code section 1327 to prohibit postconfirmation setoffs.[79]

The Chapter 11 cases upholding the discharge provisions have emphasized the government's opportunity to object to the plan[80] and the potential harm to the rehabilitative purposes of the Bankruptcy Code in instances where the tax refund

---

[75] For this purpose, a "discharged debt" has generally been interpreted to include taxes provided for in the plan, as well as any tax for which no proof of claim was filed or allowed. Consider, for example, the discussion at § 1015.4 (relating to the priority of tax claims in successive bankruptcies). *See also* discussion at § 1014.

[76] 963 F.2d 1269 (9th Cir.), *cert. denied, sub nom. Carolco Television, Inc. v. National Broadcasting Co.*, 113 S. Ct. 330 (1992). *See also Slaw Constr. Corp. v. Hughes Foulkrod Constr. Co. (In re Slaw Constr. Corp.)*, 17 B.R. 744 (Bankr. E.D. Pa. 1982). *Consider also Matter of Davis*, 889 F.2d 658 (5th Cir. 1989), *cert. denied, sub nom., Campbell v. United States*, 110 S. Ct. 2175 (1990) (permitted postconfirmation setoff; unclear whether setoff was ever challenged on discharge grounds).

[77] 1993 U.S. Dist. LEXIS 16,801 (N.D. Ill. 1992), *aff'd on other grounds*, 34 F.3d 536 (7th Cir. 1994).

[78] *But consider In re Holder*, 182 B.R. 770 (Bankr. M.D. Tenn. 1995) (held that, although the Customs Service's right of setoff was unaffected by Bankruptcy Code section 1141, Customs had waived its setoff rights when it agreed by separate order to have its claim paid as an unsecured creditor; the court noted that, by so holding, it was unnecessary for it to decide whether Customs waived its setoff rights by failing to object to confirmation of the plan).

[79] *See, e.g., United States v. Norton, supra* note 22, *In re Alexander*, 31 B.R. 389 (Bankr. S.D. Ohio 1983); *In re Hackney*, 20 B.R. 158 (Bankr. D. Idaho 1982). Subsequently, however, Chapter 13 courts had been moving in the other direction. *See, e.g., United States v. Munson*, 248 B.R. 343, 2000-1 U.S.T.C. ¶ 50,456 (C.D. Ill. 2000), *rev'g*, 241 B.R. 410 (Bankr. C.D. Ill. 1999); *In re Sedlock*, 219 B.R. 207 (Bankr. N.D. Ohio 1998); *Womack v. IRS (In re Womack)*, 188 B.R. 259 (Bankr. E.D. Ark. 1995); *United States v. Orlinski (In re Orlinski)*, 140 B.R. 600 (Bankr. S.D. Ga. 1991) (permitting postconfirmation setoff; although noting that IRS filed its motion preconfirmation, court expressly disagreed with authorities prohibiting postconfirmation setoff). *But see In re Shultz*, 2006-1 U.S.T.C. ¶ 50,332 (Bankr. 6th Cir. 2006) (2005) (affirmed bankruptcy court denial of setoff; however, it was assumed that the IRS could retain possession of the tax refund as adequate protection, pending the receipt of payment under the plan).

Where the issue is solely one of Bankruptcy Code section 524, as in the case of individual debtors in Chapter 7, most courts have permitted the subsequent setoff of prepetition overpayments against otherwise discharged taxes. *See, e.g., IRS v. Luongo (In re Luongo)*, 259 F.3d 323, 2001-2 U.S.T.C. ¶ 50,527 (5th Cir. 2001); *Davidovich v. Welton (In re Davidovich)*, 901 F.2d 1533, 1539 (10th Cir. 1990); *Conti v. United States (In re Conti)*, 50 B.R. 142, 85-2 U.S.T.C. ¶ 9497 (Bankr. E.D. Va. 1985); *Eggemeyer v. IRS (In re Eggemeyer)*, 75 B.R. 20 (Bankr. S.D. Ill. 1987) (same; right of setoff extends to individual's exempt property); *Gribben v. United States (In re Gribben)*, 158 B.R. 920 (S.D. N.Y. 1993).

[80] *See In re Newport Offshore, Ltd.*, 86 B.R. 325 (Bankr. D.R.I. 1988).

would assist the debtor's efforts to consummate a plan.[81] The Third Circuit, in *In re Continental Airlines*,[82] factually distinguished the *De Laurentiis* decision and denied the government's post-confirmation claim for setoff, stating that the Ninth Circuit had predicated its decision upon the particular facts in the case before it, including the creditor's diligent pursuit of its setoff claim before the bankruptcy court "during the entire period the reorganization plan was being considered." The creditor in *De Laurentiis* had asserted its setoff right in a timely filed proof of claim, sought relief from the automatic stay prior to confirmation and pursued its setoff right in an adversary proceeding throughout the bankruptcy case. In contrast, in *Continental Airlines*, the government made no claim for setoff until six weeks after confirmation.

In an unusual situation, the district court and Sixth Circuit in *In re Gordon Sel-Way, Inc.*[83] allowed the IRS to set off a *postconfirmation* refund for FUTA taxes against its prepetition general unsecured claim for employment tax penalties. All other general unsecured creditors had received distributions of 20 cents on the dollar. Significantly, the IRS had been engaged in lengthy litigation with the debtor over its claim, and for a period of time pending successive appeals had been held to be subordinate to all other general unsecured claims (*see* § 1015.2 below, note 97). Although in litigation with the IRS, the debtor did not maintain a reserve for the IRS's claim and, absent the tax refund, had insufficient funds to pay its professional fees and other administrative expenses. On the other hand, the tax refund was just large enough that, if the court permitted the setoff, the IRS would obtain a commensurate recovery with the other general unsecured creditors. Considering the circumstances, the district court concluded that the equities favored the IRS, and effectively blamed the debtor's failure to reserve sufficient funds for the IRS claim on its professionals. The court overcame the issue of offsetting "mutual" obligations (*i.e.*, the issue of a postconfirmation refund offsetting a prepetition claim), finding that a prepetition claim is transformed into a postpetition (postconfirmation) obligation where the plan of reorganization does not discharge the claim. In this regard, it is important to note that the reason that the claim was not discharged was that the plan was a *liquidating* plan under which no discharge is permitted under Bankruptcy Code section 1141(d)(3). The Sixth Circuit was similarly persuaded, concluding that the debtor's "manipulation of the plan of reorganization (whether intentional or not) gave the government a post-petition claim against [the debtor] for a pro-rata share of the amount that was distributed to the other class 5 creditors."

---

[81] *See, e.g., United States v. Driggs*, 185 B.R. 214 (D. Md. 1995); *United States v. Crabtree (Matter of Crabtree)*, 76 B.R. 208 (Bankr. M.D. Fla. 1987) (to permit setoff "would, of course, emasculate a specific rehabilitative purpose" of Bankruptcy Code section 1129(a)(9)(C), which permits the deferred payment of priority prepetition taxes, "in instances where the debtor has a pending tax refund claim which if it is honored might play a very important role in the Debtors' efforts to consummate a confirmed plan").

[82] *Supra* note 56.

[83] *United States v. Gordon Sel-Way, Inc. (In re Gordon Sel-Way, Inc.)*, 239 B.R. 741, 99-2 U.S.T.C. ¶ 50,849 (E.D. Mich. 1999), *aff'd*, 270 F.3d 280, 2001-2 U.S.T.C. ¶ 50,720 (6th Cir. 2001) (Sixth Circuit also upheld bankruptcy court jurisdiction over injunction action, rejecting IRS claim of sovereign immunity).

### *§1006.1.1.4 Equitable Recoupment—An Exception to Setoff Limitations*

The doctrine of equitable recoupment is similar to, and often confused with, the right of setoff. It is important, however, to distinguish the two. This is because, in contrast to the general right of setoff, recoupment is not subject to the automatic stay in bankruptcy, and thus does not require prior court approval.[84]

In non-bankruptcy federal tax litigation, the function of equitable recoupment is to overcome a statute of limitations in the furtherance of overall fairness.[85] The doctrine may be asserted, in appropriate circumstances, by either the IRS (in the case of a barred tax deficiency) or the taxpayer (in the case of a barred tax refund). Although an in-depth discussion of the contours and continued vitality of the doctrine of equitable recoupment is beyond the scope of this volume,[86] the doctrine of equitable recoupment involves the ability to raise, as a defense against a current tax refund claim (in the case of the IRS) or a current tax deficiency (in the case of the taxpayer), an otherwise barred deficiency or refund where the two tax amounts (i) arise from a single transaction, item or taxable event and (ii) involve inconsistent positions.[87] Accordingly, the doctrine is a very narrow one.[88] Moreover, within solely the income tax context, the function served by equitable recoupment has since 1938 been substantially, although not wholly, addressed by the mitigation provisions of the Internal Revenue Code.[89] Most tax cases in this area have therefore involved two

---

[84] *See, e.g., Malinowski v. New York State Dep't of Labor (In re Malinowski)*, 156 F.3d 131 (2d Cir. 1998) (the amount subject to recoupment is not considered the debtor's property). As discussed above at §1006.1.1.1, there is a line of authority based on the Seventh Circuit's decision in the *Pettibone Corporation* case, that the setoff of certain tax amounts are a type of setoff that would not be subject to the automatic stay. In addition as discussed in the introductory section to §1006.1.1, the IRS is statutorily permitted in more recent bankruptcy cases to setoff certain prepetition income tax amounts.

[85] *See, e.g., Bull v. United States*, 295 U.S. 247, 35-1 U.S.T.C. ¶9346 (1935) (seminal case); *United States v. Dalm*, 494 U.S. 596, 607-08, 90-1 U.S.T.C. ¶60,012 (1990).

[86] For an in-depth discussion of the doctrine of equitable recoupment in the tax context, *see, e.g.*, Andrews, Modern-Day Equitable Recoupment and the "Two Tax Effect:" Avoidance of the Statutes of Limitation in Federal Tax Controversies, 28 Ariz. L. Rev. 595 (1986); Willis, Some Limits of Equitable Recoupment, Tax Mitigation, and Res Judicata: Reflections Prompted by *Chertkof v. United States*, 38 Tax Law. 625 (1985). *See also* Saltzman, IRS Practice and Procedure, ¶5.04 (Rev. Second Edition).

[87] *See, e.g., Stone v. White*, 301 U.S. 532, 37-1 U.S.T.C. ¶9303 (1937); Dalm, 494 U.S. at 605 n.5; *IRS v. Pransky (In re Pransky)*, 318 F.3d 536, 2003-2 U.S.T.C. ¶50,216 (3rd Cir. 2003); *Bowen v. United States, Dept. of Treasury (In re Bowen)*, 174 B.R. 840 (Bankr. S.D. Ga. 1994). The doctrine of equitable recoupment can also arise in a two taxpayer context (such as in the case of a decedent and his estate, or possibly a trust and its beneficiary) if there is an extremely close identity-of-interest such that it would be inequitable if recoupment is not allowed. *See, e.g.*, Rev. Rul. 71-56, 1971-1 C.B. 4 (decedent and his estate).

[88] There is also a developing split among the Courts of Appeals as to whether the Tax Court, since lacking general equitable powers, can only employ equitable recoupment in the extremely limited circumstance of the same tax and the same taxable year. *Compare Mueller v. Commissioner*, 153 F.3d 302, 98-2 U.S.T.C. ¶60,325 (6th Cir. 1998) (limited), *with Estate of Branson v. Commissioner*, 264 F.3d 904, 2001-1 U.S.T.C. ¶50,622 (9th Cir. 2001) (supporting availability, but not determinative).

[89] *See* Code §1311 *et seq.* For an example where equitable recoupment did apply because the mitigation provisions were unavailable, see *Kolom v. United States*, 791 F.2d 762, 86-1 U.S.T.C. ¶9471 (9th Cir. 1986). In contrast to equitable recoupment which reduces a party's current recovery by the

different taxes, such as an excise tax and an income tax, that are affected by the same transaction or item.

The Supreme Court's decision in *Rothensies v. Electric Storage Battery Co.*[90] illustrates the limited scope of the doctrine. The taxpayer-company had paid federal excise taxes from 1919 through 1926 on its battery sales and deducted the amounts from income. The company later determined that no excise tax should have been paid and, in 1935, after a lengthy litigation, obtained a refund for the open years (1922-1926). It did not, however, include the refund in its income. The IRS timely asserted a tax deficiency. The company paid the tax, and (in 1943) sued for a refund (after its refund claim was rejected), claiming that if the prior refund was properly income that it should be permitted to recoup against the resulting income (and excess profits) tax liability the excise taxes paid in the earlier years for which a tax refund was barred by the statute of limitations (1919-1921). The district court and Court of Appeals both permitted recoupment, but the Supreme Court reversed. In effect, the Supreme Court viewed the later year battery sales as separate transactions from the earlier year sales, even though the underlying tax issue giving rise to the excise tax overpayments was the same. In concluding, the Court noted with concern the approximately 20 years that had passed since the excise taxes at issue had been paid, and stated that: "In many cases, if not most cases of asserted deficiency the items which occasion it relate to past years closed by statute, at least as closely as does the item here involved. . . . Every assessment of deficiency and each claim for refund would invite a search of the taxpayer's entire history for items to recoup. . . . We cannot approve such encroachments on the policy of the statute [of limitations] . . . ."

In a wrongly decided case, the bankruptcy court in *In re Coastal Bus and Equipment Sales, Inc.*,[91] recently utilized recoupment in favor of the IRS to permit a corporate debtor's prepetition income tax overpayments to be applied against unpaid postpetition payroll tax liabilities without regard to the automatic stay. Interestingly, the court raised the doctrine of equitable recoupment of its own accord, and when it originally asked the parties to consider the applicability of the doctrine, the IRS's conclusion was that "[s]ince different taxes and periods are involved here, and no single transaction, item, or taxable event is involved, the doctrine of recoupment has *no application* to the facts of this case" (emphasis added). Recognizing that it was adopting an interpretation more favorable to the IRS than the IRS itself espoused, the court held that "the taxes and tax years at issue here form a unified whole where recoupment is singularly appropriate," focusing on the general interdependence of a corporation's tax liability across taxable years. This is clearly contrary to the Supreme Court's decision in *Electric Storage*. Distinguishing between corporations and individ-

---

(Footnote Continued)

earlier barred amount that such party should have paid (no affirmative recovery for the barred amount is allowed)—*see, e.g., Estate of Mueller v. Commissioner*, 107 T.C. 189 (1996)—mitigation allows the other party to actually correct the prior year tax liability and obtain an affirmative recovery unlimited to the amount payable in the later year.

[90] 329 U.S. 296, 47-1 U.S.T.C. ¶9106 (1946).

[91] *Supra* note 53.

uals, the same bankruptcy court a month later refused to apply recoupment to the offsetting of prepetition overpayments and underpayments of an *individual* debtor.[92]

### § 1006.1.2 Relief from Interest and Penalties

**Interest.** No interest generally will be allowable on prepetition taxes past the filing of the bankruptcy petition, unless (1) the debtor corporation is solvent or the IRS has a lien on the debtor corporation's assets (or a right of setoff) that adequately secures both the prepetition taxes owed and any accruing interest,[93] or (2) the tax is nondischargeable (which is a fairly new concept to reorganizing corporate debtors and only applies in a very narrow set of circumstances).[94] However, no special relief is accorded for prepetition interest. In addition, the bankruptcy court cannot use its equitable powers to abate any prepetition interest properly claimed by the IRS.[95]

**Penalties for failure to pay.** In no event will any penalty imposed under Code § 6651 (failure to pay taxes) or Code § 6655 (failure to pay estimated taxes) for the failure to pay prepetition income and excise taxes be imposed for any period during which the bankruptcy case is pending (other than excise taxes for which the debtor acts as a collecting agent, *see* § 1006.3.1).[96] Accordingly, if the bankruptcy case is

---

[92] *Beaucage v. United States (In re Beaucage)* (Bankr. D. Mass.), *supra* note 54.

[93] *See* § 301, note 3; 11 U.S.C. § 502(b)(2) (claims for "unmatured interest" not allowable); IRS Manual, Part 5 (Collecting Process), Ch. 9 (Bankruptcy), § 13.21.2 (3/1/07), at ¶7; *but see infra* notes 172-173 and accompanying text (involving employment withholding taxes). The bankruptcy plan, or the parties by agreement, can provide otherwise. *See, e.g., United States v. Graham (In re Monclova Care Center, Inc.)*, 2003-1 U.S.T.C. ¶50,266 (6th Cir. 2003) (Chapter 11 plan provided that allowed priority claims were "unimpaired," which in bankruptcy parlance means that its legal rights are unaltered including, the court held, its right to statutory interest until paid; thus, the IRS was entitled to interest at the Code § 6621 rate through and after the effective date of the plan until fully paid).

[94] *See, e.g.,* discussion below at § 1014, note 7; Levin and Ranney-Marinelli, The Creeping Repeal of Chapter 11: The Significant Business Provisions of the Bankruptcy Abuse Prevention and Consumer Protection Act of 2005, 79 Am. Bankr. L.J. 603, 614-618 (2005).

[95] *In re Carlson*, 126 F.3d 915, 97-2 U.S.T.C. ¶50,702 (7th Cir. 1997), *reh'g, en banc, denied*, 1997 U.S. App. LEXIS 33969, *cert. denied*, 118 S. Ct. 1388 (1988); *Karlsson v. United States (In re Karlsson)*, 247 B.R. 321 (Bankr. M.D. Fla. 2000); *In re Vendell Healthcare, Inc.*, 222 B.R. 564 (Bankr. M.D. Tenn. 1998); *Followell v. United States (In re Gurley)*, 335 B.R. 389 (Bankr. W.D. Tenn. 2005) (also concluding that a bankruptcy court cannot abate any *penalties* properly claimed, by analogy to interest; *but see* discussion of nonfiling penalties, below). *See* Code § 6404, governing abatement of interest.

[96] Code § 6658(a)(2); *see* IRS Manual, Part 20 (Penalty and Interest), Ch. 1 (Penalty Handbook), § 2.1.6.1 (7/31/2001) (as to Code § 6651) and § 3.4.1.4 (9/12/06) (as to Code § 6655); *see also* IRS Manual, Part 5 (Collecting Process), Ch. 9 (Bankruptcy), § 4.14 (1/1/06); *see, e.g., Industrial Indemnity v. Robert Snyder*, 84-1 U.S.T.C. ¶9507 (E.D. Wash.) (facts disclose IRS only imposed penalties accrued prior to bankruptcy petition); *Woodward v. United States (In re Woodward)*, 113 B.R. 680, 90-1 U.S.T.C. ¶50,244 (Bankr. D. Or. 1990); *In re Quick*, 152 B.R. 902 and 909 (Bankr. W.D. Va. 1992). In the case of an *involuntary* bankruptcy, the IRS is also precluded from imposing such penalties on taxes incurred between the filing of the petition and the order of relief. *See* Code § 6658(a)(2). *Consider also In re CF&I Fabricators of Utah Inc.*, 148 B.R. 332, 93-1 U.S.T.C. ¶50,012 (Bankr. D. Utah 1992) (Code § 4971(a) minimum funding tax did not accrue where payment of accumulated funding deficiency was precluded by the automatic stay), *aff'd*, 179 B.R. 704 (C.D. Utah 1994), *appealed and aff'd on other issues; cf. The LTV Corp. v. IRS (In re Chateaugay Corp.)*, 146 B.R. 626 (S.D.N.Y. 1992) (Code § 4971 minimum funding tax expunged "under the terms of the automatic stay" where deadline for funding payments was after the bankruptcy filing), *vacated as moot*, 157 B.R. 74 (1993).

subsequently dismissed, such penalties can again begin to accrue for any periods of nonpayment following the date on which the dismissal order is entered.[97] In addition, in the case of a nondischargeable tax (which, as indicated above, is a concept of limited applicability to reorganizing corporate debtors), such penalties can again begin to accrue after the bankruptcy case is closed, even if the Chapter 11 plan properly provides for the deferred payment of the tax under the Bankruptcy Code beyond the closing of the case.[98]

**EXAMPLE**

On March 15, 1985, X Corporation failed to pay the $1,000 tax shown on its 1984 federal income tax return. As of March 16, 1985, a Code § 6651(a)(2) penalty of $5 is imposed (for the period March 16 to April 15), with additional accruals monthly (for a maximum of 49 months) at the rate of $5 per month until the tax is paid. If, on June 15, 1985, X Corporation files a voluntary Chapter 11 petition, the monthly accrual of the penalty would stop, and the IRS would only be permitted to impose a penalty of $15 for the three-month period preceding the bankruptcy petition.

Moreover, no penalty shall be imposed under Code § 6651 or Code § 6656 (for failure to make a required deposit of taxes) if the failure to pay by the due date (including extensions) is "due to reasonable cause and not due to willful neglect."[99] A failure to pay will be considered to be due to reasonable cause to the extent the debtor makes a "satisfactory showing that he exercised ordinary business care and prudence in providing for the payment of his tax liability and was nevertheless either unable to pay the tax or would suffer an undue hardship (as described in § 1.6161-1(b) of [the Regulations]) if he paid on the due date."[100] To establish the absence of willful

---

[97] Rev. Rul. 2005-9, 2005-6 I.R.B. 470 (interpreting the term "pending" in Code § 6658).

[98] Id.

[99] In the case of a deficiency assessment for which a notice and demand for payment has been made—in contrast to an unpaid tax shown on the return—the date as of which penalties begin to accrue (absent bankruptcy), and the date for ascertaining reasonable cause for nonpayment, is the last date specified for payment in the notice and demand. IRS Chief Counsel Advice 200543058, September 28, 2005, *reprinted at* 2005 TNT 209-27; Reg. § 301.6651-1(f), Example (1)(b), illustrating penalty computation under Code § 6651(a)(3).

[100] Reg. § 301.6651-1(c)(1). In making the determination whether the debtor exercised ordinary business care and prudence, all facts and circumstances will be considered, including an examination of the debtor's expenditures in light of the debtor's reasonably expected income (or other amounts) prior to the date prescribed for payment. Id. Proof that the debtor made reasonable efforts to conserve its assets in marketable form to satisfy its tax liability, but nevertheless was not able, will be sufficient. Id.; *see also* IRS Manual, Part 20 (Penalty and Interest), Ch. 1 (Penalty Handbook), § 1.3.1 (8/20/98) (listing common reasons given by taxpayers for nonpayment or nonfiling, and appropriate IRS considerations). For a discussion of "undue hardship" for purposes of Code § 6161, *see* § 1016.1.

neglect, the debtor must show that the failure to pay was not conscious, intentional, or with reckless indifference.[101] The debtor thus bears a "heavy burden" of proof.[102]

In *In re Pool & Varga, Inc.*,[103] reasonable cause was demonstrated (and willful neglect was not asserted) where the president of the debtor testified that sporadic payments had been made to the IRS to the best of the debtor's ability; that the IRS was not the only creditor to whom payments were not timely made; and that there were no available assets that could be liquidated or employees that could be laid off, without putting the company out of business. As a result, the penalties imposed for failure to pay income taxes for certain periods prior to filing bankruptcy were improperly assessed. Similarly, in *Glenwal-Schmidt v. United States*,[104] reasonable cause was demonstrated (and willful neglect was not asserted) where the debtor, faced with a cash shortage due to a contract dispute with the Navy over monies due and the choice of either defaulting on its contract with the Navy or depositing withheld employment taxes, opted to avoid defaulting on its contract. The court found that the debtor could not have foreseen that the Navy would not have complied with its regulations which contemplated a speedy and orderly resolution of any contract dispute. The possibility of default was considered an "undue hardship."[105]

In *C.J. Rogers, Inc. v. United States*,[106] however, the district court held that the taxpayer's financial difficulties (namely, the need to maintain progress on its jobs for General Motors, its primary customer) did not provide a reasonable cause for the nonpayment of withholding taxes and stated that the *Pool & Varga and Glenwal-Schmidt* decisions are "anomalous and contrary to established precedent." A significant factor potentially distinguishing *Rogers* from at least *Pool & Varga* is that *Rogers* involved withholding taxes whereas *Pool & Varga* involved income taxes. As the court observed, quoting from Reg. § 301.6651-1(c)(2), "what may constitute reasonable cause for nonpayment of income taxes may not constitute reasonable cause for failure to pay over" withholding taxes.

There is a developing disagreement among the various Circuit Courts of Appeals as to whether financial difficulties alone can ever constitute reasonable cause in the case of employment withholding taxes, as well as the employer's share of FICA and

---

101 *United States v. Boyle*, 469 U.S. 241, 245, 85-1 U.S.T.C. ¶ 13,602 (1985) (involved late filing of estate tax return).

102 Id.

103 86-1 U.S.T.C. ¶ 9445 (Bankr. E.D. Mich.).

104 78-2 U.S.T.C. ¶ 9610 (D.D.C.). *See also In re Arthur's Industrial Maintenance, Inc.*, 92-1 U.S.T.C. ¶ 50,242 (Bankr. W.D. Va.) (to similar effect), *appealed on other grounds.*

105 *See also In re Jensen*, 200 B.R. 5 (Bankr. D.N.H. 1996) (reliance on bankruptcy court order which disallowed portion of IRS claim but was granted without proper notice by debtor to IRS held reasonable cause for nonpayment of disallowed portion from date of order through filing of second bankruptcy, only after which was order vacated).

106 91-1 U.S.T.C. ¶ 50,297 (E.D. Mich. 1990). *See also East Wind Indus., Inc. v. United States*, 196 F.3d 499, 99-2 U.S.T.C. ¶ 50,968 (3rd Cir. 1999) (involving employment withholding taxes), *rev'g*, 33 F. Supp. 2d 339 (D. N.J. 1999), discussed in text below; *In re Woodstein-Lauderdale, Inc.*, 94-2 U.S.T.C. ¶ 50,461 (Bankr. S.D. Fla. 1994).

Medicare taxes. In *Brewery, Inc. v. United States*,[107] the Sixth Circuit considered the imposition of penalties in respect of the nonpayment of both the employee's and employer's share of FICA and Medicare taxes. First considering the employee's (withheld) portion, the court held that the taxpayer's financial difficulties could not excuse the taxpayer's willful decision "to invade the funds held in trust for the government in order to pay its creditors. We agree with the district court that such actions *cannot, as a matter of law,* constitute reasonable cause."[108] The Sixth Circuit then turned to the question of the employer's portion. Although recognizing that such taxes were not withholding taxes, the Sixth Circuit stated that the same reasoning utilized in relation to the failure to pay over the withheld taxes "applies with equal force" to the employer's portion:

> There is, in reality, no such thing as the "employer's share" since the taxes under 26 U.S.C. § 3111 inure to the benefit of the employee. Additionally, the employer's share is effectively paid for to the detriment of the employer. Most economists agree that the employer's share of social security taxes is ultimately borne by the employees in the form of lower wages . . . . We find that the employer's obligation to pay FICA and Medicare is much more closely analogous to the trust funds than to individual income tax obligations.

Similarly, no distinction was drawn in *In re Upton Printing Co.*,[109] where, in accord with the *Rogers* decision, the bankruptcy court also upheld the imposition of penalties for the employer's failure to pay FUTA taxes.

In *Fran Corp. v. United States*,[110] the Second Circuit rejected the government's position (which the government based on its reading of the Sixth Circuit's decision in *Brewery*) that financial difficulties, regardless of their cause or severity, could never justify reasonable cause for the nonpayment of withholding taxes. Nevertheless, the court recognized that the taxpayer has the heavy burden of proving that the nonpayment was due to reasonable cause and not willful neglect, and on the facts presented, concluded that such burden was not sustained.[111] Factually, the government con-

---

[107] 33 F.3d 589, 94-2 U.S.T.C. ¶ 50,435 (6th Cir. 1994) (emphasis added).

[108] *Accord In re Gordon Sel-Way, Inc.*, 95-2 U.S.T.C. ¶ 50,456 (Bankr. E.D. Mich. 1995), *appealed on other issues*, but recognizes the possibility of an equity or estoppel based exception when the government is the cause of the financial difficulty that led to the nonpayment of the taxes. *See also Norwalk Liquidating, Inc. v. United States*, 159 F. Supp. 2d 684, 2001-2 U.S.T.C. ¶ 50,557 (N.D. Ohio 2001), refusing to depart from bright-line test in *Brewery*.

[109] 186 B.R. 904, 95-2 U.S.T.C. ¶ 50,377 (Bankr. E.D. La. 1995).

[110] 164 F.3d 814, 99-1 U.S.T.C. ¶ 50,208 (2d Cir. 1999), *aff'g* 998 F. Supp. 296, 98-2 U.S.T.C. ¶ 50,533 (S.D.N.Y. 1998).

[111] The Second Circuit acknowledged that it will be the "rare case" that a penalty would not be imposed. Similarly, the district court below, after engaging in the same analysis and reaching the same conclusion, stated that "it is difficult to conceive of a precise set of circumstances, where as a matter of law, financial difficulties standing alone would justify a finding of reasonable cause, absent some unforeseeable intervening factor such as force majeure." On the other hand, the Second Circuit saw no justification for a different standard of reasonable cause in withholding tax cases than other cases.

ceded that the taxpayer had undergone severe financial difficulties, attributable in part to disputes with two separate customers (one being the State of New York), and that the taxpayer ultimately paid the tax and interest due (as well as the penalties for which it now sought a refund). Also undisputed, however, was that the taxpayer had, during the period of nonpayment, (i) continued to pay an affiliate for services provided while the affiliate continued to owe the taxpayer money on a personal loan, and (ii) incurred "lavish" and "extravagant" car rental and entertainment expenses. As a result, the Second Circuit found that the taxpayer failed to exercise ordinary business care and prudence in providing for payment of its tax liability. It made no difference that the aggregate amount of the expenditures was less than the unpaid withholding taxes.

In *East Wind Indus., Inc. v. United States,*[112] the Third Circuit similarly rejected the Sixth Circuit's "bright line" rule, and adopted the approach of the Second Circuit in *Fran Corp.* The court therefore examined all of the facts and circumstances surrounding the taxpayer's financial situation to determine whether reasonable cause existed for the taxpayer's nonpayment of employment taxes. In a split decision, the Third Circuit held that the facts presented one of the rare situations that justified the relief of penalties. The taxpayer, a defense contractor, had initially acceded to minor bribery demands of certain defense agency personnel, but subsequently refused when the demands moved to cash payments. In reprisal, the taxpayer received fewer contracts, often had completed orders falsely rejected, and received payment (if at all) only after substantial delays. Meanwhile, the taxpayer used all its available funds (and substantial personal funds lent by its controlling shareholder and one other of its officers) to pay employees essential to the continuation of the business in an effort to fulfill its government contracts and thereby obtain the funds needed to pay the IRS and its other creditors. Although the business ultimately failed, the taxpayer was able to recover enough through a settlement with the defense agencies to pay the IRS as well as other creditors. The court, in finding taxpayer's nonpayment of employment taxes legally excusable, acknowledged that the taxpayer was not entirely innocent, but viewed the illegal conduct of the defense agency personnel as the real cause of the taxpayer's financial situation and, given that the taxpayer's financial viability was entirely dependent on and controlled by the defense agencies, viewed the government as a "willing partner" in the taxpayer's floundering business.

The Second and Third Circuits have since been joined by the Seventh and Ninth Circuits and the Court of Federal Claims in rejecting the Sixth Circuit's "bright line" rule.[113]

---

[112] *Supra* note 106.

[113] *Diamond Plating Co. v. United States,* 390 F.3d 1035, 2005-1 U.S.T.C. ¶50,107 (7th Cir. 2004); *Van Camp & Bennion v. United States,* 251 F.3d 862, 868, 2001-1 U.S.T.C. ¶50,446 (9th Cir. 2001); *Q.E.D. Inc. v. United States,* 55 Fed. Cl. 140, 2003-1 U.S.T.C. ¶50,213 (Fed. Cl. 2003). For a further synthesis of the limited cases addressing financial difficulties and "reasonable cause," *see In re Hillard Dev. Corp.,* 2007 Bankr. LEXIS 1459 (Bankr. S.D. Fla. 2007); *Frances P. Harvey & Sons, Inc. v. IRS,* 2005-1 U.S.T.C. ¶50,154 (D. Mass. 2004). *See also* Raby and Raby, Payroll Tax Penalties for Doing Good and for Delegating, 105 Tax Notes 1639 (December 20, 2004).

As discussed immediately below in connection with penalties for failure to file, it is unclear whether—and, if so, the extent to which—a bankruptcy court can invoke its equitable powers to abate or otherwise limit the imposition of penalties.

**Penalties for failure to file.** Neither filing for bankruptcy nor financial difficulties is an excuse for failing to timely *file* a tax return.[114] Nevertheless, a late-filing penalty under Code §6651(a)(1) will not be imposed if the late filing is "due to reasonable cause and not due to willful neglect." A filing delay will be considered due to reasonable cause if the debtor "exercised ordinary business care and prudence and was nevertheless unable to file the return within the prescribed time."[115] In *In re Hudson Oil Co.*,[116] "reasonable cause" was established where the bankruptcy court appointed a trustee less than one month prior to the filing date, the debtor's records and those of its consolidated subsidiaries (also in bankruptcy) were in disarray, the trustee reasonably relied on accountant's advice to delay filing until a complete and accurate return could be prepared, and the trustee kept the court fully apprised of the reasons for delay.[117]

In addition, some bankruptcy courts have attempted with mixed success to employ their equitable powers to limit nonfiling penalties. For example, in *In re Sanford*,[118] the bankruptcy court (affirmed by the district court) made the "equitable decision" to diminish the penalties imposed for the debtor's nonfiling of several years' tax returns by two-thirds, rather than taking an all or nothing approach. The

---

[114] *See, e.g.*, *In re Pool & Varga, Inc.*, *supra* note 103; *Jones v. Commissioner*, 25 T.C. 1100, Dec. 21,590 (1956), *rev'd on other grounds*, 259 F.2d 300, 58-2 U.S.T.C. ¶9832 (5th Cir. 1958); *cf.* Code §6658(a).

[115] Reg. §301.6651-1(c)(1); *see also* IRS Manual, Part 20 (Penalty and Interest), Ch. 1 (Penalty Handbook), §1.3.1 (8/20/98) (listing common reasons given by taxpayers for nonpayment or nonfiling, and appropriate IRS considerations).

[116] *Supra* note 3.

[117] *See also In re O'Neil*, 79-2 U.S.T.C. ¶9618 (W.D. Va. 1979) (late-filing penalty excused where bankruptcy trustee was advised by counsel that no tax was due, but was unaware that a tax return was still required), *appealed on other issues. Consider also United States v. Quality Medical Consultants, Inc.*, 214 B.R. 246, 97-2 U.S.T.C. ¶50,632 (M.D. Fla. 1997) (late filing of information returns not excusable, but understandable, where pressing bankruptcy and operational matters—including the wrestling of control back from creditors, the fending off of the appointment of a trustee, and operational confusion caused by the bankruptcy filing—resulted in taxpayer's conscious decision to defer information returns; thus, court upheld imposition of basic Code §6721 late-filing penalty, rather than increased penalty for intentionally disregarding filing requirements); *United States v. Craddock* (*In re Craddock*), 149 F.3d 1249, 98-2 U.S.T.C. ¶50,618 (10th Cir. 1998) (upheld imposition of late-filing penalty, and reversed district court, where failure to file was due, among other things, to a combination of rapidly expanding businesses and technical problems in assimilating and organizing information in debtor's accounting system; court stated that a taxpayer "is expected in the exercise of ordinary business care and prudence ... not [to] take on such a load that he could not fulfill his own legal obligations within the required time [citations omitted]") *rev'g* 95-2 U.S.T.C. ¶50,475 (D. Col. 1995).

[118] *United States v. Sanford* (*In re Sanford*) (S.D. Fla.), *reprinted at* 91 TNT 185-13 (July 24, 1991), *rev'd*, 979 F.2d 1511 (11th Cir. 1992). *Consider In re Carlson* (7th Cir.), *supra* note 95, and *Karlsson v. United States* (*In re Karlsson*) (Bankr. M.D. Fla. 2000), *supra* note 95—both holding that a bankruptcy court (i) cannot use its equitable powers to abate prepetition interest and (ii) does not have jurisdiction under Bankruptcy Code section 505(a) (discussed at §1013 below) to abate interest, because neither the "amount" nor the "legality" of the interest is at issue—and *Followell v. United States* (*In re Gurley*), 335 B.R. 389 (Bankr. W.D. Tenn. 2005) (concluding that a bankruptcy court cannot abate any penalties properly claimed, by analogy to interest).

Eleventh Circuit reversed, finding that the nonfiling penalties imposed by Code §§6651(a)(1), 6652(a)(2), and 6654 must be waived or imposed in their entireties. In contrast, where the IRS intentionally delayed issuing a deficiency notice to the debtor for three years while it conducted a criminal investigation into the debtor's nonfiling of its tax return, which it later dropped, the bankruptcy court disallowed on equitable grounds the IRS' entire claim for interest and penalties.[119] The district court affirmed, but limited the bankruptcy court's holding to its facts.

### §1006.1.3 Voidable Prepetition Tax Elections?

Can a tax election that is irrevocable without the consent of the Commissioner be avoided in bankruptcy? Although such cases would seem rare, the Eighth Circuit has held that it is possible and other courts have followed suit. The IRS, however, continues to maintain that such an election is not avoidable.[120]

In the *Russell* case,[121] a divided Eighth Circuit held that an irrevocable election to forgo the carryback of NOLs may be avoided as a fraudulent transfer under Bankruptcy Code section 548(a)(1)(A) *if* made within one year before the bankruptcy filing and with the "actual intent to hinder, delay, or defraud any existing or future creditors."[122] (The 2005 bankruptcy reform act has since increased the one year to two years.) The Eighth Circuit remanded the case to consider whether the requisite intent was present.

The trustee in *Russell* asserted that the debtor, an individual, had elected to forgo the carryback—and, thus, the resulting tax refund—in order to increase his NOLs beyond that necessary for the debtor's bankruptcy. In that way, even after the bankruptcy, some portion of the NOLs would remain for the debtor's personal benefit,[123] whereas the tax refunds would have been used to pay creditors.[124]

In the court's view, the bankruptcy trustee's ability to avoid an "irrevocable" tax election did not undermine the tax policy that a taxpayer should not be able to escape the consequences of a prior election upon discovering that the election was imprudent, because the trustee, not the taxpayer, was seeking to avoid the election, whereas

---

119 *United States v. Clark*, 145 B.R. 275, 92-2 U.S.T.C. ¶50,416 (E.D. Ark. 1992).

120 *See, e.g.*, IRS Chief Counsel Advice 199927037, April 26, 1999 (reasserts belief that the Eighth Circuit decision in *Russell*, discussed below, is incorrect), *reprinted at* 1999 TNT 132-69.

121 *Gibson v. United States* (*In re Russell*), 927 F.2d 413, 91-1 U.S.T.C. ¶50,128 (8th Cir. 1991).

122 At the same time, the court held that a similar postpetition election could be avoided under Bankruptcy Code section 549(a) if the election was not "in the ordinary course of business" (*see* §1006.2.2 below). *See* Pollack & Goldring, Eighth Circuit Holds Bankruptcy Trustee Can Avoid "Irrevocable" Tax Elections, 3 Faulkner & Gray's Bankr. L. Rev. #2, 38 (Summer 1991).

123 *See* Code §1398(g)(1) (only applies to individual debtors).

124 To constitute a fraudulent transfer, there must be a transfer of "property" of the debtor. According to the Eighth Circuit, this property was the right to carry forward the NOL, not the potential tax refund (citing the *Prudential Lines* case, *see* §1002.4.1 above). This seems curious, however, since the effect of the election (which the trustee sought to avoid) was to forgo the tax refund and increase the NOL. More properly, the property at issue would seem to be the tax refund. In this regard, the Supreme Court has long ago held that a tax refund attributable to an NOL carryback is "property" for bankruptcy law purposes. *Segal v. Rochelle*, 382 U.S. 375 (1966).

the underlying purpose of the avoidance provisions—to protect the bankruptcy estate from improper transfers—was directly at issue. If the trustee is successful, the election is avoided *ab initio.*

On remand, the facts established that the debtor had relied on the advice of his tax advisors and had been unaware that a refund was available. Accordingly, the debtor lacked the requisite intent under Bankruptcy Code section 548(a)(1)(A) to hinder, delay, or defraud his creditors.[125]

The trustee then raised for the first time whether the debtor's election could be avoided as a "constructive" fraudulent conveyance under Bankruptcy Code section 548(a)(1)(B) (as subsequently redesignated),[126] which has no intent requirement. Under that section, a transfer of property within one year before the bankruptcy filing could be avoided *if* the debtor received less than reasonably equivalent value and either (1) was or thereby became insolvent, (2) was engaged, or about to engage, in a business or transaction with unreasonably small capital, or (3) intended to incur additional debts beyond its ability to repay. (The 2005 bankruptcy reform act has here also increased the one year to two years.) The bankruptcy court initially determined that a finding as to constructive fraud was not within the Eighth Circuit's mandate on remand; however, the district court subsequently concluded otherwise and again remanded the case for further proceedings.[127] This time the bankruptcy court conducted an evidentiary hearing, and it found that the evidence was "overwhelming that neither the debtor nor the estate received any value for carrying the NOL forward" and that the debtor was insolvent at the time of the election. The bankruptcy court thus concluded (and the district court later affirmed) that the debtor's election constituted constructive fraud and was voidable under Bankruptcy Code section 548(a)(1)(B).[128]

The Ninth Circuit, in *In re Feiler,*[129] similarly concluded, under substantially identical facts, that the debtor's election was voidable as a fraudulent conveyance under Bankruptcy Code section 548(a).[130]

---

[125] *Streetman v. United States (In re Russell)*, 154 B.R. 723, 726-728, 93-1 U.S.T.C. ¶50,309 (Bankr. W.D. Ark. 1993).

[126] Prior to June 19, 1998, this was section 548(a)(2).

[127] 1994 U.S. Dist. LEXIS 7185 (W.D. Ark.), *reh'g denied*, 1994 U.S. Dist. LEXIS 7160.

[128] *See* district court decision at 187 B.R. 287, 95-2 U.S.T.C. ¶50,453 (W.D. Ark. 1995).

[129] 218 F.3d 948, 2000-2 U.S.T.C. ¶50,579 (9th Cir. 2000), *aff'g*, 230 B.R. 164 (Bankr. 9th Cir. 1999), *aff'g*, 218 B.R. 957 (Bankr. N.D. Cal. 1998) (also held that Bankruptcy Code section 550(a) did not preclude the fraudulent conveyance action under then Bankruptcy Code section 548(a)(2), because the IRS was properly regarded as a "transferee" of the debtors' right to the NOL carryback and the related right to a tax refund).

[130] The IRS has informally considered the ability of a bankruptcy trustee to override an individual taxpayer's election to forego an immediate refund of a tax overpayment and, instead, to apply the overpayment as a (refundable) credit towards the individual's next year's taxes. The IRS noted that, in contrast to the waiver of an NOL carryback with an indeterminate future value, the tax credit generally affords the taxpayer a dollar-for-dollar benefit. *See* IRS Chief Counsel Advice 199927037, April 26, 1999, *reprinted at* 1999 TNT 132-69. *Consider Morton v. IRS (In re Metcalf)*, 2001-2 U.S.T.C. ¶50,706 (Bankr. N.D. Tex. 2001) (upheld debtor's election to apply overpayment to next year's taxes; court noted that the trustee did not contend that the election was a fraudulent transfer).

Although both *Russell* and *Feiler* involved an individual debtor, a similar issue could arise in the corporate context. For example, consider a consolidated return filed by a solvent parent corporation and a bankrupt subsidiary with NOL carryforwards. A situation analogous to the facts in *Russell* could arise if (1) the bankrupt subsidiary incurred a loss that could be carried back for a refund to a prior year in which the subsidiary had income[131] and (2) the parent, within one or two years before the bankruptcy filing (or during the bankruptcy case[132]) elected to forgo the carryback in order to increase the NOL carryforwards available to offset its future income under the consolidated return regulations for the remaining period of their consolidation.[133] An avoidable transfer of property does not occur where the parent's use of the bankrupt subsidiary's NOL carryforwards occurs by reason of the normal application of the consolidated return regulations (and the election to file consolidated was made more than a year or two before the bankruptcy filing).[134]

A case-specific example arose in the Subchapter S corporation context in *In re Trans-Lines West, Inc.*[135] In that case, less than a month prior to the debtor corporation's Chapter 11 filing, the debtor and its sole shareholder elected to revoke the debtor's Subchapter S status. By notice, the IRS confirmed the revocation. A Chapter 11 trustee was subsequently appointed. The trustee ascertained that, as a result of the debtor's status as a C corporation, the estate would incur a prohibitive tax liability upon the disposition of certain property. Thus, the trustee sought to undo the revocation of its Subchapter S status.

The trustee initially attempted to challenge the validity of the revocation,[136] failing which it sought to avoid the revocation as fraudulent conveyances under Bankruptcy Code sections 548(a)(1)(A) and 548(a)(1)(B) (as subsequently redesignated)[137] and under applicable state law, as permitted by Bankruptcy Code

---

[131] Under the consolidated return regulations, any such refund is ordinarily paid by the IRS to the common parent as agent for the group. *See* Reg. § 1.1502-77(a). However, the refund may nevertheless be property of the subsidiary's estate, absent a tax-sharing agreement providing to the contrary. *See* § 806.2.

[132] *See supra* note 122, and *In re Home America TV-Appliance-Audio, Inc.*, discussed at § 1006.2.2 below.

[133] For example, *see Nisselson v. Drew Industries Inc.* (*In re White Metal Rolling and Stamping Corp.*), 217 B.R. 981 (S.D.N.Y. 1998) (wherein the debtor subsidiary brought multiple fraudulent conveyance actions against other members of consolidated group for benefits obtained from use of debtor's NOLs and impact of prebankruptcy worthless stock deduction under Code § 382; only jurisdictional issue was currently before the court), and 222 B.R. 417 (S.D.N.Y. 1998) (dismissed tax-related actions due to failure to demonstrate that debtor's NOLs had value, particularly in light of the debtor's pending liquidation).

[134] *See, e.g., Marvel Entertainment Group Inc. v. Mafco Holdings Inc.* (*In re Marvel Entertainment Group Inc.*), 273 B.R. 58, 2002-1 U.S.T.C. ¶ 50,302 (D. Del. 2002) (so holding).

[135] *Guinn v. Lines, et al.* (*In re Trans-Lines West, Inc.*), 203 B.R. 653, 97-1 U.S.T.C. ¶ 50,252 (Bankr. E.D. Tenn. 1996). *Accord Parker v. Saunders* (*In re Bakersfield Westar, Inc.*), 226 B.R. 227 (Bankr. 9th Cir. 1998).

[136] The trustee challenged the validity of the revocation on the grounds that neither the election to revoke nor the related shareholder consent had been signed. The court held that, without the consent of the shareholders who consented to the revocation, the trustee did not have standing to challenge the validity of the revocation.

[137] *See supra* note 126.

section 544(b). The IRS filed a motion to dismiss and for summary judgment, contending that the revocation of Subchapter S status was not a "transfer of an interest of the debtor in property" under section 548 or a "conveyance" under applicable state law. The court disagreed.

Defining "property" as essentially nothing more than a collection of rights, the court concluded that the debtor did in fact possess a property interest in its Subchapter S status. The court found that Code § 1362 afforded the debtor "a guaranteed, indefinite right to use, enjoy, and dispose of [its Subchapter S] status" until terminated by the debtor in accordance with such section. In concluding that the revocation constituted a "transfer," the court relied on the definition of transfer in Bankruptcy Code section 101 and, in part, the Eighth Circuit's holding in *Russell* that an irrevocable election under the Internal Revenue Code constituted a transfer under the Bankruptcy Code. The court similarly concluded that the revocation of the debtor's Subchapter S status constituted a "conveyance" under applicable state statutes for purposes of the state law fraudulent conveyance action. The court therefore denied the IRS motion and scheduled a trial as to the issues of intent, insolvency and consideration, under both Bankruptcy Code section 548 and the state fraudulent conveyance statutes.

## *§ 1006.2 Postpetition Taxable Years*

A debtor-in-possession (or trustee) must continue to file estimated and annual federal income tax returns for the debtor corporation during the bankruptcy case, using the debtor corporation's taxpayer identification number.[138] All income and expenses of the debtor-in-possession should be included.[139] In addition, unlike prepetition taxes, the payment of which is generally suspended, all postpetition taxes generally must be paid when due.[140] The IRS may not, however, generally set off

[138] Code § 6012(b)(3), discussed *supra* note 3; Reg. § 1.6012-3(b)(4); Rev. Rul. 79-120, 1979-1 C.B. 382; *In re Sapphire S.S. Lines, Inc.*, 762 F.2d 13, 85-1 U.S.T.C. ¶9403 (2d Cir. 1985) (nonoperating trustee under prior Bankruptcy Act required to file estimated tax returns where appropriate); *but see infra* text accompanying notes 152-155 (where debtor has ceased operations and has neither assets nor income). In addition, a bankruptcy court may make the timely filing of tax returns the subject of a court order and, thus, enforceable by any sanctions that the bankruptcy court deems appropriate. *Supra* notes 5 and 6; *cf. In re Arie Enterprises, Inc.*, 116 B.R. 641 (Bankr. S.D. Ill. 1990). *See also Lopez-Stubbe v. Rodriquez-Estrada (In re San Juan Hotel Corp.)*, 847 F.2d 931, 946-949 (1st Cir. 1988) (a trustee who intentionally failed to pay taxes incurred by the bankruptcy estate was personally "surcharged" the resulting interest and penalties). In a small business bankruptcy case (one where, among other things, the debtor has no more than $2 million in noncontingent, liquidated debts), the timely filing of tax returns and the timely payment of taxes is made an affirmative duty of the debtor-in-possession. *See* 11 U.S.C. § 1116(6).

[139] Rev. Rul. 79-120, 1979-1 C.B. 382; *see In re Nab Food Services, Inc.*, 25 B.R. 221, 83-1 U.S.T.C. ¶9222 (Bankr. S.D. Ohio 1983) (interest earned on money invested by trustee during Chapter 7 case taxable to debtor corporation).

[140] *See, e.g.*, 28 U.S.C. § 960; Code §§ 6151(a), 6658(a) and 6903; 11 U.S.C. §§ 1108 (authority to operate debtor's business, unless the court, after notice and a hearing, orders otherwise) and 363(c) (authorizes use, sale and lease of estate property in ordinary course of business where authorized to operate business); *see also* 11 U.S.C. § 549 (acts out of ordinary course require court approval). In appropriate circumstances, failure to pay postpetition taxes may constitute "cause" to dismiss or

overpayments of prepetition or postpetition taxes against unpaid postpetition taxes without prior bankruptcy court approval.[141] With limited exceptions (discussed in § 1006.2.1 below), penalties will be imposed for any failure to file or failure to pay any postpetition taxes.[142]

In a Chapter 11 case, Bankruptcy Code sections 363(c) and 1108, among others, provide the requisite statutory authority for the payment of most taxes.[143] Such sections grant a debtor-in-possession (or trustee) authority to operate the debtor's business (unless the bankruptcy court orders otherwise), including the payment of postpetition expenses incurred in the ordinary course of business. In contrast, in a Chapter 7 case, a trustee has no authority to operate the debtor's business unless the bankruptcy court determines that such operation is consistent with an orderly liquidation, and in the best interest, of the estate and so orders.[144] Absent such authority, or a more specific grant of authority by the court to pay taxes (such as in response to a request for payment by the IRS, upon notice and a hearing[145]), it was held that a Chapter 7 trustee had no duty to remit any postpetition taxes to the IRS in advance of an orderly distribution of the estate's assets.[146] In one instance, the court went so far as to disallow accrued interest on postpetition taxes which were subsequently eliminated by the carryback of later year postpetition losses.[147] The 2005 bankruptcy reform act changes this result for bankruptcy cases commenced on or after October 17, 2005. Absent a specific provision of the Bankruptcy Code excusing current payment, a Chapter 7 trustee now must timely pay all postpetition taxes *unless* (i) the tax was incurred prior to the appointment of a trustee, or (ii) prior to the due date, an order of the bankruptcy court makes a finding of probable insufficiency

---

(Footnote Continued)

convert a Chapter 11 case under Bankruptcy Code section 1112(b). *See, e.g., Matter of Santiago Vela*, 87 B.R. 229, 231-232 (Bankr. D. P.R. 1988).

[141] *See* 11 U.S.C. § 553, and discussion at § 1006.1.1 above; *In re Calore Express Company, Inc., supra* note 23 (ability to setoff mutual postpetition obligations is subject to the automatic stay, as it constitutes "an act to obtain possession of property of the estate or of property from the estate or to exercise control over property of the estate" under section 362(a)(3) of the Bankruptcy Code; First Circuit reversed on other grounds); *United States v. Ferguson*, 778 F.2d 1017 (4th Cir. 1985) (in the face of a refund claim, overpayment of prepetition taxes may not be retained to pay unpaid postpetition taxes), *cert. denied sub. nom., Wilson v. United States*, 106 S. Ct. 1990 (1986); *United States v. Norton, supra* note 22; *In re Mealey*, 16 B.R. 800, 82-1 U.S.T.C. ¶ 9173 (Bankr. E.D. Pa. 1982); *see also In re Harris, supra* note 50 (setoff of overpayments disallowed after claim for refund of overpayment filed).

[142] *See, e.g., Nicholas v. United States*, 384 U.S. 678 (1966); *In re Samuel Chapman, Inc.*, 394 F.2d 340 (2d Cir. 1968). Where a Chapter 11 case is converted to a Chapter 7 liquidation, interest and penalties on postpetition taxes incurred during the Chapter 11 case do not continue to accrue after conversion. *See In re Sun Cliffe, Inc.*, 143 B.R. 789 (Bankr. D. Colo. 1992).

[143] *See also* 11 U.S.C. § 1116(6)(B) (applicable to "small business" debtors).

[144] *See* 11 U.S.C. § 721.

[145] *See* discussion of postpetition taxes at § 1010.4 below.

[146] *See, e.g., In re Quid Me Broadcasting, Inc.*, 181 B.R. 715 (Bankr. W.D.N.Y. 1995), *aff'd*, 1996 U.S. Dist. LEXIS 7581 (W.D.N.Y. 1996).

[147] Id.

of funds to pay, in full, administrative expenses of the same priority as the tax owed.[148]

As discussed at § 1015.1.1 below, a number of courts (including three Circuit Courts) had held that any income tax due for the year of the bankruptcy filing should be bifurcated between the pre- and postpetition portions of the year for purposes of determining priority of payment. In such instance, only the postpetition portion would be payable on a current basis. However, for bankruptcy cases commenced on or after October 17, 2005, any income tax due for a taxable year ending after the petition date (and during the administration of the bankruptcy case), such as the year of the bankruptcy filing, should be treated *entirely* as a postpetition tax (*see* § 1015.1.1 discussion).

### § 1006.2.1 Relief from Penalties

If the debtor corporation is unable to pay postpetition income and excise taxes (other than excise taxes for which the debtor acts as a collecting agent, *see* § 1006.3.1) because of insufficient funds, and such fact is supported by a bankruptcy court finding of "probable insufficiency of funds" to pay all postpetition expenses, the debtor corporation will be relieved from any penalties (but not interest) that would otherwise be imposed for such failure under Code § 6651 (failure to pay taxes) and Code § 6655 (failure to pay estimated taxes).[149] For this purpose, the term "funds" has been held to be a generic term and to include marketable securities, as well as cash.[150] The penalty for failure to deposit taxes imposed by Code § 6656 may also be avoided if such failure is "due to reasonable cause and not due to willful neglect." As discussed at § 1006.1.2 above, the courts are split as to whether, and in what circumstances, a debtor's financial hardships may be sufficient to establish reasonable cause. In an involuntary bankruptcy, regardless of the debtor corporation's ability to pay, no penalty under Code § 6651 or 6655 will be imposed for failure to pay postpetition income and excise taxes incurred prior to the earlier of the bankruptcy court's formal approval of the petition (called an "order for relief") or, if a trustee is appointed, the appointment of a trustee.[151]

As for relief from filing penalties, as discussed at § 1006.1.2, no penalty will be imposed under Code § 6651(a)(1) for failing to file a timely tax return if "reasonable cause" is established for the late filing. For this purpose, financial hardship is no excuse.

---

148 *See* 28 U.S.C. § 960(b) and (c), *as added by* P.L. 109-8, § 712 (2005) (the same section of the 2005 Act dispensed with a governmental unit's need to file a "request for payment" as a precondition for an administrative expense being allowed). As to the exception for insufficient funds, compare Code § 6658(a)(1), discussed in the next section, which employs a substantially identical standard for penalty relief.

149 Code § 6658(a)(1).

150 *In re Ashmun*, 182 B.R. 17, 95-2 U.S.T.C. ¶ 50,424 (Bankr. S.D. Tex. 1995).

151 Code § 6658(a)(2).

In addition, a debtor-in-possession may request relief from filing a federal income tax return if it has ceased operations and has neither assets nor income.[152] The request must be submitted to the District Director of the Internal Revenue Service for the district in which the debtor corporation has its principal place of business,[153] and within 90 days the district director must inform the debtor-in-possession whether the request has been granted or denied.[154] In determining whether the debtor has assets for this purpose, the IRS has taken the position that a lawsuit prosecuted by, or on behalf of, the debtor corporation is an asset of the corporation.[155]

### §1006.2.2 Voidable Postpetition Tax Elections?

As discussed above, a debtor-in-possession must continue to file tax returns on behalf of the debtor corporation. Does this also mean that, in connection with such filing, a debtor-in-possession is authorized to make any related tax elections it deems appropriate? Or is prior court approval required?

In the *Russell* case,[156] an individual debtor filed a voluntary petition under Chapter 11 and, initially, operated as a debtor-in-possession. During that time, the debtor filed his tax return for his last taxable year and, as he had done on his previous tax return (*see* §1006.1.3), irrevocably elected to forgo the carryback of his current year NOLs. Subsequently, a trustee was appointed and, ignoring the debtor's election, filed tax refund claims for the prior years based on a carryback of the NOLs, which was then followed by a tax refund suit.

On appeal, the Eighth Circuit held that the postpetition election could be avoided as an improper transfer of estate property under Bankruptcy Code section 549(a) *if* the election (as opposed to the filing of the tax return) was not "in the ordinary course of business."[157] The court then remanded the issue for further factual development.

On remand, the bankruptcy court noted that there were at least 250 elections permitted in the Internal Revenue Code and that a debtor would be reasonably expected to make the applicable election in connection with the filing of his tax returns.[158] Accordingly, the court concluded that, absent a showing of bad faith or fraud, a debtor's act of exercising a tax election is in the ordinary course of business.

---

152 Rev. Rul. 84-123, 1984-2 C.B. 244; *see* Rev. Proc. 84-59, 1984-2 C.B. 504 (procedure for obtaining consent).

153 Rev. Proc. 84-59, §3.01, 1984-2 C.B. 504.

154 Id. at §3.05.

155 *See* IRS Letter Ruling 8251077, September 21, 1982.

156 *Gibson v. United States (In re Russell), supra* note 121, discussed earlier at §1006.1.3 with respect to prepetition elections.

157 *See* 927 F.2d at 418; *supra* note 124 (regarding NOLs and tax refunds as "property" of the estate). The dissent in *Russell* would have procedurally dismissed the trustee's claim under Bankruptcy Code section 549 as untimely. *See* 11 U.S.C. §549(d), providing that an action or proceeding under that section must be commenced within two years after the date of the transfer sought to be avoided (but no later than the close or dismissal of the bankruptcy case).

158 *Streetman v. United States (In re Russell), supra* note 125, at 728-730.

On the facts, the court found no evidence of fraud or bad faith. The debtor had relied on the advice of its tax advisors, and it was irrelevant whether the tax advisors were negligent or unreasonably optimistic as to the benefit from any carryback or carryforward. In this regard, the court focused on the fact that the debtor nevertheless "did receive a contingent benefit in return for the election which could have benefited the estate if certain events had transpired in the future."

However, in connection with a subsequent evidentiary hearing as to whether the debtor's similar prepetition election the prior year constituted constructive fraud (*see* discussion at § 1006.1.3), the bankruptcy court found "overwhelming" evidence that "neither the debtor nor the estate received any value for carrying the NOL forward."[159] Accordingly, upon a later appeal, the district court reversed the bankruptcy court's decision (as well as its own prior ruling initially affirming such decision) and held that the debtor's election was not made in the ordinary course of business.[160]

In reaching this conclusion, the court stated that a transaction must satisfy two tests in order to be considered in the ordinary course of business. The first involves whether other similar businesses would engage in such transactions as ordinary business, and the second is whether from the vantage point of a hypothetical creditor the transaction is ordinary and consistent with the creditors' reasonable expectations (in this regard, the district court noted that the test is not one of bad faith or fraud, as the bankruptcy court had stated). Given the bankruptcy court's factual finding, the district court held that the debtor's election to forgo the tax refund violated the creditors' reasonable expectations.

As discussed above at § 1006.1.3, although *Russell* involved an individual debtor, analogous situations can arise in the corporate context (particularly in the consolidated return area). Just such a situation arose in the bankruptcy case of *Home America TV-Appliance-Audio, Inc.*, where a parent and subsidiary filed a consolidated return for the first time immediately after an involuntary bankruptcy case was commenced against the subsidiary (the parent had acquired the requisite 80 percent control for consolidation just a few months earlier). On the return, the parent elected to forgo the carryback of the subsidiary's current year NOLs for which a tax refund would have been available. As a result of the consolidated filing and election, the parent was able to use the subsidiary's current year NOLs against its current and future taxable income. Subsequently a trustee was appointed. The trustee sought to void the subsidiary's election to file consolidated returns and the parent's election to forgo the NOL carryback, on the grounds that the election was outside the ordinary course of business and, under Bankruptcy Code section 549(b) (involving transactions in an involuntary bankruptcy case during the "gap" period before the order for relief is entered), less than fair value was received therefor. In a bench decision, the bankruptcy court agreed that the elections were voidable and ordered the government to pay the refund.[161] On appeal, the district court vacated the bankruptcy court's

---

[159] *See* later district court decision at 187 B.R. 287, 95-2 U.S.T.C. ¶ 50,453 (W.D. Ark. 1995).

[160] Id.

[161] *In re Home America TV-Appliance-Audio, Inc.* (Bankr. D. Ariz. March 22, 1994), judgment reprinted at 94 TNT 87-17 and reported at 25 B.C.D. A7 (April 28, 1994); *see also* government's opening and reply briefs on appeal, filed July 18, 1994, and August 17, 1994, respectively, and

decision for failure to join the parent as a necessary party under Rule 19(a) of the Fed. Rules of Civ. Proc., such that the parent would be bound by the judgment of the court and the IRS would not be exposed to potentially duplicative litigation and inconsistent obligations.[162] The trustee subsequently filed an amended complaint joining the parent, and the bankruptcy court again granted the tax refunds. This time, the district court affirmed. On further appeal, however, the Ninth Circuit, without addressing the merits of the refund claim, held that the trustee's action was barred, since it was not brought within the two-year statute of limitations for avoidance actions under Bankruptcy Code section 549(d) (measured from the date the consolidated return was filed).[163]

Significantly, the Ninth Circuit's action in procedurally dismissing the trustee's avoidance action as untimely, even though filed within the requisite period for bringing a suit for tax refund (*i.e.*, within two years of a notice of disallowance of a timely filed refund claim), joins ranks with the dissent in the *Russell* case (*see supra* note 156). In the Ninth Circuit's view, the avoidance of the debtor's consent to file a consolidated return was a necessary predicate to the trustee's recovery of a tax refund under the Internal Revenue Code. In contrast, the Eighth Circuit's decision in *Russell* held that the trustee's action, since brought as a suit for refund, was governed exclusively by the statute of limitations for tax refunds under the Internal Revenue Code, even though the "theory underlying the refund suit may involve a § 549 unauthorized post-petition transfer."[164]

Another example of an unauthorized tax election arose in *In re Walterman Implement Inc.* in the Subchapter S corporation context.[165] In this case, an involuntary Chapter 7 petition was filed against the debtor S corporation. Despite the appointment of a trustee, the president-sole shareholder revoked the corporation's Subchapter S election shortly after the bankruptcy filing. Upon learning of the revocation, the trustee sought to have it voided. Agreeing with the trustee, the bankruptcy court held that the debtor's "right to use, benefit from, or revoke its subchapter S election

---

(Footnote Continued)

trustee's response, filed August 1, 1994. In contrast, a parent's use of a previously consolidated bankrupt subsidiary's NOLs under the normal application of the consolidated return regulations (without the assistance of a special election, such as the waiver of an NOL carryback) would not be an avoidable benefit. *See, e.g., Marvel Entertainment Group Inc. v. Mafco Holdings Inc.* (*In re Marvel Entertainment Group Inc.*), *supra* note 134 (so holding).

162 193 B.R. 929 (D. Ariz. 1995). The district court did not, however, dismiss the lawsuit, but rather remanded the case and directed that the trustee take all reasonable steps to join the parent as a party within a reasonable amount of time (or, alternatively, obtain the parent's agreement to be bound by the results of the litigation) so that the lawsuit could still proceed.

163 232 F.3d 1046, 2000-2 U.S.T.C. ¶ 50,854 (9th Cir. 2000) (describes the procedural history), *cert. denied*, 122 S. Ct. 239 (2001). The court declined to address the merits of the trustee's argument that the date of the physical filing of the consolidated return should not be the considered date of the unauthorized "transfer," and that such transfer should not occur until the tax return has been processed by the IRS, as such argument was raised for the first time only on appeal.

164 *See* 927 F.2d at 417.

165 *Hanrahan v. Walterman* (*In re Walterman Implement Inc.*), 2006 Bankr. LEXIS 921 (Bankr. N.D. Iowa 2006).

falls within the broad definition of property of the estate,"[166] and therefore declared the revocation void both as a violation of the automatic stay and as an unauthorized postpetition transfer under Bankruptcy Code section 549(a).

Looking at the possibility of avoiding an undesirable tax election from a slightly different perspective, it has been asserted that the act of *not* making an election should be avoidable thereby requiring that the election be made (even if the time for making the election had otherwise expired). This is one of the alternative forms of relief that was sought by the creditors' committee and Chapter 7 trustee in *In re Forman Enterprises, Inc.*,[167] also involving a Subchapter S corporation. In that case, the debtor S corporation had generated income in prior years and had made tax distributions to its shareholders. In the taxable year at issue, the return for which was filed after the debtor entered bankruptcy, the S corporation generated a loss which the shareholders carried back to obtain a refund of the prior year taxes. The bankruptcy court considered (1) whether, on the one hand, the shareholders were required to turn the refunds over to the S corporation for the ultimate benefit of the creditors under a theory of unjust enrichment or constructive trusts, or (2) failing that, whether the shareholders' decision to claim the tax refund, rather than waiving the loss carryback and making the loss available to offset future taxable income of the debtor allocable to the shareholders (presumably on the theory that the debtor might otherwise have to make additional tax distributions), could be avoided under Bankruptcy Code section 549(a). In each instance, the bankruptcy court held in favor of the shareholders. Observing that the NOLs and the right to use them pass automatically under the Internal Revenue Code to the S corporation shareholders, the bankruptcy court did not see how the shareholders were unjustly enriched and thus any ground for a constructive trust (or breach of fiduciary duty claim), and concluded that there was no "transfer" of "property" of the S corporation for purposes of Bankruptcy Code section 549(a). Rather, the "Debtor was merely a 'conduit' through which the NOL and the right to use it passed to [the shareholders]." The court also could not comprehend how a decision by the shareholders not to waive the loss carryback amounted to any kind of transfer.

## *§1006.3 Trust Fund Taxes*

A debtor-in-possession has a continuing duty to collect, account for, and pay over all tax monies required to be collected or withheld (generally termed "trust fund" taxes)—whether collected or withheld prepetition or postpetition or in respect

---

[166] The court observed that this same conclusion was reached, in dicta, by the Bankruptcy Appellate Panel for the Eighth Circuit in *Halverson v. Funaro* (*In re Funaro*), 263 B.R. 892, 898 (Bankr. 8th Cir. 2001).

[167] *The Official Comm. of Unsecured Creditors v. Forman* (*In re Forman Enterprises, Inc.*), 273 B.R. 408, 2002-1 U.S.T.C. ¶50,338 (Bankr. W.D. Pa. 2002) (denying the shareholders' motion to dismiss), and 281 B.R. 600 (Bankr. W.D. Pa. 2002) (holding in favor of shareholders).

of payments under a Chapter 11 plan.[168] Such taxes include income and employment withholding taxes, backup withholding, and certain excise taxes.[169]

Subject to a confirmed plan, however, a debtor-in-possession is prohibited from paying (without prior court approval) any trust fund taxes not remitted prior to the bankruptcy case (*see* § 1006.1).[170] In many cases, this may prompt the IRS to seek alternative sources of payment. In particular, as discussed at § 1006.3.2 below, the IRS may seek to collect such taxes from any responsible officers or employees of the debtor. Court approval for the payment of such taxes by the debtor-in-possession should be easily obtained, however, where the trust fund taxes have been segregated prior to the commencement of the bankruptcy case or it can otherwise be established that such taxes were in the debtor's possession at the commencement of the case and have not been expended (and in many cases is sought at the start of the bankruptcy case, *see* § 1002.2 above).[171] In such cases, some courts (including the Fifth and Ninth

---

168 *Otte v. United States*, 419 U.S. 43, 74-2 U.S.T.C. ¶9822 (1974) (withhold FICA and income taxes; IRS not required to file proof of claim for amounts required to be withheld upon subsequent payment of prepetition wage claims); *Laub Baking Co. v. United States*, 642 F.2d 196, 81-1 U.S.T.C. ¶9333 (6th Cir. 1981) (pay FUTA); *In re Armadillo Corp.*, 561 F.2d 1382, 77-2 U.S.T.C. ¶9659 (10th Cir. 1977). *See also* IRS Chief Counsel Advice Memorandum 200036043, May 17, 2000, *reprinted at* 2000 TNT 176-66 (so concluding); Howard, An Overview of the State and Federal Tax Responsibilities of Bankruptcy Trustees and Debtors, 93 Comm. L.J. 43, 56-58 (1988). Under Code § 7501, the amount of any tax collected or withheld is considered to be held "in trust for the United States," hence the term "trust fund" tax.

169 Only excise taxes imposed on the purchaser of a product or service, and thus required to be "collected," are considered trust fund taxes—such as (1) the tax on certain communication services imposed by Code § 4251; (2) the tax on certain air transportation imposed by Code §§ 4261 and 4271; and (3) the windfall profit tax on domestic crude oil imposed by Code § 4986 (repealed for oil removed on or after August 23, 1988). In contrast, the taxes imposed by Code §§ 4081 and 4091 on gasoline and aviation fuel are not trust fund taxes. *See* IRS Manual, Part 5 (Collection Process), Ch. 7 (Trust Fund Compliance), § 3.1.1 (4/13/06). As discussed below, only trust fund taxes generally carry the potential for "responsible person" liability. However, effective December 1, 1990, Congress enacted Code § 4103 also imposing personal liability on any person who willfully fails to pay the taxes imposed by Code §§ 4081 and 4091, or willfully causes the failure to pay such taxes. Effective January 1, 1994, such provision was extended to cover the Code § 4041(a)(1) tax on diesel fuel.

170 *See* 11 U.S.C. §§ 549 (prohibits postpetition transactions involving property of the estate) and 541 (defines "property of the estate"); 124 Cong. Rec. H 11,096, 11,114 (daily ed. September 28, 1978), S 17,413, 17,430-17,431 (daily ed. October 6, 1978) (legislative statements indicate that "property of the estate" includes the legal title to, but not the beneficial interest in, withheld taxes).

For a discussion of the proper handling of payroll taxes where, prior to bankruptcy, the debtor had issued checks to its employees for net wages and paid over the withholding taxes to the IRS, but, due to the bankruptcy filing, the bank dishonors the wage checks, *see* Letter Ruling 7702012130A, February 1, 1977.

171 *See, e.g.*, 124 Cong. Rec. H 11,114 (daily ed. September 28, 1978), S 17,430-17,431(daily ed. October 6, 1978) ("Where the [IRS] can demonstrate that the amounts of taxes withheld are still in the possession of the debtor at the commencement of the case, then if a trust is created, those amounts are not property of the estate. The courts should permit the use of reasonable assumptions under which the [IRS], and other tax authorities, can demonstrate that amounts of withheld taxes are still in the possession of the debtor at the commencement of the case. For example, where the debtor has commingled that amount of withheld taxes in his general checking account, it might be reasonable to assume that any remaining amounts in that account on the commencement of the case are the withheld taxes"); *Texas Comptroller of Public Accts. v. Megafoods Stores, Inc.* (*In re Megafoods Stores, Inc.*), 163 F.3d 1063 (9th Cir. 1997) (applied "lowest intermediate balance" rule to trace trust fund collections placed in a commingled account, measured from the time of collection through the

Circuits) have even permitted postpetition interest (at a rate determined under state trust law), concluding that the Bankruptcy Code provision generally prohibiting postpetition interest (*see* § 1006.1.2) does not apply to amounts that are held "in trust" and, thus, are not property of the estate.[172] In addition, both the Fifth and Ninth Circuits have upheld the current payment of such interest as an administrative expense of the bankruptcy estate because it resulted from the debtor's postpetition failure to pay over the withheld taxes.[173] Reversed on appeal, the Ninth Circuit Bankruptcy Appellate Panel had viewed such interest simply as an eighth priority unsecured claim because it related to a prepetition tax and was not an actual and necessary cost or expense of preserving the bankruptcy estate.

Because a trustee is not himself considered an "employee" for purposes of the employment withholding tax provisions, any compensation paid to the trustee would not be subject to employment tax withholding.[174] In calculating the amount of income tax to be withheld from each employee in respect of prepetition wages subsequently paid, such amount may be determined either by (1) using the current withholding tax table at the time of payment (with reference to the employee's last W-4) or (2) applying the flat rate for supplemental wage payments—which ranges from 28 percent for payments on or before August 6, 2001, down to 25 percent for payments in 2003 and after (as discussed in the footnote below),[175] but in the case of supplemen-

(Footnote Continued)

bankruptcy filing), *aff'g in part and rev'g in part*, 210 B.R. 351 (Bankr. 9th Cir. 1997); *In re Al Copeland Enters., Inc.*, 133 B.R. 837 (Bankr. W.D. Tex. 1991) (same), *appealed and aff'd on other issues*, 991 F.2d 233 (5th Cir. 1993); *see also City of Farrell v. Sharon Steel Corp.*, 41 F.3d 92 (3d Cir. 1994) (recognized that "lowest intermediate balance" rule may constitute a reasonable assumption); *In re American Int'l Airways, Inc.*, 70 B.R. 102, 87-1 U.S.T.C. ¶ 9294 (Bankr. E.D. Pa. 1987) (funds set aside by debtor prior to bankruptcy to pay withheld taxes and held in a separate bank account were only available to IRS; discusses legislative history to Bankruptcy Code section 541 as it relates to withheld taxes); *cf. Begier, Jr. v. IRS* (U.S.), discussed *supra* at § 1005.2 (also involving the American International Airways, Inc. bankruptcy); *In re Sunrise Paving, Inc.*, 204 B.R. 691 (Bankr. D. Md. 1996) (check for the payment of trust fund taxes written prior to, but not sent until after, the bankruptcy filing was not sufficient to treat commingled funds as trust fund taxes). *See also In re Russman's*, 125 B.R. 520 (Bankr. E.D. Tenn. 1991), discussed *supra* § 1005.2, note 68, involving a segregated fund for certain postpetition trust fund taxes in analogous circumstances.

[172] *See, e.g., Al Copeland Enters., Inc. v. State of Texas* (*Matter of Al Copeland Enters., Inc.*), 991 F.2d 233 (5th Cir. 1993) (postpetition interest allowed at statutory rate on sales taxes held "in trust," except for the 60-day period immediately following the due date, for which the rate of interest was limited to that earned by the debtor; under state law, no interest accrued during such 60-day period, but state ordinarily would have received a penalty payment, which payment is subordinated in bankruptcy, *see* § 1015.2); *In re Megafoods Stores, Inc.*, *supra* note 171 (9th Cir.) (followed Fifth Circuit's decision in *Al Copeland*; and reversed Appellate Panel's decision that limited rate to that earned by the debtor). *Consider also In re Goldblatt Bros., Inc.*, 61 B.R. 459 (Bankr. N.D. Ill. 1986) (non-tax case; imposed interest for period following the petition date at prejudgment rate until monies were invested by debtor and, thereafter, at rate actually earned).

[173] *Al Copeland Enters., Inc. v. State of Texas* (*Matter of Al Copeland Enters., Inc.*) (5th Cir.), *supra* note 172, at 238-240; *In re Megafoods Stores, Inc.* (9th Cir.), *supra* note 171 (also justified administrative expense treatment on the grounds that it was undeniable that the debtors benefited by keeping trust funds in their own bank account and utilizing those funds for other purposes).

[174] Rev. Rul. 69-657, 1969-2 C.B. 189; Rev. Rul. 69-500, 1969-2 C.B. 185.

[175] IRS Manual, Part 4 (Examining), Ch. 23 (Employment Tax Handbook), § 3.10.7 (March, 1, 2003), at ¶ (2) (plus current FICA withholding); *Otte v. United States*, *supra* note 168 (noting, in footnote 2 of

tal wage payments to an employee totaling over $1 million for the calendar year, is fixed at the maximum tax rate in effect for individuals (35% for 2006).[176] FICA should be withheld based on the rate in effect at the time such wages are paid.[177]

### § 1006.3.1 No Special Relief from Penalties

As discussed above at §§ 1006.1.2 and 1006.2.1, depending on whether one is dealing with prepetition or postpetition taxes, bankruptcy generally affords a corporate debtor potential relief from penalties. For example, in the case of prepetition income taxes, no penalties accrue beyond the petition and, in the case of postpetition income taxes, a special exception applies where the debtor has insufficient funds to pay the taxes. Under Code § 6658(b), however, these special relief provisions do not apply to any penalty or other addition to tax that arises from the failure to pay or deposit taxes for which the debtor acts as a collection or withholding agent (*i.e.*, "trust fund" taxes).

Thus, absent "reasonable cause," the failure to pay or deposit penalties will continue to accrue on such taxes (up to their maximum amount) until payment. In addition, as noted above, reasonable cause is generally more difficult to establish in the case of withholding taxes than in the case of income taxes.[178] Undoubtedly, the same would be true of other trust fund taxes.

---

(Footnote Continued)

the decision, these two options, and, at pp. 53-54 of the decision, relying on the trustee's ability to use a flat rate in downplaying the compliance burden to the trustee versus the interests of the IRS and the public in the collection of the taxes), *aff'g In re Freedomland, Inc.*, 480 F.2d 184, 73-2 U.S.T.C. ¶ 9504 (2d Cir. 1973). The optional flat rate for supplemental withholding payments, set forth in Reg. § 31.3402(g)-1(a)(2), is 27.5 percent for 2001, 27 percent for 2002 through May 27, 2003, and 25 percent for the remainder of 2003 and currently thereafter, *subject to* the special rate applicable to supplemental wage payments to an employee that aggregate over $1 million for a calendar year (as discussed further in the text). The current 25 percent rate is equal to, and changes with, the corresponding rate in effect under Code § 1(i)(2), but an employer can always choose to use a 28 percent rate instead.

A debtor-in-possession's employment tax reporting (Forms W-2, etc.) generally should be unaffected by an *employee's* own filing for bankruptcy. *See* IRS Notice 2006-83, 2006-40 I.R.B. 596 (October 2, 2006) (providing guidance for individuals filing bankruptcy cases under Chapter 11 of the Bankruptcy Code, but assistive as to other chapters of the Bankruptcy Code as well).

[176] American Jobs Creation Act of 2004, P.L. 108-357, § 904(b) (all persons treated as a single employer under Code § 52(a) or (b) are similarly treated as a single employer for purposes of this provision); *see also* Reg. § 31.3402(g)-1; Salam, Berard, and Wimer, A Year in Review—Hot Topics From E&Y's 2005 Employment Tax Webcast, BNA Daily Tax Report (January 30, 2006), at J-1.

[177] *See supra* note 175; Code §§ 3101 and 3102; *United States v. Cleveland Indians Baseball Co.*, 121 S. Ct. 1433, 2001-1 U.S.T.C. ¶ 50,341 (2001) (held that back wages are subject to FICA and FUTA taxes by reference to the year the wages are paid, not the year earned), *distinguishing Social Security Board v. Nierotko*, 327 U.S. 358 (1946) (interpreting use of same language in non-tax statute; held that, for purposes of determining employee benefits, a back pay award under the National Labor Relations Act to an employee who was wrongfully discharged constituted "wages" under the Social Security Act for the periods in which the wages were earned).

[178] *See supra* text accompanying notes 104-113. *See also Bossert v. United States (In re Bossert)*, 201 B.R. 553, 562-563, 96-2 U.S.T.C. ¶ 50,689 (Bankr. E.D. Wash. 1996) (upheld postpetition accrual of penalty since the debtor failed to maintain the integrity of the trust funds).

It should be noted, however, that any penalty imposed with respect to unpaid prepetition trust fund taxes (other than under Code § 3505 or 6672, *see* § 1006.3.2 below) generally should be treated as a general unsecured claim in the Chapter 11 case and, thus, subject to discharge (*see* §§ 1014 and 1015.1.4). Nevertheless, the reasoning of the Fifth Circuit in the Al *Copeland Enterprises* case,[179] which was followed by the Ninth Circuit in *In re Megafoods Stores, Inc.*,[180] suggests that, in cases where the trust fund taxes can be traced, the postpetition accrual of penalties might be treated as an administrative expense.

### § 1006.3.2 Personal Liability for Unpaid Trust Fund Taxes

As discussed below (and at § 103), the penalties for failure to collect or pay over withholding and other trust fund taxes, or to file the requisite forms or maintain the requisite records, may subject the debtor corporation and any responsible person (including the trustee) to civil and criminal penalties.[181] Of these, Code § 6672, which imposes a civil penalty on "responsible persons" for 100 percent of any trust fund taxes that should have been paid over, is generally of greatest practical concern.[182]

Liability may be imposed under Code § 6672 where the responsible person's failure to collect or pay over the accrued taxes is "willful." For this purpose, willful generally includes acting with reckless disregard. Factually, this generally means that a person that knew (or had reason to know) of the unpaid trust fund taxes and, having the means (even if directed otherwise by his superiors), failed to ensure that the taxes were paid is a responsible person to which the Code § 6672 penalty

---

179 *See supra* note 172 and accompanying text.

180 *See supra* notes 171-172 and accompanying text.

181 *See, e.g.*, Code § 6672 (100 percent of employment withholding tax imposed for "willfull" failure or failure to "truthfully" account); Code § 7202 (five years imprisonment and/or $10,000; "willful" failure); Code § 7203 (one year imprisonment, $25,000 [$100,000 for corporations]; "willful" failure); Code § 7215 (one year imprisonment and/or $5,000 imposed for failure to comply unless "due to circumstances beyond his control," including lack of funds). *See infra* text accompanying notes 225-228 and § 1014 note 16. *See also* IRS Chief Counsel Advice Memorandum 200036043, May 17, 2000, *reprinted at* 2000 TNT 176-66 (concluding that a Chapter 11 trustee can have personal liability under Code § 6672).

182 A similar provision imposing personal liability for certain *non*-trust fund excise taxes is Code § 4103. Under that provision, responsible persons who willfully fail to pay, or willfully cause the failure to pay, taxes imposed by Code § 4081 (and former Code § 4091) on gasoline and aviation fuels (effective December 1, 1990) and by Code § 4041(a)(1) on diesel fuel (effective January 1, 1994) are "jointly and severally liable" with the taxpayer for such taxes. In addition, under Code § 6206, any excess amount paid by the IRS to a taxpayer under Code §§ 6420 or 6421 for the use of gasoline for certain farming or off highway business use, or under Code § 6427(e) for the production of certain alcohol and biodiesel mixtures, are collectable as if assessed under Code § 4081. Accordingly, it appears that any persons responsible for the receipt or repayment of such excess amount may be "jointly and severally liable" for such amount under Code § 4103. This should be contrasted with Code § 6672 which imposes liability by imposing a "penalty equal to the amount of the tax" not paid. Because of this difference in approach, one must be careful in applying the authorities discussed below (such as those involving a right of contribution, particularly in light of subsequent legislative developments) to a responsible person's liability under Code § 4103. *See generally* IRS General Litigation Bulletin #383 (August 1992), 1992 GLB LEXIS 5 (discussing certain basic aspects of Code § 4103, and indicating the general intent that the two provisions be treated similarly).

applies.[183] Accordingly, the penalty does not apply if, at the time the officer or employee otherwise became a responsible person, there were no funds with which to satisfy the tax obligation—all funds on hand being encumbered (other than due to voluntary contractual obligations)—and the funds thereafter generated are not directly traceable to collections of the tax.[184]

The Tenth Circuit has recently held out some prospect of hope for the well-intentioned officer or employee who nevertheless is considered to have acted reckless under this standard, by recognizing a "reasonable cause" exception to Code §6672 liability.[185] As fashioned by the Tenth Circuit, reasonable cause for nonpayment exists if (and only if) the responsible person made reasonable efforts to protect (or pay) the accrued taxes but failed to ensure their payment due to circumstances outside his control. The factual situation before the Tenth Circuit, which was remanded for a new trial, involved an officer who upon discovering unpaid trust fund taxes gave specific directions to pay the taxes and, when he later learned that his directions had not been followed, there were no unencumbered funds.[186] The Tenth Circuit's decision has

---

[183] For a more detailed discussion of the Code §6672 penalty, *see* Saltzman, IRS Practice and Procedure, ¶¶17.07-17.11 (Revised Second Edition); Raby and Raby, Payroll Tax Penalties for Doing Good and for Delegating, 105 Tax Notes 1639 (December 20, 2004); Sheppard, Tenth Circuit Writes Its Own Responsible Person Penalty, Tax Notes (September 8, 1997); Bedikian, The Pernicious Reach of 26 U.S.C. Section 6672, 13 Va. Tax Rev. 225 (1993); Seiffert & Hudson, IRS's New Approach to Determining "Responsible" Persons for the 100% Penalty, 79 J. Taxation 144 (1993); Hertz, Personal Liabilities of the Unsuspecting Executive for Penalties Under Section 6672 and Other Nightmares, 32 Inst. on Fed. Tax'n 1171 (1974). *See also Powers v. United States*, 2001-1 U.S.T.C. ¶50,338 (2d Cir. 2001) (unpublished decision; officer subject to Code §6672 penalty even though he believed that he would have been criminally liable under state law had he failed to use available funds to pay his continuing payroll), *citing Hochstein v. United States*, 900 F.2d 543, 549 (2d Cir. 1990); *Wright v. United States*, 809 F.2d 425, 87-1 U.S.T.C. ¶9130 (7th Cir. 1987) (gross negligence is enough to establish "reckless disregard"). The procedures for administratively appealing a proposed Code §6672 penalty assessment are described in Rev. Proc. 2005-34, 2005-24 I.R.B. 1233.

[184] *See, e.g., Slodov v. United States*, 436 U.S. 238, 78-1 U.S.T.C. ¶9447 (Code §6672 penalty not imposed as later acquired funds generated in carrying on the business, not from withholding tax collections); *Michaud v. United States* (Ct. Cl. 1997), *reprinted at* 97 TNT 233-11 (officers held not liable); *Elmore v. United States*, 843 F.2d 1128, 88-1 U.S.T.C. ¶9267 (8th Cir. 1988) (finding reversible error in failing to issue jury instruction regarding encumbered and after-acquired funds); *Bell v. United States*, 355 F.3d 387, 2004-1 U.S.T.C. ¶50,118 (6th Cir. 2004) (holding that funds are encumbered "only when certain legal obligations, such as statutes, regulations, and ordinances" impede the use of the funds, citing other Circuit Court authorities; voluntary contractual obligations are not sufficient); *Honey v. United States*, 963 F.2d 1083, 92-1 U.S.T.C. ¶50,253 (8th Cir. 1992) (defining "encumbered" funds as only those funds that must be used to satisfy obligations that are superior in payment to the withheld taxes); *Bradshaw v. United States*, 71 F.3d 1517, 96-1 U.S.T.C. ¶50,028 (10th Cir. 1995) (officer originally negotiated credit facility), *withdrawn and republished at* 83 F.3d 1175, *cert. denied*, 117 S. Ct. 296 (1996).

[185] *Finley v. United States*, 123 F.3d 1342, 97-2 U.S.T.C. ¶50,613 (10th Cir. 1997) (*en banc*). *See also Howell v. United States*, 164 F.3d 523, 99-1 U.S.T.C. ¶50,144 (10th Cir. 1998) (case remanded for consideration of reasonable cause exception).

[186] In the first trial from which the appeal arose, the jury had found that the officer's actions were not willful, but the trial court had set aside the jury's verdict. *Cf. In re Nutt*, 271 B.R. 896, 2001-2 U.S.T.C. ¶50,613 (Bankr. M.D. Fla. 2001) (holding that an officer/shareholder's actions under somewhat similar circumstances were *not* "willful" where the officer undertook corrective measures upon learning of the tax deficiencies and paid a portion with personal funds), *reaff'd on remand*, 2002-2 U.S.T.C. ¶50,753 (Bankr. M.D. Fla. 2002), *aff'd*, 2003-1 U.S.T.C. ¶50,395 (M.D. Fla. 2003); *Macagnone v. United States*, 253 B.R. 99, 2000-2 U.S.T.C. ¶50,551 (M.D. Fla. 2000) (a president and 50 percent owner

been criticized and widely discussed for its rather unique approach.[187] The Second Circuit has also recognized a self-described "reasonable cause" exception, but more limited in scope.[188] Such exception provides that "a responsible person's failure to cause the withholding taxes to be paid is not willful if he believed that the taxes were in fact being paid, so long as that belief was, in the circumstances, a reasonable one."[189] However, if the responsible person subsequently becomes aware of the nonpayment while company has liquid funds, he *will* be held liable if the taxes thereafter remain unpaid (in contrast to the Tenth Circuit exception which still holds out the possibility of relief).[190] Although a "reasonable cause" exception has long been recognized by the Fifth Circuit, the Fifth Circuit has not proffered a specific definition and has cautioned that the exception "should have a very limited application."[191] And so its been, with only one known case exonerating a responsible person based on the Fifth Circuit exception.[192] Although not attempting a definition, the Fifth

(Footnote Continued)

of a corporation did *not* "willfully" fail to pay over withholding taxes where he spent all his time seeking business opportunities, meeting with investors, and seeking financing, the company had never previously been delinquent, and neither the other 50 percent owner nor the employee who prepared and filed the withholding tax returns gave him any indication that there were unpaid taxes or of any need for additional funds, as was their usual routine); *Pitts v. United States*, 2001-1 U.S.T.C. ¶50,419 (D. Ariz. 2001) (similarly so held, where plaintiff had a 20 percent interest, with other 80 percent owned by his two adult children; could control major business decisions but could not influence day-to-day operations; did not know, and would not have been expected to inquire, of delinquent employment taxes; had made substantial loans to the corporation and secured the company's line of credit with his home, and had never refused to lend money to the company when asked).

[187] *See, e.g.*, Sheppard, *supra* note 183, at 1283-1284; Raby and Raby, Trust Fund Penalties and Reasonable Cause, 102 Tax Notes 617 (February 2, 2004). "Reasonable cause" exceptions have been specifically rejected by several Circuit Courts of Appeals. *See, e.g., Olsen v. United States*, 952 F.2d 236, 241, 92-1 U.S.T.C. ¶50,036 (8th Cir. 1991); *Harrington v. United States*, 504 F.2d 1306, 1315, 74-1 U.S.T.C. ¶9772 (1st Cir. 1974); *Monday v. United States*, 421 F.2d 1210 (7th Cir.), *cert. denied*, 400 U.S. 821 (1970).

[188] *Winter v. United States*, 196 F.3d 339, 345-346, 99-2 U.S.T.C. ¶50,955 (2d Cir. 1999) (citing earlier Second Circuit decisions).

[189] *United States v. Rem*, 38 F.3d 634, 643, 94-2 U.S.T.C. ¶50,537 (2d Cir. 1994), *citing Kalb v. United States*, 505 F.2d 506, 511, 74-2 U.S.T.C. ¶9760 (2d Cir. 1974).

[190] Id.

[191] *See Newsome v. United States*, 431 F.2d 742, 746, 70-2 U.S.T.C. ¶9504, *reh'g denied*, 70-2 U.S.T.C. ¶9597 (5th Cir. 1970), *cert. denied*, 411 U.S. 986 (1971); *see also Logal v. United States*, 195 F.3d 229, 99-2 U.S.T.C. ¶50,988 (5th Cir. 1999) (no such defense may be asserted by a responsible person who knew that the withholding taxes were due, yet made a conscious decision to use corporate funds to pay other creditors).

[192] *See, e.g., Anderson v. United States*, 77-2 U.S.T.C. ¶9701 (W.D. La. 1977) (wherein the court granted a responsible officer's motion for summary judgment based on reasonable cause; officer had relied on counsel's advice not to pay over withheld taxes because the IRS would have a priority in bankruptcy); Action on Decision CC-1978-158 (May 24, 1978), 1978 AOD LEXIS 24 (distinguished *Anderson* from certain older decisions under Code §6672 involving a transportation excise tax where counsel had advised that the company was not liable for the tax; IRS Chief Counsel recommended appealing, but Solicitor General decided against it); *see also Bowen v. United States*, 836 F.2d 965, 88-1 U.S.T.C. ¶9164 (5th Cir. 1988) (wherein the Fifth Circuit, obviously unaware of the unpublished decision in *Anderson*, above, observed: "Although we have recognized conceptually that a reasonable cause may militate against a finding of willfulness, no taxpayer has yet carried that pail up the hill"); *Logal v. United States* (5th Cir. 1999), *supra* note 191 (reiterating same).

Circuit has noted that the mere delegation of authority is insufficient to establish reasonable cause, and that reasonable reliance on advice of counsel may suffice under certain (unexplained) circumstances.[193]

In another recent decision, the First Circuit considered the circumstances under which an officer-shareholder of a company would, or, as it turned out on the facts, would not be considered to have the requisite control and authority over the company's affairs to be a responsible person for purposes of Code § 6672 (even though knowing of the unpaid taxes).[194] During the relevant period, the officer (a former IRS employee) was an equal co-owner and a director of the company, was the company treasurer but did not have an office at the company, and, in fact, maintained a separate accounting practice, had check signing authority but never actually signed any checks nor had access to the company checkbook, prepared the company's quarterly withholding tax returns, was aware of the unpaid withholding taxes, and, when the company had during a prior period been delinquent in paying its withholding taxes, had negotiated an installment arrangement with the IRS (with which the company fully complied). The day-to-day management was handled by the other 50 percent shareholder, whose wife was the office manager and bookkeeper. The First Circuit identified several factors relevant to the responsible person determination, some more important than others, and ultimately concluded (in a divided decision) that, "[a]bsent a finding that [the officer]possessed *actual, exercised authority* over the company's financial matters, including the duty and power to determine which creditors to pay, as a matter of law he cannot be a responsible person."[195] The court therefore held that the officer was not a responsible person. Subsequently, however, the First Circuit affirmed the determination that an officer, who was the treasurer and chief financial officer and had significant day-to-day involvement in the company's affairs including writing checks and filing tax returns, was liable as a responsible person, *even though* the court accepted the officer's testimony that he could not have paid the taxes "without ignoring the directions of the company's highest officials and quite possibly losing his job."[196]

As discussed at § 104, a creditor or other third party may also be held responsible for a debtor's withholding taxes—where, for example, the lender pays wages directly to the employee, supplies funds to or for the account of the employer for the specific purpose of paying wages (Code § 3505), or is otherwise deemed to have control over

---

[193] *Newsome v. United States, supra* note 191, at 748 n.12; *see also Cash v. Campbell*, 346 F.2d 670, 65-1 U.S.T.C. ¶ 9428 (5th Cir. 1965) (counsel simply advising that IRS had prior lien on certain funds did not establish reasonable cause for nonpayment of withholding taxes).

[194] *Vinick v. United States*, 205 F.3d 1, 2000-1 U.S.T.C. ¶ 50,263 (1st Cir. 2000). For a discussion of other cases, *see* commentaries cited *supra* note 183.

[195] 205 F.3d at 15 (emphasis added). The IRS disagrees with the holding in *Vinick. See* Action on Decision CC-2001-02 (February 27, 2001). The First Circuit, in reaching its conclusion that the officer was not a responsible person, viewed as irrelevant and immaterial the officer's role during the company's subsequent bankruptcy, observing in part that "the bankruptcy court's oversight into the company's affairs would bear upon the degree of control that [the officer] could have had."

[196] *Lubetzky v. United States*, 393 F.3d 76, 2005-1 U.S.T.C. ¶ 50,207 (1st Cir. 2004).

the disbursement of funds by the debtor corporation to pay wages (and is therefore considered a responsible person under Code § 6672).[197]

The civil penalties imposed by Code §§ 3505 and 6672, however, are only collection devices and are, therefore, not to be exacted where the tax itself is ultimately paid.[198] Where an actual assessment of the penalty is made prior to payment of the tax by the corporation, the responsible person may be held liable for interest accruing from the date of assessment—at least to the extent interest for the same period was not paid by the corporation.[199] The IRS need not pursue all responsible persons at once.[200] Where the same penalty is assessed against multiple persons, the IRS will collect the total amount due only once.[201] However, it will not

---

[197] In appropriate circumstances, a lawyer may be a "responsible person" for purposes of Code § 6672. *See, e.g., IRS v. Blais*, 85-2 U.S.T.C. ¶ 9684 (D. Mass.) (lawyer acting under a power of attorney operated failing business); *Brown v. United States*, 464 F.2d 590, 72-2 U.S.T.C. ¶ 9568 (5th Cir. 1972), *cert. denied*, 410 U.S. 908 (1973) (attorney "nominal" president of client's corporation).

[198] *See, e.g.*, Code § 3505(c); *see also United States v. Huckabee Auto Co.*, 783 F.2d 1546, 86-1 U.S.T.C. ¶ 9268 (11th Cir. 1986) (*per curiam*); *Emshwiller v. United States*, 565 F.2d 1042, 77-2 U.S.T.C. ¶ 9744 (8th Cir. 1977).

[199] *See, e.g., Turchon v. United States*, 77 B.R. 398, 87-2 U.S.T.C. ¶ 9541 (E.D.N.Y. 1987) (officer liable for interest from the corporation's bankruptcy petition date until the petition date of his bankruptcy), *aff'd without opinion*, 841 F.2d 1116 (2d Cir. 1988); *Bradley v. United States*, 936 F.2d 707, 91-2 U.S.T.C. ¶ 50,332 (2d Cir. 1991), *aff'g* 90-1 U.S.T.C. ¶ 50,227 (D. Conn.) (officer liable for interest for the term of the corporation's bankruptcy, and for additional interest on interest thereafter).

[200] *See, e.g., Winter v. United States* (2d Cir.), *supra* note 188 (IRS may be selective so long as it does not utilize "invidious or legally impermissible criteria").

[201] IRS Manual, Part 5 (Collecting Process), Ch. 9 (Bankruptcy), § 3.9 (3/1/07), at ¶ 5 ("Withheld income and employment taxes or collected excise taxes are collected only once, whether from the business and/or from one or more of its responsible persons"); IRS Manual, Part 4 (Examining Process), Ch. 23 (Employment Tax Handbook), § 9.13 (3/1/03), at ¶ 3 ("The Service's policy is to collect the full tax only once, from the corporation or from one or more of the responsible officers"); IRS Manual, Part 8 (Appeals), Ch. 11 (Appeals Penalties), § 2.3 (9/12/06), at ¶ 5; IRS Manual, Part 5 (Collection Process), Ch. 7 (Trust Fund Compliance), § 3.1 (2/1/07), at ¶ 8 (involving collected excise taxes); former IRS Manual § 4784(4) (August 10, 1994) (also stating that "[w]here more than one penalty had been assessed with respect to the same tax, any outstanding assessments will be adjusted accordingly once the tax has been paid"); IRS Chief Counsel Advisory 200026024, June 30, 2000, *reprinted at* 2000 TNT 128-34 (explaining how each assessed person is credited with the payment of another, how excess payments are refunded, and how the IRS can recover payments erroneously refunded to the wrong responsible person); *cf.* Code § 6672(d) (granting right of contribution against other responsible persons, effective for penalties assessed after July 30, 1996); *see also Gens v. United States*, 615 F.2d 1335, 80-1 U.S.T.C. ¶ 9238 (Ct. Cl. 1980); *McCray v. United States*, 910 F.2d 1289, 90-2 U.S.T.C. ¶ 50,492 (5th Cir. 1990), *reh'g denied*, 1990 U.S. App. LEXIS 18750 (1990), *cert. denied sub nom. Scott v. United States*, 111 S. Ct. 1313 (1991); *United States v. Pomponio*, 635 F.2d 293, 298-99, 80-2 U.S.T.C. ¶ 9820 (4th Cir. 1980).

In *United States v. Estridge*, 797 F.2d 1454, 86-1 U.S.T.C. ¶ 9282 (8th Cir. 1986) (per curiam), the Eighth Circuit upheld the district court finding that the IRS's assertion of a Code § 6672 100 percent penalty against the corporate officer was not "substantially justified" and awarded him attorneys' fees and expenses under the Equal Access to Justice Act. *See* 28 U.S.C. § 2414(d)(1)(A); for post-February 1983 actions, *see* Code § 7430 (discussed at § 1007.7.4 below). The primary reason for the district court's finding was that the IRS did not diligently investigate who was responsible for paying the taxes and merely brought claims against several officers and directors in the hope that one or more of them would be found liable. In addition, IRS failed to provide the corporate officer with any specific statement of fact or law on which the IRS based its claim; failed to investigate the truth of evidence offered by the corporate officer; and gave unwarranted credence to obviously biased witnesses.

abate the assessments (and may even pursue such assessments) against the nonpaying parties until the paying party may no longer seek a refund.[202] Payments under Code § 6672 generally have been held to be nondeductible.[203]

Traditionally, most persons paying the penalty have been unsuccessful in their attempts to shift or otherwise mitigate the cost, although this will likely change over time given the 1996 enactment of a statutory right of contribution from other responsible persons (discussed below). Prior to 1996, most courts had held that the payor had no general right of contribution from other responsible persons.[204] In

---

[202] *See, e.g., USLife Title Ins. Co. of Dallas v. Harbison v. United States,* 784 F.2d 1238, 1243-45, 86-1 U.S.T.C. ¶9278 (5th Cir. 1986) (permitting continued IRS collection efforts until refund period expires); *McCray v. United States, supra* note 201; IRS Field Service Advice 199904032, November 10, 1998, *reprinted at* 1999 TNT 20-64; IRS Litigation Guideline Memorandum, dated March 14, 1986, *reprinted at* 96 TNT 155-53. *Cf. United States v. Chene (In re Chene),* 236 B.R. 69, 99-2 U.S.T.C. ¶50,720 (M.D. Fla. 1999) (erroneous refund of Code § 6672 penalty to one party did not relieve other responsible persons from liability), *rev'g,* 98-2 U.S.T.C. ¶50,797 (Bankr. M.D. Fla. 1998). *See also* IRS Legal Memorandum 200137021, September 14, 2001, *reprinted at* 2001 TNT 180-71 (amounts collected from a person subsequently determined not to be responsible can only be refunded pursuant to a timely refund claim).

[203] *See, e.g.,* Code § 162(f); *Duncan v. Commissioner,* 95-2 U.S.T.C. ¶50,547 (9th Cir. 1995) (but upheld deduction for comparable payments under state law where "willfullness" was not a precondition to liability), *aff'g in part and rev'g in part,* 66 T.C.M. 420, Dec. 49,222(M), T.C. Memo 1993-370 (related legal and accounting fees deductible under Code § 212); *Benjamin T. Smith v. Commissioner,* 34 T.C. 1100, Dec. 24,365 (1960), *aff'd per curiam,* 294 F.2d 957, 61-2 U.S.T.C. ¶9686 (5th Cir. 1961) (involved predecessor to Code § 6672); *In re Vale,* 204 B.R. 716, 738-745, 96-2 U.S.T.C. ¶50,700 (Bankr. N.D. Ind. 1996) (interest paid held nondeductible as personal interest; distinguished authorities predating Tax Reform Act of 1986); *Arrigoni v. Commissioner,* 73 T.C. 792, Dec. 36,758 (1980) (pre-1986 Act case; interest paid held deductible), *acq. and nonacq.; Estate of Ward W. Blazzard,* 62 T.C.M. 54, Dec. 47,443(M), T.C. Memo. 1991-296. However, a deduction was permitted in *First Natl. Bank of Duncanville v. United States,* 481 F. Supp. 633, 79-2 U.S.T.C. ¶9561 (N.D. Tex. 1979), where the payor had a contractual claim against the debtor corporation.

[204] These cases generally involved the Code § 6672 penalty. The primary reasons given for denying contribution were that (1) responsible persons are akin to intentional joint tortfeasors between whom no right of contribution exists under applicable state law and (2) without the ability to be solely liable, there would be little incentive for responsible persons to fulfill their statutory obligations. *See, e.g., McDermitt v. United States,* 954 F.2d 1245, 1252, 92-1 U.S.T.C. ¶50,060 (6th Cir. 1992) (involving Ohio law); *Plato v. State Bank of Alcester,* 555 N.W.2d 365 (S.D. 1996) (involving South Dakota law); *Continental Illinois Natl. Bank and Trust Co. of Chicago v. United States,* 87-2 U.S.T.C. ¶9442 (E.D. Ill.) (also held that no right of contribution under Code § 3505, even though it has no "willfulness" requirement); *Moats v. United States,* 564 F. Supp. 1330, 83-2 U.S.T.C. ¶9735 (W.D. Mo. 1983), *aff'd without opinion sub nom., United States v. Crowley,* 786 F.2d 1171 (8th Cir. 1986); *Hanhauser v. United States,* 80-1 U.S.T.C. ¶9139 (M.D. Pa.) (responsible officer sought right of contribution against lender, claiming lender was a responsible person); *Conley v. United States,* 773 F. Supp. 1176, 91-2 U.S.T.C. ¶50,431 (S.D. Ind. 1991); *Cohen v. United States,* 75-1 U.S.T.C. ¶9391 (E.D. Mich.); *DiBenedetto v. United States,* 75-1 U.S.T.C. ¶9503 (D. R.I.) (has been called the "seminal case"). *See also Sinder v. United States,* 655 F.2d 729, 81-2 U.S.T.C. ¶9612 (6th Cir. 1981) (no federal right of contribution under Code § 6672; decision predates Code § 6672(d), as discussed in text below, effective for penalties assessed after July 30, 1996).

A minority of courts have upheld a right of contribution under state law. *See, e.g., Aardema v. Fitch,* 684 N.E.2d 884 (Ill. App. Ct. 1997) (recognized right of contribution under Illinois corporate law among directors who participated in the decision not to pay over withheld employment taxes); *Swift v. Levesque,* 614 F. Supp. 172, 86-1 U.S.T.C. ¶9109 (D. Conn. 1986) (recognized right to contribution under Connecticut state law, but not a right to indemnification); *Schoot v. United States,* 664 F. Supp. 293 (N.D. Ill. 1987) (reasoning that, after the tax is paid, the IRS has no interest in who is ultimately

addition, it is questionable whether the payor would be subrogated to the rights of the IRS against the debtor or otherwise able to seek indemnification from the debtor.[205] Even if a subrogation claim is permitted, however, the payor would not be subrogated to the priority of the IRS in bankruptcy—thereby relegating the claim, in most cases, to a general unsecured claim.[206] Moreover, in *St. Paul Fire & Marine Insurance Co. v. Briggs*,[207] a Minnesota court held that an officer's liability under Code § 6672 was uninsurable as a matter of law and, accordingly, that the officer was not entitled to reimbursement under the corporation's director's and officer's liability policy. The court reasoned that, because an officer is under a legal obligation to ensure that the corporation's taxes were paid, to shift the liability to a third party would be contrary to public policy.[208] Similarly, the Seventh Circuit Court of Appeals, in *Mortenson v. National Union Fire Insurance Co.*,[209] held that the Code § 6672 penalty was an excluded loss under a provision of the directors' and officers' liability policy that excluded "fines or penalties imposed by law or other matters which may be deemed uninsurable under the law pursuant to which this policy shall be construed." Although the court's conclusion was based on the determination that a Code § 6672 penalty was properly considered a "fine or penalty" for this purpose (dismissing, both as a matter of contractual interpretation as well as substantive evaluation, any

(Footnote Continued)

responsible for the money); *Esstman v. Boyd*, 605 S.W.2d 237 (Tenn. App. 1978) (claim of contribution must be brought as a separate action from that brought by the IRS pursuant to Code § 6672). *See also Garity v. United States*, 80-1 U.S.T.C. ¶ 9407 (E.D. Mich. 1980) (suggesting that claim for indemnity might rest upon a theory of fraud or breach of contract); and authorities cited *infra* note 205; *but see, e.g., Rebelle v. United States*, 588 F. Supp. 49, 84-2 U.S.T.C. ¶ 9717 (M.D. La.) (follows majority; sharply criticizes *Garity*, calling its reasoning "unsound and unsupported by the jurisprudence or by congressional intent").

205 *Compare Levit v. Ingersoll Rand Fin. Corp. (In re Deprizio)*, 874 F.2d 1186 (7th Cir. 1989); *In re All Star Sports, Inc.*, 78 B.R. 281 (Bankr. D. Nev. 1987); *Patterson v. Yeargin (In re Yeargin)*, 116 B.R. 621 (Bankr. M.D. Tenn. 1990) (no subrogation right), and cases cited *supra* note 204; *with In re Fiesole Trading Corp.* (Bankr. D. Mass. 2004) (permitting right of subrogation under Massachusetts law), *infra* note 206; *Reid v. United States*, 83-1 U.S.T.C. ¶ 9397, 558 F. Supp. 686 (N.D. Miss. 1983) (allowed right of indemnification over against employer; reasoned that employer is primarily liable, and Code § 6672 penalty is compensatory rather than penal); *Glude v. Sterenbuch*, 133 F.3d 914 (4th Cir. 1998) (unpublished opinion), *reported in full at* 1998 U.S. App. LEXIS 410 (permitted contractual indemnification/contribution under similar reasoning; also suggested that right of contribution might exist under Maryland law); *also consider In re Franklin Press, Inc.*, 46 B.R. 523, 85-2 U.S.T.C. ¶ 9681 (Bankr. S.D. Fla. 1985) (last paragraph).

206 11 U.S.C. § 507(d), discussed *infra* at § 1015.3; *In re Fiesole Trading Corp.*, 315 B.R. 198 (Bankr. D. Mass. 2004) (permitted equitable subrogation under Massachusetts law, as circumscribed by Bankruptcy Code section 507(d), thereby allowing the responsible persons to participate as general unsecured creditors in the debtor's bankruptcy); *In re Tentex Marine, Inc.*, 83 B.R. 530 (Bankr. W.D. Tenn. 1988); *see also Singer v. District Director of Internal Revenue*, 354 F.2d 992, 66-1 U.S.T.C. ¶ 9171 (2d Cir. 1966) (Bankruptcy Act case; denied officer of a bankrupt corporation subrogation to the IRS's priority position for amounts paid under Code § 6672; did not address whether the officer would be entitled to subrogation as a general unsecured creditor, since available assets were insufficient to satisfy all priority claims).

207 464 N.W.2d 535 (Minn. App. 1990).

208 The court also noted that it would be contrary to public policy to require insurers to pay for losses due to the insured's willful acts.

209 249 F.3d 667 (7th Cir. 2001).

argument that Code § 6672 was simply a collection device and not a penalty or fine for wrongful conduct[210]), the Seventh Circuit also indicated that it was "strongly arguable" that insuring against the Code § 6672 penalty is contrary to public policy.

Also on public policy grounds, the district court, in *Alten v. Ellin & Tucker*,[211] held that, under Delaware law, an officer (and shareholder) could not recover the Code § 6672 penalty paid by him from the accounting services firm whose agreed responsibility it was to pay over the withheld taxes. In the court's view, the officer's action—whether based on breach of contract, accountant malpractice or breach of fiduciary duty—was essentially an action for indemnification for what the law regarded as a "willful" act and thus was contrary to public policy. The Fourth Circuit, however, is of the opposite view. In *Glude v. Sterenbuch*,[212] the Fourth Circuit, in an unpublished opinion, upheld a contractual arrangement between two officer/shareholders to share equally any Code § 6672 personal liability. It found "no merit" to the public policy argument, given that an officer's actions need not be egregious or with evil intent for personal liability to attach (but only knowing or reckless), and that the IRS's policy is to use Code § 6672 as solely a collection device for the tax, rather than a true penalty. Similarly, the Georgia Court of Appeals upheld a contractual indemnity from one shareholder to another as part of a settlement and transfer of the other shareholder's stock.[213] In rejecting the public policy argument, the court relied in part on Congress' decision to enact a statutory right of contribution, even though enacted subsequent to the liability at issue.

Effective for penalties assessed and paid after July 30, 1996, Congress, as part of the Taxpayer Bill of Rights 2, created a statutory right of contribution among responsible persons liable for the Code § 6672 penalty.[214] This right requires that any action to recover against another responsible person be brought in a separate proceeding from the IRS action for collection, and not as a third-party complaint.[215] But how much can the responsible person recover? The statute provides that the responsible person is entitled to recover the amount of the payment in excess of his proportionate share of the penalty. Sound easy? But how do you go about determining the number of responsible persons? It's bad enough to litigate one person's responsibility, much less a countless number of others, depending on the facts. And, how much can you recover from any single person if there are multiple other responsible parties? Can you recover more than the other person's proportionate

---

[210] The court did not view as significant the possibility of a right of contribution "among the wrongdoers."

[211] 854 F. Supp. 283 (D. Del. 1994).

[212] *Supra* note 205.

[213] *Lostocco v. D'Eramo*, 518 S.E.2d 690 (Ga. Ct. App. 1999) (5:2 decision).

[214] *See* Code § 6672(d). This section parallels in substantial part the earlier recommendations of the Association of the Bar of the City of New York. *See* Assn. of the Bar of the City of New York, Proposal to Create a Federal Right of Contribution Among "Responsible Persons" Under Section 6672 of the Internal Revenue Code, The Record (April 1992).

[215] Even prior to this provision, the courts had held that an officer seeking contribution or indemnification under state common law had to do so in a separate proceeding. *See Bellovin v. United States*, 983 F. Supp. 344, 98-1 U.S.T.C. ¶ 50,111 (E.D.N.Y. 1997).

share? One can imagine the court battles to come, with all potential responsible persons being named as defendants and making assertions against one another.[216] In one instance, a former Chief Financial Officer (CFO) brought an action for contribution against (1) the company, (2) the temporary employment agency through which he first came to work for the company (and during which period of time the tax deficiencies related), (3) an officer of an indirect shareholder of the company, who met periodically with management of the company in connection with monitoring its investment, (4) a former president and consultant of the company, (5) a managing/consulting company which provided management and consulting services to the company, and (6) the company's lending bank.[217] In most cases, the actions were dismissed on summary judgment due to the CFO's failure to present sufficient evidence of responsibility *and* willfulness (and in some cases for lack of prosecution).

Some assistance in identifying potential responsible persons is provided by Code § 6103(e)(9), which requires the IRS to disclose, upon written request, to any person it determined to be a responsible person, the name of any other persons it determined to be responsible persons, the general nature of any collection activity against such persons and the amount collected. The IRS in a court battle over the scope of its disclosure obligations under Code § 6103(e)(9) objected to an assessed officer's motion to compel disclosure of its collection activities against the corporate debtor (and its successor in interest), but did not dispute its obligation to disclose the general nature of its collection activities against the principal owner (Savite) who was similarly assessed as a responsible person.[218] The court acknowledged that Code § 6103(e)(9) did not automatically entitle a responsible person to information about the collection activities against the corporate debtor. However, in view of Savite's relationship with the corporate debtor (and its successor in interest), the court found that, as part of the general nature of the collection activities against Savite, the officer was entitled to know the general nature of any agreement the IRS may have with the corporate debtor (or its successor) "for the payment of Savite's penalty" and the amount collected under such agreements.

With few exceptions, the filing of a bankruptcy petition by (or against) a debtor does not hinder the assessment or collection of the Code §§ 3505 and 6672 penalties by the IRS (although it may impede a suit for contribution). This is true even though a debtor-in-possession is precluded from paying over trust fund taxes collected or withheld prior to the bankruptcy case without first obtaining court approval.[219]

Although upon the filing of the bankruptcy petition the IRS is automatically stayed from collecting or recovering unpaid prepetition taxes, such stay applies only

---

[216] An alternative approach proposed by various bar associations would have based contribution on relative culpability. *See, e.g.*, American Bar Assn., Comment Concerning Taxpayer Bill of Rights 2, *reprinted at*, 92 TNT 159-33 (August 5, 1992); New York State Bar Assn., Tax Section, Report on Creation of Federal Right to Contribution/Declaratory Judgment for Section 6672 Liability (October 20, 1992), reprinted at 92 TNT 222-24.

[217] *See Spade v. Star Bank*, 2003-1 U.S.T.C. ¶ 50,182 (E.D. Pa. 2002), and 2002 U.S. Dist. LEXIS 21643 (E.D. Pa. 2002).

[218] *United States v. NYS Division of the Lottery*, 97-1 U.S.T.C. ¶ 50,191 (S.D. N.Y. 1996).

[219] *See supra* notes 170-173 and accompanying text.

to the debtor corporation.[220] It does not extend to the debtor's officers. For this reason, the Eleventh Circuit and a number of lower courts have held either that the bankruptcy court lacks jurisdiction to enjoin the IRS from assessing or collecting the Code § 6672 penalty against its officers or that the debtor corporation lacks standing to seek the injunction.[221] More frequently, courts (including most Circuit Courts) have entertained the debtor corporation's motion, but have refused to invoke the broad equitable powers granted under Bankruptcy Code section 105(a) to override the Anti-Injunction Act.[222] A few lower courts, however, had early on enjoined the IRS.[223] The

---

[220] *See* 11 U.S.C. § 362(a). For bankruptcy cases commenced before October 22, 1994, the stay also applies to assessments.

[221] *See, e.g., United States v. Huckabee Auto Co., supra* note 198 (lacked jurisdiction); *Success Tool and Mfg. Co. v. United States(In re Success Tool and Mfg. Co.)*, 86-2 U.S.T.C. ¶ 9563 (N.D. Ill.) (same; "It is irrelevant that the collection of the penalty from [the principal officer and major shareholder] will affect the reorganization of the debtor"); *United States v. A&B Heating and Air Conditioning, Inc.*, 57 B.R. 360, 86-2 U.S.T.C. ¶ 9520 (Bankr. M.D. Fla. 1986) (debtor corporation lacked standing; alternatively, held that Anti-Injunction Act barred injunction against IRS); *United States v. Driscoll's Towing Service, Inc. (In re Driscoll's Towing Service, Inc.)*, 51 B.R. 990, 85-2 U.S.T.C. ¶ 9603 (S.D. Fla. 1985) (same); *J.C. Williams and Peeptite Paving Co. v. IRS*, 86-1 U.S.T.C. ¶ 9383 (Bankr. S.D. Fla.) (same); *United States v. Rayson Sports, Inc.*, 44 B.R. 280, 84-2 U.S.T.C. ¶ 9968 (N.D. Ill. 1984) (same); Dynamic Maintenance Service, Inc., No. 81-C-6640 (N.D. Ill. March 5, 1982) (Kocoras, J.).

[222] The Anti-Injunction Act prohibits any "suit for the purpose of restraining the assessment or collection of any tax," other than certain enumerated exceptions. *See* Code § 7421(a). *See, e.g., United States v. Prescription Home Health Care, Inc. (In re Prescription Home Health Care, Inc.)*, 316 F.3d 542, 2003-1 U.S.T.C. ¶ 50,163 (5th Cir. 2002) (vacated injunction precluding IRS from assessing and collecting Code § 6672 penalty from nondebtor officers); *In re LaSalle Rolling Mills, Inc. v. Department of Treasury (In re LaSalle Rolling Mills, Inc.)*, 832 F.2d 390 (7th Cir. 1987) (would not enjoin IRS from assessing Code § 6672 penalty against two officer/shareholders of the debtor, who together owned 100 percent of the debtor, even though the complaint alleged that the debtor's reorganization would be irreparably impaired both by (1) the expenditure of time that the officers would be required to devote to the proceedings with the IRS and (2) the depletion of their personal assets which had been used in part to fund the reorganization by serving as collateral for their guarantee of the debtor's borrowings); *A to Z Welding & Mfg. Co. v. United States*, 803 F.2d 932, 87-1 U.S.T.C. ¶ 9109 (8th Cir. 1987) (*per curiam*); *American Bicycle Assn. v. United States (In re American Bicycle Assn.)*, 895 F.2d 1277, 90-1 U.S.T.C. ¶ 50,104 (9th Cir. 1990); *In re Arrow Transfer and Storage Co.*, 50 B.R. 726 (E.D. Tenn. 1985), *rev'g* 85-1 U.S.T.C. ¶ 9145; *Steel Products, Inc.*, 53 B.R. 999, 85-2 U.S.T.C. ¶ 9600 (D. Wash. 1985) (would not enjoin the IRS even though bankrupt corporation was in compliance with Chapter 11 plan which called for payment of tax over six years, and even though bankruptcy court perceived penalty as threat to a successful reorganization), *rev'g* 85-1 U.S.T.C. ¶ 9439 (Bankr. E.D. Mich.); *Dore & Assocs. Contracting, Inc. v. United States (In re Dore & Assocs. Contracting, Inc.)*, 85-1 U.S.T.C. ¶ 9196 (Bankr. E.D. Mich.) (would not enjoin IRS even though officers would seek indemnification from debtor corporation, impairing ability of debtor to perform Chapter 11 plan, and Chapter 11 plan provided for payment of withholding taxes over six years); *cf. In re Becker's Motor Transportation, Inc.*, 632 F.2d 242, 246, 81-1 U.STC. ¶ 9438 (3d Cir. 1981), *cert. denied*, 450 U.S. 916 (held that Anti-Injunction Act precluded injunction against IRS collection efforts against debtor under prior Bankruptcy Act); *In re Heritage Village Church & Missionary Fellowship, Inc.*, 851 F.2d 104, 88-2 U.S.T.C. ¶ 9476 (4th Cir. 1988) (held that the Anti-Injunction Act prevented bankruptcy court from enjoining IRS revocation of debtor's tax-exempt status; presumably, this court would also consider that the Anti-Injunction Act prevents it from enjoining the collection of tax against the debtor's officers). *See* Bennett, The Bankruptcy Code and the Anti-Injunction Act: Collectibility of Employment Tax Liabilities from Nondebtor "Responsible Persons," 48 Tax Law. 349 (1995).

[223] *See, e.g., J.K. Printing Services Inc. v. United States (In re J.K. Printing Services, Inc.)*, 49 B.R. 798, 803, 85-1 U.S.T.C. ¶ 9433 (W.D. Va. 1985) (enjoined IRS from collecting Code § 6672 100 percent penalty from bankrupt corporation's president and sole stockholder since to do so would render him

reason given is generally that the debtor corporation (especially if it is a small, closely held "family corporation") will be severely, if not fatally, hampered in its reorganization efforts by any assertion and collection of the Code § 6672 penalty against its corporate officers, due to the personal efforts and/or capital resources of its corporate officers required for a successful reorganization. Most recently, the Fifth Circuit in the Prescription Home Health Care bankruptcy case vacated an injunction originally approved by a Texas bankruptcy court, in partial reliance on its broad equitable powers, and upheld by the district court. The injunction had been contained in the debtor's confirmed Chapter 11 Plan (over the government's objection) and precluded the IRS from proceeding against the debtor's president *as long as* the debtor plan payments were timely made to the IRS.[224]

In general (the preceding case being one exception), the IRS need not exhaust collection efforts against the debtor corporation (or any third-party guarantor or surety) before proceeding under Code § 6672.[225] In this regard, former IRS Manual HB 57(16), § (10)35 (January 14, 1987) provided:

(Footnote Continued)

insolvent and thwart any hope of rehabilitation for the bankrupt corporation; fact that debtor was in default on payments under Chapter 11 plan irrelevant; IRS, however, permitted to complete assessment and president's disposition of his assets restricted); *In re The Original Wild West Foods, Inc.*, 45 B.R. 202, 85-1 U.S.T.C. ¶ 9137 (W.D. Tex. 1985) (held that because the IRS's conduct in seizing and threatening to foreclose on corporate officer's property "severely impedes the debtor's reorganization efforts" and the payment of the employment withholding taxes were provided for in the debtor's Chapter 11 plan, the IRS was enjoined from collecting the Code § 6672 100 percent penalty from the officer); *In re O.H. Lewis Co.*, 40 B.R. 531, 84-2 U.S.T.C. ¶ 9987 (Bankr. D.N.H. 1984); *In re Datair Systems Corp.*, 37 B.R. 690, 84-1 U.S.T.C. ¶ 9276 (Bankr. N.D. Ill. 1984); *In re Jon Co.*, 30 B.R. 831 (Bankr. N.D. Colo. 1983). *See also William Netherly, Inc. v. United States* (*In re William Netherly, Inc.*), 85-2 U.S.T.C. ¶ 9777 (Bankr. M.D. Fla.) (although finding that debtor corporation had standing to seek injunctive relief and that the Anti-Injunction Act did not preclude such injunction, the court concluded that the IRS collection would have a minimal, if any, adverse impact on the debtor's ability to consummate its confirmed plan of reorganization; court distinguished between the need to protect the corporate officers prior to confirmation, at which point personal efforts are needed almost full time to work toward a plan of reorganization, from that generally needed after confirmation; after confirmation, the court stated, "injunctive relief is no longer justified" unless the corporate officrs' personal properties are needed to fund the plan or serve as collateral). *But see In re John Renton Young, Ltd.*, 87 B.R. 635 (D. Nev. 1988) (observing that the basic authorities on which the above cases rely have been overturned).

For a more detailed discussion of these cases, *see* Robison & Mark, Techniques to Avoid the Imposition of the Section 6672 Penalty on Officers of Bankrupt Corporations, 65 Taxes 110 (1987); Note, Bankruptcy Court Jurisdiction and the Power to Enjoin the IRS, 70 Minn. L. Rev. 1279 (1986) (favors enjoining IRS in appropriate cases).

[224] *See United States v. Prescription Home Health Care, Inc.* (*In re Prescription Home Health Care, Inc.*), *supra* note 222; *see also* briefs filed in *In Re Prescription Home Health Care, Inc.* in connection with appeal: the government's brief in support of its appeal, dated May 15, 2002, *reprinted at* 2002 TNT 117-31; debtor's brief in response, dated June 14, 2002, *reprinted at* 2002 TNT 139-45; and the government's reply brief, dated July 1, 2002, *reprinted at* 2002 TNT 139-42. Neither the bankruptcy court's action nor the district court's decision (described in the Fifth Circuit's opinion) appears to be published.

[225] *See, e.g., Balzer v. United States*, 2002-1 U.S.T.C. ¶ 50,171 (9th Cir. 2002); *Calderone v. United States*, 799 F.2d 254 (6th Cir. 1986) (restricted *McCarty, infra*, to its facts); *Cooper v. United States*, 539 F. Supp. 117, 82-1 U.S.T.C. ¶ 9296 (E.D. Va. 1982), *aff'd without opinion*, 705 F.2d 442 (4th Cir. 1983); *United States v. Pomponio* (4th Cir.), *supra* note 201; *Datlof v. United States*, 370 F.2d 655, 67-1 U.S.T.C. ¶ 9167 (3d Cir. 1967), *cert. denied*, 387 U.S. 906 (1967); *Hornsby v. United States*, 588 F.2d 952, 954, 79-1 U.S.T.C. ¶ 9188

> Where the corporation is in bankruptcy, it is not necessary that assessment of the 100-percent penalty against a responsible officer (not in bankruptcy) be delayed until the proceeding's conclusion. The automatic stay does not apply to such an assessment and the statutory period for assessment of the 100-percent penalty against responsible persons is not extended by reason of a corporate bankruptcy. Therefore prompt action should be taken so that a proper determination can be made before the statutory period for assessment of the 100-percent penalty assessment is about to expire, extensions of the period for assessment should be obtained from all parties against whom the assessment may be proposed.

Nevertheless, in 1993, the IRS discarded its prior bias which favored Code §6672 penalty assessments in Chapter 11 cases. It is now the IRS's general policy to refrain from making Code §6672 penalty assessments in Chapter 11 cases, except in those cases where the delay would jeopardize ultimate collection.[226] To this has since been added the statement that in Chapter 11 cases the assertion of the penalty "normally" (or "usually") will be withheld prior to and after confirmation of a plan unless there are indications that ultimate collection is doubtful.[227] However, the determination as to whether, and how actively, to proceed is generally within the discretion of the

(Footnote Continued)

(5th Cir. 1979); *Kelley v. Lethert*, 362 F.2d 629, 66-2 U.S.T.C. ¶9509 (8th Cir. 1966); *Bernardi v. United States*, 74-1 U.S.T.C. ¶9170 (N.D. Ill.) (Conclusion of Law #9), *aff'd*, 507 F.2d 682, 75-1 U.S.T.C. ¶9133 (7th Cir.), *cert. denied*, 422 U.S. 1042 (1974); *Roth v. United States*, 83-2 U.S.T.C. ¶9650 (S.D. Cal. 1983) (failure to timely file proof of claim did not preclude IRS from assessing Code §6672 penalty against corporate officers); *Abramson v. United States*, 39 B.R. 237 (Bankr. D.D.C. 1984) (collecting cases). *Cf. Freeland v. IRS (In re White Trailer Corporation)*, 2000 Bankr. LEXIS 1554 (Bankr. N.D. Ind. 2000) (bankruptcy court refused to equitably subordinate IRS claim where the IRS chose to go against debtor before proceeding against a potentially liable third party). *See also infra* §1014 note 16.

In limited circumstances, however—generally involving inequitable conduct by the IRS—courts have been willing to depart from the general rule. *See, e.g., McCarty v. United States*, 437 F.2d 961, 71-1 U.S.T.C. ¶9232 (Ct. Cl. 1971); *Spivak v. United States*, 370 F.2d 612, 67-1 U.S.T.C. ¶9158 (2d Cir. 1967), *cert. denied*, 387 U.S. 908 (1967) (suggesting that IRS could be stayed if IRS mislead officers); *Anderson v. United States*, (W.D. La.), *supra* note 192 (corporate officer and his attorney had asked IRS to file proof of claim, but when the IRS eventually did so the claim was barred as untimely; subsequently, the IRS assessed the Code §6672 penalty against the officer; court held that, under the circumstances, the officer, relying on his attorney's advice, justifiably assumed that the IRS would pursue the corporation's assets, which were more than sufficient). *Consider also Cash v. United States*, 961 F.2d 562, 92-1 U.S.T.C. ¶50,298 (5th Cir. 1992), *cert. denied*, 113 S. Ct. 492 (1992) (responsible officers had standing to challenge IRS failure to actively pursue collection on levied accounts receivable of the corporation but held that it was within the IRS's discretion to simply await collection of the receivables; discusses cases where the IRS has exercised sufficient "dominion and control" over seized assets to justify crediting the value of the seized assets); *In re Nece*, 139 B.R. 637, 92-2 U.S.T.C. ¶50,032 (S.D. Tex. 1992) (failure of IRS to pursue sureties even after having demanded payment under certain performance bonds did not warrant equitable exception); *Ramette v. United States (In re Bame)*, 279 B.R. 833 (Bankr. 8th Cir. 2002) (bankruptcy court require IRS and state taxing authorities, as holders of claims secured by liens on property, to first proceed against such property before participating in any distributions from the estate).

[226] IRS Manual, Part 5 (Collecting Process), Ch. 9 (Bankruptcy), §8.10 (3/1/07); former IRS Manual §5638.6 (May 5, 1993).

[227] *See, e.g.*, IRS Manual, Part 5 (Collecting Process), Ch. 9 (Bankruptcy), §8.10 (3/1/07), at ¶6.

revenue officer assigned to the matter. Accordingly, as in our prior editions, we continue to express the hope (but with an increasing expectation) that, based on the relevant considerations identified in the IRS Manual, the IRS will refrain from making any penalty assessment so long as it appears that the debtor's Chapter 11 plan will provide (and, thereafter, actually provides) for payment in full of the trust fund taxes to which the penalty relates, the bankruptcy and later the plan are proceeding in due course, and a timely extension of the statute of limitations is provided upon request.[228]

Alternatively, in an appropriate case, the responsible person may himself file for bankruptcy and thereby automatically stay the collection of the penalty (although not the assessment). Moreover, as part of his bankruptcy plan, he may be able to permanently stay collection of the penalty, subject to a later motion for reconsideration if timely payments are not made under the debtor corporation's Chapter 11 plan.[229] As discussed below (at §1016.2), although a debtor's plan may provide for the payment of tax claims in installments, the debtor may be able to direct that trust fund taxes be paid first.

## *§1006.4 Other Reporting Requirements*

A debtor-in-possession (and, if authorized to operate the debtor's business, a trustee) must file with the bankruptcy court and the IRS periodic reports and summaries of the operation of such business, including a statement of receipts and disbursements, and such other information as the court requires or, unless the court orders otherwise, that the IRS requests.[230] Any informational filings normally re-

---

[228] *See, e.g.*, prior citation, and IRS Manual, Part 5 (Collecting Process), Ch. 9 (Bankruptcy), §8.10 (3/1/07), at ¶7 (listing factors to consider in determining whether to forbear, both before and after a plan). Previously, the IRS's bias was toward assessment and collection except where there was "apparent certainty" that the taxes would be paid in full under a Chapter 11 plan. Moreover, where possible, field agents generally were encouraged to file tax liens prior to deferring collection efforts. *See* former IRS Manual §57(13)2.61:(6) (November 17, 1992). This itself represented a significant hardening of the IRS's position from a year earlier. *See, e.g.*, former IRS Manual §5754.1(4) (May 29, 1991) (assessment may be withheld if "substantial likelihood" that the IRS will be paid in full).

[229] *See, e.g.*, *United States v. Rowe*, 90-1 U.S.T.C. ¶50,005 (N.D. Ga.), emphasizing that, "once it has proper jurisdiction of all parties in the case [apparently meaning the company, the officer, and the IRS], it may formulate its orders to manage the competing interest of the Bankruptcy Code and the Internal Revenue Code" (for cases of a contrary slant, *see supra* note 225); *In re Dobbins*, 108 B.R. 638, 90-1 U.S.T.C. ¶50,011 (Bankr. W.D. Tenn. 1990) (considered the reasonable probability of payment by the company, the officer's role in the company's Chapter 11, and the potential adverse effect on the company's reorganization of a further impairment of the officer's financial condition were the officer to pay the penalty); *see also* Weiss, Bankruptcy Court Power to Enjoin the IRS from Collecting the Debtor's Taxes from Its Officers: An Analysis of Recent Developments, 1986 Ann. Survey of Bankr. L. 233, 252-256 (also suggesting that, in appropriate circumstances, both bankruptcy cases might be consolidated, *see* Advisory Committee Note to Bankruptcy Rule 1015).

[230] 11 U.S.C. §704(7) and (8); *see* 11 U.S.C. §1108 (unless the court orders otherwise, Chapter 11 trustee authorized to operate debtor's business); 11 U.S.C. §1109 (party in interest). *Consider In re Grabill Corp.*, 109 B.R. 329 (N.D. Ill. 1989) (state-created accountant privilege did not bar creditors' access to accountant's workpapers under 11 U.S.C. §704(7) where the workpapers were potentially relevant to them in connection with the bankruptcy proceeding, such as the possible "discovery of additional assets and information").

quired by the IRS, such as Forms 1099-INT and 1099-OID for interest, would presumably be covered by this provision.

## §1007 SUSPENSION OF ASSESSMENTS AND COLLECTION OF PREPETITION TAX

Upon the filing of a bankruptcy petition, the IRS (through the automatic stay) is, with limited exceptions, prohibited from collecting or recovering unpaid prepetition taxes and, for bankruptcy cases commenced before October 22, 1994, from assessing such taxes.[1] In addition, the IRS generally is stayed from taking any act to create, perfect, or enforce any lien or judgment against the debtor corporation (whether relating to unpaid prepetition or postpetition taxes).[2] The automatic stay has thus generally been

---

[1] **§1007** *See* 11 U.S.C. §§362(a)(1), (6), (b)(9) (as amended by the Bankruptcy Reform Act of 1994); *In re Greene*, 5 B.R. 785, 85-1 U.S.T.C. ¶9559 (S.D.N.Y. 1985); *Robert D. Twomey*, 82-2 U.S.T.C. ¶9687 (Bankr. W.D.N.Y.) (an assessment in violation of the stay is presumed invalid); *Debois Investment Group, Inc. v. Shamblin (In re Shamblin)*, 890 F.2d 123 (9th Cir. 1989) (voided tax sale and issuance of tax deed in violation of the stay; good faith purchaser denied a lien on the property); *Elbar Investments Inc. v. Pierce (In re Pierce)*, 2004 U.S. App. LEXIS 1316 (5th Cir. 2004) (unpublished opinion; tax sale unknowingly conducted 30 minutes after bankruptcy filing was void); *Calif. State Bd. of Equalization v. Taxel (In re Sluggo's Chicago Style, Inc.)*, 912 F.2d 1073 (9th Cir.), *cert. denied*, 111 S. Ct. 784 (1991) (cashing of a certificate of deposit given as security for prepetition sales and use taxes violated stay). *See also* IRS Manual, Part 5 (Collecting Process), Ch. 9 (Bankruptcy), §4.20 (1/1/06), at ¶10 (concluding that a taxpayer's bankruptcy filing may suspend, but does not terminate, any installment agreement between the taxpayer and the IRS under Code §6159); IRS Legal Memorandum 199920005, February 5, 1999, *reprinted at* 1999 TNT 99-61 (same).

[2] *See* 11 U.S.C. §§362(a)(2)-(5); *Lincoln Savings Bank, FSB v. Suffolk County Treasurer (In re Parr Meadow Racing Assn., Inc.)*, 880 F.2d 1540 (2d Cir. 1989), *cert. denied*, 104 S. Ct. 869 (1990) (the stay protects against liens created and perfected "by operation of law," as well as those requiring an "affirmative act"); *In re Pointer* (5th Cir.), *infra* note 112 (same); *United States v. Gold (In re Avis)*, 178 F.3d 718, 99-2 U.S.T.C. ¶50,632 (4th Cir. 1999) (split decision) (automatic stay precludes a federal tax lien filed prepetition from attaching to property acquired postpetition even though the lien would ordinarily encompass after-acquired property); *Deel v. United States (In re Deel)*, 1995 U.S. Dist. LEXIS 9251 (W.D. Va. 1995) (automatic stay not limited by Anti-Injunction Act); *but see Kocurek v. Arnold (In re Thurman)*, 163 B.R. 95, 100 (Bankr. W.D. Tex. 1994) (disagrees with *Parr Meadows* and *Pointer*).

The cases are split as to whether the issuance of a tax deed upon expiration of a debtor's redemption period violates the automatic stay where the tax sale occurred prepetition. *See, e.g., Rodgers v. Monroe County, N.Y. (In re Rodgers)*, 333 F.3d 64 (2d Cir. 2003) (delivery of deed under New York law was a ministerial act; foreclosure sale cut off debtor's legal and equitable interests); *Tax 58 v. Froehle (In re Froehle)*, 286 B.R. 94 (Bankr. 8th Cir. 2002), *citing Johnson v. First Nat'l Bank of Montevideo (In re Johnson)*, 719 F.2d 270 (8th Cir. 1983), *cert. denied*, 104 S. Ct. 184 (1984) (suggesting possible distinction based on the extent of affirmative actions necessary to confer full title postpetition); *Jackson v. Midwest Partnership (In re Jackson)*, 176 B.R. 156 (N.D. Ill. 1994) (issuance permitted, since tax purchaser held an interest in property), *rev'g*, 173 B.R. 637 (Bankr. N.D. Ill. 1994), *with In re Stewart*, 190 B.R. 846 (Bankr. C.D. Ill. 1996) (viewed tax purchaser's interest as akin to a lien, and the issuance of the tax deed as akin to perfecting the lien); *In re Donovan*, 266 B.R. 862 (S.D. Iowa 2001) (act to acquire title was the enforcement of a lien under Iowa law).

held to override the Anti-Injunction Act.[3] However, the IRS is not prohibited from renewing a previously filed lien if permitted under generally applicable law.[4]

The automatic stay generally remains in effect until the bankruptcy case is closed or dismissed, or a discharge is granted or denied, unless the bankruptcy court exercises its discretion to terminate or otherwise limit the stay.[5] In the context of a discharge pursuant to a confirmed Chapter 11 plan, the bankruptcy court's retention of jurisdiction over specified matters pursuant to the plan does not operate to extend the stay (although in certain cases the continued imposition of some form of injunction may be separately justified and provided for).[6] An appeal of an order to dismiss

---

[3] *But see Krumhorn v. United States (In re Krumhorn)*, 2002-2 U.S.T.C. ¶50,762 n.3 (N.D. Ill. 2002) (*dicta*); *cf. IRS v. Barnard (In re Kuppin)*, 335 B.R. 675, 2006-2 U.S.T.C. ¶50,502 (S.D. Ohio 2005) (relying in significant part, and erroneously, on cases discussed at §1006.3.2 above involving the inapplicability of the automatic stay to nondebtors, court broadly asserts that "Congress did not intend the Bankruptcy Code to be an exception to the application of the Anti-Injunction Act"). The Anti-Injunction Act is a provision in the Internal Revenue Code that prohibits any "suit for the purpose of restraining the assessment or collection of any tax," other than certain enumerated exceptions. *See* Code §7421(a).

[4] *See, e.g.*, 11 U.S.C. §§362(b)(3), 546(b)(1)(B); *In re O'Callaghan*, 342 B.R. 364 (Bankr. M.D. Fla. 2006); *In re Stuber*, 142 B.R. 435 (Bankr. D. Kan. 1992); *see also In re Carlson*, 126 F.3d 915 (7th Cir. 1997) (duplicate lien filing does not violate stay); IRS Legal Memorandum 200215052, February 28, 2002, *reprinted at* 2002 TNT 72-79 (refiling of lien would violate stay to the extent it constitutes an original filing against newly acquired property). In addition, if the IRS has a prior "interest in property" of the debtor, such interest may be perfected after the start of the bankruptcy case (and despite the automatic stay) if, under generally applicable law, such perfection would be effective against an intervening interest. 11 U.S.C. §§362(b)(3), 506(b)(1)(A); *see, e.g.*, H. Rep. No. 595, 95th Cong., 1st Sess. 371-372 (1977) (example of purchase money security interest); S. Rep. No. 989, 95th Cong., 2d Sess. 86-87 (1978); *In re AR Accessories Group, Inc.*, 345 F.3d 454 (7th Cir. 2003), *cert. denied sub nom. Bank One v. Wisconsin Dep't of Workforce Dev.*, 124 S. Ct. 1715 (2004); *see also* discussion in §1102.13 involving property tax liens.

[5] *See* 11 U.S.C. §362(c)-(f) (in respect of actions against property of the estate, the automatic stay remains in effect until all such property is gone; in the case of a corporation, this would generally be the confirmation date of the plan, at which point all property of the estate revests in the debtor unless the plan or confirmation order provides otherwise, *see* 11 U.S.C. §1141(b)) and discussion at §1002.4.2 above; *see, e.g., Mollo v. IRS*, 2005-1 U.S.T.C. ¶50,272 (M.D. Pa. 2005) (discharge terminated stay, even though bankruptcy case was still officially open). *See also* discussion at §1009 notes 8-10 and accompanying text (discussing whether court action is effective when order is signed, or when order is entered on the docket); *In re Best Finance Corp.*, 74 B.R. 243 (D.P.R. 1987) (debtor's consent to tax assessment without prior court approval did not waive automatic stay). By its terms, Bankruptcy Rule 6009 (derived from former Bankruptcy Rule 610 under prior Bankruptcy Act) permits the debtor-in-possession to waive the stay with respect to any proceeding or action by or against the debtor corporation before any tribunal, whether commenced prior to or after the filing of the bankruptcy petition. Presumably, Bankruptcy Rule 6009 would not apply to Tax Court proceedings. *See* 11 U.S.C. §362(a)(8) (suspends the commencement or continuation of any Tax Court proceeding "concerning the debtor"); 28 U.S.C. §2075 (procedural Bankruptcy Code provisions given priority over Bankruptcy Rules); Bienenstock, Bankruptcy Reorganizations 18 n.67 (1987) (states that "to apply Bankruptcy Rule 6009 to a Tax Court proceeding . . . would, in part, render Bankruptcy Code sections 362(a)(8) and 362(d) a nullity"); *but see* Collier Pamphlet Edition, Bankruptcy Rules 287 (1998 version) (wherein Lawrence P. King, a member of the Advisory Committee on Bankruptcy Rules of the Judicial Conference of the United States, comments that Bankruptcy Rule 6009 "is not affected by any provision in the [Bankruptcy]Code").

[6] *See, e.g., Wood v. United States (In re Wood)*, 341 B.R. 804, 2006-2 U.S.T.C. ¶50,563 (Bankr. S.D. Fla. 2006).

does not extend the automatic stay.[7] However, delayed notice to the IRS of the debtor's dismissal or discharge may result in an effective extension of the applicable statute of limitations.[8] As discussed at § 1009 below, the courts are split as to whether an order vacating a prior dismissal or discharge reinstates the automatic stay, but appear to agree that the reopening of a bankruptcy case does not resurrect the stay. In addition, many jurisdictions have entered "standing orders" (or local rules) restricting the scope of the automatic stay to permit certain limited IRS action,[9] although the validity of such orders is questionable.[10]

The automatic stay applies only to actions against the debtor corporation, not its corporate officers. Thus, it does not prevent the IRS from proceeding against corporate officers for penalties for failure to collect and pay employment withholding taxes (*see* § 1006.3.2).

---

[7] *See Olson v. Commissioner*, discussed in text accompanying *infra* § 1009 note 23; *In re Wethersfield Farms, Inc.*, 34 B.R. 435, 439 (Bankr. D. Va. 1983); *see also In re De Jesus Suez*, 721 F.2d 848 (1st Cir. 1983); *In re Bluford*, 40 B.R. 640 (Bankr. W.D. Mo. 1984).

[8] *See Richmond v. United States*, 172 F.3d 1099, 99-1 U.S.T.C. ¶ 50,352 (9th Cir. 1999) (IRS entitled to rely on Bankruptcy Rule 4006 for notice of dismissal of bankruptcy case, unless and until actual notice received; actual facts particularly sympathetic to IRS, because court clerk never entered dismissal on docket and on 13 separate occasions told the IRS that the case was still open).

[9] For example, *see* the Second Revised General Order No. 2 for the U.S. Bankruptcy Court of the Northern District of Ohio, Eastern Division entered January 15, 1982 (signed by each bankruptcy judge sitting by appointment), which modified the automatic stay to permit the IRS:

> (1) "to make income tax refunds, in the ordinary course of business, in Chapters 7, 11 and 13 cases; . . . to offset against any refund due a debtor any taxes due the United States Government; . . . to assess any tax liability satisfied by offsetting any refund, when such liability has not previously been assessed;" and
> (2) "to assess tax liabilities (income, estate, gift, excise, and employment) shown on voluntarily filed returns, agreed deficiencies/adjustments in such tax liabilities, adjustments in employment and excise tax liabilities with respect to which the debtor/taxpayer fails to lodge a timely protest, agreed penalties asserted under Code § 6672 and penalties asserted under Code § 6672, with respect to which the debtor/taxpayer fails to lodge a timely protest."

The recitals in the order justify the modifications on the grounds that the administration of bankruptcy cases and the federal tax system are unduly "hindered, burdened and delayed," due to the constant monitoring necessary under the automatic stay provisions. *See In re Dominguez*, 67 B.R. 526, 86-2 U.S.T.C. ¶ 9736 (Bankr. N.D. Ohio 1986) (setting forth, in an appendix, the full text of the order). *See also Ramirez v. Minn. Dept. of Rev. (In re Ramirez)*, 266 B.R. 441 (Bankr. D. Minn. 2001) (setoff of tax refund against uncontested tax liability permitted under local rule); *Harbaugh v. United States (In re Harbaugh)*, discussed *supra* § 1006 note 30.

[10] *See, e.g., In re Willardo*, 67 B.R. 1014 (Bankr. W.D. Mich. 1986), wherein an *en banc* panel of the bankruptcy judges for the Western District of Michigan vacated two general orders restricting the scope of the automatic stay. The panel stated that such orders directly conflicted with Bankruptcy Code section 362(d)—which details the procedures to be followed by creditors seeking relief from the stay—and did not comport with the "most basic requirements of due process." *See also California State Bd. of Equalization v. Owen (In re Owen)* (Bankr. 9th Cir. March 4, 1993), *reprinted at* 93 TNT 92-27 (unpublished memorandum decision, per curiam) (to similar effect; however, case remanded to consider possibility of granting IRS equitable relief from stay, since the period for assessment had since run); *Harris v. IRS (In re American Payroll Network, Inc.)*, 98-2 U.S.T.C. ¶ 50,680 n.10 (Bankr. N.D.N.Y. 1998) (to similar effect, but permitted IRS to rely on general order given the facts and circumstances of that case).

The Ninth Circuit (in a split decision) has also held that the automatic stay did not preclude the IRS from serving a bankruptcy trustee with a notice of levy in respect of a *creditor's* unpaid taxes, and the bankruptcy trustee from having to honor the levy with respect to any subsequent distributions, where the creditor held an allowed claim at the time of the levy and such claim constituted "property" under state law.[11]

## *§1007.1 Exceptions to Suspension of Assessments*

As part of the Bankruptcy Reform Act of 1994, Congress excluded from the automatic stay all assessments of tax.[12] Accordingly, effective for bankruptcy cases commenced on or after October 22, 1994, the IRS may immediately assess any tax deficiency.[13]

For all prior cases, the automatic stay continues to apply to assessments. In only one instance while the automatic stay is operative may the IRS assess a prepetition tax. A prepetition tax may be immediately assessed if, pursuant to a bankruptcy court determination, liability for such tax has become *res judicata* against the debtor corporation.[14] A binding determination by the Tax Court will not suffice, although in such case the IRS could request the bankruptcy court to terminate the stay. Presumably, however, any act to collect such tax would still be subject to the automatic stay.

The stay also does not prevent the IRS from issuing a statutory notice of deficiency (also called a "90-day letter") or, as discussed at §1007.2 and §1007.5, conducting a tax audit.[15] The 90-day period during which the debtor corporation is permitted to file a petition in the Tax Court will, however, not begin to run until the automatic stay is terminated, and the debtor corporation will be allowed 150 days thereafter (rather than the usual 90 days) to file the petition.[16]

It is understood that the general purpose of the 1994 amendment excluding all tax assessments from the automatic stay was to eliminate unnecessary interference with the clerical process of assessing the tax liability, which frequently results in inadvertent violations of the automatic stay. It is not intended to give the IRS a preference or priority claim any different than that to which it is otherwise entitled.[17] Nor may any tax lien generally attach by reason of such an assessment.[18] However,

---

[11] *See United States v. Hemmen*, 51 F.3d 883, 95-1 U.S.T.C. ¶50,210 (9th Cir. 1995). *Accord United States v. Ruff*, 99 F.3d 1559, 97-1 U.S.T.C. ¶50,130 (11th Cir. 1996).

[12] 11 U.S.C. §362(b)(9)(D) (added by the Bankruptcy Reform Act of 1994).

[13] *Consider Riley v. United States* (E.D. Mo.), discussed below.

[14] Code §6871(b)(2); 11 U.S.C. §505(c).

[15] 11 U.S.C. §362(b)(9).

[16] *See infra* §1009.

[17] S. Rep. No. 103-168, 103d Cong., 1st Sess. 43 (1993).

[18] *See* 11 U.S.C. §362(b)(9)(D), which permits a tax lien to attach only where the tax is nondischargeable and the property or proceeds are transferred to, or revest in, the debtor. In the case of a corporation, this may only occur in so-called liquidating bankruptcies. *See* §1014. Even then, however, the tax lien may be subordinated. *See* 11 U.S.C. §726(a)(4); *see also* 11 U.S.C. §510(c), discussed *infra* at §1015.2 (in the context of tax penalties) and at §1010 note 17 (in the context of late claims).

the fact of assessment would effect the period over which such claim could be paid under a Chapter 11 plan (*see* § 1016.1).

In *Riley v. United States*,[19] the IRS had issued against the debtor during the pendency of the automatic stay a Notice of Proposed Assessment relating to a Code § 6672 penalty and, following the bankruptcy, effected assessment. The debtor claimed that the notice was issued in violation of the automatic stay and thus void. The district court agreed, stating that the statute only excludes from the automatic stay notices of tax "deficiencies," not "penalties," and in turn invalidated the assessment as an outgrowth of the notice. On appeal, the Eighth Circuit reversed on the grounds that the issuance of the Notice of Proposed Assessment was not statutorily required and thus did not affect the validity of the later assessment. The IRS did not appeal, and the Eighth Circuit did not address, the district court's conclusion that the Notice of Proposed Assessment itself violated the stay. Significantly, since July 1, 1996, notices of proposed assessment under Code § 6672 have been statutorily required—thereby raising anew for future cases the proper treatment of such notices under the exception to the automatic stay for the issuance of a "notice of tax deficiency."

Similarly, the *Riley* case also puts at issue the scope of the exception permitting the "assessment of any *tax*" (emphasis supplied). Applying the type of "plain language" interpretation that the district court in *Riley* suggests has rather unexpected implications. For example, it is standard for the IRS to include in a statutory notice of deficiency for income taxes any tax penalties relating thereto.[20] Moreover, the Internal Revenue Code expressly provides that tax penalties (including the Code § 6672 penalty) shall be "assessed and collected in the same manner as taxes."[21] Thus, adopting the *Riley* court's reasoning, many (if not most) notices of deficiency and tax assessments would violate the automatic stay. Accordingly, such a literal interpretation reintroduces the proclivity for inadvertent violations of the automatic stay which Congress had sought to avoid. This would suggest that the exceptions to the automatic stay for a "notice of tax deficiency" and the "assessment of any tax" should be read in light of the normal meaning and application of such concepts under the Internal Revenue Code. So viewed, such exceptions would incorporate the whole of

---

[19] 192 B.R. 727, 96-1 U.S.T.C. ¶ 50,090 (E.D. Mo. 1995), *rev'd*, 118 F.3d 1220, 97-2 U.S.T.C. ¶ 50,522 (8th Cir. 1997), *reh'g, en banc, denied*, 1997 U.S. App. LEXIS 24822, *cert. denied*, 118 S. Ct. 1299 (1998).

[20] *See, e.g.*, Code § 6665(b) (subjecting certain tax penalties to notice of deficiency procedures).

[21] *See* Code § § 6665(a)(1) and 6671(a) (also applies to additions to tax and certain other liabilities); *cf.* Code § 6601(e)(1) (providing same treatment for interest).

the debtor's tax liability, inclusive of interest and penalties.[22] And at least one bankruptcy court has so held.[23]

## *§1007.2 Exceptions to Suspension of Collection*

Although any act to collect prepetition taxes is generally suspended, the IRS may file with the bankruptcy court a claim against the bankruptcy estate (called a "proof of claim," *see* §1010) or a request for payment of taxes or the taking of any other action within the bankruptcy court's jurisdiction, such as a request for a determination of the debtor corporation's tax liability.[24] Also, the Bankruptcy Code has always excluded from the automatic stay the issuance of a notice of tax deficiency. In the Bankruptcy Reform Act of 1994, Congress also expressly excluded (i) the conduct a tax audit (*see also* §1007.5), (ii) a demand for tax returns, and (iii) the issuance of a notice and demand for payment in connection with the assessment of the tax.[25] The added exceptions for tax audits and tax returns were generally viewed as a clarification of prior law.[26] Thus, a request by the IRS for an extension of the statute of limitations on assessment in connection with the conduct of an audit does not violate the automatic stay.[27] It is also the IRS's position that a request for an extension of the statute of limitations on *collection* does not violate the stay.[28]

---

[22] For bankruptcy priority purposes, most courts have concluded that interest is itself part of the claim for "taxes" (even though it may also be characterized, if need be, as a compensatory penalty). *See, e.g., Hardee v. IRS (In re Hardee)*, 137 F.3d 337, 98-1 U.S.T.C. ¶50,307 (5th Cir. 1998); *In re Larson*, 862 F.2d 112, 118-19, 88-2 U.S.T.C. ¶9590 (7th Cir. 1988); and discussion at §1015.1.5, below. In contrast, due to the separate references to, or treatment of, tax penalties for bankruptcy priority purposes, it appears that, at least for purposes of priority, the terms "tax" and "tax penalties" were perceived as distinct. *See, e.g.*, 11 U.S.C. §§503(b)(1)(C) and 507(a)(8)(G). *But consider In re Gillespie*, 96-2 U.S.T.C. ¶50,409 (Bankr. D. Minn. 1996), granting the IRS a tax priority under Bankruptcy Code section 507(a)(8) in respect of its claim, as assignee, for unpaid child support, on the grounds that Code §6305(a)(1) instructs the IRS to assess and collect the unpaid amount in the same manner, and with the same powers, "as if such amount were a tax imposed by Subtitle C," *appeal dismissed*, 1996 U.S. Dist. LEXIS 12769 (due to death of appellant).

[23] *In re Innovation Instruments, Inc.*, 228 B.R. 313, 99-1 U.S.T.C. ¶50,282 (Bankr. N.D. Fla. 1998).

[24] Code §§6213(f)(2) and 6871(c).

[25] 11 U.S.C. §362(b)(9).

[26] *See, e.g., In re Carlson* (7th Cir.), *supra* note 4 (information requests in connection with a tax audit in a pre-1994 Act case did not violate automatic stay, as such requests were simply inquiries about deficiencies rather than actions in the nature of an assessment; noted that 1994 change in respect of tax audits amounted to a codification of prior law); *In re H & H Beverage Distributors*, 850 F.2d 165 (3d Cir. 1988) (tax audit did not violate automatic stay and was consistent with exception for notices of deficiency), *cert. denied*, 488 U.S. 944 (1988); *Wood v. Commissioner*, 2005 Bankr. LEXIS 1289 (Bankr. S.D. Fla. 2005); *see also Richmond v. United States* (9th Cir.), *supra* note 8 (extension of statute of limitations was not obtained in violation of the automatic stay, since it is part of the determination of a tax deficiency and precedes the notice of deficiency).

[27] *See, e.g., Richmond v. United States* (9th Cir.), discussed in preceding footnote; *see also* IRS Legal Memorandum 200210032, December 4, 2001, *reprinted at* 2002 TNT 47-28 (request and execution of waiver of statute of limitations on assessment is part of assessment process, and thus not prohibited by the automatic stay).

[28] IRS Legal Memorandum 200221045, May 24, 2002, *reprinted at* 2002 TNT 102-78.

Although permitting tax assessments and demands for payment during the pendency of the stay, no tax lien generally may attach by reason of the assessment or demand.[29] In addition, it has been held that a Notice of Intent to Levy constitutes more than a demand for payment and thus violates the automatic stay.[30] And the IRS has similarly so concluded.[31] The Tax Court has also held that an IRS notice of adverse determination following a Code § 6330 collection due process hearing with respect to a final notice of intent to levy violates the automatic stay.[32] The notice stated that the IRS had "determined that it was appropriate to proceed with the proposed levies."[33] Although the IRS believes that the Tax Court erred in so holding, IRS Chief Counsel Notice CC-2006-019 states that "the Service generally will not challenge [such] holding in the Tax Court, especially if the notice was issued before the confirmation of a plan." The Notice is somewhat more equivocal about similar situations involving notices of adverse determination following a collection due process hearing with respect to tax liens, but indicates that the IRS nevertheless will follow such holding in most lien cases where a Tax Court petition is filed during the pendency of the automatic stay.

## *§1007.3 Immediate Assessment in Receivership Proceeding*

In contrast to a bankruptcy case, the IRS may, upon the appointment of a receiver in any receivership proceeding before any federal or state court, make an immediate assessment of any tax deficiency.[34] No statutory notice of deficiency is

---

[29] *See supra* notes 17-18 and accompanying text. *See also* IRS Chief Counsel Advice 200144029, September 26, 2001, *reprinted at* 2001 TNT 214-22 (concluding that the sending of an annual installment agreement statement does not violate the automatic stay; the statement is for information purposes only, and is not a bill).

[30] *Beverly v. Commissioner*, T.C. Memo 2005-41 (notice of intent to levy); *Jacoway v. Dept. of Treasury (In re Graycarr, Inc.)*, 330 B.R. 741 (Bankr. W.D. Alaska 2005) (same); *Foltz v. United States (In re Foltz)*, 2004 Bankr. LEXIS 738 (Bankr. M.D. Pa. 2005) (same); *Covington v. IRS (In re Covington)*, 2000-1 U.S.T.C. ¶50,344 (Bankr. D. S.C. 2000) (court consistently referred to both the Notice of Intent to Levy and the accompanying pamphlet entitled "Understanding the Collection Process").

[31] *See, e.g.*, IRS Chief Counsel Notice CC-2006-019, dated August 18, 2006 (updates and replaces Collection Due Process Handbook), at IV.E.1, *reprinted at* BNA Daily Tax Report (August 29, 2006), BNA TaxCore (advising that, in such instance, the notice "should be rescinded and any levies made in violation of the stay should be released"); IRS Chief Counsel Advice 200018005, December 23, 1999, *reprinted at* 2000 TNT 89-73 (expressed view that the issuance of a "Notice of Intent to Levy and Notice of Your Right to a Hearing"—known as a "Collection Due Process Notice" (IRS Form 1058)—violated the automatic stay).

[32] *Smith v. Commissioner*, 124 T.C. 36 (2005).

[33] *Smith*, 124 T.C. at 38. In *In re Drake*, 336 B.R. 155 (Bankr. D. Mass. 2006), *reconsid. denied*, 2006 Bankr. LEXIS 834, the bankruptcy court voided as a violation of the automatic stay the IRS issuance of a determination notice denying an individual debtor's request for innocent spouse relief and indicating the IRS "was continuing its collection activities by charging Debtor interest and the failure to pay penalty if such penalty were applicable." The court viewed the notice as "part and parcel of the collection process" (per its decision denying reconsideration), and equated such notice to the notice of adverse determination discussed in the text above with respect to a debtor's request for relief from a notice of intent to levy.

[34] Code § 6871(a).

required.[35] This means that, unlike a company in bankruptcy, a company in receivership may be unable to contest the deficiency in the Tax Court.[36] In general, to the extent any portion of such claim for taxes is allowed by the court, payment is made either from the receivership assets or, after termination of the proceedings, by the debtor corporation upon notice and demand by the IRS.[37] It may be possible, however, for the debtor corporation to work out a deferred payment arrangement with the IRS.[38]

## *§1007.4 Consolidated Returns*

It is not entirely clear how the automatic stay operates in the context of a consolidated return where not all members of the consolidated group are in bankruptcy, particularly where the common parent, but not all of its subsidiaries, are in bankruptcy.

Technically, from purely a bankruptcy perspective, the nonbankrupt members of the consolidated group—each of which is severally liable for the entire consolidated group's tax liability and its own tax liability[39]—are not debtors in the bankruptcy case and, thus, generally not subject to the automatic stay.[40] The consolidated return regulations, however, add a potential gloss, in that they provide as a general rule that the common parent is to be the sole agent for each member of the group for essentially all procedural matters and "no subsidiary shall have authority to act for or represent itself in any [such] matter."[41] Such procedural matters include the granting of extensions of time, the receipt of notices of deficiency, the receipt of notices and

---

[35] Id.

[36] *E.g., David R. Kane*, 57 T.C.M. 648, Dec. 45,751(M), T.C. Memo. 1989-272 (letter advising taxpayer of assessment of deficiencies pursuant to Code §6871 did not confer right to litigate deficiencies in Tax Court).

[37] Code §6873. *See Resyn Corp. v. United States*, 851 F.2d 660, 88-2 U.S.T.C. ¶9420 (3d Cir. 1988) (2-1) (held that postpetition interest on fraud penalties, which were assessed pursuant to Code §6871(a), accrues from the date of assessment, notice, and demand; dissent would not accrue interest until the court's determination of the validity of the penalty is final); *Resyn Corp. v. United States* (*In re Resyn Corp.*), 945 F.2d 1279, 91-2 U.S.T.C. ¶50,498 (3d Cir. 1991) (continuing the saga of the 1988 decision, held that a proof of claim was not an effective notice and demand for fraud penalties because it did not satisfy the notice requirements of Code §6303(a), *i.e.*, it was not left at the taxpayer's usual place of business or mailed to its last known address; however, absent prior notice and demand, IRS was entitled to postjudgment interest from the time the bankruptcy court entered its determination upholding the penalties).

[38] *See infra* §1017.

[39] Reg. §1.1502-6(a).

[40] *But consider United States v. Wright*, 57 F.3d 561, 95-2 U.S.T.C. ¶50,334 (7th Cir. 1995), *rev'g* 868 F. Supp. 1070, 94-2 U.S.T.C. ¶50,549 (S.D. Ind.) (involving tolling of statute of limitations on collection against the general partners of a bankrupt partnership for unpaid employment taxes of the partnership), discussed at §1008.2 below.

[41] Reg. §§1.1502-77(a)(1), (3), 1.1502-77A(a). However, where an existing consolidated group implements a holding company structure by means of a reverse acquisition, and the old common parent (now a subsidiary) continues to exist, the Tax Court has held that both the old common parent and the new common parent are agents for the consolidated group for purposes of the receipt of notices of deficiency for taxable years before the reverse acquisition. *Union Oil Co. of California v.*

demand for payment of taxes, the filing of petitions with the Tax Court, the filing of claims for refund or credit, the receipt of any refunds, and the like.[42] Applying these provisions, the Tax Court has held that, where a common parent that is in bankruptcy is prevented by the automatic stay from filing a Tax Court petition, the nonbankrupt subsidiaries in the consolidated group may not file a petition in the Tax Court for any consolidated return year.[43] And the IRS has concluded accordingly that such prohibition results in a corresponding suspension of the statute of limitations on assessment for the nonbankrupt subsidiaries as well under Code § 6503(a)(1).[44] On the other hand, the same portion of the consolidated return regulations contains the following statement:

> The Commissioner may, upon issuing to the common parent written notice that expressly invokes the authority of this provision, deal directly with any member of the group with respect to its [several] liability under section 1.1502-6 for the consolidated tax of the group, in which event such member has sole authority to act for itself with respect to that liability.[45]

Thus, it would appear that, if the sole basis for the extension of the automatic stay to the nonbankrupt subsidiaries is the "sole agency" rule, the IRS could circumvent the

---

(Footnote Continued)

*Commissioner*, 101 T.C. 130 (1993). Special rules also apply in the limited circumstances where a foreign entity is the common parent of a U.S. consolidated group. *See* Reg. § 1.1502-77(j).

[42] Reg. §§ 1.1502-77(a)(2), 1.1502-77A(a). *See also* IRS Field Service Advice, 1992 FSA LEXIS 293 (June 30, 1992) (concluding that a common parent that is a debtor-in-possession in a Chapter 11 case has authority to execute an extension of the statute of limitations on assessment on behalf of the group without prior bankruptcy court approval).

[43] *J&S Carburetor Co. v. Commissioner*, 93 T.C. 166 (1989). *Cf. Oakridge Consulting Inc. v. United States (In re Consolidated FGH Liquidating Trust)*, 2005 Bankr. LEXIS 769 (Bankr. S.D. Miss. 2005) (a liquidating trustee, acting on behalf of the debtor, a former member of a consolidated group, could not bring an action for a tax refund—even under an action seeking to recover the tax refund as property of the debtor's estate—since Reg. § 1.1502-77(a) makes the parent of the consolidated group the sole agent; the bankruptcy court was also not enamored with the prospect of determining the tax liability of non-debtors, namely, the other members of the consolidated group).

[44] IRS Field Service Advice 200203007, January 18, 2002, *reprinted at* 2002 TNT 14-93.

[45] Reg. § 1.1502-77(a)(6) (effective for taxable years beginning on or after June 28, 2002), and Reg. § 1.1502-77A(a) (last sentence, for prior taxable years), containing substantially the same provision. The regulations also provide that, if the common parent is about to be dissolved or its existence otherwise terminated, the common parent (or if the common parent fails to act, the remaining members of the consolidated group) may designate another member of the group to act in its place as agent for the group. Any designation is subject to the Commissioner's (or formerly the district director's) approval. If no substitute agent has been approved, and the Commissioner had reason to believe that the common parent's existence in fact has terminated, pre-7/28/02 regulations provided that the Commissioner could, if he deemed it advisable, deal directly with any member of the group in respect of its liability. Reg. § 1.1502-77A(d). The new regulations provide, instead, that if the common parent has a single successor that is a domestic corporation, such successor will become the substitute agent for the group upon termination of the common parent's existence. In all other circumstances, the Commissioner's designation of the substitute agent generally will control. Reg. § 1.1502-77(d), (e). *See also* Rev. Proc. 2002-43, 2002-2 C.B. 99; IRS Field Attorney Advice 20071701F, August 22, 2006, *reprinted at* 2007 TNT 83-25.

automatic stay simply by notifying the common parent that it intends to deal directly with each subsidiary.

Although, in appropriate circumstances, the bankruptcy court may enjoin an action against a nondebtor pursuant to its broad equitable powers under Bankruptcy Code section 105,[46] it remains to be seen how far (if at all) the bankruptcy courts might apply this power to restrain actions by the IRS against nonbankrupt members of a consolidated group.[47] The IRS Manual has in the past recognized that, absent a preassessment adjudication, a bankruptcy court might prohibit the IRS from initiating collection actions against nonbankrupt solvent subsidiaries of a bankrupt common parent.[48] Accordingly, the Manual recommended that in appropriate circumstances, either (1) the Department of Justice seek a partial lifting of the automatic stay to permit the common parent to file in the Tax Court or (2), alternatively, the district director notify the common parent that the IRS will deal separately with each subsidiary so as to permit the filing of a Tax Court petition by each subsidiary.[49]

---

[46] *See* Bienenstock, *supra* note 5, at 109-111; *see also In re U.I.P. Engineered Prods. Corp.*, 831 F.2d 54 (4th Cir. 1987) (criticized bankruptcy court for not enjoining third-party suit against nonbankrupt subsidiary due to subsidiary's critical role in parent company's bankruptcy); *Queenie, Ltd. v. Nygard Int'l*, 321 F.3d 282 (2d Cir. 2003) (extended the automatic stay to suspend a copyright infringement litigation against a debtor's wholly-owned subsidiary because "the adjudication of the claim . . . will have an immediate adverse economic impact on" the debtor; cited other situations where courts have extended the automatic stay to nondebtors, including where the debtor is a guarantor of the claim that is the subject of the litigation, and actions where "there is such identity between the debtor and the third-party defendant that the debtor may be said to be the real party defendant . . ."); *Teachers Ins. & Annuity Assn. of America v. Butler*, 803 F.2d 61 (2d Cir. 1986) (pursuant to its general equitable powers, bankruptcy court may extend automatic stay to nondebtor general partners of the debtor, provided that they had not made bad faith efforts to escape liability under an adverse judgment); *A.H. Robins Co. v. Piccinin*, 788 F.2d 994 (4th Cir. 1986) (employing substantially identical standard to that in *Queenie*, above); Shapiro, Non-Debtor Third Parties and the Bankruptcy Code: Is Protection Available Without Actually Filing? 95 Comm. L.J. 345 (1990); Note, Expanding the Bankruptcy Code: The Use of Section 362 and Section 105 to Protect Solvent Executives of Debtor Corporations, 58 Brooklyn L. Rev. 929 (1992) (discussing nontax cases).

[47] Consider *supra* §1006 notes 221-224 and accompanying text (most courts hold that the Anti-Injunction Act prevents bankruptcy court from enjoining the assessment or collection of taxes against nondebtors). *See also Harrison v. IRS (In re Harrison)*, 82 B.R. 557, 87-2 U.S.T.C. ¶9660 (D. Colo. 1987), holding that neither the automatic stay nor the court's general injunctive power under Bankruptcy Code section 105 could be invoked to preclude the IRS from collecting unpaid taxes from the debtor's wife with whom he filed a joint tax return; *accord Goldsby v. United States (In re Goldsby)*, 135 B.R. 611, 92-1 U.S.T.C. ¶50,118 (Bankr. E.D. Ark. 1992). In *J&S Carburetor*, the Tax Court distinguished the joint return situation from the consolidated return situation for purposes of the automatic stay in that the filing of a joint return does not create an agency relationship between spouses.

[48] *See, e.g.*, former IRS Manual, Part 5 (Collecting Process), HB 5.9 (Bankruptcy Handbook), Chapter 4.2 (2/11/99), at ¶2; former IRS Manual §(35)8(10)6(1)(a)4 (March 15, 1990).

[49] Id.

## §1007.5 *Ability to Issue Summons*

Courts have reached differing conclusions as to whether the automatic stay precludes the IRS's issuance of a summons against the debtor,[50] or against a third party,[51] for the purpose of gathering information concerning the tax obligations of the debtor. These cases may be effectively rendered moot by the Bankruptcy Reform Act of 1994, in that the Act specifically excludes tax audits from the automatic stay.[52] Presumably, this includes the IRS's right to issue an "information" summons in connection with the audit (*see* Code §7602).

## §1007.6 *Actions in Violation of Automatic Stay: Void or Voidable?*

There is a split among the Circuit Courts as to whether actions in violation of the automatic stay are void *ab initio* or are simply voidable, such that affirmative action must be taken during the bankruptcy case to void the action.[53] Most courts have held that such actions are void *ab initio*, subject to possible relief based on equitable considerations.[54] For example, many courts have granted relief from the automatic

---

[50] *Compare United States v. Moore,* 1990 U.S. App. LEXIS 13768 (5th Cir.) (issuance subject to automatic stay); *Davis v. United States* (*In re Davis*), 1991 U.S. Dist. LEXIS 20047 (E.D. Cal.) (same); *with In re Moore,* 131 B.R. 893 (Bankr. S.D. Fla. 1991).

[51] *Compare United States v. Arthur Andersen & Co.,* 623 F.2d 725, 80-1 U.S.T.C. ¶9360 (1st Cir.) (summons permitted), *cert. denied,* 449 U.S. 1021 (1980); *In re Greene, supra* note 1; *with In re Spencer,* 123 B.R. 858 (Bankr. N.D. Cal. 1991); *Jon Co. v. United States,* No. 83-K-631 (D. Colo. June 22, 1983).

[52] *See* 11 U.S.C. §362(b)(9) (as amended by the Bankruptcy Reform Act of 1994, effective for bankruptcy cases commenced on or after October 22, 1994). In this regard, *see supra* note 26 and accompanying text.

[53] The Fifth, Sixth, and Federal Circuits hold that violations are voidable, whereas the First, Second, Third, Ninth, Tenth, and Eleventh Circuits hold that violations are void *ab initio. Compare Schwartz v. United States* (*In re Schwartz*), 954 F.2d 569 (9th Cir. 1992) (assessment void; collecting cases); *Ellis v. Consolidated Diesel Elec. Corp.,* 894 F.2d 371 (10th Cir. 1990); *In re Ward,* 837 F.2d 124 (3d Cir. 1988); *48th St. Steakhouse, Inc. v. Rockefeller Group, Inc.* (*In re 48th Street Steakhouse, Inc.*), 835 F.2d 427 (2d Cir. 1987), *cert. denied,* 485 U.S. 1035 (1988); *Matthews v. Rosene,* 739 F.2d 249 (7th Cir. 1984); *Borg-Warner Acceptance Corp. v. Hall,* 685 F.2d 1306, 1308 (11th Cir. 1982); *In re Smith Corset Shops, Inc.,* 696 F.2d 971 (1st Cir. 1982); *with Bronson v. United States,* 46 F.3d 1573 (Fed. Cir. 1995) (voidable; "If the assessment does not frustrate the purpose of the automatic stay and there is no indication from Congress that the action is void, then it should be merely voidable"); *Easly v. Pettibone Michigan Corp.,* 990 F.2d 905 (6th Cir. 1992) ("we hold that actions taken in violation of the stay are invalid and voidable and shall be voided absent limited equitable circumstances"); *Sikes v. Global Marine, Inc.,* 881 F.2d 176, 178-179 (5th Cir. 1989) (violations are voidable, *but* are viewed as void until validated by the bankruptcy court), *reh'g denied, en banc,* 888 F.2d 1388 (1989).

[54] In addition to Circuit Court cases cited in note 53, *see, e.g., Bronson v. United States,* 28 Fed. Cl. 756 (1993) (held assessment void, but provided equitable relief; debtor had intentionally acted as if the IRS assessments were proper—by extending the statute of limitations and cooperating in IRS levies—until the extended assessment period had run, at which time the debtor sought to void the assessments); *Ward v. IRS* (*In re Ward*), 261 B.R. 889, 2001-1 U.S.T.C. ¶50,351 (Bankr. W.D. Va. 2001) (pre-10/94 assessment was void even though debtor never challenged the assessments until after the expiration of the statute of limitations and 9 years after bankruptcy); *United States v. White,* 325 B.R. 918, 2005-1 U.S.T.C. ¶50,391 (N.D. Ga. 2005) (to the same effect); *Olson v. United States,* 133 B.R. 1016, 91-2 U.S.T.C. ¶50,555 (D. Neb. 1991) (assessment void), *adhered to, modified on reconsideration,* 161 B.R. 45 (1992), *appealed on other grounds; Spears v. United States,* 1992 WL 130923 (N.D. Okla.) (same). Under

stay on equitable grounds where the action was without knowledge of the automatic stay and the debtor's unreasonable behavior was a contributing factor.[55] Also, some courts have granted relief for technical, nonsubstantive violations of the stay.[56] Aside from its equitable powers, the bankruptcy court may also retroactively annul (or otherwise modify) the automatic stay under Bankruptcy Code section 362(d) in certain circumstances.[57] It is in light of these powers that many courts have viewed actions in violation of the automatic stay as simply voidable.[58]

(Footnote Continued)

this interpretation, there exists a technical conflict between the automatic stay provisions and Bankruptcy Code section 549(c), which provides that the trustee "may not avoid" postpetition transfers of real property to certain good faith purchasers. Some courts have read such section as a statutory exception to the automatic stay, whereas others have required that the purchaser request relief from the stay. *See, e.g., 40235 Washington Street Corp. v. Lusardi*, 329 F.3d 1076 (9th Cir. 2003) (concluding, contrary to *dicta* in earlier Third, Fifth and even Ninth Circuit Court decisions, that section 549(c) is *not* an exception to the automatic stay, but only relates to unauthorized sales by the trustee or debtor itself); *Bustamante v. Cueva (In re Cueva)*, 371 F.3d 232 (5th Cir. 2004) (similarly so concluding); *New Orleans Airport Motel Assocs., Ltd. v. Lee (In re Servico, Inc.)*, 144 B.R. 933 (Bankr. S.D. Fla. 1992).

[55] *See, e.g., In re Smith Corset Shops, Inc., supra* note 53 (debtor could not remain "stealthily silent" when it had advance notice of the proposed action and had an agent present when the action was occurring); *Matthews v. Rosene, supra* note 53 (laches barred debtor's attempt to void a 33-month-old judgment in favor of creditor who had filed a counterclaim in a state court action initiated by the debtor); *In re Calder*, 907 F.2d 953 (10th Cir. 1990) (state court judgment not void where debtor actively participated in action and did not provide notice of bankruptcy until just before final judgment was entered); *In re Downing*, 23 B.C.D. 134 (Bankr. N.D. Okla. 1992) (to same effect); *see also* 2 Collier on Bankruptcy § 362.07 (15th ed.).

[56] *See, e.g., Harbaugh v. United States (In re Harbaugh)*, 89-2 U.S.T.C. ¶ 9608 (W.D. Pa.), *aff'd without opinion*, 902 F.2d 1560 (3d Cir. 1990) (allowed setoff without prior court approval where IRS was unaware of bankruptcy). *Cf. Soares v. Brockton Credit Union (In re Soares)*, 107 F.3d 969 (1st Cir. 1997) (purely "ministerial" acts, *i.e.*, acts that are essentially clerical in nature, do not violate stay); *Schwartz v. United States (In re Schwartz), supra* note 53, at 574-575. *But cf. infra* notes 104-106.

[57] *See, e.g.*, § 1002.4 (criteria for modifying stay); *Soares v. Brockton Credit Union (In re Soares), supra* note 56 (1st Cir.) (retroactive relief is appropriate only in circumstances in which the facts are "both unusual and unusually compelling"); *In re Kissinger*, 72 F.3d 107, 109 (9th Cir. 1995) (retroactive relief should be granted only in "extreme circumstances"); *In re Murray*, 193 B.R. 20 (Bankr. E.D. Cal. 1996) (denied IRS retroactive relief where IRS acted with continuous indifference to bankruptcy process, even though there was no harm to creditors); *In re Halas*, 194 B.R. 605 (Bankr. N.D. Ill. 1996) (granted creditor partial retroactive relief where no prior knowledge of bankruptcy), *appeal dismissed*, 199 B.R. 654 (N.D. Ill. 1996); *Goldman v. United States (In re Schield)*, 242 B.R. 1, 99-2 U.S.T.C. ¶ 50,829 (Bankr. C.D. Cal. 1999) (granted retroactive relief, without specific reference to Bankruptcy Code section 362(d), where the IRS had mistakenly believed that a prepetition offer in compromise effectuated an assignment of debtor's tax refund and that it could therefore setoff the refund without violating the automatic stay). *See also George v. United States (In re George)*, 2001 U.S. App. LEXIS 2361 (9th Cir. 2001) (unpublished opinion; relief under section 362(d) must be requested by a party in interest; court cannot act *sua sponte*).

[58] *See, e.g., Bronson v. United States, supra* note 53.

## *§1007.7 Damages for Violating Automatic Stay*

In the event of certain willful (and, possibly, even inadvertent) violations of the automatic stay, the IRS may be liable for damages.[59] As a result of changes made by the IRS Restructuring and Reform Act of 1998, a debtor's ability to recover damages differs significantly depending on whether the violation occurs after July 22, 1998.[60]

*For IRS violations of the automatic stay occurring on or before July 22, 1998,* as well as any IRS violations occurring thereafter that are *not* in connection with the collection of federal tax from the debtor, there are four potential bases for a claim for damages:

(1) the civil contempt power of the bankruptcy court;
(2) Bankruptcy Code section 362(h);
(3) Code §7430 ("Awarding of Costs and Certain Fees"); and
(4) the Equal Access to Justice Act (28 U.S.C. §2412).

However, depending on the court, some or all of these may not be available (*see* §§1007.7.2 through 1007.7.5). Prior to the Bankruptcy Reform Act of 1994, it was the IRS's position that, because of the United States' sovereign immunity and the fact that any stay violation is in connection with the determination or collection of tax, Code §7430 was the exclusive means for obtaining attorneys' fees against the IRS in bankruptcy.[61] As a general matter, most courts rejected this position.[62] Moreover, as amended by the Bankruptcy Reform Act of 1994, Bankruptcy Code section 106 waives any sovereign immunity defense in respect of most tax related actions (*see* §1005.1).

*For violations of the automatic stay by the IRS after July 22, 1998,* in connection with the collection of federal tax from the debtor, a debtor's potential bases for damages are circumscribed by Code §7433(e) ("Actions for Violations of Certain Bankruptcy Procedures"), as discussed at §1007.7.1 below. As a result, a debtor can no longer seek monetary sanctions against the IRS for contempt or seek recovery of costs under the Equal Access to Justice Act for such violations. Actual, direct economic damages are potentially recoverable only under Code §7433 or Bankruptcy Code section 362(h). And Code §7430 is now the exclusive basis for recovering attorneys' fees, as

---

[59] In *In re Innovation Instruments, Inc., supra* note 23, the bankruptcy court (although ultimately concluding that no violation of the automatic stay occurred) held that it did not have authority to disallow the IRS's claim as punishment for violating the automatic stay, and that the debtor's only recourse would be to seek damages.

[60] *See* Code §7433(e), discussed at §1007.1.1 below.

[61] *See, e.g.,* former IRS Manual §(34)(10)32 (August 26, 1992); IRS Litigation Guideline Memorandum GL-51, February 26, 1991, at part II.D.2, *reprinted at* 2000 TNT 91-42, *supplemented by* IRS Litigation Guideline Memorandum GL-51A, June 4, 1992, *reprinted at* 2000 TNT 91-43.

[62] *See, e.g., Graham v. United States* (*In re Graham*), 981 F.2d 1135, 93-1 U.S.T.C. ¶50,255 (10th Cir. 1992) ("Whether section 7430 is or is not the sole waiver of sovereign immunity for grants of attorney's fees on the merits of a case, it does not necessarily preclude a separate waiver for intermediate sanctions for procedural missteps"); *Taborski v. IRS,* 141 B.R. 959, 92-1 U.S.T.C. ¶50,281 (N.D. Ill. 1992) (Code §7430 does not preempt Bankruptcy Code section 362(h)); *In re Price,* 143 B.R. 190, 193 (Bankr. N.D. Ill. 1992) (same); *Kolb v. United States* (*In re Kolb*), 137 B.R. 29, 92-1 U.S.T.C. ¶50,255 (N.D. Ill. 1992) (Code §7430 does not preempt contempt sanctions).

well as certain other costs, from the IRS with respect to such damage actions. Exhaustion of all available administrative remedies is a prerequisite to any damage action under Code § § 7430 and 7433.

Aside from violations of the automatic stay, it should be noted that the bankruptcy court's contempt power, Code § 7430 and the Equal Access to Justice Act are also potentially available to a debtor where there are other violations of bankruptcy court procedures (*e.g.*, postdischarge collection efforts) or abuses of the bankruptcy process. For example, in appropriate cases, the IRS could be held liable for filing a frivolous or unjustified proof of claim.[63] However, with respect to any IRS violations of the postdischarge injunction after July 22, 1998, Code § § 7430 and 7433 provide the exclusive basis for recovering damages.[64]

### § 1007.7.1 Code § 7433: Damage Actions for Post-July 22, 1998, Violations

As a result of changes made by the IRS Restructuring and Reform Act of 1998, the recovery of damages with respect to any IRS violation of the automatic stay (or of the postdischarge injunction imposed by Bankruptcy Code section 542) that occurs after July 22, 1998, in connection with the collection of federal tax from the debtor is circumscribed by Code § 7433 and, in particular, Code § 7433(e).[65]

Under Code § 7433 as so amended, the debtor may, in the case of a willful violation, recover damages of up to $1 million for (i) any actual, direct economic damages sustained by the debtor as a proximate result of the IRS violation and (ii) the costs of the damage action.[66] Also, the debtor may be able to recover other reasonable litigation costs (including attorneys' fees) under Code § 7430.[67] Such actions must be brought in the bankruptcy court and, with the exception of any action for damages permitted under Bankruptcy Code section 362(h) (in the case of stay violations), are the debtor's exclusive remedy for such violations.[68] Thus, a debtor can no longer seek

---

[63] *See, e.g., In re Brickell Investment Corp.*, 922 F.2d 696, 91-1 U.S.T.C. ¶ 50,056 (11th Cir. 1991); and *infra* § 1010.1 note 21 (involving proof of claim). With respect to postdischarge collection efforts, *see supra* § 1005 notes 50-52 and accompanying text, and *infra* § 1014 note 15.

[64] *See* Code § 7433(e) and Reg. § 301.7433-1(b), (h), discussed at § 1007.7.1 below. Although actions under Bankruptcy Code section 362(h) are permitted by Code § 7433(e)(2), Bankruptcy Code section 362(h) applies by its terms only to violations of the automatic stay.

[65] Because new Code § 7433(e) only applies to violations in connection with the "collection" of federal tax, any violation of the automatic stay (or post-discharge injunction) in connection with the *determination* or *assessment* of tax is not governed by Code § 7433(e), even though the violation occurs after July 22, 1998. *Cf. Shaw v. United States*, 20 F.3d 182, 94-1 U.S.T.C. ¶ 50,254 (5th Cir. 1994), *cert. denied*, 115 S. Ct. 635 (1994). Because most actions relating to the assessment and determination of tax are no longer subject to the automatic stay for bankruptcy cases commenced on or after October 22, 1994, the practical impact of this aspect of Code § 7433(e) should be relatively minimal. As relates to tax assessments following a debtor's discharge, *see* discussion at § 1008, accompanying notes 14-15 below.

[66] Code § § 7433(b), (e).

[67] *See* Reg. § 302.7433-2(b)(2), (h).

[68] Code § 7433(e); *see also Williamson v. United States*, 2005 U.S. Dist. LEXIS 13530 (E.D. Tex. 2005) (district court declined to exercise ancillary jurisdiction, since by statute the exclusive remedy for damages was an action in the bankruptcy court).

monetary sanctions against the IRS for such violations under the bankruptcy court's equitable powers.

Prior to any award of damages under Code § 7433 or Code § 7430, the debtor must exhaust all available administrative remedies within the IRS.[69] Although the statute suggests that such remedies technically may be pursued following the filing of the petition for damages with the bankruptcy court, the regulations under Code §§ 7430 and 7433 require that any available administrative remedies be pursued prior to the filing of the petition.[70] These regulations were amended on March 25, 2003 to incorporate the provisions of Code § 7433(e), but carry a July 22, 1998, effective date.[71] The amended regulations require that an administrative claim first be filed with the Chief of the "Local Insolvency Unit" for the judicial district in which the taxpayer's bankruptcy case is pending.[72] And, except where the claim is filed within six months of the expiration of the two year period for filing an action in the bankruptcy court, the regulations prohibit the filing of an action in the bankruptcy court until after (i) the IRS has rendered its decision on the claim or (ii) six months have passed since the claim was filed.[73]

New Bankruptcy Code section 342(g)(2) effectively imposes another condition on damage actions under Code § 7433 for automatic stay violations. For bankruptcy cases filed on or after October 17, 2005, Bankruptcy Code section 342(g)(2) prohibits the imposition of any monetary penalty for a violation of the automatic stay unless the violation occurs after the IRS receives notice of the bankruptcy case (or in an involuntary case, of the order for relief) in accordance with that section.

---

[69] Code §§ 7430(b)(1), 7433(d)(1). One bankruptcy court has erroneously concluded to the contrary. *See In re Graham*, 2003-1 U.S.T.C. ¶ 50,465 (Bankr. E.D. Va. 2003).

[70] Reg. § 301.7430-1(a), (e), requiring prior compliance with administrative remedies of Reg. § 301.7433-2(e) whether the claim for damages is under Code § 7433(b) or Bankruptcy Code section 362(h); Reg. § 301.7433-1(d). Similarly, the legislative history to the 1998 Reform Act states that "[n]o person is entitled to seek civil damages in a court of law *without first exhausting* administrative remedies." S. Rep. No. 174, 105th Cong., 2d Sess. 49 (1998) (emphasis added). *See also* Treasury Dept. General Explanations of Clinton Administration's Revenue Proposals for FY 1999 (issued February 2, 1998) (wherein Code § 7433(e) was first proposed; "Jurisdiction over such cases would lie with the Bankruptcy Court, but the claimant would be required to exhaust administrative remedies at the IRS to the same extent as for other claims under section 7433").

[71] For the most part, this was expected. The language utilized in Code § 7433(e) in establishing a cause of action against the IRS for stay violations generally parallels the phrasing in Code § 7433(a) with respect to damage actions against the IRS for disregarding any provision of the Internal Revenue Code. Accordingly, it was expected that provisions similar to those in the then-existing regulations would apply, as relevant, to subsequent actions under Code § 7433(e).

[72] *See* Reg. § 301.7433-2(d), (e) (also specifies information to be contained in, or included with, the claim). Prior to these amended regulations, the IRS in the fall of 1998 instituted certain procedures intended, in part, to facilitate the prompt correction of violations of the automatic stay and postdischarge injunction, and to handle any damage claims arising from such violations. *See* Announcement 98-89, 1998-2 C.B. 460, described at § 1007.7.6 below. Presumably, despite the retroactive effective date of the new Code § 7433(e) regulations and the absence of any mention of these procedures in the regulations, prior compliance with these procedures (to the extent available) would be considered to have exhausted all available administrative remedies. *See* § 1007.7.4 below at notes 142-145. Although not identical, these procedures are very similar to those adopted in the regulations. *See* Reg. § 301.7433-2.

[73] *See* Reg. § 301.7433-2(d).

A debtor may only recover damages under Code §7433 if the IRS has "willfully" violated the automatic stay (or postdischarge injunction). Neither the Code nor the legislative history defines the term "willful." One possibility is that the term should be interpreted in furtherance of the policies and purposes of the Bankruptcy Code. In this regard, it should be noted that the term "willful" is also used in Bankruptcy Code section 362(h) with respect to the recovery of damages for stay violations, and generally has been held to mean that (1) the party knew of the automatic stay (or bankruptcy filing) and (2) the actions that violated the stay were done intentionally, although not necessarily with the specific intent to violate the stay (*see* discussion at §1007.7.3 below). Under this standard, even inadvertent violations of the automatic stay generally have been considered "willful" (although, as indicated above, the receipt of official notice of the bankruptcy case is a statutory prerequisite to recovering monetary damages for new bankruptcy cases).[74] Alternatively, it is possible that one could look to how the term willful is used for purposes of the various civil penalties imposed by the Internal Revenue Code, such as the 100% penalty imposed by Code §6672. In the latter case, "willful" generally has been held to mean acting with "intentional or reckless disregard."[75] So defined, the term is likely to be interpreted in much the same way as under Bankruptcy Code section 362(h) other than possibly in the case of inadvertent violations. So far, the courts have used the bankruptcy definition.[76]

Only "actual, direct economic damages" (meaning actual pecuniary damages[77]) and the "costs of the action" are recoverable. Injuries such as inconvenience, emotional distress, and loss of reputation are compensable only to the extent that they result in actual pecuniary damages. Such damages must be reduced by the amount that could have reasonably been mitigated by the debtor.[78] The "costs of the damage action" are limited to certain court fees and cost of witnesses (as set forth in the footnote below).[79]

---

[74] In one case, involving a violation of the *postdischarge injunction*, the bankruptcy court stated that the IRS willfully violates the injunction "if it knows the injunction is in place and intends the actions that violate the injunction." *Stewart v. United States* (*In re Stewart*), 2000-2 U.S.T.C. ¶50,623 (Bankr. S.D. Ga. 2000) (court mistakenly granted attorney fees under the Equal Access to Justice Act, rather than Code §7430, although nominal in amount); *accord Payne v. United States* (*In re Payne*), 306 B.R. 230, 237-238, 2004-1 U.S.T.C. ¶50,210 (Bankr. N.D. Ill. 2004) (appealed on different issue). The court cited as authority the Eleventh Circuit's decision in *Hardy v. United States*, 97 F.3d 1384, 1390, 96-2 U.S.T.C. ¶50,635 (11th Cir. 1996), which involved the imposition of civil contempt sanctions.

[75] *See, e.g., Phillips v. United States*, 73 F.3d 939, 942-943, 96-1 U.S.T.C. ¶50,057 (9th Cir. 1996); *Kalb v. United States*, 505 F.2d 506, 511, 74-2 U.S.T.C. ¶9760 (2d Cir. 1994), *cert. denied*, 95 S. Ct. 1981 (1975). *But consider Finley v. United States*, 123 F.3d 1342, 97-2 U.S.T.C. ¶50,613 (10th Cir. 1997) (permitting a reasonable cause defense), discussed at §1006.3.2 above.

[76] *See, e.g., In re Lowthorp*, 332 B.R. 656 (Bankr. M.D. Fla. 2005) (without discussion); *Jacoway v. Dept. of Treasury* (*In re Graycarr, Inc.*), 330 B.R. 741 (Bankr. W.D. Alaska 2005) (same).

[77] Reg. §301.7433-1(b)(1), -2(b)(1).

[78] Code §7433(d)(2).

[79] The specific costs covered are (1) fees of the clerk and marshall; (2) fees of the court reporter for all or any part of the stenographic transcript necessarily obtained for use in the case; (3) fees and disbursements for printing and witnesses; (4) fees for exemplification and copies of paper necessarily obtained for use in the case; (5) docket fees; and (6) compensation for court appointed experts and interpreters. Reg. §301.7433-1(c), -2(c).

Other reasonable litigation costs (such as reasonable attorneys' fees or the cost of any study, analysis or report prepared for the court proceeding) are not recoverable as either direct economic damages or costs of the action, but may be recoverable under Code § 7430.[80] Significantly, based on previously existing regulations, it appeared that, if the debtor sought judicial recourse under Code § 7433 because the IRS denied the debtor's administrative claim for damages on the grounds that no willful violation of the automatic stay or postdischarge injunction occurred (or the IRS failed to respond on the merits of the claim within six months), and the debtor thereafter proved that a willful violation did occur and substantially prevailed with respect to the amount of damages, the debtor would be entitled to recover its reasonable administrative and litigation costs under Code § 7430 provided *only* that it met the net worth and size requirements of Code § 7430(c)(4)(A)(ii) (*i.e.*, in the case of most corporations, not more than $7 million in net worth and not more than 500 employees) and timely filed its application for costs.[81] Thus, the IRS would not have had the chance of avoiding such costs by trying to show that its position was substantially justified. However, the regulations issued in March 2003, which are specifically applicable to these types of damage claims, allow the IRS to demonstrate that its position was substantially justified.[82]

Prior to these regulations (and the proposed regulations that preceded them), it was unclear whether the debtor could recover any costs incurred in pursuing administrative relief, other than as discussed below in connection with damage actions under Bankruptcy Code section 362(h). With respect to damage actions against the IRS under Code § 7433(a) for disregarding any provision of the Internal Revenue Code, the regulations under Code § 7430 deny any recovery for administrative costs. The new regulations clarify that, in the case of damage actions under Code § 7433(e) and Bankruptcy Code section 362(h), reasonable administrative costs (which are costs incurred in connection with pursuing the administrative claim) may be recoverable under Code § 7430 to the extent not otherwise recoverable as costs of the damage action.[83]

Any action for damages under Code § 7433 must be brought within two years after the cause of action accrues (and, as indicated above, preceded by the filing of an administrative claim that satisfies the requisite waiting period, if any).[84] The cause of action for damages accrues when the taxpayer has had a reasonable opportunity to discover all essential elements of a possible action.[85]

---

[80] Code § 7430(c)(1); Reg. § 301.7433-2(h). For a further discussion of Code § 7430, *see* § 1007.7.4 below.

[81] *See* Reg. § 301.7433-1(h) (treating the taxpayer as a "prevailing party" for purposes of Code § 7430, with the exception of the notice and net worth/size requirements).

[82] *See* Reg. § 301.7433-2(h)(1). Otherwise, this provision is identical to Reg. § 301.7433-1(h). *Cf. Baird v. United States (In re Baird)*, 2005-1 U.S.T.C. ¶ 50,173 (Bankr. M.D. Ala. 2004) (denied petition for fees since IRS position during the litigation was substantially justified).

[83] Reg. § § 301.7430-3(a)(4), -8; Reg. § 301.7433-2(h)(2)(i).

[84] Code § 7433(d)(3).

[85] Reg. § 301.7433-2(g)(2).

A claim for reasonable administrative costs under Code § 7430 must be filed within 90 days after the IRS mails to the debtor, or otherwise notifies the debtor, of its decision on its claim for damages under Code § 7433.[86] If the IRS denies a claim for administrative costs, in whole or in part, any action before the bankruptcy court to recover such costs must be brought within 90 days after the IRS mails, or otherwise furnishes, to the debtor its denial (or, in the absence of a response on the merits, within six months after the claim for was filed). Thus, the filing of an administrative claim for costs is a prerequisite to the bringing of a judicial action to recover administrative costs. Any action under Code § 7430 for reasonable litigation costs must be brought within 30 days after a final judgment in any litigation relating to the violation, including any litigation to recover damages under Code § 7433 (without any requirement that a prior administrative claim be filed with respect to such litigation costs).[87]

In lieu of an action for damages under Code § 7433, a debtor may be able to recover damages for an IRS violation of the automatic stay under Bankruptcy Code § 362(h). (Such section does not apply to violations of the postdischarge injunction.) The ability of a corporate debtor to recover damages under Bankruptcy Code section 362(h) is discussed below at § 1007.7.3. As discussed therein, there is currently a split among the Circuit Courts as to whether such section is available to corporate debtors. Accordingly, in most jurisdictions, a corporate debtor's exclusive remedy for violations of the automatic stay (as well as for violations of the postdischarge injunction) will be under Code § 7433.

Where a damage action can be brought under Bankruptcy Code section 362(h) for an IRS violation, there has come into issue whether the debtor is statutorily required to exhaust its administrative remedies before filing suit under Bankruptcy Code section 362(h) and, by implication, whether such action is subject to the $1 million cap on damages in Code § 7433.[88] Stated more technically, the question is whether an action permitted to be brought under Bankruptcy Code section 362(h) by Code § 7433(e)(2)(B) is governed by Code § 7433(b) (which imposes the $1 million cap on damages) and therefore subject to the requirement in Code § 7433(d)(1) that administrative remedies must be exhausted, which refers only to damage awards under Code § 7433(b). We believe that the answer should be no. Code § 7433(b) only applies to a "petition filed under subsection (e)." Such petition is described in Code § 7433(e)(1). Code § 7433(e)(2)(A) then goes on to provide that "[e]xcept as provided in subparagraph (B), . . . such petition shall be the exclusive remedy for recovering damages . . . ." Subparagraph (B) provides, in turn, that subparagraph (A) "shall not apply to an action under [Bankruptcy Code] section 362(h) . . . ." Thus, we believe

---

[86] *See* Reg. § 301.7430-8(e), -2(c)(2) (filed with the Chief of the Local Insolvency Unit, presumably for the district in which the debtor's bankruptcy case is pending).

[87] *See* Code § 7430(c)(4)(A)(ii), which in turn references the notice requirements of 28 U.S.C. § 2412(d)(1)(B) (as in effect on October 22, 1986). *Cf.* Reg. § 301.7433-1(h), -2(h)(1).

[88] *Compare In re Graham*, 2003-1 U.S.T.C. ¶ 50,465 (Bankr. E.D. Va. 2003) (need not exhaust), *with In re Lowthorp*, 332 B.R. 656 (Bankr. M.D. Fla. 2005) (must exhaust); *Jacoway v. Dept. of Treasury* (*In re Graycarr, Inc.*), 330 B.R. 741 (Bankr. W.D. Alaska 2005) (denied petition for damages without prejudice, for failure to exhaust administrative remedies).

that the better reading is that an action under Bankruptcy Code section 362(h) is an alternative remedy not subject to the $1 million dollar limitation in Code §7433(b) or the exhaustion of administrative remedy requirement in Code §7433(d)(1).[89]

Any recovery of administrative and litigation costs in connection with an action under Bankruptcy Code section 362(h) for an IRS stay violation may only be awarded under Code §7430.[90] In contrast to the recovery of actual damages (as just discussed), a debtor's *costs* are only recoverable if the debtor has fully exhausted its administrative remedies, which means that the debtor must have unsuccessfully made an administrative claim for *actual damages* under Code §7433.[91] In addition, as discussed above, the filing of an administrative claim for costs is a prerequisite to bringing a judicial action for such costs. Any recovery of administrative costs in connection with an action under Bankruptcy Code section 362(h) is limited to any administrative costs incurred after the commencement of the debtor's bankruptcy.[92]

### §1007.7.2 The Civil Contempt Power of the Bankruptcy Court

The majority of courts have (in cases not involving the IRS) upheld the civil contempt powers of the bankruptcy court in core matters, such as violations of the automatic stay, as an appropriate application of the bankruptcy court's equitable powers.[93] Even in a minority jurisdiction, however, it may be possible for the bankruptcy court to impose "sanctions" for stay violations (in that the stay is legislatively mandated) without technically finding the party in "contempt" of

---

[89] Reg. §301.7433-2(a)(2) also supports this conclusion. Such regulation provides: "An action under this section constitutes the exclusive remedy under the Internal Revenue Code. In addition, taxpayers . . . may maintain actions under section 362(h) of the Bankruptcy Code." No reference is made to any Internal Revenue Code imposed limitation on an action under section 362(h), other than subjecting any recovery of costs to Code §7430.

[90] Code §7433(e)(2)(B)(i).

[91] *See* Code §7430(b)(1) and Reg. §301.7430-1(a), requiring exhaustion of administrative remedies; and Reg. §301.7430-1(c)(2), requiring compliance with Reg. §301.7433-2(d) and (e) even where the damage action is ultimately brought under Bankruptcy Code section 362(h).

[92] Code §7433(e)(2)(B)(ii); Reg. §301.7433-2(h)(2)(ii).

[93] *See, e.g., In re Jove Engineering, Inc.*, 92 F.3d 1539, 96-2 U.S.T.C. ¶50,469 (11th Cir. 1996) (involving IRS); *In re Power Recovery Sys., Inc.* 950 F.2d 798, 802 (1st Cir. 1991); *Mountain America Credit Union v. Skinner (In re Skinner)*, 917 F.2d 444 (10th Cir. 1989); *Burd v. Walters (In re Walters)*, 868 F.2d 665 (4th Cir. 1989); *In re Prairie Trunk Ry.*, 125 B.R. 217, 222 (Bankr. N.D. Ill. 1991); *but compare United States v. Arkison (In re Cascade Roads, Inc.)*, 34 F.3d 756 (9th Cir. 1994) (remanding stay violation case to bankruptcy court to consider imposition of sanctions; however, the court "express[ed] no opinion at this time on the way in which the bankruptcy court, if it chooses to do so, could impose such sanctions") *with Plastiras v. Idell (In re Sequoia Auto Brokers Ltd.)*, 827 F.2d 1281 (9th Cir. 1987) (bankruptcy court must certify facts to district court to review *de novo* and determine whether to issue contempt order). *See generally* Collier on Bankruptcy ¶105.06 (15th ed.); Bankruptcy Service, L. Ed., §§11:70, 11:71; Parkinson, The Contempt Power of the Bankruptcy Court Fact or Fiction: The Debate Continues, 65 Am. Bankr. L.J. 591 (1991) (concluding that the better analysis is that no contempt power exists in the bankruptcy court). Contempt proceedings are governed by Bankruptcy Rule 9020.

court.[94] In general, a party can be held in contempt for violating the automatic stay if it acts with knowledge of the bankruptcy filing (as generally would be true in the case of the IRS, *see* § 1004 above).[95] The violation need not be willful, *i.e.*, a conscious intent to violate. Nevertheless, if the party "acted without maliciousness and had a good faith argument and belief that his actions did not violate the stay," no sanctions generally would be imposed.[96] In the case of stay violations, the courts have permitted contempt proceedings to be brought by another creditor, as well as the debtor.[97]

Several courts have imposed civil contempt sanctions on the IRS for violations of the automatic stay predating the enactment of Code § 7433(e) (*see* § 1007.7.1 above).[98] For example, the IRS was found in contempt and liable for the debtors' expenses, lost income, and reasonable attorneys' fees where it mistakenly removed a computer code and, thus, permitted collection efforts against the debtors.[99] As discussed at § 1005.1, although historically a shield, sovereign immunity should no longer be a viable defense in most tax-related actions given the 1994 amendments to Bankruptcy Code section 106. As amended, Bankruptcy Code section 106(a) waives federal sovereign immunity to most Bankruptcy Code actions (other than as to punitive damages), but imposes certain limitations on the amount of costs or attorneys' fees recoverable (*see* discussion at § 1005.1.1).[100]

---

[94] *See, e.g., Havelock v. Taxel (In re Pace)*, 159 B.R. 890 (Bankr. 9th Cir. 1993), *aff'd*, 67 F.3d 187 (9th Cir. 1995) (permitting sanctions under Bankruptcy Code section 105(a) equitable powers); *Davis v. Conter (In re Soll)*, 181 B.R. 433 (Bankr. D. Ariz. 1995).

[95] *See, e.g., In re Jove Engineering, Inc., supra* note 93, at 1555 (rejected IRS attempt to avoid responsibility by blaming computer system); *In re Ray Irwin Shafer*, 63 B.R. 194, 86-2 U.S.T.C. ¶ 9523 (Bankr. D. Kan. 1986); *Fidelity Mortg. Investors v. Camelia Builders, Inc.*, 550 F.2d 47 (2d Cir. 1976) (Bankruptcy Act case), *cert. denied*, 427 U.S. 1093, *rehg. denied*, 430 U.S. 976 (1977). *But consider In re A&J Auto Sales, Inc.*, 210 B.R. 667 (Bankr. D.N.H. 1997) (although IRS held to have knowingly violated stay, no contempt damages imposed since revenue agents acted in good faith in accordance with IRS Manual and advice of IRS Office of Special Procedures), *aff'd*, 223 F.3d 839, 98-1 U.S.T.C. ¶ 50,416 (D. N.H. 1998) (collecting cases), *reh'g denied* (June 24, 1998), *reprinted at* 98 TNT 145-8.

[96] *See, e.g., Davis v. Conter (In re Soll)*, 181 B.R. *supra* note 94; *Barnett Bank of Southeast Georgia, N.A. v. Trust Co. Bank of Southeast Georgia, N.A. (In re Ring)*, 178 B.R. 570 (Bankr. S.D. Ga. 1995). For stay violations in bankruptcy cases filed on or after October 17, 2005, no monetary penalty may be imposed unless the violation occurs after the creditor receives notice of the bankruptcy case (or in an involuntary case, of the order for relief) in accordance with Bankruptcy Code section 342. 11 U.S.C. § 342(g)(2).

[97] *See, e.g., Crysen/Montenay Energy Co. v. Esselen Assoc., Inc. (In re Crysen/Montenay Energy Co.)*, 902 F.2d 1098, 1104 (2d Cir. 1990).

[98] *See, e.g., In re Colon*, 114 B.R. 890 (Bankr. E.D. Pa. 1990) (invoked civil contempt power with respect to a municipality; held that Bankruptcy Code section 362(h) provides an additional, not the exclusive, remedy to stay violations), *app. dismissed; cf. Kolb v. United States (In re Kolb)*, 1991 Bankr. LEXIS 921 (Bankr. N.D. Ill.) (IRS held in civil contempt for violating discharge order; debtor awarded damages), *aff'd*, N.D. Ill., *supra* note 62; *United States v. Kolb*, 161 B.R. 30 (N.D. Ill. 1993) (subsequent proceeding affirming award of costs under Code § 7430); *In re Kiker*, 98 B.R. 103 (Bankr. N.D. Ga. 1988) (same); *see also In re Holland*, 70 B.R. 409 (Bankr. S.D. Fla. 1987) (IRS may be held in contempt for violating court-ordered settlement agreement).

[99] *In re Ray Irwin Shafer, supra* note 95.

[100] In a case of first impression, the First Circuit has held that Bankruptcy Code section 106(a) does not waive, as a general matter, the government's immunity against damages for emotional distress. *United States v. Torres (In re Torres)*, 432 F.3d 20, 2006-1 U.S.T.C. ¶ 50,112 (1st Cir. 2005) (involved a violation of the post-discharge injunction under Bankruptcy Code section 524, and therefore distin-

In addition, the Ninth Circuit has held that the bankruptcy court's authority to impose sanctions does not extend to an award of damages (such as for costs and attorneys' fees incurred) relating to an appeal from a prior bankruptcy court determination; rather, such amounts must be the subject of a separate motion before the appellate court, or a notice from the court, under the Federal Rules of Appellate Procedure, Rule 38 (involving frivolous appeals).[101]

For IRS violations of the automatic stay (or postdischarge injunction) after July 22, 1998, a bankruptcy court may no longer impose monetary sanctions in exercise of its equitable powers where the violation occurs in connection with the collection of federal tax.[102]

### § 1007.7.3 Bankruptcy Code Section 362(h)

In 1984, Congress enacted Bankruptcy Code section 362(h), which provides that:

> An individual injured by any willful violation of [the automatic stay] shall recover actual damages, including costs and attorneys' fees, and, in appropriate circumstances, may recover punitive damages.

Despite the reference only to "individuals," two of the seven Circuit Courts to consider the issue (namely, the Third and Fourth Circuits) have held that Bankruptcy Code section 362(h) is also available to corporate debtors.[103] These courts reason that, because the automatic stay clearly applies to all debtors, the term "individual" (which is undefined in the Bankruptcy Code, although generally used to mean a living person) should be read in this context to mean all persons protected by the automatic stay. In contrast, courts that hold otherwise generally stress the plain meaning of the word "individual" and its general usage in the Bankruptcy Code, the lack of legislative history, and the fact that section 362(h) was enacted as part of the "Consumer Credit Amendments."

---

(Footnote Continued)

guished damage actions allowed under Bankruptcy Code section 362(h) for violations of the automatic stay), *rev'g* 309 B.R. 643, 2004-2 U.S.T.C. ¶ 50,379 (Bankr. 1st Cir. 2004).

101 *State of California Empl. Dev. Dept. v. Taxel (In re Del Mission Limited)*, 98 F.3d 1147 (9th Cir. 1996).

102 *See* Code § 7433(e)(2)(A), discussed at § 1007.7.1 above.

103 *Compare Budget Service Co. v. Better Homes of Virginia, Inc.*, 804 F.2d 289 (4th Cir. 1986) (finding of civil contempt not necessary to invoke section; applied section to corporate debtor); *In re Atlantic Business & Community Corp.*, 901 F.2d 325 (3d Cir. 1990) (adopting the holding of *Better Homes* without discussion); *with In re Jove Engineering, Inc., supra* note 93 (11th Cir.) (section restricted to individuals); *Spookyworld, Inc. v. Town of Berlin (In re Spookyworld, Inc.)*, 346 F.3d 1 (1st Cir. 2003); *Johnston Envtl. Corp. v. Knight (In re Goodman)*, 991 F.2d 613, 618-620 (9th Cir. 1993) (same); *Maritime Asbestosis Legal Clinic v. LTV Steel Co. (In re Chateaugay Corp.)*, 920 F.2d 183 (2d Cir. 1990) (same); *Sosne v. Reinert & Duree, P.C. (In re Just Brakes Corporate Systems, Inc.)*, 108 F.3d 881, 884-5 (8th Cir. 1997), *cert. denied* 118 S. Ct. 364 (1997). *See also Havelock v. Taxel (In re Pace)*, 67 F.3d 187 (9th Cir. 1995) (held that a bankruptcy trustee acts as a representative of the bankruptcy estate, an entity, not as an "individual" for purposes of Bankruptcy Code section 362(h); discusses contrary case law; however, sanctions permitted under bankruptcy court's equitable powers); *In re Prairie Trunk Ry.* (Bankr. N.D. Ill.), *supra* note 93 (collecting cases; followed *Chateaugay*).

Bankruptcy Code section 362(h) imposes liability for "willful" violations of the automatic stay. For this purpose, a violation is considered "willful" if:

(1) the party knew of the automatic stay, and

(2) the actions that violated the stay were done intentionally, although not necessarily with the specific intent to violate the stay.[104]

In effect, Bankruptcy Code section 362(h) generally imposes strict liability for stay violations (although in bankruptcy cases filed on or after October 17, 2005, no monetary penalty may be imposed unless the violation occurs after receipt of notice of the bankruptcy case, or order for relief, in accordance with Bankruptcy Code section 342).[105] This should be contrasted with the "good faith" standard generally employed in contempt proceedings. Thus, with only limited exception, whether the party believed in good faith that it has a right to the property is not relevant for purposes of section 362(h), but generally would preclude contempt sanctions. In both cases, however, the IRS's size and complexity alone will not excuse an IRS violation of the stay.[106]

In a split decision, recognized by the dissent as eroding the rejection of a "good faith" defense, the Third Circuit held that a creditor's actions were not "willful" where there was persuasive legal authority supporting the creditor's position that its actions did not violate the automatic stay (although ultimately rejected by the court), and no contrary "contemporaneous interpretations" of section 362.[107] As a result, courts within the Third Circuit are more apt to be forgiving of an IRS violation if case

---

[104] *See, e.g., Geichman v. Bloom (In re Bloom)*, 875 F.2d 224, 227 (9th Cir. 1989); *Lansdale Family Rest., Inc. v. Weis Food Serv. (In re Lansdale Family Rest.)*, 977 F.2d 826, 829 (3d Cir. 1992); *Crysen/Montenay Energy Co. v. Esselen Assocs., Inc. (In re Crysen/Montenay Energy Co.)* (2d Cir.), *supra* note 97, at 1105; *Taborski v. IRS (In re Taborski)*, *supra* note 62, at 965-966 (collecting cases); *United States v. Bulson (In re Bulson)*, 117 B.R. 537, 91-1 U.S.T.C. ¶50,023 (Bankr. 9th Cir. 1991), *aff'd without opinion*, (9th Cir. Aug. 17, 1992) (*per curiam*) (IRS held liable, even though it mistakenly believed that the debtor's bankruptcy case was closed); *California State Bd. of Equalization v. Owen (In re Owen)*, *supra* note 9 (IRS held liable even though assessment was in accordance with a "standing order" of the court which was only later found invalid); *Hamrick v. United States (In re Hamrick)*, 175 B.R. 890 (W.D. N.C. 1994) (the issuance of a demand letter as a result of an "innocent clerical error" due to poor training held "inadvertent" and not intentional); *In re Boldman*, 157 B.R. 412 (D. Ill. 1993) (failure to list employer identification number on bankruptcy petition did not excuse violation); *In re McPeck*, 1991 Bankr. LEXIS 100 (Bankr. D. Minn.) (debtor entitled to damages where IRS telephoned debtor regarding payment of past taxes and to confirm the bankruptcy filing); *Pinkstaff v. United States (In re Pinkstaff)*, 974 F.2d 113 (9th Cir. 1992) (filing of a notice of tax lien constituted a "willful" violation).

[105] 11 U.S.C. §342(g)(2).

[106] *See, e.g., In re Price*, 103 B.R. 989, 993, 89-2 U.S.T.C. ¶9052 (Bankr. N.D. Ill. 1989), *aff'd*, 130 B.R. 259 (N.D. Ill. 1991), *aff'd*, 42 F.3d 1068 (7th Cir. 1994); *In re Stucka*, 77 B.R. 777 (Bankr. C.D. Cal. 1987); *In re Ray Irwin Shafer*, *supra* note 95 (contempt proceeding); *but consider Shadduck v. Rodolakis*, 221 B.R. 573, 98-2 U.S.T.C. ¶50,516 (D. Mass. 1998) (held that the "bureaucratic structure" of the IRS was no defense for purposes of section 362(h), but implicitly accepted defense for purposes of contempt motion); *Mitchell v. IRS (In re Mitchell)*, 101 B.R. 278, 89-1 U.S.T.C. ¶9293 (Bankr. W.D. Okla. 1988) (denied damages under section 362(h) for "technical, inadvertent violation of the stay," since no showing of willfulness).

[107] *University Medical Center v. Sullivan (In re University Medical Center)*, 973 F.2d 1065 (3d Cir. 1992), *reh'g, en banc, denied*, 1992 U.S. App. LEXIS 27506 (3d Cir. 1992).

law exists from which the IRS reasonably could believe that its actions would not violate the stay.

As discussed at § 1005.1.1, to the extent that the damages sought are for cost or fees, such amount may be subject to certain hourly rate and similar limitations. Moreover, for IRS violations after July 22, 1998, in connection with the collection of federal tax, some courts have required that the debtor first exhaust its administrative remedies to recover such damages under Code § 7433 (*see* § 1007.7.1 above). In addition, any damages for administrative or litigation costs may only be awarded under Code § 7430 (and administrative costs may only be awarded to the extent incurred on or after the filing date of the bankruptcy case).[108] Thus, after July 22, 1998, any costs or fees incurred with respect to such violations will only be recoverable in connection with an action under Bankruptcy Code section 362(h) if the qualification requirements under Code § 7430 are satisfied (*see* § 1007.7.4 below). In contrast, as discussed at § 1007.7.1, certain court costs may be recoverable in a damage action under Code § 7433 without regard to Code § 7430.

In addition to actual damages,[109] there is a possibility that a debtor could recover punitive damages under Bankruptcy Code section 362(h) if the debtor can show that the IRS engaged in "egregious" and "intentional misconduct." As discussed at § 1005.1.1, although the general abrogation of sovereign immunity under Bankruptcy Code section 106(a) prohibits the imposition of punitive damages against any governmental unit,[110] it is unclear whether such prohibition applies if there is an independent basis under Bankruptcy Code section 106(b) or (c) for a waiver of sovereign immunity.[111]

It should be noted that a number of courts have held that a damage action under Bankruptcy Code section 362(h) can be brought by a creditor, inasmuch as the statute is not restricted to an injured "debtor" and the purpose behind the automatic stay is to protect creditors from unequal treatment.[112] However, the Ninth Circuit (in an

---

[108] Code § 7433(e)(2)(B), discussed at § 1007.7.1 above.

[109] *See, e.g., Aiello v. Providian Financial Corp.*, 239 F.3d 876 (7th Cir. 2001) (damages for emotional injury not recoverable where no financial loss, but "might" be permitted to "top off" redress of financial injury); *United States v. Harchar*, 331 B.R. 720 (N.D. Ohio 2005) (damages for emotional distress not recoverable; considers split of authority among the Circuit Courts of Appeal); *Holden v. United States (In re Holden)*, 226 B.R. 809 (Bankr. D. Vt. 1998) (permitted individual debtor to submit evidence of mental anguish and emotional distress).

[110] *See, e.g., Flynn v. IRS (In re Flynn)*, 1995 U.S. Dist. LEXIS 5136 (S.D. Ga. 1995), *rev'g in part*, 169 B.R. 1007 (Bankr. S.D. Ga. 1994). *See also United States v. Lile (In re Lile)*, 95-1 U.S.T.C. ¶ 50,031 (5th Cir. 1994) (debtor's counsel conceded prohibition), *rev'g in* part, 161 B.R. 788 (S.D. 1993).

[111] For cases pre-dating the 1994 amendments to Bankruptcy Code section 106, *see, e.g.*, lower court decisions cited *supra* note 110 (granting punitive damages, but reversed following 1994 amendments); *Davis v. IRS*, 136 B.R. 414 (E.D. Va. 1992) (punitive damages denied; discussed standard and cites examples); *In re McPeck* (Bankr. D. Minn.), *supra* note 104 (punitive damages denied). *See also Herbert v. United States (In re Herbert)*, 98-1 U.S.T.C. ¶ 50,548 (Bankr. 9th Cir. 1998) (punitive damages denied).

[112] *Homer Natl. Bank v. Namie*, 96 B.R. 652 (W.D. La. 1989). *See also City of Farmers Branch v. Pointer (In re Pointer)*, 952 F.2d 82 (5th Cir. 1992) (discussing cases), *reh'g denied*, 1992 U.S. App. LEXIS 2724, *cert. denied*, 112 S. Ct. 3035 (1992); *McRoberts v. S.I.V.I. (In re Bequette)*, 184 B.R. 327 (Bankr. S.D. Ill. 1995) ("It is generally accepted that the remedy of § 362(h) extends to creditors as well as debtors who have sustained injuries from a violation of the stay").

"unpublished" decision) has held that, although deriving an "incidental" benefit from the automatic stay, creditors do not have standing under the Bankruptcy Code to bring an action under Bankruptcy Code section 362(h).[113]

### § 1007.7.4 Code § 7430: Recovering Costs

In general, Code § 7430 allows a taxpayer to recover reasonable costs (including reasonable attorneys' fees) with respect to any administrative or court proceeding in connection with the determination or collection of taxes if the taxpayer was the prevailing party. As discussed below, several interpretational issues are posed by this provision, and in many cases the qualification requirements (in particular, those embodied within the statutory definition of a "prevailing party") may be difficult to satisfy.

Significantly, with respect to any proceedings against the IRS for violations of the automatic stay (or the postdischarge injunction) after July 22, 1998, in connection with the collection of tax, Code § 7430 is the exclusive means by which a debtor may seek to recover certain costs (including attorneys' fees). Any such proceeding and any related action under Code § 7430 must be brought in the bankruptcy court.[114]

**Preliminary considerations.** Before undertaking a more general discussion of the qualification requirements of Code § 7430, two points bear special mention. The first is that Code § 7430 only applies to corporations that, at the time the initial proceeding against the IRS is commenced, do not have a net worth in excess of $7 million and do not have more than 500 employees. This condition is discussed further below.

The second focuses on the definition of an "administrative" or "court" proceeding. Somewhat surprisingly, the regulations applicable under Code § 7430 generally exclude from the definition of an "administrative" proceeding any proceeding in connection with collection actions, including proceedings under Code § 7433.[115] So applied, the only costs and fees that would likely be recovered under Code § 7430 in connection with a damage action for stay violations would be those incurred by the debtor in connection with a court proceeding. Such regulations, however, pre-dated the enactment of Code § 7433(e). The new regulations applicable to damage actions under Code § 7433(e) (which were issued in March 2003, but carry a July 22, 1998, effective date) confirm that an "administrative proceeding" includes the pursuit of an administrative claim for damages under Code § 7433(e) or Bankruptcy Code section 362(h).[116]

---

113 *Associated Fin. Serv. Co. of Idaho, Inc. v. First Fed. Savings and Loan Assn. (In re Franck)*, 1994 U.S. App. LEXIS 5461 (9th Cir.); *see also Barnett Bank of Southeast Georgia, N.A. v. Trust Co. Bank of Southeast Georgia, N.A. (In re Ring), supra* note 96 (although holding that the bank lacked standing under Bankruptcy Code section 362(h), the court stated that the bank would have standing to initiate civil contempt proceedings for the stay violation and seek compensation for its damages and, although citing contrary Circuit Court authority, to void the violative action).

114 *See* Code § 7433(e), discussed at § 1007.7.1 above.

115 Reg. § 301.7430-3(a), (b).

116 *See* Reg. § 301.7430-8(c).

The term "court proceeding" also may not be all that one would expect. In particular, in light of the enactment of Code § 7433(e)—which expressly subjects to Code § 7430 any award of costs or fees in connection with a bankruptcy court action for damages for certain IRS stay violations—one would expect that an action in the bankruptcy court would constitute a "court proceeding" within the meaning of Code § 7430. Nevertheless, under the state of the law as of the time of the enactment of Code § 7433(e), this was not—and may still not be—entirely clear.

Code § 7430(c)(6) defines a "court proceeding" as "any civil proceeding brought in a court of the United States (including the Tax Court and the United States Claims Court)." Interpreting the phrase "court of the United States" to mean an Article III court, the Eleventh Circuit, in a 1989 decision in *In re Brickell Investment Corp.*,[117] held that a bankruptcy court was not a court of the United States for purposes of Code § 7430. However, most other courts that considered the issue (including the Fourth and Ninth Circuits) reached the contrary conclusion.[118] These courts generally reasoned that bankruptcy courts are "units of the district court" and thus, like the district court, should be "courts" of the United States, and that the inclusion of the Tax Court evidences an intent to enlarge the scope of the statute beyond Article III courts.[119] Still more courts applied Code § 7430 without considering the jurisdictional issue.[120]

Although holding as it did, the Eleventh Circuit suggested two possible means by which an action in the bankruptcy court to recover costs might be effectively brought within the scope of Code § 7430. Viewing a request for damages under Code § 7430 as a proceeding "related to" the bankruptcy case (but not a "core" proceeding, *see* § 1013.2 below), the Eleventh Circuit stated that the bankruptcy court could submit proposed findings of fact and conclusions of law to the district court, and that the district court (which is an Article III court) could then award the fees. Or, alternatively, the bankruptcy court could, with the consent of both parties, hear and decide the issue. Acting on its own advice, the Eleventh Circuit remanded the case to

---

[117] *Supra* note 63.

[118] *See, e.g., United States v. Yochum (In re Yochum)*, 89 F.3d 661, 96-2 U.S.T.C. ¶ 50,390 (9th Cir. 1996) (Ninth Circuit; listed six reasons in support of its holding), *aff'g*, 156 B.R. 816 (D. Nev. 1993); *Grewe v. United States (In re Grewe)*, 4 F.3d 299, 93-2 U.S.T.C. ¶ 50,535 (4th Cir. 1993), *cert. denied*, 114 S. Ct. 1056 (1994); and, *e.g., Range v. United States*, 245 B.R. 266, 99-1 U.S.T.C. ¶ 50,457 (S.D. Tex. 1999); *In re Germaine*, 152 B.R. 619, 93-2 U.S.T.C. ¶ 50,372 (Bankr. 9th Cir. 1993); *Abernathy v. United States (In re Abernathy)*, 150 B.R. 688, 694, 93-1 U.S.T.C. ¶ 50,108 (Bankr. N.D. Ill. 1993); *In re Chambers*, 140 B.R. 233, 92-1 U.S.T.C. ¶ 50,183 (N.D. Ill. 1992), *recons. denied*, 92-1 U.S.T.C. ¶ 50,300; *Kreidle v. Department of Treasury (In re Kreidle)*, 145 B.R. 1007, 92-2 U.S.T.C. ¶ 50,449 (Bankr. D. Colo. 1992) (collecting cases).

[119] *See* 28 U.S.C. § 151 ("Designation of Bankruptcy Courts"). *Cf. O'Connor v. United States Dept. of Energy*, 942 F.2d 771 (10th Cir. 1991) (nontax case holding that a bankruptcy court could award costs under the Equal Access to Justice Act based, in relevant part, on the fact that the Act simply refers to "a court" or "any court" in discussing the types of courts having jurisdiction, as opposed to the phrase "court of the United States").

[120] For a collection of cases, *see In re Brickell Investment Corp., supra* note 63, at 699 n.2; *see also In re M.L. Hill*, 71 B.R. 517, 87-1 U.S.T.C. ¶ 9297 (Bankr. D. Colo. 1987); *In re McPeck, supra* note 104. *Consider also United States v. McPeck*, 910 F.2d 509, 90-2 U.S.T.C. ¶ 50,593 (8th Cir. 1990) (remanded case to consider Code § 7430; observed that, whereas Bankruptcy Code section 362(h) damages would be subject to setoff against IRS claim, amounts recovered under Code § 7430 would not).

the district court with instructions to either (i) return the case to the bankruptcy court for the submission of findings of facts and conclusions of law to the district court (which the district court subsequently did[121]), or (ii) allow the debtors to renew their application for fees directly with the district court. If the Eleventh Circuit is correct, a bankruptcy court should be able to include a "savings" clause in any decision awarding costs under Code § 7430 which would treat its decision as a submission of proposed findings of fact and conclusions of law in the event it was held to lack the requisite jurisdiction. At least one district court treated a bankruptcy court decision as reflecting proposed findings even absent a savings clause.[122] Nevertheless, it is difficult to see how the submission of proposed findings relating solely to the award of costs technically solves the jurisdictional issue, assuming there is one. Rather, it would also seem necessary to submit for consideration by the district court the bankruptcy court's original determination with respect to which costs are sought (namely, the determination that the stay was violated).

**Qualification requirements.** A taxpayer may be awarded reasonable costs under Code § 7430 only if:

(1) the administrative or court proceeding is "in connection with the determination or collection of tax";
(2) the taxpayer is the "prevailing party"; and
(3) all available administrative remedies have been exhausted.

An application for costs in connection with a court proceeding (including any earlier administrative proceeding) must be submitted to the court within 30 days of a final judgment in the proceeding.[123]

Most courts have concluded with little difficulty that an action against the IRS for violating the automatic stay is a proceeding "in connection with the determination or collection of tax" and, thus, within the basic scope of Code § 7430.[124]

---

[121] *See In re Brickell Investment Corp.*, 94-1 U.S.T.C. ¶ 50,276 (Bankr. S.D. Fla. 1993) (subsequent bankruptcy court decision submitting findings of fact and conclusions of law to the district court), and 171 B.R. 149, 94-1 U.S.T.C. ¶ 50,277 (S.D. Fla. 1994) (subsequent district court decision adopting findings and conclusions).

[122] *See, e.g., United States v. Yochum (In re Yochum)*, *supra* note 118 (district court decision subsequently affirmed by Ninth Circuit on grounds that a bankruptcy court can award damages under Code § 7430).

[123] *See* Code § 7430(c)(4)(A)(ii) and first sentence of 28 U.S.C. § 2412(d)(1)(B) (as in effect on October 22, 1986) (also describes contents of application). In addition, the Taxpayer Relief Act of 1997 imposed certain time limitations on any application made with the IRS (as opposed to a court) for reimbursement of costs relating to an administrative proceeding. Effective for administrative proceedings commenced after August 5, 1997, any such application must be filed before the 91st day after the IRS mailed its final decision as to the determination of tax liability. Code § 7430(b)(4); *see also* discussion at § 1007.7.1 above.

[124] Courts so holding include the Fourth, Eighth, Ninth, and Tenth Circuits. *See, e.g., Grewe v. United States (In re Grewe)* (4th Cir.), *supra* note 118; *United States v. McPeck* (8th Cir.), *supra* note 120; *United States v. Arkison (In re Cascade Roads, Inc.)*, 34 F.3d 756, 767-769 (9th Cir. 1994); *In re Shafer*, 148 B.R. 617 (D. Kan. 1992), *citing Graham v. United States (In re Graham)*, 981 F.2d 1135, 93-1 U.S.T.C. ¶ 50,255 (10th Cir. 1992); *In re Hanson*, 148 B.R. 584 (Bankr. E.D. Mo. 1992); *In re Kiker*, *supra* note 98 (involving violation of postdischarge injunction). This conclusion is also generally implicit in Congress's enact-

*Prevailing Party.* To be considered the "prevailing party," a taxpayer generally must demonstrate that it (1) has substantially prevailed with respect to the amount in controversy or the most significant issue (or set of issues) presented,[125] and (2) satisfies the criteria of 28 U.S.C. § 2412(d)(2)(B) (as in effect on October 22, 1986), which generally sets forth certain net worth and size requirements.[126] In addition, the IRS's position in the proceeding must not be substantially justified.[127] As discussed below, these requirements (other than the net worth and size requirements) may be disregarded in connection with certain damage actions under Code § 7433 or Bankruptcy Code section 362(h), and in connection with certain tax disputes where a qualified offer was made.

As a result of the net worth and size requirements, a corporation, partnership, trust or other organization (other than certain limited types of organizations) that has a net worth in excess of $7 million based on the acquisition cost of its assets or more than 500 employees cannot be a "prevailing party" and thus cannot recover its costs and attorneys' fees under Code § 7430.[128] Although the measurement date for this purpose is generally the inception of any administrative proceeding,[129] in the case of an action for violation of the automatic stay (where there is no administrative proceeding) it appears that the measurement date would be the commencement of the court proceeding.

The IRS has, on occasion, argued that a bankruptcy estate is not eligible to be a prevailing party, because it is not a person specifically named in 28 U.S.C. § 2412(d)(2)(B) (as in effect on October 22, 1986), and cannot be said to be an "organization." The Eleventh Circuit, in *In re Brickell Investment Corp.*,[130] rejected this position at least as it relates to debtor corporations in Chapter 11 reorganizations, on the grounds that corporations are continuing entities that existed and operated before

(Footnote Continued)

ment of Code § 7433(e) to address willful violations by the IRS of the automatic stay or postdischarge injunction in connection with the collection of tax from the debtor.

However, in *Pinkstaff v. United States (In re Pinkstaff)*, *supra* note 104, the Ninth Circuit upheld the award of attorneys' fees under the Equal Access to Justice Act (which does not apply to court proceedings governed by Code § 7430) for stay violations by the IRS, without discussing Code § 7430. *See also In re Sneller*, 153 B.R. 343 (Bankr. M.D. Ala. 1993) (Equal Access to Justice Act controlled where IRS violated postdischarge injunction), and 1993 Bankr. LEXIS 475 (1993) (costs/fees proceeding).

[125] *See, e.g., Goettee v. Commissioner*, 124 T.C. No. 17 (2005).

[126] Code § 7430(c)(4)(A), (D).

[127] Code § 7430(c)(4)(B).

[128] Code § 7430(c)(4)(A)(ii) and 28 U.S.C. § 2412(d)(2)(B) (as in effect on October 22, 1986) (contains exception for tax-exempt organizations and certain cooperatives); Reg. § 301.7430-5(f)(2); H.R. Rep. No. 1418, 96th Cong., 2d Sess. 15 (1980) (assets to be valued at acquisition cost); *Swanson v. Comm.*, 106 T.C. 76 (1996) (so holding). For a discussion of the case law relating to the computation of net worth, *see* Raby and Raby, "Net Worth" and the Shifting Burden of Proof, 2000 TNT 126-44 (June 29, 2000).

[129] *See* Reg. § 301.7430-5(f)(2) and -3(c), which provides that such date is the earlier of the issuance of a final notice of decision by IRS Appeals or a statutory notice of deficiency; *see also* flush language of Code § 7430(c)(2) (as amended by the 1998 Reform Act, effective for costs incurred after December 6, 1998), which moves such date, if earlier, to the date the first letter of proposed deficiency is sent which allows for administrative review.

[130] *Supra* note 63.

the bankruptcy and will continue to operate after. The Eleventh Circuit distinguished its earlier decision in *In re Davis*,[131] wherein it held that a Chapter 7 bankruptcy estate was not an "organization" and, thus, not an eligible "party" within the meaning of that section.

As indicated above, a taxpayer that otherwise qualifies as a prevailing party will nevertheless not be treated as a prevailing party if the IRS's position in the proceeding is substantially justified (unless one of the two special exceptions discussed below apply). With respect to proceedings commenced on or before July 30, 1996, it was the taxpayer's burden to establish that the IRS's position was "not substantially justified."[132] However, with respect to proceedings commenced after July 30, 1996, the burden has been switched such that an otherwise qualifying taxpayer will be entitled to costs unless the IRS establishes that its position was "substantially justified."[133] The Supreme Court has held, within the context of the Equal Access to Justice Act (from which Code § 7430 is derived), that the term "substantially justified" means:

> "justified in substance or in the main"-that is, justified to a degree that could satisfy a reasonable person. That is no different from the "reasonable basis both in law and fact" formulation adopted . . . by the vast majority of . . . Courts of Appeals that have addressed this issue. To be "substantially justified" means, of course, more than merely undeserving of sanctions for frivolousness . . . [134]

In making this determination with respect to costs incurred after December 6, 1998, the deciding court is directed to take into account whether the United States has lost in courts of appeal for other circuits on substantially similar issues.[135]

Under Code § 7430, the focus of this inquiry is the IRS's position "in the proceeding"—in this case, the court proceeding in which the IRS's actions are found to violate the automatic stay.[136] The courts are split as to whether the IRS's position thus encompasses the IRS's prelitigation conduct, such as the IRS's actual act of

---

131 *Gower v. Farmers Home Admin.* (*In re Davis*), 899 F.2d 1136 (11th Cir. 1990), *reh'g denied, en banc,* 908 F.2d 980 (1990), *cert. denied,* 111 S. Ct. 510 (1990). It is unclear whether in a liquidation context the Eleventh Circuit would treat the estate of a corporate debtor differently than the estate of an individual debtor (as was at issue in *In re Davis*).

132 *See* former Code § 7430(c)(4)(A)(i), (ii) (as in effect prior to amendment by the Taxpayer Bill of Rights 2). *See also In re McPeck, supra* note 104 (debtor sought to recover costs of bringing damage action under Bankruptcy Code section 362(h); court held that debtor did not "substantially prevail" because, although debtor prevailed on the issue of attorneys' fees, the IRS prevailed on the issues of other actual damages and punitive damages).

133 Code § 7430(c)(4)(B).

134 *Pierce v. Underwood*, 487 U.S. 552, 565-566 (1988) (citations omitted); *see also INS v. Jean*, 496 U.S. 154, 158 n.6 (1990) (quoting *Underwood*); *De Alto v. United States*, 42 Fed. Cl. 619, 99-1 U.S.T.C. ¶ 50,133 (1999) (applying quoted definition within the context of Code § 7430).

135 Code § 7430(c)(4)(B)(iii) (as amended by the 1998 Reform Act). *See also Foster v. United States*, 249 F.3d 1275, 2001-1 U.S.T.C. ¶ 50,392 (11th Cir. 2001) (IRS was not substantially justified in its position where "the law in this circuit was clear," even though the IRS had been successful in other circuits).

136 *See* Code § 7430(c)(7).

violating the stay.[137] This difference can be critical in cases where the IRS concedes the violation, since it is difficult to see how the IRS's "in-court" concession is not (in and of itself) substantially justified.[138]

Accordingly, the inquiry, in the case of a violation of the automatic stay, would appear to be whether the IRS knew of the stay and was substantially justified in proceeding despite such knowledge (assuming either that prelitigation conduct is relevant or the IRS denies any violation in the court proceeding). This should be contrasted with the definition of "willful" in Bankruptcy Code section 362(h), which generally ignores the reason for the IRS's action, and the "good faith" standard generally employed in contempt proceedings.

There are two special exceptions to the foregoing definition of a "prevailing party," only one of which is potentially applicable to damage actions under Code § 7433(e) or Bankruptcy Code section 362(h). Where applicable, the taxpayer will be considered the prevailing party provided only that it satisfies criteria of 28 U.S.C. § 2412(d)(2)(B) (as in effect on October 22, 1986) (namely, the net worth and size requirements) and timely files its application for costs. Thus, the taxpayer would not have to establish that it substantially prevailed, and the IRS would not have the chance to show that its position was substantially justified.

Unfortunately, the first exception, which is in the general regulations under Code § 7433, does not apply with respect to costs relating to damage actions under Code § 7433(e) or Bankruptcy Code section 362(h).[139] Under the general exception, substantial justification is no excuse where the IRS denies administrative relief on the grounds that no compensable violation occurred and thereafter loses in court.[140]

The second exception was added by the 1998 Reform Act, and applies to costs incurred by a taxpayer after December 6, 1998, where the amount of the taxpayer's tax liability is in dispute, the taxpayer previously made a "qualified offer" to settle the dispute which was rejected, *and* the court ultimately decides the dispute on its merits for an amount less than the liability which would have been determined had the IRS accepted the offer.[141]

---

[137] *Compare Lennox v. Commissioner*, 998 F.2d 244, 93-2 U.S.T.C. ¶ 50,444 (5th Cir. 1993) (determination of the "reasonableness of [the IRS's] position must include a review of the actions leading to its establishment"); *Kaufman v. Egger*, 758 F.2d 1, 85-1 U.S.T.C. ¶ 9278 (1st Cir. 1985) (included prelitigation conduct); *In re Abernathy, supra* note 118; *and In re Rasbury*, 93-1 U.S.T.C. ¶ 50,351 (N.D. Ala.), *aff'd*, 24 F.3d 159 (11th Cir. 1994); *with In re Graham, supra* note 124, at 1139; *Ewing and Thomas, P.A. v. Heye*, 803 F.2d 613, 86-2 U.S.T.C. ¶ 9768 (11th Cir. 1986) (restricted to in-court litigation position); *Huffman v. Commissioner*, 61 T.C.M. 2289, Dec. 47,266(M), T.C. Memo. 1991-144 (concluded that position of the United States in a court proceeding is generally evidenced by the answer filed by the District Counsel).

[138] *See, e.g., Unroe v. United States (In re Unroe)*, 144 B.R. 85, 92-2 U.S.T.C. ¶ 50,356 (Bankr. S.D. Ind. 1992) (IRS position was "substantially justified" where there were no prior administrative proceedings and, from the time the violation proceeding was commenced, the IRS admitted its errors, promptly returned the withheld refund, and ceased further collection efforts); *Baird v. United States (In re Baird)*, 2005-1 U.S.T.C. ¶ 50,173 (Bankr. M.D. Ala. 2004); *In re Kiker, supra* note 98.

[139] *Compare* new Reg. § 301.7433-2(h)(1) *with* Reg. § 301.7433-1(h).

[140] Reg. § 301.7433-1(h).

[141] Code § 7430(c)(4). The requirements for a "qualified offer" are set forth in Code § 7430(g) and Reg. § 301.7430-7 (effective for qualified offers after December 24, 2003), T.D. 9106. *See also* Temp. Reg.

*Exhaustion of Administrative Remedies.* Prior to the issuance of the new Code §7433(e) regulations and the related regulations under Code §7430, the IRS had instituted, on a test basis, administrative procedures for the expedited resolution of tax-related disputes in bankruptcy cases (including automatic stay violations) and the handling of damage claims for violations of the automatic stay and postdischarge injunction. These procedures are discussed further at §§1007.7.6 and 1010.5 below. Presumably, a debtor that complied with these procedures (to the extent available) would be considered to have exhausted all available administrative remedies, despite the retroactive effective date of the new regulations and the absence of any mention of these procedures in the regulations. These procedures are consistent with, but more expeditious than, the procedures in the new Code §7433(e) regulations.

The new procedures require that (1) the taxpayer submit a written claim for relief to the Chief of the "Local Insolvency Unit" for the judicial district in which the debtor's bankruptcy case is pending, describing in reasonable detail (including appropriate documentation, as specified in the regulations) the violation, the injuries sustained and the dollar amount claimed (including damages reasonably foreseeable that have not yet occurred), and (2) the IRS has either denied the claim for relief in writing or failed to act within six months.[142] Traditionally, although no longer the case, most bankruptcy courts took a practical approach toward the exhaustion of administrative remedies in the case of violations of the automatic stay. In many cases, a phone call or letter to the IRS sufficed.[143] Futile efforts, however, were not required, particularly in the presence of continued violations.[144] Where the stay violation

(Footnote Continued)

§301.7430-7T (effective for qualified offers after January 3, 2001), and before December 25, 2003, the effective date of the final regulations, T.D. 8922. *See also* Raby and Raby, Qualified Offers and Settlement of Tax Controversies, 113 Tax Notes 455 (Oct. 30, 2006); *Gladden v. Commissioner*, 120 T.C. No. 16 (2003) (a settlement entered into following a series of judicial determinations and appeals did not render the "qualified offer" exception inapplicable). Prior to formulating the Temporary Regulations, the IRS had issued a notice raising certain interpretational questions and seeking comment. *See* IRS Notice 98-55, 1998-2 C.B. 644. Also, on an interim basis, the IRS had issued instructions to its attorneys with respect to the application of this exception. *See* IRS Chief Counsel Notice, dated February 14, 2000 (and effective until February 14, 2001), *reprinted at* 2000 TNT 32-21, which superceded IRS Chief Counsel Notice, dated August 18, 1999, *reprinted at* 1999 TNT 246-19, which expired on February 14, 2000.

[142] *See* Reg. §§301.7433-2(e) (specifying contents of claim) and 301.7430-8(e). *See also* discussion at §1007.7.1 above.

[143] *See, e.g., United States v. Torres (In re Torres)*, 309 B.R. 643, 2004-2 U.S.T.C. ¶50,379 (Bankr. 1st Cir. 2004) (appealed on other issues; in absence of specific regulations, "the Debtors were left to their own designs"), *rev'g in part* 2002-1 U.S.T.C. ¶50,268 (Bankr. D. P.R. 2002); *In re Germaine* (Bankr. 9th Cir.), *supra* note 118; *Abernathy v. United States (In re Abernathy)*, *supra* note 118; *In re Jones*, 164 B.R. 543, 551 (1994). *But see, e.g., Grewe v. United States (In re Grewe)* (4th Cir.), *supra* note 118 (denied litigation costs where debtor did not pursue administrative remedies to have IRS tax lien removed before seeking bankruptcy court action for violation of postdischarge injunction).

[144] *See, e.g., In re Germaine* (Bankr. 9th Cir.), *supra* note 118, at 629 (involved continued violations; "The assertion by the IRS that the matter 'could well have been avoided by a timely phone call' in the face of these facts ignores reality"); *United States v. Yochum (In re Yochum)*, *supra* note 118 (bankruptcy court recognized the then absence of any administrative remedy in the bankruptcy context; also, IRS did not provide debtor with requisite notice or affirmatively offer any procedural remedies to the debtor).

involved the issuance of a Notice of Levy for which an administrative hearing is available under Code §6330(b), the failure to request a hearing has precluded recovery due to the failure to exhaust administrative remedies.[145]

**Recoverable costs.** Recoverable costs generally include (i) reasonable court costs, (ii) reasonable expenses of expert witnesses (although limited in compensation to the highest rate payable by the United States for expert witnesses), (iii) reasonable costs of any study, analysis or other report or project necessary for the preparation of the party's case, and (iv) reasonable attorneys' fees (subject to a maximum rate).[146]

Congress in 1996 and again in 1998 increased the maximum reimbursable rate for attorneys' fees.[147] For services rendered after December 6, 1998, the maximum hourly rate is $125/hour with mandatory cost of living increases (resulting in an hourly rate of $150/hour as of 2004) and discretionary increases for special factors, such as the limited availability of qualified attorneys for such proceeding, the difficulty of the issues present in the case, or the local availability of tax expertise (but not tax expertise in and of itself).[148] For services rendered prior to such date in proceedings commenced after July 30, 1996, the base rate is $110/hour with mandatory cost of living increases and the last two special factors do not necessarily apply.[149] Prior to such time, the base rate was $75/hour but with discretionary (rather than mandatory) increases for cost of living.

Unfortunately, in the event the taxpayer has to await recovery of its costs pending an unsuccessful appeal by the government of such award, the taxpayer is not entitled to recover postjudgment interest for the delayed payment.[150]

---

[145] *In re Parker*, 279 B.R. 596 (Bankr. S.D. Ala. 2002).

[146] *See* Code §§7430(c)(1) (definition of "reasonable litigation costs"), 7430(c)(2) (definition of "reasonable administrative costs").

[147] "Attorneys' fees" for this purpose include fees for the comparable services of any individual (whether or not an attorney) who is authorized to practice before the Tax Court or before the Internal Revenue Service. *See Cozean v. Commissioner*, 109 T.C. 227 (1997); Code §7430(c)(3)(A) (as amended by the 1998 Reform Act; effective for costs incurred after December 6, 1998, but effectively codifying prior law); *Ragan v. Commissioner*, 135 F.3d 329, 98-1 U.S.T.C. ¶50,209 (5th Cir. 1998), *cert. denied*, 119 S. Ct. 176 (1998) (accountant fees were recoverable as reasonable litigation costs, and not subject to the cap on attorney fees, to the extent such fees were for the preparation of an analysis or report that aided in taxpayer's defense).

[148] Code §7430(c)(1)(B)(iii) (as amended by the 1998 Reform Act). *See, e.g., United States v. Scheingold*, 293 F. Supp. 2d 447, 2004-1 U.S.T.C. ¶50,116 (D. N.J. 2004) (allowing higher rate for particular tax expertise; collecting cases); *United States v. Guess*, 425 F. Supp.2d 1143 (S.D. Cal. 2006); and *infra* note 149.

[149] With respect to what traditionally constituted a "special factor," *see, e.g., IRS v. In re Brickell Investment Corp.*, 1995 U.S. Dist. LEXIS 8926 (S.D. Fla. 1995) (allowed $150/hour to bankruptcy counsel), and (S.D. Fla. June 11, 1997) (same), *reprinted at* 97 TNT 134-83; *Moulton v. United States (In re Moulton)*, 195 B.R. 954 (Bankr. M.D. Fla. 1996) (government's "totally indefensible conduct" was special factor justifying $150/hour, double the then statutory rate), *aff'd*, 78 A.F.T.R.2d (RIA) 5554 (M.D. Fla. 1996). For a very narrow reading of what "special factor" means, *see Estate of Cervin v. Commissioner*, 2000 U.S. App. LEXIS 807 (5th Cir. 2000) (involving pre-12/98 services; requires attorney to have special non-legal or technical abilities).

[150] *IRS v. Brickell Investment Corp. (In re Brickell Investment Corp.)*, 1996 U.S. Dist. LEXIS 18973 (S.D. Fla. 1996).

### § 1007.7.5 The Equal Access to Justice Act

The Equal Access to Justice Act (or EAJ) (28 U.S.C. § 2412) is the predecessor of Code § 7430, and continues to apply to most civil actions against the United States other than those to which Code § 7430 applies, *i.e.*, other than administrative or court proceedings in connection with the determination or collection of tax.[151] Thus, the EAJ has limited applicability to actions involving the IRS. Nevertheless, the EAJ has been applied against the IRS where, for example, the proceeding was not considered to be in connection with the determination or collection of tax.[152] In addition, the EAJ could be implicated in a tax-related proceeding in the bankruptcy court in the event that (i) a bankruptcy court proceeding is not a proceeding for which costs are permitted under Code § 7430 but is a proceeding for which costs are permitted under the EAJ, and (ii) the proceeding is one to which Code § 7433(e) does not apply, such as a petition for damages relating to a violation of the automatic stay that occurred on or before July 22, 1998.

Although similar in form and approach, there are nevertheless meaningful differences between Code § 7430 (discussed in the preceding section) and the EAJ. A complete discussion of the EAJ is beyond the scope of this volume. However, the following provides a brief contrast of some of the similarities and differences between the two statutes.

(1) *Applicable Court Proceedings.* As discussed in the preceding section, the Eleventh Circuit has held that a bankruptcy court proceeding is not within the type of courts permitted to award costs under Code § 7430 (absent the consent of both parties). The same jurisdictional issue arises under the EAJ. Although 28 U.S.C. § 2412(a)(1) refers to "any court" rather than a "court of the United States" (as under Code § 7430), the cases similarly are divided as to whether bankruptcy courts are permitted to award costs under such statute. Here again, the Eleventh Circuit has held that they are not (and has suggested the possibility of the bankruptcy court submitting proposed findings of fact and conclusions of law to the district court, or of obtaining the consent of the parties).[153] In contrast, the Tenth Circuit has held that bankruptcy courts are permitted.[154]

---

[151] *See* 28 U.S.C. § 2412(e) (types of proceeding to which Code § 7430 applies is determined without regard to the limitations in Code § 7430(b) and Code § 7430(f); the reference to Code § 7430(f) appears to be to such section as it existed when Code § 7430 was originally enacted in 1982; later deleted, Code § 7430(f) initially provided that Code § 7430 would not apply to proceedings commenced after December 31, 1985).

[152] *See supra* note 124. In such instance, both Code § 7433(e) (which applies only to violations of the automatic stay and postdischarge injunction "in connection with any collection of Federal tax") and Code § 7430 would be inapplicable.

[153] *See In re Davis*, 899 F.2d 1136 (11th Cir.), *reh'g denied, en banc*, 908 F.2d 980, *cert. denied*, 111 S. Ct. 510 (1990); and *supra* discussion accompanying notes 117-122.

[154] *See O'Connor v. United States Dept. of Energy*, *supra* note 119. *Consider also In re Esmond*, 752 F.2d 1106 (5th Cir. 1985) (never questioned jurisdiction of bankruptcy court when it remanded case for further consideration).

(2) *Net Worth Requirement and Proper "Party."* Both statutes generally do not apply to corporations and other organizations that, at the time the civil action is commenced, have a net worth in excess of $7 million based on acquisition cost of assets or more than 500 employees.[155] In fact, Code §7430(c)(4)(A)(ii) references for this purpose the 1986 version of the EAJ. Due to these overlapping definitions, the issue as to whether, or in what circumstances, a bankruptcy estate is an eligible "party" to recover costs is the same under both statutes.

(3) *Other Qualifications for Prevailing Party.* Under Code §7430, the taxpayer is only considered a prevailing party if (i) it can establish that it substantially prevailed with respect to the amount in controversy or the most significant issue (or set of issues) presented, and (ii) the IRS's position in the proceeding is not substantially justified. The burden of proof on the latter issue is on the taxpayer for proceedings commenced on or before July 30, 1996, and on the IRS for proceedings commenced thereafter. The latter change brought the Code §7430 concept of a "prevailing" party in closer parity with the EAJ, but the two are not yet identical. For example, the EAJ has no formal requirement that the taxpayer (or equivalent person) have "substantially" prevailed (although such a concept seems implicit in many courts' holdings as to what it means to prevail). In addition, under the EAJ, the court has the right not to award costs where, for example, "special circumstances make an award unjust."[156] Also potentially different is the focus of the determination of whether the government's position is substantially justified. Under Code §7430, the courts are split as to whether the IRS's position thus encompasses the IRS's prelitigation conduct, such as the IRS's actual act of violating the stay.[157] In contrast, under the EAJ, it is clear that the act upon which the proceeding is based (*i.e.*, the actual stay violation) is taken into account,[158] although the concept of prevailing party may require that the government have maintained its position at least until the threat of litigation.[159]

(4) *Reimbursable Rate for Attorneys' Fees.* Both statutes now provide for a maximum base hourly rate for attorneys' fees of $125/hour. However, Code §7430 provides for mandatory cost-of-living adjustments, whereas the EAJ only has discretionary adjustments. In both cases, the rate can be increased for certain special factors. On the other hand, the $125/hour rate

---

155 *See* Code §7430(c)(4)(A)(ii) and 28 U.S.C. §2412(d)(2)(B) (contains exception for tax-exempt organizations and certain other organizations).

156 28 U.S.C. §2412(d)(3).

157 *See supra* discussion accompanying notes 137-138.

158 *See* 28 U.S.C. §2412(d)(2)(D), which defines "position of the United States" to mean, "in addition to the position taken by the United States in the civil action, the action or failure to act by the agency upon which the civil action is based."

159 *See, e.g., Wilderness Soc. v. Babbitt*, 5 F.3d 383 (9th Cir. 1993) (must demonstrate that the lawsuit was a material factor or played a catalytic role in bringing about desired outcome); *Citizens Coalition for Block Grant Compliance, Inc. v. City of Euclid*, 717 F.2d 964 (6th Cir. 1983).

under the EAJ has been in effect since 1996 (increased from its previous rate of $75/hour),[160] whereas such rate only went into effect under Code §7430 in 1998.

(5) *Postjudgment Interest.* Unlike Code §7430, the EAJ specifically authorizes the payment of postjudgment interest with respect to the costs awarded in the event the government unsuccessfully appeals such award.[161]

### §1007.7.6 Administrative Procedures Prior to New Code §7433(e) Regulations

Prior to the issuance of regulations under Code §7433(e) in March 2003, the IRS conducted two pilot programs. In September 1998, the IRS announced the adoption of a new initiative to facilitate the prompt correction of any IRS violations of the bankruptcy laws (such as violations of the automatic stay and postdischarge injunction), and to handle any damage claims arising from such violations.[162] The local "Special Procedures" office of the IRS Collection Division (*i.e.*, the office in the district in which the bankruptcy case is pending) coordinated the handling of violations of the automatic stay and postdischarge injunction.

The procedures implementing this initiative were to be reflected in greater detail in the next version of the IRS Manual, but never were. The initiative called for a pilot program—which remained in effect until the issuance of the regulations under Code §7433(e)—to test new administrative procedures for handling damage claims for IRS violations of the bankruptcy laws, such as claims for damages under Code §7433 or for costs under Code §7340. Under these procedures, debtors could file claims for damages with the local "Special Procedures" office. The claims had to be made in writing and had to include any supporting documentation requested by the IRS. Such claims were to be evaluated and acted upon within 60 days.

It is our understanding that this 60-day process applied only to damage claims for which the IRS violation was undisputed. In this regard, this initiative dovetailed with another test program that the IRS initiated in late 1997 in select cities, which program was intended to expedite the resolution of certain tax-related disputes in bankruptcy cases including automatic stay violation issues and most dischargeability determinations.[163] This earlier program is discussed in greater detail at §1010.5 below. Under such program, the local Special Procedures office, at the debtor's request, undertook an expedited review of the merits of the dispute. The entire review process (including any additional review by Appeals) was generally intended to take no more than 30 workdays for stay violations and no more than 65 workdays for dischargeability determinations. It is our understanding that, although such

---

[160] 28 U.S.C. §2412(d)(2)(A), new rate effective for fees awarded in connection with civil action commenced on or after March 29, 1996.

[161] 28 U.S.C. §2412(f).

[162] Announcement 98-89, 1998-2 C.B. 460. *See also* IRS Manual, Part 1 (Organization, Finance and Management), Chapter 2 (Servicewide Policies and Authorities), §52.4 (8/1/05) (Delegation Order 25-10, delegating and circumscribing authority with respect to such damage actions).

[163] *See* Announcement 97-111, 1997-47 I.R.B. 15.

program called for prompt corrective action to be undertaken by the IRS in the event of a debtor favorable determination, the corrective action envisioned did not include the payment of damages.

### §1007.8 *Tax Court May Abstain From Determination of Stay and Other Bankruptcy Laws*

Questions involving the proper application of the bankruptcy laws may arise within the context of a Tax Court proceeding. For example, the IRS has considered whether the commencement or continuation of a Tax Court proceeding was in violation of the automatic stay and thus invalid (*see* § 1009) and, within the context of a collection due process proceeding, whether a particular debt was discharged (*see* § 1014.3). In such cases, however, the bankruptcy question was considered "relatively straight forward."[164] Where, however, the case presents more complex bankruptcy questions, the Tax Court may refrain from deciding the issue in deference to the expertise and authority of the bankruptcy court, based on considerations of comity and judicial efficiency.[165]

For example, in *Meadows v. Commissioner*,[166] the taxpayer contended that the IRS's collection of tax monies from his wife by placing a nominee lien on their house, which was held solely in the wife's name, and the application of such monies to his taxes violated the automatic stay. Although the Tax Court questioned whether its authority extended to questions of IRS violations of the automatic stay (whether generally, or in a particular case, based on the particular remedy sought), it declined to so determine, instead concluding that it could defer the matter to the bankruptcy court. The Eleventh Circuit agreed, also finding that the taxpayer's contentions raised a number of wrinkles adding to the complexity (including the extent of the taxpayer's interest in the house, where the taxpayer failed to list any interest in the house in his bankruptcy schedules, and a question of laches).

## §1008 TOLLING OF ASSESSMENT AND COLLECTION STATUTE OF LIMITATIONS

Under the Internal Revenue Code, the suspension of the IRS's ability to assess or collect prepetition taxes also results in a tolling of any applicable statute of limitations on assessment and collection.[1] In a bankruptcy case, the statute of limitations on assessment and collection is tolled under Code § 6503(h) for the period during which

---

164 *See Washington v. Commissioner*, 120 T.C. 114, 124-125 (Wells, J., concurring).

165 *See, e.g., Meadows v. Commissioner*, 405 F.3d 909, 2005-1 U.S.T.C. ¶50,274 (11th Cir. 2005) (affirming Tax Court); *Washington v. Commissioner*, 120 T.C. 114, 124-125 (Wells, J., concurring).

166 *Supra* note 165.

1 **§1008** *See, e.g., Franklin v. IRS (In re Franklin)*, 78 B.R. 118, 87-2 U.S.T.C. ¶9550 (Bankr. E.D. Va. 1987) (statute of limitations on assessment was extended as a result of a statutory notice of deficiency mailed shortly before the three-year period was due to expire; subsequently, when the taxpayer filed for bankruptcy prior to the extended period expiring, the statute of limitations was tolled).

the IRS is prohibited by reason of the bankruptcy case from assessing or collecting the tax, plus an additional 60 days for assessments or six months for collections.[2] Thus, the statute of limitations for *collecting* prepetition taxes is generally tolled for the duration of the automatic stay (and for any period during which the IRS is precluded from collecting pursuant to a confirmed Chapter 11 plan, such as where the taxes will be paid over time[3]) and for six months thereafter; and, for bankruptcy cases commenced *before* October 22, 1994, the statute of limitations for *assessing* prepetition taxes is generally tolled for the duration of the automatic stay and for 60 days thereafter.[4] The application of this tolling of the statute of limitations on collection within the context of successive bankruptcies is discussed at § 1008.4 below.

This tolling operates in respect of the applicable statute of limitations as extended by any prepetition waivers, even though the waiver purports to establish a date certain for the expiration of the limitations period.[5] In contrast, the IRS Manual provides that an extension of the statute of limitations executed while the automatic

---

[2] Technically, Code § 6503(b) (discussed at *infra* note 42 and accompanying text), which provides for the tolling of the applicable statute of limitations on collections in non-Bankruptcy Code insolvency proceedings (including bankruptcy proceedings under the Bankruptcy Act), also applies to Bankruptcy Code cases. Presumably, however, Code § 6503(h), which was enacted specifically to deal with Bankruptcy Code cases, overrides Code § 6503(b) to the extent overlapping. *See* IRS Chief Counsel Advice 200522021, March 11, 2005, *reprinted at* 2005 TNT 107-40, discussing the potential continuing role of Code § 6503(b) in individual Chapter 7 bankruptcy cases.

[3] *See, e.g., United States v. Wright*, 57 F.3d 561, 95-2 U.S.T.C. ¶ 50,334 (7th Cir. 1995); *United States v. McCarthy*, 21 F. Supp. 2d 888, 98-1 U.S.T.C. ¶ 50,424 (S.D. Ind. 1998); IRS Chief Counsel Advice 200146058, November 16, 2001, *reprinted at* 2001 TNT 223-68; IRS Chief Counsel Advice 200022010, February 22, 2000, *reprinted at* 2000 TNT 108-66 (also concludes that the IRS's ability to setoff any pending tax payments under the plan against outstanding tax refunds—assuming such ability exists at all, *see* § 1006.1.1.3 above—is insufficient to end the tolling); IRS Chief Counsel Advice 200016017, February 23, 2000, *reprinted at* 2000 TNT 79-35 (same); *cf.* IRS Chief Counsel Advice 200522021, March 11, 2005, *reprinted at* 2005 TNT 107-40 (contrasting the treatment of Chapter 7 and Chapter 11 cases; concludes that the discharge injunction imposed by Bankruptcy Code section 524 exists independently of the bankruptcy case, and not "by reason of the case," and thus does not, in and of itself, operate to extend the statute of limitations under Code § 6503(h)); IRS Chief Counsel Advice 200447036, November 19, 2004, *reprinted at* 1004 TNT 225-26 (reaches similar conclusion, but would apply principles of equitable estoppel to extend the statute of limitations where a debtor obtains a revocation of a prior discharge order; involved an individual debtor in a Chapter 7 case).

[4] *Clark v. Commissioner*, 90 T.C. 68, Dec. 44,528 (1988) (tolling ends when stay is lifted even if IRS does not receive notice); *J.P. Galanis*, 92 T.C. 34, Dec. 45,432 (1989) (holds that Code § 6503(h) controls the suspension of the statute of limitations in bankruptcy cases, other than when the tax is subject to immediate assessment); *see, e.g., Workman v. United States (In re Workman)*, 90-1 U.S.T.C. ¶ 50,197 (Bankr. S.D. W. Va. 1990) (suspension of the collection period during prior bankruptcy and, under Code § 6502(a), during current proceeding brought by debtor to determine the dischargeability of the claimed taxes in the prior bankruptcy and the amount and sufficiency of such taxes); *In re Dakota Indus., Inc.*, 131 B.R. 437 (Bankr. D.S.D. 1991) (suspension of collection period); *Wekell v. United States*, 144 B.R. 503 (W.D. Wash. 1992) (same; rejected argument that collection period only tolled for the time it would have reasonably taken the IRS to petition for relief from the automatic stay), *aff'd*, 1994 U.S. App. LEXIS 324 (9th Cir. 1994).

For a discussion of the duration of the automatic stay with respect to the assessment and collection of prepetition taxes, *see* § 1007 above.

[5] *Klingshirn v. United States (In re Klingshirn)*, 147 F.3d 526, 98-2 U.S.T.C. ¶ 50,538 (6th Cir. 1998), *aff'g*, 209 B.R. 698, 97-2 U.S.T.C. ¶ 50,537 (Bankr. 6th Cir. 1997), *rev'g* 194 B.R. 154 (Bankr. N.D. Ohio 1996); *see* Reg. § 301.6502-1(d), Example. *Accord Behren v. United States*, 82 F.3d 1017, 96-1 U.S.T.C. ¶ 50,254 (11th Cir. 1996) (discussing effect of 1990 legislative extension of the general limitations

stay is in place will only be given operative effect *if* the expiration date specified in the waiver is later than the date the limitations period would have otherwise expired as extended by Code § 6503(h). In such event, the date specified in the waiver controls, and Code § 6503(h) has no practical effect.[6]

For bankruptcy cases commenced *on or after* October 22, 1994, tax assessments are no longer subject to the automatic stay (*see* § 1007). As a result, the statute of limitations on assessment generally will continue to run unaffected by the bankruptcy (and independent of any "bar date" for filing proofs of claim). However, upon the issuance of a notice of deficiency, the statute of limitations on assessment will be suspended under Code § 6503(a)(1).[7] As discussed below at § 1008.3, such suspension will itself last for the duration of the automatic stay plus at least 60 days thereafter (and generally longer). This results from the fact that the assessment period is suspended during the period in which a Tax Court petition may be filed (generally 90 days), which period is itself suspended in the case of a deficiency proceeding for the duration of the automatic stay plus 60 days. Whether the debtor intends to file a petition in the Tax Court or, in the interim, obtains a determination of its taxes in the bankruptcy court is irrelevant. Similarly, when there is a previously pending Tax Court proceeding which is stayed by the bankruptcy case (*see* § 1009), the statute of limitations on assessment will remain suspended under Code § 6503(a)(1) until the stay terminates or is lifted as to the Tax Court proceeding and there is a final decision by the Tax Court.[8] For example, in *Freytag v. Commissioner*,[9] the Tax Court held that the assessment period remained suspended, despite a determination of the tax dispute by the bankruptcy court, until such time as the Tax Court enters its decision—even if simply to dismiss the case or to declare the bankruptcy court's determination *res judicata*—and such decision becomes final.

---

(Footnote Continued)

period for collection from six to 10 years); *Kaggen v. IRS*, 57 F.3d 163, 95-1 U.S.T.C. ¶ 50,304, *adhered to on reh'g*, 71 F.3d 1018, 95-2 U.S.T.C. ¶ 50,635 (2d Cir. 1995) (same).

[6] IRS Manual, Part 4 (Examining Process), Ch. 27 (Bankruptcy), § 4.2.1 (5/25/99), at ¶ 3. The IRS Restructuring Reform Act of 1998, P.L. 105-206—which amended Code § 6502(a)(2) to limit the circumstances in which a waiver of the *collection* period could be obtained—also contained a non-code "sunset" provision governing the continued effect of waivers of the collection period executed prior to January 1, 2000. Under this sunset provision, the collection period expires not later than December 31, 2002, or the end of the original collection period, unless the waiver was obtained in connection with the granting of an installment agreement, in which event the collection period expires 90 days after the date specified in the waiver. *See* Act § 3461. The foregoing limitations are embodied in Reg. § 301.6502-1, as of September 6, 2006. *See* comments on the original proposed regulations (REG-148701-03) by a technical advisor in the IRS Taxpayer Advocate Service, *reprinted at* 2005 TNT 111-19 (June 10, 2005), including certain legislative history underlying the statutory change. *See also* IRS Legal Memorandum 200126575, September 18, 2001, *reprinted at* 2001 TNT 204-26.

[7] *See* Rev. Rul. 2003-80, 2003-29 I.R.B. 83. An assessment made during such suspension is invalid. *See, e.g.*, IRS Field Service Advice 200137010, June 4, 2001, *reprinted at* 2001 TNT 180-18.

[8] *See also* IRS Chief Counsel Notice, dated December 1, 1998, *reprinted at* 1999 TNT 64-59 (explaining effect of bankruptcy on statute of limitations on assessment).

[9] 110 T.C. 35 (1998).

Because the automatic stay does not prohibit the assessment of *postpetition* taxes (regardless of when the bankruptcy case was commenced),[10] there is no general tolling of the statute of limitations for the assessment of such taxes. Significantly, however, the automatic stay suspends the filing of a Tax Court proceeding with respect to postpetition taxes of a corporate debtor, just as it does for prepetition taxes (*see* § 1009). Accordingly, the statute of limitations for the assessment of postpetition taxes will be suspended in the same manner as discussed in the preceding paragraph for prepetition taxes in bankruptcy cases commenced on or after October 22, 1994.

As discussed at § 1006.2 above, a debtor-in-possession in a Chapter 11 case generally is required to pay its postpetition taxes in the ordinary course. In the event the debtor fails to pay such taxes, the IRS may file a request for payment with the bankruptcy court and take other appropriate judicial action. Due to the automatic stay, however, no IRS tax lien will have attached to the debtor's property, and the IRS will be precluded from enforcing any judgment against the debtor without bankruptcy court approval.[11] As discussed above, Code § 6503(h) tolls the statute of limitations on collection for the period during which the IRS is prohibited by reason of the bankruptcy case from collecting the tax, plus six months thereafter. In view of the partial nature of the proscriptions on the IRS's ability to collect postpetition taxes, it would seem that no suspension of the applicable statute of limitations on collection should occur so long as adequate judicial remedies otherwise remain available under the facts and circumstances. The collection period appropriately is suspended, however, if the IRS is required to await payment of the tax under the Chapter 11 plan.[12]

The IRS has taken the position that the tolling of the collections period generally continues unless and until the debtor has "substantially defaulted" on its payments under the Chapter 11 plan. In this regard, the IRS has cautioned, at various times, that the debtor generally should not be considered to be in substantial default unless (1) the debtor has missed a series of plan payments and has ceased making any payments under the plan, and (2) the IRS has sent the debtor notice giving the debtor a brief period to cure (such as 15 to 30 days) and the debtor has failed to do so. Once the debtor is in substantial default, it is the IRS's view that all tax payments under the plan, including any deferred payments with respect to priority tax claims (*see* § 1016.1 below), become immediately collectible.[13]

Turning back to the statute of limitations on assessments, it is logical to assume that in originally enacting the tolling provisions of Code § 6503(h) in 1980, at which time any tax assessments during the bankruptcy case generally were stayed (even

---

[10] *See* 11 U.S.C. § 362(a)(1), (6) (only staying any act to assess, or the taking of any administrative action with respect to, claims that arose prepetition).

[11] *See* 11 U.S.C. § 362(a)(3), (4) and (b)(9)(D).

[12] *See supra* note 3.

[13] *See, e.g.*, IRS Chief Counsel Advice 200146058, November 16, 2001, *reprinted at* 2001 TNT 223-68; IRS Chief Counsel Advice 200022010, February 22, 2000, *reprinted at* 2000 TNT 108-66; IRS Chief Counsel Advice 200016017, February 23, 2000, *reprinted at* 2000 TNT 79-35 (same). *But consider In re Decker's General Contracting, Inc.* (Bankr. D. N.J. August 28, 2000), No. 97-15083 (JHW) (consent order) (court increased rate of repayment to IRS, but did not require immediate repayment in full, where debtor missed several successive payments to the IRS; court indicated that any subsequent failure would result in the reopening and conversion of the case to Chapter 7).

though there may have been no disagreement as to the amount owed), Congress believed that the IRS would have the continued ability to assess any unpaid taxes *following* the confirmation of the debtor's Chapter 11 plan and emergence from bankruptcy. This is, of course, tempered by the fact that the plan and the Bankruptcy Code may provide for the discharge of the debtor's liability for certain taxes and for the imposition of a post-discharge injunction under Bankruptcy Code section 524(a). However, to the extent payment of such taxes is provided under the plan (whether over time or otherwise), one would reasonably expect that the IRS could effectuate the assessment of an otherwise allowable tax claim following confirmation of the plan, so long as the statute of limitations remains open. Moreover, this would seem to naturally follow from the fact that, for pre-October 17, 2005 bankruptcy cases, Bankruptcy Code section 1129(a)(9)(C) utilizes the assessment date as the starting date for the fixed period over which a debtor is permitted to pay prepetition priority tax claims under a Chapter 11 plan. Consistent with such provision, most plans in such bankruptcy cases technically require an assessment as a predicate to payment even though the tax claim is an allowed claim. It would therefore be surprising if confirmation of a Chapter 11 plan, and the post-discharge injunction of Bankruptcy Code section 524(a), cut off the ability of the IRS to assess an otherwise valid (and agreed) tax claim. Yet, that is precisely what one bankruptcy court held.[14] The bankruptcy court reasoned that the plan discharged the old tax debt, and substituted for it a new contractual obligation; that the old debt, having been discharged, was no longer subject to assessment; and that any assessment and collection of such taxes, other than as provided by the plan, was enjoined by the post-discharge injunction. Subsequently, the decision was vacated as moot, apparently due to a consensual resolution between the debtor and the IRS. Not surprisingly, one can find barely a mention of this decision by courts in the 15 years since (although raised by counsel from time to time). In the one case where it was discussed, and where the issue was again relevant, the court severely criticized this position.[15] In an articulate and common sense discussion, the court found such position untenable and clearly inconsistent with the workings of, and the Congressional intent behind, the Bankruptcy Code and the related Tax Code provisions. Harmonizing the two Codes, the court concluded that the tax payment obligations under the plan maintain the characteristics of the underlying tax claim, and that the plan necessarily permits the IRS, or otherwise confers the right, to assess such taxes within the applicable statute of limitations (assuming the debtor does not have some other basis for objecting to the tax claim).

---

[14] *In re Flanigan's Enter., Inc.*, 75 B.R. 446 (Bankr. S.D. Fla. 1987), *vacated as moot*, 117 B.R. 724 (Bankr. S.D. Fla. 1988) (referencing an unpublished order of the district court dismissing all appeals as moot and remanding the case).

[15] *United States v. Conston, Inc. (In re Conston, Inc.)*, 181 B.R. 769 (D. Del. 1995) (involving the priority tax status of an IRS tax claim upon a second bankruptcy of the debtor). Similarly, *see* the discussion at § 1015.4 below (involving the priority status of tax claims in successive bankruptcies). *Consider also* IRS Chief Counsel Advice 20014011, June 5, 2001, *reprinted at* 2001 TNT 200-37 (assessment simply reflects the IRS's judgment of what taxes are owed and does not create the tax liability since, under Code § 6501(a), a collection proceeding in court can be brought without an assessment so long as it's brought within the statute of limitations for assessment).

## *§1008.1 Possible Exceptions to Tolling of Assessment Period*

As discussed above, the assessment period for prepetition taxes is generally tolled for the duration of the automatic stay (plus 60 days) for bankruptcy cases commenced *before* October 22, 1994, due to the inability of the IRS to assess such taxes while the automatic stay is in effect. The following discusses certain possible, or asserted, exceptions to this general rule.

Prior to 1993, the IRS Manual raised the possibility that, even though the automatic stay prohibited the assessment of prepetition taxes, the statute of limitations on assessment may *not* be tolled by the bankruptcy case *unless or until* a notice of deficiency is issued. In 1993, however, the IRS revised its discussion to state that "it makes no difference whether a statutory notice is required or not."[16] The accompanying transmittal letter described this as a clarifying change.[17] The prior discussion read as follows:

> it is our litigating position that IRC 6503(i) [now (h)] suspends the period of limitation on assessment for the period during which the Service is prohibited under the Bankruptcy Code from making the assessment, *i.e.*, until the automatic stay is lifted, plus sixty days; however, see below as to taxes subject to the deficiency procedures . . . . Because a credible position can be advanced that the statute of limitations is not suspended until issuance of the notice of deficiency, issuance of a notice of deficiency should not be delayed because of the fact of bankruptcy.[18]

Although the IRS Manual provided no further explanation of the issue, the "credible position" flows from the literal language of Code §6503(h).[19] Code §6503(h) only suspends the statute of limitations "for the period during which the Secretary is prohibited by reason of [the bankruptcy] case." As indicated, the IRS is precluded by the automatic stay (for bankruptcy cases commenced *before* October 22, 1994) from assessing any prepetition tax against a debtor corporation. However, even outside of bankruptcy, the IRS is generally precluded from making an assessment of any taxes that are subject to the deficiency procedures of Code §6211 *et seq.* (including income, estate, gift, and certain excise taxes) until a notice of deficiency is issued (and for at least 90 days thereafter). Thus, it has been argued that, until a notice of deficiency is issued, the IRS is *not* prohibited from making an assessment of such taxes "by reason of the bankruptcy case," because the IRS was *already* precluded from making an assessment by reason of the deficiency procedures of the Internal Revenue Code.

---

[16] Former IRS Manual §8(15)13.3(2)(a) (2/25/93). *See also* IRS Manual, Part 8 (Appeals), Ch. 15 (Appeals Bankruptcy Cases), §1.1.2.1 (6/27/05), at ¶ 2(A) (later revision; although the statement no longer appears, the substance is unchanged); IRS Litigation Guideline Memorandum GL-28, August 25, 1998, *reprinted at* 2000 TNT 91-27 (also taking that position, citing Clark *v. Commissioner, supra* note 4, but still cautioning "the recognition of the legal principle of this guideline is not yet well settled").

[17] MT 8-227 (2-25-93).

[18] Former IRS Manual §4583.21(8) (3/2/90 and 6/29/92); *see also* former IRS Manual §8(15)13:(3)(b) (10/20/95) (to same effect).

[19] *Cf.* IRS Litigation Guideline Memorandum GL-28, August 25, 1998, *supra* note 16.

Under this interpretation, even if the IRS filed a proof of claim in the debtor's bankruptcy, the assessment period could expire during the bankruptcy case unless a statutory notice of deficiency is issued. This appears directly contrary to the legislative intent[20] and is inconsistent with the applicable case law.[21]

However, the IRS's apparent fear becomes more real as relates to the running of the statute of limitations against the nonbankrupt members of a consolidated group where the common parent is in bankruptcy. As discussed at § 1007.4, although the automatic stay in the common parent's bankruptcy case may prohibit the IRS from assessing the common parent, even if only on behalf of the nonbankrupt members of the group, the IRS may be able to assess the nonbankrupt subsidiaries directly by simply notifying the common parent of its intent to do so. Accordingly, a "credible" (and persuasive) position exists that Code § 6503(h) would not operate with respect to such subsidiaries and that the statute of limitations continues to run with respect to such subsidiaries until a notice of deficiency is issued either to each subsidiary or the common parent.[22] A possible alternative analysis is presented by the Seventh Circuit's decision in *United States v. Wright*,[23] discussed at § 1008.2 below.

To protect against this risk, the IRS Manual had advised that either an extension of the statute be obtained or that a notice of deficiency be issued prior to the expiration of the normal three-year assessment period.[24]

A further risk to the IRS involves the extent to which periods of limitations on assessment referred to in sections of the Internal Revenue Code other than Code §§ 6501 and 6502 are suspended during bankruptcy. This risk is illustrated by the bankruptcy court decision in *In re Leland*.[25] In that case, the debtors had invested in several tax shelter partnerships. Prior to filing bankruptcy, the debtors entered into a closing agreement with the IRS resolving their tax liabilities with respect to such partnerships. Under Code § 6229(f), the IRS had one year from the date of the agreement to assess the tax. Before the IRS assessed, the debtors filed for bankruptcy. In deciding to grant the IRS relief from the automatic stay in order to assess, the bankruptcy court concluded that, unlike the period of limitations in Code §§ 6501 and 6502 to which Code § 6503(h) specifically applies, Code § 6503(h) does not extend the period of limitations in Code § 6229(f) (nor, at such time, did any other provision). Thus, the court believed that after the one-year period in Code § 6229(f) expired, the statute of limitations on assessment would run.

---

[20] *See* S. Rep. No. 1035, 96th Cong., 2d Sess. 50-51 (1980); H.R. Rep. No. 833, 96th Cong., 2d Sess. 45 (1980).

[21] *See* cases cited in *supra* note 4.

[22] *See* Code § 6503(a)(2) (notice of deficiency to common parent suspends statute of limitations as to all members); IRS Field Service Advice 200203007 (September 28, 2001) (Issue 4A; notice of deficiency to a common parent in bankruptcy suspends statute of limitations as to nonbankrupt members).

[23] 57 F.3d 561, 95-2 U.S.T.C. ¶ 50,334 (7th Cir. 1995).

[24] Former IRS Manual § 8(15)13: (3)(b) (April 14, 1992). *See also* IRS Manual, Part 4 (Examining Process), Ch. 27 (Bankruptcy), § 3.3.1 (5/25/99), at ¶ 4(A), stating that a notice of deficiency generally will be issued in all bankruptcy cases for all open prepetition years when deficiencies have been determined but not assessed.

[25] 160 B.R. 834 (Bankr. E.D. Cal. 1993).

Arguably, however, the statute of limitations was tolled.[26] Although Code § 6229 is entitled "Period of Limitations for Making Assessments," it does not in and of itself operate as a statute of limitations. Rather, it ensures that the otherwise applicable assessment period "shall not expire before" a given date. This is in contrast to Code § 6501(a), which limits the assessment period and prohibits subsequent collection proceedings absent a timely assessment. Moreover, Code § 6501(o) expressly cross-references Code § 6229, stating: "For extension of period in the case of partnership items . . . , see section 6229." Thus, it appears that Code § 6229 simply operates to keep open the assessment period under Code § 6501, which should then be further extended by Code § 6503(h).[27]

In the Taxpayer Relief Act of 1997, Congress clarified the operation of Code § 6229(f) with respect to a partner in bankruptcy by expressly suspending the limitations period in Code § 6229(f) for the same period during which the statute of limitations on assessments is suspended under Code § 6503(h).[28] The legislative history cautions that no inference was intended by such clarification as to the proper interpretation of prior law.[29]

## *§ 1008.2 Possible Exceptions to Tolling of Collection Period*

As discussed at § 1007.4 and in the prior section with respect to the statute of limitations on assessment, the IRS may be able to proceed against the nonbankrupt members of a consolidated group even though the common parent is in bankruptcy, simply by notifying the common parent of its intent to do so. Logically, it would seem to follow that the statute of limitations on collection continues to run with respect to such members. As discussed above, Code § 6503(h) only tolls the statute of limitations on collection for the period during which the IRS is prohibited from collecting "by reason of [the bankruptcy] case."

A similar line of reasoning had been adopted by the district court in *United States v. Wright*[30] as relates to the derivative liability of general partners for the unpaid employment taxes of a bankrupt partnership. In that case, the IRS took the position that the partnership's bankruptcy also operated to toll the statute of limitations on collection against the general partners, who themselves were not in bankruptcy. The district court disagreed on the grounds that the IRS was not prohibited by reason of

---

[26] *Cf. Andersen v. United States*, 62 F.3d 1428, 95-2 U.S.T.C. ¶ 50,467, *cert. denied*, 116 S. Ct. 925 (1996), *aff'g* 94-1 U.S.T.C. ¶ 50,215 (N.D. Okla. 1994).

[27] *See AD Global Fund, LLC v. United States*, 481 F.3d 1351 (Fed. Cir. 2007), *aff'g* 67 Fed. Cl. 657 (Fed. Cl. 2005) (discusses conflicting authorities); and *Rhone-Poulenc Surfactants and Specialties, L.P. v. Commissioner*, 114 T.C. 533 (2000) (reviewed decision, with three judges dissenting), so concluding. For a discussion of the arguments for and against Code § 6229 as a separate statute of limitations, *see* IRS Litigation Memorandum 199905040, September 25, 1998, *reprinted at* 1999 TNT 25-19.

[28] Code § 6229(h) (effective for any taxable years for which the statute of limitations had not expired on or before August 5, 1997).

[29] Conference Report, 105th Cong., 1st Sess. 394 (1997).

[30] 868 F. Supp. 1070, 94-2 U.S.T.C. ¶ 50,549 (S.D. Ind. 1994), *rev'd*, 57 F.3d 561, 95-2 U.S.T.C. ¶ 50,334 (7th Cir. 1995).

the partnership's Chapter 11 case from pursuing the partners, but the Seventh Circuit reversed. Relying on its prior decision in *United States v. Associates Commercial Corp.*,[31] which involved a similar tolling provision under Code § 6503(b) (applicable in non-bankruptcy situations where the assets of the taxpayer are in the control or custody of a court), the Seventh Circuit held that the statute of limitations for collection actions against persons derivatively liable for taxes (here, the general partners) is coextensive with the statute of limitations for the taxpayer (here, the partnership).[32]

The Seventh Circuit's analysis in *Wright* yields interesting possibilities in the context of consolidated return groups, depending on whether a member's several liability for the entire group's tax liability is viewed as a "derivative" liability for this purpose. Arguably, this would mean that the statute of limitations may be tolled as to a non-bankrupt member's several liability for the portion of the group's tax liability relating to the bankrupt members, but not for the portion of the group tax liability relating to the nonbankrupt members.

## *§ 1008.3 Plus 60 Days . . . or, Would You Believe, 180 Days?*

As mentioned above, Code § 6503(h) tolls the statute of limitations on assessment for the period during which the IRS is prohibited from assessing the tax by reason of the bankruptcy case *plus* an additional 60 days. However, a technical reading of the Code—formally adopted by the IRS in Rev. Rul. 2003-80[33]—leads to a potential double, or for bankruptcy cases commenced before October 22, 1994, triple counting of the additional 60-day period where a statutory notice of deficiency is issued and the period for filing a Tax Court petition is tolled by the bankruptcy case.

**Pre-10/22/94 Bankruptcy Cases: Triple Counting.** As discussed below (at § 1009.2), just as the statute of limitations is tolled for the period of the automatic stay plus 60 days for bankruptcy cases commenced *before* October 22, 1994, so is the filing period for Tax Court petitions. It is this additional 60-day extension of the Tax Court filing period that gives rise in such cases to the potential for a second 60-day extension of the statute of limitations on assessment beyond the period of the automatic stay. This results from the fact that, independent of the automatic stay and the tolling of the statute of limitations under Code § 6503(h), an extension of the Tax Court filing period results in a similar extension of the statute of limitations on assessment and collection under Code § 6503(a)(1).[34] Thus, where the Tax Court filing

---

[31] 721 F.2d 1094, 1096-1098 (7th Cir. 1983).

[32] The Seventh Circuit acknowledged that not all Circuit Courts were necessarily in accord with its decision in *Associates Commercial Corp.*, citing the Ninth Circuit's decision in *United States v. Harvis Constr. Co.*, 857 F.2d 1360, 1364-1365 (9th Cir. 1988). However, the court's decision in *Harvis*, which involved the collection period for a lender's liability under Reg. § 31.3505-1(d)(1), rested upon the court's technical reading of that regulation and thus appears limited in scope. The Seventh Circuit's decision in *Wright* was favorably cited by the Supreme Court in *United States v. Galletti*, 124 S. Ct. 1528, 2004-1 U.S.T.C. ¶ 50,204 (2004).

[33] 2003-29 I.R.B. 83.

[34] *See* Reg. § 301.6503(a)-1(a); *see also* Code § 6213(a) (assessment or collection action suspended until expiration of Tax Court filing period).

period is also tolled by the automatic stay, *both* Code § 6503(h) and Code § 6503(a)(1) independently toll the statute of limitations on assessment for the term of the automatic stay plus an additional 60 days. The potential for a third additional 60-day period results from the fact that Code § 6503(a)(1) itself tacks on a further 60-day period.[35]

It appears clear from the statutory scheme that this potential triple counting of the additional 60-day periods was not intended. Nonetheless, the IRS has long taken the position that the additional 60-day periods are cumulative.[36] Under this interpretation, if the Tax Court filing period was tolled by a pre-10/22/94 bankruptcy case, the statute of limitations on assessment would have been effectively tolled for the period of the automatic stay plus up to 270 days—*i.e.*, the 90-day filing period (or, if shorter, the period remaining as of the commencement of the bankruptcy case), the 60-day extension of the filing period, the additional 60 days under Code § 6503(h), and the 60 days tacked on by Code § 6503(a)(1).

**Current Bankruptcy Cases: Double Counting.** For bankruptcy cases commenced *on or after* October 22, 1994, the additional 60-day period under Code § 6503(h) should no longer be implicated to the extent that the automatic stay no longer applies to tax assessments (*see* § 1007.1). However, the doubling up of the 60-day extension of the Tax Court filing period and the 60-day period tacked on by Code § 6503(a)(1) still exists,[37] as illustrated in Rev. Rul. 2003-80.

## *§ 1008.4 Successive Bankruptcies*

The IRS, in Chief Counsel Advice 200346006,[38] considered the period for which the statute of limitations on collection is tolled under Code § 6503(h) where the debtor has successive bankruptcies, with the second bankruptcy filing occurring less than six months after the completion of the first bankruptcy. As discussed above (in the first part of this § 1008), Code § 6503(h)(2) generally operates to toll the statute of limitations on collection for the duration of the automatic stay and for any additional for

---

[35] *See United States v. Fingers (In re Fingers)*, 170 B.R. 419, 94-2 U.S.T.C. ¶ 50,434 (S.D. Cal. 1994), illustrating the combination of the 60-day periods under Code § 6503(h) and Code § 6503(a)(1) where the Tax Court case was concluded prior to the bankruptcy case and the bankruptcy case commenced before 10/22/94. *See also* IRS Manual, Part 4 (Examining Process), Ch. 27 (Bankruptcy), § 4.2.1 (5/25/99), at ¶ 7 (pre-10/22/94 bankruptcy cases), and § 4.3 (5/25/99), at ¶ 3(A) (later bankruptcy cases), providing a similar illustration where the Tax Court filing period expired and no assessment was made prior to the bankruptcy case, and then illustrates the same sequence of events in the context of a post-10/21/94 bankruptcy case.

[36] IRS Manual, Part 4 (Examining Process), Ch. 27 (Bankruptcy), § 4.2.1 (5/25/99), at ¶ 9; IRS Litigation Guideline Memorandum GL-28, August 25, 1998, *reprinted at* 2000 TNT 91-27 (illustrating the application of this position); Rev. Rul. 2003-80, 2003-29 I.R.B. 83; *see also* former IRS Manual HB 48(13)2, § 220(4) (December 20, 1993), § 4583.21(8) (June 29, 1992).

[37] *See* IRS Manual, Part 4 (Examining Process), Ch. 27 (Banruptcy), § 4.3 (5/25/99), at ¶ 3(B); IRS Chief Counsel Notice, dated December 1, 1998 (explaining effect of bankruptcy on statute of limitations on assessment), *reprinted at* 1999 TNT 64-59; *see also* IRS Manual, Part 4 (Examining Process), Ch. 27 (Bankruptcy), § 4.2.1 (5/25/99), at ¶¶ 8-10 (discussing pre-10/22/94 bankruptcy cases).

[38] *Reprinted at* 2003 TNT 221-39 (issuance date of Advice was redacted, but is clearly in 2003).

which collection is enjoined by the Chapter 11 plan, *plus* six months thereafter. A second bankruptcy can therefore occur while the statute of limitations pertaining to the collection of taxes predating the first bankruptcy is still tolled. In such event, is the IRS still entitled to an extension of the statute of limitations for the "unused" portion of the additional six-month period attributable to the first bankruptcy as of the second bankruptcy filing, as well as the additional six-month period attributable to the second bankruptcy once the second bankruptcy is over? The Advice concludes no. The Advice explains that, in effect, the suspension period relating to the first bankruptcy overlaps and continues to run concurrent with the suspension period relating to the second bankruptcy, rather than being consecutive periods.[39]

A similar issue was considered in a subsequent Chief Counsel Advice, although in respect of the suspension of the Tax Court filing period under Code § 6213(f)(1) and its resulting effect on the limitations period for assessments. In Chief Counsel Advice 200521030,[40] the IRS considered the period for which the statute of limitations on assessment is tolled when the IRS issues a statutory notice of deficiency while the debtor's first bankruptcy case is pending, the case is then dismissed, and a second bankruptcy case is commenced within 60 days thereafter. As discussed above (at the beginning of § 1008), the assessment period is suspended during the period for which a Tax Court petition may be filed (generally 90 days), which period is itself suspended under Code § 6213(f)(1) in the case of deficiency proceedings for the duration of the automatic stay and for 60 days thereafter. Accordingly, the issue was whether the "unused" portion of the additional 60-day suspension of the Tax Court filing period as of the commencement of the second bankruptcy case operates to extend the assessment period following the second bankruptcy case. First observing that the additional 60-day suspension period properly runs prior to the normal 90-day filing period (based on the plain language of the statute and on several Tax Court decisions[41]), the Advice concludes—consistent with (although without citing) the prior Chief Counsel Advice—that the unused portion of the 60-day period is *not* added on after the second bankruptcy case (in addition to the 60-day suspension period attributable to that case), but runs concurrent with the suspension period relating to the second bankruptcy case.

## *§1008.5 Other Insolvency Proceeding*

In an insolvency proceeding other than a bankruptcy case where the assets of a debtor corporation are in the control or custody of a federal or state court, the statute of limitations on collections (not assessment) shall be tolled during the period of the

---

[39] In reaching this conclusion, the IRS relied on case law addressing an analogous issue where the collection period is tolled due to the submission of successive offers in compromise. *See, e.g., United States v. Newman*, 405 F.2d 189, 194 n.6 (5th Cir. 1968); *United States v. Malkin*, 317 F.Supp. 612, 614 n.4. (E.D.N.Y. 1970); *United States v. Morgan*, 213 F. Supp. 137, 139-140 (S.D. Tex. 1962).

[40] April 6, 2005, *reprinted at* 2005 TNT 103-17.

[41] *See, e.g., Clevenger v. Commissioner*, T.C. Memo 1998-37, *aff'd*, 176 F.3d 482, 99-1 U.S.T.C. ¶50,538 (9th Cir. 1999); *Howard v. Commissioner*, T.C. Memo 1998-300; *Zimmerman v. Commissioner*, 105 T.C. 220 (1995).

court's control or custody, plus an additional six months thereafter.[42] The statute of limitations on assessments is tolled only for the period from the commencement of the proceeding until 30 days after the IRS receives notice of the receiver's appointment or authorization to act.[43]

## §1009 SUSPENSION OF TAX COURT PROCEEDINGS

Upon the filing of the bankruptcy petition, the Bankruptcy Code (pursuant to the automatic stay) suspends any pending proceeding before the Tax Court "concerning" the debtor,[1] but as to bankruptcy cases commenced on or after October 17, 2005, only with respect to proceedings "concerning a corporate debtor's tax liability for a taxable period the bankruptcy court may determine."[2] It also prohibits the debtor corporation from starting any new proceeding, whether in respect of pre- or postpetition taxes.[3] Any petition filed during the stay is invalid and, to be effective, must be refiled after

---

[42] Code §6503(b). For a brief discussion of Code §6503(b), as well as its overlapping and subordinate role to Code §6503(h) in bankruptcy cases, *see* IRS Chief Counsel Advice 200522021, March 11, 2005, *reprinted at* 2005 TNT 107-40.

[43] *See* Code §6872 (tolls statute of limitations only where notice required under Reg. §301.6036-1, discussed *supra* §1004 note 1, but in no event more than two years).

[1] **§1009** 11 U.S.C. §362(a)(8); 124 Cong. Rec. H 11,110-111 (daily ed. Sept. 28, 1978) (statement of Rep. Edwards), S 17,426-28 (daily ed. Oct. 6, 1978) (statement of Sen. DeConcini) (explains that one of the purposes of the stay is to allow the bankruptcy judge to determine which court should determine the merits of the tax claim; the stay also allows a debtor or trustee time to assess its options). *Consider Kovitch v. Commissioner*, 128 T.C. No. 9 (2007), and IRS Chief Counsel Advice 200621018, January 24, 2006, *reprinted at* 2006 TNT 103-49 (both to similar effect: automatic stay does not prohibit a debtor from intervening into a spouse's Tax Court case involving relief from joint and several liability, nor thereafter preclude such proceeding from continuing, since the proceeding does not directly affect or "concern" the tax liability of the debtor).

[2] *See* P.L. 109-8, §709 (2005). As amended, Bankruptcy Code section 362(a)(8) only suspends Tax Court proceedings concerning *individual* debtors with respect to *prepetition* taxes, and no longer applies to non-corporate, non-individual debtors. Accordingly, any Tax Court proceedings involving prepetition taxes of non-corporate, non-individual debtors apparently are stayed only if considered under Bankruptcy Code section 362(a)(1) to be a continuation of a proceeding "against" the debtor (*see* discussion at §1009.4).

[3] Id.; *Halpern v. Commissioner*, 96 T.C. No. 46 (1991). It has been held that a Tax Court proceeding to determine the propriety of a Final Partnership Administrative Adjustment with respect to a *debtor partnership* ultimately "concerns" the *income tax* liability of the partners, not the partnership, and is therefore not stayed by the partnership's bankruptcy filing. *See, e.g., Madison Recycling Assoc. v. IRS (In re Madison Recycling Assoc.)*, 2001-1 U.S.T.C. ¶50,361 (E.D. Ky. 2001), *aff'd per curiam*, 2002-2 U.S.T.C. ¶50,626 (6th Cir. 2002); *1983 W. Reserve Oil & Gas Co. v. Commissioner*, 95 T.C. 51 (1990) (same), *aff'd without published op.*, 995 F.2d 235 (9th Cir. 1993); *see also Computer Programs Lambda, Ltd. v. Commissioner*, 89 T.C. 198, Dec. 44,072 (1987) (automatic stay precluded debtor from filing a notice partner petition with the Tax Court; debtor's "partnership items" converted to "nonpartnership items" upon its filing for bankruptcy, resulting in the termination of its status of tax matter partner and effectively removing the debtor as a party to any partnership proceeding in the Tax Court). *See* Temp. Reg. §301.6231(a)(7)-1T(l)(4) in conjunction with Temp. Reg. §301.6231(c)-7T(a). In contrast, a partnership level *employment tax* proceeding "concerns" the tax liability of the partnership, rather than its partners, and thus is not stayed by a bankruptcy of its partners. *People Place Auto Hand Carwash LLC v. Commissioner*, 126 T.C. No. 19 (2006).

the stay terminates.[4] Similarly, a decision entered by the Tax Court during the stay is invalid and may be vacated.[5] Thus, in the context of a Tax Court proceeding, the automatic stay operates against the debtor corporation as well as the IRS.[6]

The automatic stay remains in effect until the close or dismissal of the bankruptcy case or, in a Chapter 11 case, until a discharge is granted or denied (which generally occurs upon confirmation of the Chapter 11 plan, *see* § 1014), unless the bankruptcy court lifts the stay to permit the Tax Court proceeding to continue.[7] For this purpose, the date on which the bankruptcy court enters the order of dismissal or

---

[4] *See, e.g., Thompson v. Commissioner*, 84 T.C. 645, Dec. 42,014 (1985); *McClamma v. Commissioner*, 76 T.C. 754, Dec. 37,899 (1981); *Archie McRoy Nichols v. Commissioner*, 55 T.C.M. 1071, Dec. 44,831(M), T.C. Memo. 1988-257; *Glickman v. Commissioner*, 51 T.C.M. 1265, Dec. 43,133(M), T.C. Memo. 1986-258; *Ever Clean Services, Inc.*, 45 T.C.M. 349, Dec. 39,576(M), T.C. Memo. 1982-726 (Tax Court petition filed during stay cannot be "reinstated" by court; new filing required after stay terminated); *Reagoso v. Commissioner*, 66 T.C.M. 850, Dec. 49,307(M), T.C. Memo. 1993-450, *aff'd*, 74 A.F.T.R.2d ¶ 94-5426 (3d Cir. 1994) (Tax Court petition held invalid even though IRS waited until expiration of filing period to seek dismissal; petition could not be validated by a retroactive lifting of the stay); *Zaklama v. Commissioner*, T.C. Memo. 1997-170 (annulment of bankruptcy case and automatic stay did not restore Tax Court's jurisdiction over dismissed petition which had become final in the interim and was properly dismissed based on the facts at the time); *Cassel v. Commissioner*, T.C. Memo. 2006-132 (IRS may raise jurisdictional issue at any time). *But consider In re Ulrich* (Bankr. E.D. La.), *reprinted at* 93 TNT 7-67 (wherein the bankruptcy court granted the debtor retroactive relief from the automatic stay in an effort to validate an earlier Tax Court petition filed in violation of the stay).

[5] *See, e.g., Adkins v. Commissioner*, T.C. Memo. 2005-260 (granted IRS leave to file motion to vacate a stipulated decision that had become final, and declared decision to be void as in violation of the stay).

[6] In a startling decision that disregards the plain language of Bankruptcy Code section 362(a)(8), overlooks the function of the automatic stay with respect to Tax Court proceedings as described in the legislative statements of the sponsors of the 1978 Bankruptcy Code and ignores the prior case law, one bankruptcy court held that Bankruptcy Code section 362(a) does not stay the commencement or continuation of a Tax Court proceeding by the debtor. *In re Thompson* (Bankr. S.D. Ga. Sept. 3, 1999), *reprinted at* 1999 TNT 192-13. Such decision is clearly wrong and should not be relied upon. Similarly, *see* discussion of Bankruptcy Rule 6009, at § 1007 note 4 above.

[7] 11 U.S.C. § 362(c)(2); *see, e.g., Bigelow v. Commissioner*, 65 F.3d 127 (9th Cir. 1995); *Zimmerman v. Commissioner*, 105 T.C. No. 15 (1995) (suspension of filing period ended when debtor's discharge was granted, even though debtor did not receive notice of the discharge until several months later); *Moody v. Commissioner*, 95 T.C. 655, Dec. 47,100 (1990) (automatic stay lifted upon confirmation of Chapter 11 plan, even though certain creditor claims remained; bankruptcy court could have provided for continuation of the stay, but did not); *Sanford v. Commissioner*, T.C. Memo. 1992-182 (to same effect); *Zamarello v. Commissioner*, 62 T.C.M. 913, Dec. 47,665(M), T.C. Memo. 1991-494; *Smith v. Commissioner*, 96 T.C. No. 2 (1991) (a settlement agreement approved by the bankruptcy court and waiving the debtor's right to discharge was the equivalent of a "denial" of discharge so as to terminate the automatic stay; although the case involved an individual debtor in a Chapter 7 case, Bankruptcy Code section 1141(d)(4) provides a similar operative provision for Chapter 11 cases); *Noli v. Commissioner*, 860 F.2d 1521, 88-2 U.S.T.C. ¶ 9595 (9th Cir. 1988) (bankruptcy court granted relief from the stay and permitted Tax Court to render judgment where bankruptcy petitions were filed as an indirect method of avoiding a decision in the Tax Court). *Consider also Richmond v. United States*, 97-2 U.S.T.C. ¶ 50,587 (S.D. Cal. 1997) (as relates to tolling of statute of limitations, IRS was entitled to rely on Bankruptcy Rule 4006 for notice of dismissal of bankruptcy case, unless and until actual notice otherwise received; contrast Tax Court decision in *Zimmerman* above); *W. Jaye Ford*, 62 T.C.M. 293, Dec. 47,509(M), T.C. Memo. 1991-354 (Tax Court proceeding not stayed where the debtor failed to rebut the IRS's contention that the debtor's bankruptcy case had ended). For circumstances under which the IRS may wish to have the stay lifted to allow a Tax Court litigation to proceed, *see* IRS Manual, Part 34 (General Litigation), Ch. 3.1 (Procedures in Bankruptcy Cases), § 2.1 (8/11/04), at ¶ 2.

discharge—viewed by some courts as the date the order is signed by the judge,[8] and by other courts as the date the order is docketed[9]—generally terminates the automatic stay, regardless of whether the order has been appealed or a motion to vacate is pending.[10] A further stay may be granted by the bankruptcy court or the appellate court pending the appeal of an order of dismissal or discharge.[11] Although the Tax Court has twice held that the reinstatement of a bankruptcy case and the vacating of a prior order of dismissal or discharge does not reimpose the automatic stay absent an express indication from the bankruptcy court to the contrary,[12] the Bankruptcy Appellate Panel for the Tenth Circuit and at least two bankruptcy courts have held otherwise.[13] In addition, the Tax Court has held (and bankruptcy courts appear to agree) that the reopening of a bankruptcy case does not resurrect the automatic stay, although the bankruptcy court could issue an express order staying any Tax Court proceeding pursuant to Bankruptcy Code section 105 (*see* § 1013.5).[14]

## *§1009.1 Consolidated Returns*

As discussed above (at § 1007.4), the Tax Court, in *J&S Carburetor*, held that in the context of a consolidated return where the common parent is in bankruptcy, the nonbankrupt subsidiaries are precluded from filing a Tax Court petition for any consolidated return year.[15] The basis for the court's decision was the fact that, under

---

[8] *See, e.g., Saunders v. United States (In re Saunders)*, 240 B.R. 636, 99-1 U.S.T.C. ¶ 50,445 (S.D. Fla. 1999).

[9] *See, e.g., Olson v. Commissioner, infra* at § 1009.2; *United States v. Breaux*, 2000-1 U.S.T.C. ¶ 50,286 (E.D. La. 2000) (even though entry was 18 months late due to a bankruptcy clerk's oversight), *motion for recons. denied*, 2000 U.S. Dist. LEXIS 5292 (E.D. La. 2000).

[10] *See* id. (involved appeal of order of dismissal); *Douglass v. Commissioner*, T.C. Memo. 1997-272 (1997) (involved pending motion to vacate order of discharge); *see* 11 U.S.C. § 362(c)(2)(B) (the "stay continues until the earliest of . . . the time the case is dismissed, or . . . the time a discharge is granted or denied"). *See also Schulman v. IRS (In re Schulman)*, 105 F.3d 666 (9th Cir. 1996), full decision at 1996 U.S. App. LEXIS 33301 (unpublished decision; counsel's ignorance or mistake as to significance of discharge was no excuse for late filing of Tax Court petition).

[11] *See* Bankruptcy Rule 8005 (discussing the manner and circumstances in which a motion for a stay pending appeal may be made).

[12] *Kieu v. Commissioner*, 105 T.C. 387 (1995) (involved order vacating an individual debtor's nondischarge under Chapter 7); *Guerra v. Commissioner*, 110 T.C. 271 (1998) (involved order vacating prior dismissal of debtor's Chapter 7 case).

[13] *Diviney v. Nationsbank of Texas, N.A. (In re Diviney)*, 225 B.R. 762 (Bankr. 10th Cir. 1998) (Chapter 13 case); *In re Nail*, 195 B.R. 922, 929 n.10 (Bankr. N.D. Ala. 1996) (Chapter 13 case; also so holding); *In re Hakim* (Bankr. N.D. Cal. Aug. 12, 1999) (Chapter 7 case), *reprinted at* 1999 TNT 169-5.

[14] *See Allison v. Commissioner*, 97 T.C. No. 36 (1991) (retracting prior statements to the contrary); *In re Trevino*, 78 B.R. 29 (Bankr. M.D. Pa. 1987). For earlier statements to the contrary, *see Kimmerling v. Commissioner*, 58 T.C.M. 138, Dec. 46,023(M), T.C. Memo. 1989-501; *cf. Terrell v. Commissioner*, 59 T.C.M. 1020, Dec. 46,681(N), T.C. Memo. 1990-323. *Consider also Krumhorn v. United States*, 2002-2 U.S.T.C. ¶ 50,762 (N.D. Ill. 2002) (bankruptcy court stay of IRS enforcement actions pending debtor's appeal of an adverse determination regarding the nondischargeability of its tax liability violates the Anti-Injunction Act, Code § 7421).

[15] *J&S Carburetor Co. v. Commissioner*, 93 T.C. 166 (1989). *See also* IRS Field Service Advice 200203007, September 28, 2001, *reprinted at* 2002 TNT 14-93 (question 4). This is in contrast to the rule for spouses, where there is no similar agency concept precluding the nonbankrupt spouse from

the consolidated return regulations, the common parent had the exclusive authority to file a Tax Court petition and conduct proceedings before the Tax Court on behalf of the group.[16] In addition, the court observed:

> Although not determinative, we note that our disposition of [the Government's]motion avoids an anomalous result. Here, neither the Government nor any of the corporations in bankruptcy requested the bankruptcy court to lift the stay. Thus, if we were to deny [the Government's] motion [to dismiss the petitions by the nonbankrupt subsidiaries for lack of jurisdiction], this Court and the bankruptcy court (exercising its jurisdiction to decide tax issues under [Bankruptcy Code section 505]) each might proceed to decide the consolidated corporate tax liability issue, a result contrary to the exercise of judicial economy and consistency.[17]

The Tax Court did not consider, however, other potential ramifications of its decision. For example, as discussed at § 1007, can the IRS now assess the nonbankrupt subsidiaries or institute collection actions? What if the IRS notifies the common parent that it will deal directly with each subsidiary, as it is permitted to do under the consolidated return regulations? Assuming each subsidiary could thereafter file a petition in the Tax Court, could the common parent enjoin the subsidiaries from doing so on the grounds that it undermines the bankruptcy court's preemptive jurisdiction over the common parent's tax liability and, in the words of the Tax Court, is "contrary to the exercise of judicial economy and consistency"? Conversely, what results should obtain if the subsidiaries, rather than the common parent, are in bankruptcy?

## *§1009.2 Tolling of Tax Court Filing Period*

**Deficiency proceedings.** A Tax Court petition must ordinarily be filed within 90 days from the date the IRS mails the debtor corporation a statutory notice of deficiency.[18] Because Tax Court filings during the automatic stay are suspended, the 90-day filing period is also tolled.[19] Following the termination of the stay, an extra 60

---

(Footnote Continued)

proceeding; or in the partnership area, where the status of the "tax matters partner" terminates when the partner files for bankruptcy, thereby avoiding a stay of the Tax Court proceedings. *See, e.g., McClamma v. Commissioner, supra* note 4 (spouses); *Smee v. Commissioner*, T.C. Memo 1997-364 (same); *Tempest Assocs. Ltd. v. Commissioner*, 94 T.C. No. 49 (1990) (tax matters partner).

[16] Reg. § 1.1502-77A(a) (effective for taxable years beginning before June 28, 2002); *see also* Reg. § 1.1502-77(a)(1), (2)(x) (effective for taxable years beginning on or after June 28, 2002).

[17] 93 T.C. at 170.

[18] *See* Code § 6213(a).

[19] *See* Code § 6213(f)(1) (filing period is suspended "for the period during which the debtor is prohibited by reason of [the bankruptcy] case from filing a petition in the Tax Court with respect to such deficiency, and for 60 days thereafter"); and beginning discussion to § 1009.

days is added to the suspension period.[20] After the stay terminates, the filing period will therefore equal 60 days plus the unexpired portion of the 90-day filing period remaining as of the filing date of the bankruptcy petition.[21] As a result, where a statutory notice of deficiency was issued during the stay, the debtor-in-possession would have 150 days after the stay terminates in which to file the Tax Court petition.[22]

In *Olson v. Commissioner*,[23] the debtors filed a Chapter 11 petition on March 1, 1982. On December 21, 1982, the IRS issued a statutory notice of deficiency. On January 27, 1984, the bankruptcy court issued an order dismissing the bankruptcy case and, on January 31, 1984, entered the order of dismissal on its docket. On February 7, 1984, the debtors filed a motion for reconsideration of the order of dismissal, which was denied on February 17, 1984. Immediately thereafter, on February 23, 1984, the debtors filed an appeal to the district court, followed on February 27, 1984, with a motion for a stay pending the appeal. On March 13, 1984, the district court denied the motion for stay and, on August 21, 1984, affirmed the bankruptcy court's order of dismissal. On August 22, 1984, the debtors filed a petition with the Tax Court. Because the Tax Court petition was filed more than 150 days after the bankruptcy court entered its order dismissing the bankruptcy case (actually 204 days) the debtors' petition was dismissed.[24] The Tax Court noted that it was not deciding the issue of whether the 150-day period was tolled by the motion for reconsideration of the order of dismissal or during the pendency of the motion for a stay pending the appeal, since even with such periods (totalling 25 days) excluded, the elapsed period was more than 150 days.

For a discussion of the interplay between the tolling period for Tax Court filings and the suspension of the statute of limitations on assessment, *see* §§1008.3 and 1008.4 above.

**Other proceedings—A trap for the unwary.** Over time, Congress has expanded the Tax Court's jurisdiction to cover various non-deficiency proceedings. Such proceedings include petitions for review of adverse administrative determinations involving the filing of a tax lien,[25] a notice of intent to levy against the debtor's assets,[26] certain requests for the abatement of interest,[27] the employment status of one or more

[20] Id.; *see, e.g., Brannon v. Commissioner*, 56 T.C.M. 371, Dec. 45,102(M), T.C. Memo. 1988-472 (bankruptcy court cannot order further extension of filing period).

[21] *See Howard v. Commissioner*, T.C. Memo 1998-300 (involving successive bankruptcies and thus multiple 60-day extensions).

[22] Id.; Rev. Rul. 2003-80, 2003-29 I.R.B. 83 (Situation A).

[23] 86 T.C. 1314, Dec. 43,137 (1986).

[24] The Tax Court in *Olson* took the position that the order of dismissal is not considered "entered" until docketed. However, not all courts agree. *See supra* note 8.

[25] Code §§6320(c), 6330(d) (and, in certain cases, to the district court).

[26] Code §6330(d) (and, in certain cases, to the district court).

[27] Code §6404(h).

individuals,[28] and an individual taxpayer's request for relief from joint and several liability with respect to a joint return.[29]

The Tax Court in *Drake v. Commissioner*[30] and in the companion case of *Prevo v. Commissioner*[31] considered the implications of the automatic stay with respect to the respective debtor's petition for review, filed during the bankruptcy case, of an IRS determination upholding the filing of a tax lien (*Prevo*) and of an IRS denial of the individual debtor's request for relief from joint and several liability (*Drake*). In both cases, the Tax Court easily concluded that the automatic stay—which expressly bars "the commencement or continuation of a proceeding before the United States Tax Court concerning the debtor" (including with respect to individual debtors for pre-October 17, 2005 bankruptcy cases)—applied to such petitions, and that the court therefore lacked jurisdiction to consider the merits of the appeals. More significantly, though, the Tax Court found that, unlike in the case of deficiency proceedings governed by Code § 6213, the period for filing an appeal with the Tax Court under Code § 6330(d) with respect to tax liens and levy actions, and under Code § 6015(e) with respect to an individual's joint and several liability, is *not* tolled during the period of the stay. As a result, in both cases the Tax Court determined that the statutory appeal period expired while the automatic stay was pending, effectively eliminating the debtor's ability to obtain Tax Court review of the IRS's determination.[32]

The Tax Court, in *Prevo*, acknowledged that the debtor had "fallen victim to a trap for the unwary," but concluded that any remedy "must originate with Congress." Significantly, the notice of determination in *Prevo* had been issued shortly before the debtor's bankruptcy filing. Although the notice of determination in *Drake* was issued after the debtor's bankruptcy filing, the Tax Court was not asked nor did it consider whether the issuance of the notice by the IRS was itself a violation of the automatic stay.

Subsequently, in *Smith v. Commissioner*,[33] the Tax Court was again presented with a determination notice issued after a debtor's bankruptcy filing, in this instance with respect to earlier notices of intent to levy. Recognizing the debtor's predicament if the debtor's petition for Tax Court review was dismissed for being in violation of the automatic stay, this time the court, *sua sponte*, questioned whether the determination notice was issued in violation of the stay, and held that it was. As a result, if

---

[28] Code § 7436(a).

[29] Code § 6015(e).

[30] 123 T.C. 320.

[31] 123 T.C. 326.

[32] The court in *Prevo* noted that Code § 6330(d) as then in effect (which, in cases where the Tax Court did not have jurisdiction of the underlying tax liability, allowed appeals to the district court) provided, in part, that "[i]f a court determines that the appeal was to an incorrect court, a person shall have 30 days after the court determination to file such appeal with the correct court." However, it expressly refrained from determining whether, under the circumstances, the Tax Court was an "incorrect" court. In the Pension Protection Act of 2007, Congress provided the Tax Court exclusive jurisdiction over all appeals. Code § 6330(d)(1), *as amended by* P.L. No. 109-280, § 855(a) (2007).

[33] 124 T.C. 36 (2005).

following the debtor's bankruptcy (or an earlier lifting of the stay) the IRS still wanted to proceed to levy against the debtor's assets, it would have to issue new notices of intent to levy from which the debtor could again seek IRS reconsideration and subsequent Tax Court review. Although the IRS believes that the *Smith* decision was wrongly decided, IRS Chief Counsel Notice CC-2006-019 states that "the Service generally will not challenge the *Smith* holding in the Tax Court" and, in similar situations involving levies, generally will rescind the determination notice without prior court action. The Notice is somewhat more equivocal about comparable situations involving tax liens, but nevertheless indicates that the IRS will follow *Smith* in most lien cases where the debtor files a Tax Court petition during the pendency of the automatic stay.

Not all non-deficiency proceedings present the "trap" described above. For example, the provisions governing determinations of employment status expressly incorporate the principles of Code §6213(f)(1), which applies to deficiency proceedings.[34] A similar tolling provision would be appropriate for other non-deficiency proceedings.

In those cases where the debtor is unable to obtain or otherwise preserve its right to a Tax Court review, the debtor may be able to challenge the IRS determination in the bankruptcy court.[35]

## *§1009.3 Preemption of Tax Court Jurisdiction by Bankruptcy Court*

When a Tax Court proceeding is pending at the time the bankruptcy petition is filed, the bankruptcy court may effectively preempt the Tax Court's jurisdiction by keeping the automatic stay in effect and deciding the merits of the debtor corporation's Tax Court petition itself (*see* §1013).[36] The bankruptcy court's decision is then binding on the Tax Court with respect to the stayed Tax Court proceeding under the doctrine of issue preclusion or *res judicata*.[37] In addition, the bankruptcy court may

---

[34] Code §7436(d)(1).

[35] *See Drake* at n.4 (citing two cases involving an individual debtor's joint and several liability). The debtor in *Drake* subsequently did petition the bankruptcy court. In a further twist, the bankruptcy court held that the IRS determination was itself issued in violation of the automatic stay and thus void. *In re Drake*, 336 B.R. 155 (Bankr. D. Mass. 2006), *reconsid. denied*, 2006 Bankr. LEXIS 834.

[36] *See* 11 U.S.C. §§362(a)(8) and 505(a)(1); *cf.* Code. §6871(c)(1). *See also Valley Die Cast Corp. v. Comm.*, T.C. Memo. 1983-103 (1983) (unchallenged IRS proof of claim in debtor's bankruptcy case, as to which the confirmation of the bankruptcy case served as a final judgment, was determinative of the debtor's tax liability; thus, pending Tax Court case, that was stayed during the debtor's bankruptcy case, was subsequently dismissed); *Wood v. Commissioner*, 328 B.R. 880 (Bankr. S.D. Fla. 2005) (Tax Court properly had jurisdiction, since debtor had previously received a discharge thereby causing the automatic stay to terminate; absent the stay, the bankruptcy court may share jurisdiction with other courts), *reh'g denied*, 2005 Bankr. LEXIS 1749 (Bankr. S.D. Fla. 2006).

[37] *See Freytag v. Commissioner*, 110 T.C. 35, 39-41 (1998), which also discusses the effect of this interplay on the suspension of the debtor's statute of limitations on assessment (*see* §1008). *Accord Brumlik v. Commissioner*, T.C. Memo 1998-201.

decide the merits of any earlier Tax Court petition for which a default judgment was entered prior to the IRS's filing its answer.[38]

Moreover, even if the bankruptcy court lifts the automatic stay and lets the Tax Court proceeding continue, the bankruptcy court still retains concurrent jurisdiction to resolve the tax liability of the debtor. Thus, the bankruptcy court may, in its discretion, still undertake to decide the merits of the tax case—such as where the Tax Court proceeding is unduly delayed.[39] In the event that the Tax Court ultimately decides the matter prior to the bankruptcy court, there is conflicting authority as to whether the bankruptcy court would be bound by the Tax Court's determination under the doctrine of *res judicata*.[40]

## *§1009.4 Suspension of Tax Court Appeal*

**Suspension of filed appeal.** Two Circuit Courts have considered the application of the automatic stay to Tax Court appeals that had already been filed when the bankruptcy commenced, reaching different conclusions.[41]

The Fifth Circuit first considered the issue in *Freeman v. Commissioner*.[42] There, the debtors (who had filed a Chapter 11 petition ten days after filing their notice of appeal) moved to vacate the Fifth Circuit's earlier decision regarding the dismissal of their Tax Court petition, arguing that the automatic stay precluded the Fifth Circuit from originally proceeding with the appeal. The Fifth Circuit—omitting any reference to Bankruptcy Code section 362(a)(8), which specifically suspends the "commencement or continuation of a proceeding before the United States Tax Court concerning the debtor"—stated that, under the more general provision of Bankruptcy Code

---

[38] *See* discussion at §1013; 124 Cong. Rec. H 11,110 (daily ed. September 28, 1978) (statement of Rep. Edwards), S 17, 427-17,428 (daily ed. October 6, 1978) (statement of Sen. DeConcini).

[39] *See United States v. Wilson*, 974 F.2d 514, 92-2 U.S.T.C. ¶50,510 (4th Cir. 1992), *cert. denied*, 113 S. Ct. 1352 (1993). *Cf. United States v. Olson (In re Olson)*, (9th Cir. February 14, 1992), reprinted at 92 TNT 50-33 (10 months after debtors commenced a postbankruptcy refund suit in district court challenging the underlying assessment, the debtors filed an action in the bankruptcy court also challenging the assessment and requesting a determination of dischargeability; held that the bankruptcy court did not abuse its discretion under Bankruptcy Code section 105(a) in staying the IRS's prosecution of the district court proceedings).

[40] *Compare Doerge v. United States (In re Doerge)*, 181 B.R. 358, 364 (1995) (which, in the fact pattern described in the text, held that the Tax Court's decision was *res judicata*), *citing* 3 Colliers on Bankruptcy ¶505.03 (15th ed. 1994); legislative statements cited *supra* note 1 (also so stating), *with Mantz v. Calif. State Board of Equal. (In re Mantz)*, 343 F.3d 1207 (9th Cir. 2003) (concluding that the doctrine of *res judicata* does *not* preclude a bankruptcy court from redetermining a debtor's tax liability that was the subject of an adjudication that became final postpetition, at least where the matter was not pending appeal or in the appeal filing period at the time of the bankruptcy petition; rejected legislative statements to the contrary in light of the plain language of Bankruptcy Code section 505(a) authorizing the bankruptcy court to determine any tax "whether or not" previously adjudicated and carving out only pre-bankruptcy adjudications; collecting cases).

[41] *See also Roberts v. Commissioner*, 175 F.3d 889, 99-1 U.S.T.C. ¶50,511 (11th Cir. 1999), discussed below (although noting that it was not deciding whether a filed Tax Court appeal was stayed, the court disagreed with the Ninth Circuit that a Tax Court proceeding was within the ambit of section 362(a)(1) of the Bankruptcy Code).

[42] 799 F.2d 1091 (5th Cir. 1986).

section 362(a)(1), the automatic stay only precluded the commencement or continuation of proceedings "against the debtor." The Fifth Circuit then held that, as the Tax Court proceeding of which the appeal was obviously a continuation was commenced by (and not against) the debtor, the prior appellate proceeding was *not* stayed.

In contrast, the Ninth Circuit, in *Delpit v. Commissioner*,[43] concluded that, because the Tax Court proceeding was simply a continuation of the administrative proceedings initiated by the IRS against the taxpayer prepetition (*i.e.*, a tax audit), any appeal of the Tax Court proceeding was stayed under Bankruptcy Code section 362(a)(1). The Ninth Circuit rejected as "faulty" the reasoning in *Freeman*, since it failed to examine the entirety of the proceeding to determine whether they were in fact initiated "against the debtor." In addition, the Ninth Circuit observed that the Fifth Circuit in *Freeman* technically addressed only the first clause of Bankruptcy Code section 362(a)(1), and that the appeal would also be stayed under the second clause—which stays the commencement or continuation of any action or proceeding against the debtor to recover a prepetition claim.

The Ninth Circuit had previously concluded that Tax Court appeals were not stayed under the more specific language of Bankruptcy Code section 362(a)(8), since that section expressly applies only to the continuation of a proceeding *before* the Tax Court and not to proceedings before the court of appeals.[44] Observing that the provisions of Bankruptcy Code section 362(a) frequently overlap and that its prior holding was limited to section 362(a)(8), the Ninth Circuit had "no difficulty" reconciling its earlier decision.

**Suspension of filing period.** In *Roberts v. Commissioner*,[45] the Eleventh Circuit considered whether the automatic stay operated to suspend the 90-day period during which a notice of appeal from a Tax Court decision may be filed. The court held that it did not. The Eleventh Circuit disagreed with the Ninth Circuit, in Delpit, that a Tax Court proceeding is a mere continuation of an administrative proceeding against the debtor. "[I]t is clear that a Tax Court proceeding is properly to be characterized as an independent judicial proceeding" commenced by (and not against) the debtor. Thus, the Eleventh Circuit held that Bankruptcy Code section 362(a)(1) did not apply. As for Bankruptcy Code section 362(a)(8), the court agreed with the IRS that the Tax Court retains jurisdiction over the Tax Court case during the appeal period, and that the Tax Court decision does not become final until the appeal period has expired, but nevertheless concluded that the appeal period was not part of the "proceeding before" the Tax Court. The court explained that a judicial "proceeding" within the meaning of section 362(a) ends once the decision is rendered, and does not include ministerial acts or automatic occurrences that entail no deliberation, discretion or judicial involvement.

Although not suspended by the automatic stay, the appeal period was extended by approximately 30 days under Bankruptcy Code section 108(b). Such section ensures that a debtor or trustee has at least 60 days after the commencement of the

---

[43] 18 F.3d 768, 94-1 U.S.T.C. ¶ 50,127 (9th Cir. 1994).

[44] *See Cheng v. Commissioner*, 938 F.2d 141, 91-2 U.S.T.C. ¶ 50,346 (9th Cir. 1991).

[45] *Supra* note 41.

bankruptcy or, in an involuntary bankruptcy, after the order for relief to make certain filings. Unfortunately, this was still not sufficient under the circumstances to render the debtor's notice of appeal (which was filed approximately four months after the start of the bankruptcy case) timely.

### *§1009.5 Receivership Proceeding*

In the case of a receivership proceeding, Code §6871(c)(2) precludes the commencement of a new proceeding in the Tax Court after the appointment of a receiver.[46] If a Tax Court proceeding is already pending, both the court overseeing the receivership proceeding and the Tax Court have jurisdiction.[47] In contrast, once a bankruptcy petition is filed, the bankruptcy case takes precedence (*see generally* §1009.3 above).[48]

## §1010 IRS PROOF OF CLAIM

Like any other creditor, the IRS must file a proof of claim with the bankruptcy court for any unpaid prepetition taxes in order to participate as a creditor in a bankruptcy case under Chapter 11 with respect to such taxes.[1] The date by which this must be done is called the "bar date" and is established by the court (subject to extension for cause) after the start of the bankruptcy case.[2] However, the Bankruptcy Code ensures the IRS a minimum of 180 days in which to file a claim (for bankruptcy cases commenced on or after October 22, 1994).[3] In addition, the IRS will be deemed to have filed a proof of claim (absent an actual filed claim) for any unpaid taxes identified in the debtor's schedule of liabilities that are not listed as disputed, contingent or unliquidated.[4] Any claim for prepetition taxes due to an excessive allowance of a "quickie" refund (or tentative carryback adjustment) received during

---

46 *See, e.g., Dennis C. Levine*, 54 T.C.M. 1064, Dec. 44,322(M), T.C. Memo. 1987-564 (1987) (it is irrelevant that only a portion of the taxpayer's assets is under control of the receiver).

47 *See* Code §6871(c)(1); Reg. §301.6871(b)-1(b); *David R. Kane*, 93 T.C. 782 (1989); *cf.* S. Rep. No. 1035, 96th Cong., 2d Sess. 46-47, 50 (1980).

48 *See, e.g., Gilchrist v. General Electric Capital Corp.*, 262 F.3d 295 (4th Cir. 2001) (so holding in connection with the imposition of the automatic stay).

1 **§1010** Bankruptcy Rule 3003(c)(2); *see, e.g., In re Milton*, 1990 Bankr. LEXIS 952 (Bankr. S.D. Cal.) (IRS claim listing amounts owed as "unknown" was not a valid proof of claim).

2 *See* Bankruptcy Rule 3003(c)(3). For a discussion of post-bar date amendments and late claims, *see* discussion below (this section) and at §1010.2; *see also In re International Horizons, Inc.*, 85-1 U.S.T.C. ¶9212 (11th Cir.), discussed *infra* at §1014.1. The bar date operates independently of, and does not dispense with the need to also comply with, any applicable statute of limitations for assessment or collection of the tax. *See* 11 U.S.C. §502(b)(1); *In re Brac Group, Inc.*, 2004 Bankr. LEXIS 1087 (Bankr. D. Del. 2004).

3 11 U.S.C. §502(b)(9); Bankruptcy Rule 3003.

4 11 U.S.C. §1111(a); Bankruptcy Code section 3002(c)(2); *see also Cohen v. United States (In re Cohen)*, 198 B.R. 382, 96-2 U.S.T.C. ¶50,608 (Bankr. S.D. Fla. 1996) (subsequently filed IRS claim superseded scheduled amounts, even though IRS failed to claim all amounts listed in the schedules). *But consider ATD Corp. v. Advantage Packaging, Inc. (In re ATD Corp.)*, 352 F.3d 1062 (6th Cir. 2003), which leaves

the bankruptcy case is treated as an administrative expense (*see* §1010.4 below) and, thus, is not subject to the general bar date for prepetition claims.[5] Also, as discussed below, the absence of a proof of claim does not necessarily affect a filed IRS lien.

Although the IRS has in the past ordinarily used its own form of proof of claim (*see* Form 6338, "Proof of Claim for Internal Revenue Taxes"), the IRS Manual now advises use of a computer-generated "Form B10," the official bankruptcy form.[6] The proof of claim must be filed by an authorized IRS representative; however, the IRS's filing of a proof of claim is not the commencement of a "civil action" requiring prior permission (or delegation) of the Secretary of the Treasury and the Attorney General under Code §7401.[7]

The types of prepetition taxes (including interest and penalties) included on the form are generally broken down between secured claims, unsecured priority claims (*see* §1015), and general unsecured claims.[8] Where the debtor is a member of a consolidated group, the amount claimed will be based on the tax owing by the entire group and not just the debtor company.[9] The IRS Chief Counsel's office has also recommended that, when unpaid taxes are the subject of a previously accepted offer-in-compromise for which amounts are still payable as of the petition date, a contingent proof of claim be filed for the full amount of the underlying tax liability to

(Footnote Continued)

open the possibility that the bankruptcy court could require that proofs of claim be filed even for scheduled claims as to which there is no dispute, provided the creditors receive adequate notice.

5 *See* 11 U.S.C. §503(b)(1)(B)(ii).

6 IRS Manual, Part 5 (Collecting Process), Ch. 9 (Bankruptcy), §13.6 (3/1/07), at ¶1. In certain cases, other bankruptcy court pleadings, or possibly even the issuance of a notice of deficiency during the bankruptcy case, might constitute an "informal" proof of claim. *See, e.g., Campbell v. U.S. (In re Campbell)*, 99-1 U.S.T.C. ¶50,169 (Bankr. 9th Cir. 1998); *In re International Horizons, Inc.* (11th Cir.), *supra* note 2 (raising possibility that notice of deficiency might suffice); and discussion above at §1005.1.2 note 28. However, the IRS is not required to send a notice of deficiency before filing a proof of claim. *See, e.g., Carroll v. United States*, 41 F.3d 668 (11th Cir. 1994) (*per curiam*) (unpublished decision), *reprinted in full at* 94 TNT 246-23, *reh'g, en banc, denied*, 46 F.3d 72 (1995), *cert. denied*, 116 S. Ct. 26 (1995).

7 *Bozich v. IRS (In re Bozich)*, 97-1 U.S.T.C. ¶50,217 (Bankr. D. Ariz. 1996), *aff'd*, 99-2 U.S.T.C. ¶50,721 (D. Ariz. 1999); *see also In re Bozich*, 212 B.R. 354 (Bankr. D. Ariz. 1997) (subsequent decision granting IRS partial summary judgment as to IRS agent's authority to file proof of claim).

8 *See* IRS Manual, Part 5 (Collecting Process), Ch. 9 (Bankruptcy), §13.20 (3/1/06), at ¶3. For the treatment of interest and penalties in respect of a secured tax claim, *see* §301 note 2 above (interest), and §1015 at note 4 below (penalties). For a discussion of the reclassification of secured claims where the value of the liened property is less than the purported secured claims, *see* IRS Litigation Guideline Memorandum, "Reclassification of Lien Claims in Bankruptcy," dated May 2, 1994, at 96 TNT 155-63. *See also In re Offshore Diving & Salvaging, Inc.*, 226 B.R. 185, 98-2 U.S.T.C. ¶50,593 (Bankr. E.D. La. 1998) (order entered in earlier bankruptcy fixing amount of IRS's secured claim controlled in subsequent bankruptcy).

9 *See, e.g.*, IRS Manual, Part 8 (Appeals), Ch. 15 (Appeals Bankruptcy Cases), §1.4.1 (6/27/05), at ¶3. Similarly, if the debtor were a general partner in a partnership, the amount claimed generally would include any unpaid partnership level taxes (such as employment or other transactional taxes) for which the IRS is seeking to hold the debtor liable. The extent to which a general partner can be held liable for partnership debts generally depends on applicable state law. *See, e.g., United States v. Galletti*, 124 S. Ct. 1528, 2004-1 U.S.T.C. ¶50,204 (2004) (IRS need not individually assess a partner in order to hold the partner liable for employment tax liabilities assessed against the partnership); IRS Chief Counsel Notice CC-2005-003 (January 19, 2005), *reprinted at* 2005 TNT 14-18 (discussing *Galletti*).

protect against the possibility that the debtor does not assume the accepted offer as an executory contract (and that the claim so indicates).[10] The IRS is not required to attach any supporting documentation to a proof of claim when filed, unless the claim arises from a contractual agreement.[11] However, a bankruptcy court may impose sanctions for filing a frivolous or unjustified proof of claim.[12]

Although the absence of a proof of claim does not impede any tax lien filed (perfected) prior to the commencement of the bankruptcy case,[13] a debtor in Chapter 11 may be able to void (or "strip") the lien under Bankruptcy Code section 506(d) to the extent the lien exceeds the value of the liened property.[14] In addition, the

---

[10] IRS Chief Counsel Advice 200027050, May 16, 2000, *reprinted at* 2000 TNT 132-66 (concludes that an offer-in-compromise is not a "personal service contract" that cannot be assumed, despite the condition that the taxpayer continue to comply with the tax laws for five years); IRS Chief Counsel Advice 200015037, February 8, 2000, *reprinted at* 2000 TNT 74-56 (offer-in-compromise does not convert tax liability into a contractual claim; both case law and the language of the offer-in-compromise form, IRS Form 656, are cited in support of this conclusion).

[11] *See, e.g., In re Los Angeles Int'l Airport Hotel Assoc.*, 106 F.3d 1479 (9th Cir. 1997) (*per curiam*) (Bankruptcy Rule 3001(c) only requires that documentation be attached where the claim or interest "is based on a writing," not a statute; a written assessment of the tax is not itself the basis for the claim, but simply the enforcement of a pre-existing statutory obligation); *In re Boehm*, 255 B.R. 686, 2000-2 U.S.T.C. ¶50,779 (Bankr. E.D. Ky. 2000) (IRS entitled to priority tax claim for Code §6672 penalty, even though proof of claim simply identified "type of tax" as a "civil penalty" and did not identify it as a trust fund recovery or attach any supporting documentation); *In re Shaver*, 2000-1 U.S.T.C. ¶50,171 (Bankr. E.D. Tenn. 1999) (collecting cases); *In re Catron*, 198 B.R. 905 (Bankr. M.D.N.C. 1996); *United States v. Braunstein (In re Pan)*, 209 B.R. 152, 97-2 U.S.T.C. ¶50,581 (D. Mass. 1997). *See also Gill v. Indian Wells Estates, Inc. (In re Indian Wells Estates, Inc.)*, 96-2 U.S.T.C. ¶50,521 (9th Cir. 1996) (unpublished decision; involved IRS claim for interest; IRS later provided substantiation in defense of trustee's objection on the merits); *Neilson v. United States (In re Olshan)*, 356 F.3d 1078, 2004-1 U.S.T.C. ¶50,143 (9th Cir. 2004) (allowance of IRS claim is not an all or nothing determination dependent on the IRS proving the accuracy of the amount specified in the claim; rather, the normal burden of proof rules applicable outside bankruptcy apply, *see* §1013.4 below).

Query, whether the IRS would be required to attach any installment agreement. *See* IRS Legal Memorandum 199920005, February 5, 1999 (concluding that a taxpayer's bankruptcy filing may suspend, but does not terminate, any installment agreement between the taxpayer and the IRS under Code §6159), *reprinted at* 1999 TNT 25-19.

[12] *See* authorities cited *infra* note 21.

[13] 11 U.S.C. §§506(d) and 522(c)(2); *see, e.g., In re Tarnow*, 749 F.2d 464 (7th Cir. 1984); *cf. Dewsnup v. Timm*, 502 U.S. 410 (1992) (Chapter 7 case; lien for amount in excess of value of liened property is not voidable under Bankruptcy Code section 506(d)); *In re Southwest Equip. Rental, Inc.*, 1993 Bankr. LEXIS 1554 (Bankr. E.D. Tenn.) (IRS lien attached to postpetition recoveries from preference and fraudulent conveyance actions); *see also Ryan v. Homecomings Financial Network*, 253 F.3d 778 (4th Cir. 2001) (Chapter 7 case; denied the "strip-off" of a lien with respect to property as to which senior liens have exhausted the value, finding no principled distinction from the situation in *Dewsnup*, wherein the Supreme Court prohibited the "strip-down" of a creditor's lien in a Chapter 7 case when the lien retained some value); *Talbert v. City Mortgage Servs. (In re Talbert)*, 344 F.3d 555 (6th Cir. 2003) (same); *Laskin v. First Nat'l Bank of Keystone (In re Laskin)*, 222 B.R. 872 (Bankr. 9th Cir. 1998) (same); *Hoekstra v. United States (In re Hoekstra)*, 255 B.R. 285, 2000-2 U.S.T.C. ¶50,857 (E.D. Va. 2000), *rev'g*, 253 B.R. 193, 2000-1 U.S.T.C. ¶50,490 (Bankr. E.D. Va. 2000) (Chapter 7; bankruptcy court had permitted a "strip-off" of an IRS lien; the district court reversed because the tax lien was still partially secured by other personal property of the debtor).

[14] *See, e.g., Wade v. Bradford*, 39 F.3d 1126 (10th Cir. 1994) (lien stripping permitted); *Dever v. IRS (In re Dever)*, 164 B.R. 132 (Bankr. C.D. Cal. 1994); *but see Taffi v. United States (In re Taffi)*, 1993 U.S. Dist. LEXIS 15073 (C.D. Cal. 1993) (not permitted), *rev'd on other grounds*, 68 F.3d 306 (9th Cir. 1995) (split decision), *aff'd, en banc*, 96 F.3d 1190 (9th Cir. 1996); *Blue Pac. Car Wash, Inc. v. St. Croix County (In re*

continued existence of such lien postconfirmation may depend upon the treatment of the lien in the Chapter 11 plan or confirmation order (*see* § 1014 below). On the other hand, the IRS may be able to file an otherwise secured claim as an unsecured (priority) creditor and forgo its lien (such as where the payout period for priority unsecured claims is more favorable than for secured claims).[15]

If the IRS fails to file a timely proof of claim, the debtor or any person who may be liable with the debtor (including a co-debtor, surety, or guarantor) may file a proof of claim on behalf of the IRS within 30 days after the bar date.[16] In general, it will be rare that a corporate debtor seeks to employ this procedure since any prepetition taxes for which a proof of claim is not filed are generally dischargeable (*see* § 1014). This procedure may be useful, however, where, for example, there are current or former members of the debtor's consolidated group that would have continuing several liability for any discharged taxes of the debtor.

It should be noted that late filed claims are treated differently in Chapter 7 cases than in Chapter 11 cases. In Chapter 7 cases, Bankruptcy Code section 726(a) expressly provides for distributions with respect to late-filed claims. Accordingly, even though former Bankruptcy Rule 3002 provided that only filed claims were "allowed" and provided time limits for filing, most courts had upheld distributions to late claims in Chapter 7 cases, although generally on a subordinated basis.[17] Effective for bankruptcy cases commenced on or after October 22, 1994, Bankruptcy Code section 502(b)(9) expressly permits distributions to late claims in Chapter 7 in

---

(Footnote Continued)

*Blue Pac. Car Wash, Inc.*), 150 B.R. 434 (W.D. Wis. 1992). This is not the case in Chapter 7. *See Dewsnup v. Timm, supra* note 13. Also, a creditor's election under Bankruptcy Code section 1111(b) to retain the benefit of the full lien but forgo any deficiency claim will preempt the debtor's ability to strip the lien. *See Wade v. Bradford, supra; cf. 680 Fifth Ave. Assocs. v. Mutual Benefit Life Ins. Co.* (*In re 680 Fifth Ave. Assocs.*), 29 F.3d 95 (2d Cir. 1994).

[15] *Herckner v. United States*, 2005-2 U.S.T.C. ¶ 50,600 (D. N.J. 2005) (unpublished decision; holding that the IRS could; discusses contrasting authorities).

[16] *See* 11 U.S.C. § 501(b), (c); Bankruptcy Rules 3004 and 3005. *See also In re Kilen*, 129 B.R. 538, 91-2 U.S.T.C. ¶ 50,361 (Bankr. N.D. Ill. 1991), discussed *infra* at § 1013.3.2; *In re Kolstad*, 928 F.2d 171, 91-1 U.S.T.C. ¶ 50,190 (5th Cir. 1991) (IRS allowed to amend proof of claim filed on its behalf by the debtor), *reh'g denied en banc*, 936 F.2d 571, *cert. denied*, 112 S. Ct. 419 (1992); *In re Stoiber*, 160 B.R. 307 (Bankr. N.D. Ohio 1993) (disallowed amendment on equitable grounds, distinguishing *Kolstad*), *aff'd*, 1993 U.S. Dist. LEXIS 18,759 (N.D. Ohio).

[17] *See, e.g., United States v. Cardinal Mine Supply, Inc.*, 916 F.2d 1087 (6th Cir. 1990). For cases commenced prior to October 22, 1994, an interesting interpretational issue under Bankruptcy Code section 726(a)(1) is whether, and to what extent, late filed priority claims are granted a first priority in distribution along side timely filed priority claims. *Compare United States v. Vecchio* (*In re Vecchio*), 20 F.3d 555 (2d Cir. 1994) (concluding all late claims, but remanded case to bankruptcy court to consider equitable subordination); *United States v. Towers* (*In re Pacific-Atlantic Trading Co.*), 33 F.3d 1064 (9th Cir. 1994) (same, at least where the claim is filed before distributions are made); *In re Davis*, 81 F.3d 134 (11th Cir. 1996) (to same effect); *Cooper v. Internal Revenue*, 167 F.3d 857 (4th Cir. 1999) (same; adopts Second Circuit opinion as its own); *In re Michael A. Rago*, 1992 Bankr. LEXIS 1855 (Bankr. N.D. Ill.) (suggesting all late claims); *with IRS v. Century Boat Co.* (*In re Century Boat Co.*), 986 F.2d 154 (6th Cir. 1993) (only claims filed late for lack of notice, absent factors warranting equitable subordination; clarifies the Sixth Circuit decision in *Cardinal Mine Supply*); *United States v. Simon* (*In re Burnham, Connolly, Oesterle and Henry*), 1996 U.S. App. LEXIS 26634 (6th Cir. 1996) (reaffirming its view); *United States v. Waindel* (*In re Waindel*), 65 F.3d 1307 (5th Cir. 1995). For subsequent cases, such section expressly grants a first priority to any claim filed before the trustee begins distributions.

accordance with Bankruptcy Code section 726(a).[18] Under section 726(a)(1), any late-filed priority claims will maintain their priority if filed before the earlier of (i) the date the trustee commences final distributions or (ii) for bankruptcy cases commenced on or after October 17, 2005, 10 days after the mailing of the Chapter 7 trustee's final report to the creditors.[19] No similar provision is made for unexcused late claims in Chapter 11, although a late-filed claim may be permitted on equitable grounds (*see* discussion at § 1010.2). This is consistent with prior law.[20] The strict adherence to the bar date in Chapter 11 cases addresses a reorganizing debtor's need for finality as to the extent of any potential claims in connection with the formulation of its plan, and the desire to expedite reorganization proceedings.

## *§1010.1 "Capping" (or Estimating) Tax Claims*

In many cases, the amount stated in the initial proof of claim filed by the IRS may be inflated if the IRS has been unable, or has had insufficient time, to audit the debtor.[21] Moreover, even if the claim accurately reflects the amount the IRS believes to be owing (or is amended to so reflect), the claimed amount generally will be

---

[18] *See also* Bankruptcy Rule 3002, as amended December 1, 1996.

[19] *See also* discussion of late claims at *infra* note 48. A Chapter 7 trustee is generally considered to commence distributions upon the *approval* of his final report and accounting by the bankruptcy court. *See, e.g., Security State Bank v. IRS (In re Van Gerpen)*, 267 F.3d 453 (5th Cir. 2001); *Andersen v. Baer (In re Andersen)*, 275 B.R. 922 (Bankr. 10th Cir. 2002), *rev'g*, 266 B.R. 498 (Bankr. D. Kan. 2001).

[20] *See* 2 Collier on Bankruptcy ¶ 57.27 (14th ed.).

[21] *See, e.g.*, IRS Manual, Part 5 (Collecting Process), Ch. 9 (Bankruptcy), § 13.20.1 (3/1/07), at ¶ 3 (advising that the initial proof of claim be based on as much information as possible to avoid filing an inflated claim); *In re Limited Gaming of America, Inc.*, 213 B.R. 369 (Bankr. N.D. Okla. 1997) (IRS bankruptcy specialist testified that it was IRS policy to file estimated claims rather than requesting an extension of the bar date). *See also* former IRS Manual § 57(13)2.35:(7)(c) (December 7, 1988), advising against the filing of a "large *unliquidated* proof of claim that is not supported by available information" (emphasis added). Subsequently, the IRS substituted the word "estimated" for "unliquidated"—former IRS Manual § 57(13)2.35:(8)(c) (March 16, 1995)—and has since substituted "unassessed" for "estimated." IRS Manual, Part 5 (Collecting Process), Ch. 9 (Bankruptcy), § 13.20.1 (3/1/07), at ¶ 1. *See also* IRS Manual, Part 34 (General Litigation), Ch. 3.1 (Procedures in Bankruptcy Cases), § 3.3 (8/11/04) (Significant Bankruptcy Case Program), advising that "[e]very effort should be made to insure that the initial claims filed are as accurate and complete as possible even if estimates are necessary," and that "[i]n order to avoid the potential of misleading the bankruptcy court, any claim which is still under audit should be so labeled."

*Consider also Hamilton v. United States (In re Hamilton)*, 104 B.R. 525 (Bankr. M.D. Ga. 1989) (IRS sanctioned, and debtor awarded his attorneys' *fees*, where IRS filed a proof of claim that incorrectly listed certain taxes as unpaid, even though it promptly amended the claim in line with debtor's objections); *In re McAllister*, 123 B.R. 393 (Bankr. D. Or. 1991) (filing of precautionary claim for income taxes based only upon an investigation that revealed no tax returns had been filed for the years at issue warranted imposition of sanctions); IRS Chief Counsel Advice 200048044, October 17, 2000, *reprinted at* 2000 TNT 233-59 (advising that the IRS "must make a reasonable inquiry prior to filing a proof of claim for taxes and must believe that the claim is well grounded in fact;" and recognizing the bankruptcy court's ability to impose sanctions); *see also* § 1007.7 (discussing bankruptcy court contempt power and Code § 7430); *In re M.L. Hill*, 71 B.R. 517, 87-1 U.S.T.C. ¶ 9297 (Bankr. D. Colo. 1987) (awarded legal fees to debtor; held that settlement of IRS claim after hearings before the bankruptcy court came within statutory requirements of Code § 7430). *Cf. M.L. Powers v. Commissioner*, 100 T.C. 457 (unjustified assessment).

disputed by the debtor. Where a settlement cannot be reached, and a substantive resolution of the open issues could involve protracted or time-consuming litigation and have a significant impact on the debtor's reorganization, the bankruptcy court may be required to estimate the claim for certain bankruptcy purposes (possibly including for distribution purposes) with the objective of imposing a reasonable "cap" on the amount recoverable.

Bankruptcy Code section 502(c)(1) requires that any "contingent or unliquidated claim" be estimated, for purposes of allowance, where the fixing or liquidation of the claim "would unduly delay the administration of the case." The terms "contingent" and "unliquidated" are not defined in the Bankruptcy Code. Nevertheless, all courts appear to agree that a claim is "contingent" if the debtor's legal duty to pay only comes into existence upon the occurrence or happening of an extrinsic event[22] and that a claim is considered "liquidated" if it is "readily ascertainable."[23] The debate has therefore been over whether a debt is readily ascertainable when there exists a genuine and substantial dispute as to liability and amount.[24]

Arguably, in a general sense, any proof of claim for unassessed taxes is an "unliquidated" claim, unless previously agreed to by the debtor. In fact, in *In re King*,[25] when it suited the government's interest, the government early on took precisely this position:

> The government argues . . . that it is standard practice for the IRS to assert unliquidated or estimated claims in bankruptcy proceedings. In this case, the claim is for an estimated, or unassessed, deficiency which has been determined by an audit of the debtors' tax return.[26]

---

[22] *See, e.g., Fostvedt v. Dow (In re Fostvedt)*, 823 F.2d 305, 306 (9th Cir. 1987).

[23] *See, e.g., Slack v. Wilshire Ins. Co. (In re Slack)*, 187 F.3d 1070 (9th Cir. 1999) (holding that "a debt is liquidated if the amount is readily ascertainable, notwithstanding the fact that the question of liability has not been finally decided").

[24] *See, e.g.*, id. (discussing various court positions; viewed debt as readily determinable depending on whether it was easily calculable, although still subject to litigation, or whether an extensive hearing would be required to determine the amount); and authorities cited *infra* note 29. To illustrate the interpretive confusion, *compare In re Sylvester*, 19 B.R. 671 (Bankr. 9th Cir. 1982) (dispute did not render claim unliquidated; court reasoned that, because the definition of "claim" in Bankruptcy Code section 101(5) includes any right of payment, whether or not "contingent," "unliquidated," or "disputed," the three terms were intended to be distinct concepts); *In re Albano*, 55 B.R. 363 (N.D. Ill. 1985) (also contrasts language in Bankruptcy Code section 303(b)(1), referring to a claim that is "not contingent as to liability or the subject of a bona fide dispute"); *with In re Lambert*, 43 B.R. 913 (Bankr. D. Utah 1984) (concluded that the terms "contingent," "unliquidated," and "disputed" were overlapping and interlinking concepts). *See also Comprehensive Accounting Corp. v. Pearson (In re Pearson)*, 773 F.2d 751 (6th Cir. 1985).

[25] 102 B.R. 184 (Bankr. D. Neb. 1989), *rev'd on other grounds*, 91-2 U.S.T.C. ¶50,553 (D. Neb.). Interestingly, rather than involving the estimation of claims, the debtors were attempting to have the IRS claim disallowed on the theory that Bankruptcy Code section 502(c)(1) provided for the only circumstances under which estimated claims would be allowable in bankruptcy and that an "estimated" tax claim was neither contingent nor unliquidated. Without deciding the contingent or unliquidated nature of the tax claim, the bankruptcy court rejected the debtors' argument as to the role of Bankruptcy Code section 502(c)(1).

[26] 102 B.R. at 187. *See also In re Imperial Corp. of America*, 91-2 U.S.T.C. ¶50,342 (Bankr. D. Cal.) (court estimated IRS claims for prepetition and postpetition taxes), discussed below. *Cf. In re Century Vault*

However, the IRS generally takes the contrary position.[27]

Numerous courts have considered the question of a tax claim's status as "contingent or unliquidated" under Bankruptcy Code section 109(e) for purposes of determining an individual debtor's eligibility for relief under Chapter 13 of the Bankruptcy Code. Many of these cases involved facts peculiar to the Chapter 13 eligibility issue.[28] As to the others, it now appears that most courts view disputed tax claims as noncontingent and nonliquidated for purposes of section 109(e), except, possibly, where the claim itself purports to be an estimate; however, a minority still exists.[29] In one case, the court held that an IRS claim for tax shelter related penalties

(Footnote Continued)

*Co.*, 416 F.2d 1035, 1040 (3d Cir. 1969) (state tax claim was "in the nature of an unliquidated claim" where state had only roughly computed debtor's taxes; involved Bankruptcy Act predecessor); IRS Manual, Part 5 (Collecting Process), Ch. 9 (Bankruptcy), §13.20.1 (3/1/07), at ¶2 (stating that the proof of claim "can include both assessed (i.e., the exact amount owing has been determined) and unassessed amounts").

[27] In the estimation context, *see, e.g.*, the briefs filed in *In re The Drexel Burnham Lambert Group Inc.* (Bankr. S.D.N.Y.), in support and opposition to the debtors' motion "Pursuant to Sections 505(a) and 502(c) to Determine IRS Tax Claims Through Estimation," Chapter 11, 90 Civ. 6954 (MP), Return Date March 28, 1991. In that case, although the court (in a bench decision) approved the debtors' motion and scheduled the estimation hearings, a settlement was ultimately reached between the debtors and the IRS. Similarly, *see In re Baldwin-United Corp.*, 79 B.R. 321, 332 (Bankr. S.D. Ohio 1987) (involved IRS tax claims, totalling over $450 million and involving thousands of transactions dating back many years; court had expressed intent to commence estimation hearings if a settlement, without which no plan was possible, could not be reached).

[28] For example, in *In re Hutchens*, 69 B.R. 806 (Bankr. E.D. Tenn. 1987), the taxes at issue were assessed prior to the bankruptcy case but not disputed until afterwards, leading the court to believe that the dispute was for the sole purpose of characterizing the debt as "unliquidated" so that the individual would be eligible for Chapter 13 relief.

[29] *Compare In re Elrod*, 178 B.R. 5 (Bankr. N.D. Okla. 1995) ("a claim is liquidated when the amount can be readily determined with precision and capable of ascertainment by reference to an agreement or simple mathematical computation. If a determination of the amount requires judgment, discretion or interpretation of applicable statutes, then it is unliquidated"; accordingly, the court held that a tax claim, which the IRS itself labeled an "estimated liability" and would require an evidentiary hearing, was unliquidated); *In re Harbaugh*, 153 B.R. 54 (Bankr. D. Idaho 1993) (claim for tax and interest considered unliquidated to the extent resolution of dispute would require an evidentiary hearing; even then, however, debtor's liquidated claims exceeded Chapter 13 eligibility limit); *Matter of Verdunn*, 160 B.R. 682 (Bankr. M.D. Fla. 1993) (tax liabilities were not readily determinable from the documents before the court, and were therefore deemed unliquidated), *aff'd*, 187 B.R. 996 (M.D. Fla. 1995), *rev'd*, 89 F.3d 799 (11th Cir. 1996) (holding that tax liability set forth in notice of deficiency was liquidated, including assertion of fraud penalties, since based on tax statutes, even though Tax Court proceeding pending; a debt is unliquidated "[i]f the amount of the debt is dependent . . . upon the future exercise of discretion, not restricted by specific criteria"); *Mazzeo v. United States (In re Mazzeo)*, 131 F.3d 295 (2d Cir. 1997) (agrees with Eleventh Circuit; held that responsible person liability as reflected in a notice of deficiency was liquidated; court did not address the status of the IRS's "estimated" claim); *United States v. May*, 211 B.R. 991 (M.D. Fla. 1997) (reached opposite result to that of Eleventh Circuit, but was apparently not aware of earlier Eleventh Circuit decision); *with Barcal v. Laughlin (In re Barcal)*, 213 B.R. 1008 (Bankr. 8th Cir. 1997) (whether a tax claim is liquidated does not depend on "the extent of the dispute nor the amount of evidence required to establish the claim, but whether the process for determining the claim is fixed, certain, or otherwise determined by a specific standard"); *Hounsom v. United States*, 325 B.R. 319 (M.D. Fla. 2005) (same; followed Eleventh Circuit decision in *Verdunn*; held that it was irrelevant the IRS had not issued a notice of deficiency as of the petition date); *with United States v. Dallas*, 157 B.R. 912, 93-1 U.S.T.C. ¶50,352 (S.D. Ala. 1993) (dispute irrelevant; the fact that the tax was previously assessed did not appear to bear on the court's

unassessed at the time of the Chapter 13 filing was a "contingent nonliquidated claim" by comparing the tax penalties to tort claims.[30] The court placed considerable emphasis on the fact that the IRS, even outside bankruptcy, bore the burden of proof on the threshold issue of culpability (*i.e.*, that the debtor engaged in the prohibited conduct) in the same way that the plaintiff in a tort action—which the courts have held to be both "contingent" and "unliquidated"—bears the burden on the issue of negligence.[31]

On the more helpful side, Bankruptcy Code section 502(i) expressly contemplates that tax claims may be subject to estimation under Bankruptcy Code section 502(c)(1).[32]

Ultimately, whether a disputed tax claim is considered a "contingent or unliquidated" claim for purposes of Bankruptcy Code section 502(c)(1) may come down to a technical nicety, given that Bankruptcy Code section 502(c)(1) does not *prohibit* estimation of liquidated claims; rather, it requires the estimation of contingent and unliquidated claims.[33] Thus, it would seem that a disputed tax claim that is definitionally held to be a "liquidated" claim can still be subject to estimation, in the discretion of the court, if the resolution of the dispute would unduly delay the administration of the case.

In appropriate cases, the estimation process may serve as an alternative (or adjunct) to litigation (*see* § 1013 below). In contrast to litigation, the estimation process generally addresses the substantive issues in an accelerated and summary fashion with the objective of imposing a reasonable "cap" on the amount recoverable, so as to allow the bankruptcy case to proceed more quickly and efficiently. Unless expressly limited in scope (*e.g.*, solely for purposes of determining the extent to which a holder of a disputed claim can vote in respect of a proposed Chapter 11 plan), the estimation process generally imposes a substantive cap on liability for *actual* distribution purposes. Subject to the cap, the substantive issues may then be addressed in due course.[34] In certain cases, however, the estimation process will effectively resolve the

(Footnote Continued)

decision). *See also In re Madison*, 168 B.R. 986 (D. Haw. 1994) (held that tax claim was liquidated where a notice of deficiency had been issued, even though Tax Court case was pending). *See also* cases cited *supra* note 24; Annotation, Classification of Debt as Liquidated, Unsecured, or Contingent, for Purposes of Determining Debtor's Eligibility Under § 109(e) of 1978 Bankruptcy Code, 95 A.L.R. Fed. 793.

[30] *In re Robertson*, 143 B.R. 76 (Bankr. N.D. Tex. 1992). *But see In re Slack* (9th Cir.), *supra* note 23 (observing that tort claims have even been held to be liquidated in certain cases), and *Matter of Verdunn* (11th Cir.), *supra* note 29 (asserted fraud penalties were a liquidated claim).

[31] Arguably, the burden of proof outside bankruptcy loses its significance in the context of Bankruptcy Code section 502(c) where the issue becomes the resolution of the tax claim in bankruptcy rather than the status of the claim at the inception of the bankruptcy. *See* § 1013.4, discussing burden of proof in bankruptcy.

[32] Bankruptcy Code section 502(i) provides that priority tax claims arising postpetition "shall be allowed under subsection (a), (b) or (c) of this section . . . the same as if such claim" arose prepetition.

[33] *Cf. In re King*, *supra* note 25.

[34] *See, e.g.*, Colliers on Bankruptcy ¶ 502.04[3] (15th ed.); Bienenstock, Bankruptcy Reorganizations 635-638 (1987 with 1989 Supp.). *See also* discussion of estimation proceedings in *United States v. Sterling Consulting Corp. (In re Indian Motocycle Co., Inc.)*, 261 B.R. 800 (Bankr. 1st Cir. 2001). *Cf.* 28

substantive issue. For example, in the *Imperial Corporation* case,[35] the bankruptcy court estimated the IRS claim for prepetition taxes at zero. In that case, the debtor and the IRS agreed to a summary procedure in which each side was limited to 1/2 hours of direct or cross-examination and one half hour for opening statements and closing arguments. Direct evidence was submitted by way of declaration with supporting exhibits, and examination of declarants was limited to cross-examination. Testimony of rebuttal witnesses was also offered, subject to agreed time limitations. Moreover, although the court applied the standard burden of proof for proof of claims in bankruptcy (thus placing the initial burden of going forward on the debtor and the ultimate burden of persuasion on the IRS, *but see* discussion at § 1013.4 below for subsequent developments with respect to the burden of proof in bankruptcy cases), it noted that at least one bankruptcy court has held that an estimated tax claim is not entitled to even a *prima facie* presumption of validity.[36] Subsequently, upon motion by the debtor, the bankruptcy court declared the notice of deficiency that had previously been issued to the debtor to be of no further force or effect and ordered the IRS to withdraw the notice (even though a Tax Court petition was already pending).[37]

Finally, it should be noted the estimation process is not necessarily limited to claims for prepetition taxes but also may apply to postpetition taxes. For example, in the *Imperial Corporation* case, the bankruptcy court also was "required" to estimate the tax claims of the IRS arising out of certain postpetition transactions, because the confirmed Chapter 11 plan "committed to pay any tax attributable to events occurring prior to the confirmation date" and the creditors' committee and the debtor "had agreed to withhold distribution under the plan until an estimation of the amount of any such obligation could be made and its priority determined." The authority for estimation proceedings with respect to postpetition taxes, however, probably does not rest in Bankruptcy Code section 502(c), given that section 502 as a whole generally speaks only to prepetition claims. Rather, courts that have focused on the issue of authority generally have relied on their more general authority in Bankruptcy Rules 7016 and 9014 to regulate the manner in which evidence is presented in a contested hearing, and have adapted the procedures employed under Bankruptcy Code section 502(c).[38] In *In re MacDonald,* the bankruptcy court also cautioned against utilizing the estimation process in the case of postpetition administrative claims to set

(Footnote Continued)

U.S.C. § 157(b)(2)(B) (only estimation proceedings in respect of a personal injury tort or wrongful death claim are expressly excluded from the bankruptcy court's "core" jurisdiction for distribution purposes).

[35] *In re Imperial Corp. of America, supra* note 26.

[36] Id. at n.1, *citing In re Mobile Mfg. Co.,* slip op. (Bankr. D. Utah May 8, 1985).

[37] *See* IRS Field Service Advice 1999-566 (Fall/Winter 1991) (clear from comparison of facts that the field service advice involved the *Imperial Corporation* case; recommended appeal of the orders nullifying the notice of deficiency, given that the IRS was still challenging confirmation of the debtor's Chapter 11 plan, but refrained from making any recommendation with respect to the propriety of the estimation hearing because of the possibility that, upon remand, an actual litigation on the merits could result in unfavorable precedent to the IRS on the substantive issues, some of which were "very sensitive"), *reprinted at* 1999 TNT 20-109.

[38] *See, e.g., In re MacDonald,* 128 B.R. 161 (Bankr. W.D. Tex. 1991) (non-tax case).

a cap on the ultimate amount of the allowed claim (since such claims are generally entitled to full payment), in contrast to simply assisting in the evaluation of the feasibility of a given plan.[39] The Bankruptcy Appellate Panel for the First Circuit similarly took this view in *In re Indian Motocycle Co., Inc.*,[40] and reversed a bankruptcy court's estimation of a postpetition tax liability. In that case, the debtor corporation was in Chapter 7 and the purpose for estimating the tax liability was to establish the cash escrow that would be maintained for such liability and thus effectively cap its recovery. In this circumstance, the Bankruptcy Appellate Panel concluded that "proper statutory construction requires that [the]administrative tax liability be determined according to the provisions of § 505", including section 505(b) which provides a prompt determination procedure for postpetition taxes for which a tax return is filed (*see* § § 1011 and 1013 below).[41]

## *§1010.2 Post-Bar Date Amendments and Late Claims*

In general, a proof of claim may be amended to increase as well as decrease the amount claimed. However, where the bar date has passed, a bankruptcy court generally will permit the IRS to amend its (timely filed) claim only if the amendment relates to such claim (*i.e.*, does not state a new claim) and does not jeopardize the administration of the Chapter 11 case or confirmation of a plan. Not surprisingly, courts have differed as to what constitutes a new claim.[42] At a minimum, the courts

---

[39] Id. at 167-168.

[40] *United States v. Sterling Consulting Corp.* (*In re Indian Motocycle Co., Inc.*), 261 B.R. 800, 808-810 (Bankr. 1st. Cir. 2001).

[41] Consider *also In re Indus. Comm. Electrical Inc.*, 304 B.R. 24, 33, 2004-1 U.S.T.C. ¶50,228 (Bankr. W.D. Mass. 2004) (stating, *in dicta*, that "[t]here is no comparable provision for estimating contingent or unliquidated administrative expenses"), *rev'd on other grounds*, 319 B.R. 35 (D. Mass. 2005).

[42] *Compare In re International Horizons, Inc.* (11th Cir.), *supra* note 2 (amended proof of claim for income taxes held to constitute a new claim and, thus, was disallowed, since original claim was only for employment withholding taxes); *United States v. Owens*, 84 B.R. 361 (E.D. Pa. 1988) (disallowed as untimely the portion of an amended claim relating to 1981 federal income taxes, since original proof of claim for federal income taxes did not include such year); *and United States v. Baker* (*In re Baker*), 129 B.R. 607 (E.D. Mo. 1991) (same, but noting split of authority); *with Menick v. Hoffman*, 205 F.2d 365, 53-2 U.S.T.C. ¶9506 (9th Cir. 1953) (permitting an amendment of the type rejected in *International Horizons*; taxes involved were also for different years); *and In re Bajac Const. Co.*, 100 B.R. 524 (Bankr. E.D. Cal. 1989). *See generally* IRS Litigation Guideline Memorandum GL-23, June 21, 1990, *reprinted at* 2000 TNT 91-24 (discussing this split in authorities).

*See, e.g., In re Miss Glamour Coat Co.*, 80-2 U.S.T.C. ¶9737 (S.D.N.Y.) (identifying five factors for a bankruptcy court to consider in determining whether to allow a post-bar date amendment); *In re Stavriotis*, 103 B.R. 1005 (Bankr. N.D. Ill. 1989) (overview of differing approaches to post-bar date amendments; disallowed amended claim where debtor had inadequate prior notice of the claim or its magnitude—approximately $2,500,000 compared to an original claim of approximately $11,000—and the amended claim included an additional year; the fact that an audit was ongoing was not sufficient notice), *aff'd*, 129 B.R. 527 (N.D. Ill. 1991), *aff'd*, 977 F.2d 1202, 93-1 U.S.T.C. ¶50,081 (7th Cir. 1992); *Highlands Ins. Co., Inc. v. Alliance Operating Corp.* (*In re Alliance Operating Corp.*), 60 F.3d 1174 (5th Cir. 1995) (held that any amendment of a claim to reclassify its priority constitutes a new claim); *United States v. Berger* (*In re Tanaka Brothers Farms, Inc.*), 36 F.3d 996 (10th Cir. 1994) (IRS permitted to amend claim for employment taxes four-fold in accord with debtor's actually filed returns, despite having knowledge prior to the bar date that claim would have to be substantially increased, where original

(Footnote Continued)

claim was clearly labeled "estimated" and was based on the debtor's quarterly and prior period returns); *In re Telephone Co. of Central Fla.*, 308 B.R. 579, 2004-1 U.S.T.C. ¶50,226 (Bankr. M.D. Fla. 2004) (to similar effect, where the amount stated in the original claim was stamped "pending examination" and the IRS audit was still in its initial stages, even though the IRS was aware of and failed to object to the debtor's assertions and projections in its disclosure statement that the amount ultimately owing would be less than the estimated amount claimed); *In re Gilley*, 288 B.R. 901, 2003-1 U.S.T.C. ¶50,156 (Bankr. M.D. Fla. 2002) (adhering to Eleventh Circuit authority treating each tax year as a new claim, but discusses authorities more generally); *In re Limited Gaming of America, Inc., supra* note 21 (did not permit IRS to amend reinstated claim over seventy-fold from $5,000 to over $351,000, where tax return was timely filed and IRS, by denoting amount as "unassessed," did not clearly identify it as an estimate); *Jackson v. IRS (In re Jackson)*, 220 B.R. 273, 98-1 U.S.T.C. ¶50,208 (Bankr. W.D. Va. 1998) (permitted amendment of "estimated" IRS claim to include additional periods and other taxes, where the debtor had knowledge of the potential claim and the IRS was the only creditor; also, as to the inclusion of additional periods with respect to a claimed 100% penalty under Code §6672, the court analogized to Federal Rule of Civil Procedure 15(c)(2), which permits an original pleading to be amended when the amended claim "arose out of the conduct, transaction, or occurrence set forth or attempted to be set forth in the original pleading;" in this case, the conduct or occurrence was the individual debtor's ongoing acts or omissions with respect to the nonpayment of a controlled corporation's trust fund taxes); *In re McFarlin*, (Bankr. E.D. Ark. June 4, 1992), *reprinted at* 92 TNT 143-17 (discussing varying approaches); *United States v. Norris Grain Co.*, 131 B.R. 747 (M.D. Fla. 1990) (court disallowed post-bar date amendment increasing original claim by $1.7 million, since IRS had adequate notice of the liability before the bar date and delay was attributable to IRS's negligence, but allowed an amendment for taxes where the tax return was not due until after the bar date and the debtor had tentatively estimated such taxes at zero), *aff'd without opinion*, 969 F.2d 1047 (11th Cir. 1992); *In re Goodman*, 261 B.R. 415, 2001-1 U.S.T.C. ¶50,450 (Bankr. N.D. Tex. 2001) (IRS permitted to amend claim one year after confirmation of Chapter 13 plan to reflect amount shown on taxpayer's earlier filed return, even though the return was filed prior to the IRS's original claim, since no surprise to the debtor and no apparent prejudice to other creditors); *In re Sage-Dey, Inc.*, 170 B.R. 46 (Bankr. N.D.N.Y. 1994) (discusses split of authority; allowed FICA taxes for prior period given the "continuous nature" of such taxes; accordingly, the court stated that its "finding today is limited in its application . . . to amendments for FICA and FUTA tax liabilities accued prior to the time period listed in the original proof of claim"); *In re Waindel*, 166 B.R. 87 (Bankr. S.D. Tex. 1993) (original claim for 1990 income taxes did not provide sufficient proof that IRS intended to hold debtor liable for prior taxable years), *aff'd in relevant part*, 65 F.3d 1307 (5th Cir. 1995); *In re Osborne*, 159 B.R. 570 (Bankr. C.D. Cal. 1993), *aff'd without opinion*, 167 B.R. 698 (Bankr. 9th Cir. 1994) (permitted IRS to "dramatically" increase original claim for income taxes and to add a subsequent taxable year, where amendment was within one year of original claim and the original claim disclosed that the amounts listed were only estimates; rejected attempt to add claim for payroll taxes, distinguishing the Ninth Circuit's decision in *Menick*), *appealed on other issues*; *Metro Transportation Co.*, 117 B.R. 143 (Bankr. E.D. Pa. 1990) (state workmen's compensation fund could not amend claim after bar date to claim priority, where no new factors justified change and plan was based on original classification); *In re Hudson Oil Co.*, 100 B.R. 72 (Bankr. D. Kan. 1989) (rejected amendment claiming late-filing penalty, even though original claim was filed before the debtor's return, because the IRS knew of the late filing at the time of its original claim; in *dicta*, the court distinguished an amendment for negligent or substantial understatement penalties, because these penalties could not be known before either the filing of a return or an audit); Berryman, Filing Post Bar Date Amendments of Tax Claims: A Definite Maybe, The Bankr. Strategist 3 (December 1990). *See also In re Fidelity America Financial Corp. v. IRS*, 91-1 U.S.T.C. ¶50,161 (Bankr. E.D. Pa.) (IRS granted additional time to file an amended claim, even though original claim was arbitrary and without rational foundation).

*Also consider Johnson v. United States (In re Johnson)*, 85-2 U.S.T.C. ¶9811 (Bankr. E.D. Pa.) (bankruptcy trustee denied standing to request a declaratory judgment as to the timeliness of an amended IRS proof of claim; the court stated that, because the trustee would not be in violation of its duties if the IRS proof of claim was paid pursuant to court order, the trustee lacked a sufficient personal stake; alternatively, the court held that the amended proof of claim, although filed after the bar date, was a proper amendment).

generally permit an amended proof of claim to be filed subsequent to the bar date so long as the tax classification and taxable period were included in a timely filed proof of claim and the debtor was aware that the amount claimed may change.[43] Several courts have disallowed a post-bar date amendment increasing the amount of a previously claimed tax where the magnitude of the increase was unexpected.[44] Courts are generally more reluctant to permit amendments after confirmation of the debtor's Chapter 11 plan, and may require that the IRS also seek reconsideration of the confirmation order to permit the amendment.[45] In addition, in Chapter 11 cases, a late filed claim may be excused on equitable grounds.[46] Some courts have found excusable neglect where a taxing authority, although receiving notice of the debtor's bankruptcy, has no reason to suspect that a tax liability exists until after the bar date and then reasonably promptly files, or asks the bankruptcy court for leave to file, its claim.[47] In contrast, in Chapter 7 cases, most courts take a harder line as to late

---

[43] *See supra* note 42. *See also* IRS Manual, Part 5 (Collecting Process), Ch. 9 (Bankruptcy), § 13.21 (3/1/06), at ¶ 2 (takes the position that a withholding tax claim for one period may be amended to add a claim for another period of the same year); *but*, to the contrary, *see Ginley v. United States (In re Johnson)*, 901 F.2d 513, 90-2 U.S.T.C. ¶ 50,413 (6th Cir. 1990) (rejecting post-bar date amendment adding withholding and FICA taxes for a new tax period). In *In re CF&I Fabricators of Utah, Inc.* (Bankr. D. Utah August 16, 1994), *reprinted at* 94 TNT 183-9, *aff'd on other issues*, 1995 U.S. Dist. LEXIS 7367 (D. Utah 1995), the court disallowed an IRS amended claim for alternative minimum tax (AMT) for taxable years for which the original claim showed a zero liability. Although the original claim disclosed that the IRS might conduct a future audit of such years, the sole purpose stated for an audit was the possible elimination of any NOL carryforwards that the debtor might attempt to claim. There was no mention of a possible AMT, which the court stated, "[a]lthough . . . part of the same generic category as an income tax, . . . is a separate and distinct calculation and tax." The court therefore found the disclosure insufficient to put the debtors (who it recognized were sophisticated taxpayers), the court, "or even the IRS" on notice of a possible AMT.

[44] *See, e.g., In re Stavriotis, supra* note 42; *In re Limited Gaming of America, Inc., supra* note 21; *United States v. Norris Grain Co., supra* note 42; *but see In re Osborne, supra* note 42.

[45] *Holstein v. Brill*, 987 F.2d 1268 (7th Cir. 1993) (post-confirmation amendments should only be granted with compelling reason); *United States v. Carr*, 142 B.R. 351 (D. Neb. 1992) (required to seek reconsideration of the confirmation order); *GMAC Mortgage Corp. of Iowa v. Gold (In re Gold)*, 1995 U.S. Dist. LEXIS 17051, *4 (E.D. Pa. 1995) (amendment denied); *but see In re The Telephone Co. of Central Florida*, 308 B.R. 579 (Bankr. M.D. 2004) (permitting amendment in light of debtor's knowledge that proof of claim would be amended). In certain cases where a plan is promptly proposed and confirmed, it is possible that confirmation could occur prior to the bar date, in which event no special dispensation should be needed. *See, e.g., In re Grogan*, 158 B.R. 197 (Bankr. E.D. Cal. 1993) (Chapter 13; confirmation did not preempt bar date).

[46] *See Pioneer Investment Services Co. v. Brunswick Assocs. L.P.*, discussed *supra* § 1002 note 59; *see also* 8 Collier on Bankruptcy ¶ 3003.05[4][a] (15th ed.); *In re SC Corporation*, 265 B.R. 660 (Bankr. D. Conn. 2001) (late filing of tax claim was not due to "excusable neglect" where taxing authority knowingly took risk that debtor's pre-bankruptcy estimated tax payments might not be sufficient to cover the debtor's tax liability for the year preceding the bankruptcy, for which no tax return had been filed as of the bar date); *In re Intelligent Medical Imaging, Inc.*, 262 B.R. 142 (Bankr. S.D. Fla. 2001) (IRS proof of claim, filed after the bar date and after confirmation, which had the effect of amending the debtor's scheduled amounts, was treated as a late claim; although late filing was due to attorney error, court denied claim due to prejudice to other creditors); and cases cited *supra* at note 41 (since every disallowed post-bar date amendment becomes, by definition, a late claim). Of course, the lack of proper notice of the bar date may justify a late filing. *See* similar discussion at § 1014 (dischargeability) and § 1004 (IRS should automatically receive notice of bar date).

[47] *See, e.g., In re PT-1 Communications, Inc.*, 292 B.R. 482 (Bankr. E.D. N.Y. 2003) (although the Massachusetts Dept. of Revenue (MDOR) had received notice of the bankruptcy filing of the debtor,

claims.[48] However, as discussed in the introductory section to § 1010, the stakes are slightly different in Chapter 7, in that the penalty (if any) for filing a late claim in a Chapter 7 case generally is subordination, not disallowance. Of course, depending on the extent of the estate's assets, subordination may be functionally equivalent to a disallowance.

In general, the IRS may withdraw its claim as of right by filing a notice of withdrawal.[49] However, where an objection to the claim was filed or an adversary proceeding against the IRS commenced, or where the IRS has participated significantly in the case (including having accepted or rejected the Chapter 11 plan), the IRS may withdraw its claim only with court approval, after notice and a hearing.[50]

---

(Footnote Continued)

an out-of-state corporation, and certain affiliates, and the bankruptcy schedules filed by one of the affiliates disclosed the MDOR as a creditor, the bankruptcy court stated that "it would be unreasonable . . . to expect the MDOR to divine" from annual reports filed with a different state agency that sales taxes were owing; accordingly, court permitted the MDOR's late claim, even though filed almost a year after the bar date, where it only became aware of any taxable sales 3$^1/_2$ months earlier).

[48] *See* 8 Collier on Bankruptcy ¶ 3002.05[l] (15th ed.); *compare* Bankruptcy Rule 3002(c)(1) (Chapter 7; permitting extension of time for government claims only if request is filed before bar date) *with* Bankruptcy Rule 3003(c)(3) (Chapter 11; no similar limitation); *see also In re Ohio Movers & Storage, Inc.*, 118 B.R. 533 (Bankr. N.D. Ohio 1990) (IRS was not permitted to file a late claim even though the delay was due to an incorrect employer identification number included on the debtor's bankruptcy petition and notice of bar date). *Cf. United States v. United States (In re Chavis)*, 47 F.3d 818 (6th Cir. 1995) (applying and contrasting Chapter 7 cases to Chapter 13 cases; cites somewhat conflicting circuit court authority). *See also Gardenhire v. IRS (In re Gardenhire)*, 209 F.3d 1145, 2000-1 U.S.T.C. ¶ 50,376 (9th Cir. 2000) (strictly enforcing 180-day deadline in Chapter 13 cases under Bankruptcy Rules 3002(c) and 9006(b), despite equitable arguments), *rev'g*, 220 B.R. 376 (Bankr. 9th Cir. 1998) (Bankruptcy Appellate Panel had equated such deadline to a statute of limitations and applied the doctrine of equitable tolling; in applying the doctrine, the panel had required a higher level of diligence than would suffice for purposes of "excusable neglect" under the rules); *In re Hernandez*, 2004 Bankr. LEXIS 378 (Bankr. S.D. Fla. 2004) (strictly enforced 180-day deadline against IRS in a Chapter 13 case, even though the IRS's late filing solely resulted from its lack of notice); *but see, e.g., IRS v. Hilderbrand*, 245 B.R. 287, 2000-1 U.S.T.C. ¶ 50,250 (M.D. Tenn. 2000) (decided prior to Ninth Circuit decision in *Gardenhire*, the bankruptcy court held in accord with the earlier Bankruptcy Appellate Panel decision); *In re Danielson*, 981 F.2d 296 (7th Cir. 1992) (applying "excusable neglect" standard with respect to claims filed by the debtor on behalf of the IRS after the 30-day period specified in Bankruptcy Code section 501(c)), *reh'g denied*, 1993 U.S. App. LEXIS 260; IRS Chief Counsel Advice 200304009, October 7, 2002, *reprinted at* 2003 TNT 17-57 (discussing the common law concept of "equitable tolling" as applied to the 180-day deadline for government claims within Chapter 13 cases, and three situations in which a bankruptcy court should be able to utilize its general equitable powers under Bankruptcy Code section 105 to allow a late claim).

[49] Bankruptcy Rule 3006.

[50] Id.; *Bishop v. United States (In re Leonard)*, 112 B.R. 67 (Bankr. D. Conn. 1990) (IRS claim for Code § 6672 penalty related to three different companies constituted three separate claims); *cf. Fairchild v. IRS (In re Fairchild)*, 969 F.2d 866 (10th Cir. 1992) (debtor's objection could not be withdrawn after the IRS had filed its answer); *In re Wotkyns*, 274 B.R. 690 (Bankr. S.D. Tex. 2002) (debtor could not withdraw objection, even though outcome of litigation had since become predetermined in light of Supreme Court decision issued one day before trial). *See also United States v. Bushnell*, 96-2 U.S.T.C. ¶ 50,472 (D. Ver. 1996), discussed *infra* at § 1013.3.2.

## §1010.3 *Timing of Objection to IRS Claim*

Although a complete discussion of the government's internal rules for handling proofs of claims is beyond the scope of this volume, one item that has a direct bearing on the timing of a debtor's objection to an IRS proof of claim deserves special mention.

According to the IRS Manual, the IRS (rather than the Department of Justice) generally has sole authority to settle, compromise, or reduce any proof of claim for the first six months of a bankruptcy case (subject to possible extension upon request by the IRS).[51] However, after an objection is filed (or the debtor files a complaint to have the bankruptcy court determine its tax liability), settlement authority shifts (with minor exception) to the Department of Justice, Tax Division (or, in certain cases, to the U.S. Attorney). In addition, area counsel will immediately refer to the Department of Justice any matter that is then at IRS Appeals.[52] Appeals will cease working on the case, unless the government's attorney of record requests that Appeals retain the case for settlement or otherwise concurs in such action.[53] In cases not at Appeals, the IRS may retain limited settlement authority if the debtor-in-possession agrees that any hearing on the objection will be deferred until 30 days after negotiations cease. The IRS's settlement authority in such circumstances is restricted to the "criteria ordinarily used by revenue agents or revenue officers in settling cases."[54] If it appears that the matter cannot be resolved without consideration of litigating hazards, the matter must be immediately referred to the Department of Justice.[55]

In certain cases, the IRS Manual provides for the implementation of expedited procedures within the IRS, such as in the case of significant (or "large") bankruptcy cases.[56] These include prepackaged bankruptcies, cases that involve disputed amounts of over $1 million, previously assessed amounts of over $10 million, or

---

[51] *See* IRS Manual, Part 8 (Appeals), Ch. 15 (Appeals Bankruptcy Cases), §1.2.3 (6/27/05), and Exhibit 8.15.1-1 (6/27/05); IRS Manual, Part 34 (General Litigation), Ch. 3.1 (Procedures in Bankruptcy Cases), §1.7 (8/11/04), at ¶7. Any settlement that takes into account litigating hazards must be evidenced by a closing agreement.

[52] *See* IRS Manual, Part 8 (Appeals), Ch. 15 (Appeals Bankruptcy Cases), §1.3.1 (6/27/05) and Exhibit 8.15.1-1 (6/27/05); IRS Manual, Part 8 (Appeals), Ch. 20 (Appeals Records and Processing Manual), §7.5.3 (1/31/02), at ¶2; IRS Manual, Part 34 (General Litigation), Ch. 3.1 (Procedures in Bankruptcy Cases), §1.7 (8/11/04), at ¶7.

[53] As a procedural matter, regardless of whether Appeals continues to work toward a settlement at the government attorney's request, Appeals is directed to issue a notice of deficiency (if one has not been issued and is appropriate) and to close the case. Thereafter, if the government attorney wants to keep the case out of a litigation mode, he may request that Appeals reopen the case. IRS Manual, Part 8 (Appeals), Ch. 15 (Appeals Bankruptcy Cases), §1.3.1 (6/27/05); IRS Manual, Part 34 (General Litigation), Ch. 3.1 (Procedures in Bankruptcy Cases), §1.7 (8/11/04), at ¶7.

[54] IRS Manual, Part 8 (Appeals), Ch. 15 (Appeals Bankruptcy Cases), Exhibit 8.15.1-1 (6/27/05); IRS Manual, Part 34 (General Litigation), Ch. 3.1 (Procedures in Bankruptcy Cases), §1.7 (8/11/04), at ¶7.

[55] Id.

[56] *See* IRS Manual, Part 34 (General Litigation), Ch. 3.1 (Procedures in Bankruptcy Cases), §3 (Significant Bankruptcy Case Program) (8/11/04) (permits referral to field counsel to assist in identifying cases that require coordination of examination issues on an expedited basis); IRS Manual, Part 8 (Appeals), Ch. 15 (Appeals Bankruptcy Cases), §§1.4 and 1.4.1 (6/27/05) (emphasizes need to quickly identify and process "large bankruptcy" cases, and to coordinate with area counsel).

assets of $50 million or more; cases that present difficult postconfirmation tax issues; and any cases that are otherwise identified as having special significance (such as where a large group of taxpayers may be affected, a potential for notoriety exists, or the debtor is in a business that is part of the Industry Specialization Program or the Coordinated Examination Program). The implementation of such expedited procedures is within the IRS's discretion. In addition, in accordance with Code § 7123, added by the IRS Restructuring and Reform Act of 1998, the IRS has issued Revenue Procedure 99-28,[57] which provides a method by which a taxpayer may be able to request "early referral" by Appeals with respect to individual issues where the issue has been fully developed at the audit level. However, early referral is not by right; the IRS case/group manager may reject a request for early referral (subject only to the taxpayer's right to request a conference with the case/group manager's supervisor).

From 1997 until early 2003, the IRS had implemented in select areas a test program to expedite, at the debtor's request, the resolution of tax-related disputes in bankruptcy cases.[58] Under this program, the Office of Special Procedures within the Collection Division of the IRS and, if necessary, Appeals conducted a prompt review of the dispute. Appeals had substantial settlement authority. In all, the process generally was expected to take no more than 30 workdays. This expedited process could be used even after an objection to an IRS proof of claim had been filed or the debtor had filed a complaint with the bankruptcy court to determine its tax liability. The program apparently was terminated due to disuse.

The above expedited procedures and programs, as well as others, are discussed further at § 1010.5.

It should also be noted that a proof of claim that is allowed by order of the bankruptcy court, even if uncontested, constitutes a final judgment on the merits and thus can bar a subsequent litigation under the principles of *res judicata*.[59] This is in contrast to the general status of a proof of claim, which is deemed allowed unless a party in interest objects, with no time set for objections.[60] In such instance, due to the possibility that an objection might still be filed, finality may only come with time, and not before the debtor has been discharged and possibly the bankruptcy case is

---

[57] 1999-2 C.B. 109.

[58] *See* IRS Announcement 97-111, 1997-47 I.R.B. 15.

[59] *See, e.g., EDP Medical Computer Systems Inc. v. United States*, 480 F.3d 621 (2d Cir. 2007), *aff'g* 2005 U.S. Dist. LEXIS 29062 (E.D. N.Y. 2005) (interestingly, after the claim was allowed but prior to payment, the government entered into a stipulation with the majority shareholder and certain others seemingly waiving its proof of claim against the debtor; however, no objection to the payment of the claim was pursued until more than a year after the claim was actually paid and the bankruptcy case was closed; the Second Circuit upheld the payment; the Second Circuit did not directly address the waiver, whereas the lower court expressly treated the assertion of waiver as an untimely objection to the allowance of the proof of claim rather than viewing the waiver as a subsequent independent act, and stated that one "cannot relitigate issues that could have been raised by filing an objection to the claim during the bankruptcy proceeding"); *Siegel v. Fed. Home Loan Mtg. Corp.*, 143 F.3d 528-531 (9th Cir. 2002); *Bank of Lafayette v. Baudoin (In re Baudoin)*, 981 F.2d 736, 742 (5th Cir. 1993).

[60] 11 U.S.C. § 502(a).

closed.[61] Accordingly, most Chapter 11 plans specify an outside date by which objections to proofs of claims must be filed.

## *§1010.4 Claims for Postpetition Taxes*

Postpetition taxes are generally treated as administrative expenses (*see* §1015.1.1 below) and therefore, to the extent incurred in the ordinary course of the debtor's business, are generally payable currently.[62] In addition, the IRS may file (and, where, for whatever reason, the debtor in a bankruptcy case commenced before October 17, 2005, does not pay its taxes in the ordinary course, the IRS must file) a request for payment of any such unpaid postpetition taxes with the court (*see* Form 6338-A, "Request for Payment of Internal Revenue Taxes").[63] The court, after notice and a hearing, may authorize payment of such taxes.[64] Also treated as an administrative expense and in the same fashion as postpetition taxes is any excessive allowance of a "quickie" refund (or tentative carryback adjustment) received during the bankruptcy case (regardless of whether it relates to a pre- or postpetition year).[65]

Upon request of the debtor or the proponent of the Chapter 11 plan, the court may fix a bar date (generally a date after the confirmation of the plan) by which administrative expense claims must be filed.[66] There is no statutorily imposed mini-

---

[61] *See, e.g.*, cases cited *supra* note 59, and *County Fuel Co. v. Equitable Bank Corp.*, 832 F.2d 290 (4th Cir. 1987).

[62] *See, e.g., supra* §1006.2 and discussion at §1015.1.1; *see also* IRS Manual, Part 5 (Collecting Process), Ch. 9 (Bankruptcy), §13.13 (3/1/06).

[63] 11 U.S.C. §503(a) and (b)(1)(D) (the latter provision eliminates the need of any governmental authority to request payment of a postpetition tax as a precondition for administrative expense treatment for bankruptcy cases commenced on or after October 17, 2005); IRS Manual, Part 5 (Collecting Process), Ch. 9 (Bankruptcy), §13.6 (3/1/07), at ¶3 (same forms also used to claim "involuntary gap" taxes in an involuntary bankruptcy, *see* §1015.1.2); *cf. In re Howard Indus., Inc.*, 225 B.R. 388, 97-2 U.S.T.C. ¶50,989 (Bankr. S.D. Ohio 1997) (failure to include taxes in request for payment in original bankruptcy precluded later collection). Some courts also have required, prior to their acting on the request, that the request for payment comply with normal motion procedures (including a proof of service). *See In re Glen Eden Hospital Inc.*, 172 B.R. 538 (Bankr. ED Mich. 1994).

[64] *See* 11 U.S.C. §503(b). *See, e.g., In re Tom Cat Enterprises, Inc.*, 90-1 U.S.T.C. ¶50,300 (Bankr. M.D. Fla.) (allowing IRS application for payment of postpetition income tax withholding and FICA); *cf. In re Quid Me Broadcasting, Inc.*, 181 B.R. 715 (Bankr. W.D.N.Y. 1995), *aff'd*, 1996 U.S. Dist. LEXIS 7581 (W.D.N.Y. 1996) (found absence of current payment justified in the case of a non-operating trustee under Chapter 7; court described the inequity, and the potential liability of the trustee, of paying taxes currently where there may be insufficient assets to pay all administrative claims), discussed at §1006.2.

[65] *See* 11 U.S.C. §503(b)(1)(B)(ii). *See also* discussion of quickie refunds at §1012.1 below.

[66] If a Chapter 11 case is converted to a Chapter 7 liquidation, a further bar date may be set to request payment for administrative expenses (including taxes) incurred during the Chapter 11 case. *See* Bankruptcy Rule 1019(6) (effective December 1, 1999; also clarifies that government units will have at least 180 days from the date of conversion). However, the conversion does not create a new petition date. *Lee v. United States*, 274 B.R. 893 (Bankr. D. Md. 2001). Prior to the change in Bankruptcy Rule 1019(6), and still applicable for filings prior to December 1999, it had been held that the filing of a "request for payment" for such expenses (rather than a "proof of claim") was insufficient to establish the claim. *See, e.g., Ginley v. United States (In re Johnson), supra* note 43; *In re Lissner Corp.*, 1990 Bankr. LEXIS 724 (Bankr. N.D. Ill.).

mum period for such a bar date, as there is for the filing of prepetition claims by the IRS (and other governmental authorities).[67] Any request filed after such bar date may be permitted by the court only for cause.[68] As discussed above at § 1010.1, it is unclear whether the bankruptcy court has the authority to estimate postpetition tax claims. In general, all administrative expenses are of equal priority.[69]

## § 1010.5 *Expedited IRS Examination/Appeals Process*

As mentioned at § 1010.3 above, the IRS will, of its own accord, often implement expedited procedures with respect to pending IRS examinations in the case of significant (or "large") bankruptcy cases. In addition, Congress, in the IRS Restructuring and Reform Act of 1998, enacted Code § 7123. Such section requires the IRS to establish procedures for early referrals of issues from examination to Appeals and, as to any issue unresolved at Appeals, for nonbinding mediation (at either party's request) or binding arbitration (if both parties agree). In certain limited cases, early referrals and mediation were already permitted under pre-existing IRS procedures. The IRS has since taken steps to implement more expansive procedures. For example, in Revenue Procedure 99-28,[70] the IRS has prescribed the method by which a taxpayer generally may request early referral of an unagreed issue that has been fully developed at the audit level, where the remaining issues in the case are not expected to be completed before Appeals could resolve the early referral issue. Significantly, a request for early referral is subject to the approval of the case/group manager (with the taxpayer's only recourse in the event the request is rejected being a conference with the manager's supervisor). Issues for which early referral is *not* permitted under any circumstance include issues that are designated for litigation by the Office of the Chief Counsel or are part of a "whipsaw" transaction.

In addition, in November 1998, the IRS announced the expansion of its mediation program (which was previously limited to Coordinated Examination Program cases) to include factual issues—such as valuation, reasonable compensation and transfer pricing—involving examination adjustments of $1 million or more that are at the Appeals level.[71] This expansion was initially to be in effect for a two-year test

---

[67] *See* 11 U.S.C. § 502(b)(9) and Bankruptcy Rule 3003 (providing for a minimum period of 180 days for the filing of prepetition claims). *Cf. United States v. Official Comm. of Unsecured Creditors of Indus. Comm. Electrical, Inc. (In re Indus. Comm. Electrical, Inc.)*, 319 B.R. 35, 46-47, 2005-1 U.S.T.C. ¶ 50,312 (D. Mass. 2005) (IRS filed a "protective" administrative claim with respect to a postpetition quickie refund, following which, upon objection by the debtors, the bankruptcy court gave the IRS 111 days to audit the debtor and prepare for trial; the debtors had sought a shorter time and the IRS requested 90 days; upon subsequent review, the district court indicated that 180 days would have been more appropriate, in view of the 180 day audit period in Bankruptcy Code section 505(b), but did not fault the bankruptcy court since the IRS did not initially request the additional time).

[68] 11 U.S.C. § 503(a) (effective for bankruptcy cases commenced on or after October 22, 1994).

[69] *See infra* § 1015 note 3. Where the Chapter 11 case is converted to a Chapter 7 liquidation, however, postconversion administrative expenses have priority. *See* 11 U.S.C. § 726(b).

[70] 1999-2 C.B. 109, *superseding* Rev. Proc. 96-9, 1996-1 C.B. 575 (which involved early referrals with respect to cases in the Coordinated Examination Program).

[71] Announcement 98-99, 1998-2 C.B. 650.

period, but was extended through January 15, 2002.[72] On July 1, 2002, the IRS formally established an Appeals mediation process in Rev. Proc. 2002-44, and expanded the availability of mediation.[73] Mediation is now generally available for any issues, legal or factual, without regard to dollar amount, including Industry Specialization Program issues and Appeals Coordinated Issues. Mediation may be sought, however, only after settlement discussions at Appeals have proven unsuccessful and, in general, only when all issues for which mediation is not being requested have been resolved. In addition, mediation is not available for issues designated for litigation or docketed in any court, collection cases, issues for which mediation "would not be consistent with sound tax administration" (such as those contrary to direct authority), frivolous issues or cases where the taxpayer has not acted in good faith during settlement negotiations.

The IRS has also tested what it calls "fast-track" mediation or dispute resolution, and officially made permanent two such programs. The first program, titled "Fast Track Mediation," was originally introduced on July 1, 2000,[74] and made permanent in June 2003.[75] It is jointly administered by the Small Business/Self-Employed Compliance Division (SB/SE) and the Office of Appeals. This program does not supplant other dispute resolution options in the event a resolution is not achieved. The program is structured to resolve issues within an average of 30 to 40 days, but is only intended to apply after an issue has been fully developed. In general, this program is available for all cases over which SB/SE has jurisdiction that are not docketed or designated for litigation or are collection cases—including offers in compromise, responsible-person liability cases, and collection due process cases—where the resolution does not depend on hazards of litigation. In this process, an appeals officer serves as a mediator to resolve disputes while cases are still at examination or are in collection.

The second program, titled "Fast Track Settlement," was originally introduced on November 14, 2001 (with the title "LMSB Fast Track Dispute Resolution Pilot Program"),[76] and was also made permanent in June 2003.[77] For cases within the jurisdiction of the IRS's Large and Mid-Size Business Division (LMSB), this program

---

[72] Announcement 2001-9, 2001-1 C.B. 357. The IRS had in early 2000 informally announced its intent to expand the program to include disputes of any dollar size. *See* BNA Daily Tax Report (May 17, 2000), at G-4. Although this was not done at the time, it clearly provided an indication of the IRS's direction for the program.

[73] 2002-26 I.R.B. 10.

[74] *See* BNA Daily Tax Report (May 17, 2000), at G-4; IR-2000-57 (August 15, 2000), 2000 IRB LEXIS 259 ("Redesigned Appeals Division Begins Work at IRS"; initially restricted to small dollar deficiency and offer in compromise cases, and responsible person liability cases); IR-2002-80 (June 26, 2002) (expanded test program to small business and self-employed taxpayers). When originally introduced, this program was restricted to Denver, Hargor, Houston, and Jacksonville.

[75] Rev. Proc. 2003-41, 2003-1 C.B. 1047; IR-2003-72 (June 3, 2003), 2003 I.R.B. LEXIS 225.

[76] *See* BNA Daily Tax Report (November 15, 2001), at L-8; IR-2001-109 (November 14, 2001), 2001 I.R.B. LEXIS 427. The procedures for implementing, and requesting participation in, the pilot program were described in Notice 2001-67, 2001-2 C.B. 544.

[77] Rev. Proc. 2003-40, 2003-1 C.B. 1044; IR-2003-72 (June 3, 2003), 2003 I.R.B. LEXIS 225. *See generally* Weinstein and Packman, Fast Track Settlement—On the Fast Track, But to Where? A Practical Guide to the Program, 103 J. Tax'n 288 (2005).

is administered by the LMSB and the Office of Appeals. In April 2005, but more formally in August 2006, this program was expanded on a test basis within select areas to cases within the Small Business/Self-Employed Division (SB/SE), to be administered jointly by the SB/SE and the Office of Appeals.[78] The fast track settlement program is generally limited to cases that are not designated for litigation, but can be expanded depending on the circumstances and operational needs of the case. In this instance, the program is structured to handle issues within a 120-day time frame. This program also does not preclude other dispute resolution alternatives in the event a settlement is not reached. Unlike Fast Track Mediation, it appears that hazards of litigation can appropriately be taken into account under this program.

In connection with making these two programs permanent, the IRS also announced a pilot fast track program for tax exempt bonds, titled "Tax Exempt Bond Mediation Dispute Resolution Pilot Program" (TEB Mediation), to provide issuers of tax exempt debt a greater opportunity to expedite the resolution of cases within the IRS's Tax Exempt Bond organization.[79]

Back in 2001, the IRS also initiated a "Comprehensive Case Resolution" pilot program.[80] This program was intended to permit large businesses to obtain, through an IRS team process, an expedited and comprehensive resolution of all years under examination by the LMSB, in Appeals and in docketed Tax Court cases.[81] Participation in this program was initially limited to a select few during the test period. The status of this program is unclear.

In Announcement 2000-4,[82] the IRS instituted a procedure permitting binding arbitration of certain factual issues (such as valuation and reasonable compensation) for a two-year test period beginning January 18, 2000, but was thereafter extended through June 20, 2003,[83] and, we understand, has been continued on an informal basis. In addition, the IRS has expanded the scope of issues which may be subject to arbitration, including substantiation of Code § 162 expenses, but excluding issues similar to those excluded from mediation under Rev. Proc. 2002-44, above. Arbitration can be requested only after the normal Appeals process and only if all other issues have been resolved. Arbitration is optional, and must be approved by the appeals officer (or team chief), as well as a succession of others in the Appeals

---

78 *See* IRS Announcement 2006-61, 2006-36 I.R.B. 390, *corrected by* IRS Announcement 2006-97, 2006-50 I.R.B. 1108; Stratton, Fast-Track Settlement Now Available to Small Businesses, 2005 TNT 82-2 (April 28, 2005) (reporting on the Commissioner's signing of Delegation Order 4.25 authorizing the SB/SE to participate in the program). Apparently, the expanded use by SB/SE got off to a slow start. *See* BNA Daily Tax Report #81 (April 27, 2006), at G-1, and BNA Daily Tax Report #218 (November 14, 2005), at G-8. Under the original program, fast track settlement was only available to cases within SB/SE on a select, discretionary basis. *See* § 3.02 of Rev. Proc. 2003-40, 2003-1 C.B. 1044.

79 *See* Announcement 2003-36, 2003-1 C.B. 1093; IR-2003-72 (June 3, 2003), 2003 I.R.B. LEXIS 225; IR-2003-73 (June 3, 2003), 2003 I.R.B. LEXIS 226. This pilot program has been extended through July 3, 2007. Announcement 2006-43, 2006-27 I.R.B. 48.

80 *See* BNA Daily Tax Report (January 12, 2001), at L-73; IR-2001-5 (January 11, 2001), 2001 I.R.B. LEXIS 9.

81 *See* Notice 2001-13, 2001-1 C.B. 514.

82 2001-1 C.B. 296.

83 Announcement 2002-60, 2002-2 C.B. 28.

division. If approved, the terms of the arbitration (within the parameters of the procedure) will be negotiated and set forth in a formal executed agreement. A model agreement is included as an exhibit to the Announcement.

The LMSB also implemented, as of December 4, 2002, a streamlined examination process called the Limited Issue Focused Examination (LIFE, for short).[84] Under this initiative, the taxpayer and the IRS enter into a formal agreement governing key aspects of the examination, including among other things, establishing dollar limits below which the IRS will agree not to raise issues and the taxpayer will agree not to file claims, agreeing to deadlines for information, etc., and obtaining the IRS's commitment to use appropriate issue resolution processes throughout the examination. A form of the agreement is available on the IRS website (noted above), along with answers to frequently asked questions and what the IRS calls the Facts of LIFE.

Moreover, the IRS has instituted programs intended to resolve issues on a *pre-filing* tax return basis. These programs have so far been limited to taxpayers within the jurisdiction of the LMSB.[85]

**Test Program to Expedite Resolution of Tax-Related Disputes in Bankruptcy Cases Terminated.** On November 6, 1997, the IRS commenced a special test program to expedite the resolution of tax-related disputes in bankruptcy cases. The initial test of the program was scheduled to last for six to 12 months but ultimately remained in effect until early 2003, when it was finally terminated (apparently due to disuse). During the test period, the program was available only in Arizona, Indiana, Massachusetts and the Texas counties comprising the Houston IRS District. The program is described in IRS Announcement 97-111,[86] and provided for a prompt and thorough review of the debtor's dispute by the IRS with an opportunity for settlement. The entire review process generally was intended to take no more than about 30 workdays. The program did not alter existing bankruptcy court jurisdiction or procedures.

Due to confidentiality concerns, only the debtor (or trustee) could use this expedited process. Competing creditors, as well as others, had to use other existing procedures. In addition, the debtor had to be in bankruptcy at the time the process was initiated (except in limited circumstances where the bankruptcy was closed but the debtor believed that IRS actions were inconsistent with bankruptcy court orders).

This process could be used to resolve an array of tax-related issues. These were: preferences, setoff and refund issues, automatic stay violations, proof of claim and administrative claim issues, and most dischargeability determinations.[87]

---

[84] IR-2002-133 (December 4, 2002), *reprinted at* 2002 TNT 234-7. Certain changes were made to the program in 2003 based on interim feedback. *See* the IRS website at http://www.irs.gov/businesses/article/0,,id=103618,00.html.

[85] *See, e.g.*, Rev. Proc. 2007-17, 2007-4 I.R.B. 368, *superseding* Rev. Proc. 2005-12, 2005-2 I.R.B. 311 (pre-filing agreement program); Announcement 2005-87, 2005-50 I.R.B. 1144 (reporting on Compliance Assurance Process (CAP) pilot program); Bennett, Nolan Gives First Glimpse of LMSB Compliance Assurance Pilot Program, 2005 TNT 14-3 (January 24, 2005).

[86] 1997-47 I.R.B. 15.

[87] The IRS, on September 25, 1998, also initiated a pilot program to handle any claims for damages with respect to IRS violations of the automatic stay or postdischarge injunction. *See* Announcement 98-89, 1998-2 C.B. 460, discussed at §1007.7.6 above. Although seemingly overlapping the 1997

Here is how the process worked. The debtor generally had to contact, either in writing or by telephone, the IRS Office of Special Procedures in the district in which the bankruptcy was pending (*see* Announcement for addresses and phone numbers). The debtor had to provide:

(1) copies of its bankruptcy court documents (presumably, the bankruptcy petition and the bankruptcy court's order for relief);

(2) any unfiled, past-due income tax returns; and

(3) any other documents or information relevant to the IRS's review of the dispute.

Special Procedures was to begin its review within two business days of receiving all documentation, and complete its initial review within 10 business days (unless additional information was required). If the initial determination was adverse, the debtor could request that Special Procedures review its decision. This second review was to be completed within five business days. If its decision was still adverse, Special Procedures would so inform the debtor by letter and include with the letter an appeal request form. (Only after there had been a second review by Special Procedures could the debtor go to Appeals.) The debtor had 10 business days in which to complete and timely mail back the form in order to go to Appeals.

Appeals was to complete its review within 10 business days of receiving the case (45 business days for dischargeability determinations), unless extended by agreement. Appeals had substantial settlement authority, and could consider hazards of litigation. Appeals was to inform the debtor of its decision by letter (and describe any corrective actions to be taken). If the decision was adverse, no further administrative recourse with respect to the dispute would be available to the debtor through the IRS.

During this process, the debtor was provided an opportunity to confer with Special Procedures and Appeals (generally by telephone). Where the decision of Special Procedures or Appeals was favorable, actions to correct the matter had to be commenced immediately (within three business days in the case of Appeals) and completed within 30 business days.

This expedited process could be used even after the debtor filed an objection to an IRS proof of claim or commenced an adversary proceeding against the IRS in the bankruptcy court (but not after the issue had already been litigated before the bankruptcy court).

---

(Footnote Continued)

program in certain respects, it was our understanding that the 1998 program was only implicated after any dispute regarding the fact of the violation had already been resolved (which is the province of the existing program) and the only issue that remained was the determination of damages, if any. This program was terminated in early 2003, in connection with the issuance of final regulations under Code § 7433(e) providing for the handling of such damage claims. *See* § 1007.7 above.

## § 1011 REQUEST FOR PROMPT DETERMINATION OF POSTPETITION TAX LIABILITY

Section 505(b) of the Bankruptcy Code allows the debtor-in-possession, even prior to the closing of the bankruptcy case, to request a prompt determination by the IRS of its tax liability in respect to any *unpaid* postpetition tax for a completed taxable year for which a tax return has been filed.[1] If the payment of the tax shown on the return is made at the time the return is filed (or the return shows an NOL), the IRS will only determine whether a further tax payment is due; it generally will not rule on the correctness of the original filing or on the amount of the remaining NOL.

Revenue Procedure 2006-24 provides that, from and after May 30, 2006, any request for a prompt determination must be submitted (in duplicate) together with an exact copy of the debtor corporation's tax return to the Centralized Insolvency Operation, as more particularly outlined in the Revenue Procedure.[2] A return will not be accepted by the IRS as a valid return if the penalty-of-perjury certification is stricken, deleted, or modified. If the request is incomplete for any reason, all the documents received will be returned with an explanation identifying the missing items (following which the submission process can begin anew). In accordance with changes made to section 505(b) as part of the 2005 bankruptcy reforms, the clerk of the bankruptcy court in each district must now maintain a listing of the designated

---

[1] **§ 1011** *See* 11 U.S.C. § 505(b); Rev. Proc. 2006-24, 2006-22 I.R.B. 943 (for requests on and after May 30, 2006); Rev. Proc. 81-17, 1981-1 C.B. 688 (for requests before May 30, 2006); 124 Cong. Rec. H 11,111 (daily ed. September 28, 1978) (statement of Rep. Edwards), S 17,427-17,428 (daily ed. October 6, 1978) (statement of Sen. DeConcini). *See also In re Goldblatt Bros., Inc.*, 106 B.R. 522 (Bankr. N.D. Ill. 1989), discussed *infra* in this section; IRS Manual, Part 4 (Examining Process), Ch. 27 (Bankruptcy), § 5.3 (8/27/99), at ¶ 1 (stating that section 505(b) procedure does not apply to *information* returns, such as IRS Form 1065 for partnerships); *Kellogg v. United States (In re Southwestern States Marketing Corp.)*, 95-1 U.S.T.C. ¶ 50,057 (N.D. Tex. 1994), *aff'd*, 82 F.3d 413, 96-1 U.S.T.C. ¶ 50,165 (5th Cir. 1996) (section 505(b) procedure did not preclude the IRS from subsequently denying the trustee's claimed refund as shown on the filed tax return; nor did the issuance of an "accepted as filed" letter estop the IRS from denying the refund claim); *In re Weisberg*, 226 B.R. 172 (Bankr. E.D. Pa. 1998) (expressing view that section 505(b) does not foreclose IRS from subsequently assessing debtor for an excessive refund; *but see* discussion at the end of § 1012.1).

[2] Rev. Proc. 2006-24, § 3, 2006-22 I.R.B. 943. Prior thereto, the guidelines for filing a request for prompt determination were set forth in Revenue Procedure 81-17, 1981-1 C.B. 688, and required that the request be submitted to the IRS District Director for the district in which the bankruptcy case was pending. *See also* legislative statements cited *supra* note 1; *In re Flaherty*, 169 B.R. 267 (Bankr. D. N.H. 1994) (must file with the special procedures unit of the District Director, as specified in Rev. Proc. 81-17; request included with debtor's originally filed return not sufficient); *but see*, with respect to bankruptcy cases commenced before October 17, 2005, *In re PT-1 Communications, Inc., et al.*, 2007-1 U.S.T.C. ¶ 50,330 (Bankr. E.D. N.Y. 2006) (following the IRS's elimination of the position of District Director, it was reasonable for the debtors to submit their request with the normal filing of their tax return at the applicable IRS Service Center); *United States v. Leonard (In re Carie Corp.)*, 128 B.R. 266 (D. Ala. 1989) (upheld filing of request at the IRS Service Center where debtor's tax returns are usually filed and taxes are usually paid, since statute "is not precise [and] . . . does not put the typical trustee (who may well not be an attorney or a tax accountant) on notice that a filing is expected at some place other than where taxes are usually collected"); *Eller Industries, Inc. v. Indian Motorcycle Mfg., Inc.*, 2000 U.S. Dist. LEXIS 5528 (D. Col. 2000) (section 505(b) determination upheld even though the trustee apparently only filed the tax returns and the request with the bankruptcy court, with service of process to the IRS).

address to which a request for prompt determination must be sent with respect to any taxing authority and where any information with respect to additional requirements is located.[3] Presumably, for the IRS, the designated address will be consistent with the IRS's revenue procedure. For bankruptcy cases commenced on or after October 17, 2005, section 505(b) requires that the request be submitted at the address maintained by the clerk,[4] and in accordance with any other requirements referenced in the listing.

The IRS has 60 days following the submission of the request (which will only be considered to occur when the IRS has received a complete submission in accordance with its Revenue Procedure[5]) to notify the debtor-in-possession that the return has been selected for audit.[6] If an audit is conducted, the IRS must complete the audit and notify the debtor-in-possession of any tax due within 180 days after the request was submitted (or within such additional time as the bankruptcy court permits).[7]

If the audit results in a proposed tax deficiency, the debtor-in-possession has the choice of (1) paying the deficiency, (2) challenging the determination and asking the bankruptcy court to resolve the dispute, or (3) presumably (although this is not expressly stated in the Bankruptcy Code) requesting the bankruptcy court to lift the stay and, upon the issuance of a statutory notice of deficiency, challenging the determination in the Tax Court.[8]

Unless the tax return was fraudulent or contained a material misrepresentation, payment of the tax due (as agreed to with the IRS or as finally determined by the court) will discharge "the trustee, the debtor, and any successor to the debtor" from any further liability for such tax (including interest and penalties).[9] In addition, for bankruptcy cases commenced on or after October 17, 2005, the discharge also applies

---

[3] 11 U.S.C. § 505(b)(1)(A), *as amended by* P.L. 109-8, § 703 (2005).

[4] Absent an express designation, a debtor-in-possession may send the request to the address where its tax return is filed or where a protest would be filed with such taxing authority. 11 U.S.C. § 505(b)(1)(B), *as amended by* P.L. 109-8, § 703 (2005).

[5] Rev. Proc. 2006-24, § 3, 2006-22 I.R.B. 943.

[6] 11 U.S.C. § 505(b)(2)(A)(i), *as amended by* P.L. 109-8, § 703 (2005) (formerly subsection (b)(1)(A)). The IRS has stated that it will also affirmatively notify the debtor-in-possession within 60 days if the return is being accepted as filed. Rev. Proc. 2006-24, § 3, 2006-22 I.R.B. 943.

[7] 11 U.S.C. § 505(b)(2)(A)(ii), *as amended by* P.L. 109-8, § 703 (2005) (formerly subsection (b)(1)(B)); Rev. Proc. 2006-24, § 3.04, 2006-22 I.R.B. 943. *See In re Hudson Oil Co.*, 100 B.R. 72 (Bankr. D. Kan. 1989) (IRS substantially complied with time requirements where the court order granting additional time was ambiguous and, even upon a strict reading, the IRS notice was only two days late).

[8] 11 U.S.C. § 505(b).

[9] Id.; *Grassgreen v. United States (In re Grassgreen)*, 200 B.R. 696, 96-2 U.S.T.C. ¶ 50,688 (Bankr. M.D. Fla. 1996) (omission on amended return of the tax due on the original return was not a misrepresentation nor did it mislead the IRS), *aff'd in part and rev'd in part*, 221 B.R. 975 (M.D. Fla. 1998) (reversal on other issues); *In re Carie Corp., supra* note 2 (also discharged liability for any previously unasserted interest and penalties); *United States v. McLemore (In re Estes)*, 87 B.R. 52 (M.D. Tenn. 1988) ("In that the interest, penalties and additional taxes arising from an alleged arithmetical error are all defined as 'taxes,' the trustee and the debtors herein are entitled to discharge with regard to such items"). Only interest and penalties relating to the tax at issue are discharged. *See United States v. Farm Loan Services, Inc. (Farm Loan Services, Inc.)*, 153 B.R. 234, 93-1 U.S.T.C. ¶ 50,343 (W.D. Wis. 1992) (discharge for corporate income taxes did not discharge penalty under Code § 6722 for trustee's failure to furnish the employee copy of Form W-2).

to "the estate" due to a legislative change. Prior to such change, several courts (including the Fifth Circuit, in the context of a corporate debtor) had held that the assets of the bankruptcy estate (as distinguished from the postbankruptcy liability of the debtor) are not discharged under this procedure, at least where there is no adjudication of the tax liability.[10] Thus, the IRS could come in at any time prior to confirmation and assert a deficiency (including interest and penalties) for any postpetition year. This result was supported by a plain reading of the statute (which differentiates between the debtor and the bankruptcy estate) and by the legislative history, at least in the individual context.[11] One bankruptcy court recently took exception with these cases and held that the bankruptcy estate (despite not being expressly identified in the list of discharged persons) is also discharged. The court pointed out that none of the prior cases considered the impact of Bankruptcy Code section 558, which provides that "[t]he estate shall have the benefit of any defense available to the debtor as against any entity other than the estate, including statutes of limitation . . . ."[12] In the court's view, this provision confers upon the estate the benefit of the limitations period created by section 505(b). The court also considered significant that each of the prior cases arose under Chapter 7 where the debtor has a separate existence from the bankruptcy estate, in contrast to a Chapter 11 case where the estate and the debtor-in-possession are inseparable "from an economic standpoint." Although the court did not distinguish between individual and corporate debtors, both the Bankruptcy Code and the Internal Revenue Code treat an individual and his bankruptcy estate as separate taxpayers, each liable for its own tax,[13] whereas in the corporate context, the estate has no independent tax status; rather, the corporate debtor continues to file as the taxpayer (*see* § 1003). Thus, for this reason as well, it could be argued that the discharge of a corporate debtor should also discharge the estate.[14]

Because a request for a prompt determination can be made only for a completed taxable year for which a return has been filed, and because a number of months must

---

10 *See Kellogg v. United States (In re West Texas Marketing Corp.)*, 54 F.3d 1194 (5th Cir. 1995) (corporate debtor in Chapter 7), *cert. denied*, *aff'g* 94-1 U.S.T.C. ¶ 50,063 (N.D. Tex. 1994), *aff'g* 155 B.R. 399 (Bankr. N.D. Tex. 1993); *In re Fondiller*, 125 B.R. 805 (N.D. Cal. 1991) (estate of individual debtor was not a "successor to the debtor" and legislative history did not require a contrary conclusion; "real focus" of section was to protect the trustee from personal liability), *rev'g* 1990 Bankr. LEXIS 709 (Bankr. N.D. Cal.); *In re Rode*, 119 B.R. 697 (Bankr. E.D. Mo. 1990) (same); *In re Vale*, 204 B.R. 716, 725-726 (Bankr. N.D. Ind. 1996) (follows foregoing cases); *In re Grassgreen*, 221 B.R. 975 (M.D. Fla. 1998) (same); *In re Goodrich*, 215 B.R. 638, 98-1 U.S.T.C. ¶ 50,183 (Bankr. D. Mass. 1997) (same, with discussion); *In re Edwards*, 2003-2 U.S.T.C. ¶ 50,671 (Bankr. E.D. Pa. 2003) (same, with discussion).

11 *Cf.* 11 U.S.C. § 505(b) with 11 U.S.C. § 505(c) (separately referring to "the estate, the debtor, or a successor to the debtor"). *See* S. Rep. No. 989, 95th Cong., 2d Sess. 68 (1978); 124 Cong. Rec. H 11,111 (daily ed. September 28, 1978) (statement of Rep. Edwards), S 17,427-17,428 (daily ed. October 6, 1978) (statement of Sen. DeConcini).

12 *In re PT-1 Communications, Inc., et al.*, *supra* note 2.

13 *See* Code § § 1398, 1399 (federal); 11 U.S.C. § § 346(b), (c) (state and local).

14 *See also* Klee & Wallace, Tax Procedure Considerations in Chapter 11 Reorganizations, Tax'n for Law at 293 (March/April 1992). It does not appear that this line of reasoning was previously considered by the courts. *See, e.g.*, *Kellogg v. United States (In re West Texas Marketing Corp.)* (5th Cir.), *supra* note 10 (concluding only that the estate of a corporate debtor is not a "successor to the debtor").

be allowed for the determination process to be completed, the debtor-in-possession generally will not be able to apply this prompt-determination procedure to the last couple of taxable years of its bankruptcy case prior to confirming a plan. As a result, at least in the context of a reorganizing Chapter 11 case, the debtor-in-possession may not be able to obtain a meaningful discharge of liability in the bankruptcy proceeding for its postpetition taxes for these later years (*see* § 1014), although as discussed below the reorganized debtor may be able to utilize the prompt determination procedure for such years *following* confirmation of the plan and the filing of any necessary returns. It is possible, however, that the debtor might obtain a declaratory judgment as to its tax liability for these later years.[15] Alternatively, the debtor may impose an administrative "bar date" (*see* § 1010.4) or otherwise attempt to obtain a discharge or fix the amount of such taxes pursuant to a confirmed plan (although where timely challenged, attempts to short-circuit the process through the plan have generally failed).[16]

In addition, an appealing case can be made that the prompt-determination process should be available even postconfirmation for all postpetition periods through (and including) the effective date of the plan.[17] This is arguably consistent with the legislative intent of providing a mechanism whereby a final determination of the trustee's liability for administrative period taxes could be obtained, and the trustee, the debtor, and any successor to the debtor could be discharged from any further liability for such taxes.[18] Moreover, such a result would further the general purposes of the Bankruptcy Code to the extent the amount or value of the consideration received by a creditor would be significantly reduced by any additional taxes

---

[15] *See, e.g., In re Goldblatt Bros., Inc., supra* note 1, discussed *infra* at § 1013.3. *Contrast In re Callan* (Bankr. D. Ala. March 13, 1992), *reprinted at* 92 TNT 84-58, discussed *infra* at § 1013. *See also* Wallace, Representing a Failing Business, 44 Maj. Tax Plan. 406.3 (1992).

[16] *But see IRS v. Taylor (In re Taylor)*, 132 F.3d 256, 98-1 U.S.T.C. ¶ 50,130 (5th Cir. 1998), *rev'g* 204 B.R. 10, 97-1 U.S.T.C. ¶ 50,259 (E.D. Tex. 1996) (plan provision had provided that "[p]ursuant to 11 U.S.C. § 505, Debtor is not indebted for any claims in this class" and had discharged all tax claims in the class that might be owed to the IRS, including, in particular, any potential Code § 6672 liability of the individual debtor; both the bankruptcy court and the district court had held that the IRS was bound by plan provision, given that the IRS had not objected to the plan or confirmation and had participated in the bankruptcy by filing and later withdrawing a protective proof of claim for income taxes; the Fifth Circuit reversed, holding that the confirmation of a plan does not itself invoke a tax determination), *reh'g denied, en banc*, 140 F.3d 1040 (5th Cir. 1998), also discussed *infra* at § 1014; *Varela v. Dynamic Brokers, Inc. (In re Dynamic Brokers, Inc.)*, 293 B.R. 489 (Bankr. 9th Cir. 2003) (court rejected debtor's attempt to include in its Chapter 11 plan a provision fixing at a reduced amount a creditor's claim that was previously scheduled by the debtor in a fixed, undisputed amount), also discussed at § 1014.

[17] *But consider Holly's, Inc. v. City of Kentwood (In re Holly's, Inc.)*, 172 B.R. 545, 560-561 (Bankr. W.D. Mich.) (property taxes assessed on the effective date of the plan were not within court's jurisdiction; although the court partially relied on the fact that the plan only provided for the discharge of preconfirmation claims, it stated that any attempt in the plan to have extended the discharge to debts incurred through the effective date would have been counter to the discharge of claims permitted by Bankruptcy Code section 1141(d), which the court read as limited to preconfirmation claims; the court also raised due process concerns), *appealed on other issues*.

[18] *See* H. Rep. No. 595, 95th Cong., 1st Sess. 356 (1977); and S. Rep. No. 989, 95th Cong., 2d Sess. 67-68 (1978), reflecting Congress's intent to codify the referee's decision (and, thus, reverse the result) in *In re Statmaster Corp.*, 465 F.2d 978, 72-2 U.S.T.C. ¶ 9649 (5th Cir. 1972). *See also* legislative statements cited *supra* note 11.

payable for such periods. A narrower view of the legislative history is also possible given the legislative history's focus on tax returns *filed by* the trustee (or debtor-in-possession). In most cases where the debtor's existence continues postconfirmation, the return for the plan year will be filed by the *reorganized debtor*—suggesting that the prompt-determination procedure generally may be unavailable to fix the immediate tax liability impact of the plan itself.

However, consider *In re Van Dyke*,[19] wherein the bankruptcy court permitted a refund action to be brought under Bankruptcy Code section 505(a) for a pre-confirmation taxable year by the trustee of a liquidating trust established pursuant to a liquidating Chapter 11 plan. The court relied in part on the Sixth Circuit's 2001 decision in *In re Gordon Sel-Wey, Inc.*,[20] which rejected the IRS's argument that Bankruptcy Code section 505(b) can only be invoked by a Chapter 11 trustee or debtor-in-possession, and thus that Bankruptcy Code section 505(a) was so limited.[21] In addition, the court in *Van Dyke* observed that the liquidating trustee was (1) acting for the benefit of the estate and any recovery would inure to the benefit of the debtor's unsecured creditors under the confirmed plan, and (2) in the confirmation order, expressly delegated the responsibility of dealing with the bankruptcy estate's tax liability for the years at issue and given all of the rights of a debtor-in-possession. Similar delegations of responsibility (often expressly authorizing the liquidating trustee to request a prompt determination of a debtor corporation's post-petition taxes) are relatively common in liquidating Chapter 11 plans.

Adopting a broader interpretation of Bankruptcy Code section 505(b), the bankruptcy court in *In re Goldblatt Bros., Inc.*[22] held (and the government agreed) that the unsecured creditors' committee could invoke the prompt determination procedure with respect to an account established pursuant to a Chapter 11 plan for the benefit of creditors and administered by the committee, even though Bankruptcy Code section 505(b) only refers to requests filed by the trustee (or debtor-in-possession) and even though it was several years after confirmation. The court reasoned that, despite confirmation, the account and the unsecured creditors' committee (which also had responsibility for evaluating and contesting any unresolved claims) were still essential parts of the bankruptcy estate.[23]

---

[19] *Schroeder v. United States (In re Van Dyke)*, 275 B.R. 854, 2002-1 U.S.T.C. ¶50,270 (Bankr. C.D. Ill. 2002).

[20] *Gordon Sel-Way, Inc. v. United States (In re Gordon Sel-Way, Inc.)*, 270 F.3d 280, 2001-2 U.S.T.C. ¶50,720 (6th Cir. 2001). *See also* discussion at §1013 below.

[21] *Cf. Center for Advanced Mfg. & Technology v. Wrightco Technologies, Inc. (In re Center for Advanced Mfg. & Technology)*, 331 B.R. 649 (Bankr. W.D. Pa. 2005), *appeal denied*, 2006 U.S. Dist. LEXIS 6389 (W.D. Pa. 2006) (permitting the reorganized debtor to initiate and pursue avoidance actions that were preserved in the debtor's plan).

[22] *Supra* note 1, discussed *infra* at §1013.2 and §1013.3.1.

[23] *See also In re Scott Cable Communications, Inc.*, 227 B.R. 596 (Bankr. D. Conn. 1998) ("Memorandum and Order on Objection to Confirmation"), also discussed at §1002.8.1 above, wherein the debtor corporation proposed a prepackaged liquidating Chapter 11 plan that attempted to stage the sale of its assets to occur only after confirmation of the plan so that the tax incurred upon the sale would not be an administrative expense of the bankruptcy case. The bankruptcy court rejected the debtor's position and held that, under the circumstances, the administrative period encompassed the postconfirmation sale of the assets. Such circumstances (each of which would alone have been

Because any discharge granted under Bankruptcy Code section 505(b) only applies to unpaid taxes, the IRS would not be barred from reexamining a tax return as to which a request for a prompt determination was made either in connection with a subsequent claim for refund or in order to challenge a subsequent use of a preconfirmation NOL against postconfirmation income.[24] Such reexamination could presumably take into account unreported income, as well as improperly claimed deductions and credits.[25]

**EXAMPLE**

On January 1, 1982, X Corporation, a calendar year taxpayer, filed a petition under Chapter 11. For 1981 and 1982, X Corporation's tax returns showed an NOL of $75x and $50x, respectively. For 1983, X Corporation filed a tax return showing an NOL (prior to applying its NOLs from 1981 and 1982) of $10x. X Corporation was discharged in 1984. Because Bankruptcy Code section 505(b) only applies to unpaid taxes for completed postpetition taxable years for which a tax return has been filed, a prompt determination of X corporation's tax liability may only be requested for 1982 and 1983. If the IRS proposes no tax deficiency, X Corporation would be discharged from paying any taxes for such postpetition taxable years. If subsequently, however, the IRS discovers that X Corporation had unreported income and had taken improper deductions in 1982 totalling $145x, it appears that the IRS could reduce X Corporation's NOLs for 1981, 1982, and 1983 to zero, but could not collect the remaining $10x

(Footnote Continued)

sufficient in the court's view) included the fact that the debtor sought, for the period through the sale, to obtain an effective extension of the automatic stay with respect to the assets, that the sale and the plan were interdependent parts of one transaction ("[n]o one part [of which] can stand without the other") and that no business purpose was served by requiring the sale to follow confirmation. Although not at issue in *Scott Cable*, the bankruptcy court's analysis would support the conclusion that, in the context of a liquidating Chapter 11 plan, the debtor may properly obtain a prompt determination of its postconfirmation tax liability. For similar support, *see Boston Regional Medical Center, Inc. v. Reynolds (In re Boston Regional Medical Center, Inc.)*, 410 F.3d 100 (1st Cir. 2005) (upholding the bankruptcy court's post-confirmation jurisdiction in the case of a liquidating Chapter 11 plan), discussed at § 1013 below. *But consider In re PT-1 Communications, Inc., et al., supra* note 2 (the court, in *dicta*, viewed the liquidating trust in that case as a "successor to the debtor and debtor in possession" so as to benefit from the debtors' earlier discharge under Bankruptcy Code section 505(b)).

[24] Although the legislative history to Bankruptcy Code section 505(b) is silent in this regard, the explanatory statements made in Congress regarding Bankruptcy Code section 1141(d) (the general discharge provision) stated that the IRS is not prohibited "from disallowing any tax benefit claimed after the reorganization if the item originated in a deduction, credit, or other item improperly reported before the reorganization occurred." 124 Cong. Rec. H 11,114 (daily ed. September 28, 1978) (statement of Rep. Edwards), S 17,431 (daily ed. October 6, 1978) (statement of Sen. DeConcini). *See also Firsdon v. United States*, 95 F.3d 444, 449 n.7 (6th Cir. 1996).

[25] Id. *Cf.* IRS Field Service Advice 200039007, June 23, 2000, *reprinted at* 2000 TNT 191-44 (involving an individual debtor; concluded that a postbankruptcy NOL could be carried back, for purposes of reducing the amount of the NOL, to a taxable year for which any tax liability was discharged).

deficiency, nor could it use such deficiency to reduce an NOL for a subsequent taxable year not claimed until after the discharge under Bankruptcy Code section 505(b).

## § 1012 REFUND PROCEDURES IN BANKRUPTCY

Bankruptcy proceedings generally have little impact on the normal rules for obtaining refunds of federal taxes, except in two areas: (1) the IRS's ability to set off (or credit) a tax refund or overpayment against existing prepetition tax liabilities (*see* § § 1006.1.1 and 1012.1) and (2) the time period in which a suit for refund may be filed (*see* § 1012.2).[1]

### *§ 1012.1 Quickie Refunds*

A debtor-in-possession has the same right to obtain a "quickie refund" of prior year income taxes as does a nonbankrupt corporation.[2] Where the tax return shows an NOL, ITC, capital loss, or research credit carryover, the corporation (or, in bankruptcy, the debtor-in-possession or trustee) may request from the IRS a quickie refund of any past taxes refundable on account of such losses or credits (or it may obtain an adjustment of such taxes if still unpaid).[3] The IRS must act upon the application within 90 days after the later of the date the application was filed or the last day of the month in which the tax return for the loss year was due (including extensions).[4] The application may be denied, in whole or in part, only if it contains material omissions or errors of computation.[5]

---

[1] **§ 1012** *See also* IRS Legal Memorandum 200130041, June 14, 2001, *reprinted at* 2001 TNT 146-78 (a deposit made in connection with an offer in compromise must be returned upon the taxpayer's filing for bankruptcy, as it is the IRS's view that a bankruptcy filing renders the offer unprocessable, *see* § 1016.1 below).

[2] No expedited refund procedure exists for excess employment tax deposits, although tax deposits that are made using the Electronic Tax Payment System may, in certain cases, be able to be returned or reversed under the Automated Clearing House rules. *See* IRS Legal Memorandum 200152045, November 15, 2001, *reprinted at* 2001 TNT 251-30; Rev. Proc. 98-32, § § 9-10, 1998-1 C.B. 935.

[3] Code § 6411(a); Reg. § § 1.6411-(a) and 1.1502-78 (special consolidated return rules). For a discussion of the interplay between Code § § 6411 and 6164 (allowing the postponement of a current tax payment based on expected NOLs), *see* Beghe, Tax Planning for the Financially Troubled Corp., 52 Taxes 795, 805-807 (1974).

[4] Id.

[5] Reg. § 1.6411-3(c). Although the 90-day period is statutorily mandated, no apparent sanctions are imposed under the Internal Revenue Code if the IRS fails to act within such period. *See, e.g., Kellogg v. United States* (*In re Southwestern States Marketing Corp.*), 95-1 U.S.T.C. ¶ 50,057 (N.D. Tex. 1994), *aff'd*, 82 F.3d 413, 96-1 U.S.T.C. ¶ 50,165 (5th Cir. 1996). However, in *In re Rozel Industries, Inc.*, 120 B.R. 944, 948 (Bankr. N.D. Ill. 1990), the bankruptcy court deemed the IRS to have effected a setoff of the refund claim when it failed to respond to the request, thereby stopping the accrual of interest on offsetting prepetition tax liabilities. In addition, in appropriate circumstances, the imposition of sanctions may be within the bankruptcy court's equitable powers. Consider, for example, the original bankruptcy court decision in *Midway Indus. Contractors, Inc., infra* note 7. *See also* § § 1013.5 (regarding the scope of

In addition, the IRS is ordinarily permitted to credit the amount of any refund claim against any tax (or installment) then due from the taxpayer and to refund only the remainder.[6] As discussed at § 1006.1.1, however, while the automatic stay is pending, the IRS is generally (absent prior court approval[7]) precluded from effecting a setoff of any postpetition tax overpayments against unpaid prepetition taxes and, although considerably less clear, may be precluded from effecting a setoff of prepetition tax overpayments.[8] Absent relief from the automatic stay, the IRS would, upon request, generally be entitled under Bankruptcy Code section 362(d) to "adequate protection" of its interest in the tax refund.[9] The IRS recently issued Rev. Rul. 2007-53 and Temp. Reg. § 1.6411-3T which include among the tax liabilities to be offset in determining the available refund any unassessed tax liabilities set forth in a statutory notice of deficiency *or* in a proof of claim filed in a bankruptcy proceeding. The premise for this is that the notice and claim represent a specific administrative determination of the nature and amount of a tax liability that is entitled to a presumption of correctness, and thus reflect a liability that is currently due. The IRS did not address the potential implications of the automatic stay with respect to any such offset.

Any portion of a quickie refund (or tentative carryback adjustment) that is subsequently determined to have been excessive following a full audit of the return is

---

(Footnote Continued)

the bankruptcy court's equitable powers), 1005.1 (addressing sovereign immunity) and 1007.7 (discussing damages for violating the automatic stay).

[6] Code § 6411(b); Reg. § § 1.6411-3(d)(3); Temp. Reg. § 1.6411-3T; *see also* Code § 6402(a).

[7] *Consider Weems v. United States (In re The Custom Center, Inc.)*, 163 B.R. 309 (Bankr. E.D. Tenn. 1994) (involved a quickie refund for which application was made prebankruptcy, but was receivable postpetition; court declined to make a final determination as to whether to require an immediate refund or to permit setoff until the parties had had a further opportunity to brief the issue; court suggested that the administrative priority generally accorded an excessive refund might not apply where the refund is based on a carryback of prepetition losses).

[8] *But consider United States v. Midway Indus. Contractors, Inc. (In re Midway Industrial Contractors, Inc.)*, 178 B.R. 734 (N.D. Ill. 1995) (applying an expansive interpretation of the Seventh Circuit's decision in the *Pettibone Corporation* case, discussed at § 1006.1.1.1 above, the District Court held that the reduction of a quickie refund claim by outstanding employment tax liabilities for late deposits was not a type of "setoff" precluded by the Bankruptcy Code), *rev'g*, 167 B.R. 139, 94-1 U.S.T.C. ¶ 50-268 (Bankr. N.D. Ill. 1994) (the bankruptcy court had held that the failure to issue the tax refund within the statutory 90-day period demonstrated an intent to set off in violation of the automatic stay, and awarded attorney's fees to the debtor; however, the bankruptcy court thereafter modified the automatic stay to permit setoff, finding that the IRS's interest in the tax refund was not otherwise adequately protected; the court did not discuss the considerations raised below in the text). *Cf. Security Pac. Natl. Bank v. United States (In re Siebert Trailers, Inc.)*, 132 B.R. 37, 91-2 U.S.T.C. ¶ 50,308 (Bankr. E.D. Cal. 1991) (debtor had entered into stipulation allowing the IRS to set off a tentative refund subject to secured creditor's right to bring the current proceeding to determine if the creditor's security interest preempted any setoff; held for IRS; creditor's right to refund was derivative of the rights of the debtor and thus subject to the IRS's right of setoff). *See also* IRS to Give Leslie Fay $13.7M Tax Refund For 1992, The Daily Bankruptcy Review, December 23, 1993. For a discussion of whether a particular tax overpayment is a pre- or postpetition obligation, *see* § 1006.1.1 above at notes 34-39.

[9] *See also* 11 U.S.C. § 506(a), which treats a creditor's claim, which is otherwise unsecured, as a secured claim to the extent such claim is subject to setoff under Bankruptcy Code section 553 (involving mutual prepetition debts).

treated as an administrative expense of the bankruptcy (regardless of whether it relates to a pre- or postpetition year), and thus entitled to priority in payment.[10]

### EXAMPLE

On November 1, 1998, the IRS assessed L Corporation, a calendar year taxpayer, $100x in tax deficiencies as a result of an audit of L's 1993 and 1994 tax returns. For 1996 and 1997, L paid taxes of $60x and $40x, respectively. During 1998, L's business underwent a severe downturn, resulting in a substantial NOL for the year, and on March 1, 1999, L filed a petition under Chapter 11. Immediately prior to the bankruptcy filing, L filed IRS Form 1139, carrying back its 1998 NOL, and claiming a quickie refund for the full $100x of 1996 and 1997 taxes.

If the bankruptcy court grants the IRS permission to setoff the $100x refund, L will no longer have a tax deficiency, nor will it have available the cash from the refund. Assuming that the IRS promptly audits L's 1996 through 1998 taxable years and determines that the refund should only have been $75x, the IRS will have an administrative expense claim for the repayment of the $25x excess—which would be payable upon consummation of the Chapter 11 plan out of L's other available funds (assuming it has any), if not sooner.

In contrast, if the IRS is required to remit the $100x refund, L will have use of the refund and will still owe $100x in prepetition taxes, which it presumably will pay over time under a confirmed Chapter 11 plan. Assuming again that the IRS promptly audits L and determines that the refund should only have been $75x, the IRS will (as above) have an administrative expense claim for the repayment of the $25x excess. Only in this case, L could (in an all perfect world) simply repay the $25x out of the original $100x refund. Thus, L would retain $75x of the refund monies, while the IRS awaited payment of the $100x tax deficiency under L's Chapter 11 plan. Even assuming that L is required to apply the net refund in payment of the tax deficiency (under, say, an "adequate protection" order), L would still have preserved the ability to pay the remaining $25x net deficiency over time.

In general, an application for a quickie refund (or tentative carryback adjustment) must be filed (on Form 1139) after the tax return for the loss year, but within 12 months after the end of such year.[11] Where the loss year is a short year due to the company having joined a new consolidated group, the 12 month period is measured

---

[10] *See* §1015 (priority of tax claims); 11 U.S.C. §503(b)(1)(B)(ii) (regarding administrative expense treatment).

[11] Code §6411(a), (b); Reg. §1.6411-1(b)(1); Reg. §1.1502-78(e).

from the end of the taxable year of the new group.[12] If, however, the application period would terminate within 60 days after the filing of a voluntary bankruptcy petition (or, in the case of an involuntary petition, after the court's formal approval of the petition, called an "order for relief"), Bankruptcy Code section 108(b) operates to extend the application period to the end of such 60-day period.

Because an application for a quickie refund does not constitute a claim for refund,[13] a denial of the application cannot be used as grounds for a subsequent suit for refund. Conversely, the IRS's allowance of a quickie refund (or tentative carryback adjustment) does not preclude the IRS from reexamining the return.[14] As mentioned above, any tax subsequently determined to be payable due to an excessive allowance of a quickie refund received during bankruptcy is treated as an administrative expense of the bankruptcy—regardless of whether it relates to a pre- or postpetition year.[15]

Query whether the prompt determination procedure in Bankruptcy Code section 505(b), discussed at § 1011 above, could be used to accelerate finality of the amount of a quickie refund. Such procedure applies "for any tax incurred during the administration of the case by submitting a tax return for such tax . . . ." Given that the Bankruptcy Code treats any tax due as a result of an excessive allowance of a quickie refund as an administrative expense, it appears appropriate to treat such tax as "incurred during the administration of the case."[16] In such event, we would hope the filing of the Form 1139, together with the tax return(s) for the year(s) to which the loss was carried back, would satisfy the requirement that the debtor submit a tax return.

---

[12] Reg. § 1.1502-78(e)(2). Thus, this extension only applies to a corporation that, immediately before joining the new group, was either (1) not part of another consolidated group or (2) the common parent of another consolidated group. Id.

[13] Reg. § 1.6411-1(b)(2); *VDO-ARGO Instruments, Inc. v. United States*, 83-2 U.S.T.C. ¶ 9605 (Ct. Cl. 1983) (an application for quickie refund does not constitute an informal claim for refund); *Sherman Kamens v. United States*, 83-2 U.S.T.C. ¶ 9540 (D. Mo. 1983) (same); *Morse v. United States*, 80-2 U.S.T.C. ¶ 9496 (Ct. Cl. 1980) (same).

[14] Reg. § 1.6411-1(b)(2); *Union Equity Cooperative Exchange*, 58 T.C. 397, Dec. 31,410 (1972), *aff'd on other grounds*, 481 F.2d 812, 73-2 U.S.T.C. ¶ 9534 (10th Cir. 1973), *cert. denied*, 94 S. Ct. 457 (1974).

[15] *See* 11 U.S.C. § 503(b)(1)(B)(ii) and discussion at § 1015.1.1.

[16] *Consider United States v. Official Comm. of Unsecured Creditors of Indus. Comm. Electrical, Inc.* (*In re Indus. Comm. Electrical, Inc.*), 319 B.R. 35, 42, 2005-1 U.S.T.C. ¶ 50,312 (D. Mass. 2005) (implying such potential). Although the bankruptcy court in *In re Weisberg*, 226 B.R. 172 (Bankr. E.D. Pa. 1998), concluded otherwise, its reasoning was that the obligation to return an excessive refund is different than a tax liability owing and, thus, not within the scope of section 505(b). This fails to recognize, however, that a quickie refund is simply a tentative carryback adjustment, and that any recovery by the IRS presupposes a prior determination of tax due by the IRS, as demonstrated by the three ways that the IRS can recover an excess allowance relating to a quickie refund. These are (1) a summary assessment (similar to that employed for mathematical errors on a taxpayer's return, and which itself is an assessment of tax due), (2) the issuance of a notice of tax deficiency (as is often done), and (3) an action for erroneous refund under Code § 7405 (which effectively requires, in the quickie refund context, a prior determination by the IRS that there was still tax due—otherwise there would be nothing to return). *See generally* Saltzman, IRS Practice and Procedure (rev. 2nd Ed.), at ¶ 11.03.

## §1012.2 *Claims and Suits for Refund*

Quickie refunds aside, a corporation seeking a refund (or credit) from the IRS generally must first file a claim for refund. Any claim for a refund filed after the commencement of the bankruptcy case, whether on an original return (for a postpetition taxable year), an amended return, or otherwise, should be filed with the district director of the IRS for the district in which the bankruptcy case is pending.[17]

A suit for refund may then be filed only after (1) the IRS has disallowed the claim for refund or (2) six months have passed since the filing of the claim.[18] In bankruptcy, the six-month waiting period is reduced to 120 days.[19] The filing of a claim for refund, however, as well as the 120-day waiting period are dispensed with where the refund results from an offset or counterclaim to a proof of claim, or a request for payment of taxes, filed by the IRS with the bankruptcy court.[20] Where a tax refund

---

[17] *See* Rev. Proc. 81-18, 1981-1 C.B. 688.

[18] Code §6532(a)(1); *see also Texaco, Inc. v. Louisiana Land and Exploration*, 113 B.R. 924, 938-939 (M.D. La. 1990) (according to magistrate's report, a suit filed before 120 days may be cured by supplemental pleading under Rule 15(d) of the Federal Rules of Civil Procedure). In the case of an originally filed return claiming a tax overpayment, the application of such overpayment contrary to the taxpayer's instructions should be treated as the disallowance of a claim for refund. *See, e.g., United States v. Ryan (In re Ryan)*, 64 F.3d 1516, 95-2 U.S.T.C. ¶50,519 (11th Cir. 1995); *Kiesner v. IRS (In re Kiesner)*, 194 B.R. 452, 96-1 U.S.T.C. ¶50,139 (Bankr. E.D. Wis. 1996). For a further discussion of what constitutes a notice of disallowance, *see* IRS Chief Counsel Advice 200203002, August 3, 2001, *reprinted at* 2002 TNT 14-98 (concluding that a letter stating a refund claim could not be "processed" did not constitute a notice of disallowance).

[19] Code §6532(a)(5); 11 U.S.C. §505(a)(2)(B). *See Murray Indus., Inc. v. United States (In re Murray Indus.)*, 106 B.R. 284 (Bankr. M.D. Fla. 1989) (other Internal Revenue Code requirements unaffected; because a refund suit was a "related" not a "core" proceeding, the bankruptcy court only had limited nonbinding jurisdiction to hear the suit unless the government consented).

[20] Rev. Proc. 81-18, §2.02, 1981-1 C.B. 688; 124 Cong. Rec. H 11,110 (daily ed. September 28, 1978) (statement of Rep. Edwards), S 17,427 (daily ed. October 6, 1978) (statement of Sen. DeConcini); *United States v. Kearns*, 177 F.3d 706, 99-1 U.S.T.C. ¶50,573 (8th Cir. 1999) (allowed offset, even though no claim for refund had been filed and statutory period for doing so had passed, where the IRS claimed additional taxes based on previously unreported income for monies embezzled by the debtor, and the offset—principally the debtor's tax savings from deducting his restitution payments—also arose out of the embezzlement; the court carefully avoided addressing whether the prior passage of the statutory period for filing a refund claim could, on other facts, impede a debtor's ability to offset previously unclaimed tax savings for taxable years not covered by the proof of claim), *rev'g*, 219 B.R. 823 (Bankr. 8th Cir. 1998); *United States v. Henderson (In re Guardian Trust Co.)*, 260 B.R. 404, 2000-2 U.S.T.C. ¶50,777 (S.D. Miss. 2000) (upheld bankruptcy court's jurisdiction over trustee's claim for an offset arising out of an asserted NOL carryback from one of the same taxable years for which the IRS had filed a claim for tax deficiencies, even though an administrative claim for refund would not have been timely; relied on *Kearns* decision); *In re Dunhill Medical, Inc.*, 96-1 U.S.T.C. ¶50,276 (Bankr. D.N.J. 1996) (offset must still be asserted within the applicable statute of limitations for filing a claim for refund); *Michaud v. United States*, 206 B.R. 1, 97-1 U.S.T.C. ¶50,292 (D. N.H. 1997) (permitted actual cash refund, not simply offset, where the tax liability that the IRS originally claimed to be owing was ultimately determined to be zero); *cf. Texaco, Inc. v. Louisiana Land and Exploration*, *supra* note 18, at 928. *Consider also In re Maley* (Bankr. W.D.N.Y.), *reprinted at* 93 TNT 20-24 (court treated as a proper claim for refund the debtor's objection to the IRS's postconfirmation motion to convert or dismiss the debtor's Chapter 11 case due to the debtor's failure to pay the IRS's prepetition claim, and measured the 120-day waiting period from the filing of the objection, where the debtor asserted that he was actually due a refund and the court's decision on the jurisdictional issues was unavoidably delayed; however, the court limited any refund that might otherwise be allowable to

claim has been filed and disallowed, the suit for refund generally must be filed within two years from the date the notice of disallowance is mailed.[21] As discussed below, this period may be extended in bankruptcy.

Under Bankruptcy Code section 108, the statute of limitations for filing a claim for refund or suit for refund may be extended where such claim or suit relates to a prepetition tax payment and the statute of limitations has not expired before the filing of the bankruptcy petition.[22] In such case, the statute of limitations for filing a *claim for refund* will expire the later of the date at which it would ordinarily expire or 60 days after a voluntary petition is filed (or, in an involuntary bankruptcy, after the order for relief is filed).[23] Although Bankruptcy Code section 108 also operates to extend the statute of limitations for filing a *suit for refund*—until the later of the date at which it would ordinarily expire or two years after a voluntary petition is filed (or, in an involuntary bankruptcy, after the order for relief is filed)[24]—as discussed at § 1013 below, once a claim for refund has been properly filed and the requisite waiting period has been satisfied, it is possible (depending on the circuit, the type of tax, and the facts) that a suit for refund may be brought under Bankruptcy Code section 505(a) at any time, irrespective of the applicable statute of limitations.

One bankruptcy court had effectively fashioned a further exception to the statute of limitations for a *claim for refund*, but was reversed on later appeal by the Fifth

---

(Footnote Continued)

that necessary to pay preconfirmation creditors in full and professional fees relating to the objection); *Schroeder v. United States (In re Van Dyke)*, 275 B.R. 854, 2002-1 U.S.T.C. ¶ 50,270 (Bankr. C.D. Ill. 2002) (permitting suit for refund in a non-offset situation under alternative theories, including a broad reading of the *Kearns* decision).

[21] Code § 6532(a)(1), (2), (4) (may be extended by written agreement with the IRS, but is not otherwise extended by any reconsideration or action by the IRS following the notice of disallowance); *Marcinkowsky v. United States*, 206 F.3d 1419, 2000-1 U.S.T.C. ¶ 50,320 (Fed. Cir. 2000). *Consider Cooper v. United States*, 99-2 U.S.T.C. ¶ 50,877 (W.D. N.C. 1999) (suit for refund was held timely when filed within two years of the disallowance of a "perfected" claim for refund, which related back to a previously filed "protective" claim for refund; although a notice of disallowance had been issued with respect to the protective claim more than two years prior to the suit for refund, the court found that the IRS had rescinded such disallowance); *Ihnen v. United States*, 272 F.3d 577, 2001-2 U.S.T.C. ¶ 50,786 (8th Cir. 2001) (taxpayer estopped from pursuing a refund claim where there was a prior tax settlement agreement and the IRS could no longer assess; observed that other circuit courts might conclude differently).

[22] 11 U.S.C. § 108(a) and (b); *see, e.g., In re Qual Krom South, Inc.*, 119 B.R. 327 (Bankr. S.D. Fla. 1990); *In re Carter*, 125 B.R. 832, 91-1 U.S.T.C. ¶ 50,133 (Bankr. D. Kan. 1991) (involving claim for refund).

[23] 11 U.S.C. § 108(b); *see, e.g., Valory v. United States*, 97-2 U.S.T.C. ¶ 50,805 (N.D. Cal. 1997), *aff'd*, 98-2 U.S.T.C. ¶ 50,659 (9th Cir. 1998) (unpublished decision); *In re Howard Indus., Inc.*, 170 B.R. 358, 94-2 U.S.T.C. ¶ 50,417 (Bankr. S.D. Ohio 1994). Bankruptcy Code section 108(b) has also been held to extend a taxpayer's right of redemption under Code § 6337 for real property sold at a tax sale. *See In re Cooke*, 127 B.R. 784 (Bankr. W.D.N.C. 1991).

[24] 11 U.S.C. § 108(a); *see TLI, Inc. v. United States*, 100 F.3d 424, 96-2 U.S.T.C. ¶ 50,655 (5th Cir. 1996) (holding that a tax refund claim, although a prerequisite to the filing of a suit for refund, does not itself "commence an action" and thus is not covered by the longer filing extension permitted by section 108(a) of the Bankruptcy Code), also discussed at *infra* note 27. In view of a 2005 statutory change to section 505(a) of the Bankruptcy Code, a suit for refund with respect to *ad valorem* property taxes must be brought within the applicable time frame under nonbankruptcy law. 11 U.S.C. § 505(a)(2)(C) (effective for bankruptcy cases commenced on or after October 17, 2005).

Circuit Court of Appeals. In *In re Armstrong*,[25] the IRS was engaged in an audit of the debtor as of the commencement of the bankruptcy case. The IRS later issued an assessment against the debtor, which the debtor disputed and litigated. Ultimately, but after the statute of limitations for filing a claim for refund had expired, the IRS agreed with the debtor that no additional taxes were owing and that the debtor had in fact overpaid its taxes by $126,240. The bankruptcy court, although recognizing that the statute of limitations for refund claims had expired, nevertheless held that the overpayment constituted property of the estate, which the IRS was compelled to turn over to the bankruptcy trustee under Bankruptcy Code section 542(a). In the bankruptcy court's view, this followed from the fact that, as of the commencement of the bankruptcy case, the debtor's interest in any refund of prepetition taxes for the year under audit was itself property of the estate, which thereafter simply became liquidated in amount. Acknowledging the resulting tension between the Internal Revenue Code and the Bankruptcy Code, the bankruptcy court stated that:

> This reading of the codes is limited to the facts and circumstances of this case; specifically the liquidation of an overpayment in a fixed amount of money by agreement of the United States and the taxpayer following the commencement of litigation . . . . Had that not occurred, the trustee would have had to file a claim with the IRS consistent with the limitations period in the Internal Revenue Code.

The Fifth Circuit disagreed, and held that the filing requirements (and thus the limitations period) for refunds under Code § 6511 were controlling. The Fifth Circuit based its decision on the fact that other provisions of the Bankruptcy Code anticipated compliance with the refund mechanism of Code § 6511;[26] that Bankruptcy Code section 108 expressly provides relief from certain statutes of limitations,[27] and that, in relation to Bankruptcy Code section 542(a), Code § 6511 is the more specific provision. In this latter regard, the court stated that, "§ 542(a) is a provision of general application, relating to all property in which the estate has a continuing interest, while § 6511 creates and circumscribes a taxpayer's (and therefore the bankruptcy estate's) interest in a refund."

---

[25] *McCullough v. United States* (*In re Armstrong*), 217 B.R. 192, 97-2 U.S.T.C. ¶ 50,973 (Bankr. N.D. Tex. 1997), *rev'd on appeal, sub. nom. United States v. Neary* (*In re Armstrong*), 206 F.3d 465, 2000-1 U.S.T.C. ¶ 50,269 (5th Cir. 2000). The Fifth Circuit decision indicates that the bankruptcy court decision was affirmed by the district court, but no citation to the district court's action has been found.

[26] *Citing* 11 U.S.C. § 505(a)(2)(B) (conferring bankruptcy court jurisdiction over a refund only where, as discussed above and at § 1013 below, the bankruptcy trustee first "properly requests" such refund from the governmental unit and either 120 days has expired or the request has been denied).

[27] Although not particularly relevant to its discussion of section 108, the court overstated its earlier holding in *TLI, Inc. v. United States, supra* note 24. In that decision, the Fifth Circuit held that Bankruptcy Code section 108(a) did not operate to extend the statute of limitations for a claim for refund, but expressly noted (in footnote 2 of its decision) that "§ 108(b) may very well apply to an administrative tax refund claim due prior to any litigation." It did *not* hold, as suggested in its decision in *In re Armstrong*, that neither Bankruptcy Code section 108(a) nor 108(b) applies to filings of administrative claims under the Internal Revenue Code.

In *In re Smith*,[28] the Eighth Circuit Court of Appeals rejected a similar assertion that a turnover action could be employed in the absence of a timely refund claim.[29] In that case, the IRS had applied the debtor's overpayment of his personal income taxes in partial satisfaction of an outstanding Code § 6672 penalty assessment for unpaid withholding taxes. Both the bankruptcy court and district court held that the debtor was not liable for the penalty, but did not order a refund of the credited amount. Nor did the debtor or the bankruptcy trustee file (or otherwise seek a refund) of the credited amount. The government initially appealed the district court decision, but subsequently sought to have the entire case declared moot on the grounds that the time within which the debtor could seek a refund had long since passed and that the IRS had decided not to pursue the unsatisfied portion of the original assessment. In reply, the debtor asserted that the appeal still had practical significance because the bankruptcy trustee could still file a turnover proceeding against the IRS for repayment of the money. The Eighth Circuit disagreed, and found the preclusive language of Code § 7422(a) determinative of the issue. Such section provides that:

> *No suit or proceeding shall be maintained in any court* for the recovery of any internal revenue tax alleged to have been erroneously or illegally assessed or collected, or of any penalty claimed to have been collected without authority, or of any sum alleged to have been excessive or in any manner wrongfully collected, *until a claim for refund or credit has been duly filed* with the Secretary, according to the provisions of law in that regard, and the regulations of the Secretary established in pursuance thereof [emphasis added].

In yet another case, the liquidating trustee in *In re Consolidated FGH Liquidating Trust*,[30] acting on behalf of the debtor, a former member of a consolidated tax group, sought to utilize a turnover action as justification for bringing an action for a tax refund in lieu of the common parent of the consolidated group. The bankruptcy court concluded, in accordance with the consolidated return regulations, that the common parent was the only person authorized to seek the tax refund for the group.[31] (The court was also not enamored with the prospect of determining the tax liability of non-debtors, namely, the other members of the consolidated group.)

It is also important to be aware that, where the IRS has filed a proof of claim in the bankruptcy case, any adjustments to the claim must be raised by timely objection (or other appropriate motion), either during the bankruptcy case or within any additional period permitted by the plan or confirmation order. A case on point is

---

[28] *Smith v. United States (In re Smith)*, 921 F.2d 136 (8th Cir. 1990), *substituted opinion at* 1990 U.S. App. LEXIS 19136 (contains minor corrections).

[29] *Consider also United States v. Ryan (In re Ryan)* (11th Cir.), *supra* note 18, wherein the IRS raised and argued the issue, but the Eleventh Circuit did not have to address it given that it concluded that the debtor's filing of its original tax return claiming a tax overpayment that the IRS applied contrary to the debtor's instructions constituted a timely claim for refund.

[30] *Oakridge Consulting Inc. v. United States (In re Consolidated FGH Liquidating Trust)*, 325 B.R. 564, 2005-2 U.S.T.C. ¶ 50,448 (Bankr. S.D. Miss. 2005).

[31] *See* Reg. § 1.1502-77(a), discussed at § 1007.4 above.

*Puckett v. United States.*[32] In that case, the IRS had filed a proof of claim (and amendments) for several prepetition and postpetition taxable years. The debtors' Chapter 11 plan specifically provided for such taxes and, in accordance with the plan, the debtors paid all the postpetition taxes and the portion of the prepetition taxes for which the IRS had a priority claim. Subsequently, the debtors filed several claims for refund and thereafter a suit for refund, asserting certain additional deductions and seeking to apply certain NOL carryovers incurred in taxable years prior to, and during, the bankruptcy case. The court held that, because the confirmation of a Chapter 11 plan constitutes a final judgment on the merits of any creditor claims allowed in accordance with the plan, the debtors were barred under the principles of *res judicata* from pursuing the tax refunds.[33]

## § 1013 BANKRUPTCY COURT JURISDICTION OVER DEBTOR'S TAX LIABILITY

A bankruptcy court has as its central purpose the successful financial rehabilitation of the debtor corporation. The bankruptcy court will also be familiar with the affairs of the debtor and with the plan for its rehabilitation. As a result, a debtor corporation may find the bankruptcy court a better place than any other court in which to resolve tax disputes.

Pursuant to Bankruptcy Code section 505(a), the bankruptcy court may determine the amount or legality of any tax claim against the debtor (including any addition to tax, fine, or penalty relating to a tax), whether incurred prepetition or postpetition and whether or not previously assessed or paid.[1] A decision by the bankruptcy court as to the debtor corporation's tax liability is fully binding on the debtor corporation and cannot thereafter be relitigated in any tribunal.[2]

---

[32] 99-2 U.S.T.C. ¶ 50,637 (S.D. Tex. 1999), *aff'd*, 213 F.3d 636, 2000-1 U.S.T.C. ¶ 50,439 (5th Cir. 2000) (unpublished opinion), *cert. denied*, 121 S. Ct. 759 (2001).

[33] Consider also, *Johnston v. Commissioner*, 461 F.3d 1162 (9th Cir. 2006) (taxpayer could not apply NOLs from other audit years to reduce a tax liability agreed to in a settlement agreement with the IRS where such use of the NOLs was not preserved in the agreement).

[1] **§ 1013** 11 U.S.C. § 505(a)(1). *See, e.g., United States v. Smith (In re Smith)*, 158 B.R. 813, 93-2 U.S.T.C. ¶ 50,656 (Bankr. 9th Cir. 1993) (motion for order requiring State Lottery Commission to remit lottery winnings without reduction for applicable federal withholding taxes was not a proceeding "to determine the amount or legality of any tax"); *see also IRS v. Sulmeyer (In re Grand Chevrolet, Inc.)*, 153 B.R. 296 (C.D. Cal. 1993), and *Inter Urban Broadcasting of Cincinnati, Inc. v. Lewis (In re Inter Urban Broadcasting of Cincinnati, Inc.)*, 180 B.R. 153 (Bankr. E.D. La. 1995), discussed *infra* § 1013.3. As the use of the word "may" indicates, it is generally within the bankruptcy court's discretion to abstain from determining the merits of any tax claim. *See* discussion at § 1013.1; *see also In re Franklin*, 78 B.R. 118 (Bankr. E.D. Va. 1987) (court declined to consider allegation of faulty assessment where debtor had opportunity to file in Tax Court and did not raise request in its complaint to the bankruptcy court).

For a discussion of the ability (or inability) of a debtor to obtain relief from interest and penalties, *see* §§ 1006.1.2 (prepetition taxes), 1006.2.1 (postpetition taxes) and 1006.3.1 (trust fund taxes).

[2] S. Rep. No. 833, 96th Cong., 2d Sess. 48 (1980); *see, e.g., Florida Peach Corp. v. Commissioner*, 90 T.C. 678, Dec. 44,689 (1988) (bankruptcy court tax decision binding even though Chapter 11 case subsequently dismissed); *Samuel Leroy Bostian*, 62 T.C.M. 1337, Dec. 47,775(M), T.C. Memo. 1991-589 (same); *In re Pine Knob Investment*, 20 B.R. 714 (Bankr. E.D. Mich. 1982). A bankruptcy court order upholding (or "allowing") an IRS proof of claim constitutes a final and appealable judgment. *See, e.g.,*

In general, this broad grant of authority means that the bankruptcy court may rule on a debtor's challenge to a previously assessed (but unpaid) tax liability even if the time period for challenging the assessment has expired under applicable non-bankruptcy law. Inevitably, though, this concept proves to be the rare exception, rather than the rule.[3]

As discussed below, the bankruptcy court may not rule on a tax claim that has been previously adjudicated in a contested proceeding before a judicial or administrative tribunal of competent jurisdiction before the commencement of the bankruptcy case.[4] Nor, in bankruptcy cases commenced on or after October 17, 2005, may

---

(Footnote Continued)

Circuit Court cases discussed at end of § 1010.3 above, and *Samuel Leroy Bostian*, 62 T.C.M. 1337, *supra*. For a brief discussion of the binding effect of a court approved settlement agreement, *see* discussion *infra* at notes 71-80; *see also Schwab v. United States (In re Shop N' Go Partnership)*, 261 B.R. 810 (Bankr. M.D. Pa. 2001) (concluding that "a settlement agreement entered into as part of a Chapter 11 plan proceeding and affirmed through a court order has a similar effect as a confirmed plan"; thus, in absence of any objection or timely appeal of the affirming order or of fraud in the procurement of the order, the debtor's settlement agreement with the IRS was binding even though the payment provisions were arguably inconsistent with the prioritization of claims in the Bankruptcy Code and the Plan).

In general, a bankruptcy court's declared findings of facts in an order confirming a debtor corporation's Chapter 11 plan are not determinative of such facts in a later IRS tax dispute that was not before the court at the time. *See, e.g., Dycoal Inc. v. IRS (In re Dycoal Inc.)*, 327 B.R. 220, 2005-2 U.S.T.C. ¶ 50,554 (Bankr. W.D. Pa. 2005) *aff'd*, 2006 U.S. Dist. LEXIS 25078 (W.D. Pa. 2006) (IRS not bound by findings of facts in confirmation order purporting to establish factual predicates for Code § 29 tax credits for pre-confirmation periods), discussed at § 1014.1 below.

[3] Such belated challenges were relatively common in the local property tax area, but (as discussed in the text below) are no longer possible in the property tax context for bankruptcy cases commenced on or after October 17, 2005. *See, e.g., New Haven Projects L.L.C. v. City of New Haven (In re New Haven Projects L.L.C.)*, 225 F.3d 283 (2d Cir. 2000) (recognized broad grant of jurisdiction, but upheld bankruptcy court's right to abstain from redetermining two-year to six-year-old property tax assessments where reduction would result in a "windfall" to the debtor and an insider secured creditor to the prejudice of the city and the tax lien purchasers, and the amount of unsecured debt was *de minimis*), *cert. denied*, 121 S. Ct. 1093 (2001); *In re AWB Associates, G.P.*, 144 B.R. 270 (Bankr. E.D. Pa. 1992) (upheld jurisdiction to redetermine seven-year-old property taxes previously unchallenged by the debtor; acknowledged that at some point the staleness of the tax years may become relevant); and other authorities cited *infra* note 8 (which contrast the treatment of unpaid taxes with that of tax refunds); *In re WUS Corporation*, 1998 U.S. Dist. LEXIS 13754 (D.N.J. 1998) (debtor may challenge property tax assessments that were the basis for creditor's secured claim, but were assessed prior to debtor's ownership of the property); *Eddyville Corp. v. Ulster County*, 1998 U.S. Dist. LEXIS 2735 (S.D.N.Y. 1998) (upheld bankruptcy court's denial of debtor's motion to redetermine six years of unpaid property taxes assumed by debtor in connection with the debtor's recent purchase of the property from a bankrupt affiliate while the property was pending foreclosure); *Allison v. United States (In re Allison)*, 232 B.R. 195, 99-1 U.S.T.C. ¶ 50,285 (Bankr. D. Mont. 1998) (refusing to entertain debtor's action with respect to propriety of IRS levies where underlying tax assessments were over a decade old, the IRS levies were themselves several years old and no claim for refund had been filed; as one of several reasons given for its refusal, the court asserted that section 505(a) "must be read in light of the federal statutes granting appeal rights of tax assessments to taxpayers;" additional reasons given included laches by estoppel, efficient administration of the bankruptcy estate and fairness to the creditors and the bankruptcy trustee), *aff'd*, 242 B.R. 705, 99-1 U.S.T.C. ¶ 50,522 (D. Mont. 1999) (sanctions allowed), *judgment vac'd*, 2000-2 U.S.T.C. ¶ 50,768 (9th Cir. 2000) (vacated district court judgment due to untimely appeal).

[4] 11 U.S.C. § 505(a)(2)(A); *see* discussion accompanying notes 19-25 below, and authorities *infra* at § 1102.11 note 123. In a recent 2005 district court decision, this restriction was interpreted to include

the bankruptcy court rule on an *ad valorem* tax claim relating to real or personal property if the statutory period for contesting or redetermining the tax under nonbankruptcy law has expired.[5] In addition, a bankruptcy court may not disregard a time limit that relates to the grant of a statutory privilege, such as a charitable tax exemption which is conditioned upon the making of a timely application.[6]

A bankruptcy court also may not rule on a claim for refund unless (1) a refund claim has been properly filed with the IRS and the necessary waiting period for filing the refund suit has expired (*see also* § 1012.2) or (2) the refund claim has been disallowed by the IRS.[7] Although the limitation on suits for refund appears relatively straightforward, the treatment of tax refunds has engendered considerable confusion in the case law. Nevertheless, except in certain limited circumstances, it is clear that the timely filing of a refund claim with the IRS is a precondition to a bankruptcy court determination of the refund.[8] Most courts have treated a request for a tax

---

(Footnote Continued)

certain pre-bankruptcy administrative proceedings where there was an "opportunity" for judicial review. *See Central Valley AG Enterprises v. United States*, 326 B.R. 807, 2005-2 U.S.T.C. ¶ 50,612 (E.D. Cal. 2005), discussed below in text. For other case discussions, *see In re TMI Growth Properties*, 109 B.R. 403 (Bankr. N.D. Cal. 1990) (upheld reconsideration of a debtor's property tax assessment, despite an earlier *postpetition* determination by the assessment appeals board; restriction in Bankruptcy Code section 505(a)(2)(A) only applies to prepetition determinations; moreover, the debtor was acting in good faith and presented evidence of an unduly high tax assessment that "outweigh[ed] the court's desire to honor the county's assessment acs a matter of comity"); *Mantz v. Calif. State Board of Equal. (In re Mantz)*, 343 F.3d 1207 (9th Cir. 2003) (concluding that the doctrine of *res judicata* does *not* preclude a bankruptcy court from redetermining a debtor's tax liability that was the subject of an adjudication that became final postpetition, at least where the matter was not pending appeal or in the appeal filing period at the time of the bankruptcy petition); *Bunyan v. United States (In re Bunyan)*, 354 F.3d 1149, 2004-1 U.S.T.C. ¶ 50,128 (9th Cir. 2004) (claim was previously adjudicated even though the tax matter at issue was not raised and determined in the prior proceeding *until* the Court of Appeals level). Although Bankruptcy Code section 505(a)(2)(A) is often said to be "jurisdictional in nature," it is also well recognized as embodying the common law concepts of *res judicata*. Accordingly, like the defense of *res judicata*, some courts view such provision as an affirmative defense that may be lost if not timely raised. *See, e.g., In re El Tropicano, Inc.*, 128 B.R. 153, 156-157 (Bankr. W.D. Tex. 1991). *But see infra* note 13 and accompanying text, considering the same issue in the context of the limitation on the court's jurisdiction under Bankruptcy Code section 505(a)(2)(B).

[5] 11 U.S.C. 505(a)(2)(C). This effectively reverses the case law discussed in note 3, *supra*. It also appears that the reference to "nonbankruptcy" law precludes any limited extensions of time under Bankruptcy Code section 108 (see discussion at § 1012.2).

[6] *See, e.g., Metropolitan Dade County v. Kapila (In re Home and Housing of Dade County, Inc.)*, 220 B.R. 492 (S.D. Fla. 1997) (involving use tax; distinguishes a procedural statute of limitations relating to the amount of an assessment from a time limit relating to a substantive entitlement).

[7] 11 U.S.C. § 505(a)(2)(B). *See also* Code § 7422(a) (quoted in full in the preceding section). It may therefore be relevant in a given case whether the monies remitted were in fact tax "payments" or simply "deposits" intended to preclude the accrual of interest and penalties. *See, e.g., IRS v. Pransky*, 261 B.R. 380, 2001-1 U.S.T.C. ¶ 50,440 (D.N.J. 2001), *aff'd* and *rem'd*, 318 F.3d 536, 2003-1 U.S.T.C. ¶ 50,216 (3d Cir. 2003). *See also* Rev. Proc. 2005-18, 2005-13 I.R.B. 798 (setting forth procedures for making, withdrawing or identifying deposits to suspend the running of interest on potential underpayments).

[8] *See also* discussion at § 1012.2 above (discussing statute of limitations and interaction of the Bankruptcy Code); *City of Jersey City v. Mocco (In re Mocco)*, 2002 U.S. Dist. LEXIS 18592 (D.N.J. 2002) (only "requires the debtor to *properly request a refund*, not to *properly prosecute*" such claim).

Most of the law in this area, and the genesis of considerable confusion, involves property tax abatements (in bankruptcy cases pre-dating the 2005 statutory change in the Bankruptcy Court's

"credit" in the same manner.[9] As discussed at § 1012, the necessity of first filing a claim for refund is dispensed with where the refund arises by way of offset or counterclaim.[10] Nevertheless, some courts (including the Third Circuit) have held that the offset or counterclaim must still be asserted within the applicable statute of limitations for claims for refund.[11] One possible exception to the need for a timely

---

(Footnote Continued)

jurisdiction for *ad valorem* claims) and stems from Judge Queenan's decision in *Ledgemere Land Corp.*, which he subsequently refuted in *Cumberland Farms. Compare, e.g., City of Perth Amboy v. Custom Distribution Services, Inc.* (*In re Custom Distribution Services, Inc.*), 224 F.3d 235, 243-44 (3rd Cir. 2000) (involved New Jersey property tax; court did not have jurisdiction to refund excess payments since tax had not been contested in accordance with state law); *In re Venture Stores, Inc.*, 2002 U.S. App. LEXIS 25242 (3d Cir. 2002) (involved Texas property taxes; same); *In re Farmland Indus., Inc.*, 336 B.R. 415 (Bankr. W.D. Mo. 2005) (citing as comparative support the Eighth Circuit decision in *Kearns, infra* note 13); *Constable Terminal Corp. v. City of Bayonne, New Jersey* (*In re Constable Terminal Corp.*), 222 B.R. 734 (Bankr. D. N.J. 1998) (to same effect; follows *Cumberland Farms*), *aff'd*, 246 B.R. 181 (D. N.J. 2000), *aff'd, without op.*, 281 F.3d 220 (3rd Cir. 2001); *Cumberland Farms, Inc. v. Town of Barnstable, et al.* (*In re Cumberland Farms, Inc.*), 175 B.R. 138 (Bankr. D. Mass. 1994) (after considering legislative history, Judge Queenan reversed his original position in *Ledgemere Land Corp.*, in respect of property taxes); *In re St. John's Nursing Home, Inc.*, 169 B.R. 795 (D. Mass. 1994) (ruled contrary to *Ledgemere Land Corp.* with respect to property taxes and required timely filing; discussing authorities, including Third Circuit's unpublished opinion in *Continental Airlines, infra*), *with In re Ledgemere Land Corp.*, 135 B.R. 193 (Bankr. D. Mass. 1991) (Queenan, J.) (contrasting the treatment of federal income tax refunds with property tax abatements, and upholding jurisdiction over property tax abatements despite absence of timely filing).

*See also In re Continental Airlines, Inc.*, 8 F.3d 811 (3d Cir. 1993) (unpublished opinion) (involving Denver sales and use tax), *cert. denied*, 114 S. Ct. 1297 (1994), *rev'g in part and aff'g in part* 149 B.R. 76, 80-81, 89 (D. Del. 1993) (although the district court ultimately upheld the need for timely filing, as to claims for refund as well as tax credit, it did so not so much on jurisdictional grounds but, rather, as a matter of substantive compliance with the time limitations of state law), *aff'g* 138 B.R. 430, 433-434 (Bankr. D. Del. 1992); *In re Qual Krom South, Inc.*, 119 B.R. 327 (Bankr. S.D. Fla. 1990), discussed below. The bankruptcy court decision in *Qual Krom South* has been often cited and highly criticized for its rather unusual reasoning. Although upholding the federal statute of limitations on refund claims, the court did so based on a narrow construction of the court's general grant of authority under Bankruptcy Code section 505(a), rather than on the more specific rule for refunds in Bankruptcy Code section 505(a)(2)(B). Under the bankruptcy court's reasoning, the bankruptcy court's jurisdiction would be subject to all types of statutes of limitation, whether relating to unpaid taxes or refund claims. Such a pervasive limitation, however, was clearly not intended. *See, for example, Roberts v. Sullivan County* (*In re Penking Trust*), 196 B.R. 389, 395-398 (Bankr. E.D. Tenn. 1996) (involving property taxes; also discusses the status of tax payments "under protest"); *see also supra* note 3.

In contrast, consider *In re Swan*, 152 B.R. 28 (Bankr. W.D.N.Y. 1992), implying that the bankruptcy court may have it within its equitable discretion to consider a refund suit despite an improperly filed refund claim. Similarly, consider *Schroeder v. United States* (*In re Van Dyke*), 275 B.R. 854, 2002-1 U.S.T.C. ¶ 50,270 (Bankr. C.D. Ill. 2002) (permitting suit for refund in a non-offset situation under alternative theories, including a broad reading of the *Kearns* decision, discussed *infra* note 11).

[9] *See, e.g., In re Dunhill Medical, Inc.*, 96-1 U.S.T.C. ¶ 50,276 (Bankr. D.N.J. 1996) (credit and refund treated alike for purposes of Bankruptcy Code section 505(a)(2)(B)); *In re Continental Airlines, Inc., supra* note 8; *Constable Terminal Corp. v. City of Bayonne* (*In re Constable Terminal Corp.*), *supra* note 8 (both bankruptcy and district courts).

[10] *See supra* § 1012 note 20.

[11] *See, e.g., City of Perth Amboy v. Custom Distribution Services, Inc.* (*In re Custom Distribution Services, Inc.*) (3rd Cir.), *supra* note 8; *In re Dunhill Medical, Inc., supra* note 9 (*see* sections "III" and "IV" of decision); *In re Bowen*, 1994 Bankr. LEXIS 1604 (Bankr. S.D. Ga.). *Cf. In re Nottingham*, 2005-2 U.S.T.C. ¶ 50,479 (Bankr. C.D. Ill. 2005) (no amount legally subject to setoff by debtor where period to claim refund or credit had expired); *Constable Terminal Corp. v. City of Bayonne* (*In re Constable Terminal*

filed claim for refund is where a prepetition tax was (with court permission) paid postpetition. In such event, some courts have viewed a debtor's later action to reduce the tax to be part of the normal claims adjustment process, rather than in the nature of a refund claim, and therefore not subject to the same preconditions as a claim for refund or credit.[12] Although not entirely clear, it appears that the absence of a timely filed claim for refund or tax credit (where otherwise required) is a jurisdictional bar which can be raised as a defense at any time during the proceeding or on appeal, rather than a procedural or affirmative defense that may be lost if not timely raised.[13] Once the refund claim is timely filed and the requisite waiting period is satisfied, the case law developed in the state and local property tax area (pre-dating the 2005 statutory change in the bankruptcy court's jurisdiction) generally supports the ability of the bankruptcy court to rule on the refund claim irrespective of any generally applicable statute of limitations for suits for refund, in view of the bankruptcy court's

(Footnote Continued)

*Corp.*), *supra* note 8; *In re Gibson*, 176 B.R. 910 (Bankr. Or. 1994) (statute of limitations barred setoff of contract damage claim against tax debt).

*But see United States v. Kearns*, 177 F.3d 706, 99-1 U.S.T.C. ¶50,573 (8th Cir. 1999) (allowed offset even though no claim for refund had been filed and statutory period for doing so had passed, where the IRS claimed additional taxes based on previously unreported income for monies embezzled by the debtor, and the offset—principally the debtor's tax savings from deducting his restitution payments—also arose out of the embezzlement; the court carefully avoided addressing whether the prior passage of the statutory period for filing a refund claim could, on other facts, impede a debtor's ability to offset previously unclaimed tax savings for taxable years not covered by the proof of claim), *rev'g*, 219 B.R. 823 (Bankr. 8th Cir. 1998); *United States v. Henderson (In re Guardian Trust Co.)*, 2000-2 U.S.T.C. ¶50,777 (S.D. Miss. 2000) (upheld bankruptcy court's jurisdiction over trustee's claim for an offset arising out of an asserted NOL carryback from one of the same taxable years for which the IRS had filed a claim for tax deficiencies, even though an administrative claim for refund would not have been timely; the district court, relying on the Eighth Circuit's decision in *Kearns*, held that jurisdiction was justified since the IRS had already committed itself to expending resources for the tax years at issue, and, thus, no additional litigation burden would be imposed).

[12] *See, e.g., MCorp Financial, Inc. v. Harris County (In re MCorp Financial, Inc.)*, 216 B.R. 596 (Bankr. S.D. Tex. 1996) (involved real estate taxes); *150 North Street Assoc. Ltd. L.P. v. City of Pittsfield*, 184 B.R. 1 (Bankr. D. Mass. 1995) (same).

[13] *See, e.g., City of Perth Amboy v. Custom Distribution Services, Inc. (In re Custom Distribution Services, Inc.)*, *supra* note 8 (jurisdictional; Third Circuit reversed district court holding to the contrary); *Graham v. United States (In re Graham)*, 981 F.2d 1135, 1138, 93-1 U.S.T.C. ¶50,255 (10th Cir. 1992) (held that bankruptcy court erred in awarding tax refund because Bankruptcy Code section 505(a)(2)(B) and Code §7422(a) "are nonwaivable jurisdictional requirements," and stated that, until a timely claim for refund is filed, the government has not waived its sovereign immunity). *Cf. United States v. Kearns (In re Kearns)*, 219 B.R. 823, 98-1 U.S.T.C. ¶50,315 (Bankr. 8th Cir. 1998) (involves individual debtor; viewed Bankruptcy Code section 505(a)(2)(B) as a jurisdictional bar; similarly considered the filing of a timely claim as a precondition to waiving sovereign immunity; lack of subject matter jurisdiction may be raised at any stage of proceeding), *rev'd*, 177 F.3d 706, 99-1 U.S.T.C. ¶50,573 (8th Cir. 1999) (Eighth Circuit disagreed with Appellate Panel as to the need for a timely filed claim in certain cases of offset, *see supra* note 11). Consider also the following cases discussing whether the timely filing requirement is jurisdictional or procedural, but did not involve an untimely defense. *Compare United States v. Ryan (In re Ryan)*, 64 F.3d 1516, 1520-1521, 95-2 U.S.T.C. ¶50,519 (11th Cir. 1995) (discussing jurisdictional significance of a timely filed claim in the bankruptcy context); *In re Dunhill Medical, Inc. supra* note 9 (same); *In re Qual Krom South, Inc., supra* note 8; *with* district court decision in *In re Continental Airlines, Inc., supra* note 8. *But cf. In re El Tropicano, Inc., supra* note 4 (Bankruptcy Code section 505(a)(2)(A) is not a jurisdictional bar, but rather an affirmative defense that may be lost if not timely raised).

broad grant under Bankruptcy Code section 505(a) to determine any tax liability of the debtor "whether or not paid."[14] Nevertheless, such courts generally have considered the relative equities in determining whether to entertain actions brought several years after the original tax assessment and payment.[15] Moreover, it is uncertain whether the reasoning of such cases properly extends to federal tax refunds. For example, in *In re Pransky*,[16] the Third Circuit applied the normal two-year statute of limitations on refund suits in Code § 6532 without any discussion of any potential Bankruptcy Code interplay.

Another potential limitation on the bankruptcy court's jurisdiction in tax refund actions is whether the debtor's suit for refund is a "core" or "non-core" proceeding under 28 U.S.C. § 157(a). As discussed further at § 1013.2 below, a bankruptcy court has general jurisdiction over any civil proceeding that is at least "related to" the bankruptcy case. However, unless the proceeding constitutes a "core" proceeding or the parties otherwise consent, the bankruptcy court's power to dispose of the proceeding is limited to hearing the case and submitting proposed findings of fact and conclusions of law to the district court for *de novo* review. A "core" proceeding generally includes matters concerning the allowance or disallowance of prepetition claims or otherwise affecting the adjustment of the debtor-creditor relationship. Thus, most (if not all) proceedings involving prepetition tax claims are "core" proceedings. In contrast, a suit for tax refund may not involve an offsetting claim against the debtor for unpaid taxes and, even when it does, may *not* be considered a "core" proceeding.

For example, in an unusual procedural set of facts, the individual debtor, in *Dunmore v. United States*,[17] brought a refund action in the district court with respect to certain prepetition taxes following its discharge in bankruptcy, as to which the IRS alleged certain offsets. In the process, the IRS also raised certain bankruptcy specific issues that the district court determined were best resolved by the original bankruptcy court. Accordingly, the matter was referred back to the bankruptcy court to

---

[14] *See, e.g., In re Poiroux*, 167 B.R. 980 (Bankr. S.D. Ala. 1994), and the case law referenced *supra* at note 3, which—as relates to bankruptcy cases commenced before October 17, 2005—generally holds that the lapse of the debtor's right to protest or appeal an outstanding state or local tax assessment is not binding on the bankruptcy court. *But see CGE Shattuck LLC v. Town of Jaffrey (In re CGE Shattuck LLC)*, 272 B.R. 514 (Bankr. D. N.H. 2001) (debtor did not "properly request" a tax refund where it failed to appeal a decision of the town selectmen and the statute of limitations for doing so had expired). *Also consider* 11 U.S.C. § 106(a)(5), discussed *supra* at § 1005.1 (stating that the waiver of sovereign immunity contained in that section does not "create any substantive claim for relief or cause of action not otherwise existing" under the Bankruptcy Code or applicable nonbankruptcy law).

[15] *See, e.g., Delafield 246 Corp. v. The City of New York (In re Delafield 246 Corp.)*, 2007 Bankr. LEXIS 1389 (Bankr. S.D. N.Y. 2007) (under appropriate circumstances, abstention can be proper even where an alternative remedy is no longer available); Report of the American Bar Association Task Force Concerning the Tax Recommendation of the National Bankruptcy Review Commission (April 15, 1997), p. 132, *reprinted at* 97 TNT 90-22 ("The Bankruptcy Courts have in the past . . . exercised appropriate discretion in determining which tax issues need be resolved to provide an orderly completion of the pending [bankruptcy]case"). *Cf.* cases cited *supra* note 3.

[16] *IRS v. Pransky* (*In re Pransky*), 318 F.3d 536, 2003-1 U.S.T.C. ¶ 50,216 (3d Cir. 2003); *see also In re Smythe*, 306 B.R. 218, 2004-1 U.S.T.C. ¶ 50,180 (Bankr. N.D. Ohio 2004), *citing Pransky*.

[17] 358 F.3d 1107 (9th Cir. 2004).

resolve such issues. After resolving such issues, the bankruptcy court (rather than referring the matter back to the district court) proceeded to trial on the refund action, ultimately dismissing the debtors' refund claim with prejudice for failure to prosecute. The debtor appealed. Although recognizing there existed contrary authority, the Ninth Circuit held that the debtor's refund actions were *not* "core" proceedings, since such actions did not depend on the Bankruptcy Code for their existence and could proceed in another court. The Ninth Circuit acknowledged that the Sixth Circuit, in *In re Gordon Sel-Way, Inc.*,[18] had held that a tax refund claim with an alleged IRS offset was a "core" proceeding since the outcome could affect the adjustment of a debtor-creditor relationship, but believed that a debtor's right to an adjudication of its refund by an Article III (district) court should not depend on whether or not the IRS asserts an offset. As a "non-core" proceeding, the bankruptcy court could only propose findings of fact and conclusions of law to the district court. Accordingly, the Ninth Circuit remanded the case to the district court, holding that the bankruptcy court had abused its discretion in dismissing the debtor's refund actions.

As indicated above, under Bankruptcy Code section 505(a), the Bankruptcy Court may not rule on any tax claim for which there was a prebankruptcy adjudication by a judicial or administrative tribunal of competent jurisdiction. A tax claim has been previously "adjudicated" if judgment has been entered and has become final.[19] This includes a Tax Court decision rendered pursuant to the stipulation of the parties.[20] Accordingly, if judgment has not been entered, the bankruptcy court may preempt another court's jurisdiction and determine the debtor's tax liability.[21] In addition, a default judgment will generally not preclude a redetermination by the bankruptcy court.[22] However, a default judgment entered in a Tax Court proceeding after the IRS has filed its answer is binding on the bankruptcy court.[23] A judgment that, as of the commencement of the bankruptcy case, is appealable (or on appeal)

---

[18] *Gordon Sel-Way, Inc. v. United States (In re Gordon Sel-Way, Inc.)*, 270 F.3d 280, 2001-2 U.S.T.C. ¶50,720 (6th Cir. 2001).

[19] *See, e.g., Mantz v. Calif. State Board of Equal. (In re Mantz)*, 343 F.3d 1207 (9th Cir. 2003) (reversing bankruptcy and district courts); *cf. infra* notes 23 and 24.

[20] *See, e.g., IRS v. Teal (In re Teal)*, 16 F.3d 619 (5th Cir. 1994) (irrelevant that the stipulation did not specifically address the legality of the penalty in question, but simply fixed the amount); *Baker v. IRS (In re Baker)*, 74 F.3d 906 (9th Cir. 1996) (similarly concluding), *cert. denied*, 116 S. Ct. 1683 (1996); *Graham v. IRS (In re Graham)*, 94 B.R. 386, 397 (Bankr. E.D. Pa. 1988); *Dufault v. United States (In re Dufault)*, Case No. 89-61431, Adv. No. 90-6065 (Bankr. N.D. Ind. April 24, 1992).

[21] *See* 11 U.S.C. §362(a)(8), and discussion at §1009.2.

[22] *In re Tapp*, 16 B.R. 315 (Bankr. D. Alaska 1981) ("contested" proceeding generally excludes default judgment); *In re Buchert*, 1987 U.S. Dist. LEXIS 7550 (N.D. Ill. 1987); *cf. City of Jersey City v. Mocco (In re Mocco)* (D.N.J.), *supra* note 8 (held that a *dismissal* of an action under New Jersey state law did not constitute a previous adjudication; distinguished *Northbrook Partners, infra,* which analogized a dismissal to a default judgment, since under New Jersey law a default judgment did not necessarily have preclusive effect); *but see Northbrook Partners LLP v. County of Hennepin (In re Northbrook Partners LLP)*, 245 B.R. 104 (Bankr. D. Minn. 2000) (analogizing a dismissal to a default judgment which, under the governing state law, had preclusive effect, the court held that a dismissal of a prior state court action amounted to a previous adjudication).

[23] *Von Tempske v. United States (In re Von Tempske)*, 1989 Bankr. LEXIS 1415 (Bankr. N.D. Ga.); 124 Cong. Rec. H 11,110 (daily ed. September 28, 1978) (statement of Rep. Edwards), S 17,427 (daily ed. October 6, 1978) (statement of Sen. DeConcini).

and thus not yet final will not bar reconsideration by the bankruptcy court (subject to *res judicata* considerations).[24]

One district court, in a 2005 decision,[25] gave a more expansive reading to the concept of a prebankruptcy adjudication. In that case, a partnership in which the debtor corporation was a substantial indirect partner was the subject of a partnership level audit and administrative appeal governed by Code §§6621-6234 (a so-called "TEFRA proceeding," named for the enacting legislation) that resulted in the issuance of a Notice of Final Partnership Administrative Adjustment (FPAA). The FPAA provided each of the partners with the opportunity to challenge the adjustments in the Tax Court, the filing period for which expired prior to the debtor's filing for bankruptcy. Although no Tax Court review was ever sought, the district court held that the adjustments had been previously adjudicated. The court stated that the "partners fully participated in the proceedings described by TEFRA up to the point of the issuance of the FPAA" and that "the critical point is that [the debtor] could have, under the terms of TEFRA, proceeded to judicial review of the FPAA."

Although an action for the determination of taxes under Bankruptcy Code section 505(a) is generally commenced by the debtor-in-possession (or trustee), most courts have held that such section is not so restricted and that such an action may be commenced, in appropriate circumstances, by any party in interest including the post-reorganization debtor or its successor.[26] In general, an action for a determination of taxes arises either by filing an objection to a previously filed claim or initiating an

---

[24] *See, e.g., City Vending of Muskogee, Inc. v. Oklahoma Tax Comm'n*, 898 F.2d 122, 125 (10th Cir.), *cert. denied*, 498 U.S. 823 (1990); *In re Freytag*, 93-2 U.S.T.C. ¶50,531 (Bankr. N.D. Tex. 1993), *aff'd*, 173 B.R. 330, 94-2 U.S.T.C. ¶50,456 (N.D. Tex. 1994) (holding that a Tax Court judgment that was on appeal when the bankruptcy petition was filed was not a complete "adjudication"; however, upon becoming final, *res judicata* barred the bankruptcy court from reconsidering debtor's tax liability); *Lipetzky v. Dept. of Rev. (In re Lipetsky)*, 64 B.R. 431 (Bankr. D. Mont. 1986) (property tax assessment held not fully "adjudicated" where appeal from decision of State Tax Appeals Board was still pending); *but see In re The Railroad Street Partnership*, 255 B.R. 644 (Bankr. N.D.N.Y. 2000).

[25] *Central Valley AG Enterprises v. United States*, 326 B.R. 807, 2005-2 U.S.T.C. ¶50,612 (E.D. Cal. 2005).

[26] *See, e.g., Gordon Sel-Way, Inc. v. United States (In re Gordon Sel-Way, Inc.)* (6th Cir.), *supra* note 18 (involved a debtor's postconfirmation claim for a tax refund); *IRS v. Luongo (In re Luongo)*, 259 F.3d 323, 2001-2 U.S.T.C. ¶50,527 (5th Cir. 2001) (2:1 decision) (to same effect); *Schroeder v. United States (In re Van Dyke)* (Bankr. C.D. Ill.), *supra* note 8 (involved a postconfirmation trustee of a liquidating trust established pursuant to a liquidating Chapter 11 plan and which, in the confirmation order, was delegated the responsibility of dealing with the bankruptcy estate's tax liability for specified years and given all of the rights of a debtor-in-possession); *United States v. Official Comm. of Unsecured Creditors of Indus. Comm. Electrical, Inc. (In re Indus. Comm. Electrical, Inc.)*, 319 B.R. 35, 53, 2005-1 U.S.T.C. ¶50,312 (D. Mass. 2005) (creditors' committee took over prosecution of objection to IRS claim). *See also* discussion at §1013.2 (tax liability of nondebtors). *Consider also Commodore Int'l, Ltd. v. Gould (In re Commodore Int'l, Ltd.)*, 262 F.3d 96 (2d Cir. 2001) (non-tax case, holding that a creditors' committee may obtain standing to pursue a debtor's claims (i) if the committee has the debtor's consent and the court finds that the litigation is in the best interests of the estate and necessary and beneficial to the fair and efficient resolution of the bankruptcy case," as well as (ii) if the debtor "unjustifiably failed to bring suit or abused its discretion in not suing;" but recognized that many bankruptcy courts only permit such creditor actions in the latter situation); *Smart World Technologies, LLC v. Juno Online Services, Inc. (In re Smart World Technologies, LLC)* 423 F.2d 166 (2d Cir. 2005) (to same effect; under the circumstances, creditors did *not* have standing to settle an adversary proceeding over the debtor's objection).

adversary proceeding (*see* § 1004 above). In some cases, debtors have attempted to sidestep this process by fixing the amount of, or otherwise addressing, the tax claim in their Chapter 11 plan; however, where timely challenged, such attempts have generally failed.[27]

It should be noted, however, that Bankruptcy Code section 505(a) does not confer jurisdiction over postconfirmation taxes unrelated to the bankruptcy. Moreover, some circuit courts of appeals have held that the bankruptcy court's postconfirmation jurisdiction is limited exclusively to matters pertaining to the implementation or execution of the plan.[28] Thus, a former debtor cannot use the bankruptcy court as a second Tax Court.[29] For example, in *In re Callan*,[30] the former debtors filed a motion under Bankruptcy Code section 505(a) seeking a tax refund of postconfirmation federal fuel taxes. The court held that it no longer had jurisdiction because the taxes at issue did not arise from the activities of the estate and, as such, the debtors were no longer acting as debtors-in-possession akin to "trustees." The court further agreed that the IRS's "sovereign immunity is not waived in this contested proceeding which involves postconfirmation taxes which are not specifically alluded to in the confirmed plan." In contrast, in *In re Eagle Bus Manufacturing, Inc.*,[31] the bankruptcy court held it had jurisdiction over similar postconfirmation refund claims. There, however, the court found that, because the IRS's retention of such refunds (and interest) "will allow the Service to effectively satisfy its prepetition tax claims with post-Confirmation Date refunds . . . in violation of section 553" of the Bankruptcy Code (governing setoffs), the refund "claims directly affect the bankruptcy estate."

In *In re Holly's, Inc.*,[32] the debtor returned to the bankruptcy court to seek a determination of certain postpetition property taxes assessed preconfirmation, as well as a property tax assessed on the effective date of the plan. Although the court ultimately concluded that it was precluded by the plan from considering any of the assessments, since the period provided for in the plan for filing objections to claims had expired, the court initially determined that it did not have jurisdiction over the property tax assessed on the effective date. In the court's view, the fact that the tax was assessed on the effective date was of no significance, since the plan itself did not

---

[27] *See* cases at § 1011 note 16 above, and discussion at § 1014.1 below.

[28] *See, e.g., Bank of Louisiana v. Craig's Stores of Texas, Inc.* (*In re Craig's Stores of Texas, Inc.*), 266 F.3d 388 (5th Cir. 2001) (non-tax case; adopting the more restrictive view, and briefly discussing the split among the circuit courts of appeal). According to the Fifth Circuit in *Craig Stores of Texas* (and taking such case into account), the Second, Fifth, Seventh and Eighth Circuits adhere to the more restrictive view, whereas the Third, Sixth and Tenth Circuits (at least in concept) take a broader approach. The First Circuit has drawn a distinction between reorganizing bankruptcies (such as in *Craig Stores of Texas*) and liquidating Chapter 11 bankruptcies, as discussed below in the text. *Boston Regional Medical Center, Inc. v. Reynolds* (*In re Boston Regional Medical Center, Inc.*), 410 F.3d 100 (1st Cir. 2005).

[29] *See, e.g., In re Maley* (Bankr. W.D. N.Y.), *reprinted at* 93 TNT 20-24. *Cf. Allis-Chalmers Corp. v. Goldberg* (*In re Hartman Material Handling Systems, Inc.*), 141 B.R. 802, 92-2 U.S.T.C. ¶ 50,325 (Bankr. S.D. N.Y. 1992), discussed at § 1002.8.

[30] Bankr. D Ala. (March 13, 1992), *reprinted at* 92 TNT 84-85.

[31] Bankr. S.D. Tex., Case No. 90-00985-B-11, memorandum opinion, entered Sept. 22, 1993.

[32] 172 B.R. 545 (Bankr. W.D. Mich. 1994), *aff'd*, 178 B.R. 711 (W.D. Mich. 1995) (only appealed as to preconfirmation taxes).

effect a discharge of such taxes (as the discharge only related to preconfirmation taxes)—nor, in its view, could it have. According to the court, a plan may only narrow, and cannot enlarge upon, the general discharge of Bankruptcy Code section 1141(d). The court also cited "common sense and notions of due process." These same notions of due process, along with the fact that the tax was never considered during the plan preparation or confirmation process, lead the court to conclude that the tax was unrelated to the bankruptcy.

In contrast, in *In re Dutch Masters Meats, Inc.*,[33] the bankruptcy court held that, given the broad language of the plan regarding the court's retention of jurisdiction over the determination of matters pertinent to the reorganization, it had jurisdiction to hear the debtor's request for an injunction prohibiting the IRS from collecting postconfirmation employment tax deficiencies from the debtor. The court's factual findings disclose that the IRS intended to levy on the debtor's accounts receivable and that the IRS's actions had already jeopardized the debtor's reorganization in that a significant creditor had, as a result, deemed its loan in default and indicated its intention to enforce its lien. (The court thereafter denied the debtor's request on the merits.)

In *In re Boston Regional Medical Center, Inc.*,[34] the First Circuit considered the extent of a bankruptcy court's postconfirmation jurisdiction within the context of a liquidating Chapter 11 plan, and held that "when a debtor (or a trustee acting to the debtor's behoof) commences litigation designed to marshal the debtor's assets for the benefit of its creditors pursuant to a liquidating plan of reorganization, the compass of related to jurisdiction persists undiminished after plan confirmation." At issue was the bankruptcy court's ability to interpret and enforce a bequest to the debtor hospital that only became known postconfirmation. The court reasoned that the general post-confirmation concerns over unrelated actions—that the court would become the focal point for all types of post-bankruptcy litigation for years to come that only have tangential relationship to the bankruptcy and would unfairly advantage the reorganizing debtor—did not exist where the debtor corporation's sole continuing purpose pursuant to the plan was to liquidate its assets and distribute the proceeds to its creditors, whereas there existed a "strong" federal policy in favor of the expeditious liquidation of debtor corporations and the distribution of their assets.

Even where the bankruptcy court otherwise has jurisdiction, the district court has the power, under 28 U.S.C. § 157(d), to remove any pending action from the bankruptcy court to the district court, either on its own motion or on a timely motion of any party, for cause shown. Moreover, the same section provides that, on timely motion by any party, the district court must remove any action if it determines that the resolution of such action requires consideration of both bankruptcy and "other laws of the United States regulating organization or activities affecting interstate commerce." However, the legislative history cautions (and the courts have so held) that such provision should be narrowly construed so as not to become an "escape

---

[33] 182 B.R. 405, 95-1 U.S.T.C. ¶ 50,224 (Bankr. M.D. Pa. 1995).

[34] *Boston Regional Medical Center, Inc. v. Reynolds (In re Boston Regional Medical Center, Inc.)*, 410 F.3d 100 (1st Cir. 2005).

hatch" through which most bankruptcy matters could be removed to the district court.[35]

For example, the IRS in *In re CM Holdings, Inc.*[36] argued successfully that the tax issues involved necessitated the mandatory withdrawal of the pending action from the bankruptcy court to the district court. At issue was the deductibility of interest on nonrecourse insurance policy loans obtained in connection with Corporate-Owned Life Insurance (COLI) policies under Code §§163(a) and 264 (for policies issued prior to 1996). The court stated that removal of the action was mandatory where the consideration of federal laws outside the Bankruptcy Code are "substantial and material," such that there is required a "meaningful consideration" of the federal law and not just a straightforward "simple application" of federal law to the facts of the case. The court noted that some courts might require that the law in dispute be either one of first impression or in sharp conflict with competing provisions of the Bankruptcy Code. Nevertheless, the court held that, under both formulations, removal was mandatory in that the tax issues involved would require meaningful consideration (as evidenced by the existence of an adverse technical advice memorandum) and were matters of first impression.[37]

## *§1013.1 Jurisdiction Is Discretionary*

The bankruptcy court, although empowered to determine the merits of any tax claim, generally may abstain and leave the tax claim in abeyance.[38] The only apparent

---

[35] *See* 130 Cong. Rec. H 1849-50 (daily ed. March 21, 1984); *see also* S. Rep. No. 55, 98th Cong., 1st Sess. 16 (1983). For a discussion of 28 U.S.C. §157(d), *see* 1 Collier on Bankruptcy ¶3.01 (15th ed.); IRS Litigation Guideline Memorandum, "Withdrawal of the Reference to the Bankruptcy Court—Defending 100% Penalty Assessments in Bankruptcy," dated September 23, 1991, *reprinted at* 96 TNT 155-66. *See also Scharffenberger v. United States*, 2006 U.S. Dist. LEXIS 91548 (W.D. Pa. 2006) (IRS motion to remove action was untimely when brought more than 10 months after the issues were known, where there was prejudice to the estate and no justification for the delay).

[36] *IRS v. CM Holdings, Inc. (In re CM Holdings, Inc.)*, 221 B.R. 715 (D. Del. 1998).

[37] For other cases considering this question, *see, e.g., United States v. G-I Holdings, Inc. (In re G-I Holdings, Inc.)*, 295 B.R. 222, 2003-2 U.S.T.C. ¶50,535 (D. N.J. 2003) (mandatory removal was appropriate where the primary issue was an issue of first impression involving the applicability of Code §707 versus §721, which would necessarily require substantial and material consideration of competing nonbankruptcy legal standards; the court also observed that close to a billion dollars in tax liability was at issue); *United States v. Heller Healthcare Finance, Inc. (In re Numed Healthcare, Inc.)*, 2001 U.S. Dist. LEXIS 19264 (M.D. Fla. 2001) (denied government motion to remove to district court a dispute involving competing liens); *Central Valley AG Enterprises v. United States*, 326 B.R. 807, 2005-2 U.S.T.C. ¶50,612 (E.D. Cal. 2005) (noting that it had previously withdrawn from the bankruptcy court an action to determine the legality of a lease-stripping tax shelter).

[38] 28 U.S.C. §1334(c)(1); Bankruptcy Rule 5011(b) (bankruptcy court can make findings, conclusions, and recommendations on abstention, but ultimate disposition is vested in district court); *see, e.g., Arkansas Corp. Commissioner v. Thompson*, 313 U.S. 132 (1941); *New Haven Projects L.L.C. v. City of New Haven (In re New Haven Projects L.L.C.)* (2d Cir.), *supra* note 3 (upheld bankruptcy court abstention with respect to redetermination of multiple year property tax assessments where only *de minimis* benefit to other creditors, aside from insiders); *Queen v. United States* (4th Cir. January 20, 1993) (unpublished decision), *reprinted at* 94 TNT 21-24; *Smith v. United States (In re Smith)*, 122 B.R. 130 (Bankr. M.D. Fla. 1990) (abstention appropriate only where interests of the creditors and the debtor would be served; Bankruptcy Rule 5011 not implicated where decision is to permit continua-

exception to this general rule is where the tax dispute results from the IRS's prompt determination of the debtor's tax liability pursuant to Bankruptcy Code section 505(b) (*see* § 1011 above). In addition, to avoid undue delay, the bankruptcy court may be required to estimate the tax claim (*see* § 1010.1). Alternatively, the bankruptcy court may, on request of the debtor or the IRS, terminate the stay and permit the debtor's tax liability to be determined by another court.[39] Although the bankruptcy court is not compelled to terminate the stay, a debtor's request to have its tax liability determined by the Tax Court is not likely to be denied. More frequently, however, it will be the IRS who requests relief from the automatic stay, given that bankruptcy judges are generally less experienced in tax matters and are generally viewed as having a pro-debtor bias.[40] Also, until recently, a debtor might also have benefited from a potentially different burden of proof in bankruptcy cases (*see* § 1013.4 below).

In *In re Hunt*,[41] the debtors and the IRS were still in the early stages of preparing for trial in the Tax Court when the debtors filed voluntary petitions for reorganization under Chapter 11. The filing automatically stayed the continuation of the Tax Court case. Shortly thereafter, the debtor filed a "Motion for Determination of Tax Liability Pursuant to 11 U.S.C. § 505;" in response, the IRS moved to have the stay modified to permit the Tax Court case to continue. In deciding whether to hear the tax case or to lift the stay, the court considered the following factors:

(1) the extent to which the debtors actively contest the assessment;
(2) the need to ensure prompt and orderly administration of the bankruptcy estate;
(3) the complexity of the tax issues and the "special expertise" of the Tax Court;
(4) the potential "whipsaw effect" to the IRS where, as here, there are related cases not before the court (the court observed that the potential whipsaw effect could, in this case, be avoided in the Tax Court since the related cases were already docketed and could be consolidated);

(Footnote Continued)

tion of Tax Court proceeding, rather than simply to hold the tax claim in abeyance); *In re Fairchild Aircraft Corp.*, 124 B.R. 488 (Bankr. W.D. Tex. 1991) (rejected abstention motion, despite prior *postpetition* adjudication of property tax valuation, since the matter was properly before the bankruptcy court and did not challenge "the overall valuation methodology used by the appraisal district," nor otherwise affect the amount of taxes payable by other taxpayers); *Northbrook Partners LLP v. County of Hennepin (In re Northbrook Partners LLP)* (Bankr. D. Minn.), *supra* note 22 (abstained from deciding property tax valuation case). *See also Millsaps v. United States (In re Millsaps)*, 133 B.R. 547 (Bankr. M.D. Fla. 1991) (burden on court's docket constituted an additional factor favoring abstention), *aff'd*, 138 B.R. 87 (M.D. Fla. 1991).

[39] 11 U.S.C. § 362(d).

[40] *See* IRS Manual, Part 34 (General Litigation), Ch. 3.1 (Procedures in Bankruptcy Cases), § 2.1 (8/11/04), at ¶ 2 (factors that the IRS considers in deciding whether to request a lifting of the stay on Tax Court litigation); *see also In re Sheffield*, 225 B.R. 234 (Bankr. E.D. Okla. 1997) (court lifted stay at request of IRS to allow Tax Court proceeding to continue where bankruptcy case was filed within seven weeks of trial date); *United States v. Matthew*, 232 B.R. 554 (Bankr. D. Conn. 1999) (court denied IRS's request to lift stay where debtor would be forced to litigate in a different state and possibly have to hire new counsel).

[41] 95 B.R. 442, 89-1 U.S.T.C. ¶¶ 9231 and 9232 (Bankr. N.D. Tex 1989) (identical cases involving two brothers and their spouses).

(5) the burden on the bankruptcy court's docket; and
(6) the fact that a trial before the bankruptcy court adds a potential layer of review (*i.e.*, the district court), thereby extending the time for ultimate resolution.

Balancing these factors and taking into account the magnitude of the proposed deficiency (over $250 million including interest), the court lifted the stay to permit the parties to prepare for—but, at least initially, not to proceed to—trial before the Tax Court. The court conditioned the further lifting of the stay on the parties progressing toward trial in a "meaningful manner" and upon their announcement that they are ready for trial. To ensure the debtors' compliance, the court cautioned that "[a]ppropriate actions will be taken if [they] do not diligently progress toward preparation for trial . . . ."[42]

In *Pursue Energy Corp. v. Mississippi State Tax Commission*,[43] the debtor had filed for bankruptcy relief under Chapter 11 promptly after receiving three assessments from the Mississippi State Tax Commission totaling approximately $11 million. The Tax Commission thereafter filed a proof of claim. However, by motion, the Tax Commission requested that the bankruptcy court abstain from resolving the claim and/or grant relief from the automatic stay so that the assessments could be resolved in administrative and judicial proceedings under state law. The bankruptcy court denied both requests, and the district court affirmed.[44] Most of the factors considered by the two courts (although set forth with greater delineation than in *Hunt*) are subsumed within the factors described above. Other factors included:

- the likelihood that the commencement of the bankruptcy case involves forum shopping;
- the presence in the proceeding of nondebtor parties; and
- the possibility of prejudice to other parties in the action.

In this case, the bankruptcy court observed that no state proceeding had yet commenced, and that the state process would have subjected the debtor to possibly

---

[42] 95 B.R. at 448 n.14; *see also New Haven Projects L.L.C. v. City of New Haven* (*In re New Haven Projects L.L.C.*) (2d Cir.), *supra* note 3; *D'Alessio v. IRS* (*In re D'Alessio*), 181 B.R. 756 (Bankr. S.D.N.Y. 1995) (abstention held inappropriate where tax issues were not complex and could be resolved sooner and the bankruptcy case could be closed following a resolution of the tax issues); *In re Huddleston*, 75 A.F.T.R.2d ¶95-482 (Bankr. W.D. La. 1994) (jurisdiction retained); *Universal Life Church, Inc. v. United States* (*In re Universal Life Church, Inc.*), 127 B.R. 453 (E.D. Cal. 1991) (bifurcated tax issues, retaining jurisdiction as to some and allowing Tax Court proceeding to continue as to others), *aff'd*, 965 F.2d 777 (9th Cir. 1992); *Noli v. Commissioner*, 860 F.2d 1521, 88-2 U.S.T.C. ¶9595 (9th Cir. 1988).

[43] 338 B.R. 283 (S.D. Miss. 2005) (the bankruptcy court's decision is unpublished but described in the district court's opinion).

[44] The district court also concurred with the bankruptcy court's initial conclusion that the determination of the Tax Commission's claim was a "core" proceeding under 28 U.S.C. §157(a), noting that only in a "non-core" proceeding is a federal court required to abstain from hearing a state law claim or cause of action for which there is no independent jurisdiction other than the bankruptcy case, "if an action is commenced, and can be timely adjudicated, in a State forum of appropriate jurisdiction." *See* 28 U.S.C. §1334(c)(2); *see also* discussion of "core" and "non-core" proceedings in the preceding section, above.

four levels of administrative and judicial review. As such, the bankruptcy court concluded (and the district court concurred) that the tax issue could be determined faster and more efficiently in the bankruptcy court. Moreover, state law would have required the debtor to first pay the full tax liability in connection with an appeal, which the court considered particularly unfair to the unsecured creditors (despite the Tax Commission's suggestion that special accommodations could be made) in view of the amount involved and the fact that the unsecured creditors could not participate in the state proceedings. The court also discounted, in view of the substantial amount involved, the Tax Commission's concern that the debtor in filing for bankruptcy was simply forum shopping.

In *In re Wheadon*,[45] the debtor had received a discharge under Chapter 7, and the case was closed. Subsequently, the IRS issued a notice of deficiency to the debtor for certain prepetition years. Two days after the debtor timely filed a petition with the Tax Court, he also filed an adversary proceeding in the bankruptcy court for a determination of his tax liability for the years in question and its dischargeability in the earlier bankruptcy. The bankruptcy court reopened the debtor's bankruptcy case for the sole purpose of considering the debtor's request.

Identifying the threshold issue—from both a tax and dischargeability perspective—as being the statute of limitations on assessment (complicated by certain tolling events and an issue of fraud), the court abstained from deciding the issue and left the parties to proceed in the Tax Court. If and when the dischargeability issue again became relevant—that is, if the IRS won in the Tax Court—the debtor could again reopen the case and raise the issue with the bankruptcy court.

The principal considerations cited by the court in reaching its decision were: (1) the "general proposition" that complicated, technical tax disputes should be decided by the Tax Court, given its well-developed expertise (citing *Hunt*); (2) the estate had no assets to distribute so that fixing the tax liability had no bearing on the administrative function in bankruptcy; (3) the only two parties affected by this dispute were the debtor and the IRS; and (4) the dispute would "almost certainly" have gone into litigation even if the debtor had not filed for bankruptcy.[46]

In contrast to *Wheadon*, where the bankruptcy court reopened the debtor's bankruptcy case to consider the debtor's request, in *Plachter v. United States*,[47] the debtor's postconfirmation motion for a determination that certain prepetition tax liabilities were discharged upon confirmation was dismissed for lack of jurisdiction. The court in *Plachter* rejected the debtor's contention that the bankruptcy case was still open, finding that the confirmation order only preserved postconfirmation

---

[45] 1990 Bankr. LEXIS 1978 (Bankr. D. Minn.).

[46] *See also Zack v. United States*, 224 B.R. 601, 98-2 U.S.T.C. ¶50,756 (E.D. Mich. 1998) (abstention held appropriate under somewhat analogous circumstances); *Cain v. United States*, 142 B.R. 785 (Bankr. W.D. Tex. 1992) (also a Chapter 7 "no asset" case where case had been previously closed; although "extenuating circumstances" justified bankruptcy court's retention of jurisdiction over debtor's two complaints for a determination of its tax liability for several prepetition taxable years, the bankruptcy court was "unwilling" to retain jurisdiction where only the debtor would be benefited and prior to the bankruptcy the debtor had chosen not to seek administrative or Tax Court review).

[47] 1992 U.S. Dist. LEXIS 17234 (S.D. Fla.), *aff'd*, 39 F.3d 323 (11th Cir. 1994) (*per curiam*).

jurisdiction until the plan was substantially consummated, which it was. We would question whether, as in *Wheadon*, the bankruptcy court could have "reopened" the bankruptcy case pursuant to Bankruptcy Code section 350(b) (*see* discussion at §1002.9 above).

## *§1013.2 Tax Liability of Nondebtors*

Several courts (including the Second, Fifth, Ninth, and Eleventh Circuits) have held that the bankruptcy court's jurisdiction to resolve tax claims extends only to claims against the debtor or the estate, not against its officers (or any other third party).[48] Although Bankruptcy Code section 505(a) is not by its terms so restricted, such courts have relied principally on the legislative history.[49] Thus, such courts have held that the bankruptcy court may not resolve claims of the IRS against officers of the debtor corporation for failure to pay employment withholding taxes, even if the debtor corporation's Chapter 11 plan provides for those claims to be satisfied fully.[50]

Although the Third Circuit in *Quattrone Accountants, Inc. v. IRS*[51] reached a similar result in an analogous situation, in doing so it concluded that the jurisdiction of the bankruptcy court was not limited per se to tax claims against the debtor. In its view, the specific grant of authority in Bankruptcy Code section 505(a)—which, the

---

[48] *See, e.g., In re Brandt-Airflex Corp.*, 843 F.2d 90, 88-1 U.S.T.C. ¶9258 (2d Cir. 1988) (involved liability of lender under Code §3505; in so holding, the court stated that "[t]his is particularly true in the present case because even if [the lender] were liable for the withholding taxes, the mere fact of its liability could have no practical impact on [the debtor's] reorganization plan"); *United States v. Prescription Home Health Care, Inc. (In re Prescription Home Health Care, Inc.)*, 316 F.3d 542, 2003-1 U.S.T.C. ¶50,163 (5th Cir. 2002) (vacated injunction precluding IRS from assessing and collecting Code §6672 penalty from nondebtor officers); *American Principals Leasing Corp. v. United States*, 904 F.2d 477, 90-1 U.S.T.C. ¶50,292 (9th Cir. 1990) (involved liability of nondebtor partners for the activities of a debtor partnership); *United States v. Huckabee Auto Co.*, 783 F.2d 1546, 86-1 U.S.T.C. ¶9268 (11th Cir. 1986) (involved corporate officer's liability under Code §6672); *Holland Indus., Inc. v. United States (In re Holland Indus., Inc.)*, 103 B.R. 461 (Bankr. S.D.N.Y. 1989) (involved tax liens imposed on property of corporate officers liable under Code §6672, which property was to be contributed to the debtor under the debtor's proposed plan); *In re Vermont Fiberglass, Inc.*, 88 B.R. 41 (D. Vt. 1988) (sought to invoke Bankruptcy Code section 505(a) to require IRS to apply tax payments held to be involuntary to trust fund portion of debtor's tax liability, thereby reducing officer's tax liability); *but see, e.g, In re Major Dynamics, Inc.*, 14 B.R. 969, 81-2 U.S.T.C. ¶9766 (Bankr. S.D. Cal. 1981).

*See also Hoffman v. United States*, 130 B.R. 526 (W.D. Wis. 1991) (bankruptcy trustee's liability under Code §6672 could not be declared by bankruptcy court because the trustee was not a debtor, nor did he have any controversy with the bankruptcy estate or with any of the estate's creditors over an asset of the estate); *In re American Motor Club, Inc.*, 139 B.R. 578 (Bankr. E.D.N.Y. 1992) (denied former officer/director's motion seeking a determination of the debtor's tax liability for unpaid withholding taxes, and an order authorizing the debtor's payment of such liability).

[49] *See* H. Rep. No. 595, 95th Cong., 1st Sess. 356 (1977) (refers to "liability of the debtor"); S. Rep. No. 989, 95th Cong., 2d Sess. 67 (1978) (same); *see also* 124 Cong. Rec. H 11,110 (daily ed. September 28, 1978) (statement of Rep. Edwards) (tax "of the debtor or the estate"), S 17,426-17,427 (daily ed. October 6, 1987) (statement of Sen. DeConcini) (same).

[50] *See also United States v. Regas (In re Earnest S. Regas, Inc.)*, 1993 U.S. Dist. LEXIS 12324 (D. Nev.) (bankruptcy court did not have jurisdiction to order release of officers and directors over IRS objection as part of corporate settlement of trust fund liability).

[51] 895 F.2d 921, 90-1 U.S.T.C. ¶50,103 (3d Cir. 1990).

court agreed, addresses only the debtor's tax liability—was intended to clarify certain aspects of prior law without limiting the bankruptcy court's general jurisdiction.

Pursuant to 28 U.S.C. § 157(a), a bankruptcy court has general jurisdiction over any civil proceeding that is at least "related to" the bankruptcy case.[52] It has been held that a proceeding is "related to" a bankruptcy case when "the outcome of that proceeding could conceivably have any effect on the estate being administered."[53] Under 28 U.S.C. § 157, a bankruptcy court's jurisdiction in proceedings that are "related to" the bankruptcy case but do not also constitute "core" proceedings is limited to proposing findings of fact and conclusions of law that are submitted to the district court for *de novo* review, unless the parties otherwise consent.[54] Examples of "core" proceedings—as to which the bankruptcy court may enter a binding determination—include matters concerning the administration of the estate, allowance or disallowance of claims, orders to turn over property, preference or avoidance actions, and confirmation of the Chapter 11 plan (as well as any other proceeding affecting the liquidation of the assets of the estate or the adjustment of the debtor-creditor or the equity holder relationship, except certain tort claims).[55] Thus, a determination of the debtor's own tax liability is almost always a "core" proceeding; it makes no difference that such determination may impact, and possibly bind, nondebtors.[56]

---

[52] *See also* 28 U.S.C. § 1334(b).

[53] *Quoting Pacor, Inc. v. Higgins*, 743 F.2d 984, 994 (3d Cir. 1984) (original in italics). This formulation of the bankruptcy court's general jurisdiction under 28 U.S.C. § 157 has been adopted by most circuit courts, although with varying results. *See, e.g., Michigan Employment Security Commission v. Wolverine Radio Co. (In re Wolverine Radio Co.)*, 930 F.2d 1132, 1142 n.15 (6th Cir. 1991) (collecting cases), *reh'g denied*, 1991 U.S. App. LEXIS 15,283, *cert. dismissed*, 112 S. Ct. 1605 (1992); *Randall & Blake, Inc. v. Evans, et al. (In re Canion)*, 196 F.3d 579 (5th Cir. 1999). *But see In re Holly's, Inc., supra* note 32 (involving postconfirmation jurisdiction). The Seventh Circuit has interpreted "related to" jurisdiction somewhat more narrowly than most circuits, requiring more than "mere possibility" that the dispute affects the amount of property available for distribution or the allocation of property among creditors. *See, e.g., In re Xonics, Inc.*, 813 F.2d 127, 131 (7th Cir. 1987); *In re Management Control Systems, Inc.*, 99-2 U.S.T.C. ¶ 50,766 (Bankr. S.D. Ind. 1999). However, most courts recognize that what is "conceivable" similarly may become too attenuated at times to support jurisdiction. *See, e.g.*, Wolverine Radio, 930 F.2d at 1142; *In re McGuirl*, 2002-1 U.S.T.C. ¶ 50,276 (Bankr. D.C. 2001). If a sufficient connection existed at the filing of the particular proceeding, but ceases to exist during the proceeding (such as where the debtor no longer has any assets available to satisfy any resulting claim), the bankruptcy court may be divested of subject matter jurisdiction and required to dismiss the action. *Enterprise Bank v. Eltech, Inc. (In re Eltech, Inc.)*, 313 B.R. 659 (Bankr. W.D. Pa. 2004) (so concluding based on Third Circuit authorities).

[54] *See In re Johnson*, 960 F.2d 396, 403 (4th Cir. 1992) ("The substantial weight of authority indicates that a party can impliedly consent to entry of judgment by the bankruptcy court in a non-core related matter"; express consent is not necessary).

[55] 28 U.S.C. § 157(b)(2). *Consider In re Franklin*, 1990 U.S. Dist. LEXIS 16402 (W.D. Mo. 1990) (upheld bankruptcy court's approval of a settlement agreement providing for (1) the sale of certain property in which the estate had a part interest and (2) an allocation of the tax liability from the sale that provides that *neither party* would be liable for tax on the portion of the property owned by the other party; given that the settlement permitted the trustee to dispose of property in which the estate only had a part interest, the district court concluded that, "in this case, the [tax] liability of the nondebtor is sufficiently related to the bankruptcy case to permit the Bankruptcy Court's jurisdiction").

[56] *See ACME Music Company, Inc. v. IRS (In re ACME Music Company, Inc.)*, 196 B.R. 925, 96-2 U.S.T.C. ¶ 50,391 (Bankr. W.D. Pa. 1996). *Consider also Illinois v. Raleigh (In re Stoecker)*, 179 B.R. 532,

In *Quattrone Accountants*, both the debtor accounting firm and its principal officer (also a part owner) were potentially liable under Code § 6672 for the unpaid withholding taxes of one of the firm's clients. Although the Third Circuit believed the bankruptcy court had power to determine the tax liability of the principal officer if the liability was "related to" the debtor's bankruptcy, the court concluded that it was not so "related." In reaching this conclusion, the Third Circuit noted:

> the fact remains that [the] debtor is jointly and severally liable for the 100% penalty, and, given this fact combined with the highly contingent nature of [the officer's] actually paying a portion of [the client's] tax liability, we cannot conclude that a determination of [the officer's] tax liability under Section 6672 would conceivably have any effect on the bankrupt estate.[57]

In contrast, the Third Circuit, in *In re Kaplan*,[58] found that it was within the bankruptcy court's jurisdiction to consider the debtors' motion to compel the IRS to reallocate tax payments made by a related nondebtor corporation first to the payment of the corporation's unpaid withholding taxes, given that such payments would reduce the debtors' acknowledged liability under Code § 6672. (However, the court thereafter concluded that debtors' motion could not be sustained under the bankruptcy court's grant of equitable authority in Bankruptcy Code section 105, *see* § 1013.5 below.)

Closely resembling the issue of officer liability for a debtor's unpaid taxes, the Third Circuit, in *Belcufine v. Aloe*,[59] was presented with an action by the employees of the debtor seeking to hold the debtor's officers personally liable under Pennsylvania law for the nonpayment of wages. The employees' action had initially been filed in state court, but had been successfully removed by the officers first to the district court and then to the bankruptcy court, following the filing by the officers of a third party complaint against the debtor for indemnification under the debtor's by-laws. The bankruptcy court proceeded to find in favor of the officers, and the district court affirmed. Challenging the bankruptcy court's jurisdiction, the employees argued that the officers' indemnification claims against the debtor were barred under the Bankruptcy Code and were a collusive attempt to manufacture jurisdiction. The Third Circuit dismissed the officers' arguments, readily recognizing that an indemnification claim could have a conceivable effect on the bankruptcy estate and observing that the question of whether claims are barred is uniquely within the jurisdiction of the bankruptcy court. The Third Circuit also found no evidence of collusion.

(Footnote Continued)

541 (N.D. Ill. 1995) (bankruptcy court could determine nondebtor corporation's use tax liability as one means of establishing individual debtor's responsible person liability).

[57] 895 F.2d at 927, n.4. *Cf. United States v. Heller Healthcare Finance Inc.* (*In re Numed Home Healthcare*), 2002-1 U.S.T.C. ¶ 50,383 (Bankr. M.D. Fla. 2002) (concluded, under any interpretation of the jurisdictional reach of Bankruptcy Code section 505(a), that it could not determine a creditor's liability for the debtor's unpaid withholding taxes under Code § 3505).

[58] *IRS v. Kaplan* (*In re Kaplan*), 104 F.3d 589, 97-1 U.S.T.C. ¶ 50,169 (3d Cir. 1997).

[59] 112 F.3d 633 (3d Cir. 1997).

In *Michigan Employment Security Commission v. Wolverine Radio Company*, the Sixth Circuit adopted the analysis of Third Circuit in *Quattrone Accountants* and upheld a bankruptcy court's authority to resolve a tax dispute involving a nondebtor.[60]

In *Wolverine Radio*, the debtor, pursuant to its confirmed Chapter 11 plan, sold its broadcasting business "free and clear" of all liens and other interests and indemnified the purchaser against any damages arising out of the debtor's operations. Subsequently, the purchaser was notified by the Michigan Employment Security Commission (MESC) that, due to the debtor's employment history, its "contribution rate" to the employment security fund would be substantially higher than for new employers, and of certain other charges. Upon motion by the debtor, the bankruptcy court entered an order enforcing its earlier confirmation order and prohibiting the MESC from assigning the debtor's experience rating to the purchaser. In upholding the bankruptcy court's jurisdiction, the Sixth Circuit relied extensively on the Third Circuit's analysis in *Quattrone Accountants*, similarly concluding that Bankruptcy Code section 505(a) did not limit the bankruptcy court's general jurisdiction over a nondebtor's tax liability. In holding that the purchaser's tax dispute was at least "related to" the debtor's bankruptcy and, thus, within the bankruptcy court's general jurisdiction under 28 U.S.C. § 157, the Sixth Circuit stated that—due to the contractual indemnification over against the debtor, the fact that the debtor may thus be bound by the outcome of the dispute and the fact that the MESC had filed a claim in the debtor's bankruptcy and thus obtained creditor status—it could not conclude that the dispute would have no "conceivable effect" on the debtor.[61] It then also concluded that the debtor's motion was (in form and substance) a core proceeding under 28 U.S.C. § 157, because it involved "issues which arose because of the bankruptcy proceeding—the dischargeability of debts and the confirmation of a plan—and because [the debtor] asserts a right based on bankruptcy law," namely, the right under Bankruptcy Code section 363(f) to sell property "free and clear." Thus, it was within the bankruptcy court's juisdiction to enter judgment on the motion. (On the substantive issue, the Sixth Circuit disagreed with the bankruptcy court, and affirmed the district court which held that the MESC could take into account the debtor's prior employment history.)

---

60 *Supra* note 53.

61 *Cf. Pacor, Inc. v. Higgins, supra* note 53, at 995-996 (potential third-party claim for indemnification did not support jurisdiction where issues involved in underlying action could be relitigated by the debtor with respect to any subsequent indemnification claim and the plaintiff in such action had not filed a claim against the debtor); *see also Marlow v. United States* (*In re Julien Co.*), 136 B.R. 760 (Bankr. W.D. Tenn. 1991) (tax case). The Sixth Circuit recognized, however, that the "conceivable effect" standard must be applied with the caveat that situations may arise where an extremely tenuous connection to the estate would not satisfy the jurisdictional requirement. Wolverine Radio, *supra* note 53, at 1142. Query whether the decision in *Quattrone Accountants* would have turned out differently had the officer sought indemnification from the debtor? As discussed at § 1006.3.2, it is unclear whether an officer has a right to indemnification from the debtor for liability under Code § 6672. *Consider also Randall & Blake, Inc. v. Evans, et al.* (*In re Canion*) (5th Cir.) *supra* note 53 (raising equivalent considerations in affirming a bankruptcy court's denial of jurisdiction in a non-tax case).

Query, whether the Sixth Circuit would have reached a different result had the MESC not filed a claim in the debtor's bankruptcy?[62] Consider, for example, Bankruptcy Code section 106 (discussed at § 1005.1), which provides for a limited waiver of a government's sovereign immunity in bankruptcy cases.[63]

In *Illinois v. Schechter*,[64] the State of Illinois asserted personal liability against a Chapter 11 trustee for unpaid hotel and use taxes, arguing in part that the trustee had breached his fiduciary duty to pay over the taxes. The district court upheld the bankruptcy court's jurisdiction to determine the trustee's liability on the grounds that any claim for breach of the trustee's fiduciary duty could only "arise" out of the provisions of the Bankruptcy Code and thus was a "core" proceeding.

In *In re Plymouth House Health Center Inc.*,[65] the debtor challenged certain real estate tax assessments for which it was contractually responsible under a lease arrangement. The amount of such taxes was being held in a separate account, pending the bankruptcy court's determination. The bankruptcy court held that the tax dispute was clearly "related to" the debtor's bankruptcy case and thus within the court's jurisdiction, since the debtor's estate would directly benefit from any reduction in the taxes.

In *In re Labrum & Doak*,[66] a Pennsylvania district court upheld a bankruptcy court's jurisdiction to consider a bankrupt partnership's proposed allocation of so-called "recapture" income among current and former partners, none of whom were debtors.[67] The IRS argued that the allocation could only affect the tax liability of the

---

[62] In accord with *Wolverine* and involving analogous facts, but without the debtor indemnity, *see* the bankruptcy court decision in *In re Eveleth Mines, LLC*, 312 B.R. 634 (Bankr. D. Minn. 2004) (bankruptcy court had "core" jurisdiction over proceeding brought by nondebtor purchaser; also concluded that state could take into account debtor's pre-sale history in assessing a production tax against purchaser), *rev'd*, 318 B.R. 682 (Bankr. 8th Cir. 2004). The bankruptcy court's decision was subsequently reversed by the Bankruptcy Appellate Panel for the Eighth Circuit, however, on the grounds that the "state" Tax Injunction Act (28 U.S.C. § 1341) barred the bankruptcy court from exercising it jurisdiction as there was a "plain, speedy, and efficient" remedy available under state law (even though such remedy could take as long as two years, and even though it was unclear whether the state courts would give proper deference to the bankruptcy court's sale order). In this regard, it should be observed that in *Eveleth Mines* the action in the bankruptcy court was brought by the nondebtor, and the debtor had no continuing interest, whereas in *Wolverine* the debtor brought the action and had an interest in the outcome. *Consider* also discussion at § 1102.4.

[63] *See also MDFC Equipment Leasing Corp. v. Robbins (In re Interstate Motor Freight System)*, 62 B.R. 805 (Bankr. W.D. Mich. 1986) (the fact that a nondebtor's tax liability may be within the court's general jurisdiction is not alone sufficient; one must also find "an express waiver of sovereign immunity necessary for this court to make decisions as to nondebtor taxpayers that would be binding upon the United States"; the court concluded that Bankruptcy Code section 106 did not provide the necessary waiver, as it only waives sovereign immunity with regard to the interests of the debtor or the estate); *United States v. Zellers (In re CNS, Inc.)*, 225 B.R. 198, 2000-2 U.S.T.C. ¶ 50,846 (N.D. Ohio 2000) (to same effect).

[64] 195 B.R. 380 (N.D. Ill. 1996).

[65] Memorandum decision, dated Sept. 10, 2004 (Bankr. ED. Pa.), Ch. 11 No. 03-19135F, *reprinted at* BNA TaxCore (Nov. 17, 2004).

[66] 2000 U.S. Dist. LEXIS 12066 (E.D. Pa. 2000), *aff'g*, 222 B.R. 749 (Bankr. E.D. Pa. 1998) (within Third Circuit).

[67] The so-called "recapture" income involved in this case relates to the application of Code § 467 to a lease with increasing rent, and refers to the portion of the partnership's net income that, during the

partners and thus was not "related to" the partnership's bankruptcy case. The district court (as did the bankruptcy court) disagreed, given the partnership's affirmative obligation under the Internal Revenue Code (subject to the imposition of penalties for failure to perform) to file information returns and statements reflecting the proper allocation of tax liability, and further held that the allocation was significant to the administration of the bankruptcy case and thus a "core" proceeding (presumably due to the partnership's position that the former partner's who received the earlier tax benefits had an actual or implied obligation to bear their appropriate share of the subsequent "recapture" income).[68]

In *In re Goldblatt Bros., Inc.,*[69] the bankruptcy court took a more expansive view of Bankruptcy Code section 505(a). There, the unsecured creditors' committee sought a declaratory judgment that an account established pursuant to a confirmed Chapter 11 plan for the benefit of creditors, and administered by the committee (including evaluating and contesting the allowability of any claims payable out of the fund), was not required to pay federal and state income tax and file tax returns. In holding that the tax liability of the account was within the subject matter jurisdiction of the court, the court first concluded that the dispute was a core proceeding and, thus, within its general jurisdiction under 28 U.S.C. § 157. The court decided it was a core proceeding because the account was an integral part of the debtor's plan (serving as an efficient vehicle for the processing of disputed claims) and any tax due would proportionately reduce distributions to general unsecured creditors.

The court then addressed the question of whether it had jurisdiction to decide the dispute under Bankruptcy Code section 505(a). Recognizing that most courts have read Bankruptcy Code section 505(a) as limiting the bankruptcy court's general jurisdiction to the determination of the tax liability of the debtor, the court nonetheless concluded that it had jurisdiction under Bankruptcy Code section 505(a) to determine the tax liability of the account *even if* it was found to be a separate taxable entity from the debtor. The court observed that the legislative history to Bankruptcy Code section 505(a) sometimes referred to the tax liability of the "debtor" and other times to the "debtor or the estate," and, therefore, it cautioned against an overly restrictive interpretation of the court's jurisdiction based on such terms. Rather, it asserted that, "in light of the legislative purpose of § 505, Congressional drafters were referring to the collection of [a] debtor's assets to be used to satisfy its creditors' claims." The court concluded that, because the account operates for that purpose, it was certainly part of the bankruptcy "estate." The court then observed that under its holding:

---

(Footnote Continued)

latter part of the lease, would have been offset by rental expense but for the spreading of such expense under Code § 467 to earlier years of the lease with lower rental payments.

[68] This should be contrasted with the Ninth Circuit's decision in *American Principals Leasing Corp., supra* note 48, which arguably can be distinguished both on the law (the present case being within the Third Circuit and governed by the principles of *Quattrone Accountants*) and on the facts (the tax matter at issue in that case apparently involving the application of the "at risk" rules of Code § 465 at the partner level, and arguably not proper partnership reporting or other partnership level consequences).

[69] 106 B.R. 522 (Bankr. N.D. Ill. 1989).

> the parameters of a bankruptcy court's jurisdiction over the subject matter of federal and state taxation under [Bankruptcy Code section] 505(a)(1) corresponds with general principles governing a bankruptcy court's power to adjudicate at least core matters under 28 U.S.C. § 157.[70]

**Consolidated return.** In the context of a consolidated return group where the common parent is in bankruptcy, it would seem that a substantive determination of the group's tax liability by the bankruptcy court should be binding upon the IRS as to all group members, regardless of whether they are in bankruptcy. This is due to the fact that, under the consolidated return regulations, the common parent generally has the exclusive authority to represent the consolidated group in tax litigation matters (*see* § 1007.4).[71]

Moreover, it is possible that even where the bankruptcy court's determination purports to be binding on the IRS as to some, but not all, the members of the group—such as where the common parent is not in bankruptcy, but other members are—the IRS may nevertheless be bound by such determination as to all members of the group. This result is premised on the principles of *res judicata* and collateral estoppel and has been referred to by some courts as the doctrine of "judicial estoppel." A similar situation can arise where the bankruptcy court approves a settlement of the tax dispute that reflects the IRS's position on the substantive tax issues involved. As discussed below, the bankruptcy court's approval of the settlement may be treated as an effective adjudication of the underlying tax issues.

The Sixth Circuit's decision in *Reynolds v. Commissioner*[72] illustrates the potential application of the doctrine of judicial estoppel in the case of a bankruptcy settlement.

---

[70] Id. at 529. *But consider Portfolio Lease Funding Corp. v. Seagate Technology, Inc. (In re Atlantic Computer Systems, Inc.)*, 163 B.R. 704 (Bankr. S.D.N.Y. 1994) (assets transferred to Liquidating and Reserve Trusts established under the debtor's plan were no longer considered part of the bankruptcy estate; accordingly, the fact that a pending litigation involving two nondebtors could result in an additional claim for distributions from the Trusts did not have any "conceivable effect" on the bankruptcy estate so as to support subject matter jurisdiction). We question whether the result in *Atlantic Computer Systems* would have been different had the Chapter 11 plan expressly provided that the Liquidating and Reserve Trusts were to be treated as successors in interest to the debtor's estate. Moreover, literally read, the court's reasoning would appear to preclude even postconfirmation jurisdiction over the claims reconciliation process presumably continued by the Trusts—a seemingly unintended result.

[71] *Cf. McQuade v. Commissioner*, 84 T.C. 137, Dec. 41,859 (1985), involving a husband (*H*) and wife (*W*) who had filed joint returns. *H* died shortly after filing bankruptcy. Thereafter, the IRS issued both a separate and joint notice of deficiency to *W*, individually, and as executrix of *H*'s estate. On behalf of *H*'s estate, *W* litigated the proposed deficiency in the bankruptcy court, after which the bankruptcy court concluded that "the McQuades" (jointly) had no federal tax liability for the years at issue. Although *W* was neither in bankruptcy nor a named party to the litigation, the Tax Court held that the IRS was collaterally estopped from relitigating *W*'s tax liability for such years. The Tax Court found that *W* had exercised sufficient control over the litigation and had a sufficient financial stake so as not to be considered "a stranger to the cause," that the bankruptcy court had before it both deficiency notices and other documents relating to *W*'s liability, and that the issues involved were exactly the same. *Consider also Lone Star Life Ins. Co. v. Commissioner*, T.C. Memo 1997-465 (decision of IRS to deal directly with subsidiary, as permitted by Treas. Reg. § 1.1502-77(a), did not preclude subsidiary from also allowing its common parent to continue to act as its agent).

[72] 861 F.2d 469, 88-2 U.S.T.C. ¶ 9591 (6th Cir. 1988).

In *Reynolds*, the IRS was "judicially estopped" from asserting that sales proceeds received by the taxpayer's ex-wife from certain leasehold interests were actually attributable to the taxpayer, where during the ex-wife's bankruptcy case the IRS entered into a stipulation of settlement with the ex-wife wherein the IRS took the position (and, in substantial part, the ex-wife conceded) that the sales proceeds were properly those of the ex-wife, and such stipulation was approved and ordered by the bankruptcy court. In so holding, the Sixth Circuit, in a split decision, stated that "when a bankruptcy court—which must protect the interest of all creditors—approves a payment from the bankruptcy estates on the basis of a party's assertion of a given position, that, in our view, is sufficient 'judicial acceptance' to estop the party from later advancing an inconsistent position." Moreover, the court stated that, in considering a proposed settlement, the bankruptcy court is charged with an affirmative obligation to apprise itself of the underlying facts and to make an independent judgment as to whether the compromise is fair and equitable.

In a subsequent decision, the Sixth Circuit clarified that the application of judicial estoppel is limited to those situations where the stipulation of settlement or court order contains admissions or findings of law or fact, in contrast to a settlement that simply fixes the tax liability owed.[73] For example, in *Reynolds*, the IRS admitted that the sales proceeds were those of the ex-wife, implicitly exonerating the taxpayer.

Another case in which preclusion concepts have been applied to a settlement agreement is *In re Donahue*.[74] In *Donahue*, the IRS filed a claim in the debtor's bankruptcy case asserting that certain expenditures of the debtor's wholly owned corporation constituted constructive distributions to the debtor. The debtor objected (in the form of a motion for summary judgment), claiming that the IRS's position was fundamentally inconsistent with the resolution of the deductibility of such expenditures by the corporation in an earlier Tax Court case. The IRS and the corporation had in that case reached a settlement partially allowing and partially disallowing the corporation a deduction for such expenditures, which was stipulated to the Tax Court and embodied in the Tax Court's decision. Relying in part on the Sixth Circuit decision in *Reynolds*, the bankruptcy court concluded:

(1) that a settlement embodied in a judicial decision that resulted in an "actual and necessary" determination of the issues is entitled to the same *res judicata*/collateral estoppel effect as a litigated result and should not be equated to a mere contract between the parties; and

(2) that preclusion concepts not only apply when the parties in a subsequent proceeding are identical to the parties in a prior proceeding, but also apply

---

[73] *Teledyne Indus., Inc. v. NLRB*, 911 F.2d 1214, 1218 (6th Cir. 1990), *reh'g denied, en banc*, 1990 U.S. App. LEXIS 22,065. *See also In re Matunas*, 261 B.R. 129, 2001-1 U.S.T.C. ¶50,388 (Bankr. D. N.J. 2001) (applying claim preclusion concepts to stipulated agreement of tax liability approved by the bankruptcy court; discusses case law); *Barrett-Crofoot Investments, Inc. v. Commissioner*, 67 T.C.M. 2166 (1994) (distinguishing *Reynolds*).

[74] *Donahue v. United States (In re Donahue)*, 107 B.R. 146, 89-2 U.S.T.C. ¶9618 (Bankr. S.D. Ohio 1989).

to nonparties "whose legal rights and obligations are intrinsically intertwined and dependent upon the results obtained in the prior proceeding."

Accordingly, in light of the specificity of the amounts stated in the settlement and noting the control relationship between the debtor and the corporation, the court held that the IRS was precluded from asserting that the amounts previously allowed as corporate expenses in the Tax Court settlement were now constructive distributions to the debtor.

Presenting a further perspective on the issue is the Tax Court decision in *Kroh v. Commissioner*,[75] which was reviewed by the court (with two judges dissenting). In that case, an earlier bankruptcy court settlement relating to a husband's (H's) joint return tax liability did not preclude the IRS from proceeding against the wife (W) for the full uncompromised amount of the liability. The settlement agreement set forth the amount owed by H by year without any apparent admissions or findings of fact.

Before considering the principles of *res judicata* and collateral estoppel, the Tax Court concluded that the settlement agreement was not binding on W as a matter of tax, bankruptcy, or contract law. Relying on its earlier decision in *Dolan v. Commissioner*,[76] upholding separate assessments against a husband and wife filing a joint return, the Tax Court concluded that the IRS had separate causes of action against W and H that could be independently litigated and compromised. Moreover, the Tax Court observed that the bankruptcy court had no jurisdiction over W's tax liability because W had made "no showing [that H's] title 11 proceedings could not be administered without having the bankruptcy court determine her tax liability,"[77] and it pointed out that the settlement agreement only referred to "the debtor" and thus, by its terms, did not purport to bind W. The Tax Court therefore concluded that the IRS had "no choice" but to proceed against W separately and was not, as a general matter, barred from doing so.

The Tax Court then considered whether the principles of *res judicata* or collateral estoppel applied. In holding they did not, the court found that a husband and wife's joint return liability also were separate causes of action for *res judicata* purposes; that a joint return does not create privity; that W was not a party to, nor did she participate in, H's "bankruptcy proceedings" (presumably referring only to the tax proceedings) in any way; and that the bankruptcy court's approval of the settlement agreement only constituted a "pro forma acceptance" of the settlement agreement and, accordingly, that the bankruptcy court did not actually decide any disputed issue with respect to the merits of W's claim.

Disagreeing with the majority on virtually every point including the preclusive effect of the settlement agreement, the dissent would have held that *res judicata* applies. Neither the majority nor the dissent discussed the Sixth Circuit's decision in *Reynolds*.

---

[75] 98 T.C. 383 (1992).

[76] 44 T.C. 420 (1965).

[77] *Citing Tavery v. United States*, 897 F.2d 1032, 1033, 90-1 U.S.T.C. ¶50,121 (10th Cir. 1990).

To what extent the *Kroh* decision has relevance in consolidated return situations, aside from its treatment of the settlement agreement is not entirely clear.[78] As noted earlier,[79] the concept of "agency" does not exist in the joint return context, whereas in the consolidated return context the common parent generally acts as the "sole agent" for the group. Moreover, the common parent generally has direct or indirect control over all members of the group—the notable exceptions being former members and members for whom a trustee or receiver has been appointed. In this regard, it should be noted that the Tax Court distinguished the *McQuade* case,[80] wherein the IRS *was* collaterally estopped from proceeding against the wife, from the *Kroh* case, based on the extent of the wife's participation in the earlier proceedings in the bankruptcy court. In *McQuade*, the wife (although not herself in bankruptcy) controlled the earlier proceedings, whereas in *Kroh* the wife did not participate at all. (In addition, the *McQuade* case involved an actual determination by the bankruptcy court, in contrast to a settlement agreement.) This again raises the question in the consolidated return context as to what happens if the IRS District Director notifies the parent that it will deal directly with the subsidiary, in which event the regulations say the subsidiary has "full authority to act for itself" (*see* § 1007.4 above). If the subsidiary is still controlled by the common parent, would the requisite "control" exist for *res judicata* or collateral estoppel purposes (assuming a current determination of the subsidiary's consolidated return liability) to bar the IRS from proceeding anew against the common parent or other members of the group and relitigating the tax liability?

Presenting a different aspect of the interplay of consolidated returns, the liquidating trustee in *In re Consolidated Liquidating FGH Trust*,[81] acting on behalf of the debtor, a former member of a consolidated tax group, sought to utilize a turnover action—which seeks to recover property of the estate from a third party—as justification for bringing an action for a tax refund in lieu of the common parent of the consolidated group. The bankruptcy court concluded, in accordance with the consolidated return regulations, that the common parent was the only person authorized to seek the tax refund for the group. The court was also not enamored with the prospect of determining the tax liability of non-debtors, namely, the other members of the consolidated group.

---

[78] *Consider, e.g., Valley Die Cast Corp. v. Commissioner*, T.C. Memo. 1983-103 (unchallenged IRS proof of claim in a subsidiary's bankruptcy case, as to which the confirmation of the bankruptcy case served as a final judgment, was determinative of the subsidiary's tax liability, but not the other members of the consolidated group); IRS Field Service Advice 1999-811 (c. 1993) (discussing the criteria of *Kroh* within the context of a potential consolidated group; however, relationship of the debtor and the asserted common parent at the time of the debtor's bankruptcy case is unclear from the redacted facts), *reprinted at* 1999 TNT 45-97.

[79] *Supra* § 1009 note 15.

[80] Discussed *supra*, at note 71.

[81] *Oakridge Consulting Inc. v. United States (In re Consolidated FGH Liquidating Trust)*, 325 B.R. 564, 2005-2 U.S.T.C. ¶ 50,448 (Bankr. S.D. Miss. 2005).

## *§1013.3 Declaratory Judgments*

Although declaratory judgments on federal tax issues are generally prohibited by the Declaratory Judgment Act (28 U.S.C. §2201),[82] an express exception applies in the case of "a proceeding under section 505 or 1146 of title 11."[83] Thus, if an actual controversy over federal taxes is otherwise within its jurisdiction, a bankruptcy court may enter a final judgment declaring the rights and other legal relations of any interested party seeking such declaration, whether or not alternative relief could be sought.[84] No similar exception applies in the case of receiverships.[85]

For example, in *In re Goldblatt Bros., Inc.* (also discussed in the preceding section),[86] the bankruptcy court upheld its authority to issue a declaratory judgment as to whether an account established pursuant to a confirmed Chapter 11 plan and administered by the unsecured creditors' committee was required to pay federal and state income tax and file tax returns. In doing so, the court made clear that the filing of a tax return, and the use of the prompt determination procedure of Bankruptcy Code section 505(b) (which the government agreed could be invoked by the creditors' committee, although it was not specifically named therein and although it was several years after confirmation), were not prerequisites to the court's jurisdiction. *See* §1011 above. The court found particularly persuasive the fact that a contrary result would render meaningless—other than for taxes for which no return is required—the express exception permitting declaratory judgments in section 505 proceedings,

---

[82] *See generally* 10A Wright, Miller & Kane, Federal Practice and Procedure, Civil 3d, §2751 *et seq.* (1998 with Supp.). Actions under section 7428 of the Internal Revenue Code (relating to the status and classification of tax-exempt organizations) are specifically permitted.

[83] Consider also *In re Becker's Motor Transportation, Inc.*, 632 F.2d 242, 81-1 U.S.T.C. ¶9348 (3d Cir. 1981), *cert. denied*, 101 S. Ct. 1358 (1981) (holding that bankruptcy court had power to issue declaratory judgments under prior Bankruptcy Act, because a bankruptcy court as then established was not definitionally a court to which the Declaratory Judgment Act applied). Although proceedings under Bankruptcy Code section 1146 are excepted from the general prohibition against declaratory judgments with respect to federal taxes, such section contains special tax provisions generally applicable only to state and local taxes. The inclusion of this section thus appears to be a remnant of the original House and Senate versions of that section, wherein such section also applied to federal taxes. The reference to federal taxes was deleted in the final version. *See* §1101.

[84] *See generally In re McGuirl, supra* note 53. In contrast to federal taxes, a federal court's jurisdiction to issue declaratory judgments as to state tax matters is generally predicated on the absence of an adequate remedy under state law. *See* cases cited at 28 U.S.C.A. §2201, Notes of Decisions #522. *Compare Agnew v. Franchise Tax Board (In re Sharon Steel Corp.)*, 118 B.R. 30 (Bankr. W.D. Pa. 1990) (bankruptcy court could consider the "proposed decombination" of the debtor and its wholly owned subsidiary for purposes of the California Unitary Tax, even though no assessment was made and no proof of claim was filed; former Bankruptcy Code section 106(c) abrogated sovereign immunity); *with IRS v. Sulmeyer (In re Grand Chevrolet, Inc.)*, 153 B.R. 296 (C.D. Cal. 1993), discussed below (holding that the bankruptcy court could *not* authorize the consolidation of several commonly controlled corporations for *federal* tax purposes).

[85] *See, e.g., Sterling Consulting Corp. v. United States*, 245 F.3d 1161 (10th Cir. 2001) (so held even though the bankruptcy court in a related case purported to cede jurisdiction to the receivership court).

[86] *See supra* note 69 and accompanying text.

which exception was enacted contemporaneously with the enactment of the section 505(b) procedure.[87]

Nevertheless, in order to expedite the resolution of the tax issue, the court required, as a condition to considering the tax issue, that the committee in fact file tax returns (which had already been prepared) and commence the prompt determination procedure of Bankruptcy Code section 505(b). While the IRS examination was pending, the court would then consider the substantive issue of whether the account was subject to tax. If the answer was yes, the filing of the tax returns and the request for a prompt determination would expedite the proper assessment of tax; and, if the answer was no, the prompt determination procedure would become moot.[88]

Similarly, in *In re Amoskeag Bank Shares, Inc.*,[89] the bankruptcy court held that it had authority to rule on a declaratory judgment motion (originally filed by the Chapter 7 trustee but subsequently joined in and pursued by the principal creditor of the estate) as to the trustee's employment tax obligations with respect to pending distributions to general unsecured creditors, and the district court so affirmed. The court rejected the IRS's assertion that there could be no determination of taxes unless and until a tax return was filed, given the practicality that the trustee needed to know the liability in advance (in particular the employer's portion) so as to effectuate a

---

[87] Although not mentioned by the court, the original House proposal would have permitted declaratory judgments only in "proceedings under section 505(c) or 1146(d)" of the Bankruptcy Code. *See* H.R. Rep. No. 595, 95th Cong., 1st Sess. § 251 (1977). Section 1146(d) has since been redesignated section 1146(b). *See* P.L. 109-8 (2005).

[88] *Contrast United States v. Sterling Consulting Corp.* (*In re Indian Motocycle Co., Inc.*), 261 B.R. 800 (Bankr. 1st Cir. 2001) (held that bankruptcy court does not have jurisdiction to estimate administrative tax liability; noted availability of the prompt determination procedure under Bankruptcy Code section 505(b); did not address bankruptcy court's ability to consider action under Bankruptcy Code section 505(a) in advance of a completed audit by the IRS); *Feldman v. Maryland Natl. Bank* (*In re Wills*), 46 B.R. 333, 334, 85-1 U.S.T.C. ¶ 9222 (Bankr. D. Md. 1985) (denying request for determination where the prompt determination procedure of Bankruptcy Code section 505(b) was more appropriate); *Dycoal Inc. v. IRS* (*In re Dycoal Inc.*), 327 B.R. 220, 2005-2 U.S.T.C. ¶ 50,554 (Bankr. W.D. Pa. 2005), *aff'd*, 2006 U.S. Dist. LEXIS 25078 (W.D. Pa. 2006), discussed in text below. *See also Scharrer v. Dept. of Treasury* (*In re American Leasing and Acceptance Corp. of Lakeland*), 228 B.R. 755, 98-1 U.S.T.C. ¶ 50,113 (Bankr. M.D. Fla. 1997) (debtor had not claimed interest deductions with respect to certain payments for certain years, but had for later years; the IRS allowed the later year deductions, but disagreed as to amount; the IRS made no change to the early years, nor was an amended return filed claiming the deductions; yet, in conjunction with challenging the amount of the later year deduction, the liquidating trustee of the debtor's estate sought the bankruptcy court's declaration that the early year payments should also have been deducted as interest; although the court recognized that there appeared to be no justiciable controversy with respect to the early years, the court stated that "[f]or the sake of judicial economy," it would consider the issue and not await the filing of an amended return and a possible challenge by the IRS), *rev'd on other grounds*, 229 B.R. 210, 99-1 U.S.T.C. ¶ 50,404 (Bankr. M.D. Fla. 1999). *Also consider In re Franklin, supra* note 55, wherein the government asserted that a bankruptcy court order approving an allocation of tax liability in the context of a settlement agreement violated the doctrine of sovereign immunity, in that the bankruptcy court did not have authority to make federal tax determinations unless (1) the government filed a claim for the tax or (2) the trustee filed a tax return and followed the prompt determination procedure of Bankruptcy Code section 505(b). In upholding the bankruptcy court's jurisdiction, the district court stated: "Significantly, the Bankruptcy Court did not assess or determine an amount of tax owed. If it had, then 11 U.S.C. Section 505(b) would provide the proper method for determining the amount of a tax claim."

[89] *Bezanson v. United States* (*In re Amoskeag Bank Shares, Inc.*), 215 B.R. 1 (Bankr. D.N.H. 1997), *aff'd in part and rev'd in part*, 239 B.R. 653, 98-2 U.S.T.C. ¶ 50,746 (D. N.H. 1998).

complete and final distribution of all estate funds in an efficient and expeditious manner.

In the *Holywell* case,[90] discussed below and at § 902.1, the liquidating trustee of a trust created pursuant to a Chapter 11 plan sought and obtained a similar declaratory judgment. Although the Supreme Court subsequently reversed on the merits, the IRS never questioned the court's jurisdiction to rule on the issue.[91]

In contrast, in *In re Grand Chevrolet, Inc.*,[92] a trustee sought a declaratory judgment authorizing him to file a consolidated federal income tax return for several commonly controlled corporations that, for bankruptcy purposes, had already been substantively consolidated. Reversing the bankruptcy court, the district court held that the bankruptcy court lacked jurisdiction on the alternative grounds that (1) no "actual controversy" existed (since the trustee had nothing "more than a belief" that the IRS would deny consolidated status)[93] and (2) the relief sought was not within the court's authority under Bankruptcy Code section 505(a) and thus not within the exception to the Declaratory Judgment Act for section 505 proceedings. As to the latter point, the district court stated that section 505(a) only authorized bankruptcy courts to determine the "amount or legality" of any tax; it did not authorize bankruptcy courts to deal with tax issues in a vacuum, unrelated to the determination of a "tax liability." In this regard, the court's analysis seems to come down to the fact that the trustee never suggested and put into issue how much tax would be owed if tax consolidation were allowed, nor otherwise explained the impact of tax consolidation on its ultimate tax liability, but, rather, simply contended that separate reporting would substantially defeat the purpose of bankruptcy consolidation, be inequitable, and result in undue expense without any guarantee of accuracy.

---

[90] *Holywell Corp. v. Smith*, 112 S. Ct. 1021, 92-1 U.S.T.C. ¶ 50,110 (1992).

[91] *See also Holywell Corp. v. United States*, 229 F.2d 1142 (4th Cir. 2000) (unpublished decision), *reported in full at* 2000-2 U.S.T.C. ¶ 50,710 (concluding prior adjudication was *res judicata* and that bankruptcy court's exercise of jurisdiction over liquidating trust's tax liability was not manifest error given the fact, in the present appeal, that both parties presented reasonable arguments for their respective positions that jurisdiction did or did not exist), *cert. denied*, 121 S. Ct. 1192 (2001). At least one district court has granted declaratory relief in an analogous nonbankruptcy situation involving two testamentary trusts where the question was who, as between the trusts and their beneficiaries, should pay the tax on certain asset sales by the trusts. *See Dominion Trust Co. of Tennessee v. United States*, 786 F. Supp. 1321, 92-1 U.S.T.C. ¶ 50,136 (M.D. Tenn. 1991), *appealed and aff'd on other issues*, 1993 U.S. App. LEXIS 27,023 (6th Cir. 1993). Even though the IRS had yet taken no action to collect the tax, the court found that an "actual controversy" existed because the due date for filing the (still unfiled) tax returns had passed (a fact that similarly existed in both the *Goldblatt* and *Holywell* cases). Moreover, the court found that the general prohibition against declaratory judgments "with respect to Federal taxes" did not apply. The court observed that such prohibition was only intended to preclude the circumvention of the Anti-Injunction Act (*see* Code § 7421) through a request for declaratory relief and thus only bars declaratory relief "for the purpose of restraining the assessment or collection of any tax" (the scope of the Anti-Injunction Act). In the court's view, the issue of "who" pays a tax—in contrast to whether the tax is due at all—was not such a restriction.

[92] *IRS v. Sulmeyer (In re Grand Chevrolet, Inc.), supra* note 1.

[93] For a discussion of the "actual controversy" requirement, *see* § 1013.3.1 below. In this regard, it is interesting to note that the corporations involved, although commonly controlled, were not affiliated within the meaning of Code § 1504.

Similarly, the bankruptcy court in *In re Inter Urban Broadcasting of Cincinnati, Inc.*[94] found that a debtor's action in so far as it requested a declaration that certain purported stock transfers did not have any effect upon its status as an S corporation, and sought a court order reinstating its S status, suffered from the same deficiency as the trustee's action in *Grand Chevrolet*. Accordingly, the court dismissed the action against the United States and the IRS.

In *In re Dycoal Inc.*,[95] the debtor corporation, several years following the confirmation of its Chapter 11 plan, had sought a declaratory judgment from the bankruptcy court that certain synthetic fuels qualified for preconfirmation tax credits under Code § 29, even though the debtor had not yet filed any pre- or postconfirmation tax returns utilizing such credits. The bankruptcy court (affirmed by the district court) held, as alternative grounds, that there was no existent tax liability predicated upon the use of such credits, that the action was not ripe for determination as the IRS had not yet disallowed the credits or challenged certain court findings upon which the debtor sought to rely, and that the action involved a postconfirmation tax liability outside the purview of section 505(a).[96]

### § 1013.3.1 Plan-Related Issues

It is unclear whether a bankruptcy court may, pursuant to its declaratory judgment power, declare the federal income tax consequences of a Chapter 11 plan. The *Goldblatt and Amoskeag Bank Shares* cases (discussed in the preceding section) would suggest it can. However, other cases, such as the Fifth Circuit decision in *In re Wingreen Company* and the bankruptcy court decision in the *Allis-Chalmers* case (both discussed below), suggest the contrary.

In *Wingreen*,[97] the bankruptcy trustee had informally proposed a plan of reorganization under Chapter X of the then Bankruptcy Act, but had not yet presented it to the court or the government. One of the important features of the plan was a provision by which the reorganized corporation could take advantage of the debtor's $2.5 million NOL carryforward. Accordingly the trustee requested a ruling from the IRS on the amount and availability of any loss carryforwards, but the IRS declined to rule, responding that the matter was under study. The trustee then asked the court to direct the IRS "to show cause whether, under the proposed plan of reorganization[,] the continuing and reorganized corporation would have available to it the full tax loss carry forward benefits available to the debtor or a lesser benefit, and whether the ruling would be binding on the Service."[98] Over the government's objection, the

---

94 *Supra* note 1.

95 *Dycoal Inc. v. IRS (In re Dycoal Inc.)*, 327 B.R. 220, 2005-2 U.S.T.C. ¶ 50,554 (Bankr. W.D. Pa. 2005), *aff'd*, 2006 U.S. Dist. LEXIS 25078 (W.D. Pa. 2006).

96 For a discussion of the bankruptcy court's limited jurisdiction over postconfirmation taxes, *see* the opening discussion of § 1013 above.

97 *United States v. Brock (In re Wingreen Company)*, 412 F.2d 1048, 69-2 U.S.T.C. ¶ 9511 (5th Cir. 1969).

98 Id. at 1050.

district court required that, within 45 days, the IRS conduct an audit to determine the amount, extent, and duration of the debtor's NOL carryforwards, if any.

The Fifth Circuit reversed the district court's order, holding that the district court had no jurisdiction to enter it. Although the Fifth Circuit could have simply held that the district court order granted a form of declaratory relief that was specifically precluded by the Declaratory Judgment Act as then in effect (there being no specific exception at that time for federal tax proceedings in bankruptcy cases), it also provided the following reasoning:

> The order directs a ruling by the Internal Revenue Service on the relationship of the Bankruptcy Act and the Internal Revenue Code, including a determination of the tax consequences of a proposed plan of reorganization regarding the availability to a hypothetical continuing and reorganized corporation of a possible net operating loss carryover *in futuro*. This in effect constitutes an attempt by the trustee to receive a declaratory judgment, yet there is no "actual controversy" between the Service and any taxpayer.[99]

As to the portion of the order directing the IRS to audit the taxpayer, the court also concluded that the IRS had no specific duty to do so and, thus, could not be required to do so.

Although on one level the above quoted reasoning might be dismissed as *dicta*, it nevertheless raises serious questions as to the practical utility of the bankruptcy court's declaratory judgment power. Assuming that the result in *Wingreen* is sound—namely, that an informally proposed plan of reorganization is not a proper basis for a declaratory judgment—how far does the *Wingreen* reasoning extend? If it is limited to its facts, such that the Fifth Circuit might conclude differently if presented with a formally filed or an approved plan of reorganization, that would be one thing.[100] However, the court's conclusion—that "there is no 'actual controversy' between the Service and any taxpayer"—does not appear so limited. Taken to an extreme, this type of reasoning could, as a practical matter, eliminate the ability of a debtor to obtain declaratory judgments with respect to most plan-related federal tax issues (and would be in direct conflict with the courts' holdings in the *Goldblatt* and *Amoskeag Bank Shares* cases).

---

[99] Id. at 1052 (citations omitted).

[100] In this regard, consider *In re Franklin, supra* notes 55 and 88, wherein the government asserted that the matter at issue—an allocation of tax liability for the proposed sale of certain property in which the estate only had a part interest (*see* note 55)—involved "no case or controversy because the government had not made a claim against the estate for the sale of [the property]—the reason being that no sale of the property had been made." The court disagreed, finding that the "allocation of potential tax liability relates to the Trustee's ability to dispose of property not owned by the estate (11 U.S.C. § 725 (1990)) and to administer a settlement plan." *But see Official Comm. of Unsecured Creditors of Antonelli v. United States* (*In re Antonelli*), 1992 Bankr. LEXIS 2369 (Bankr. D. Md. 1992) (denied request for a declaratory judgment as to the application of the transfer tax exemption of Bankruptcy Code section 1146(c)—now section 1146(a)—with respect to anticipated postconfirmation sales by a liquidating trust provided for in a proposed Chapter 11 plan; court was "mindful" that its decision could delay confirmation efforts and complicate the negotiation process).

More recently, in a 1992 decision, the bankruptcy court in the *Allis-Chalmers* case[101] concluded, on the facts, that it was not within its jurisdiction to rule on whether Code § 269 precluded the postconfirmation availability of the Chapter 11 debtor's NOL carryforwards. In contrast to *Wingreen*, here the debtor had sought postconfirmation declaratory relief.

Shortly after the debtor emerged from bankruptcy, the IRS notified the reorganized debtor that its future use of NOLs might be challenged under Code § 269. The IRS thereafter issued regulations under Code § 269 "clarifying" that Code § 269 could apply to creditor takeovers of a bankrupt corporation and that a bankruptcy court's finding for plan confirmation purposes that the principal purpose for filing the Chapter 11 plan was not tax avoidance (which the bankruptcy court in this case had earlier determined) was not controlling for Code § 269 purposes.[102] In response, the debtor sought various forms of relief from the bankruptcy court.

First, the debtor asserted that the bankruptcy court's earlier finding of no tax avoidance for purposes of confirmation barred a subsequent Code § 269 challenge under the principles of *res judicata* or collateral estoppel.[103] However, as discussed at § 1002.8, the court concluded that *res judicata* did not apply and that the IRS could not be collaterally estopped from making a subsequent Code § 269 challenge "to attempts to use the NOLs after transactions not specifically contemplated in [the debtor's] plan of reorganization." Thus, the court left open the prospect that *res judicata* or collateral estoppel could apply in other cases where the use of the NOLs was more immediate and specifically contemplated by a debtor's plan.

Next, the debtor asked the court to rule on the applicability of Code § 269 and the regulations to the creditors' acquisition pursuant to the debtor's Chapter 11 plan. It is here that the court held that it lacked jurisdiction.

The court pointed out that, under the Declaratory Judgment Act, in order for it to issue a declaratory judgment with respect to federal taxes the requested relief must be within the court's authority under Bankruptcy Code section 505 or 1146. In concluding that section 505 did not apply, the court was extremely sensitive to the limits on its jurisdiction as to postconfirmation events. The court commented that "any tax," as used in Bankruptcy Code section 505(a), did not mean any tax of any entity at any point in time. The court also observed that the debtor was seeking an advance ruling since it had not yet attempted to use its NOLs (and might never use them) and that "any ruling would have to consider postconfirmation events which were not even known at the time of confirmation to determine a speculative future tax liability of the debtor." Hence, the court concluded that "a § 269 action had not ripened at the time of confirmation (and still has not ripened)" and added that: "Such a ruling

---

101 *Allis-Chalmers Corp. v. Goldberg (In re Hartman Material Handling Systems, Inc.), supra* note 29.

102 These regulations are discussed at § 509.1.

103 The debtor also asserted that the IRS should be equitably estopped from subsequently applying Code § 269, given that the IRS did not raise the issue when it issued to the debtor prior to confirmation a private letter ruling on certain Code § 382(1)(5) issues. Although the court stated that the issue was premature, it nevertheless noted the difficulty that the debtor would have in maintaining such a claim given the "no other opinion" language in the ruling and the fact that the disclosure statement accompanying the plan warned of the Code § 269 risk.

would establish a precedent for a former debtor to return to bankruptcy court to have any and all of its future tax consequences determined." The court noted that only Bankruptcy Code section 1146(d), since redesignated section 1146(b) (discussed below), provides for prospective tax determinations resembling the relief sought by the debtor, but that such section only applies for state and local tax purposes and appears to contemplate only a preconfirmation determination.

Finally, the court viewed the relief sought by the debtor as "closely analogous" to the position taken by the liquidating trustee in the *Holywell* case[104] and rejected by the Supreme Court (*see also* § 902.1) with respect to the binding effect of a confirmed Chapter 11 plan. The liquidating trustee had taken the position that he was not responsible for postconfirmation taxes on certain liquidating sales by the liquidating trust, arguing in part that the IRS, as a creditor in the debtor's bankruptcy, was precluded from seeking payment of the tax since the Chapter 11 plan (which created the trust) did not specifically provide for any taxes. The Supreme Court disagreed, stating that, even if a confirmed Chapter 11 plan binds all creditors with respect to preconfirmation claims (*see* § 1014.1 below), "we do not see how it can bind the United States or any other creditor with respect to postcon firmation claims," and noting that the Bankruptcy Code definition of "creditor" for this purpose spoke in terms of preconfirmation claims.

Resembling more closely the *Allis-Chalmers* case is the *McLean Industries* case.[105] Decided prior to *Allis-Chalmers*, that case also involved a confirmed Chapter 11 plan and the effect of the same Code § 269 regulations on the future availability of the debtor's NOL carryforwards (its "primary asset"), although at that time the regulations were only in proposed form. Moreover, in a letter ruling obtained by the debtors in connection with their plan, the IRS raised the possibility of a Code § 269 determination in the future.[106] The court acknowledged that the proposed regulations, "if adopted, would affect the Debtors by precluding their use of the NOLs."[107]

Although the court did not view the debtors' motion as requesting a declaratory judgment as to the debtors' tax liability (and denied the motion on other grounds, *see* § 1002 note 85 above), the court nevertheless commented on whether, if the debtors had wanted such a tax determination, such request would have presented a "justiciable case or controversy" under Article III of the U.S. Constitution.[108] Concluding that it would not, the court stated:

---

[104] *Holywell Corp. v. Smith* (S. Ct.), *supra* note 90.

[105] 132 B.R. 267, 91-2 U.S.T.C. ¶50,465 (S.D.N.Y. 1991).

[106] *See* IRS Letter Ruling 9019036, February 9, 1990.

[107] *See* then Prop. Reg. § 1.269-3(d). The proposed retroactive effective date of this section of the regulations was changed in the final version. As finalized, this section only applies to bankruptcy plans confirmed after August 14, 1990, the date the proposed regulations were released. Accordingly, the final version does not apply to the *McLean Industries* bankruptcy.

[108] The concept of "case or controversy" for such purpose is the same as the "actual controversy" requirement in the Declaratory Judgment Act. *See, e.g., Public Service Comm'n v. Wycoff Co.*, 73 S. Ct. 236, 240 (1952); *Harris Trust & Savings Bank v. E-II*, 926 F.2d 636 (7th Cir. 1991), *reh'g denied*, 1991 U.S. App. LEXIS 8606, *cert. denied*, 112 S. Ct. 192 (1991); *In re Kilen*, 129 B.R. 538, 91-2 U.S.T.C. ¶50,761 (Bankr. N.D. Ill. 1991).

> This Court will not render an advisory opinion as to the possible danger to the Debtors' NOLs because such a threat remains purely hypothetical at this juncture. A court can only determine an issue that presents a "real, substantial controversy between parties having adverse legal interests, a dispute definite and concrete, not hypothetical or abstract." . . . Until the [proposed] regulations are officially promulgated, there can be no concrete controversy concerning the Debtors' tax situation . . . .
> In the future, if the proposed regulations are ultimately adopted, then the appropriate issue would be whether a retroactive application of the I.R.C. would divest the Debtors of their NOLs. Additional issues would involve jurisdictional conflicts between the tax authorities and the bankruptcy courts.

Thus, the *McLean Industries* court never reached the jurisdictional issues that the *Allis-Chalmers* court in part found determinative. It should be noted, however, that the two courts apparently had different views as to what it would take to create an "actual controversy." The *McLean Industries* court apparently believed that the ultimate adoption of the regulations, as proposed, would have supplied the necessary controversy even absent any current income against which the NOLs could be used,[109] whereas the *Allis-Chalmers* court believed the existence of such income to be an essential element. Early on, the Supreme Court focused on the difficulty in distinguishing between an "abstract question" and an "actual controversy" as contemplated by the Declaratory Judgment Act:

> The difference . . . is necessarily one of degree, and it would be difficult, if it would be possible, to fashion a precise test for determining in every case whether there is such a controversy. Basically, the question in each case is whether the facts alleged, under all the circumstances, show that there is a *substantial controversy*, between parties having adverse legal interests, of *sufficient immediacy* and *reality* to warrant the issuance of a declaratory judgment.[110]

As discussed below at § 1013.3.2, the bankruptcy court in the *Kilen* case found a "sufficient immediacy and reality" in the debtor's need "to insure that his confirmed plan is implemented as intended." In that case, all events had occurred necessary to

---

[109] It should be noted that, although the court asserted that the proposed regulation, "if adopted, would affect the debtors by precluding their use of the NOLs," this conclusion is not necessarily clear from the face of the regulation. As proposed (and subsequently adopted), the regulation creates a strong presumption of tax avoidance if the level of the debtor's business operations during or subsequent to the bankruptcy is considered "insignificant." *Supra* note 107, and discussions at §§ 508.5 and 509.1. Thus, under the regulations, there are certain factual issues—namely, the level of business operations and the ability to rebut the presumption—which would appear to require the court to make a factual and legal determination. Whether the court considered these factual issues susceptible to a declaratory judgment, or simply relied on the unchallenged factual assertions of the debtors in their underlying brief, is unclear.

[110] *Golden v. Zwickler*, 394 U.S. 103, 108 (1969), *quoting Maryland Casualty Co. v. Pacific Coal & Oil Co.*, 312 U.S. 270, 273 (1941) (emphasis added).

establish the debtor's liability other than an actual or proposed assessment by the IRS. Moreover, as previously discussed, the district court in the *Amoskeag Bank Shares* case upheld a declaratory judgment motion with respect to a Chapter 7 trustee's employment tax obligations with respect to *pending* distributions to general unsecured creditors that were certain to occur.[111]

Following on the heels of the *Allis-Chalmers* case, the bankruptcy court in the *Monarch Capital* bankruptcy case denied a motion seeking a determination of certain plan related tax issues even though the plan was pending confirmation.[112] In addition to Code § 269, the tax issues raised were (i) the application of Code § 382(l)(5) in a consolidated return context, (ii) the sufficiency of the stock being issued for purposes of the "nominal or token" test to the stock-for-debt exception, (iii) the status of the reorganized debtor as a life insurance company under the Internal Revenue Code, and (iv) the status of the notes being issued as "debt" for federal income tax purposes. In what amounts to a one-paragraph decision, the court ruled from the bench that neither Bankruptcy Code section 505(a) (due to the lack of an actual controversy) nor the court's equitable authority under Bankruptcy Code section 105 ("I don't see that there's that absolute necessity for a ruling or for an action that 105 contemplates") supported the motion. Counsel had indicated, during the course of oral argument, that it would be prepared to opine as to four of the five tax issues (Code § 382(l)(5) being the exception). And the plan proponents acknowledged, in response to the court's inquiry, that they were prepared to go forward with confirmation even absent a determination.

In a 2006 decision in the *United Airlines (UAL)* bankruptcy case, the bankruptcy court likewise denied the debtors' request for an order declaring that certain plan distributions to Union employees would not be "wages" for federal income tax purposes.[113] Engaging in a close examination of the role of Bankruptcy Code section 505(a)—including the location and interplay of section 505(a) with other provisions in the Bankruptcy Code (which it found compelling), the legislative history of section 505(a) (which it found confirmatory), policy considerations (which it found two-sided), and relevant case law (which it found, at best, unsettled)—the bankruptcy court concluded that section 505(a) does not grant bankruptcy courts the power to determine the tax consequences of a Chapter 11 plan.[114] The court did not comment upon or even reference the *Amoskeag Bank Shares* case upholding the bankruptcy

---

[111] *See also In re Labrum & Doak* (E.D. Pa.), *supra* note 66, at *20-*21 (upholding a declaratory judgment motion to approve a debtor partnership's proposed allocation of income among current and former partners, and determining the matter to be a "core" proceeding in view of the significance of the issue to the estate and the confirmability of the debtor's Chapter 11 plan).

[112] *See In re Monarch Capital Corp.* (Bankr. D. Mass.), Chapter 11, Case No. 91-41379-JFQ, "Joint Motion of Plan Proponents to Determine Certain Federal Tax Consequences of the Plan in Furtherance of Confirmation," dated June 3, 1992; and the government's reply, dated June 22, 1992 (to which it attached the *Allis-Chalmers* decision); hearing held and motion denied, on June 25, 1992 (Queenan, J.).

[113] *In re UAL Corporation*, 336 B.R. 370 (Bankr. N.D. Ill. 2006).

[114] Having so concluded, the court found it unnecessary to decide whether the requested determination presented a constitutional "case or controversy."

court's jurisdiction to determine a very similar request by a Chapter 7 trustee in the context of a final distribution.

In sum, the above line of cases starting with *Allis-Chalmers* casts a serious blow to a debtor's ability to gain the certainty desired as to the federal income tax consequences of a Chapter 11 plan. Alone, the *Allis-Chalmers* decision leaves room for hope. In contrast to the potentially sweeping holding in the *Wingreen* case, the bankruptcy court's opinion in *Allis-Chalmers* does not purport to address a debtor's ability to obtain a declaratory judgment on the multitude of tax issues that can arise in the plan context for which the facts are known at the time of confirmation. The future availability of a debtor's NOLs under Code § 269 is only one potential tax issue (albeit frequently of considerable and determinative importance).[115] Also at issue may be the current taxability of various plan transactions, as well as numerous other tax issues with an immediate or known impact. There is a chance that when presented with these other issues some bankruptcy courts will conclude that it is within their jurisdiction to resolve them.[116] As demonstrated, though, by the *Monarch Capital* case and the more recent decision in the *UAL* bankruptcy case, debtors will not have an easy time of it. One can venture to say that a debtor's likelihood of success will

---

[115] Even then, as discussed at § 1002.8, the collateral estoppel effect of confirmation on a debtor's ability to use its NOLs postconfirmation against projected income from an on-going business is arguably outside the court's opinion. In *In re Dycoal Inc.*, also discussed in the introductory section of § 1013, the debtor sought a plan-related determination several years after confirmation as to the future availability of certain Code § 29 fuel credits. *Dycoal Inc. v. IRS (In re Dycoal Inc.)*, 327 B.R. 220, 2005-2 U.S.T.C. ¶ 50,554 (Bankr. W.D. Pa. 2005), *aff'd*, 2006 U.S. Dist. LEXIS 25078 (W.D. Pa. 2006). The bankruptcy court (affirmed by the district court) held that it did not have jurisdiction under section 505(a) due, among other things, to the absence of any existing (and more particularly preconfirmation) tax liability or IRS challenge, nor could such jurisdiction be supplied by the bankruptcy court's equitable authority under Bankruptcy Code section 105 or 1123(b)(5) (*see* § 1013.5 below). The district court also rejected the debtor's claim that the feasibility of the plan was dependent upon the availability of the Code § 29 credits and consequently that the IRS was bound by certain findings of fact in the bankruptcy court's confirmation order relating to such credits. The court concluded that such a determination "is neither required [on the facts] nor appropriate under" Bankruptcy Code section 1129(a)(11) (the feasibility condition for plan confirmation) or 1142(a) (implementation of the plan by the reorganized debtor).

[116] In addition to several cases discussed in the text, *see, e.g.*, *McCorkle v. Georgia (In re McCorkle)*, 209 B.R. 703 (Bankr. M.D. Ga. 1997) (court held that it had jurisdiction to determine whether, at such future time as the State's current lien expired, the State could refile its lien or was precluded from doing so due to the debtor's personal discharge; in the court's view, the "immediacy and reality" of the adverse interests was clear, given that the outcome could affect the debtor's decision to abandon his home to the bank or to keep it); *In re Pflug*, 146 B.R. 687, 92-2 U.S.T.C. ¶ 50,586 (Bankr. E.D. Va. 1992) (wherein the bankruptcy court expressed doubt whether it was within its jurisdiction to entertain an individual debtor's motion to compel the bankruptcy trustee to file tax returns not yet due since the motion "essentially requests an advisory opinion on prospective transactions," but nevertheless ruled on the issue "since it raises an important question concerning a Chapter 7 trustee's duty with respect to income tax reporting of forgiveness of indebtedness income"); *Scharrer v. Dept. of Treasury (In re American Leasing and Acceptance Corp. of Lakeland)*, *supra* note 88 ("for the sake of judicial economy" court ruled on liquidating trustee's summary judgment motion for a tax determination prior to the filing of an amended return formally asserting the tax position and any adverse action by the IRS).

increase as the dependency of the debtor's plan on a favorable resolution of the tax issues increases.[117]

Sympathetic to the debtor's plight, the *Allis-Chalmers* court expressed the need for legislative action (footnotes omitted):[118]

> Through the [Code § 269]Regulations, the IRS has highlighted an unfortunate loophole in the finality of the reorganization process and the need for reconciliation and modification of the relevant statutes. The degree of uncertainty in the current statutory scheme jeopardizes the viability of many reorganizations. It is essential that a reorganizing company know how to structure its reorganization to preserve its tax benefits. In many cases, this certainty will be necessary to determine the feasibility of a plan. *See* § 1129(a)(11) . . . .
>
> . . . Indeed, the Regulations suggest an ill-fated system for all involved. While the IRS may take some satisfaction in the outcome in this case as it may mean that some favorable tax attributes are never used, its sister governmental organizations may not view the IRS's endeavors with the same glee. The government as a major creditor in many mega cases has an interest in successful reorganizations. The PBGC and the Environmental Protection Agency, for example, will be harmed along with all other creditor types. The government safety net agencies and the courts, furthermore, may find that they have more customers from liquidating companies than anticipated.

As previously mentioned, the issue of declaratory judgments and plan feasibility was specifically addressed for state and local tax purposes in Bankruptcy Code section 1146(d), since redesignated section 1146(b). Such section permits the bankruptcy court to authorize the proponent of a plan to request from the appropriate state and local taxing authorities a determination, limited to questions of law, of the tax effect of the plan; and, in the event of an adverse determination or upon the passage of 270 days, permits the court to declare such effect.[119] According to legislative statements at the time of enactment, the import of this provision is that:

> the power of the bankruptcy court to declare the tax effects of the plan is limited to issues of law and not to questions of fact such as the allowance of specific deductions. Thus, the bankruptcy court could declare whether the reorganization qualified for tax free status under State or local tax

---

[117] We recommend, as well, to the reader the following articles: Jacobs, The Bankruptcy Court's Emergence as Tax Dispute Arbiter of Choice, 45 Tax Law. 971, 1013-1016 (1992); Sheppard, New Tax Avoidance Regs Avoid Bankruptcy Court, 92 TNT 8-8 (January 13, 1992); Faber, The Declaratory Powers of Bankruptcy Courts to Determine the Federal Tax Consequences of Chapter 11 Plans, 3 Am. Bankr. Inst. Law Rev. 407 (1994).

[118] 141 B.R. at 813-14.

[119] *See also* discussion at § 1102.17; Collier on Bankruptcy ¶ 8.03[c] (15th ed.).

rules, but it could not declare the dollar amount of any tax attributes that survive the reorganization.[120]

Although, as originally proposed, this provision would have applied also to federal taxes, the reference to federal taxes here (as elsewhere in section 1146) was deleted in the final bill (*see* § 1101 below). In its report to Congress, the National Bankruptcy Review Commission recommended that this provision also apply to federal taxes.[121] Although no change has yet been made to Bankruptcy Code section 1146(b), Congress in the 2005 bankruptcy reforms expanded the comparable section in Chapter 12 of the Bankruptcy Code (applicable to certain family farmers or fisherman) to cover federal taxes.[122]

### § 1013.3.2 Prepetition Tax Issues

In the *Kilen* case,[123] the bankruptcy court considered whether it had the power to resolve a tax dispute ostensibly created by the debtor pursuant to Bankruptcy Code section 501(c). As discussed at § 1010, Bankruptcy Code section 501(c) permits a debtor to file a proof of claim on behalf of the IRS where the IRS fails to do so.

In *Kilen*, the debtor (an individual) had set aside, as part of his Chapter 11 plan, some $640,000 to satisfy his potential personal liability to the IRS pursuant to Code § 6672 for unpaid trust fund taxes of several controlled corporations. However, the IRS had filed a proof of claim for taxes owed by only one of the corporations (although many of the corporations had admitted to owing the taxes in the schedules of liabilities filed in their respective bankruptcy cases). This left the debtor in the position that, if no proof of claim was filed for the taxes owed by the other corporations and the IRS asserted such claim after the bankruptcy, the money set aside would have been distributed to the debtor's general unsecured creditors and the debtor would remain personally liable since, as an individual, his liability under Code § 6672 would not be discharged. To prevent this result, the debtor filed a proof of claim on behalf of the IRS for such taxes, pursuant to Bankruptcy Code section 501(c) and, immediately thereafter, objected to the claim, asking the court to declare either that the amount of the liability was zero or that he was not a "responsible person" within the meaning of Code § 6672 and, thus, not liable for such taxes. The IRS opposed the motion, contending that, without an actual or proposed assessment, "there is no actual case or controversy between the parties that is ripe for hearing and determination."

---

[120] 123 Cong. Rec. H 11,115 (daily ed. September 28, 1978) (statement of Rep. Edwards), S 17,432 (daily ed. October 6, 1978) (statement of Sen. DeConcini).

[121] National Bankruptcy Review Commission Final Report (October 20, 1997), Recommendation 3.2.5, at pp. 811-817.

[122] *See* 11 U.S.C. § 1231(b), *as amended by* P.L. 109-8, § 1003(b) (2005) (formerly section 1231(d) of the Bankruptcy Code). *See also* Rev. Proc. 2006-52, 2006-48 I.R.B. 995 (describing the procedure for requesting IRS determinations under the expanded provision).

[123] *Supra* note 108.

Rejecting the IRS's arguments to the contrary, the bankruptcy court held that, given the magnitude of the potential harm to the debtor and the fact that the events and conduct upon which the claim was based already occurred, the relief sought was "ripe" for consideration and that an "actual controversy" existed. In addressing the debtor's need for relief, the court stated:

> Kilen needs declaratory relief under § 505, *i.e.*, to have this Court determine what, if anything, he owes the IRS for trust fund liability, in order to insure that his confirmed plan is implemented as intended and the priority tax claims satisfied ahead of the claims of nonpriority unsecured creditors.

The court also found that the debtor's use of Bankruptcy Code section 501(c) was consistent with bankruptcy policy and with Bankruptcy Act precedent and concluded that "Section 501 . . . in effect empower[s] the debtor to create an actual controversy by filing a proof of claim on behalf of the creditor and then turning around and opposing allowance of the claim."

As discussed at § 1010, it generally will be rare that a corporate debtor files a proof of claim on behalf of the IRS since, in contrast to the case of an individual debtor, any unpaid prepetition taxes of a corporate debtor for which a proof of claim has not been filed generally are dischargeable. However, any person who may be liable for such taxes with the debtor (such as a former member of the debtor's consolidated group) similarly may file a claim on behalf of the IRS where the IRS fails to do so.

In *In re Schwartz*,[124] the bankruptcy court was presented with a situation similar to that in *Kilen*, but where the debtor, rather than filing a proof of claim on behalf of the IRS, simply filed an adversary proceeding in the bankruptcy court against the IRS (and the New Jersey Division of Taxation) seeking a determination that he was not liable as a "responsible person" within the meaning of the respective tax statutes. What is also striking about the case is that the IRS had not suggested to the debtor that he might be liable, nor had it commenced an investigation to determine whether the debtor had any such liability. However, the IRS readily admitted that it was possible that it could conduct such an investigation sometime in the future. Also, the New Jersey Division of Taxation had in one instance already determined the debtor to be a responsible person under its tax statutes. Thus, the bankruptcy court viewed as real the possibility that the debtor could have substantial liability. Moreover, the court, discussing *Kilen*, did not view the filing of the proof of claim under Bankruptcy Code section 501(c) as essential to the holding in that case. Rather, in the bankruptcy court's view, what was critical in *Kilen* was the expansive definition of a "claim" under the Bankruptcy Code which includes unliquidated and contingent claims, the equally expansive jurisdiction of the bankruptcy court under Bankruptcy Code section 505(a) to deal with such claims, and the debtor's need for immediate relief to ensure the successful implementation of its Chapter 11 plan. Finding a similar need, and based on its review of other relevant authorities, the bankruptcy court concluded

---

[124] 192 B.R. 90 (Bankr. D.N.J. 1996).

that an "actual controversy" existed between the debtor, on the one hand, and the IRS and the New Jersey Division of Taxation, on the other hand.

The situation in *United States v. Bushnell*[125] presents a third variation on the theme. In this case, the IRS had in fact issued a notice of proposed liability and filed a proof of claim (the issue here being transferee, rather than responsible person, liability), in reaction to which the debtor commenced the present proceeding to determine its liability. Subsequently, however, in response to a previously filed protest by the debtor, IRS Appeals determined that the debtor in fact had no liability. The IRS thus sought to withdraw its proof of claim, but "without prejudice." Wanting to ensure finality, the debtor pursued its action and obtained summary judgment. The IRS argued, among other things, that the debtor's action should be dismissed due to the absence of a case or controversy. The district court found that the bankruptcy court properly exercised its jurisdiction in adjudicating the debtor's tax liability, given that the IRS had originally submitted to the court's jurisdiction by filing its claim and, despite its attempted withdrawal, sought to maintain the right to reassert the claim at a later date.

## *§1013.4 Burden of Proof*

Burden of proof issues with respect to taxes can arise in many different situations—such as through an objection to a proof of claim, an action against the IRS to turn over assets, or an action for a declaratory judgment. Depending on the context, the party having the "burden of going forward" and the ultimate "burden of persuasion" may differ.[126]

**Proof of claim.** As to proofs of claim, Bankruptcy Rule 3001(f) provides that "[a] proof of claim executed and filed in accordance with these rules shall constitute *prima facie* evidence of the validity and amount of the claim." Thus, in the case of an objection to a proof of claim, the initial burden of going forward and introducing evidence is on the debtor (or any other objecting party).[127]

Prior to the Supreme Court's decision in *Raleigh v. Illinois Department of Revenue*,[128] in May 2000, courts were divided as to whether the debtor or the taxing authority bore the ultimate burden of persuasion in such cases.[129] As discussed

---

[125] 96-2 U.S.T.C. ¶50,472 (D. Vt. 1996).

[126] *Compare, e.g.*, discussion in text *with* Code §7422(e) (burden generally on taxpayer in tax refund actions). *See also* Porter, Burdens of Proof in Bankruptcy Court, 17 Colo. Law. 251 (February 1988); Cash, Dickens and Ward-Vaughn, Burden of Proof and the Impact of Code Sec. 7491 in Civil Tax Disputes, 80 Taxes 33 (2002); Khadiri, The Burden of Proof in Court Proceedings Under I.R.C. §7491: Separating Fact From Fiction, Tax Mgmt. Memo. (October 15, 1998); Clukey, Examining the Limited Benefits of the Burden of Proof Shift, 1999 TNT 20-136 (February 1, 1999).

[127] *See also Brown v. United States (In re Brown)*, 82 F.3d 801, 97-2 U.S.T.C. ¶50,559 (8th Cir. 1996) (debtor must present "substantial evidence" to overcome initial burden).

[128] 120 S.Ct. 1951 (2000), *aff'g*, 179 F.3d 546 (7th Cir. 1999).

[129] For a further discussion of the various lines of authorities and a collection of cases, *see In re Premo*, 90-2 U.S.T.C. ¶50,396 (Bankr. E.D. Mich. 1990); and *Kranzdorf v. IRS (In re Fidelity America Corp.)*, 1990 Bankr. LEXIS 1857 (Bankr. E.D. Pa. 1990), *opinion withdrawn*. *See also* Jenks, The Tax Collector in Bankruptcy Court: The Government's Uneasy Role as a Creditor in Bankruptcy, 71 Taxes

below, the Supreme Court in *Raleigh* held that a taxpayer's burden of proof is a matter of substantive law and thus unaltered in bankruptcy.

At least four different positions had previously emerged from the cases:

(1) A taxing authority was treated no differently than any other creditor. Accordingly, unlike the rule outside bankruptcy, once the debtor produced evidence rebutting the *prima facie* effect of the proof of claim, the burden of persuasion rested with the taxing authority.[130]

(2) The nonbankruptcy rule applied. Accordingly, the burden of persuasion was generally on the debtor.[131] Effective for taxable periods or events

(Footnote Continued)

847 (1993); Martin, Burden of Persuasion: The Overlooked Defense to Tax Claims, 21 Cal. Bankr. J. 117 (1993).

[130] *See, e.g., Franchise Tax Board v. MacFarlane (In re MacFarlane)*, 83 F.3d 1041 (9th Cir. 1996), *cert. denied*, 117 S. Ct. 1243 (1997) (involved deductibility of bad debts); *In re Fidelity Holding Co., Ltd.*, 837 F.2d 696 (5th Cir. 1988) (involved state sales and use tax); *In re Placid Oil Co.*, 988 F.2d 554 (5th Cir. 1993) (involved deductibility of pre- and postpetition bankruptcy related expenses; *see* Chapter 13); *Fullmer v. United States*, 962 F.2d 1463, 92-1 U.S.T.C. ¶50,237 (10th Cir. 1992) (applied bankruptcy rule without discussion); *Izzo v. IRS*, 2000-1 U.S.T.C. ¶50,273 (Bankr. W.D. Pa. 2000) (narrowly construing Third Circuit decision in *Resyn, infra* note 131); *In re Forte*, 234 B.R. 607, 99-2 U.S.T.C. ¶50,568 (Bankr. E.D. N.Y. 1999) ("courts in this district have followed the Fifth, Ninth and Tenth Circuits"; involved status as S corporation shareholder and disallowed deductions); *In re Avien, Inc.*, 390 F. Supp. 1335 (E.D.N.Y. 1975) (involved city income tax), *aff'd*, 532 F.2d 273 (2d Cir. 1976); *In re Dakota Indus., Inc.* (Bankr. D.S.D.), 131 B.R. 437 (Bankr. D.S.D. 1991) (involved employment taxes); *United States v. Craddock (In re Craddock)*, 95-2 U.S.T.C. ¶50,475 (D. Col. 1995) (IRS had the ultimate burden of proving negligence for purposes of the Code §6653 negligence penalty; however, the debtor bore the ultimate burden of proving "reasonable cause" exception under Code §6651, as the court viewed such relief "in the nature of an affirmative defense"); *In re Hudson Oil Co.*, 100 B.R. 72 (Bankr. D. Kan. 1989) (but similarly imposed burden on debtor to establish "reasonable cause" exception under Code §6651); *In re L.G.J. Restaurant, Inc.*, 27 B.R. 455 (Bankr. E.D.N.Y. 1983) (involved state sales tax); *Thompson v. United States (In re Waston)*, 456 F. Supp. 432, 79-1 U.S.T.C. ¶9283 (S.D. Ga. 1979); *In re American Electric Const. Inc.*, 1990 Bankr. LEXIS 2252 (Bankr. S.D. Ohio) (involved an IRS "request for payment" of administrative expense claims); *In re Federated Dept. Stores, Inc.*, 135 B.R. 950, 92-1 U.S.T.C. ¶50,097 (Bankr. S.D. Ohio 1992), *aff'd*, 171 B.R. 603 (S.D. Ohio 1994) (involved deductibility of "white knight" break-up fees; also cited equitable factors); *see also United States v. Rasbury (In re Rasbury)*, 141 B.R. 752 (N.D. Ala. 1992) (involved employee status; found that *Terrell, infra* note 131, should be limited to its facts); *Arndt v. United States (In re Arndt)*, 158 B.R. 863 (Bankr. D. Fla. 1993) (also involved employee status). *Cf. In re Premo, supra* note 129; *In re Unimet*, 74 B.R. 156 (Bankr. N.D. Ohio 1987); *In re Imperial Corp. of America*, 91-2 U.S.T.C. ¶50,342 (Bankr. D. Cal.) (estimation proceeding); *In re Compass Marine Corp.*, 1992 WL 207671 (Bankr. E.D. Pa.) (suggesting that the Third Circuit decision in *Resyn, infra* note 131, should be narrowly construed).

The Eighth Circuit also appears to support the burden of persuasion on the IRS. *Compare Brown v. United States (In re Brown), supra* note 127 (favorably cited *Placid Oil*, but ultimately held that taxpayer failed to overcome initial presumption of validity), *with Gran v. IRS (In re Gran)*, 964 F.2d 822, 92-1 U.S.T.C. ¶50,283 (8th Cir. 1992) (the bankruptcy court had shifted burden to IRS; the Eighth Circuit declined to reach the burden of proof issue, since the bankruptcy court further held that the government had established its claim by convincing evidence), *and In re Uneco, Inc.*, 532 F.2d 1204, 76-1 U.S.T.C. ¶9326 (8th Cir. 1976) (Bankruptcy Act case; imposed burden on debtor without discussion of conflict with bankruptcy rule). Many of the above cases are also factually consistent with the third position in that no valid assessment was made.

[131] *See, e.g., Raleigh v. Illinois (In re Stoecker)* (7th Cir.), *supra* note 128 (involved responsible person liability under Illinois use tax); *IRS v. Levy (In re Landbank Equity Corp.)*, 973 F.2d 265 (4th Cir. 1992) (where Form 870 was previously filed; involved deduction for bad debts), *rev'g* 130 B.R. 28 (E.D. Va.

(including examinations) beginning or occurring after June 9, 1998, Code §7491(a) changes the nonbankruptcy rule and generally shifts the burden of persuasion to the IRS in tax cases where the taxpayer (i) in the case of a corporation, partnership, or trust, satisfies the net worth and size requirements of Code §7430(c)(4)(A)(ii) (*i.e.*, not more than $7 million in net worth based on acquisition cost of assets and not more than 500 employees),[132] (ii) has complied with any relevant substantiation requirements under the Code, and (iii) has cooperated with reasonable requests of the IRS for information, witnesses, meetings and interviews.[133]

(3) The nonbankruptcy rule applied only if a valid tax assessment had been made. Accordingly, if a prepetition tax assessment was made, the burden of

---

(Footnote Continued)

1991); *Resyn Corp. v. United States*, 851 F.2d 660, 88-2 U.S.T.C. ¶9420 (3d Cir. 1988) (without discussion of conflict with bankruptcy rule); *United States v. Charlton*, 2 F.3d 237, 93-2 U.S.T.C. ¶50,469 (7th Cir. 1993) (same); *Thinking Machines Corporation v. New Mexico Tax'n & Rev. Dept.*, 211 B.R. 426 (D. Mass. 1997) (involved sales tax); *In re Duffy*, 95-1 U.S.T.C. ¶50,110 (Bankr. E.D. Cal. 1994) (involved debt/equity issue); *In re Terrell*, 75 B.R. 291, 87-1 U.S.T.C. ¶9269 (N.D. Ala. 1987) (involved Code §6672 penalty; adopted government briefs), *aff'd*, 835 F.2d 1439 (11th Cir. 1987); *United States v. Macagnone (In re Macagnone)*, 240 B.R. 444, 99-2 U.S.T.C. ¶50,681 (M.D. Fla. 1999) (involved Code §6672 penalty); *In re Rose*, 89-2 U.S.T.C. ¶9533 (Bankr. E.D. Ark. 1989) (involved disallowed deductions); *Cobb v. United States (In re Cobb)*, 135 B.R. 640 (Bankr. D. Neb. 1992) (reconciles Bankruptcy Rule); *In re Arthur's Industrial Maintenance, Inc.*, 93-1 U.S.T.C. ¶50,092 (W.D. Va. 1993) (involved application of credits, computation of interest and penalties, and "reasonable cause" for nonpayment of taxes).

Not surprisingly, the IRS stated that it agreed with, and would advocate, the position of the Fourth Circuit in *In re Landbank Equity Corp.* and, within the Fifth Circuit, would attempt to distinguish the Fifth Circuit's decision in *In re Placid Oil Co.*, *supra* note 130, on its facts (although it was unclear on what basis). Action on Decision CC-1995-004, April 17, 1995, 1995-16 I.R.B. 4.

[132] *See* Reg. §301.7430-5(f), and discussion of Code §7430 at §1007.7.4 above. Based on the regulations under Code §7430, such requirements are tested as of the earlier of the issuance of a final notice of decision by IRS Appeals or a statutory notice of deficiency. *See* Reg. §§301.7430-5(f)(2), -3(c); *see also* flush language of Code §7430(c)(2) (as amended by the 1998 Reform Act), effective for costs incurred after December 6, 1998, moves such date, if earlier, to the date on which the first letter of proposed deficiency is sent which allows for administrative review. However, in the context of a bankruptcy, the IRS may file a proof of claim prior to the occurrence of either of such events (assuming such events occur at all). Query whether the filing date of the proof of claim will control.

[133] The legislative history indicates that a "necessary element of cooperating . . . is that the taxpayer must exhaust his or her administrative remedies (including any appeal rights provided by the IRS)." H.R. Conf. Rep. 599, 105th Cong., 2d Sess. 57 (1988). *See* generally "Excerpts From IRS Description of Impact of IRS Reform Act With Actions Necessary to Implement Specific Provisions," BNA Daily Tax Report (Sept. 8, 1998), at L-1; Congressional Research Service Report on Code §7491 (March 9, 1999), *reprinted at* 1999 TNT 52-62; Cash, Dickens and Ward-Vaughn, *supra* note 126; Clukey, *supra* note 126; Khadiri, *supra* note 126. If all of the above conditions are satisfied, *and* the taxpayer provides "credible evidence" with respect to the factual matter at issue, the burden of persuasion with respect to such issue shifts to the government. *See, e.g.*, *Higbee v. Commissioner*, 116 T.C. 438 (2001) (applying the meaning of "credible evidence" in the legislative history, which requires "the quality of evidence which, after critical analysis, the court would find sufficient upon which to base a decision on the issue if no contrary evidence were submitted"); *Griffin v. Commissioner*, 315 F.3d 1017, 2003 U.S.T.C. ¶50,186 (8th Cir. 2003) (*per curiam*) (same; taxpayer's uncorroborated testimony was sufficient to satisfy the "credible evidence" requirement); *United States v. Official Comm. of Unsecured Creditors of Indus. Comm. Electrical, Inc. (In re Indus. Comm. Electrical, Inc.)*, 319 B.R. 35, 53, 2005-1 U.S.T.C. ¶50,312 (D. Mass. 2005) (discusses what is necessary to constitute "credible evidence" within a bankruptcy court proceeding where a debtor's entire tax liability for a particular year is effectively in dispute due to the IRS's filing of a protective claim).

persuasion was generally borne by the debtor; however, in other cases, the burden of persuasion rested with the taxing authority.[134]

(4) The choice between the competing policies of the bankruptcy and nonbankruptcy rules was made on an *ad hoc* basis based on the particular facts and circumstances involved in the case (including, for example, which party presumably had the peculiar means of knowledge as to the facts at hand).[135] In practice, however, this position tended to be just a rationalization for the adoption by a court of one of the first three positions.

This divergence of views similarly reflected the position of the courts with respect to a taxing authority's request for the payment of postpetition taxes,[136] with the exception that when it came to postpetition taxes some courts also imposed the initial burden of going forward on the claimant.[137]

Reacting to the conflicting case law, and recognizing the arguments for and against the various positions, the National Bankruptcy Review Commission, in its report to Congress in October 1997, recommended that the Bankruptcy Code be amended to "clarify" that the burden of proof rules (and related presumptions) applicable to tax controversies outside bankruptcy are equally applicable to the determination of tax claims in bankruptcy.[138]

The debate finally reached the Supreme Court in *Raleigh v. Illinois Department of Revenue*.[139] The Illinois Department of Revenue sought to impose "responsible officer" liability on the debtor for unpaid use tax. The Department issued to the debtor

---

[134] *See, e.g., United States v. Kontaratos*, 36 B.R. 928, 84-1 U.S.T.C. ¶9208 (D. Me. 1984); *In re Coleman American Cos., Inc.*, 26 B.R. 825 (Bankr. D. Kan. 1983); *In re Twomey*, 24 B.R. 799, 82-2 U.S.T.C. ¶9687 (Bankr. W.D.N.Y. 1982) (involved Code §6672 penalty); *Associated Bicycle Service, Inc. v. United States (In re Bicycle Service, Inc.)*, 128 B.R. 436, 443-444, 91-1 U.S.T.C. ¶50,134 (Bankr. N.D. Ind. 1991); *D'Alessio v. IRS (In re D'Alessio)*, *supra* note 42 (does not discuss what happens absent assessment); *consider also In re Unimet*, *supra* note 130 (IRS asserted burden shifted once a statutory notice of deficiency or assessment is issued; however, no assessment was made and court held that, even if the alleged statutory notice of deficiency applied to the issues raised, it was inequitable to shift the burden since the notice was not sent until the eve of trial); *In re BKW Systems, Inc.*, 90-1 U.S.T.C. ¶50,139 (Bankr. D.N.H. 1989) (incorrectly suggesting that, absent assessment, burden of *going forward* also shifts to the government); *but see In re Terrell*, *supra* note 131 (adopting government's brief criticizing this rule, in part on the basis that the proof of claim serves as a substitute for assessment in bankruptcy cases, which, at the time, was generally precluded by the automatic stay).

[135] *See, e.g., In re Premo*, *supra* note 129 (involves Code §6672 penalty; ultimately adopted general bankruptcy rule "in part as a means of promoting uniformity, if only within the Sixth Circuit"); *Kranzdorf v. IRS*, discussed *supra* note 129; *In re Wilhelm*, 173 B.R. 398, 94-2 U.S.T.C. ¶50,485 (Bankr. E.D. Wis. 1994) (involved farm related expenses; concluding that both the IRS and the debtor had equal access to the facts, court placed burden of persuasion on the IRS). *See also Abel v. United States (In re Abel)*, 200 B.R. 816, 96-2 U.S.T.C. ¶50,498 (E.D. Pa. 1996) (involved Code §6672 penalty; considered facts and circumstances, but within the more general backdrop of the competing policies and the Third Circuit decision in *Resyn*, *supra* note 131; imposed burden on debtor).

[136] *See, e.g., In re American Electric Const., Inc.*, 1990 Bankr. LEXIS 2252 (Bankr. S.D. Ohio 1990) (did not distinguish).

[137] *See Fullmer v. United States (In re Fullmer)* (10th Cir.), *supra* note 130.

[138] National Bankruptcy Review Commission Final Report (October 20, 1997), Recommendation 3.2.5, at pp. 811-817 (discusses competing considerations).

[139] *Supra* note 128.

a Notice of Penalty Liability (which, under Illinois law, has the effect of shifting the burden of production and persuasion to the responsible officer) and filed a proof of claim with the bankruptcy court. The trustee in bankruptcy objected to the claim, and asserted that the Department bore the burden of persuasion with respect to its claim. Due to the lack of factual evidence, the burden of proof was critical to the determination of liability.

In a unanimous decision, the Supreme Court held that the burden of proof on a tax claim in bankruptcy "remains where the substantive tax law puts it"—meaning, in this case, on the taxpayer and therefore on the trustee in bankruptcy. The Court justified its holding on several grounds, including (i) that the burden of proof is a "substantive" and essential element of the claim itself and that the validity of claims and property rights in bankruptcy (in contrast to the allowance of claims) is generally left to state law; (ii) the traditional rationales supporting the general imposition of the burden on the taxpayer (including access to information and encouraging compliance with the tax laws),[140] (iii) the absence of any indication that Congress intended to alter the burden of proof for tax claims; and (iv) the uniformity and equality provided by ensuring that the same burden of proof applies whether the bankruptcy court undertakes the determination of the tax claim or lets the claim be determined by another court.[141]

Although the Court's decision factually involves a state tax claim, the decision applies with equal force to federal tax claims. The Court's analysis effectively undercuts the reasoning of the various lower courts that had held to the contrary in the context of federal tax claims and is in accord with the Fourth Circuit's 1992 opinion in *In re Landbank Equity Corporation*,[142] which involved a federal tax claim.[143] The Fourth Circuit similarly emphasized that matters of proof (including burdens and presump-

---

[140] The Court acknowledged that a trustee might have less access to the facts than the taxpayer, but noted that the trustee takes custody of the taxpayer's records and may have greater access to the taxpayer than the government.

[141] Also illustrative of the Supreme Court's concern regarding inequality (although not used as an example by the Court) was the potential for the party bearing the ultimate burden of persuasion to be different depending on whether the debtor stylized his objection to a proof of claim in the form of an objection (where the taxing authority might have the burden of proof) or, instead, in the form of an affirmative motion to determine tax liability (where the burden of proof traditionally has been recognized to be on the debtor, as the moving party). In a questionable decision, at least one bankruptcy court, although acknowledging that the debtor's motion was the equivalent of an objection, held that the debtor was stuck with his form and, thus, as the moving party, bore the burden of persuasion. *See In re Carden*, 98-2 U.S.T.C. ¶50,686 (Bankr. E.D. La. 1998) (debtor was held to his form). Other courts had been more willing to look beyond the form. *See, e.g., In re Carson*, 227 B.R. 148 (S.D. Ind. 1998) (court recognized that the debtor's "Section 505(a)(1) motion certainly amounted to an objection to the United States' proof of claim," and that, had it come down to the burden of proof, the burden of proof rules applicable to objections to tax claims (which were admittedly unclear) would have controlled).

[142] *Supra* note 131.

[143] For post-Supreme Court decisions, *see, e.g., Moser v. United States* (*In re Moser*), 2002-1 U.S.T.C. ¶50,170 (4th Cir. 2002); *IRS v. CM Holdings, Inc.* (*In re CM Holdings, Inc.*), 254 B.R. 578, 2000-2 U.S.T.C. ¶50,791 (D. Del. 2000); *In re Treacy*, 255 B.R. 656, 2000-2 U.S.T.C. ¶50,776 (Bankr. E.D. Pa. 2000); *In re Aboody*, 250 B.R. 1, 2000-2 U.S.T.C. ¶50,556 (Bankr. D. Mass. 2000) (but also recognizing that the burden of proof may shift to the IRS under Code §7491(a), discussed above).

tions) are properly considered part of the substantive law and found nothing in the Bankruptcy Code that expressed a policy or intent to change any such aspect of federal tax law.

**Proving tax avoidance purpose of Chapter 11 plan.** As mentioned earlier, the government bears the burden of proof in any hearing under Bankruptcy Code section 1129(d) as to whether the principal purpose of the Chapter 11 plan is tax avoidance (*see* § 1002.8.1 note 87). In addition, as discussed in Chapter 5 (at § 509.1), the regulations under Code § 269 take the position that a determination under Bankruptcy Code section 1129(d) that the principal purpose is not tax avoidance is not controlling for Code § 269 purposes. The preamble to the regulations states as the principal justification for this position the differing burden of proof, citing the Restatement (Second) of Judgments § 28(4).[144]

Query, whether similar reasoning would not also limit the *res judicata* or collateral estoppel effect of any substantive tax issue favorably resolved by the bankruptcy court where, prior to the Supreme Court's decision in *Raleigh*, the court shifted the burden of proof to the government? For example, assume the bankruptcy court held that certain expenses could be amortized over the life of a debt that extends beyond the bankruptcy case. Can the IRS relitigate the same issue for a postbankruptcy year with respect to the same expense? If so, can the bankruptcy court nevertheless enjoin the IRS from doing so on the theory that the future amortization deductions are "property of the estate"? (Consider, for example, the *Prudential Lines* case, discussed at § § 508.2.4 and 1002.4.1.)

## *§1013.5 Bankruptcy Court's Broad Equitable Powers*

In furtherance of the basic objectives of the Bankruptcy Code, the bankruptcy court is empowered with broad equitable powers.[145] In general, the statutory basis for the court's equitable powers is Bankruptcy Code section 105(a), although other provisions of the Bankruptcy Code also may confer equitable authority for specific purposes. Bankruptcy Code section 105(a) provides:

> The Court may issue any order, process, or judgment that is necessary or appropriate to carry out the provisions of [the Bankruptcy Code]. No provision of [the Bankruptcy Code] shall be construed to preclude the court from, sua sponte, taking any action or making any determination necessary or appropriate to enforce or implement court orders or rules, or to prevent an abuse of process.

The bankruptcy court's equitable powers are not limitless, however.[146] The basic limitation is contained in Bankruptcy Code section 105(a) itself in that it only grants

---

144 *But consider Allis-Chalmers Corp. v. Goldberg* (*In re Hartman Material Handling Systems, Inc.*), *supra* note 29, at n.14, asserting that the burden of proof may not always differ.

145 *See generally* Collier on Bankruptcy ¶ 105 (15th ed.); Bankruptcy Service, L Ed, § § 11:63 *et seq.*

146 *See, e.g., United States v. Energy Resources*, 495 U.S. 545 (1990); *Norwest Bank Worthington v. Ahlers*, 485 U.S. 197 (1988).

the bankruptcy court the equitable power to carry out the "provisions" of the Bankruptcy Code. Thus, the bankruptcy court cannot, in order to achieve equity, issue an order contrary to the specific provisions of the Bankruptcy Code.[147]

In addition, a bankruptcy court's exercise of its equitable powers may be inappropriate if the action conflicts with a nonbankruptcy law. For example, as discussed at § 1006.3.2, most courts have refused to invoke the bankruptcy court's equitable powers to override the Anti-Injunction Act and thereby enjoin IRS assessment or collection actions against a debtor's officers for the debtor's unpaid withholding taxes under Code § 6672. In contrast, the Anti-Injunction Act frequently will not act as a bar in the case of IRS actions against the debtor itself. This is best exemplified by the automatic stay imposed by the Bankruptcy Code, which, as discussed above, enjoins any act to collect, assess (for bankruptcy cases commenced before October 22, 1994), or recover unpaid prepetition taxes.[148]

In *United States v. Energy Resources Co.*,[149] the Supreme Court acknowledged the limitations on a bankruptcy court's broad equitable powers, but, in that case, held that such limitations had not been transgressed. There, the Supreme Court held that a bankruptcy court had the authority to order the IRS to apply tax payments made pursuant to a corporate debtor's Chapter 11 plan first to outstanding trust fund taxes—thereby eliminating any personal liability of its officers under Code § 6672—if the bankruptcy court determined that such designation "is necessary to the success of a reorganization plan." Although the Bankruptcy Code does not explicitly authorize such designation, the Court found ample authority in Bankruptcy Code section 105 and in Bankruptcy Code section 1123(b)(5), which permits a reorganization plan to include "any . . . appropriate provision not inconsistent with the applicable provisions of this title."

Rejecting the IRS's arguments to the contrary, the Supreme Court observed that what the IRS really wanted was the "added protection not specified in the [Bankruptcy] Code itself" that, if the bankruptcy court was incorrect in its judgment that the reorganization plan would succeed, it might still obtain payment of the entire tax debt by having the nontrust fund liabilities paid before the trust fund liabilities (for which the officers may be personally liable). Moreover, in reaction to the IRS's assertion that such designation would undermine Code § 6672 as an alternative

---

[147] *See, e.g.*, *Raleigh v. Illinois Department of Revenue* (S. Ct.), *supra* note 128, at 1957: "[T]he scope of a bankruptcy court's equitable power must be understood in the light of the principle of bankruptcy law discussed already, that the validity of a claim is generally a function of underlying substantive law. Bankruptcy courts are not authorized in the name of equity to make wholesale substitution of underlying law controlling the validity of creditors' entitlements, but are limited to what the Bankruptcy Code itself provides."

[148] *But see, e.g.*, *In re Heritage Village Church & Missionary Fellowship, Inc.*, 851 F.2d 104, 88-2 U.S.T.C. ¶ 9476 (4th Cir. 1988) (Anti-Injunction Act prevented bankruptcy court from enjoining IRS revocation of debtor's exempt status); *IRS v. Barnard (In re Kuppin)*, 335 B.R. 675, 2006-2 U.S.T.C. ¶ 50,502 (S.D. Ohio 2005) (relying in significant part on cases involving the inapplicability of the automatic stay to nondebtors, asserts that "Congress did not intend the Bankruptcy Code to be an exception to the application of the Anti-Injunction Act"); *Krumhorn v. United States* (*In re Krumhorn*), 2002 U.S. Dist. LEXIS 17956 (N.D. Ill. 2002) (asserts, in *dicta*, that automatic stay does not override Anti-Injunction Act).

[149] *Supra* note 146, also discussed at § 1016.2.

source of collection for trust fund taxes, the Court observed that, rather than preventing the collection of trust fund taxes, the designation, in fact, required that such taxes be paid first. Accordingly, the Court found that the bankruptcy court had not transgressed any limitation on its broad powers.

As a variation on *Energy Resources*, joint debtors, faced with a partially secured and partially unsecured IRS claim for both trust fund and nontrust fund taxes, sought a court order allocating the security to the trust fund portion of the claim.[150] By so doing, the trust fund taxes would be satisfied in full, whereas the nontrust fund taxes (as nonpriority unsecured taxes) would only receive partial payment. In contrast, were the trust fund taxes unsecured, the IRS would receive full payment of all taxes since the trust fund taxes would be priority unsecured taxes. The Tenth Circuit affirmed the bankruptcy court denial of the debtors' request, distinguishing *Energy Resources*. The court observed that in *Energy Resources* all taxes were to be paid in full and that the only issue was the order in which the taxes would be paid.

In another case, the Third Circuit rejected an individual debtor's attempt to employ *Energy Resources* to compel the retroactive allocation of tax payments of a related nondebtor corporation to the payment of the corporation's unpaid trust fund taxes for which the debtor also had liability under Code § 6672.[151] The court considered of greatest relevance the fact that the corporation was, at the time of the payment, not itself in bankruptcy and thus did not have at stake its own Chapter 11 reorganization (although this seems to misdirect the focus of the inquiry as relates to the individual debtors). In addition (and, we believe, more significantly), the court stated that the IRS lacked the usual protections of a Chapter 11 reorganization to assure payment of the corporation's nontrust fund taxes (such as priority status and nondischargeability), at the time the payments were made. Although the corporation itself subsequently filed for bankruptcy and filed its own motion to compel the allocation, the court observed that the corporation had no pending plan of reorganization and that, to approve a reallocation of prepetition tax payments, would amount to an improper extension of the time applicable to preferential transfers under Bankruptcy Code section 547.

---

[150] *Bates v. United States (In re Bates)*, 974 F.2d34, 92-2 U.S.T.C. ¶ 50,582 (10th Cir. 1992); *accord In re Haas*, 162 F.3d 1087, 99-1 U.S.T.C. ¶ 50,178 (11th Cir. 1998) (similar facts); *In re Lybrand*, 2006-1 U.S.T.C. ¶ 50,217 (Bankr. W.D. Ark. 2006) (similar facts but involving postconfirmation setoff; IRS permitted to setoff against non-priority unsecured portion of its claims even though setoff would cause the debtor's plan to fail); *but see In re Moore*, 200 B.R. 687 (Bankr. D. Oregon 1996) (holding to contrary on substantially identical facts involving postconfirmation setoff; does not discuss *Bates*); *United States v. Martinez*, 2007 U.S. Dist. LEXIS 6163 (M.D. Pa. 2007) (Chapter 13 case to similar effect), *upon remand from* 2007 Bankr. LEXIS 1168 (M.D. Pa. 2007) (remanded so that bankruptcy court could explain its reasoning). *See also Small Business Admin. v. Preferred Door Co. (In re Preferred Door Co.)*, 990 F.2d 547 (10th Cir. 1993) (debtor could not reclassify postpetition interest and penalties as general unsecured claims on the basis of *Energy Resources*), *but consider* § 1015.2, discussing the possibility of subordinating tax penalties; *Kiesner v. IRS (In re Kiesner)*, 194 B.R. 452, 96-1 U.S.T.C. ¶ 50,139 (Bankr. E.D. Wis. 1996) (denied individual debtor's motion to reallocate IRS's setoff of tax overpayments first to nondischargeable trust fund taxes on the basis of *Energy Resources*). With respect to the reclassification of a partially secured IRS tax claim, *see also* IRS Litigation Guideline Memorandum GL-50, May 2, 1994, *reprinted at* 2000 TNT 91-41.

[151] *IRS v. Kaplan (In re Kaplan)*, *supra* note 58.

Other situations in which bankruptcy courts have exercised their equitable powers in furtherance of tax objectives include the following:

(1) to permanently enjoin the claiming of a worthless stock deduction by a controlling shareholder that would otherwise result in limitations upon the debtor's NOLs under Code § 382 (*see* § 1002.4);
(2) to restrict trading in claims in order to preserve the debtor's ability to maximize the postreorganization value of its NOLs under Code § 382(1)(5) (*see* § 1002.4.1);
(3) to eliminate the remedial voting rights on otherwise excludable Code § 1504(a)(4) preferred stock of a consolidated bankrupt subsidiary in order to prevent such stock from becoming voting stock and, thus, deconsolidating the subsidiary (*see* § 804.1);[152]
(4) to enforce the automatic stay and discharge provisions of the Bankruptcy Code, in appropriate cases, by finding the IRS in contempt and liable for damages (*see* § 1007.7.2);
(5) to require the IRS to consider a debtor's offer in compromise in accordance with the normal procedures and policies applicable to non-debtors (although some courts have refused to do so, *see* § 1016.1.2);
(6) to enforce the debtor's obligation to file tax returns and, in absence thereof, to find the debtor in contempt and subject to appropriate sanctions (*see* § 1006.1); and
(7) to temporarily enjoin a state court tax proceeding where the bankruptcy court reopened the debtor's Chapter 7 case to determine the dischargeability of the state taxes.[153]

Other situations in which bankruptcy courts have *refused* to exercise their equitable powers include:

(1) to abate any prepetition interest properly claimed by the IRS (*see* § 1006.1.2);
(2) to issue a postconfirmation declaratory judgment to the debtor, such as along the lines of Bankruptcy Code section 1129(d), that the principal purpose of the debtor's reorganization plan was not tax avoidance (*see* §§ 1002.8.1 and 1013.3);
(3) to alter the burden of proof with respect to tax claims from that under nonbankruptcy law (*see* § 1013.4, discussing the Supreme Court's decision in *Raleigh v. Illinois Department of Revenue*); and
(4) in most Chapter 7 and liquidating Chapter 11 cases, to designate tax payments first to the payment of trust fund taxes (*see* § 1016.2).

---

[152] The court in that case also based its authority on the principles of section 303 of the Delaware Corp. Law, which permits court ordered amendments to the capital stock of a Delaware corporation in connection with a plan of reorganization. *See In re Federated Dept. Stores, Inc.*, 1991 Bankr. LEXIS 743 (Bankr. S.D. Ohio), *aff'd*, 133 B.R. 886 (S.D. Ohio 1991).

[153] *Mass. Dept. of Rev. v. Crocker (In re Crocker)*, 362 B.R. 49 (Bankr. 1st Cir. 2007) (injunction facilitated the bankruptcy court's proper exercise of its jurisdiction).

As to whether a bankruptcy court might be willing to employ its equitable powers to extend the automatic stay to nonbankrupt members of the debtor's consolidated group, *see* the consolidated return discussion at § 1007.4. In addition, in the *Continental Airlines* bankruptcy case, Continental Airlines requested the bankruptcy court to invoke its equitable powers, in conjunction with Bankruptcy Code section 554 (which permits the abandonment of property of inconsequential value and benefit to the estate), to extinguish its interest in the worthless stock of its also bankrupt subsidiary (Eastern Air Lines) and, thus, deconsolidate the subsidiary (*see* discussion at § 804.1). Subsequently, Continental Airlines entered into a stipulation and order with Eastern Air Lines,[154] which order was appealed by the Department of Labor.[155] The appeal was later withdrawn.

It should be noted that, because appellate courts are extremely reluctant to employ equitable considerations where not previously presented and considered by the trial court, one should be careful to raise the potential application of the bankruptcy court's equitable powers in its initial papers in the bankruptcy court and to present a factual foundation for such position.[156]

## § 1014 DISCHARGEABILITY OF TAX CLAIMS

Bankruptcy Code section 1141(d) provides that a debtor corporation in a Chapter 11 case is, in general, discharged from all taxes incurred prior to the confirmation of the Chapter 11 plan that are not provided for in the Chapter 11 plan or order confirming the plan, unless the plan provides for liquidation of all or substantially all of the debtor's property and the debtor does not engage in business after the consummation of the plan.[1] As discussed below, the 2005 bankruptcy reform bill has cut back in certain limited instances on the general corporate discharge.

The discharge is generally effective upon the entry of the confirmation order, unless the Chapter 11 plan or confirmation order provide otherwise.[2] In contrast, the consummation or effective date of the Chapter 11 plan generally occurs only some time after the confirmation date, usually when the appeal period for the confirmation

---

[154] *See In re Continental Airlines, Inc.*, Ch. 11, Case Nos. 90-932 through 90-984, Stipulation and Order, dated December 26, 1991.

[155] *See* amicus curiae brief filed by the Pension Benefit Guaranty Corp. in support of Department of Labor's appeal, dated April 17, 1992.

[156] *See, e.g., Quenzer v. United States (In re Quenzer)*, 19 F.3d 163 (5th Cir. 1993) (rejected IRS position under Bankruptcy Code section 105, since not considered by lower courts, and record devoid of any factual findings justifying exercise of equitable powers).

[1] **§ 1014** *See* 11 U.S.C. § 1141(d)(3). *See also Holly's, Inc. v. City of Kentwood (In re Holly's, Inc.)*, 172 B.R. 545 (Bankr. W.D. Mich.), *appealed on other issues* (asserting that a Chapter 11 plan cannot extend such discharge to debts incurred through the effective date of the plan), and text accompanying *supra* § 1013 note 32. Although Bankruptcy Code section 1141 technically has a third requirement, namely that the debt would have been denied a discharge under Chapter 7, because corporations are not granted a discharge under Chapter 7, the third requirement is automatically satisfied. For a discussion of certain potential ramifications of deferring the date of discharge, particularly to unsecured creditors, *see* Ahart and Meadows, Deferring Discharge in Chapter 11, 70 Am. Bankr. L.J. 127 (1996).

[2] *United States v. White*, 466 F.3d 1241 (11th Cir. 2006).

order has expired or appeals have been completed. Accordingly, unless the plan or confirmation order provides that the discharge does not occur until the plan becomes effective, the creditors may substantively lose their claims if the plan is disallowed on appeal and, at the very least, the time of the discharge will become separated from the consummation of the plan. Chapter 11 plans are therefore generally drafted to align the discharge event with the effectiveness of the plan.

To satisfy Bankruptcy Code section 1141(d)'s conditions for discharge, it appears that the business continued need not be the same as that conducted by the debtor prior to the discharge. Although Bankruptcy Code section 1141(d) appears to be self-contained, for a discharge of any claim to be effective, due process (or, in the case of governmental entities, concepts of fundamental fairness) requires that proper notice be made to the holder of the claim.[3] Because the IRS should automatically receive notice of the commencement of the bankruptcy case, the bar date for filing claims, and the confirmation hearing (*see* § 1004), these due process requirements will usually be met with respect to federal tax claims.[4] However, incomplete or false notice may render the notice inadequate.[5]

Despite the breadth of its language, Bankruptcy Code section 1141(d) generally will not operate to effectively discharge liability for postpetition taxes and most prepetition taxes for which claims are filed. This is because: Bankruptcy Code section 1141(d) applies only to the extent it does not conflict with the Chapter 11 plan; Bankruptcy Code section 1129(a)(9) requires the payment of all priority claims to be provided for in the Chapter 11 plan (*see* § 1016); and all postpetition taxes (to the extent not discharged pursuant to Bankruptcy Code section 505(b)), and many prepetition taxes, are treated as priority claims (*see* § 1015). With respect to prepetition

---

[3] *See generally United States v. State Street Bank and Trust Co.* (*In re Scott Cable Comm., Inc.*), 259 B.R. 536, 543-45 (D. Conn. 2001); Bienenstock, Bankruptcy Reorganizations, at Ch. 16, nn. 304-306 (and accompanying text) (1987); *Hairopoulos v. United States*, 118 F.3d 1240, 97-2 U.S.T.C. ¶ 50,568 (8th Cir. 1997) (Chapter 13 case) (burden of establishing that creditor received appropriate notice rests with debtor; a letter properly addressed and mailed is presumed to have been delivered; however, debtor could not prove timely mailing or receipt of notice of conversion from Chapter 7 to Chapter 13, bar date or confirmation hearing).

[4] *See, e.g., In re Penn. Cent. Transp. Co.*, 771 F.2d 762 (3d Cir. 1985) (notice of claims filing procedure sufficient), *cert. denied*, 474 U.S. 1033 (1985); *Reliable Electric Co. v. Olson Constr. Co.*, 726 F.2d 620 (10th Cir. 1984) (held creditor's claim nondischargeable, since no formal notice of confirmation hearing received); *Broomall Indus., Inc. v. Data Designs Logic Systems, Inc.*, 786 F.2d 401, 406 (Fed. Cir. 1986) (actual notice of creditor does not obviate debtor's obligation to provide formal notice within the meaning of the Bankruptcy Code; in certain instances, notice by publication will suffice); *see also In re American Properties, Inc.*, 30 B.R. 247 (Bankr. D. Kan. 1983) (claim not dischargeable where known creditor did not receive formal notice of bar date). *Cf. In re Moseley*, 74 B.R. 791, 801-803 (Bankr. C.D. Cal. 1987) (Chapter 13 case; additional IRS claim was barred by confirmation order; because Chapter 13 plan specified amount to be received by IRS and was timely served on the IRS, it was irrelevant that the IRS had not received notice of the bar date for filing proofs of claim or of the first meeting of creditors).

[5] *Cf. In re Trembath*, 205 B.R. 909, 914-915, 97-2 U.S.T.C. ¶ 50,738 (Bankr. N.D. Ill. 1997) (Chapter 13 case). *Consider also Calif. Franchise Tax Bd. v. Joye*, 2007 U.S. Dist. LEXIS 24855 (N.D. Ca. 2007) (discussing principle of "fundamental fairness" and concluding that notice was inadequate where the state taxing authority was scheduled as a creditor only in a nominal amount and the debtor did not file its tax return until after the claims bar date; court observed that this was not a situation where the state could have determined the debtor's tax liability absent the tax return).

taxes, however, the plan will usually limit the debtor's liability, at most, to that contained in a properly filed (or amended) proof of claim, with the result that the debtor is effectively discharged of liability only above such amounts. In contrast, for postpetition taxes not discharged under Bankruptcy Code section 505(b), the plan will usually contain only a general statement providing for payment in full without setting a limit on liability.[6]

In a major shift in the bankruptcy policy toward corporations reorganizing in bankruptcy, the 2005 bankruptcy reform bill added new section 1141(d)(6) which, among other things, denies a corporate debtor a discharge from any tax or customs duty with respect to the debtor if the debtor either (i) made a fraudulent return or (ii) willfully attempted in any manner to evade or defeat the tax or duty.[7] This provision parallels the exception to discharge applicable to individuals under Bankruptcy Code section 523(a)(1)(C). In the case of a corporation, the corporation is, in effect, permanently burdened with a claim due to the actions of officers and/or directors who are probably no longer with the company. Historically, this has been considered counter to, and outweighed by, the bankruptcy policies favoring "fresh starts" and corporate reorganizations. In contrast, the comparable provision for individuals ensures that the responsible individual bears the repercussions of his or her own actions.

Within the individual context, the determination of what type of conduct is necessary to constitute a willful attempt to evade or defeat a tax has been subject to considerable litigation. Such cases are naturally dependent on the facts and circumstances, but generally require more than a mere willful failure to pay taxes—such as also the failure to file tax returns or an attempt to conceal income or assets.[8] It remains to be seen what type of conduct will suffice in the corporate context.

---

[6] Where, however, a confirmed plan erroneously contains no provision for postpetition, preconfirmation tax liabilities, the IRS may nevertheless be bound by the terms of the plan, assuming that prior to confirmation it had due notice and opportunity to be heard on the terms of the proposed plan but did not object. *See* discussion at § 1014.1.

[7] 11 U.S.C. § 1141(d)(6)(B), *as added by* P.L. 109-8, § 708 (2005) (effective for bankruptcy cases commenced on or after October 17, 2005). If a tax claim is nondischargeable, it is likely that any *postpetition* interest similarly will be nondischargeable. In such event, even if the postpetition interest is not an "allowable" claim under Bankruptcy Code section 502(b)(2) and thus cannot participate in any distributions under the plan, it would nevertheless be collectable from any available assets of the debtor corporation postbankruptcy. *Cf. Ward v. Board of Equalization of California (In re Artisan Woodworkers)*, 204 F.3d 888, 2000-1 U.S.T.C. ¶ 50,270 (9th Cir. 2000) (involving individual debtor in Chapter 11); *Stacy v. United States (In re Stacy)*, 249 B.R. 683, 2000-1 U.S.T.C. ¶ 50,481 (Bankr. W.D. Va. 2000) (same).

New section 1141(d)(6) also excepts from discharge any debt described in Bankruptcy Code section 523(a)(2)(A) or (B) (involving amounts obtained in a false or fraudulent manner) that is owed to a federal, state or local government, or to a person that pursued an action against the corporate debtor on the government's behalf under 31 U.S.C. § 3721 *et seq.* or any similar state statute. 11 U.S.C. § 1141(d)(6)(A). *See generally* Levin and Ranney-Marinelli, The Creeping Repeal of Chapter 11: The Significant Business Provisions of the Bankruptcy Abuse Prevention and Consumer Protection Act of 2005, 79 Am. Bankr. L.J. 603 (2005).

[8] *See, e.g., Gardner v. United States (In re Gardner)*, 360 F.3d 551, 2004-1 U.S.T.C. ¶ 50,196 (6th Cir. 2004) (denied discharge where debtor concealed his assets by using bank accounts in others' names); *United States v. Fretz (In re Fretz)*, 244 F.3d 1323, 2001-1 U.S.T.C. ¶ 50,308 (11th Cir. 2001) (denied discharge where debtor intentionally did not file his tax returns and pay his taxes); *Griffith v. United States (In re Griffith)*, 206 F.3d 1389, 2000-1 U.S.T.C. ¶ 50,317 (11th Cir.), *cert. denied*, 121 S.Ct. 73 (2000)

As in the case of the discharge granted by Bankruptcy Code section 505(b), the discharge granted by Bankruptcy Code section 1141(d) does not establish the validity of the debtor corporation's preconfirmation NOLs. The statute does not specifically address this issue. However, the legislative statements made in the House and Senate prior to enactment of the statute state that:

> [Bankruptcy Code section 1141(d)] does not prohibit a tax authority from disallowing any tax benefit claimed after the reorganization if the item originated in a deduction, credit, or other item improperly reported before the reorganization occurred.[9]

Although it may be possible to argue that the IRS may only disallow a preconfirmation NOL because of "improperly reported" deductions and credits, in contrast to "unreported" income (for which a timely proof of claim was not filed with the bankruptcy court), such a reading of the legislative history appears unduly restrictive.[10]

**EXAMPLE**

> On January 1, 1982, X Corporation, a calendar year taxpayer, filed a petition under Chapter 11. For 1981 and 1982, X Corporation's tax returns showed an NOL of $75x and $50x, respectively. For 1983, X Corporation incurred an NOL (prior to applying its NOLs from 1981 and 1982) of $10x. On January 1, 1984, the bankruptcy court confirmed X Corporation's Chapter 11 plan. Under Bankruptcy Code section 1141(d), unless otherwise provided in the Chapter 11 plan or in the order confirming the plan, X Corporation would be discharged from paying any further taxes for preconfirmation taxable years. If, subsequently, however, the IRS discov-

---

(Footnote Continued)

(denies discharge for willful attempt to evade the *payment* of taxes even if there was no attempt to evade the *assessment* of the tax), *overruling Haas v. Internal Revenue Service (In re Haas)*, 48 F.3d 1153, 95-1 U.S.T.C. ¶50,200 (11th Cir. 1995); *Tudisco v. United States (In re Tudisco)*, 183 F.3d 133, 99-2 U.S.T.C. ¶50,669 (2d Cir. 1999) (denied discharge where in addition to failing to pay and failing to file, the debtor provided his employer with a false IRS Form W-4); *Roper v. Barclay (In re Roper)*, 2003 Bankr. LEXIS 615 (Bankr. 8th Cir. 2003) (granted discharge where debtor willfully failed to pay his taxes but timely filed his returns).

[9] 124 Cong. Rec. H 11,114 (daily ed. Sept. 28, 1978) (statement of Rep. Edwards); 124 Cong. Rec. S 17,431 (daily ed. October 6, 1978) (statement of Sen. DeConcini). For a discussion of the weight to be accorded legislative statements, *see supra* § 1005 note 68.

[10] *See, e.g.*, 11 U.S.C. §§ 1141(d) (refers to a discharge of all "debts"), 101(12) ("debt" defined as liability for any "claim"), 101(5) ("claim" broadly defined as any "right to payment"). Should Bankruptcy Code section 524(a)(2) (which provides that a discharge operates as an injunction against, among other things, any act "to collect, recover or offset" any discharged debt as a personal liability) be read to preclude an offset of unreported income to reduce a preconfirmation NOL? We believe not. *Cf.* IRS Field Service Advice 200039007, June 23, 2000, *reprinted at* 2000 TNT 191-44 (involving an individual debtor; concluded that a postbankruptcy NOL could be carried back, for purposes of reducing the amount of such NOL, to a taxable year for which any tax liability was discharged).

ers that X Corporation had unreported income and had taken improper deductions in 1982 totalling $145x, it appears that the IRS could reduce X Corporation's preconfirmation NOLs to zero, but could not collect the remaining $10x deficiency, nor could it use such deficiency to reduce a postconfirmation NOL since X Corporation's liability for such tax deficiency was discharged.

In *In re Taylor*,[11] the Fifth Circuit Court of Appeals rejected an individual debtor's attempt to use its Chapter 11 plan as a vehicle to obtain a substantive tax determination that no priority tax liabilities were owing to the IRS. The debtor had included in the plan an affirmative finding that, pursuant to Bankruptcy Code section 505, it was not indebted to the IRS for any such claims. In reaching its conclusion, the court relied extensively on Fifth Circuit Chapter 13 authorities involving a secured creditor's continued secured status under circumstances where, despite the creditor having filed a proof of claim indicating its secured status, and despite the absence of any objection to the claim, the Chapter 13 plan attempted to treat the creditor as unsecured.[12] The court observed that such authorities held that the plan could not substitute for an objection to the secured claim as it did not place the creditor on proper notice of a challenge to its claim, and that therefore the creditor's lien remained valid. Following such cases, the court similarly concluded that a debtor could not use a Chapter 11 plan to circumvent the tax determination process and obviate the need to directly contest the IRS's claim.

Similarly, the Bankruptcy Appellate Panel of the Ninth Circuit rejected a debtor's attempt to include in its Chapter 11 plan a provision reducing the amount of a creditor's claim that was previously scheduled by the debtor in a fixed, undisputed amount.[13] Although the court expressly refrained from holding that a plan could never be used to object to a creditor's claim, the court held that the essence of the claims objection procedures must be complied with, including that the creditor receive specific notice (not buried in a plan provision or disclosure statement) of at least the quality of specificity as would be provided in a straightforward claim objection, and the same opportunity to litigate one-on-one. Because the claim at issue was one scheduled by the debtor, the court also observed that the debtor could have amended its schedules to list such claim as "disputed," but in such event would still have had to provide specific notice of the amendment to the creditor at which point the creditor probably would have filed an actual proof of claim.

**Postdischarge injunction.** Pursuant to Bankruptcy Code section 524(a)(2), the IRS is enjoined from taking any action to collect, recover, or offset any discharged

---

[11] *IRS v. Taylor (In re Taylor)*, 132 F.3d 256, 98-1 U.S.T.C. ¶50,130 (5th Cir. 1998), *reh'g, en banc, denied*, 140 F.3d 1040 (5th Cir. 1998).

[12] *See, e.g., Sun Finance Co. v. Howard (In re Howard)*, 972 F.2d 639 (5th Cir. 1992); *Simmons v. Savell (In re Simmons)*, 765 F.2d 547 (5th Cir. 1985).

[13] *Varela v. Dynamic Brokers, Inc. (In re Dynamic Brokers, Inc.)*, 293 B.R. 489 (Bankr. 9th Cir. 2003) (non-tax case). In the court's words: "Neither the statute nor the rules say, 'oh, by the way, we can also sandbag you by sneaking an objection into a reorganization plan and hoping you do not realize that we can use this device to circumvent the claim objection procedure mandated by the rules.'" Id. at 497.

taxes as a recourse (personal) liability of the debtor.[14] As discussed at §§1005.1 and 1007.7, where the IRS attempts to assess and collect such taxes (whether intentionally or through a clerical error), it may be held liable for damages.[15] However, as discussed at §1006.1.1.3, notwithstanding the seemingly absolute injunction imposed by Bankruptcy Code section 524(a)(2) and the general discharge of Bankruptcy Code section 1141, the courts are divided as to whether, or under what circumstances, a postconfirmation setoff of a mutual prepetition debt would be permitted. As discussed at the end of §1008, the IRS should not be precluded from assessing any tax provided for in the Chapter 11 plan for which the statute of limitations has not expired, solely for purposes of fixing such liability in its records consistent with the plan.

The IRS is also not precluded from invoking appropriate remedies to collect any taxes provided for in the plan as to which the debtor has subsequently defaulted in payment (*see* §1002.9 above). Moreover, notwithstanding that the Chapter 11 plan provides for installment payments in full satisfaction of the debtor corporation's obligation for unpaid withholding taxes and timely payment is being made under the plan, most courts have held that the IRS is not precluded (prior to obtaining full recovery) from asserting the Code §6672 100-percent penalty against the corporate officers.[16]

---

[14] *But see* IRS Legal Memorandum 200150007, September 5, 2001 *reprinted at* 2001 TNT 242-32 (concluding that the reinstatement of an IRS lien that self-releases does not violate the postdischarge injunction, but noting that the IRS's priority status relative to competing liens cannot be reinstated); *Global Sales Corp v. United States*, discussed *infra* note 17. *See also In re Weichman*, 2002-1 U.S.T.C. ¶50,256 (Bankr. N.D. Ill. 2001) (IRS's delay in releasing tax liens following payment of tax claim did not violate postdischarge injunction because IRS did not commit an affirmative act to collect).

[15] *See* Code §7433(e) (discussed at §1007.7.1), allowing damages for willful violations of postdischarge injunction occurring after July 22, 1998 in connection with the collection of federal tax. With respect to violations occurring on or before July 22, 1998, *see, e.g., Hardy v. United States*, 97 F.3d 1384 (11th Cir. 1996); *In re Torres*, 309 B.R. 643, 2002-1 U.S.T.C. ¶50,268 (Bankr. D. P.R. 2002), *aff'd in part and rev'd in part*, 309 B.R. 643 (Bankr. 1st Cir. 2004), *rev'd in part*, 432 F.3d 20, 2006-1 U.S.T.C. ¶50,112 (1st Cir. 2005); *In re Moulton*, discussed *supra* §1005 note 31, and text accompanying §1005 notes 47-49; *Global Sales Corp. v. United States*, Case No.5a 85-00147 JB, Adv. No.SA91-3511 JB (Bankr. C.D. Cal. May 8, 1992). For pre-*Nordic Village* cases, *see, e.g., In re McCullough*, 86-2 U.S.T.C. ¶9584 (Bankr. E.D. Pa.); *Conti v. United States*, 50 B.R. 142, 85-2 U.S.T.C. ¶9497 (Bankr. E.D. Va. 1985); *Bryant v. United States* (*In re Bryant*), 1991 U.S. Dist LEXIS 13093 (D. Kan.); *Kolb v. United States* (*In re Kolb*), 137 B.R. 29, 92-1 U.S.T.C. ¶50,255 (N.D. Ill. 1992); *In re Kiker*, 98 B.R. 103 (Bankr. N.D. Ga. 1988) (collecting cases).

[16] *See* cases cited *supra* §1006 notes 221-224 and accompanying text; *see also Smith v. United States*, 894 F.2d 1549, 90-1 U.S.T.C. ¶50,134 (11th Cir. 1990) (officer of bankrupt company liable for full amount of unpaid withholding taxes, even though IRS agreed to partial payment under company's Chapter 11 plan); *Skouras v. United States*, 93-2 U.S.T.C. ¶50,380 (S.D.N.Y.), *aff'd*, 26 F.3d 13 (2d Cir. 1994) (to similar effect); *United States v. Davel*, 669 F. Supp. 924, 87-2 U.S.T.C. ¶9462 (D. Wis. 1987) (receipt of the president's personal note in satisfaction of bankrupt corporation's obligation for unpaid withholding taxes pursuant to a Chapter 11 plan did not preclude IRS from asserting the Code §6672 penalty against the president—in addition to asserting its contractual rights under the note—when the note went into default).

*But consider Ramette v. United States* (*In re Bame*), 279 B.R. 833 (Bankr. 8th Cir. 2002) (bankruptcy court requires IRS and state taxing authorities, as holders of claims secured by liens on property, to first proceed against such property before participating in any distributions from the estate); *In re Jukel*, Case No. 99-13833 (JHW) (D. N.J. July 23, 2002), *reprinted at* 2002 TNT 162-22 (letter opinion; an individual debtor sought to have the employment withholding taxes of a related corporation paid out

**Extinguishment of tax liens.** Bankruptcy Code section 1141(c) provides that postconfirmation, except in those cases where the debtor would be denied a discharge, or unless the Chapter 11 plan or confirmation order provides otherwise, "*the property dealt with by the plan* is free and clear of all *claims and interests* of creditors [and] equity security holders . . . " (emphasis added). Thus, it would seem, and most courts (including circuit courts of appeals) have held, that a lien, which Bankruptcy Code section 101(37) defines as a "charge against or *interest in property* to secure payment of a debt or performance of an obligation" (emphasis added), generally will be extinguished upon confirmation of the Chapter 11 plan absent a contrary provision in the plan or order.[17] This conclusion has also been justified on the practical grounds that the plan process would be greatly complicated were a debtor required to challenge each and every lien prior to submitting a plan.[18] In addition, in *Johnson v. Home State Bank,* the Supreme Court held that, for purposes of the Bankruptcy Code, a "claim" includes a mortgage lien.[19]

Although a number of cases decided prior to *Johnson* held otherwise and concluded that, absent a contrary provision in the plan or order,[20] a previously perfected lien will survive the bankruptcy case (even if the debtor's recourse liability is

(Footnote Continued)

of her bankruptcy estate in view of her liability as a responsible person; initially the bankruptcy court agreed and enjoined the IRS from taking any collection actions against the corporate taxpayer for such taxes; subsequently however, the bankruptcy court determined that, due to the failure of the IRS to file a claim in the bankruptcy, the bankruptcy estate was precluded from paying such taxes).

17 *See, e.g., Universal Suppliers, Inc. v. Regional Building Systems, Inc. (In re Regional Building Systems, Inc.)*, 254 F.3d 528 (4th Cir. 2001); *In re Penrod*, 50 F.3d 459 (7th Cir. 1995), discussed *infra* in this section; *FDIC v. Union Entities (In re Be-Mac Transport Co.)*, 83 F.3d 1020 (8th Cir. 1996) (follows Seventh Circuit decision in *Penrod*); *American Bank and Trust Co. v. Jardine Ins. Serv. Texas, Inc. (In re Barton Indus., Inc.)*, 104 F.3d 1241 (10th Cir. 1997) (same); *In re Hurricane R.V. Park, Inc.*, 185 B.R. 610 (Bankr. D. Utah 1995); *Board of County Commissioners of Saline County, Kansas v. Coleman American Properties, Inc. (In re American Properties, Inc.)*, 30 B.R. 239 (Bankr. D. Kan. 1983); *In re Eagle Bus Mfg., Inc.*, Case No. 90-00985-B-11, Adv. Pro. 93-2157-B (Bankr. S.D. Tex. August 10, 1994) (also discusses the concept of property "dealt with" by the plan); *see also In re Henderberg*, 108 B.R. 407 (Bankr. N.D.N.Y. 1989) (discussing contrary authorities). *Consider also Global Sales Corp. v. United States, supra* note 15 ("self-releasing language" in liens did not operate as a release where confirmed plan provided for continuation of the lien until full payment was made); *Gen. Elec. Capital Corp. v. Dial Business Forms, Inc. (In re Dial Business Forms, Inc.)*, 341 F.3d 738 (8th Cir. 2003) (priority of competing liens established in a confirmed Chapter 11 plan remains valid despite later lapse of the creditors' financing statements under state law).

18 *See, e.g., Minstar, Inc. v. Plastech Research, Inc. (In re Arctic Enterprises, Inc.)*, 68 B.R. 71 (D. Minn. 1986).

19 111 S. Ct. 2150 (1991). *Accord 680 Fifth Ave. Assocs. v. Mutual Benefit Life Ins. Co. (In re 680 Fifth Ave. Assocs.)*, 29 F.3d 95 (2d Cir. 1994). In *Johnson*, the issue was whether a mortgage lien that passed through a prior Chapter 7 bankruptcy unaffected (although the individual debtor's personal liability was discharged) was a claim subject to inclusion in a subsequent Chapter 13 reorganization plan. The Court held it was.

20 In this regard, several courts have held that a Chapter 11 plan that classifies an otherwise secured claim as either an "unsecured" or "priority" claim (which, by its nature, is an unsecured claim, *see* § 1015) also operates to extinguish the creditor's lien, absent a timely objection to the plan (and assuming due notice of the confirmation hearing). *See, e.g., In re Henderberg, supra* note 17; *cf. In re Rankin*, 141 B.R. 315 (Bankr. W.D. Tex. 1992) (debtor was judicially estopped from denying proper classification due to prior representations made to the court at the confirmation hearing and relied on by the taxing authorities).

discharged), such decisions are questionable and arguably in error.[21] And so the Seventh Circuit, in *In re Penrod*,[22] has specifically held. Nevertheless, the Seventh Circuit also stated in *dicta*—and has since been followed by the Eighth and Tenth Circuits—that, where the plan and order are silent as to the treatment of a secured creditor's lien, the lien will only be extinguished if the creditor has participated in the bankruptcy case.

In the Seventh Circuit's view, unless the creditor participated in the bankruptcy, its lien would not be "property dealt with by the plan" within the meaning of Bankruptcy Code section 1141(c) and thus not extinguished. According to the court, such participation could include, for example, the filing of a proof of claim (which the creditor in that case had done), a motion to lift the automatic stay or even a proof of claim filed on its behalf by the debtor or another creditor pursuant to Bankruptcy Code section 501(c).[23] This presents a strained reading of Bankruptcy Code section 1141(c). A more natural reading of that section (which the Seventh Circuit acknowledged, but dismissed) would be to read the word "property" as referring only to property of the estate. It is the estate's property, not the creditor's lien, which is to be "free and clear of all claims and interests of creditors [and]equity security holders." This is consistent with the legislative history.[24] This would suggest that it should make no difference whether the secured creditor participated in the bankruptcy case (although the creditor must still have received proper notice, as discussed earlier in this section). No similar distinction was drawn by the Fourth Circuit in *In re Regional Building Systems, Inc.*,[25] which has since also concluded that a creditor's lien not expressly provided for in a Chapter 11 plan or confirmation order is extinguished.

Although *Regional Building Systems* also involved a creditor that actively participated in the plan, the Fourth Circuit focused extensively on the phrase "property dealt with by the plan" in distinguishing its earlier, seemingly contrary holding in the

---

[21] *See, e.g., Relihan v. Exchange Bank*, 69 B.R. 122 (S.D. Ga. 1985) (concluding that a "claim" is distinct from a "lien," each having its own separate definition, and that it would be "odd" for Congress to have used the undefined term "interest" to mean "lien" when it could have used the defined term and avoided uncertainty); *Dillard v. United States*, 118 B.R. 89 (Bankr. N.D. Ill. 1990) (no discussion of Bankruptcy Code section 1141). Much of the confusion in the case law arises due to Bankruptcy Code section 506(d), which generally precludes the avoidance of perfected liens regardless of whether a proof of claim is filed. *See supra* § 1010 note 13.

For a comprehensive discussion of the lien survival doctrine and the extinguishment of tax liens in bankruptcy, *see* Richards, Property Taxes in Bankruptcy: Section 546(b), Section 506(c) and Lien Survival, J. Bankr. L. and Prac. 277, 302-316 (1993).

[22] *Supra* note 17, at 463.

[23] *But see Sterling Packaging Corp. v. Systec Corp.* (*In re Sterling Packaging Corp.*), 265 B.R. 701 (Bankr. W.D. Pa. 2001), distinguishing *In re Penrod* where the secured creditor's claim remained in dispute at the time that the plan was confirmed, and as a result, the plan was also silent as to the treatment of the creditor's claim. The court also could not determine how the plan dealt with the property that was the subject of the creditor's lien and thus concluded that it did not deal with it.

[24] *See* H. Rep. No. 595, 95th Cong., 1st Sess. 418 (1977) (" . . . the confirmation of a plan vests all of the *property of the estate* in the debtor and releases it from all claims and interests of creditors, equity security holders and general partners"; emphasis supplied); S. Rep. No. 989, 95th Cong., 2d Sess. 129 (1978) (same).

[25] *Universal Suppliers, Inc. v. Regional Building Systems, Inc.* (*In re Regional Building Systems, Inc.*), *supra* note 17.

Chapter 13 context. In the Chapter 13 context, the Fourth Circuit had held that the initiation of an adversary proceeding is a necessary prerequisite to modifying or extinguishing a lien and cannot be circumvented by the confirmation process.[26] The court emphasized that, unlike the focus of Bankruptcy Code section 1141(c) on cleansing the estate's property dealt with under the plan, Bankruptcy Code section 1327(c) provides, in general, only that any property vesting in the debtor shall be free and clear of "any claim or interest of any creditor provided for" by the plan. This difference in focus, the court explained, was entirely consistent with the type of certainty necessary in the more complicated reorganizations governed by Chapter 11, from the perspective of both current creditors (who are being asked to vote on the plan) and prospective lenders (who would be faced with the risk of unidentified parties asserting liens against postconfirmation assets).

Even if a court were to accept the Seventh Circuit's proposition, however, it may be possible to draft the plan to ensure that a nonparticipating creditor's lien is extinguished. For example, in *In re Winchell*,[27] it was sufficient that the plan and order expressly provide that, upon confirmation, "all property of the estate" shall vest in the debtor free and clear of all claims, liens and encumbrances.

## *§1014.1 IRS Bound by Chapter 11 Plan and Confirmation Order*

Unless one of the exceptions to the general discharge provision of Bankruptcy Code section 1141(d) discussed above applies, the IRS (like any other creditor) is generally bound by the terms of the debtor corporation's Chapter 11 plan and the order confirming the plan.[28] The following are a few examples.[29] For a discussion of the potential *res judicata*/collateral estoppel effects of confirmation on the IRS's later

---

[26] *Cen-Pen Corporation v. Hanson*, 58 F.3d 89 (4th Cir. 1995) (2:1 decision); *see also Deutchman v. Internal Revenue (In re Deutchman)*, 192 F.3d 457, 99-2 U.S.T.C. ¶50,852 (4th Cir. 1999) (adhering to *Cen-Pen Corp.*). *Accord In re Taylor* (5th Cir.), *supra* note 11.

[27] *Winchell v. Town of Wilmington*, 200 B.R. 734 (Bankr. D. Mass. 1996). *But consider In re Be-Mac Transport Co.* (8th Cir.), *supra* note 17 (wherein the bankruptcy court had, prior to confirmation, wrongly disallowed the FDIC's secured claim without first considering the validity of the lien).

[28] 11 U.S.C. §1141(a). *See, e.g., Miller v. United States*, 363 F.3d 999, 2005-1 U.S.T.C. ¶50,252 (9th Cir. 2004) (but holding that a plan that is ambiguous as to a material term may be interpreted by a reviewing court); *In re Penn-Dixie Indus., Inc.*, 32 B.R. 173 (Bankr. S.D.N.Y. 1983); *In re Henderberg* (Bankr. N.D.N.Y.), *supra* note 17, at 411 (collecting cases); *United States v. Victor*, 121 F.3d 1383, 97-2 U.S.T.C. ¶50,539 (10th Cir. 1997); *G.E. Capital Corp. v. General Business Forms, Inc. (In re General Business Forms, Inc.)*, 273 B.R. 594 (Bankr. 8th Cir. 2002) (lien subordination language in plan controlled over state law priorities); *cf. In re Pardee*, 193 F.3d 1083 (9th Cir. 1999) (Chapter 13 case); *United States v. Richman (In re Talbot)*, 124 F.3d 1201, 97-2 U.S.T.C. ¶50,624 (10th Cir. 1997) (Chapter 13 case). *See also Corbett v. Macdonald Moving Services, Inc.*, 124 F.3d 82 (2d Cir. 1997) (not involving governmental entity, but discusses *res judicata* effect of plan; terms of plan operated to discharge parent of debtor from any multi-employer pension plan "withdrawal liability" over and above that specifically provided for in the Chapter 11 plan).

[29] *See also Martin v. United States (In re Martin)*, 150 B.R. 43 (Bankr. S.D. Cal. 1993) (IRS bound by agreed procedures set forth in plan for resolving open tax years), *appeal dismissed as moot*, (S.D. Cal. June 7, 1994), *reprinted at* 94 TNT 132-12; *In re River City Hotel Corp.*, 191 B.R. 371 (Bankr. E.D. Tenn. 1995) (shareholder could not revoke debtor's S corporation status where the creditor's confirmed plan assumed the sale of assets by an S corporation, as the debtor's own disclosure statement for its

ability to challenge the postconfirmation use of the debtor's tax benefits under Code § 269, *see* § § 1002.8 and 1013.3.1.

**Noncompliance with payment provisions of Bankruptcy Code.** In *In re St. Louis Contracting Company,*[30] the bankruptcy court confirmed a plan that contained no provision for postpetition, preconfirmation tax liabilities. Although the IRS had received notice of the terms of the proposed plan and disclosure statement, it did not attend the hearing on the plan or otherwise object. Nor did it attend or object at the confirmation hearing. Although the IRS claimed that it did not receive notice of the confirmation hearing, there was ample evidence to support the fact that the debtor had, consistent with its normal practice, sent a notice to the IRS. Accordingly, the court concluded that the IRS could not now (182 days after the entry of the confirmation order) object to the plan, even though the confirmation order was not in compliance with the applicable provisions of the Bankruptcy Code. The court stressed the importance of finality in corporate reorganizations, particularly where, as here, the plan entailed a third-party infusion of capital. The court added however, that a bankruptcy court could revoke a confirmation order procured by fraud if requested by a party in interest before 180 days after the entry of the order (*see* § 1002.9).

Similarly, in *In re St. Louis Freight Lines, Inc.,*[31] the court confirmed a Chapter 11 plan that provided that all postpetition, preconfirmation employment withholding taxes and the employer's related portion of such taxes would be paid (exclusive of interest and penalties) in cash within 60 days of confirmation of the plan. The IRS, subsequent to confirmation of the plan, argued that it was entitled to receive the interest and penalties on such taxes, as well as the taxes themselves. The court concluded that, although the IRS was theoretically entitled to such interest and penalties as a priority claim, the IRS was bound by the terms of the plan as confirmed. It was irrelevant that the plan ultimately provided the IRS with less than that to which it was otherwise legally entitled.[32]

---

(Footnote Continued)

competing plan acknowledged; also, in light of the shareholder's prior conduct and agreements in the case, shareholder was held estopped from attempting to revoke the S election).

Similarly, debtors must also beware the binding effect of the plan and confirmation order in dealing with filed tax claims. *See, e.g., Puckett v. United States,* 99-2 U.S.T.C. ¶ 50,637 (S.D. Tex. 1999), *aff'd,* 213 F.3d 636, 2000-1 U.S.T.C. ¶ 50,439 (4th Cir. 2000), *cert. denied* 121 S. Ct. 759 (2001), discussed at § 1012.2 above.

[30] 1990 U.S. Dist. LEXIS 822; *see also Custom Arc Mfg., Inc. v. United States* (*In re Custom Arc Mfg., Inc.*), 125 B.R. 843 (Bankr. M.D. Fla. 1991) (IRS bound by plan that did not provide for interest on IRS claim, even though claim asserted that postpetition interest "may be payable"; IRS did not raise issue until two years after confirmation); *Burrell v. Marion, Mass.* (*In re Burrell*), 2006 Bankr. LEXIS 1344 (Bankr. 1st Cir. 2006) (Chapter 13 case; Town bound by confirmed plan that treated its secured claim as a priority unsecured claim, without entitlement to postpetition interest due to the Town's failure to timely claim such interest). *But consider In re Escobedo,* 28 F.3d 34 (7th Cir. 1994) (held that a Chapter 13 plan that did not include mandatory provisions providing for full payment of priority claims was invalid and not *res judicata* as to the omitted claims).

[31] 45 B.R. 546 (Bankr. E.D. Mich. 1984).

[32] It may also be asserted that, by failing to object to confirmation of the plan, the IRS implicitly accepted the lesser payment provided by the plan. *Cf. United States v. LaForgia* (*In re LaForgia*), 1999 Bankr. LEXIS 563 (Bankr. M.D. Pa. 1999) (Chapter 13 case) (so held, based on the right of a priority

Not all courts have been so accepting, however, instead viewing such a provision as an improper attempt to reduce the amount of a creditor's claim without the specificity of notice and opportunity to be heard provided for objections to claims under the Bankruptcy Rules.[33]

In addition, the fact that a plan provides for postconfirmation sales and does not provide for the payment of tax on such sales will not bind the IRS. As discussed at § 1013.3, the Supreme Court in the *Holywell* case, on essentially these facts, stated that, even if the plan binds creditors as to claims that arose before confirmation, "we do not see how it can bind the United States or any other creditor with respect to postconfirmation claims," noting that the Bankruptcy Code definition of "creditor" for this purpose spoke in terms of preconfirmation claims.[34] In contrast, the Fourth Circuit, in *State of Maryland v. Antonelli Creditors' Liquidating Trust*,[35] viewed as distinguishable the situation where the plan expressly provides that certain postconfirmation claims or sales shall be exempt from transfer tax (rather than remaining silent), and has more than a frivolous basis for the position.

One bankruptcy court had the following caution for creditors, debtors and debtors' counsel:[36]

> As a preliminary matter, this Court finds the intentional insertion of a plan provision that bypasses clear and unambiguous language of the Bankruptcy Code and controlling case law is unacceptable, and poten-

(Footnote Continued)

creditor, under Bankruptcy Code section 1322(a)(2), to agree to a different treatment of its claim); and *see* 11 U.S.C. § 1129(a)(9) (similarly permits a priority creditor, in the context of a Chapter 11 plan, to agree to a treatment of its claim different than that otherwise required). *But see In re Luarks*, 301 B.R. 352, 2003-2 U.S.T.C. ¶ 50,646 (Bankr. D. Kan. 2003) (Chapter 13 case; effectively rejecting such position in the case of priority tax claims, at least in the case of individual debtors where such claims are supposed to be nondischargeable).

[33] *See, e.g., United States v. Smith(In re Smith)*, 142 B.R. 862 (Bankr. E.D. Ark. 1992) (Chapter 13 case), *quoting Fireman's Fund Mortgage Corp. v. Hobdy (In re Hobdy)*, 130 B.R. 318, 321 (Bankr. 9th Cir. 1991): "We do not believe the need for finality of confirmed plans extends to circumstances present in this case: where a debtor misuses, whether or not intentionally, the plan confirmation process to reduce a valid claim without the requisite notice and opportunity to be heard [under Bankruptcy Rules 3007 and 9014, with respect to objections to claims]."

[34] *See also United States v. State Street Bank and Trust Co.* (Bankr. D. Del.), *infra* note 44 (citing the *Holywell* case for this proposition). The Supreme Court cited as comparative support for this latter proposition the definition of "claim" in Bankruptcy Code section 101(10), which other courts have pointed out generally encompasses only *prepetition* claims. *See, e.g., Dycoal Inc. v. IRS (In re Dycoal Inc.)*, 327 B.R. 220, 2005-2 U.S.T.C. ¶ 50,554 (Bankr. W.D. Pa. 2005), *aff'd*, 2006 U.S. Dist. LEXIS 25078 (W.D. Pa. 2006), discussed later in this section.

[35] 123 F.3d 777 (4th Cir. 1997), *citing Celotex Corp. v. Edwards*, 115 S. Ct. 1493, 1501 (1995). The *Antonelli Creditors'* case is discussed further at § 1102.15 below.

[36] *In re Luarks* (Bankr. D. Kan.), *supra* note 32, at 360 (citations omitted) (Chapter 13 case; although the IRS had received notice of the confirmed plan and did not object to or appeal confirmation, the court held inapplicable a footnote in the plan that treated a portion of the IRS's priority tax claims as unsecured claims; among the reasons given were (1) the relative promptness in which the issue was raised after confirmation, (2) the ability to redress the IRS's harm without impairing the debtor's fresh start, (3) the fact that the claims were priority claims entitled to payment in full under the Bankruptcy Code and nondischargeable, and (4) the ambiguous nature of the plan treatment under the circumstances).

> tially sanctionable . . . . This Court must rely on the fact that counsel appearing before it are officers of the Court and are ethically obligated to inform the Court if they are aware of the existence of a plan provision that renders the plan nonconfirmable . . . .
>
> Finally this Court would be remiss . . . not to warn creditors that they may not fail to take an active role to protect their claims, then later complain that plan provisions were inconsistent with the Code . . . . The possibility that a debtor's counsel could be sanctioned for the inclusion of improper plan provisions will be little recompense for the discharge of the creditor's debt for failing to protect its rights by a timely objection.

**Late claim.** In *In re International Horizons, Inc.*,[37] the debtor corporations filed voluntary petitions for reorganization under Chapter 11 on March 20, 1981. The "bar date" for filing all proofs of claims was set as August 31, 1981, and the IRS was sent timely notice. In May and June of 1981, the IRS filed proofs of claims for employment withholding taxes totalling approximately $69,000. Although on October 15, 1980, before the debtor corporations filed in bankruptcy, an audit conference had been held between the IRS and one of the debtor corporations regarding the corporation's 1974 and 1975 tax returns, no proof of claim for federal income taxes was filed prior to the bar date nor was there any indication that a proof of claim would be filed. On December 28, 1981, which was after the bar date, the IRS issued a statutory notice of deficiency for corporate income taxes of approximately $15,250,000, but still filed no proof of claim.

On January 22, 1982, the debtor corporations filed a disclosure statement indicating that they would "vigorously" contest the asserted deficiency and that all unfiled claims as of the bar date should be discharged without payment. On November 2, 1982, the IRS amended its prior proof of claim, adding a claim for federal income taxes for 1974 and 1975 in excess of $20,000,000. The IRS, however, did not object to the Chapter 11 plan (even though it was "[a]ware that debtors' plan was unviable should its claims prevail"), and, on December 15, 1982, the plan was confirmed.

In March 1983, the debtor corporations filed an objection to the IRS's amended proof of claim and moved for summary judgment, which was granted. The IRS on appeal put forward several arguments, all of which the Eleventh Circuit rejected. The Eleventh Circuit held that the amended proof of claim for federal income taxes was in actuality a new claim, not merely an amendment to the original claim for employment withholding taxes, and therefore concluded that the filing of the claim for federal income taxes was time-barred. The Eleventh Circuit rejected the IRS's argument that the filing of the amended claim for federal income taxes was merely a method of perfecting an informal proof of claim. The court said that mere notice of a potential claim is insufficient. The statutory notice of deficiency (which arguably could suffice) was not received until after the bar date. The IRS argued that the debtor corporations had waived their right to object to the claim when they allowed the plan

---

[37] 751 F.2d 1213, 85-1 U.S.T.C. ¶9212 (11th Cir. 1985). *See generally* discussion of post-bar date amendments and late claims at § 1010.2 above.

to be confirmed without objection. The Eleventh Circuit rejected this argument as well, since the plan disclosed that only timely filed claims would be paid.

**Upgrading unsecured debt to secured debt.** In *In re Scott Cable Communications, Inc.*,[38] the debtor was in bankruptcy for the second time. At the time of its first bankruptcy case, the debtor had both unsecured public debentures and unsecured subordinated notes, totalling approximately $94 million. Pursuant to the Chapter 11 plan in that case, the holders of the public debentures and subordinated notes collectively received cash, new secured PIK notes and 99 percent of the common stock of the reorganized company. The notes and stock were shared in different proportions. The new secured notes had an original principal amount of approximately $39 million with interest at the rate of 16 percent per annum (payable semi-annually in additional notes), and a security interest in all of the reorganized company's assets.

The plan contemplated the likelihood of a sale of the company's assets within approximately three years, with the belief that, given a reasonable period of time to market the company, the value of its assets could be maximized for the benefit of its creditors. The disclosure statement accompanying the plan stated that there was no assurance that a sale would generate sufficient value to pay the new secured notes or any taxes resulting from the sale (which could be substantial), and that it may be necessary at such time to again file for bankruptcy. As contemplated, the debtor, approximately 18 months later, entered into an agreement to sell substantially all of its assets, and in connection therewith, filed a second bankruptcy case along with a prepackaged liquidating Chapter 11 plan.

The debtor estimated that taxes from the sale of its assets would be approximately $37 million. Recognizing that the taxes would be an administrative expense of the bankruptcy if incurred during the Chapter 11 case and thus entitled to payment in full under a Chapter 11 plan with insufficient assets left over to pay the secured notes,[39] the debtor proposed to close the sale postconfirmation and took the position that the resulting taxes were not administrative expenses that had to be provided for under the plan. In the debtor's view, such taxes would be a nonbankruptcy liability of the liquidating company payable only to the extent of any assets remaining after completion of all distributions in accordance with the Chapter 11 plan, which would be none. The IRS objected, and in a separate decision, the bankruptcy court held that the taxes would still qualify as administrative expenses and that the proposed liquidating plan was nonconfirmable.[40] The debtor therefore proceeded with the sale in bankruptcy, with the expectation that the case would be converted from Chapter 11 to Chapter 7. Under Chapter 7, holders of secured debt are generally entitled to be

---

[38] *United States v. State Street Bank and Trust Co. (In re Scott Cable Comm., Inc.)*, 232 B.R. 558, 99-1 U.S.T.C. ¶50,513 (Bankr. D. Conn. 1999), *rev'd*, 259 B.R. 536 (D. Conn. 2000); and Disclosure Statement, dated August 17, 1998, for the Prepackaged Liquidating Chapter 11 Plan for Scott Cable Communications, Inc., Case No. 98-51923.

[39] *See* 11 U.S.C. § 1129(a)(9)(A).

[40] *See In re Scott Cable Comm., Inc.*, 227 B.R. 596, 600, 99-1 U.S.T.C. ¶50,288 (Bankr. D. Conn. 1998) (also held that the plan was nonconfirmable because the principal purpose of the plan was tax avoidance), discussed at § 1002.8.1 above.

paid first out of the proceeds of their collateral, even if the debtor would be left with insufficient assets to pay its administrative expenses.[41] Accordingly, the IRS sought to equitably subordinate the new secured notes or otherwise characterize them as equity.

Initially, the bankruptcy court held that the IRS's challenge was barred, under the doctrine of *res judicata*, by the confirmation order in the debtor's prior bankruptcy case. Although the IRS did not file a proof of claim in that case, it did request and receive a copy of the disclosure statement and plan, which specifically disclosed the possibility of a later sale and the possibility that any sales proceeds might be insufficient to satisfy the new secured notes as well as any resulting tax liability. Accordingly, the court held that the IRS had adequate notice and opportunity to raise any objections to the prior plan and, in view of the potential pecuniary harm to the IRS, had standing in the prior case to object to the secured status being granted the previously unsecured claims. Thus, the IRS could have sought a court order subordinating the new secured notes to any tax liability incurred upon a sale of the assets. Having failed to do so then, the bankruptcy court stated that it could not do so now.

On appeal, the district court reversed, concluding that in the prior bankruptcy case the IRS did not receive notice reasonably calculated, under the circumstances, to inform it that its rights might be modified by the plan. The court observed that the IRS, even though sophisticated, was entitled to assume that it would receive full and fair disclosure. In the court's view, there was nothing in the prior plan or disclosure statement which would have raised a "red flag" or suggested to the IRS (particularly since the IRS was not then a creditor) that the note holders' position would be improved relative to claims by the IRS or that the IRS's pecuniary interest could be adversely affected.[42] The court also took note that the debtor had in large print cautioned that there was no assurance that the IRS would not challenge any or all of the tax consequences of the plan.[43] For similar reasons, the bankruptcy court on remand denied a summary judgment motion by the trustee for the note holders which asserted that the confirmation order in the prior bankruptcy case was final and could not be challenged by the IRS.[44]

---

41 *See* H. Rep. No. 595, 95th Cong., 1st Sess. 382-383 (1977) (explaining operation of Bankruptcy Code section 725); S. Rep. No. 989, 95th Cong., 2d Sess. 96 (1978) (same). This is also true outside of bankruptcy. *See* discussion of 31 U.S.C. § 3713, at § 1017 below.

42 *Contrast United States v. Sterling Consulting Corp. (In re Indian Motorcycle Co. Inc.)*, 289 B.R. 269, 2003-1 U.S.T.C. ¶ 50,210 (Bankr. 1st Cir. 2003) (involving an IRS challenge to a previously approved settlement agreement between the debtor and a third party under somewhat analogous, but not so egregious, circumstances; court entertained the IRS's challenge but upheld the settlement agreement in such instance).

43 On remand, the bankruptcy court (located in Connecticut) transferred venue over further proceedings in this matter to the Delaware district court which presided over the debtor's first bankruptcy case, viewing such court as the more appropriate forum to interpret and apply the prior plan. *United States v. State Street Bank and Trust Co. (In re Scott Cable Comm., Inc.)*, 263 B.R. 6 (Bankr. D. Conn. 2001). *See also United States v. State Street Bank and Trust Co. (In re Scott Cable Comm., Inc.)*, 2002 Bankr. LEXIS 183 (Bankr. D. Del. 2002) (allowing debtor to intervene in the Delaware proceeding between the IRS and the note holders).

44 *United States v. State Street Bank and Trust Co.*, 303 B.R. 35 (Bankr. D. Del. 2003).

**Findings of fact in confirmation order.** In *In re Dycoal Inc.,*[45] the debtor corporation and several affiliated entities sought *unsuccessfully* to bind the IRS to certain factual findings in the bankruptcy court's order confirming the debtor's Chapter 11 plan. The confirmation order had included findings of fact that purported to establish all factual predicates necessary to a determination that synthetic fuel produced by entities in which the debtor and its affiliates had ownership interests generated preconfirmation Code § 29 tax credits. Several years following confirmation, the debtor filed an adversary action in the bankruptcy court seeking to enforce the confirmation order as against the IRS (even though no pre- or postconfirmation tax return had as yet been filed utilizing such credits[46]).

Citing the Supreme Court's decision in *Holywell,* discussed briefly above in this section, and other cases, the bankruptcy court explained that, as relates to the tax matter in question, the IRS was not a party-in-interest as to whom the confirmed plan and confirmation order is binding under Bankruptcy Code section 1141(a) (such as creditors in respect of prepetition claims).[47] The bankruptcy court acknowledged that the confirmed plan and confirmation order could also be binding against a third party who appears and participates in a litigation dealt with by the plan or order (or possibly is in privity with such a person) so as to make such person a party to the order and bound by the doctrine of *res judicata,* but that was clearly not the situation in question. And the district court so affirmed.[48]

The district court also rejected the debtor's assertion that the feasibility of the debtor's Chapter 11 plan was dependent upon the availability of the Code § 29 tax credits and thus that the IRS was bound by certain findings of fact in the bankruptcy court's confirmation order relating to such credits, concluding that such a determination "is neither required [on the facts] nor appropriate under" Bankruptcy Code section 1129(a)(11) (the feasibility condition for plan confirmation) or 1142(a) (implementation of the plan by the reorganized debtor).

**Subsequent dismissal of case.** Even if the Chapter 11 case is later dismissed,[49] the plan may have a lasting effect. For example, in *In re Compco Corp.,*[50] the debtor's plan had been confirmed and substantially fulfilled. Due to unexpected financial difficulties, however, the debtor failed to make (nor could it make in the future) the required payments to the Illinois Department of Revenue in respect of its priority claim. Based on the grounds that the debtor's failure constituted a material default

---

[45] *Dycoal Inc. v. IRS (In re Dycoal Inc.)*, 327 B.R. 220, 2005-2 U.S.T.C. ¶ 50,554 (Bankr. W.D. Pa. 2005), *aff'd*, 2006 U.S. Dist. LEXIS 25078 (W.D. Pa. 2006). Involving facets of the same issue, *see* the discussion of *Allis Chalmers Corp. v. Goldberg (In re Hartman Material Handling Systems, Inc.)*, 141 B.R. 802, 92-2 U.S.T.C. ¶ 50,325 (Bankr. S.D. N.Y. 1992), at §§ 1002.8.1 and 1013.3.1 above.

[46] The bankruptcy court partially, although not exclusively, relied on this fact in rejecting the debtor's alternative request for a declaratory judgment under Bankruptcy Code section 505(a) that it qualified for the tax credit (*see* § 1013.3.1 above).

[47] The bankruptcy court relied heavily on *In re Union Golf of Florida, Inc.*, 242 B.R. 51 (Bankr. M.D. Fla. 1998), and the decisions cited therein.

[48] 2006 U.S. Dist. LEXIS 25078 (W.D. Pa. 2006).

[49] *See* § 1002.9 above.

[50] 1990 Bankr. LEXIS 38 (Bankr. N.D. Ill.).

with respect to the plan, the Department of Revenue moved to convert the case (to Chapter 7) or dismiss the case pursuant to Bankruptcy Code section 1112(b)(8).

The court concluded that the dismissal of the debtor's Chapter 11 case was appropriate. The court found that the plain language of Bankruptcy Code section 1112(b)(8) contemplates that the bankruptcy court has jurisdiction to convert or dismiss a Chapter 11 case even after confirmation of a plan in the event of a material default; and that Bankruptcy Rule 3020(d) (permitting postconfirmation orders necessary to administer the estate) clearly contemplates the continued jurisdiction of the bankruptcy court following confirmation, whether or not the plan so provides. Moreover, the court easily concluded that the debtor's failure constituted a material default: "It would make no sense that a plan must provide for full payment [of priority claims] in order to be confirmed but a failure to carry through such a required term of the plan does not constitute a material default."[51]

The court also considered the debtor's concern that, pursuant to Bankruptcy Code sections 348 and 349, the effect of a dismissal (or conversion) would be to undo all transactions undertaken in reliance on the confirmed plan and ultimately concluded that it had "the plenary power to craft the order of dismissal in such a way that the legitimate expectations of parties under the Plan would be protected." In this regard, the court stated that:

> Other courts dealing with the question of the continued validity of plan transactions upon conversion or dismissal have interpreted the relevant Code Sections as not undoing the effect of transactions consummated pursuant to a confirmed plan. . . . The rule fashioned by these courts is that transactions entered into in reliance upon a confirmed plan will not be undone upon conversion or dismissal; the effect of confirmation is seen to be an irrevocable determination of the rights of the parties affected by the plan.
>
> Furthermore, the provisions of Bankruptcy Code § 348 [for conversions] and § 349 [for dismissals] give the bankruptcy court sufficient leeway to provide appropriate relief to protect vested expectations flowing from the confirmation of the plan. Both § 348(b) and § 349(b) are prefaced by the language "unless the court, for cause, orders otherwise."[52]

---

[51] In contrast, the court distinguished the situation where unsecured creditors were to receive 50 cents per dollar of claim under the plan, but ultimately receive only 10 cents. In that case, the court stated, the plan would still have been confirmable had the plan only provided for a 10 cent payment in the first place.

[52] To similar effect, H. Rep. No. 595, 95th Cong., 1st Sess. 337-38 (1977); S. Rep. No. 989, 95th Cong., 2d Sess. 48-9 (1978). *See, e.g., United States v. Standard State Bank*, 91 B.R. 874 (D. Mo. 1988) (dismissal of Chapter 11 case and confirmed plan only given prospective effect; accordingly, IRS lien was not reinstated), *aff'd on other grounds*, 905 F.2d 185 (8th Cir. 1990); *Amer. Bank and Trust Co. v. United States (In re Barton Indus., Inc.)*, 159 B.R. 954 (Bankr. W.D. Okla. 1993) (to same effect), *appealed on other issues*; *Twin City Pipe Trade Service Assn. v. IRS (In re Burner Services & Combustion Control Co.)*, 1992 U.S. Dist. LEXIS 12259 (D. Minn.) (to same effect); *In re Lopez Development, Inc.*, 154 B.R. 607 (Bankr. S.D. Fla. 1993) (subsequent dismissal did not undo transfer tax exemption under then Bankruptcy Code section 1146(c), now section 1146(a), for properties already sold pursuant to the confirmed plan); *In re Depew*, 115 B.R. 965, 970 (Bankr. N.D. Ind. 1989). *Cf. Schwab v. United States (In re Shop N' Go*

However, the basic purpose of Bankruptcy Code section 349, and thus the general effect of dismissal, is to undo the bankruptcy case, as far as practicable.[53] Accordingly, not all aspects of the plan may be preserved.[54]

## §1014.2 *Consolidated Returns*

Where the Chapter 11 debtor files a consolidated return with solvent, non-Chapter 11 corporations, the discharge of the debtor's tax liability may be but an empty victory. Under the consolidated return regulations, the common parent and each subsidiary that was a member of the consolidated group for any part of the

(Footnote Continued)

*Partnership*), 261 B.R. 810 (Bankr. M.D. Pa. 2001) (a settlement agreement with the IRS that was entered into in connection with the confirmation of the Chapter 11 plan was not undone by the subsequent conversion of bankruptcy case to Chapter 7). *See also* IRS Legal Memorandum 199924006, March 12, 1999 (discussing the IRS's ability to reapply tax payments received in the context of a dismissed Chapter 13 case, as between trust fund and non-trust fund taxes), *reprinted at* 1999 TNT 118-79.

In addition, despite a dismissal of a bankruptcy case, most courts (including several Circuit Courts) have upheld continuing bankruptcy court jurisdiction over related proceedings, based on fairness and judicial economy. *See, e.g., Fidelity & Deposit Co. of Maryland v. Morris* (*In re Morris*), 950 F.2d 1531, 1534 (11th Cir. 1992) (decision to retain jurisdiction is "left to the sound discretion of the bankruptcy court or the district court, depending upon where the adversary proceeding is pending"; collecting cases); *In re Statistical Tabulating Corp., Inc.*, 60 F.3d 1286 (7th Cir. 1995), *cert. denied*, 116 S. Ct. 815 (1996) (dismissal of bankruptcy case could not deprive the district court of jurisdiction over an appeal arising from an earlier bankruptcy court order regarding the priority of competing liens, nor could the bankruptcy court refuse jurisdiction on remand, since the matter arose out of the underlying bankruptcy proceeding itself rather than a separate adversary proceeding, and the issue was not mooted by the dismissal of the bankruptcy case); *Kieslich v. United States* (*In re Kieslich*), 258 F.3d 968 (9th Cir. 2001) (*per curiam*) (unpublished decision; government considered to waive challenge to bankruptcy court's retention of jurisdiction since it never objected to such retention before the bankruptcy court), *rev'g*, 243 B.R. 871 (D. Nev. 1999) (held that the bankruptcy court abused its discretion in retaining jurisdiction of a related proceeding and vacated the bankruptcy court's decision; although the proceeding had been pending for two years at the time the bankruptcy case was dismissed, only limited discovery had been conducted by the parties; the fact that the bankruptcy court had since rendered a decision on the merits was of no importance; however, the fact that it took the bankruptcy court four years to do so strengthened the districts court's view that (i) a more expedient resolution of the matter would have been achieved, with no unfairness to the parties and only minimal inconvenience, had the bankruptcy court not retained jurisdiction, and (ii) the bankruptcy court should have realized as much); *Smith v. Commercial Banking Corp.* (*In re Smith*), 866 F.2d 576, 579-580 (3d Cir. 1989); *In re Boch*, 1997 Bankr. LEXIS 1896 (Bankr. M.D. Pa. 1997); *Tankson v. Yao, Ltd.* (*In re Tankson*), 1992 Bankr. LEXIS 275 (Bankr. N.D. Ill. 1992); *Florida Peach Corp. v. Commissioner*, 90 T.C. 678 (1988).

[53] H. Rep. No. 595, 95th Cong., 1st Sess. 337-338 (1977); S. Rep. No. 989, 95th Cong., 2d Sess. 48-9 (1978).

[54] *Compare In re Southern California College of Chiropractic* (Bankr. C.D. Cal. Nov. 20, 1992), *reprinted at* 93 TNT 15-19 (despite subsequent dismissal of confirmed Chapter 11 case, no interest was allowed on the IRS's tax claim for the period of the bankruptcy); *with In re Whitmore*, 154 B.R. 314 (Bankr. D. Nev. 1993) (Chapter 13 case permitting interest in a similar situation; court's holding purports to rest on the court's interpretation of Bankruptcy Code section 349(b), and not necessarily on the fact that, in the case of an individual debtor, postpetition interest on a nondischargeable tax claim continues to accrue against the debtor personally).

consolidated return year is severally liable for the group's tax liability.[55] This liability is unaffected by agreements among the members of the group.[56] Accordingly, even though one member of the group has received a discharge in bankruptcy, the non-Chapter 11 members may remain liable for the group's entire tax liability with respect to the taxable years for which the bankrupt member was discharged. Although it may be argued that the group's tax liability should be reduced by that portion allocable to the bankrupt member, we can find no support for such position. In fact, the authorities support the contrary position.[57]

As a further wrinkle, does postpetition interest continue to accrue while one member of the group is in bankruptcy? The answer appears to be yes, even though as to the bankrupt member such postpetition interest generally would be a disallowed claim and, therefore, discharged.[58]

Accordingly, where a consolidated return group consists both of bankrupt and nonbankrupt companies, careful consideration should be given to bringing the solvent companies into the bankruptcy. Upon confirmation, the outstanding tax liability (probably reduced due to the additional assets now available in the bankruptcy) would then be discharged as to the entire group.

## *§1014.3 Tax Court Generally Cannot Determine Dischargeability*

The Tax Court lacks the requisite subject matter jurisdiction in deficiency proceedings to determine whether tax claims were discharged under the Bankruptcy

---

[55] Reg. §1.1502-6(a).

[56] Reg. §1.1502-6(c).

[57] *See, e.g.*, 11 U.S.C. §524(e) ("discharge of a debt of the debtor does not affect the liability of any other entity on, or the property of any other entity for, such debt," other than as to certain community property; derived from section 16 of the prior Bankruptcy Act); *cf.* 11 U.S.C. §509 (generally allows subrogation claim by guarantors, sureties and persons jointly and severally liable with the debtor to be filed in the bankruptcy to the extent of any payment made to the creditor; no relief, however, is granted as against the creditor); Bankruptcy Rule 3005(a) (permitting a claim by persons subrogated under Bankruptcy Code section 509 to be filed prior to making payment in certain instances where the creditor has failed to file). *See also* National Bankruptcy Review Commission Final Report (October 20, 1997), Recommendation 2.4.13 ("Release of Claims Against Nondebtor Parties"), at pp. 534-540.

[58] *See, e.g.*, *Metro Commercial Real Estate, Inc. v. Antonio Reale*, 968 F. Supp. 1005 (E.D. Pa. 1997) (general partner remained liable for postpetition interest on prepetition obligation of bankrupt partnership, even though, under Bankruptcy Code section 502(b)(2), such interest was not an allowable claim as against the partnership), *aff'd without op.*, 156 F.3d 1225 (3d Cir. 1998); *Household Finance Corp. v. Hansberry*, 20 B.R. 870 (Bankr. S.D. Ohio 1982) (Chapter 13 case; nondebtor cosignatory liable for postpetition interest). *But see El Paso Ref. v. IRS*, 205 B.R. 497, 97-1 U.S.T.C. ¶50,386 (W.D. Tex. 1996) (holding directly contrary to *Metro Commercial* on similar facts), *rev'g* 192 B.R. 144 (Bankr. W.D. Tex. 1996); *also consider Aetna Business Credit, Inc. v. Hart Ski Mfg. Co., Inc.*, 7 B.R. 465 (Bankr. D. Minn. 1980) (holding that a guarantor is not liable for postpetition interest that was not an allowable claim in the debtor's bankruptcy).

Code.[59] Accordingly, in *Neilson v. Commissioner*,[60] the Tax Court held that it could not decide whether the proposed deficiencies had been *discharged* in the bankruptcy case, but that it could decide the *merits* of the proposed deficiencies (*see* § 1009).[61] However, the Tax Court does have the requisite jurisdiction to determine the dischargeability of a tax claim in connection with an appeal of a collection due process determination by the IRS under Code § 6330(d), whether involving a taxpayer's right to a hearing after the filing of a tax lien (Code § 6320) or before the IRS proceeds with the collection of taxes by levy (Code § 6330).[62] In addition, if after the bankruptcy case is closed, the debtor desires a determination of whether a particular tax claim was discharged in the bankruptcy, the debtor can still file a complaint with the bankruptcy court (as well as any appropriate nonbankruptcy forum, *e.g.*, a district court).[63] Though, according to the district court in *Somma v. United States*,[64] such a determination must await at least the issuance of a statutory notice of deficiency; a notice of proposed deficiency (*i.e.*, the issuance of a "30-day" letter) will not suffice.

---

[59] *Neilson v. Commissioner*, 94 T.C. 1 (1990); *Terrell v. Commissioner*, 59 T.C.M. 1020, Dec. 46,681(M), T.C. Memo. 1990-323; *see also Graham v. Commissioner*, 75 T.C. 389, Dec. 48,988(M) (1980) (Bankruptcy Act case); *Deason v. Commissioner*, 35 T.C.M. 978, Dec. 33,930(M), T.C. Memo. 1976-224, *aff'd*, 590 F.2d 1377, 79-1 U.S.T.C. ¶ 9269 (5th Cir. 1979). But consider *In re Cassidy*, 892 F.2d 637, 90-1 U.S.T.C. ¶ 50,023 (7th Cir. 1990), *cert. denied* (taxpayer barred by doctrine of "judicial estoppel" from relitigating issue of dischargeability of his tax debts after Court of Appeals determined that such debts were not dischargeable; this was so even though the issue was first raised on appeal and the Tax Court below had no jurisdiction to consider the issue).

[60] *Supra* note 59.

[61] *See also* IRS Field Service Advice 1999-565 (undated) (advised that pending Tax Court proceeding should be brought to conclusion on the merits, even though underlying tax liability had been discharged; recommended use of a stipulated decision reflecting entire amount of pre-discharged iability), *reprinted at* 1999 TNT 20-110; IRS Field Service Advice 200007013, February 18, 2000, *reprinted at* 2000 TNT 35-51 (concluded that the taxpayers' prior discharge was still effective, even though the taxpayers' thereafter pursued to final judgment a previously commenced Tax Court proceeding, including a subsequent appeal and remand).

[62] *See Washington v. Commissioner*, 120 T.C. 114 (2003) (involving a lien proceeding); *Swanson v. Commissioner*, 121 T.C. 111 (2003) (involving the collection of taxes by levy); *Richardson v. Commissioner*, T.C. Memo 2003-154 (same); IRS Legal Memorandum 200213007, November 28, 2001, *reprinted at* 2002 TNT 62-49 (involving the collection of taxes by levy). In contrast, the Tax Court cannot review a taxpayer's substantive tax liability as part of a Code § 6330(d) proceeding, unless the taxpayer did not receive a statutory notice of deficiency or otherwise have an opportunity to dispute its tax liability. Code § 6330(c)(2); *see, e.g., Kendricks v. Commissioner*, 124 T.C. 69 (2005) (taxpayer had prior opportunity to dispute its tax liability where the IRS filed a proof of claim in the taxpayer's earlier bankruptcy case); *Sabath v. Commissioner*, T.C. Memo. 2005-222 (same).

[63] *See* Bankruptcy Rule 4007(a), (b), and accompanying Advisory Committee Notes, reprinted at Collier Pamphlet Edition, Bankruptcy Rules 240 (1998 version); *see also* 11 U.S.C. § 350(b), discussed at § 1002.9; *In re Wheadon* (Bankr. D. Minn.), discussed at § 1013.1; *In re Becker's Motor Transportation, Inc.*, 632 F.2d 242, 81-1 U.S.T.C. ¶ 9348 (3d Cir. 1981), *cert. denied*, 450 U.S. 916 (1981) (Bankruptcy Act case); *cf. In re Workman*, 90-1 U.S.T.C. ¶ 50,197 (Bankr. S.D. W. Va.).

[64] 93-1 U.S.T.C. ¶ 50,120 (N.D. Ohio 1993).

## §1015 PRIORITY OF TAX CLAIMS

In general, unsecured tax claims are granted a priority status in bankruptcy.[1] The effect of priority status is twofold. First, it entitles the holder to assurances of full payment prior to the time lower priority or nonpriority unsecured claims are paid. Second, payment of unsecured claims above the eighth priority must generally be made in cash on the effective date of the Chapter 11 plan.[2] Moreover, tax claims treated as first priority, or after the 2005 bankruptcy reform changes, second priority, administrative expense claims—which, particularly after the 2005 changes, includes secured claims as well as unsecured claims—generally have to be paid on a current basis during the bankruptcy case to the extent incurred in the ordinary course of business (*see* §1010.4 above). Within each priority, distributions under a plan generally must be made pro rata.[3] Unsecured claims not accorded a priority generally are referred to as "general unsecured claims."

Of course, valid perfected liens generally will have priority over unsecured claims in respect of the property they encumber, at least in Chapter 11 cases.[4] In

---

[1] **§1015** A "tax" for this purpose may include charges not ordinarily viewed in terms of a tax. *See, e.g., LTV Steel Co., Inc. v. Shalala (In re Chateaugay Corp.)*, 53 F.3d 478 (2d Cir. 1995) (held premiums due under the Coal Industry Retiree Health Benefit Act were "taxes"); *In re Leckie Smokeless Coal Company*, 99 F.3d 573 (4th Cir. 1996) (same), *cert. denied*, 117 S. Ct. 1251 (1997); *United Mine Workers of America 1992 Benefit Plan v. Rushton (In re Sunnyside Coal Company)*, 146 F.3d 1273 (10th Cir. 1998) (same).

[2] *See* §1016; 11 U.S.C. §1129(a)(9).

[3] *Missouri v. Ross*, 299 U.S. 72 (1936); *see, e.g.*, 11 U.S.C. §726(b); *In re Duby*, 98 B.R. 126 (Bankr. D.R.I. 1989); *see also Bishop v. United States (In re Leonard)*, 132 B.R. 226 (Bankr. D. Conn. 1991) (holding that Bankruptcy Code section 726(b), which requires pro rata payment among claims of the same priority, did not require that a creditor who receives payment in respect of multiple claims apply the payments received pro rata among such claims).

[4] *See United States v. Ron Pair Enterprises, Inc.*, 109 S. Ct. 1026 (1989), discussed in §301 at note 2, holding that Bankruptcy Code section 506(b) permits postpetition interest on oversecured tax claims (but not fees, costs, or other charges). In addition, it has been held that Bankruptcy Code section 506(b) does not permit secured status for any postpetition accrual of "penalties" on oversecured tax claims. *See In re Parr Meadow Racing Assn., Inc.*, 880 F.2d 1540 (2d Cir. 1989), *cert. denied*, 110 S. Ct. 869 (1990); *In re Pointer*, 952 F.2d 82 (5th Cir. 1992); *In re Brentwood Outpatient, Ltd.*, 43 F.3d 256 (6th Cir. 1994), *cert. denied*, 115 S. Ct. 1824 (1995); *see also* IRS Chief Counsel Advice 199945042, August 2, 1999, *reprinted at* 1999 TNT 219-66. Due to a statutory change in 2005, however, this is no longer the case for state tax claims in bankruptcy cases commenced on or after October 17, 2005; in these cases, any reasonable fees, costs or other charges (including penalties) accruing postpetition under a state statute with respect to a tax claim are also permitted secured status. No such Bankruptcy Code impediment existed, however, with respect to the inclusion of prepetition penalties in a taxing authority's secured claim. *See, e.g., In re Nunez*, 317 B.R. 666 (Bankr. E.D. Pa. 2004); *Aguilar v. United States (In re Aguilar)*, 312 B.R. 394 (D. Ariz. 2003) (prepetition interest and penalties properly included in secured claim); *Murphy v. IRS (In re Murphy)*, 279 B.R. 163 (Bankr. M.D. Pa. 2002). For a discussion of the IRS's litigation stance with respect to the reclassification of a partially secured IRS tax claim, *see* IRS Litigation Guideline Memorandum GL-50, May 2, 1994, *reprinted at* 2000 TNT 91-41. For a varied priority accorded secured tax claims in Chapter 7 cases, *see* 11 U.S.C. §724(b), discussed briefly at §1005.4 note 101.

For a discussion of tax liens in and out of bankruptcy, *see* Elliot, Federal Tax Collections, Liens and Levies (1995 with Supp.); Saltzman, IRS Practice and Procedure, Chapters 14-15 (Rev. Second Edition); St. James, Federal Tax Liens—Making Bankruptcy Attractive to Creditors, 46 Bus. Law. 157 (1990).

contrast, many unperfected liens (including an unperfected IRS tax lien, *see* § 1005.4) and even certain perfected liens may be voided pursuant to Bankruptcy Code section 544 or 545. In addition, pursuant to Bankruptcy Code section 506(c), a debtor-in-possession may recover from property securing a claim the reasonable and necessary costs and expenses of preserving or disposing of such property, to the extent of any benefit to the secured creditor.[5] This provision may work both for and against the IRS. For example, in one case, an IRS recovery on a secured claim was reduced by a share of the litigating costs incurred in preserving its collateral.[6] On the other hand, in another case, the payment of postpetition employment taxes was upheld as an appropriate charge against a recovery by a third-party lender who stood to realize significantly more from the sale of the collateral (a business) as a going concern than as a liquidation of assets.[7]

## *§ 1015.1 Unsecured Priority Tax Claims*

### § 1015.1.1 Administrative Expense Tax Claims

Traditionally, claims that constituted administrative expenses of the bankruptcy estate were called "first priority" claims, because they ranked first in the hierarchy of claims under section 507(a) of the Bankruptcy Code. Although as part of the 2005 bankruptcy reform changes, effective for bankruptcy cases commenced on or after October 17, 2005, administrative expense claims have been lowered to a second priority behind domestic support obligations (such as child support), this change has no practical significance in corporate bankruptcies absent very unusual circumstances.

Administrative expense claims expressly include:

(1) unless specifically designated an eighth priority claim under Bankruptcy Code section 507(a)(8), any claim for taxes (including employment taxes)

---

[5] The Supreme Court, in *Hartford Underwriters Insurance Co. v. Union Planters Bank, N.A.*, 120 S. Ct. 1942 (2000), held that another creditor does not have standing to bring an action under Bankruptcy Code section 506(c) where any recovery would belong solely to the creditor. A footnote in the Court's opinion, however, specifically left open the possibility that a creditor might bring a derivative claim in the name of the debtor-in-possession (or bankruptcy trustee) for the benefit of the estate as a whole, such that any recovery would be distributed by the estate in accordance with normal Bankruptcy Code priorities. 102 S. Ct. at 1951 n.5. For a more detailed discussion of Bankruptcy Code section 506(c), *see* Carlson, Surcharge and Standing: Bankruptcy Code Section 506(c) *After Hartford Underwriters*, 76 Am. Bankr. L. J. 43 (2002).

As part of the 2005 bankruptcy reforms, Congress sought to clarify that the payment of *ad valorem* property taxes was a proper surcharge under Bankruptcy Code section 506(c), and thus would always satisfy the benefits test. However, the actual change is somewhat ambiguous on the latter point. *See* P.L. 109-8, § 712(d)(2) (2005).

[6] *See In re Council* (Bankr. E.D. Cal.), *vacated and remanded on other grounds*, 1991 Bankr. LEXIS 1327 (Bankr. 9th Cir. 1991).

[7] *See United States v. Boatmen's First Natl. Bank of Kansas City*, 5 F.3d 1157 (8th Cir. 1993) (IRS permitted to recover postpetition payroll taxes, interest and penalties; *but see supra* note 5, discussing recent limits on direct action by creditors, such as the IRS).

incurred by the estate during the bankruptcy case (*i.e.*, postpetition taxes), or for any penalties, fines, and additions to tax related to such tax;[8] and

(2) any claim attributable to an excess allowance of a quickie refund (or tentative carryback adjustment), which allowance was made after the filing of the bankruptcy petition.[9]

More generically, administrative expense claims include the actual, necessary costs and expenses of preserving the debtor's estate. However, the administrative expense treatment of the above tax claims is expressly provided for regardless of the benefit or detriment to the bankruptcy estate.[10] Most (but not all) courts have held that a claim for interest on postpetition taxes, although not specifically enumerated in the statute, is also granted administrative expense status.[11]

Thus, a corporate debtor's postpetition taxes generally will be administrative expenses of the estate.[12] Whether a tax is "incurred" postpetition is principally a

---

[8] 11 U.S.C. §507(a)(1); 11 U.S.C. §503(b)(1)(B)(i) and (C) (no specific mention of interest); *United States v. Friendship College, Inc.*, 737 F.2d 430, 84-2 U.S.T.C. ¶9629 (4th Cir. 1984) (withholding taxes on postpetition wages, and related interest and penalties, are first priority administrative expense claims); 124 Cong. Rec. H 11,112 (daily ed. September 28, 1978) (statement of Rep. Edwards) (withholding taxes on postpetition wages granted first priority), S 17,428 (daily ed. October 6, 1978) (statement of Sen. DeConcini); *see also Official Creditors Committee v. Tuchinsky (In re Major Dynamics, Inc.)*, 897 F.2d 433, 90-1 U.S.T.C. ¶50,317 (9th Cir. 1990) (holding that no Code §7501 trust is created with respect to postpetition withholding taxes and that distribution of the withheld funds are subject to the priorities set out in the Bankruptcy Code); *In re Mariner Enters. of Pensacola, Inc.*, 173 B.R. 771 (Bankr. N.D. Fla. 1994) (unpaid postpetition withholding entitled to administrative expense status).

[9] 11 U.S.C. §507(a)(1); 11 U.S.C. §503(b)(1)(B)(ii).

[10] In *United States v. Chris-Marine, U.S.A., Inc. (In re Chris-Marine, U.S.A., Inc.)*, 321 B.R. 63 (M.D. Fla. 2004), the United States unsuccessfully argued for an expansion of administrative expense treatment under Bankruptcy Code section 503(b) to encompass the continued accrual of a "coercive fine" imposed pre-bankruptcy for the failure to produce documents sought by the IRS where "policy considerations" so dictate, based on the Eleventh Circuit's decision in *Alabama Surface Mining Comm. v. N.P. Mining Co., Inc.*, 963 F.2d 1449, 1455 (11th Cir. 1992) (involving the continued accrual of a per diem fine relating to surface mining).

[11] *See* discussion at §1015.1.5. However, where the Chapter 11 case is subsequently converted to a Chapter 7 liquidation, interest and penalties on taxes incurred during the Chapter 11 case no longer accrue and postconversion expenses have priority. *See* 11 U.S.C. §726(b), *and In re Sun Cliffe, Inc.*, 143 B.R. 789 (Bankr. D. Colo.), *citing Nicholas v. United States*, 384 U.S. 678 (1966). Moreover, some courts have relegated any interest accruing during the preconversion Chapter 11 period to a fifth priority under Bankruptcy Code section 726(a)(5), although most courts have not. *Compare Rupp v. United States (In re Rocky Mountain Refractories)*, 208 B.R. 709, 97-2 U.S.T.C. ¶50,579 (Bankr. 10th Cir. 1997) (no change in priority), *United States v. Cranshaw (In re Allied Mechanical Serv., Inc.)*, 885 F.2d 837, 89-2 U.S.T.C. ¶9578 (11th Cir. 1989) (same); *United States v. Ledlin (In re Mark Anthony Constr., Inc.)*, 886 F.2d 1101, 89-2 U.S.T.C. ¶9550 (9th Cir. 1989) (same), *with In re Hospitality Assoc. of Laurel*, 212 B.R. 188, 97-2 U.S.T.C. ¶50,716 (Bankr. D.N.H. 1997) (fifth priority). A similar conflict exists with respect to postconversion interest, *i.e.*, postpetition interest on administrative expenses incurred during the Chapter 7 case. *See, e.g., United States v. Yellin (In re Weinstein)*, 272 F.3d 39, 2002-1 U.S.T.C. ¶50,111 (1st Cir. 2001) (first priority), *rev'g*, 251 B.R. 174 (Bankr. 1st Cir. 2000), *aff'g*, 237 B.R. 4 (Bankr. D. Mass. 1999) (both lower courts had said fifth priority).

[12] In certain circumstances, depending on the provisions of the Chapter 11 plan and confirmation order, even postconfirmation taxes may be considered administrative expenses. *See, e.g., In re Scott Cable Communications, Inc.*, 227 B.R. 596 (Bankr. D. Conn. 1998) ("Memorandum and Order on Objection to Confirmation"), discussed at §§1002.8, 1011 and 1014.1 above (held that administrative

function of when the events giving rise to the tax occurred, rather than when the tax is payable.[13] For example, an income tax for a taxable year ending before the bankruptcy filing is not an administrative expense, even though the due date is after the filing. As discussed below, such a tax is specifically accorded an eighth priority. Also potentially affecting the priority of a tax liability is whether the debtor's liability for such tax is a direct or secondary liability.[14]

It should be observed that a penalty "relating to a tax of a kind [that constitutes an administrative expense]" is itself entitled to administrative expense treatment. This implicitly excludes penalties that relate to conduct—such as the Code § 6700 penalty for promoting abusive tax shelters[15] and the "minimum funding tax" under Code § 4971 that is treated as penalty for bankruptcy purposes[16]—as well as penalties relating to the filing of many (but possibly not all) information statements. By contrast, a penalty arising under Code § 6656 due to a debtor's failure to make its tax deposit electronically (although timely paid by check) was held to be related to the tax and hence an administrative expense.[17] The court, in that case, stated that

---

(Footnote Continued)

expense period would include a postconfirmation sale of substantially all of the debtor's assets that was approved preconfirmation and an integral part of the debtor's plan of liquidation).

[13] *See, e.g.*, 124 Cong. Rec. H 11,112 (daily ed. September 28, 1978) (statement of Rep. Edwards), S 17,428 (daily ed. October 6, 1978) (statement of Sen. DeConcini); *In re Overly-Hautz Co.*, 57 B.R. 932, 937 (Bankr. N.D. Ohio 1986) (involving prepetition excise taxes under Code § 4971), *appealed on other issues, citing United States v. Redmond*, 36 B.R. 932 (D. Kan. 1984); and the discussion below.

[14] *See* discussion of *Imperial Corporation case, infra* at text accompanying notes 36-39. In addition, the district court in *In re Grothues* held that a corporate tax liability asserted against an individual debtor based on an alter ego or nominee theory was not a claim for the underlying tax, since the debtor was not directly liable for such taxes, but was only an equitable claim for the amount owed. Thus, the IRS's claim for such taxes was not considered by the district court a priority "tax" claim under Bankruptcy Code section 507(a)(8). The Fifth Circuit reversed, however, observing that an alter ego theory is just one of several ways to pierce the corporate veil under state law, and thus concluding that a finding of alter ego does not alter the IRS's underlying claim for unpaid taxes. *Grothues v. IRS (In re Grothues)*, 226 F.3d 334 (5th Cir. 2000), *rev'g*, 245 B.R. 828 (W.D. Tex. 1999). On the other hand, a debtor-in-possession's liability under Code § 6672 for unpaid withholding taxes of another person that became payable during the bankruptcy case may not be considered to be "incurred by the estate" and thus an administrative expense. *Cf. In re Rainey*, 257 B.R. 792 (Bankr. W.D. Va. 2001) (involving the liability of an individual debtor's bankruptcy estate for corporate sales and use taxes under a state "responsible person" statute).

[15] *See* IRS Litigation Guideline Memorandum GL-36, April 24, 1998, *reprinted at* 2000 TNT 91-33.

[16] *See In re Unitcast, Inc.*, 214 B.R. 1010, 98-1 U.S.T.C. ¶ 50,109 (Bankr. N.D. Ohio 1997), *aff'd*, 219 B.R. 741, 98-1 U.S.T.C. ¶ 50,294 (Bankr. 6th Cir. 1998) (a Code § 4971 minimum funding *tax* that was incurred postpetition but which for bankruptcy purposes is viewed as a "penalty," was not entitled to administrative priority because the penalty did not relate to a tax incurred by the estate; the court cited both the plain language of the statute, as well as the fact that the minimum funding deficiencies giving rise to the penalty predominantly occurred prepetition); IRS Chief Counsel Advice 200005001, October 13, 1999, *reprinted at* 2000 TNT 25-55 (Issue 4, to same effect; however, in Issues 1 and 2, the IRS concluded that, unlike the Code § 4971 minimum funding tax, the Code § 4980 excise tax on pension plan reversions should be respected as a "tax," and not viewed as a "penalty," for priority purposes—*see* authorities at note 53 below—and that the status of the tax as an administrative expense should depend solely on when the reversion occurs, not the period over which the earnings accumulated tax-free).

[17] *United States v. Servint Corp. (In re Servint Corp.)*, 298 B.R. 579, 2003-2 U.S.T.C. ¶ 50,643 (Bankr. E.D. Va. 2003).

"[g]enerally, a penalty relates to a tax when it is assessed in connection with the failure of the taxpayer to pay the tax in the time or manner or at the place required by law."[18] Moreover, it is the IRS's position that a penalty—such as the Code § 4971 minimum funding tax, mentioned above—may independent of the above relationship test still obtain administrative priority if it can be shown that the penalty is an actual and necessary cost of preserving the estate.[19] In the case of the Code § 4971 minimum funding tax, the IRS's argument is that the debtor-in-possession has a continuing obligation to operate its business in accordance with federal pension laws, and that any penalty incurred for failing to do so is (to coin a phrase) necessarily attendant to that obligation.

There is conflicting case law as to whether administrative expense claims in bankruptcy cases commenced before October 17, 2005, include secured, as well as unsecured, tax claims (*see* § 1016 note 3 below). However, for subsequent bankruptcy cases, both secured and unsecured claims will qualify for administrative expense treatment.[20]

Pursuant to Bankruptcy Code section 554, a bankruptcy trustee (or debtor-in-possession) may "abandon" any property of the estate back to the debtor that is burdensome, or of inconsequential value and benefit, to the estate after notice and a hearing. In the case of a corporation, this presents somewhat of a metaphysical result since the estate and the debtor are a single taxpayer for income tax purposes. Maybe for this reason, cases involving abandonments by debtor corporations or their trustee are rare. Nevertheless, one such abandonment occurred in *In re Mailman Steam Carpet Cleaning, Inc.*[21] At issue in that case was whether the property taxes incurred with respect to the abandoned property following the conversion of the bankruptcy case to Chapter 7 but before the property was abandoned were an administrative expense of the bankruptcy estate. The bankruptcy court held they were, since the trustee had control of the property during that period and provided no reasonable explanation for having waited two years to abandon the property. None of the property taxes following the abandonment, however, would be considered incurred by the estate and thus administrative expenses. Nor would it seem that any such taxes would be valid claims against the bankruptcy estate. However, any unpaid tax presumably would continue to be a nondischarged liability of the corporate entity, and thus could have continuing significance to a reorganizing debtor.

**Year of filing.** Of practical significance in most bankruptcies is the proper priority to be accorded income taxes for the year of the bankruptcy filing, where all or

---

[18] Id. at 581.

[19] IRS Chief Counsel Notice CC-2006-007, dated December 22, 2005, *reprinted at* 2005 TNT 247-10 (relying on various non-tax cases involving state environmental laws and federal labor laws). *But see In re Unitcast, Inc.* (Bankr. 6th Cir.), *supra* note 16 ("Penalties that relate to a tax of a type [entitled to administrative priority] are the only penalties given administrative priority by the Bankruptcy Code").

[20] 11 U.S.C. §§ 503(b)(1)(B)(i), *as amended by* P.L. 109-8, § 712(b) (2005); in conjunction with 11 U.S.C. § 507(a)(1).

[21] *Mailman Steam Carpet Cleaning, Inc. v. Salem* (*In re Mailman Steam Carpet Cleaning, Inc.*), 256 B.R. 240 (Bankr. D. Mass. 2000).

part of the tax is attributable to the prepetition portion of the year. Should the entire tax be considered an administrative expense, given that the tax depends on the entire year's activities and is not determinable until the end of the year? Or should the tax liability be allocated between the prepetition and postpetition periods?

For bankruptcy cases commenced *on or after* October 17, 2005, the answer is relatively clear: The entire tax should be considered an administrative expense. As part of the 2005 bankruptcy reform legislation, section 507(a)(8)(A)—pertaining to unsecured prepetition income taxes accorded an eighth priority—was amended to apply only to taxable years *ending on or before* the petition date.[22] As a result, it should no longer be the case that all or part of a debtor corporation's income tax liability for the year of filing is considered an eighth priority claim, and thus expressly excluded from administrative expense treatment under Bankruptcy Code section 503(b)(1)(B). Interestingly, the change is not commented upon, or alluded to, in the description that accompanied the legislation (or any earlier versions of the legislation).[23] Although presumably intended to end the court debate (discussed below) with respect to the priority of the year-of-filing income tax liability, the legislation does not technically address the issue of when an income tax is considered "incurred" by a bankruptcy estate—a precondition to administrative expense treatment. As discussed below, some lower courts have held that an income tax liability is incurred as it accrues. If these courts are correct, a literal application of the change would have the absurd (and untenable) result of turning any prepetition period income tax liability for the year of filing into a general unsecured claim, as it would no longer qualify as either an eighth priority claim or an administrative expense claim.[24]

For *pre*-October 17, 2005 bankruptcy cases, the year-of-filing issue for income taxes remains contentious. Surprisingly, relatively few cases have historically considered the issue. The IRS generally maintains that the entire tax should be considered

---

[22] 11 U.S.C. § 507(a)(8)(A), *as amended by* P.L. 109-8, § 705(1) (2005).

[23] The National Bankruptcy Review Commission, in its report to Congress in October 1997, had recommended treating a corporate debtor's entire income tax liability for the year of filing as an administrative expense, but had also recommended giving the debtor an election to close its taxable year as of the date of the bankruptcy filing. The election would have created two "short" years, one entirely prepetition and one entirely postpetition. National Bankruptcy Review Commission Final Report (October 20, 1997), Recommendation 4.2.33, at pp. 973-974. Such election would have been similar to that currently permitted under Code § 1398(d) for individuals. For a discussion of several alternative proposals, *see* Chambers, Split Priority Bankruptcy Claims, 98 TNT 239-77 (December 14, 1998).

The presence of an elective closing of the year would have required the corporate debtor to engage in a cost/benefit analysis. One benefit of closing the year would have been the ability to defer the payment of the prepetition period taxes beyond the effective date of the Chapter 11 plan (*see* § 1016.1). On the other hand, closing the year could distort the tax results of companies with seasonal businesses (potentially creating a loss in one period and increased income in the other), and would shorten the company's carryover period for losses by one year. This reduction in the carryover period could prove particularly significant in the case of NOL carrybacks which generally may be carried back only two taxable years.

[24] For a discussion of the consequences of this change in wording and prior law, see Germain, Income Tax Claims in the Year of Bankruptcy: A Congressionally Created Quagmire, 59 Tax Law. 329 (2006).

an administrative expense.[25] The principal support for treating the entire year's tax liability as an administrative expense is the explanatory statements made by sponsors of the Bankruptcy Code at the time of enactment. Such statements state that, in determining priority, an income tax should be considered to be "incurred" as of the last day of the taxable year.[26] Thus, a tax for the year of filing would be considered incurred postpetition. Nevertheless, an increasing number of courts—including the Eighth, Ninth, and Eleventh Circuits—have bifurcated the tax liability.[27]

Some of the lower courts initially focused on the Senate Report discussion of administrative expenses—which states that taxes incurred by the estate include "taxes on capital gains from sales of property by the trustee and taxes on income *earned* by the estate during the case"—and thus concluded that an income tax is "incurred" as the *income* actually accrues.[28] It is unclear, however, whether the general proposition of the Senate Report is appropriately applied to income taxes for the year of filing, particularly when one considers that the Senate version of the

---

[25] *See* IRS Manual, Part 5 (Collecting Process), Ch. 9 (Bankruptcy), § 13.20 (3/1/06), at ¶ 2(A), (C) (maintaining position except in Circuits where the Court of Appeals has held otherwise); IRS Chief Counsel Advice 199907016, December 22, 1998 (same), *reprinted at* 1999 TNT 34-33.

[26] 124 Cong. Rec. H 11,112 (daily ed. September 28, 1978) (statement of Rep. Edwards), S 17,428 (daily ed. October 6, 1978) (statement of Sen. DeConcini). *See, e.g., In re Gonzalez*, 112 B.R. 10 (Bankr. E.D. Tex. 1989); *cf.* legislative history to the Bankruptcy Tax Act of 1980, S. Rep. No. 1035, 96th Cong., 2d Sess. 26 (1980) (discussing the effect of an individual's election under Code § 1398(d) to close his taxable year as of his bankruptcy filing); H. Rep. No. 833, 96th Cong., 2d Sess. 21 (1980) (same); *Moore v. IRS (In re Moore)*, 132 B.R. 533, 91-2 U.S.T.C. ¶ 50,390 (Bankr. W.D. Pa. 1991) (individual's income tax liability for entire taxable year of the bankruptcy filing was a postpetition obligation of the individual); *but see In re Johnson*, 190 B.R. 724, 95-2 U.S.T.C. ¶ 50,611 (Bankr. D. Mass. 1995) (distinguishing result under Code § 1398). *Consider also In re International Match Corp.*, 79 F.2d 203 (2d Cir.), *cert. denied*, 296 U.S. 652 (1935) (Bankruptcy Act case, involving "accrual" of franchise tax liability).

[27] *See, e.g., United States v. Hillsborough Holdings Corp. (In re Hillsborough Holdings Corp.)*, 116 F.3d 1391, 97-2 U.S.T.C. ¶ 50,542 (11th Cir. 1997), *aff'g* 1995 WL 795113 (M.D. Fla. 1995), *aff'g* 156 B.R. 318 (Bankr. M.D. Fla. 1993) (taxpayer prorated tax for the year); *Towers v. United States (In re Pacific-Atlantic Trading Co.)*, 64 F.3d 1292 (9th Cir. 1995), *aff'g* in part 160 B.R. 136 (N.D. Cal. 1993) (on facts, entire year's income was earned prepetition); *Missouri Dept. of Rev. v. L. J. O'Neill Shoe Co. (In re L. J. O'Neill Shoe Co.)*, 64 F.3d 1146 (8th Cir. 1995), *aff'g sub nom. Hy-Test, Inc. v. Missouri Dept. of Rev. (In re Interco, Inc.)*, 143 B.R. 707 (Bankr. E.D. Mo. 1992) (allowing as administrative expenses "only the portions of the claims that reasonably can be viewed to relate to or further the bankruptcy proceedings"); *Matter of O.P.M. Leasing Services, Inc.*, 68 B.R. 979 (Bankr. S.D.N.Y. 1987) (distinguishes pre-Bankruptcy Code law); *In re Prime Motor Inns, Inc.*, 144 B.R. 554 (Bankr. S.D. Fla. 1992) (entire tax allocable to prepetition sale of assets; generally relied on cases involving excise taxes and wage withholding); *United States v. Simon (In re Bondi's Valu-King, Inc.)*, 126 B.R. 47, 50-51 (N.D. Ohio 1991). *See also Bayly Corp. v. Skeen*, 163 F.3d 1205 (10th Cir. 1998) (favorably citing several of the above authorities in connection with a dispute over the priority status of a PBGC claim for unfunded pension plan benefits).

Bifurcation similarly appears to be the rule applied to tax refunds. Although an income tax refund resulting from tax overpayments during the year has been generally held to accrue at the end of the taxable year—*see, e.g., Harbaugh v. United States (In re Harbaugh)*, 89-2 U.S.T.C. ¶ 9608 (W.D. Pa. 1989), *aff'd without opinion*, 902 F.2d 1560 (3d Cir. 1990)—in cases thus far involving individual debtors, bankruptcy courts have for the year of the bankruptcy filing allocated the tax refund between the prepetition and postpetition portions of the year. *See, e.g., Barowsky v. Serelson (In re Barowsky)*, 946 F.2d 1516 (10th Cir. 1991); *In re Haedo*, 211 B.R. 149 (Bankr. S.D.N.Y. 1997); and *supra* text accompanying notes 37-42 at § 1006.1.1.

[28] S. Rep. No. 989, 95th Cong., 2d Sess. 66 (1978) (emphasis added).

Bankruptcy Code also included a provision that would have expressly treated income taxes as incurred on the last day of the year for all purposes of the Bankruptcy Code.[29] This rule, although not adopted for *all purposes* was, according to the sponsors, still to apply for purposes of the priority rules. For this reason, the Ninth Circuit acceded to the proposition that income taxes were incurred on the last day of the year (but, for the reasons discussed below, nevertheless bifurcated the tax liability). Both the Eighth and Eleventh Circuits offered no view.

However, all three Circuit Courts, and also the various lower courts, have held that, regardless of when incurred, taxes attributable to income earned during the prepetition portion of the year of filing are specifically accorded an eighth (formerly a seventh) priority, and therefore are not an administrative expense. Specifically, such courts concluded that such taxes are within the plain reading of Bankruptcy Code section 507(a)(8)(A)(iii) (as in effect prior to the 2005 Act changes), which grants an eighth priority to claims for income taxes that are "not assessed before, but assessable . . . after, the commencement of the case." Each of the Circuit Courts dismissed the government's argument that to adopt such a reading would also mean that the postpetition period taxes, as well as any taxes payable for taxable years entirely during the administrative period, would be eighth priority tax claims.[30] Acknowledging the absurdity of this result, such courts concluded, based on the structure of the statute and the legislative history, that eighth priority treatment was only intended to deal with prepetition taxes and should be read consistent with that intent. In addition, the Ninth Circuit, and some of the lower courts, observed that, by narrowly construing the administrative priority and treating prepetition period taxes as eighth priority claims, the reorganization policies of the Bankruptcy Code are advanced, particularly given the debtor's ability to defer the payment of such taxes under a plan (*see* § 1016.1 below).[31]

Although this also makes the income tax attributable to the prepetition period a tax for which a proof of claim generally must be filed by the bar date, the IRS may be permitted to file a late claim where it had no prior notice that a potential tax for such period might be due.[32]

In light of the foregoing decisions requiring bifurcation in pre-October 17, 2005 bankruptcy cases, the factual issue of how to allocate the year's tax liability becomes critical. Although the factual allocation of the tax was not an issue in the case, the

---

[29] *See* S. 2266, 95th Cong., 2d Sess. § 346(a)(1) (1978), as reported by the Senate Judiciary Committee and the Senate Finance Committee. *See also Hy-Test, Inc. v. Missouri Dept. of Revenue (In re Interco Inc.), supra* note 27.

[30] The Bankruptcy Code defines the term "claim" to include any "right to payment, whether or not . . . fixed, contingent matured [or] unmatured." 11 U.S.C. § 101(5)(A); *see also* H. Rep. No. 595, 95th Cong., 1st Sess. 309 (1977) (the term "claim" encompasses "all legal obligations of the debtor, no matter how remote or contingent"); S. Rep. No. 989, 95th Cong., 2d Sess. 21 (1978) (same).

[31] *See, e.g., Towers v. United States (In re Pacific-Atlantic Trading Co.), supra* note 27 (Ninth Circuit decision); *Hy-Test, Inc. v. Missouri Dept. of Revenue (In re Interco Incorporated), supra* note 27.

[32] *See In re Prime Motor Inns, Inc.*, 147 B.R. 605 (Bankr. S.D. Fla. 1992) (permitting late claim; court stated that the debtors could have included a narrative statement in their schedules "that possible state [income] taxes might be due, although the precise amount of those taxes was not yet determinable"); *see also* discussions at § § 1010.2 (late claims) and 1014 (discharge).

Ninth Circuit's decision discloses that the trustee in that case had allocated the year's gross income based on a pure tracing and, although this point is less clear, presumably did the same for deductions.[33] The result of this allocation was that all of the debtor's net income for the year and, thus, the entire tax liability for the year was attributable to the prepetition period. The IRS did not contest the allocation. In the case before the Eleventh Circuit, the taxpayer "prorated" the tax for the year; however, the basis for such allocation—whether based on the number of days or, for example, relative income, which would be closer to a true tracing—is unclear from the Eleventh Circuit and lower court decisions.[34]

In addition, although not dealt with in any of the cases, the determination of the amount of taxes payable for the prepetition or postpetition period may be complicated by any prepetition payments of estimated taxes for the year. For example, are such payments automatically prorated between the prepetition and postpetition portions of the year, on the grounds that the payments were advance payments of tax for the *entire* year;[35] or can they be allocated to the prepetition portion of the year, particularly where the amount paid was based on annualized prebankruptcy results?

**Consolidated return liability.** In the *Imperial Corporation* case,[36] the bankruptcy court held that the IRS's claim for postpetition taxes against the debtor arising out of the debtor's several liability for the federal income taxes of its consolidated subsidiary was not entitled to first priority status but, rather, was a general unsecured claim. Although incurred postpetition, the bankruptcy court held that the debtor's liability was in the nature of a surety and not a liability for taxes "incurred by the estate,"[37] and that the IRS had not met its burden of showing that the liability was "an actual and necessary cost and expense of preserving" the estate.[38] Accordingly, the liability was not entitled to an administrative priority, nor could the liability qualify as an eighth priority tax claim (see below) since it did not relate to a prepetition taxable

---

33 *See In re Pacific-Atlantic Trading Co.*, 64 F.3d at 1296 n.6.

34 *See In re Hillsborough Holdings Corp.*, 116 F.3d at 1396 n.2, and 156 B.R. at 15-16. *See also* Todres, Corporate Bankruptcy: Treatment of Filing Year Income Tax—A Suggested Approach, 9 Am. Bankr. Inst. L. Rev. 523 (2001) (advocating the use of a proration based on number of days in all cases).

35 *Consider* discussion of estimated taxes in *In re Halle*, 132 B.R. 186, 91-1 U.S.T.C. ¶50,121 (D. Colo. 1991) (Chapter 13 case); *In re Michaelson*, 200 B.R. 862 (Bankr. D. Minn. 1996) (Chapter 13 case; estimated tax payments based on prior year's income could not serve as basis for allocating tax liability for the year of the bankruptcy filing).

36 91-2 U.S.T.C. ¶50,342 (Bankr. D. Cal. 1991).

37 *Cf. Ndosi v. State of Minn.*, 950 F.2d 1376 (8th Cir. 1991) (interpreting the phrase "earned from the debtor" in Bankruptcy Code section 507(a)(7)(D), now section 507(a)(8)(D)). *Consider also* discussion at *supra* note 14.

38 *See* 11 U.S.C. §503(b)(1)(A), which provides that administrative expenses include "the actual, necessary costs and expenses of preserving the estate." The bankruptcy court recognized that it might be argued that the transaction giving rise to the tax liability (namely, advances by the Resolution Trust Corp. to the debtor's savings and loan subsidiary) somehow preserved the subsidiary's value as an asset of the estate, but was not persuaded that this produced a sufficient benefit to the "estate as a whole" to justify an administrative priority for the tax liability.

year. Not surprisingly, the IRS believes that Imperial Corporation was wrongly decided, and continues to claim administrative priority in bankruptcy cases.[39]

### §1015.1.2 Third Priority Tax Claims

Third (formerly second) priority tax claims include claims for taxes incurred in the ordinary course of the debtor's business following an involuntary bankruptcy petition and prior to the earlier of (1) the bankruptcy court's formal approval of the petition (called an "order for relief") or (2) the appointment of a trustee.[40] Such claims are frequently called "involuntary gap" claims.

### §1015.1.3 Employment Taxes Relating to Pending Wage Claims (Fourth and Eighth Priority)

Wages accorded a fourth (formerly a third) priority are those earned during the 180-day period prior to filing the bankruptcy petition or the cessation of the debtor corporation's business, whichever is earlier, up to a maximum of $10,000 for each individual.[41] To the extent a claim for an employee's share of employment taxes relates to wages of the type described, such claim will also be granted a fourth priority.[42]

Pursuant to Bankruptcy Code section 507(a)(8)(D), claims for the employer's share of employment taxes relating to third priority-type wages are granted an eighth priority, as are the employee's share and employer's share of employment taxes relating to wages (other than fourth priority-type wages) earned before the bankruptcy petition if the tax return for such taxes was due (with extensions) after three years before the date of the filing of the bankruptcy petition.[43]

Nevertheless, there is some confusion as to the priority accorded the payment of the employer's share of employment taxes on wage claims that are treated as general

---

[39] IRS Field Service Advice 1999-539 (undated) (detailed discussion), *reprinted at* 1999 TNT 15-119. *See also* IRS Field Service Advice 1999-566 (c. Fall/Winter 1991) (advice given to the field in the *Imperial Corporation* case shortly after the bankruptcy court rendered its decision), *reprinted at* 1999 TNT 20-109.

[40] *See* 11 U.S.C. §507(a)(3), *as amended by* P.L. 109-8 (2005) (2005 Act changed priority from second to third for bankruptcy cases commenced on or after October 17, 2005); 11 U.S.C. §502(f).

[41] *See* 11 U.S.C. §507(a)(4), *as amended by* P.L. 109-8 (2005) (2005 Act changed priority from third to fourth, and increased time period from 90 days, for bankruptcy cases commenced on or after April 20, 2005; maximum dollar amount has been periodically increased from $2,000 for bankruptcy cases commenced before October 22, 1994).

[42] Id.; S. Rep. No. 989, 95th Cong., 2d Sess. 68-73 (1978); 124 Cong. Rec. H 11, 112 (daily ed. September 28, 1978) (statement of Rep. Edwards), S 17,428 (daily ed. October 6, 1978) (statement of Sen. DeConcini). *Cf. Otte v. United States*, 419 U.S. 43 (1974) (Bankruptcy Act case; same result).

[43] *See also State of Texas v. Pierce (In re Pierce)*, 935 F.2d 709 (5th Cir. 1991) (involved state unemployment taxes on wages paid more than 90 days before bankruptcy but otherwise within priority period); *In re Stafford Dawson*, 1999 Bankr. LEXIS 1603 (Bankr. W.D. Va. 1999) (to similar effect, but involving FUTA taxes and employer's share of FICA; unclear whether wages were paid prepetition or still owing); *Paulson v. United States (In re Paulson)*, 152 B.R. 46 (Bankr. W.D. Pa. 1992); *In re Lackawanna Detective Agency, Inc.*, 82 B.R. 336 (Bankr. D. Del. 1988).

unsecured claims. As written, Bankruptcy Code section 507(a)(8)(D) makes such taxes an eighth priority claim (in that no tax return is due for such taxes until after the wage claims are paid). Thus, even though such taxes cannot, as a practical matter, be paid in advance of any payments to general wage claims—since no liability for such taxes exists until the wages are paid—the full payment of the employer's share would have to be factored into any distributions available to general unsecured claims (resulting in a potentially circular calculation), subject to the ability of the debtor to spread the payment of such taxes over six years, like any other eighth priority claim (*see* § 1016.1).

In contrast, the legislative history states that the employer's share of employment taxes on any amounts payable with respect to general wage claims is itself treated as a general unsecured claim.[44] This has created some speculation that the employer's share would be part of the pool of general unsecured claims and share pro rata in any distributions (also resulting in a potentially circular calculation). Thus, it would be possible that the full amount of the employer's share would not be paid. However, the legislative statements made at the time of enactment go on to say that, "[i]n calculating the amounts payable as general wage claims, the trustee must pay the employer's share of employment taxes on such wages."[45] Although not the model of clarity, a fair reading of this statement would, like the statute, seem to require full payment of the employer's share (although not necessarily in cash). Read this way, the practical differences between the legislative history and the statute would potentially relate to the timing and the form of the payment.

### § 1015.1.4 Eighth Priority Tax Claims

In addition to certain employment tax claims discussed above, other eighth priority tax claims include unsecured tax claims for:[46]

(1) income or gross receipts taxes (*i.e.*, taxes "on or measured by income or gross receipts") with respect to taxable years ending on or before the date of the filing of the petition in bankruptcy and for which a tax return, if required, was either last due (with extensions) within three years before the petition date, or due after the petition date;[47]

---

[44] *Supra* note 42.

[45] 124 Cong. Rec. H 11,112 (daily ed. September 28, 1978) (statement of Rep. Edwards), S 17,428 (daily ed. October 6, 1978) (statement of Sen. DeConcini).

[46] Originally, when the Bankruptcy Code was enacted in 1978, these tax claims were accorded a "sixth" priority. This was changed in 1984 to a "seventh" priority, and then in 1994 to an "eighth" priority.

[47] 11 U.S.C. § 507(a)(8)(A)(i) (literal wording of statute is to tax returns "last due . . . after three years before" the petition date); *Wood v. United States (In re Wood)*, 866 F.2d 1367, 89-1 U.S.T.C. ¶ 9283 (11th Cir. 1989) (irrelevant that tax return was actually *filed* more than three years before the filing of the bankruptcy petition, since the final *due date* with extensions was within the three-year period); (*Padden v. IRS (In re Padden)*, 1997 Bankr. LEXIS 1895 (Bankr. M.D. Pa. 1997) (same); *Roth v. United States (In re Roth)*, 89-1 U.S.T.C. ¶ 9302 (Bankr. D. Neb. 1988) (priority unaffected by conversion from Chapter 11 to Chapter 7). *Cf. Savaria v. United States (In re Savaria)*, 317 B.R. 395 (Bankr. 9th Cir. 2004)

(2) income and gross receipts taxes (including any transferee liability) assessed within 240 days prior to the filing of the petition in bankruptcy (which period is extended to include the period for which there was an offer of compromise pending or in effect, plus 30 days thereafter, provided with respect to *pre*-October 17, 2005 bankruptcy cases, such offer of compromise was made within 240 days after the assessment);[48]

---

(Footnote Continued)

(statutory time reference in Bankruptcy Code section 523(a)(1)(B) to returns last due "after two years before" the petition date includes tax returns due *after* the petition date).

[48] *See* 11 U.S.C. § 507(a)(8)(A)(ii), as in effect before and after the 2005 Act changes, P.L. 109-8, § 705(1); 124 Cong. Rec. H 11,112 (daily ed. September 28, 1978) (statement of Rep. Edwards), S 17,428 (daily ed. October 6, 1978) (statement of Sen. DeConcini); *McKowen v. United States*, 370 F.3d 1023, 2005-1 U.S.T.C. ¶ 50,242 (10th Cir. 2004) (upheld priority tax treatment for a transferee liability for income taxes, citing the Tax Court's decision in *Hamar v. Comm.*, 42 T.C. 867 (1964), involving the equivalent issue under the Bankruptcy Act; in that case, the Tax Court observed that, even though "the liability of a transferee may not be a tax liability in the ordinary sense, nevertheless it is a liability for a tax;" the Tenth Circuit specifically considered and rejected the bankruptcy court's decision in *Pert*, below), *aff'g*, 263 B.R. 618, 2001-2 U.S.T.C. ¶ 50,538 (D. Col. 2001) (consistent with congressional statements, upheld priority treatment), *rev'g*, 2001-1 U.S.T.C. ¶ 50,211 (Bankr. D. Col. 2001); *but see Pert v. United States (In re Pert)*, 201 B.R. 316, 96-2 U.S.T.C. ¶ 50,681 (Bankr. M.D. Fla. 1996) (rejecting treatment of transferee liability as a priority tax claim, without discussing congressional statements to the contrary). *See also Brown v. IRS (In re Brown)*, 1991 Bankr. LEXIS 1002 (Bankr. N.D. Ohio 1991) (example of 240-day rule).

For examples of the operation of the extension of time for offers in compromise, *see, e.g., Frey v. IRS (In re Frey)* (Bankr. E.D. La.), *reprinted at* 88 TNT 219-6 (September 30, 1988) (IRS priority lapsed 30 days after first offer in compromise was rejected; increase in offer one year later, following collection actions by the IRS, was considered a new offer); *Aberl v. United States (In re Aberl)*, 159 B.R. 792 (Bankr. N.D. Ohio 1993) (offer made before date of assessment, but not rejected until afterwards, did not extend 240-day period—note that the 2005 bankruptcy reforms change this outcome; also held that an "appeal" of a previously rejected offer did not extend the 240-day period), *aff'd*, 175 B.R. 915 (N.D. Ohio 1994), *aff'd*, 78 F.3d 241 (6th Cir. 1996); *In re Genung*, 220 B.R. 505, 98-1 U.S.T.C. ¶ 50,328 (Bankr. N.D.N.Y. 1998) (offer that was rejected by the IRS but "appealed" by the debtor was still considered "pending" for purposes of extending the 240-day period; the court distinguished *In re Aberl, supra*, based on language added in 1992 to IRS Form 656—the official form for making an offer in compromise—with respect to a taxpayer's general waiver of the statutes of limitation on assessment and collection during a pending offer; the added language provides that "[i]f there is an appeal with respect to this offer, the offer shall be deemed pending until the date the Appeals office formally accepts or rejects this offer in writing"); *Nader v. United States (In re Nader)*, 99-2 U.S.T.C. ¶ 50,824 (Bankr. E.D. Pa. 1999) (same); *United States v. Donovan*, 348 F.3d 509, 2003-2 U.S.T.C. ¶ 50,705 (6th Cir. 2003) (similarly concluding based on the language in IRS Form 656 that an offer is not officially withdrawn until an authorized IRS official acknowledges the withdrawal in writing); *Hobbs v. United States (In re Hobbs)*, 97-1 U.S.T.C. ¶ 50,127 (Bankr. N.D. Iowa 1996) (both sides treated an "appeal" of a previously rejected offer as extending 240-day period; priority denied for other reasons); *Colish v. United States (In re Colish)*, 239 B.R. 260, 99-2 U.S.T.C. ¶ 50,906 (Bankr. E.D. N.Y. 1999) (priority period not extended by pre-assessment offer in compromise); *Callahan v. United States (In re Callahan)*, 168 B.R. 272 (Bankr. D. Mass. 1993) (declined to extend period for the time that a second offer in compromise was outstanding); *Romagnolo v. United States (In re Romagnolo)*, 195 B.R. 801, 96-1 U.S.T.C. ¶ 50,301 (Bankr. M.D. Fla. 1996) (an offer in compromise which was not "processable" under the criteria set out in the IRS Manual, but which the IRS initially began processing and then stopped when it realized its mistake, was not considered "pending" for purposes of the 240-day rule until it was amended and conformed with the Manual); *In re Howell*, 120 B.R. 137 (Bankr. 9th Cir. 1990) (debtor could not rely on an incorrect assessment date supplied by an IRS employee at the IRS "800 number").

Effective for offers in compromise pending on or made after December 31, 1999, Code § 6331(k)(1) expressly prohibits the IRS from levying upon a taxpayer's property with respect to any

(3) except as discussed below, income and gross receipts taxes (including any transferee liability) still assessable but not yet assessed[49] and—for bankruptcy cases commenced on or after October 17, 2005—only for taxes with respect to taxable years ending on or before the filing of the petition in bankruptcy;

(4) certain property taxes;[50]

---

(Footnote Continued)

tax for which an offer in compromise is "pending" (commencing on the date the offer is accepted for processing) and, if the offer is rejected, for 30 days thereafter. If the rejection is appealed within such 30-day period, the prohibition remains in effect during the appeal. While such prohibition is in effect, the applicable statute of limitations on collection is suspended. Code § 6331(k)(3), (i)(5). The prohibition would not apply, however, if the IRS determines that collection is in jeopardy. Code § 6331(a). The enactment of Code § 6331(k)(1) substantially codifies the IRS practice since 1992. *See In re Genung, supra;* and *In re Nader, supra.* The IRS has since expounded, in Rev. Proc. 2003-71, 2003-36 I.R.B. 517, on the circumstances under which it considers an offer in compromise to be "pending" for tax purposes.

For when a tax is considered to be "assessed," *see, e.g., Hartman v. United States (In re Hartman)*, 110 B.R. 951, 90-1 U.S.T.C. ¶ 50,163 (D. Kan. 1990) (tax "assessed" on date IRS Form 3552 was issued to taxpayers, not the date of the notice of deficiency); *In re Shotwell*, 120 B.R. 163 (Bankr. D. Or. 1990) (quoting Reg. § 301.6203-1, held that "date of assessment is the date the summary record is signed by an assessment officer"); *Lilly v. United States (In re Lilly)*, 194 B.R. 885 (Bankr. D. Idaho 1996) (execution of Form 870-AD, waiving restrictions on assessment and collection, did not constitute the assessment; a tax is assessed only when the IRS enters the assessment pursuant to Code § 6203); *Roberts v. Commissioner*, 118 T.C. 365 (2002) (IRS may use either a computer generated form known as Revenue Accounting Control System (RACS) Report 006 or Form 23C to make an assessment; Form 4340, "Certificate of Assessments, Payments, and Other Specified Matters," properly establishes assessment absent an irregularity in the IRS's assessment procedure). The IRS Penalty Handbook defines "assessment date" as "[t]he date Form 23C is executed by the assessment officer," and in the definition of "23C Date" states that an "[a]ssessment is accomplished when the assessment officer schedules the liability and signs the assessment register (Form 23C, Assessment Certificate, Summary Record of Assessments)." IRS Manual, Part 20 (Penalty and Interest), Ch. 1 (Penalty Handbook), Exhibit 20.1.1.6-8 (8/20/98). *See also Frary v. United States (In re Frary)*, 117 B.R. 541 (Bankr. D. Alaska 1990) (court rejected debtor's argument that, where the IRS made multiple assessments for the same year, the final assessment should "relate back" to the earlier assessments and thus fall outside the 240-day period); *Hardie v. United States (In re Hardie)*, 204 B.R. 944, 97-2 U.S.T.C. ¶ 50,883 (S.D. Tex. 1996) (entry of Tax Court decision is not an assessment; assessment does not occur until IRS records the assessment and thus issues its certificate of assessment). Consistent with the foregoing authorities, and as discussed *infra* at § 1016.1.1 n. 6, the mere filing of a tax return showing an amount due (for which no payment is remitted) does not constitute a "self-assessment." Only the IRS can "assess" a tax.

[49] *See* 11 U.S.C. § 507(a)(8)(A)(iii), including the opening language to section 507(a)(8)(A) both before and after the 2005 Act changes, P.L. 109-8, § 705(1); 124 Cong. Rec. H 11,112 (daily ed. September 28, 1978) (statement of Rep. Edwards), S 17,429 (daily ed. October 6, 1978) (statement of Sen. DeConcini); *McKowen v. United States (In re McKowen), supra* note 48 (consistent with congressional statements, held that a transferee liability claim for income taxes was an eighth priority tax claim), *rev'g*, 2001-1 U.S.T.C. ¶ 50,211 (Bankr. D. Colo. 2001); *but see Pert v. United States (In re Pert), supra* note 48 (rejecting treatment of transferee liability as a priority tax claim, without discussing congressional statements to the contrary). *See also Wines v. United States (In re Wines)*, 122 B.R. 804 (Bankr. S.D. Fla. 1991) (taxes were still assessable since six-year statute of limitations for assessment applied, and tolled for period of Tax Court proceeding).

[50] For a discussion of the priority accorded unsecured property taxes, *see* Chapter 11 at § 1102.13.

(5) taxes required to be collected or withheld and for which debtor is liable in whatever capacity ("trust fund" taxes);[51]
(6) excise taxes (including gasoline and special fuel taxes, truck taxes, and, possibly, sales and use tax[52]) on a prepetition transaction for which a return is either (i) last due (with extensions) within three years before the date of the filing of the bankruptcy petition, or due after the petition date or (ii) not required and the transaction occurred within three years before the petition date;[53]

---

[51] 11 U.S.C. § 507(a)(8)(C); *see, e.g., Illinois Dept. of Rev. v. Hayslett/Judy Oil, Inc.*, 426 F.3d 899 (7th Cir. 2005) (Illinois Motor Fuel Tax is a "trust fund" tax, and not simply an "excise" tax, since, by statute, it is a tax collected by the distributor and not part of the retailer's sale price); *Shank v. Washington State Dept. of Rev. (In re Shank)*, 792 F.2d 829 (9th Cir. 1986) (held that sales taxes collected from customers are "trust fund" taxes, not "excise" taxes—in contrast to those owed personally by the debtor—with the result that seventh (now eighth) priority status will always be granted, rather than being limited to those sales taxes collected within approximately three years prior to bankruptcy); *DeChiaro v. NYS Tax Commission*, 760 F.2d 432 (2d Cir. 1985) (same); *Rosenow v. State of Illinois Dept. of Revenue*, 715 F.2d 277 (7th Cir. 1983) (same); *In re Taylor Tobacco Enterprises, Inc.*, 106 B.R. 441 (E.D.N.C. 1989) (includes sales tax "required to be," but not actually, collected); *see also Groetken v. State of Illinois (In re Groetken)*, 843 F.2d 1007 (7th Cir. 1988) (Illinois' Occupation Tax is not a "trust fund" tax since imposed directly on retailer; interestingly, the court held that the tax was *both* a gross receipts tax and an excise tax). *See also In re LMS Holding Co.*, 149 B.R. 684 (Bankr. N.D. Okla. 1993) (holding that the phrase "in whatever capacity" includes a person who is liable for such taxes as a transferee); *Mosbrucker v. United States (In re Mosbrucker)*, 198 F.3d 250, 99-2 U.S.T.C. ¶ 50,883 (8th Cir. 1999) (also includes responsible person liability under Code § 6672); *In re Thomas*, 222 B.R. 742 (Bankr. E.D. Pa. 1998) (holding similarly; collecting cases); 124 Cong. Rec. H 11,112 (daily ed. September 28, 1978) (statement of Rep. Edwards), S 17,429 (daily ed. October 6, 1978) (statement of Sen. DeConcini) (expressly recognizing priority of "responsible person" liabilities); *but see In re Total Employment Company Inc.*, 2003 Bankr. LEXIS 1147 (Bankr. M.D. Fla. 2003) (asserting that amounts due under Code § 3505(a) are not taxes but are "a sum equal to the taxes" and thus not entitled to priority), *rev'd on other grounds*, 305 B.R. 333, 2004-1 U.S.T.C. ¶ 50,177 (M.D. Fla. 2004).

[52] *See In re Tapp*, 16 B.R. 315 (Bankr. D. Alaska 1981); 124 Cong. Rec. H 11,113 (daily ed. September 28, 1978) (statement of Rep. Edwards), S 17,429-17,430 (daily ed. October 6, 1978) (statement of Sen. DeConcini); *Trustees of the Trism Liquidating Trust v. IRS (In re Trism, Inc.)*, 2004 Bankr. LEXIS 900 (Bankr. 8th Cir. 2004) (tax imposed by Code § 4481 on the operation of heavy motor vehicles on highways is an "excise" tax, not a fee; discusses breadth of the definition of "excise tax" and "transaction"); *Garrow Oil Corp. v. Bork (In re Bork)*, 147 B.R. 734 (Bankr. E.D. Wis. 1992) (held federal and Wisconsin motor fuel taxes were "excise" taxes). However, most sales taxes are also "collected" taxes entitled to priority under Bankruptcy Code section 507(a)(8)(C) without regard to time periods. *See supra* note 51.

[53] *See* 11 U.S.C. § 507(a)(8)(E) (as relates to filed returns, the literal wording of statute is to tax returns "last due . . . after three years before" the petition date); 124 Cong. Rec. H 11,113 (daily ed. September 28, 1978) (statement of Rep. Edwards), S 17,429-17,430 (daily ed. October 6, 1978) (statement of Sen. DeConcini); *In re Edmiston*, 36 B.R. 1 (Bankr. D. Kan. 1982) (invoked three-year prepetition restriction).

In addition, a federal "tax" that resembles a penalty may be considered a penalty for priority purposes. *See, e.g., United States v. Reorganized CF&I Fabricators of Utah, Inc.*, 116 S. Ct. 2106, 96-1 U.S.T.C. ¶ 50,322 (1996) (minimum funding tax imposed by Code § 4971 held to be a noncompensatory "penalty"), *aff'g in relevant part and rev'g in part*, 53 F.3d 1155, 95-2 U.S.T.C. ¶ 50,632 (10th Cir. 1995). *Also compare United States v. Mansfield Tire & Rubber Co. (In re Mansfield Tire & Rubber Co.)*, 942 F.2d 1055, 91-2 U.S.T.C. ¶ 50,419 (6th Cir. 1991), *cert. denied*, 112 S. Ct. 1165 (1992) (pre-dating the Supreme Court's decision in *CF&I Fabricators*, the Sixth Circuit had held that the Code § 4971 minimum funding tax was an "excise tax" for priority purposes; concluding that, unlike so-called state and local "taxes," once Congress has called something a "tax," the courts are not free to decide that its "essential characteristic" is that of a "penalty" for priority purposes), *rev'g*, 120 B.R. 862 (N.D.

(7) certain custom duties;[54] and

(8) any compensatory penalty relating to any of the foregoing claims.[55]

An income tax claim for this purpose should include a claim based on the debtor's several liability for income taxes attributable to other members of its consolidated group. As discussed at § 1015.1.1, the bankruptcy court in the *Imperial Corporation* case held, in a similar situation involving *postpetition* taxes, that the IRS's tax claim based on the debtor's several liability *was not* entitled to an administrative priority as a postpetition "tax" liability, because the underlying tax was not "incurred by the estate." Rather, the debtor was acting in the nature of a surety. However, no similar language appears in the statutory description of eighth priority income tax claims. This difference is underscored by the fact that the bankruptcy court also considered whether the IRS's tax claim would qualify as an eighth (then seventh) priority claim and, in concluding that it would not, made no mention of the several liability. Rather, the court analyzed the statutory language and concluded that only prepetition income taxes could qualify for eighth priority status.

In addition, the Fifth Circuit has held that a tax liability asserted against a debtor based on the debtor being a nominee for, or alter ego of, another corporation retains its status and priority as a *tax* claim.[56] In contrast, the district court had held that the claim was only an equitable claim for the amount owed rather than a claim for the tax itself, and thus not a tax claim entitled to priority treatment.

A tax need only qualify under one of the above numbered paragraphs to be granted an eighth priority. Thus, an income or gross receipts tax that fails to qualify

---

(Footnote Continued)

Ohio 1990); *In re C-T of Virginia, Inc.*, 977 F.2d 137, 93-1 U.S.T.C. ¶ 50,022 (4th Cir. 1992), *cert. denied*, 113 S. Ct. 1644 (1993) (tax imposed by Code § 4980 on pension plan reversions held to be an excise tax, not a "penalty"); *United States v. Plan Comm. of Juvenile Shoe Corp. of Am. (In re Juvenile Shoe Corp. of America)*, 99 F.3d 898, 96-2 U.S.T.C. ¶ 50,642 (8th Cir. 1996) (same), *aff'g* 180 B.R. 206 (E.D. Mo. 1995) (same), *rev'g* 166 B.R. 404 (Bankr. E.D. Mo. 1994); *with United States v. Dumler (In re Cassidy)*, 983 F.2d 161, 93-1 U.S.T.C. ¶ 50,006 (10th Cir. 1992) (tax imposed by Code § 72(t) on early withdrawals from retirement plans held to be a noncompensatory "penalty"); *In re Airlift Intl., Inc.*, 90-2 U.S.T.C. ¶ 50,358 (S.D. Fla.) (same); *cf. Matter of Unified Control Systems, Inc.*, 586 F.2d 1036 (5th Cir. 1978) (Bankruptcy Act case; Code § 4941 excise tax on private foundations was a "penalty," not a tax). Consistent with the foregoing authorities, the IRS has concluded that the excise tax imposed on a disqualified person by Code § 4975(a) for engaging in a prohibited transaction would be considered a "penalty" for priority purposes. IRS Chief Counsel Advice 200109010, November 24, 2000, *reprinted at* 2001 TNT 43-70.

[54] *See* 11 U.S.C. § 507(a)(8)(F).

[55] *See* 11 U.S.C. § 507(a)(8)(G); 124 Cong. Rec. H 11,113 (daily ed. September 28, 1978) (statement of Rep. Edwards), S 17,429-17,430 (daily ed. October 6, 1978) (statement of Sen. DeConcini); *see also* Code § 6658, discussed *supra* at § 1006.1.2 (precluding certain late-payment penalties on prepetition taxes past the filing of the bankruptcy petition). *In re Patco Photo Corp.*, 82 B.R. 192, 88-1 U.S.T.C. ¶ 9173 (Bankr. E.D.N.Y. 1988) (fines and penalties relating to prepetition federal income taxes not compensatory); *In re Hernando Appliances, Inc.*, 41 B.R. 24 (N.D. Miss. 1983) (same). *See also State of Washington v. Hovan, Inc. (In re Hovan, Inc.)*, 96 F.3d 1254 (9th Cir. 1996) (rejected argument that a tax penalty based on a percentage of the tax due should be treated as compensatory up to the amount of costs and expenses incurred in collection).

[56] *See Grothues v. IRS (In re Grothues)*, *supra* note 14 (reversing district court).

under paragraph (1) could still qualify under paragraphs (2) or (3).[57] For example, even if a tax return for income taxes was due more than three years prior to the filing of a petition in bankruptcy, if a tax deficiency for such year could still be assessed—because the statute of limitations on assessment has been waived—but has not yet been assessed, the resulting tax claim would be entitled to an eighth priority pursuant to paragraph (3).

In determining the due date of an income tax return for purposes of the three-year time limitation in paragraph (1), the IRS in a Chief Counsel Advice explained that the "timely filing" rule in Code §7503 (that treats a tax return for which the due date falls on a weekend or legal holiday as timely filed if filed on the next weekday) does *not* change the technical due date of the return.[58] In Rev. Rul. 2007-59, the IRS similarly stated that a postponement of the time to file a tax return under Code §7508A due to a declared disaster or a terroristic or military action (or in the case of an individual, under Code §7508 due to service in a combat zone) does not change the "due date, including extension" of an income tax return for purposes of the three-year time limitation. This is in contrast to a normal three-month or six-month extension of time for filing under Code §6081.[59]

A tax claim is not entitled to priority pursuant to paragraph (3), however, if it is for "a tax of a kind specified in [Bankruptcy Code] section 523(a)(1)(B) or 523(a)(1)(C)." Although Bankruptcy Code section 523(a) lists those debts from which an *individual* debtor is not discharged, the reference to individuals is only to be found in the introductory language to that section. Read alone, sections 523(a)(1)(B) and (C)—which pertain to taxes for which either no tax return,[60] a late return (filed within

---

[57] *See, e.g., Long v. United States (In re Long)*, 1999 Bankr. LEXIS 1869 (Bankr. 6th Cir. 1999); *Longley v. United States*, 66 B.R. 237, 86-2 U.S.T.C. ¶9710 (Bankr. N.D. Ohio 1986); *Daniel v. United States (In re Daniel)*, 170 B.R. 466 (Bankr S.D. Ga. 1994), *amended*, 1994 Bankr. LEXIS 1592. We observe that, in connection with certain statutory changes made to paragraph (2) as part of the 2005 bankruptcy reforms, the connecting "; or" between paragraph (2) and paragraph (3) was replaced with a period. This appears to have been inadvertent, and without any intent to change the relationship between the three paragraphs. *See* 11 U.S.C. §507(a)(8)(A), as in effect immediately before and after the 2005 Act changes, P.L. 109-8, §705(1).

[58] IRS Chief Counsel Advice 200603001, December 10, 2003, *reprinted at* 2006 TNT 14-13.

[59] *See also In re Viego*, 224 B.R. 570 (Bankr. E.D. N.C. 1997) (individual debtor applied for an "automatic" extension to file his federal income tax return but failed to satisfy the necessary payment conditions; nevertheless, the bankruptcy court held that the IRS was not precluded from granting, and in fact granted, the debtor an extension, and that as a result, it was the extended filing date that governed the determination of priority); *Kimball v. United States (In re Kimball)*, 2001-1 U.S.T.C. ¶50,230 (D. Mass. 2001), *aff'd*, 2002-1 U.S.T.C. ¶50,307 (D. Mass. 2002) (to same effect); *United States v. McDermott (In re McDermott)*, 286 B.R. 913, 2002-2 U.S.T.C. ¶50,741 (M.D. Fla. 2002), *rev'g*, 2002-1 U.S.T.C. ¶50,139 (Bankr. M.D. Fla. 2001) (debtor's request for a filing extension was effective, and not rendered moot, even though the debtor subsequently filed on time and thus did not benefit from the extension; application also contained inaccurate tax information).

[60] This generally includes cases where the debtor failed to file a return but the IRS subsequently filed a "substitute return" on behalf of the debtor under Code §6020(b). *See, e.g., Villalon v. United States (In re Villalon)*, 253 B.R. 837, 2000-2 U.S.T.C. ¶50,753 (Bankr. N.D. Ohio 2000); *In re Pruitt*, 107 B.R. 764 (Bankr. D. Wyo. 1989); *Gushue v. IRS (In re Gushue)*, 126 B.R. 202, 91-1 U.S.T.C. ¶50,223 (Bankr. E.D. Pa. 1991); *cf. Colsen v. United States (In re Colson)*, 446 F.3d 836, 2006-1 U.S.T.C. ¶50,300 (8th Cir. 2006) (although acknowledging contrary Fourth, Sixth and Seventh Circuit Court authority, held that tax returns filed by the debtor after IRS had prepared substitute returns were valid

two years of the filing of the bankruptcy petition) or a fraudulent return was filed, or with respect to which the debtor willfully attempted in any manner to evade or defeat the tax—are not limited to taxes incurred by individuals. Thus, it is possible that tax claims for such taxes are deprived of priority status, whether or not incurred by an individual debtor.[61] This would give the phrase "a tax of a kind specified in" its most literal meaning. This interpretation is not supportable from a policy (or equitable) perspective, however, and has been rejected by the courts.[62] Only when the debtor is an individual does it make sense to deprive such tax claims of priority status. This is due to the fact that, in the case of an individual debtor, such tax claims are nondischargeable and, thus, must ultimately be paid out of the individual's personal assets to the extent there are insufficient assets in the estate to pay such claims.[63] As a result, it is generally the individual, not the government, that effectively is penalized by the loss of priority status. In the case of a corporate debtor, however, the reverse would be true, because (other than in a liquidating bankruptcy and, after the 2005 bankruptcy reforms, limited other cases) the corporate debtor is granted a discharge to the extent its assets are insufficient to satisfy all general unsecured claims (*see* § 1014 above). Nevertheless, query whether the 2005 change exempting from the corporate discharge (although not by express cross-reference) taxes of the type covered by Bankruptcy Code section 523(a)(1)(C) would alter this result?[64] Presumably not.

Under certain circumstances, the time limitations that apply for purposes of determining a tax claim's priority status (such as the 3-year period for tax return filing in the case of certain income, gross receipts or excise taxes and the 240-day period in the case of certain income tax assessments) may be extended. The issue of extensions frequently arises in the context of successive bankruptcies, where the IRS's ability to collect the tax was impeded by the prior bankruptcy of the debtor, as discussed at § 1015.4 below. Similarly, other situations may arise where the IRS's ability to collect is impeded, such as where the debtor prior to filing bankruptcy (i) applies for a taxpayer assistance order (TAO) under Code § 7811, (ii) requests a formal hearing under Code § 6330(a) with respect to a proposed IRS levy, or (iii) submits an offer in compromise under Code § 7122. In the case of a TAO, it is the

---

(Footnote Continued)

"returns," concluding that "the honesty and genuineness of the filer's attempt to satisfy the tax laws should be determined from the face of the form itself, not from the filer's delinquency or the reasons for it"); *Izzo v. United States (In re Izzo)*, 287 B.R. 158, 2003-1 U.S.T.C. ¶ 50,190 (Bankr. E.D. Mich. 2002) (amended returns filed by a debtor after the IRS filed "substitute" returns constituted validly filed returns for this purpose, since the amended returns reflected a different tax liability (*albeit* lower) than the IRS accepted the returns, and there was no evidence that the returns were not a reasonable and honest attempt to comply with the tax laws). This case law regarding substitute returns was codified by the bankruptcy reforms in 2005. *See* 11 U.S.C. § 523(a) (flush language at end), *as amended by* P.L. 109-8, § 714 (2005).

[61] *Cf.* IRS Publication 908, Bankruptcy (Sept. 1994) (exception stated as if it applies to all debtors).

[62] *See, e.g., Matter of O.P.M. Leasing Services, Inc.* (Bankr. S.D.N.Y.), *supra* note 27, at 983, *citing In re Trafalgar Assoc.*, 53 B.R. 693, 696 (Bankr. S.D.N.Y. 1985).

[63] *See, e.g.*, S. Rep. No. 1106, 95th Cong., 2d Sess. 22 n.19 (1978); *In re Muina*, 75 B.R. 192 (Bankr. S.D. Fla. 1987).

[64] *See* 11 U.S.C. § 1141(d)(6), *as added by* P.L. 109-8, § 708 (2005), discussed above at § 1014.

IRS's policy (although not statutorily required) to refrain from all collection activity while the application is pending, unless it determines that enforcement is required to protect the government's interest.[65] However, in the case of a formal Code § 6330(a) hearing or a pending offer in compromise, the IRS is only prohibited from pursuing the levy; other modes of collection may be pursued, if available.[66] For bankruptcy cases commenced *on or after* October 17, 2005, an automatic extension of the applicable time limitations (also called "lookback periods") is provided for any period during which the IRS is prohibited under applicable nonbankruptcy law from collecting a tax as a result of "a request by the debtor for a hearing and an appeal of any collection action taken or proposed against the debtor," plus 90 days.[67] This would appear to encompass a request for a formal Code § 6330(a) hearing (in contrast to a so-called "equivalent hearing"[68]), but depending on the circumstances, might not reach an *application* for a TAO or an offer in compromise.

In contrast, for prior bankruptcy cases, the Supreme Court in *Young v. United States* held that an extension of the time limitations depends on the traditional principles of equitable tolling (*see* discussion at § 1015.4 below). In the aftermath of *Young*, the IRS Chief Counsel's office in a Chief Counsel Advice considered whether the time limitations should be extended for the period during which an offer in compromise was pending.[69] Recognizing that Congress had expressly granted an extension of time for offers in compromise in the case of the 240-day lookback period applicable to certain tax assessments, the Advice concludes that it would be inconsistent to utilize equitable tolling to suspend the general 3-year lookback period for income tax return filings. The Advice then goes on to conclude that, even if it was *not* determined to be inconsistent, "in our view, equitable tolling of the 3-year lookback period is simply not appropriate where the Service has other remedies it may exercise to protect or collect the tax liability." The latter conclusion would apply equally to a formal Code § 6330(a) hearing.[70]

---

[65] *See* former IRS Manual HB 1.2.7.9, Chapter 3.5.8(1) (4/30/98).

[66] *See* Code §§ 6330(e) and 6331(k).

[67] 11 U.S.C. § 507(a)(8) (flush language at end), *as amended by* P.L. 109-8, § 705(2) (2005) (also provides for an automatic extension in the case of successive bankruptcies, *see infra* § 1015.4; applies to all taxing authorities).

[68] *See* Reg. § 301.6330-1(i).

[69] IRS Chief Counsel Advice 200404049, January 5, 2004, *reprinted at* 2004 TNT 16-13.

[70] Prior to *Young*, it was likely that the IRS would seek an extension of the applicable time limitations, at least in the case of a TAO or a Code § 6330(a) hearing, whenever necessary to preserve priority status. *See* IRS Chief Counsel Advice 199910043, January 14, 1999, *reprinted at* 1999 TNT 49-100. In the referenced Advice, the Chief Counsel's office concluded, based on the then case law, that it was within the bankruptcy court's general equitable authority under Bankruptcy Code section 105(a) to suspend the applicable time limitations in the case of a TAO or a Code § 6330(a) hearing, and that practical or legal constraints on the IRS's collection activity would be factors to be considered by the court in the IRS's favor when determining the equities.

### §1015.1.5 Interest on Tax Claims

Prepetition interest on a prepetition tax claim is generally considered entitled to the same priority as the tax claim,[71] even if computed at the higher rate applicable to large corporate underpayments under Code §6621(c).[72] Interest on postpetition taxes is generally treated as an administrative expense of the bankruptcy.[73] Some courts, however, have disallowed claims for interest on postpetition taxes.[74] Also, as referenced in the footnote below, additional considerations may be relevant in Chapter 7 cases.[75]

---

[71] Two avenues of reasoning have been used: First, that despite the deletion of the specific mention of interest from Bankruptcy Code section 507(a)(8), there is no evidence that Congress intended to treat interest on a tax claim differently than the claim itself. Second, that a claim for interest is a compensatory penalty. *See, e.g., Hardee v. IRS (In re Hardee)*, 137 F.3d 337, 98-1 U.S.T.C. ¶50,307 (5th Cir. 1998) (concluded that interest is part of tax claim, as well as being a compensatory penalty); *In re Larson*, 862 F.2d 112, 88-2 U.S.T.C. ¶9590 (7th Cir. 1988) (interest is part of tax claim); *Jones v. United States (In re Garcia)*, 955 F.2d 16 (5th Cir. 1992) (held that interest was a compensatory penalty without deciding whether it was also part of tax claim); *In re Patco Photo Corp., supra* note 55 (relying on both rationales); *United States v. H.G.D. & J. Mining Co. (In re H.G.D. & J. Mining Co.)*, 74 B.R. 122, 87-1 U.S.T.C. ¶9344 (S.D. W. Va. 1987), *aff'd without opinion*, 836 F.2d 546, 547 (4th Cir. 1987); *In re Healis*, 49 B.R. 939 (Bankr. M.D. Pa. 1985) (denied priority status to prepetition interest where underlying tax claim not entitled to priority, even though adhering to reasoning that interest is a compensatory penalty); *In re Divine*, 127 B.R. 625, 91-1 U.S.T.C. ¶50,273 (Bankr. D. Minn. 1991) (same); *In re Leonard E. Treister*, 52 B.R. 735, 85-2 U.S.T.C. ¶9672 (Bankr. S.D.N.Y.); *In re Palmer*, 86-2 U.S.T.C. ¶9592 (N.D. Tex.); *In re Hernando Appliances, Inc., supra* note 55; *contra In re Razorback Ready Mix Concrete Co.*, 45 B.R. 917 (E.D. Ark. 1984).

[72] *See, e.g., Hardee v. IRS (In re Hardee)* (5th Cir.), *supra* note 71 (involving increased interest under former Code §6621(c) on substantial underpayments attributable to tax-motivated transactions); *In re Hall*, 191 B.R. 814, 96-1 U.S.T.C. ¶50,031 (Bankr. D. Alaska 1995) (same).

[73] 11 U.S.C. §507(a)(1); 11 U.S.C. §503(b)(1)(B)(i) and (b)(1)(C) (no specific mention of interest); *United States v. Friendship College, Inc.* (4th Cir.), *supra* note 8 (held interest and penalties on postpetition taxes are administrative expenses); *United States v. Flo-Lizer, Inc. (In re Flo-Lizer, Inc.)*, 916 F.2d 363 (6th Cir. 1990); *United States v. Cranshaw (In re Allied Mechanical Services, Inc.)* (11th Cir.), *supra* note 11; *United States v. Ledlin (In re Mark Anthony Constr., Inc.)* (9th Cir.), supra note 11; *In re Patco Photo Corp., supra* note 55; *In re Berkshire Family Restaurant, Inc.*, 86-2 U.S.T.C. ¶9589 (Bankr. E.D. Pa. 1986); *In re Thompson*, 85-1 U.S.T.C. ¶9243 (Bankr. N.D. Ohio). *See also In re Gould & Eberhardt Gear Machinery Corp.*, 80 B.R. 614 (D. Mass. 1987) (interest on Chapter 7 postpetition taxes were administrative expenses since delay in payment did not result from time-consuming procedures of administering bankruptcy case or by virtue of any court order deferring payment); *In re Injection Molding Corp.*, 95 B.R. 313, 89-1 U.S.T.C. ¶9256 (Bankr. M.D. Pa. 1989) (allowed interest on postpetition taxes at Code §6621 rate); *In re Cooper*, 124 B.R. 797 (Bankr. D. Neb. 1990) (allowed interest on postpetition property taxes at statutory rate). *See also* Ruotolo, Recovery of Interest on Postpetition Taxes Under Section 503 of the Bankruptcy Code, 64 Am. Bankr. L.J. 427 (1990).

[74] *In re H&C Enterprises*, 35 B.R. 352 (D. Idaho 1983) (focuses on legislative history and concluded that the omission of a reference to interest in 11 U.S.C. §503(b)(1)(B) was intentional); *In re Stack Steel & Supply*, 28 B.R. 151 (W.D. Wash. 1983) (same); *In re Lumara Foods of America, Inc.*, 50 B.R. 809 (Bankr. N.D. Ohio 1985) (same); *In re Luker*, 1993 U.S. Dist. LEXIS 17283 (N.D. Okla.), *aff'g* 148 B.R. 946 (Bankr. N.D. Okla. 1992) (arguably would have allowed the portion of the postpetition interest relating to the period preceding the imposition of a trustee upon a sufficient showing when the taxes were incurred; court relied in part on the pre-Bankruptcy Code Supreme Court decision in *Nicholas v. United States*, 384 U.S. 678 (1966)).

[75] For example, in *In re Quid Me Broadcasting, Inc.*, 1996 U.S. Dist. LEXIS 7581 (W.D.N.Y. 1996), *aff'g* 181 B.R. 715 (Bankr. W.D.N.Y. 1995), involving a non-operating Chapter 7 trustee, the court disallowed the IRS claim for accrued interest on postpetition taxes which were subsequently eliminated by

### § 1015.1.6 Erroneous Refunds or Credits; ITC Recapture

Other than certain excess allowances of a quickie refund (or tentative carryback adjustment) which are expressly granted administrative expense status (*see* § 1005.1.1), a claim for an erroneous refund or credit is granted the same priority as a claim for the tax to which such credit or refund relates.[76] The Bankruptcy Code does not specifically address the classification of a claim for an erroneous refund that results from the miscrediting of monies due to another taxpayer (so-called "nonrebate" erroneous refunds), and thus does not directly relate to a tax of the debtor. In *In re Jackson,*[77] in a situation involving the miscrediting of an income tax refund of

(Footnote Continued)

the carry back of later-year postpetition losses, because the trustee was precluded by the Bankruptcy Code from paying such taxes on a current basis. The court recognized, on the facts presented, that it did not have to consider the circumstance where net taxes were still owing. In addition, *consider In re National Automatic Sprinkler Co. of Oregon,* 86-2 U.S.T.C. ¶9620 (Bankr. D. Or. 1986), wherein the bankruptcy court distinguished, for Chapter 7 purposes, the rationale upon which courts in Chapter 11 cases decided the priority of interest on postpetition taxes (whether or not such courts ultimately granted then first priority treatment). The court held that, because Bankruptcy Code section 726(a)(5) expressly designated interest on administrative claims in Chapter 7 cases as a fifth priority add-on claim, interest on postpetition taxes was similarly relegated to such priority. However, the First Circuit Court of Appeals has held that such interest should be treated as a so-called "first priority" (and since 2005, technically second priority) administrative expense. *See United States v. Yellin (In re Weinstein)* (1st Cir.), *supra* note 11 (reversing decision of the Bankruptcy Appellate Panel, which had agreed with the bankruptcy court). A similar issue arises with respect to postpetition interest accruing prior to conversion of a case from Chapter 11 to Chapter 7, with most courts according then first priority administrative expense treatment. *See* authorities cited *supra* note 11. *See also* IRS Chief Counsel Advice 200205045, December 12, 2001, *reprinted at* 2002 TNT 23-68 (acknowledging that the interest accruing *post*-conversion on preconversion administrative expenses is properly relegated under Bankruptcy Code section 726(a)(5) to a fifth priority add-on claim).

[76] 11 U.S.C. § 507(c) (amended in 1984 to add the reference to "same priority" in lieu of the more general concept of treating such claim "the same as" a claim for the related tax). *See, e.g., United States v. Frontone,* 383 F.3d 656 (7th Cir. 2004), *reh'g denied, en banc,* 2004 U.S. App. LEXIS 24621 (7th Cir. 2004) (involved an individual debtor; an IRS claim for the recovery of an erroneous refund of the debtor's own tax payments—a so-called "rebate" refund—was (i) entitled to priority treatment under section 507(c) and (ii) nondischargeable since the claim constituted a "tax" claim; the court distinguished the treatment of "nonrebate" erroneous refunds, such as that involved in the *Jackson* case, *infra,* as non-tax claims); *Jackson v. United States (In re Jackson),* 253 B.R. 570 (M.D. Ala. 2000) (involved individual debtor; held that grant of "same priority" applies only for purposes of receiving payment from the bankruptcy estate and does not serve to render a claim for the recovery of an erroneous refund of monies properly due a *different* taxpayer—a "nonrebate" refund—nondischargeable as if the claim itself were tax claim; also discussed in text above), *contrasting Bleak v. United States,* 817 F.2d 1368 (9th Cir. 1987) (applying provision prior to 1984 amendment); *In re Coleman American Moving Services, Inc.,* 20 B.R. 267 (Bankr. D. Kan. 1981) (excess allowance of a quickie refund *received prepetition* is an "erroneous" refund within the scope of section 507(c) of the Bankruptcy Code).

*Consider also In re Campbell,* 1990 Bankr. LEXIS 2922 (Bankr. D. Colo. 1990) (IRS was entitled to the immediate repayment of an erroneous refund where the refund, even though relating to a prepetition taxable year, occurred postpetition; because the refund occurred postpetition, the court did not view the IRS as a "creditor" seeking to collect a claim, since a creditor is defined under Bankruptcy Code section 101 as an entity that has a claim against the debtor that arose *before* the bankruptcy case; in the court's view, the IRS was simply a person who paid the debtor "its money in error" and thus was entitled to repayment).

[77] *United States v. Jackson (In re Jackson),* 241 B.R. 473, 1999 Bankr. LEXIS 1381 (Bankr. M.D. Ala. 1999), *rev'd on other grounds,* 253 B.R. 570 (M.D. Ala. 2000) (*see supra* note 76).

another taxpayer, the bankruptcy court held that the erroneous refund should relate to the taxable year in which the debtor received it. Thus, because the income tax refund occurred only two years prior to the debtor's bankruptcy, the IRS's claim for the return of the erroneous refund was treated as an eighth priority claim.

A claim for an investment tax credit recapture (even if triggered by a postpetition disposition) is granted the same priority as the tax to which it relates would have been granted.[78]

## *§1015.2 Subordination of Tax Penalties*

Prior to two 1996 Supreme Court decisions, most courts (including four Circuit Courts) had, pursuant to Bankruptcy Code section 510(c)(1), applied the "principles of equitable subordination" to subordinate in payment to other general unsecured creditors an IRS claim for noncompensatory (or "nonpecuniary loss") penalties—such as a negligence or fraud penalty imposed under Code § 6653—in the context of a liquidating Chapter 11 plan.[79] On the same basis, the Sixth Circuit and several other courts had subordinated in payment administrative expense claims for noncompensatory tax penalties.[80]

However, in two back-to-back decisions (discussed below), the Supreme Court effectively curtailed (except in rare circumstances) the ability of bankruptcy courts to subordinate tax penalties under Bankruptcy Code section 510(c)(1) without a finding of inequitable conduct.[81] The Court, however, left open the possibility that the subordination of prepetition tax penalties in a liquidating Chapter 11 could be sustained without reliance on section 510(c)(1), under other provisions of the Bankruptcy Code.

**Pre-Supreme Court decisions.** The Seventh Circuit, in *In re Virtual Network Services Corp.*,[82] was the first Circuit Court originally to consider the issue. The trustee in that case had filed an amended Chapter 11 plan providing for a straight liquidation of the company. The IRS thereafter filed a proof of claim that included approxi-

---

[78] H. Rep. No. 595, 95th Cong., 1st Sess. 357-358 (1977); *see* 11 U.S.C. § 502(i).

[79] *See, e.g., Virtual Network Services Corp. v. United States (In re Virtual Network Services Corp.)*, 902 F.2d 1246 (7th Cir. 1990), *aff'g*, 98 B.R. 343 (N.D. Ill. 1989); *In re Schultz Broadway Inn, Ltd.*, 912 F.2d 230 (8th Cir. 1990); *Burden v. United States (In re Burden)*, 917 F.2d 115 (3d Cir. 1990) (Chapter 13 case; followed *Virtual Network*; remanded issue, because district court had automatically subordinated IRS claims for prepetition penalties without considering the equities involved); *United States v. Reorganized CF&I Fabricators of Utah, Inc. (In re CF&I Fabricators of Utah, Inc.)* (10th Cir.), 53 F.3d 1155, 95-2 U.S.T.C. ¶ 50,632 (10th Cir. 1995), *rev'd in relevant part and aff'd in part*, 116 S. Ct. 2106, 96-1 U.S.T.C. ¶ 50,322 (1996); *In re Quality Sign Co.*, 51 B.R. 351 (Bankr. S.D. Ind. 1985). Moreover, some courts have reclassified certain federal "taxes" as noncompensatory "penalties" and then considered whether to subordinate such taxes under equitable subordination principles. *See* cases cited at note 53.

[80] *See United States v. Noland (In re First Truck Lines, Inc.)*, 48 F.3d 210, 95-1 U.S.T.C. ¶ 50,187 (6th Cir. 1995), *reh'g, en banc, denied*, 1995 U.S. App. LEXIS 16557, *rev'd*, 116 S. Ct. 1524, 96-1 U.S.T.C. ¶ 50,252 (1996); and cases cited *infra* notes 90-92.

[81] *See United States v. Noland, supra* note 80; *United States v. Reorganized CF&I Fabricators of Utah, Inc., supra* note 53.

[82] *Supra* note 79.

mately $63,000 of prepetition (noncompensatory) tax penalties, which the IRS identified as a general unsecured claim. The trustee objected, contending that such claim should be subordinated to other general unsecured claims.[83]

In upholding the trustee's objection and subordinating the IRS claim for tax penalties, the Seventh Circuit concluded (1) that "Bankruptcy Code section 510(c)(1) authorizes courts to equitably subordinate claims to other claims on a case-by-case basis without requiring in every instance inequitable conduct on the part of the creditor . . . " and (2) that the equities in the present case favored subordination.

The court relied in substantial part on the statements by the sponsors of the Senate and House bills, which stated that:

> [U]nder existing law, a claim is generally subordinated only if [the] holder of such claim is guilty of inequitable conduct, *or the claim itself is of a status susceptible to subordination, such as a penalty*.[84]

In evaluating the equities for and against subordination, the court focused on "fairness to the creditors." The equities cited by the Seventh Circuit as supporting subordination included the fact that all other unsecured creditors had suffered actual cash losses and, similar to the IRS, were innocent of any wrongdoing; that the IRS had waited "too long" to collect its debt;[85] and that the debtor was in a "unique situation" in that it had attempted reorganization but had since sold most of its assets and filed a liquidation plan. In addition, the district court speculated that similar equities may underlie the congressional decision to expressly subordinate noncompensatory penalties in Chapter 7 liquidation proceedings.[86]

In *In re Schultz Broadway Inn, Ltd.*,[87] the Eighth Circuit factually took the *Virtual Network* decision one step further by subordinating the IRS penalties to general unsecured claims of insiders, as well as other creditors. The court rejected the

---

[83] The decision discloses that the amount available for distribution to unsecured creditors was only 15-30 percent of the total amount of their claims. 902 F.2d at 124. Accordingly, subordinating the IRS claim for tax penalties would probably result in no payment on the IRS claim.

[84] 124 Cong. Rec. H 11,095 (daily ed. September 28, 1978) (statement of Rep. Edwards) (emphasis added); 124 Cong. Rec. S 17,412 (daily ed. October 6, 1978) (statement of Sen. DeConcini) (same). Although the court agreed that a "tax claim would rarely be subordinated under this provision" (as stated in the legislative notes to the statute), it did not consider a claim for tax penalties that are punitive in nature to be a "tax claim" in the sense intended. In contrast, in *Mansfield Tire & Rubber Co., supra* note 53, the Sixth Circuit refused to subordinate a claim for federal excise taxes that were properly classified as "taxes" even though they had characteristics of a penalty.

[85] Interestingly, the Seventh Circuit attributed this factor to the district court, but the district court decision made no mention of it. Rather, it simply stated that "because the loss has fallen on the government, and because it offers no justification for passing it on to other innocent creditors, the government must bear the loss." 98 B.R. at 352. Moreover, it is not entirely clear what delay the Seventh Circuit was referring to, although, as indicated above, the IRS proof of claim was not filed until after the trustee filed its amended plan to liquidate the company.

[86] 98 B.R. at 352; *see* 11 U.S.C. § 726(a). It should be noted that the Seventh Circuit and district court decisions stopped short of requiring that the Chapter 7 priorities be followed in every instance in a liquidating Chapter 11 case. *See also In re Burden, supra* note 79. *But consider In re Independent Refining Corp.*, 65 B.R. 622, 626 n.3 (Bankr. S.D. Tex. 1986).

[87] *Supra* note 79.

government's opposing arguments as untimely, since the government had not raised the insider issue at either the bankruptcy court or district court level. The court stated that, although an appropriate case may arise where a bankruptcy court, after consideration of the relative equities, may determine that a nonpecuniary loss claim should be subordinated to the actual loss claims of some but not all creditors, the government bears the burden of directly bringing such equitable considerations to the bankruptcy court's attention.

In *CF&I Fabricators*,[88] the Tenth Circuit also upheld the subordination of tax penalties, relying in meaningful part on the decisions of the Seventh and Eighth Circuits, as well as the similar decisions of other Circuits. In evaluating the equities, the Tenth Circuit referred to the bankruptcy court's finding that other general unsecured creditors—including the Pension Benefit Guaranty Corporation (PBGC), which would be paying pension benefits under the debtor's terminated and underfunded pension plans—would recover only a small percentage of their claims. Adding to the sense of injustice, the bankruptcy court observed that the penalty in question was the tax imposed by Code § 4971 for the debtor's failure to make its required pension plan contributions.[89] Thus, the bankruptcy court reasoned, and the Tenth Circuit agreed, that permitting equal treatment for the tax penalty claim would advance neither the purposes of the Bankruptcy Code nor the provisions of the Internal Revenue Code that gave rise to the penalty.

The principles of equitable subordination under Bankruptcy Code section 510(c)(1) had also been applied (most prominently, by the Sixth Circuit in *United States v. Noland*) to subordinate *postpetition* tax penalties—in one case, to other administrative claims;[90] in another, to the status of a general unsecured claim;[91] and in still another, to all general unsecured claims.[92] In *Noland*, the issue arose in the context of a Chapter 11 case that had been converted to Chapter 7. The Sixth Circuit placed considerable emphasis on various statements by the House and Senate bill

---

[88] *Supra* note 79.

[89] The Tenth Circuit had earlier in its decision agreed with (and the Supreme Court subsequently affirmed) the treatment of the Code § 4971 minimum funding tax as a "penalty" for bankruptcy purposes. *See supra* note 53.

[90] *See In re Import & Mini Car Parts, Ltd., Inc.*, 136 B.R. 178 (Bankr. N.D. Ind. 1991) (converted Chapter 7 case; subordinated penalties, but not accrued interest, on preconversion, postpetition taxes to other Chapter 11 administrative claims). In a subsequent proceeding in the same bankruptcy case, the bankruptcy court rejected the trustee's further attempt to subordinate the tax itself (as well as the interest) to his expenses. Although it did so on the basis of *res judicata*, the court also considered doubtful the validity of the trustee's theory for subordination: namely that the trustee's expenses were somehow worthier or more deserving of payment. *Walker v. United States* (*In re Import & Mini Car Parts, Ltd., Inc.*) (Bankr. N.D. Ind. Dec. 17, 1992), *reprinted at* 93 TNT 21-27.

[91] *See United States v. Noland* (*In re First Truck Lines, Inc.*) (6th Cir.), *supra* note 80 (Chapter 7 case), *aff'g*, 1993 U.S. Dist. LEXIS 14006 (S.D. Ohio 1993), *aff'g*, 141 B.R. 621 (Bankr. S.D. Ohio 1992), but subsequently reversed by the Supreme Court. *But see In re Greensboro Lumber Co.*, 183 B.R. 316, 95-1 U.S.T.C. ¶ 50,259 (Bankr. M.D. Ga. 1995) (refusing to subordinate administrative expense claim for tax penalties due to the absence of inequitable conduct, without discussing the line of cases cited in this section).

[92] *See Unger v. United States* (*In re CMC Elecs. Corp.*), 166 B.R. 382 (Bankr. E.D. Mo. 1993) (involved postpetition penalties for improperly submitted Form W-2s).

sponsors (including the statement quoted above), and the general unfairness of providing equal or higher treatment to a noncompensatory claim than to claims of innocent creditors arising from the extension of value. The Sixth Circuit also observed that Bankruptcy Code section 726(a) (which generally incorporates the priorities under Bankruptcy Code section 507 for purposes of paying claims in Chapter 7), includes the caveat: "Except as provided in section 510 of this title . . . ".

Similar principles of equitable subordination to those discussed above had also been applied by some courts to secured claims.[93]

**1996 Supreme Court decisions.** Reversing both the Sixth Circuit's decision in *Noland* and the Tenth Circuit's decision in *CF&I Fabricators,* the Supreme Court unanimously held that bankruptcy courts cannot categorically subordinate noncompensatory tax penalties under the guise of the principles of equitable subordination.

The Supreme Court criticized both Circuits for engaging in effectively legislative decisions by reexamining the general fairness of the priority provisions, and observed that the distinction between compensatory and noncompensatory claims ran directly contrary to Congress' general policy judgment as to the treatment accorded tax penalties. It made no difference whether the general treatment so accorded be as an administrative expense (as in the case of *Noland*) or a general unsecured claim (as in the case of *CF&I Fabricators*). Although the Court recognized that the principles of equitable subordination may allow a bankruptcy court to reorder the priority of a tax penalty in a given case, it emphasized that exceptions to the general statutory scheme are permitted only when "justified by particular facts."[94]

The Court viewed any reliance on the remarks of the congressional sponsors with respect to the subordination of penalties as misguided.[95] The Court, however, stopped short of deciding that equitable subordination required inequitable conduct. In *Noland*, the Court expressly left the issue open:

> Given our conclusion that the Sixth Circuit's rationale was inappropriately categorical in nature, we need not decide today whether a bankruptcy court must always find creditor misconduct before a claim may be equitably subordinated. We do not hold that (in absence of a need to reconcile conflicting congressional choices) the circumstances that prompt

---

[93] 11 U.S.C. § 510(c)(2); *see* legislative statements cited *supra* note 84 ("The fact that such a claim may be secured is of no consequence to the issue of subordination"). *See also In re Manchester Lakes Assocs.*, 117 B.R. 221 (Bankr. E.D. Va. 1990) (denying secured status to prepetition tax penalties under the guise of Bankruptcy Code section 506(b) and then equitably subordinating the unsecured claim); *Retail Marketing Corp. v. United States (In re Mako)*, 135 B.R. 902 (E.D. Okla. 1991) (upheld bankruptcy court's decision to deprive penalty portion of IRS claim of secured status), *aff'd*, 135 B.R. 902 (E.D. Okla. 1991) (but did so on equitable subordination grounds), *rev'd*, 99 F.3d 1150 (10th Cir. 1996), reprinted in full at 97-1 U.S.T.C. ¶ 50,166 (following the Supreme Court's decisions in *Noland* and *CF&I Fabricators*, discussed below in the text). *But consider Cennamo v. United States (In re Cennamo)*, 147 B.R. 540 (Bankr. C.D. Cal. 1992) (wherein equitable subordination of secured IRS tax penalties was denied where subordination would only benefit individual debtor, not innocent creditors). However, in *In re Divine*, *supra* note 71, the court refused to subordinate secured penalty claims in the absence of inequitable conduct. *Accord In re Burgess*, 171 B.R. 227, 94-2 U.S.T.C. ¶ 50,442 (Bankr. E.D. Tex., 1994).

[94] *Noland*, 116 S. Ct. at 1527 (citation omitted).

[95] Id. at 1528.

> a court to order equitable subordination must not occur at the level of policy choice at which Congress itself operated in drafting the Bankruptcy Code.[96]

The Court similarly did not pursue the issue in *CF&I Fabricators*. It appears to have dismissed, without comment, the fact-specific findings of the bankruptcy court cited by the Tenth Circuit, and the rather intriguing circumstances involved in that case—namely, the interplay between the PBGC as creditor and the IRS, with the IRS seeking recovery on a tax penalty for the debtor's failure to fund its pension plan.

Thus, the circumstances, if any, under which a noncompensatory tax penalty claim can be equitably subordinated under Bankruptcy Code section 510(c)(1), without a finding of inequitable conduct, are unclear and presumably rare.[97] There remains, however, the possibility of an independent basis for subordination. The Supreme Court in *CF&I Fabricators* expressly did not pass on (1) whether the penalty claim at issue was not substantially similar to other unsecured claims and, thus, should not be classified with other general unsecured claims for distribution purposes; and (2) whether, at least in the case of a liquidating Chapter 11 plan, bankruptcy courts may be guided by the priorities accorded claims in Chapter 7 cases, with the result that prepetition noncompensatory tax penalty claims could be subordinated.[98]

Lower courts have since applied the basic holdings of *Noland* and *CF&I Fabricators* to preclude as well the general subordination under Bankruptcy Code section 510(c)(1) of the tax penalty portion of secured claims.[99]

The National Bankruptcy Review Commission, in its report to Congress in October 1997, has recommended the adoption of legislation subordinating prepetition (but apparently not postpetition) noncompensatory tax penalties to general unsecured claims in Chapter 11 cases.[100]

---

[96] Id. (citation omitted).

[97] *See, e.g., Gordon Sel-Way, Inc. v. United States*, 217 B.R. 221, 97-2 U.S.T.C. ¶50,942 (E.D. Mich. 1997) (equitable subordination denied; the court observed that, given the Supreme Court's limited holding, the law within the Sixth Circuit remained, based on the Circuit Court decision in *Noland*, that creditor misconduct was not necessarily required for equitable subordination but "is to be determined on a case-by-case basis, focusing on fairness to all of the creditors involved"; however, the "mere inequities" in bankruptcy priority is not enough). *Cf. Harris v. IRS (In re American Payroll Network, Inc.)*, 98-2 U.S.T.C. ¶50,680 (Bankr. N.D.N.Y. 1998) (concluding, in connection with a discussion of equitable subordination within the context of an asserted setoff, that within the Second Circuit, some proof of the creditor's inequitable behavior is necessary), *citing Kelleran v. Andrijevic*, 825 F.2d 692, 697 (2d Cir. 1987), *cert. denied*, 484 U.S. 1007 (1988).

[98] *CF&I Fabricators*, 116 S. Ct. at 2115.

[99] *See, e.g., In re Mako* (10th Cir.), *supra* note 93; *Kerth v. Ozark Construction (In re North Port Assoc., Inc.)*, 1997 Bankr. LEXIS 1086 (Bankr. E.D. Mo. 1997).

[100] *See* National Bankruptcy Review Commission Final Report (October 20, 1997), Recommendation 4.2.36, at pp. 978-979.

## *§1015.3 Subrogation Claim*

Under Bankruptcy Code section 507(d), the holder of a subrogation claim relating to a fourth priority or eighth priority tax claim is not subrogated to the tax claim's priority status; instead, the holder is treated as a general unsecured creditor.[101] No similar rule applies in the case of an administrative expense tax claim.[102] Thus, the holder of a subrogation claim in such instance would be entitled to claim administrative expense treatment.

## *§1015.4 Successive Bankruptcies*

In successive bankruptcies, the issue may arise whether a tax claim that was a priority claim in the first bankruptcy can still qualify for priority status in the second bankruptcy. Assume, for example, that the IRS had a withholding tax claim against a corporate debtor, that such claim was provided for in the debtor's first Chapter 11 plan and that the debtor is again in bankruptcy. As discussed at §1015.1.4 above, a prepetition withholding tax claim generally is entitled to an eighth priority. In *Official Committee of Unsecured Creditors of White Farm Equipment Company v. United States*,[103] the district court held, on these facts, that the first bankruptcy "discharged" the priority debt (even though providing for full payment) and substituted therefor a new undertaking that became a general unsecured claim in the second bankruptcy. On appeal, however, the Seventh Circuit reversed and upheld priority status.[104] Finding nothing in the statutory language or legislative history compelling the district court's conclusion, the Seventh Circuit stated that it merely strove to interpret the statute "so as to ensure that the delicate balance of the priority and discharge

---

[101] *See supra* §1006 note 206; *Aetna Casualty and Surety Co. v. Chateaugay Corp.* (*In re Chateaugay Corp.*), 89 F.3d 942 (2d Cir. 1996); *In re Fiesole Trading Corp.*, 315 B.R. 198 (Bankr. D. Mass. 2004) (discussing the applicable standard for subrogation under Bankruptcy Code section 507(d) where a debtor corporation's withholding tax liability is satisfied through payments by the "responsible individuals" under the Code §6672 100% penalty); *Creditor's Committee v. Massachusetts Dept. of Revenue*, 105 B.R. 145 (D. Mass. 1989); *In re Kaldis*, 122 B.R. 54 (Bankr. S.D. Tex. 1990); *In re Brickel Assoc., Inc.*, 170 B.R. 140 (Bankr. W.D. Wis. 1994) (Treasury could not by regulation change a subrogation claim for customs duties into an assignment in order to assign its priority); *In re Chalk Line Mfg.*, 181 B.R. 605 (Bankr. N.D. Ala. 1995) (same); *see also* Collier Pamphlet Edition, 1 Bankruptcy Code 265 (1990/1991 version). Such section, however, does not prevent the holder from benefiting from a related tax lien. *See, e.g., United Bank of Arizona v. Watkins Oil Service, Inc.* (*In re Watkins Oil Service, Inc.*), 100 B.R. 7 (Bankr. D. Ariz. 1989).

For rules relating to the establishment of a subrogation claim in the case of a codebtor, surety or guarantor, *see* Bankruptcy Code section 509. *See also In re Chateaugay Corp.* (2d Cir.), *supra*; *Mason v. Pennsylvania Dept. of Revenue* (*In re Davis*), 145 B.R. 499 (Bankr. W.D. Pa. 1992) (held that partners that are liable for taxes of the partnership are considered "codebtors" and that, under Bankruptcy Code section 509(b)(2), payment of the tax by one partner does not result in subrogation rights, although the partner may have a right of contribution against the other partner); *Garrow Oil Corp. v. Bork* (*In re Bork*), *supra* note 52 (discussing the concept of subrogation).

[102] *See, e.g., In re Trasks' Charolais*, 84 B.R. 646 (Bankr. D.S.D. 1988).

[103] 111 B.R. 158 (N.D. Ill. 1990).

[104] 943 F.2d 752 (7th Cir. 1991), *cert. denied*, 112 S. Ct. 1292 (1992).

scheme established by the [Bankruptcy] Code is not skewed by the unanticipated development of serial Chapter 11 filings."[105]

In contrast, the Third Circuit commented that "the holding in *White Farm* may be contrary to the legislative intent underlying" the discharge provisions of Bankruptcy Code section 1141 with respect to corporate debtors and, therefore, considered the Seventh Circuit's interpretation in *White Farm* "debatable."[106] Subsequently, however, several lower courts (including within the Third Circuit) have in fact dismissed the Third Circuit's comment as *dicta* and inconclusive,[107] and have held that a bankruptcy discharge affects only the debtor's legal obligation to pay and "does not alter the priority character of the underlying claim, even as embodied in the treatment of the claim in a chapter 11 plan."[108]

Under the Seventh Circuit's position and the position of these lower courts, income, gross receipts and excise taxes entitled to eighth priority status in an earlier bankruptcy also continued to be entitled to priority status in a second bankruptcy so long as any time limitations (or so-called "lookback periods") are satisfied.[109] In such instance, the issue generally became whether the time limitations (often 3 years, and in one instance 240 days) were extended by the period of the first bankruptcy plus, possibly, some additional period.

Although relatively few cases considered the extension of time limitations for priority status with respect to *corporate* debtors in this context, cases involving *individual* debtors (as to whom priority taxes generally are nondischargeable) were abundant and finally, in 2002, reached the Supreme Court in *Young v. United States*[110]

---

[105] Id. at 757. *Cf. Archer v. Warner*, 123 S. Ct. 1462 (2003) (settlement agreement relating to certain fraud claims that was entered into prebankruptcy did not change the inherent nature of any debt obligation created by the settlement agreement from being one "obtained by . . . false pretenses, a false representation, or actual fraud").

[106] *In re Benjamin Coal Co.*, 978 F.2d 823 (3d Cir. 1992) (administrative priority of non-tax claim not preserved following confirmed plan, even though case subsequently converted from Chapter 11 to Chapter 7).

[107] *In re R.J. Reynolds-Patrick County Memorial Hospital, Inc.*, 305 B.R. 243 (Bankr. W.D. Va. 2003) (character of underlying tax claim survives discharge; involved withholding taxes); *United States v. Conston, Inc.* (*In re Conston, Inc.*), 181 B.R. 769 (D. Del. 1995) (same, but involved income taxes; "What the [Third Circuit] did hold was that the bankruptcy created characteristic of priority does not, *of its own accord*, survive confirmation of the plan and automatically resurrect itself in a future Title 11 proceeding . . . . [The Third Circuit] therefore did not address the issue presented by [the debtor in this case]—does confirmation change the 'type of claim' so as to eliminate the characteristics that would permit the claim to qualify for priority treatment in a subsequent Chapter 11 proceeding;" emphasis added); *In re Sprouse-Reitz Stores, Inc.*, 177 B.R. 679 (Bankr. D. Or. 1994) (same, but involved withholding and sales taxes). None of these cases considered the issue discussed below, regarding the extension of any time limitations applicable for priority treatment.

[108] *In re R.J. Reynolds-Patrick County Memorial Hospital, Inc.* (Bankr. W.D. Va.), *supra* note 107, at 248.

[109] 943 F.2d at 757.

[110] 122 S. Ct. 1036, 2002-2 U.S.T.C. ¶50,257 (2002). *See also* Weil, Taxpayers Cannot Hide in Bankruptcy: The Supreme Court's Decision in *Young*, 96 J. Taxn. 282 (2002).

For cases pre-dating the Supreme Court's decision that considered the extension of time limitations with respect to a corporate debtor, *see In re Affiliated Food Stores, Inc.* and *In re Offshore Diving & Salvaging*, discussed *infra* in text accompanying notes 118-119.

Illustrating how the priority rules would apply to an income tax accorded a seventh (now eighth) priority in an earlier bankruptcy, and whose priority in the second bankruptcy depends on the

—which, as discussed below, adopted a form of "automatic" tolling. Meanwhile, there was pending in Congress legislation that would provide for an automatic suspension in the case of successive bankruptcies. This legislation was adopted in 2005, effective for bankruptcy cases commenced on or after October 17, 2005, and is discussed at § 1015.4.2 below. Although similar in concept, the tolling under *Young* and the new statutory suspension can result in different periods of overall extension.

### § 1015.4.1 Pre-10/17/2005 Bankruptcy Cases: The *Young* Decision

Decided in early 2002, the Supreme Court in *Young v. United States*[111] unanimously held that the three-year time period relevant for determining the eighth priority of certain income tax and gross receipt claims—and by implication the other time limitations embodied in the priority provisions of Bankruptcy Code section 507(a)(8)—were limitations periods subject to traditional principles of equitable tolling. Moreover, in applying such principles to successive bankruptcies, the Court adopted a form of "automatic" tolling.

The fact pattern before the Court was the back-to-back filings by a husband and wife of a Chapter 7 case, concurrently with (in fact one day prior to) the dismissal of the debtors' Chapter 13 case. Absent the tolling of the three-year time period for the income tax claim at issue, the IRS would have had a general unsecured claim for such taxes in the debtors' Chapter 7 case, even though it had a priority claim in the prior bankruptcy case and had been precluded by the automatic stay from collecting the taxes during the pendency of that case. Applying the principles of equitable tolling, the Court stated:

> Tolling is in our view appropriate regardless of [the debtors'] intentions when filing back-to-back Chapter 13 and Chapter 7 petitions—whether

---

(Footnote Continued)

bankruptcy filing being within three years of the due date for the tax return, the Seventh Circuit in *White Farm* had stated, in *dicta* (emphasis added), that:

> If three years have elapsed by the time the second Chapter 11 proceeding is filed, such a claim would lose its section 507 priority. *Our reading of the statute neither extends nor extinguishes the priority accorded claims under section 507.*

In view of the Supreme Court's decision in *Young*, the Seventh Circuit's own later decision in *Montoya v. United States* (*In re Montoya*), 965 F.2d 554, 92-2 U.S.T.C. ¶ 50,435 (7th Cir. 1992) (acknowledging that an extension of the three year time period was consistent with the court's own philosophy that the "delicate balance of the priority and discharge scheme" of the Bankruptcy Code should not be "skewed by the unanticipated development of serial Chapter 11 filings"), and the Seventh Circuit's only limited consideration of the issue of time extensions in *White Farm* (since the issue was not before it), this passage should be accorded no weight.

*But consider In re LMS Holding Co., supra* note 51 (where the "second" bankruptcy was that of the entity that acquired the first debtor's assets pursuant to the first debtor's bankruptcy plan, and assumed the first debtor's liability to pay priority tax claims over six years, including certain FICA, FUTA, and excise taxes; although granting continued priority to the FICA and FUTA taxes, the excise taxes were beyond the applicable three-year priority period; it appears that no extension of the three-year period was tacked on for the first bankruptcy).

[111] *Supra* note 110.

> the Chapter 13 petition was filed in good faith or solely to run down the lookback period. In either case, the IRS was disabled from protecting its claim during the pendency of the Chapter 13 petition, and this period of disability tolled the three-year lookback period when the [debtors] filed their Chapter 7 petition.[112]

Thus, the Court's decision focuses on the purpose and function of the limitations period, and is not dependent on the fact that the debtor is an individual or on the debtor's intent.

As discussed below, the Supreme Court's decision still left unresolved, and even raised anew, certain ancillary issues—which remain relevant for bankruptcy cases commenced before October 17, 2005.

**Pre-Supreme Court decisions.** Prior to the Supreme Court's decision, six Circuit Courts of Appeals had similarly adopted "automatic" tolling, although not necessarily based on the principles of equitable tolling. Four employed a strained reading of the tolling provision in Bankruptcy Code section 108(c), incorporating the safeguards of Code § 6503(h) (which tolls the statute of limitations on collections for any period during which collection is precluded by reason of a bankruptcy case and for six months thereafter).[113] One relied on the general equitable powers of the bankruptcy court under Bankruptcy Code section 105(a) and looked to such other tolling provisions as reflections of Congressional intent.[114] And one, the First Circuit in the lower court decision in the *Young* case, employed equitable concepts but did not expressly rely on Bankruptcy Code section 105(a).[115]

---

112 122 S. Ct. at 1041.

113 *See, e.g., In re Brickley*, 70 B.R. 113, 87-1 U.S.T.C. ¶ 9313 (Bankr. 9th Cir. 1987) (*per curiam*) (three-year period in then Bankruptcy Code section 507(a)(7)(A)(i) extended for the period described in Code § 6503(b); *see supra* § 1008 notes 2 and 42, with respect to nondischargeable federal taxes, where the IRS's ability to collect from the individual debtor is impeded by an earlier bankruptcy case involving such debtor; court reasoned that safeguards of Bankruptcy Code section 108(c), which extends the statute of limitations for creditors whose actions against the debtor are hampered by the automatic stay and which is intended to incorporate the tolling provisions of Code § 6503(b), would be rendered ineffective in the absence of such an extension); *West v. United States (In re West)*, 5 F.3d 423 (9th Cir. 1993), *cert. denied*, 114 S. Ct. 1830 (1994) (adopted the reasoning of *Brickley*; suspended the 240-day period of then Bankruptcy Code section 507(a)(7)(A)(ii) for the period of debtor's prior bankruptcy case, which was voluntarily dismissed, and by reason of Code § 6503(h) for six months thereafter); *Waugh v. IRS (In re Waugh)*, 109 F.3d 489, 97-1 U.S.T.C. ¶ 50,304 (8th Cir. 1997), *cert. denied*, 118 S. Ct. 80 (1997); *In re Taylor*, 81 F.3d 20, 96-1 U.S.T.C. ¶ 50,151 (3d Cir. 1996); *Montoya v. United States (In re Montoya)* (7th Cir.), *supra* note 110 (held that three-year time period was also extended for period following the first bankruptcy after the IRS's claim was disallowed until it was reinstated).

Going even further, the bankruptcy court in *In re Townsent*, 187 B.R. 230 (Bankr. W.D. Tenn. 1995), had held (without regard to any time limitations) that the IRS's income tax claim retained its priority status in the debtor's second bankruptcy.

114 *In re Richards*, 994 F.2d 763, 93-1 U.S.T.C. ¶ 50,344 (10th Cir. 1993) (upheld suspension of 240-day period as an appropriate use of the bankruptcy court's equitable powers under Bankruptcy Code section 105; suspension was consistent with Congress's intent, as reflected in the statutory priorities and in the tolling provisions of Bankruptcy Code section 108 and Code § 6503(h), that the government have the benefit of certain time periods to pursue its collection efforts).

115 *Young v. United States (In re Young)*, 233 F.3d 56, 2000-2 U.S.T.C. ¶ 50,868 (1st Cir. 2000), *aff'd*, 122 S. Ct. 1036, 2002-2 U.S.T.C. ¶ 50,257 (2002).

In contrast, three Circuit Courts of Appeals had concluded that no basis existed for an automatic extension, but recognized that an extension may be permitted on equitable grounds, depending on the facts of the particular case (with the burden on the IRS to prove than an extension was justified).[116] Factors generally taken into account included whether the debtor abused the system through the successive filings and whether the IRS had sufficient opportunity to collect the tax.[117]

In *In re Affiliated Food Stores, Inc.*,[118] a Texas district court applied the foregoing authorities to a corporate debtor and, being within the Fifth Circuit, remanded the case for a determination of the equities. The court did not discuss, nor did it suggest, any distinction between discharged and nondischargeable taxes or between corporate and individual debtors. The case involved a relatively common fact pattern. The IRS had filed a timely priority tax claim for income taxes in the debtor's first bankruptcy. Under the debtor's confirmed plan, the tax claim was discharged and the amount owed was payable in installments over approximately six years (as permitted by the Bankruptcy Code, *see* § 1016.1 below). Any attempt by the IRS to obtain earlier payment was prohibited by the plan. Prior to the IRS having been paid in full, the debtor filed its second bankruptcy case. In remanding the case to the bankruptcy court, the district court recognized that the IRS had no opportunity to collect the taxes owed to it since the commencement of the debtor's first bankruptcy (due

---

[116] *Quenzer v. United States (In re Quenzer)*, 19 F.3d 163 (5th Cir. 1993); *Palmer v. United States*, 219 F.3d 580, 2000-2 U.S.T.C. ¶ 50,588 (6th Cir. 2000), *rev'g*, 228 B.R. 880, 99-1 U.S.T.C. ¶ 50,238 (Bankr. 6th Cir. 1999) (2:1 decision); *Morgan v. United States (In re Morgan)*, 182 F.3d 775, 99-2 U.S.T.C. ¶ 50,712 (11th Cir. 1999) (but holding that "the equities will generally favor the government"), *remanded to* 2000-1 U.S.T.C. ¶ 50,851 (Bankr. N.D. Ga 2000) (upon remand, bankruptcy court tolled priority period for IRS claims relating to some but not all years; even though no evidence of dilatory conduct or bad faith was attributed to the debtor, court tolled the period where the IRS had only 70 days between the date of assessment and the filing of the debtor's first bankruptcy, which lasted over four years). *See also United States v. Messer (In re Messer)*, 2000-2 U.S.T.C. ¶ 50,609 (S.D.N.Y. 2000); *In re Tarulla*, 1999 Bankr. LEXIS 1738 (Bankr. N.D.N.Y. 1999).

A similar approach was taken by the Bankruptcy Appellate Panel for the Ninth Circuit in the case of state taxes. *See Gurney v. State of Ariz. Dept. of Rev. (In re Gurney)*, 192 Bankr. 529 (Bankr. 9th Cir. 1995) (distinguished *Brickley, supra* note 113, because Arizona did not have an equivalent provision to Code § 6503(b) or (h), but nevertheless allowed an extension based on the particular equities of the case).

[117] *See, e.g., In re Turner*, 195 B.R. 476, 96-2 U.S.T.C. ¶ 50,352 (Bankr. N.D. Ala. 1996); *Nolan v. United States (In re Nolan)*, 205 B.R. 885, 97-2 U.S.T.C. ¶ 50,990 (Bankr. M.D. Tenn. 1997), *aff'd*, 98-1 U.S.T.C. ¶ 50,362 (M.D. Tenn. 1998); *Clark v. IRS (In re Clark)*, 184 B.R. 728 (Bankr. N.D. Tex. 1995) (facts justified tolling). *See also United States v. Gilmore*, 226 B.R. 567, 98-2 U.S.T.C. ¶ 50,506 (E.D. Tex. 1998) (affirmed bankruptcy court denial of tolling where IRS failed to affirmatively request equitable relief during pendency of bankruptcy case).

[118] *United States v. Colvin (In re Affiliated Food Stores, Inc.)*, 222 B.R. 799, 98-1 U.S.T.C. ¶ 50,327 (N.D. Tex. 1998) (second time remanding), *appeal dismissed*, 174 F.3d 198 (5th Cir. 1999); and *United States v. Colvin*, 203 B.R. 930 (N.D. Tex. 1996) (initial remand, to same effect; court stated that, "[w]ith only one or two exceptions, courts addressing the issue [of tolling on equitable grounds] have held that the time periods for priority under 507(a)(7)(i) and (ii) should be tolled during intervals when the IRS is legally prohibited from collecting the funds owed"). On remand, the bankruptcy court denied tolling on equitable grounds, but the district court subsequently reversed. The district court based its determination on the prolonged period for which the IRS was prevented from collecting the taxes and the inequitable conduct of the trustee (whether or not amounting to bad faith or dilatory conduct). 265 B.R. 433 (N.D. Texas 2001).

initially to the automatic stay and thereafter to the provisions of the debtor's plan), and strongly hinted that such fact alone was sufficient to justify tolling on equitable grounds.

In *In re Offshore Diving & Salvaging, Inc.*,[119] the bankruptcy court and district court, also within the Fifth Circuit, similarly applied equitable concepts to a corporate debtor. Although the district court agreed with the IRS that misconduct on the part of the debtor was not essential to permit tolling, the IRS had offered no facts in support of the relative equities of its position, whereas the debtor showed that the IRS in fact benefited from the first bankruptcy. The debtor pointed out that going into the first bankruptcy, the IRS had only a junior lien position of negligible value, that the plan had provided for payment of 100 percent of the IRS's priority claims over time, and that the second bankruptcy filing did not occur until two years and four months afterwards (by which time the facts showed that the IRS had been paid over $^1/_3$ of its priority claims). Accordingly, the district court agreed with the bankruptcy court that the IRS failed to establish that the equities justified tolling the priority period.

The National Bankruptcy Review Commission, in its report to Congress in October 1997, recommended legislation extending the relevant time periods for eighth priority status in the case of successive bankruptcies.[120]

**Ancillary and related issues.** Prior to the Supreme Court's decision, courts adhering to the automatic extension of the applicable priority periods in successive bankruptcies had also generally upheld, where relevant, an extension of up to an additional six-month period.[121] This was consistent with the fact that the courts of appeals had generally justified the extension of the priority period (either directly or indirectly) by reference to the suspension of the statute of limitations on collections under Code §6503(h) (discussed at §1008). However, the Supreme Court's decision in *Young* relies exclusively on the principles of equitable tolling, with not even a passing reference to Code §6503(h). Thus, it remains to be seen whether or to what extent—in pre-October 17, 2005 bankruptcy cases wherein the *Young* decision continues to be controlling—courts will be willing, in the aftermath of the *Young* decision, to grant an additional extension of time to the IRS beyond the period of the prior bankruptcy case. Meanwhile, the IRS has instructed its agents, in view of the

---

[119] 99-1 U.S.T.C. ¶50,560 (Bankr. E.D. La. 1999) (involved employer taxes), *aff'd*, 1999 U.S. Dist. LEXIS 16664 (E.D. La. 1999).

[120] *See* National Bankruptcy Review Commission Final Report (October 20, 1997), Recommendation 4.2.5, at pp. 951-952.

[121] *See, e.g., Savini v. United States*, 260 B.R. 689, 2001-1 U.S.T.C. ¶50,432 (D. N.J. 2001) (IRS entitled to additional six-month extension); *In re Dodson*, 191 B.R. 869, (Bankr. D. Or. 1996) (although the debtor had already been through two bankruptcies and was on its third, the IRS was not entitled to a full additional six-month suspension of time for each of the previous two bankruptcies, but in each case was limited to the lesser of six months or the number of days that elapsed before the succeeding bankruptcy; the court justified its conclusion on equitable grounds); *Daniel v. United States (In re Daniel)*, 227 B.R. 675, 98-1 U.S.T.C. ¶50,320 (Bankr. N.D. Ind. 1998) (applied same approach as in *Dodson* to the number of additional six-month periods permitted in the case of four successive bankruptcies). *But see In re Avila*, 228 B.R. 63, 99-1 U.S.T.C. ¶50,274 (Bankr. D. Mass. 1999) (extended three-year period for prior bankruptcies, but held that there was no support in the statute or legislative history for permitting an additional six months).

reasoning in *Young*, that the priority period "should not be computed by including an additional six months, based on I.R.C. 6503(h)."[122]

In addition, the IRS has espoused the view that the applicable priority period should be extended for all periods during which it is precluded by reason of a debtor's bankruptcy from taking collection action, including under the terms of the debtor's confirmed Chapter 11 plan where payment is to be made over time.[123] Although the IRS last considered this position prior to the Supreme Court's decision, it is in accord with the Supreme Court's application of the principles of equitable tolling.

### § 1015.4.2 Current (Post-2005 Act) Bankruptcy Cases: Statutory Suspension

For bankruptcy cases commenced on or after October 17, 2005, the Bankruptcy Code now provides for an automatic suspension of the applicable time periods under Bankruptcy Code section 507(a)(8), governing the priority of unsecured tax claims, in the case of successive bankruptcies. Accordingly, in the event of a second bankruptcy, the applicable priority period (including the 240-day period for offers in compromise) is suspended for any time during which collection proceedings were stayed by a prior bankruptcy case *or* during which collection was precluded under a confirmed bankruptcy plan, plus 90 days.[124] Not apparent, though, is how the 90-day extension applies where the debtor has been through bankruptcy at least twice before: Is the 90-day extension a singular addition, regardless of the number of prior bankruptcies? Or, is it added to the period of each prior bankruptcy?[125]

### § 1015.4.3 Other Continuing Priority Considerations

Whatever the appropriate extension of time where there is a prescribed time period for priority status, a "first priority" administrative tax claim that for some reason goes unpaid from the first bankruptcy will *not* retain its administrative expense status in a second bankruptcy, but may be able to qualify as an eighth priority tax claim (depending on the type of tax and whether any applicable time limitations are satisfied[126]). This is because each bankruptcy creates its own "estate" and generally only those taxes both *incurred by* the estate and not qualifying for

---

122 IRS Chief Counsel Notice CC-2002-023, dated May 9, 2002, *reprinted at* 2002 TNT 100-41.

123 IRS Legal Memorandum 200102002, August 15, 2000, *reprinted at* 2001 TNT 10-63.

124 11 U.S.C. § 507(a)(8) (both as part of the language of subparagraph (A)(ii) and in the flush language at end of the subsection), *as amended by* P.L. 109-8, § 705(2) (2005).

125 *Consider* the treatment of multiple add-on periods under prior case law, noted in the preceding section under "Ancillary and related issues;" and in the context of extensions of the statute of limitations under Internal Revenue Code § 6503(h), discussed above at § 1008.4.

126 *See, e.g., In re Brensing*, 337 B.R. 376 (Bankr. D. Kan. 2006) (Chapter 13 case, involving pre-2005 Act years; priority period tolled under *Young* for the period of the first bankruptcy during which the postpetition taxes were owing, because the IRS was automatically stayed under Bankruptcy Code section 362(a)(3) and (4) from collecting the taxes).

eighth priority treatment are entitled to administrative expense status.[127] A "former" administrative tax claim would clearly fail the first predicate and may fail the second predicate as well.

A different issue was presented in the *Monroe Cigar* case.[128] There, the issue was whether, upon the debtor's default on its first Chapter 11 plan, the IRS could properly secure the payment of its priority tax claim from the first bankruptcy, thereby becoming a secured creditor in the debtor's second Chapter 11 case. Weighing the policy considerations as expressed in *White Farm,* the district court held that it could. The court left open whether a different balance might be reached where the first plan did not provide for full payment of the IRS's claim, such that the IRS was claiming more in the second bankruptcy as a result of its new secured status.

## §1016 PAYMENT OF TAX CLAIMS

An allowed unsecured tax claim entitled to priority (*see* discussion at §1015) must generally be paid in cash on the effective date of the Chapter 11 plan.[1] There are two general exceptions to this rule, as discussed below at §1016.1. In addition, as discussed at §1016.2, when deferred payment is permitted, the debtor may be able to apply any installment payments first to the portion of such claim, if any, for unpaid trust fund taxes.

All payments under a Chapter 11 plan remain subject to applicable withholding, *e.g.*, employment tax (*see* §§1006.3 and 1015.1.3) or back-up withholding.[2]

---

[127] *Cf. In re Benjamin Coal Co.* (3d Cir.), *supra* note 106 (administrative priority of non-tax claim not preserved following confirmed plan, even though case subsequently converted from Chapter 11 to Chapter 7; court discussed the Seventh Circuit's decision in *White Farms* and questioned, but did not conclude, whether the general character of a tax claim would continue for priority purposes); *In re Jamesway Corp.*, 202 B.R. 697 (Bankr. S.D.N.Y. 1996) (involving lease rejection claims seeking then first priority status from first bankruptcy to the next); *see also In re Occhipinti*, 98-1 U.S.T.C. ¶50,112 (Bankr. M.D. Fla. 1997) (individual debtor, Chapter 13 case; although questionable, the court concluded that the time limitations for eighth priority tax treatment should also be extended in the case of unpaid postpetition tax liabilities from a former bankruptcy case, even though the IRS could have sought payment during the former bankruptcy case).

[128] *United States v. W.F. Monroe Cigar Co. (In re W.F. Monroe Cigar Co.)*, 166 B.R. 110 (N.D. Ill. 1994) (reversing bankruptcy court). *Also consider Omega Corp., Inc. v. United States (In re Omega Corp., Inc.)*, 173 B.R. 830 (Bankr. D. Conn. 1994) (permitting IRS tax lien filing where debtor had defaulted under its Chapter 11 plan and subsequently entered into a Form 2504 and a related letter agreement providing for a new payment schedule).

[1] **§1016** 11 U.S.C. §1129(a)(9). Special rules are provided for tax claims against bankrupt (or insolvent) financial institutions and trust companies, a substantial portion of whose business consists of receiving deposits and making loans and discounts, whereby no tax shall be assessed or collected that would diminish the institutions' assets necessary for full payment of all its depositors. *See* §1017.

[2] *See, e.g.*, IRS Letter Ruling 8938019, June 23, 1989 (discusses information reporting and backup withholding); *see also* IRS Letter Ruling 8916007, January 11, 1989 (information reporting).

## §1016.1 Permitted Deferrals

In certain cases, a debtor may be able to defer the payment of a tax claim beyond the effective date of the Chapter 11 plan.

### §1016.1.1 Bankruptcy Code Authorized Deferrals

The provisions of the Bankruptcy Code permitting the deferral of payments with respect to prepetition secured tax claims and eighth priority tax claims underwent significant change in the Bankruptcy Abuse Prevention and Consumer Protection Act of 2005. Accordingly, the terms under which a debtor corporation may defer payment with respect to claims of these types differ depending on whether or not the bankruptcy case commenced on or after October 17, 2005. These provisions—both new and old—are discussed below.

**Pre-10/17/2005 bankruptcy cases.** For bankruptcy cases commenced *before* October 17, 2005, no mandatory payment scheme is provided for secured claims, except possibly in the case of postpetition secured claims (which may have to be paid as an administrative expense claim on the effective date of the plan).[3] Accordingly, nothing in the Bankruptcy Code mandates that a secured claim be paid prior to unsecured claims; rather, upon objection, the debtor must be able to establish that the treatment provided is fair and equitable.[4]

Pursuant to Bankruptcy Code section 1129(a)(9)(C), as effective for pre-10/17/2005 bankruptcy cases, unsecured prepetition tax claims entitled to an eighth priority may be paid over a period not to exceed six (6) years following the

[3] *Compare, e.g., In re Boston Harbor Marina Co.*, 157 B.R. 726 (Bankr. D. Mass. 1993) (held that only *unsecured* postpetition taxes are properly treated as a then first priority administrative expense claim); *In re Florida Engineered Constr. Products Corp.*, 157 B.R. 698 (Bankr. M.D. Fla. 1993) (same); *In re Broadway 704-706 Assoc.*, 154 B.R. 44 (Bankr. S.D.N.Y. 1993) (secured status is not elective; city could not opt to be treated as a then first priority unsecured claim in order to obtain full payment on the effective date), *with In re Moltech Power Systems, Inc.*, 296 B.R. 63 (Bankr. N.D. Fla. 2003) (secured postpetition property taxes entitled to then first priority administrative expense treatment); *City of New York v. R. H. Macy & Co. (In re R. H. Macy & Co.)*, 176 B.R. 315 (S.D.N.Y. 1994) (same; so holding under plain reading of statute); *In re Soltan*, 234 B.R. 260, 269-272 (Bankr. E.D. N.Y. 1999) (same; but cautions that "[t]his conclusion would not apply to post-petition real property taxes applicable to real property of the estate which is not administered by the Trustee"). The 2005 bankruptcy legislation also made clear for post-effective date bankruptcy cases that administrative expense claims had to be paid on the effective date of the plan, whether secured or unsecured. *See* 11 U.S.C. §§503(b)(1)(B)(i), *as amended by* P.L. 109-8, §712(b) (2005); in conjunction with 11 U.S.C. §§507(a)(1), 1129(a)(9)(A).

[4] *See* 11 U.S.C. §1129(b)(2)(A) (describing "fair and equitable" standard); *see, e.g., United States v. TM Building Products, Ltd.*, 231 B.R. 364, 98-2 U.S.T.C. ¶50,845 (S.D. Fla. 1998) (permitted secured claims to be paid at such time "when funds are available without adversely impacting the cash flow needs of the company," with the bankruptcy court retaining jurisdiction over the matter in the event it appeared that the debtor was unreasonably avoiding its obligations); *United States v. Creamer*, 195 B.R. 154 (M.D. Fla. 1996) (upholding extended payout of secured claims under one debtor's plan, but rejecting an extended payout under a second debtor's plan); *In re Rotella*, 1994 Bankr. LEXIS 436 (Bankr. N.D.N.Y. 1994) (upheld payment over 30 years of IRS claim secured by residence); *In re Haas*, 195 B.R. 933 (Bankr. S.D. Ala. 1996) (debtor agreed to extend statute of limitations on collection with respect to 30-year payout of IRS secured claim), *aff'd*, 1997 U.S. Dist. LEXIS 23095 (S.D. Ala. 1997), *rev'd and remanded on other issues*, 162 F.3d 1087, 99-1 U.S.T.C. ¶50,178 (11th Cir. 1998).

date on which the tax liability was assessed.[5] Although nominally six years, because the deferral period is measured from the date of assessment (rather than from the effective date of the plan), the actual deferral period frequently will be significantly shorter than six years, and sometimes could be longer.

**EXAMPLE**

X Corp. is a calendar year taxpayer. On June 30, 1989, the IRS assessed X for unpaid 1984 income taxes. Six months later, on January 1, 1990, X filed for bankruptcy under Chapter 11. X thereafter timely filed its federal income tax return for its 1989 taxable year (its last prepetition year). The return disclosed a $50x tax liability, but explained that payment of the tax was prohibited by the Bankruptcy Code. On January 1, 1992, X's confirmed Chapter 11 plan became effective. The plan provides for the deferred payment of all eighth priority taxes in accordance with Bankruptcy Code section 1129(a)(9)(C).

Since, as of the effective date, 2½ years have passed since the 1984 taxes were assessed, the period over which such taxes will be payable is limited to 3½ years (six years less the period since the date of assessment). In contrast, because the IRS was prohibited by the automatic stay from assessing X's 1989 tax liability (even though X admitted such tax was due on its tax return),[6] X will have a full six years over which to pay that tax. (In fact, the period could be even longer than six years if the IRS failed to immediately assess such tax at the time the plan became effective and the automatic stay terminated.[7]) For bankruptcy cases commenced on or after October 22, 1994, the IRS is no longer prohibited by the automatic stay from assessing any tax at any time during the bankruptcy case (*see* § 1007.1).

---

[5] The courts are divided as to whether the IRS may set off against the payment stream any subsequently claimed refund for prepetition taxes (or any other prepetition amounts due from the U.S. government), *see supra* § 1006.1.1.3. Also, care should be taken in drafting the plan to make sure to use the term "allowed claim" (rather than terms such as "debt" or "liability") when what is intended to be satisfied is only the actual amount claimed. *Cf. Burford v. IRS (In re Burford)*, 231 B.R. 913, 99-1 U.S.T.C. ¶ 50,423 (Bankr. N.D. Tex. 1999) (the term "debt" was held to refer to the full tax liability underlying the IRS's claim, inclusive of postpetition interest, even though such interest would not have been an allowable claim in the bankruptcy case).

[6] Technically speaking, there is no such thing as a "self-assessment." Rather, an assessment requires an official act by the IRS. *See, e.g.,* Code § 6201, which provides that the "Secretary shall assess all taxes determined by the taxpayer . . . as to which returns or lists are made under this title." *See also United States v. Goldstein*, 2005 U.S. Dist. LEXIS 29753 (S.D. Tex. 2005); *In re O'Leary*, 72-1 U.S.T.C. ¶ 9287 (W.D. Wis. 1972) (so holding). *Cf. California State Bd. of Equalization v. Owen (In re Owen)* (Bankr. 9th Cir. March 4, 1993), *reprinted at* 93 TNT 92-27 (reached similar conclusion under California sales and use tax statute).

[7] *See* discussion at § 1008 above, accompanying notes 11 and 14.

There is no statutory rule under this provision requiring equal periodic payments (such as monthly or annually), although a bankruptcy court may require it.[8] However, any deferred payment must provide for a payment of interest to ensure that the government receives the full value of its allowed claim as of the effective date of the plan.[9] In determining the appropriate interest rate (which prior to the 2005 changes discussed in the next part was not statutorily set), courts generally consider the prevailing market rate for a loan having a term equal to the payout period, taking into account the quality of the security and risk of subsequent default.[10] Decisions vary, however, as to what interest rate best approximates the "prevailing market

---

[8] *See, e.g., In re Volle Electric Inc.*, 132 B.R. 365 (Bankr. C.D. Ill. 1991), *aff'd*, 139 B.R. 451 (C.D. Ill. 1992) (permitted regular monthly payments reducing the principal by about 30 percent with a balloon payment at the end of the fourth year, where the primary secured creditor was treated similarly and general unsecured claims were discounted by 50 percent and paid semiannually over five years with no interest); *In re Gregory Boat Co.*, 144 B.R. 361 (Bankr. E.D. Mich. 1992) (approved one-year delay before amortizing tax claims over final five years, even though general unsecured creditors would receive immediate payment; applied standards of "good faith" and "feasibility"); *In re Sanders Coal & Trucking, Inc.*, 129 B.R. 516 (Bankr. E.D. Tenn. 1991) (approved no payments on principal until the 37th month); *In re Snowden's Landscaping Co.*, 110 B.R. 56 (Bankr. S.D. Ala. 1990) (permitted graduated quarterly payments where unsecured claims were similarly paid); *In re Mason and Dixon Lines, Inc.*, 71 B.R. 300 (Bankr. M.D.N.C. 1987) (required equal monthly payments; equated debtor's proposal—a balloon payment, with interest payable annually—to a forced loan). *See also* IRS Litigation Guideline Memorandum, "Payments of Priority Taxes Under Bankruptcy Code Section 1129(a)(9)(C) by Methods Other than Equal Monthly or Quarterly Payments of Principal and Interest," dated November 22, 1993, *reprinted at* 96 TNT 155-70.

[9] *In re Burgess Wholesale Mfg. Opticians, Inc.*, 721 F.2d 1146, 83-2 U.S.T.C. ¶9727 (7th Cir. 1983), *rev'g and remanding* 24 B.R. 554, 82-2 U.S.T.C. ¶9629 (N.D. Ill. 1982); *see* 11 U.S.C. §1129(a)(9)(C). *See also In re Weaver Potato Chip Co., Inc.*, 2003 Bankr. LEXIS 706 (Bankr. D. Neb. 2003) (plan provision precluding payment of postpetition interest only speaks to period from the petition date to the confirmation date); *United States v. Arrow Air, Inc. (In re Arrow Air, Inc.)*, 101 B.R. 332, 89-1 U.S.T.C. ¶9305 (S.D. Fla. 1989) (payment made 11 months after the effective date of the plan where plan provided for payment "[o]n the Effective Date of the Plan or as soon thereafter as is feasible . . . in cash in full"; court interpreted "in full" to mean with interest); *In re Collins*, 184 B.R. 151 (Bankr. N.D. Fla. 1995) (to same effect, where delay was due to litigation over the IRS's claim which had been disallowed by the bankruptcy court but subsequently allowed by the Eleventh Circuit; the court discarded as ambiguous the plan language providing for payment "upon the allowance . . . by final Order of the Bankruptcy Court" since the bankruptcy court initially *dis* allowed the claim, at which point the payment provision read substantially identical to that in *Arrow Air*); *cf. In re Fawcett*, 758 F.2d 588, 85-2 U.S.T.C. ¶9752 (11th Cir. 1985); *United States v. White Farm Equip. Co.*, 157 B.R. 117 (N.D. Ill. 1993) (IRS not entitled to postconfirmation interest where the plan was a liquidating plan that simply provided for payment of allowed claims at the time they became allowed without postconfirmation interest); *In re Mansfield Tire & Rubber Co.*, 152 B.R. 477, 93-1 U.S.T.C. ¶50,233 (Bankr. N.D. Ohio 1993) (IRS entitled to postconfirmation interest for period between effective date and resolution of claim, since the plan provided for postconfirmation interest on "allowed" claims which the plan defined as claims for which "no objection *has been interposed*" within the applicable period, and the trustees' objection was not filed until postconfirmation; although the objection was timely, court considered the definitional language ambiguous and suggested that better wording would have been to refer to claims for which "no objection has been [, or may be,] interposed" within the applicable period).

[10] *See, e.g., United States v. Neal Pharmacal Co.*, 789 F.2d 1283, 86-1 U.S.T.C. ¶9427 (8th Cir. 1986); *Grundy Natl. Bank v. Tandem Mining Corp.*, 754 F.2d 1436, 1441 (4th Cir. 1985); *Memphis Bank and Trust Co. v. Whitman*, 692 F.2d 427, 431 (6th Cir. 1982); *In re Milspec, Inc.*, 82 B.R. 811, 88-1 U.S.T.C. ¶9263 (Bankr. E.D. Va. 1988).

rate" for a loan of comparable risk and term.[11] Some bankruptcy courts have applied the Code § 6621 rate on underpayments[12] or some variation thereof.[13] The IRS has often taken the position that the Code § 6621 rate is the market rate for federal tax claims in bankruptcy and generally will not object to the use of such rate even if it is less than the prevailing commercial rate.[14] Floating rates generally have been viewed as inconsistent with the requirement under Bankruptcy Code section 1129(a)(9)(C) that the present value be determined "as of the effective date of the plan."[15] Although

---

[11] *See, e.g., United States v. Camino Real Landscape Maintenance Contractors* (*In re Camino Real Landscape Maintenance Contractors*), 818 F.2d 1503, 88-1 U.S.T.C. ¶ 9225 (9th Cir. 1988) (upheld a lower court's use of the rate on Treasury obligations plus a net 1 percent to account for risk and the quality of the security; reversed two other lower courts which applied the rate on Treasury obligations without considering the creditworthiness of the debtor; and rejected the government's position that Code § 6621 rate was necessarily the correct rate, although recognizing that it may be a relevant factor); *United States v. Southern States Motor Inns, Inc.*, 709 F.2d 647 (11th Cir. 1983), *cert. denied*, 104 S. Ct. 1275 (1984) (reversed lower court which had applied Code § 6621 rate less one percent for rehabilitation aspects of plan); *Mississippi State Tax Comm. v. Lambert* (*In re Lambert*), 194 F.3d 679 (5th Cir. 1999) (held that the proper rate is a rate "equivalent to the rate the debtor would have to pay to borrow the same amount from the commercial loan market"); *In re Haskell*, 252 B.R. 236 (Bankr. M.D. Fla. 2000) (applied "coerced loan" approach to establish market rate; concluded that statutory rate of 18 percent was appropriate given the debtor's financial condition); *In re Connecticut Aerosols*, 42 B.R. 706 (D. Conn. 1984) (rate established by 28 U.S.C. § 1961(a) for interest on judgments in federal court); *In re Tacoma Recycling, Inc.*, 23 B.R. 547 (Bankr. W.D. Wash, 1982) (same); *In re Bay Area Services*, 26 B.R. 811 (Bankr. M.D. Fla. 1982) (current prevailing prime rate plus 10 percent adjustment for inflation). The determination, therefore, must be made on a case-by-case basis. The market rate approach might not be applicable, however, in certain circumstances, such as if the debt arises from an agreement reflecting a bargained-for rate of interest. In such case, the bargained-for rate of interest may be appropriate.

[12] *See, e.g., Architectural Design, Inc. v. IRS* (*In re Architectural Design, Inc.*), 59 B.R. 1019, 86-1 U.S.T.C. ¶ 9409 (W.D. Va. 1986) (upheld bankruptcy determination that the relevant market interest rate with respect to preferred payments on unsecured tax claims was the interest rate applicable to delinquent tax payments under Code § 6621; rejected federal judgment interest rate under 28 U.S.C. § 1961, which is based on treasury bill rates); *In re Healis*, 49 B.R. 939 (Bankr. M.D. Pa. 1985) (applied Code § 6621 rate under substantially identical language in Chapter 13 of the Bankruptcy Code); *In re Stafford*, 24 B.R. 840, 82-2 U.S.T.C. ¶ 9706 (Bankr. C.D. Kan. 1982). In *Architectural Design*, the court stated that, although the Code § 6621 rate on underpayments is a relevant factor, it should not necessarily be the exclusive measure of the rate that will provide the government with the present value of its claim. The reasons stated include that the Code § 6621 rate will lag from 3½ to 9½ months behind actual market rates and that it ignores (1) variations between the length of the payment period, (2) the quality of the security (if any) and (3) the risk of default. *See also* Southern States (11th Cir.), *supra* note 11, at 651-652; *In re Connecticut Aerosols*, *supra* note 11, at 710; *In re Milspec, Inc.*, *supra* note 10 (Treasury bill rate also relevant factor); *In re Bay Area Services*, *supra* note 11, at 814; *In re Moore*, 25 B.R. 131, 134 (Bankr. N.D. Tex. 1982).

[13] *See, e.g., In re Fi-Hi Pizza, Inc.*, 40 B.R. 258 (Bankr. D. Mass. 1984) (Code § 6621 rate as periodically adjusted plus 2.5 percent for risk component).

[14] *See, e.g.,* former IRS Manual § 57(13)5.5:(2) (December 5, 1986), and cases cited *supra* notes 9 and 10.

[15] *United States v. Neal Pharmacal Co.* (8th Cir.), *supra* note 10 (rejected a rate equal to that paid on 13-week Treasury bills at the time of each quarterly payment, as well as the use of a floating rate); *In re Fisher*, 29 B.R. 542, at 551-552 (Bankr. D. Kan. 1983) (rejecting floating rate and present value analysis under similar language in Chapter 13 of the Bankruptcy Code). In *In re Fi-Hi Pizza, Inc.*, *supra* note 13, at 271, however, the court found a variable rate to be appropriate. Noting that it might be suggested that the certainty of a fixed rate at confirmation is necessary, the court stated that the use of a variable base rate (*e.g.*, the prime rate) had become standard commercial practice, and suggested

Bankruptcy Code section 1129(a)(9)(C) only applies to the unsecured portion of a tax claim, the IRS is similarly entitled to interest on deferred payments of the secured portion of its claim under Bankruptcy Code section 1129(a)(7).[16]

**Current (post-2005 Act) bankruptcy cases.** For bankruptcy cases commenced *on or after* October 17, 2005, administrative expense claims must be paid as of the effective date of the Chapter 11 plan (unless the parties otherwise agree), whether or not secured.[17] However, any prepetition secured tax claim generally may be paid over time, provided that the debtor is able to establish (upon objection) that the plan's treatment is fair and equitable.[18] The single statutory exception applies to any secured tax claim which, but for its secured status, would be classified as an eighth priority unsecured claim. Such claims are entitled to be paid in the same manner and over the same period as eighth priority tax claims (discussed below).[19]

Under Bankruptcy Code section 1129(a)(9)(C), as amended by the 2005 Act, an unsecured prepetition tax claim accorded an eighth priority generally may be paid in "regular" installments in cash over a period not to exceed five (5) years from the *petition date* (or in the case of an involuntary bankruptcy, the date of the order for relief). Thus, the longer the bankruptcy, the shorter the post-bankruptcy period over which the tax payments may be spread. Moreover, the statute requires that the payment schedule be no less favorable than that provided to the most favored nonpriority unsecured claim (other than so-called "convenience" claims, which are smaller amount claims generally paid in cash on the effective date).

(Footnote Continued)

that: "if the feasibility of any plan would come into question because of the utilization of a variable rather than a fixed rate on state taxes, the Court probably should have second thoughts about the feasibility of a debtor, in such a thin cash-flow position, having a confirmable plan." Id. at 272.

[16] *See, e.g., Till v. SCS Credit Corp.*, 124 S. Ct. 1951 (2004) (Chapter 13 case; concluding, in a plurality opinion, that a "formula approach" should be used to determine the applicable interest rate, beginning with the national prime rate and adjusting accordingly to take into account such things as the circumstances of the estate, the nature of the security, and the duration and feasibility of the plan, with the evidentiary burden on the creditor; the Court observed that "when picking a cram down rate in a Chapter 11 case, it might make sense to ask what rate an efficient market would produce," given the lending market for debtor-in-possession financing); *Bank of Montreal v. Official Comm. of Unsecured Creditors (In re American HomePatient, Inc.)*, 420 F.3d 559 (6th Cir. 2005) (held that, in the chapter 11 context, a market interest rate should be applied if there exists an efficient market; otherwise, the "formula approach" endorsed by the *Till* plurality should be employed); *In re Dominick*, 244 B.R. 51 (Bankr. N.D. N.Y. 2000) (involving secured real property tax; applied Treasury rate on instruments with comparable repayment schedules plus a premium to reflect taxing authority's risk), *applying Key Bank N.A. v. Milham (In re Milham)*, 141 F.3d 420 (2d Cir. 1998), *cert. denied*, 119 S. Ct. 169 (1998) (involved consensual lien); *In re Clarksville Hospitality Corp.*, 1996 Bankr. LEXIS 340 (Bankr. D. Mass. 1996) (employing a market rate analysis).

[17] *See* 11 U.S.C. § § 503(b)(1)(B)(i), *as amended by* P.L. 109-8, § 712(b) (2005); in conjunction with 11 U.S.C. § § 507(a)(1), 1129(a)(9)(A).

[18] *See supra* note 4.

[19] 11 U.S.C. § 1129(a)(9)(D), *as added by* P.L. 109-8, § 710(3) (2005). This is consistent with the recommendation of the National Bankruptcy Review Commission, in its report to Congress in October 1997. National Bankruptcy Review Commission Final Report (October 20, 1997), Recommendation 4.2.10, at p. 955. *See generally* Jenks, The Bankruptcy Abuse Prevention and Consumer Protection Act of 2005: Summary of Tax Provisions, 79 Am. Bankr. L.J. (December 2005), at I.G.

The implications of this "most-favored-unsecured-class" provision are far from clear. For example, does a small recovery to general unsecured creditors payable in full in cash on the effective date (or as is generally said, as soon as practicable thereafter) mean that all priority tax claims, and consequently most or all secured tax claims, must also be paid in full on the effective date? Or, as would be more reasonable, does it mean that if the general unsecured creditors receive, say, a 2% recovery all in cash on the effective date, then each priority tax claim must receive at least a 2% cash payment on the effective date, with the potential for paying in regular installments the remaining 98%? Alternatively, what if the general unsecured creditors receive 10 year bonds that are readily tradable? Is this better or worse than the right to receive regular installments over a period that will necessarily be less than five years, where the receivable is not readily tradable? Or what if general unsecured creditors receive payment on the effective date in stock or warrants? Does it make a difference if there is or is not a ready market for the stock or warrants?

Also, neither the statute nor the legislative history indicates the maximum "regular" installment period. Traditionally, many plans provided for one year installments or less. The National Bankruptcy Review Commission would have specifically required either monthly or quarterly payments,[20] but this seems clearly to have been rejected by Congress in favor of a more flexible standard. This makes sense particularly in industries that are cyclical and thus may have slow (low-cash) periods during the year.

Any deferred payment plan also must provide for the payment of interest such that, according to the statute, the total value of the installment payments, as of the effective date of the plan, equals the allowed amount of the tax claim.[21] That being said, the Bankruptcy Code elsewhere provides that the interest rate shall be the rate determined under applicable nonbankruptcy law as of the calendar month in which the plan is confirmed.[22] Thus, for IRS tax claims, the rate would be the Code § 6621 rate adjusted, if appropriate, for the increase under Code § 6621(c) for large corporate deficiencies. But the rate would be a fixed rate, rather than the quarterly floating rate to which the IRS would normally be entitled on tax deficiencies.

---

[20] In an effort to reduce litigation, the National Bankruptcy Review Commission had recommended amending Bankruptcy Code section 1129(a)(9)(C) to (1) require periodic payments (either monthly or quarterly); (2) fix the interest rate (for all taxing authorities) at the Code § 6621 underpayment rate (without regard to the higher rate for large corporate deficiencies), and (3) begin counting the permitted six-year deferral from the petition date (or order for relief). National Bankruptcy Review Commission Final Report (October 20, 1997), Recommendation 4.2.34, at pp. 976-978. As discussed below, the Bankruptcy Code does fix the interest rate, but at the applicable nonbankruptcy rate rather than simply the basic Code § 6621 rate. In any event, we can only speculate that the present section 1129(a)(9)(C) will engender as much, if not more, litigation than its predecessor due to the most-favored-unsecured-claims provision.

[21] 11 U.S.C. § 1129(a)(9)(C)(i).

[22] 11 U.S.C. § 511(a) and (b).

Failure to make timely payments in accordance with the payment schedule in the Chapter 11 plan could result in the acceleration of all payments, as well as other sanctions and the possible dismissal or conversion of the case to Chapter 7.[23]

### § 1016.1.2 Consensual Payment Arrangements, Offers in Compromise, and "Compromise" Chapter 11 Plans

Even in circumstances where the Bankruptcy Code generally requires payment on the effective date, the debtor may file a request with the IRS to extend under Code § 6161(a)(1) the time for payment of an allowed income tax claim up to 18 months and, in certain exceptional cases, up to 30 months.[24] An extension will only be granted if the debtor files the request for extension prior to the due date of the tax payments and demonstrates undue hardship. Presumably, the due date of any tax payment shall be determined pursuant to the Chapter 11 plan, regardless of whether such tax had been previously assessed. To demonstrate undue hardship, a mere declaratory statement will not suffice. Actual facts must be disclosed demonstrating substantial financial loss, *e.g.*, the need to sell property at a sacrifice price in order to make the tax payment.[25]

The debtor also may be able to work out a negotiated payment arrangement with the IRS. Code § 6159 expressly authorizes (but generally does not require) the IRS to enter into a written agreement allowing for installment payments if such agreement "will facilitate collection of such liability."[26]

It has long been the IRS's general policy, however, not to entertain a formal "offer in compromise" under the authority of Code § 7122 of a Chapter 11 debtor's tax liability under the IRS's normal procedures.[27] Moreover, since February 1997 (with the exception of the last three months of 1999), the IRS has taken the position

---

[23] *See* discussion at § 1002.9 above; *In re Decker's General Contracting, Inc.* (Bankr. D. N.J. August 28, 2000), No. 97-15083 (JHW) (consent order), *reprinted* at 2000 TNT 215-59.

[24] *See* Code § 6161(c) (also applicable to receivership proceedings); Reg. § 1.6161-1(a)(2); 11 U.S.C. § 1129(a)(9) (provides exception to payment on effective date where different treatment arranged between the debtor and claim holder).

[25] Reg. § 1.6161-1(b) (sale at current market price is not ordinarily undue hardship); *In re Pool & Varga, Inc.*, 86-1 U.S.T.C. ¶ 9445 (Bankr. E.D. Mich.) (debtor's inability to pay taxes without terminating its business constituted undue hardship); IRS Technical Advice Memorandum 8008002, November 2, 1979 (refused to reconsider district director's finding that inability to use the state tax deduction for federal income taxes paid in year payment was due does not constitute undue hardship).

[26] Code § 6159(a) (effective November 11, 1988); IRS Manual, Part 5 (Collection Process), Ch. 14 (Installment Agreements), § 1.1 (7/12/05); Prop. Reg. § 301.6159-0 *et seq.* (published on March 2, 2007). In addition, such section specifies the circumstances under which the IRS may modify or terminate such an agreement, including those cases requiring prior taxpayer notice. Code § 6159(b). Prior to Code § 6159, the IRS policy regarding installment agreements was embodied in Policy Statement P-5-14 (revoked July 11, 1989). *See also* News Release IR-87-80 (and discussion of "GAO report #2").

[27] *See, e.g.*, former IRS Manual § 57(10)(13).(12)14(1) (9/22/94) (Part V, Collection Activity) (stating that, because all priority taxes are required to be paid in full in Chapter 11, offers in compromise are "generally" not considered in such cases, but that "a compromise of the liability may be appropriate [if] the failure to compromise may lead the taxpayer to a Chapter 7 where the Service is likely to receive much less than the amount offered").

that any offer in compromise submitted by a taxpayer in bankruptcy cannot be processed, other than (in the case of non-individuals) where the Chapter 11 plan is in default and cannot be cured or modified.[28] At the same time, the IRS Manual recognizes that, in rare cases, it may be in the government's best interests to accept a compromising (deficient) plan when the circumstances are similar to those for which an offer in compromise in a non-bankruptcy context would be accepted (such as an inability to fully pay the claim and the government receiving little or nothing in a Chapter 7).[29] Over time, the IRS's position with respect to offers in compromise has become the focus of increasing litigation. The first decisions were in June 1999. In twin decisions by a bankruptcy court presiding over two separate bankruptcy cases, the court held that the IRS's restrictive policy with respect to formal offers in compromise was discriminatory and prohibited by the Bankruptcy Code.[30] The court therefore held that the IRS must consider the debtor's offer in compromise in accordance with the procedures set forth in Code § 7122, *without regard to whether the applicant has filed bankruptcy*.[31] On the other hand, the court acknowledged that the final acceptance or rejection of the offer is discretionary, subject to the limited guidelines set forth in the statute (which involve certain basic allowances for individuals).[32]

In reaction to such decisions, the IRS initially revised the application form for offers in compromise to allow for offers by taxpayers in bankruptcy (provided that the debtor obtains a lifting of the automatic stay to permit the IRS to research the

---

[28] *See* Stipulation of Facts (#9) in *In re Chapman*, discussed immediately below at *infra* note 30. *See also* Instructions to IRS Form 656 (Offer in Compromise) (2/99 rev.) (under heading "Specific Instruction on How to Submit Types of Offers") and (8/2003 rev.) (under the "Offer in Compromise Application Fee Worksheet"); IRS Manual, Part 5 (Collection Process), Ch. 8 (Offer in Compromise), § 10.2.1 (5/26/99), (2/4/2000), (11/30/01), (5/15/04), (11/15/04), and (9/1/05) and § 11.3, at ¶ 3 (9/1/05) (so providing); IRS Manual, Part 5 (Collecting Process), Ch. 9 (Bankruptcy), § 4.9 (3/1/07) (same).

[29] *See* IRS Manual, Part 5 (Collecting Process), Ch. 9 (Bankruptcy), § 8.14.2 (3/1/07), at ¶ 7, and § 4.9 (3/1/07), at ¶ 4(b) (latitude for defaulted plans added here); former IRS Manual, Part 5 (Collecting Process), HB 5.9 (Bankruptcy Handbook), Chapter 9.4.2 (2/11/99), at ¶ 6 (stating that "[t]he circumstances would be similar to those of an offer in compromise, such as an inablility to fully pay the claim and the Government receiving little or nothing in a *Chapter 7*"); IRS Legal Memorandum 200037047, July 21, 2000 ("Offers in Compromise—Effect of Bankruptcy on Processability"), *reprinted at* 2000 TNT 181-51 (recognizing such authority); and former IRS Manual § 57(10)(13).(12)14(1) (9/22/94) (Part V, Collection Activity) (quoted at *supra* note 27). *See also* IRS Manual, Part 5 (Collection Process), Ch. 8 (Offer in Compromise), § 10.2.2 (5/26/99), (2/4/2000), (5/15/04), (11/15/04), and (9/1/05) (discussing offers in compromise before bankruptcy).

[30] *Chapman v. United States* (*In re Chapman*), 99-2 U.S.T.C. ¶ 50,690 (Bankr. S.D. W.Va. 1999), *citing* 11 U.S.C. § 525(a) (generally prohibiting discriminatory treatment by governmental authorities); *Mills v. United States* (*In re Mills*), 240 B.R. 689 (Bankr. S.D. W.Va. 1999) (twin decision to *Chapman*; decided by the same judge and dated the same day).

[31] The bankruptcy court found unpersuasive the IRS's concerns that, by considering and investigating the debtor's offer, the IRS would somehow be violating the automatic stay. In this regard, the court took notice of the fact that it had, in other cases, held that the debtor's submission of an offer constitutes an implicit agreement by the debtor to be subjected to additional scrutiny.

[32] *See also In re Davison*, 156 B.R. 600 (Bankr. E.D. Ark. 1993) (bankruptcy court could not force IRS to *accept* offer in compromise).

offer).[33] However, less than three months later (effective for offers after December 31, 1999), the IRS reinstated its policy not to process such offers and revised the application form accordingly.[34] Reinforcing such action, the IRS Chief Counsel's office subsequently informed its local districts, in a detailed legal memorandum, of its conclusion (and litigating position) that the IRS's policy is not in violation of the Bankruptcy Code and that the IRS cannot be compelled by a bankruptcy court to consider offers by taxpayers in bankruptcy.[35]

Not surprisingly, the IRS thereafter again found itself defending its restrictive policy before a bankruptcy court. Although the bankruptcy court this time held that the IRS's policy was not among the types of governmental discrimination specifically precluded by the Bankruptcy Code, the court nevertheless concluded that "the subject policy directly conflicts with the policies *underlying* the Bankruptcy Code in general and the reorganization provisions of Chapter 11 in particular . . . ."[36] The IRS was therefore ordered to process and consider the debtor's offer in compromise in accordance with normal procedures *and policies* applicable to taxpayers not in bankruptcy.[37] This decision was followed by a similar decision of another bankruptcy court.[38] Both decisions were subsequently affirmed as a valid exercise of the bankruptcy court's equitable authority under Bankruptcy Code section 105(a).

In July 2004, the IRS Office of the Chief Counsel issued a notice explaining the IRS's policy with respect to offers in compromise in bankruptcy, and reasserted once again its view that bankruptcy court orders directing the IRS to alter its offer in compromise program, and its normal process for administering bankruptcy cases and considering compromise plans, go beyond the authority granted to bankruptcy courts under section 105 of the Bankruptcy Code.[39] In the IRS's view, such orders are in the nature of writs of mandamus, which are only appropriate upon a showing of a clear right to the relief sought or a clearly defined duty to act.

---

[33] *See* IRS Legal Memorandum 200011046, January 4, 2000, *reprinted at* 2000 TNT 54-89; Instructions to IRS Form 656 (Offer in Compromise) (9/99 rev.).

[34] IRS Legal Memorandum 200011046, January 4, 2000, *supra* note 33; Instructions to IRS Form 656 (Offer in Compromise) (1/2000 rev.). *See also* Instructions to IRS Form 656 (Offer in Compromise) (8/2003 rev.), (7/2004 rev.) and (2/2007 rev.).

[35] IRS Legal Memorandum 200037047. *See also* IRS Legal Memorandum 200126003, February 5, 2001, *reprinted at* 2001 TNT 127-27 (concluding that, although presenting litigating hazards, the IRS could decline to consider an offer in compromise with respect to tax liabilities that are the subject of a defaulted Chapter 11 plan, and that the decision whether or not to consider an offer in a particular case should be based on policy concerns).

[36] *Macher v. United States (In re Macher)*, 2003 Bankr. LEXIS 633 (Bankr. W.D. Va. 2003) (emphasis added), *aff'd*, 303 B.R. 798, 2004-1 U.S.T.C. ¶50,114 (W.D. Va. 2003).

[37] The court here also acknowledged that it could not (nor was it asked to) compel the IRS to compromise tax liabilities which, in the case of an individual debtor, are nondischargeable (*i.e.*, priority tax liabilities).

[38] *Holmes v. United States*, 298 B.R. 477, 2003-2 U.S.T.C. ¶50,685 (Bankr. M.D. Ga. 2003), *aff'd*, 309 B.R. 824 (M.D. Ga. 2004).

[39] IRS Chief Counsel Notice CC-20040205 (July 12, 2004), *reprinted at* 2004 TNT 135-10. Accordingly, the Chief Counsel has recommended issuing a nonacquiescence with respect to *In re Macher, supra* note 36. AOD 2004-3.

Declaring the offer in compromise program to be "inherently incompatible" with the time frames in bankruptcy, the notice explains that the IRS's Insolvency Office is responsible for considering payment proposals in bankruptcy, usually in the form of a proposed plan. For a compromise plan to be accepted, the debtor must demonstrate that it is in the Government's best interests to accept less than what is otherwise statutorily required. According to the notice, to be considered, the plan may not provide for the payment of claims with lower priority, and all income that is not necessary for the continued production of income must be committed to the plan. Other factors that the IRS may take into account include (but are not limited to) whether the taxpayer has the ability to pay the IRS's claims as required by the Bankruptcy Code; whether the debtor is in compliance with tax return filing requirements; the extent of the debtor's previous noncompliance with filing or payment requirements; whether other creditors with the same priority (such as state taxing authorities) are accepting less than full payment; whether the IRS would receive more in liquidation; and the debtor's ability to dismiss the bankruptcy case and submit an administrative offer in compromise (*e.g.*, where the IRS is the only real creditor in the case).

This time the IRS met with greater success in the bankruptcy courts. In one case, by the time the issue came before the court, the IRS had already referred the offer to the Department of Justice (DOJ) for consideration and the DOJ, having considered it, had already rejected it. Also, counsel for the IRS had indicated that, had the IRS itself considered the offer, it would simply have reaffirmed the determination made by the DOJ on the same basis. In light of these circumstances, the court denied the debtor's motion.[40] In a second case, the bankruptcy court agreed that it was within its equitable powers under Bankruptcy Code section 105(a) to order the IRS to consider the debtor's offer in compromise, but in so holding stated: "In this case, the IRS may *either* process an offer in compromise . . . *or* take seriously its stated position that it will, in good faith, consider accepting less than the bankruptcy code requires in a Chapter 13 plan" (emphasis added).[41] Thus, the court permitted the IRS to do what it effectively said it would do in the July 2004 Chief Counsel notice. The IRS finally achieved full success in *In re 1900 M Restaurant Associates Inc*,[42] which was subsequently affirmed on all grounds by the district court. In this case, it was the bankruptcy court's view that, other than in very limited circumstances, the IRS had the discretionary right whether or not to consider an offer, and that the court could not, absent a clear nondiscretionary duty, compel the IRS to process the debtor's offer in compromise. Moreover, the court was persuaded by the IRS's reasons in the July 2004 Chief Counsel notice for handling any proposed compromise within the plan process, and therefore, did not consider the IRS's refusal to process the debtor's offer in compromise an abuse of discretion. The court also, as an alternative ground, and

---

40 *In re Kline*, 2004 Bankr. LEXIS 1748 (Bankr. N.D. N.Y. 2004).

41 *In re Peterson*, 317 B.R. 532, 2005-1 U.S.T.C. ¶50,142 (Bankr. D. Neb. 2004), *reconsid. denied*, 321 B.R. 259, 2005-1 U.S.T.C. ¶50,142 (Bankr. D. Neb. 2004).

42 *1900 M Restaurant Assoc. Inc. v. United States* (*In re 1900 M Restaurant Assoc. Inc.*), 319 B.R. 302, 2005-1 U.S.T.C. ¶50,313 (Bankr. D.C. 2005), *aff'd*, 2007-1 U.S.T.C. ¶50,116 (D.C. 2007). *Accord In re Uzialko*, 339 B.R. 579 (Bankr. E.D. Pa. 2006); *In re Shope*, 347 B.R. 270 (Bankr. S.D. Ohio 2006).

similar to the first case described above, observed that the debtor had already proposed a plan reflecting its offer and that the DOJ had already evaluated and rejected it. As such, the court concluded that the debtor had already achieved its desired end, "even though not employing the means the debtor desired."

Offers in compromise are discussed further at § 1017 below.

## *§ 1016.2 Paying Trust Fund Taxes First*

As previously discussed (at §§ 103, 104, and 1006.3.2), a 100 percent penalty is imposed on any responsible person—generally, officers or employees of the debtor, as well as certain creditors—who willfully fails to collect, account for, or pay over any withholding (or "trust fund") tax to the IRS. Accordingly, where a tax claim is to be paid in installments, it is frequently in the interests of the officers of the debtor (and possibly certain creditors) to ensure that any tax payments first go to pay the trust fund portion of the claim, thereby limiting their personal liability. In a Chapter 11 case, a debtor may designate how a tax payment is applied if the bankruptcy court determines "this designation is necessary to the success of a reorganization plan."[43]

Ordinarily, the ability of a debtor to designate how a tax payment to the IRS is applied—such as to "trust fund" or nontrust fund taxes—depends on whether the payment is considered "voluntarily" or "involuntarily" made by the taxpayer.[44] If voluntary, the debtor's designation governs; if involuntary, the debtor's designation will not be honored, and the IRS generally will allocate the payment first to nontrust fund taxes.[45] Consistent with the IRS position, the majority of circuit courts consider-

---

[43] *United States v. Energy Resources Co.*, 110 S. Ct. 2139, 90-1 U.S.T.C. ¶ 50,281 (1990), *aff'g* 871 F.2d 223, 89-1 U.S.T.C. ¶ 9249 (1st Cir. 1989). In Chapter 7 cases, most courts have disallowed any designation by the debtor. *See* discussion below.

[44] *See, e.g.*, Rev. Proc. 2002-26, 2002-15 I.R.B. 746, *superseding*, Rev. Rul. 79-284, 1979-2 C.B. 83; *Muntwyler v. United States*, 703 F.2d 1030, 83-1 U.S.T.C. ¶ 9275 (7th Cir. 1983); *Elms v. United States*, 1994 U.S. App. LEXIS 30559 (6th Cir.).

[45] IRS Manual, Part 5 (Collection Process), Ch. 7 (Trust Fund Compliance), § 4.3 (4/13/06); IRS Policy Statement P-5-60 (February 2, 1993), *reprinted in* IRS Manual (CCH) 1305-14; *see also* IRS Manual, Part 5 (Collecting Process), Ch. 5 (Insolvencies, Decedents Estates and Estate Taxes), § 4.9 (6/23/05) (first apply payments to taxes for which the statutory period for collection is about to expire and then those for which the statutory period for assessing the 100 percent penalty has expired); IRS Chief Counsel Advice 200720015, March 13, 2007 (involving application of pre-2003 payments where 100 percent penalty was previously assessed); IRS Chief Counsel Advice 199905021, December 14, 1998, *reprinted at* 1999 TNT 25-20 (IRS takes the position that it retains the right to apply payments under an installment agreement in the manner that best protects the government); IRS Legal Memorandum 200044011, July 31, 2000, *reprinted at* 2000 TNT 215-52 (taxpayer cannot compel IRS to reapply payments made under an installment agreement). Where voluntary payment is made *without* any designation, the allocation of the payment is generally within the IRS's discretion and the taxpayer ordinarily cannot subsequently impose an allocation upon the IRS. *See, e.g.*, *Sotir v. United States*, 978 F.2d 29, 92-2 U.S.T.C. ¶ 50,548 (1st Cir. 1992), *cert. denied*, 113 S. Ct. 1388 (1993); *Davis v. United States*, 961 F.2d 867, 878, 92-1 U.S.T.C. ¶ 50,292 (9th Cir. 1992), *cert. denied*, 113 S. Ct. 969 (1993); *Pinto v. United States*, 228 F. Supp. 2d 908, 2002-2 U.S.T.C. ¶ 50,724 (Bankr. N.D. Ill. 2002) (IRS could reapply undesignated payment as it deemed to be in its best interests); *cf. United States v. Ryan (In re Ryan)*, 64 F.3d 1516 (11th Cir. 1995) (voluntary payment rule does not extend to overpayments due to excessive withholding); *but see In re Deer Park, Inc.* (9th Cir.), discussed below in this section. This discretion was upheld even where the undesignated check was in the amount of the tax shown due

ing the issue had held that any tax payment pursuant to a bankruptcy court order or a Chapter 11 plan is an "involuntary" payment.[46]

In *United States v. Energy Resources Co.*, however, the Supreme Court affirmed the First Circuit's decision, holding that, "whether or not the payments at issue are rightfully considered to be involuntary, the bankruptcy court has authority to order the IRS to apply the payments to trust fund liabilities if the bankruptcy court determines that this designation is necessary to the success of a reorganization plan."[47] Although there is no express provision in the Bankruptcy Code to this effect, the Court found ample authority in the broad equitable powers granted by the Bankruptcy Code.[48] Accordingly, whether a debtor can direct that a tax payment first be applied to outstanding trust fund taxes must be determined on a case-by-case basis.[49]

As fashioned by the First Circuit, the relevant inquiry is:

---

(Footnote Continued)

on an accompanying *income tax* return. Although the return was filed late and the check originally bounced and had to be presented for payment a second time, there is no indication that these facts affected the court's decision. *Windover v. Commissioner*, T.C. Summ. Op. 2007-50. However, where the payment accompanies the taxpayer's quarterly *employment tax* return and is sufficient to satisfy the tax shown due, it will first be applied to that quarter's employment taxes. *Cf.* IRS Manual, Part 5 (Collection Process), Ch. 7 (Trust Fund Compliance), § 4.3 (4/13/06); *see* former IRS Manual § 56(18)3.1 (November 21, 1989). Similarly, if it can be established that a tax deposit was in the amount required to be deposited under the regulations for the period made, the deposit will first be applied to that period's employment taxes. IRS Manual, Part 5 (Collection Process), Ch. 7 (Trust Fund Compliance), § 4.3 (4/13/06); former IRS Manual § 56(18)3.2(2) (May 5, 1993). *See also In re Ledin*, 179 B.R. 721 (Bankr. M.D. Fla. 1995). In addition, under new Code § 6656(e) and Rev. Proc. 99-10, 1999-1 C.B. 272 (for deposits after January 18, 1999 with respect to deposit periods ending on or before December 31, 2001) and Rev. Proc. 2001-58, 2001-50 I.R.B. 579 (for deposit periods beginning on or after January 1, 2002), a taxpayer may within 90 days of receiving a penalty notice for multiple failure-to-deposit penalties within a single return period, designate the deposit period(s) to which its late payment (or credit) is to be applied. *See also* CCH Tax Strategy Bulletin: Many Employers Can Benefit From Penalty Payment Designations, CCH Std. Fed. Tax Rpts, *Taxes on Parade*, Vol. 86, Issue No. 36, Rep. 32 (August 5, 1999).

[46] *See* Pollack & Goldring, Unpaid Trust Fund Taxes in Chapter 11 Cases: A New Decision But No More Certainty, 1 Faulkner & Gray's Bankr. L. Rev. #2, 48 (Summer 1989). The Tenth Circuit has since joined the Third, Sixth, and Ninth Circuits in so holding. *See Fullmer v. United States (In re Fullmer)*, 962 F.2d 1463, 92-1 U.S.T.C. ¶ 50,237 (10th Cir. 1992).

[47] *Supra* note 43. *See In re North Star Graphics Group, Inc.*, Bankr. No. 90-5720-F30-11, 1990 Bankr. LEXIS 2520 (Bankr. S.D. Ind. November 9, 1990) (placing burden of proof on debtor).

[48] *See* 11 U.S.C. §§ 105, 1123(b)(5). *See also* § 1013.5 above, discussing the potential application of *Energy Resources* in other contexts.

[49] A similar facts and circumstances approach was taken by the Eleventh Circuit in *In re A & B Heating & Air Conditioning, Inc.*, 823 F.2d 462, 87-2 U.S.T.C. ¶ 9454 (11th Cir. 1987), *vacated and remanded*, 108 S. Ct. 1724 (1988), *reinstated*, 861 F.2d 1538 (11th Cir. 1988), *and subsequently rendered moot* (due to the deletion of the designation provision from the Chapter 11 plan), 878 F.2d 1311 (11th Cir. 1989). The Eleventh Circuit, however, had carefully framed its decision within the rubric of the voluntary/involuntary distinction. *See* Pollack & Goldring, *supra* note 46, at 49-50.

*See also Neier v. United States*, 127 B.R. 669, 91-1 U.S.T.C. ¶ 50,234 (D. Kan. 1991) (IRS permitted to reallocate involuntary bankruptcy payments to nontrust fund taxes where original allocation was within the IRS's discretion).

> upon consideration of the reorganization plan as a whole, in so far as the particular structure or allocation of payments increases the risk that the IRS may not collect the total tax debt [including nontrust fund taxes], is that risk nonetheless justified by an offsetting increased likelihood of rehabilitation, *i.e.*, increased likelihood of payment to creditors who might otherwise lose their money?[50]

In the two cases consolidated in the First Circuit's decision, the court upheld the debtor's allocation. In addition to the bankruptcy judge's assessment in each case that the risk of harm to the IRS was slight, a principal factor cited by the court in both instances was the presence of a third-party infusion of capital. Not surprisingly, other courts have reached differing conclusions. More often than not, courts have rejected the debtor's allocation.[51]

Moreover, almost all courts have rejected any designation of tax payments in a liquidating Chapter 11 case (or in a Chapter 7 liquidation) since, by definition, the

---

[50] 871 F.2d at 234; *see* Note, The Solution to the Trust Fund Tax Problem in Chapter 11 Bankruptcy Proceedings: In re Energy Resources, Inc., 43 Tax Law. 837 (1990) (discussing First Circuit decision); IRS Litigation Guideline Memorandum GL-49, January 25, 1991, *reprinted at* 2000 TNT 91-40 (discussing IRS litigation strategy after *Energy Resources* decision).

[51] Those allowing a debtor to designate include: *Compass Marine Services, Inc. v. United States* (*In re Compass Marine Services, Inc.*), 2002-1 U.S.T.C. ¶50,439 (Bankr. E.D. La. 2002) (the efforts of the president/controlling shareholder and other family members had significantly contributed to a successful reorganization, and were likely to continue to do so; also, the president had paid a portion of the tax debt out of personal funds, and his wife was working without salary); *In re M. C. Tooling Consultants, Inc.*, 165 B.R. 590, 93-2 U.S.T.C. ¶50,618 (Bankr. D.S.C. 1993) (president testified of constant harassment by the IRS about his personal liability for unpaid trust taxes and his resulting inability to concentrate on business operations); *United States v. R.L. Himes & Assocs., Inc.* (*In re R.L. Himes & Assocs., Inc.*), 152 B.R. 198 (S.D. Ohio 1993) (even though bankruptcy court did not set forth specific findings of fact, but simply indicated its reliance on the debtor's representations that the designation was essential to the debtor's ability to reorganize); *In re Florida Dental Management, Inc.*, 106 B.R. 738 (Bankr. M.D. Fla. 1989); *United States v. APT Indus., Inc.*, 128 B.R. 145, 92-2 U.S.T.C. ¶50,450 (W.D.N.C. 1992) (approved postconfirmation order directing application of all tax payments under the plan, including those already made); *cf. New Terminal Stevedoring, Inc. v. M/V Belnor*, 728 F. Supp. 62 (D. Mass. 1989) (nonbankruptcy case). *See also In re Klaska*, 152 B.R. 248 (Bankr. C.D. Ill. 1993) (where the IRS, as a matter of principle, objected to an individual debtor's designation of payments first to *non*-trust fund taxes; designation resulted in the debtor's former partner, who was currently making payments of the trust fund taxes, paying a larger share of such taxes).

Courts rejecting a debtor's designation have generally reasoned (more from a policy than a factual perspective) that any enhancement of a successful reorganization is highly speculative, whereas there is a clear potential for abuse by the debtor's officers. *See, e.g., United States v. Vokes Equip., Inc.* (*In re Vokes Equip., Inc.*), 1993 U.S. Dist. LEXIS 8435 (S.D. Fla. 1993), adopting magistrate's recommendation and report, at 1993 U.S. Dist. LEXIS 5579; *In re Mold Makers, Inc.*, 109 B.R. 845, 91-1 U.S.T.C. ¶50,047 (Bankr. N.D. Ill. 1991); *In re Gilley Consulting Engineers, Inc.*, 105 B.R. 734, 90-1 U.S.T.C. ¶50,031 (Bankr. N.D. Ga. 1990). *See also In re Oyster Bar of Pensacola, Inc.*, 201 B.R. 567 (Bankr. N.D. Fla. 1996) (debtor presented no testimony or evidence in support, but simply argued that the allocation would prove an effective incentive to management; court observed that the same might be said of no allocation).

Although the designation issue is generally raised as to prepetition taxes, the issue has also been raised with respect to postpetition taxes. *See, e.g., In re ABA Recovery Service, Inc.*, 110 B.R. 484, 90-1 U.S.T.C. ¶50,080 (Bankr. S.D. Cal. 1990) (upheld trustee allocation of tax payments to postpetition trust fund taxes incurred during his tenure); *see also infra* note 52.

designation is not necessary for a successful reorganization.[52] However, in *In re Deer Park, Inc.*,[53] the Bankruptcy Appellate Panel of the Ninth Circuit (affirmed by the Ninth Circuit Court of Appeals in a divided opinion) upheld a bankruptcy court order directing the IRS to reallocate all tax payments first to trust fund taxes even though the debtor's Chapter 11 plan contemplated a liquidation.[54] The panel explained that, even in the context of a liquidation, the continuing participation of the debtor's principals and officers in a planned, orderly liquidation may be necessary to maximize recovery to creditors; this distinguished, the panel said, a Chapter 11 liquidation from a Chapter 7 liquidation, wherein a trustee is automatically appointed. In this instance, the assets of the estate (a ski facility) had been sold for a partially contingent payment keyed to whether the purchaser reopened the property for downhill skiing within 10 years, and the debtor's controlling shareholder and former president (with his experience with the facility, and his contacts with the purchaser, the Forest Service, and the local planning agencies) was seen as the person most likely to bring about the reopening of the facility, thereby maximizing the creditors' recovery.[55]

---

[52] *See, e.g.*, *United States v. Pepperman*, 976 F.2d 123, 92-2 U.S.T.C. ¶50,465 (3d Cir. 1992), *rev'g*, 1991 U.S. Dist. LEXIS 14598 (D. N.J. 1991) (Chapter 7; leaves open whether there may be some "unusual circumstances" that might justify designation in a Chapter 7 case); *United States v. Kare Kemical, Inc.* (*In re Kare Kemical, Inc.*), 935 F.2d 243, 91-2 U.S.T.C. ¶50,389 (11th Cir. 1991); *In re Frank Meador Buick, Inc.*, 946 F.2d 885 (4th Cir. 1991) (Chapter 7), full opinion at 1991 U.S. App. LEXIS 24802; *Jehan-Das, Inc. v. United States* (*In re Jehan-Das, Inc.*), 925 F.2d 237, 91-2 U.S.T.C. ¶50,319 (8th Cir. 1991), *cert. denied*, 112 S. Ct. 55 (1991) (involving unpaid postpetition withholding taxes); *In re Tillery Mechanical Contractors, Inc.*, 319 B.R. 695 (Bankr. S.D. Ala. 2004) (rejecting the attempt by the husband and wife owners of the debtor corporation, who were also the principal officers of the debtor prior to its conversion to Chapter 7, to have the court direct the debtor corporation's tax payments first to trust fund taxes in furtherance of their own "fresh start" in their individual bankruptcy cases); *In re Educare Centers of Arkansas, Inc.*, 104 B.R. 106 (Bankr. W.D. Ark. 1989); *In re The Looking Glass Ltd.*, 113 B.R. 463 (Bankr. N.D. Ill. 1990) (Chapter 7), and cases cited therein.

[53] 136 B.R. 815 (Bankr. 9th Cir. 1992), *aff'd*, 10 F.3d 1478 (9th Cir. 1993). Accord *In re 20th Century Enters., Inc.*, 1994 Bankr. LEXIS 260 (Bankr. N.D. Miss.); *In re Flo-Lizer, Inc.*, 164 B.R. 79 (Bankr. S.D. Ohio 1993), *aff'd*, 164 B.R. 749 (S.D. Ohio 1994).

[54] Neither the Court of Appeals' majority nor dissenting opinion in *Deer Park* discussed the Court of Appeals' earlier unpublished decision in *In re Equipment Fabricators, Inc.*, decided in the same year. *Sonntag v. United States* (*In re Equipment Fabricators, Inc.*), 1993 U.S. App. LEXIS 6778 (9th Cir. 1993). In that case, also involving a Chapter 11 liquidation, three different Circuit Court judges upheld the reversal of a bankruptcy court order directing that the estate's distribution in respect of unpaid postpetition taxes first be applied to taxes incurred since the current trustee's appointment (so as to satisfy all unpaid withholding taxes during that period and effectively eliminate the trustee's liability for such taxes). Nevertheless, the equitable factors mentioned in the text and in note 55 *infra*, and the fact that *Equipment Fabricators* involved a trustee's failure to remit *postpetition* withholding taxes, distinguish the two cases. For a critical discussion of the Ninth Circuit's decision in *Deer Park*, *see* Camp, Avoiding the *Ex Post Facto* Slippery Slope of *Deer Park*, 3 Am. Bankr. L. Rev. 329 (1995) (author is an attorney with the Office of the Chief Counsel of the IRS).

[55] Moreover, the reallocation of prior payments (in contrast to a designation of future payments) was justified in that the debtor's former president had relied on the satisfaction of the trust fund taxes and the release of his personal liability in staying on to manage the liquidation without compensation, and that it was only due to a clerical error in the amount of the IRS's claim provided for under the plan (which the IRS quickly discovered, but did not disclose) and after all tax payments under the plan had been made that the IRS asserted personal liability against him.

Similarly, in *In re Poydras Manor, Inc.*,[56] the bankruptcy court approved a liquidating plan's marshalling of tax payments first to trust fund taxes where the debtor's major asset was its "certificates of need" issued by the state relating to its operation as a nursing home, the transferable value of such certificates would be lost if the debtor's operations were not continued pending a sale, and the two principals of the debtor (who performed many functions at the nursing home) were the only persons who could keep the business running. In an attempt to distinguish *Deer Park*, the IRS pointed out that the two principals in this case were already being paid for their services and, thus, did not need the additional incentive provided by the allocation provision. The bankruptcy court rejected this distinction, first on the grounds that the testimony showed that the amount being paid was considerably below market value and, second, because the principals' continued participation was necessary to return the maximum value to the creditors.

In addition, in another case, it was held that court-approved designations are justified during the course of a bankruptcy case where "good faith attempts" at reorganization are made even though such attempts ultimately fail.[57]

In short, the Supreme Court decision merely rekindled, rather than clarified, the designation issue. It is therefore possible that this issue may be a subject of future legislation.[58]

Considering a slightly different allocation issue, the bankruptcy court, in *In re Steeley*,[59] held that, even after the debtor defaulted under his Chapter 11 plan, the IRS was required to continue to apply (as it had always done) any undesignated payments by the debtor to taxes owing under the debtor's plan and in accordance with the provisions of the plan, rather than to any postconfirmation taxes owing by the debtor. However, the court permitted any amounts obtained by the IRS pursuant to a notice of levy, which sought payment for both taxes owing under the plan and postconfirmation taxes to be applied to the postconfirmation taxes first, as such amounts were neither payments under the plan nor voluntary.

## §1017 PRIORITY AND PAYMENT OF TAX CLAIMS—INSOLVENT DEBTORS OUTSIDE BANKRUPTCY

**Priority.** Although a detailed discussion of the priority of payment in insolvency situations outside bankruptcy is beyond the scope of this volume, debts (including taxes) owed to the United States government generally come first. Specifically, 31 U.S.C. §3713 (often called the "insolvency priority statute") provides that, in the case

---

[56] 242 B.R. 603 (Bankr. E.D. La. 2000).

[57] *United States v. Metzger* (*In re T. M. Products Co.*), 1992 U.S. Dist. LEXIS 9404 (S.D. Fla. 1992) (but not after attempts at reorganization cease; upheld standing of officer to object to IRS motion to change debtor's prior designations), *remanding*, 118 B.R. 131 (Bankr. S.D. Fla. 1990).

[58] *See* Pollack & Goldring, *supra* note 46, at 50-51; *see also* S. 84, 101st Cong., 1st Sess. §201 (1989) (proposed legislation; would have amended the Bankruptcy Code to provide: "Payments of taxes under [title 11] to a governmental unit may be applied by the governmental unit in a manner that preserves alternative source of collection, if any").

[59] 1996 Bankr. LEXIS 699 (Bankr. D. Idaho 1996).

of an insolvent debtor, debts owed to the United States government are to be paid before any other creditor if either:

(1) the debtor without enough property to pay all debts makes a voluntary assignment of property;
(2) property of the debtor, if absent (*e.g.*, where the debtor has absconded with the property), is attached; or
(3) an act of bankruptcy is committed.[1]

No statutory exception is provided, except for bankruptcy cases.[2] Thus, this priority rule applies generally to all insolvent debtors outside bankruptcy, whether or not in receivership or any similar insolvency proceeding. As a means of enforcement, any receiver, officer, or other fiduciary of the debtor, as well as any controlling person, who, knowing of the government's debt, violates the priority accorded the government under this statute is personally liable to the extent of the proscribed payment.[3] For this purpose, knowledge means either actual knowledge of the debt or notice of such facts as would put a reasonably prudent person on inquiry as to the

---

[1] **§1017** 31 U.S.C. §3713(a)(1)(A). The concept of "an act of bankruptcy" is a carryover from the old Bankruptcy Act and is not used in the current Bankruptcy Code. Arguably, the historic meaning continues to apply. *See Jonathan's Landing, Inc. v. Townsend*, 960 F.2d 1538, 1543 (11th Cir. 1992), so holding. *Accord Law Offices of Jonathan Stein v. Cadle Co.*, 87 F. Supp.2d 1015, 99-2 U.S.T.C. ¶50,845 (C.D. Cal. 1999), *aff'd*, 250 F.3d 716, 2001-1 U.S.T.C. ¶50,411 (9th Cir. 2001), *cert. denied*, 122 S. Ct. 215 (2001). For an excellent discussion of 31 U.S.C. §3713, *see* Elliot, Federal Tax Collections, Liens and Levies Ch. 19 (1995 with Supp.); *see also* explanation of R.S. §3466 (the predecessor to the current statute) and related authorities at Stand. Fed. Tax Rep. (CCH) ¶41,790 (1999); Saltzman, IRS Practice and Procedure at ¶¶16.07-16.09 (Rev. Second Edition); former IRS Manual §(34)918 (November 13, 1996).

[2] 31 U.S.C. §3713(a)(2). *See, e.g.*, IRS Legal Memorandum 200210063, January 31, 2002, *reprinted at* 2002 TNT 47-27 (concluding that a receiver in a state insolvency proceeding has an affirmative duty under §3713 to ensure that the government is paid first, even when the IRS filed a claim in the state proceeding and failed to object to the receiver's proposed distribution, which the court then approved).

[3] 31 U.S.C. §3713(b); *see, e.g.*, *Want v. Commissioner*, 280 F.2d 777, 783, 60-2 U.S.T.C. ¶11,956 (2d Cir. 1960) (fiduciary must have had notice of claim to be held liable); *United States v. Spitzer*, 261 F. Supp. 754 (S.D. N.Y. 1966) (even shareholders who direct or control the corporation's payments can be held personally liable); Elliot, *supra* note 1, at ¶19.11. The government generally has six years, from the date of the improper payment or act, to bring an enforcement action. *United States v. Moriarty*, 8 F.3d 329 (6th Cir. 1993). However, under Code §6901(a)(1)(B) and (c)(3), it appears that the IRS may have effectively up to 10 years or more in which to assess liability under 31 U.S.C. §3713(b) for unpaid income taxes.

existence of the unpaid claim of the United States.[4] In various forms, this statute has been around for over 200 years.[5]

In addition, it is possible that a person who receives a payment in violation of the statutory priority of the United States, even though having no knowledge of the violation, may be required to disgorge the payment. This occurred, for example, in the receivership of *Indian Motorcycle Manufacturing, Inc.*,[6] even though the receiver also had no knowledge of an unpaid federal tax liability at the time it made the payment, the payment was authorized by the court, and due to subsequent litigation over the tax liability, several years had passed since the payment was made.

Despite the seeming absolute priority created by the statute, there are several recognized statutory and common law exceptions. As discussed below, these include third-party secured claims having priority under Code § 6323, claims of bank depositors to the extent Code § 7507 applies, and claims of policyholders with respect to insurance companies in receivership. Some courts have also found that the government's priority under the statute does not reach assets that are the subject of a constructive trust.[7]

---

[4] *See, e.g., Leigh v. Commissioner*, 72 T.C. 1105, 1109-1110 (1979). *See also Irving Trust Co. v. Commissioner*, 36 B.T.A. 146 (1937), acq. 1937-2 C.B. 15 (no duty to inquire unless facts presented that would put a reasonable person on notice); *Little v. Commissioner*, 113 T.C. No. 31 (1999) (executor with no legal expertise or prior experience in the administration of estates, who in good faith relied on attorney's erroneous advice that estate had no tax liabilities, was not liable for violating priority; although executor had received various Forms 1099 and W-2, the executor acted prudently in giving such information to the estate's attorney and reasonably relied on the attorney's advice).

[5] *See* 1 Stat. 29, 42 (1789). Other statutes may also impose personal liability on officers or directors. For example, *see Hudgins v. IRS*, 132 B.R. 115, 91-2 U.S.T.C. ¶ 50,397 (E.D. Va. 1991) (director of corporation whose existence was terminated for failure to pay annual Virginia registration fees became trustee for the terminated corporation's assets and was personally liable for post-termination conduct of the business (including federal taxes) to the extent not related to the process of winding up the corporation's affairs); *Mason v. United States*, No. 1:91-cv-227-ODE (N.D. Ga. September 30, 1992) (Texas law to similar effect).

[6] *In re Receivership Estate of Indian Motorcycle Mfg., Inc.*, 2006 U.S. Dist. LEXIS 61497, *amended*, 2006 U.S. Dist. LEXIS 52182 (D. Colo. 2006).

[7] *Compare Brown v. Coleman*, 566 A.2d 1091 (Ct. App. Md. 1989) (held that IRS's claim for unpaid income taxes, attributable to monies fraudulently obtained in a so-called "Ponzi" scheme, had priority in a receivership over the claims of the victims, where it could not be established under state law that the taxpayer's assets were held in constructive trust for the victims; as an aside, the court asserted that, even in circumstances where a constructive trust can be established, it is "doubtful" that Congress intended to allow the United States' priority under § 3713 to be defeated by the imposition of such a constructive trust), *with SEC v. Credit Bancorp Inc.*, 138 F. Supp. 2d 512 (S.D.N.Y. 2001) (under somewhat similar circumstances to *Coleman*, held that most of the receivership estate's assets were held in constructive trust for the victims, and that the insolvency priority statute did not apply to such assets since a transfer of the assets by the receiver to the victims "will be a transfer of property from a possessor to its owners"), *rev'd*, 297 F.3d 127 (2d Cir. 2002) (decision violated Declaratory Judgment Act); *and* IRS Chief Counsel Advice 200110007, November 22, 2000, *reprinted at* 2001 TNT 48-50 (property obtained by the government pursuant to a criminal indictment and forfeiture action, was placed in receivership pending its disposition and distribution to defrauded investors in accordance with a court's earlier restitution order; IRS concluded that it probably did not have a priority claim against such property under the insolvency priority statute; the IRS also thought it likely that a court would hold that the existence of a constructive trust would defeat the insolvency priority statute). Some receivership estates have also been held to constitute a "qualified settlement

(1) *Federal Tax Lien Act; Code § 6323.* One of the more controversial aspects of the government's seeming priority has long been in the area of secured claims, where the statute purports (and had often been held) to override senior secured claims. Significantly, the government had maintained that, under the statute, an unsecured tax claim could take priority over a secured claim irrespective of the provisions of the Federal Tax Lien Act of 1966 (Code § § 6321-6327). However, the Supreme Court, in 1998, in *United States v. Estate of Romani,*[8] held that the more specific provisions of the Tax Lien Act control. Thus, in *Estate of Romani,* a judgment creditor's properly perfected lien on all of the debtor's property (consisting of real property) retained its priority over the government's subsequently filed tax liens, despite the insolvency of the debtor. In addition to judgment liens, Code § 6323(a) also recognizes the priority of any previously perfected security interest or mechanics lien. Also, under Code § 6323(b) and (c), the priority of various creditor liens are recognized even as against a previously filed tax lien (including certain previously committed commercial financing transactions and certain liens where the creditor did not have prior notice or knowledge of the tax lien). To the extent the priorities established in the Tax Lien Act do not address certain liens, the risk of an overriding federal priority remains.

For example, in *Straus v. United States,*[9] the Seventh Circuit considered, in light of *Estate of Romani,* whether the insolvency priority statute operated to override earlier in time state tax liens, at least where the state had not taken title or possession of the debtor's property or perfected a lien in real property. The court held that the insolvency priority statute controlled. However, in *Burke v. United States,*[10] the Massachusetts Dept. of Employment and Training (which had a prior perfected lien) persuaded a Massachusetts Superior Court that the Supreme Court in *Estate of Romani* intended to protect all creditors with perfected interests against secret federal liens. This represents a distinct minority view.

Also, in *Law Offices of Jonathan A. Stein v. Cadle Co.,*[11] the Ninth Circuit held that the Tax Lien Act does not determine the priority of a federal judgment under Code § 6332(d) against a person who fails or refuses to honor a levy, whether or not that person is the taxpayer—and who, in this case, was the taxpayer's employer. Thus, the court held that, under the insolvency priority statute, the IRS's judgment against the employer had priority over a prior filed third party judgment.

(2) *Code § 7507.* Code § 7507 provides another specific exception to the government's priority in insolvency cases. This section applies in the case of any financial institution or trust company that ceases to do business by reason of insolvency (or

(Footnote Continued)

fund" under Reg § 1.468B-1, which is itself treated as a separate taxable entity. *See United States v. Brown,* 2003 U.S. App. LEXIS 13714 (10th Cir. 2003).

[8] 118 S. Ct. 1478, 98-1 U.S.T.C. ¶ 50,368 (1998).

[9] 196 F.3d 862 (7th Cir. 1999), *aff'g,* 98-2 U.S.T.C. ¶ 50,855 (N.D. Ill. 1998). *Cf. United States v. Saidman,* 231 F.2d 503 (D.C. Cir. 1956) (a District of Columbia Code provision that has the status of a federal law and gives priority to "local" D.C. taxes controlled over the predecessor to the current insolvency priority statute).

[10] (Mass. Sup. Court, Plymouth Dec. 22, 1998), *reprinted at* 1999 TNT 26-12.

[11] *Supra* note 1.

bankruptcy) and a substantial portion of the business of which consisted of receiving deposits and making loans and discounts.[12] In such cases, Code § 7507 generally provides that no tax (other than employment taxes) shall be assessed, collected, or paid until such time as the payment of the tax will not diminish the assets necessary for the full payment of all its depositors.[13]

(3) *Insurance Receiverships.* In addition, the Supreme Court has held that a state priority statute governing insolvent insurance companies will preempt the federal insolvency priority statute to the extent it protects policyholders, given that Congress has delegated to the states the regulation of the "business of insurance."[14] Accordingly, state priority afforded to the insurance claims of policyholders and to the costs and expenses of administering the proceeding or liquidation will be respected.[15] However, the federal (not the state) statute will govern the priority of government claims vis-à-vis employee claims and claims of general creditors.

**Payment.** The potential for deferring tax payments outside bankruptcy is similar to that in bankruptcy (*see* § 1016.1 above), with the exception of the potential five- or six-year deferral allowed under Bankruptcy Code section 1129(a)(9)(C).[16] In addition, the debtor may propose an "offer in compromise" pursuant to the IRS's authority

---

[12] *See, e.g.*, Rev. Rul. 88-18, 1988-1 C.B. 402 (applies to thrifts); IRS Letter Ruling 9044046, August 3, 1990 (applies to state chartered industrial loan company); IRS Letter Ruling 9102014, October 11, 1990 (does not apply to trust company that only acted as a fiduciary under a trust indenture or as a paying agent). The IRS also has released a series of field service advice memoranda discussing various qualification issues. *See, e.g.*, FSA 1998-175, March 1, 1992 (consolidated bank subsidiaries acquired by the FDIC in connection with the bank's closure did not qualify), *reprinted at* 98 TNT 173-62; FSA 1998-173, April 10, 1992 (bank that participated in a FDIC assisted transaction did not qualify), *reprinted at* 98 TNT 173-61; FSA 1998-179, June 18, 1992 (effect of consolidated return filing, and RTC payment of depositors), *reprinted at* 98 TNT 173-63; FSA 1998-187, September 9, 1992 (bank under FDIC receivership did not qualify), *reprinted at* 98 TNT 173-64; FSA 1999-568 (undated) (imposition of FDIC receivership due to failure to meet regulatory capital requirements, without proof of insolvency, did not qualify), *reprinted at* 1999 TNT 20-112; FSA 1999-1175, April 15, 1992 (bank qualified), *reprinted at* 1999 TNT 110-59; FSA 1999-1176, September 29, 1992 (IRS did not consider an arranged sale of substantially all of bank's assets by FDIC to be a "cessation" of the bank's business, but because some depositors remained unsatisfied, the Chief Counsel recommended settlement), *reprinted at* 1999 TNT 110-60.

[13] *See* Code § 7507(a) (generally requiring cessation of business), (b) (also applies where depositors' claims are satisfied with assets held in a segregated fund).

[14] *United States Dept. of Treasury v. Fabe*, 113 S. Ct. 2202 (1993). *See also Garcia v. Island Program Designer, Inc.*, 4 F.3d 57 (1st Cir. 1993) (deadline imposed for filing proofs of claim in state insurance company proceeding does not apply to claims of the United States, since the filing deadline was not necessary for the protection of the policyholders).

[15] *See North Carolina v. United States*, 97-2 U.S.T.C. ¶ 50,811 (E.D.N.C. 1997) (administrative expenses includes all taxes, including AMT, arising after the entry of the Order of Liquidation), aff'd, 139 F.3d 892, 98-1 U.S.T.C. ¶ 50,342 (4th Cir. 1998) (unpublished decision); *cf. Greene v. United States*, 440 F.3d 1304 (Fed. Cir. 2006) (older version of Arizona insurance liquidation statute, in effect at the time that a disqualified insurance company became insolvent, did not specify the priority of federal claims and therefore was preempted by the federal insolvency priority statute).

[16] Currently, failure to pay penalties are not alleviated by entering into an installment agreement with the IRS. However, legislation has been considered in the past to change this result. *See* Draft Report on "The Taxpayer Bill of Rights Act of 1991," approved by House Ways and Means Subcommittee on Oversight November 13, 1991, reprinted in BNA Daily Tax Report #220, November 14, 1991 at L-5,6.

under Code §7122, although for offers made on or after July 16, 2006, a lump-sum offer (including offers involving five or fewer installments) requires an upfront payment of 20 percent of the offer, and a deferred payment plan requires an initial installment payment at the time of the offer and continued installment payments while the offer is pending.

Until relatively recently, a tax liability could *only* be compromised if there was (1) doubt as to liability or (2) doubt as to collectibility.[17] To establish doubt as to collectibility, the IRS considers the taxpayer's equity in property (generally based on "fire sale" prices less any prior liens) and earning capacity; thus, a kind of insolvency has been required. Neither hardship, sympathy nor equitable considerations has traditionally been a basis for compromise.[18] This finally changed with the issuance of new regulations in July 1999, as discussed below.

In January 1992, the Commissioner issued Policy Statement P-5-100, which reflected an initial change in the IRS's philosophy regarding offers in compromise. The policy statement states that the IRS will accept an offer in compromise "when it is unlikely that the tax liability can be collected in full and the amount offered reasonably reflects collection potential . . . . The ultimate goal is a compromise which is in the best interests of both the taxpayer and the Service." In this regard, the IRS recognizes that it will often be in its best interest to accept payment of a lesser sum over a shorter period of time.[19]

In a further move to liberalize the IRS's offer-in-compromise program, Congress in the IRS Restructuring and Reform Act of 1998 directed Treasury to prescribe internal guidelines for determining whether an offer-in-compromise is adequate,[20] and to permit additional factors (such as equity, hardship, and public policy) to be taken into account in considering an offer, at least in the case of individual taxpayers.[21]

Acting upon Congress' directive, the IRS, in May 1999, revised the IRS Manual and, in July 1999, issued new temporary regulations, supplanting the prior regulations under Code §7122 (which had been substantially unchanged since 1960).[22] These regulations were finalized on July 18, 2002. The regulations recognize three general grounds upon which an offer-in-compromise may be based: (1) doubt as to liability, (2) doubt as to collectibility and (3) promoting effective tax administration. The first two restate the two traditional grounds for compromise. The third repre-

---

[17] Former Reg. §301.7122-1(a).

[18] Attorney General Opinion #7, dated October 2, 1934, reprinted at XIII-2 C.B. 445.

[19] *See* IRS memorandum to its field offices, dated April 13, 1992, *reprinted at* 92 TNT 106-60. *See also* Traylor, Lying Down with the Lion: The Internal Revenue Service's Offer in Compromise Program, 67 N.Y. St. B.J. 26 (Feb. 1995). Legislation proposed by the House Ways and Means Committee in November 1993 as part of a technical corrections and simplification bill (H.R. 3419, §833), but never enacted, would have incorporated the "best interests" standard into the statute.

[20] Code §7122(d), *as redesignated by* P.L. 109-222 (May 17, 2006).

[21] H.R. Conf. Rep. 599, 105th Cong., 2d Sess. 111 (1988). *See also* "Excerpts From IRS Description of Impact of IRS Reform Act With Actions Necessary to Implement Specific Provisions," BNA Daily Tax Report (September 8, 1998), at L-1, 3.

[22] *See* Temp. Reg. §301.7122-1T; and former IRS Manual, Part 5 (Collections), HB 5.8 (Offer in Compromise Handbook), now at Part 5 (Collection Process), Ch. 8 (Offer in Compromise).

sents a significant change in the law and covers situations where, although collection of the full tax liability could be achieved:

- in the case of individuals, collection of the full tax liability would create an economic hardship;[23] or
- regardless of hardship or type of taxpayer, exceptional circumstances exist such that "collection of the full liability would undermine public confidence that the tax laws are being administered in a fair and equitable manner" (this requires that the taxpayer identify compelling public policy or equity considerations sufficient to justify a compromise, and can show that the compromise is appropriate even though a similarly situated taxpayer may have paid his liability in full).[24]

In each instance, it must also be determined that the compromise of the liability would not undermine general compliance with the tax laws (such as where the taxpayer has a history of noncompliance with filing and payment requirements). The final regulations apply to offers pending or submitted on or after July 18, 2002.[25]

Although not specifically stated in the final regulations, the preamble to the regulations makes clear that "economic hardship . . . is not a basis for compromise for non-individuals under the final regulations."[26] In contrast, the temporary regulations had included an example applying economic hardship in the case of business (non-individual) taxpayers "in the event that a standard for evaluating economic hardship with respect to non-individuals could be developed."[27] However, the IRS

---

[23] The term "economic hardship" is given its meaning under Reg. §301.6343-1, which regulation provides as general justification for a release of levy that the levy create "an economic hardship due to the financial condition of an individual taxpayer," and discusses economic hardship in those terms. *See* Reg. §301.7122-1(b)(3)(i); Reg. §301.6343-1(b)(4). *See also* IRS Chief Counsel Advice 200131029, July 2, 2001, *reprinted at* 2001 TNT 151-21, and IRS Chief Counsel Advice 200128054, May 29, 2001, *reprinted at* 2001 TNT 136-77 (although the field is required to obtain an opinion from the Chief Counsel before compromising a tax liability based on hardship, it need not follow Counsel's recommendation so long as a basis for compromise exists).

[24] *See* Reg. §301.7122-1(b)(3)(ii). For a further discussion of the scope of this provision, *see* IRS Chief Counsel Advice 200043046, July 19, 2000, *reprinted at* 2000 TNT 210-58.

[25] Reg. §301.7122-1(k). For a discussion of the nature and effect of an offer in compromise, possible collateral agreements that the IRS may require, and the procedure for submitting an offer, *see* Rev. Proc. 2003-71, 2003-36 I.R.B. 517; Salzman, *supra* note 1, at §15.03. *See also* IRS Chief Counsel Advice 200133040, June 13, 2001, *reprinted at* 2001 TNT 161-23 (concluding that a collateral agreement as part of a compromise is permitted); IRS Chief Counsel Advice 200119052, March 16, 2001, *reprinted at* 2001 TNT 93-47, *clarifying* IRS Chief Counsel Advice 200119003, July 25, 2000, *reprinted at* 2001 TNT 93-46 (discussing the effect of a compromise by one spouse on the joint and several liability of the other spouse).

[26] *See* Preamble to T.D. 9007, *reprinted at* DTR Daily Tax Report No. 139 (July 19, 2002), at L-8.

[27] *See* Preamble to T.D. 9007. *See also* Temp. Reg. §301.7122-1T(b)(4)(iv)(D), Example 4 (which begins with "Taxpayer is a business . . ." and concludes that compromise would be appropriate where the taxpayer's financial condition results from an embezzlement loss, the seizure of the taxpayer's accounts receivable would cause the taxpayer to go out of business, and the taxpayer has a good overall compliance history; lending a bit of confusion, however, the example also states that the taxpayer "reviewed and signed employment tax returns and signed checks," suggesting that the taxpayer is in fact an individual). *See also* Dougherty and Hill, Corporate Offers-in-Compromise, 1 Corp. Bus. Tax'n Monthly #6, 14 (2000) (discussing offers under the temporary regulations).

and Treasury ultimately concluded that, in the case of non-individuals, an economic hardship standard would not necessarily promote effective tax administration, and "would raise the issue of whether the Government should be foregoing the collection of taxes to support a nonviable business."[28]

In February 1999, the IRS revised the form used for submitting an offer in compromise (IRS Form 656) to permit taxpayers to elect between three payment options: all cash (payable within 90 days), short-term deferred payments (payable within two years), and long-term deferred payments (payable within the statutory collections period, generally up to 10 years).[29] Subsequently, the IRS also announced a fixed monthly payment option, that would wrap all amounts owed to the IRS (including interest on the deferred payments) into a single fixed monthly payment.[30] An important aspect to bear in mind in electing a deferred payment option is that a later default generally will cause the entire original tax liability, including penalties and accrued interest, to be reinstated.[31]

As indicated above, for offers on or after July 16, 2006, an initial payment must be made with the offer (in addition to any user fee), and IRS Form 656 has since been revised to reflect this requirement. This requires, in the case of a so-called "lump sum" offer (including offers providing for five or fewer installments), a non-refundable down payment of 20 percent of the offer, and in the case of a proposed periodic payment plan (of six or more installments), an initial installment payment at the time of the offer with continued installment payments while the offer is pending.[32] The application of these "good faith" payments (such as between tax and interest, or by tax period) can be specified by the taxpayer.[33]

---

28 *See* Preamble to T.D. 9007. The regulations do permit non-individuals to demonstrate that compelling public policy or equity considerations justify a compromise.

29 *See also* IRS Manual, Part 5 (Collection Process), Ch. 8 (Offer in Compromise), § 1.9.4 (9/1/05).

30 *See* IRS News Release, dated December 29, 1999 (IR-1999-105).

31 *See* Instructions to IRS Form 656 (Offer in Compromise) (2/2007 rev.); *see also* IRS Service Center Advice 200110029, January 26, 2001, *reprinted at* 2001 TNT 48-48.

32 Code § 7122(c)(1), *as added by* P.L. 109-222 (May 17, 2006).

33 Code § 7122(c)(2)(A), *as added by* P.L. 109-222 (May 17, 2006).

# 11

# State and Local Tax Aspects of Bankruptcy



## §1101 PREEMPTION BY BANKRUPTCY CODE

For corporations involved in bankruptcy proceedings, the Bankruptcy Code affects the procedures for reporting and paying state and local taxes. The procedures prescribed for state and local taxes are for the most part the same as for federal taxes and, to the extent that state and local tax laws are in conflict with the Bankruptcy Code provisions, the latter will prevail.

The Bankruptcy Code not only affects the procedures for reporting and collecting state and local taxes, it affects the substance of state and local tax laws as well. The substantive provisions have a curious history. The people working on the revision of the bankruptcy law in the 1970s had contemplated that the new Bankruptcy Code would simultaneously reform both the bankruptcy law (including the procedural aspects of tax collection) and the substantive tax consequences of bankruptcy transactions.[1] The legislation they introduced in Congress contained comprehensive provisions to govern the substantive federal, state, and local tax consequences of bankruptcy transactions. These proved controversial, however. As a result, although Congress did include many of the new substantive tax provisions in the Bankruptcy Code when the Code was enacted in 1978, Congress limited their impact to state and

[1] **§1101** *See* The Report of the Commission on the Bankruptcy Laws of the United States (Parts I and II), H.R. Doc. No. 93-137, 93d Cong., 1st Sess. (1973); Klee, Legislative History to the New Bankruptcy Law, 28 DePaul L. Rev. 941 (1979); Plumb, The Tax Recommendations of the Commission on the Bankruptcy Laws—Tax Procedures, 88 Harv. L. Rev. 1360 (1975); Plumb, The Tax Recommendations of the Commission on the Bankruptcy Laws—Income Tax Liabilities of the Estate and the Debtor, 72 Mich. L. Rev. 937 (1974); Plumb, The Tax Recommendations of the Commission on the Bankruptcy Laws—Priority and Dischargeability of Tax Claims, 59 Cornell L. Rev. 991 (1974); Plumb, The Tax Recommendations of the Commission on the Bankruptcy Laws—Reorganizations, Carryovers, and the Effects of Debt Reduction, 29 Tax L. Rev. 229 (1974).

local taxes and did not make them applicable for federal tax purposes.[2] The study of new federal substantive rules continued until new federal rules were finally adopted in the Bankruptcy Tax Act of 1980. These differed in some respects from the provisions that were adopted in 1978 in the Bankruptcy Code for state and local tax purposes and covered a broader range of issues, but Congress did not amend the Bankruptcy Code provisions to conform them to the 1980 law.

Because many state and local tax laws conform to the federal income tax law by incorporating many of the federal computations of taxable income, the state and local tax consequences of bankruptcy transactions in such jurisdictions may invoke three sets of substantive tax rules: (1) the federal rules in the 1980 Act (and subsequent tax acts), which will govern federal computations and the portion of the state and local computations that adopt the federal concepts; (2) the nonconforming portion of the state and local tax laws; and (3) the Bankruptcy Code provisions that govern state and local substantive tax consequences. Presumably the Bankruptcy Code provisions will apply only where the first two sets of rules produce a harsher state and local tax result for the taxpayer than the Bankruptcy Code provisions would produce. In 2005, as part of a comprehensive bankruptcy reform bill, substantial changes were finally made to the provisions of the Bankruptcy Code addressing substantive state and local tax consequences of bankruptcy to bring them into greater conformity with the federal tax rules.[3]

The general power of a state to tax a company in bankruptcy, whether conducting a business or in the process of liquidating, was confirmed by the Supreme Court in *California State Board of Equalization v. Sierra Summit*.[4] Moreover, the Court acknowledged Congress's authority to create an exemption to state taxation, but cautioned that "a court must proceed carefully when asked to recognize an exemption from state taxation that Congress has not clearly expressed."[5]

In *Sierra Summit*, the Court considered 28 U.S.C. § 960, which provides that "any officers and agents conducting any business under authority of a United States court shall be subject to all federal, state, and local taxes applicable to such business to the same extent as if it were conducted by an individual or corporation." At issue was whether a bankruptcy liquidation sale was exempt from state sales tax on the grounds that Section 960 subjected a bankruptcy trustee to tax only if he "conducted a business." In upholding the state sales tax, the court stated that:

> Read most naturally, the statute evinces an intention that a State be permitted to tax a bankruptcy estate notwithstanding an intergovernmental immunity objection that might be interposed . . . . Nothing in the plain language of the statute, its legislative history, or the structure of the Bankruptcy Code indicates that Congress intended to exclude taxes on the

---

[2] *See* 11 U.S.C. § 346(a), as in effect prior to the 2005 bankruptcy reform changes; and 11 U.S.C. § 346(k)(2), *as amended by* P.L. 109-8, § 719 (2005). *See also In re Page*, 163 B.R. 196 (Bankr. D. Kan. 1994). For an interesting discussion of the politics relating to the tax provisions of the Bankruptcy Code, *see* Asofsky, Towards a Bankruptcy Tax Act of 1993, 51 NYU Inst. Fed. Tax'n § 13.02 (1993).

[3] For a brief history of the reform legislation, *see* § 1001 above.

[4] 109 S. Ct. 2228 (1989).

[5] Id. at 2234, *quoting Rockford Life Ins. Co. v. Illinois Dept. of Revenue*, 482 U.S. 182 (1987).

liquidation process from those taxes the States may impose on the bankrupt estate.[6]

Section 960 was further clarified as part of the 2005 bankruptcy reforms, by expressly requiring the timely payment of all taxes imposed in respect of a business being conducted under authority of a United States court other than in certain enumerated exceptions, all pertaining to bankruptcy. These are (i) where payment of the tax is otherwise excused under a specific provision of the Bankruptcy Code, (ii) in a Chapter 7 case, as to taxes incurred prior to the appointment of a Chapter 7 trustee, or having timely obtained a bankruptcy court order declaring the probable inability of the estate to pay administrative expenses in full, and (iii) with respect to property taxes on certain abandoned property (as discussed in the preceding footnote).[7]

## §1102 STATE AND LOCAL TAX PROCEDURE IN BANKRUPTCY

As just mentioned, the Bankruptcy Code provides procedural rules for reporting and collecting state and local taxes that are essentially the same as the rules it provides for federal tax purposes. These rules include the following:

### *§1102.1 Same Taxable Entity*

No new or separate taxable entity is created. The debtor corporation remains taxable in the same manner as if the bankruptcy case had not been commenced.[1]

### *§1102.2 Reporting for Prepetition Periods*

In respect of any prepetition taxable year for which a tax return was not filed, the debtor-in-possession in a Chapter 11 case must file all tax returns,[2] and supply the state or local taxing authority with any information the taxing authority requires with

---

[6] Id. at 2234-2235; *see also Anerinbex, Inc. v. International Decaffeinated Corp.* (*In re Anerinbex, Inc.*), 110 B.R. 575 (Bankr. M.D. Fla. 1990) (declined to apply *Sierra Summit* retroactively); *cf.* 11 U.S.C. §1146(a), discussed *infra* at §1102.15. *See also Obuchowski v. State of Vermont* (*In re Henry*), 135 B.R. 6 (Bankr. D. Vt. 1991) (upholding imposition of Vermont gains tax on dispositions of property by Chapter 7 trustee). The Tenth Circuit, in an unpublished decision, held that section 960 did not require the payment of postpetition property taxes in respect of property that was subsequently abandoned by a Chapter 7 trustee pursuant to Bankruptcy Code section 554 and therefore not considered part of the bankruptcy estate. *Butler v. Shanor*, 70 F.3d 1282, 1995 WL 699016 (10th Cir. 1995). A 2005 amendment to section 960 codifies this position, but only in situations where the abandonment occurs within a reasonable period of time after the property tax lien attaches. *See* 28 U.S.C. §960(b)(1), *as added by* P.L. 109-8, §712(a) (2005).

[7] *See* 28 U.S.C. §960(b) and (c), *as added by* P.L. 109-8, §712(a) (2005).

[1] **§1102** The relevant provisions were amended and redesignated as part of the 2005 bankruptcy reform changes. For pre-October 17, 2005 bankruptcy cases, *see* 11 U.S.C. §346(c)(1) and (h); *cf.* 11 U.S.C. §346(g)(1)(A) and (B)—all as in effect prior to the 2005 changes. For subsequent cases, *see* 11 U.S.C. §346(a) and (b), *as amended by* P.L. 109-8, §719 (2005); in conjunction with Code §1399.

[2] *See* 11 U.S.C. §346(c)(2), as in effect prior to the 2005 bankruptcy reform changes; and 11 U.S.C. §346(b) and (k)(1), *as amended by* P.L. 109-8, §719 (2005). Unless otherwise indicated, references herein

respect to any unfiled tax returns in light of the condition of the debtor corporation's books and records and the availability of the information.[3]

## *§1102.3 Reporting for Postpetition Periods*

During the bankruptcy case, a debtor-in-possession generally must file any tax return that the debtor corporation would have filed had there been no bankruptcy case and pay any tax shown thereon.[4] In a Chapter 7 (liquidation) case, it is unnecessary in a pre-October 17, 2005 bankruptcy case to file state or local tax returns for a tax on or measured by income if the debtor corporation has no net taxable income for the entire period of the bankruptcy case.[5] Otherwise, normal yearly returns are required.[6] Presumably, such returns may be filed without penalty at the termination of the Chapter 7 case. It would also seem, in keeping with the general intent of netting income and losses for the entire period of a Chapter 7 case, that no interest should accrue and be payable in respect of any postpetition taxes that, on an annual basis, would have been payable but, on a cumulative basis, need not be paid due to subsequent postpetition losses.[7] In addition, in Chapter 7 bankruptcy cases commenced on or after October 17, 2005, current *payment* of postpetition taxes is not required if (i) the tax was incurred prior to the appointment of the Chapter 7 trustee, or (ii) prior to the due date, an order of the bankruptcy court contains a finding of probable insufficiency of funds to pay in full administrative expenses of equal priority as the tax owed.[8]

---

(Footnote Continued)

to a "debtor-in-possession" generally apply equally to a bankruptcy "trustee." *See* 11 U.S.C. §§1107, 1108.

[3] 11 U.S.C. §1106(a)(6).

[4] 11 U.S.C. §346(c)(2), as in effect prior to the 2005 bankruptcy reform changes; and 11 U.S.C. §346(b) and (k)(1), *as amended by* P.L. 109-8, §719 (2005); 28 U.S.C. §960, *as amended by* P.L. 109-8, §712(a) (2005). *See also* 11 U.S.C. §521(j)(1) (added as part of the 2005 changes, this section allows a taxing authority to request an order converting or dismissing the bankruptcy cases unless the debtor timely files all tax returns due after the commencement of the bankruptcy case—including for any prepetition period—and requires that the court dismiss or convert the case unless the debtor files the return within 90 days of the request); 11 U.S.C. §1108 (authority to operate debtor's business; includes payment of postpetition expenses incurred in ordinary course); 11 U.S.C. §549 (acts out of ordinary course).

[5] 11 U.S.C. §728(b), as in effect prior to the 2005 bankruptcy reform changes. This rule was not adopted for federal tax purposes. *But cf.* IRS position in Rev. Rul. 84-123, 1984-2 C.B. 244 (permitting a debtor relief from filing a tax return if it has ceased operations and has neither assets nor income), discussed at §1006.2.1.

[6] Id. *See, e.g.*, Mass. Dept. of Rev. Directive 06-1, Prac. & Proc. (February 16, 2006) (explaining the Massachusetts tax reporting obligations for Chapter 7 trustees).

[7] *Cf. In re Quid Me Broadcasting, Inc.*, 1996 U.S. Dist. LEXIS 7581 (W.D.N.Y. 1996), *aff'g* 181 B.R. 715 (Bankr. W.D.N.Y. 1995) (holding that IRS was not entitled to interest upon similar facts where the Chapter 7 trustee was not authorized to operate the debtor's business and thus had no duty or authorization to remit any postpetition taxes in advance of an orderly distribution of the estate's assets); *see also* Goldring and Richards, Current Developments in State and Local Bankruptcy Taxation, 50 Tax Law. 539, 565-567 (1997).

[8] 28 U.S.C. §960(c), *as added by* P.L. 109-8, §712(a) (2005).

A debtor-in-possession (or, if authorized to operate the debtor corporation's business, a trustee) must file with the bankruptcy court and with any state or local taxing authority periodic reports and summaries of the operation of the debtor's business, including a statement of receipts and disbursements, and such other information as the court requires or, unless the court orders otherwise, as the taxing authority may request.[9]

## *§1102.4 Payment of Prepetition Taxes Prohibited; Responsible Person Liability*

Absent court approval, a debtor-in-possession is prohibited from remitting any prepetition taxes, including any state or local taxes required to be withheld or collected prior to the bankruptcy case with respect to salaries, commissions, sales, dividends, interest or other payments (so-called trust fund taxes).[10]

Accordingly, officers and employees involved in the remittance of trust fund taxes and other "responsible" persons should be aware that most states have personal liability (or 100 percent penalty) statutes comparable to Code §6672 (*see* §§103 and 1006.3.2) for the failure to remit trust fund taxes—although, in many cases, without regard to whether the failure was "willful." Similarly, many states have lender liability statutes for unpaid employee withholding taxes of a borrower comparable to Code §3505 (*see* §104). Therefore, to avoid potential officer (and creditor) liability, all unpaid trust fund taxes should, if possible, be remitted prior to the bankruptcy case.[11]

In a case of first impression, the bankruptcy court in the *Macy* case granted a preliminary injunction against several states seeking to collect unpaid employee withholding and sales tax from current and former officers and employees of Macy, which the court "contemplated to remain in effect until the resolution of the States' tax claims within Debtors' reorganization cases."[12] The court, in an unpublished

---

[9] 11 U.S.C. §704(7) and (8), redesignated in the 2005 reform bill as §704(a)(7) and (8); *see* 11 U.S.C. §1108 (unless the court orders otherwise, trustee authorized to operate debtor's business); 11 U.S.C. §1109 (party in interest).

[10] *See* 11 U.S.C. §549, discussed at §1006.1. Arguably, any accrual of a failure-to-pay penalty beyond the petition date would be contrary to the automatic stay. *Cf. United States v. Chris-Marine, U.S.A., Inc.* (*In re Chris-Marine, U.S.A., Inc.*), 321 B.R. 63 (M.D. Fla. 2004).

[11] *See Begier, Jr. v. IRS*, 110 S. Ct. 2258, 90-1 U.S.T.C. ¶50,294 (1990), discussed at §1005.2. The applicability of the *Begier* case depends in part on whether the unpaid tax, although generally termed a "trust fund" tax, is actually considered to be held "in trust" under governing law. *See, e.g., In re Lakeside Community Hospital, Inc.*, 1996 Bankr. LEXIS 66 (Bankr. N.D. Ill. 1996) (Illinois withholding statute held comparable to federal statute in *Begier*); *Taylor v. Adams* (*In re Nash Concrete Form Co.*), 159 B.R. 611 (D. Mass. 1993) (same regarding Massachusetts withholding statute); *City of Farrell v. Sharon Steel Corp.*, 41 F.3d 92 (3d Cir. 1994) (although statute did not create trust, Pennsylvania case law established trustee/trust relationship where one acts as agent; court saw no difference between statutory trust in *Begier* and common law trust; remanded to consider tracing of funds into commingled account). In addition, not all taxes for which an officer may be held liable are "trust fund" taxes. For example, some states impose officer liability for a corporation's failure to pay use taxes. *See, e.g., In re Unger*, 1993 WL 33296 (N.Y. Tax App.) (involving New York use tax).

[12] *See R. H. Macy & Co. v. Commonwealth of Pennsylvania, et al.* (*In re R. H. Macy & Co.*), Ch. 11, Case No. 92 B 40477 (BRL), Adv. Proc. No. 92-9881A (Bankr. S.D.N.Y.), preliminary injunction granted December 8, 1992; and Findings of Fact and Conclusions of Law, docketed March 11, 1993 (appeal

decision, held that the injunction was supportable under *both* the automatic stay and the court's equitable powers. The court found, among other things, that Macy, not the officers, was the real party-in-interest, and that the states' collection efforts were blatant attempts to circumvent the automatic stay (*see* § 1102.7 below) and force Macy into paying prepetition taxes in advance of a plan. As discussed at § 1006.3, virtually all courts have held that the federal Anti-Injunction Act (Code § 7421) precludes the bankruptcy court from enjoining IRS actions against a debtor's officers under Code § 6672. Although there is a similar anti-injunction statute for state tax purposes, known as the "Tax Injunction Act" (28 U.S.C. § 1341), it is not identical. Specifically, the existence of a "plain, speedy and efficient remedy" is a precondition to the state Tax Injunction Act but not the federal Anti-Injunction Act.[13] According to the bankruptcy court in the *Macy* case, this effectively required that Macy be able to participate in and assert control over the tax proceedings against its employees, which Macy could not do.

Subsequently, the bankruptcy court in the *McCrory Corporation* bankruptcy case[14] reached substantially the same conclusion on similar facts. On appeal, however, the district court reversed,[15] finding unpersuasive and insupportable McCrory's asserted need to be able to intervene in any such proceedings against the employees. The district court also concluded that, although having somewhat different language, the Tax Injunction Act and the Anti-Injunction Act should be interpreted in a harmonious manner.

In a given instance, an officer or an employee may be able to raise as a valid defense against a state action for unpaid trust fund taxes the absence of personal jurisdiction, assuming his only meaningful nexus with the state was in his capacity as a corporate officer or employee.[16]

In addition, it has been quite common for a corporate debtor's Chapter 11 plan to include a postconfirmation injunction and/or a nondebtor release prohibiting third parties from pursuing the debtors' directors, officers, employees and agents (directly or indirectly) with respect to any pre-confirmation claims against the debtors (except to enforce their rights under the plan). These provisions are often heavily negotiated with the various creditors' and equity committees. Not surprisingly, taxing authorities have been very sensitive to such provisions and, where spotted, generally seek and, in most cases, obtain express carve-outs. In addition, the validity of such

(Footnote Continued)

filed, but rendered moot by subsequent confirmation of Chapter 11 plan). *See generally* Note, Expanding the Bankruptcy Code: The Use of Section 362 and Section 105 to Protect Solvent Executives of Debtor Corporations, 58 Brooklyn L. Rev. 929 (1992) (discussing nontax cases).

13 *See Enochs v. Williams Packing & Navigation Co.*, 370 U.S. 1, *reh'g denied*, 370 U.S. 965 (1962).

14 *See McCrory Corp. v. Ohio*, 212 B.R. 229 (S.D.N.Y. 1997) (reversing unpublished bankruptcy court decision).

15 *Id.*

16 *Cf. United States v. Flack* (S.D. Ohio 1997), *reprinted at* 97 TNT 42-33 (involving IRS action under Code § 6672; held that status as corporate officer did not vest Ohio federal court with personal jurisdiction).

injunctions have been challenged over time,[17] with several Circuit Court of Appeals finding such injunctions impermissible. Others have allowed them (at least in situations not involving a taxing authority) when integral to the Chapter 11 plan, or have not yet considered the issue. However, any challenge to the propriety of such an injunction or third party release generally should be made with the bankruptcy court in connection with confirmation.[18] In *In re Eichner*,[19] a debtor corporation's confirmed Chapter 11 plan included such an injunction. Nevertheless, the New York State Division of Taxation issued notices of determination for unremitted corporate sales and use taxes against several of the debtor's officers. The officers challenged such notices at the state level, in part, on the basis that the notices were issued in violation of the injunction, and that the validity of the bankruptcy court's injunction (in contrast to the enforcement of the injunction) was not properly within the state tax tribunal's jurisdiction. The State Division of Tax Appeals agreed on both accounts.

## *§1102.5 Sovereign Immunity; Avoidance Actions*

A debtor-in-possession's ability to recover state and local taxes paid or satisfied shortly before the bankruptcy in respect of preexisting tax debts is similar in many respects to that described at §1005 for federal tax purposes. However, one significant difference that exists with respect to taxes imposed by state governments, which may have far-reaching bankruptcy implications beyond the context of avoidance and turnover actions, is the immunity from suit in federal court accorded to such governmental units under the Eleventh Amendment to the Constitution. The Supreme Court recently addressed the breadth and scope of such state immunity in the bankruptcy context in *Central Virginia Community College v. Katz.*[20]

### §1102.5.1 Before There Was *Katz*

Prior to the amendment of Bankruptcy Code section 106 in 1994 (*see* §1005.1.3), the Supreme Court in *Hoffman v. Connecticut Department of Income Maintenance*[21] held that, in the context of an action to recover taxes and other monies paid to the State of Connecticut, former section 106(c) did not act as a waiver of Connecticut's Eleventh Amendment immunity because Congress did not make its intention to abrogate such immunity unmistakably clear in the language of the statute. In response to the decision in *Hoffman*, and the Supreme Court's decision in *Nordic Village*,[22] Congress

---

[17] For a discussion of the relevant authorities, *see* Colliers on Bankruptcy (15th Ed.), at ¶¶105.03[2], 524.05, and 1141.02[4].

[18] *See id.* at ¶1141.02[4].

[19] DTA Nos. 819327-9, 2004 N.Y. Tax LEXIS 216 (NYS Div. of Tax Appeals) (Oct. 21, 2004).

[20] 126 S. Ct. 990 (2006).

[21] 109 S. Ct. 2818 (1989) (plurality opinion; Justice Scalia, concurring, based his decision on the grounds that Congress lacked the power to abrogate Eleventh Amendment immunity pursuant to the Bankruptcy Clause of the Constitution); *see also United States v. Nordic Village*, 112 S. Ct. 1011, 92-1 U.S.T.C. ¶50,109 (1992), discussed at §1005.1.3.

[22] *See supra* note 21.

amended section 106 as part of the Bankruptcy Reform Act of 1994 and made more explicit the waiver or, more accurately as relates to the states, the abrogation of sovereign immunity in injunctive and declaratory actions for monetary relief, thereby overruling *Hoffman* and *Nordic Village*. (The provisions of Bankruptcy Code section 106 are discussed in detail at §1005.1.) In the aftermath of the 1994 amendment, the constitutionality of Bankruptcy Code section 106 as relates to the states was litigated before numerous courts.[23]

The challenge to Bankruptcy Code section 106 focused predominantly, but not exclusively, on section 106(a), which purports to abrogate Eleventh Amendment immunity as to most Bankruptcy Code actions involving tax claims without any affirmative action by the taxing authority. The courts initially found that amended section 106(a) withstood attack on the grounds that Congress satisfied both of the criteria necessary to abrogate Eleventh Amendment immunity: first, under the rationale of the Supreme Court's decision in *Pennsylvania v. Union Gas Co.*,[24] that the Bankruptcy Clause of Article I of the Constitution, which grants Congress the power to establish uniform laws regarding bankruptcies, allows Congress to abrogate the states' immunity; and, second, that Congress made its intent to abrogate the states' immunity unmistakably clear on the face of newly-amended section 106. The courts' fundamental reliance on *Union Gas*, however, was called into serious question by the Supreme Court's 1996 decision in *Seminole Tribe of Florida v. Florida*.[25]

The *Seminole* case involved the issue of whether Congress had the power to abrogate the Eleventh Amendment immunity of the states pursuant to the Indian Commerce Clause of Article I of the Constitution. Directly confronting its prior decision in *Union Gas*, the Supreme Court found that the decision contained questionable reasoning and was a solitary departure from the established principle of law that the bounds of Article III, which sets forth the permissible scope of federal court jurisdiction, cannot be expanded by Congress operating pursuant to any constitutional provision other than the Fourteenth Amendment. Consequently, the Supreme Court overruled *Union Gas*, and held that "[t]he Eleventh Amendment restricts the judicial power under Article III, *and Article I cannot be used to circumvent the constitutional limitations placed upon federal jurisdiction*."[26] The Seminole Tribe's suit against the state of Florida was therefore barred by Florida's Eleventh Amendment immunity. Justice Stevens, in his dissenting opinion, asserted that the Court's holding extends beyond the bounds of the issues raised by the Seminole Tribe and would prevent

---

[23] *See, e.g., In re Merchants Grain, Inc.*, 59 F.3d 630 (7th Cir. 1995), *vacated and remanded*, 116 S. Ct. 1411 (1996); *In re HPA Assoc.*, 191 B.R. 167 (Bankr. 9th Cir. 1995); *In re J.F.D. Enterprises, Inc.*, 183 B.R. 342 (Bankr. D. Mass. 1995); *In re York-Hannover Developments, Inc.*, 181 B.R. 271 (Bankr. E.D.N.C.), *aff'd*, 190 B.R. 62 (E.D.N.C. 1995) (vacated and remanded by the Fourth Circuit for decision in light of *Seminole; see infra* note 35 for case on remand), *dismissed on remand*, 201 B.R. 137 (Bankr. E.D. N.C. 1996).

[24] 491 U.S. 1 (1989), *overruled by Seminole Tribe of Florida v. Florida*, 116 S. Ct. 1114 (1996). In *Union Gas*, the Supreme Court had held that the Interstate Commerce Clause of Article I of the Constitution was a sufficient grant of constitutional authority to allow Congress to abrogate Eleventh Amendment immunity.

[25] 116 S. Ct. 1114 (1996).

[26] Id. at 1131-1132 (emphasis added).

Congress from providing a federal forum in which to enforce against the states, *inter alia*, the federal bankruptcy laws.[27]

The Fourth Circuit in *In re Creative Goldsmiths of Washington, D.C., Inc.*[28] was the first Circuit Court to address in a published opinion the constitutionality of Bankruptcy Code section 106 in light of *Seminole*. The issue before the Fourth Circuit was whether the State of Maryland was protected by the Eleventh Amendment from suit by a bankruptcy trustee to avoid as a preference the debtor's payment of income taxes immediately prior to the filing of a bankruptcy petition. The trustee argued that the Bankruptcy Clause of Article I of the Constitution and, additionally, the Fourteenth Amendment to the Constitution confer upon Congress the power to abrogate Eleventh Amendment immunity and, that because Congress was acting pursuant to such provisions of the Constitution when it amended section 106(a) in 1994, section 106(a) was effective to abrogate the State of Maryland's Eleventh Amendment immunity with respect to the preference action. The trustee also argued that, pursuant to section 106(b), the State was deemed to have waived any such immunity when it filed a proof of claim in the debtor's case for sales and withholding taxes because such claim for sales and withholding taxes arose out of the same transaction or occurrence as the events that gave rise to the trustee's action to recover the income taxes.

With respect to section 106(a), the Fourth Circuit, relying on *Seminole*, concluded that such section is unconstitutional as it applies to the states because Congress is not empowered to use the Bankruptcy Clause of Article I to circumvent the Eleventh Amendment restrictions on federal jurisdiction. The court stated that there is no evidence that Congress passed the 1994 amendments to the Bankruptcy Code pursuant to the Fourteenth Amendment or sought to preserve the core values enumerated in the Amendment.

The Fourth Circuit similarly concluded that section 106(b) is unconstitutional because it is not within Congress' power to abrogate Eleventh Amendment immunity by "deeming" a waiver. However, consistent with the provisions of section 106(b), the court found that, under common law, a state may voluntarily subject itself to bankruptcy court jurisdiction if a representative of the state (who is authorized under state law to file a proof of claim in the debtor's bankruptcy case) files such a claim

---

[27] *See* id. at 1134 (Stevens, J., dissenting). Justice Stevens also observed that, because federal jurisdiction over these federal laws is exclusive, the effect of the Court's holding would be to deny any remedy for state violations of the federal bankruptcy laws. In response, the Court noted that (i) it had never awarded relief against a state under any of the federal bankruptcy laws and (ii) contrary to Justice Stevens' assertions, several avenues remain open for ensuring state compliance with federal law, such as injunctive relief under *Ex parte Young*, 209 U.S. 123 (1908) (*see infra* note 95), in order to remedy a state officer's ongoing violation of federal law. *See* 116 S. Ct. at 1131 n.16. *See also infra* note 97, discussing jurisdiction of state court with respect to federal bankruptcy matters.

[28] *Scholssberg v. Maryland* (*In re Creative Goldsmiths of Washington, D.C., Inc.*), 119 F.3d 1140 (4th Cir. 1997), *cert. denied*, 118 S. Ct. 1517 (1998). After its decision in *Seminole*, the Supreme Court granted certiorari in the *Merchants Grain* case (*supra* note 23)—wherein the Seventh Circuit (in this pre-*Seminole* decision) had held that a state did not have Eleventh Amendment immunity from suit by a Chapter 11 trustee to recover alleged preferential transfers to the state—and vacated the judgment of the Seventh Circuit and remanded the case for further consideration in light of *Seminole*. *See Ohio Agricultural Commodity Depositors Fund v. Mahern*, 116 S. Ct. 1411 (1996), *vacating and remanding* 59 F.3d 630 (7th Cir. 1995).

and the claim arises out of the same transaction or occurrence that is the basis for the debtor's claim against the state. Thus, the substance of section 106(b)—the "same transaction or occurrence" requirement—remains the pertinent law. The Fourth Circuit concluded that the State of Maryland's proof of claim for sales and withholding taxes did not arise out of the same transaction or occurrence as the trustee's action against Maryland to recover income taxes and therefore did not operate as a waiver of the State's Eleventh Amendment immunity.[29] The court also examined whether, under state law, Maryland independently waived its Eleventh Amendment immunity by defending against the trustee's action to recover income taxes and concluded that no such waiver occurred.

Consistent with *Creative Goldsmiths*, the Third,[30] Fifth,[31] Seventh,[32] Ninth and Eleventh Circuits,[33] and numerous lower courts concluded that section 106(a) was an unconstitutional attempt by Congress to abrogate Eleventh Amendment immunity pursuant to the Bankruptcy Clause of Article I.[34] Not all such courts, however,

---

[29] The Fourth Circuit did not address the applicability of section 106(c), which provides for a waiver of Eleventh Amendment immunity when a state and debtor have offsetting claims, because the trustee failed to assert such a right of setoff.

[30] *See In re Sacred Heart Hosp. of Norristown*, 133 F.3d 237 (3d Cir. 1998); *Vegliante v. New Jersey* (*In re Vegliante*), 2002 U.S. App. LEXIS 15855 (3d Cir. 2002) (unpublished), *cert. denied*, 123 S. Ct. 885 (2003).

[31] *See In re Fernandez*, 123 F.3d 241 (5th Cir.), *corrected and reh'g denied*, 130 F.3d 1138 (5th Cir. 1997).

[32] *Nelson v. La Crosse County District Attorney* (*In re Nelson*), 301 F.3d 820 (7th Cir. 2002).

[33] *See, e.g.*, *Georgia Higher Educ. Assistance Corp. v. Crow* (*In re Crow*), 394 F.3d 918 (11th Cir. 2004), *reh'g denied, en banc*, 159 Fed.Appx. 183 (11th Cir. July 15, 2005); *In re Light*, 87 F.3d 1320 (9th Cir. 1996) (an unpublished decision), full decision at 1996 WL 341112 (no discussion of Fourteenth Amendment as a potential source of congressional power for enacting the 1994 amendments to section 106); *In re Mitchell*, 209 F.3d 1111 (9th Cir. 2000) (same); *In re Elias*, 218 B.R. 80 (Bankr. 9th Cir. 1998), *aff'd*, 216 F.3d 1082 (9th Cir. 2000) (same), *In re Lapin*, 226 B.R. 637 (Bankr. 9th Cir. 1998) (expressly rejecting the Fourteenth Amendment as a potential source of congressional power for enacting the 1994 amendments to section 106); *Wilks v. United States* (*In re Wilks*), 2000-2 U.S.T.C. ¶50,644 (9th Cir. 2000), *aff'g*, 99-1 U.S.T.C. ¶50,535 (Bankr. 9th Cir. 1999). Interestingly, in *Schulman v. California* (*In re Lazar*), 237 F.3d 967 (9th Cir. 2001), *cert. denied*, 122 S. Ct. 458 (2001), the Ninth Circuit, although finding it unnecessary to address the question of the constitutionality of sections 106(a) and (b) on the matter before it, implied that it had never considered the issue. Yet, the Ninth Circuit directly addressed the issue eight months earlier in *In re Mitchell*. A reasonable explanation for this oversight is that the briefs in the *Lazar* case were submitted, and oral argument occurred, almost a year *before* the Ninth Circuit's decision in *Mitchell*, and the *Lazar* court figured that it was unnecessary to update the research since it was not going to address the issue. The Second Circuit considered the constitutionality of section 106(c) (*see infra* text accompanying note 52), but made clear that it did not need to decide, and was not deciding, the constitutionality of section 106(a) or section 106(b). *See Ossen v. Dept. of Social Services* (*In re Charter Oak Associates*) (2d Cir.), *infra* note 52, at 764.

[34] In addition to the Third, Fifth, Seventh, Ninth and Eleventh Circuits, the Sixth and Tenth Circuits, as well as the Tenth Circuit Bankruptcy Appellate Panel, had the opportunity to address the constitutionality of section 106(a) in light of *Seminole*. The Tenth Circuit Bankruptcy Appellate Panel similarly held that section 106(a) was unconstitutional. *See Straight v. Wyoming Dept. of Transp.* (*In re Straight*), 248 B.R. 403 (Bankr. 10th Cir. 2000) (split decision); *Chandler v. State of Oklahoma* (*In re Chandler*), 251 B.R. 872 (Bankr. 10th Cir. 2000). However, the Tenth Circuit Court of Appeals expressly declined to address the issue and each decided the case before it on other grounds. *See Innes v. Kansas State University* (*In re Innes*), 184 F.3d 1275 (10th Cir. 1999), *cert. denied*, 120 S. Ct. 1530 (2000); *Wyoming Dep't of Transp. v. Straight* (*In re Straight*), 143 F.3d 1387 (10th Cir. 1998), *cert. denied*, 119 S. Ct. 446 (1998). In contrast, as discussed in the text below, the Sixth Circuit Court of Appeals is the only circuit court to have upheld the constitutionality of section 106(a).

addressed the Fourteenth Amendment as a source of congressional power for this purpose.[35]

Notwithstanding the Supreme Court's decision in *Seminole,* some courts concluded that the abrogation of Eleventh Amendment immunity in the bankruptcy context is constitutional. Most notable in this regard is the decision of the Sixth Circuit in *Hood v. Tennessee Student Assistance Corp.,*[36] which concluded, in the context of an adversary proceeding initiated by an individual debtor against a state agency to determine the dischargeability of a student-loan, that the states ceded their sovereignty with respect to federal bankruptcy matters as part of the overall plan at the Constitutional Convention.[37] Expressly rejecting as unpersuasive the decisions of the

---

[35] Lower courts holding that Congress lacked the power to abrogate Eleventh Amendment immunity pursuant to either the Bankruptcy Clause of Article I or the Fourteenth Amendment: *see, e.g., Skandalakis v. Geeslin (In re Geeslin),* 303 B.R. 533 (M.D. Ga. 2004); *Powers v. Alaska Comm. on Post-Secondary Education (In re Powers),* 301 B.R. 90 (Bankr. W.D. Okla. 2003) (involved dischargeability of a student loan; the same issue was subsequently considered by the Supreme Court in *Hood,* discussed *infra* in the text, and held not to be a "suit" against the state within the Eleventh Amendment); *In re MicroAge Corp.,* 288 B.R. 842 (Bankr. D. Az. 2003); *Levin v. N.Y. Dept. of Health (In re Levin),* 284 B.R. 308 (Bankr. S.D. Fla. 2002); *In re Dodson,* 259 B.R. 635 (Bankr. E.D. Tenn. 2001); *Bakst v. State of New Jersey (In re Ross),* 234 B.R. 199 (Bankr. S.D. Fla. 1999); *United States v. State of Nebraska (In re Doiel),* 228 B.R. 439 (D. S. Dak. 1998); *In re Justice,* 224 B.R. 631 (Bankr. S.D. Ohio 1998); *In re Christie,* 218 B.R. 27 (Bankr. D.N.J. 1998), *vacated on other grounds,* 222 B.R. 64 (Bankr. D.N.J. 1998); *In re C.J. Rogers, Inc.,* 212 B.R. 265 (E.D. Mich. 1997); *Kish v. Verniero,* 1997 WL 471911 (D.N.J. 1997); *In re Mueller,* 211 B.R. 737 (Bankr. D. Mont. 1997); *In re NVR, LP,* 206 B.R. 831 (Bankr. E.D. Va. 1997), *rev'd on other grounds,* 222 B.R. 514, *vacated in relevant part,* 189 F.3d 442 (4th Cir. 1999), *cert. denied,* 120 S. Ct. 936 (2000); *In re Tri-City Turf Club, Inc.,* 203 B.R. 617 (Bankr. E.D. Ky. 1996). Lower courts not addressing the Fourteenth Amendment issue: *see, e.g., In re Martinez,* 196 B.R. 225 (D. Puerto Rico 1996); *In re Koehler,* 204 B.R. 210 (Bankr. D. Minn. 1997); *In re Charter Oaks Associates,* 203 B.R. 17 (Bankr. D. Conn. 1996), *aff'd,* 361 F.3d 760 (2d Cir. 2004) (Second Circuit affirmed unpublished district court decision on the narrow issue of the constitutionality of section 106(c), *see infra* text accompanying note 52; district court had affirmed the bankruptcy court's decision); *In re Lush Lawns, Inc.,* 203 B.R. 418 (Bankr. N.D. Ohio 1996); *In re York-Hannover Developments, Inc.,* 201 B.R. 137 (Bankr. E.D.N.C. 1996); *Ellenberg v. Board of Regents of the Univ. Systems of Georgia (In re Midland Mechanical Contractors, Inc.),* 200 B.R. 453 (Bankr. N.D. Ga. 1996).

[36] *Hood v. Tennessee Student Assistance Corp. (In re Hood),* 319 F.3d 755 (6th Cir. 2003), *aff'd on other grounds,* 541 U.S. 440 (2004). The Sixth Circuit has also held that the government bears the burden of proof in sovereign immunity cases. *J.S. Haren Co. v. Macon Water Authority,* 2005 U.S. App. LEXIS 22498 (6th Cir. 2005).

[37] *See also Katz v. Central Virginia Comm. College (In re Wallace's Bookstore, Inc.),* 2004 U.S. App. LEXIS 16199 (6th Cir. 2004) *(per curiam)* (applying *Hood* without any substantive analysis), *aff'd,* 126 S. Ct. 990 (2006) (the Supreme Court's decision in this case is the landmark decision, discussed at § 1102.5.2 below, that ultimately undermined the *Seminole* case in the bankruptcy area); *H.J. Wilson Co. v. Comm'r of Revenue (In re Service Merchandise Co.),* 333 F.3d 666 (6th Cir. 2003) (adopting reasoning of the Sixth Circuit decision in *Hood*), *reh'g denied, en banc,* 2003 U.S. App. LEXIS 19032, *cert. denied,* 124 S. Ct. 2388 (2004); *Quality Stores, Inc. v. Vermont Dept. of Taxes (In re Quality Stores, Inc.),* 324 B.R. 631 (Bankr. W.D. Mich. 2005) (same), *aff'd,* 354 B.R. 840 (W.D. Mich. 2006); *Flores v. Ill. Dept. of Public Health (In re Flores),* 300 B.R. 599 (Bankr. D. Vt. 2003) (same); *but see In re Nelson* (7th Cir.), *supra* note 32 (finding this position "clearly untenable"); *In re ABEPP Acquisition Corp.,* 215 B.R. 513 (Bankr. 6th Cir. 1997) (earlier decision of Sixth Circuit Bankruptcy Appellate Panel appearing to express tacit support for the position that section 106(a) is unconstitutional); *In re MicroAge Corp.* (Bankr. D. Ariz.), *supra* note 35 (rejecting *Hood*); *State of Alabama v. Lewis,* 279 B.R. 308 (S.D. Ala. 2002) (same); *In re Claxton,* 273 B.R. 174 (Bankr. N.D. Ill. 2002) (same). *See also* Gerson, A Bankruptcy Exception to Eleventh Amendment Immunity: Limiting the Seminole Tribe Doctrine, 74 Am. Bankr. L. J. 1 (2000) (challenging the extension of *Seminole* to the bankruptcy context).

Third, Fourth, Fifth, Seventh and Ninth Circuits (referenced above), which held that section 106(a) was unconstitutional, the Sixth Circuit held that, by ceding their sovereignty, states granted Congress the power to abrogate their immunity under the Bankruptcy Clause of Article I of the Constitution. The enactment of section 106(a) was the constitutional exercise of such power by Congress.

The Supreme Court granted *certiorari* in *Hood,* but ultimately concluded that it didn't need to decide the broader constitutional question addressed by the Sixth Circuit because "a bankruptcy court's discharge of a student loan does not implicate a State's Eleventh Amendment immunity."[38] Drawing a sharp distinction between *in rem* and *in personam* jurisdiction, the Court held that the undue hardship (discharge) determination sought by the debtor was not a "suit in law or in equity" against a state for purposes of the Eleventh Amendment:

> No matter how difficult Congress has decided to make the discharge of student loan debt, the bankruptcy court's jurisdiction is premised on the *res,* not on the *persona;* that States were granted the presumptive benefit of nondischargeability [in the case of student loans] does not alter the court's underlying authority. A debtor does not seek monetary damages or any affirmative relief from a State by seeking to discharge a debt; nor does he subject an unwilling State to a coercive judicial process. He seeks only a discharge of his debts.[39]

The Court cautioned, however, that "[t]his is not to say, 'a bankruptcy court's *in rem* jurisdiction overrides sovereign immunity,' . . . but rather that the court's exercise of its *in rem* jurisdiction to discharge a student loan debt is not an affront to the sovereignty of the State. Nor do we hold that every exercise of a bankruptcy court's *in rem* jurisdiction will not offend the sovereignty of the State."[40]

Although adopting varying rationales, numerous lower courts similarly overcame a state's assertion of sovereign immunity. For example, a few lower courts concluded that the 1994 amendment of section 106(a) was a valid exercise of congressional authority under the Fourteenth Amendment.[41] Also, some courts held that a

---

[38] *Hood v. Tennessee Student Assistance Corp.* (*In re Hood*) (U.S.), *supra* note 36, at 445.

[39] Id. at 450. Similarly, *see Goldberg v. Ellett* (*In re Ellett*), 254 F.3d 1135 (9th Cir.), *amended,* 2001 U.S. App. LEXIS 19184 (9th Cir. 2001) ("the bankruptcy court exercises jurisdiction over the *res* of the bankruptcy estate when it issues its discharge order, not *in personam* jurisdiction over the estate's creditors"), *cert. denied,* 534 U.S. 1127 (2002); *In re Bliemeister* (Bankr. D. Ariz), *infra* note 42 (reaching same conclusion); *In re Sae Young Westmont-Chicago, L.L.C.,* 276 B.R. 888 (Bankr. N.D. Ill. 2002) (held that Eleventh Amendment does not extend to *in rem* proceedings, such as an action by a debtor to assume and assign a lease under which a state is the lessee); and contrasting cases *infra* at note 84. Given that the only harm that could be visited upon the State was the discharge of its claim, the Supreme Court in *Hood* gave no dispositive weight to the fact that the present discharge action was required to be brought by means of an adversary proceeding (which requires the filing of a summons and complaint), rather than by motion.

[40] *Hood v. Tennessee Student Assistance Corp.* (*In re Hood*) (U.S.), *supra* note 36, at 450 n.5.

[41] *See, e.g., Willis v. State of Oklahoma* (*In re Willis*), 230 B.R. 619 (Bankr. E.D. Okla. 1999); *In re Straight,* 209 B.R. 540 (D. Wyo. 1997), *aff'd,* 143 F.3d 1387 (10th Cir. 1998), *cert. denied,* 119 S. Ct. 446 (1998) (on appeal, the Tenth Circuit did not address the constitutionality issue); *In re Wilson,* 258 B.R. 303 (Bankr. S.D. Ga. 2001); *In re Burke,* 203 B.R. 493 (Bankr. S.D. Ga. 1996), *aff'd,* 146 F.3d 1313 (11th

state's sovereign immunity does not extend to the federal bankruptcy laws, distinguishing the Supreme Court's decision in *Seminole* on the basis that, unlike the commerce clause, the Constitution expressly authorizes Congress to establish "uniform laws" governing bankruptcy.[42] Another court concluded that, in the context of a preference action initiated by the debtor to avoid a state's attachment of the debtor's assets, section 106(a) was not unconstitutional as the preference action did not require personal jurisdiction over the state and that jurisdiction therefore rested with the bankruptcy court.[43]

As with the divergent judicial opinions regarding the constitutionality of section 106(a), courts reached differing conclusions with respect to the constitutionality of sections 106(b) and 106(c).[44] As discussed above, the Fourth Circuit (in *Creative*

(Footnote Continued)

Cir. 1998) (on appeal, the Eleventh Circuit did not address the constitutionality issue), *cert. denied*, 119 S. Ct. 2410 (1999); *In re Headrick*, 203 B.R. 805 (Bankr. S.D. Ga. 1996), *aff'd sub nom., In re Burke*, 146 F.3d 1313 (11th Cir. 1998) (on appeal, the Eleventh Circuit did not address the constitutionality issue), *cert. denied*, 119 S. Ct. 2410 (1999); *In re Southern Star Foods, Inc.*, 190 B.R. 419 (Bankr. E.D. Okla. 1995); *see also* "United States Memorandum of Law in Support of the Constitutionality of 11 U.S.C. § 106" (Jan. 8, 1997), *filed in In re NVR, LP, supra* note 35.

[42] *See, e.g., Bliemeister v. Indus. Comm. of Ariz. (In re Bliemeister)*, 251 B.R. 383 (Bankr. D. Ariz. 2000) (so holding, even though within the Ninth Circuit; also held that Eleventh Amendment immunity does not extend to *in rem* proceedings, such as a dischargeability determination, and that state had effectively waived its sovereign immunity by not raising it as a defense until after the substantive hearing on the debtor's motion), *aff'd*, 296 F.3d 858 (9th Cir. 2002) (agreed that state had waived immunity); *Gray v. Florida State Univ. (In re Dehon, Inc.)*, 327 B.R. 38 (Bankr. D. Ma. 2005) (involved a preference action; court concluded that the Eleventh Amendment is not a bar to bankruptcy court jurisdiction because the framers of the Constitution "intended that the Constitution would alienate States' sovereign immunity with regard to bankruptcy matter upon ratification").

[43] *See In re O'Brien*, 216 B.R. 731 (Bankr. D. Vt. 1998) (although the court held that the debtor's adversary proceeding did not violate the Eleventh Amendment, it nevertheless dismissed the adversary proceeding on the condition that the debtor be allowed to bring suit in state court).

[44] With respect to section 106(b), *compare In re Straight* (10th Cir.), *supra* note 34 (section 106(b) is constitutional); *Orion Refining Corp. v. Dept. of Rev., State of Louisiana (In re Orion Refining Corp.)*, 2004 Bankr. LEXIS 2312 (Bankr. M.D. La. 2004) (same); *Nana's Petroleum, Inc. v. Clark (In re Nana's Petroleum, Inc.)*, 234 B.R. 838 (Bankr. S.D. Fla 1999) (same); *In re Charter Oaks Associates, supra* note 33 (concluding that section 106(b) does not conflict with the underpinnings of *Seminole*) *with In re Creative Goldsmiths of Washington, D.C., Inc.* (4th Cir.), *supra* note 28 (section 106(b) is unconstitutional); *In re Rose*, 215 B.R. 755 (Bankr. W.D. Mo. 1997) (section 106(b) is unconstitutional); *In re NVR, LP, supra* note 35 (concluding that section 106(b) is unconstitutional to the extent that it attempts to alter Eleventh Amendment immunity); *In re C.J. Rogers, Inc., supra* note 35 (section 106(b) is unconstitutional).

With respect to section 106(c), *see In re Charter Oaks Associates* (2d Cir.), discussed *infra* in the text; *In re MicroAge Corp.* (Bankr. D. Az.), *supra* note 35 (concluding that bankruptcy court has authority under section 106(c) to litigate the amount of the debtor's setoff claim); and *In re NVR, LP, supra* note 35 (bankruptcy court concluded that section 106(c) is unconstitutional to the extent that it attempts to alter Eleventh Amendment immunity).

The Supreme Court addressed the issue of an "implied" or "constructive" waiver of state sovereign immunity in *College Savings Bank v. Florida Prepaid Postsecondary Education Expense Board*, 119 S. Ct. 2219 (1999). In this case, which involved an action in federal court by College Savings against a Florida state agency for alleged violations of the Lanham Act—a federal law creating a private right of action against any person, including states and state instrumentalities, who make false representations in commerce—College Savings argued that the State of Florida "impliedly" or "constructively" waived its immunity from Lanham Act suit by voluntarily promoting its college

*Goldsmiths*) concluded that section 106(b) was unconstitutional because it is not within Congress' power to abrogate Eleventh Amendment immunity by "deeming" a waiver. In *In re Straight,*[45] however, the Tenth Circuit expressly rejected the analysis of *Creative Goldsmiths* as "unpersuasive," reasoning that, unlike the universal abrogation of immunity contained in section 106(a), the narrower waiver contained in section 106(b) "does not pretend to abrogate a state's immunity, it merely codifies an existing equitable circumstance under which a state can choose to preserve its immunity by not participating in a bankruptcy proceeding or to partially waive that immunity by filing a claim."[46] The First Circuit reached a similar conclusion in *Arecibo Community Health Care, Inc. v. Puerto Rico,*[47] holding that section 106(b) "draws on the well-established principle of equity that a state waives its Eleventh Amendment immunity by availing itself of the jurisdiction of the federal courts."[48] Courts split much along these same lines. However, the cases all appear to have agreed that the substance of section 106(b) is consistent with the common law, and that one always has the common law to fall back on.[49] For this reason, many courts declined to address the constitutionality of section 106(b), and instead chose in the first instance to base the state's waiver on the common law—in particular, the Supreme Court's decision in *Gardner v. New Jersey,*[50] which held that, when a state files a proof of claim in a bankruptcy proceeding, it waives its sovereign immunity with respect to such claim and any objections to such claim.[51]

---

(Footnote Continued)

tuition plan across state lines and allegedly using false and misleading advertising that impaired similar programs promoted by College Savings. The Supreme Court rejected this argument, stating that "the most that can be said with certainty is that the State has been put on notice that Congress intends to subject it to suits brought by individuals. That is very far from concluding that the State made an 'all together voluntary' decision to waive its immunity." In *Arecibo Community Health Care, Inc. v. Puerto Rico,* 270 F.3d 17 (1st Cir. 2001), the First Circuit concluded that section 106(b) (which waives sovereign immunity in connection with a filed proof of claim) is not predicated on "constructive waiver" and therefore, notwithstanding *College Savings,* the provision is constitutional.

[45] *Supra* note 34.

[46] 143 F.3d at 1392. *Accord In re Nana's Petroleum, Inc., supra* note 44.

[47] *Supra* note 44.

[48] 270 F.3d at 27.

[49] The only case found that suggests anything to the contrary is *State of New Jersey v. Mocco,* 206 B.R. 691 (D.N.J. 1997), in which the court stated in *dicta* that "based on *Seminole* the State would have retained its sovereign immunity if it had appropriately filed a proof of claim." Id. at 693. This statement, however, should be given little credence as it appears that the court failed to consider the common law rule that would apply absent section 106(b).

[50] 329 U.S. 565 (1947).

[51] *See, e.g., State of Montana v. Goldin* (*In re Pegasus Gold Corp.*), 394 F.3d 1189 (9th Cir. 2005); *California Franchise Tax Board v. Jackson* (*In re Jackson*), 184 F.3d 1046 (9th Cir. 1999); *In re Lazar* (9th Cir.), *supra* note 33; *In re Burke* 146 F.3d 1313 (11th Cir. 1998), *cert. denied* 119 S.Ct. 2410 (1999); *Ind. Dept. of Rev. v. Williams,* 301 B.R. 871 (S.D. Ind. 2003) (by filing a proof of claim, the State became subject to bankruptcy court's jurisdiction to declare the State in contempt for prior attempted collections of the claimed taxes in violation of the automatic stay); *but see Grubbs Construction Co. v. Florida Dept. of Rev.* (*In re Grubbs Construction Co.*), 321 B.R. 346 (Bankr. M.D. 2005) (although State waived Eleventh Amendment immunity by filing proof of claim, debtor's fraudulent transfer action under Bankruptcy Code section 544 was dismissed because such action was founded upon a state statute as to which the factual predicate for suit was not satisfied). *See also California v. Hurleston* (*In re Harleston*), 275 B.R. 546, 552 (Bankr. 9th Cir. 2002) ("[W]hen a state waives immunity as to one action,

With respect to section 106(c), the Second Circuit, in *In re Charter Oak Associates*,[52] similarly held that such section was an appropriate codification of the so-called waiver-of-litigation doctrine pursuant to which a state should be considered to have voluntarily submitted itself to the court's jurisdiction in respect of any permissive (as well as compulsory) counterclaims that could serve to reduce the state's recovery under its proof of claim, and thus held that section 106(c) passed constitutional muster. The Second Circuit expressly declined to adopt the Fourth Circuit's narrower view in *Creative Goldsmiths* that the Eleventh Amendment only permits compulsory counterclaims in such circumstance (although the Fourth Circuit did not specifically consider section 106(c) in its opinion). The Second Circuit does not appear to have considered, however, the fact that section 106(c) does not, by its terms, require the filing of a proof of claim, but only the existence of a claim (*see* § 1005.1.2 above).

In reaction to the states' increasing claims of sovereign immunity, it was speculated that further Congressional action might be necessary to ensure state compliance with the bankruptcy laws. To this end, the National Bankruptcy Review Commission—which was established by Congress pursuant to the Bankruptcy Reform Act of 1994 to investigate and evaluate possible bankruptcy reforms, and which issued its report to Congress in October 1997—observed that the Eleventh Amendment does not prevent the federal government from commencing suit against a state in federal court, but only private parties.[53] Accordingly, the Commission raised the possibility of specifically authorizing the United States trustee as its representative (whose objective it currently is to ensure the fair administration of the bankruptcy laws) to commence suit in the bankruptcy court against states to enforce compliance with the bankruptcy laws.[54] Alternatively, query whether Congress could condition the receipt by a state of federal funds under various existing or future federal programs upon a state's consent to affirmative jurisdiction in federal bankruptcy cases consistent with the provisions of Bankruptcy Code section 106.[55]

---

(Footnote Continued)

its waiver extends to ancillary suits to enforce orders entered in that action"), *aff'd*, 331 F.3d 699 (9th Cir. 2003).

[52] *Ossen v. Dept. of Social Services (In re Charter Oak Associates)*, 361 F.3d 760 (2d Cir. 2004), *cert. denied*, 125 S. Ct. 408 (2004); *see also* section 106(c) cases cited *supra* note 44.

[53] National Bankruptcy Review Commission Final Report (October 20, 1997), pp. 913-914; *see West Virginia v. United States*, 479 U.S. 305, 312 n.4 (1987) ("States have no sovereign immunity as against the Federal Government."). The Commission's report is available through the Government Printing Office website at www.access.gpo.gov. *See* Chapter 10, at § 1001 note 5.

[54] In *In re Lapin*, *supra* note 33, in response to a state taxing authority's attempt to collect discharged taxes, the debtor filed a contempt action against the state for violation of the discharge injunction and claimed that, notwithstanding the Eleventh Amendment, the bankruptcy court had jurisdiction over the state because the court (and not the debtor) is enforcing the discharge order (*i.e.*, the action is not between the state and a private party, but instead is between the state and the federal court). Although acknowledging that such an argument has "surface appeal," the Ninth Circuit Bankruptcy Appellate Panel rejected the argument, noting that the debtor failed to cite any authority in support of its position.

[55] *See* Goldring and Richards, Current Developments in State and Local Bankruptcy Taxation, *supra* note 7, at 546; Plumb, The Tax Recommendations of the Commission on the Bankruptcy Laws—Tax Procedures, 88 Harv. L. Rev. 1360, 1474 (1974); *see also College Savings Bank v. Florida Prepaid Postsecondary Education Expense Board* (S. Ct.), *supra* note 44 (which distinguished a constructive

### §1102.5.2 *Katz* and Its Progeny

After sidestepping an opportunity to resolve the constitutional debate over Bankruptcy Code section 106 and the abrogation of state sovereign immunity in 2004 in the *Hood* case (discussed in the preceding section), the Supreme Court again considered the question in *Central Virginia Community College v. Katz*,[56] and this time addressed the application of its earlier decision in *Seminole*[57] to bankruptcy cases.

In *Katz*, the debtor, prior to the filing of its bankruptcy petition, did business with and made certain cash payments to four state-supported schools. Following its bankruptcy filing, the bankruptcy trustee filed an adversary proceeding against the state-sponsored schools to recover the cash payments as preferential transfers. As a defense to the preference action, the schools claimed immunity under the Eleventh Amendment. The bankruptcy court rejected the Eleventh Amendment immunity claims and, on appeal, the district court and Sixth Circuit, finding that the schools raised the exact arguments rejected by the Sixth Circuit in *Hood*, affirmed.

In considering the constitutional question, and similarly rejecting the state's immunity defense, the Supreme Court in a five-to-four decision acknowledged that *dicta* contained in its 1996 decision in *Seminole* reflected an assumption that the holding in that case—that Congress lacked the power to abrogate the Eleventh Amendment immunity of the states pursuant to the Indian Commerce Clause of Article I of the Constitution—would also apply to the Bankruptcy Clause of Article I of the Constitution. "Careful study and reflection have convinced [the Court], however, that that assumption was erroneous."[58] Reviewing at length the history of bankruptcy laws prior to, and at the time of, the Constitutional Convention, the Court concluded that the waiver of the states' sovereign immunity was "effected in the plan of the Convention, not by statute:"[59]

> The ineluctable conclusion, then, is that States agreed in the plan of the Convention not to assert any sovereign immunity defense they might have had in proceedings brought pursuant to "Laws on the subject of Bankruptcies." The scope of this consent was limited; the jurisdiction exercised in bankruptcy proceedings was chiefly *in rem*—a narrow jurisdiction that does not implicate state sovereignty to nearly the same degree as other kinds of jurisdiction. But while the principal focus of the bankruptcy proceedings is and was always the res, some exercises of bankruptcy courts' powers—issuance of writs of habeas corpus included—unquestionably involved more than mere adjudication of rights in a res. In ratifying the Bankruptcy Clause, the States acquiesced in a subordina-

---

(Footnote Continued)

waiver from a Spending Clause-based appropriations of federal funds to states that treats the states acceptance of the funds as an agreement to waive immunity); *In re Innes*, *infra* note 93.

56 *Supra* note 20.

57 *Supra* note 25.

58 126 S. Ct. at 996.

59 Id. at 1005.

> tion of whatever sovereign immunity they might otherwise have asserted in proceedings necessary to effectuate the *in rem* jurisdiction of the bankruptcy courts.
>
> * * *
>
> Neither our decision in *Hood*, which held that States could not assert sovereign immunity as a defense in adversary proceedings brought to adjudicate the dischargeability of student loans, nor the cases upon which it relied . . . rested on any statement Congress had made on the subject of state sovereign immunity. Nor does our decision today. The relevant question is not whether Congress has ''abrogated'' States' immunity in proceedings to recover preferential transfers. The question, rather, is whether Congress' determination that States should be amenable to such proceedings is within the scope of its power to enact ''Laws on the subject of Bankruptcies.'' We think it beyond peradventure that it is.[60]

Accordingly, in hindsight, Bankruptcy Code section 106 does not abrogate a state's sovereign immunity, as that was already done by the states themselves as relates to "Laws on the subject of Bankruptcies" when they approved the Constitution. Rather, section 106 delineates the particular bankruptcy laws or circumstances under which a state may be subject to suit in bankruptcy. That being said, the analysis has not been made any easier.

In effect, *Katz* necessitates a two prong analysis (in no specified order): (1) Is a proceeding against a state authorized by section 106, and (2) does the proceeding involve aspects of debtor-creditor relations or the debtor's estate proper to the administration and enforcement of a bankruptcy system.[61] To illustrate the latter concept, the Supreme Court in *Katz* observed that an action seeking only a determination that a transfer by a debtor is a voidable preference, is an *in rem* proceeding involving a bankruptcy estates rights in property. (In addition, as discussed in the preceding section, and articulated in *Hood*, an *in rem* proceeding is not in any event protected by a state's Eleventh Amendment immunity.) On the other hand, an action seeking a turnover to the bankruptcy estate of the preference amount, "although ancillary to and in furtherance of the court's *in rem* jurisdiction, might itself involve *in personam* process."[62] "Whatever the appropriate appellation," the Court stated, "those who crafted the Bankruptcy Clause would have understood it to give Congress the power to authorize courts to avoid preferential transfers."[63] Other than by reference to the history and purpose of the bankruptcy laws, the Supreme Court

---

[60] Id. at 1004-05 (citations omitted; footnotes omitted).

[61] *See, e.g., Florida Dept. of Rev. v. Omine (In re Omine)*, 485 F.3d 1305, 1317-1319, 1322 (11th Cir. 2007) (however, Black, J., dissenting, asserted that "after Katz, the entire statutory scheme in § 106(a)(1) through (a)(4) is unnecessary and inapplicable to suits against a state in proceedings necessary to effectuate a bankruptcy court's *in rem* jurisdiction").

[62] Id. at 1001.

[63] Id. at 1001-02.

provides little (if any) guidance as to identifying an *in personam* proceeding falling within the auspices of the bankruptcy laws.[64]

Lower courts have already begun to apply the reasoning of *Katz* to the countless types of proceedings inherent in the bankruptcy process. For example, in the context of a Chapter 7 proceeding, the Fifth Circuit held that "[w]hatever uncertainty there may be as to the outer limits of the holdings of *Katz* and *Hood*, at the very least they together establish beyond cavil that an *in rem* bankruptcy proceeding brought merely to obtain the discharge of a debt or debts by determining the rights of various creditors in a bankruptcy estate . . . in no way infringes the sovereignty of a state as a creditor."[65] Similarly, a proceeding to determine the dischargeability of a restitution order issued in a criminal proceeding has been held to be an *in rem* proceeding subject to bankruptcy court jurisdiction.[66] It has also been held that states are not permitted to assert the defense of sovereign immunity to a number of suits identified in section 106(a), including proceedings to recover a preferential transfer pursuant to section 547,[67] to turnover property of the bankruptcy estate pursuant to section 542,[68] to determine the right of the debtor to a tax refund pursuant to section 505,[69] and to determine a discrimination claim pursuant to section 525.[70] Lower courts have also begun to address proceedings that arguably implicate *in personam* jurisdiction. For example, in the context of an adversary proceeding against a state for damages and sanctions for violation of the automatic stay, the Eleventh Circuit held that, "pursuant to *Katz*, actions to force a creditor to honor the automatic stay are the types of 'proceedings necessary to effectuate the *in rem* jurisdiction of the bankruptcy court'," thereby preventing the state's assertion of a sovereign immunity defense.[71] Any monetary awards against the state for violation of the automatic stay, however, continued to be subject to the limitation on punitive damages contained in section 106(a)(3).[72] In contrast, it has been held that an action seeking specific performance of a confirmed Chapter 11 plan and injunctive relief against a state exceeds the limits of

---

[64] Interestingly, the Court commented that "Petitioners do not dispute that [the ability to recover a voidable preference] has been a *core aspect* of the administration of bankruptcy estates since at least the 18th century." Id. at 1002 (emphasis added). Query whether, by analogy, this means that any proceeding considered to be a "core" proceeding within the meaning of 28 U.S.C. § 157(b)(2) (identifying core proceedings arising under title 11 that may be heard and determined by a bankruptcy judge, *see* §§ 1013 and 1013.1 above) should withstand a state's claim of sovereign immunity?

[65] *State of Texas v. Soileau (In re Soileau)*, 488 F.3d 302, 307 (5th Cir. 2007); *see also In re Davis*, 340 B.R. 767 (Bankr. E.D. Tex. 2006) (entry of a discharge order in a Chapter 7 case is an *in rem* proceeding binding upon a state creditor).

[66] *Burghart v. Douglas County (In re Burghart)*, 2006 Bankr. LEXIS 916 (Bankr. Kan. 2006).

[67] *Chattanooga State Tech. Comm. College v. Johnson (In re North American Royalties, Inc.)*, 2006 U.S. Dist. LEXIS 13034 (E.D. Tenn. 2006).

[68] *See In re Automotive Professionals, Inc.*, 2007 Bankr. LEXIS 2177 (Bankr. N.D. Ill. 2007); *Kids World of America, Inc. v. State of Georgia (In re Kids World of America, Inc.)*, 349 B.R. 152 (Bankr. W.D. Ky. 2006).

[69] *See Vermont Dept. of Taxes v. Quality Stores, Inc. (In re Quality Stores, Inc.)*, 354 B.R. 840 (W.D. Mich. 2006).

[70] *See The Maryland Port Administration v. Premier Automotive Services, Inc. (In re Premier Automotive Services, Inc.)*, 343 B.R. 501 (Bankr. Md. 2006).

[71] *In re Omine, supra* note 61, at 1314.

[72] *See* id. at 1317; *but consider* discussion at § 1005.1.1.

a bankruptcy court's *in rem* jurisdiction where the state's obligations were not specified in the plan, but rather a matter of a separate agreement entered into after confirmation of the plan and governed by state law.[73]

Guidance with respect to applying the analytical approach to sovereign immunity jurisprudence set forth in *Katz* should not be limited to this post-*Katz*, evolving body of case law. Following the Supreme Court's 2004 decision in *Hood*, in which the Court drew a sharp distinction between *in rem* and *in personam* jurisdiction, lower courts began assessing the *in rem* nature of many types of proceedings inherent in the bankruptcy process. For example, it has been held that an action by a debtor under Bankruptcy Code section 505 to determine a debtor's liability for personal and real property taxes is an *in rem* proceeding and, therefore, not a "suit" within the meaning of the Eleventh Amendment.[74] It has also been held that an adversary proceeding to void as a preference certain fees paid to a state agency is an *in rem* action within the bankruptcy court's jurisdiction.[75] The court acknowledged that the Eleventh Amendment may prevent a direct monetary recovery from the state (*i.e.*, an action that would require the court to exercise *in persona* jurisdiction), but concluded that alternate remedies, such as setoff against claims of the state, were within its *in rem* jurisdiction. Although the court subsequently vacated its decision, it did so as part of a settlement between the parties in lieu of an extended appeal.[76]

Many decisions that pre-date *Hood* may also be instructive with respect to the potential scope of the Supreme Court's decision in *Katz*. For example, consistent with the holding in *Hood*, several courts (including the Fourth Circuit) have held that, notwithstanding the Eleventh Amendment, a bankruptcy court has the authority to bind a state to a confirmed Chapter 11 plan or to discharge taxes.[77] It has also been

---

[73] *Emerald Casino, Inc. v. The Illinois Gaming Board*, 482 F.3d 926 (7th Cir. 2007).

[74] *Florida Furniture Indus., Inc. v. Mahaffey* (*In re Florida Furniture Indus., Inc.*), 342 B.R. 838 (Bankr. M.D. Fla. 2005); *In re Cable & Wireless USA, Inc.*, 331 B.R. 568 (Bankr. D. Del. 2005); *In re Lake Worth Generation, LLC*, 318 B.R. 894 (Bankr. S.D. Fla. 2004).

[75] *Official Comm. of Unsecured Creditors of 360Networks (USA) Inc. v. The Public Utilities Commission of the State of Calif.* (*In re 360Networks (USA) Inc.*), 316 B.R. 797 (Bankr. S.D. N.Y. 2004), *vacated* 2005 WL 3957809 (Bankr. S.D. N.Y. 2005).

[76] *See* Memorandum of Law in Support of Motion to Vacate, dated July 28, 2005, Case No. 01-13721 (ALG), Adv. Pro. No. 03-04316 (ALG).

[77] *See State of Maryland v. Antonelli Creditors' Liquidating Trust*, 123 F.3d 777 (4th Cir. 1997) (bankruptcy court has authority to bind state to confirmed plan that exempts certain property transfers from taxation in accordance with then Bankruptcy Code section 1146(c), now section 1146(a); action was not brought as an adversary proceeding, but arose out of a motion to approve the confirmation order), discussed at § 1102.15 below; *In re Hechinger Inv. Co. of Delaware*, 254 B.R. 306 (Bankr. D. Del. 2000), *aff'd*, 276 B.R. 43 (D. Del. 2002) (same); *In re Linc Capital, Inc.*, 280 B.R. 640 (Bankr. N.D. Ill. 2002) (same); *In re Ellett* (9th Cir.), *supra* note 39 ("[W]e hold that a bankruptcy court's discharge order is binding on a State, despite the State's election not to share in the recovery of the bankruptcy estate's assets by filing a proof of claim"); *Sorenson v. Artiglio* (*In re Artiglio*), 2001 U.S. App. LEXIS 15723 (9th Cir. 2001) (court applied its analysis in *In re Ellett* to similar facts); *In re Burkhardt*, 220 B.R. 837 (Bankr. D. N.J. 1998) (bankruptcy court has authority to discharge taxes in connection with Chapter 13 plan confirmation). As discussed below, this does not necessarily mean that the bankruptcy court can entertain an action by the debtor against the state in an effort to enforce or discharge the plan. This may depend on the circumstances under which such an action arises (assuming the state has not otherwise waived its sovereign immunity with respect to such action, such as by having previously filed a proof of claim with respect to the tax in question).

held that the Eleventh Amendment does not prevent a debtor from raising a prior discharge in bankruptcy as a defense to an action commenced by a state against the debtor,[78] nor does it prevent the adjudication of the dischargeability of a tax where the state filed the adversary proceeding in issue.[79] By contrast, if the bankruptcy action in issue is an adversary proceeding commenced by the debtor against a state (as opposed to other non-adversarial actions commenced in a bankruptcy proceeding), the Eleventh Amendment may be implicated if not within the constitutional waiver found in *Katz*.[80] For example, courts traditionally have held that a debtor could not bring an action against a state in the bankruptcy court to determine the prior discharge of a state tax in order to obtain a refund of the tax, even if the debtor stopped short of asking the court to declare the refund[81]—the fact that the court's determination would be *res judicata* in a subsequent action or claim against the state for a tax refund is considered tantamount to a money judgment.[82] It appears, though, that this may not be an impediment after *Katz*.[83] Presumably no longer in doubt after the Supreme Court's decisions in *Hood* and *Katz*, there previously appeared to be disagreement about whether the bankruptcy court could entertain a dischargeability motion or action by the debtor if the tax had *not* yet been paid and no proof of claim

---

[78] *See State of Texas v. Walker*, 142 F.3d 813 (5th Cir. 1998), *cert. denied*, 119 S. Ct. 865 (1999).

[79] *See Dekalb Cty. Div. of Family and Children Services v. Platter (In re Platter)*, 140 F.3d 676 (7th Cir. 1998).

[80] *See, e.g., State of Texas v. Walker* (5th Cir.), *supra* note 25 (in *dicta*, the Fifth Circuit stated that certain adversary proceedings directly against a state that has not filed a proof of claim may be barred by the Eleventh Amendment); *Taylor v. State of Georgia (In re Taylor)*, 249 B.R. 571 (Bankr. N.D. Ga. 2000). *Cf. Tenn. Student Assistance Corp. v. Hood* (S. Ct.), *supra* note 36 (no dispositive weight given to the fact that the discharge action in question was required to be brought by means of an adversary proceeding, since the substance of the action was still purely a discharge); *NVR Homes, Inc. v. Clerks of the Circuit Courts (In re NVR, LP)*, 189 F.3d 442, 451-452 (4th Cir. 1999), *cert. denied*, 120 S. Ct. 936 (2000) (stated that whether a "contested matter" initiated under Bankruptcy Rule 9014 constitutes a "suit" under the Eleventh Amendment depends on the procedure and substance of the motion, including degree of coercion, whether remedy would require jurisdiction over state, and whether the demand is specific or limits the state to the role of any other creditor); *In re Nana's Petroleum, Inc., supra* note 44 (claim objection required to be in form of an adversary proceeding is not a "suit in law or equity" for purposes of the Eleventh Amendment); *In re Merry-Go-Round Enterprises, Inc.*, 227 B.R. 775 (Bankr. D. Md. 1998) (objection to proof-of-claim is not a "suit in law or equity" for purposes of the Eleventh Amendment); *In re Polygraphex Systems, Inc.*, 275 B.R. 408 (Bankr. M.D. Fla. 2002) (same); *In re Barrett Refining Corp.*, 221 B.R. 795 (Bankr. W.D. Okla. 1998) (Eleventh Amendment did not bar bankruptcy court from adjudicating a state's proof of claim because such an adjudication does not constitute a "suit in law or equity" within the meaning of the Eleventh Amendment). *But see In re O'Brien, supra* note 43 (court held that adversary proceeding initiated by the debtor did not violate the Eleventh Amendment).

[81] *See, e.g., In re Mitchell* (9th Cir.) *supra* note 33; *Murphy v. Michigan Guaranty Agency*, 271 F.3d 629 (5th Cir. 2001) (concurring with the Ninth Circuit's reasoning in *Mitchell*); *In re Ross, supra* note 35; *In re Doiel, supra* note 35.

[82] *See, e.g., NVR Homes, Inc. v. Clerks of the Circuit Courts (In re NVR, LP)* (4th Cir.), *supra* note 80, discussed at § 1102.15 below (Eleventh Amendment precluded action against state tax authorities to determine applicability of the exemption from transfer taxes under then Bankruptcy Code section 1146(c), now section 1146(a), where debtor had a pending refund claim with the state, since resolution would have the effect of a monetary judgment).

[83] *See supra* note 69 and accompanying text.

was filed by the state in the bankruptcy proceeding.[84] Ample controversy also existed with respect to a bankruptcy court's ability (i) to determine the amount of a corporate debtor's tax liability under section 505 of the Bankruptcy Code or the state tax consequences of a plan under section 1146(b) of the Bankruptcy Code (*see* § 1102.17 below);[85] (ii) to impose sanctions against a state taxing authority for viola-

---

[84] *Compare In re Collins*, 173 F.3d 924 (4th Cir. 1999) (bankruptcy court has authority to reopen Chapter 7 proceeding and determine dischargeability of judgment debt owed to a state; no payments had been made on the debt in the interim, although garnishment proceedings had been commenced), *cert. denied*, 120 S. Ct. 785 (2000); *In re Ranstrom*, 215 B.R. 454 (Bankr. N.D. Cal. 1997) (bankruptcy court has authority to determine whether a Chapter 7 debtor's tax debts were discharged); *In re Bliemeister* (Bankr. D. Ariz.), *supra* note 42 (dischargeability proceeding qualifies for *in rem* exception to Eleventh Amendment immunity); *with May v. United States (In re May)*, 248 F.3d 1165 (8th Cir. 2001) (*per curiam*), *reported in full at* 2001 U.S. App. LEXIS 3825 (adversary proceeding to determine dischargeability of taxes dismissed where state had not yet filed a proof of claim); *In re Sacred Heart Hospital of Norristown*, 204 B.R. 132 (E.D. Pa. 1997) (court dismissed action by debtor seeking declaratory judgment that claims filed by debtor with a state agency were timely filed; Third Circuit affirmed); *In re Mitchell* (9th Cir.), *supra* note 33 (adversary proceeding initiated by Chapter 7 debtor against state to determine dischargeability of unpaid taxes was barred by Eleventh Amendment; the court did not perceive any "rational" difference between a court order that precludes the collection of a tax to one that requires a state to pay a refund, the court also distinguished between a general discharge order, which does not invoke *in personam* jurisdiction, and an adversary proceeding, where a summons is served on the state—such that the state is required to respond to the debtor's motion—and observed that, in Collins, the discharge action was not brought as an adversary proceeding); *In re Chandler* (Bankr. 10th Cir.), *supra* note 34 (follows *Mitchell*; court acknowledged that had the discharge action been brought as a motion to clarify or enforce a discharge order, as opposed to an adversary proceeding, the result may have been different); *Taylor v. State of Georgia (In re Taylor)* (Bankr. N.D. Ga.), *supra* note 80 (employed reasoning similar to *Mitchell*); *United States v. Gosselin*, 252 B.R. 854 (D. Mass. 2000) (complaint seeking to discharge state income tax was barred; analyzed Fourth Circuit authorities and similarly distinguished *Collins* based on the absence of an adversary proceeding in that case), *aff'd*, 276 F.3d 70 (1st Cir. 2002) (court did not reach issue of constitutionality of section 106(a)). *Consider also Goldberg v. Ellett (In re Ellett)* (9th Cir.), *supra* note 39 (holding, as discussed below, that, under *Ex parte Young*, the bankruptcy court had jurisdiction to determine the dischargeability of unpaid state taxes and enjoin state officers from engaging in collection efforts); *Wilson v. Cumis Ins. Society, Inc. (In re Wilson)*, 246 B.R. 600 (Bankr. E.D. Ark. 2000) (same). Note that many of cases that have held section 106(a) unconstitutional have involved dischargeability motions, but did not have presented whether such a motion was a prohibited "suit" within the meaning of the Eleventh Amendment. *See, e.g., In re Elias, supra* note 33 (at Bankruptcy Appellate level).

[85] *Compare In re Mitchell*, 222 B.R. 877 (Bankr. 9th Cir. 1998) (held that it could not rule on a debtor's dischargeability motion since it would also require resolving debtor's substantive dispute as to its tax liability; state had not filed a proof of claim in the Chapter 7 case), *aff'd* (9th Cir.), *supra* note 33; *In re Sacred Heart Hosp. of Norristown* (E.D. Pa.), *supra* note 84 (court dismissed action by debtor seeking declaratory judgment that claims filed by debtor with a state agency were timely filed; the court stated as alternative grounds for dismissal that declaratory actions were not exempt from the need for a waiver and that the action more closely resembled an action for monetary recovery), *aff'd*, 133 F.3d 237 (3d Cir. 1998); *Metromedia Fiber Network, Inc. v. Various State and Local Taxing Authorities (In re Metromedia)*, 299 B.R. 251, 271 (Bankr. S.D. N.Y. 2003) (Hardin, J.) (held that a section 505(a) property tax proceeding was an *in personam* proceeding precluded by the Eleventh Amendment, not an *in rem* proceeding; decided prior to the Supreme Court's decision in *Hood*, discussed at § 1102.5.1 above, it is unclear whether the bankruptcy court's reasoning is still valid), *with In re Psychiatric Hospitals of Florida, Inc.*, 216 B.R. 660 (M.D. Fla. 1998) (action to determine property tax liability pursuant to section 505 is not barred by Eleventh Amendment). *Consider In re A.H. Robins Company, Inc.*, 251 B.R. 312 (Bankr. E.D. Va. 2000) (debtor sought a determination, several years after confirmation, that state NOLs of the debtor were transferred from the debtor to a successor corporation; in the interim, two states had disallowed the carryover and issued a tax assessment, which the debtor paid and then filed

tions of the automatic stay or the postdischarge injunction imposed by Bankruptcy Code section 524;[86] and (iii) to order the repayment by a state of voidable preferences or the turnover by the state of bankruptcy estate property.[87] These should no longer be in debate after *Katz*.

The waiver by the states of sovereign immunity in the bankruptcy context in connection with the Constitutional Convention may not be the only potential source of waiver in a particular case. As discussed above, either under section 106(b) or under the common law, a state may waive its Eleventh Amendment immunity by filing a proof of claim (such waiver being effective with respect to any claim by the debtor against the state arising out of the same transaction or occurrence).[88] If a state has waived its Eleventh Amendment immunity by filing a proof of claim, the waiver cannot be vitiated by the state's withdrawal of its claim[89] or by the conversion of the bankruptcy proceeding from a Chapter 11 to a Chapter 7 case.[90] Other possible sources of waiver of Eleventh Amendment immunity also exist. Under the so-called

(Footnote Continued)

for a refund; debtor asserted that it was seeking a clarification of the confirmation order as it related to the transfer of the debtor's property, here in the form of the NOL, to the successor corporation; the court held that the states were immune from suit given the adversary nature of the action and the substantive effect of the action being a refund, and that the desired ruling could not be given without first determining the treatment and status of the NOLs under the state law).

[86] *See Skandalakis v. Geeslin (In re Geeslin)* (M.D. Ga.), *supra* note 35 (Eleventh Amendment bars a contempt proceeding against state official for violation of automatic stay); *In re Lapin, supra* note 33 (Eleventh Amendment bars bankruptcy court from imposing sanctions for violation of discharge order); *In re Ranstrom* (Bankr. N.D. Cal.), *supra* note 84 (court dismissed, due to state's Eleventh Amendment immunity, damage claim for state's violation of debtor's discharge); *In re Lush Lawns, Inc., supra* note 35 (no injunctive relief for state's violation of automatic stay unless state files a proof of claim or otherwise participates in the bankruptcy proceeding). *Cf. Ind. Dept. of Rev. v. Williams* (S.D. Ind.), *supra* note 51.

[87] *See, e.g., Hoffman v. Connecticut Dept. of Income Maint.* (S. Ct.), *supra* note 21 (Justice Scalia, concurring); *In re ABEPP Acquisition Corp.* (Bankr. 6th Cir.), *supra* note 37 (turnover action cannot be used as a surrogate for an action for monetary relief in order to circumvent Eleventh Amendment immunity); *In re Ross, supra* note 35 (adversary proceeding to determine bankruptcy estate's right to a state tax refund and to compel turnover prohibited by Eleventh Amendment). In addition, even if a refund or turnover of funds is not affirmatively sought, the bankruptcy court similarly cannot entertain a declaratory action against a state knowing that it could act as *res judicata* in a subsequent action or claim against the state for a tax refund. *See supra* note 82.

*See generally* Gibson, Sovereign Immunity in Bankruptcy: The Next Chapter, 70 Am. Bankr. L.J. 195 (1996); Cordry, A Tale of Two Sovereigns: Will The Bankruptcy Code Survive Seminole?, Norton Bankr. L. Advisor, May 1996, at 1 (Ms. Cordry is counsel for the National Association of Attorneys General); Browning, Who Can Waive State Immunity, 15 Am. Bankr. Inst. J. 10 (1997) (Mr. Browning is the Assistant Attorney General for the State of Texas); Browning, Tough Bankruptcy Issues Under the Eleventh Amendment, 7 J. Bankr. Law and Prac. 219 (1998). For a continuing discussion and debate of the implications of *Seminole* in the bankruptcy context, *see* Bankruptcy Court Decisions, Weekly News and Comment (May 14, 1996) and subsequent issues.

[88] *See also* § 1005.1.2 above, discussing the effect of affirmative actions by a state that may constitute an "informal" proof of claim.

[89] *See In re Barrett Refining Corp., supra* note 80 (holding that, once a waiver of Eleventh Amendment immunity has been made, "it cannot be undone"). *Stanley v. Student Loan Services, Inc. (In re Stanley)*, 273 B.R. 907 (Bankr. N.D. Fla. 2002) (same).

[90] *See In re White*, 139 F.3d 1268 (9th Cir. 1998) (holding that conversion from Chapter 11 to Chapter 7 "does not constitute the commencement of a new case for purposes of sovereign immunity but merely represents a change in the statutory chapter pursuant to which the case would proceed").

recoupment doctrine of waiver, notwithstanding the unconstitutionality of section 106, if a debtor files an action against a state and, in response thereto, the state files a counterclaim against the debtor, the state has waived its Eleventh Amendment immunity with respect to any claims asserted against it by the debtor that arise out of the same transaction or occurrence upon which the state's counterclaim is based, but only to the extent of the state's counterclaim.[91] The state's conduct in merely defending against the debtor's action generally is not sufficient to invoke the doctrine; rather, the state must affirmatively assert a counterclaim against the debtor.[92] A state also may waive its Eleventh Amendment immunity by entering into an agreement with the federal government that requires the state to participate in certain bankruptcy proceedings,[93] or by entering into an agreement with the debtor prior to the debtor's bankruptcy filing whereby the state agrees to resolve any disputes relating to the agreement in federal court.[94]

Moreover, under the *Ex parte Young* doctrine, a debtor should be able to bring an injunctive action to remedy a state officer's continuing violation of the bankruptcy laws (even absent a waiver of Eleventh Amendment immunity) so long as the relief sought is prospective in nature.[95] *Ex parte Young* cannot be used to obtain retrospec-

---

[91] *See In re Koehler, supra* note 35.

[92] *See* id.; *In re Mueller, supra* note 35; *Kish v. Verniero, supra* note 35; *May v. Missouri Dept. of Rev.* (*In re May*), 251 B.R. 714 (Bankr. 8th Cir. 2000), *aff'd* (8th Cir.), *supra* note 84; *but see Schulman v. California State Water Resources Control Bd.* (*In re Lazar*), 200 B.R. 358 (Bankr. C.D. Cal. 1996) (holding that a general appearance by a state waives Eleventh Amendment immunity), *aff'd in part and rev'd in part,* 237 F.3d 967 (9th Cir.), *cert. denied,* 122 S. Ct. 458 (2001).

[93] *See, e.g., In re Innes,* 207 B.R. 953 (Bankr. D. Kan. 1997) (agreement by state with federal agency to pursue collection of student loans in bankruptcy cases of student-borrowers waived state's Eleventh Amendment immunity), *aff'd,* 184 F.3d 1275 (10th Cir. 1999), *cert. denied,* 120 S. Ct. 1530 (2000).

[94] *See In re Magnolia Venture Capital Corp.,* 218 B.R. 843 (S.D. Miss. 1997) (bankruptcy court had jurisdiction where state agreed in pledge agreement to resolve any disputes relating to pledged assets in courts within Mississippi, whether state or federal); *Mid-Continent Electric, Inc. v. Florida* (*In re Mid-Continent Electric, Inc.*), 278 B.R. 601 (Bankr. M.D. Fla. 2002) ("It is well established that the defense of sovereign immunity does not protect a state agency from an action arising out of a breach of an express or implied covenant or condition of an express written contract entered into with statutory authority").

[95] *See Ex parte Young, supra* note 27; *see also Seminole Tribe of Florida v. Florida, supra* note 24, at 1131 n.16, 1132-1133 (in *Seminole,* the Indian Gaming Regulatory Act at issue contained specific remedial provisions and, therefore, *Ex parte Young* was inapplicable); *Deposit Insurance Agency v. Superintendent of Banks of the State of New York (In re Deposit Insurance Agency),* 482 F.3d 612 (2d Cir. 2007) (*Ex Parte Young* applies to prevent state officials from failing to turnover assets of bankrupt debtors); *Dairy Mart Convenience Stores, Inc. v. Nickel* (*In re Dairy Mart Convenience Stores, Inc.*), 411 F.3d 367 (2nd Cir. 2005) (*Ex Parte Young* applies to prevent state officials from continuing to violate the extension of time permitted by Bankruptcy Code section 108 for processing a claim of the debtor for reimbursement of certain expenses that was filed after the normal due date under state law); *In re Ellett, supra* note 39 (bankruptcy court has jurisdiction under *Ex parte Young* to determine discharge of state taxes and enjoin state officer from engaging in collection efforts; debtor did not seek monetary recovery); *In re Lazar, supra* note 33 (discussing the application of *Ex parte Young* in the bankruptcy context); *Berkelhammer v. Novella* (*In re Berkelhammer*), 279 B.R. 660 (Bankr. S.D. N.Y. 2002) (*Ex parte Young* applies to prevent state official's "continuing violation of a fundamental provision of the Bankruptcy Code: section 525(a)'s prohibition of certain kinds of discrimination contrary to the Bankruptcy Code's fresh start policy"); *In re LTV Steel Company, Inc.,* 264 B.R. 455 (Bankr. N.D. Ohio 2001) (*Ex parte Young* applies in action by debtor to prevent state official from pursuing tax collection efforts and to cause official to remove tax liens from the debtor's property; removal of the tax liens would

tive relief.[96] If successful, such an action would expose the state official to the full remedial power of a federal court, including presumably contempt sanctions. In addition, even if the Eleventh Amendment prevents a debtor from bringing suit directly against a state in bankruptcy court, the debtor may be able to maintain such a suit in state court, assuming that a traditional remedial avenue exists pursuant to which the suit may be brought that does not implicate sovereign immunity concerns (*e.g.*, a tax refund action). It is unclear whether the Eleventh Amendment would bar an action brought in state court solely based on a cause of action arising under the federal bankruptcy laws.[97]

Political subdivisions of a state, such as counties or municipal corporations, that are not agencies of the state—and which do not have the benefit of Eleventh Amendment immunity[98]—continue to be subject to section 106.

---

(Footnote Continued)

not have the same effect as a money judgment against the state); *In re Schmitt*, 220 B.R. 68 (Bankr. W.D. Mo. 1998) (stating, in *dicta*, that "actions under *Ex parte Young* against state officials to obtain a determination of dischargeability—to obtain injunctive relief—are appropriate"); *In re Neary*, 220 B.R. 864 (Bankr. E.D. Pa. 1998) (same); *but see In re ABEPP Acquisition Corp., supra* note 37 ("The principles of *Ex parte Young* are inapplicable to suits which are essentially to recover money from a state"). *See also* Brubaker, Of State Sovereign Immunity and Prospective Remedies: The Bankruptcy Discharge as Statutory *Ex Parte Young* Relief, 76 Am. Bankr. L.J. 461 (2002) (detailed analysis in support of the position that entry of a discharge order by a federal bankruptcy court, in and of itself, is permissible *Ex parte Young* relief and violation of such order by a state official is sanctionable, notwithstanding the sovereign immunity of the state).

[96] *See In re Guiding Light Corp.*, 217 B.R. 493 (Bankr. E.D. La. 1998) (*Ex parte Young* cannot be used to require a turnover of assets pursuant to Bankruptcy Code section 547, because to do so would be to grant a request for retrospective relief); *CSX Transportation, Inc. v. Board of Public Works of West Virginia*, 138 F.3d 537 (4th Cir. 1998) ("An injunction against the future collection of the illegal taxes, even those that already have been assessed, is prospective, and therefore available under the *Ex parte Young* doctrine"), *cert. denied*, 119 S. Ct. 63 (1998).

[97] In a 1999 decision, the Supreme Court, in *Alden v. Maine*, 119 S. Ct. 2240 (1999), considered whether Congress had the power pursuant to the commerce clause of Article I of the Constitution to subject non-consenting states to private actions for damages in the state's own courts. In this case, a group of individuals initially filed suit in federal district court against the State of Maine seeking damages for alleged violations of the Fair Labor Standards Act, which was enacted pursuant to the commerce clause and authorized a private right of action in any federal or state court of competent jurisdiction for certain violations of the Fair Labor Standards Act. In light of the Supreme Court's decision in *Seminole*, the federal district court dismissed the suit and the First Circuit affirmed. In response, the plaintiff's filed essentially the same suit in a Maine state court. That suit was also dismissed on the grounds of sovereign immunity. On *certiorari*, the Supreme Court affirmed, concluding that Article I of the Constitution does not vest Congress with the power to subject non-consenting states to private suits for damages in their own courts (but suggested that suits for declaratory and injunctive relief could be brought against state officers). In *In re Lenke*, the bankruptcy court concluded that a state court should have jurisdiction to determine whether a debt has been discharged, and the scope of that discharge. *Lenke v. Tischler (In re Lenke)*, 249 B.R. 1 (Bankr. D. Ariz. 2000); *see also New England Power & Marine, Inc. v. Town of Tyngsborough (In re Middlesex Power Equipment & Marine, Inc.)*, 292 F.3d 61 (1st Cir. 2002) (state court could determine effect of bankruptcy court sale order with respect to the release of liens). *Consider also* the following decisions decided prior to the *Alden* case: *In re Elias* (Bankr. 9th Cir.), *supra* note 33 ("State courts are required to enforce applicable federal law in cases brought before them"); *Charles Brewer, Trustee for Value-Added Communications, Inc. Liquidation Trust v. State of New York*, No. M-56296 (N.Y. Ct. Cl. Mar. 25, 1998) (federal statute can give rise to common law cause of action within the jurisdiction of state court).

[98] *See, e.g., Mt. Healthy City School District Board of Education v. Doyle*, 429 U.S. 274 (1977); *NVR Homes, Inc. v. Clerks of the Circuit Courts (In re NVR, LP)* (4th Cir.), *supra* note 80 (vacated lower court

## §1102.6 *Postpetition Trust Fund Taxes*

A debtor-in-possession must remit all taxes required to be withheld or collected with respect to postpetition payments. With respect to payments on prepetition claims that are made at the termination of the bankruptcy case, the claim for the withholding amounts must be given the same priority and be paid at the same time as the claim from which such amount was withheld, unless the court otherwise provides (*see also* discussion at § 1015.1.3). In the case of postpetition payments, the withholding amounts must be paid at the time and in the manner required by state or local law.[99]

## §1102.7 *Effect of Automatic Stay*

The automatic stay applies, with limited exceptions, to (i) the collection and recovery of state and local prepetition taxes and (ii) for pre-October 22, 1994 bankruptcy cases, the assessment of prepetition taxes.[100] Specifically excluded are:

- a notice of deficiency and (for bankruptcy cases commenced on or after October 22, 1994) the conduct of a tax audit, a demand for tax returns, and a notice and demand for payment in connection with the assessment of a tax (although no tax lien may attach by reason of the assessment or demand);[101]
- the creation or perfection of an ad valorem property tax lien where the taxing authority either has a prior "interest in [the] property" or (in bankruptcy cases

(Footnote Continued)

decision with respect to states, but ruled on substantive issue with respect to counties); *Hanfling v. State Comp. Ins. Fund of California (In re ATG, Inc.)*, 311 B.R. 810 (Bankr. N.D. Cal. 2004) (State Compensation Insurance Fund was not entitled to Eleventh Amendment protection); *Walsh v. Pennsylvania (In re Tylka)*, 317 B.R. 672 (Bankr. W.D. Pa. 2004) (State Employees Retirement Board was not an "alter ego" of the state entitled to Eleventh Amendment protection); *Blue Cactus Post, L.C. v. Dallas County Appraisal District (In re Blue Cactus Post, L.C.)*, 229 B.R. 379 (Bankr N.D. Tex. 1999) (local appraisal district not entitled to Eleventh Amendment protection); *In re Merry-Go-Round Enterprises, Inc., supra* note 80 (county taxing authority not entitled to Eleventh Amendment protection).

[99] 11 U.S.C. § 346(f), redesignated in the 2005 reform bill as § 346(h); *see also* 28 U.S.C. § 960(b) *as added by* P.L. 109-8, § 712(a) (2005).

[100] *See* 11 U.S.C. § 362 and the discussion of the automatic stay at § 1007.

[101] In *In re H & H Beverage Distributors*, 850 F.2d 165 (3d Cir. 1988), *cert. denied*, 488 U.S. 944 (1988), *rev'g* 79 B.R. 205 (1987), the Third Circuit held that a sales tax audit did not violate the automatic stay and that "notices of audit assessment" issued by the Commonwealth of Pennsylvania for certain prepetition sales taxes constituted notices of deficiency, rather than actual assessments—and, thus, were not barred by the automatic stay—since the notice was equivalent to a federal notice of deficiency and did not itself create a lien against the debtor. At a minimum, no lien could be created until the Commonwealth filed the amount of liability with the prothonotary (the chief clerk of the court). *See also In re Fasgo, Inc.*, 58 B.R. 99 (E.D. Pa. 1986) (involved "notices of assessment/determination" for certain prepetition liquid fuels and oil franchise taxes also issued by the Commonwealth of Pennsylvania); *Cavanagh v. Calif. Unemployment Ins. Appeals Board*, 118 Cal. App. 4th 83 (Cal. App. 3d Dist. 2004) (involved tax assessments for California unemployment insurance contributions and other tax liabilities, with respect to which a petition for reassessment could be filed prior to the assessments becoming final and any lien ordinarily attaching).

commenced on or after October 22, 1994) the due date for the property tax is postpetition (*see* § 1102.13.2 below);[102]

- for bankruptcy cases commenced on or after October 17, 2005, the creation or perfection of a statutory lien for a special tax or special assessment on real property (whether or not ad valorem) due postpetition;[103] and
- for bankruptcy cases commenced on or after October 17, 2005, the setoff of a prepetition income tax refund against a prepetition tax liability would be permitted if allowable under nonbankruptcy law, except if there is a pending action to determine the amount or legality of the tax liability, in which event the taxing authority may hold the refund pending the resolution of the action (unless the court, upon motion and a hearing, grants the taxing authority adequate protection for its secured claim).[104]

The automatic stay remains in effect until either the bankruptcy case terminates, a discharge is granted or denied or, following a request by the state or local taxing authority, the bankruptcy court decides to terminate the stay.[105] Although the automatic stay expressly operates to stay the commencement or continuation of a proceeding before the U.S. Tax Court, there is no similar express provision for state tax court proceedings initiated by the debtor-in-possession.[106] Nevertheless, where the state tax court proceeding is a "continuation" of an administrative proceeding initiated by the state or local taxing authority against the debtor, the subsequent state court proceeding may be stayed regardless of who initiated it (unless the debtor-in-possession chooses to proceed).[107]

The applicability and effect of the automatic stay may become a matter of dispute within the context of a state court proceeding and thus become the subject of a final state court decision. Nevertheless, the Ninth Circuit Court of Appeals has held, *en banc*, that a state court's decision can be collaterally attacked in the bankruptcy court.[108]

---

[102] 11 U.S.C. §§ 362(b)(18), 546(b)(1).

[103] 11 U.S.C. § 362(b)(18), *as amended by* P.L. 109-8, § 1225 (2005).

[104] 11 U.S.C. § 362(b)(26). *See* § 1006.1.1 above, discussing this provision.

[105] *See* 11 U.S.C. § 362(c)-(f). A debtor-in-possession, however, may, in certain instances, effectively waive the protection of the automatic stay. *See* Bankruptcy Rule 6009 (permits debtor-in-possession to prosecute, defend or commence any proceeding or action before any tribunal); *but consider In re Otto, infra* note 107.

[106] *See Carson Pirie Scott & Co. v. County of Dakota*, File Nos. C7-90-7005, C6-91/6205 (Minn. Tax Ct. April 15, 1992). In addition, *see Front Office Associates, Inc v. Clark (In re Front Office Associates, Inc.)*, 142 B.R. 24 (Bankr. D.R.I. 1992) (state interagency advisory opinion regarding the validity of a state tax lien on the debtor's property did not violate debtor's automatic stay).

[107] *Compare Delpit v. Commissioner*, 94-1 U.S.T.C. ¶ 50,127 (9th Cir. 1994), and other cases discussed at § 1009.4 (reaching differing conclusions as to whether a federal Tax Court proceeding is a "continuation" of the audit process); *In re Otto*, DTA No. 818778, 2004 N.Y. Tax LEXIS 181 (NYS Div. of Tax Appeals) (Sept. 2, 2004) (administrative law judge determination was a nullity because automatic stay was in effect; stated that stay could not be waived by agreement of the parties), *reconsidered and reissued due to change in facts*, 2005 N.Y. Tax LEXIS 10 (January 20, 2005). *See also* Bankruptcy Rule 6009 (permitting a debtor-in-possession or trustee to prosecute, defend or commence any action or proceeding, with or without court approval).

[108] *Gruntz v. County of Los Angeles (In re Gruntz)*, 202 F.3d 1074 (9th Cir. 2000).

## *§1102.8 Tolling of Statutes of Limitations*

Pursuant to Bankruptcy Code section 108(c), it appears that most statutes of limitations on *collection* will be tolled for the period during which the state or local taxing authority is prohibited by the automatic stay from collecting the tax.[109] However, no similar Bankruptcy Code provision appears to toll the statute of limitations on *assessment*.[110] Accordingly, whether the applicable assessment period is tolled for the period (if any) during which the automatic stay is in effect may depend on state and local law. As discussed above, the automatic stay prohibits the "assessment" of prepetition taxes in bankruptcy cases commenced *before* October 22, 1994. Most state and local taxing authorities extend the assessment period in the case of federal adjustments—effectively obtaining the benefit of the federal tolling provisions for assessments. In many (if not most) cases, however, there is no bankruptcy-related tolling provision of the assessment period for nonfederal adjustments. Accordingly, in such cases, the statute of limitations may expire even though the taxing authority may be prohibited from assessing the tax. In some cases, however, it is possible that the act of assessment necessary for statute of limitations purposes may constitute a "notice of deficiency," rather than a formal "assessment," for purposes of the automatic stay and thus not be stayed.[111] In addition, a state or local taxing authority might argue that the filing of a proof of claim during the assessment period is tantamount to an assessment for statute of limitations purposes, or that the statute of limitations should be extended on equitable grounds.[112] The latter arguments were made by the City of New York and rejected in *In re Brac Group, Inc.*[113]

## *§1102.9 Filing of Proof of Claim*

Like any other creditor (including the IRS), state and local taxing authorities must file a proof of claim with the bankruptcy court for any prepetition taxes in order to participate as creditor in a bankruptcy case under Chapter 7 or 11 (although, in certain cases, such a filing will be deemed made based on the debtor's schedule of liabilities as filed with the court). All governmental authorities have a minimum of 180 days after the date of the order for relief in which to file a proof of claim (for bankruptcy cases commenced on or after October 22, 1994), but otherwise must abide

---

[109] *See also City of Bridgeport v. Debek*, 554 A.2d 728 (Conn. 1989) (under Bankruptcy Act predecessor to Bankruptcy Code section 108(c), a landowner's bankruptcy suspended statutory period for municipality to enforce tax liens).

[110] *See* 11 U.S.C. § 108 ("Extensions of time"). Bankruptcy Code sections 108(a) and (b) only apply to extensions of time benefitting the debtor, and Bankruptcy Code section 108(c) only applies to periods "for commencing or continuing a civil action in a court."

[111] *See* § 1102.7 above; consider, for example, *H & H Beverage Distributors and Fasgo, supra* note 101.

[112] For a discussion of the bankruptcy court's equitable powers, *see* Chapter 10 at § 1013.5.

[113] 2004 Bankr. LEXIS 1087 (Bankr. D. Del. 2004) (held that the City had to comply with own procedures, which required the issuance of a notice of deficiency in a specified manner as a predicate for an assessment; the filing of the proof of claim did not suffice, even though containing the self-serving statement that the City "has made the assessment of the tax set forth herein by way of [the] proof of claim pursuant to [City's] Administrative Code").

by the "bar date" established by the bankruptcy court for filing a claim.[114] The rules governing the filing of proofs of claims (including post-bar date amendments and late claims) are discussed further at § 1010 above.

A "claim" for this purpose includes any right to payment, whether or not such right is contingent, unliquidated or disputed.[115] Thus, a proof of claim must be timely filed to protect even contingent, and currently unknown, claims. This has posed a particular problem for states in respect of so-called piggyback claims.

Most state income tax statutes "piggyback" on the federal income tax laws, and most state taxing authorities rely on the results of federal income tax audits for purposes of adjusting the federal income tax numbers in a taxpayer's state tax return. To this end, such states generally require that the taxpayer inform the state, either by written notice or possibly by the filing of an amended return, of the results of any federal income tax audits. Some states also require that the taxpayer provide written notice of the commencement of the audit. In general, this process proves cost-efficient for the states because it prevents duplication of audits and allows state auditors to focus on purely state audit issues. The general audit process is disrupted by the bankruptcy of the taxpayer. As a result of the bankruptcy, the normal statute of limitations for tax collections is effectively overridden by the general need for the state to file a proof of claim with the bankruptcy court by the bar date. However, given that most states are in a reactive mode when it comes to federal audit adjustments, many states often fail to preserve their right to recover on their potential piggyback claims by timely filing with the bankruptcy court.

In *In re Circle K Corp.*,[116] the bankruptcy court was presented with one such situation involving the State of Montana. The IRS had commenced an audit of Circle K's prepetition tax years prior to Circle K's bankruptcy filing. Montana claimed that it did not receive notice of the federal audit as required by state law. However, it did receive notice of the bankruptcy filing and the bar date for filing proofs of claim, and was aware that it was scheduled as holding an unliquidated tax claim. Yet it failed to file a proof of claim. The IRS completed its audit two months prior to confirmation of Circle K's Chapter 11 plan, but, for unexplained reasons, the audit results were not reported to Montana until after the plan was confirmed, discharging all unfiled claims. Montana asserted that it should not be barred from collecting its piggyback

---

114 *See* 11 U.S.C. § 502(b)(9); Bankruptcy Rules 3002(c)(1) and 3003. It is important that proper notice of the bar date be provided to the taxing authority. *See, e.g., United States Small Bus. Admin v. Bridges*, 894 F.2d 108, 111-13 (5th Cir. 1990) (discussing notice requirements where "an extensive, bureaucratic agency is involved as a creditor in a bankruptcy proceeding," and collecting cases); *United States v. Yale Transport Corp.*, 184 F. Supp. 42, 47 (S.D. N.Y. 1960) (Bankruptcy Act case; "notice of bankruptcy proceedings should be reasonably calculated to come to the attention of that branch of the Government familiar with the claims involved and which exercises functions with respect thereto"); *Calif. Franchise Tax Bd. v. Joye*, 2007 U.S. Dist. LEXIS 24855 (N.D. Ca. 2007) (concluded that notice was inadequate where the state taxing authority was scheduled as a creditor in a nominal amount but the debtor did not file its tax return until after the claims bar date; court observed that this was not a situation where the state could have determined the debtor's tax liability absent the tax return).

115 *See* 11 U.S.C. § 101(5).

116 *Circle K Convenience Stores, Inc. v. The State of Montana Dept. of Rev.* (*In re Circle K Corp.*), 198 B.R. 784 (Bankr. D. Ariz. 1996).

claim, because it had not received sufficient notice of the pending federal audit and audit results. The bankruptcy court disagreed, explaining the situation as follows:

> [Montana]complains debtor failed to fully comply with state law in reporting the IRS audit. That may be true. Regardless, for bankruptcy purposes, it is federal, not state, law which defines the requisite notice to be afforded creditors.
>
> The Montana authority is a sophisticated taxing entity, presumably versed in bankruptcy. When apprised it has an unliquidated claim in a pending bankruptcy, and must act by a date certain, it should do so. At a minimum, the department could have filed a contingent tax claim, reserving the right to amend when it completed its own review or heard concerning audit results.
>
> In short, debtor listed the department as holding an unliquidated claim. Montana had an obligation to do something. Given this clear notice, Montana ignored the proceedings at its peril.[117]

To be paid any postpetition (administrative period) taxes not paid by the debtor-in-possession in the ordinary course, a state or local taxing authority must file a "request for payment" with the bankruptcy court for bankruptcy cases commenced before October 17, 2005 (*see* § 1010.4 above).[118]

## *§1102.10 Prompt Audit of Postpetition Tax Years*

The debtor-in-possession, prior to the close of the bankruptcy case, may request a prompt determination of any unpaid tax liability for a completed postpetition taxable year, or any other tax incurred during the administration of the bankruptcy case, for which a tax return has been filed.[119] Unless a tax return is fraudulent or contains a material misrepresentation, the debtor-in-possession and the debtor corporation (as well as any successor corporation) are discharged from any future liability for such unpaid taxes, upon payment of the tax either (a) as shown on the tax return, if the state or local taxing authority fails to comply with the time restrictions during which it may examine the debtor's return and notify the debtor of any additional tax due, (b) as determined by the state or local taxing authority, or (c) if the result of the state or local taxing authority's examination is disputed, as determined by the bankruptcy court after notice and hearing.[120]

In accordance with changes made to section 505(b) as part of the 2005 bankruptcy reforms, the clerk of the bankruptcy court in each district must now maintain

---

[117] Id. at 790 (citations omitted).

[118] *See* P.L. 109-8, § 712 (2005), changing this result for subsequent bankruptcy cases.

[119] 11 U.S.C. § 505(b). Besides the prompt audit procedure sanctioned by the Bankruptcy Code, there may be state or local statutes or administrative procedures permitting requests for expedited audits in certain cases. *See, e.g.,* New York City Dept. of Finance, Statement of Audit Procedure 04-01-AU (March 17, 2004).

[120] Id.

a listing of the designated address to which a request for prompt determination must be sent with respect to any taxing authority and where any information with respect to additional requirements can be located.[121] For bankruptcy cases commenced on or after October 17, 2005, section 505(b) requires that the request be submitted at the address maintained by the clerk, and in accordance with any other requirements referenced in the listing.[122] Absent an express designation, a debtor-in-possession may send the request to the address where the tax return is filed or where a protest would be filed with such taxing authority.

The ability of a debtor-in-possession to request a prompt examination and the scope of the resulting discharge are discussed further at § 1011 above.

## *§ 1102.11 Adjudication of Tax Claims*

Subject to considerations of sovereign immunity (*see* § 1102.5), the bankruptcy court has the power to rule on the merits of any tax claim against the debtor corporation (including any interest, fine or penalty) unless such claim has been previously contested and adjudicated by a judicial or administrative tribunal of competent jurisdiction before the commencement of the bankruptcy proceeding.[123]

---

[121] 11 U.S.C. § 505(b)(1)(A), *as amended by* P.L. 109-8, § 703 (2005).

[122] 11 U.S.C. § 505(b)(1)(B), *as amended by* P.L. 109-8, § 703 (2005).

[123] 11 U.S.C. § 505(a). *See, e.g., City of Perth Amboy v. Custom Distribution Services, Inc.* (*In re Custom Distribution Services, Inc.*), 224 F.3d 235 (3rd Cir. 2000) (bankruptcy court has jurisdiction to adjudicate state tax claims); *In re Stoecker*, 179 F.3d 546, 549 (7th Cir. 1999) (same), *appealed and aff'd on other issues*, 120 S.Ct. 1951 (2000); *City Vending of Muskogee v. Oklahoma Tax Com'n*, 898 F.2d 122 (10th Cir. 1990) (claims were considered "previously adjudicated" where previously protested before the state tax commission, and state law provided for a hearing and a right to appeal to the state court; in one case, the protest was decided on pleadings and, in the other, the court considered irrelevant the fact that the commission did not have jurisdiction to consider debtor's constitutional arguments); *Texas Comptroller of Public Accounts v. Trans State Outdoor Advertising Co., Inc.* (*In re Trans State Outdoor Advertising Co., Inc.*), 140 F.3d 618 (5th Cir. 1998) (proceeding before an Administrative Law Judge, where rules of evidence applied and witnesses testified under oath and could be subpoenaed, was an adjudication by an administrative or judicial tribunal, *even though* the judge was selected by the State Comptroller and any decision had to be approved by the Comptroller); *Cody, Inc. v. County of Orange* (*In re Cody, Inc.*), 338 F.3d 89 (2d Cir. 2003) (denial of property tax grievance complaints by Town Board of Assessors, which could hear testimony under oath and compel the taxpayer to appear, constituted a prior adjudication, even though subject to *de novo* review); *Delafield 246 Corp. v. The City of New York (In re Delafield 246 Corp.)*, 2007 Bankr. LEXIS 1389 (Bankr. S.D. N.Y. 2007) (state law preclusion rules govern the determination of whether there has been a prior final judgment on a particular issue, citing Second Circuit authorities); *In re Mirant Corp.*, 2006 Bankr. LEXIS 1125 (Bankr. N.D. Tex. 2006) (bankruptcy court initially deferred ruling on certain significant tax claims in the hope the claims would be resolved in state court proceedings; however, after two years and a failed settlement, the court determined that it could no longer wait); *Pontes v. Cunha* (*In re Pontes*), 310 F. Supp. 2d 447 (D.R.I. 2004) (bankruptcy court has jurisdiction to adjudicate state and local tax claims); *In re TMI Growth Properties*, 109 B.R. 403 (Bankr. N.D. Cal. 1990) (upheld reconsideration of a debtor's property tax assessment, despite a prior postpetition determination by the assessment appeals board; *see* § 1013 note 4); *In re El Tropicano, Inc.*, 128 B.R. 153 (Bankr. W.D. Tex. 1991) (settlement agreement between the debtor and the local appraisal district regarding the debtor's property tax valuation held to constitute a pre-bankruptcy "adjudication"); *In re A.H. Robins Co.*, 126 B.R. 227 (Bankr. E.D. Va. 1991) (an assessment which, pursuant to state statute, became final and nonappealable after 60 days absent a prior taxpayer petition could be challenged in the bankruptcy court, since the assessment had not been previously adjudicated); *In re 499 W. Warren Street Associates, Ltd. Partnership*, 143 B.R.

Also, with respect to *ad valorem* property taxes in bankruptcy cases commenced on or after October 17, 2005, the time period under state or local law for contesting or redetermining such claims must not have expired.[124] With respect to a suit for refund, the bankruptcy court cannot determine the matter until the earlier of (a) disallowance of the claim for refund upon which the suit is based by the state or local taxing authority, or (b) the passage of 120 days since the debtor properly filed such claim.[125] Nevertheless, a suit for refund generally may be adjudicated despite the absence of a prior claim for refund if the refund results from an offset or counterclaim to a proof of claim, or a request for payment, filed by the state or local taxing authority with the bankruptcy court.[126] The bankruptcy court's jurisdiction over tax claims and refund actions is discussed further at §§1012.2 and 1013 above.

If the debtor corporation desires, it may pursue the adjudication of a state or local taxing authority's tax claim using normal non-bankruptcy procedures. No prior bankruptcy court approval is necessary.[127] Moreover, where the time period in which to initiate any judicial action or proceeding challenging a state or local tax assessment (including a suit for refund) commences prior to the filing of the debtor's bankruptcy petition, but expires afterward, Bankruptcy Code section 108(a) ensures that a debtor-in-possession has at least two years from the entry of the bankruptcy filing (or, in the case of an involuntary bankruptcy, from the entry of the order for relief) to initiate the action or proceeding.[128] Other time periods for filing pleadings, claims, notices or

---

(Footnote Continued)

326 (Bankr. N.D.N.Y. 1992) (to similar effect); *Ledgemere Land Corp. v. Town of Ashland (In re Ledgemere Land Corp.)*, 135 B.R. 193 (Bankr. D. Mass. 1991) (abatement requests that were denied by the town's board of assessors without a hearing were not adjudicated "before" a judicial or administrative "tribunal"); *In re AWB Associates, G.P.*, 144 B.R. 270 (Bankr. E.D. Pa. 1992) (upheld jurisdiction to redetermine seven-year-old property taxes previously unchallenged by the debtor; acknowledged that at some point the staleness of the tax years may become relevant; pre-dated 2005 change in the bankruptcy court's jurisdiction). *Consider also Marcellus Wood & Trucking, Inc. v. Michigan Employment Sec. Comm. (In re Marcellus Wood & Trucking, Inc.)*, 158 B.R. 650 (Bankr. W.D. Mich. 1993) (claim was held "previously adjudicated" where, following a hearing and testimony under oath, a state referee denied the debtor's late request for a redetermination of its contribution rate finding that "good cause" did not exist, and the Employment Security Board of Review affirmed); *In re WUS Corporation*, 1998 U.S. Dist. LEXIS 13754 (D. N.J. 1998) (procedural dismissals of earlier actions did not address propriety of property tax assessments and thus did not preclude a later redetermination by the bankruptcy court).

124 11 U.S.C. §505(a)(2)(C), *as added by* P.L. 109-8, §701(b) (2005).

125 11 U.S.C. §505(a)(2)(B). *See* discussion at §1013.

126 124 Cong. Rec. H 11,110 (daily ed. September 28, 1978) (statement of Rep. Edwards), S 17,427 (daily ed. October 6, 1978) (statement of Sen. DeConcini).

127 *See* Bankruptcy Rule 6009.

128 *See, e.g., Rudin v. Tax Comm. of the City of N.Y. (In re Olympia & York Maiden Lane Co., LLC)*, 233 B.R. 662 (Bankr. S.D.N.Y. 1999) (time in which to commence a court action challenging New York City property tax assessment kept open for a minimum of two years under Bankruptcy Code section 108(a), even though normal statutory period is significantly shorter); *CGE Shattuck LLC v. Town of Jaffrey (In re CGE Shattuck LLC)*, 272 B.R. 514 (Bankr. D. N.H. 2001) (property tax "appeal" from adverse decision of town's selectmen constituted the commencement of an "action" entitled to the minimum two-year filing period in Bankruptcy Code section 108(a), since review by selectmen was "simply an administrative procedure that must be followed prior to the taxpayer being eligible to proceed to a judicial or quasi-judicial forum"). *See also* discussion at §1012.2 above.

similar things (such as a claim for refund) are also extended where the bankruptcy filing interrupts the applicable filing period, but in those situations the debtor-in-possession is only ensured a minimum of 60 days to make the filing.[129]

## *§1102.12 Dischargeability of Tax Claims*

The same rules of dischargeability of tax claims apply for state and local tax purposes as were described at § 1014 for federal tax purposes. However, in certain cases, the enforcement of such rules may be made more difficult due to the state's Eleventh Amendment immunity (*see* § 1102.5 above).

## *§1102.13 Priority of Tax Claims*

Unsecured state and local tax claims are given the same priority as similar federal tax claims (*see* § 1015). A "tax" for this purpose may include state charges not ordinarily viewed in terms of a tax. For example, in certain cases, "premiums" paid to a state workers' compensation fund may be considered an "excise tax" entitled to an eighth priority.[130] Other examples are noted in the footnote below.[131] Also at issue

---

[129] 11 U.S.C. § 108(b).

[130] *Compare New Neighborhoods, Inc. v. West Virginia Workers' Comp. Fund*, 886 F.2d 714 (4th Cir. 1989) (unpaid premiums to West Virginia fund treated as an excise tax; discusses contrary authorities); *In re Suburban Motor Freight, Inc.*, 998 F.2d 338 (6th Cir. 1993) (applied analysis in *New Neighborhoods*, held unpaid premium to Ohio fund was an excise tax); *North Dakota Workers Comp. Bureau v. Voightman (In re Voightman)*, 239 B.R. 380 (Bankr. 8th Cir. 1999) (same, but involving North Dakota fund); *with In re Metro Transportation Co.*, 117 B.R. 143 (Bankr. E.D. Pa. 1990) (not an excise tax since participation in the Pennsylvania fund is not compulsory); *Brock v. Washington Metropolitan Area Transit Authority*, 796 F.2d 481 (D.C. Cir. 1986), *cert. denied*, 107 S. Ct. 1887 (1987) (involving District of Columbia fund). The Supreme Court has held that unpaid premiums do *not* constitute contributions to an employee benefit plan entitled to priority under Bankruptcy Code section 507(a)(5) (as renumbered by the 2005 reform bill). *Howard Delivery Service v. Zurich American Ins. Co.*, 126 S. Ct. 2105 (2006). In addition, the Sixth Circuit held that *reimbursements* to Ohio fund for benefits paid to workers for which premiums were unpaid or company was self-insured were *not* entitled to priority as an excise tax. *Ohio Bureau of Workers' Comp. v. Yoder (In re Suburban Motor Freight, Inc.)*, 36 F.3d 484 (6th Cir. 1994). Contrasting the Ohio fund, the Ninth Circuit, in *Industrial Comm. of Arizona v. Camilli (In re Camilli)*, 94 F.3d 1330 (9th Cir. 1996), *cert. denied*, 117 S. Ct. 953 (1997), held that mandatory contributions to an Arizona fund which bore the sole burden of compensating employees of uninsured employers were excise taxes entitled to priority. On the other hand, the Ninth Circuit, in *George v. Uninsured Employers Fund (In re George)*, 361 F.3d 1157 (9th Cir. 2004), held that a reimbursement claim by the California Uninsured Employers Fund for payment to an injured employee was *not* an excise tax (nor, in the court's view, was the payment sought with respect to "a transaction," in that the claim arose due to the company's *failure* to obtain insurance).

[131] Other examples include various state uninsured motor vehicle assessments, *Williams v. Motley*, 925 F.2d 741 (4th Cir. 1991) (Virginia assessments held, an "excise tax"; but service fee held to be a penalty); *Waldo v. Montana (In re Waldo)*, 1997 U.S. App. LEXIS 3219 (9th Cir. 1997) (same, Montana); various state unemployment compensation contributions, *In re Continental Minerals Corp.*, 132 B.R. 757 (Bankr. D. Nev. 1991) (held, an "employment tax"); *In re Northeastern Ohio General Hosp. Assn.*, 126 B.R. 513, 515 (Bankr. N.D. Ohio) (status as employment tax was "undisputed"); *In re Williams*, 183 B.R. 43 (Bankr. E.D.N.Y.), *aff'd*, 188 B.R. 331 (E.D.N.Y. 1995); contributions to Massachusetts's uncompensated care pool, *Boston Regional Medical Center, Inc. v. Mass. (In re Boston Regional Medical Center, Inc.)*, 365 F.3d 51 (1st Cir. 2004) (held "excise tax"); contributions to Massachusetts's labor

may be the classification of the tax—such as whether the tax is a tax "on or measured by income or gross receipts," an "excise tax," or otherwise—due to the differing treatment accorded different taxes.[132] In a case of first impression, one court held that the former New York real property gains tax was a tax "on or measured by income," even though it could not be said to be an "income tax" as such term is generally used.[133] In another instance, one bankruptcy court recently held that the Texas corporate franchise tax—which was capital based, and thus could not qualify as an income or gross receipts tax[134]—was nevertheless an "excise tax" for priority purposes.[135] As to certain taxes, it will also be necessary to ascertain when the tax was "assessed," which will vary depending on state and local law.[136] As to excise taxes for

(Footnote Continued)

shortage fund, *In re Ludlow Hospital Society, Inc.*, 216 B.R. 312 (Bankr. D. Mass. 1997) (same); and Oregon's highway use tax, *Oregon v. Arrow Transportation Co. of Delaware*, 229 B.R. 456 (D. Ore. 1999) (same), *rev'g*, 227 B.R. 183 (Bankr. D. Ore. 1998).

Other examples of charges that are *not* "taxes" within the meaning of the Bankruptcy Code include vehicle registration fees under the multi-state International Registration Plan, *Burlington Motor Carriers Inc. v. Indiana Dept. of Rev. (In re Burlington Motor Holdings Inc.)*, 235 B.R. 741, *recons. denied*, 1999 Bankr. LEXIS 1545 (Bankr. D. Del. 1994); and the obligation of a non-profit employer to *reimburse* New Jersey for unemployment benefits (in contrast to an up-front obligation to pay premiums or make contributions), *In re United Healthcare System, Inc.*, 396 F.3d 247 (3d Cir. 2005), *cert. denied*, 126 S. Ct. 62 (2005); *Mich. Unemployment Ins. Agency v. Boyd (In re Albion Health Serv.)*, 360 B.R. 599 (Bankr. 6th Cir. 2007).

132 *See, e.g., In re O.P.M. Leasing Services, Inc.*, 60 B.R. 679, 681 (Bankr. S.D.N.Y. 1986) (Texas franchise tax which was imposed based on value of capital, but only took into account the portion of such capital allocable to Texas based on relative gross receipts, was not a tax "on or measured by gross receipts" because the apportionment had "no impact on the measurement of the tax as it relates to capital"); *In re Raiman*, 172 B.R. 933 (Bankr. 9th Cir. 1994) (California tax imposed quarterly on a retailer's gross receipts, less certain exclusions, was a tax "on or measured by gross receipts"). *See also In re Labrum & Doak, LLP*, 1999 Bankr. LEXIS 490 (Bankr. E.D. Pa. 1999) (noted that, although the issue is not free from doubt, the debtor had conceded that the New York City commercial rent tax is an "excise" tax).

133 *In re Williams*, 173 B.R. 459 (Bankr. E.D.N.Y. 1994), *aff'd*, 188 B.R. 331 (E.D.N.Y. 1995). Contrast *995 Fifth Avenue Assoc., L.P. v. New York State Dept. of Tax'n and Finance (In re 995 Fifth Avenue Assoc., L.P.)*, *infra* note 156, distinguishing the gains tax from a "stamp or similar tax" for purposes of then Bankruptcy Code section 1146(c), now section 1146(a).

134 *See In re O.P.M. Leasing Services, Inc.* (Bankr. S.D. N.Y.), *supra* note 132.

135 *In re National Steel Corp.*, 321 B.R. 901 (Bankr. N.D. Ill. 2005); *cf. In re Pemberton Pub, Inc.*, 29 B.R. 519 (Bankr. D. Mass. 1983) (Massachusetts corporate franchise tax accepted by the court as an excise tax without discussion). The court in *National Steel* concluded, based on a review of various court decisions interpreting the term "excise tax" in different contexts, that an "excise tax" includes (in the words of *Black's Law Dictionary*) an obligation "imposed on the performance of an act, the engaging in an occupation, or the enjoyment of a privilege" and thus encompasses the Texas franchise tax. Because the priority accorded an excise tax in Bankruptcy Code section 508(a)(8)(E) speaks in terms of an excise tax "on . . . a transaction," the court also considered the breadth of the term "transaction" and concluded that, in the case of a franchise tax, the transaction is the exercise of the privilege to conduct business in Texas, thereby obtaining the benefits that such privilege confers.

136 *See, e.g., King v. Franchise Tax Board of the State of California (In re King)*, 961 F.2d 1423 (9th Cir. 1992) (involving California Franchise Tax); *Harris v. United States*, 228 B.R. 740 (Bankr. D. Ariz. 1998) (involving Arizona income tax; assessment became final when time period for all appeals of proposed assessment expired, not later when collection notices were issued); *O'Connell v. Minn. Dept. of Rev. (In re O'Connell)*, 246 B.R. 332 (Bankr. 8th Cir. 2000) (Minnesota state law definition of "assessment"—which looked to the date of the tax return filing—was not controlling; rather, assessment occurs

which no return is due, the focus is solely on when the transaction giving rise to the tax liaiblity occurred.[137]

### § 1102.13.1 Prepetition Taxes on or Measured by Income or Gross Receipts: Additional Considerations

As discussed at § 1015.1.4, an eighth priority is accorded to unsecured claims for prepetition taxes on or measured by income or gross receipts in three circumstances:

(1) a tax for which a tax return, if required, is last due (with extensions) within three years before the petition date, or due after the petition date;[138]
(2) when the tax is assessed within 240 days prior to the filing of the bankruptcy petition (which period is extended to include the period for which an offer of compromise is pending or in effect, plus 30 days thereafter, provided with respect to pre-October 17, 2005 bankruptcy cases such offer of compromise was made within 240 days after the assessment);[139] and
(3) when the tax is still assessable but not yet assessed.[140]

In many cases, priority will be easily determinable on the basis that the tax in question is still assessable at the time of the bankruptcy. However, when the tax has been previously assessed, the priority of the tax will depend on whether it was assessed within 240 days of the bankruptcy (subject to extension for an offer of compromise) or whether the taxpayer was required to file a tax return for such tax within three years of the bankruptcy.

---

(Footnote Continued)

when, looking to state law, the tax debt is finally determined on an equivalent basis to an IRS assessment); *Florida Dept. of Rev. v. General Dev. Corp. (In re General Dev. Corp.)*, 165 B.R. 691 (S.D. Fla. 1994); *In re Williams*, 183 B.R. 43 (Bankr. E.D.N.Y.), *aff'd*, 188 B.R. 331 (E.D.N.Y. 1995). *See also La. Dept. of Rev. and Tax'n v. Lewis*, 199 F.3d 249 (5th Cir. 2000) (what matters is when the state actually assessed the tax, not when the state should have assessed the tax if it had followed correct procedures; thus, later date of assessment controlled). It is also possible, depending on state law, that a state may commence collection proceedings in respect of a filed tax return for which the tax was shown but not paid without making a technical "assessment" of the tax. In the case of income taxes, this means that the tax may be considered unassessed, but still assessable, as of the commencement of the bankruptcy case for purposes of qualifying as an eighth priority claim under Bankruptcy Code section 507(a)(8)(A)(iii), despite prior collections actions. *See Lamborn v. United States (In re Lamborn)*, 181 B.R. 98 (Bankr. N.D. Okla. 1995), *supplemented*, 204 B.R. 999 (1997), so holding.

[137] *See* 11 U.S.C. § 507(a)(8)(E)(ii). *See, e.g., Deroche v. Ariz. Indus. Comm. (In re Deroche)*, 272 F.3d 1289 (9th Cir. 2001) (Arizona worker's compensation benefits payable by an uninsured debtor did not constitute a priority claim where the employee's injury occurred more than three years prior to the filing of the bankruptcy case); *Bliemeister v. Indus. Comm. of Ariz. (In re Bliemeister)*, 251 B.R. 383 (Bankr. D. Ariz. 2000), *aff'd*, 296 F.3d 858 (9th Cir. 2002) (same).

[138] 11 U.S.C. § 507(a)(8)(A)(i).

[139] 11 U.S.C. § 507(a)(8)(A)(ii).

[140] 11 U.S.C. § 507(a)(8)(A)(iii) (in the case of individual debtors, this provision does not apply to any taxes that are nondischargeable under Bankruptcy Code section 523(a)(1)(B) or (C), *see* discussion at § 1015.1.4). For bankruptcy cases commenced on or after October 17, 2005, this provision is limited to taxes with respect to taxable years ending on or before the filing of the petition in bankruptcy. *See* § 1015.1.1 above, discussing the priority accorded income taxes for the year of the bankruptcy filing.

As a result, an often raised issue is whether an amended return or other written notice required to be filed under state or local law with respect to the impact of federal audit adjustments is a "required" return for this purpose.[141] Where state law requires the filing of a formal amended return, the courts generally have held that such return is a required return with respect to such adjustments.[142] Conversely, where state law only requires the taxpayer "to report" the federal changes and any corrections, most (but not all) courts hold that such report does not constitute a required return.[143] Caught somewhere in the middle, due to its hybrid nature, is a statute that provides for an amended return but permits the taxpayer to give other written notice instead.[144] As a result, where a statute provides for an amended return but permits the tax commissioner by regulation or otherwise to accept other notice or information, the determination of whether a return is "required" will depend in significant part on the commissioner's exercise of its authority.[145]

---

[141] A similar reference to a required return appears in Bankruptcy Code section 523(a)(1)(B). Applicable only to individuals, such section provides that taxes of a kind entitled to second or eighth priority are nondischargeable if the tax is one "with respect to which a return, if required" was not filed or was filed late and within two years of the bankruptcy. Most of the cases that have considered the issue of amended returns arise under, or in conjunction with, Bankruptcy Code section 523.

[142] *See, e.g., Gambone v. State of Ohio Dept. of Taxation*, 223 B.R. 611 (Bankr. N.D. Ohio 1998); *Kansas Dept. of Revenue v. Morgan (In re Morgan)*, 209 B.R. 531 (Bankr. D. Kan. 1997); *Giacci v. United States*, 1997 Bankr. LEXIS 1640 (Bankr. S.D. Ohio 1997) (involved Ohio statute); *In re Cohn*, 96 B.R. 827 (Bankr. N.D. Ill. 1988) (Illinois statute required filing of amended return "or such other form as the Department may by regulations prescribe;" held that the amended return was a required return). *Cf. In re Fernandez*, 188 B.R. 34 (Bankr. D. Nev. 1995) (involved state requirement to file amended return for gain recognized on principal sale of residence where new residence not purchased within two years). *But consider Dyer v. Georgia Dept. of Revenue (In re Dyer)*, 158 B.R. 904 (Bankr. W.D.N.Y. 1993) (involved Georgia statute; concluded that not every return that a state requires creates a new, or renewed, obligation; however, "the Debtor must show that he filed some return, at some appropriate time, which disclosed all of his income"; thus, the court would distinguish between an amended return that includes previously unreported income and one that corrects improperly claimed deductions). The fact that a tax return may not be required if the taxpayer's income is below a minimum amount will not prevent the tax return from being a required return unless the debtor's income was in fact below such amount. *See, e.g., Humble v. State of Louisiana (In re Humble)*, 209 B.R. 54 (Bankr. E.D. La. 1997).

[143] *Compare California Franchise Tax Board v. Jackson (In re Jackson)*, 184 F.3d 1046 (9th Cir. 1999) (California statute as then in effect required notification of federal changes and state tax impact but not amended return; held, that the required notice or report was not a required return; in the court's view, the word "return" has a very specific and plain meaning when it comes to taxes); *California Franchise Tax Bd. v. Jerauld (In re Jerauld)*, 208 B.R. 183 (Bankr. 9th Cir. 1997) (same), *aff'd without op.*, 189 F.3d 473 (9th Cir. 1999); *and Blackwell v. Virginia Dept. of Taxation (In re Blackwell)*, 115 B.R. 86, 89 (Bankr. W.D. Va. 1990) (Virginia statute required the taxpayer to "report" federal changes but did not specify method, nor was there any regulation specifying the method; held, not equivalent to requiring a return), *with Blutter v. United States (In re Blutter)*, 177 B.R. 209, 210 (Bankr. S.D.N.Y. 1995) (New York State statute requiring that a taxpayer file a report of the federal changes was equivalent to requiring a return; in either case, by not filing "the debtor has failed to file information with the state which would alert it to the debtor's underpayment of tax"). *Also consider Lamborn v. United States (In re Lamborn)*, *supra* note 136, discussed below in text.

[144] *See, e.g., Lamborn v. United States (In re Lamborn)*, *supra* note 136, discussed below in text.

[145] *Compare In re Cohn*, *supra* note 142 (court observed that the statute simply gave the tax commissioner authority to change the form, but there was no indication that it had done so), *with Olson v. United States (In re Olson)*, 174 B.R. 543 (Bankr. D.N.D. 1994) and 1994 Bankr. LEXIS 1364 (Bankr. D.N.D. 1994) (North Dakota statute required either an amended return or such "other

A "hybrid" statute was considered by the bankruptcy court in *In re Lamborn.*[146] In that case, the debtors had filed amended Oklahoma returns reflecting an increase in income as a result of a federal audit, but because Oklahoma law provided taxpayers with the alternative of a written notification, the bankruptcy court considered the status of such a notice in determining whether a return was "required" or simply optional. In the court's view, the notice amounted to an "informal" tax return and should be so treated. The court could not discern any rational purpose or policy for having the priority status of a state's taxes dependent on whether the state required a formal or informal return. Accordingly, the court held that the concept of "a return" should be construed liberally to include effective substitutes for a formal return that may be permitted under state law, such as the written notification permitted by Oklahoma. As noted above, not all courts would agree.

As an additional ground for priority status, the bankruptcy court in *Lamborn* considered if and when the taxes shown on the amended returns were assessed. The debtors claimed that the taxes should be considered assessed either at the time they filed the amended returns (*i.e.*, self-assessed), or when Oklahoma commenced collection actions, both of which occurred more than 240 days before the bankruptcy case, and therefore outside the priority period. Under state law, however, an assessment required a specific official act. And it was, in Oklahoma's view, only that act which fixes the amount of tax owed by a taxpayer. Oklahoma maintained that the fact that it sought to collect an amount *admitted* to be owed did not mean that it agrees that such amount is *all* that is owing. Oklahoma thus argued that its actions to collect the tax shown on the amended returns did not constitute an assessment. The bankruptcy court agreed with Oklahoma that the taxes were still assessable at the time of the bankruptcy, despite Oklahoma's prior collection actions.

Another issue recently considered by at least one court is whether, as to an *initial* return, a "required" return is (1) a debtor specific concept that depends on whether the debtor, under its particular facts and circumstances, is required to file a return (*e.g.*, whether the debtor's gross income exceeds any minimum state tax filing threshold) or (2) a general concept that depends solely on whether the type of tax is one that in the particular jurisdiction generally requires the filing of a tax return. In *In re Carlin*,[147] the bankruptcy court concluded that the more rational reading is to focus solely on the type of tax.

As the foregoing discussion illustrates, the treatment of state tax claims—whether relating to federal adjustments, the timing of assessments,[148] or other-

(Footnote Continued)

information as required by the tax commissioner" and, in fact, told the taxpayer in writing with respect to certain of the tax years in question that no amended return was necessary given the information already obtained from the IRS; the court held that the wording of the statute made it relatively clear that the state could alter the form of the notice and, thus, it could not be said that a return was required).

[146] *Supra* note 136.

[147] *Carlin v. United States (In re Carlin)*, 318 B.R. 556, 2005-1 U.S.T.C. ¶50,215 (Bankr. D. Kan. 2004), *aff'd on other grounds*, 328 B.R. 221 (Bankr. 10th Cir. 2005).

[148] *See also supra* note 136; and federal authorities at § 1015.1.4 note 46.

wise[149]—will differ from state to state. Each applicable state's laws should be carefully examined.

### §1102.13.2 Priority Accorded Property Taxes

The treatment of property taxes has engendered considerable litigation. Unless specifically accorded an eighth priority, *unsecured* property taxes "incurred" during the bankruptcy case are granted a first (or technically, after the 2005 changes, a second[150]) priority and considered an administrative expense.[151] If "assessed" (or in bankruptcy cases commenced on or after October 17, 2005, "incurred") prior to the filing of the bankruptcy petition and last payable without penalty not earlier than one year prior to the filing of the petition, unsecured property taxes are granted an eighth

---

[149] For a discussion of the classification of a tax as a "tax on or measured by income or gross receipts," see the preceding section.

[150] First priority now goes to domestic support obligations, an item of no significance in corporate bankruptcies absent special circumstances.

[151] 11 U.S.C. §§507(a)(1), 503(b)(1)(B)(i) and (C); *see also Black v. Peoples Heritage Savings Bank* (*In re Martin*), 106 B.R. 334 (Bankr. D. Me. 1989). For a discussion of property taxes for which the debtor has responsibility as lessee (rather than directly), *see* §1102.13.3 below. For a discussion of the treatment accorded postpetition property taxes where the property has been "abandoned" under Bankruptcy Code section 554 from the bankruptcy estate back to the debtor (which in the corporate context are often thought of as the same taxable entity), *see Mailman Steam Carpet Cleaning, Inc. v. Salem* (*In re Mailman Steam Carpet Cleaning, Inc.*), 256 B.R. 240 (Bankr. D. Mass. 2000), and the discussion in Chapter 10 at §1015.1.1 above.

priority.[152] "Property taxes" have been broadly construed, in certain cases, to include water rents and garbage fees.[153]

A property tax will, however, be considered a *secured* claim, even though the lien arises postpetition, where the taxing authority either has a prior "interest in [the] property"[154] or (in bankruptcy cases commenced on or after October 22, 1994) the due

---

[152] 11 U.S.C. § 507(a)(7)(B); *In re New England Carpet Co.*, 26 B.R. 934, 940-941 (Bankr. D. Vt. 1983); *see Perpetual American Bank, FSB v. District of Columbia (In re Carlisle Court, Inc.)*, 36 B.R. 209 (Bankr. D. D.C. 1983) (rejects interpretation of 11 U.S.C. § 502(i) that would reclassify postpetition property tax claims as then seventh priority claims); *In re Pioneer Title Building*, 133 B.R. 822 (Bankr. W.D. Tex. 1991) (Bankruptcy Code section 502(b)(3), which limits property tax claim to value of estate's interest in the property, does not apply to postpetition property tax claim); *Universal Seismic Association, Inc. v. Harris County (In re Universal Seismic Associates, Inc.)*, 2002 U.S. App. LEXIS 6434 (5th Cir. 2002) (Bankruptcy Code section 502(b)(3) limits value of property tax claim to the gross value of the property at the inception of the bankruptcy case).

Under Bankruptcy Code section 506(c), a debtor-in-possession "may recover from property securing an allowed secured claim the reasonable, necessary costs and expenses of preserving, or disposing of, such property to the extent of any benefit to the holder of such claim." *See, e.g., In re Erie Hilton Joint Venture*, 125 B.R. 140 (Bankr. W.D. Pa. 1991) (applied to property taxes for the period following the lifting of the automatic stay to permit creditor to foreclose). Query whether this provision permits a debtor to deduct from the proceeds of a creditor's collateral sold during a bankruptcy case any outstanding real property and personal property taxes, even though such taxes would otherwise have been unsecured claims? Both the courts and, for bankruptcy cases commenced on or after October 17, 2005, the statute say yes. However, prior to the statutory change, the debtor first had to establish a direct benefit to the holder (which is generally difficult); the incidental benefit of general public services is insufficient. *See, e.g., United Jersey Bank v. Miller (In re C.S. Assoc.)*, 29 F.3d 903 (3d Cir. 1994) (direct benefit not proven); *Treasurer of Snohomish Cty., Wash. v. Seattle-First Natl. Bank (In re Glasply Marine Inds., Inc.)*, 971 F.2d 391 (9th Cir. 1992) (same). This does not appear to be the case after the statutory change. *See also* Jenks, The Bankruptcy Abuse Prevention and Consumer Protection Act of 2005: Summary of Tax Provisions, 79 Am. Bankr. L.J. (December 2005), at I.E., n.26.

Consistent with the literal language of Bankruptcy Code section 506(c), the Supreme Court, in *Hartford Underwriters Insurance Company v. Union Planters Bank, N.A.*, 120 S. Ct. 1942 (2000), held that only the debtor-in-possession or trustee was authorized to bring an action under Bankruptcy Code section 506(c) to surcharge a secured creditor's collateral. However, the Court specifically left open the possibility that a creditor—rather than bringing an action for its sole benefit—might bring a derivative claim in the name of the debtor-in-possession or the trustee for the benefit of the estate as a whole (such that any recovery would be distributed by the estate in accordance with normal Bankruptcy Code priorities). 102 S. Ct. at 1951 n.5. For a more detailed discussion of Bankruptcy Code section 506(c), *see* Carlson, Surcharge and Standing: Bankruptcy Code Section 506(c) After *Hartford Underwriters*, 76 Am. Bankr. L. J. 43 (2002).

[153] *See, e.g., In re New England Carpet Co., supra* note 152, at 936 (1983) (water rents); *In re Ayala*, 35 B.R. 651 (Bankr. D. Utah 1983) (garbage fees; facts indicate that garbage fees charged even if county garbage collection services not used); *but see, e.g., In re Lorber Ind. of Cal., Inc.*, 675 F.2d 1062, 1067 (9th Cir. 1982) (California industrial sewer user fees held not property taxes under prior Bankruptcy Act; court reasoned that use of sewer system was voluntary, even though no practical alternative may exist, and that the fees were charges for services rendered); *In re Adams*, 40 B.R. 545 (E.D. Pa. 1984) (water and sewer rents of a nature similar to that in *New England Carpet* held not property taxes, relying on *Lorber*), *rev'g*, 17 B.R. 742 (Bankr. E.D. Pa. 1982).

[154] *See* 11 U.S.C. § 546(b)(1). *See also* § 1007 note 3. There is a conflict in the courts as to what constitutes such a prior "interest in property." The extent of this conflict, however, has been reduced significantly by the Bankruptcy Reform Act of 1994, which now exempts from the automatic stay the creation or perfection of a statutory lien for any ad valorem property tax imposed by a local government (or the District of Columbia) that comes due postpetition. 11 U.S.C. § 362(b)(18), effective for bankruptcy cases commenced on or after October 22, 1994. For cases addressing this issue, *see, e.g., In re AR Accessories Group, Inc.*, 345 F.3d 454 (7th Cir. 2003), *cert. denied sub nom. Bank One v. Wisconsin Dep't of Workforce Dev.*, 2004 U.S. LEXIS 2399 (2004); *Lincoln Savings Bank, FSB v. Suffolk County*

date for the property tax is postpetition.[155] Since one suspects that in all states the tax lien for *real* property claims will arise no later than the due date of the tax, the effect of these two rules together is to permit most (but not all[156]) real property taxes to become secured claims and to place secured mortgage lenders in the same general position in respect of a local government's right to obtain payment of real property taxes as in an out-of-court workout or foreclosure proceeding. In contrast, the point at which a tax lien arises with respect to *personal* property taxes often varies from state to state. A claim for prepetition property taxes (whether or not secured) will be disallowed to the extent it exceeds the value of the estate's interest in the property.[157]

In general, secured claims may be paid over time (with interest).[158] The two principal exceptions are (1) postpetition secured claims that constitute administrative expense claims, and therefore generally must be paid on the effective date of the Chapter 11 plan, and (2) secured tax claims in bankruptcy cases commenced on or after October 17, 2005 that, absent their security, would be treated as an eighth priority tax claim, and thus must comply with the deferred payment conditions applicable for eighth priority tax claims.[159] Administrative expense status is generally accorded all postpetition taxes, both secured and unsecured, in bankruptcy cases commenced on or after October 17, 2005,[160] whereas for pre-October 17, 2005 bankruptcy cases, some courts have held that only unsecured postpetition taxes can qualify as administrative expenses.[161]

---

(Footnote Continued)

*Treasurer* (*In re Parr Meadow Racing Assn., Inc.*), 880 F.2d 1540 (2d Cir. 1989), *cert. denied*, 110 S. Ct. 869 (1990) (permitted postpetition lien where town assessors valued property "as of" a date prior to the bankruptcy petition; however, property taxes for all subsequent postpetition years were unsecured); *Makoroff v. The City of Lockport*, New York, 916 F.2d 890 (3d Cir. 1990) (contrary to the Second Circuit's decision in *Parr Meadow*, the Third Circuit required that the lien, although fixed postpetition, actually relate back and become effective as of a date prior to the bankruptcy case); *Maryland National Bank v. Mayor & City Council of Baltimore*, 723 F.2d 1138 (4th Cir. 1983) (upheld liens as to all postpetition property taxes, since county's "interest in property" was "ever-present"). *See also Mutual Ins. Co. of New York v. County of Fresno* (*In re D. Papagni Fruit Co.*), 132 B.R. 42 (Bankr. E.D. Cal. 1991) (discussed relative merits of different approaches); *In re Boston Harbor Marina Co.*, 157 B.R. 726 (Bankr. D. Mass. 1993) (same); *In re Summit Ventures, Inc.*, 135 B.R. 483 (Bankr. D. Vt. 1991) (same).

155 *See* 11 U.S.C. § 362(b)(18), discussed *supra* note 154. This is similarly true, in bankruptcy cases commenced on or after October 17, 2005, for special taxes or other special assessments on real property, whether or not ad valorem. 11 U.S.C. § 362(b)(18), *as amended by* P.L. 109-8, § 1225 (2005).

156 *See, e.g., United States Leather, Inc. v. City of Milwaukee* (*In re United States Leather, Inc.*), 271 B.R. 306 (Bankr. E.D. Wis. 2001) (tax lien for prepetition Wisconsin water and sewer charges that came into existence postpetition and was not retroactively effective as of the beginning of the year was avoidable).

157 *See* 11 U.S.C. § 502(b)(3); *City of Grand Rapids v. Arrene Properties Corp.* (*In re Arrene Properties Corp.*), 1989 U.S. Dist. LEXIS 17687 (W.D. Mich. 1989) (involved personal property taxes assessed against a leasehold interest); *In re Pioneer Title Building, Ltd.*, 133 B.R. 822 (Bankr. W.D. Tex. 1991) (Bankruptcy Code section 502(b)(3) held not applicable to postpetition property taxes).

158 11 U.S.C. § 1129(a)(9)(D), *as added by* P.L. 109-8, § 710(3) (2005).

159 *See* discussion at § 1102.14 below.

160 11 U.S.C. § 503(b)(1)(B)(i), *as amended by* P.L. 109-8, § 712(b) (2005).

161 *Compare, e.g., In re Boston Harbor Marina Co.*, *supra* note 154 (only *unsecured* postpetition taxes); *In re Florida Engineered Constr. Products, Corp.*, 157 B.R. 698 (Bankr. M.D. Fla. 1993) (same); *In re Broadway 704-706 Associates*, 154 B.R. 44 (Bankr. S.D.N.Y. 1993) (secured status is not elective; city

Although the statutory priority accorded to unsecured property taxes may be simply stated, the courts have had considerable difficulty in determining whether a real or personal property tax in respect of the year of the bankruptcy filing is properly accorded administrative expense treatment or an eighth priority. Consistent with the statutory scheme, most courts have adopted an "all or nothing" approach and have grappled with the factual and legal issue as to whether the property tax was "incurred" or "assessed" pre- or postpetition. The principal difficulty has stemmed from the fact that the "assessment" process for property tax purposes generally spans several months, with the tax often becoming effective (for personal liability or lien purposes) as of a date prior to the date the tax is fixed and notice is given. As a result, the decisions have varied as to whether the proper date is the effective date of the tax, the date on which the tax rate is set and the amount is fixed, or some other date.[162] Moreover, under the approach taken by some courts, the date that a property tax is

---

(Footnote Continued)

could not opt to be treated as a first priority unsecured claim in order to obtain full payment on the effective date), *with City of New York v. R. H. Macy & Co.* (*In re R. H. Macy & Co.*), 176 B.R. 315 (S.D.N.Y. 1994) (secured postpetition property taxes also entitled to first priority administrative expense treatment under plain reading of statute); *In re Soltan*, 234 B.R. 260, 269-272 (Bankr. E.D. N.Y. 1999) (same; but cautions that "[t]his conclusion would not apply to post-petition real property taxes applicable to real property of the estate which is not administered by the Trustee").

[162] *See, e.g., In re Fairchild Aircraft Corp.*, 124 B.R. 488 (W.D. Tex. 1991) (holding the term "assessed" refers to the *act* of assessment, rather than the effective date; thus, the tax was not "assessed" until after the tax rate was set); *In re Grivas*, 123 B.R. 876 (Bankr. S.D. Cal. 1991) ("escaped" property tax for back taxes was classified as a then seventh priority claim; the taxes were held to be assessed" under state law as of the lien date, which occurred prior to bankruptcy, even though the taxes were not entered on the tax rolls—and the assessment process was not completed "for the purpose of enforcing the collection" of taxes—until after the petition date).

Most recently, the Sixth Circuit in *City of White Plains v. A & S Galleria Real Estate, Inc.* (*In re Federated Dept. Stores, Inc.*), 270 F.3d 994 (6th Cir. 2001)—reaching the same conclusion as the district court in *In re R.H. Macy, infra*, and also involving New York City real property taxes—held that a property tax is "incurred" during the bankruptcy case if *in personam* liability for such taxes attaches during the case, such that the estate would continue to have liability for such taxes under applicable law even if the property was transferred mid-year to a third party. The Sixth Circuit similarly concluded that a property tax is "assessed" on the date that personal liability attaches, interpreting the concept of assessment as applying to the taxpayer's responsibility to pay the tax, and not to when the property's value is determined. Thus, the property taxes at issue were not "incurred" or "assessed" for priority purposes until the taxes were "levied" (which was also the date the taxes became due and payable). Prior to that time, the City only had an *in rem* interest. *See also In re R. H. Macy & Co.*, 157 B.R. 548 (S.D.N.Y. 1993) (involved New York City real property tax; held that *Parr Meadow* analysis, which involved whether a creditor had a prepetition "interest in property" for lien purposes, *see supra* note 154, did not apply for priority purposes; instead, the court believed that the more relevant date was the date as of which an enforceable *personal* obligation arose, which the court identified as the due date of the tax; case remanded for further consideration); *In re Broadway 704-706 Assoc., supra* note 161 (to similar effect).

Also, consider the Fourth Circuit decisions in *Forsyth County & City of Winston-Salem Tax Collector v. Burns*, 891 F.2d 286 (4th Cir. 1989) (unpublished decision, wherein the Fourth Circuit held that the property tax at issue was "incurred" on the date the tax rate was set; noted that result might be different for lien purposes) and *In re Members Warehouse, Inc.*, 991 F.2d 116 (4th Cir. 1993) (*per curiam*) (wherein the Fourth Circuit held that a prepetition payment and levy was not voidable, even though the property was subsequently sold prior to the fiscal year to which the property tax related, since the tax was "incurred" on the earlier date that the personal property was listed and lien arose; distinguished earlier 1989 decision in *Forsyth County* and rejected reasoning to the extent of any inconsistency).

"assessed" (which governs eighth priority status for pre-October 17, 2005 bankruptcy cases) may differ from the date the tax is "incurred" (which is relevant for first priority status). For example, a few courts have simply bifurcated the year and allocated the property tax on a ratable basis between the pre- and postpetition periods, even when the assessment date occurs postpetition.[163] This can (and has) lead to the absurd result that the property tax allocable to the prepetition portion of the year technically does not qualify for eighth priority treatment, since it was not assessed *before* the bankruptcy, whereas the same property tax owing for the preceding year would qualify. The 2005 bankruptcy reform act attempts to avoid some of the confusion by focusing on when a property tax is "incurred" for purposes of *both* administrative expense and eighth priority status.[164]

Also potentially at issue when it comes to prepetition property taxes, whether secured or unsecured, is the priority or treatment accorded to accrued interest, due to the high rate at which such interest accrues in many states (18 percent annually in some cases). As discussed at § 1015.1.5, *prepetition* interest on an unsecured prepetition tax claim is generally accorded the same priority as the basic tax claim. This is in contrast to the treatment of noncompensatory penalties (*i.e.*, true penalties that are not intended to compensate for the lost use of tax monies), which are not entitled to priority treatment. In the case of a secured tax claim, interest generally is permitted to accrue on a secured basis *postpetition* to the extent sufficient value exists in the underlying property. This is not the case, however, for noncompensatory penalties. Any postpetition accrual of a non-compensatory penalty would be relegated, at best,

---

(Footnote Continued)

However, both the Third and Fifth Circuits have held, on substantially similar facts, that a debtor's liability for personal property tax was "incurred" prepetition when the debtor's liability under state law first attached, even though the tax rate was not set and "assessment" did not occur until postpetition and, in the case before the Third Circuit, a tax lien did not arise until postpetition. In both cases, the record ownership and valuation was fixed or otherwise effective prepetition (as well as, in the case before the Fifth Circuit, the tax lien). *West Virginia State Dept. of Tax & Rev. v. IRS (In re Columbia Gas Trans. Corp.)*, 37 F.3d 982 (3d Cir. 1994), *aff'g*, 146 B.R. 114 (Bankr. D. Del. 1992) (to reach this result, the bankruptcy court equated the concept of "incurred" to when a "claim" within the meaning of the Bankruptcy Code first arose); *Midland Central Appraisal Dist. v. Midland Indus. Serv. Corp. (In re Midland Indus. Serv. Corp.)*, 35 F.3d 164 (5th Cir. 1994), *cert. denied*, 115 S. Ct. 1359 (1995).

In addition, some courts have focused on when a "claim" arose for bankruptcy purposes. *See, e.g., In re T&T Roofing and Sheet Metal, Inc.*, 156 B.R. 780 (Bankr. N.D. Tex. 1993) (City of Balch Springs personal property tax held "assessed" as of the effective date of the assessment, not the later date when the tax is actually determined; in court's view, no other result appropriately reconciled the various provisions of the Bankruptcy Code, including the broad definition of a "claim" in Bankruptcy Code section 101(5)); and the bankruptcy court in the *Columbia Gas* case, *supra*.

Further illustrating the lack of uniformity in outcome, even if not necessarily in approach, are two 1996 cases involving personal property taxes in Maryland. *Compare In re Garfinkels*, 203 B.R. 814 (Bankr. D.C. 1996) (administrative expense); *with In re Wang Zi Cashmere Products*, 202 B.R. 228 (Bankr. D. Md. 1996) (involving equivalent facts, held eighth priority). For a helpful discussion, *see* Richards, The Priority of Property Taxes in Bankruptcy, 3 J. Bankr. Prac. 431 (1994).

[163] *See, e.g., In re 7003 Bissonnet, Inc.*, 153 B.R. 455 (Bankr. S.D. Tex. 1992); *In re Brent Explorations, Inc.*, 91 B.R. 104 (Bankr. D. Colo. 1988). For a nonbifurcation example, consider the Third and Fifth Circuit decisions in the *Columbia Gas* and *Midland Industries* cases, *supra* note 162.

[164] *See* P.L. 109-8, § 706 (2005), replacing "assessed" with "incurred" in Bankruptcy Code section 507(a)(8)(B). For a brief summary of the property tax laws of select states for priority purposes, *see* Jenks, Ridgway and Purnell, 790 T.M., Corporate Bankruptcy, at V.D.3.b.(3).

to a general unsecured claim.[165] The secured status of any *prepetition* accrual of penalties is not affected. Due to the generally inferior treatment of penalties, the question presented where the statutory rate of interest is high is whether a portion of such interest is in fact penal, rather than compensatory, in nature and thus should be treated as a noncompensatory "penalty" for bankruptcy purposes. In one recent case, involving a secured Florida personal property tax, the court determined that the appropriate rate of "interest" was the "current government rate" of 9 percent, rather than the special 18 percent rate for property tax deficiencies.[166] Although new Bankruptcy Code section 511, added in 2005, requires the use of a state or local taxing authority's normal deficiency rate of interest for certain purposes, such as wherever the Bankruptcy Code specifically requires the payment of interest or employs a present value concept, section 511 does not appear to alter a debtor's ability to challenge the compensatory nature of a state or local taxing authority's interest claim for priority purposes.

### § 1102.13.3 Pass Through of Property Taxes as Lease Payments

When considering the priority of property taxes, it is important to distinguish between property taxes imposed directly on the debtor or its property (which are discussed in the preceding paragraphs) and property taxes that the debtor, as lessee, contractually agrees to reimburse. In the latter case, the courts are split as to whether a lessor's reimbursement claim represents a prepetition obligation or a postpetition obligation where the underlying tax arises prior to the bankruptcy, but the reimbursement payment becomes due postpetition.[167] Under Bankruptcy Code section 365(d)(3), any postpetition obligations arising under an unexpired lease for nonresidential real property generally must be paid on a current basis unless, and until, the lease is rejected.[168]

---

[165] *See* 11 U.S.C. § 506(b), and authorities discussed at § 1015 note 4, above.

[166] *In re Mulberry Phosphates, Inc.*, 283 B.R. 347 (Bankr. M.D. Fla. 2002), *relying on In re Koger Properties, Inc.*, 172 B.R. 351 (Bankr. M.D. Fla. 1994). The decision does not indicate the source of the "current government rate."

[167] Technically, it is the order for relief, rather than the bankruptcy petition, that serves as the relevant focal point. In the case of a voluntary bankruptcy, the date of the order for relief and the bankruptcy petition are the same; however, in an involuntary bankruptcy, the date of the order for relief generally occurs shortly afterward.

[168] *Compare In re Handy Andy Home Improvement Centers, Inc.*, 144 F.3d 1125 (7th Cir. 1998) (first Circuit Court opinion to address the issue; held that payment obligation should be regarded as arising day-by-day over the period of the lease to which the tax relates, regardless of the billing date; accordingly, the full payment obligation arose prepetition); *El Paso Props. Corp. v. Gonzalez (In re Furr's Supermarkets, Inc.)*, 283 B.R. 60 (Bankr. 10th Cir. 2002); *Child World, Inc. v. The Campbell/Massachusetts Trust (In re Child World, Inc.)*, 161 B.R. 571 (S.D.N.Y. 1993) (same); *In re Ames Dept. Stores, Inc.*, 136 B.R. 353 (Bankr. S.D.N.Y. 1992) (obligation arose prepetition, not when payment was due under lease); *In re Hills Stores Co.* (Bankr. S.D.N.Y.) (Brozman, J.) (bench decision, read into the record on July 23, 1991) (to same effect; applied the analysis in *Parr Meadow*, *supra* note 154, for purposes of determining when the underlying tax obligation arose; had no need to address pro-ration); *with Centerpoint Props. v. Montgomery Ward Holding Corp. (In re Montgomery Ward Holding Corp.)*, 268 F.3d 2005 (3d Cir. 2001) (2:1 decision; obligation arises when debtor is billed, even if landlord's obligation to pay underlying taxes accrued prepetition); *Montrose v. Northeast Consumer Technology Stores, Inc. (In re Appliance Store,*

In addition, if and when a debtor-in-possession decides to assume the lease, the debtor must compensate the lessor "for any actual pecuniary loss" resulting from any payment default, including as a result of the debtor's bankruptcy filing.[169] Query, whether this means that the debtor is responsible for any interest and penalties that the lessor incurs with respect to the late payment of any property taxes that, under the lease, would have been the debtor's obligation to pay but for the bankruptcy filing? Also whether it makes a difference if the lessor had the wherewithal to pay the tax but failed to do so?

## *§1102.14 Payment of Tax Claims*

Unless otherwise agreed to by the state or local taxing authority and the debtor-in-possession, a second (formerly first) priority administrative expense claim must be paid in cash on the effective date of the plan (if not required to be paid sooner in the ordinary course).[170] Administrative expense status is generally accorded all postpetition taxes, both secured and unsecured, in bankruptcy cases commenced on or after October 17, 2005, whereas for pre-October 17, 2005 bankruptcy cases, some courts have held that only unsecured postpetition taxes can qualify as administrative expenses.[171]

An unsecured eighth priority tax claim also must be paid in full but generally may be paid over time (with interest). For pre-October 17, 2005 bankruptcy cases, this period cannot exceed six years following the date on which the tax liability was assessed and the post-effective date interest on the deferred payments is computed using a market rate of interest.[172] In contrast, for subsequent bankruptcy cases, the deferred payment period is limited to five years following the commencement of the bankruptcy cases, the rate of post-effective date interest is fixed at the applicable deficiency rate under state or local law as of the confirmation date, and the payments must be made "in a manner not less favorable than the most favored nonpriority unsecured claim provided by the plan" other than so-called "convenience" claims (*see* §1016.1 above).[173]

---

(Footnote Continued)

*Inc.*), 148 B.R. 234 (Bankr. W.D. Pa. 1992) (obligation arose when payment was due under lease); *Inland's Monthly Income Fund, L.P. v. Duckwall-Alco Stores, Inc.* (*In re Duckwall-Alco Stores, Inc.*), 150 B.R. 965 (D. Kan. 1993) (same); *In re R. H. Macy & Co.*, 152 B.R. 869 (Bankr. S.D.N.Y. 1993), *aff'd*, 1994 WL 482948 (S.D.N.Y. 1994); *In re Almac's, Inc.*, 167 B.R. 4 (Bankr. D.R.I. 1994) (portion of property tax allocable on a pro rata basis, by month, to postpetition period payable when due under lease). *See Newman v. McCrory Corp.* (*In re McCrory Corp.*), 210 B.R. 934 (S.D.N.Y. 1997) (collecting cases).

169 *See* 11 U.S.C. §365(b)(1).

170 *See* 11 U.S.C. §1129(A); and 11 U.S.C. §503(b)(1)(B)(i) (administrative expense provision), *as amended by* P.L. 109-8, §712(b) (2005); in conjunction with 11 U.S.C. §507(a)(2), formerly, prior to the 2005 Act, §507(a)(1).

171 *See supra* note 161.

172 *See* 11 U.S.C. §1129(a)(9)(C), as in effect before amendment by P.L. 109-8, §710 (2005); *In re Burgess Wholesale Mfg. Opticians, Inc.*, 721 F.2d 1146, 83-2 U.S.T.C. ¶9727 (7th Cir. 1983).

173 *See* 11 U.S.C. §1129(a)(9)(C), *as amended by* P.L. 109-8, §710 (2005); 11 U.S.C. §511, *added by* P.L. 109-8, §704 (2005).

Similarly, secured tax claims generally may be paid over time (with interest) unless, as discussed above, the claim constitutes an administrative expense claim.[174] For bankruptcy cases commenced on or after October 17, 2005, the deferral conditions applicable to eighth priority claims also apply to secured claims that, absent the security, would be treated as eighth priority tax claims.[175]

## *§1102.15 Exemption from Stamp, Transfer, and Similar Taxes*

Under section 1146(a) of the Bankruptcy Code—formerly section 1146(c), and often referred to herein accordingly—state and local governments may not impose any stamp tax or similar tax on the issuance, transfer, or exchange of a security or the making or delivery of an instrument of transfer under a Chapter 11 plan confirmed by the bankruptcy court.[176] A stamp or similar tax includes a tax imposed on the transfer of real estate,[177] as well as a mortgage recording tax.[178] The Second Circuit has held that this provision does *not* apply to a tax imposed at the time of transfer on the transferor's gain (such as the former New York real property gains tax) as it is not a "stamp or similar tax."[179] In addition, two lower courts have held that sales and use

---

[174] *See* 11 U.S.C. §1129(a)(9)(D), *as added by* P.L. 109-8, §710(3) (2005) (plan requirements).

[175] *See* 11 U.S.C. §1129(a)(9)(C), *as amended by* P.L. 109-8, §710 (2005).

[176] 11 U.S.C. §1146(c) (also applies to federal taxes). This provision is derived from section 267 of the prior Bankruptcy Act. H.R. Rep. No. 595, 95th Cong., 1st Sess. 421-422 (1977). For a discussion of the history and application of this exemption, *see* Goldring, The Bankruptcy Code's Tax Exemption for Sales During Chapter 11 Reorganizations, 2 Corp. Tax'n #4, p. 55 (November/December 1989).

[177] *See, e.g., City of New York v. Jacoby-Bender, Inc. (In re Jacoby-Bender, Inc.)*, 758 F.2d 840 (2d Cir. 1985) (relief from New York City transfer tax on sale of building in Chapter 11 case); *NVR Homes, Inc. v. Clerks of the Circuit Courts (In re NVR, LP)* (4th Cir.), *supra* note 80 (involved Maryland and Pennsylvania real estate transfer taxes); *Delaware Director of Revenue v. CCA Partnership*, 72 B.R. 765 (D. Del. 1987) (purchaser of real estate from a Chapter 11 debtor held exempt from the Delaware Realty Transfer Tax), *aff'd without opinion*, 833 F.2d 303 (3d Cir. 1987); *In re Cantrup*, 53 B.R. 104 (Bankr. D. Colo. 1985) (irrelevant that transfer tax imposed on transferee rather than debtor); *In re Jacoby-Bender, Inc.*, 34 B.R. 60 (Bankr. E.D. N.Y. 1983) (tax on recording of a deed was a stamp or similar tax; exemption nevertheless denied for lack of a confirmed plan); *In re Lopez Dev., Inc.*, 154 B.R. 607 (Bankr. S.D. Fla. 1993) (dismissal of Chapter 11 case following confirmation of the plan did not undo tax exemption for properties already sold).

[178] *See, e.g., City of New York v. Baldwin League of Indep. Schools (In re Baldwin League of Indep. Schools)*, 110 B.R. 125 (S.D. N.Y. 1990). *See also* Goldring, *supra* note 7. As discussed below, the courts have differentiated between mortgage recording taxes incurred by the debtor and those incurred by a person purchasing property from the debtor.

[179] *995 Fifth Avenue Assoc., L.P. v. New York State Dept. of Tax'n and Finance (In re 995 Fifth Avenue Assoc., L.P.)*, 963 F.2d 503 (2d Cir. 1992), *cert. denied*, 113 S. Ct. 395 (1992) (the factors distinguishing the gains tax from a "stamp or similar tax" were that: (1) the tax was contingent on the transferor's recognizing a gain on the transfer; (2) the amount of the tax was a percentage of the gain, rather than the consideration paid; and (3) the tax rate of 10 percent greatly exceeded the rate normally imposed by a stamp or similar tax of one percent or less), *rev'g* 127 B.R. 533 (S.D.N.Y. 1991), 116 B.R. 384 (Bankr. S.D.N.Y. 1990) (among the reasons given by the lower courts in reaching the opposite conclusion were that payment of the gains tax was a precondition to the recording of the deed and that the gain on the sale of one property could not be offset against a loss on the sale of another property); *see also In re Jacoby-Bender*, 40 B.R. 10 (Bankr. E.D.N.Y. 1984) (gains tax not exempt), *appealed on other issues. But see Sheffel v. New York (In re Lehal Realty Associates)*, 133 B.R. 9 (Bankr. S.D.N.Y. 1991) (decided prior to Second Circuit decision). *Consider also* Rev. Rul. 80-121, 1980-1 C.B. 44 (concluded,

taxes are not exempt taxes,[180] although language encompassing such taxes is sometimes included within bankruptcy court exemption orders.[181]

**Under a confirmed plan.** Several courts also have considered what it means for a transfer of real property to be "under a plan confirmed" by the bankruptcy court and thus exempt from real estate transfer tax. The Second Circuit, in *In re Jacoby-Bender, Inc.*,[182] held that the plan need not include specifics about the transfer (or, apparently, even mention the transfer), so long as the transfer serves to execute or effectuate the confirmed plan. In that case, the confirmed plan simply mentioned that the necessary funding for the plan would be provided through a sale of a building owned by the debtor. No other specifics were given, and subsequent bankruptcy court approval was required to authorize the sale. In concluding that the subsequent sale was "under" the Chapter 11 plan, the Second Circuit observed that "Congress's apparent purpose in enacting Section 1146 was to facilitate reorganizations through giving tax relief, a purpose served equally well when the reorganization plan leaves details to be settled in the future."[183] The court also expressed the view that a "sale in general, following on confirmation of a plan, serves to make the plan effective."[184]

Some courts have applied the section 1146(a) exemption to preplan sales—the most recent being the Eleventh Circuit Court of Appeals in a 2007 decision.[185] Such

---

(Footnote Continued)

for federal income tax purposes, that the Vermont land gains tax was a transfer tax, not an income tax).

[180] *See In re GST Telecom, Inc.*, 2002 U.S. Dist. LEXIS 4662 (D. Del. 2002) (Washington State use tax, imposed at 6.5% rate, was "too large to qualify as a stamp or similar tax;" citing *995 Fifth Avenue, supra* note 179 in support), and Linden Hill Associates Limited Partnership, Md. Tax Court No. 424 (December 15, 1989) (did not apply to Maryland sales and use tax since tax was not imposed on a written instrument of transfer). This is one of several areas where the states, through the National Association of Attorneys General (NAAG), have undertaken to coordinate their positions. *See* Cordry, The Incredible Expanding § 1146(c), 21-JAN Am. Bankr. Inst. J. 10 (2003) (the author is in-house counsel for the NAAG).

[181] *See, e.g., In re A.H. Robins Co.*, 88 B.R. 742, 754 (E.D. Va. 1988) (joint memorandum of district judge and bankruptcy judge), and *In re 222 Liberty Associates*, Bankr. No. 88-11535S (Bankr. E.D. Pa. March 19, 1990) (confirmation order). *See generally* Goldring, *supra* note 176, at 59.

[182] *See City of New York v. Jacoby-Bender, Inc.* (*In re Jacoby-Bender, Inc.*) (2d Cir.), *supra* note 177.

[183] 758 F.2d at 842. *See also NVR Homes, Inc. v. Clerks of the Circuit Courts* (*In re NVR, LP*) (4th Cir.), *supra* note 80 (citing *Jacoby-Bender* with approval); *Baltimore County, Md. v. IHS Liquidating LLC* (*In re Integrated Health Services Inc.*), 2006 U.S. Dist. LEXIS 8403 (D. Del. 2006) (plan provided that the debtor's interest in its headquarters property shall be transferred to a liquidating trust, subject to a mortgage lien; such transfer effectively unraveled a prior "synthetic lease" and necessitated a transfer of title by the lessor-mortgage holder to the liquidating trust; citing *Jacoby-Bender*, the court held that the transfer by the lessor-mortgage holder was "under" the plan).

[184] 758 F.2d at 842.

[185] *See, e.g., Fla. Dept. of Rev. v. Piccadilly Cafeterias, Inc. (In re Piccadilly Cafeterias, Inc.)*, 484 F.3d 1299 (11th Cir. 2007), *petition for cert. filed* (8/30/2007), discussed below; *In re Permar Provisions, Inc.*, 79 B.R. 530 (Bankr. E.D.N.Y. 1987) (sale of real property prior to even a proposed Chapter 11 plan was exempt from transfer tax because "in all probability" the trustee's plan of liquidation would not have been confirmed without the sale); *City of New York v. Smoss Enterprises Corp.* (*In re Smoss Enterprises Corp.*), 54 B.R. 950 (E.D.N.Y. 1985) (preconfirmation sale of real property, pursuant to a prepetition contract entered into over a year before the sale, held exempt from transfer tax where the debtor's Chapter 11 liquidation plan was conditioned upon, and depended entirely on, the sale), *aff'd without op.*, 1986 U.S. App. LEXIS 28677 (2d Cir. 1986), *cert. denied*, 107 S. Ct. 110 (1986); *City of New York v.*

cases have done so where the transfers were "essential" or "necessary" to the consummation of the plan and, thus, in the court's view, properly considered to be part of the plan ultimately confirmed. The Fourth Circuit Court of Appeals, in a 1999 decision,[186] took exception to this line of cases, and held that the statute, by requiring that the transfer be "under" the confirmed plan, only exempts transfers occurring *after* confirmation of the plan. In the court's view, this result flowed from the plain meaning of the word "under"—meaning to be "subordinate" to or "authorized by." One judge, disagreeing that the statute was clear on its face, concurred in the court's holding on the grounds that a Congressionally conferred exemption from state and local taxation should be narrowly construed and that the court's reading was a reasonable one. Subsequently, both a Delaware and Illinois bankruptcy court and the Delaware district court declined to follow the Fourth Circuit's lead, finding the Fourth Circuit's reasoning unpersuasive.[187] Also of the view that the statutory language was unclear (in the absence of traditional temporal language, such as "at any time after"), the Delaware courts believed (and the Illinois court similarly expressed)

(Footnote Continued)

*Baldwin League of Indep. Schools* (*In re Baldwin League of Indep. Schools*), *supra* note 178 (pre-confirmation mortgage financing was a "reasonably necessary step in consummating the plan," as it provided the sole source of funding). This is another area that the states have targeted for litigation. *See* Cordry, *supra* note 180. These two cases (both within the Second Circuit) were subsequently distinguished, in a 2002 decision, by another New York district court, which held that section 1146(c) (as it was then designated) does *not* exempt transfers that take place before a plan of reorganization "has been drafted." The court expressly refrained from deciding whether section 1146(c) exempts a transfer that "occurs after a plan has been introduced but not yet confirmed," or is otherwise unavailable to liquidating corporations. *N.Y.C. Dept. of Finance v. 310 Associates, L.P.* (*In re 310 Associates, L.P.*) (Cedarbaum, J.), 282 B.R. 295 (S.D.N.Y. 2002). However, in a 2003 decision, involving a pre-plan sale of substantially all of the assets of Bethlehem Steel, a bankruptcy court within the same district agreed with the earlier two cases andapproved the section 1146(c) exemption provision in the sale order. *In re Bethlehem Steel Corporation*, Ch. 11 Case No. 01-15288 (BRL) (Lifland, J.) (Bankr. S.D.N.Y.) (April 22, 2003 bench ruling). A subsequent decision, also within the same district, provides strong support for the application of the exemption to transfers prior to the filing of a plan, but did not have to directly address that issue. *See In re Beulah Church of God in Christ Jesus, Inc.*, 316 B.R. 41 (Bankr. S.D.N.Y. 2004) (Drain, J.) (upholding application of exemption to a pre-confirmation sale of assets; a proposed plan had been filed prior to the sale of assets).

[186] *NVR Homes, Inc. v. Clerks of the Circuit Courts* (*In re NVR, LP*) (4th Cir.), *supra* note 80, *vacating in part, aff'g in part and rev'g in part*, 222 B.R. 514 (E.D. Va. 1998) (lower courts had held that the ongoing purchase and sale of real estate lots over the course of the approximately 1$^1/_2$ year bankruptcy were "essential to the formulation, confirmation and consummation of the Confirmed Plan" and, thus, exempt from transfer tax; the district court observed that the sales allowed the debtor to reduce prepetition debt during the bankruptcy by more than $50 million and facilitated a public debt offering that was a precondition to the plan's confirmation, thereby enabling the debtor to remain a viable operation and avoid liquidation).

[187] *In re Linc Capital, Inc.*, (Bankr. N.D. Ill.), *supra* note 77 (exempted pre-plan transfer "conditional upon confirmation of the Debtor's plan of reorganization entered into evidence at the sale hearing, and effective upon entry of order confirming such plan"); *Baltimore County v. Hechinger Inv. Co. of Del., Inc.* (*In re Hechinger Inv. Co. of Del., Inc.*), 254 B.R. 306 (Bankr. D. Del. 2000) (held that preplan sales that are "essential to or an important component of the plan process" qualify for the exemption; required an escrow of a portion of the sale proceeds pending confirmation of a plan; later reversed by Third Circuit), *aff'd*, 276 B.R. 43 (D. Del. 2002) (Sleet, J.) (preplan "transfers must be necessary or essential to confirmation"), *rev'd*, 2003 U.S. App. LEXIS 14449 (3d Cir. 2003). The same Delaware district court judge, as in *Hechinger Investment Co.*, so held again, two days later, in *In re GST Telecom, Inc.* (D. Del.) (Sleet, J.), *supra* note 180.

that a broader interpretation was more consistent with the realities of the plan process and the purpose of the exemption. On appeal, the Third Circuit (in a divided decision) reversed the Delaware district court, and agreed with the Fourth Circuit that preplan transfers are *not* exempt under section 1146(c) (as it was then designated).[188] Similarly, a subsequent Illinois district court decision (involving a different Chapter 11 debtor than in the earlier Illinois bankruptcy court decision referred to above) agreed with the Third and Fourth Circuits.[189]

Disagreeing with the Third and Fourth Circuits, the Eleventh Circuit's reasoning is similar to that of the Delaware courts (although not specifically cited in the opinion).[190] In response to the State of Florida's admonitions regarding a narrow construction of the exemption, the Eleventh Circuit stated that it also had to be mindful not to construe the statute too narrowly so as to abrogate the purpose of the exemption—particularly in light of the principle that a remedial statute such as the Bankruptcy Code should be liberally construed. The court thus observed that "it is just as probable that a debtor may need to close a sale as a condition precedent to the parties' willingness to proceed with confirmation of a plan as it is for the parties" to confirm a plan and then pursue a sale. Accordingly, the Eleventh Circuit held that the exemption "may apply to *those* pre-confirmation transfers that are necessary to the consummation of a confirmed plan of reorganization, which, at the very least, requires that there be some nexus between the pre-confirmation sale and the confirmed plan."[191] The State of Florida has filed a petition for *certiorari* with the Supreme Court. Within the New York Southern District, the courts are currently split as to the applicability of the exemption to preplan transfers *at least* where, at the time of transfer, no plan has been drafted and filed with the court.[192] A further bankruptcy court decision within the same district presents a respectful opposing view to that of the Third and Fourth Circuits.[193] Although the bankruptcy court in that case approved the application of the exemption to preplan transfers, the court did not have to directly address the pre-filed plan controversy (there having already been a proposed plan on file). Nevertheless, the court's reasoning strongly supports the absence of any distinction.

**Non-debtor involvement and benefit.** The courts have also been sensitive of the extent to which the transfer in question directly involves the debtor or otherwise facilitates the consummation of the Chapter 11 plan. For example, the Fourth Circuit,

---

[188] *In re Hechinger Inv. Co. of Del., Inc.* (3d Cir.), *supra* note 185.

[189] *Illinois v. National Steel Corp.*, 2003 U.S. Dist. LEXIS 15695 (N.D. Ill. 2003).

[190] Interestingly, the Eleventh Circuit had to do a little bit of back peddling, since it had seemingly approved of the Third and Fourth Circuit's interpretations in an earlier decision on a "somewhat similar issue" in *State of Florida v. T.H. Orlando Ltd. (In re T.H. Orlando Ltd.)*, 391 F.3d 1287, 1291 (11th Cir. 2004), *reh'g, en banc, denied* 2005 U.S. App. LEXIS 9157 (2005).

[191] The Eleventh Circuit did not consider whether the factual context in which the issue arose satisfied this standard, since the issue raised on appeal was solely whether, as a matter of law, section 1146(c) could properly be applied to preplan transfers.

[192] *Compare In re 310 Associates, L.P.* (S.D.N.Y.), discussed *supra* note 185, *with In re Bethlehem Steel Corporation* (Bankr. S.D.N.Y.), *supra* note 185.

[193] *In re Beulah Church of God in Christ Jesus, Inc.* (Bankr. S.D. N.Y.), *supra* note 185.

in *In re Eastmet Corp.*,[194] held that section 1146(c) does not exempt a purchaser of property under a confirmed Chapter 11 plan from a recording tax imposed in connection with the financing of the purchase, at least where the plan does not address the purchaser's method of financing, the lenders are not parties to the plan and the debtor is not a party to the financing.

Also on the basis that the sale at issue was between nondebtors, the bankruptcy court in *In re Kerner Printing Co., Inc.*,[195] denied the application of the exemption in the following situation. The debtor was a lessee of certain condominium units in New York City, with a one-dollar purchase option. Pursuant to the terms of the confirmed Chapter 11 liquidating plan, the debtor was deemed to exercise its purchase option and thereafter transfer all right, title and interest in the three units to a third party (namely, the debtor's principal mortgage lender or its designee) free and clear of all liens and encumbrances other than existing mortgages. Under the plan, the third party, in its sole discretion, would be authorized to sell the units within at most six years. Any sale proceeds remaining after payment of the mortgages and costs of sale would be returned to the debtor for distribution in accordance with the plan. The City challenged the plan provision purporting to exempt from the City's real property transfer tax the future sale by the third party (but not the transfer to or from the debtor), on the grounds that such sale was between nondebtors. The Bankruptcy Court agreed with the City, rejecting the argument that the third party was simply acting as a sales agent, in that the third party "has complete control over how, when, or to whom" the units would be sold, subject only to certain time constraints.

In contrast, the district court in *State of Maryland v. Antonelli Creditors' Liquidating Trust*[196] held that section 1146(c) would exempt from transfer tax any postbankruptcy transfers of real property by a liquidating trust established under the debtors' confirmed Chapter 11 plan. The court distinguished *Kerner Printing* in that, in *Antonelli Creditors' Liquidating Trust*, the liquidating entity was a new entity created and operating under the plan, was controlled by a committee of trustees comprised of six creditors and one representative of the debtors, had as its sole purpose the orderly liquidation of the bankruptcy estate for distribution to all the debtors' creditors, and would terminate when all transfers were completed. In contrast, the "liquidating" entity in *Kerner Printing* was the principal creditor most likely to benefit from the subsequent transfers.

The district court viewed the liquidating trust, both "theoretically and practically," as an extension of the debtors. The court justified this conclusion, in part, on the basis that the liquidating trust furthered the public's interest in sound and

---

[194] *Mensh v. Eastern Stainless Corp.* (*In re Eastmet Corp.*), 907 F.2d 1487 (4th Cir. 1990) (also held that no exemption was available under Maryland state law). *See also In re Amsterdam Avenue Development Assocs.*, 103 B.R. 454 (Bankr. S.D.N.Y. 1989) (same); *In re Bel-Aire Investments, Inc.*, 142 B.R. 992 (Bankr. M.D. Fla. 1992) (postsale refinancing of properties obtained by purchaser in conjunction with the refinancing of properties retained by debtor did not support purchaser's exemption from recording taxes; the court observed that the refinancing benefited the purchaser as well as the debtor and that it "was not the only option available" to the purchaser); *City of New York v. Baldwin League of Indep. Schs.* (*In re Baldwin League of Independent Schools*), *supra* note 178.

[195] 188 B.R. 121 (Bankr. S.D.N.Y. 1995).

[196] 191 B.R. 642 (D. Md. 1995), *aff'd, in part on other grounds*, 123 F.3d 777 (4th Cir. 1997).

efficient administration of bankruptcy estates. The liquidating trust eliminated the need to prolong the bankruptcy cases during the liquidation process, which would have entailed the concomitant increase in the expenditure of the debtors' assets and the bankruptcy court's time. Accordingly, the court did not view the subsequent sale by the liquidating trust as involving a transfer between nondebtors.

On appeal, the Fourth Circuit affirmed the district court's decision but on procedural grounds which are equally noteworthy and, in part, bear on the substantive application of the exemption. Significantly, each of the three taxing authorities that challenged the applicability of the exemption were served copies of the debtors' Chapter 11 plan as prepetition creditors, which expressly provided that any transfers by the liquidating trust would be exempt from transfer tax. The accompanying disclosure statement also included a complete listing of the debtors' properties and their location. None of the taxing authorities objected to confirmation of the debtors' Chapter 11 plan, nor did they appeal the confirmation order.[197] In fact, it was not until one year after the sales by the liquidating trust, and after the recording of the sales without the payment of transfer taxes, that the taxing authorities sought payment of the taxes from the liquidating trust. The Fourth Circuit held that each of the taxing authorities, having had sufficient notice of both the plan and confirmation to put them on legal notice as to claimed exemption, were barred from collaterally attacking the plan and confirmation order.

In addition, the Fourth Circuit rejected the taxing authorities' argument that the bankruptcy court exceeded its jurisdiction in confirming the plan with the claimed exemption. In this regard, the court observed that the jurisdictional issue was not whether the court misconstrued section 1146(c) in applying it to liquidating trusts, but whether the exemption was "related to" the bankruptcy case, which it clearly was. However, to dispel any argument that the court order had only "a frivolous pretense to validity" and thus was without binding force, the court carefully considered the arguments favoring exemption. In particular, the court focused on the limitations of its earlier decision in *In re Eastmet Corp.* (discussed above), pointing out that, in the present case, the sales by the liquidating trust were required by, and an integral part of, the plan and that the sole function of the liquidating trust was to effectuate the debtors' sale of its assets to third parties and the distribution of the proceeds to creditors. Thus, despite the liquidating trust being a nondebtor entity, the Fourth Circuit found that it was "entirely reasonable"—and "far from" frivolous—to conclude that transfers by the liquidating trust were transfers under the debtors' Chapter 11 plan. The court stayed clear of reaching the ultimate merits of the issue. The Eleventh Circuit Court of Appeals, in *In re T.H. Orlando Ltd.*,[198] subsequently found the Fourth Circuit's reasoning in this regard to be persuasive of the substantive

---

[197] Moreover, two of the three taxing authorities (State of Maryland and Montgomery County) had been the subject of a preconfirmation declaratory judgment motion by the debtors (which was dismissed as premature) with respect to the exemption provision in the plan, and thus had specific notice of the provision. This proved to be a critical fact at the district court level. Given such prior notice, the district court had held that the State and county were bound by the plan regardless of the merits of their challenge. It was only as to the challenge by the third taxing authority (Baltimore County) that the district court proceeded to rule on the merits.

[198] *State of Florida v. T.H. Orlando Ltd.* (*In re T.H. Orlando Ltd.*) (11th Cir.), *supra* note 190.

conclusion. In that case, the only lender willing to refinance the debtors' reorganization conditioned its offer to lend on the agreement of the adjacent hotel owner (a nondebtor) to refinance its hotel at the same time. The neighboring owner agreed ("solely as an accommodation to the debtors"), and the plan made clear that such refinancing was a necessary part of the plan. The Eleventh Circuit concluded that the plain language of section 1146(c) exemption encompasses any transfer authorized by the plan that is necessary to the plan's consummation, and that there is nothing in the plain language of section 1146(c) that otherwise precludes its application to nondebtors.[199]

**Binding effect of court declared exemption.** The Fourth Circuit in *Antonelli Creditors' Liquidating Trust* (discussed above) also rejected the taxing authorities' assertion that the bankruptcy court's confirmation order was not binding on them because of the immunity accorded the states under the Eleventh Amendment. The court pointed out that such immunity does not affect the force of the bankruptcy court's order, but, rather, the ability of a state to be haled into federal court (*see* § 1102.5 above). However, because the federal courts have exclusive jurisdiction over the federal bankruptcy laws, if a state chooses to challenge the bankruptcy court's order, as was done in this case, it must submit to federal jurisdiction.

The Fourth Circuit had an opportunity to refine its view of the application of section 1146(c) in *In re NVR, LP*.[200] In that case, the debtor sought a refund of state and local real estate transfer and recordation taxes previously paid, claiming exemption under Bankruptcy Code section 1146(c) and the provisions of its Chapter 11 plan incorporating such exemption. The Maryland and Pennsylvania taxing authorities declined such refund, following which the debtor requested the bankruptcy court declare that the debtor's continual purchases and sales of real property during the bankruptcy case were exempt under section 1146(c) and the plan. The bankruptcy court so held, but, in response to the States' Eleventh Amendment defense, stated that its decision was binding only as to the collection of local and *not* state transfer tax. The district court reversed (or, more accurately, nullified) the bankruptcy court's Eleventh Amendment finding as to the States. In the district court's view, the debtor's declaratory action was not a "suit" against any state; rather, the debtor's action was a request to clarify the intended coverage of the plan's exemption provision (in accordance with the court's retention of jurisdiction over the plan). The notice provided to the States did not compel them to appear, although they could if desired. Thus, the debtor's action was entirely proper. However, the district court made clear

---

[199] *See also Baltimore County, Md. v. IHS Liquidating LLC (In re Integrated Health Services Inc.)* (D. Del.), *supra* note 183, involving the unraveling of a "synthetic lease" under which the debtor was in form the leasee but in substance the property owner. In furtherance of the debtor's Chapter 11 plan, the lessor-mortgage holder transferred title to the property to a liquidating trust established under the debtor's plan. The court held that the transfer to the trust was exempt under section 1146(c), even though involving a non-debtor. The court equated the transfer to the initial transfer of the condominium units in *Kerner Printing Co.* (discussed earlier in the text) to the debtor and then from the debtor to its lender or the lender's designee, which the court in that case held to be exempt. (The problematic transfer in *Kerner Printing Co.* was the intended future sale by the lender.)

[200] *NVR Homes, Inc. v. Clerks of the Circuit Courts (In re NVR, LP)* (4th Cir.), *supra* note 80, *vacating in part, aff'g in part and rev'g in part*, 222 B.R. 514 (E.D. Va. 1998), also discussed at *supra* note 186 and accompanying text.

that, in so concluding, it neither reached nor decided whether the bankruptcy court's order interpreting the exemption is binding "in any way" on the States. That question, the court stated, "is appropriately left to the court or state agency to which [the debtor] must apply for a refund."[201] The States then appealed to the Fourth Circuit.

The Fourth Circuit disagreed with the district court. Acknowledging that the debtor's motion to determine whether the real estate transfers in question were exempt from state and local transfer and recordation taxes under section 1146(c) was not in and of itself an action that compelled the States to appear in federal court, the Fourth Circuit nevertheless held that the substantive effect of the action must also be considered and that, in this light, the proceeding constituted a "suit in law or equity" within the meaning of the Eleventh Amendment. The Fourth Circuit observed that, in contrast to the situation in *Antonelli Creditors' Liquidating Trust*, the debtor here had paid the taxes and was seeking a determination that would constitute an improper advisory opinion absent the bankruptcy court's ability to order the refund of the taxes. Thus, the court concluded that the debtor's action was in fact one in which the adjudication depended on the court's jurisdiction over the States, that the debtor "clearly sought a determination that the [S]tates owed [the debtor] money—repayment of exempt transfer and recordation taxes—and [that] a favorable decision would require that a federal court raid Maryland's and Pennsylvania's treasuries." Accordingly, the Fourth Circuit held that the debtor's action as to the States was barred by the Eleventh Amendment, and vacated the district court's decision in this regard. Because local governments have no Eleventh Amendment immunity, the Fourth Circuit proceeded to address the substantive application of section 1146(c) in relation to the local taxing authorities. Presumably, the Fourth Circuit's conclusion that an action as to the States was barred would no longer be correct in light of the Supreme Court's subsequently declared view, in *Central Virginia Community College v. Katz* (discussed at § 1102.5 above), as to the limited nature of a state's sovereign immunity in bankruptcy cases.

In *In re Hechinger Investment Co. of Delaware*,[202] the State of Maryland again attempted to defend against a bankruptcy court's adjudication of the section 1146(c) exemption—in this case the action arose (as in *Antonelli Creditors' Liquidating Trust*) in advance of the tax payment. The State tried a slightly new twist, arguing that the defending character of a "suit" against a state is one that, looking to the substance of the action, would result in a loss to the state, either because the state would have to affirmatively turn over money or property (as in *NVR*), or because the state's interest would be adversely affected, such as preventing it from collecting revenue. Predating the *Katz* decision, both the Delaware bankruptcy court and district court firmly rejected this position, employing the Fourth Circuit's analysis in *Antonelli Creditors' Liquidating Trust*. The courts also asserted that Maryland's position could

---

[201] *Cf. In re Lehal Realty Assocs.*, *supra* note 179 (decided prior to the 1994 Act changes to Bankruptcy Code section 106; bankruptcy court had jurisdiction to determine scope of exemption under section 1146(c) but could not order state to refund taxes already paid due to state's Eleventh Amendment immunity).

[202] *Supra* note 185.

arguably amount to a "constitutional immunity from federal law," which it found untenable.[203]

**Exemptions under state or local law.** Some state and local authorities have also issued guidance with respect to the application of section 1146(c) in particular situations. For example, the Florida Department of Revenue, in a Technical Assistance Advisement (which operates like to a private letter ruling), concluded that the execution and recordation of substitute, replacement or additional collateral for certain cash flow notes previously issued pursuant to a confirmed Chapter 11 plan, and the renewal or modification of the original notes and mortgages by the debtor (other than in connection with additional advances), were exempt from both the Florida Documentary Stamp Tax and Intangible Tax under section 1146(c) of the Bankruptcy Code.[204]

Aside from the Bankruptcy Code, state and local statutes may provide their own bankruptcy exceptions.[205]

## §1102.16 Exemption from State Tax Bulk Sales Statutes

In *In re Missouri Precision Castings, Inc.*,[206] the issue arose whether, pursuant to the Missouri bulk sales statute, a purchaser of a business from a bankruptcy trustee would have successor liability for unpaid *pre-existing* taxes (including income taxes) of the debtor. Interpreting the bulk sales statute in conjunction with the bankruptcy trustee's status as a lien creditor pursuant to Bankruptcy Code section 544(a), the bankruptcy court held that a sale by the bankruptcy trustee free and clear of all liens

---

203 *But consider In re Mitchell* (9th Cir.), *supra* note 33, at 1117 (concluding that a dischargeability proceeding against a state was barred by the Eleventh Amendment, because a decision for the debtors "would effectively prevent the state from collecting monies otherwise due to it"). The State, as an alternative to its Eleventh Amendment immunity argument, argued that the debtor's action violated the state Tax Injunction Act (*see* generally §1102.4 above). Both courts rejected this position as well, on the grounds that (i) Bankruptcy Code section 505(a) allows the court to determine the "amount or legality of any tax . . . whether or not previously assessed . . ." (*see* §1102.11 above), which includes a determination under section 1146(c), (ii) section 1146(c) is itself a tax exemption, and thus the bankruptcy court would not be enjoining the State's collection of a tax, but enforcing a tax exemption, and (iii) by the same accord, there was no "plain, speedy and efficient remedy" under state law.

204 Supplement to Fla. Tech. Assist. Adv. 94(M)-006, *reprinted at* 94 STN 148-11. Prior to the Fourth Circuit's decision in *In re NVR, LP* (discussed *supra* at note 177), the Florida Department of Revenue had also issued technical advice exempting preplan transfers in accord with *Permar Provisions* and *Smoss Enterprises, supra* note 185—Fla. Tech. Assist. Adv. 93(M)-008, *reprinted at* 1993 WL 591441—and despite the Fourth Circuit's decision, still exempted pre-plan transfers under its regulations. *See* Fla. Tech. Assist Adv. 06M-001 (January 30, 2006). *See also* Fla. Tech. Assist. Adv. 94(M)-002 (determining not to impose a tax on the transfer of a warranty deed from a third party to the debtor's nonbankrupt subsidiary, as it appeared too difficult and costly since (i) the debtor was instrumental in providing and obtaining the financing for the subsidiary and might be viewed by the bankruptcy court as a *de facto* party to the deed and (ii) the bankruptcy court was out-of-state). Nevertheless, the Florida Department of Revenue proceeded to challenge preplan transfers and lost in *In re Piccadilly Cafeterias* (11th Cir.), *petition for cert. filed*, *supra* note 185.

205 *See, e.g.*, New York Tax Law §1405(b)(8) (exempting from the New York State Real Estate Transfer Tax all conveyances in bankruptcy).

206 *Checkett v. Benton (In re Missouri Precision Castings Inc.)*, 128 B.R. 544 (Bankr. W.D. Mo. 1991).

(and following notice to all creditors, including the Missouri Department of Revenue) amounted to the "enforcement" of a "lien" by a lien creditor within the meaning of the bulk sales statute and, thus, pursuant to the statute, no successor liability would attach.

In contrast, in *State of Ohio v. B/G 98 Co., LLC*,[207] an Ohio Court of Appeals held that a sale by a Chapter 11 debtor did *not* qualify for any recognized exception to successor liability for unpaid taxes under Ohio law, including an apparent exception for judicial sales. In the Ohio court's view, a judicial sale was one in which the court (rather than the debtor) was considered to be the vendor, and this did not appear to be the case in a court-supervised sale under Bankruptcy Code section 363, the governing provision for sales of assets in bankruptcy.[208] The court acknowledged that under the former Bankruptcy Act the bankruptcy court itself was conceived to be the seller when property of the bankruptcy estate was sold.

Still, many state tax bulk sales statutes contain specific exemptions for transfers in bankruptcy.[209]

## *§1102.17 Determination of Tax Consequences of Plan*

The proponent of a Chapter 11 plan may request (with the bankruptcy court's approval) a ruling from a state or local taxing authority declaring the state or local tax effects of the plan. If the proponent either (a) receives a response from the state or local taxing authority with which it disagrees, or (b) has not received a response within 270 days after such request, the bankruptcy court may declare the state or local tax effects of the plan.[210] Any ruling or determination is limited to questions of law.[211] Accordingly, the ruling or determination cannot address questions of fact, such as the incurrence of specific deductions or the dollar amount of any tax attributes that survive the reorganization.[212]

The practical utility of this provision is greatly limited by the fact that it only applies to state and local (and not federal taxes), and generally requires at least a 9-10 month lead time. Moreover, it remains to be seen what effect a state's Eleventh

---

[207] 2001 Ohio App. LEXIS 757 (Ct. App. Ohio 2001).

[208] In addition, the purchaser made the argument that any successor liability was negated by the express provisions of the bankruptcy court order. However, the court found sufficient evidence surrounding the parties' reduction in purchase price in conjunction with the bankruptcy court's approval (which reduction, testimony showed, equaled the amount of the debtor's unpaid taxes) to preclude summary judgment on such basis.

[209] *See, e.g.*, New York Tax Law §537.1(a)(4) (excluding from definition of "bulk sale," under the sales and use tax, any sales by "trustees in bankruptcy or any public officer under judicial process"); Rhode Island Gen. Laws §44-11-29(b) (1964) (exempting sales by "trustees in bankruptcy"; the Division on Taxation has confirmed, by private letter, that this includes sales by debtors-in-possession).

[210] 11 U.S.C. §1146(b), formerly §1146(d). No similar provision exists for federal tax purposes. *See* discussion at Chapter 10, §1013.3.

[211] Id.

[212] 124 Cong. Rec. H11,115 (daily ed. September 28, 1978) (statement of Rep. Edwards), S17,432 (daily ed. October 6, 1978) (statement of Sen. DeConcini).

Amendment immunity will have (if any) on the bankruptcy court's ability to declare the state tax effects of a plan (*see* § 1102.5).

In addition to the special procedural rules for bankruptcy transactions provided in the Bankruptcy Code, state and local tax laws may contain their own special procedural provisions. For example, it is generally the policy of most states, following the commencement of a bankruptcy case, to grant release from penalties imposed for failure to pay prepetition taxes.

## § 1103 SUBSTANTIVE STATE AND LOCAL TAX ASPECTS OF BANKRUPTCY

The special tax provisions of the Bankruptcy Code relating to the substantive state and local tax aspects of a bankruptcy case are intended to create a balance between bankruptcy and tax policy.[1] These provisions included, when the Bankruptcy Code was enacted in 1978, rules relating to the tax-free status of a bankruptcy reorganization and the consequences of COD income. By placing certain substantive tax aspects in the Bankruptcy Code, uniformity is created among all states, significantly reducing the uncertainty of state and local tax consequences. Another goal of the provisions is to minimize the out-of-pocket tax consequences of bankruptcy restructuring transactions, thereby allowing a debtor corporation to devote its assets to rehabilitating its business. States may provide more beneficial rules. These provisions were substantially revised as part of a comprehensive reform bill in 2005, with the principal objective of creating greater conformity with the federal income tax rules.[2] However, among the changes was the removal of *any* provision addressing the tax-free status of a bankruptcy reorganization.

### *§ 1103.1 Tax-Free Status of Bankruptcy Reorganization in Pre-10/17/05 Bankruptcy Cases*

Bankruptcy Code section 346(g)(1)(C), as in effect for bankruptcy cases commenced *before* October 17, 2005, provides that for state and local law purposes neither gain nor loss shall be recognized on a transfer by a debtor corporation in a Chapter 11 proceeding to an affiliate participating in a joint plan with the debtor, or to a successor of the debtor under the plan, "except to the extent that such transfer results in the recognition of gain or loss under section 371 of the Internal Revenue Code of 1986."

Code § 371 was repealed for federal income tax purposes by the Bankruptcy Tax Act of 1980.[3] Presumably this does not affect the application of Bankruptcy Code

---

[1] **§ 1103** H.R. Rep. No. 595, 95th Cong., 1st Sess. 274 (1977).

[2] *See* § 1101, at note 3; and P.L. 109-8, § 719 (2005) (reflecting a total rewrite of Bankruptcy Code sections 346, 728 and part of 1146).

[3] *See* Code § 370 (Code § 371 no longer applicable to proceedings commenced after October 1, 1979).

section 346(g)(1)(C), but nonetheless the meaning of its reference to Code § 371 is less than entirely clear.

In reorganizations to which it applied, Code § 371 required the transferor corporation to recognize gain (but not loss) to the extent of any boot that it received but did not distribute to its shareholders or creditors.[4] The section applied to Chapter X proceedings under the prior Bankruptcy Act but not to Chapter XI proceedings.[5] And, while Code § 371 had its own rather relaxed continuity of interest and business rules, it did not apply unless these rules were met.[6]

Does the reference in Bankruptcy Code section 346(g)(1)(C) to "the recognition of gain or *loss under* section 371" (emphasis added) mean only that gain will be recognized to the transferor to the extent the transferor does not distribute boot to shareholders or creditors, whether or not the transaction would have qualified under Code § 371? Or does it mean that the nonrecognition rule will not apply at all unless the transaction would have qualified under Code § 371, and even then it will not apply to the extent boot is not distributed?

The use of the word "under" suggests the first interpretation, but the reference to "loss" suggests the second. There is no guidance in the legislative history. If the second interpretation prevails, then the tax advisor will have to determine whether Code § 371 would have applied to the transaction if it were still law. And, since the distinction between Chapter X and Chapter XI proceedings was not continued in the Bankruptcy Code, there would be the further question as to whether Code § 371 should be considered for this purpose to apply to all Chapter 11 proceedings under the Bankruptcy Code, or only to those that could have been treated as Chapter X proceedings under the old law. A sensible practical answer to the latter question would be to treat all Chapter 11 proceedings as so qualifying, but one must recognize that the law is not always construed in a practical way.

Bankruptcy Code section 346(g)(1)(C)(2) goes on to say that the transferee "of a transfer of a kind specified in this subsection shall take the property transferred with the same character, and with the transferor's basis [except as adjusted for COD income] and holding period." The question under this provision is what is meant by "a transfer of a kind specified in this subsection"? Does it include any transfer described in Bankruptcy Code section 346(g)(1)(C), whether or not it would have qualified under Internal Revenue Code § 371? This is the same question as the one we have just been discussing, and there is no guidance on the answer.

These are the only references in the tax portion of the Bankruptcy Code to two-company reorganizations (and, as indicated above, only apply to bankruptcy cases commenced *before* October 17, 2005). The Bankruptcy Code contains no limitations on the way that state and local governments can tax the creditors or shareholders of a debtor involved in a two-company bankruptcy transaction. Nor does it say anything about the carryover of NOLs to the successor corporation. This is left to be deter-

---

[4] *See* Code § 371; Reg. §§ 1.371-1 *et seq.* For an excellent discussion of many of these rules, *see* Tillinghast and Gardner, Acquisitive Reorganizations and Chapters X and XI of the Bankruptcy Act, 26 Tax L. Rev. 663 (1971).

[5] *See* GCM 34230 (November 28, 1969).

[6] *Supra* note 4.

mined by local law.[7] In this regard, it should be noted that many states and localities do not permit NOL carryovers of any kind, even to the corporation that incurred the loss.

## *§1103.2 State and Local Tax Consequences of COD Income*

Bankruptcy Code section 346(j) generally provides that, for state or local tax purposes, income is not to be realized by the estate, the debtor corporation or a successor to the debtor by reason of the cancellation of debt in a bankruptcy case—with the concomitant cost of attribute reduction. From this general perspective, the Bankruptcy Code's basic attitude toward COD is unchanged by the 2005 bankruptcy reform bill. But, as is often said, the devil is in the details. Although section 346(j) has always had attribute reduction provisions similar to those in Code §108, there have been significant differences (as discussed below). For new bankruptcy cases, section 346(j) adopts a purer form of conformity with the federal income tax treatment of COD.

### §1103.2.1 Current (Post-2005 Act) Bankruptcy Cases: Code §108 Rules

For bankruptcy cases commenced *on or after* October 17, 2005, Bankruptcy Code section 346(j) provides that, for purposes of any state or local law imposing a tax on or measured by income, no COD income is realized by the estate, debtor corporation or any successor "except to the extent, if any, that such income is subject to tax under the Internal Revenue Code of 1986."[8] This effectively incorporates the various exclusions and exceptions to COD income in Code §108, as well as the various rules for measuring the amount of COD income—including those in Code §108(e)(10) (utilizing issue price concepts) and the potentially differing treatment of recourse and nonrecourse debt in connection with the transfer of the underlying property.

Moreover, section 346(j) incorporates the attribute reduction rules in Code §108(b), by providing that, whenever the Internal Revenue Code requires that the excluded COD income be applied to reduce tax attributes of the debtor corporation, a similar reduction shall be made under state or local law to the extent such state or local law recognized such attributes.[9] Only after such available attributes are absorbed—presumably employing federal concepts such as the "liability limitation" under Code §1017(b)(2) in the case of basis reductions—can state or local law provide for the reduction of other attributes with respect to any excluded COD income not yet applied.[10]

---

[7] *See, e.g., American Home Products Corp. v. Tracy*, 2003 Ohio 1521 (Ohio Ct. App. 2003); *A. H. Robins Co., Inc. v. Director, Div. of Taxation*, 2002 N.J. Tax LEXIS 5 (N.J. Tax Ct. 2002), *aff'd*, 365 N.J. Super. 472, 839 A.2d 914 (N.J. Super. Ct. App. Div. 2004), *aff'd*, 182 N.J. 77, 861 A.2d 131 (N.J., Sup. Ct. 2004). For an earlier proceeding in the bankruptcy court, *see In re A. H. Robins Co., Inc., supra* §1102.5, note 85 (action dismissed due to state's Eleventh Amendment immunity).

[8] 11 U.S.C. §346(j)(1), *as amended by* P.L. 109-8, §719 (2005).

[9] 11 U.S.C. §346(j)(2), *as amended by* P.L. 109-8, §719 (2005).

[10] Id.

### §1103.2.2 Pre-10/17/05 Bankruptcy Cases: Bankruptcy Code Rules

For bankruptcy cases commenced *before* October 17, 2005, Bankruptcy Code section 346(j) provides a self-contained set of rules for the exclusion of COD income and attribute reduction. These rules bear various similarities to the federal rules, but also have significant differences (in some cases as a result of the interim repeal of the complimentary federal rule, such as the repeal in 1994 of the federal stock-for-debt exception to the realization of COD income).

Subject to the "equity security-for-debt" and capital contribution exceptions (discussed below), the attribute reductions required by section 346(j) as applicable to pre-10/17/05 bankruptcy cases are as follows:

(1) *No Reduction Required if No Prior Tax Benefit Generated.* No reduction for COD is required if (a) the cancelled liability consisted of "items of a deductible nature" that had not yet been deducted,[11] or (b) when originally paid or accrued, the cancelled liability gave rise to an NOL carryover that expired unused prior to the taxable year of cancellation.[12]

(2) *Disallowance of Current/Future Deductions Related to Cancelled Debt.* Consistent with (1) above, no current or future deduction is allowed with respect to any cancelled liability.[13] For example, interest cancelled in the year it accrued will not be deductible. In addition, in computing any capital loss (but apparently not gain) incurred on a disposition of an asset, the basis of such asset must be reduced by any liability incurred in connection with the asset's acquisition.[14] It also appears that the debtor should be disallowed future depreciation deductions in respect of such tax basis (up to the amount of the cancelled liability) so long as it continues to hold the asset. This can leave the debtor in somewhat of a quandary as to the extent of any reduction in its NOLs and tax basis under (3) and (4) below, since such reductions exclude any COD that resulted in a disallowance of a current or future deduction. Is the reduction a one-time adjustment? Or must the debtor continually readjust the amount of its remaining NOLs and tax basis (with the potential need to file multiple amended returns) until the full amount of its disallowed deductions and losses for future years is firmly established, or it has no remaining NOLs or available tax basis to be reduced? Were the debtor simply required to reduce the tax basis of the affected asset for both gain and loss purposes, the adjustment would be fixed and determinable at the time of cancellation. Yet this is not what the statutory language seems to suggest, and the legislative history offers no guidance.

---

[11] A clear example is a liability for accrued interest owed by a cash basis debtor. The full meaning of the reference to "items of a deductible nature," however, is unclear. *See* Bryan, Cancellation of Indebtedness by Issuing Stock in Exchange: Challenging the Congressional Solution to Debt-Equity Swaps, 63 Tex. L. Rev. 89, 102 (1984); Berenson, Bankruptcy—Tax Accounting, Tax Returns and Congressional Revision: H.R. 9973, 9 Tax Advisor 298, 300 (1978) (quoting from a report prepared by a subcommittee of the House Judiciary Committee).

[12] 11 U.S.C. §346(j)(4), as in effect prior to the 2005 changes.

[13] 11 U.S.C. §346(j)(2), as in effect prior to the 2005 changes.

[14] 11 U.S.C. §346(j)(2), as in effect prior to the 2005 changes.

### EXAMPLE

Bankrupt corporation acquired land in 1984 at a cost of $1,000, for which it paid $900 down with a note for the remaining $100. During the bankruptcy case, the $100 note is cancelled and, in the same taxable year, the land is sold for $850. Bankrupt corporation has only a $50 loss; the $100 note is excluded from basis for purposes of the loss computation.

(3) *Reduction in NOLs.* To the extent the COD incurred exceeds the deductions and losses described in (2), any remaining COD reduces the debtor corporation's current NOL, if any, and NOL carryovers to the current taxable year.[15] The Bankruptcy Code does not specify the order in which NOLs and NOL carryovers are reduced; presumably, they would be reduced in the order incurred. (As mentioned above, not all states and localities permit NOL carryovers.)

(4) *Reduction in Basis of Property; Election to Recognize Income.* Any COD remaining after the adjustments provided in (2) and (3) will either (a) reduce the basis of the debtor's property, but not below the debtor's total preexisting liabilities still remaining after the cancellation of debt, or (b) to the extent that the debtor elects, result in taxable income, but not in excess of the amount of the reduction in basis that would have been required to be made in the absence of the election. The basis reduction applies not only to the debtor corporation but also to any other corporation that carries over the debtor's basis.[16]

Bankruptcy Code section 346(j)(7) (as in effect for bankruptcy cases commenced before October 17, 2005), although awkwardly worded, contains an equity-security-for-debt exception to COD. Generally speaking, the equity-security-for-debt exception is the counterpart to the stock-for-debt exception for federal income tax purposes. Nevertheless, the two should not be confused. First, the general scope of the two exceptions obviously differ: The stock-for-debt exception (which has since been generally repealed) only applied, if at all, if "stock" was used, whereas the equity-security-for-debt exception also permits the use of certain equity securities such as warrants. Second, the equity-security-for-debt exception will in general not apply with respect to "items of a deductible nature" (such as accrued but unpaid interest), whereas the stock-for-debt exception could apply (*see* § 302). Accordingly, the equity-security-for-debt exception will at times be broader than, and at other times be narrower than, the traditional stock-for-debt exception.

In general, the equity-security-for-debt exception provides that no COD will be created where an equity security of the debtor corporation (or its successor) is issued in satisfaction of the debtor corporation's debt. Similarly, no COD will generally be

---

[15] 11 U.S.C. § 346(j)(3), as in effect prior to the 2005 changes. *Consider Ill. Dept. of Rev. v. Envirodyne Ind. Inc.*, 2006 U.S. Dist. LEXIS 80154 (N.D. Ill. 2006) (although the court correctly held that this rule does not preclude the carryback of prepetition NOLs against prepetition income, the court in its explanation incorrectly stated that the filing of the bankruptcy petition was "the event eliminating the losses;" rather, the event is the discharge or cancellation of debt, which only occurs later in the bankruptcy case).

[16] *See* 11 U.S.C. § 346(g)(1)(C)(2), as in effect prior to the 2005 changes, discussed *supra* at § 1103.1.

created upon a contribution to capital of any debt by an equity security holder.[17] An equity security includes for this purpose (1) any share in a corporation, whether or not transferable or denominated as "stock," or any similar security, and (2) any warrant or right to purchase, sell, or subscribe to such an equity interest (other than a right to convert).[18] Does this mean that preferred stock, if respected as stock, will always qualify as an equity security? No guidance is given. Nevertheless, it would appear that Congress, in this regard, was attempting to expand upon, rather than narrow, the stock-for-debt exception applicable for federal income tax purposes.[19] Thus, at a minimum, preferred stock should qualify as an equity security in those cases where the use of preferred stock would also have qualified for purposes of the stock-for-debt exception (*see* § 504A.3).

The equity security-for-debt and capital-contribution exceptions, however, in general, do not apply to the extent that the debt exchanged consists of items of a deductible nature (whether or not previously deducted).[20] This would include, for example, a liability for services or accrued interest. If, however, the exchange of an equity security for debt has the same effect as the making of a cash payment equal to the value of the equity security, then, with respect to any portion of a cancelled liability of a deductible nature, the equity-security-for-debt exception will apply in an amount equal to the fair market value of the equity security attributable to such portion of the cancelled liability.[21] In other words, the use of an equity security to satisfy, say, accrued but unpaid interest may be respected as a payment of such accrued interest in an amount equal to the fair market value of the equity security exchanged therefor, with no resulting COD consequences for such portion.[22] This rule, when taken in conjunction with the rule discussed earlier providing that no attribute reduction or COD income will result from cancellation of a liability of a deductible nature that did not generate a prior tax benefit, will have the following consequences for cash basis and accrual basis debtors in bankruptcy cases commenced before October 17, 2005.

A cash-basis debtor will generally be entitled to a current deduction in an amount equal to the fair market value of the equity security exchanged for the deductible portion of a cancelled liability and will have no attribute reduction (or COD income) for the remainder of such portion, if any. In contrast, an accrual basis debtor, to the extent that it had previously deducted the liability (and such liability is not reflected in an expired unused NOL), will generally have attribute reduction (or COD income) in an amount equal to the excess, if any, of the deductible portion of

---

[17] 11 U.S.C. § 346(j)(7), as in effect prior to the 2005 changes.

[18] 11 U.S.C. § 101(16).

[19] *Cf.* Plumb, The Tax Recommendations of the Commission on the Bankruptcy Laws—Reorganizations, Carryovers, and the Effects of Debt Reduction, 29 Tax L. Rev. 229, at 274 (1974) (indicating that accepted formulation of stock-for-debt exception was to be adopted; discussion, however, refers to an exchange of equity security for debt).

[20] This would include, for example, a liability for services or accrued interest. The full meaning of the reference to "items of a deductible nature," however, is unclear. *Supra* note 9.

[21] 11 U.S.C. § 346(j)(7)(B), as in effect prior to the 2005 changes.

[22] *See* S. Rep. No. 989, 95th Cong., 2d Sess. 47 (1978).

the cancelled liability over the fair market value of the equity security exchanged therefor. In the end, both the cash basis and accrual basis debtor will generally have claimed, after offset by the amount of any attribute reduction (or COD income), a net deduction equal in amount to the fair market value of the equity security exchanged for the deductible portion of the cancelled liability.[23]

---

[23] Id.

# 12

# Liquidating Bankruptcies



## §1201 INTRODUCTION

When all else fails and it becomes apparent that the failing company cannot be returned to viable status through the device of reorganization, the failed company will have to be liquidated. In this circumstance, the attention of the tax advisor shifts away from efforts to provide the optimum tax treatment for the creditors and shareholders and to preserve the NOLs and other tax attributes of the company for use in its reorganized business, and focuses instead simply on minimizing corporate level taxes on the liquidation of the failed company's assets.

Where the liquidating plan involves modification or transfer of the company's debt, there is a potential risk that the IRS may take the position that a Code §382 ownership change has taken place, thereby impairing the company's NOLs. *See* §1202.1 below.

## §1202 UTILIZATION OF CARRYOVERS

One device for minimizing tax at the corporate level is the use of the failed company's NOLs and other carryovers. In earlier days when these could be carried forward for only five or seven years, it was quite possible for many of these carryovers—most of which may have been created in years before the bankruptcy proceeding commenced—to expire before the final liquidation of assets occurred. Now that these benefits can last for 15 to 20 years, this is unlikely to be the case. However, as we have seen, COD income can cause a reduction in these attributes. The stock-for-debt exception to COD income, which existed before 1995 (*see* §504A), did not apply in liquidating bankruptcies. Interestingly enough, it can be argued that COD income never arises in a liquidating bankruptcy (whether under Chapter 7 or Chapter 11), at least until the end of the case, because the Bankruptcy Code provides that the debt is never discharged in such a case.[1] However, there is no authority that holds that this conclusion applies as a matter of law for COD purposes. The cases that do exist on the timing of COD income all suggest that the question of *when* COD income arises is a factual issue, and that debt cancellation occurs when a definitive event takes place that indicates the debt will never be paid. These cases are discussed at § 404.8 above. Two of these cases, the *Friedman* and the *Alpert* cases, involving S corporation liquidating bankruptcies, held that the COD income did not arise until the bankruptcy was wound up, even though for some time before it had seemed fairly clear that the debts would not be paid. The courts in these cases stated that throughout the bankruptcy case the trustee actively administered the estate, collecting and distributing monies, such that it could not be said that a definitive event had occurred until the termination of the bankruptcy. Another of these cases, the *Coburn* case, held that even though the creditor abandoned the collateral and made no effort to collect on the loan, the COD probably would not arise until the future date when the statute of limitations on enforcement of the loan expired. However, as even these cases state that the issue is a question of fact, caution would suggest that liquidating transactions should be planned in such a way as to minimize the harm that might arise if COD income were held to occur.

This puts a special premium on timing the sequence of asset dispositions in relation to the realization of any COD income. As we pointed out at § 404, COD income of companies in bankruptcy reduces the NOLs for the year of the debt cancellation and the NOL carryovers to future years, but this occurs only after the tax for the year of cancellation has been determined.[2] This means that if the debt cancellation does not occur until the last year in which asset dispositions take place, the COD income should not reduce the amount of NOLs available to shelter any gains from the asset dispositions.

## *§1202.1 The* **Integrated Resources** *Bankruptcy and Later Authorities*

Liquidating bankruptcies usually involve no changes in the terms of the outstanding debt or stock. There is merely an orderly liquidation of the assets, and the proceeds are applied to the debt in accordance with the priorities of the various classes of debt. Where there are direct or indirect modifications in the debt structure, however, potential problems may arise.

In late 1993, the IRS filed an objection to a proposed Chapter 11 liquidating bankruptcy plan in the *Integrated Resources* case, which illustrates the potential scope of some of these problems.[3] The plan had been filed by a group of creditors. Both the

---

[1] **§ 1202** *See* 11 U.S.C. §§ 727(a)(1), 1141(d)(3). *See also* New York State Bar Association, Tax Section, Committee on Bankruptcy, Report on Suggested Bankruptcy Tax Rulings, 50 Tax Notes 631, 639 (February 11, 1991).

[2] *See* Code § 108(b)(4)(A).

[3] Memorandum filed for hearing date of November 29, 1993, In re Integrated Resources, Inc., Case No. 90 B 10411 (C.B.)(Bankr. S.D.N.Y.). For an earlier ruling in which the IRS expressly did not rule on the question whether a substantial modification of debt that remained deeply under water caused the debt to become equity, *see* IRS Letter Ruling 9146030, August 15, 1991.

stock and the debt of Integrated Resources, the debtor, were substantially under water. The IRS asserted that the assets would have to appreciate two to three times before even the debt could be paid in full. The debtor had significant NOLs and it was also expected to realize substantial income in the future from contract rights that it held. Even after realization of this income, it was expected that nothing would be available for the stockholders and the creditors would not be paid in full. The plan proposed that no change be made in the outstanding stock, and that no new stock be issued. It also proposed that no change be made in the outstanding debt, but that this debt be transferred by the creditors to liquidating trusts in exchange for certificates of beneficial interest (CBIs). The more senior creditors would have a choice of obtaining some cash instead of CBIs for their debt or of receiving less cash but also getting the CBIs. The cash would be supplied by certain of the major creditors, who agreed to purchase for cash anything from 25 percent to 100 percent of the more senior CBIs. The parties presumably assumed that because neither the stock of the debtor nor the debt instruments of the debtor themselves would be changed, there would not be any debt cancellation or ownership change of the debtor as a result of consummation of the plan. Thus, the NOLs would be preserved and could be used against future income.

The IRS felt that the plan involved an indirect modification of the debtor's capital structure, and filed an objection against the plan. The proponents then withdrew the plan. The IRS asserted that issuance of the CBIs would constitute the issuance of an interest that should be treated as stock of the debtor for Code § 382 purposes under the regulation described at § 508.2.2.3 above, and that the stock itself should be treated as "not stock" under the regulation discussed at § 508.2.2.2 above. This would produce a Code § 382 ownership change of the debtor. As a result, the IRS asserted that the debtor's NOLs would become largely useless, and not only would the proposed disclosure statement be inadequate for failing to state this, but the plan itself would not be feasible because it would not have provided adequately for the payment of corporate level taxes.

The IRS alternatively asserted that the plan would result in a constructive material modification of the existing debt that might produce substantial COD income. In this regard, the IRS asserted that one could not consider the new debt to have a face amount greater than the amount that the creditors might realistically expect to receive in satisfaction of it. Since the IRS did not discuss the possible application of the stock-for-debt exception to COD income in this portion of its argument, the IRS apparently presented this argument as an alternative to the first argument, and in this alternative assumed that none of the existing debt should be considered as having been converted into stock (or, at least, not the type of stock that would qualify for the stock-for-debt exception).

Finally, the IRS objected to the fact that the plan did not require the dissolution of the debtor after all of its assets had been realized and distributed. The IRS said that if the debtor corporation could remain in existence after that point, it might become a shell that continued to have unused NOLs and other tax benefits. The IRS asserted that allowing this to happen could indicate that the principal purpose of the plan was the avoidance of taxes, which under Bankruptcy Code § 1129(d) would prevent the court from confirming the plan.

An interesting contrast to the position taken by the IRS in the *Integrated Resources* bankruptcy case is provided by a recent private letter ruling.[4] Here, a consolidated group of companies had filed a Chapter 11 bankruptcy proceeding. Later deciding that its liabilities substantially exceeded its assets, the debtors proposed a "liquidating" Chapter 11 plan, pursuant to which the assets of the debtors would be liquidated and the debtors would cease to survive. Rather than distributing their assets to a liquidating or similar fund of some kind, the debtors planned to retain them during the liquidation process, and distribute them or their proceeds to the creditors ultimately found to be entitled to them. If anything were to remain after paying all of the debtors' creditors (considered unlikely), such excess would be paid to the shareholders of the parent. The group had considerable NOLs, which it hoped to use against any gains arising during the liquidation process. The plan provided that the parent's shares of stock would be converted into newly issued shares having identical terms to the shares given up, but with the new shares being deposited into a trust that severely limited their transferability. The ruling held that this conversion and deposit would not constitute an owner shift for purposes of Code §382(g), and that the interests of the creditors would not be considered "stock" for purposes of Code §382. Thus, the IRS ruled that neither the confirmation nor the consummation of the bankruptcy plan would result in an ownership change under Code §382, thereby preserving the NOLs for use against the liquidation of the assets. The ruling did not address the COD implications of the plan.

## §1203 LIBERALIZED OLD CODE §337 RULES

Before the repeal of old Code §337 by the Tax Reform Act of 1986, the twelve-month liquidation under Code §337 was another tool available to the tax advisor for sheltering the corporation from tax on asset dispositions.[1] Such repeal is generally effective for liquidations completed after 1986.[2] Old Code §337 treatment, however, is still available for liquidations completed during 1987 if pursuant to a plan of liquidation adopted before August 1986.[3] This provision may have the effect of grandfathering 1987 liquidations of corporations in Chapter 7 proceedings commenced before August 1986.[4] In addition, a pared-down version of old Code §337 may be available to certain closely held corporations (valued at not more than $10 million) for liquidations completed before 1989.[5]

Prior to the Bankruptcy Tax Act of 1980, Code §337 was not available to insolvent companies. The IRS had ruled that Code §337 did not apply unless there

---

[4] IRS Letter Ruling 200445020, November 12, 2003, *supplemented by* IRS Letter Ruling 200509001, March 11, 2004.

[1] **§1203** *See. e.g.*, explanation of the twelve-month liquidation rules as they applied prior to repeal by the Tax Reform Act of 1986 at Stand. Fed. Tax Rep. (CCH) ¶16,227.

[2] *See* Tax Reform Act of 1986, Pub. L. No. 99-514, §633(a)(1).

[3] Id. at §633(c)(1)(A).

[4] *See infra* note 10.

[5] *See* Tax Reform Act of 1986, §633(d).

was a distribution to the shareholders of the corporation.[6] This position was reminiscent of the holding that Code § 332 does not apply unless there is a distribution to all of the stockholders of the corporation,[7] although there was far less reason in the statutory language to read insolvent companies out of Code § 337.[8] The Bankruptcy Tax Act of 1980 overruled the IRS position by adding Code § 337(g), which extended Code § 337 to plans of complete liquidation adopted in a Title 11 case or in a receivership, foreclosure, or similar proceeding in a federal or state court. Code § 337(g) added two special rules for the application of Code § 337 in such a case. First, the period of nonrecognition, which commenced on the adoption of the plan of liquidation and normally terminated 12 months thereafter, would, for a plan of liquidation adopted in a bankruptcy or similar case, not end until the case terminated.[9] The plan of complete liquidation, however, must have been adopted after commencement of the case.[10] The effect of this rule was that the period of nonrecognition could extend for a much longer time than 12 months. The second special rule was that the Code § 337 benefit did not extend to property acquired after adoption of the liquidation plan, except for inventory sold in bulk to one person in one transaction.[11]

Because Code § 337 did not eliminate the tax on recapture items (such as depreciation, tax benefit and other recaptures), the debtor's NOLs and ITCs were still useful in sheltering the bankrupt corporation from tax on these items even if Code § 337 was utilized.

As mentioned above, the Tax Reform Act of 1986 repealed old Code § 337, subject to certain grandfathering provisions. Except where the applicability of old Code § 337 is preserved by the grandfathering provisions, tax planning for liquidating bankrupt-

---

[6] Rev. Rul. 56-387, 1956-2 C.B. 189; Rev. Rul. 73-264, 1973-1 C.B. 178.

[7] *See* discussion at § 802.

[8] The IRS rulings on the inapplicability of old Code § 337 to insolvent companies were criticized in Bittker & Eustice, Federal Income Taxation of Corporations and Shareholders § 11.64 (4th ed. with Supp.).

[9] Code § 337(g)(2), prior to amendment by Pub. L. No. 99-514. For a discussion of this provision as it applied to the adoption of a plan of liquidation for a corporation in bankruptcy, *see* Tatlock, 466 T.M., Bankruptcy and Insolvency: Tax Aspects and Procedure, A-48 to A-49 (1985); Asofsky, Reorganizing Insolvent Corporations, 41 Inst. on Fed. Tax'n §§ 5, 5.06[4] (1983) [hereafter cited as Asofsky, Reorganizing]; Hyman, Martin & Montali, Tax Aspects of Corporate Debt Exchanges, Recapitalizations, and Discharges, California Continuing Education of the Bar, Taxation Series Program Material, 10-11, 67-69 (1982); Asofsky, Bacon, Hyman, Klee, Ruge, Singer & Tatlock, Conference on The Bankruptcy Tax Act of 1980, 39 Inst. on Fed. Tax'n §§ 57, 57.09[8] at 57-133 to 57-135 (1981) [hereafter cited as Bankruptcy Tax Conference].

[10] *See* H.R. Rep. No. 833, 96th Cong., 2d Sess. 37 (1980); S. Rep. No. 1035, 96th Cong., 2d Sess. 41-42 (1980); Asofsky, Reorganizing, *supra* note 9, at § 5.06[4] (indicates that it would appear appropriate in most Chapter 7 cases to deem the plan of liquidation to be adopted on the date that the bankruptcy court enters its order accepting the Chapter 7 petition and, in most Chapter 11 cases, on the date the bankruptcy court confirms the Chapter 11 plan of reorganization); Hyman, Martin & Montali, *supra* note 9, at 10-11, 67-69 (states that the IRS has, at least in one unreported case, accepted the argument that the plan of liquidation was adopted automatically and simultaneously with the filing of the bankruptcy petition); Bankruptcy Tax Conference, *supra* note 9, at § 57.09[8] at 57-133 to 57-135 (remarks of Paul H. Asofsky and Kenneth N. Klee).

[11] *See* Code § 337(g)(1), prior to amendment by Pub. L. No. 99-514.

cies will now revert to where it largely was before the liberalizing changes made by the Bankruptcy Tax Act of 1980. The planner will want to ensure that any net gains to be realized from asset sales take place before NOLs are destroyed by debt cancellation.

# 13

# Deductibility of Expenses During Bankruptcy



## §1301 BANKRUPTCY EXPENSES

Rev. Rul. 77-204[1] held that the trustee's expenses of operating the debtor's business in either a reorganizing or liquidating bankruptcy were deductible. However, it held that in a reorganizing bankruptcy the costs and expenses incurred with respect to the institution and administration of the bankruptcy proceeding itself were not deductible since they were capital expenditures that would benefit the corporation in future years. With respect to the liquidating bankruptcy, on the other hand, the ruling held that, although the costs of selling assets must be charged against the proceeds of sale, the expenses of liquidation, including the costs and expenses incurred with respect to the institution and administration of the liquidating bankruptcy proceeding itself, were fully deductible.

As the prior chapters of this volume illustrate, the transactions that occur in a Chapter 11 bankruptcy restructuring are many and diverse in nature. The petition in bankruptcy must be filed; the assets and liabilities of the company must be identified and marshalled; claims against the company must be defended; causes of action held by the company must be prosecuted; assets may be sold; creditors' committees and shareholders' committees must be dealt with; bankruptcy court approvals must be obtained for many activities involved in the continued operation of the bankrupt business, including certain acquisitions and dispositions of assets and payment of certain liabilities; periodic reports must be filed with the bankruptcy court; periodic reports may also have to be filed with other government agencies; a bankruptcy plan must be formulated; old debt may be retired; new debt may be issued; stock may be cancelled or issued; profitable businesses may be acquired; tax advice will be sought; and tax returns will have to be filed.

Rev. Rul. 77-204 does not contain any detailed analysis of the myriad transactions that occur during bankruptcy. Rather, the only facts stated in the ruling were

---

[1] **§1301** 1977-1 C.B. 40.

that (1) a corporation had filed a petition for reorganization under Chapter X of the old Bankruptcy Act, (2) a trustee had been appointed by the bankruptcy court, (3) the trustee had incurred business expenses for the continued operation of the corporation's business, and (4) the trustee had also incurred various other costs and expenses in connection with the "institution and administration" of the Chapter X proceeding. No indication was given as to the nature of these various expenses, nor as to what the Chapter X plan of reorganization provided.

The ruling applied the following line of reasoning: First, the deductibility of the administrative expenses incurred by the trustee depends upon the extent to which corporations "in general" are allowed to deduct expenses "connected with a reorganization." Second, the ordinary and necessary business expenses incurred by the trustee in the operation of the business are deductible under Code § 162, just as if no Chapter X proceeding had been instituted. Third, since expenses "connected with a reorganization" generally are not deductible under Code § 162 because they are capital expenditures that will benefit the corporation in future years, the expenses incurred "with respect to the institution and administration of the Chapter X proceeding" are not deductible since they are capital expenditures that will benefit the corporation in future years.

In analyzing the statements made in the ruling and the validity of its conclusions, one must take care to avoid being confused by the fact that the concepts of "reorganization" and "administrative expenses" have sharply different meanings in the bankruptcy field than in the tax field. These different meanings given to the same words can all too easily create a confused analysis leading to an errorneous conclusion. A Chapter X or Chapter 11 case is called a "reorganization" by bankruptcy practitioners even if it does not involve a "reorganization" in the tax sense or even if it does not end up involving any change whatsoever in the capital structure of the company. Similarly, section 503(b) of the Bankruptcy Code defines "administrative expenses" for bankruptcy purposes as including almost all expenses incurred by the company after commencement of the bankruptcy case, including costs of running the business, taxes, costs of an examiner, professional fees, expenses incurred by creditors' and shareholders' committees, expenses of preserving assets, and expenses of buying and selling assets. In the tax world, the concept of "administrative expenses" tends to connote only overhead or housekeeping expenditures. Rev. Rul. 77-204 did not pay adequate attention to the way these words are used differently under the bankruptcy law than under the tax law.

For its generalization that "reorganization" expenses are generally capital in nature, Rev. Rul. 77-204 cited one ruling and three cases. The ruling is Rev. Rul. 73-580,[2] which dealt with a nonbankrupt corporation that had a policy of expansion through acquisitions. The ruling held that the corporation must capitalize the portion of its expenses that were attributable to mergers and acquisitions that had been consummated but could deduct as Code § 165 losses the costs attributable to acquisition plans that were abandoned. This ruling simply rests on the familiar rule that expenses of issuing stock are to be treated as a nondeductible reduction in the

---

[2] 1973-2 C.B. 86.

proceeds from the stock issuance, and the other expenses of acquiring property are capitalizable (in a taxable acquisition they are added to the basis of the property acquired, and in a tax free reorganization they become a nonamortizable intangible with an indefinite useful life[3]).

The first case cited was *Bush Terminal Buildings Co.*,[4] which involved expenses incurred in a bankruptcy plan that extended the payment dates for the company's debt. The plan did not provide for any issuance of equity. Although the expenses of issuing new debt or of extending old debt should generally be amortizable over the life of the new or modified debt,[5] the court specifically noted that it did not have this question before it. The only question before it was whether such expenses were immediately deductible. The court correctly held they were not. This holding does not, however, support a broad generalization that bankruptcy "reorganization" expenses are "not deductible."[6]

The second case cited was *Chicago, Milwaukee, St. Paul & Pacific R.R. Co. v. United States*,[7] which involved expenses indirectly relating to the issuance of stock under a bankruptcy plan. The court disallowed a deduction for these expenses.

The third case cited was *Denver & Rio Grande Western R.R. Co.*,[8] where the bankruptcy order required the debtor company to reimburse its bond indenture trustee for services rendered and for all expenses incurred in foreclosing on certain collateral. The court disallowed a deduction for these expenses. This case, unlike the preceding authorities, seems wrong; and not surprisingly, a reading of the case shows that its holding was based on a legal doctrine that has since been overruled. The doctrine is the "clean slate" doctrine of *Willingham v. United States*.[9] Although this doctrine was still potentially alive when Rev. Rul. 77-204 was issued, soon thereafter

---

[3] However, there is some authority to the effect that the acquirer's capitalized expenses (other than its expenses of issuing stock) in a tax-free acquisitive reorganization can be deducted when the target is liquidated or all its assets are sold, rather than the later date when the acquirer is liquidated. *See McCrory Corp. v. United States*, 651 F.2d 828, 81-2 U.S.T.C. ¶9499 (2d Cir. 1981), in which the taxpayer company acquired assets of another company for stock in a statutory merger. Subsequently, after the acquired assets were sold, the taxpayer deducted the expenses relating to the merger. The IRS disallowed the deduction, viewing the expenses generically as reorganization expenses. The Second Circuit disagreed and held that all expenses relating to the purchase of the assets in the merger were properly deductible, and only the specific costs of issuing the stock in the merger could not be deducted. This case was cited with apparent approval by the Supreme Court in its *INDOPCO* opinion, cited at note 23 below.

[4] 7 T.C. 793, Dec. 15,382 (1946), *acq.* 1947-2 C.B. 1.

[5] *See Great Western Power Co. v. Commissioner*, 297 U.S. 543, 36-1 U.S.T.C. ¶9185 (1936) (nonbankruptcy case; expense of exchanging new bonds for old bonds must be capitalized, but is amortizable over the term of the new bonds).

[6] *See also International Bldg. Co. v. United States*, 97 F. Supp. 595, 51-1 U.S.T.C. ¶9164 (E.D. Mo. 1951), *aff'd*, 199 F.2d 12, 52-2 U.S.T.C. ¶9485 (8th Cir. 1952), *rev'd on other grounds*, 345 U.S. 502, 53-1 U.S.T.C. ¶9366 (1953), which on similar facts relied on *Bush Terminal*.

[7] 404 F.2d 960, 69-1 U.S.T.C. ¶9125 (Cl. Ct. 1969).

[8] 38 T.C. 557, Dec. 25,595 (1962), *acq.* 1963-2 C.B. 4.

[9] 289 F.2d 283, 61-1 U.S.T.C. ¶9401 (5th Cir. 1961), *cert. denied*, 368 U.S. 8 (1961).

it was relegated to oblivion. It was rejected by the Tax Court,[10] abandoned by the IRS[11] and, finally, overruled by Congress.[12]

Neither Rev. Rul. 77-204 nor the authorities it cited provide a detailed analysis regarding which of the myriad activities that go on during a bankruptcy case should be considered capital in nature. Nor do they adequately address the question of the extent to which costs that must be capitalized need to be treated as a separate intangible asset with an indeterminate life that cannot be deducted until the bankrupt corporation liquidates, or instead whether they can be allocated to a portion of the case that has a limited life such as the issuance of debt and can thus be amortized. It is unfortunate that Rev. Rul. 77-204 did not provide a more transactional analysis and did not address these questions.[13]

Rev. Rul. 77-204 seems inconsistent with Rev. Rul. 68-48,[14] dealing with a bankrupt partnership. Here the IRS did provide more transactional detail. In this ruling the IRS stated that even though the bankruptcy trustee did not continue to operate the partnership business, the compensation of attorneys and accountants retained by the trustee was deductible under Code § 212 to the extent it was for the production of income, management of property, or determination of tax. The ruling specifically held that such deductible expenses included the "usual cost of administration, including the referee's compensation, statutory compensation for the trustee and for the bankrupt's attorney, the trustee's bond premium, and charges of court reporting and transcripts." It also held that filing costs originally paid by the petitioning creditors and compensation for the attorneys of the petitioning creditors could be deducted by the trustee to the extent the bankrupt estate was liable to reimburse the creditors for these items.[15] Perhaps the two rulings can be harmonized by viewing Rev. Rul. 68-48 as though it dealt with a liquidating bankruptcy.

Unfortunately, the lack of specificity in Rev. Rul. 77-204 has encouraged IRS agents to take an aggressive position toward disallowing expenses incurred during a corporate bankruptcy case, often asserting that all expenses that would not have been incurred but for the bankruptcy are nondeductible.

---

[10] *See Jacqueline, Inc. v. Commissioner*, 36 T.C.M. 1363, Dec. 34,668(M), T.C. Memo. 1977-340; and *Daytona Beach Kennel Club, Inc. v. Commissioner*, 69 T.C. 1015, Dec. 35,072 (1978).

[11] *See* Technical Advice Memorandum 7953017 (Sept. 27, 1979).

[12] *See* S. Rep. No. 1035, 96th Cong., 2d Sess. 37 (1980); H. Rep. No. 833, 96th Cong., 2d Sess. 32 (1980).

[13] *See* Bittker & Eustice, Federal Income Taxation of Corporations and Shareholders ¶ 5.06[2][b] (7th ed.).

[14] 1968-1 C.B. 301.

[15] Code § 212 and Code § 162 are to be read "*in pari materia* with respect to the capital-ordinary distinction." *See Woodward v. Commissioner*, 397 U.S. 572, 574 n.3, 70-1 U.S.T.C. ¶ 9348 (1970).

Because Code § 162 actually allows a broader range of expenses to be deducted, Congress in the Bankruptcy Tax Act of 1980 enacted Code § 1398(h)(1) to ensure that bankrupt individuals could deduct as broad a range of administrative and related expenses as could corporations. *See* S. Rep. No. 1035, 96th Cong., 2d Sess. 29 (1980).

The IRS position was repeated—and if anything extended—in a 1991 technical advice memorandum,[16] which dealt with a bankruptcy proceeding that was commenced primarily for the purpose of settling tort claims that had arisen out of the taxpayer's trade or business. Citing Rev. Rul. 77-204, as its guiding authority, the technical advice memorandum states that the ordinary and necessary business expenses incurred in the operation of the taxpayer's business, including those related to the handling of the tort claims, are deductible under Code § 162, "to the same extent they would have been if the bankruptcy proceeding had not been instituted *to the extent the expenses were not incurred with respect to the institution and administration of the bankruptcy proceeding*" (emphasis added), whereas all of the expenses incurred with respect to the institution and administration of the bankruptcy proceeding are to be capitalized. The specific holding of the technical advice memorandum would appear to be (although the language is something less than totally clear) that the expenses for handling tort claims would be deductible only to the extent to which they related to proceedings in courts other than the bankruptcy court, and would not be deductible to the extent to which they related to the resolution of tort claims in the bankruptcy court. Such a distinction—which is based on form rather than substance—has nothing to recommend it.

Too great a willingness to find expenses nondeductible because a bankruptcy "reorganization" is involved does not serve either tax policy or bankruptcy policy. Tax policy generally requires that one look behind the word "reorganization" to the specific transactions involved, and encourages looking to the substance of a transaction. Bankruptcy policy encourages the use of bankruptcy proceedings to revive the affairs of the debtor. Applying a more rigorous approach to bankruptcy than to nonbankruptcy workouts undermines both policies. For example, take the case of a troubled corporation that only needs to extend the terms and otherwise modify its debt and uses a bankruptcy proceeding to do this. If this debt modification were done outside bankruptcy, none of the cost would be treated as an unamortizable intangible capital asset with an unlimited life. Instead, it would be amortized over the life of the debt. If this same modification is done through use of a bankruptcy proceeding, why should any part of the cost be treated differently? The substance seems the same, the entire transaction results only in the exchange of new debt for old debt.

The IRS approach was unfortunately rewarded by the bankruptcy court in the *Placid Oil Company* case.[17] Here the debtor company in a bankruptcy case (1) sold down some of its assets, (2) reduced the number of its employees, and (3) modified the terms of its debt. No stock was issued. The IRS disallowed deductions for essentially all the professional expenses incurred by the company during the bankruptcy case. The company asked the bankruptcy court to adjudicate the disallowance.

The first issue addressed by the bankruptcy court was the burden of proof. The IRS argued that the burden of proof should fall entirely on the taxpayer, as it would if

---

[16] IRS Letter Ruling 9204001, May 13, 1991. Compare the *Hillsborough Holdings* case described below in note 22, in which the tort litigation was apparently all conducted outside the bankruptcy court.

[17] *In re Placid Oil Company*, 92-1 U.S.T.C. ¶¶ 50,049 and 50,050 (Bankr. N.D. Tex. 1990), *aff'd*, 92-1 U.S.T.C. ¶ 50,051 (N.D. Tex. 1991).

the matter were contested in the Tax Court. The bankruptcy court disagreed, holding that in any proceeding before the bankruptcy court involving a contested claim, including a tax claim, the debtor has the initial burden of going forward to refute the claim, but once the debtor has carried that initial burden, the ultimate burden of proof lies with the claimant against the estate (here, the IRS).[18] The court then held that the taxpayer had not satisfied its initial burden because it had not introduced enough evidence to allow the court to determine which expenses were deductible and which were not.[19]

In the course of its opinion, the court accepted the IRS view that "reorganization" expenses are capital in nature; and it concluded that Placid's case involved a "reorganization" because it effectuated a contraction of Placid's corporate structure, including a reduction of its work force, the sale of substantial assets, and the restructuring of its debt. This is an extraordinarily broad view of what, in a tax rather than a bankruptcy sense, represents a "reorganization."

The court gave little indication where it would have drawn the line between deductible and nondeductible expenses had the taxpayer submitted more adequate proof, except to say that it would have permitted a current deduction for the cost of bankruptcy proceedings that go to the day-to-day operation of the business, including objections to claims as to current amounts due or eligible for credit, and motions to use cash collateral for day-to-day operations. On the other hand, the court indicated that the cost of services rendered to the creditors' committee, and negotiations for the payment of debt through a plan over an extended period of time, would constitute capital items. Nor did the court address the question whether any of the capitalized items might be amortizable.

On appeal, the Court of Appeals for the Fifth Circuit disagreed with the lower courts.[20] The Court of Appeals concluded the bankruptcy court had erred in holding that *Placid Oil* had not satisfied its burden of initial proof. It reversed and remanded the case for further proceedings, including, if need be, the introduction of additional evidence. In the course of its opinion, the Court of Appeals made clear it also disagreed as a matter of substance with the narrow view of deductibility taken by the bankruptcy court. It said:

> On remand, the Bankruptcy Court should not bind itself by a sweeping characterization that Placid's bankruptcy proceedings were "in substance" a "reorganization," with the result that all Placid's bankruptcy-related fees and expenses must be capitalized to an intangible asset without amortization. I.R.C. section 368. On remand, the Bankruptcy

---

[18] There had been a split between the circuits on this burden of proof issue, which the Supreme Court resolved in 2000 by holding that the Bankruptcy Code does not change the burden of proof that is provided for in the applicable substantive tax law. *Raleigh v. Illinois Dept. of Revenue*, 120 S. Ct. 1951, 2000-1 U.S.T.C. ¶50,498 (S. Ct. 2000).

[19] For a discussion of the burden of proof issue in bankruptcy cases, *see* Chapter 10 at §1013.4.

[20] *In the Matter of Placid Oil Co.*, 988 F.2d 55, 93-1 U.S.T.C. ¶50,234 (5th Cir.), *reh'g denied*, 4 F.3d 992 (1993). The IRS has non-acquiesced in the holding that the government had the ultimate burden of proof. 1995-2 C.B. 2. The Supreme Court has subsequently agreed with the IRS on this point. *Raleigh v. Illinois Dept. of Revenue*, *supra* note 18.

> Court should analyze all the fees and expenses to identify them as: (1) currently deductible; (2) amortizable over the period of the useful life of the underlying transaction or event; and (3) allocated to nonamortizable intangible assets . . . . [citations omitted]For example, professional fees and expenses that are related to restructuring a specific debt and therefore conferred a specific long-term benefit are to be capitalized with an amortization period equivalent to the useful life of that underlying transaction. Included in the Bankruptcy Court's task on remand is to distinguish between professional fees and expenses for initiating and administering the bankruptcy proceedings, as opposed to those fees and expenses that are directly related to a particular asset or debt transaction.

The IRS, however, won an important acceptance of its "but for" argument—*i.e.*, its argument that all expenses that would not have been incurred but for the bankruptcy filing create an intangible asset with an unlimited useful life—in *Hillsborough Holdings Corp. v. United States*.[21] Here the taxpayer filed for bankruptcy because asbestos personal injury claims that had been made against it had prevented it from refinancing its debt or selling assets to reduce its debt. During the bankruptcy proceeding, the taxpayer's debt and equity interests were restructured. The taxpayer argued that since the purpose of the bankruptcy proceeding was to allow it to continue to defend its business against the attack by the asbestos personal injury claimants, all professional fees related to the bankruptcy proceeding should be deductible.

The court agreed that the costs of defending against the asbestos cases were fully deductible. But it also accepted the IRS "but for" argument that all expenses that would not have been incurred "but for" the bankruptcy were nondeductible and had to remain capitalized for the remainder of the taxpayer's existence. The court reasoned that bankruptcy expenses were extraordinary rather than ordinary expenses and thus had to be capitalized; that capital expenditures usually result in a long term benefit; and that if there is no ascertainable specific asset created by them or if they have no ascertainable limited useful life, the capital expenditure will ordinarily be deductible only when the corporation is dissolved. The court added that a capital expenditure that confers an intangible benefit on the corporation, such as "creating or enhancing goodwill or enabling the business's continued survival, is neither amortizable nor depreciable."[22]

Applying these tests, the court then held that all professional fees paid by the taxpayer for the various creditors' committees (which the debtor is required to pay by

---

[21] 99-1 U.S.T.C. ¶50,514 (Bankr. M.D. Fla. 1999), and subsequent proceeding at 2003-1 U.S.T.C. ¶50,394 (Bankr. M.D. Fla. 2003).

[22] A test so general as to require capitalization of expenditures that enable "the business's continued survival" is likely to obscure rather than clarify what a more careful transactional analysis would reveal. Surely the corporation's continued survival would be threatened if it did not pay its regular operating payroll expenses, or its asbestos litigation expenses, yet the court allows deductibility for these items. Such an overly broad word formula hinders rather than helps in arriving at a proper result.

the Bankruptcy Code) had to be capitalized, even if they related to claims disputes or sales of assets or ordinary business activities, because they would not have been incurred "but for" the bankruptcy. On the other hand, the court treated the taxpayer's noncreditor professional fees somewhat differently. It allowed deductions for these, for example, if they related to claims disputes or sales of assets or ordinary business activities. Yet, it required capitalization of these if they related to items that would not have been incurred "but for" the bankruptcy, including fee applications, and work on the various bankruptcy plans. With respect to work on the bankruptcy plans, the court even disallowed deductibility for work on plans that were abandoned (even though the court did allow deductions for abandonment of items that were not related to the bankruptcy), treating all bankruptcy related expenses as a single event that should not be subdivided.

The Supreme Court's opinion in *INDOPCO, Inc. v. Commissioner*[23] was cited by the *Hillsborough* court in support of its position. The *INDOPCO* opinion is troublesomely vague, and has caused a great deal of confusion. Here, the Court required capitalization of investment banking and legal fees incurred by a target corporation that was taken over in a friendly acquisition. The Court found that the acquisition, and therefore these expenses, produced a substantial future benefit for the target corporation because of the resources of the acquiring corporation and the synergy that became available to it from the acquisition, and because of the expense savings that would come from no longer being a public corporation with many shareholders.

In reaching its conclusion, the Court rejected (as a misreading of the *Lincoln Savings* case)[24] the taxpayer's argument that an expenditure needs to be capitalized only if it creates a separate and distinct asset. The Court then concluded that if the expenditure produces a "significant" future benefit it must be capitalized. The Court also said that the presence of a merely "incidental" future benefit from an expenditure does not warrant capitalization. By formulating the test in this manner, the Court emphasized its heavily factual nature. Nothing in the opinion suggests that a transactional analysis should not be applied to the facts of each particular case to determine which of the expenses should be capitalized (and of those, which can be amortized) and which should be expensed. The Court's citation with apparent approval of the *McCrory* case[25] supports this conclusion. We believe the Court felt that in its *INDOPCO* opinion it was simply affirming prior law while eliminating a misinterpretation of *Lincoln Savings*, and in the prior law, this exercise of tracing was well recognized. This view is also supported by the fact that as one of the building blocks for its position in the *Placid Oil* case, the Fifth Circuit noted that in *INDOPCO* the Supreme Court had observed that the distinctions between current and capital expenditures are ones of degree rather than kind and that each case must be decided according to its specific facts. This view is also supported by the Supreme Court's

---

[23] 112 S. Ct. 1039, 92-1 U.S.T.C. ¶50,113 (1992). In the lower courts, this case was known as the *National Starch and Chemical Corp.* case.

[24] *Commissioner v. Lincoln Savings & Loan Assn.*, 403 U.S. 345, 71-1 U.S.T.C. ¶9476 (1971).

[25] *Supra* note 3.

subsequent opinion in *Newark Morning Ledger Co. v. United States*.[26] There the Court also emphasized that the distinction between capital expenditures that are amortizable (such as the subscriber accounts in that case) and those that are not (such as goodwill) is a factual rather than a legal issue; and in support of allowing amortization in the *Newark* case the Court quoted from *INDOPCO* the statement that "the Code endeavors to match expenses with the revenues of the taxable period to which they are properly attributable, thereby resulting in a more accurate calculation of net income for tax purposes . . . ."

In response to the *Newark* type of litigation, Congress in 1993 adopted Code § 197, which allows an amortization deduction for the cost of certain intangibles, including goodwill. However, this provision is unlikely to apply to most of the items that arise in the context of bankruptcy cases. With a few limited exceptions, Code § 197 applies only where the intangible is acquired in connection with the acquisition of assets constituting a trade or business or a substantial portion thereof. It does not apply where what is involved is merely the capital restructuring of an existing business.

As mentioned above, the "significant future benefit" test used in the *INDOPCO* opinion created a great deal of confusion. It led the IRS to take quite aggressive positions in many instances. It also led to inconsistency and increased disputes between taxpayers and the IRS. Happily, the Treasury decided to address these problems. In January 2002, it issued a formal notice of its intention to do this by issuing regulations under Code § 263(a) designed to provide greater certainty and reduce compliance costs in this area.[27] The notice set out the general principles and standards the Treasury proposed to apply in the regulations, and solicited suggestions. After reviewing the various comments it received in response to this request, the Treasury on December 2, 2002, issued proposed regulations under Code §§ 263, 167, and 446,[28] and on January 5, 2004 it issued final regulations §§ 1.167(a)-3(b), 1.263(a)-4, 1.263(a)-5, and 1.446-5.[29] These are effective for transactions occurring on or after December 31, 2003.

In the Explanation issued with the proposed regulations, the Treasury observed that the pre-*INDOPCO* standard of requiring capitalization for expenditures that create a "separate and distinct intangible asset" had not created the same level of uncertainty and controversy as the "significant future benefit" standard articulated in *INDOPCO*. Accordingly, the proposed and final Code § 263 regulations retained the "separate and distinct intangible asset" test, but as for a "significant future benefit"

---

[26] 113 S. Ct. 1670, 93-1 U.S.T.C. ¶ 50,228 (1993).

[27] *See* Notice of Proposed Rulemaking, Guidance Regarding Deduction and Capitalization of Expenditures, *reprinted at* 2002 TNT 13-7 (January 17, 2002).

[28] Guidance Regarding Deduction and Capitalization of Expenditures, 67 Fed. Reg. 77701 (December 19, 2002).

[29] Guidance Regarding Deduction and Capitalization of Expenditures, 69 Fed. Reg. 436 (January 5, 2004). These regulations are analyzed in detail in Yale, The Final *INDOPCO* Regulations, 105 Tax Notes 435 (October 25, 2004). The IRS has issued a series of Revenue Procedures relating to making accounting changes to conform to the regulations. *See* Rev. Proc. 2005-9, 2005-2 I.R.B. 303, as *modified by* Rev. Proc. 2005-17, 2005-13 I.R.B. 797.

standard, the Explanation said that such a standard does not provide the certainty and clarity necessary for compliance with, and sound administration of, the law; and, thus, retaining this concept as a separate standard would lead to continued uncertainty and controversy. The proposed (and final) regulations specifically list many intangible categories or items for which they require capitalization, and although the Explanation noted that the future benefit concept underlies many of these specific items, the concept itself is not retained as a separate standard; and if in the future the IRS decides there are other transactions that should be added to the listings, this will be done by later published guidance, and with only prospective effect. This approach is explicitly provided for in § 1.263(a)-4(b)(1) and (2) of the final regulations.

The final regulations under Code § 263 are divided into two parts. The first part, Reg. § 1.263(a)-4, deals only with the creation or acquisition of intangible assets, and covers the capitalization of both the direct costs of purchasing or otherwise acquiring or producing such an asset,[30] and the transactional costs involved in making such an acquisition, described in the regulation as costs to "facilitate" the acquisition or creation.[31]

The second part of the regulations, Reg. § 1.263(a)-5, carves out from the scope of the first part amounts paid or incurred for the acquisition of a trade or business, a change in the capital structure of a business entity, and certain other transactions, including bankruptcy reorganizations. Specifically, the transactions covered by the second part include (1) an acquisition or disposition of assets constituting a trade or business, (2) an acquisition of an ownership interest in a business entity if the taxpayer and the entity are related after the acquisition within the meaning of Code § 267(b) or 707(b), (3) an acquisition (except by the taxpayer) of an ownership interest in the taxpayer, (4) a restructuring, recapitalization, or reorganization of the capital structure of a business entity (including under Code §§ 368 or 355), (5) a transfer under Code § 351 or 721, (6) a formation of a disregarded entity, (7) an acquisition of capital, (8) a stock issuance, (9) a borrowing, or (10) the writing of an option.[32] This second part of the regulations differs from the first part in that (a) it deals with the acquisition in these transactions of not just intangible but also tangible assets and (b) on the other hand, it deals only with "facilitating" or indirect costs, not the direct or purchase price costs themselves.

The regulations define "facilitating" costs (to be distinguished from the purchase price itself) for a transaction as an amount paid in the process of investigating or otherwise pursuing the transaction (including an amount paid to determine the value or price to be paid in the transaction).[33] The regulations contain several provisions designed to limit the types of events that are to be considered "facilitative" of the transaction. For example, the regulations provide that the fact that an amount would (or would not) have been paid "but for" the transaction is relevant but not determina-

---

[30] Reg. § 1.263(a)-4(c) and (d).

[31] Reg. § 1.263(a)-4(e).

[32] Reg. § 1.263(a)-5(a).

[33] Reg. §§ 1.263(a)-5(b)(1), -4(e)(1).

tive.[34] Examples given in the regulations of costs that are not to be considered facilitative of another transaction, even though they would not have been incurred "but for" that other transaction, include costs: to facilitate the disposal of assets unwanted in a merger; to facilitate a distribution of stock required by law or regulatory or judicial mandate in connection with another transaction; to facilitate a borrowing in connection with another covered transaction such as a stock or asset acquisition; or to facilitate the integration of the taxpayer's business with an acquired business, such as costs to relocate personnel or equipment, to downsize and pay severance benefits to terminated employees, to integrate information systems and financial statements and to eliminate redundancies in the combined businesses.[35]

For certain defined taxable or nontaxable acquisitions of businesses,[36] the regulations provide a helpful bright-line test for determining the point in time when activities in the process of investigating or pursuing the transaction will need to begin being considered "facilitative."[37] The general rule provided here is that such activities will be considered "facilitative" only if they are performed on or after the earlier of (a) the date a letter of intent, exclusivity agreement, or similar written communication (other than a confidentiality agreement) is executed by representatives of both parties, or (b) the date the material terms of the transaction are approved by the taxpayer's board of directors or, if this is not required, the date the contract is executed. This general rule specifically does not apply, however, to what are described as "inherently facilitative amounts." These "inherently facilitative amounts" must be capitalized even if they precede the bright-line dates. They are defined as amounts paid for: (i) obtaining an appraisal, formal written evaluation, or fairness opinion; (ii) structuring the transaction, including negotiating the structure and obtaining tax advice on it; (iii) preparing and reviewing the documents to effectuate the transaction, such as merger or purchase agreements; (iv) obtaining regulatory approval (and Reg. § 1.263(a)-5(l) Examples 1 and 15 make clear this includes SEC stock registration); (v) obtaining shareholder approval (proxy costs, etc.); and (vi) costs of conveying property (*e.g.*, transfer taxes and title registration fees). The Explanation to the final regulations observes that this definition of inherently facilitative payments should not be construed broadly to bring most due diligence into the "facilitative" category; "general due diligence costs are intended to be addressed by the bright-line test, not the inherently facilitative rules."

A provision that is very helpful in both acquisitive and non-acquisitive transactions is a rule which provides that employee compensation (including bonuses and commissions), and overhead costs, are to be treated as amounts that do not facilitate the acquisition of an asset covered by the regulations.[38] This rule applies regardless of

---

[34] *Ibid.*

[35] Reg. § 1.263(a)-5(c), (l) Example 6.

[36] The covered transactions are taxable acquisitions of assets constituting a trade or business, taxable acquisitions of ownership interests in a trade or business, and certain "A," "B," "C," and "D" reorganizations. This provision does not refer to recapitalizations or "G" reorganizations.

[37] Reg. § 1.263(a)-5(e).

[38] Reg. §§ 1.263(a)-4(e)(4), -5(d). These provisions also give the taxpayer considerable flexibility, on a transaction by transaction basis, to choose to capitalize some or all of these expenses if it wishes.

the percentage of the employee's time that is allocable to capital transactions. Thus, the Explanation to the regulations when in proposed form noted, capitalization is not required for compensation that is paid to an employee who works full time on merger transactions. The final regulations extend this treatment by treating as employee compensation certain amounts paid to persons who are not employees. This includes annual compensation paid to a director for attendance at regular (but not special) board or committee meetings. It includes payments to non-employees (including the employer of these non-employees) for secretarial, clerical, or similar administrative support services (other than services involving the preparation and distribution of proxy solicitations and other documents seeking shareholder approval of an acquisitive or restructuring transaction). In the case of a consolidated return group, it also includes payments by one member of the group to another member for services performed by an employee of the latter.

Of special interest to readers of this book, the regulations also provide a special rule for bankruptcy reorganization costs.[39] This provides that an amount paid by a debtor to institute or administer a Chapter 11 proceeding constitutes an amount paid to facilitate a reorganization, "regardless of the purpose for which the proceeding is instituted." The provision specifically states that this includes an amount paid to prepare and file a bankruptcy petition, to obtain an extension of the exclusivity period, to formulate plans of reorganization under Chapter 11, to analyze plans of reorganization formulated by another party in interest, or to contest or obtain approval of a Chapter 11 plan. However, the provision adds that an amount paid to operate its business during a Chapter 11 proceeding (including, the Explanation says, the types of costs described in Rev. Rul. 77-204) is not an amount paid to institute or administer the proceeding and does not facilitate a reorganization. The rule also says that capitalization is not required for amounts paid by a taxpayer to defend against the commencement of an involuntary bankruptcy proceeding. Finally, the rule provides that "amounts specifically paid to formulate, analyze, contest or obtain approval of the portion of a plan of reorganization under Chapter 11 that resolves tort liabilities of the taxpayer do not facilitate a reorganization . . . if the amounts would have been treated as ordinary and necessary business expenses under section 162 had the bankruptcy proceeding not been instituted." The reference to the "portion of a plan of reorganization under Chapter 11" would seem clearly to include proceedings in the bankruptcy court, and not just those in other courts or venues, that relate to such tort liability. The costs of the bankruptcy proceeding itself can be seen as an extra layer of procedural and administrative expense that would not have been incurred if the transactions had occurred outside bankruptcy, and this provision seems clearly to allow these extra expenses to be deducted to the extent they relate to deductible tort matters. This would seem to be confirmed by Reg. § 1.263(a)-5(l), Example 18, where a bankruptcy petition is filed in order to deal with tort claims. Outside counsel prepares the petition; and in addition prepares the plan of reorganization and an analysis of the protections provided under the plan, attends hearings about the plan before the bankruptcy court, and defends against motions by creditors

---

[39] Reg. § 1.263(a)-5(c)(4).

and tort claimants to strike the plan. The Example says that the portions of these items (other than the preparation of the bankruptcy petition itself) that deal with the tort liability are not to be treated as amounts that facilitate the reorganization. We would hope that the IRS would apply in the same way the provision that says amounts paid to facilitate a borrowing are not to be treated as facilitating another transaction (other than the borrowing itself),[40] although, because this provision is not mentioned in the special bankruptcy rule, this is less clear.

We believe this exception included in the bankruptcy rule in the final regulations for tort matters is an important step in the right direction. We hope that the Treasury and the courts will give further thought to extending this approach to other aspects of bankruptcy. It seems too facile, and factually inaccurate, to view bankruptcy expenses as always creating some amorphous intangible asset that lasts forever. Rather than viewing the bankruptcy proceeding as being the primary event and all the financing and other transactions as being secondary, we would argue that it is more transactionally realistic to view the bankruptcy proceeding as merely being facilitative, and thus secondary, to the transactions that occur during it. If such a focus were adopted, the bankruptcy expenses would be allocated among the transactions that it was instituted to facilitate, and treated for tax purposes accordingly.

The regulations simultaneously issued under Code § 167[41] extend safe-harbor 15-year amortization to certain of the intangible facilitative costs covered by the new Reg. § 1.263(a)-4, but not to amounts required to be capitalized under Reg. § 1.263(a)-5. The Code § 167 regulations provide that amounts required to be capitalized in taxable acquisitive transactions are added by the acquirer to the basis of the asset acquired, and amounts required to be capitalized by a seller in a taxable sale of assets are applied by the seller as a reduction of the amount realized. Debt expenses are to be amortized, as provided in Reg. § 1.446-5. The final regulations do not address the treatment of amounts required to be capitalized in most other transactions to which Reg. § 1.263(a)-5 applies. The Explanation accompanying the final Code § 167 regulations notes that these unaddressed transactions include amounts required to be capitalized in tax-free transactions, costs of a target in a taxable stock acquisition, and stock issuance costs. It then adds that "the IRS and Treasury Department intend to issue separate guidance to address the treatment of these amounts and will consider at that time whether such amounts should be eligible for the 15-year safe harbor amortization period described in § 1.167(a)-3." We would hope that the treatment of bankruptcy reorganization costs would be reexamined as part of that process.[42]

It may be useful here to list the types of transactions that occur in (as well as outside of) bankruptcy, together with an indication of the way they have been treated under general tax principles. We suggest that the same results should apply whether they occur in a bankruptcy case or in a nonbankruptcy workout.

---

[40] Reg. § 1.263(a)-5(c)(1).

[41] Reg. § 1.167(a)-3(b).

[42] For a further discussion of the treatment of bankruptcy costs under the foregoing regulations, *see* Jenks, Ridgway, and Prunell, 790 T.M., Corporate Bankruptcy, at VI.D.

**Preparation of financial statements, business plans, projections and periodic audits.** The ordinary expenses of auditing a company's records, and of preparing financial statements, business plans and projections are generally deductible.[43] The same is true of expenses of directors' meetings, advice to officers and directors, and legal expenses for the recovery of fees improperly allowed to an attorney by a receivership court.[44]

**Installing an accounting system.** The cost of installing an accounting system is deductible.[45] So is the cost of hiring an efficiency expert to study the company's operations and install a new operations system.[46]

**Selling assets.** Expenses incurred in selling capital assets are treated as an offset to the selling price of the asset, and thus in effect are deductible when the asset is sold.[47]

**Compliance with government regulations.** Although the initial registering with government agencies may not always be deductible, the general cost of compliance with their rules and regulations ordinarily is deductible.[48]

**Identifying assets and liabilities.** The cost of identifying liabilities and assets is generally deductible.[49]

**Investigating fraudulent conduct of officers.** The cost of investigating the alleged misconduct of corporate officers is generally deductible.[50]

**Issuing or exchanging debt.** Expenses incurred in issuing debt or exchanging new debt for old debt is generally amortizable over the life of the new debt.[51]

**Stock issuance and related expenses.** Stock issuance expenses and the cost of registering stock with the SEC are nondeductible, nonamortizable expenses.[52] How-

---

[43] *Ellis Banking Co. v. Commissioner*, 688 F.2d 1376, 82-2 U.S.T.C. ¶9630 (11th Cir. 1982), *cert. denied*, 463 U.S. 1207 (1983).

[44] *Missouri-Kansas Pipe Line Co.*, 3 T.C.M. 15 (1944), *aff'd*, 148 F.2d 460 (3d Cir. 1945).

[45] Schlosser Bros., Inc., 2 B.T.A. 137, Dec. 558 (1925).

[46] *See* IRS Letter Ruling 7906011, Oct. 25, 1978.

[47] *Woodward v. Commissioner*, 397 U.S. 572, 574-5, 70-1 U.S.T.C. ¶9348 (1970); Reg. §1.263(a)-2(e). This treatment is confirmed by Reg. §1.263(a)-5(g)(2)(ii) for taxable sales of assets by the target, including by way of merger or consolidation, but these regulations specifically decline to deal with the treatment of costs by the target for taxable sales of stock representing a business.

[48] *See* Rev. Rul. 65-13, 1965-1 C.B. 87 (in contrast to the initial cost of registering with the SEC, the cost of obtaining the necessary information for, and of filing semi-annual reports in connection with an employee stock option offering were deductible as ordinary and necessary expenses); *Pacific Great Products Co. v. Commissioner*, 17 T.C. 1097 (1952), *acq.* 1952-2 C.B. 3, *appealed on other issues*, 219 F.2d 862 (9th Cir. 1955) (compliance with food and drug laws). Reg. §1.263(a)-5(a) provides that one must capitalize the costs of facilitating a stock issuance or an acquisition of capital or a borrowing, and Reg. §1.263(a)-5(l), Examples 1 and 15 provide that the payments to outside counsel for registering stock with the SEC are to be treated as amounts paid to facilitate the issuance of stock.

[49] *See Arc Realty Company v. Commissioner*, 34 T.C. 484, Dec. 24,230 (1960), *acq.* 1960-2 C.B. 3, *appealed on other issues*, 295 F.2d 98 (8th Cir. 1961); *Walsh v. United States*, 78-2 U.S.T.C. ¶9615 (N.D. Tex. 1978).

[50] *Lomas & Nettleton Co. v. United States*, 79 F. Supp. 886, 48-2 U.S.T.C. ¶9362 (D.C. Conn. 1948).

[51] *Great Western Power Co. v. Commissioner*, 297 U.S. 543, 36-1 U.S.T.C. ¶9185 (1936). *See also* Reg. §§1.263(a)-5(a)(9), (c)(1) and 1.446-5.

[52] *See McCrory Corp. v. United States*, *supra* note 3; *Consumers Water Co. v. United States*, 369 F. Supp. 939, 74-1 U.S.T.C. ¶9189 (D. Me. 1974). Reg. §1.263(a)-5(a)(8) provides that costs facilitating the

ever, stock transfer fees, and the expenses connected with proxy solicitations, shareholder relations, and preparing annual reports are currently deductible.[53]

**Abandoned plans of restructuring.** Expenses of formulating a separate proposed plan of recapitalization or acquisition that is ultimately abandoned and not used are generally deductible.[54] There can be a question, however, as to whether the costs involved relate to a separate plan, or are part of a single plan. The IRS has taken the position that a plan is not separate unless both the abandoned plan and the completed plan could have been completed; if they are mutually exclusive alternative methods of reaching but a single objective, then the cost of the abandoned plan should be capitalized as part of the plan that was completed.[55] This same approach is taken in Reg. § 1.263(a)-5(c)(8). The case law supports such a formulation of the rule where the mutually exclusive alternative plans are being considered simultaneously[56] or where it is difficult to determine how to tell which expenses did not benefit the plan that was ultimately adopted.[57] However, where this is not the case, the case law supports an abandonment deduction for the costs of the abandoned plans.[58] As

(Footnote Continued)

issuance of stock have to be capitalized, and Reg. § 1.263(a)-5(l), Examples 1 and 15 provide that this includes registering stock with the SEC.

53 *See* Bittker & Eustice, *supra* note 13, at ¶ 5.04[9] n. 155. However, Reg. § 1.263(a)-5(c)(7) provides that, whereas amounts paid to a registrar or stock transfer agent are normally deductible, such amounts paid with respect to an acquisitive or reorganization transaction are treated as facilitative payments that have to be capitalized. Similarly, costs of proxy solicitations for an acquisitive or reorganization transaction would presumably be facilitative amounts required to be capitalized under Reg. § 1.263(a)-5(a).

54 *See* Rev. Rul. 73-580, 1973-2 C.B. 86; *Sibley, Lindsay & Curr Co. v. Commissioner*, 15 T.C. 106, Dec. 17,788 (1950), *acq.* 1951-1 C.B. 3.

55 *See* Technical Advice Memorandum 9402004 (Jan. 14, 1994); Technical Advice Memorandum 200512021 (December 29, 2004) (fee to terminate one merger in order to do a different merger with a different corporation; involved a pre-Reg. § 1.263-5(c)(8) year).

56 *Libson Shops, Inc. v. Koehler*, 55-1 U.S.T.C. ¶ 9458 (E.D. Mo. 1955) (different plans for combining 16 corporations into one); *aff'd on other issues*, 229 F.2d 220, 56-1 U.S.T.C. ¶ 9216 (8th Cir. 1956), 353 U.S. 382, 57-1 U.S.T.C. ¶ 9691 (1957); *Sibley, Lindsey & Curr Co. v. Commissioner, supra* note 4; *Haspel v. Commissioner*, 62 T.C. 59, Dec. 32,549 (1974) (two architects' plans for same hotel); *Arthur T. Galt*, 19 T.C. 892, Dec. 19,491 (1953), *aff'd on other issues*, 216 F.2d 41, 54-2 U.S.T.C. ¶ 9457 (7th Cir. 1954) (property to be leased to one lessee successfully leased to one of several prospects; cost of pursuing other prospects had to be capitalized into successful lease); *Larsen v. Commissioner*, 66 T.C. 478, Dec. 33,881 (1976), *acq.* 1977-1 C.B. 1 (abandonment deduction allowed for unsuccessful lease efforts for part of property where other part was successfully leased; all of the leases could have been executed and were not mutually exclusive).

57 *Frankford-Quaker Grocery Co. v. United States*, 353 F. Supp. 93, 73-1 U.S.T.C. ¶ 9297 (E.D. Pa. 1973); *Arthur T. Galt*, supra note 56; *Libson Shops, Inc.*, supra note 56.

58 In Haspel, supra note 56, the court said an abandonment deduction would have been allowed if the first architect's plans had been completely abandoned and subsequently a second architect had submitted alternative plans for the hotel; *Bredingen v. Commissioner*, 6 B.T.A. 335, *acq.* VI-2 C.B. 1 (deduction allowed for abandoned architect's plans despite fact that same architect later submitted other plans for the building that was built); *Tobacco Products Export Corp. v. Commissioner*, 18 T.C. 1100, Dec. 19,208 (1952), *nonacq.* 1955-2 C.B. 11 (deduction allowed for alternative plans for removing asset from corporation, which abandoned plans were not presented simultaneously with plan that was later adopted); *Portland Furniture Manufacturing Co. v. Commissioner*, 30 B.T.A. 579 (1934), *nonacq.* XIII-2 C.B. 33 (deduction allowed for abandonment of plans for merger of several corporations even though in the next year a subsequent plan for merging some of these corporations was adopted). The

mentioned above,[59] the bankruptcy court in the *Hillsborough* case took the view that in a bankruptcy proceeding no deduction can be taken for abandoned bankruptcy plans or restructuring plans, accepting the IRS argument that a bankruptcy is a unitary capital event that cannot be subdivided. This latter approach would seem to be modified by Reg. § 1.263(a)-5(c)(8), which provides that an amount paid to terminate or facilitate the termination of an agreement to enter into an acquisitive or reorganization transaction constitutes an amount paid to facilitate a second transaction only if the transactions are mutually exclusive, and, similarly, an amount paid to facilitate the making of an acquisitive or reorganization transaction will be treated as an amount paid to facilitate a second transaction only if the two are mutually exclusive. In general, the approach of the Reg. § 1.263(a)-5 provisions, as discussed above, is to separate rather than integrate transactions.

(Footnote Continued)

question whether the foregoing abandonment principle applies to expenses of unsuccessful efforts to resist a hostile takeover was considered in both *United States v. Federated Dept. Stores, Inc.*, 171 B.R. 603 (S.D. Ohio 1994) and in *A.E. Staley Mfg. Co.*, 105 T.C. No. 14 (1995). The Court found that the taxpayer had adequately proved separateness in *Federated.* In *Staley*, the Tax Court had reached the contrary conclusion. But on appeal, the Court of Appeals for the Seventh Circuit held that separateness had been proven. *A.E. Staley Manufacturing Co. v. Commissioner*, 119 F.3d 482, 97-2 U.S.T.C. ¶ 50,521. The Seventh Circuit opinion seems inconsistent with the approach taken in Technical Advice Memorandum 9402004, *supra* note 55.

[59] *See Hillsborough Holdings Corp. v. United States*, *supra* note 21.

# Table of Cases

*All references are to sections.*

## D

## E

## F

## G

## H

## I

## J

## K

## L

M

## N

## O

## P

## Q



## R

## S

## T

## U

## V



## W

## X



## Y



## Z

# Table of Internal Revenue Code Sections

*All references are to sections.*

# Table of Bankruptcy Code Sections

*All references are to sections.*

# Table of Bankruptcy Rules

*All references are to sections.*

# Table of Regulations

*All references are to sections.*

**Final Regulations**

## Temporary Regulations

### Proposed Regulations

# Table of IRS Letter Rulings

*All references are to sections.*

# Table of Revenue Rulings

*All references are to sections.*

# Table of Technical Advice Memoranda

*All references are to sections.*

# Table of General Counsel's Memoranda

*All references are to sections.*

# Table of the IRS Manual

*All references are to sections.*

# Table of IRS Notices

*All references are to sections.*



**Internal Revenue News Releases**

# Table of Revenue Procedures

*All references are to sections.*

# Table of IRS Field Service Advice, Chief Counsel Advice, and Legal Memoranda

*All references are to sections.*

**Field Service Advice**



**IRS Chief Counsel Advice**

### IRS Legal Memoranda



### IRS Service Center Advice

# Table of Miscellaneous References

*All references are to sections.*

# Bibliography

Advisory Committee Notes to Bankruptcy Rule 3007, *reprinted at* Collier Pamphlet Edition, Bankruptcy Rules 129 (1992 version).

Ahart & Meadows, Deferring Discharge in Chapter 11, 70 Am. Bankr. L.J. 127 (1996).

ALI, Federal Income Tax Project, Subchapter C (1982).

American Bar Association, Comments Concerning Taxpayer Bill of Rights 2, 92 TNT 159-33 (Aug. 5, 1992).

American Bar Association Task Force Report on Proposals Before the National Bankruptcy Review Commission (dated Apr. 15, 1997), *reprinted at* 97 TNT 90-22.

American Bar Association, Tax Section, Comments Concerning Notice 2003-65 Under Section 382 of the Internal Revenue Code Regarding the Treatment of Recognized Built-In Gains and Losses, April 29, 2005, *reprinted in* BNA Daily Tax Report (May 3, 2005), BNA Tax Core.

American Bar Association, Tax Section, Comments Concerning Subchapter C No-Net-Value Regulations Proposals (April 24, 2006), *reprinted at* 2006 TNT 79-16 (April 25, 2006).

American Bar Association, Tax Section, Comments Regarding Transfers of Assets and Stock Following a Reorganization (February 7, 2005), *reprinted at* 2005 TNT 26-7 (February 9, 2005).

American Bar Association, Tax Section, Committee on Corporate Stockholder Relationships, Legislative Recommendation No. 1985-1 (to Amend Section 382) (Feb. 6, 1985).

American Bar Association, Tax Section, Committee on Corporate Stockholder Relationships, Legislative Recommendation No. 1984-6 (to Modify "G" Reorganization Provisions) (Jul. 23, 1984).

American Bar Association, Tax Section, Committee on Liens, Levies, Limitations and Bankruptcy, Legislative Recommendation No. 1983-12 and Report on the Bankruptcy Tax Act of 1980 (June 23, 1983).

American Bar Association, Tax Section, Report on the Tax Provisions of H.R. 3150, 51 Tax Law 635 (1998).

Andrews, Modern-Day Equitable Recoupment and the "Two Tax Effect:" Avoidance of the Statutes of Limitation in Federal Tax Controversies, 28 Ariz. L. Rev. 595 (1986).

Annot., Classification of Debt as Liquidated, Unsecured, or Contingent, for Purposes of Determining Debtor's Eligibility Under Sec. 109(e) of 1978 Bankruptcy Code, 95 A.L.R. Fed. 793.

Annot., Liability of Federal Equity Receivers, or Trustees Under Bankruptcy Act, for Payment of State and Local Taxes Accruing During the Period of Their Possession and Control, 85 L. Ed. 656 (1941).

Arrow, Bankruptcy Relief Against Governmental Entities, 47 Consumer Fin. L.Q. Rep. 25 (1993).

Asofsky, Discharge of Indebtedness in Bankruptcy After the Bankruptcy Tax Act of 1980, 27 St. Louis U. L.J. 583 (1983).

Asofsky, A Guide to the Tax Treatment of Contingent Payment Debt Instruments, 56 NYU Inst. on Fed. Tax'n, Chapter 5 (1998).

Asofsky, An Historical Look at the Stock-for-Debt Exception, 56 Tax Notes 1091 (Aug. 24, 1992).

Asofsky, Reorganizing Insolvent Corporations, 41 Inst. on Fed. Tax'n § 5 (1983).

Asofsky, Towards a Bankruptcy Tax Act of 1993, 51 NYU Inst. Fed. Tax'n § 13.02 (1993)

Asofsky, Uncertain Limits: The Stock-For-Debt Exception to Discharge of Indebtedness Income, 1 Corp. Tax'n 59 (1988).

Asofsky, Bacon, Hyman, Klee, Ruge, Singer & Tatlock, Conference on the Bankruptcy Tax Act of 1980, 39 Inst. on Fed. Tax'n § 57 (1981).

Asofsky & Tatlock, Bankruptcy Tax Act Alters Treatment of Bankruptcy and Discharging Debts, 54 J. Tax'n 106 (1981).

Asofsky & Tatlock, Reorganizations, Procedures and Corporate Taxes Greatly Affected by Bankruptcy Tax Act, 54 J. Tax'n 170 (1981).

Association of the Bar of the City of New York, Limited Liability Companies and Bankruptcy, 51 The Record 46 (1996).

Association of the Bar of the City of New York, Proposal to Create a Federal Right of Contribution Among "Responsible Persons" Under Section 6672 of the Internal Revenue Code, The Record (Apr. 1992).

Association of the Bar of the City of New York, Response to Certain Proposals Made to the National Bankruptcy Review Commission Relating to Tax Issues, 52 The Record 418 (1997).

Axelrod, The Basis for Using E&P in Consolidated Return Basis Adjustments, 12 J. Corp. Tax'n 228 (1985).

Axelrod, What's "Reasonable" Before the Consolidated COD Regulations?, 115 Tax Notes 745 (May 21, 2007).

Bacon, Rescue Planning for the Failing or Bankrupt Company, 61 Taxes 931 (1983).

Bacon & Adrion, Taxable Events: The Aftermath of Cottage Savings, 59 Tax Notes 1227, 1385 (May 31, 1993).

Bacon & Billinger, Analyzing the Operation and Tax Effects of the New Bankruptcy Act, 50 J. Tax'n 76 (1979).

Bacon, Krupsky, Hyman, Klee & Asofsky, Tax Planning for the Financially Troubled Company, 36 Major Tax Plan 14-1 (1984).

Bacon & Tomasulo, Net Operating Loss and Credit Carryovers: The Search for Corporate Identity, 20 Tax Notes 835 (Sept. 12, 1983).

Baird & Jackson, Corporate Reorganizations and the Treatment of Diverse Ownership Interests: A Comment on Adequate Protection of Secured Creditors in Bankruptcy, 51 U. Chicago L. Rev. 97 (1984).

Banoff, Tax Aspects of Real Estate Refinancing and Debt Restructuring: The Best and Worst of Times, 64 Taxes 926 (1986).

Barr, The Availability of Net Operating Loss Carryovers Following Taxable Changes of Ownership: Section 382(a) of the Internal Revenue Code, 38 Inst. on Fed. Tax'n § 5 (1980).

Barry, The Foreign Aspects of Code Sec. 382: Searching for Answers in a Troubled Global Economy, 80 Taxes 153 (2002).

Beck, Is Compromise of a Tax Liability Itself Taxable? A Problem of Circularity in the Logic of Taxation, 14 Va. Tax, Rev. 153 (1994).

Beghe, Tax Planning For the Financially Troubled Corporation, 52 Taxes 795 (1974).

Beller, "D" Reorganizations and Dropdowns: An Uneasy Match, 90 Tax Notes 1757 (June 21, 1999).

Berdan & Arnold, Displaying the Debtor in Possession: The Requisites for and Advantages of the Appointment of a Trustee in Chapter 11 Proceedings, 67 Marq. L. Rev. 457 (1984).

Berenson, Bankruptcy—Tax Accounting, Tax Returns and Congressional Revision: H.R. 9973, 9 Tax Advisor 298 (1978).

Berenson & Blank, The Bankruptcy Tax Act of 1980 (Part 1), 12 Tax Advisor 68 (1981).

Berquist & Groff, Reorganizing the Financially Troubled Corporation After The Bankruptcy Tax Act of 1980, 36 Tax L. Rev. 517 (1981).

Berryman, Filing Post Bar Date Amendments of Tax Claims: A Definite Maybe, The Bankr. Strategist 3 (Dec. 1990).

Bienenstock, Bankruptcy Reorganizations, 632 Practicing Law Institute (1987 with 1989 Supp.).

Bittker, B., & J. Eustice, Federal Income Taxation of Corporations and Shareholders, 506(2) (7th ed. with Supp.).

Blanchard, Hooker and Vogel, Underwater Assets and Insolvent Corporations: Reflections on Treasury's Recently Proposed Regulations and Related Matters, 59 Tax Law. 107 (2005).

Blanchard, Jr., The Single Entity Theory of the Consolidated Section 382 Regulations: A Study in Complexity, 69 Taxes 915 (1991).

Blanchard, Jr., The Taxation of Federally Assisted Acquisitions of Troubled Financial Institutions, 44 Tax Law. 1037 (1991).

Blanchard, Jr., Bennett, and Speer, The Deductibility of Investments in Financially Troubled Subsidiaries and Related Federal Income Tax Considerations, 80 Taxes 91 (2002).

Blastin, Bankruptcy Taxation: Succession to Tax Attributes Generated by a Professional Corporation Upon Its Bankruptcy Liquidation, 10 J. Corp. Tax'n 335 (1984).

Bloom, Certain Preferred Stock Gets the "Boot"—But Does It Fit? 88 J. Tax'n 69 (1998).

Bloom, The Resurrection of a Dormant Doctrine: Continuity of Business Enterprise, 7 J. Corp. Tax'n 315 (1981).

Bowen & Sheffield, Section 269 Revisited, 61 Taxes 881 (1983).

Bowmar, The Bankruptcy Trustee as "Bona Fide Purchaser" Under Section 545(2) Against Federal Tax Liens on Personal Property, 29 Unif. Comm. Code L.J. 168 (1996).

Braubach, Insolvency Reorganizations Under the Bankruptcy Tax Act of 1980, 8 J. Corp. Tax'n 91 (1981).

Brock, The Forthcoming Built-In Regulations: Issues for the Government to Address, 95 Tax Notes 97 (Apr. 1, 2002).

Brod, Exercise Caution in Forming Section 337 Liquidating Trusts, 59 Taxes 44 (1980).

Brod, Section 337 Liquidating Trusts Revisited—The IRS Revises Rev. Proc. 79-1, 59 Taxes 286 (1981).

Browning, Tough Bankruptcy Issues Under the Eleventh Amendment, 7 J. Bankr. Law and Prac. 219 (1998).

Browning, Who Can Waive State Immunity, 15 Am. Bankr. Inst. J. 10 (1997).

Brubaker, Of State Sovereign Immunity and Prospective Remedies: The Bankruptcy Discharge as Statutory Ex Parte Young Relief, 76 Am. Bankr. L.J. 461 (2002).

Bryan, Cancellation of Indebtedness by Issuing Stock in Exchange: Challenging the Congressional Solution to Debt-Equity Swaps, 63 Tex. L. Rev. 89 (1984).

Calvin & Farias, When Can Holders of Defaulted Debt Cease Accruing Interest Income?, J. Tax'n 378 (Dec. 1990).

Camp, Avoiding the Ex Post Facto Slippery Slope of Deer Park, 3 Am. Bankr. L. Rev. 329 (1995).

Camp, Carryovers of Net Operating Losses Following Changes in Corporate Ownership, 43 Inst. on Fed. Tax'n § 3 (1984).

Carlson, Surcharge and Standing: Bankruptcy Code Section 506(c) After Hartford Underwriters, 76 Am. Bankr. L. J. 43 (2002).

Carrington, Capitalization After INDOPCO and into the New Millennium, 93 Tax Notes 813 (Nov. 5, 2001).

Cash, Dickens, and Ward-Vaughn, Burden of Proof and the Impact of Code Sec. 7491 in Civil Tax Disputes, 80 Taxes 33 (2002).

CCH Std. Fed. Tax Rpts, Taxes on Parade, Vol. 86, Issue No. 36, Rep. 32 (Aug. 5, 1999).

CCH Tax Strategy Bulletin: Many Employers Can Benefit From Penalty Payment Designations.

Chambers, Split Priority Bankruptcy Claims, 98 TNT 239-77 (Dec. 14, 1998).

Cieri, Fitzgerald, & Miller, Forum Shopping, First Day Orders, and Case Management Issues in Bankruptcy, 1 DePaul Bus. & Comm. L.J. 515 (2003).

Clukey, Examining the Limited Benefits of the Burden of Proof Shift, 1999 TNT 20-136 (Feb. 1, 1999).

Collier on Bankruptcy (15th ed.).

Collier on Bankruptcy Taxation.

Cordy, A Tale of Two Sovereigns: Will The Bankruptcy Code Survive Seminole?, Norton Bankr. L. Advisor, May 1996, at 1.

Cordry, The Incredible Expanding § 1146(c), 21-JAN Am. Bankr. Inst. J. 10 (2003).

Costello, The Troubled Business Venture—Dealing with the New Bankruptcy Reorganization and Cancellation of Indebtedness Provisions, 40 Inst. on Fed. Tax'n § 43 (1982).

Cowan, Recent Cases Reflect Continuing IRS Uncertainties About COD Income from Contingent Debt, 84 J. Tax'n 261 (1996).

Crestol, J., K. Hennessey & A. Rua, The Consolidated Tax Return (1973).

Cuff, Indebtedness of a Disregarded Entity, 81 Taxes 303 (2003).

Culp & Marsh, Avoiding Cancellation of Debt Income Where the Liability is Disputed, 74 J. Tax'n 288 (1991).

Cummings, The Disregarded Entity Is and Isn't Disregarded, 99 Tax Notes 743 (May 5, 2003).

Cummings and Hanson, New Limitations on Corporate Built-in Losses, 107 Tax Notes 1553 (June 20, 2005).

Dahlberg and Miles, Built-in Gain of Foreign Corporations, 47 Tax Notes 1217 (June 4, 1990).

Daley & Friedel, Section 108 Attribute Reduction for Consolidated Groups (Parts 1 & 2), 31 J. Corp. Tax'n (Jan./Feb. 2004; Mar./Apr. 2004).

Del Negro, Liquidating Trusts—Their Nature and Uses, 38 Inst. on Fed. Tax'n § 23 (1980).

Deming, Personal Liability of Corporate Officers for Failure to Pay Over Withheld Taxes, 3 Tax Ideas ¶ 28,013 (1978).

Department of the Treasury, I.R.S. Publication 908, Bankruptcy (Sept. 1994).

Dicello, Fielding & Teel, Litigation of Tax Controversies in Bankruptcy Proceedings, (Jan. 24, 1987) (outline presented at midyear meeting of the American Bar Association, Tax Section).

Disregarded Entity Is and Isn't Disregarded, The, 99 Tax Notes 743 (May 5, 2003).

Dooher, Contingent Liabilities and the Insolvency Exception to Cancellation of Debt Income: Merkel v. Comm'r, 39 Tax Mgmt. Memo. 195 (1998).

Dooher, Recovering Attorneys Fees and Other Costs Incurred in Tax Controversies: Recent Developments, 33 Tax Mgmt. Mem. 13 (June 29, 1992).

Dooher, Review of the Tax Aspects of Real Estate Foreclosures and Workouts 91 Tax Mgmt. Mem. 220-221 (1985).

Dougherty & Hill, Corporate Offers-in-Compromise, 1 Corp. Bus. Tax'n Monthly #6, 14 (2000).

Douglas-Hamilton, Creditor Liabilities Resulting from Improper Interference with the Management of a Financially Troubled Debtor, 31 Bus. Law. 343 (1975).

Douglas-Hamilton, When Are Creditors in Control of Debtor Companies?, 26 Prac. Law. (no. 7) 61 (1980).

Dubroff, A, J. Blanchard, Jr., J. Broadbent, K. Duvall, Federal Income Taxation of Corporations Filing Consolidated Tax Returns (2d ed.).

Eisenberg, Limitations on Importation and Transfer of Built-in Losses: Untangling the New Basis Adjustment Rules, 107 Tax Notes 869 (May 16, 2005).

Elliot, Federal Tax Collections, Liens and Levies (1995 with Supp.).

Eustice, Cancellation of Indebtedness and the Federal Income Tax: A Problem of Creeping Confusion, 14 Tax L. Rev. 223 (1959).

Eustice, Cancellation of Indebtedness Redux The Bankruptcy Tax Act of 1980 Proposals—Corporate Aspects, 36 Tax L. Rev. 1 (1980).

Eustice, A Case Study in Technical Tax Reform: Section 361, or How Not To Revise a Statute, 35 Tax Notes 282 (Apr. 20, 1987).

Eustice, Federal Income Taxation of Corporations and Shareholders (5th ed. 1988 Supp. No. 1).

Eustice, The Tax Reform Act of 1984: A Selective Analysis (1984).

Eustice & Portney, The Destiny of Net Operating Losses, 22 San Diego L. Rev. 115 (1985).

Evans & Gallagher, INDOPCO—The Treasury Finally Acts, 80 Taxes 47 (2002).

Faber, The Declaratory Powers of Bankruptcy Courts to Determine the Federal Tax Consequences of Chapter 11 Plans, 3 Am. Bankr. Inst. Law Rev. 407 (1994).

Faber, Net Operating Losses in Corporate Reorganizations Revisited in 1979, 38 Inst. on Fed. Tax'n § 4 (1979).

Falk, Recovering Prepetition Levies and Seizures by the IRS, 4 Faulkner & Gray's Bankr. L. Rev. #1, 21 (Spring 1992).

Ferguson, Profiting from Tax Losses, 60 Taxes 1010 (1982).

Fortgang & King, The 1978 Bankruptcy Code: Some Wrong Policy Decisions, 56 N.Y.U. L. Rev. 1148 (1981).

Fortgang & Mayer, Developments in Trading Claims and Taking Control of Corporations in Chapter 11, 13 Cardozo L. Rev. 1 (1991).

Friedel, Final Consolidated Return Regs. Preventing Loss Duplication: Worse Than Useless (Parts 1 & 2), 33 J. Corp. Tax'n #4 and #5 (July/Aug. and Sept./Oct. 2006).

Friedman, Debt Exchanges After Rev. Rul. 2004-78, 105 Tax Notes 979 (November 15, 2004).

Gallagher, How to Resolve Corporate Chapter 11 Reorganization Tax Issues, 10 The Practical Law. 57 (1996).

Gelfeld & Lobl, Tax Planning Opportunities for Debtor Corporations in Chapter 11 Proceedings, 91 Comm. Law. J. 417 (1986).

Germain, Avoiding Phantom Income in Bankruptcy: A Proposal for Reform, 5 Florida Tax Rev. 249 (2001).

Gibson, Sovereign Immunity in Bankruptcy: The Next Chapter, 70 Am. Bankr. L.J. 195 (1996).

Ginsburg, Future Payment Sales After the 1980 Revision Act, 39 Inst. on Fed. Tax'n § 43 (1981).

Ginsburg, Rethinking the Tax Law in the New Installment Sales World, 59 Taxes 886 (1981).

Ginsburg & Levin, Mergers, Acquisitions and Buyouts, § 605 (Aspen, May 2000 ed.).

Glicklich, Section 384: Less Left for Loss Corporations, 16 J. Corp. Tax'n 23 (Spring, 1989).

Goldman, Joining or Leaving an Affiliated Group Which Files a Consolidated Return: A Checklist for the Agreement, 36 Tax L. Rev. 199 (1981).

Goldring, The Bankruptcy Code's Tax Exemption for Sales During Chapter 11 Reorganizations, 2 Corp. Tax'n 55 (Nov./Dec. 1989).

Goldring, Modifying Debt and Its Consequences, Vol. 20 Tax Strategies for Corporate Acquisitions, Dispositions, Spin-Offs, Joint Ventures, Financing, Reorganizations and Restructurings (Prac. Law Inst. 2006).

Goldring & Feiner, Section 382 Ownership Change, 66 Taxes 427, 619, and 803 (June, Sept., and Nov. 1988).

Goldring & Mayo, Lenders Beware: Potential Liability for Unpaid Employment Taxes, 4 J. Bank Tax'n #1 (Fall 1990).

Goldring & Richards, Current Developments in State and Local Bankruptcy Taxation, 50 Tax Law. 539, 565-567 (1997).

Goldring & Sontag, Life After the Final Regulations: Consolidated Section 382 and SRLY, Vol. 27 Tax Strategies for Corporate Acquisitions, Dispositions, Spin-Offs, Joint Ventures, Financing, Reorganizations and Restucturings (Prac. Law Inst. 2006).

Gravis & Koger, If at First You Don't Succeed . . . : An Alternative Remedy After Nordic Village, 66 Am. Bankr. L.J. 423, 427-429 (1992).

Guidance Regarding Deduction and Capitalization of Expenditures, 67 Fed. Reg. 77701 (Dec. 19, 2002).

Haims & Schaumberger, Restructuring the Overleveraged Company, 48 Tax Notes 91 (Jul. 2, 1990).

Heinlen, The ABC's of Cancellation of Indebtedness Income and Attribute Reduction, 40 Inst. on Fed. Tax'n § 42 (1982).

Henderson, Controlling Hyperlexis—The Most Important "Law and . . . ," 43 Tax Law. 177, 186-191 (1989).

Henderson, Developing a Tax Strategy For the Failing Company, 63 Taxes 952 (1985).

Henderson, Side Effects of Leaving a Consolidated Return Group, 27 Inst. on Fed. Tax'n 711 (1969).

Henderson, Tax Planning for Taxable Stock Acquisitions Under the Section 338 Temporary Regulations, 38 Maj. Tax Plan. Ch. 2 (1986).

Heng & Parker, Tax-Free Debt Repurchase Using Stock-for-Debt Exchanges, 60 Taxes 527 (1982).

Henry, Reissuance Revisited, 42 Tax Notes 91 (Jan. 2, 1989).

Hertz, Personal Liabilities of the Unsuspecting Executive for Penalties Under Section 6672 and Other Nightmares, 32 Inst. on Fed. Tax'n 1171 (1974).

Hill, Toward a Theory of Bankruptcy Tax: A Statutory Coordination Approach, 50 Tax Law. 103 (1996).

Hipple, Special Tax Provisions of the Bankruptcy Reform Act of 1978, 1979 Ann. Survey of Bankr. Law 127 (1979).

Hirsch, The Bankruptcy Tax Act of 1980, Tax Mgmt. Mem. 81-7, p. 2 (1981).

Hoffenberg, Owner Shifts and Fluctuations in Value: A Theory of Relativity, 106 Tax Notes 1446 (March 21, 2005).

Hoffer, Give Them My Regards: A Proposal for Applying the COD Rules to Disregarded Entities, 107 Tax Notes 327 (April 18, 2005).

Howard, An Overview of the State and Federal Tax Responsibilities of Bankruptcy Trustees and Debtors, 93 Comm. L.J. 43, 56-58 (1988).

Huber, Lubozynski & Pallerro, Consolidated Return Temp. Regs. Modernize SRLY Treatment for Credits and Create OFL Problems, 89 J. Tax'n 12 (1998).

Hyman & Hoffman, Consolidated Returns: Summary of Tax Considerations in Acquisition of Common Parent or Subsidiary Member of Affiliated Group, 33 Tax Law. 383 (1980).

Hyman, Martin & Montali, Tax Aspects of Corporate Debt Exchanges, Recapitalizations, and Discharges, California Continuing Education of the Bar, Advanced Taxation Series Program Material (1982).

Jacobs, The Bankruptcy Court's Emergence as Tax Dispute Arbiter of Choice, 45 Tax Law. 971, 1008 (1992).

Jacobs, Escrows and Their Consequences, 39 Inst. on Fed. Tax'n § 5 (1980).

Jacobs, Tax Treatment of Corporate Net Operating Losses and Other Tax Attribute Carryovers, 5 Va. Tax Rev. 701 (1986).

Jacobson & Law, Federal "Tax Collection" Procedures: Recent Developments and Emerging Trends to Remedy 'Abusive' Tactics Used in the Collection of Income Tax Liabilities, 38 Tax Mgmt. Memo. 147 (May 26, 1997).

Jenks, The Tax Collector in Bankruptcy Court: The Government's Uneasy Role as a Creditor in Bankruptcy, 71 Taxes 847 (1993).

Jenks, The Bankruptcy Abuse Prevention and Consumer Protection Act of 2005: Summary of Tax Provisions, 79 Am. Bankr. L.J. (December 2005), at I.G.

Jenks, Ridgway, & Purnell, 790 T.M. Corporate Bankruptcy (2004 ed.).

Jerome, Blauner & Drain, Bankruptcy Courts Impose New Roadblocks to Claims Trading, 4 Faulkner & Gray's Bankr. L. Rev. #1, 30 (Spring 1992).

Joint Committee on Taxation, Explanation of Technical Corrections to the Tax Reform Act of 1984 and Other Recent Legislation 42 (May 13, 1987).

Joint Committee on Taxation, Federal Income Tax Aspects of Mergers and Acquisitions (JCS-6-85), Mar. 29, 1985.

Joint Committee on Taxation, General Explanation of the Economic Recovery Tax Act of 1981 (Aug. 1, 1981).

Joint Committee on Taxation, General Explanation of the Revenue Provisions of the Deficit Reduction Act of 1984 (Dec. 31, 1984).

Joint Committee on Taxation, General Explanation of the Tax Reform Act of 1986 (May 14, 1986).

Joint Committee on Taxation, Special Limitations on the Use of Net Operating Loss Carryovers and Other Tax Attributes of Corporations (JCS-16-85) (May 21, 1985).

Joint Committee on Taxation, Staff Description of Amendment Proposing Additional Tax Law Changes and Tax Increases to H.R. 4333 (Jul. 13, 1988).

Kahn and Kahn, Prevention of Double Deductions of a Single Loss: Solutions in Search of a Problem, 26 Va. Tax Rev. 1 (2006).

Kies, Taking a Fresh Look at the Stock-for-Debt Exception, 56 Tax Notes 1619 (Sept. 21, 1992).

Kirschner, Kusnotz, Solarsh & Gatarz, Prepackaged Bankruptcy Plans: The Deleveraging Tool of the '90s In the Wake of OID and Tax Concerns, 21 Seton Hall L. Rev. 643 (1991).

Klee, Legislative History of the New Bankruptcy Law, 28 DePaul L. Rev. 941 (1979).

Kliegman, Troubled Thrift Reorganizations—The Short Happy Life of Section 368(a)(3)(D), 64 Taxes 281 (1986).

Koger & True, The Final Word on Excusable Neglect?, 98 Comm. L.J. 21 (1993).

Krane, Preserving the Tax Attributes of Financially Troubled Corporations, 53 Taxes 802 (1975).

Krieger, Tax Accounting: Sub S Debt and The Bankruptcy Tax Act, 8 J. Corp. Tax'n 162 (1981).

Krupsky, Take Over of a Bankruptcy Company by a Single Major Creditor, 36 Major Tax Plan.

Kusnetz, Loss of Control—The Clash of Codes in the Battle Over a Debtor's Net Operating Losses, Tax Review Paper #243 (Nov. 13, 2006).

Larson, The Bankruptcy Court Overlooks Tax Law in In re Prudential Lines, Inc.: An NOL Should Not Be a Property of a Bankruptcy Estate, 29 Willamette L. Rev. 23 (1993).

Lassila & Putnam, The Discharge of "Qualified Business Indebtedness": Should the Section 108(d)(4) Election Be Made? 36 Tax Executive 365 (1984).

Lawniczak, Courts Defining Ordinary Course of Business in a Preference Case More Liberally, 31 Bankr. Ct. Dec. (LRP Pub., Aug. 12, 1997), at p. 3.

Leeds, The IRS Expands Business Purpose Requirement for Transfers to Corporations, 29 J. Corp. Tax'n 3 (2002).

Levin & Rocap, A Transactional Guide to Federal Tax Aspects of Restructuring Troubled Corporation Debt, 52 Tax Notes 1177 (Sept. 2, 1991).

Levin & Ranney-Marinelli, The Creeping Repeal of Chapter 11: The Significant Business Provisions of the Bankruptcy Abuse Prevention and Consumer Protection Act of 2005, 79 Am. Bankr. L.J. 603 (2005).

Lewis, Recognizing Discharge of Indebtedness Income on Bond-for-Bond Recapitalizations, 45 J. Tax'n 370 (Dec. 1976).

Libin, Continuity of Business Enterprise: The New Regulations, 39 Inst. on Fed. Tax'n § 4 (1980).

Lipton, Debt-Equity Swaps for Parent-Subsidiary: A Current Analysis of a Useful Technique, 59 J. Tax'n 46 (1983).

Lipton, The Section 1001 Debt Modification Regulations: Problems and Opportunities, 85 J. Tax'n 216 (1996).

Lipton, Section 1274 and COD Income Due to Modification of the Interest Rate in a Debt Instrument, 68 Taxes 504 (Jul. 1990).

Lipton, The Tax Consequences to a Debtor from the Transfer of Its Indebtedness, 69 Taxes 939 (Dec. 1991).

Lipton, The Tax Court's New Standard for Testing Contingent Liabilities—Will it Work? 88 J. Tax'n 150 (1998).

Lipton & Bots, Gitlitz & Winn, Petitioners, v. Commissioner of Internal Revenue, Respondent, 28 J. Tax'n 3 (Jan./Feb. 2001).

Los Angeles County Bar Association, Taxation Section, Corporate Tax Committee, Recommendations for Regulations to be Promulgated Under Section 382(h)(6), 2003 TNT 94-130 (May 15, 2003).

Los Angeles County Bar Association, Taxation Section, Corporate Tax Committee, Report on Restructuring the Debt of Financially Troubled Companies, 2003 TNT 94-126 (May 15, 2003).

Lundgren, Liability of a Creditor in a Control Relationship with Its Debtor, 67 Marq. L. Rev. 523 (1984).

Luria & Donald, 88-4th T.M., Cancellation of Indebtedness—Sections 108 and 1017 (1981).

Mandel, Lender Beware: Tax Planning for Troubled Loans in Troubled Times, 80 Taxes 77 (2002).

McBurney, the Consolidated Return Regs.' Loss Disallowance Rule—When Is It Vulnerable? 90 J. of Tax'n 20 (Jan. 1999).

McCurley & Simon, FIRREA Changes the Rules Governing Acquisitions of Troubled Financial Institutions, 45 Tax Notes 617 (Oct. 30, 1989).

McQueen, C., & J. Williams, Federal Tax Aspects of Bankruptcy (1997).

Makel & Chadwick, Lender Liability for a Borrower's Unpaid Payroll Taxes, 43 Bus. Law. 507 (1988).

Metzer, An Effective Use of Plain English—The Evolution and Impact of Section 368(a)(1)(F), 32 Tax Law. 703 (1979).

Miller & Tanenbaum, High Court Clarifies "Excusable Neglect," Natl. L.J. (May 24, 1993).

Mirsky, Reorganizing a Going Business: Eliminating Divisions and Subsidiaries That are Generating Losses; Consolidated Return Considerations, 34 Inst. on Fed. Tax'n 629 (1976).

Mirsky & Willens, The Bankruptcy Tax Act of 1980, 59 Taxes 145 (1981).

Mombrun & Johnson, Loss Disallowance Post-Rite Aid: The IRS and Treasury Revisit the Treatment of Subsidiary Stock Losses, 81 Taxes 21 (2003).

Morris, Imposition of Transfer Limitations on Claims and Equity Interests During Corporate Debtor's Chapter 11 Case to Preserve the Debtor's Net Operating Loss Carryforward: Examining the Emerging Trend, 77 Am. Bankr. L.J. 285 (2003).

National Association of Bond Lawyers, Committee on General Federal Tax Matters, Tax Analysis of "Reissue" Questions Arising From Changes in Bond Terms (undated and unpublished memorandum).

National Bankruptcy Conference Bankruptcy Code Review Project, presented at ALI-ABA Conference, June 10-12, 1993 (Bankruptcy Reform Circa 1993).

National Bankruptcy Review Commission Final Report (Oct. 20, 1997).

Needham, The "Item of Income" Exclusion of Section 382(h)(6)(A)—An Expansion of the Built-in Gain Rule, 51 Tax Notes 373 (Apr. 22, 1991).

New York State Bar Association, Tax Section, Report of the Committee on Bankruptcy, The Stock-for-Debt Exception to the Tax Treatment of Income >From Discharge of Indebtedness (Dec. 20, 1983).

New York State Bar Association, Tax Section, Report on Advance Notice of Proposed Rulemaking on Deduction and Capitalization of Expenditures Connected with Intangibles, Jul. 25, 2002.

New York State Bar Association, Tax Section, Report on Application of the IRC Sections 6111 and 6112 Material Advisor Rules to Law and Accounting Firms (May 5, 2006), *reprinted at* 2006 TNT 88-79 (May 8, 2006).

New York State Bar Association, Tax Section, Report on Creation of Federal Right to Contribution/Declaratory Judgment for Section 6672 Liability, 92 TNT 222-24 (Oct. 20, 1992).

New York State Bar Association, Tax Section, Report on Distributions Following Tax-Free Reorganizations (May 19, 2004), 2004 TNT 99-28 (May 21, 2004).

New York State Bar Association, Tax Section, Report on Notice 2004-37 (November 18, 2004), *reprinted at* 2004 TNT 226-13 (November 23, 2004).

New York State Bar Association, Tax Section, Report on Proposed Legislation to Amend the Market Discount Rules of Sections 1276-78 (June 22, 1999).

New York State Bar Association, Tax Section, Report on Proposed Regulations Regarding Continuity of Interest and Pre-Closing Stock Value Fluctuation (November 29, 2004), *reprinted at* 2004 TNT 233-12 (December 3, 2004).

New York State Bar Association, Tax Section, Report on Proposed Regulations Regarding Organizations, Reorganizations and Liquidations Involving Insolvent Corporations (January 20, 2006), *reprinted at* 2006 TNT 15-10 (January 24, 2006).

New York State Bar Association, Tax Section, Report on Related Party Debt Acquisitions Under Section 108(e)(4) of the Code (Apr. 12, 1984).

New York State Bar Association, Tax Section, Report on Section 597 Proposed Regulations, 58 Tax Notes 769 (Feb. 8, 1993).

New York State Bar Association, Tax Section, Report on the Taxation of Shareholder Rights Plans (Jul. 15, 1988).

New York State Bar Association, Tax Section, Report on Temporary Regulation § 1.337(d)-2T and Proposed Regulation § 1.1502-35T, 2003 TNT 43-35 (Feb. 28, 2003).

New York State Bar Association, Tax Section, Report on "Tracking Stock" Arrangements, 43 Tax L. Rev. 51 (1987).

New York State Bar Association, Tax Section, Ad Hoc Committee, Report on Proposed Original Issue Discount Regulations, 34 Tax Notes 363 (Jan. 26, 1987).

New York State Bar Association, Tax Section, Committee on Bankruptcy, Report on Acquisitions of Discount Debt by Related Parties Under the New Section 108(e)(4) Regulation, 52 Tax Notes 211 (Jul. 8, 1991).

New York State Bar Association, Tax Section, Committee on Bankruptcy, Report on Related Party Debt Acquisitions Under Section 108(e)(4) of the Code (Apr. 13, 1984).

New York State Bar Association, Tax Section, Committee on Bankruptcy, Report on Reorganizations Under Section 368(a)(1)(G); Recommendations for Proposed Regulations (Oct. 25, 1985).

New York State Bar Association, Tax Section, Committee on Bankruptcy, Report on Suggested Bankruptcy Tax Revenue Rulings, Tax Notes (Feb. 11, 1991).

New York State Bar Association, Tax Section, Committee on Bankruptcy and Insolvency, Report on Certain Provisions of H.R. 5043 (The "Bankruptcy Tax Act of 1979") Amending Subchapter C (Corporate Distributions and Adjustments) of the Internal Revenue Code of 1954 (Oct., 1979).

New York State Bar Association, Tax Section, Committee on Bankruptcy and Insolvency, Report on Suggested Regulation and Statutory Amendment Projects Relating to The Bankruptcy Tax Act of 1980 (Jul. 21, 1981), Tax Notes Doc. 81-7903.

New York State Bar Association, Tax Section, Committee on Bankruptcy and Losses, Report on Reorganizations Involving Insolvent Subsidiaries (Nov. 7, 2003), 101 Tax Notes 761 (Nov. 10, 2003).

New York State Bar Association, Tax Section, Committee on Net Operating Losses, The New Operating Loss Provisions of the House-Passed Version of H.R. 3838 (May 12, 1986), 31 Tax Notes 1217 (June 23, 1986).

New York State Bar Association, Tax Section, Committee on Reorganizations, Report on Temporary Regulations § 1.368-2T Relating to "A" Reorganizations Involving Disregarded Entities (May 26, 2004), 2004 TNT 103-12 (May 27, 2004).

Newton & Wertheim, Examining the Impact from the Repeal of the Stock-for-Debt Exception, 3 Am. Bankr. Inst. 355 (1995).

Nicholls, Cottage Savings: More S&L Problems?, 45 Tax Lawyer 727 (1992).

Nicholls, Net Operating Loss and Section 382, 22 Tax Notes 609 (Feb. 13, 1984).

Noffke, Discharge of Indebtedness Under the Bankruptcy Tax of 1980, 60 Taxes 635 (1982).

Note, An Examination of the Section 108 Statutory Insolvency Exclusion and Its Definition of "Assets" as Applied in Carlson v. Commissioner, 55 Tax Law. 329 (2001).

Note, Availability of Tax-Free Reorganization Treatment for Mergers Involving Hybrid Securities: Paulsen v. Commissioner, 39 Tax Law. 349 (1986).

Note, Bankruptcy and Turnover Proceedings Against the IRS: A Path Toward Reorganization and Rehabilitation Fraught with Pitfalls, 4 Whittier L. Rev. 87 (1982).

Note, Bankruptcy Court Jurisdiction and the Power to Enjoin the IRS, 70 Minn. L. Rev. 1279.

Note, Challenges to Enforceability of a Debt Do Not Trigger the Contested Liability Exception to the Discharge-of-Indebtedness Income Rule: Preslar v. Commissioner, 53 Tax Lawyer 535 (2000).

Note, Compensation for Time Value as Part of Adequate Protection During the Automatic Stay in Bankruptcy, 50 Univ. of Chicago L. Rev. 305 (1983).

Note, Debt-Equity Swaps, 37 Tax Law. 677 (1984).

Note, Discharge of Indebtedness and the Bankruptcy Tax Act of 1980: An Economic Benefit Approach, 50 Fordham L. Rev. 104 (1981).

Note, Discharge of Nonrecourse Liability Versus Discharge of Third Party Indebtedness: Friedland v. Commissioner, 55 Tax Law. 917 (2002).

Note, Excise Taxes in Bankruptcy: United States v. Mansfield Tire and Rubber Co. Holds Congress to Its Word, 12 Va. Tax Rev. 513 (1993).

Note, Expanding the Bankruptcy Code: The Use of Section 362 and Section 105 to Protect Solvent Executives of Debtor Corporations, 58 Brooklyn L. Rev. 929 (1992).

Note, Jersey Shore State Bank v. United States: Lender Liability and Notice—When a Summons Is Enough, 7 Va. Tax Rev. 179 (1987).

Note, Post-Petition Interest on Tax Claims in Bankruptcy Proceedings, 36 Tax Law. 793 (1983).

Note, The Solution to the Trust Fund Tax Problem in Chapter 11 Bankruptcy Proceedings: In re Energy Resources, Inc., 43 Tax Law. 837 (1990).

Note, Supreme Court Decisions in Taxation: 1988 Term—United States v. Ron Pair Enterprises, 43 Tax Law. 475, 488-489 (1990).

Note, Tax Payments: Are They Voidable Preferences in Low-Asset Bankruptcies? 10 Cardozo L. Rev. 341 (1988).

Note, Taxation: Lender Liability Under I.R.C. §3505(a), 39 Okla. L. Rev. 348 (1986).

Notice of Proposed Rulemaking, Guidance Regarding Deduction and Capitalization of Expenditures, *reprinted at* 2002 TNT 13-7 (Jan. 17, 2002).

Olson & Bailine, How Do the Ownership Change Rules Affect Consolidated Returns? 3 Corp. Tax'n 4 (Jul./Aug. 1990).

Parker, The Innocent Civilians in the War Against NOL Trafficking: Section 382 and High-Tech Start-up Companies, 9 Va. Tax Rev. 625 (1990).

Parkinson, The Contempt Power of the Bankruptcy Court Fact or Fiction: The Debate Continues, 65 Am. Bankr. L.J. 591 (1991).

Peaslee, Discharge of Debt Through Its Acquisition by a Person Related to the Debtor—An Analysis of Section 108(e)(4), 37 Tax L. Rev. 193 (1982).

Peaslee, Modifications of Nondebt Financial Instruments as Deemed Exchanges, 95 Tax Notes 737 (Apr. 29, 2002).

Peaslee & Cohen, Section 382 as Amended by the Tax Reform Act of 1986, 33 Tax Notes 849 (Dec. 1, 1986).

Peaslee & Levy, Section 382 and Separate Tracking, 56 Tax Notes 1779 (Sept. 28, 1992).

Peel, F., Consolidated Tax Returns (3d ed.).

Peischel, Adjustments to the Value of a Loss Corporation for Purposes of Section 382, 30 Crop. Tax'n 3 (2003).

Phelan & Jernigan, OID and Claim Allowance—Will the Pengo Lingo Reduce the LTV Risk? Faulkner & Gray's Bankruptcy Law Rev. 5 (Winter 1992).

Phelan & Sharp, Kick 'Em While They're Down—A Taxation and Bankruptcy Critique of the Technical and Policy Aspects of the Bankruptcy Tax Act of 1980, 35 Sw. L.J. 833 (1981).

Phelan & Sharp, Practical Tax Problems and Solutions in Bankruptcy Cases, 1981 S.M.U. Symp. Fed. Tax. 141 (1981).

Pisem & Glicklich, Was the Bankruptcy Court Lost at Sea? Prudential Lines Collides with the Internal Revenue Code, 48 Tax Notes 1553 (Sept. 17, 1990).

Plumb, The Bankruptcy Tax Act, 33 Major Tax Plan. 800 (1981).

Plumb, The Federal Income Tax Significance of Corporate Debt: A Critical Analysis and a Proposal, 26 Tax L. Rev. 369 (1971).

Plumb, The Tax Recommendations of the Commission on the Bankruptcy Laws—Income Tax Liabilities of the Estate and the Debtor, 72 Mich. L. Rev. 935 (1974).

Plumb, The Tax Recommendations of the Commission on the Bankruptcy Laws—Priority and Dischargeability of Tax Claims, 59 Cornell L. Rev. 991 (1974).

Plumb, The Tax Recommendations of the Commission on the Bankruptcy Laws—Reorganizations, Carryovers, and the Effects of Debt Reduction, 29 Tax L. Rev. 227 (1974).

Plumb, The Tax Recommendations of the Commission on the Bankruptcy Laws—Tax Procedures, 88 Harv. L. Rev. 1360 (1975).

Pollack, How Section 108 Election Permits Debt Cancellation Income to be Minimized, 62 J. Tax'n 226 (1985).

Pollack & Goldring, Can Cancellation of Indebtedness Income Be Avoided with Parent Stock? 2 Corp. Tax'n 18 (Jan./Feb. 1990), 3 Corp. Tax'n 12 (Jul./Aug. 1990).

Pollack & Goldring, Eighth Circuit Holds Bankruptcy Trustee Can Avoid "Irrevocable" Tax Elections, 3 Faulkner & Gray's Bankr. L. Rev. 38 (Summer 1991).

Pollack & Goldring, Filing for Bankruptcy Can Alter Tax Consequences of Numerous Transactions, 66 J. Tax'n 330 (1987).

Pollack & Goldring, The Stock for Debt Exception—New Restrictions on the Use of Preferred Stock, 2 Faulkner & Gray's Bankr. L. Rev. #4, p. 41 (Winter 1991).

Pollack & Goldring, Unpaid Trust Fund Taxes in Chapter 11 Cases: A New Decision But No More Certainty, 1 Faulkner & Gray's Bankr. L. Rev. #2, at 48 (Summer 1989).

Pollack, Goldring & Gelbfish, Uncollectible Original Issue Discount: To Accrue or Not to Accrue, 84 J. Tax'n 157 (Mar. 1996).

Ponikvar and Kestenbaum, Aspects of the Consolidated Group in Bankruptcy: Tax Sharing and Tax Sharing Agreements, 58 Tax Law. 803 (2005).

Porter, Burdens of Proof in Bankruptcy Court, 17 Colo. Law. 251 (Feb. 1988).

Practising Law Inst., Bankruptcy Tax Act of 1980, Course Handbook Series No. 248 (1981).

Rabinowitz & Jacobson, Reorganization of the Bankrupt Corporation Under IRC 368(a)(1)(G): Panacea or Placebo, 42 Inst. on Fed. Tax'n § 10 (1984).

Rabinowitz & Rubin, The Bankruptcy Act of 1980—H.R. 5043, Proposals for New Tax Treatment for Debtors and Creditors, 57 Taxes 911 (1979).

Raby & Raby, Do Contingent Liabilities Count for Section 108 Insolvency?, Tax Notes (Jan. 12, 1998).

Raby & Raby, Measuring Assets and Liabilities for DOI Purposes, 85 Tax Notes 77 (Oct. 4, 1999).

Raby & Raby, "Net Worth" and the Shifting Burden of Proof, 2000 TNT 126-44 (June 29, 2000).

Raby & Raby, Payroll Tax Penalties for Doing Good and for Delegating, 105 Tax Notes 1639 (December 20, 2004).

Raby & Raby, Qualified Offers and Settlement of Tax Controversies, 113 Tax Notes 455 (Oct. 30, 2006).

Raby & Raby, Stock Ownership Tax Attribution and Siblings, 106 Tax Notes 675 (February 7, 2005).

Raby & Raby, Trust Fund Penalties and Reasonable Cause, 102 Tax Notes 617 (Feb. 2, 2004).

Rapisardi, Bad Faith Chapter 11 Filings—An Elusive and Undefined Concept, N.Y.L.J. (Jan. 20, 2000).

Remeikis, Debt/Equity Considerations and Deep Discount Bonds, 41 Inst. on Fed. Tax'n § 6 (1983).

Richards, The Priority of Property Taxes in Bankruptcy, 3 J. Bankr. L. & Prac. 431 (1994).

Richards, Property Taxes in Bankruptcy: Section 546(b), Section 506(c) and Lien Survival, 2 J. Bankr. L. & Prac. 277, 302-316 (1993).

Richman, More Equal Than Others: State Sovereign Immunity Under the Bankruptcy Code, 21 Rutgers L.J. 603 (1990).

Robison & Mark, Techniques to Avoid the Imposition of the Section 6672 Penalty on Officers of Bankrupt Corporations, 65 Taxes 110 (1987).

Ross, Exempt Assets and the Calculation of Insolvency Under § 108: Carlson v. Commissioner, Tax Mgmt. Mem. (June 21, 2001).

Ruge, The Bankruptcy Tax Act (Public Law 96-589) Part I: Tax Treatment of Discharge of Indebtedness—Bankruptcy, Insolvent and Solvent Debtors, 39 Inst. on Fed. Tax'n (Part II) § 40 (1981).

Ruotolo, Recovery of Interest on Postpetition Taxes Under Section 503 of the Bankruptcy Code, 64 Am. Bankr. L.J. 427 (1990).

Salem, How to Use Net Operating Losses Effectively Under the New Consolidated Return Regulations, 26 J. Tax'n 270 (1967).

Salem, LDR: Light at the End of the Tunnel?, 105 Tax Notes 1273 (November 29, 2004).

Salem, Judicial Deference, Consolidated Returns and Loss Disallowance—Could LDR Survive a Court Challenge?, 43 Tax Executive 167 (1991).

Saltzman, M., IRS Practice and Procedure (Rev. Second Edition).

Schler, Consolidated Return Loss Disallowance: Conceptual Issues, 95 Tax Notes 899 (May 6, 2002).

Schler, The Sale of Property for a Fixed Payment Note: Remaining Uncertainties, 41 Tax L. Rev. 209 (1986).

Schler, LDR: What to Do?, 105 Tax Notes 1585 (December 13, 2004).

Scranton, Corporate Transactions Under the Bankruptcy Tax Act of 1980, 35 Tax Law. 49 (1981).

Seifert & Hudson, IRS's New Approach to Determining "Responsible" Persons for the 100% Penalty, 79 J. Tax'n 144 (1993).

Seto, The Function of the Discharge of Indebtedness Doctrine: Complete Accounting in the Federal Income Tax System, 51 Tax Law Rev. 199 (1996).

Shakow, The Stock-for-Debt De Minimis Exception, 41 Tax Notes 1325 (Dec. 19, 1988).

Shapiro, Non-Debtor Third Parties and the Bankruptcy Code: Is Protection Available Without Actually Filing?, 95 Comm. L.J. 345 (1990).

Sheinfeld & Caldwell, Taxes: An Analysis of The Bankruptcy Code and The Bankruptcy Tax Act of 1980, 55 Am. Bankr. L.J. 97 (1981).

Sheppard, Elect Your Subsidiary Loss, 104 Tax Notes 894 (August 30, 2004).

Sheppard, Elect Your Subsidiary Loss, Part 2, 106 Tax Notes 1129 (March 7, 2005).

Sheppard, How to Avoid COD Income, and How Not To Do It, 90 TNT 222-5 (Oct. 31, 1990).

Sheppard, New Tax Avoidance Regs. Avoid Bankruptcy Court, 92 TNT 8-8 (Jan. 13, 1992).

Sheppard, Preserving NOL Carryovers in Bankruptcy: The Progeny of Prudential Lines, 91 TNT 182-9 (Aug. 30, 1991).

Sheppard, Rethinking Tax Collection in Bankruptcy, 75 Tax Notes 1051 (May 26, 1997).

Sheppard, Tenth Circuit Writes Its Own Responsible Person Penalty, Tax Notes (Sept. 8, 1997).

Sheppard, Why Bankrupts May Still Owe Taxes, and Other Anomalies, 43 Tax Notes 941 (May 22, 1989).

Shmuel Vasser, Waiver of Foreign Sovereign Immunity Under Bankruptcy Code § 106, N.Y.L.J. (June 5, 2003).

Silberberg, Consolidated Section 382: The Proposed Regulations 69 Taxes 395 (Jul. 1991).

Silverman & Keyes, An Analysis of the New Ownership Regs. Under Section 382, 68 J. Tax'n 68, 142, and 300 (Feb., Mar., & May 1988) and 69 J. Tax'n 42 (Jul. 1988).

Silverman & Keyes, How Stock Acquisitions Will Trigger Section 384, J. Tax'n 74 (Feb. 1990).

Silverman & Keyes, Limiting Built-In Gains and Losses After Asset Acquisitions, 72 J. Tax'n 238 (Apr. 1990).

Silverman & Keyes, New Limitation on NOL Carryovers Following the Tax Reform Act: Parts I and II, 66 J. Tax'n 194, 259 (1987).

Silverman & Weinstein, The New Continuity of Interest/Continuity of Business Enterprise Regs., 80 Tax Notes (Jul. 20, 1998).

Silverman & Zarlenga, Rite Aid: A Tough Pill for the Government to Swallow, 94 Tax Notes 1343 (Mar. 11, 2002).

Simmons, Bankruptcy: Sixth Circuit Answers the Question, "When Is an Excise Tax an Excise Tax?" 55 Tax Notes 82 (Apr. 6, 1992).

Simon, Compound Complexity: Accounting for Built-In Gains and Losses Under the AMT After an Ownership Change, 107 Tax Notes 477 (April 25, 2005).

Smith & Sobol, New Rev. Rul. Says 'Timmm-Berrr' to Built-In Gains Tax for Natural Resource Companies, 96 J. Tax'n 46 (2002).

Sniderman, Gallagher & Joshowitz, A Tax Overview of Troubled Company Debt Restructuring, 21 Tax Advisor 199 (Apr. 1990).

Soble, Eggersten & Bernstein, Pension-Related Claims in Bankruptcy, 56 Am. Bankr. L.J. 155 (1982).

Solinga, A Survey of Legal Factors Helpful in Establishing the Principal Motivation Requirements of Section 269, 64 Taxes 302 (1986).

Soukup, The Continuity-of-Proprietary-Interest Doctrine and Thrift Institution Mergers, 12 J. Corp. Tax'n 141 (1985).

Steinberg & Fruchter, Bankruptcy Code Section 502(d): Back Door to Avoidance, 28 Unif. Comm. Code L. J. 73 (1995).

Stone & Jacobs, An Analysis of the Net Operating Loss and Excess Credit Carryforwards Under H.R. 3838, 31 Tax Notes 725 (May 19, 1986).

Strobel & Strobel, The Effect on Earnings and Profits of the Forgiveness of Indebtedness Pursuant to Discharge in Bankruptcy, 12 J. Corp. Tax'n 359 (1985).

Tatlock, Bankruptcy and Insolvency: Tax Aspects and Procedure, 466 T.M.

Thompson, Planning for the Loss Corporation: The Interaction Among Code Sections 269, 381, Old and New Sections 382 and the Consolidated Return Regulations, 31 Major Tax Plan. 223 (1979).

Tillinghast & Gardner, Acquisitive Reorganizations and Chapters X and XI of the Bankruptcy Act, 26 Tax L. Rev. 663 (1971).

Todres, Corporate Bankruptcy: Treatment of Filing Year Income Tax—A Suggested Approach, 9 Am. Bankr. Inst. L. Rev. 523 (2001).

Treasury Department General Explanations of Clinton Administration's Revenue Proposals for FY 1999 (issued Feb. 2, 1998).

Vogel & Hering, New Loss Disallowance Regulations—Welcome to the Age of Tracing and Appraisals, 96 J. Tax'n 327 (2002).

Wallace, Representing a Failing Business, 44 Maj. Tax Plan 406.03 (1992).

Watts, Corporate Acquisitions and Divisions Under The Bankruptcy Tax Act: The New "G" Type Reorganization, 59 Taxes 845 (1981).

Weinstein and Packman, Fast Track Settlement—On the Fast Track, But to Where? A Practical Guide to the Program, 103 J. Tax'n 288 (2005).

Weiss, Bankruptcy Court Power to Enjoin the IRS from Collecting the Debtor's Taxes from Its Officers: An Analysis of Recent Developments, 1986 Ann. Survey of Bankr. L. 233, 252-256.

White, Loss Disallowance Regulations Flanked? 41 Tax Mgmt. Memo. 248 (2000).

Wilkins & Hyde, NCNB Texas Ruling Breaks New Ground, 40 Tax Notes 1417 (Sept. 26, 1988).

Willens, A 'Solvent' Liquidation Can Be Taxable, 115 Tax Notes 581 (May 7, 2007).

Willens, Applying the New 'Continuity of Interest' Regulations, 72 BNA Daily Tax Report (April 16, 2007).

Willens, "Bruno"-Type Bankruptcy Arrangement Secures IRS Seal of Approval, BNA Daily Tax Rep. (Jan. 5, 2004), J-1.

Willens, Conseco's Worthless Stock Loss Appears to Withstand Scrutiny, BNA Daily Tax Report #5 (January 9, 2006).

Willens, Determining Deductibility of a 'Premium' in Equity-for-Debt Exchanges, BNA Daily Tax Report (Nov. 8, 2006).

Willens, Formal Bankruptcy Proceedings Can Improve Tax Consequences Where Debtors See Potential Cancellation of Indebtedness Income, BNA Daily Tax Report (Feb. 21, 2007).

Willens, Good News in Gauging Existence of an "Ownership Change," BNA Daily Tax Report (Jan. 27, 2003).

Willens, Securing an Ordinary Loss Deduction for Worthless Holding Company Stock, BNA Daily Tax Report (March 22, 2007).

Willens, When Siblings Are Regarded as Strangers, 110 Tax Notes 1099 (March 6, 2006).

Willis, Some Limits of Equitable Recoupment, Tax Mitigation, and Res Judicata: Reflections Prompted by *Chertkof v. United States*, 38 Tax Law. 625 (1985).

Winston, What Is Section 1504(a)(4) Preferred Stock? 76 Tax Notes 111 (Jul. 7, 1997).

Winterer, "Reissuance" and Deemed Exchanges Generally, 37 Tax Law. 509 (1984).

Witt & Albergotti, G Reorganization Offers Simple, Effective Way to Acquire Bankrupt Corporations, 61 J. Tax'n 90 (1985).

Witt & Lyons, An Examination of the Tax Consequences of Discharge of Indebtedness, 10 Va. Tax Rev. 1, 111 (1990).

Woll, Post Bruno's Bankruptcy Planning: An Analysis of Taxable Emergence Structures, 4 DePaul Bus. & Comm. L.J. 277 (2006).

Wood, Rulings Make Qualified Settlement Funds More Attractive, 111 Tax Notes 673 (May 8, 2006).

Wootton, Section 382 After the Tax Reform Act of 1986, 64 Taxes 874 (1986).

Wright, Miller & Cooper, Federal Practice and Procedure, Civil 3d (1998 ed. with Supp.).

Yale, The Final *INDOPCO* Regulations, 105 Tax Notes 435 (October 25, 2004).

Yates, Prop. Regs. on Consolidated 382 and Related Matters Balanced But Complex (Parts I and II), 74 J. Tax'n 364, 75 J. Tax'n 18 (1992).

Yates, Vogel, Hering & Hoffenberg, The Final Factor—Temp. Reg. 1.1502-35T Takes a New Approach to Barring Duplicated Losses, 98 J. Tax'n 263 (2003).

# Index

*All references are to sections.*

## A

## B

## C

## D

## E

## F



## G

## Q



## R

## U



## W